Online

Online Learning Center

Within the book's Web site, there is a password-protected Online Learning Center for Garrison. Adopters of **Managerial Accounting, 9/E,** will have full access to select pages of text, graphics, PowerPoint® slides, exercises, as well as online testing and grading. The McGraw-Hill content is so comprehensive that you needn't change a thing, but you can still customize if you wish. You can delete content, add a personal course syllabus, provide Internet links, or integrate your own material.

McGraw-Hill Learning Architecture

This Web-based software offers an easier way to administer your course. Use it to post homework, assign quizzes, even track your students' progress—all from your computer.

Student collaboration is also made easier thanks to an embedded e-mail system that lets you instantly answer questions and form student discussion groups.

Online Learning Center **features**

For the student

- Provides Learning Objectives, Key Terms, and chapter summaries from the text.
- Flashcards*—The flashcards are designed to help students learn the major concepts.
- Readiness Assessment Tests*—Each chapter contains a 10 question, objective assessment test to ensure student comprehension.
- "What If" exercises*—These interactive Excel spreadsheets require students to solve an initial problem. Students can then change variables and see how it impacts the solution.
- Spreadsheet Application Templates (SPATS)—Select end-of-chapter problems in the text may be solved using these templates that can be downloaded from the Online Learning Center.
- Additional Internet exercises*—These additional problems require students to go onto the Web to solve them.

* New content only found on the Online Learning Center.

For the Instructor

- Create a course homepage and/or online course using PageOut
- Access an online gradebook and quizzing ability
- Form synchronous discussion groups
- Create your own Web links

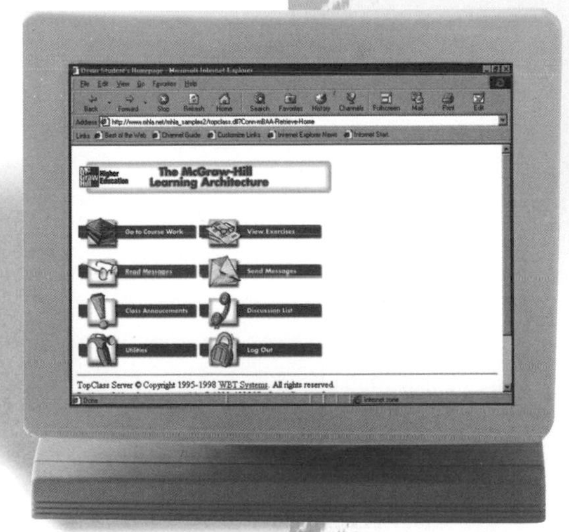

P.L.U.S. Edition
(Professional Learning Unit System)

Managerial Accounting

P.L.U.S. Edition
(Professional Learning Unit System)

Managerial Accounting

NINTH EDITION

RAY H. GARRISON, D.B.A., CPA
Professor Emeritus
Brigham Young University

ERIC W. NOREEN, PH.D., CMA
University of Washington
and
INSEAD

Boston Burr Ridge, IL Dubuque, IA Madison, WI
New York San Francisco St. Louis Bangkok Bogotá
Caracas Lisbon London Madrid Mexico City Milan
New Delhi Seoul Singapore Sydney Taipei Toronto

Dedication: To our families and to our many colleagues who use this book.

McGraw-Hill Higher Education

A Division of The ***McGraw-Hill*** *Companies*

MANAGERIAL ACCOUNTING

This book is printed on acid-free paper.

domestic 1 2 3 4 5 6 7 8 9 0 VNH/VNH 9 0 9 8 7 6 5 4 3 2 1 0 9
international 1 2 3 4 5 6 7 8 9 0 VNH/VNH 9 0 9 8 7 6 5 4 3 2 1 0 9

ISBN 0-256-26073-7 (student ed.)
ISBN 0-07-109249-8 (annotated instructor's ed.)

Vice president/Editor-in-chief: *Michael W. Junior*
Publisher: *Jeffrey J. Shelstad*
Sponsoring editor: *Stewart Mattson*
Developmental editor: *Tracey Klein Douglas*
Senior marketing manager: *Rhonda Seelinger*
Project manager: *Pat Frederickson*
Senior production supervisor: *Heather D. Burbridge*
Designer: *Kiera Cunningham*
Senior photo research coordinator: *Keri Johnson*
Photo researcher: *Martin Levik*
Supplement coordinator: *Rose Hepburn/Carol Loreth*
Compositor: *GAC Indianapolis*
Typeface: *10/12 Times Roman*
Printer: *Von Hoffmann Press, Inc.*

Library of Congress Cataloging-in-Publication Data

Garrison, Ray H.
Managerial accounting / Ray H. Garrison, Eric W. Noreen.—9th ed.
p. cm.
Includes index.
ISBN 0-256-26073-7 (student ed.).—ISBN 0-07-109249-8 (annotated instructor's ed.)
1. Managerial accounting. I. Noreen, Eric W. II. Title.
HF5657.4.G37 2000
658.15'1—dc21 99-12837

INTERNATIONAL EDITION

http://www.mhhe.com

Author Biography

RAY H. GARRISON is *emeritus* Professor of Accounting at Brigham Young University, Provo, Utah. He received his B.S. and M.S. degrees from Brigham Young University and his D.B.A. degree from Indiana University.

As a certified public accountant, Professor Garrison has been involved in management consulting work with both national and regional accounting firms. He has published articles in *The Accounting Review, Management Accounting,* and other professional journals. Innovation in the classroom has earned Professor Garrison the Karl G. Maeser Distinguished Teaching Award from Brigham Young University.

ERIC W. NOREEN is a globe-trotting academic who has held appointments at institutions in the United States, Europe, and Asia. He is currently Professor of Accounting at the University of Washington and Visiting Price Waterhouse Professor of Management Information & Control at INSEAD, an international graduate school of business located in France.

He received his B.A. degree from the University of Washington and MBA and Ph.D. degrees from Stanford University. A Certified Management Accountant, he was awarded a Certificate of Distinguished Performance by the Institute of Certified Management Accountants.

Professor Noreen has served as Associate Editor of *The Accounting Review* and the *Journal of Accounting and Economics*. He has numerous articles in academic journals including: the *Journal of Accounting Research; The Accounting Review;* the *Journal of Accounting and Economics; Accounting Horizons; Accounting, Organizations and Society; Contemporary Accounting Research;* the *Journal of Management Accounting Research;* and the *Review of Accounting Studies*. He is a frequent presenter at workshops and conferences throughout the world.

Professor Noreen teaches management accounting at the undergraduate, masters, and doctoral levels and has won a number of awards from students for his teaching.

Preface

This text is designed for a one-term course in managerial accounting after students have already completed one or two terms of basic financial accounting. *Managerial Accounting* is concerned with how a manager should use accounting data within his or her organization. Managers need information to carry out three essential functions in an organization: (1) planning operations, (2) controlling activities, and (3) making decisions. The purpose of *Managerial Accounting* is to show what kind of information is needed, where this information can be obtained, and how this information can be used by managers as they carry out their planning, controlling, and decision-making responsibilities.

A paramount objective of *Managerial Accounting* has always been to provide a clear and balanced presentation of relevant subject matter. This focus on relevance continues in the ninth edition with coverage of current topics such as the balanced scorecard, activity-based costing and management, and the theory of constraints. In recognition of the widespread application of managerial accounting concepts, many examples and problems deal with not-for-profit, service, retail, and wholesale organizations as well as with manufacturing organizations. In short, the watchwords for this edition of *Managerial Accounting* have again been *relevance, balance,* and a continued tradition of *clarity.*

Organization and Content

As in the prior editions, flexibility in meeting the needs of courses varying in length, content, and student composition continues to be a prime concern. Sufficient text material is available to permit the instructor to choose topics and depth of coverage as desired. Appendices, parts of chapters, or even (in some cases) whole chapters can be omitted without adversely affecting the continuity of the course. The Solutions Manual gives a number of alternatives for organizing the course.

New in This Edition

The ninth edition builds on the success of the eighth edition. Changes are motivated by a desire to make the material even more accessible and relevant to students. The popular "Managerial Accounting in Action" dialogues involving businesspeople in lifelike settings have been expanded. "Focus on Current Practice" boxes have been updated and new ones added throughout the book. New chapter openers help students relate chapter concepts with the real world. Where feasible, technical material has been simplified to make it clearer and easier to learn and new Internet exercises have been added to the end of each chapter.

As in prior editions, special attention has been given to the exercise, problem, and case material in the book. Users will again find a wide range of assignment material with various levels of difficulty.

Three major changes have been made in the organization and content of the book. The activity-based costing chapter has been completely rewritten to emphasize decision making and has been moved so that it follows the chapter on variable costing. The material on the cost of quality has been moved to an appendix at the end of the text. And new material on the balanced scorecard has been added to Chapter 10.

Many small "polishing" changes have been made throughout the book to improve flow, comprehension, and readability. However, change has not been made simply for the sake of change. Rather, the revision has been completed with a single thought in mind—to make the ninth edition of *Managerial Accounting* the most up-to-date and teachable text available in its field. Technology advances are reflected in the Presentation Manager CD ROM, free student CD ROM, Online Learning Center, and telecourse.

The Texty and McGuffey awards are a further reflection of the excellence of this product. Awarded by the Text and Academic Authors Association, these awards recognize works for their excellence in the areas of content, presentation, appeal, and teachability.

Specific Chapter Enhancements

All of the chapters have been improved and updated in various ways in this edition. The following table summarizes the most significant of these changes:

Chapter	Major Content Changes in This Edition
Chapter 2	More emphasis has been placed on service companies.
Chapter 3	The schedule of cost of goods manufactured has been simplified to make it easier to understand and to construct. Under- or overapplied overhead is now allocated among ending inventories and Cost of Goods Sold on the basis of the amount of overhead applied during the period in the ending balances of the accounts rather than on the basis of their gross ending balances. A new appendix covers the controversy over the choice of the level of activity in the denominator of the predetermined overhead rate.
Chapter 5	This was Chapter 6 in the eighth edition and has been revised and updated.
Chapter 6	This was Chapter 7 in the eighth edition and has been revised and updated.
Chapter 7	This was Chapter 8 in the eighth edition and has been revised and updated.
Chapter 8	This new chapter covers activity-based costing. The ABC material in the text has been completely rewritten to emphasize decision making in both service and manufacturing companies.
Chapter 10	The balanced scorecard has been added to the chapter and integrated with the material on operating performance measures.
Chapter 11	Much greater emphasis is given to the control of overhead costs in service companies.
Chapter 12	The chapter has been reorganized. The discussion of decentralization now comes first, followed by the segment margin. The transfer pricing appendix has been completely rewritten with a new approach based on the economics of negotiated transfer prices.
Chapter 14	The preference ranking material that was previously in Chapter 15 has been brought forward to Chapter 14.
Chapter 15	The MACRS depreciation material has been simplified.
Chapter 18	Trend analysis now includes time-series plots of data. The gross margin percentage has been added while extraordinary items and diluted earnings per share have been dropped.
Pricing Appendix	A new section stresses the role of the price elasticity of demand in setting prices. The contribution approach to cost-plus pricing has been dropped. The drawbacks of using the absorption costing approach to cost-plus pricing are given more coverage.
Quality Appendix	This cost of quality material has been extracted from Chapter 5 in the eighth edition.

Instructor Supplements

New!

PRESENTATION MANAGER CD-ROM ISBN 0072304022
This is your all-in-one resource. It contains the Instructor's Manual, Test Bank, transparencies, PowerPoint, and video clips—organized by concept and chapter. Thanks to the Presentation Manager, you can create a multimedia presentation that incorporates video, transparencies, and PowerPoint slides.

INSTRUCTOR'S RESOURCE GUIDE AND VIDEO GUIDE ISBN 0256260745
These extensive chapter-by-chapter lecture notes can serve as a base for classroom presentation. They also provide useful ways of presenting key concepts and ideas. An "assignment grid" for each chapter indicates the topics covered by each exercise, problem, and case. The video guide provides a brief overview of the key points and length of the video segments. It also provides questions to promote classroom discussion.

PROFESSIONAL LEARNING UNIT SYSTEM (P.L.U.S.) EDITION
ISBN 0071092498
This special Instructor's Edition contains annotations in the margins to help you plan your lessons. There are five types of marginal annotations: Instructor's Notes, Reinforcing Problems, In the Real World, Suggested Readings, and Check Figures.

SOLUTIONS MANUAL AND DISK ISBN 007109248X
This supplement contains completely worked-out solutions to all assignment material and a general discussion of the use of group exercises. In addition, the manual contains suggested course outlines and a listing of exercises, problems, and cases scaled as to difficulty.

SOLUTIONS TRANSPARENCIES ISBN 0071092501
These transparencies feature completely worked-out solutions to all assignment material. Their boldface type is large enough for the back row of any lecture hall. Masters of these transparencies are available in the Solutions Manual.

TEACHING TRANSPARENCY MASTERS ISBN 007109251X
Contains a comprehensive set of over 260 teaching transparencies covering every chapter that can be used for classroom lectures and discussion.

READY SHOWS (PowerPoint® Slide Version 7) ISBN 0256260869
Prepared by Jon Booker, Charles Caldwell, Susan Galbreath, and Richard Rand, all of Tennessee Technical University, these slides offer a great visual complement for your lectures. A complete set of slides covers each objective and key topic of the text.

READY SLIDES ISBN 0256260826
These four-color acetates are produced from the Ready Shows. The Ready Slides and Ready Shows were prepared by Jon Booker of Tennessee Technological University.

COMPUTEST (Windows ISBN 0256260850 and MAC ISBN 0256260842)
This test bank is now delivered in the Diploma Shell, new from Brownstone. Use it to make different versions of the same test, change the answer order, edit and add questions, and conduct online testing.

TEST BANK ISBN 025626077X
Nearly 2,000 questions are organized by chapter and include true/false, multiple-choice, computational problems, and essay.

TELETEST

By calling a toll-free number, you can specify the content of exams and have a laser-printed copy of the exams mailed to you.

CHECK FIGURES ISBN 0071092528

This list of check figures gives key answers for selected problems and cases.

SPREADSHEET APPLICATION TEMPLATE SOFTWARE (SPATS)

ISBN 0072345306

Prepared by Jack Terry of ComSource Associates, Inc., these Excel templates offer solutions to the Student SPATS version.

VIDEO LIBRARY

Designed to strengthen your classroom presentations, grab student interest, and add variety to your students' learning process, these six volumes of videos include international and service examples to go along with numerous manufacturing examples.

INSTRUCTOR'S MANUAL TO ACCOMPANY MANAGERIAL ACCOUNTING USING EXCEL 97 ISBN 0072295325

This supplement provides teaching tips and solutions for use with this product.

New!

LECROY CENTER TELECOURSE An exciting new Telecourse has been developed in partnership with the LeCroy Center. New videos and a student guide have been created for this text. Visit http://dallas.dcccd.edu for more details.

Student Supplements

New!

STUDENT CD-ROM (Shrink-wrapped free with *Managerial Accounting,* 9/E)

ISBN 0072324120

Students can use this software's tutorial features for added learning opportunities, or click on a video clip for a real-world look relating to chapter material.

WORKBOOK/STUDY GUIDE ISBN 0071092463

This study aid provides suggestions for studying chapter material, summarizes essential points in each chapter, and tests students' knowledge using self-test questions and exercises.

READY NOTES ISBN 0256260818

This booklet provides Ready Slide exhibits in a workbook format for efficient note taking.

STUDENT LECTURE AID ISBN 0072324139

Much like the Ready Notes, this booklet offers a hard-copy version of all the Teaching Transparencies. Students can annotate the material during the lecture and take notes in the space provided.

WORKING PAPERS ISBN 0256260761

This study aid contains forms that help students organize their solutions to homework problems.

SPATS ISBN 0072324120

Prepared by Jack Terry of ComSource Associates, Inc., this spreadsheet-based software uses Excel to solve selected problems and cases in the text. These selected problems and cases are identified in the margin of the text with an appropriate icon.

MANAGERIAL ACCOUNTING USING EXCEL 97 ISBN 0072296291

Prepared by Ali Peyvandi and Nancy Hongola, both of California State University at Fresno, this product incorporates spreadsheets into a managerial accounting course with a four-step process:

- Provides students with a brief introduction to the computer.
- Introduces students to an Excel spreadsheet and its functions.
- Asks students to solve managerial accounting problems using Excel templates.
- Requires students to solve managerial accounting problems by creating a spreadsheet from scratch.

KJC MANUFACTURERS, INC. ISBN 007030744X

Prepared by Leland Mansuetti of Sierra College, this manual practice set contains a narrative of transactions for a manufacturing company. KJC is a small corporation that manufactures patio furniture. Its records include Sales Journal, a Cash Receipts Journal, a Voucher System, General Ledger, and Accounts Receivable Ledger. Estimated completion time is 15 to 20 hours.

RAMBLEWOOD MANUFACTURING, INC. (Windows ISBN 0256221383 and CD-ROM ISBN 0072348151)

This computerized practice set was prepared by Leland Mansuetti and Keith Weidkamp, both of Sierra College, and has been completely updated. This software simulates the operations of a company that manufactures customized fencing. It can be used to illustrate job-order costing systems with JIT inventory in a realistic setting. The entire simulation requires 10 to 14 hours to complete. A new feature prevents files from being transferred from one disk to another without detection. It is available on 3.5" diskettes and the CD-ROM, Windows platform.

COMMUNICATION FOR ACCOUNTANTS: EFFECTIVE STRATEGIES FOR STUDENTS AND PROFESSIONAL ISBN 0070383901

Authored by Maurice Hirsch of Southern Illinois University-Carbondale and Susan Gabriel and Rob Anderson, both of St. Louis University, this brief and inexpensive handbook addresses the need for accountants to communicate effectively through both writing and speaking.

Features

CHAPTER OPENERS

Chapter content reflects the real world, so it seems only appropriate that the chapter openers do as well. That's why new business examples now start every chapter. They are designed to engage the reader and place upcoming material in a real-world context.

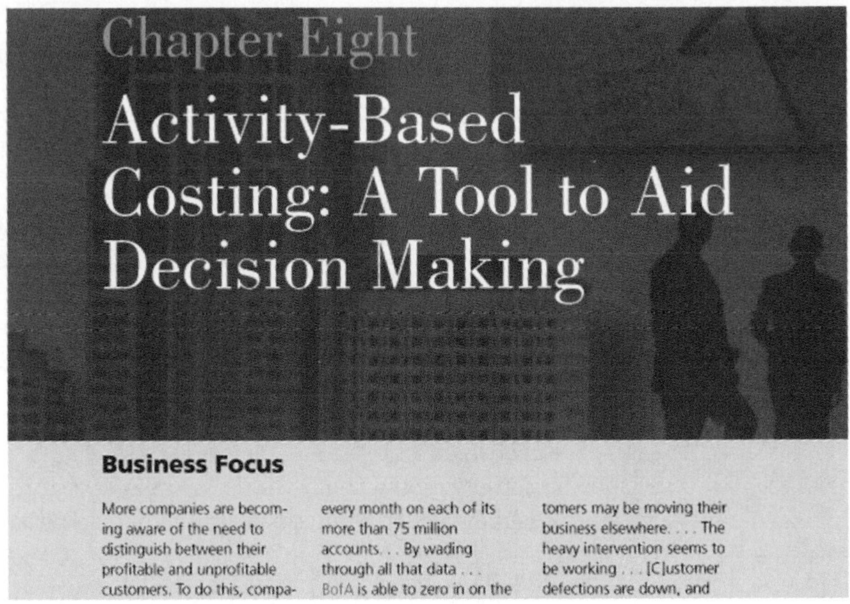

Chapter Eight

Activity-Based Costing: A Tool to Aid Decision Making

Business Focus

More companies are becoming aware of the need to distinguish between their profitable and unprofitable customers. To do this, companies every month on each of its more than 75 million accounts. . . By wading through all that data . . . BofA is able to zero in on the customers may be moving their business elsewhere. . . . The heavy intervention seems to be working . . . [C]ustomer defections are down, and

FOCUS ON CURRENT PRACTICE BOXES

Managerial Accounting's real-world orientation is further strengthened with updated boxes containing actual companies and how they use, or are affected by, the concepts discussed in the related chapters. Anywhere from two to nine examples per chapter show how managerial accounting is used in actual business practice.

Focus on Current Practice

Japanese law makes it difficult to lay off or fire workers or to hire away employees from competitors. Exemptions may be granted to the no-layoff rule—particularly for small companies—but this rule effectively ties an employee to a single company for life. As a result, labor is commonly regarded as a fixed cost in Japan. This reduces the ability of Japanese companies to adjust costs in response to peaks and valley in the business cycle, but there are advantages to this system. "Since Japanese workers enjoy lifetime job guarantees, they see no downside risk in helping employers improve productivity. In fact, they embrace new technology because they

MANAGERIAL ACCOUNTING IN ACTION BOXES

These are vignettes involving businesspeople in lifelike settings. They are frequently used to introduce core concepts and stimulate interest. They are essential to, and an integral part of, reading and understanding the text. Real products and services that students can relate with are used as much as possible.

Managerial Accounting in Action

THE ISSUE

Samantha Trivers, president of Double Diamond Skis, was worried about the future of the company. After a rocky start, the company had come out with a completely redesigned ski called The Ultimate. It was made of exotic materials and featured flashy graphics. Exhibit 4–5 illustrates how this ski is manufactured. The ski was a runaway best seller—particularly among younger skiers—and had provided the company with much-needed cash for two years. However, last year a dismal snowfall in the Rocky Mountains had depressed sales, and Double Diamond was once again short of cash. Samantha was worried that another bad ski season would force Double Diamond into bankruptcy.

Just before starting production of next year's model of The Ultimate, Samantha called Jerry Madison, the company controller, into her office to discuss the reports she would need in the coming year.

SPREADSHEET INTEGRATION

ABC and budgeting are functions for which most managerial accountants use spreadsheets. Therefore, exhibits in these chapters appear as Microsoft® Excel spreadsheet screen captures. This unique feature helps students recognize the importance of spreadsheets as an ABC and budgeting tool and shows how they look in a spreadsheet.

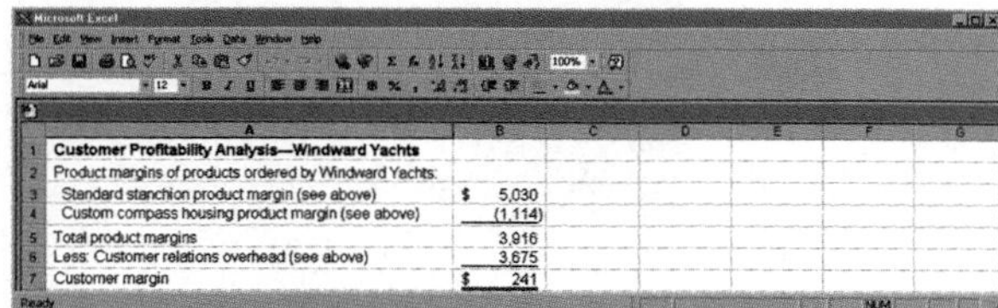

	A	B
1	**Customer Profitability Analysis—Windward Yachts**	
2	Product margins of products ordered by Windward Yachts:	
3	Standard stanchion product margin (see above)	$ 5,030
4	Custom compass housing product margin (see above)	(1,114)
5	Total product margins	3,916
6	Less: Customer relations overhead (see above)	3,675
7	Customer margin	$ 241

MORE INCLUSION OF SERVICE COMPANY EXAMPLES

Special attention to real-world examples has always been a priority in *Managerial Accounting*. Where appropriate, the authors use service company examples in the text.

END-OF-CHAPTER MATERIAL

Solid, reliable end-of-chapter exercises, problems, and cases continue to respond to AECC and AACSB recommendations. This includes group projects, writing assignments, and ethics content.

INTERNET EXERCISES

Garrison and Noreen have always embraced new technology to help students learn. That's why Internet exercises have been added to the end-of-chapter material. A new World Wide Web logo points out which exercises or problems require students to investigate a company online. All URLs are accessible as hot links from the text's web site (www.mhhe.com/garrison).

NEW DESIGN

Clear presentation is always important, and the ninth edition doesn't ignore function for the sake of aesthetics. A contemporary design offers new real-world Chapter Openers, redesigned logos in the margins, as well as other engaging features—like boxed material that is integrated within the text, and color-coded chapter openers that reflect the division of chapters into parts.

Discussions and examples ranging from ethics to the real world are identified in the margin of the text by an appropriate icon.

World Wide Web
Indicates an end-of-chapter exercise requiring research on the Internet.

International
Represents discussions with an international dimension.

Writing
Represents an exercise that offers a chance for students to hone their written communication skills.

Spreadsheet Application Template Software (SPATS)
Identifies selected end-of-chapter material that may be solved using these spreadsheet templates.

Ethics
Found in margin whenever ethical issues are discussed.

Real World
Appears in margin when an actual company is discussed in the text.

WEB PAGE

A dynamic, extensive web site has been developed for students and instructors. See the inside cover of this text for details or visit www.mhhe.com/garrison.

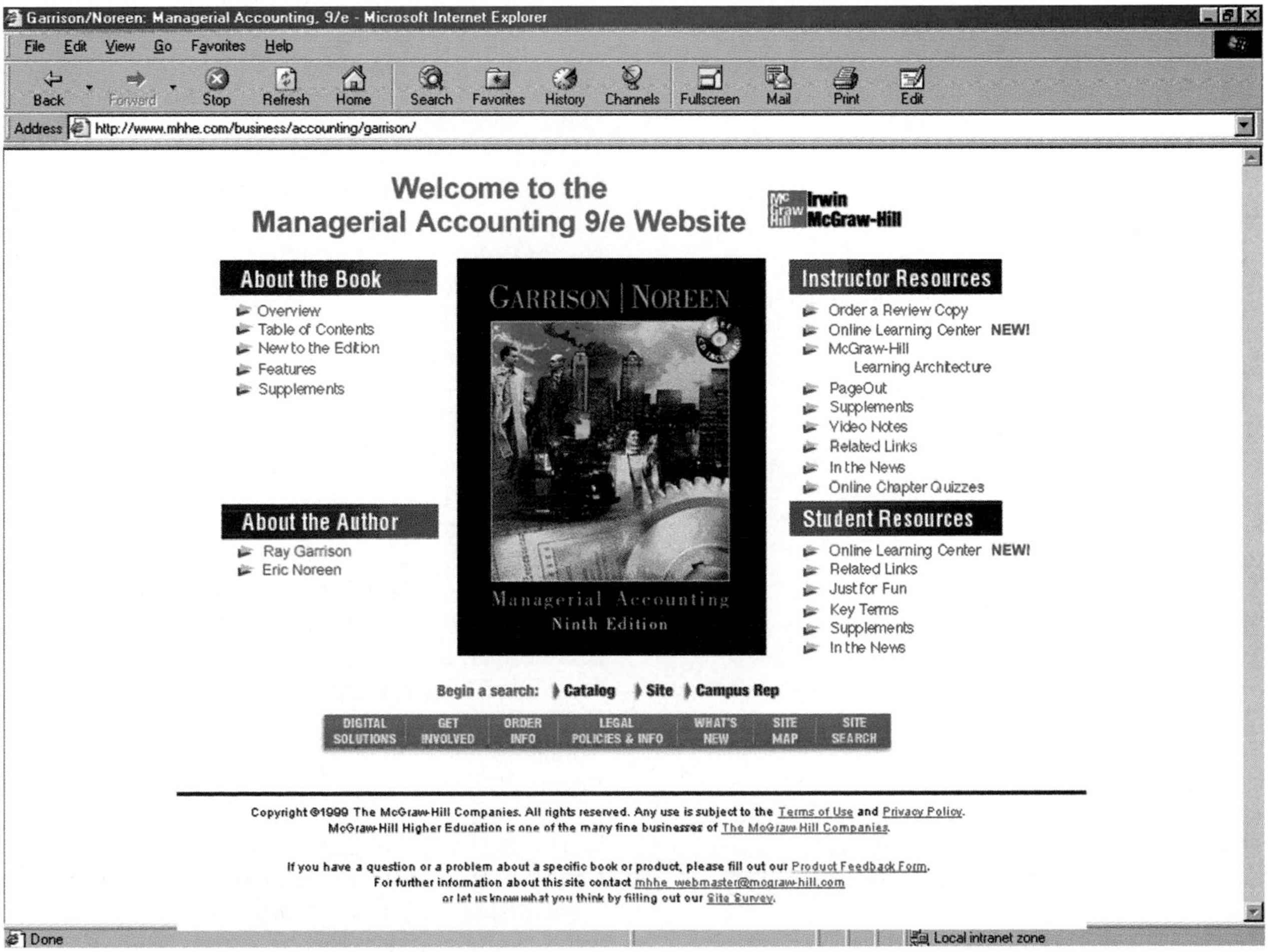

Garrison/Noreen: Managerial Accounting, 9/e - Microsoft Internet Explorer

File Edit View Go Favorites Help

Back Forward Stop Refresh Home Search Favorites History Channels Fullscreen Mail Print Edit

Address http://www.mhhe.com/business/accounting/garrison/

Welcome to the
Managerial Accounting 9/e Website

Irwin McGraw-Hill

About the Book
- Overview
- Table of Contents
- New to the Edition
- Features
- Supplements

About the Author
- Ray Garrison
- Eric Noreen

GARRISON | NOREEN
Managerial Accounting
Ninth Edition

Instructor Resources
- Order a Review Copy
- Online Learning Center NEW!
- McGraw-Hill Learning Architecture
- PageOut
- Supplements
- Video Notes
- Related Links
- In the News
- Online Chapter Quizzes

Student Resources
- Online Learning Center NEW!
- Related Links
- Just for Fun
- Key Terms
- Supplements
- In the News

Begin a search: Catalog Site Campus Rep

DIGITAL SOLUTIONS | GET INVOLVED | ORDER INFO | LEGAL POLICIES & INFO | WHAT'S NEW | SITE MAP | SITE SEARCH

If you have a question or a problem about a specific book or product, please fill out our Product Feedback Form.
For further information about this site contact mhhe_webmaster@mcgraw-hill.com
or let us know what you think by filling out our Site Survey.

Done Local intranet zone

Development Focus and Acknowledgments

Suggestions have been received from many of our colleagues throughout the world who have used the prior edition of *Managerial Accounting.* This is vital feedback that we rely on in each edition. Each of those who have offered comments and suggestions has our thanks.

The efforts of many people are needed to develop and improve a text. Among these people are the survey respondents, consultants, and reviewers who point out areas of concern, cite areas of strength, and make recommendations for change. In this regard, the following professors provided feedback that was enormously helpful in preparing the ninth edition of *Managerial Accounting:*

Reviewers
Betty Jo Browning, Bradley University
Alan Czyzewski, Indiana State University
Deborah Davis, Hampton University
James Emig, Villanova University
Harriet Farney, University of Hartford
Jackson Gillespie, University of Delaware
Joe Goetz, Louisiana State University
Art Goldman, University of Kentucky
David Jacobson, Salem State College
Holly Johnston, Boston University
Lisa Martin, Western Michigan University
Michael O'Neill, Seattle Central Community College
Leonardo Rodriguez, Florida International University
Eldon Schafer, University of Arizona
Soliman Soliman, Tulane University

Consultants
Wagdy Abdallah, Seton Hall University
Sheila Ammons, Austin Community College
Mohamed Bayou, University of Michigan—Dearborn
Suzanne Breitenbach, Keller Graduate School of Business
Thomas Buttros, Indiana University at Kokomo
Larry Carney, Fontbonne College
Robert Close, Consumnes River College
Gail Cook, University of Wisconsin—Parkside
Jeremy Cripps, Heidelberg College
Patricia Doherty, Boston University
Pete Dorff, Kent State University
Alan Doyle, Pima College
Sheila Handy, Lafayette College
Thomas Hoar, Houston Community College
Bonnie Holloway, Lake-Sumter Community College
Susan Hughes, Butler University
Phillip Jones, University of Richmond
Carol Keller, Coastal Carolina University
Janice Klimek, Missouri Western State College
Terry Lindenberg, Rock Valley College
Lawrence Logan, University of Massachusetts—Dartmouth
Rex Mahlman, Northwestern Oklahoma State University
Carol Mannino, Milwaukee School of Engineering
Duncan McDougall, Plymouth State College
Noel McKeon, Florida Community College
David Morris, North Georgia College and State University
Doug Moses, Naval Postgraduate School
Kevin Nathan, Oakland University
Kathy Otero, University of Texas at El Paso
Michael Pearson, Kent State University
Vaughan Radcliffe, Case Western Reserve University
David Remmele, University of Wisconsin—Whitewater
John Roberts, St. John's River Community College
Don Schwartz, National University
Mayda Shorney, St. Gregory's University
Donald Simons, Frostburg State University
Parvez Sopariwala, Grand Valley State University
Mel Stinnett, Oklahoma Christian University
Ephraim Sudit, Rutgers University—Newark
Kimberly Temme, Maryville University
Nicole Turner, Florida Community College—Jacksonville
Kiran Verma, University of Massachusetts—Boston
Lee Warren, Boston College
Ronald Wood, Pittsburg State University
Martha Woodman, University of Vermont

Survey Respondents
L. M. Abney, LaSalle University
Robert Appleton, University of North Carolina—Wilmington
Leonard Bacon, California State University, Bakersfield
Larry Bitner, Hood College
Jay Blazer, Milwaukee Area Technical College
Nancy Bledsoe, Millsaps College
William Blouch, Loyola College
Eugene Blue, Governor State University
Casey Bradley, Troy State University
Marley Brown, Mt. Hood Community College
Myra Bruegger, Southeastern Community College
Francis Bush, Virginia Military Institute
Rebecca Butler, Gateway Community College
June Calahan, Redlands Community College

Elizabeth Cannata, Stonehill College
John Chandler, University of Illinois—Champaign
Lawrence Chin, Golden Gate University
Carolyn Clark, St. Joseph's University
Joanne Collins, California State University—Los Angeles
Judith Cook, Grossmont College
Charles Croxford, Merced College
Jill Cunningham, Santa Fe Community College
Richard Cummings, Benedictine College
G. DiLorenzo, Gloucester County College
John Gill, Jackson State University
Michael Farina, Cerritos College
M. A. Fekrat, Georgetown University
W. L. Ferrara, Stetson University
James Franklin, Troy State University Montgomery
David Gibson, Hampden-Sydney College
James Gravel, Husson College
Linda Hadley, University of Dayton
Anita Hape, Farrant County Jr. College
Dan Hary, Southwestern Oklahoma State University
Susan Hass, Simmons College
Robert Hayes, Tennessee State University
James Hendricks, Northern Illinois University
Nancy Thorley Hill, DePaul University
Kathy Ho, Niagra University
Ronald Huntsman, Texas Lutheran University
Wayne Ingalls, University of Maine College
Martha Janis, University of Wisconsin—Waukesha
Sanford Kahn, University of Cincinnati
Christopher Kwak, Ohlone College
Michael Kulper, Santa Barbara City College
Greg Kordecki, Clayton College and State University
Robert Larson, Penn State University
Barry Lewis, Southwest Missouri State University
Joan Litton, Ferrum College
G. D. Lorenzo, Gloucester Community College
Bob Mahan, Milligan College
Leland Mansuetti, Sierra College
Laura Morgan, University of New Hampshire
Anthony Moses, Saint Anselm College
Daniel Mugavero, Lake Superior State University
Presha Neidermeyer, Union College
Eustace Phillip, Emmanuel College
Anthony Piltz, Rocky Mountain College
H. M. Pomroy, Elizabethtown College
Alan Porter, Eastern New Mexico University
Barbara Prince, Cambridge Community College
Ahmad Rahman, La Roch College
Joan Reicosky, University of Minnesota—Morris
Gary Ross, College of the Southwest
Martha Sampsell, Elmhurst College
Roger Scherser, Edison Community College
Deborah Shafer, Temple College
Ola Smith, Michigan State University
John Snyder, Florida Technical
Alice Steljes, Illinois Valley Community College
Joseph Ugras, LaSalle University
Edward Walker, University of Texas—Pan American
Frank Walker, Lee College
Robert Weprin, Lourdes College
Brent Wickham, Owens Community College
Geri Wink, University of Texas at Tyler
James Wolfson, Wilson College

We are grateful for the outstanding support from Irwin/McGraw-Hill. In particular, we would like to thank Jeff Shelstad, publisher; Stewart Mattson, sponsoring editor; Tracey Douglas, developmental editor; Rhonda Seelinger, senior marketing manager; Pat Frederickson, project manager; Heather Burbridge, senior production supervisor; Kiera Cunningham, designer; Rose Hepburn and Carol Loreth, supplements coordinators; and Keri Johnson, senior photo research coordinator. Special thanks go to Loretta Scholten who has always done a superb job of fine-tuning the text.

We would also like to thank Sheila Handy, Lafayette College; Thomas Hoar, Houston Community College; Marvin Bouillon, Iowa State University; Larry Deppe, Weber State University and Robert Dunn, Auburn University for their valuable contributions. Finally, we would like to thank Geeta Chemuduri, Angela Engebretsen, Chris McCormick, Maria Reagin, and Barbara Schnathorst for working so hard to ensure an error-free ninth edition.

We are grateful to the Institute of Certified Management Accountants for permission to use questions and/or unofficial answers from past Certificate in Management Accounting (CMA) examinations. Likewise, we thank the American Institute of Certified Public Accountants, the Society of Management Accountants of Canada, and the Chartered Institute of Management Accountants (United Kingdom) for permission to use (or to adapt) selected problems from their examinations. These problems bear the notations CMA, CPA, SMA, and CIMA respectively.

Ray H. Garrison
Eric Noreen

Brief Contents

Contents

PART THREE The Capstone: Using Cost Data in Decision Making

Chapter Thirteen Relevant Costs for Decision Making 614

Chapter Fourteen Capital Budgeting Decisions 666

Chapter One

Managerial Accounting and the Business Environment

Business Focus

"When Wendelin Wiedeking became chief of Porsche in 1992, the marque seemed destined for the junkyard. Sales that year plunged to 14,362 cars, one-fourth their 1986 peak. Losses mounted to $133 million. Most industry insiders believed that the company couldn't survive on its own . . .

"Change didn't come easily. But Wiedeking's determination overcame Porsche's stubborn traditionalism. He hired two Japanese efficiency experts . . . They immediately tackled a wasteful inventory of parts stacked on shelves all over the three-story Stuttgart factory. One of the experts handed Wiedeking a circular saw. While astounded assembly workers watched, he moved down an aisle and chopped the top half off a row of shelves.

"That was only the start . . . A revamped assembly process will turn out the new 911 [Carrera model] in just 60 hours, vs. 120 for its predecessor. Developing a new model, a process that used to drag on for seven years, now takes just three. Porsche uses 300 parts suppliers, down from nearly 1,000. And a quality-control program has helped reduce the number of defective parts by a factor of 10." As a consequence of these, and other actions, the company's sales have more than doubled to about 34,000 cars, and earnings were about $55 million in the latest fiscal year.

Source: David Woodruff, "Porsche Is Back—And Then Some," Business Week, *September 15, 1997, p. 57. Reprinted with permission of the McGraw-Hill Companies.*

Learning Objectives

After studying Chapter 1, you should be able to:

1 Describe what managers do and why they need accounting information.

2 Identify the major differences and similarities between financial and managerial accounting.

3 Explain the basic characteristics of just-in-time (JIT).

4 Describe the total quality management (TQM) approach to continuous improvement.

5 Explain the basic ideas underlying process reengineering.

6 Describe how the theory of constraints (TOC) can be used to focus improvement efforts.

7 Discuss the impact of international competition on businesses and on managerial accounting.

8 Describe the role the controller plays in a decentralized organization.

9 Explain the importance of ethical standards in an advanced market economy.

Managerial accounting is concerned with providing information to managers—that is, people *inside* an organization who direct and control its operations. In contrast, **financial accounting** is concerned with providing information to stockholders, creditors, and others who are *outside* an organization. Managerial accounting provides the essential data with which organizations are actually run. Financial accounting provides the scorecard by which a company's past performance is judged.

Because it is manager oriented, any study of managerial accounting must be preceded by some understanding of what managers do, the information managers need, and the general business environment. Accordingly, the purpose of this chapter is to briefly examine these subjects.

The Work of Management and the Need for Managerial Accounting Information

objective 1

Describe what managers do and why they need accounting information.

Every organization—large and small—has managers. Someone must be responsible for making plans, organizing resources, directing personnel, and controlling operations. This is true of the Bank of America, the Peace Corps, the University of Illinois, the Catholic Church, and the Coca-Cola Corporation, as well as the local 7-Eleven convenience store. In this chapter, we will use a particular organization—Good Vibrations, Inc.—to illustrate the work of management. What we have to say about the management of Good Vibrations, Inc., however, is very general and can be applied to virtually any organization.

Good Vibrations, Inc., runs a chain of retail outlets that sell a full range of music CDs. The chain's stores are concentrated in Pacific Rim cities such as Sydney, Singapore, Hong Kong, Beijing, Tokyo, and Vancouver, British Columbia. The company has found that the best way to generate sales, and profits, is to create an exciting shopping environment. Consequently, the company puts a great deal of effort into planning the layout and decor of its stores—which are often quite large and extend over several floors in key downtown locations. Management knows that different types of clientele are attracted to different kinds of music. The international rock section is generally decorated with bold, brightly colored graphics, and the aisles are purposely narrow to create a crowded feeling much like one would experience at a popular nightclub on Friday night. In contrast, the classical music section is wood-paneled and fully sound insulated, with the rich, spacious feeling of a country club meeting room.

Managers at Good Vibrations, Inc., like managers everywhere, carry out three major activities—*planning, directing and motivating,* and *controlling.* **Planning** involves selecting a course of action and specifying how the action will be implemented. **Directing and motivating** involves mobilizing people to carry out plans and run routine operations. **Controlling** involves ensuring that the plan is actually carried out and is appropriately modified as circumstances change. Management accounting information plays a vital role in these basic management activities—but most particularly in the planning and control functions.

Planning

The first step in planning is to identify alternatives and then to select from among the alternatives the one that does the best job of furthering the organization's objectives. The basic objective of Good Vibrations, Inc., is to earn profits for the owners of the company by providing superior service at competitive prices in as many markets as possible. To further this objective, every year top management carefully considers a range of options, or alternatives, for expanding into new geographic markets. This year management is considering opening new stores in Shanghai, Los Angeles, and Auckland.

When making this and other choices, management must balance the opportunities against the demands made on the company's resources. Management knows from bitter experience that opening a store in a major new market is a big step that cannot be taken lightly. It requires enormous amounts of time and energy from the company's most experienced, talented, and busy professionals. When the company attempted to open stores in both Beijing and Vancouver in the same year, resources were stretched too thinly. The result was that neither store opened on schedule, and operations in the rest of the company suffered. Therefore, entering new markets is planned very, very carefully.

Among other data, top management looks at the sales volumes, profit margins, and costs of the company's established stores in similar markets. These data, supplied by the management accountant, are combined with projected sales volume data at the proposed new locations to estimate the profits that would be generated by the new stores. In general, virtually all important alternatives considered by management in the planning process have some effect on revenues or costs, and management accounting data are essential in estimating those effects.

After considering all of the alternatives, Good Vibrations, Inc.'s top management decided to open a store in the burgeoning Shanghai market in the third quarter of the year, but to defer opening any other new stores to another year. As soon as this decision was made, detailed plans were drawn up for all parts of the company that would be involved in the Shanghai opening. For example, the Personnel Department's travel budget was increased, since it would be providing extensive on-the-site training to the new personnel hired in Shanghai.

As in the Personnel Department example, the plans of management are often expressed formally in **budgets,** and the term *budgeting* is applied to generally describe this part of the planning process. Budgets are usually prepared under the direction of the **controller,** who is the manager in charge of the Accounting Department. Typically, budgets are prepared annually and represent management's plans in specific, quantitative terms. In addition to a travel budget, the Personnel Department will be given goals in terms of new hires, courses taught, and detailed breakdowns of expected expenses. Similarly, the manager of each store will be given a target for sales volume, profit, expenses, pilferage losses, and employee training. These data will be collected, analyzed, and summarized for management use in the form of budgets prepared by management accountants.

Directing and Motivating

In addition to planning for the future, managers must oversee day-to-day activities and keep the organization functioning smoothly. This requires the ability to motivate and effectively direct people. Managers assign tasks to employees, arbitrate disputes, answer questions, solve on-the-spot problems, and make many small decisions that affect customers and employees. In effect, directing is that part of the managers' work that deals with the routine and the here and now. Managerial accounting data, such as daily sales reports, are often used in this type of day-to-day decision making.

Controlling

In carrying out the **control** function, managers seek to ensure that the plan is being followed. **Feedback,** which signals whether operations are on track, is the key to effective control. In sophisticated organizations this feedback is provided by detailed reports of various types. One of these reports, which compares budgeted to actual results, is called a **performance report.** Performance reports suggest where operations are not proceeding as planned and where some parts of the organization may require additional attention. For example, before the opening of the new Shanghai store in the third quarter of the year, the store's manager will be given sales volume, profit, and expense targets for the fourth quarter of the year. As the fourth quarter progresses, periodic reports will be made in which the actual sales volume, profit, and expenses are compared to the targets. If the actual results fall below the targets, top management is alerted that the Shanghai store requires more attention. Experienced personnel can be flown in to help the new manager, or top management may come to the conclusion that plans will have to be revised. As we shall see in following chapters, providing this kind of feedback to managers is one of the central purposes of managerial accounting.

The End Results of Managers' Activities

As a customer enters one of the Good Vibrations stores, the results of management's planning, directing and motivating, and control activities will be evident in the many details that make the difference between a pleasant and an irritating shopping experience. The store will be clean, fashionably decorated, and logically laid out. Featured artists' videos will be displayed on TV monitors throughout the store, and the background rock music will be loud enough to send older patrons scurrying for the classical music section. Popular CDs will be in stock, and the latest hits will be available for private listening on earphones. Specific titles will be easy to find. Regional music, such as CantoPop in Hong Kong, will be prominently featured. Checkout clerks will be alert, friendly, and efficient. In short, what the customer experiences doesn't simply happen; it is the result of the efforts of managers who must visualize and fit together the processes that are needed to get the job done.

The Planning and Control Cycle

The work of management can be summarized in a model such as the one shown in Exhibit 1–1. The model, which depicts the **planning and control cycle,** illustrates the smooth flow of management activities from planning through directing and motivating, controlling, and then back to planning again. All of these activities involve decision making, so it is depicted as the hub around which the other activities revolve.

Exhibit 1–1 The Planning and Control Cycle

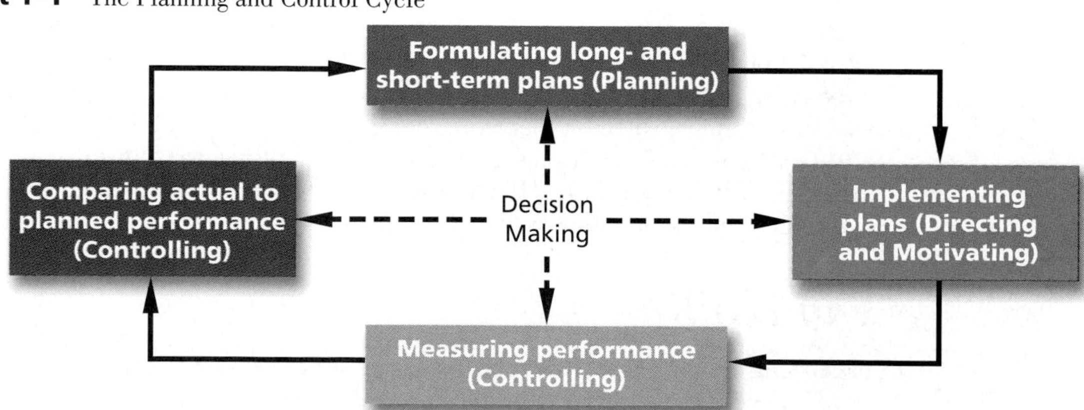

Comparison of Financial and Managerial Accounting

objective 2

Identify the major differences and similarities between financial and managerial accounting.

Financial accounting reports are prepared for the use of external parties such as shareholders and creditors, whereas managerial accounting reports are prepared for managers inside the organization. This contrast in basic orientation results in a number of major differences between financial and managerial accounting, even though both financial and managerial accounting rely on the same underlying financial data. These differences are summarized in Exhibit 1–2.

As shown in Exhibit 1–2, in addition to the difference in who the reports are prepared for, financial and managerial accounting also differ in their emphasis between the past and the future, in the type of data provided to users, and in several other ways. These differences are discussed in the following paragraphs.

Exhibit 1–2 Comparison of Financial and Managerial Accounting

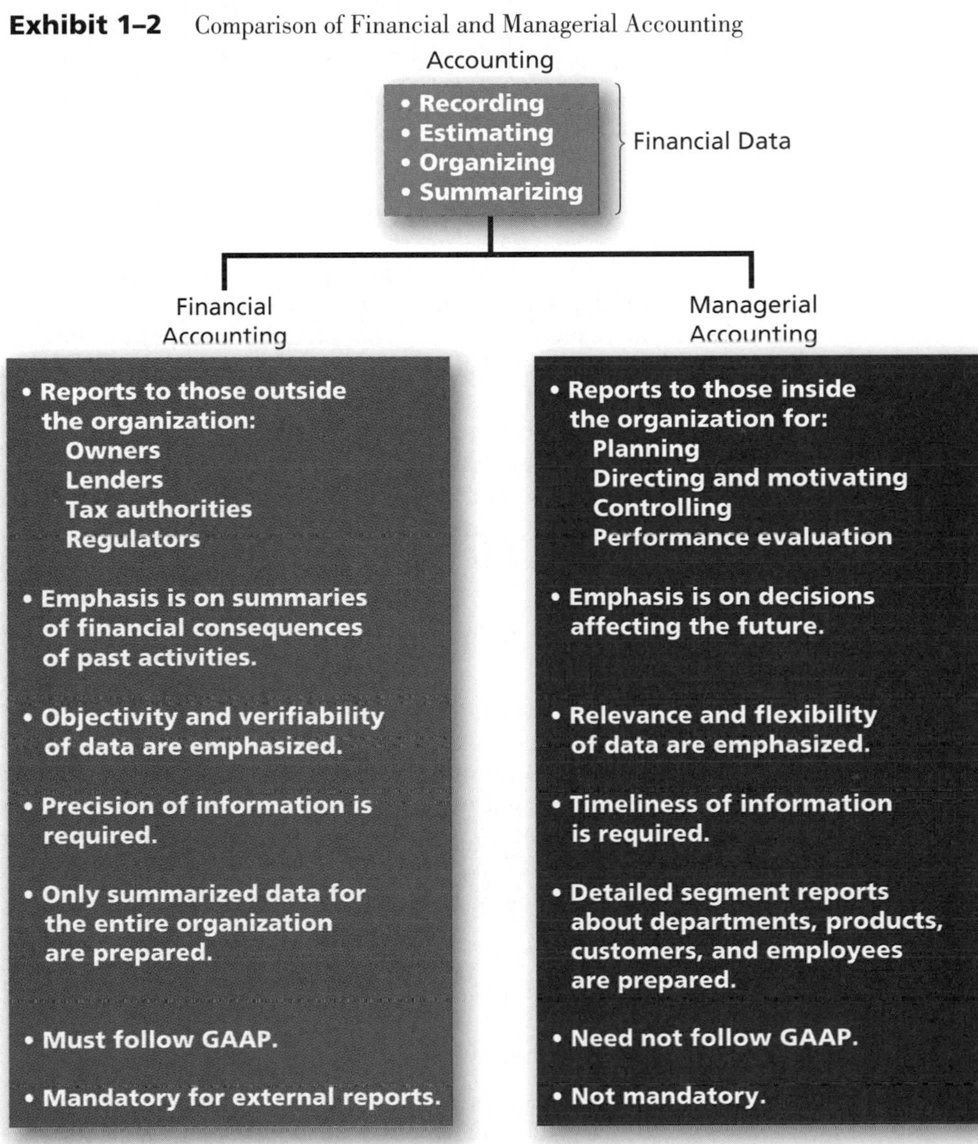

Emphasis on the Future

Since *planning* is such an important part of the manager's job, managerial accounting has a strong future orientation. In contrast, financial accounting primarily provides summaries of past financial transactions. These summaries may be useful in planning, but only to a point. The difficulty with summaries of the past is that the future is not simply a reflection of what has happened in the past. Changes are constantly taking place in economic conditions, customer needs and desires, competitive conditions, and so on. All of these changes demand that the manager's planning be based in large part on estimates of what will happen rather than on summaries of what has already happened.

Relevance and Flexibility of Data

Financial accounting data are expected to be objective and verifiable. However, for internal uses the manager wants information that is relevant even if it is not completely objective or verifiable. By relevant, we mean *appropriate for the problem at hand.* For example, it is difficult to verify estimated sales volumes for a proposed new store at Good Vibrations, Inc., but this is exactly the type of information that is most useful to managers in their decision making. The managerial accounting information system should be flexible enough to provide whatever data are relevant for a particular decision.

Less Emphasis on Precision

Timeliness is often more important than precision to managers. If a decision must be made, a manager would much rather have a good estimate now than wait a week for a more precise answer. A decision involving tens of millions of dollars does not have to be based on estimates that are precise down to the penny, or even to the dollar. Estimates that are accurate to the nearest million dollars may be precise enough to make a good decision. Since precision is costly in terms of both time and resources, managerial accounting places less emphasis on precision than does financial accounting. In addition, managerial accounting places considerable weight on nonmonetary data. For example, information about customer satisfaction is of tremendous importance even though it would be difficult to express such data in a monetary form.

Segments of an Organization

Financial accounting is primarily concerned with reporting for the company as a whole. By contrast, managerial accounting focuses much more on the parts, or **segments,** of a company. These segments may be product lines, sales territories, divisions, departments, or any other categorization of the company's activities that management finds useful. Financial accounting does require some breakdowns of revenues and costs by major segments in external reports, but this is a secondary emphasis. In managerial accounting, segment reporting is the primary emphasis.

Generally Accepted Accounting Principles (GAAP)

Financial accounting statements prepared for external users must be prepared in accordance with generally accepted accounting principles (GAAP). External users must have some assurance that the reports have been prepared in accordance with some common set of ground rules. These common ground rules enhance comparability and help reduce fraud and misrepresentation, but they do not necessarily lead to the type of reports that would be most useful in internal decision making. For example, GAAP requires that land be stated at its historical cost on financial reports. However, if management is considering moving a store to a new location and then selling the land the store currently sits on, management would like to know the current market value of the land—a vital piece of information that is ignored under GAAP.

Managerial accounting is not bound by generally accepted accounting principles. Managers set their own ground rules concerning the content and form of internal reports. The only constraint is that the expected benefits from using the information should outweigh the costs of collecting, analyzing, and summarizing the data. Nevertheless, as we shall see in subsequent chapters, it is undeniably true that financial reporting requirements have heavily influenced management accounting practice.

Managerial Accounting—Not Mandatory

Financial accounting is mandatory; that is, it must be done. Various outside parties such as the Securities and Exchange Commission (SEC) and the tax authorities require periodic financial statements. Managerial accounting, on the other hand, is not mandatory. A company is completely free to do as much or as little as it wishes. There are no regulatory bodies or other outside agencies that specify what is to be done, or, for that matter, whether anything is to be done at all. Since managerial accounting is completely optional, the important question is always, "Is the information useful?" rather than, "Is the information required?"

Expanding Role of Managerial Accounting

Managerial accounting has its roots in the industrial revolution of the 19th century. During this early period, most firms were tightly controlled by a few owner-managers who borrowed based on personal relationships and their personal assets. Since there were no external shareholders and little unsecured debt, there was little need for elaborate financial reports. In contrast, managerial accounting was relatively sophisticated and provided the essential information needed to manage the early large-scale production of textiles, steel, and other products.[1]

After the turn of the century, financial accounting requirements burgeoned because of new pressures placed on companies by capital markets, creditors, regulatory bodies, and federal taxation of income. Johnson and Kaplan state that "many firms needed to raise funds from increasingly widespread and detached suppliers of capital. To tap these vast reservoirs of outside capital, firms' managers had to supply audited financial reports. And because outside suppliers of capital relied on audited financial statements, independent accountants had a keen interest in establishing well-defined procedures for corporate financial reporting. The inventory costing procedures adopted by public accountants after the turn of the century had a profound effect on management accounting."[2]

As a consequence, for many decades, management accountants increasingly focused their efforts on ensuring that financial accounting requirements were met and financial reports were released on time. The practice of management accounting stagnated. In the early part of the century, as product lines expanded and operations became more complex, forward-looking companies such as Du Pont, General Motors,

[1] A. D. Chandler, *The Visible Hand: The Managerial Revolution in American Business* (Cambridge, MA: Harvard University Press, 1977).

[2] H. Thomas Johnson and Robert S. Kaplan, *Relevance Lost: The Rise and Fall of Management Accounting* (Boston, MA: Harvard Business School Press, 1987), pp. 129–30.

and General Electric saw a renewed need for management-oriented reports that was separate from financial reports.[3] But in most companies, management accounting practices up through the mid-1980s were largely indistinguishable from practices that were common prior to World War I. In recent years, however, new economic forces have led to many important innovations in management accounting. These new practices will be discussed in later chapters.

The Changing Business Environment

The last two decades have been a period of tremendous foment and change in the business environment. Competition in many industries has become worldwide in scope, and the pace of innovation in products and services has accelerated. This has been good news for consumers, since intensified competition has generally led to lower prices, higher quality, and more choices. However, the last two decades have been a period of wrenching change for many businesses and their employees. Many managers have learned that cherished ways of doing business don't work anymore and that major changes must be made in how organizations are managed and in how work gets done. These changes are so great that some observers view them as a second industrial revolution.

This revolution is having a profound effect on the practice of managerial accounting—as we will see throughout the rest of the text. First, however, it is necessary to have an appreciation of the ways in which organizations are transforming themselves to become more competitive. Since the early 1980s, many companies have gone through several waves of improvement programs, starting with just-in-time (JIT) and passing on to total quality management (TQM), process reengineering, and various other management programs—including in some companies the theory of constraints (TOC). When properly implemented, these improvement programs can enhance quality, reduce cost, increase output, eliminate delays in responding to customers, and ultimately increase profits. They have not, however, always been wisely implemented, and there is considerable controversy concerning the ultimate value of each of these programs. Nevertheless, the current business environment cannot be properly understood without an appreciation of what each of these approaches attempts to accomplish. Each is worthy of extended study, but we will discuss them only in the broadest terms. The details are best handled in operations management courses.

Just-in-Time (JIT)

objective 3

Explain the basic characteristics of just-in-time (JIT).

When companies use the **just-in-time (JIT)** production and inventory control system, they purchase materials and produce units only as needed to meet actual customer demand. In a JIT system, inventories are reduced to the minimum and in some cases are zero. For example, the Memory Products Division of Stolle Corporation in Sidney, Ohio, slashed its work in process inventory from 10,000 units to 250 units by using JIT techniques.[4]

The JIT approach can be used in both merchandising and manufacturing companies. It has the most profound effects, however, on the operations of manufacturing companies, which maintain three classes of inventories—*raw materials, work in process,* and *finished goods.* **Raw materials** are the materials that are used to make a product. **Work in process** inventories consist of units of product that are only partially

[3] H. Thomas Johnson, "Management Accounting in an Early Integrated Industrial: E. I. du Pont de Nemours Powder Company, 1903–1912," *Business History Review,* Summer 1975, pp. 186–87.

[4] Nabil Hassan, Herbert E. Brown, Paula M. Sanders, and Nick Koumoutzis, "Stolle Puts World Class into Memory," *Management Accounting,* January 1993, pp. 22–25.

complete and will require further work before they are ready for sale to a customer. **Finished goods** inventories consist of units of product that have been completed but have not yet been sold to customers.

Traditionally, manufacturing companies have maintained large amounts of all three kinds of inventories to act as *buffers* so that operations can proceed smoothly even if there are unanticipated disruptions. Raw materials inventories provide insurance in case suppliers are late with deliveries. Work in process inventories are maintained in case a workstation is unable to operate due to a breakdown or other reason. Finished goods inventories are maintained to accommodate unanticipated fluctuations in demand.

While these inventories provide buffers against unforeseen events, they have a cost. In addition to the money tied up in the inventory, experts argue that the presence of inventories encourages inefficient and sloppy work, results in too many defects, and dramatically increases the amount of time required to complete a product. None of this is obvious—if it were, companies would have long ago reduced their inventories. Managers at Toyota are credited with the insight that large inventories often create more problems than they solve, and Toyota pioneered the JIT approach.

THE JIT CONCEPT Under ideal conditions, a company operating a just-in-time system would purchase *only* enough materials each day to meet that day's needs. Moreover, the company would have no goods still in process at the end of the day, and all goods completed during the day would have been shipped immediately to customers. As this sequence suggests, "just-in-time" means that raw materials are received *just in time* to go into production, manufactured parts are completed *just in time* to be assembled into products, and products are completed *just in time* to be shipped to customers.

Although few companies have been able to reach this ideal, many companies have been able to reduce inventories to only a fraction of their previous levels. The result has been a substantial reduction in ordering and warehousing costs, and much more effective operations.

How does a company avoid a buildup of parts and materials at various workstations and still ensure a smooth flow of goods when JIT is in use? In a JIT environment, the flow of goods is controlled by a *pull* approach. The pull approach can be explained as follows: At the final assembly stage, a signal is sent to the preceding workstation as to the exact amount of parts and materials that will be needed *over the next few hours* to assemble products to fill customer orders, and *only* that amount of parts and materials is provided. The same signal is sent back through each preceding workstation so that a smooth flow of parts and materials is maintained with no appreciable inventory buildup at any point. Thus, all workstations respond to the pull exerted by the final assembly stage, which in turn responds to customer orders. As one worker explained, "Under a JIT system you don't produce anything, anywhere, for anybody unless they *ask* for it somewhere *down*stream. Inventories are an evil that we're taught to avoid." The pull approach is illustrated in Exhibit 1–3.

The pull approach described above can be contrasted to the *push* approach used in conventional manufacturing systems. In conventional systems, when a workstation completes its work, the partially completed goods are "pushed" forward to the next workstation regardless of whether that workstation is ready to receive them. The result is an unintentional stockpiling of partially completed goods that may not be completed for days or even weeks. This ties up funds and also results in operating inefficiencies. For one thing, it becomes very difficult to keep track of where everything is when so much is scattered all over the factory floor.

Another characteristic of conventional manufacturing systems is an emphasis on "keeping everyone busy" as an end in itself. This inevitably leads to excess inventories—particularly work in process inventories—for reasons that will be more fully explored in a later section on the theory of constraints. In JIT, the traditional emphasis

Exhibit 1–3 JIT Pull Approach to the Flow of Goods

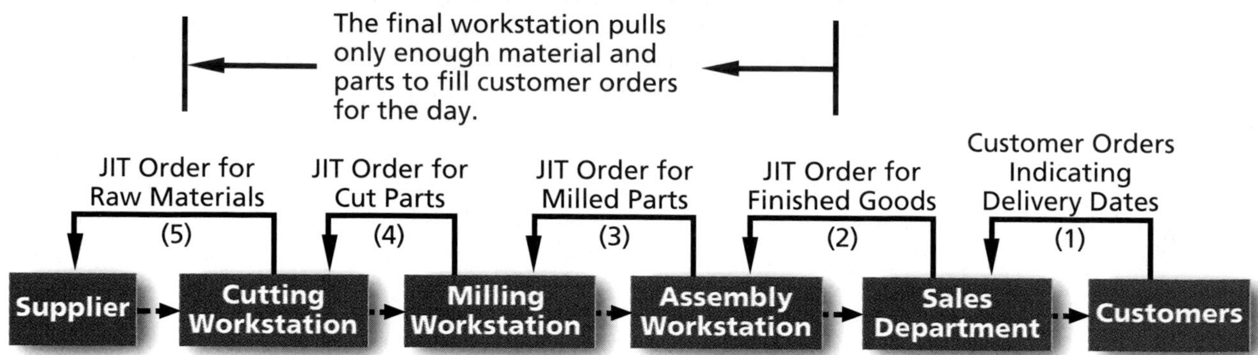

on keeping everyone busy is abandoned in favor of producing only what customers actually want—even if that means some workers are idle.

Focus on Current Practice

McDonald's new just-in-time (JIT) system called "Made for You" is "plainly an answer to the charge that made-to-order food from rivals such as Burger King and Wendy's tastes fresher." McDonald's franchisees often cook burgers and other food in batches which then sit around, losing flavor and freshness. The objective of the new system, which costs about $25,000 to install in a restaurant, is to serve each customer with the freshest food possible within 90 seconds of ordering. To design the new "Made for You" system, McDonald's carefully studied JIT manufacturing systems like Toyota's.

"The moment a Big Mac is ordered, a computer screen in the kitchen tells one of the workers to start assembling it. Meanwhile, by monitoring the flow of orders, the computer also estimates future demand, indicating when to start cooking things (like fries) that cannot be squeezed into the 90-second slot.

" 'Made for You' should help cut stock costs, and there may be some staff savings. But the proof of the pudding will, so to speak, be in the burgers."[5] ■

JIT Purchasing Any organization with inventories—retail, wholesale, distribution, service, or manufacturing—can use *JIT purchasing.* Under JIT purchasing:

1. *A company relies on a few ultrareliable suppliers.* IBM, for example, eliminated 95% of the suppliers from one of its plants, reducing the number from 640 to only 32. Rather than soliciting bids from suppliers each year and going with the low bidder, the dependable suppliers are rewarded with long-term contracts.
2. *Suppliers make frequent deliveries in small lots just before the goods are needed.* Rather than deliver a week's (or a month's) supply of an item at one time, suppliers must be willing to make deliveries as often as several times a day, and in the

[5] "McJITers," *The Economist,* April 4, 1998, p. 70.

exact quantities specified by the buyer. Undependable suppliers who do not meet delivery schedules are weeded out. Dependability is essential, since a JIT system is highly vulnerable to any interruption in supply. If a single part is unavailable, the entire assembly operation may have to be shut down. Or, in the case of a merchandising company, if the supplier allows inventories to get down to zero, customers may be turned away unsatisfied.

3. *Suppliers must deliver defect-free goods.* Because of the vulnerability of a JIT system to disruptions, defects cannot be tolerated. Indeed, suppliers must become so reliable that incoming goods do not have to be inspected.

Companies that adopt JIT purchasing often realize substantial savings from streamlined operations. Note that a company does not have to eliminate all inventories to use the JIT approach. Indeed, retail organizations must maintain some inventories or they couldn't operate. But the amount of time a product spends on a shelf or in a warehouse can be greatly reduced.

Focus on Current Practice

Dell Computer Corporation has finely tuned its just-in-time (JIT) system so that an order for a customized personal computer that comes in over the Internet at 9 A.M. can be on a delivery truck to the customer by 9 P.M. the following day. In addition, Dell's low-cost production system allows it to underprice its rivals by 10% to 15%. This combination has made Dell the envy of the personal computer industry and has enabled the company to grow at five times the industry rate.

How does the company's JIT system deliver lower costs? "While machines from Compaq and IBM can languish on dealer shelves for two months, Dell doesn't start ordering components and assembling computers until an order is booked. That may sound like no biggie, but the price of PC parts can fall rapidly in just a few months. By ordering right before assembly, Dell figures its parts, on average, are 60 days newer than those in an IBM or Compaq machine sold at the same time. That can translate into a 6% profit advantage in components alone."[6] ■

KEY ELEMENTS IN A JIT SYSTEM In addition to JIT purchasing, four key elements are usually required for the successful operation of a JIT manufacturing system. These elements include improving the plant layout, reducing the setup time needed for production runs, striving for zero defects, and developing a flexible workforce.

Improving Plant Layout To properly implement JIT, a company typically must improve the manufacturing flow lines in its plant. A *flow line* is the physical path taken by a product as it moves through the manufacturing process as it is transformed from raw materials to completed goods.

Traditionally, companies have designed their plant floors so that similar machines are grouped together. Such a functional layout results in all drill presses in one place, all lathes in another place, and so forth. This approach to plant layout requires that work in process be moved from one group of machines to another—

[6] Gary McWilliams, "Whirlwind on the Web," *Business Week,* April 7, 1997, p. 134.

Exhibit 1–4 Plant Layout in a JIT System

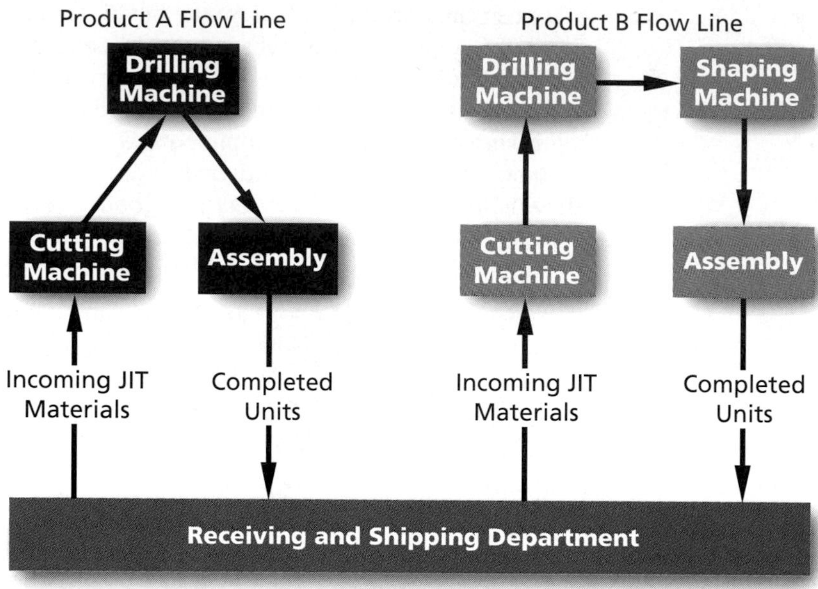

Exhibit 1–5 Example of a Manufacturing Cell

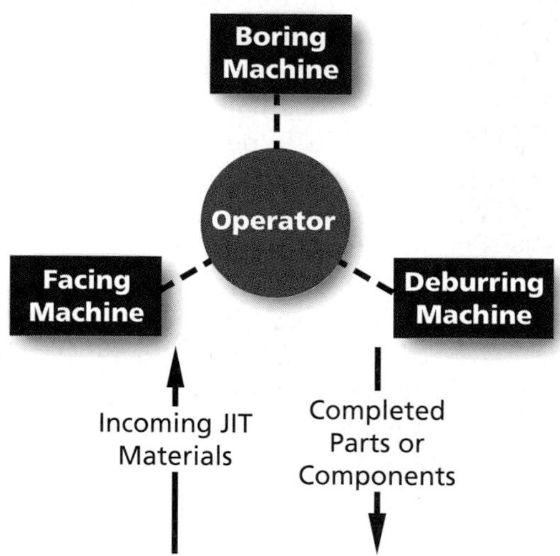

frequently across the plant or even to another building. The result is extensive material-handling costs, large work in process inventories, and unnecessary delays.

In a JIT system, all machines needed to make a particular product are often brought together in one location. This approach to plant layout creates an individual "mini" factory for each separate product, frequently referred to as a *focused factory* or as a "factory within a factory." The flow line for a product can be straight, as shown earlier in Exhibit 1–3, or it can be in a U-shaped configuration as shown in Exhibit 1–4. The key point is that all machines in a product flow line are tightly grouped together so that partially completed units are not shifted from place to place all over the factory. *Manufacturing cells* are also often part of a JIT product flow line. In a *cell,* a single worker operates several machines. An example of a cell is illustrated in Exhibit 1–5.

The focused factory approach allows workers to focus all of their efforts on a product from start to finish and minimizes handling and moving. After one large manufacturing company rearranged its plant layout and organized its products into individual flow lines, the company determined that the distance traveled by one product had been decreased from 3 miles to just 300 feet. Apart from reductions in handling, this more compact layout makes it much easier to keep track of where a particular job is in the production process.

As the accompanying Focus on Current Practice box illustrates, an improved plant layout can dramatically increase *throughput,* which is the total volume of production through a facility during a period, and it can dramatically reduce **throughput time** (also known as **cycle time**), which is the time required to make a product.

Focus on Current Practice

American Standard uses cell manufacturing to cut inventories and reduce manufacturing time. At its plant in Leeds, England, it used to take as much as three weeks to manufacture a vacuum pump and another week to process the paperwork for an order. Therefore, customers had to place orders a month in advance. "Today Leeds . . . has switched to manufacturing cells that do everything from lathing to assembly in quick sequence. The result is a breakthrough in speed. Manufacturing a pump now takes just six minutes."[7] ■

Reduced Setup Time **Setups** involve activities—such as moving materials, changing machine settings, setting up equipment, and running tests—that must be performed whenever production is switched over from making one type of item to another. For example, it may not be a simple matter to switch over from making ½-inch brass screws to making ¾-inch brass screws on a manually controlled milling machine. Many preparatory steps must be performed, and these steps can take hours. Because of the time and expense involved in such setups, many managers believe setups should be avoided and therefore items should be produced in large batches. For example, one batch of 400 units requires only one setup, whereas four batches of 100 units each would require four setups. The problem with big batches is that they create large amounts of inventory that must wait for days, weeks, or even months before further processing at the next workstation or before they are sold

One advantage of a dedicated flow line, such as the one illustrated in Exhibit 1–4, is that it requires fewer setups. If equipment is dedicated to a single product, setups are largely eliminated and the product can be produced in any batch size desired. Even when dedicated flow lines are not used, it is often possible to slash setup time by using techniques such as *single-minute-exchange-of-dies.* A die is a device used for cutting out, forming, or stamping material. For example, a die is used to produce the stamped metal door panels on an automobile. A die must be changed when it wears out or when production is switched to a different product. This changeover can be time-consuming. The goal with *single-minute-exchange-of-dies* is to reduce the amount of time required to change a die to a minute or less. This can be done by simple techniques such as doing as much of the changeover work in advance as possible rather than waiting until production is shut down.[8] When such techniques are followed, batch sizes can be very small.

---

[7] Shawn Tully, "Raiding a Company's Hidden Cash," *Fortune,* August 22, 1994, pp. 82–87.

[8] Shigeo Shingo and Alan Robinson, *Modern Approaches to Manufacturing Improvement: The Shingo System* (Cambridge, MA: Productivity Press, 1990).

Smaller batches reduce the level of inventories, make it easier to respond quickly to the market, reduce cycle times, and generally make it much easier to spot manufacturing problems before they result in a large number of defective units.

Zero Defects and JIT Defective units create big problems in a JIT environment. If a completed order contains a defective unit, the company must ship the order with less than the promised quantity or it must restart the whole production process to make just one unit. At minimum, this creates a delay in shipping the order and may generate a ripple effect that delays other orders. For this and other reasons, defects cannot be tolerated in a JIT system. Companies that are deeply involved in JIT tend to become zealously committed to a goal of *zero defects.* Even though it may be next to impossible to attain the zero defect goal, companies have found that they can come very close. For example, Motorola, Allied Signal, and many other companies now measure defects in terms of the number of defects per *million* units of product.

In a traditional company, parts and materials are inspected for defects when they are received from suppliers, and quality inspectors inspect units as they progress along the production line. In a JIT system, the company's suppliers are responsible for the quality of incoming parts and materials. And instead of using quality inspectors, the company's production workers are directly responsible for spotting defective units. A worker who discovers a defect is supposed to punch an alarm button that stops the production flow line and sets off flashing lights. Supervisors and other workers then descend on the workstation to determine the cause of the defect and correct it before any further defective units are produced. This procedure ensures that problems are quickly identified and corrected, but it does require that defects are rare—otherwise there would be constant disruptions to the production process.

Flexible Workforce Workers on a JIT line must be multiskilled and flexible. Workers are often expected to operate all of the equipment on a JIT product flow line. Moreover, workers are expected to perform minor repairs and do maintenance work when they would otherwise be idle. In contrast, on a conventional assembly line a worker performs a single task all the time every day and all maintenance work is done by a specialized maintenance crew.

BENEFITS OF A JIT SYSTEM Many companies—large and small—have employed JIT with great success. Among the major companies using JIT are Bose, Goodyear, Westinghouse, General Motors, Hughes Aircraft, Ford Motor Company, Black and Decker, Chrysler, Borg-Warner, John Deere, Xerox, Tektronix, and Intel. The main benefits of JIT are the following:

1. Working capital is bolstered by the recovery of funds that were tied up in inventories.
2. Areas previously used to store inventories are made available for other, more productive uses.
3. Throughput time is reduced, resulting in greater potential output and quicker response to customers.
4. Defect rates are reduced, resulting in less waste and greater customer satisfaction.

As a result of benefits such as those cited above, more companies are embracing JIT each year. Most companies find, however, that simply reducing inventories is not enough. To remain competitive in an ever changing and ever more competitive business environment, companies must strive for *continuous improvement.*

Focus on Current Practice

Just-in-time (JIT) systems have many advantages, but they *are* vulnerable to unexpected disruptions in supply. A production line can quickly come to a halt if essential parts are unavailable. Toyota, the developer of JIT, found this out the hard way. One Saturday, a fire at Aisin Seiki Company's plant in Aichi Prefecture stopped the delivery of all brake parts to Toyota. By Tuesday, Toyota had to close down all of its Japanese assembly lines. By the time the supply of brake parts had been restored, Toyota had lost an estimated $15 billion in sales.[9] ■

Total Quality Management (TQM)

objective 4

Describe the total quality management (TQM) approach to continuous improvement.

The most popular approach to continuous improvement is known as *total quality management.* There are two major characteristics of **total quality management (TQM):** (1) a focus on serving customers and (2) systematic problem solving using teams made up of front-line workers. A variety of specific tools are available to aid teams in their problem solving. One of these tools, **benchmarking,** involves studying organizations that are among the best in the world at performing a particular task. For example, when Xerox wanted to improve its procedures for filling customer orders, it studied how the mail-order company L. L. Bean processes its customer orders.

THE PLAN-DO-CHECK-ACT CYCLE Perhaps the most important and pervasive TQM problem-solving tool is the *plan-do-check-act (PDCA) cycle,* which is also referred to as the Deming Wheel.[10] The **plan-do-check-act cycle** is a systematic, fact-based approach to continuous improvement. The basic elements of the PDCA cycle are illustrated in Exhibit 1–6. The PDCA cycle applies the scientific method to problem solving. In the Plan phase, the problem-solving team analyzes data to identify possible causes for the problem and then proposes a solution. In the Do phase, an experiment is conducted. In the Check phase, the results of the experiment are analyzed. And in the Act phase, if the results of the experiment are favorable, the plan is implemented. If the results of the experiment are not favorable, the team goes back to the original data and starts all over again.

AN EXAMPLE OF TQM IN PRACTICE Sterling Chemicals, Inc., a producer of basic industrial chemicals, provides a good example of the use of TQM.[11] Among many other problems, the company had been plagued by pump failures. In one year, a particular type of pump had failed 22 times at an average cost of about $10,000 per failure. The company first tried to solve the problem using a traditional, non-TQM approach. A committee of "experts"—in this case engineers and manufacturing

---

[9] "Toyota to Recalibrate 'Just-in-Time,' " *International Herald Tribune,* February 8, 1997, p. 9.

[10] Dr. W. Edwards Deming, a pioneer in TQM, introduced many of the elements of TQM to Japanese industry after World War II. TQM was further refined and developed at Japanese companies such as Toyota.

[11] The information about Sterling Chemicals in this section was taken from Karen Hopper Wruck and Michael C. Jensen, "Science, Specific Knowledge, and Total Quality Management," *Journal of Accounting and Economics* 18 (1994), pp. 247–87. The quotations are from pages 260 and 261 of this article and are used with permission.

Exhibit 1–6 The Plan-Do-Check-Act Cycle

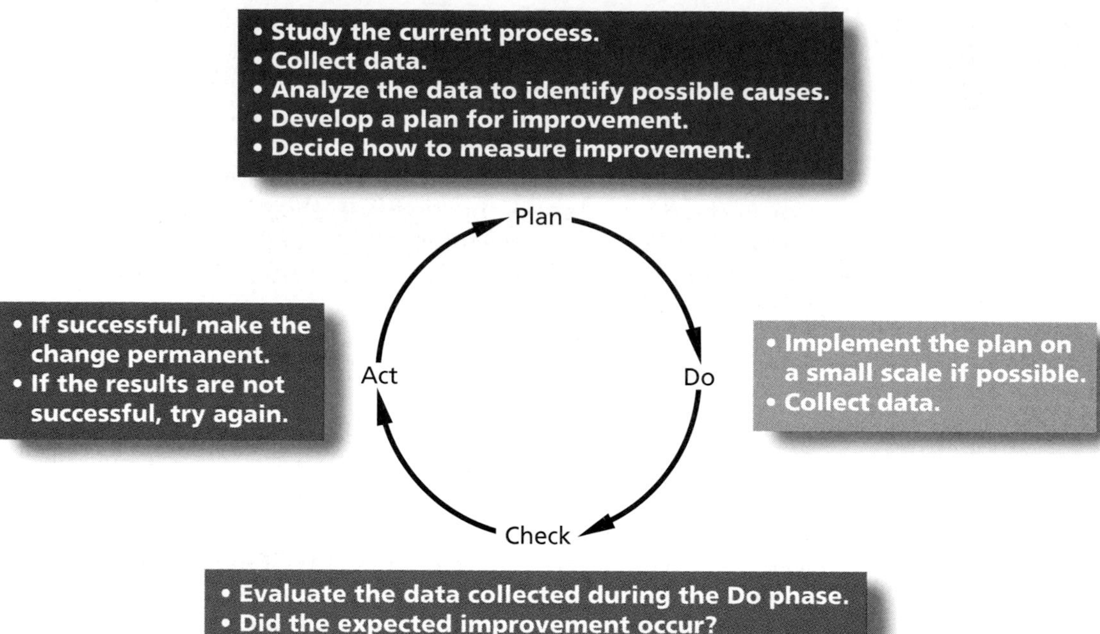

supervisors—was appointed to solve the problem. A manager at Sterling Chemicals describes the results:

> This team immediately concluded that each of the 22 pump failures . . . was due to a special or one-of-a-kind cause. There was some finger pointing by team members trying to assign blame. Maintenance engineers claimed that production personnel didn't know how to operate the pumps, and production supervisors blamed maintenance people for poor repair work.

One year later, a TQM team was formed to tackle the same pump failure problem. The team consisted primarily of hourly workers with hands-on experience working with the pumps. A Sterling Chemicals manager describes what happened:

> Based on their knowledge and the data they had collected, the team brainstormed and listed 57 theories that potentially explained the high pump failure rates. The team reviewed and edited the brainstorming list, testing each theory against the data. Through this process, they reduced the brainstorming list to four potential causes of failure: i) the pump seal installation procedure, ii) pump suction pressure, iii) excessive pump vibration, and iv) missing or broken equipment upstream from the pump.
>
> They then experimented to determine which of these causes were important determinants of pump failure. Testing the pump suction theory rejected it as a cause of failure. The broken or missing equipment theory was eliminated through inspection. Since testing the two remaining theories required making changes and observing the results of those changes over time, the team developed recommendations to address [them] both . . . The recommendations were implemented . . . Since then we have had no pump failures.

Notice how the plan-do-check-act cycle was used to solve this pump failure problem. Instead of bickering over who was responsible for the problem, the team began by collecting data. They then hypothesized a number of possible causes for the problem, and these hypotheses were checked against the data. Perhaps the most important feature of TQM is that "it improves productivity by encouraging the use of science in decision-making and discouraging counter-productive defensive behavior."[12]

---

[12] Ibid., p. 247.

TQM IS WIDELY USED Thousands of organizations have been involved in TQM and similar programs. Some of the more well-known companies are American Express, AT&T, Cadillac Motor Car, Corning, Dun & Bradstreet, Ericsson of Sweden, Federal Express, GTE Directories, First National Bank of Chicago, Florida Power and Light, General Electric, Hospital Corporation of America, IBM, Johnson & Johnson, KLM Royal Dutch Airlines, LTV, 3M, Milliken & Company, Motorola, Northern Telecom of Canada, Phillips of the Netherlands, Ritz Carlton Hotel, Texas Instruments, Westinghouse Electric, and Xerox. As this list illustrates, TQM is international in scope and is not confined to manufacturing. Indeed, a survey by the American Hospital Association of 3,300 hospitals found that 69% have launched quality-improvement programs. For example, Intermountain Healthcare's LDS Hospital in Salt Lake City is using total quality management techniques to reduce infection rates among surgery patients and the toxic side effects of chemotherapy.[13]

An important element of TQM is its focus on the customer. The accounting and consulting firm KPMG Peat Marwick periodically surveys its customers' satisfaction with its services. The firm's CEO points out that it costs four times as much to gain a new customer as to keep an old customer, and the most satisfied customers are generally the most profitable customers for the firm. "For each complaint that you hear, there are fifty you don't hear. If you don't monitor clients' satisfaction, you may find out about their dissatisfaction as they walk out the door."[14]

In sum, TQM provides tools and techniques for continuous improvement based on facts and analysis; and if properly implemented, it avoids counterproductive organizational infighting.

Focus on Current Practice

TQM is not just a big company phenomenon. Penril DataComm is a Maryland designer and producer of data communications equipment. Before embarking on TQM, defect rates were so high that the company was reworking or scrapping one-third of everything it made. Applying TQM techniques resulted in an 81% decrease in defects, an 83% decrease in failures in the first three months of use, and a 73% decrease in first-year warranty repairs. TQM is credited with taking the company "from the brink of financial disaster" to excellent financial health.[15] ■

Focus on Current Practice

Many total quality management companies insist that their suppliers also embark on TQM. McDevitt Street Bovis, a construction services firm based in Charlotte, North Carolina, was forced to adopt TQM by a major client. Despite initial ignorance of TQM, the firm quickly developed its own version of TQM and applied it to more than 40 projects—with very good

[13] Ron Wilson, "Excising Waste: Health-Care Providers Try Industrial Tactics in U.S. to Cut Costs," *The Wall Street Journal Europe,* November 10, 1993, p. 1, 8.

[14] Jon C. Madonna, "A Service Company Measures, Monitors and Improves Quality," *Leadership and Empowerment for Total Quality,* The Conference Board Report No. 992 (New York, 1992), pp. 9–11.

[15] "Poor Quality Nearly Short Circuits Electronics Company," *Productivity,* February 1993, pp. 1–3.

results. One specific benefit is that the firm has not had a single construction-related lawsuit after adopting TQM, and as a consequence legal expenses have been cut in half. And every client whose project was managed using TQM has awarded the company additional business.[16] ■

Process Reengineering

objective 5

Explain the basic ideas underlying process reengineering.

Process reengineering is a more radical approach to improvement than TQM. Instead of tweaking the existing system in a series of incremental improvements, in **process reengineering** a *business process* is diagrammed in detail, questioned, and then completely redesigned in order to eliminate unnecessary steps, to reduce opportunities for errors, and to reduce costs. A **business process** is any series of steps that are followed in order to carry out some task in a business. For example, the steps followed to make a large pineapple and Canadian bacon pizza at Godfather's Pizza are a business process. The steps followed by your bank when you deposit a check are a business process. While process reengineering is similar in some respects to TQM, its proponents view it as a more sweeping approach to change. One difference is that while TQM emphasizes a team approach involving people who work directly in the processes, process reengineering is more likely to be imposed from above and to use outside consultants.

Process reengineering focuses on *simplification* and *elimination of wasted effort.* A central idea of process reengineering is that *all activities that do not add value to a product or service should be eliminated.* Activities that do not add value to a product or service that customers are willing to pay for are known as **non-value-added activities.** For example, moving large batches of work in process from one workstation to another is a non-value-added activity that can be eliminated by redesigning the factory layout as discussed earlier in the section on JIT. To some degree, JIT involves process reengineering as does TQM. These management approaches often overlap.[17]

Process reengineering has been used by many companies to deal with a wide variety of problems. For example, the EMI Records Group was having difficulty filling orders for its most popular CDs. Retailers and recording stars were rebelling—it took the company as much as 20 days to deliver a big order for a hit CD, and then nearly 20% of the order would be missing. Small, incremental improvements would not have been adequate, so the company reengineered its entire distribution process with dramatic effects on on-time delivery and order fill rates.[18] Another example is provided by Reynolds & Reynolds Co. of Dayton, Ohio, which produces business forms. Filling an order for a customer used to take 90 separate steps. By reengineering, the number of steps was slashed to 20 and the time required to fill an order was cut from three weeks to one week.[19] Massachusetts General Hospital is even using process reengineering to standardize and improve surgical procedures.[20]

---

[16] Luther P. Cochrane, "Not Just Another Quality Snow Job," *The Wall Street Journal,* May 24, 1993, p. A10.

[17] Activity-based costing and activity-based management, both of which are discussed in Chapter 8, can be helpful in identifying areas in the company that could benefit from process reengineering.

[18] Glenn Rifkin, "EMI: Technology Brings the Music Giant a Whole New Spin," *Forbes ASAP,* February 27, 1995, pp. 32–38.

[19] William M. Bulkeley, "Pushing the Pace: The Latest Big Thing at Many Companies Is Speed, Speed, Speed," *The Wall Street Journal,* December 23, 1994, pp. A1, A7.

[20] George Anders, "Required Surgery: Health Plans Force Even Elite Hospitals to Cut Costs Sharply," *The Wall Street Journal,* March 8, 1994, pp. A1, A6.

AN EXAMPLE OF PROCESS REENGINEERING Racing Strollers, Inc., of Yakima, Washington, provides an interesting illustration of process reengineering at work. The company originated the three-wheeled stroller for joggers in 1984.[21] While the company was still the market leader, there was growing concern about losing ground to competitors—some of whom were selling strollers for half the price charged by Racing Strollers. Mary Baechler, the president of Racing Strollers, felt that a radical approach such as process reengineering was required to keep Racing Strollers competitive.

Mary Baechler describes the results of using process reengineering on a very simple task—receiving orders over the fax machine:

> Take faxes. Pretty simple, right? Not at our place! We had 15 steps just to get a fax from the fax machine to the computers, where an order would be entered into our accounting program. (Laugh all you want, but you probably do something similar at your place.) A fax would come in. We'd log it into a fax book. (Someone once told us to do that for legal reasons.) A copy of each fax would be saved for me. (Someone once told me I should glance at all faxes.) It all added up to those 15 steps. Only after a lot of work did we reduce the number to 4.
>
> That was just one area, and it's typical of what we found throughout the company. If you were to look at all those steps for a fax, every one originally had a purpose. The process was very much like a tribal superstition, though, since the original reason for each step had disappeared long ago. What was even worse was that no one could remember who started many of the steps. I had no idea why we were doing them, and everybody else thought they were what I wanted done!

Note that Racing Strollers is a comparatively young company. The situation is typically much worse at older companies—a step may have been introduced into a process many years ago to handle a problem that has long since disappeared and no one can remember.

THE PROBLEM OF EMPLOYEE MORALE A recurrent problem in process reengineering is employee resistance. The cause of much of this resistance is the fear that people may lose their jobs. Workers reason that if process reengineering succeeds in eliminating non-value-added activities, there will be less work to do and management may be tempted to reduce the payroll. Process reengineering, if carried out insensitively and without regard to such fears, can undermine morale and will ultimately fail to improve the bottom line (i.e., profits). As with other improvement projects, employees must be convinced that the end result of the improvement will be more secure, rather than less secure, jobs. Real improvement can have this effect if management uses the improvement to generate more business rather than to cut the workforce. If by improving processes the company is able to produce a better product at lower cost, the company will have the competitive strength to prosper. And a prosperous company is a much more secure employer than a company that is in trouble.

Focus on Current Practice

Process reengineering that is imposed from above and that results in disruptions and layoffs can lead to cynicism. Eileen Shapiro, a management consultant, says that "reengineering as often implemented can erode the bonds of trust that employees have toward their employers. Nevertheless,

[21] The information in this section about Racing Strollers, Inc., was taken from an article by Mary Baechler. Reprinted with permission, *Inc.* magazine, May 1995. Copyright 1995 by Goldhirsh Group, Inc., 38 Commercial Wharf, Boston, MA 02110.

many companies reengineer at the same time that they issue mission statements proclaiming, 'Our employees are our most important asset,' or launch new initiatives to increase 'employee involvement.' As one senior executive, a veteran of reengineering, muttered recently while listening to his boss give a glowing speech about working conditions at their organization, 'I sure wish I worked for the company he is describing.' "[22] ■

The Theory of Constraints (TOC)

objective 6

Describe how the theory of constraints (TOC) can be used to focus improvement efforts.

A **constraint** is anything that prevents you from getting more of what you want. Every individual and every organization faces at least one constraint, so it is not difficult to find examples of constraints. You may not have enough time to study thoroughly for every subject *and* to go out with your friends on the weekend, so time is your constraint. United Airlines has only a limited number of loading gates available at its busy O'Hare hub, so its constraint is loading gates. Vail Resorts has only a limited amount of land to develop as homesites and commercial lots at its ski areas, so its constraint is land.

Since a constraint prevents you from getting more of what you want, the **theory of constraints (TOC)** maintains that effectively managing the constraint is a key to success. For example, United Airlines should concentrate on quickly turning around its aircraft on the ground so they do not tie up precious gates. Delays on the ground decrease the number of flights that can be flown out of O'Hare and therefore result in lost business for United.

AN EXAMPLE OF TOC A simple example will be used to illustrate the role of a constraint. ProSport Equipment, Inc., manufactures aluminum tennis rackets on the production flow line that is sketched in Exhibit 1–7. Each workstation has a particular capacity that, in this case, may be stated in terms of the maximum number of rackets processed in a week. For example, the aluminum extruding workstation can extrude enough aluminum each week to build as many as 2,500 tennis rackets.

Suppose the company could sell as many as 2,100 rackets each week. All of the workstations except frame assembly and stringing are capable of producing this many rackets in a week. The capacity in stringing is 2,000 rackets per week, but since the capacity in frame assembly is only 1,800 rackets per week, no more than 1,800 complete tennis rackets can be processed per week. The capacity of frame assembly is the constraint, or *bottleneck.* The capacity (and rate of output) of the entire operation can be no more than the capacity of the bottleneck, which is 1,800 rackets per week. Therefore, if the company wants to increase its output, it must increase the capacity of this particular workstation.[23]

There are several ways the capacity of the constraint can be increased. These will be discussed in detail in Chapter 13. As one example, the capacity of the frame assembly can be increased by improving the frame assembly process so that it requires less time. Thus, TQM and process reengineering efforts can be leveraged by targeting the constraint.

---

[22] Eileen Shapiro, "Theories Don't Pull Companies in Conflicting Directions. Managers Do," *Harvard Business Review,* March–April 1997, p. 142.

[23] If demand was less than 1,800 tennis rackets per week, there would not be a production constraint. However, there would still be a constraint of some type. For example, the company's constraint might be a poor logistical system that limits how many tennis rackets can be distributed in a timely fashion to retailers. All businesses that are organized to make a profit face at least one constraint.

Exhibit 1–7 A Flowchart of an Aluminum Tennis Racket Production Line

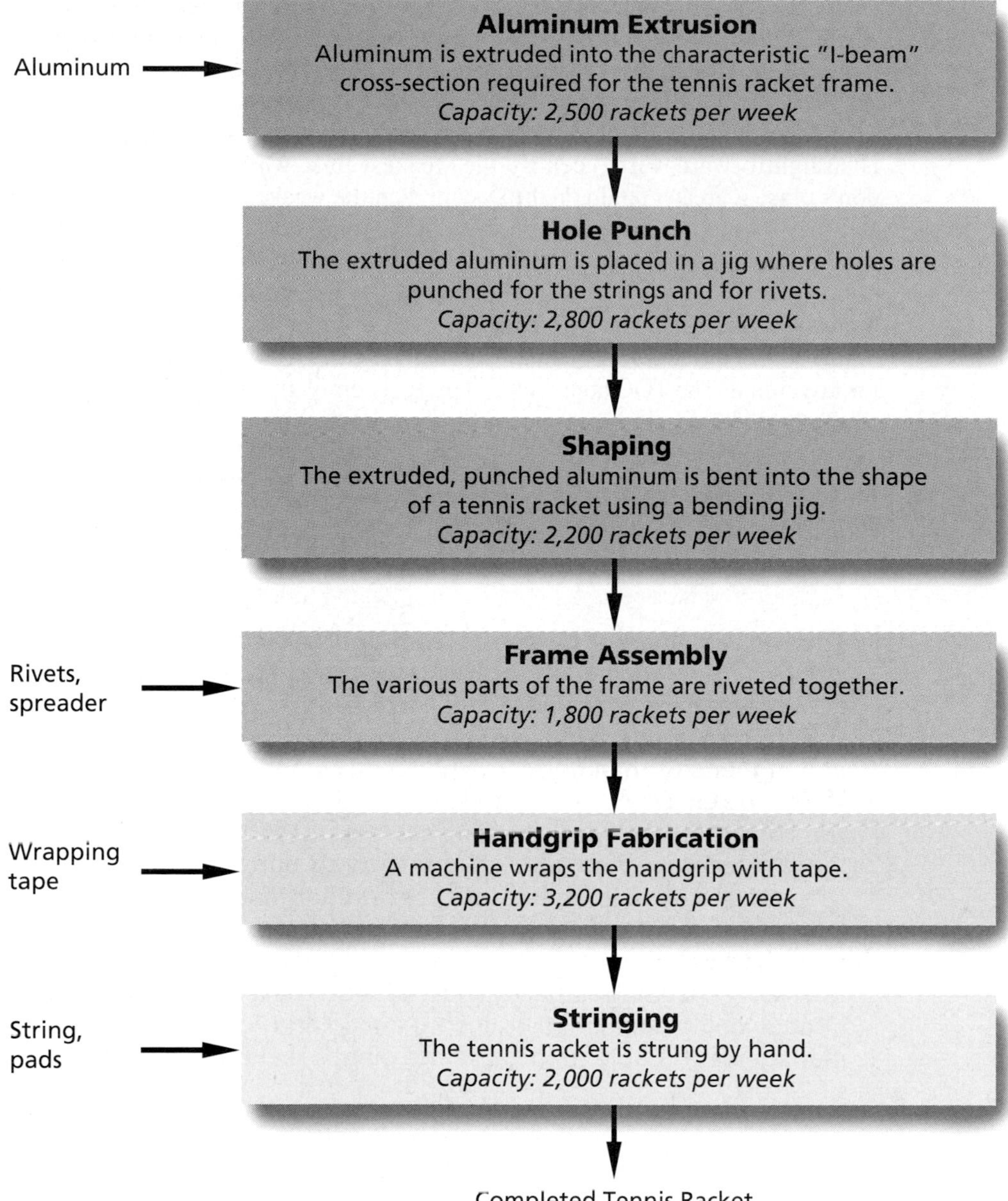

Consider what would happen if process reengineering were used to improve one of the *nonconstraints.* Suppose, for example, that the handgrip fabrication process is improved so that it requires only half as much time. Will this increase profits? The answer is "Probably not." Handgrip fabrication already has plenty of excess capacity—it is capable of processing 3,200 rackets per week, but demand is only 1,900 rackets. Speeding up this process will simply create more excess capacity. Unless resources can now be shifted from handgrip fabrication to the constraint area (frame assembly) or unless spending can be cut in the handgrip fabrication work center, there will be no increase in profits. In contrast, if the processing time were cut in half in frame assembly, which is the constraint, the company could produce and sell more tennis rackets. The margins on the additional tennis rackets would go straight to the bottom line as additional profits.

TOC AND CONTINUOUS IMPROVEMENT In TOC, an analogy is often drawn between a business process—such as the tennis racket production line—and a chain. If you want to increase the strength of a chain, what is the most effective way to do this? Should you concentrate your efforts on strengthening the strongest link, the largest link, all the links, or the weakest link? Clearly, focusing effort on the weakest link will bring the biggest benefit.

Continuing with this analogy, the procedure to follow in strengthening the chain is straightforward. First, identify the weakest link, which is the constraint. Second, don't place a greater strain on the system than the weakest link can handle. Third, concentrate improvement efforts on strengthening the weakest link. Fourth, if the improvement efforts are successful, eventually the weakest link will improve to the point where it is no longer the weakest link. At this point, the new weakest link (i.e., the new constraint) must be identified, and improvement efforts must be shifted over to that link. This simple sequential process provides a powerful strategy for continuous improvement. The TOC approach is a perfect complement to TQM and process reengineering—it focuses improvement efforts where they are likely to be most effective.

Focus on Current Practice

The Lessines plant of Baxter International makes medical products such as sterile bags. Management of the plant is acutely aware of the necessity to actively manage its constraints. For example, when materials are a constraint, management may go to a secondary vendor and purchase materials at a higher cost than normal. When a machine is the constraint, a weekend shift is often added on the machine. If a particular machine is chronically the constraint and management has exhausted the possibilities of using it more effectively, then additional capacity is purchased. For example, when the constraint was the plastic extruding machines, a new extruding machine was ordered. However, even before the machine arrived, management had determined that the constraint would shift to the blenders once the new extruding capacity was added. Therefore, a new blender was already being planned. By thinking ahead and focusing on the constraints, management is able to increase the plant's real capacity at the lowest possible cost.[24] ■

International Competition

objective 7

Discuss the impact of international competition on businesses and on managerial accounting.

Over the last several decades, competition has become worldwide in many industries. This has been caused by reductions in tariffs, quotas, and other barriers to free trade; improvements in global transportation systems; and increasing sophistication in international markets. These factors work together to reduce the costs of conducting international trade and make it possible for foreign companies to compete on a more equal footing with local firms.

[24] Eric Noreen, Debra Smith, and James Mackey, *The Theory of Constraints and Its Implications for Management Accounting* (Montvale, NJ: The IMA Foundation for Applied Research, Inc., 1995), p. 67.

The movement toward freer trade has been most dramatic in the European Union (EU). The EU has grown from a very small free-trade zone involving a few basic commodities such as coal and steel in the late 1950s to a free-trade zone of over a dozen European nations involving almost unlimited movement of goods and services across national borders. This vast, largely unified market has a population of over 375 million, as compared with over 268 million in the United States and about 125 million in Japan. Many of the countries in the EU are adopting a common currency called the euro, which should make trading within the EU even easier. The euro will fully replace traditional currencies such as the French franc, the German mark, and the Italian lira in July 2002. The relatively new North American Free Trade Association (NAFTA) trading block, which consists of Canada, the United States, and Mexico, has a combined population in excess of 395 million.

Such reductions in trade barriers have made it easier for agile and aggressive companies to expand outside of their home markets. As a result, very few firms can afford to be complacent. A company may be very successful today in its local market relative to its local competitors, but tomorrow the competition may come from halfway around the globe. As a matter of survival, even firms that are presently doing very well in their home markets must become world-class competitors. On the bright side, the freer international movement of goods and services presents tremendous export opportunities for those companies that can transform themselves into world-class competitors. And, from the standpoint of consumers, heightened competition promises an even greater variety of goods, at higher quality and lower prices.

What are the implications for managerial accounting of increased global competition? It would be very difficult for a firm to become world-class if it plans, directs, and controls its operations and makes decisions using a second-class management accounting system. An excellent management accounting system will not by itself guarantee success, but a poor management accounting system can stymie the best efforts of people in an organization to make the firm truly competitive.

Throughout this text we will highlight the differences between obsolete management accounting systems that get in the way of success and well-designed management accounting systems that can enhance a firm's performance. It is noteworthy that elements of well-designed management accounting systems have originated in many countries. More and more, managerial accounting has become a discipline that is worldwide in scope.

Focus on Current Practice

Global competition sometimes comes from unexpected sources. Companies in the former Soviet bloc in Central and Eastern Europe are rapidly raising the quality of their products to Western standards and are beginning to provide stiff competition. The Hungarian company Petofi Printing & Packaging Co., a maker of cardboard boxes, wrappers, and other containers, provides a good example. "Only a few years ago, Petofi's employees drank beer at work. Flies buzzing in open windows got stuck in the paint and pressed into the paperboard. Containers were delivered in the wrong colors and sizes." Under the Communist system, the company's customers didn't dare complain, since there was no other source for their packaging needs.

The company was privatized after the fall of the Soviet system, and the company "began overhauling itself, leapfrogging Western companies with state-of-the-art machinery. It whipped its workforce into shape with a combination of inducements and threats." Now, most of its products are exported. PepsiCo, for example, buys Petofi wrappers for Cheetos and Ruffles snacks and claims that Petofi's quality compares very favorably with Western suppliers. PepsiCo's buyer states, "They have filled the gap between competitive quality and best cost."[25] ■

Organizational Structure

Since organizations are made up of people, management must accomplish its objectives by working *through* people. Presidents of companies like Good Vibrations, Inc., could not possibly execute all of their company's strategies alone; they must rely on other people. This is done by creating an organizational structure that permits *decentralization* of management responsibilities.

Decentralization

Decentralization is the delegation of decision-making authority throughout an organization by providing managers at various operating levels with the authority to make decisions relating to their area of responsibility. Some organizations are more decentralized than others. Because of Good Vibrations, Inc.'s geographic dispersion and the peculiarities of local markets, the company is highly decentralized.

Good Vibrations, Inc.'s president (also called chief executive officer or CEO) sets the broad strategy for the company and makes major strategic decisions such as opening stores in new markets, but much of the remaining decision-making authority is delegated to managers on various levels throughout the organization. These levels are as follows: The company has a number of retail stores, each of which has a store manager as well as a separate manager for each section such as international rock and classical/jazz. In addition, the company has support departments such as a central Purchasing Department and a Personnel Department. The organizational structure of the company is depicted in Exhibit 1–8.

The arrangement of boxes shown in Exhibit 1–8 is called an **organization chart.** The purpose of an organization chart is to show how responsibility has been divided among managers and to show formal lines of reporting and communication, or *chain of command.* Each box depicts an area of management responsibility, and the lines between the boxes show the lines of formal authority between managers. The chart tells us, for example, that the store managers are responsible to the operations vice president. In turn, the latter is responsible to the company president, who in turn is responsible to the board of directors. Following the lines of authority and communication on the organization chart, we can see that the manager of the Hong Kong store would ordinarily report to the operations vice president rather than directly to the president of the company.

Informal relationships and channels of communication often develop outside the formal reporting relationships on the organization chart as a result of personal contacts between managers. The informal structure does not appear on the organization chart, but it is often vital to effective operations.

[25] Dana Milbank, "New Competitor: East Europe's Industry Is Raising Its Quality and Taking on West," *The Wall Street Journal,* September 21, 1994, pp. A1, A7.

Exhibit 1–8 Organization Chart, Good Vibrations, Inc.

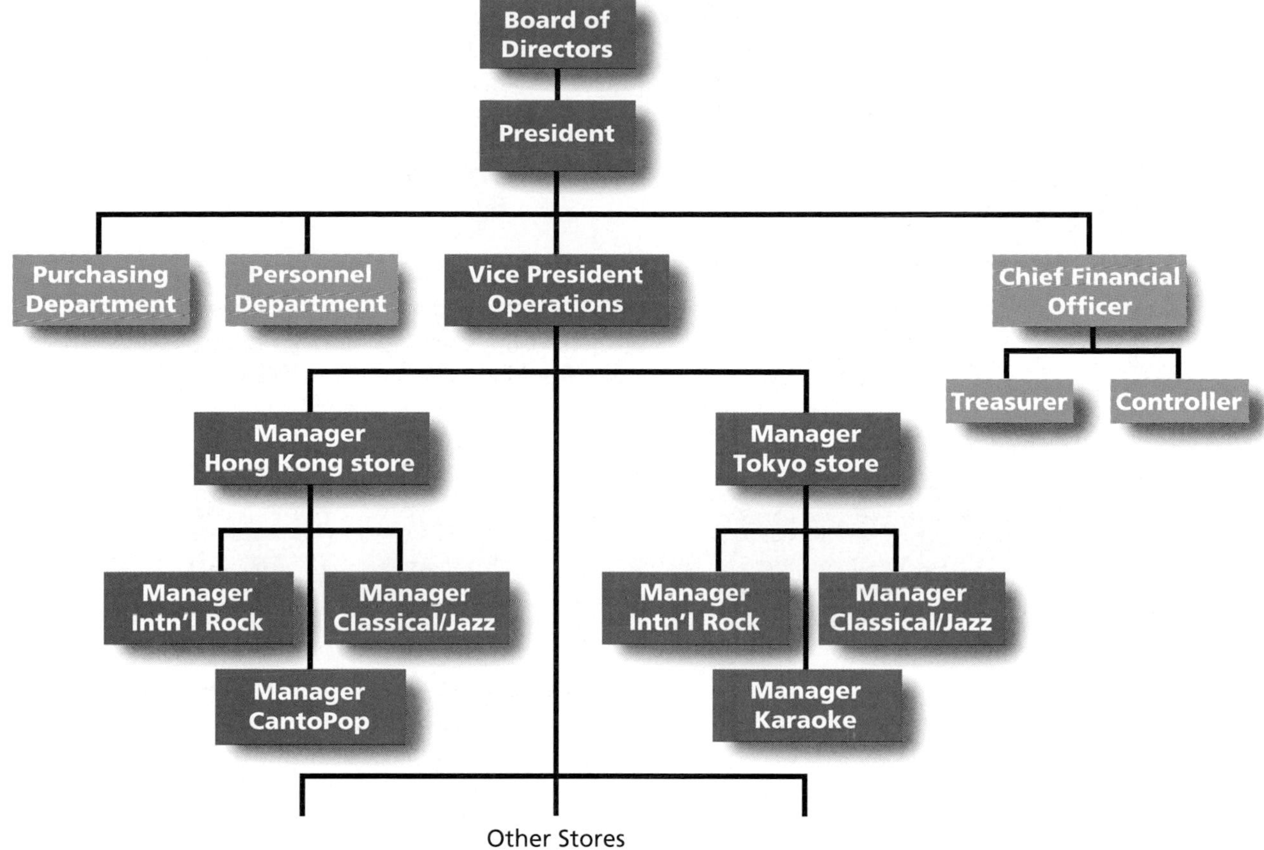

Line and Staff Relationships

An organization chart also depicts *line* and *staff* positions in an organization. A person in a **line** position is *directly* involved in achieving the basic objectives of the organization. A person in a **staff** position, by contrast, is only *indirectly* involved in achieving those basic objectives. Staff positions *support* or provide assistance to line positions or other parts of the organization, but they do not have direct authority over line positions. Refer again to the organization chart in Exhibit 1–8. Since the basic objective of Good Vibrations, Inc., is to sell recorded music at a profit, those managers whose areas of responsibility are directly related to the sales effort occupy line positions. These positions, which are shown in a darker color in the exhibit, include the managers of the various music departments in each store, the store managers, the operations vice president, and members of top management.

By contrast, the manager of the central Purchasing Department occupies a staff position, since the only function of the Purchasing Department is to support and serve the line departments by doing their purchasing for them.

objective 8

Describe the role the controller plays in a decentralized organization.

The Controller

As previously mentioned, in the United States the manager in charge of the accounting department is usually known as the *controller*. The controller is the member of the top-management team who is given the responsibility of providing relevant and timely data to support planning and control activities and of preparing financial statements for external users.

Exhibit 1–9 Organization of the Controller's Office

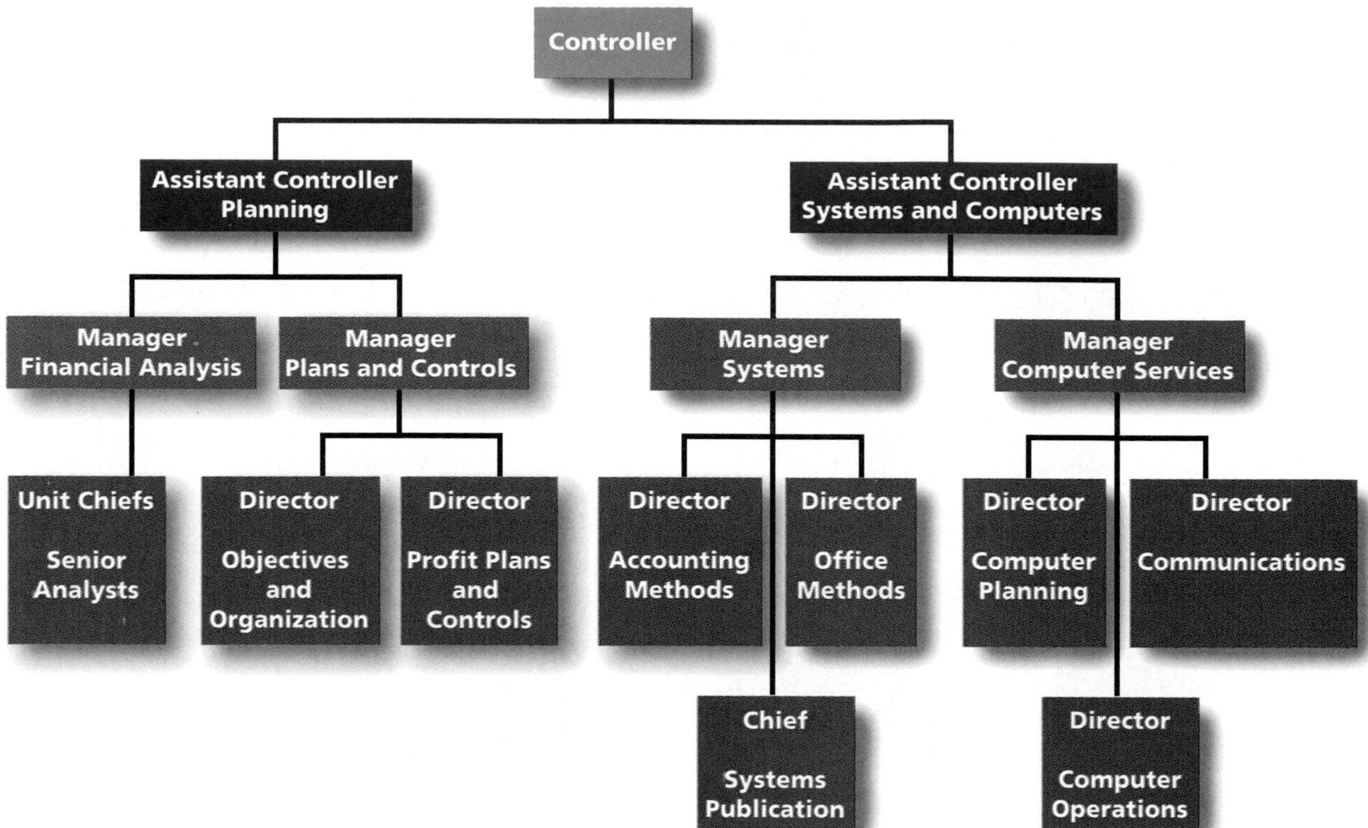

The organization of a typical controller's office is shown in Exhibit 1–9. From that organization chart we see that the controller's office combines a number of important functions including, quite often, management of the company's computer services. Because the controller becomes familiar with all parts of a company's operations by working with managers throughout the company, it is not unusual for the controller's office to be a stepping-stone to the top position in a company.

Professional Ethics

objective 9

Explain the importance of ethical standards in an advanced market economy.

In recent years, many concerns have been raised regarding ethical behavior in business and in public life. Allegations and scandals of unethical conduct have been directed toward managers in virtually all segments of society, including government, business, charitable organizations, and even religion. Although these allegations and scandals have received a lot of attention, it is doubtful that they represent a wholesale breakdown of the moral fiber of the nation. After all, hundreds of millions of transactions are conducted every day that remain untainted. Nevertheless, it is important to have an appreciation of what is and is not acceptable behavior in business and why. Fortunately, the Institute of Management Accountants (IMA) of the United States has developed a very useful ethical code called the *Standards of Ethical Conduct for Practitioners of Management Accounting and Financial Management.* Even though the standards were specifically developed for management accountants, they have much broader application.

Code of Conduct for Management Accountants

The IMA's Standards of Ethical Conduct for Practitioners of Management Accounting and Financial Management is presented in full in Exhibit 1–10. There are two parts to the standards. The first part provides general guidelines for ethical behavior. In a nutshell, the management accountant has ethical responsibilities in four broad areas: first, to maintain a high level of professional competence; second, to treat sensitive matters with confidentiality; third, to maintain personal integrity; and fourth, to be objective in all disclosures. The second part of the standards gives specific guidance concerning what should be done if an individual finds evidence of ethical misconduct within an organization. We recommend that you stop at this point and read the standards in Exhibit 1–10.

Exhibit 1–10
Standards of Ethical Conduct for Practitioners of Management Accounting and Financial Management

Practitioners of management accounting and financial management have an obligation to the public, their profession, the organization they serve, and themselves, to maintain the highest standards of ethical conduct. In recognition of this obligation, the Institute of Management Accountants has promulgated the following standards of ethical conduct for practitioners of management accounting and financial management. Adherence to these standards, both domestically and internationally, is integral to achieving the Objectives of Management Accounting. Practitioners of management accounting and financial management shall not commit acts contrary to these standards nor shall they condone the commission of such acts by others within their organizations.

Competence. Practitioners of management accounting and financial management have a responsibility to:

- Maintain an appropriate level of professional competence by ongoing development of their knowledge and skills.
- Perform their professional duties in accordance with relevant laws, regulations, and technical standards.
- Prepare complete and clear reports and recommendations after appropriate analysis of relevant and reliable information.

Confidentiality. Practitioners of management accounting and financial management have a responsibility to:

- Refrain from disclosing confidential information acquired in the course of their work except when authorized, unless legally obligated to do so.
- Inform subordinates as appropriate regarding the confidentiality of information acquired in the course of their work and monitor their activities to assure the maintenance of that confidentiality.
- Refrain from using or appearing to use confidential information acquired in the course of their work for unethical or illegal advantage either personally or through third parties.

Integrity. Practitioners of management accounting and financial management have a responsibility to:

- Avoid actual or apparent conflicts of interest and advise all appropriate parties of any potential conflict.
- Refrain from engaging in any activity that would prejudice their ability to carry out their duties ethically.
- Refuse any gift, favor, or hospitality that would influence or would appear to influence their actions.
- Refrain from either actively or passively subverting the attainment of the organization's legitimate and ethical objectives.
- Recognize and communicate professional limitations or other constraints that would preclude responsible judgment or successful performance of an activity.

Exhibit 1–10
Standards of Ethical Conduct for Practitioners of Management Accounting and Financial Management *(continued)*

- Communicate unfavorable as well as favorable information and professional judgments or opinions.
- Refrain from engaging in or supporting any activity that would discredit the profession.

Objectivity. Practitioners of management accounting and financial management have a responsibility to:

- Communicate information fairly and objectively.
- Disclose fully all relevant information that could reasonably be expected to influence an intended user's understanding of the reports, comments, and recommendations presented.

Resolution of Ethical Conflict. In applying the standards of ethical conduct, practitioners of management accounting and financial management may encounter problems in identifying unethical behavior or in resolving an ethical conflict. When faced with significant ethical issues, practitioners of management accounting and financial management should follow the established policies of the organization bearing on the resolution of such conflict. If these policies do not resolve the ethical conflict, such practitioner should consider the following courses of action:

- Discuss such problems with the immediate superior except when it appears that the superior is involved, in which case the problem should be presented initially to the next higher managerial level. If a satisfactory resolution cannot be achieved when the problem is initially presented, submit the issues to the next higher managerial level.
- If the immediate superior is the chief executive officer, or equivalent, the acceptable reviewing authority may be a group such as the audit committee, executive committee, board of directors, board of trustees, or owners. Contact with levels above the immediate superior should be initiated only with the superior's knowledge, assuming the superior is not involved. Except where legally prescribed, communication of such problems to authorities or individuals not employed or engaged by the organization is not considered appropriate.
- Clarify relevant ethical issues by confidential discussion with an objective advisor (e.g., IMA Ethics Counseling Service) to obtain a better understanding of possible courses of action.
- Consult your own attorney as to legal obligations and rights concerning the ethical conflict.
- If the ethical conflict still exists after exhausting all levels of internal review, there may be no other recourse on significant matters than to resign from the organization and to submit an informative memorandum to an appropriate representative of the organization. After resignation, depending on the nature of the ethical conflict, it may also be appropriate to notify other parties.

*Institute of Management Accountants, formerly National Association of Accountants, *Statements on Management Accounting: Objectives of Management Accounting,* Statement No. 1B, New York, NY, June 17, 1982 as revised in 1997.

The ethical standards provide sound, practical advice for management accountants and managers. Most of the rules in the ethical standards are motivated by a very practical consideration—if these rules were not generally followed in business, then the economy would come to a screeching halt. Consider the following specific examples of the consequences of not abiding by the standards:

- Suppose employees could not be trusted with confidential information. Then top managers would be reluctant to distribute confidential information within the company. As a result, decisions would be based on incomplete information and operations would deteriorate.
- Suppose employees accepted bribes from suppliers. Then contracts would tend to go to suppliers who pay the highest bribes rather than to the most competent suppliers. Would you like to fly in an aircraft whose wings were made by the subcontractor who was willing to pay the highest bribe to a purchasing agent? What would happen to the airline industry if its safety record deteriorated due to shoddy workmanship on contracted parts and assemblies?

- Suppose the presidents of companies routinely lied in their annual reports to shareholders and grossly distorted financial statements. If the basic integrity of a company's financial statements could not be relied on, investors and creditors would have little basis for making informed decisions. Suspecting the worst, rational investors would pay less for securities issued by companies. As a consequence, less funds would be available for productive investments and many firms might be unable to raise any funds at all. Ultimately, this would lead to slower economic growth, fewer goods and services, and higher prices.

As these examples suggest, if ethical standards were not generally adhered to, there would be undesirable consequences for everyone. Essentially, abandoning ethical standards would lead to a lower standard of living with lower-quality goods and services, less to choose from, and higher prices. In short, following ethical rules such as those in the Standards of Ethical Conduct for Practitioners of Management Accounting and Financial Management is not just a matter of being "nice"; it is absolutely essential for the smooth functioning of an advanced market economy.

Company Codes of Conduct

"Those who engage in unethical behavior often justify their actions with one or more of the following reasons: (1) the organization expects unethical behavior, (2) everyone else is unethical, and/or (3) behaving unethically is the only way to get ahead."[26]

To counter the first justification for unethical behavior, many companies have adopted formal ethical codes of conduct. These codes are generally broad-based statements of a company's responsibilities to its employees, its customers, its suppliers, and the communities in which the company operates. Codes rarely spell out specific do's and don'ts or suggest proper behavior in a specific situation. Instead, they give broad guidelines.

Unfortunately, the single-minded emphasis placed on short-term profits in some companies may make it seem like the only way to get ahead is to act unethically. When top managers say, in effect, that they will only be satisfied with bottom-line results and will accept no excuses, they are asking for trouble. See the accompanying Focus on Current Practice box concerning Sears, Roebuck & Company's automobile service centers for a vivid example.

Focus on Current Practice

Top managers at Sears, Roebuck & Company created a situation in its automotive service business that led to unethical actions by its front-line employees.[27]

> Consumers and attorneys general in more than 40 states had accused the company of misleading customers and selling them unnecessary parts and services, from brake jobs to front-end alignments. It would be a mistake, however, to see this situation . . . in terms of any one individual's moral failings. Nor did management set out to defraud Sears customers . . .
>
> In the face of declining revenues, shrinking market share, and an increasingly competitive market, . . . Sears management attempted to spur performance of its auto centers . . .

---

[26] Michael K. McCuddy, Karl E. Reichardt, and David Schroeder, "Ethical Pressures: Fact or Fiction?" *Management Accounting,* April 1993, pp. 57–61.

[27] Reprinted by permission of *Harvard Business Review.* Excerpt from Lynn Sharp Paine, "Managing for Organizational Integrity," *Harvard Business Review,* March–April 1994. Copyright © 1994 by the President and Fellows of Harvard College. All rights reserved.

The company increased minimum work quotas and introduced productivity incentives for mechanics. The automotive service advisers were given product-specific sales quotas—sell so many springs, shock absorbers, alignments, or brake jobs per shift—and paid a commission based on sales. According to advisers, failure to meet quotas could lead to a transfer or a reduction in work hours. Some employees spoke of the "pressure, pressure, pressure" to bring in sales.

This pressure-cooker atmosphere created conditions under which employees felt that the only way to satisfy top management was by selling customers products and services they didn't really need.

Shortly after the allegations against Sears became public, CEO Edward Brennan acknowledged management's responsibility for putting in place compensation and goal-setting systems that "created an environment in which mistakes did occur." ■

Codes of Conduct on the International Level

The *Guideline on Ethics for Professional Accountants,* issued in July 1990 by the International Federation of Accountants (IFAC), governs the activities of *all* professional accountants throughout the world, regardless of whether they are practicing as independent CPAs, employed in government service, or employed as internal accountants.[28] In addition to outlining ethical requirements in matters dealing with competence, objectivity, independence, and confidentiality, the IFAC's code also outlines the accountant's ethical responsibilities in matters relating to taxes, fees and commissions, advertising and solicitation, the handling of monies, and cross-border activities. Where cross-border activities are involved, the IFAC ethical requirements must be followed if these requirements are stricter than the ethical requirements of the country in which the work is being performed.[29]

In addition to professional and company codes of ethical conduct, accountants and managers in the United States are subject to the legal requirements of *The Foreign Corrupt Practices Act of 1977.* The Act requires that companies devise and maintain a system of internal controls sufficient to ensure that all transactions are properly executed and recorded. The Act specifically prohibits giving bribes, even if giving bribes is common practice in the country in which the company is doing business.

The Certified Management Accountant (CMA)

Management accountants who possess the necessary qualifications and who pass a rigorous professional exam earn the right to be known as a *Certified Management Accountant (CMA).* In addition to the prestige that accompanies a professional designation, CMAs are often given greater responsibilities and higher compensation than those who do not have such a designation. Information about becoming a CMA and the

[28] A copy of this code can be obtained on the International Federation of Accountants' web site www.ifac.org.

[29] *Guideline on Ethics for Professional Accountants* (New York: International Federation of Accountants, July 1990), p. 23.

CMA program can be accessed on the Institute of Management Accountants' (IMA) web site www.imanet.org or by calling 1-800-638-4427.

To become a Certified Management Accountant, the following four steps must be completed:

1. File an Application for Admission and register for the CMA examination.
2. Pass all four parts of the CMA examination within a three-year period.
3. Satisfy the experience requirement of two continuous years of professional experience in management and/or financial accounting prior to or within seven years of passing the CMA examination.
4. Comply with the Standards of Ethical Conduct for Practitioners of Management Accounting and Financial Management.

Summary

Managerial accounting assists managers in carrying out their responsibilities, which include planning, directing and motivating, and controlling.

Since managerial accounting is geared to the needs of the manager rather than to the needs of outsiders, it differs substantially from financial accounting. Managerial accounting is oriented more toward the future, places less emphasis on precision, emphasizes segments of an organization (rather than the organization as a whole), is not governed by generally accepted accounting principles, and is not mandatory.

The business environment in recent years has been characterized by increasing competition and a relentless drive for continuous improvement. Several approaches have been developed to assist organizations in meeting these challenges—including just-in-time (JIT), total quality management (TQM), process reengineering, and the theory of constraints (TOC).

JIT emphasizes the importance of reducing inventories to the barest minimum possible. This reduces working capital requirements, frees up space, reduces throughput time, reduces defects, and eliminates waste.

TQM involves focusing on the customer, and it employs systematic problem solving using teams made up of front-line workers. Specific TQM tools include benchmarking and the plan-do-check-act (PDCA) cycle. By emphasizing teamwork, a focus on the customer, and facts, TQM can avoid the organizational infighting that might otherwise block improvement.

Process reengineering involves completely redesigning a business process in order to eliminate non-value-added activities and to reduce opportunities for errors. Process reengineering relies more on outside specialists than TQM and is more likely to be imposed by top management.

The theory of constraints emphasizes the importance of managing the organization's constraints. Since the constraint is whatever is holding back the organization, improvement efforts usually must be focused on the constraint in order to be really effective.

Most organizations are decentralized to some degree. The organization chart depicts who works for whom in the organization and which units perform staff functions rather than line functions. Accountants perform a staff function—they support and provide assistance to others inside the organization.

Ethical standards serve a very important practical function in an advanced market economy. Without widespread adherence to ethical standards, the economy would slow down dramatically. Ethics are the lubrication that keep a market economy functioning smoothly. The Standards of Ethical Conduct for Practitioners of Management Accounting and Financial Management provide sound, practical guidelines for resolving ethical problems that might arise in an organization.

Key Terms for Review

At the end of each chapter, a list of key terms for review is given, along with the definition of each term. (These terms are printed in boldface where they are defined in the chapter.) Carefully study each term to be sure you understand its meaning, since these terms are used repeatedly in the chapters that follow. The list for Chapter 1 follows.

Benchmarking A study of organizations that are among the best in the world at performing a particular task. (p. 17)

Budget A detailed plan for the future, usually expressed in formal quantitative terms. (p. 5)

Business process A series of steps that are followed in order to carry out some task in a business. (p. 20)

Constraint Anything that prevents an organization or individual from getting more of what it wants. (p. 22)

Control The process of instituting procedures and then obtaining feedback to ensure that all parts of the organization are functioning effectively and moving toward overall company goals. (p. 5)

Controller The manager in charge of the accounting department in an organization. (p. 5)

Controlling Ensuring that the plan is actually carried out and is appropriately modified as circumstances change. (p. 4)

Cycle time See *Throughput time.* (p. 15)

Decentralization The delegation of decision-making authority throughout an organization by providing managers at various operating levels with the authority to make key decisions relating to their area of responsibility. (p. 26)

Directing and motivating Mobilizing people to carry out plans and run routine operations. (p. 4)

Feedback Accounting and other reports that help managers monitor performance and focus on problems and/or opportunities that might otherwise go unnoticed. (p. 5)

Financial accounting The phase of accounting concerned with providing information to stockholders, creditors, and others outside the organization. (p. 4)

Finished goods Units of product that have been completed but have not yet been sold to customers. (p. 11)

Just-in-time (JIT) A production and inventory control system in which materials are purchased and units are produced only as needed to meet actual customer demand. (p. 10)

Line A position in an organization that is directly related to the achievement of the organization's basic objectives. (p. 27)

Managerial accounting The phase of accounting concerned with providing information to managers for use in planning and controlling operations and in decision making. (p. 4)

Non-value-added activity An activity that consumes resources or takes time but that does not add value for which customers are willing to pay. (p. 20)

Organization chart A visual diagram of a firm's organizational structure that depicts formal lines of reporting, communication, and responsibility between managers. (p. 26)

Performance report A detailed report comparing budgeted data to actual data. (p. 6)

Plan-do-check-act (PDCA) cycle A systematic approach to continuous improvement that applies the scientific method to problem solving. (p. 17)

Planning Selecting a course of action and specifying how the action will be implemented. (p. 4)

Planning and control cycle The flow of management activities through planning, directing and motivating, and controlling, and then back to planning again. (p. 6)

Process reengineering An approach to improvement that involves completely redesigning business processes in order to eliminate unnecessary steps, reduce errors, and reduce costs. (p. 20)

Raw materials Materials that are used to make a product. (p. 10)

Segment Any part of an organization that can be evaluated independently of other parts and about which the manager seeks financial data. Examples include a product line, a sales territory, a division, or a department. (p. 8)

Setup Activities that must be performed whenever production is switched over from making one type of item to another. (p. 15)

Staff A position in an organization that is only indirectly related to the achievement of the organization's basic objectives. Such positions are supportive in nature in that they provide service or assistance to line positions or to other staff positions. (p. 27)

Theory of constraints (TOC) A management approach that emphasizes the importance of managing constraints. (p. 22)

Throughput time The time required to make a completed unit of product starting with raw materials. Throughput time is also known as cycle time. (p. 15)

Total quality management (TQM) An approach to continuous improvement that focuses on customers and using teams of front-line workers to systematically identify and solve problems. (p. 17)

Work in process Units of product that are only partially complete and will require further work before they are ready for sale to a customer. (p. 10)

Questions

1–1 What is the basic difference in orientation between financial and managerial accounting?

1–2 What are the three major activities of a manager?

1–3 Describe the four steps in the planning and control cycle.

1–4 What function does feedback play in the work of the manager?

1–5 Distinguish between line and staff positions in an organization.

1–6 What are the major differences between financial and managerial accounting?

1–7 In a just-in-time (JIT) system, what is meant by the pull approach to the flow of goods, as compared to the push approach used in conventional systems?

1–8 How does the plant layout differ in a company using JIT as compared to a company that uses a more conventional approach to manufacturing? What benefits accrue from a JIT layout?

1–9 Identify the benefits that can result from reducing the setup time for a product.

1–10 How does a workforce in a JIT facility differ from the workforce in a conventional facility?

1–11 What are the major benefits of a JIT system?

1–12 Explain how the plan-do-check-act cycle applies the scientific method to problem solving.

1–13 Why is process reengineering a more radical approach to improvement than total quality management?

1–14 How can process reengineering undermine employee morale?

1–15 Why does the theory of constraints emphasize managing constraints?

1–16 Why is adherence to ethical standards important for the smooth functioning of an advanced market economy?

Exercises

E1–1 Listed below are a number of terms that relate to organizations, the work of management, and the role of managerial accounting:

Budgets	Controller
Decentralization	Directing and motivating
Feedback	Financial accounting
Line	Managerial accounting
Nonmonetary data	Performance report
Planning	Precision
Staff	

Choose the term or terms above that most appropriately complete the following statements:

1. A position on the organization chart that is directly related to achieving the basic objectives of an organization is called a ___________ position.
2. When ___________ , managers oversee day-to-day activities and keep the organization functioning smoothly.
3. The plans of management are expressed formally in ___________ .
4. ___________ consists of identifying alternatives, selecting from among the alternatives the one that is best for the organization, and specifying what actions will be taken to implement the chosen alternative.
5. A ___________ position provides service or assistance to other parts of the organization and does not directly achieve the basic objectives of the organization.
6. The delegation of decision-making authority throughout an organization by allowing managers at various operating levels to make key decisions relating to their area of responsibility is called ___________ .
7. Managerial accounting places less emphasis on ___________ and more emphasis on ___________ than financial accounting.
8. ___________ is concerned with providing information for the use of those who are inside the organization, whereas ___________ is concerned with providing information for the use of those who are outside the organization.
9. The accounting and other reports coming to management that are used in controlling the organization are called ___________ .
10. The manager in charge of the accounting department is generally known as the ___________ .
11. A detailed report to management comparing budgeted data against actual data for a specific time period is called a ___________ .

E1–2 Listed below are a number of terms that relate to just-in-time, total quality management, process reengineering, and theory of constraints:

Benchmarking	Business process
Constraint	Frequent
Just-in-time	Nonconstraint
Non-value-added activities	Plan-do-check-act cycle
Process reengineering	Pull
Setup	Total quality management

Choose the term or terms above that most appropriately complete the following statements:

1. To successfully operate a JIT system, a company must learn to rely on a few suppliers who are willing to make ___________ deliveries.
2. ___________ is an incremental approach to improvement, whereas ___________ tends to be a much more radical approach that involves completely redesigning business processes.
3. A production system in which units are produced and materials are purchased only as needed to meet actual customer demand is called ___________ .
4. In just-in-time, the flow of goods is controlled by what is described as a ___________ approach to manufacturing.

5. Increasing the rate of output of a ____________ as the result of an improvement effort is unlikely to have much effect on profits.
6. ____________ involves studying the business processes of companies that are considered among the best in the world at performing a particular task.
7. The activities involved in getting equipment ready to produce a different product are called a ____________ .
8. The theory of constraints suggests that improvement efforts should be focused on the company's ____________ .
9. The ____________ is a systematic, fact-based approach to continuous improvement that resembles the scientific method.
10. In process reengineering, two objectives are to simplify and to eliminate ____________.
11. A ____________ is any series of steps that are followed in order to carry out some task in a business.

E1–3 The management at Megafilters, Inc., has been discussing the possible implementation of a just-in-time (JIT) production system at its Illinois plant, where oil and air filters are manufactured. The Metal Stamping Department at the Illinois plant has already instituted a JIT system for controlling raw materials inventory, but the remainder of the plant is still discussing how to proceed with the implementation of this concept. The Metal Stamping Department implemented JIT with no advance planning, and some of the other department managers have become uneasy about adopting JIT after hearing about the problems that have arisen.

Robert Goertz, manager of the Illinois plant, is a strong proponent of the JIT approach. He recently made the following statement at a meeting of all departmental managers:

> We will all have to make many changes in the way we think about our employees, our suppliers, and our customers if we are going to be successful in using JIT procedures. Rather than dwelling on some of the negative things you have heard from the Metal Stamping Department, I want each of you to prepare a list of things we can do to make a smooth transition to the JIT approach for the rest of the plant.

Required

1. The JIT approach has several characteristics that distinguish it from conventional production systems. Describe these characteristics.
2. For the JIT approach to be successful, Megafilters, Inc., must establish appropriate relationships with its suppliers. Describe these relationships under JIT.

(CMA, adapted)

E1–4 Mary Karston was hired by a popular fast-food restaurant as an order-taker and cashier. Shortly after taking the job, she was shocked to overhear an employee bragging to a friend about shortchanging customers. She confronted the employee who then snapped back: "Mind your own business. Besides, everyone does it and the customers never miss the money." Mary didn't know how to respond to this aggressive stance.

Required

What would be the practical consequences on the fast-food industry and on consumers if cashiers generally shortchanged customers at every opportunity?

Problems

P1–5 Preparing an Organization Chart Bristow University is a large private school located in the Midwest. The university is headed by a president who has five vice presidents reporting to him. These vice presidents are responsible for, respectively, auxiliary services, admissions and records, academics, financial services (controller), and physical plant.

In addition, the university has managers over several areas who report to these vice presidents. These include managers over central purchasing, the university press, and the university bookstore, all of whom report to the vice president for auxiliary services; managers over computer services and over accounting and finance, who report to the vice president for financial services; and managers over grounds and custodial services and over plant and maintenance, who report to the vice president for physical plant.

The university has four colleges—business, humanities, fine arts, and engineering and quantitative methods—and a law school. Each of these units has a dean who is responsible to the academic vice president. Each college has several departments.

Required

1. Prepare an organization chart for Bristow University.
2. Which of the positions on your chart would be line positions? Why would they be line positions? Which would be staff positions? Why?
3. Which of the positions on your chart would have need for accounting information? Explain.

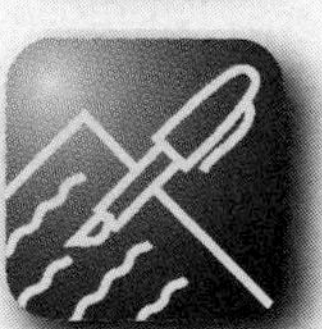

P1–6 Ethics and the Manager Richmond, Inc., operates a chain of department stores located in the northwest. The first store began operations in 1965, and the company has steadily grown to its present size of 44 stores. Two years ago, the board of directors of Richmond approved a large-scale remodeling of its stores to attract a more upscale clientele.

Before finalizing these plans, two stores were remodeled as a test. Linda Perlman, assistant controller, was asked to oversee the financial reporting for these test stores, and she and other management personnel were offered bonuses based on the sales growth and profitability of these stores. While completing the financial reports, Perlman discovered a sizable inventory of outdated goods that should have been discounted for sale or returned to the manufacturer. She discussed the situation with her management colleagues; the consensus was to ignore reporting this inventory as obsolete, since reporting it would diminish the financial results and their bonuses.

Required

1. According to the Standards of Ethical Conduct for Practitioners of Management Accounting and Financial Management, would it be ethical for Perlman *not* to report the inventory as obsolete?
2. Would it be easy for Perlman to take the ethical action in this situation?

(CMA, adapted)

P1–7 JIT; Process Reengineering Snedden Products manufactures athletic equipment, including footballs. The footballs are manufactured in several steps, which are listed below:

a. Leather and other materials are received at a centrally located dock where the materials are checked to be sure they conform to exacting company standards. Rejected materials are returned to the supplier.
b. Acceptable materials are transported to a stores warehouse pending use in production.
c. A materials requisition form is issued, and materials are transferred from the stores warehouse to the Cutting Department where all cutting equipment is located.
d. Since the Cutting Department cuts materials for a variety of products, the leather is placed on large pallets and stationed by the appropriate machines.
e. The leather and other materials are cut to proper shape, with the operator taking care to cut all sections of a football from a single piece of leather. Waste materials are placed in a bin, and at the end of each day the materials are sorted to reclaim the items that can be used in manufacturing other products.
f. Each cut item of material is examined by one of three checkers to ensure uniformity of cut, thickness of the leather, and direction of the grain. Rejected pieces are tossed in the scrap bin.
g. Cut materials are placed on pallets and transferred to the Centralized Sewing Department, where the pallets are placed in a staging area.
h. Materials are taken from the pallets, the company's name and logo are stamped into one section of each set of cut pieces, and the pieces are then sewed together.
i. The sewn pieces are placed in bins, which are then transferred to the staging area of the Assembly Department.
j. An operator in the Assembly Department installs a lining in the football, stitches the ball closed with a stitching machine, and then inflates it.

k. The completed footballs are placed on a conveyor belt that passes by another set of checkers. Each ball is checked for uniformity of shape and for other potential defects.
l. Completed footballs are boxed and transferred to the finished goods warehouse.

Required Assume that the company adopts JIT inventory practices and establishes individual product flow lines. Explain what changes would have to be made in manufacturing procedures and prepare a sketch of how the football product flow line would be arranged.

P1–8 Line and Staff Positions Special Alloys Corporation manufactures a variety of specialized metal products for industrial use. Most of the revenues are generated by large contracts with companies that have government defense contracts. The company also develops and markets parts to the major automobile companies. It employs many metallurgists and skilled technicians because most of its products are made from highly sophisticated alloys.

The company recently signed two large contracts; as a result, the workload of Wayne Washburn, the general manager, has become overwhelming. To relieve some of this overload, Mark Johnson was transferred from the Research Planning Department to the general manager's office. Johnson, who has been a senior metallurgist and supervisor in the Research Planning Department, was given the title "assistant to the general manager."

Washburn assigned several responsibilities to Johnson in their first meeting. Johnson will oversee the testing of new alloys in the Product Planning Department and be given the authority to make decisions as to the use of these alloys in product development; he will also be responsible for maintaining the production schedules for one of the new contracts. In addition to these duties, he will be required to meet with the supervisors of the production departments regularly to consult with them about production problems they may be experiencing. Washburn is expecting that he will be able to manage the company much more efficiently with Johnson's help.

Required

1. Positions within organizations are often described as having (a) line authority or (b) staff authority. Describe what is meant by these two terms.
2. Of the responsibilities assigned to Mark Johnson as assistant to the general manager, which tasks have line authority and which have staff authority?
3. Identify and discuss the conflicts Mark Johnson may experience in the production departments as a result of his new responsibilities.

(CMA, adapted)

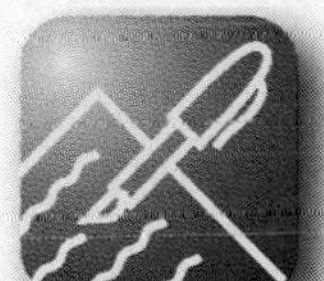

P1–9 Ethics; Just-in-Time (JIT) Purchasing (The situation described below was adapted from a case published by the Institute of Management Accountants' Committee on Ethics.*)

WIW is a publicly owned corporation that makes various control devices used in the manufacture of mechanical equipment. J.B. is the president of WIW, Tony is the purchasing agent, and Diane is J.B.'s executive assistant. All three have been with WIW for about five years. Charlie is WIW's controller and has been with the company for two years.

J.B.: Hi, Charlie, come on in. Diane said you had a confidential matter to discuss. What's on your mind?

Charlie: J.B., I was reviewing our increased purchases from A-1 Warehouse Sales last week and wondered why our volume has tripled in the past year. When I discussed this with Tony he seemed a bit evasive and tried to dismiss the issue by stating that A-1 can give us one-day delivery on our orders.

J.B.: Well, Tony is right. You know we have been trying to implement just-in-time and have been trying to get our inventory down.

Charlie: We still have to look at the overall cost. A-1 is more of a jobber than a warehouse. After investigating orders placed with them, I found that only 10% are delivered from their warehouse and the other 90% are drop-shipped from the manufacturers. The average

---

* Neil Holmes, ed., "Ethics," *Management Accounting* 73, no. 8 (February 1992), p. 16. Used (and adapted) by permission.

markup by A-1 is 30%, which amounted to about $600,000 on our orders for the past year. If we had ordered directly from the manufacturers when A-1 didn't have an item in stock, we could have saved about $540,000 ($600,000 × 90%). In addition, some of the orders were late and not complete.

J.B.: Now look, Charlie, we get quick delivery on most items, and who knows how much we are saving by not having to stock this stuff in advance or worry about it becoming obsolete. Is there anything else on your mind?

Charlie: Well, J.B., as a matter of fact, there is. I ordered a Dun & Bradstreet credit report on A-1 and discovered that Mike Bell is the principal owner. Isn't he your brother-in-law?

J.B.: Sure he is. But don't worry about Mike. He understands this JIT approach. Besides, he's looking out for our interests.

Charlie (to himself): This conversation has been enlightening, but it doesn't really respond to my concerns. Can I legally or ethically ignore this apparent conflict of interests?

Required

1. Would Charlie be justified in ignoring this situation, particularly since he is not the purchasing agent? In preparing your answer, consider the IMA's Standards of Ethical Conduct in Exhibit 1–10.
2. State the specific steps Charlie should follow to resolve this matter.

P1–10 Ethics Refer to the Focus on Current Practice box concerning Sears, Roebuck & Company's automotive service business on pages 31 and 32. Suppose all automotive service businesses routinely followed the practice of attempting to sell customers unnecessary parts and services.

Required

1. How would this unethical behavior affect customers? How might customers attempt to protect themselves against this unethical behavior?
2. How would this unethical behavior probably affect profits and employment in the automotive service industry?

Group Exercises

GE1–11 Ethics on the Job Ethical standards are very important in business, but they are not always followed. If you have ever held a job—even a summer job—describe the ethical climate in the organization where you worked. Did employees work a full day or did they arrive late and leave early? Did employees honestly report the hours they worked? Did employees use their employer's resources for their own purposes? Did managers set a good example? Did the organization have a code of ethics and were employees made aware of its existence? If the ethical climate in the organization you worked for was poor, what problems, if any, did it create?

IE1–12 Management Accounting Profession The Institute of Management Accountants' (IMA) web site at www.imanet.org contains a great deal of information about the organization and the management accounting profession. Answer the following questions by accessing data on that web site. (Many of the questions can be answered by going to the Student Facts Kit.)

Required

1. What is the mean total compensation for an IMA member in your age group who does not have a CMA or CPA? For an IMA member in your age group who has a CMA? Who has a CPA? Who has both a CMA and a CPA?
2. What is the average salary in your state for a member of the IMA?
3. In which industry is the average salary for a member of the IMA the highest? The lowest?
4. Where is the nearest chapter of the IMA? Does this chapter have its own web site? If so, access the web site and note what services the chapter provides to its members.
5. Does the IMA have any scholarships for which you might qualify?

6. What is the nature of the CMA exam? Is it an essay exam, a multiple-choice exam, or some combination of the two? When may you take the exam?

IE1–13 Malcolm Baldrige National Quality Award The National Quality Program maintains a web site at www.quality.nist.gov that provides information about the prestigious Malcolm Baldrige National Quality Award.

Required

1. What is the Malcolm Baldrige National Quality Award?
2. What organizations are recent winners of the award? What industries are they from?
3. Is any evidence presented on the web site that winners of the award are more successful than other organizations?
4. Awards are currently given in three categories: business, education, and health care. Briefly describe the criteria that are used for awarding the education award. Do the criteria require that specific goals be met in terms of achievement on standardized tests or other measures of performance?

IE1–14 Business Process Reengineering ProSci, a business process reengineering publishing and research organization, has its web home page at www.prosci.com. Among other things, this web site contains a tutorial concerning business process reengineering and a yellow pages directory of consultants and other specialists in the field. Use information gleaned from this web site to answer the following questions:

Required

1. Were most early attempts at business process reengineering successful?
2. Who should be on a business process reengineering team?
3. Why is top-management support necessary for a successful implementation of business process reengineering?
4. How can consultants sometimes unintentionally create barriers to successful implementation of business process reengineering?

IE1–15 Just-in-Time (JIT) Suppliers JIT Manufacturing Incorporated is a just-in-time supplier of medical and industrial products to other companies. The company maintains a web site at www.jitmfg.com where the company's products and services are described.

Required

1. How often can customers pull items from JIT Manufacturing Incorporated's stocks?
2. How does JIT Manufacturing Incorporated ensure that it is able to fill customer orders? What information does JIT Manufacturing require from its customers?
3. In return for its services, what does JIT Manufacturing Incorporated ask of its customers?

Chapter Two
Cost Terms, Concepts, and Classifications

Business Focus

Terri, the owner of a retail florist shop, has been trying to decide for some time whether she should continue to use a local courier service to deliver flowers to customers or buy a delivery truck and use one of her employees to make the deliveries. At a recent family Thanksgiving dinner, she brought up the subject of the delivery truck with her brother-in-law, who fancies himself as an expert on all management subjects. He grabbed this opportunity to impress on Terri his understanding of costs.

In rapid-fire succession, Terri's brother-in-law told her that the fees paid to the courier to deliver flowers are a variable cost and a period cost, but the costs of the flowers are product costs rather than period costs, even though the flower costs are also variable costs. On the other hand, the depreciation of the delivery truck would be a fixed cost and a period cost. And while the fuel for the truck would be a variable cost and a differential cost, the wages of the person making the deliveries would be a fixed cost, not a differential cost, and would involve an opportunity cost. At this point, Terri excused herself—pleading that she had to help in the kitchen.

Terri felt that her brother-in-law's comments were more confusing than helpful, but she knew that she could no longer put off the decision about the delivery truck. She would have to think carefully about her costs and determine what costs should be considered in this decision.

Learning Objectives

After studying Chapter 2, you should be able to:

1 Identify and give examples of each of the three basic cost elements involved in the manufacture of a product.

2 Distinguish between product costs and period costs and give examples of each.

3 Prepare a schedule of cost of goods manufactured in good form.

4 Explain the flow of direct materials cost, direct labor cost, and manufacturing overhead cost from the point of incurrence to sale of the completed product.

5 Identify and give examples of variable costs and fixed costs, and explain the difference in their behavior.

6 Define and give examples of direct and indirect costs.

7 Define and give examples of cost classifications used in making decisions: differential costs, opportunity costs, and sunk costs.

8 (Appendix 2A) Properly classify labor costs associated with idle time, overtime, and fringe benefits.

As explained in Chapter 1, the work of management focuses on (1) planning, which includes setting objectives and outlining how to attain these objectives; and (2) control, which includes the steps to take to ensure that objectives are realized. To carry out these planning and control responsibilities, managers need *information* about the organization. From an accounting point of view, this information often relates to the *costs* of the organization.

In managerial accounting, the term *cost* is used in many different ways. The reason is that there are many types of costs, and these costs are classified differently according to the immediate needs of management. For example, managers may want cost data to prepare external financial reports, to prepare planning budgets, or to make decisions. Each different use of cost data demands a different classification and definition of costs. For example, the preparation of external financial reports requires the use of historical cost data, whereas decision making may require current cost data.

In this chapter, we discuss many of the possible uses of cost data and how costs are defined and classified for each use. Our first task is to explain how costs are classified for the purpose of preparing external financial reports—particularly in manufacturing companies. To set the stage for this discussion, we begin the chapter by defining some terms commonly used in manufacturing.

General Cost Classifications

Costs are associated with all types of organizations—business, nonbusiness, manufacturing, retail, and service. Generally, the kinds of costs that are incurred and the way in which these costs are classified depends on the type of organization involved. Managerial accounting is as applicable to one type of organization as to another. For this reason, we will consider in our discussion the cost characteristics of a variety of organizations—manufacturing, merchandising, and service.

Our initial focus in this chapter is on manufacturing companies, since their basic activities include most of the activities found in other types of business organizations. Manufacturing companies such as Texas Instruments, Ford, and Kodak are involved in acquiring raw materials, producing finished goods, marketing, distributing, billing, and almost every other business activity. Therefore, an understanding of costs in a manufacturing company can be very helpful in understanding costs in other types of organizations.

In this chapter, we develop cost concepts that apply to diverse organizations. For example, these cost concepts apply to fast-food outlets such as Kentucky Fried Chicken, Pizza Hut, and Taco Bell; movie studios such as Disney, Paramount, and United Artists; consulting firms such as Andersen Consulting and McKinsey; and your local hospital. The exact terms used in these industries may not be the same as those used in manufacturing, but the same basic concepts apply. With some slight modifications, these basic concepts also apply to merchandising companies such as Wal-Mart, The Gap, 7-Eleven, Nordstrom, and Tower Records that resell finished goods acquired from manufacturers and other sources. With that in mind, let us begin our discussion of manufacturing costs.

objective 1

Identify and give examples of each of the three basic cost elements involved in the manufacture of a product.

Manufacturing Costs

Most manufacturing companies divide manufacturing costs into three broad categories: direct materials, direct labor, and manufacturing overhead. A discussion of each of these categories follows.

DIRECT MATERIALS The materials that go into the final product are called **raw materials.** This term is somewhat misleading, since it seems to imply unprocessed natural resources like wood pulp or iron ore. Actually, raw materials refer to any materials that are used in the final product; and the finished product of one company can become the raw materials of another company. For example, the plastics produced by Du Pont are a raw material used by Compaq Computer in its personal computers.

Direct materials are those materials that become an integral part of the finished product and that can be physically and conveniently traced to it. This would include, for example, the seats Boeing purchases from subcontractors to install in its commercial aircraft. Also included is the tiny electric motor Panasonic uses in its CD players to make the CD spin.

Sometimes it isn't worth the effort to trace the costs of relatively insignificant materials to the end products. Such minor items would include the solder used to make electrical connections in a Sony TV or the glue used to assemble an Ethan Allen chair. Materials such as solder and glue are called **indirect materials** and are included as part of manufacturing overhead, which is discussed later in this section.

DIRECT LABOR The term **direct labor** is reserved for those labor costs that can be easily (i.e., physically and conveniently) traced to individual units of product. Direct labor is sometimes called *touch labor,* since direct labor workers typically touch the product while it is being made. The labor costs of assembly-line workers, for example, would be direct labor costs, as would the labor costs of carpenters, bricklayers, and machine operators.

Labor costs that cannot be physically traced to the creation of products, or that can be traced only at great cost and inconvenience, are termed **indirect labor** and treated as part of manufacturing overhead, along with indirect materials. Indirect labor includes the labor costs of janitors, supervisors, materials handlers, and night security guards. Although the efforts of these workers are essential to production, it would be either impractical or impossible to accurately trace their costs to specific units of product. Hence, such labor costs are treated as indirect labor.

In some industries, major shifts are taking place in the structure of labor costs. Sophisticated automated equipment, run and maintained by skilled indirect workers, is increasingly replacing direct labor. In a few companies, direct labor has become such a minor element of cost that it has disappeared altogether as a separate cost category. More is said in later chapters about this trend and about the impact it is having on cost systems. However, the vast majority of manufacturing and service companies throughout the world continue to recognize direct labor as a separate cost category.

MANUFACTURING OVERHEAD **Manufacturing overhead,** the third element of manufacturing cost, includes all costs of manufacturing except direct materials and direct labor. Manufacturing overhead includes items such as indirect materials; indirect labor; maintenance and repairs on production equipment; and heat and light, property taxes, depreciation, and insurance on manufacturing facilities. A company also incurs costs for heat and light, property taxes, insurance, depreciation, and so forth, associated with its selling and administrative functions, but these costs are not included as part of manufacturing overhead. Only those costs associated with *operating the factory* are included in the manufacturing overhead category.

Various names are used for manufacturing overhead, such as *indirect manufacturing cost, factory overhead,* and *factory burden.* All of these terms are synonymous with *manufacturing overhead.*

Manufacturing overhead combined with direct labor is called **conversion cost.** This term stems from the fact that direct labor costs and overhead costs are incurred in the conversion of materials into finished products. Direct labor combined with direct materials is called **prime cost.**

Nonmanufacturing Costs

Generally, nonmanufacturing costs are subclassified into two categories:

1. Marketing or selling costs.
2. Administrative costs.

Marketing or selling costs include all costs necessary to secure customer orders and get the finished product or service into the hands of the customer. These costs are often called *order-getting and order-filling costs.* Examples of marketing costs include advertising, shipping, sales travel, sales commissions, sales salaries, and costs of finished goods warehouses.

Administrative costs include all executive, organizational, and clerical costs associated with the *general management* of an organization rather than with manufacturing, marketing, or selling. Examples of administrative costs include executive compensation, general accounting, secretarial, public relations, and similar costs involved in the overall, general administration of the organization *as a whole.*

Product Costs versus Period Costs

objective 2

Distinguish between product costs and period costs and give examples of each.

In addition to the distinction between manufacturing and nonmanufacturing costs, there are other ways to look at costs. For instance, they can also be classified as either *product costs* or *period costs.* To understand the difference between product costs and period costs, we must first refresh our understanding of the matching principle from financial accounting.

Generally, costs are recognized as expenses on the income statement in the period that benefits from the cost. For example, if a company pays for liability insurance in advance for two years, the entire amount is not considered an expense of the year in which the payment is made. Instead, one-half of the cost would be recognized as an expense each year. The reason is that both years—not just the first year—benefit from the insurance payment. The unexpensed portion of the insurance payment is carried on the balance sheet as an asset called prepaid insurance. You should be familiar with this type of *accrual* from your financial accounting coursework.

The *matching principle* is based on the accrual concept and states that *costs incurred to generate a particular revenue should be recognized as expenses in the same period that the revenue is recognized.* This means that if a cost is incurred to acquire or make something that will eventually be sold, then the cost should be recognized as an expense only when the sale takes place—that is, when the benefit occurs. Such costs are called *product costs.*

Product Costs

For financial accounting purposes, **product costs** include all the costs that are involved in acquiring or making a product. In the case of manufactured goods, these costs consist of direct materials, direct labor, and manufacturing overhead. Product costs are viewed as "attaching" to units of product as the goods are purchased or manufactured, and they remain attached as the goods go into inventory awaiting sale. So initially, product costs are assigned to an inventory account on the balance sheet. When the goods are sold, the costs are released from inventory as expenses (typically called cost of goods sold) and matched against sales revenue. Since product costs are initially assigned to inventories, they are also known as **inventoriable costs.**

We want to emphasize that product costs are not necessarily treated as expenses in the period in which they are incurred. Rather, as explained above, they are treated as expenses in the period in which the related products *are sold.* This means that a product cost such as direct materials or direct labor might be incurred during one period but not treated as an expense until a following period when the completed product is sold.

Period Costs

Period costs are all the costs that are not included in product costs. These costs are expensed on the income statement in the period in which they are incurred, using the usual rules of accrual accounting you have already learned in financial accounting. Period costs are not included as part of the cost of either purchased or manufactured goods. Sales commissions and office rent are good examples of the kind of costs we are talking about. Neither commissions nor office rent are included as part of the cost of purchased or manufactured goods. Rather, both items are treated as expenses on the income statement in the period in which they are incurred. Thus, they are said to be period costs.

As suggested above, *all selling and administrative expenses are considered to be period costs.* Therefore, advertising, executive salaries, sales commissions, public relations, and other nonmanufacturing costs discussed earlier would all be period costs. They will appear on the income statement as expenses in the period in which they are incurred.

Exhibit 2–1 contains a summary of the cost terms that we have introduced so far.

Exhibit 2–1 Summary of Cost Terms

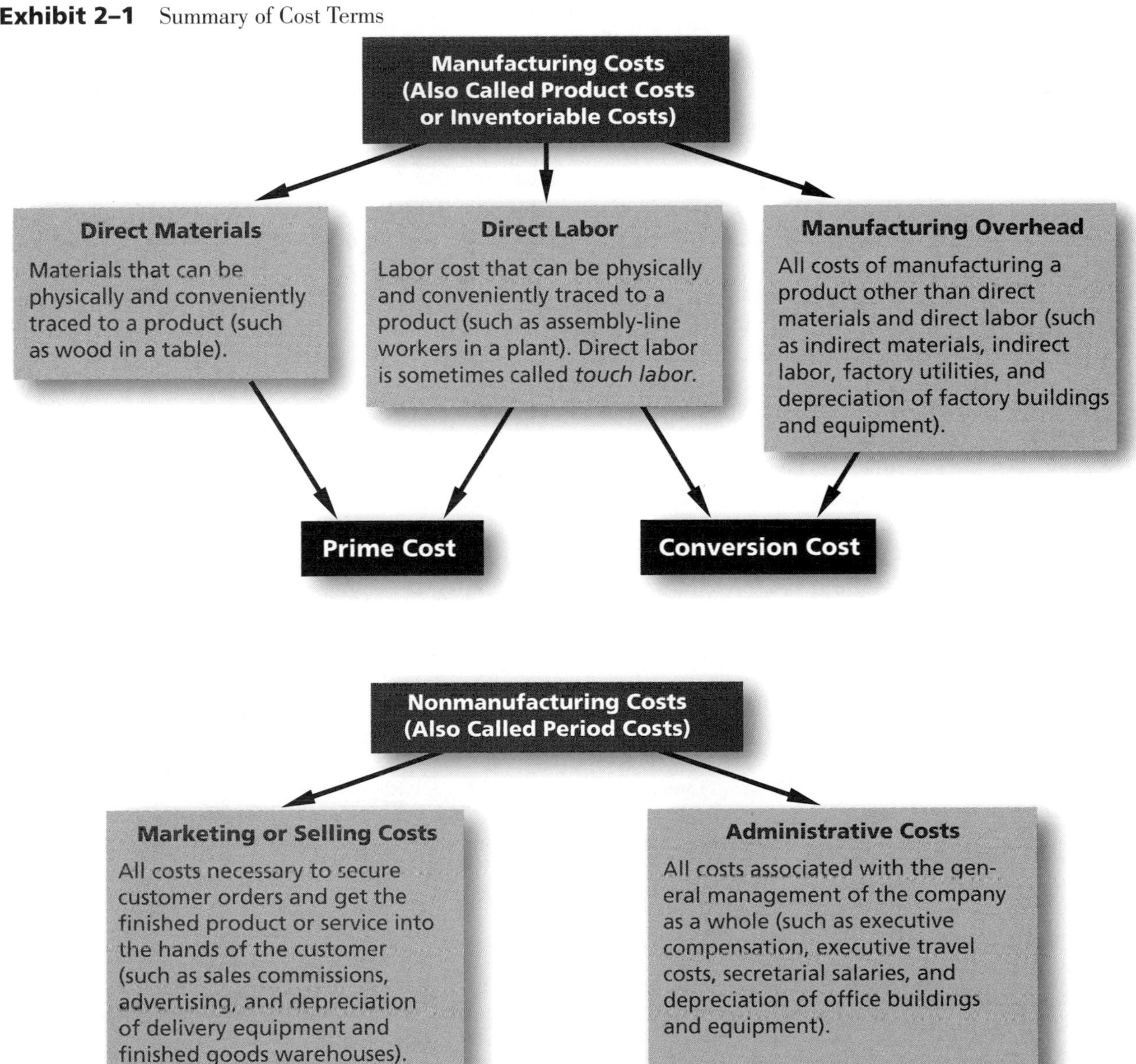

Cost Classifications on Financial Statements

In your prior accounting training, you learned that firms prepare periodic financial reports for creditors, stockholders, and others to show the financial condition of the firm and the firm's earnings performance over some specified interval. The reports you studied were probably those of merchandising companies, such as retail stores, which simply purchase goods from suppliers for resale to customers.

The financial statements prepared by a *manufacturing* company are more complex than the statements prepared by a merchandising company. Manufacturing companies are more complex organizations than merchandising companies because the manufacturing company must produce its goods as well as market them. The production process gives rise to many costs that do not exist in a merchandising company, and somehow these costs must be accounted for on the manufacturing company's financial statements. In this section, we focus our attention on how this accounting is carried out in the balance sheet and income statement.

The Balance Sheet

The balance sheet, or statement of financial position, of a manufacturing company is similar to that of a merchandising company. However, there are differences in the inventory accounts. A merchandising company has only one class of inventory—goods purchased from suppliers that are awaiting resale to customers. By contrast, manufacturing companies have three classes of inventories—*raw materials, work in process,* and *finished goods.* As discussed in Chapter 1, *work in process* consists of goods that are only partially completed, and *finished goods* consist of goods that are ready to be sold. The breakdown of the overall inventory figure into these three classes of inventories is usually provided in a footnote to the financial statements.

We will use two companies—Graham Manufacturing and Reston Bookstore—to illustrate the concepts discussed in this section. Graham Manufacturing is located in Portsmouth, New Hampshire, and makes precision brass fittings for yachts. Reston Bookstore is a small bookstore in Reston, Virginia, specializing in books about the Civil War.

The footnotes to Graham Manufacturing's Annual Report reveal the following information concerning its inventories:

Graham Manufacturing Corporation
Inventory Accounts

	Beginning Balance	Ending Balance
Raw Materials	$ 60,000	$ 50,000
Work in Process	90,000	60,000
Finished Goods	125,000	175,000
Total inventory accounts	$275,000	$285,000

Graham Manufacturing's raw materials inventory consists largely of brass rods and brass blocks. The work in process inventory consists of partially completed brass fittings. The finished goods inventory consists of brass fittings that are ready to be sold to customers.

In contrast, the inventory account at Reston Bookstore consists entirely of the costs of books the company has purchased from publishers for resale to the public. In merchandising companies like Reston, these inventories may be called *merchandise inventory.* The beginning and ending balances in this account appear as follows:

Reston Bookstore
Inventory Account

	Beginning Balance	Ending Balance
Merchandise Inventory	$100,000	$150,000

The Income Statement

Exhibit 2–2 compares the income statements of Reston Bookstore and Graham Manufacturing. For purposes of illustration, these statements contain more detail about cost of goods sold than you will generally find in published financial statements.

At first glance, the income statements of merchandising and manufacturing firms like Reston Bookstore and Graham Manufacturing are very similar. The only apparent difference is in the labels of some of the entries that go into the computation of the cost of goods sold figure. In the exhibit, the computation of cost of goods sold relies on the following basic equation for inventory accounts:

Exhibit 2–2 Comparative Income Statements: Merchandising and Manufacturing Companies

MERCHANDISING COMPANY
Reston Bookstore

Sales		$1,000,000
Cost of goods sold:		
Beginning merchandise inventory	$100,000	
Add: Purchases	650,000	
Goods available for sale	750,000	
Deduct: Ending merchandise inventory	150,000	600,000
Gross margin		400,000
Less operating expenses:		
Selling expense	100,000	
Administrative expense	200,000	300,000
Net income		$ 100,000

The cost of merchandise inventory purchased from outside suppliers during the period. (→ Add: Purchases)

MANUFACTURING COMPANY
Graham Manufacturing

Sales		$1,500,000
Cost of goods sold:		
Beginning finished goods inventory	$125,000	
Add: Cost of goods manufactured	850,000	
Goods available for sale	975,000	
Deduct: Ending finished goods inventory	175,000	800,000
Gross margin		700,000
Less operating expenses:		
Selling expense	250,000	
Administrative expense	300,000	550,000
Net income		$ 150,000

The manufacturing costs associated with the goods that were finished during the period. (See Exhibits 2–4 and 2–5 for details.) (→ Add: Cost of goods manufactured)

Basic Equation for Inventory Accounts

$$\text{Beginning balance} + \text{Additions to inventory} = \text{Ending balance} + \text{Withdrawals from inventory}$$

The logic underlying this equation, which applies to any inventory account, is illustrated in Exhibit 2–3. During a period, there are additions to the inventory account through purchases or other means. The sum of the additions to the account and the beginning balance represents the total amount of inventory that is available for use during the period. At the end of the period, all of the inventory that was available must either be in ending inventory or must have been withdrawn from the inventory account.

These concepts are applied to determine the cost of goods sold for a merchandising company like Reston Bookstore as follows:

Cost of Goods Sold in a Merchandising Company

$$\text{Beginning merchandise inventory} + \text{Purchases} = \text{Ending merchandise inventory} + \text{Cost of goods sold}$$

or

$$\text{Cost of goods sold} = \text{Beginning merchandise inventory} + \text{Purchases} - \text{Ending merchandise inventory}$$

The cost of goods sold for a manufacturing company like Graham Manufacturing is determined as follows:

Cost of Goods Sold in a Manufacturing Company

$$\text{Beginning finished goods inventory} + \text{Cost of goods manufactured} = \text{Ending finished goods inventory} + \text{Cost of goods sold}$$

or

$$\text{Cost of goods sold} = \text{Beginning finished goods inventory} + \text{Cost of goods manufactured} - \text{Ending finished goods inventory}$$

To determine the cost of goods sold in a merchandising company like Reston Bookstore, we only need to know the beginning and ending balances in the Merchandise Inventory account and the purchases. Total purchases can be easily determined in a merchandising company by simply adding together all purchases from suppliers.

Exhibit 2–3 Inventory Flows

To determine the cost of goods sold in a manufacturing company like Graham Manufacturing, we need to know the *cost of goods manufactured* and the beginning and ending balances in the Finished Goods inventory account. The **cost of goods manufactured** consists of the manufacturing costs associated with goods that were *finished* during the period. The cost of goods manufactured figure for Graham Manufacturing is derived in Exhibit 2–4, which contains a *schedule of cost of goods manufactured.*

Schedule of Cost of Goods Manufactured

objective 3
Prepare a schedule of cost of goods manufactured in good form.

At first glance, the **schedule of cost of goods manufactured** in Exhibit 2–4 appears complex and perhaps even intimidating. However, it is all quite logical. Notice that the schedule of cost of goods manufactured contains the three elements of product costs that we discussed earlier—direct materials, direct labor, and manufacturing overhead. The total of these three cost elements is *not* the cost of goods manufactured, however. The reason is that some of the materials, labor, and overhead costs incurred during the period relate to goods that are not yet completed. The costs that relate to goods that are not yet completed are shown in the work in process inventory figures at the bottom of the schedule. Note that the beginning work in process inventory must be added to the

Exhibit 2–4 Schedule of Cost of Goods Manufactured

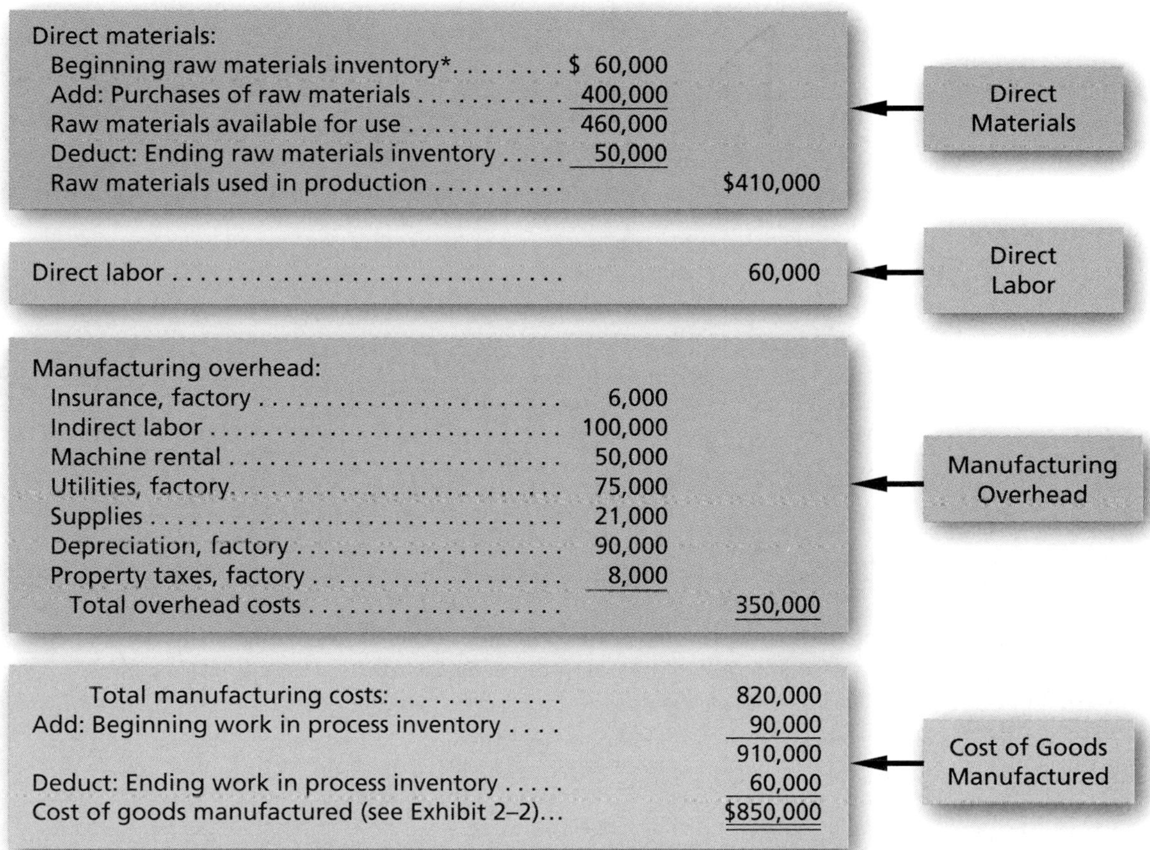

Direct materials:		
Beginning raw materials inventory*	$ 60,000	
Add: Purchases of raw materials	400,000	
Raw materials available for use	460,000	
Deduct: Ending raw materials inventory	50,000	
Raw materials used in production		$410,000
Direct labor		60,000
Manufacturing overhead:		
Insurance, factory	6,000	
Indirect labor	100,000	
Machine rental	50,000	
Utilities, factory	75,000	
Supplies	21,000	
Depreciation, factory	90,000	
Property taxes, factory	8,000	
Total overhead costs		350,000
Total manufacturing costs:		820,000
Add: Beginning work in process inventory		90,000
		910,000
Deduct: Ending work in process inventory		60,000
Cost of goods manufactured (see Exhibit 2–2) . . .		$850,000

*We assume in this example that the Raw Materials inventory account contains only direct materials and that indirect materials are carried in a separate Supplies account. Using a Supplies account for indirect materials is a common practice among companies. In Chapter 3, we discuss the procedure to be followed if *both* direct and indirect materials are carried in a single account.

Exhibit 2–5 An Alternative Approach to Computation of Cost of Goods Sold

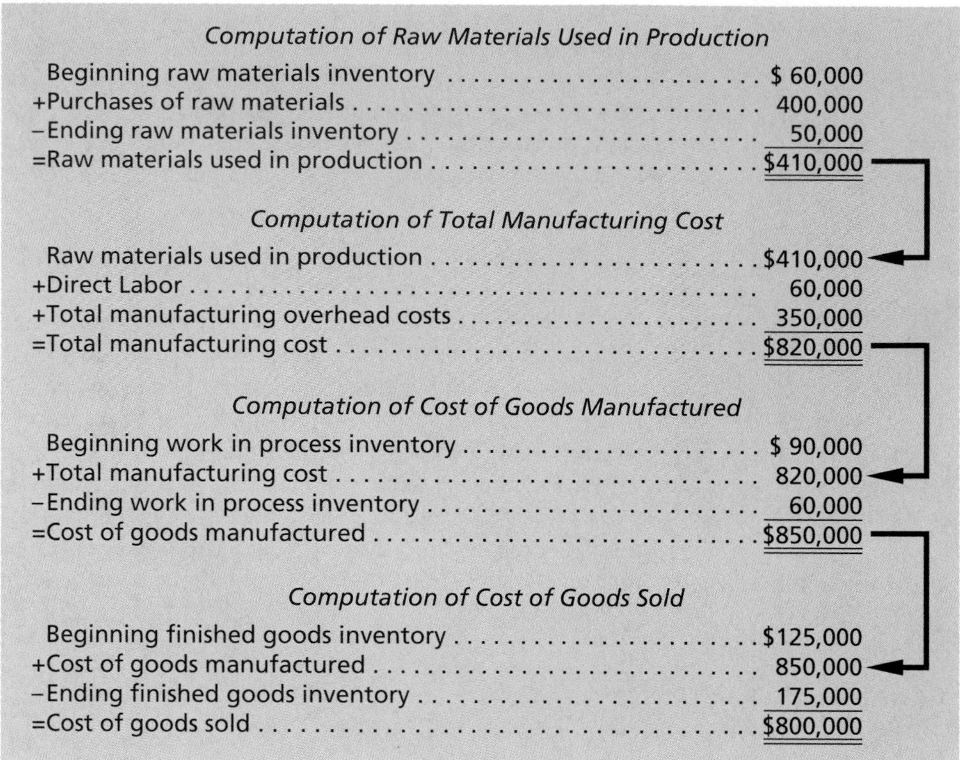

Computation of Raw Materials Used in Production	
Beginning raw materials inventory	$ 60,000
+Purchases of raw materials	400,000
−Ending raw materials inventory	50,000
=Raw materials used in production	$410,000
Computation of Total Manufacturing Cost	
Raw materials used in production	$410,000
+Direct Labor	60,000
+Total manufacturing overhead costs	350,000
=Total manufacturing cost	$820,000
Computation of Cost of Goods Manufactured	
Beginning work in process inventory	$ 90,000
+Total manufacturing cost	820,000
−Ending work in process inventory	60,000
=Cost of goods manufactured	$850,000
Computation of Cost of Goods Sold	
Beginning finished goods inventory	$125,000
+Cost of goods manufactured	850,000
−Ending finished goods inventory	175,000
=Cost of goods sold	$800,000

manufacturing costs of the period, and the ending work in process inventory must be deducted, to arrive at the cost of goods manufactured.

The logic underlying the schedule of cost of goods manufactured and the computation of cost of goods sold is laid out in a different format in Exhibit 2–5. To compute the cost of goods sold, go to the top of the exhibit and work your way down using the following steps:

1. Compute the raw materials used in production in the top section of the exhibit.
2. Insert the total raw materials used in production ($410,000) into the second section of the exhibit, and compute the total manufacturing cost.
3. Insert the total manufacturing cost ($820,000) into the third section of the exhibit, and compute the cost of goods manufactured.
4. Insert the cost of goods manufactured ($850,000) into the bottom section of the exhibit, and compute the cost of goods sold.

Product Costs—A Closer Look

objective 4

Explain the flow of direct materials cost, direct labor cost, and manufacturing overhead cost from the point of incurrence to sale of the completed product.

Earlier in the chapter, we defined product costs as consisting of those costs that are involved in either the purchase or the manufacture of goods. For manufactured goods, we stated that these costs consist of direct materials, direct labor, and manufacturing overhead. To understand product costs more fully, it will be helpful at this point to look briefly at the flow of costs in a manufacturing company. By doing so, we will be able to see how product costs move through the various accounts and affect the balance sheet and the income statement in the course of producing and selling products.

Exhibit 2–6 illustrates the flow of costs in a manufacturing company. Raw materials purchases are recorded in the Raw Materials inventory account. When raw materials are used in production, their costs are transferred to the Work in Process inventory account as direct materials. Notice that direct labor cost and manufacturing overhead cost are added directly to Work in Process. Work in Process can be viewed most

Exhibit 2–6 Cost Flows and Classifications in a Manufacturing Company

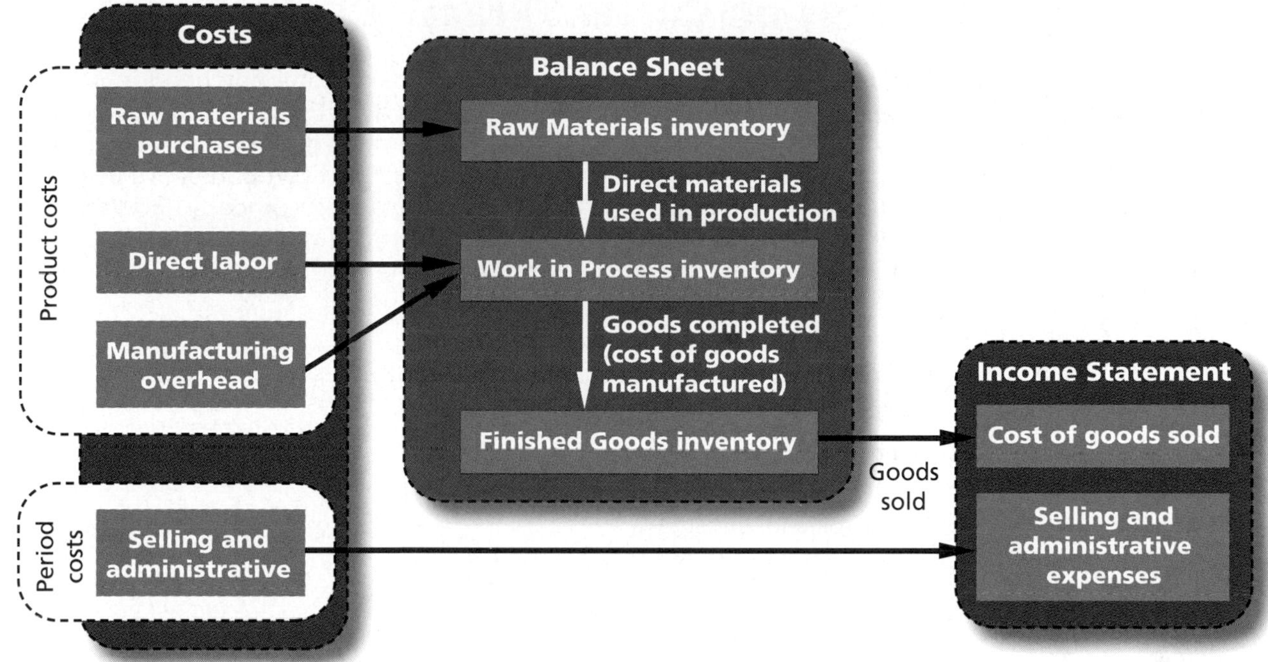

simply as an assembly line where workers are stationed and where products slowly take shape as they move from one end of the assembly line to the other. The direct materials, direct labor, and manufacturing overhead costs added to Work in Process in Exhibit 2–6 are the costs needed to complete these products as they move along this assembly line.

Notice from the exhibit that as goods are completed, their cost is transferred from Work in Process into Finished Goods. Here the goods await sale to a customer. As goods are sold, their cost is then transferred from Finished Goods into Cost of Goods Sold. It is at this point that the various material, labor, and overhead costs that are required to make the product are finally treated as expenses.

Inventoriable Costs

As stated earlier, product costs are often called inventoriable costs. The reason is that these costs go directly into inventory accounts as they are incurred (first into Work in Process and then into Finished Goods), rather than going into expense accounts. Thus, they are termed *inventoriable costs. This is a key concept in managerial accounting, since such costs can end up on the balance sheet as assets if goods are only partially completed or are unsold at the end of a period.* To illustrate this point, refer again to the data in Exhibit 2–6. At the end of the period, the materials, labor, and overhead costs that are associated with the units in the Work in Process and Finished Goods inventory accounts will appear on the balance sheet as part of the company's assets. As explained earlier, these costs will not become expenses until later when the goods are completed and sold.

As shown in Exhibit 2–6, selling and administrative expenses are not involved in the manufacture of a product. For this reason, they are not treated as product costs but rather as period costs that go directly into expense accounts as they are incurred.

Focus on Current Practice

United Colors of Benetton, an Italian apparel company headquartered in Ponzano, is unusual in that it is involved in all activities in the "value chain" from clothing design through manufacturing, distribution, and ultimate sale to customers in Benetton retail outlets. Most companies are involved in only one or two of these activities. Looking at this company allows us to see how costs are distributed across the entire value chain. A recent income statement from the company contained the following data:

	Billions of Italian Lire	**Percent of Net Sales**
Net sales	2,768	100.0%
Cost of sales	1,721	62.2
Selling and general and administrative expenses:		
Payroll and related cost	166	6.0
Distribution and transport	57	2.1
Sales commissions	115	4.2
Advertising and promotion	120	4.3
Depreciation and amortization	42	1.5
Other expenses	275	9.9
Total selling and general and administrative expenses	775	28.0%

Even though this company spends large sums on advertising and runs its own shops, the cost of sales is still quite high in relation to the net sales—62% of net sales. And despite the company's lavish advertising campaigns, advertising and promotion costs amounted to only a little over 4% of net sales. (Note: One U.S. dollar was worth about 1,600 Italian lire at the time of this financial report.)

An Example of Cost Flows

To provide a numerical example of cost flows in a manufacturing company, assume that a company's annual insurance cost is $2,000. Three-fourths of this amount ($1,500) applies to factory operations, and one-fourth ($500) applies to selling and administrative activities. Therefore, $1,500 of the $2,000 insurance cost would be a product (inventoriable) cost and would be added to the cost of the goods produced during the year. This concept is illustrated in Exhibit 2–7, where $1,500 of insurance cost is added into Work in Process. As shown in the exhibit, this portion of the year's insurance cost will not become an expense until the goods that are produced during the year are sold—which may not happen until the following year or even later. Until the goods are sold, the $1,500 will remain as part of the asset, inventory (either as part of Work in Process or as part of Finished Goods), along with the other costs of producing the goods.

By contrast, the $500 of insurance cost that applies to the company's selling and administrative activities will go into an expense account immediately as a charge against the period's revenue.

Thus far, we have been mainly concerned with classifications of manufacturing costs for the purpose of determining inventory valuations on the balance sheet and cost

Exhibit 2–7 An Example of Cost Flows in a Manufacturing Company

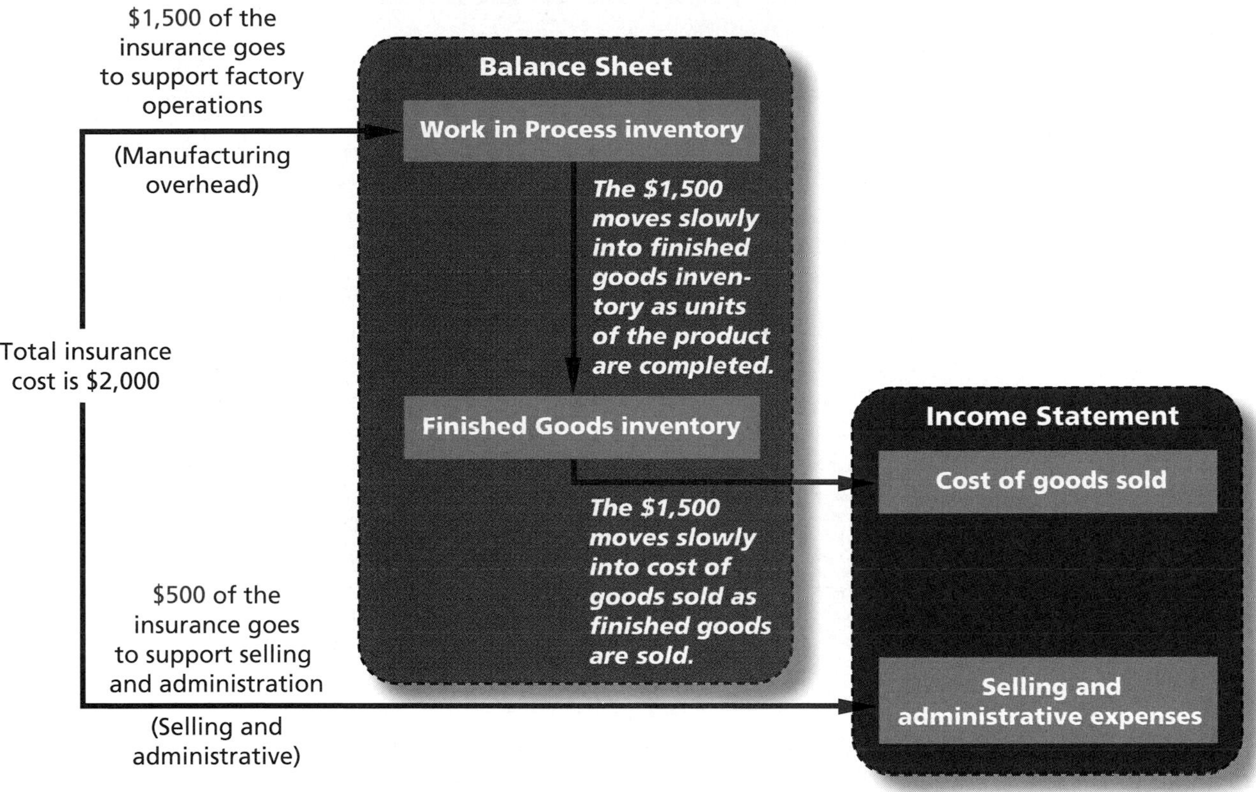

of goods sold on the income statement of external financial reports. There are, however, many other purposes for which costs are used, and each purpose requires a different classification of costs. We will consider several different purposes for cost classifications in the remaining sections of this chapter. These purposes and the corresponding cost classifications are summarized in Exhibit 2–8. To maintain focus, we suggest that you refer back to this exhibit frequently as you progress through the rest of this chapter.

Focus on Current Practice

Planet Hollywood International, Inc., provides an interesting contrast to United Colors of Benetton, which was featured in the previous Focus on Current Practice box. Planet Hollywood develops and operates theme restaurants that provide a "unique dining and entertainment experience in a high-energy environment." Restaurants are located at high-profile locations and have spectacular design features. At Benetton customers ultimately are buying clothing; at Planet Hollywood, customers are buying both food and entertainment. This difference has a dramatic effect on how costs are distributed across the value chain. The following data have been taken from a Planet Hollywood annual report:

	Millions of U.S. Dollars	Percent of Net Sales
Direct sales revenues	347	100.0%
Cost of sales	93	26.8
Other expenses:		
Operating expenses	157	45.2
General and administrative expenses	20	5.8
Depreciation and amortization	27	7.8
Total other expenses	204	58.8%

Direct comparisons with Benetton are complicated by differences in accounting methods. For instance, Benetton separately reports advertising and promotion expenses, whereas Planet Hollywood does not. Nevertheless, the difference in cost of sales as a percent of sales is striking. At Benetton, the cost of sales percentage is in excess of 62%, whereas at Planet Hollywood it is less than 27%. However, the difference is largely due to how Planet Hollywood accounts for its cost of sales. Planet Hollywood includes only the cost of food and beverages in its cost of sales. So roughly speaking, the cost of the food and beverages is about 27% of the tab at the restaurant and about 45% of the tab is for entertainment (i.e., the operating expenses). The rest covers general expenses and profits.

Exhibit 2–8 Summary of Cost Classifications

Purpose of Cost Classification	Cost Classifications

Preparing external financial statements	• Product costs (inventoriable)
	  • Direct materials
	  • Direct labor
	  • Manufacturing overhead
	• Period costs (expensed)
	  • Nonmanufacturing costs
	    • Marketing or selling costs
	    • Administrative costs

Predicting cost behavior in response to changes in activity	• Variable cost (proportional to activity) • Fixed cost (constant in total)
Assigning costs to cost objects such as departments or products	• Direct cost (can be easily traced) • Indirect cost (cannot be easily traced; must be allocated)
Making decisions	• Differential cost (differs between alternatives) • Sunk cost (past cost not affected by a decision) • Opportunity cost (forgone benefit)

Cost Classifications for Predicting Cost Behavior

objective 5

Identify and give examples of variable costs and fixed costs, and explain the difference in their behavior.

Quite frequently, it is necessary to predict how a certain cost will behave in response to a change in activity. For example, a manager at AT&T may want to estimate the impact a 5% increase in long-distance calls would have on the company's total electric bill or on the total wages the company pays its long-distance operators. **Cost behavior** means how a cost will react or respond to changes in the level of business activity. As the activity level rises and falls, a particular cost may rise and fall as well—or it may remain constant. For planning purposes, a manager must be able to anticipate which of these will happen; and if a cost can be expected to change, the manager must know by how much it will change. To help make such distinctions, costs are often categorized as variable or fixed.

Variable Cost

A **variable cost** is a cost that varies, in total, in direct proportion to changes in the level of activity. The activity can be expressed in many ways, such as units produced, units sold, miles driven, beds occupied, lines of print, hours worked, and so forth. A good example of a variable cost is direct materials. The cost of direct materials used during a period will vary, in total, in direct proportion to the number of units that are produced. To illustrate this idea, consider the Saturn Division of GM. Each auto requires one battery. As the output of autos increases and decreases, the number of batteries used will increase and decrease proportionately. If auto production goes up 10%, then the number of batteries used will also go up 10%. The concept of a variable cost is shown in graphic form in Exhibit 2–9.

It is important to note that when we speak of a cost as being variable, we mean the *total* cost rises and falls as the activity level rises and falls. This idea is presented below, assuming that a Saturn's battery costs $24:

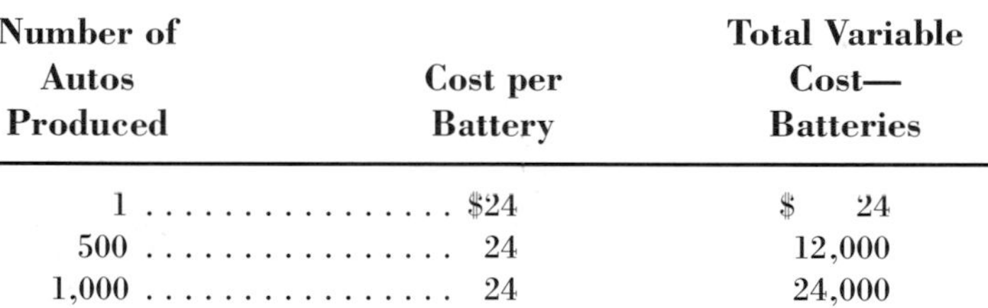

Number of Autos Produced	Cost per Battery	Total Variable Cost—Batteries
1	$24	$ 24
500	24	12,000
1,000	24	24,000

Exhibit 2–9 Variable and Fixed Cost Behavior

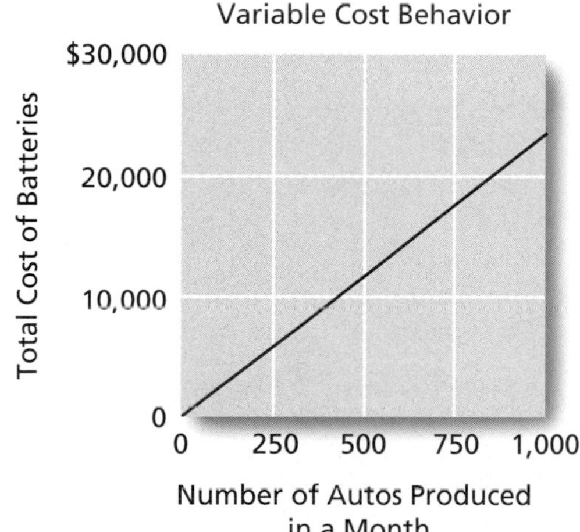

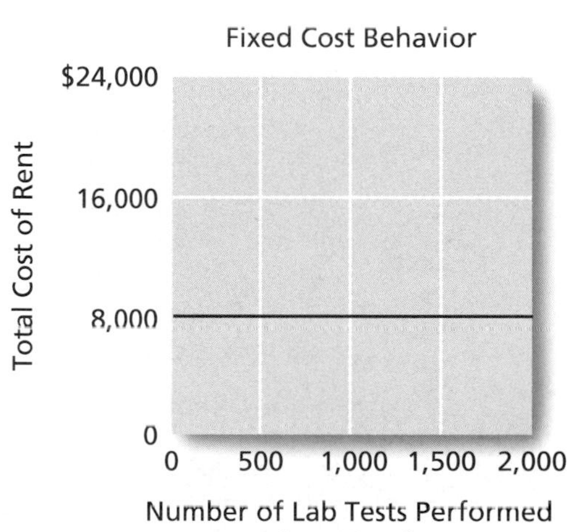

One interesting aspect of variable cost behavior is that a variable cost is constant if expressed on a *per unit* basis. Observe from the tabulation above that the per unit cost of batteries remains constant at $24 even though the total amount of cost involved increases and decreases with activity.

There are many examples of costs that are variable with respect to the products and services provided by a company. In a manufacturing company, variable costs include items such as direct materials and some elements of manufacturing overhead such as lubricants, shipping costs, and sales commissions. For the present we will also assume that direct labor is a variable cost, although as we shall see in Chapter 6, direct labor may act more like a fixed cost in many situations. In a merchandising company, variable costs include items such as cost of goods sold, commissions to salespersons, and billing costs. In a hospital, the variable costs of providing health care services to patients would include the costs of the supplies, drugs, meals, and perhaps nursing services.

The activity causing changes in a variable cost need not be how much output is produced or sold. For example, the wages paid to employees at a Blockbuster Video outlet will depend on the number of hours the store is open and not strictly on the number of videos rented. In this case, we would say that wage costs are variable with respect to the hours of operation. Nevertheless, when we say that a cost is variable, we ordinarily mean it is variable with respect to the volume of revenue-generating output—in other words, how many units are produced and sold, how many videos are rented, how many patients are treated, and so on.

Fixed Cost

A **fixed cost** is a cost that remains constant, in total, regardless of changes in the level of activity. Unlike variable costs, fixed costs are not affected by changes in activity. Consequently, as the activity level rises and falls, the fixed costs remain constant in total amount unless influenced by some outside force, such as price changes. Rent is a good example of a fixed cost. Suppose the Mayo Clinic rents a machine for $8,000 per month that tests blood samples for the presence of leukemia cells. The $8,000 monthly rental cost will be sustained regardless of the number of tests that may be performed during the month. The concept of a fixed cost is shown in graphic form in Exhibit 2–9.

Very few costs are completely fixed. Most will change if there is a large enough change in activity. For example, suppose that the capacity of the leukemia diagnostic machine at the Mayo Clinic is 2,000 tests per month. If the clinic wishes to perform more than 2,000 tests in a month, it would be necessary to rent an additional machine, which would cause a jump in the fixed costs. When we say a cost is fixed, we mean it is fixed within some *relevant range*. The **relevant range** is the range of activity within which the assumptions about variable and fixed costs are valid. For example, the assumption that the rent for diagnostic machines is $8,000 per month is valid within the relevant range of 0 to 2,000 tests per month.

Fixed costs can create difficulties if it becomes necessary to express the costs on a per unit basis. This is because if fixed costs are expressed on a per unit basis, they will react *inversely* with changes in activity. In the Mayo Clinic, for example, the average cost per test will fall as the number of tests performed increases. This is because the $8,000 rental cost will be spread over more tests. Conversely, as the number of tests performed in the clinic declines, the average cost per test will rise as the $8,000 rental cost is spread over fewer tests. This concept is illustrated in the table below:

Monthly Rental Cost	Number of Tests Performed	Average Cost per Test
$8,000	10	$800
8,000	500	16
8,000	2,000	4

Exhibit 2–10
Summary of Variable and Fixed Cost Behavior

	Behavior of the Cost (within the relevant range)	
Cost	**In Total**	**Per Unit**
Variable cost	Total variable cost increases and decreases in proportion to changes in the activity level.	Variable costs remain constant per unit.
Fixed cost	Total fixed cost is not affected by changes in the activity level within the relevant range.	Fixed costs decrease per unit as the activity level rises and increase per unit as the activity level falls.

Note that if the Mayo Clinic performs only 10 tests each month, the rental cost of the equipment will average $800 per test. But if 2,000 tests are performed each month, the average cost will drop to only $4 per test. More will be said later about the problems created for both the accountant and the manager by this variation in unit costs.

Examples of fixed costs include straight-line depreciation, insurance, property taxes, rent, supervisory salaries, administrative salaries, and advertising.

A summary of both variable and fixed cost behavior is presented in Exhibit 2–10.

Cost Classifications for Assigning Costs to Cost Objects

objective 6
Define and give examples of direct and indirect costs.

Costs are assigned to objects for a variety of purposes including pricing, profitability studies, and control of spending. A **cost object** is anything for which cost data are desired—including products, product lines, customers, jobs, and organizational subunits. For purposes of assigning costs to cost objects, costs are classified as either *direct* or *indirect.*

Direct Cost

A **direct cost** is a cost that can be easily and conveniently traced to the particular cost object under consideration. The concept of direct cost extends beyond just direct materials and direct labor. For example, if Reebok is assigning costs to its various regional and national sales offices, then the salary of the sales manager in its Tokyo office would be a direct cost of that office.

Indirect Cost

An **indirect cost** is a cost that cannot be easily and conveniently traced to the particular cost object under consideration. For example, a Campbell Soup factory may produce dozens of varieties of canned soups. The factory manager's salary would be an indirect cost of a particular variety such as chicken noodle soup. The reason is that the factory manager's salary is not caused by any one variety of soup but rather is incurred as a consequence of running the entire factory. *To be traced to a cost object such as a particular product, the cost must be caused by the cost object.* The factory manager's salary is called a *common cost* of producing the various products of the factory. A **common cost** is a cost that is common to a number of costing objects but cannot be traced to them individually. A common cost is a particular type of indirect cost.

A particular cost may be direct or indirect, depending on the cost object. While the Campbell Soup factory manager's salary is an *indirect* cost of manufacturing chicken noodle soup, it is a *direct* cost of the manufacturing division. In the first case, the cost object is the chicken noodle soup product. In the second case, the cost object is the entire manufacturing division.

Cost Classifications for Decision Making

objective 7

Define and give examples of cost classifications used in making decisions: differential costs, opportunity costs, and sunk costs.

Costs are an important feature of many business decisions. In making decisions, it is essential to have a firm grasp of the concepts *differential cost, opportunity cost,* and *sunk cost.*

Differential Cost and Revenue

Decisions involve choosing between alternatives. In business decisions, each alternative will have certain costs and benefits that must be compared to the costs and benefits of the other available alternatives. A difference in costs between any two alternatives is known as a **differential cost.** A difference in revenues between any two alternatives is known as **differential revenue.**

A differential cost is also known as an **incremental cost,** although technically an incremental cost should refer only to an increase in cost from one alternative to another; decreases in cost should be referred to as *decremental costs.* Differential cost is a broader term, encompassing both cost increases (incremental costs) and cost decreases (decremental costs) between alternatives.

The accountant's differential cost concept can be compared to the economist's marginal cost concept. In speaking of changes in cost and revenue, the economist employs the terms *marginal cost* and *marginal revenue.* The revenue that can be obtained from selling one more unit of product is called marginal revenue, and the cost involved in producing one more unit of product is called marginal cost. The economist's marginal concept is basically the same as the accountant's differential concept applied to a single unit of output.

Differential costs can be either fixed or variable. To illustrate, assume that Nature Way Cosmetics, Inc., is thinking about changing its marketing method from distribution through retailers to distribution by door-to-door direct sale. Present costs and revenues are compared to projected costs and revenues in the following table:

	Retailer Distribution (present)	Direct Sale Distribution (proposed)	Differential Costs and Revenues
Revenues (V)	$700,000	$800,000	$100,000
Cost of goods sold (V)	350,000	400,000	50,000
Advertising (F)	80,000	45,000	(35,000)
Commissions (V)	–0–	40,000	40,000
Warehouse depreciation (F)	50,000	80,000	30,000
Other expenses (F)	60,000	60,000	–0–
Total	540,000	625,000	85,000
Net income	$160,000	$175,000	$ 15,000

V = Variable; F = Fixed.

According to the above analysis, the differential revenue is $100,000 and the differential costs total $85,000, leaving a positive differential net income of $15,000 under the proposed marketing plan.

The decision of whether Nature Way Cosmetics should stay with the present retail distribution or switch to door-to-door direct selling could be made on the basis of the net incomes of the two alternatives. As we see in the above analysis, the net income under the present distribution method is $160,000, whereas the net income under door-to-door direct selling is estimated to be $175,000. Therefore, the door-to-door direct distribution method is preferred, since it would result in $15,000 higher net income. Note that we would have arrived at exactly the same conclusion by simply focusing on the differential revenues, differential costs, and differential net income, which also show a $15,000 advantage for the direct selling method.

In general, only the differences between alternatives are relevant in decisions. Those items that are the same under all alternatives and that are not affected by the decision can be ignored. For example, in the Nature Way Cosmetics example above, the "Other expenses" category, which is $60,000 under both alternatives, can be ignored, since it has no effect on the decision. If it were removed from the calculations, the door-to-door direct selling method would still be preferred by $15,000. This is an extremely important principle in management accounting that we will return to in later chapters.

Focus on Current Practice

An Annual Report of CBS states: "One of television's fastest-growing segments is the export of news and entertainment programming to overseas markets, and CBS Enterprises had a superlative year selling its program inventory to more than 300 outlets in nearly 100 countries. The export business has mushroomed, reflecting both the global spread of privately owned commercial television, which is supplanting a handful of state-controlled channels, and the expansion of international satellite capacity and distribution . . . As a result, international markets for CBS have become an increasingly important profit center, particularly with the buildup of CBS Entertainment's incremental program production. . . . CBS's international revenues rose by more than 20 percent compared with the prior year, led by the global distribution of CBS News programming and foreign sales of *Rescue 911®* and *Dr. Quinn, Medicine Woman.*" The revenue on foreign sales of CBS's programming is almost pure profit. There is very little *incremental cost* since the programming was already produced for the U.S. market.

Opportunity Cost

Opportunity cost is the potential benefit that is given up when one alternative is selected over another. To illustrate this important concept, consider the following examples:

Example 1

Vicki has a part-time job that pays her $100 per week while attending college. She would like to spend a week at the beach during spring break, and her employer has agreed to give her the time off, but without pay. The $100 in lost wages would be an opportunity cost of taking the week off to be at the beach.

Example 2

Suppose that Neiman Marcus is considering investing a large sum of money in land that may be a site for a future store. Rather than invest the funds in land, the company could invest the funds in high-grade securities. If the land is acquired, the opportunity cost will be the investment income that could have been realized if the securities had been purchased instead.

Example 3

Steve is employed with a company that pays him a salary of $20,000 per year. He is thinking about leaving the company and returning to school. Since returning to school would require that he give up his $20,000 salary, the forgone salary would be an opportunity cost of seeking further education.

Opportunity cost is not usually entered in the accounting records of an organization, but it is a cost that must be explicitly considered in every decision a manager makes. Virtually every alternative has some opportunity cost attached to it. In example 3 above, for instance, if Steve decides to stay at his job, there still is an opportunity cost involved: it is the greater income that could be realized in future years as a result of returning to school.

Sunk Cost

A **sunk cost** is a cost *that has already been incurred* and that cannot be changed by any decision made now or in the future. Since sunk costs cannot be changed by any decision, they are not differential costs. Therefore, they can and should be ignored when making a decision.

To illustrate a sunk cost, assume that a company paid $50,000 several years ago for a special-purpose machine. The machine was used to make a product that is now obsolete and is no longer being sold. Even though in hindsight the purchase of the machine may have been unwise, no amount of regret can undo that decision. And it would be folly to continue making the obsolete product in a misguided attempt to "recover" the original cost of the machine. In short, the $50,000 originally paid for the machine has already been incurred and cannot be a differential cost in any future decision. For this reason, such costs are said to be sunk and should be ignored in decisions.

Summary

In this chapter, we have looked at some of the ways in which managers classify costs. How the costs will be used—for preparing external reports, predicting cost behavior, assigning costs to cost objects, or decision making—will dictate how the costs will be classified.

For purposes of valuing inventories and determining expenses for the balance sheet and income statement, costs are classified as either product costs or period costs. Product costs are assigned to inventories and are considered assets until the products are sold. At the point of sale, product costs become cost of goods sold on the income statement. In contrast, following the usual accrual practices, period costs are taken directly to the income statement as expenses in the period in which they are incurred.

In a merchandising company, product cost is whatever the company paid for its merchandise. For external financial reports in a manufacturing company, product costs consist of all manufacturing costs. In both kinds of companies, selling and administrative costs are considered to be period costs and are expensed as incurred.

For purposes of predicting cost behavior—how costs will react to changes in activity—managers commonly classify costs into two categories—variable and fixed. Variable costs, in total, are strictly proportional to activity. Thus, the variable cost per unit is constant. Fixed costs, in total, remain at the same level for changes in activity that occur within the relevant range. Thus, the average fixed cost per unit decreases as the number of units increases.

For purposes of assigning costs to cost objects such as products or departments, costs are classified as direct or indirect. Direct costs can be conveniently traced to the cost objects. Indirect costs cannot be conveniently traced to cost objects.

For purposes of making decisions, the concepts of differential costs and revenue, opportunity cost, and sunk cost are of vital importance. Differential cost and revenue are the cost and revenue items that differ between alternatives. Opportunity cost is the benefit that is forgone when one alternative is selected over another. Sunk cost is a cost that occurred in the past and cannot be altered. Differential cost and opportunity cost should be carefully considered in decisions. Sunk cost is always irrelevant in decisions and should be ignored.

These various cost classifications are *different* ways of looking at costs. A particular cost, such as the cost of cheese in a taco served at Taco Bell, could be a manufacturing cost, a product cost, a variable cost, a direct cost, and a differential cost—all at the same time.

Review Problem 1: Cost Terms

Many new cost terms have been introduced in this chapter. It will take you some time to learn what each term means and how to properly classify costs in an organization. To assist in this learning process, consider the following example: Porter Company manufactures furniture, including tables. Selected costs associated with the manufacture of the tables and the general operation of the company are given below:

1. The tables are made of wood that costs $100 per table.
2. The tables are assembled by workers, at a wage cost of $40 per table.
3. Workers assembling the tables are supervised by a factory supervisor who is paid $25,000 per year.
4. Electrical costs are $2 per machine-hour. Four machine-hours are required to produce a table.
5. The depreciation cost of the machines used to make the tables totals $10,000 per year.
6. The salary of the president of Porter Company is $100,000 per year.
7. Porter Company spends $250,000 per year to advertise its products.
8. Salespersons are paid a commission of $30 for each table sold.
9. Instead of producing the tables, Porter Company could rent its factory space out at a rental income of $50,000 per year.

In the following tabulation, these costs are classified according to various cost terms used in the chapter. *Carefully study the classification of each cost.* If you don't understand why a particular cost is classified the way it is, reread the section of the chapter discussing the particular cost term. The terms *variable cost* and *fixed cost* refer to how costs behave with respect to the number of tables produced in a year.

Solution to Review Problem 1

	Variable Cost	Fixed Cost	Period (selling and administrative) Cost	Product Cost: Direct Materials	Product Cost: Direct Labor	Product Cost: Manufacturing Overhead	To Units of Product: Direct	To Units of Product: Indirect	Sunk Cost	Opportunity Cost
1. Wood used in a table ($100 per table)	X			X			X			
2. Labor cost to assemble a table ($40 per table) . . .	X				X		X			
3. Salary of the factory supervisor ($25,000 per year)		X				X		X		
4. Cost of electricity to produce tables ($2 per machine-hour)	X					X		X		
5. Depreciation of machines used to produce tables ($10,000 per year)		X				X		X	X*	
6. Salary of the company president ($100,000 per year)		X	X							
7. Advertising expense ($250,000 per year)		X	X							
8. Commissions paid to salespersons ($30 per table sold)	X		X							
9. Rental income forgone on factory space										X†

*This is a sunk cost, since the outlay for the equipment was made in a previous period.

†This is an opportunity cost, since it represents the potential benefit that is lost or sacrificed as a result of using the factory space to produce tables. Opportunity cost is a special category of cost that is not ordinarily recorded in an organization's accounting books. To avoid possible confusion with other costs, we will not attempt to classify this cost in any other way except as an opportunity cost.

Review Problem 2: Schedule of Cost of Goods Manufactured and Income Statement

The following information has been taken from the accounting records of Klear-Seal Company for last year:

Selling expenses	$ 140,000
Raw materials inventory, January 1	90,000
Raw materials inventory, December 31	60,000
Utilities, factory	36,000
Direct labor cost	150,000
Depreciation, factory	162,000

Purchases of raw materials	$ 750,000
Sales	2,500,000
Insurance, factory	40,000
Supplies, factory	15,000
Administrative expenses	270,000
Indirect labor	300,000
Maintenance, factory	87,000
Work in process inventory, January 1	180,000
Work in process inventory, December 31	100,000
Finished goods inventory, January 1	260,000
Finished goods inventory, December 31	210,000

Management wants to organize these data into a better format so that financial statements can be prepared for the year.

Required

1. Prepare a schedule of cost of goods manufactured as in Exhibit 2–4.
2. Compute the cost of goods sold.
3. Using data as needed from (1) and (2) above, prepare an income statement.

Solution to Review Problem 2

1.

KLEAR-SEAL COMPANY
Schedule of Cost of Goods Manufactured
For the Year Ended December 31

Direct materials:		
Raw materials inventory, January 1	$ 90,000	
Add: Purchases of raw materials	750,000	
Raw materials available for use	840,000	
Deduct: Raw materials inventory, December 31	60,000	
Raw materials used in production		$ 780,000
Direct labor		150,000
Manufacturing overhead:		
Utilities, factory	36,000	
Depreciation, factory	162,000	
Insurance, factory	40,000	
Supplies, factory	15,000	
Indirect labor	300,000	
Maintenance, factory	87,000	
Total overhead costs		640,000
Total manufacturing costs		1,570,000
Add: Work in process inventory, January 1		180,000
		1,750,000
Deduct: Work in process inventory, December 31		100,000
Cost of goods manufactured		$1,650,000

2. The cost of goods sold would be computed as follows:

Finished goods inventory, January 1	$ 260,000
Add: Cost of goods manufactured	1,650,000
Goods available for sale	1,910,000
Deduct: Finished goods inventory, December 31	210,000
Cost of goods sold	$1,700,000

3.

KLEAR-SEAL COMPANY
Income Statement
For the Year Ended December 31

Sales		$2,500,000
Less cost of goods sold (above)		1,700,000
Gross margin		800,000
Less selling and administrative expenses:		
Selling expenses	$ 140,000	
Administrative expenses	270,000	
Total expenses		410,000
Net income		$ 390,000

Key Terms for Review

Administrative costs All executive, organizational, and clerical costs associated with the general management of an organization rather than with manufacturing, marketing, or selling. (p. 46)

Common costs A common cost is a cost that is common to a number of costing objects but cannot be traced to them individually. For example, the wage cost of the pilot of a 747 airliner is a common cost of all of the passengers on the aircraft. Without the pilot, there would be no flight and no passengers. But no part of the pilot's wage is caused by any one passenger taking the flight. (p. 59)

Conversion cost Direct labor cost plus manufacturing overhead cost. (p. 45)

Cost behavior The way in which a cost reacts or responds to changes in the level of business activity. (p. 57)

Cost object Anything for which cost data are desired. Examples of possible cost objects are products, product lines, customers, jobs, and organizational subunits such as departments or divisions of a company. (p. 59)

Cost of goods manufactured The manufacturing costs associated with the goods that were finished during the period. (p. 51)

Differential cost A difference in cost between any two alternatives. Also see *Incremental cost.* (p. 60)

Differential revenue The difference in revenue between any two alternatives. (p. 60)

Direct cost A cost that can be easily and conveniently traced to the particular cost object under consideration. (p. 59)

Direct labor Those factory labor costs that can be easily traced to individual units of product. Also called *touch labor.* (p. 45)

Direct materials Those materials that become an integral part of a finished product and can be conveniently traced into it. (p. 45)

Fixed cost A cost that remains constant, in total, regardless of changes in the level of activity within the relevant range. If a fixed cost is expressed on a per unit basis, it varies inversely with the level of activity. (p. 58)

Incremental cost An increase in cost between two alternatives. Also see *Differential cost.* (p. 60)

Indirect cost A cost that cannot be easily and conveniently traced to the particular cost object under consideration. (p. 59)

Indirect labor The labor costs of janitors, supervisors, materials handlers, and other factory workers that cannot be conveniently traced directly to particular products. (p. 45)

Indirect materials Small items of material such as glue and nails. These items may become an integral part of a finished product but are traceable to the product only at great cost or inconvenience. (p. 45)

Inventoriable costs Synonym for *product costs.* (p. 46)

Manufacturing overhead All costs associated with manufacturing except direct materials and direct labor. (p. 45)

Marketing or selling costs All costs necessary to secure customer orders and get the finished product or service into the hands of the customer. (p. 46)

Opportunity cost The potential benefit that is given up when one alternative is selected over another. (p. 61)

Period costs Those costs that are taken directly to the income statement as expenses in the period in which they are incurred or accrued; such costs consist of selling (marketing) and administrative expenses. (p. 47)

Prime cost Direct materials cost plus direct labor cost. (p. 45)

Product costs All costs that are involved in the purchase or manufacture of goods. In the case of manufactured goods, these costs consist of direct materials, direct labor, and manufacturing overhead. Also see *Inventoriable costs.* (p. 46)

Raw materials Any materials that go into the final product. (p. 45)

Relevant range The range of activity within which assumptions about variable and fixed cost behavior are valid. (p. 58)

Schedule of cost of goods manufactured A schedule showing the direct materials, direct labor, and manufacturing overhead costs incurred for a period and assigned to Work in Process and completed goods. (p. 51)

Sunk cost Any cost that has already been incurred and that cannot be changed by any decision made now or in the future. (p. 62)

Variable cost A cost that varies, in total, in direct proportion to changes in the level of activity. A variable cost is constant per unit. (p. 57)

Appendix 2A: Further Classification of Labor Costs

objective 8

Properly classify labor costs associated with idle time, overtime, and fringe benefits.

Labor costs often present difficult problems of segregation and classification. Although companies vary considerably in how they break down labor costs, the following subdivisions represent the most common approach:

Direct Labor	Indirect Labor (part of manufacturing overhead)	Other Labor Costs
(Discussed earlier)	Janitors	Idle time
	Supervisors	Overtime premium
	Materials handlers	Labor fringe benefits
	Night security guards	
	Maintenance workers	

The costs listed in the Indirect Labor and Other Labor Costs columns are representative of the kinds of costs that one might expect to find under these classifications. The costs in the Other Labor Costs column require further comment.

Idle Time

Idle time represents the costs of direct labor workers who are unable to perform their assignments due to machine breakdowns, materials shortages, power failures, and the like. Although direct labor workers are involved, the costs of idle time are treated as part of manufacturing overhead cost rather than as part of direct labor cost. The reason is that managers feel that such costs should be spread over *all* the production of a period rather than just over the jobs that happen to be in process when breakdowns and the like occur.

To give an example of how the cost of idle time is computed, assume that a press operator earns $12 per hour. If the press operator is paid for a normal 40-hour workweek but is idle for 3 hours during a given week due to breakdowns, labor cost would be allocated as follows:

Direct labor ($12 × 37 hours)	$444
Manufacturing overhead (idle time: $12 × 3 hours)	36
Total cost for the week	$480

Overtime Premium

The overtime premium paid to *all* factory workers (direct labor as well as indirect labor) is usually considered to be part of manufacturing overhead and is not assigned to any particular order. At first glance this may seem strange, since overtime is always spent working on some particular order. Why not charge that order for the overtime cost? The reason is that it would be considered unfair to charge an overtime premium against a particular order simply because the order *happened* to fall on the tail end of the daily scheduling sheet.

To illustrate, assume that two batches of goods, order A and order B, each takes three hours to complete. The production run on order A is scheduled early in the day, but the production run on order B isn't scheduled until late in the afternoon. By the time the run on order B is completed, two hours of overtime have been logged in. The necessity to work overtime was a result of the fact that total production exceeded the regular time available. Order B was no more responsible for the overtime than was order A. Therefore, managers feel that all production should share in the premium charge that resulted. This is considered a more equitable way of handling overtime premium in that it doesn't penalize one run simply because it happens to occur late in the day.

Let us again assume that a press operator in a plant earns $12 per hour. She is paid time and a half for overtime (time in excess of 40 hours a week). During a given week, she works 45 hours and has no idle time. Her labor cost for the week would be allocated as follows:

Direct labor ($12 × 45 hours)	$540
Manufacturing overhead (overtime premium: $6 × 5 hours)	30
Total cost for the week	$570

Observe from this computation that only the overtime premium of $6 per hour is charged to the overhead account—*not* the entire $18 earned for each hour of overtime work ($12 regular rate × 1.5 = $18).

Labor Fringe Benefits

Labor fringe benefits are made up of employment-related costs paid by the employer and include the costs of insurance programs, retirement plans, various supplemental unemployment benefits, and hospitalization plans. The employer also pays the employer's share of Social Security, Medicare, workers' compensation, federal employment tax, and state unemployment insurance. These costs often add up to as much as 30% to 40% of base pay.

Many firms treat all such costs as indirect labor by adding them in total to manufacturing overhead. Other firms treat the portion of fringe benefits that relates to direct labor as additional direct labor cost. This approach is conceptually superior, since the fringe benefits provided to direct labor workers clearly represent an added cost of their services.

Questions

2–1 What are the three major elements of product costs in a manufacturing company?

2–2 Distinguish between the following: (a) direct materials, (b) indirect materials, (c) direct labor, (d) indirect labor, and (e) manufacturing overhead.

2–3 Explain the difference between a product cost and a period cost.

2–4 Describe how the income statement of a manufacturing company differs from the income statement of a merchandising company.

2–5 Of what value is the schedule of cost of goods manufactured? How does it tie into the income statement?

2–6 Describe how the inventory accounts of a manufacturing company differ from the inventory account of a merchandising company.

2–7 Why are product costs sometimes called inventoriable costs? Describe the flow of such costs in a manufacturing company from the point of incurrence until they finally become expenses on the income statement.

2–8 Is it possible for costs such as salaries or depreciation to end up as assets on the balance sheet? Explain.

2–9 What is meant by the term *cost behavior?*

2–10 "A variable cost is a cost that varies per unit of product, whereas a fixed cost is constant per unit of product." Do you agree? Explain.

2–11 How do fixed costs create difficulties in costing units of product?

2–12 Why is manufacturing overhead considered an indirect cost of a unit of product?

2–13 Define the following terms: differential cost, opportunity cost, and sunk cost.

2–14 Only variable costs can be differential costs. Do you agree? Explain.

2–15 (Appendix 2A) Mary Adams is employed by Acme Company. Last week she worked 34 hours assembling one of the company's products and was idle 6 hours due to material shortages. Acme's employees are engaged at their workstations for a normal 40-hour week. Ms. Adams is paid $8 per hour. Allocate her earnings between direct labor cost and manufacturing overhead cost.

2–16 (Appendix 2A) John Olsen operates a stamping machine on the assembly line of Drake Manufacturing Company. Last week Mr. Olsen worked 45 hours. His basic wage rate is $10 per hour, with time and a half for overtime (time worked in excess of 40 hours per week). Allocate Mr. Olsen's wages for the week between direct labor cost and manufacturing overhead cost.

Exercises

E2–1 Following are a number of cost terms introduced in the chapter:

Variable cost	Product cost
Fixed cost	Sunk cost
Prime cost	Conversion cost
Opportunity cost	Period cost

Choose the term or terms above that most appropriately describe the cost identified in each of the following situations. A cost term can be used more than once.

1. Lake Company produces a tote bag that is very popular with college students. The cloth going into the manufacture of the tote bag would be called direct materials and classified as a ____________ cost. In terms of cost behavior, the cloth could also be described as a ____________ cost.
2. The direct labor cost required to produce the tote bags, combined with the manufacturing overhead cost involved, would be known as ____________ cost.
3. The company could have taken the funds that it has invested in production equipment and invested them in interest-bearing securities instead. The interest forgone on the securities would be called ____________ cost.
4. Taken together, the direct materials cost and the direct labor cost required to produce tote bags would be called ____________ cost.
5. The company used to produce a smaller tote bag that was not very popular. Some three hundred of these smaller bags are stored in one of the company's warehouses. The amount invested in these bags would be called a ____________ cost.
6. The tote bags are sold through agents who are paid a commission on each bag sold. These commissions would be classified by Lake Company as a ____________ cost. In terms of cost behavior, commissions would be classified as a ____________ cost.
7. Depreciation on the equipment used to produce tote bags would be classified by Lake Company as a ____________ cost. However, depreciation on any equipment used by the company in selling and administrative activities would be classified as a ____________ cost. In terms of cost behavior, depreciation would probably be classified as a ____________ cost.
8. A ____________ cost is also known as an inventoriable cost, since such costs go into the Work in Process inventory account and then into the Finished Goods inventory account before appearing on the income statement as part of cost of goods sold.
9. The salary of Lake Company's president would be classified as a ____________ cost, since the salary will appear on the income statement as an expense in the time period in which it is incurred.
10. Costs can often be classified in several ways. For example, Lake Company pays $5,000 rent each month on its factory building. The rent would be part of manufacturing overhead. In terms of cost behavior, it would be classified as a ____________ cost. The rent can also be classified as a ____________ cost and as part of ____________ cost.

E2–2 A product cost is also known as an inventoriable cost. Classify the following costs as either product (inventoriable) costs or period (noninventoriable) costs in a manufacturing company:

1. Depreciation on salespersons' cars.
2. Rent on equipment used in the factory.
3. Lubricants used for maintenance of machines.
4. Salaries of finished goods warehouse personnel.
5. Soap and paper towels used by factory workers at the end of a shift.
6. Factory supervisors' salaries.
7. Heat, water, and power consumed in the factory.
8. Materials used in boxing units of finished product for shipment overseas. (Units are not normally boxed.)
9. Advertising outlays.
10. Workers' compensation insurance on factory employees.
11. Depreciation on chairs and tables in the factory lunchroom.
12. The salary of the switchboard operator for the company.
13. Depreciation on a Lear Jet used by the company's executives.
14. Rent on rooms at a Florida resort for holding of the annual sales conference.
15. Attractively designed box for packaging breakfast cereal.

E2–3 The Devon Motor Company produces automobiles. During April, the company purchased 8,000 batteries at a cost of $10 per battery. Devon withdrew 7,600 batteries from the storeroom during the month. Of these, 100 were used to replace batteries in autos being used by the company's traveling sales staff. The remaining 7,500 batteries withdrawn from the storeroom were placed in autos being produced by the company. Of the autos in production during April, 90% were completed and transferred from work in process to finished goods. Of the cars completed during the month, 30% were unsold at April 30.

There were no inventories of any type on April 1.

Required

1. Determine the cost of batteries that would appear in each of the following accounts at April 30:
   a. Raw Materials.
   b. Work in Process.
   c. Finished Goods.
   d. Cost of Goods Sold.
   e. Selling Expense.
2. Specify whether each of the above accounts would appear on the balance sheet or on the income statement at April 30.

E2–4 Below are a number of costs that are incurred in a variety of organizations.

Required

Classify each cost as being variable or fixed with respect to the number of units of product or services sold by the organization.

	Cost Behavior	
Cost Item	**Variable**	**Fixed**

Place an *X* in the appropriate column for each cost to indicate whether the cost involved would be variable or fixed with respect to the number of units of products or services sold by the organization.

1. X-ray film used in the radiology lab at Virginia Mason Hospital in Seattle.
2. The costs of advertising a Madonna rock concert in New York City.
3. Depreciation on the Planet Hollywood restaurant building in Hong Kong.
4. The electrical costs of running a roller coaster at Magic Mountain.
5. Property taxes on your local cinema.
6. Commissions paid to salespersons at Nordstrom.
7. Property insurance on a Coca-Cola bottling plant.
8. The costs of synthetic materials used to make Nike running shoes.
9. The costs of shipping Panasonic televisions to retail stores.
10. The cost of leasing an ultra-scan diagnostic machine at the American Hospital in Paris.

E2–5 The following cost and inventory data are taken from the accounting records of Mason Company for the year just completed:

Costs incurred:	
Direct labor cost	$ 70,000
Purchases of raw materials	118,000
Indirect labor	30,000
Maintenance, factory equipment	6,000
Advertising expense	90,000
Insurance, factory equipment	800
Sales salaries	50,000
Rent, factory facilities	20,000
Supplies	4,200
Depreciation, office equipment	3,000
Depreciation, factory equipment	19,000

continued

	Beginning of the Year	End of the Year
Inventories:		
Raw materials	$ 7,000	$15,000
Work in process	10,000	5,000
Finished goods	20,000	35,000

Required

1. Prepare a schedule of cost of goods manufactured in good form.
2. Prepare the cost of goods sold section of Mason Company's income statement for the year.

E2–6 Below are listed various costs that are found in organizations.

1. Hamburger buns in a McDonald's outlet.
2. Advertising by a dental office.
3. Apples processed and canned by Del Monte Corporation.
4. Shipping canned apples from a Del Monte plant to customers.
5. Insurance on a Bausch & Lomb factory producing contact lenses.
6. Insurance on IBM's corporate headquarters.
7. Salary of a supervisor overseeing production of circuit boards at Hewlett-Packard.
8. Commissions paid to Encyclopedia Britannica salespersons.
9. Depreciation of factory lunchroom facilities at a General Electric plant.
10. Steering wheels installed in BMWs.

Required

Classify each cost as being either variable or fixed with respect to the number of units sold. Also classify each cost as either a selling and administrative cost or a product cost. Prepare your answer sheet as shown below.

	Cost Behavior		Selling and Administrative	Product
Cost Item	Variable	Fixed	Cost	Cost

Place an *X* in the appropriate columns to show the proper classification of each cost.

E2–7 (Appendix 2A) Paul Clark is employed by Aerotech Products and assembles a component part for one of the company's product lines. He is paid $10 per hour for regular time and time and a half (i.e., $15 per hour) for all work in excess of 40 hours per week.

Required

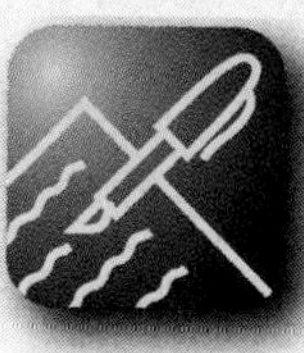

1. Assume that during a given week Paul is idle for five hours due to machine breakdowns and that he is idle for four more hours due to material shortages. No overtime is recorded for the week. Allocate Paul's wages for the week between direct labor cost and manufacturing overhead cost.
2. Assume that during the following week Paul works a total of 48 hours. He has no idle time for the week. Allocate Paul's wages for the week between direct labor cost and manufacturing overhead cost.
3. Paul's company provides an attractive package of fringe benefits for its employees. This package includes a retirement program and a health insurance program. So far as direct labor workers are concerned, explain two ways that the company could handle the costs of fringe benefits in its cost records.

E2–8 (Appendix 2A) Several days ago you took your TV set into a shop to have some repair work done. When you later picked up the set, the bill showed a $75 charge for labor. This charge represented two hours of service time—$30 for the first hour and $45 for the second.

When questioned about the difference in hourly rates, the shop manager explained that work on your set was started at 4 o'clock in the afternoon. By the time work was completed two hours later at 6 o'clock, an hour of overtime had been put in by the repair technician. The second hour therefore contained a charge for an "overtime premium," since the company had to pay the repair technician' time and a half for any work in excess of eight hours per day. The shop manager further explained that the shop was working overtime to "catch up a little" on its backlog of repairs, but it still needed to maintain a "decent" profit margin on the technicians' time.

Required

1. Do you agree with the shop's computation of the service charge on your job?
2. Assume that the shop pays its technicians $14 per hour for the first eight hours worked in a day and $21 per hour for any additional time worked in a day. Prepare computations to show how the cost of the repair technician's time for the day (nine hours) should be allocated between direct labor cost and general overhead cost on the shop's books.
3. Under what circumstances might the shop be justified in charging an overtime premium for repair work on your set?

Problems

P2–9 Cost Identification Wollogong Group Ltd. of New South Wales, Australia, acquired its factory building about 10 years ago. For several years the company has rented out a small annex attached to the rear of the building. The company has received a rental income of $30,000 per year on this space. The renter's lease will expire soon, and rather than renewing the lease, the company has decided to use the space itself to manufacture a new product.

Direct materials cost for the new product will total $80 per unit. To have a place to store finished units of product, the company will rent a small warehouse nearby. The rental cost will be $500 per month. In addition, the company must rent equipment for use in producing the new product; the rental cost will be $4,000 per month. Workers will be hired to manufacture the new product, with direct labor cost amounting to $60 per unit. The space in the annex will continue to be depreciated on a straight-line basis, as in prior years. This depreciation is $8,000 per year.

Advertising costs for the new product will total $50,000 per year. A supervisor will be hired to oversee production; her salary will be $1,500 per month. Electricity for operating machines will be $1.20 per unit. Costs of shipping the new product to customers will be $9 per unit.

To provide funds to purchase materials, meet payrolls, and so forth, the company will have to liquidate some temporary investments. These investments are presently yielding a return of about $3,000 per year.

Required Prepare an answer sheet with the following column headings:

			Product Cost					
Name of the Cost	Variable Cost	Fixed Cost	Direct Materials	Direct Labor	Manufacturing Overhead	Period (selling and administrative) Cost	Opportunity Cost	Sunk Cost

List the different costs associated with the new product decision down the extreme left column (under Name of the Cost). Then place an *X* under each heading that helps to describe the type of cost involved. There may be *X*'s under several column headings for a single cost. (For example, a cost may be a fixed cost, a period cost, and a sunk cost; you would place an *X* under each of these column headings opposite the cost.)

P2–10 Supply Missing Production and Cost Data Supply the missing data in the following cases. Each case is independent of the others.

S

	Case 1	Case 2	Case 3	Case 4
Direct materials	$ 4,500	$ 6,000	$ 5,000	$ 3,000
Direct labor	?	3,000	7,000	4,000
Manufacturing overhead	5,000	4,000	?	9,000
Total manufacturing costs	18,500	?	$20,000	?
Beginning work in process inventory	2,500	?	3,000	?
Ending work in process inventory	?	1,000	4,000	3,000
Cost of goods manufactured	$18,000	$14,000	$?	$?

continued

	Case			
	1	2	3	4
Sales	$30,000	$21,000	$36,000	$40,000
Beginning finished goods inventory	1,000	2,500	?	2,000
Cost of goods manufactured	?	?	?	17,500
Goods available for sale	?	?	?	?
Ending finished goods inventory	?	1,500	4,000	3,500
Cost of goods sold	17,000	?	18,500	?
Gross margin	13,000	?	17,500	?
Operating expenses	?	3,500	?	?
Net income	$ 4,000	$?	$ 5,000	$ 9,000

P2–11 Allocating Labor Costs (Appendix 2A) Mark Hansen is employed by Eastern Products, Inc., and works on the company's assembly line. Mark's basic wage rate is $10 per hour. The company's union contract states that employees are to be paid time and a half (i.e., $15 per hour) for any work in excess of 40 hours per week.

Required

1. Suppose that in a given week Mark works 46 hours. Compute Mark's total wages for the week. How much of this amount would be allocated to direct labor cost? To manufacturing overhead cost?
2. Suppose in another week that Mark works 48 hours but is idle for 3 hours during the week due to machine breakdowns. Compute Mark's total wages for the week. How much of this amount would be allocated to direct labor cost? To manufacturing overhead cost?
3. Eastern Products, Inc., has an attractive package of fringe benefits that costs the company $3 for each hour of employee time (either regular time or overtime). During a particular week, Mark works 50 hours but is idle for 2 hours due to material shortages. Compute Mark's total wages and fringe benefits for the week. If the company treats all fringe benefits as part of manufacturing overhead cost, how much of Mark's wages and fringe benefits for the week would be allocated to direct labor cost? To manufacturing overhead cost?
4. Refer to the data in (3) above. If the company treats that part of fringe benefits relating to direct labor as added direct labor cost, how much of Mark's wages and fringe benefits for the week will be allocated to direct labor cost? To manufacturing overhead cost?

P2–12 Cost Classification Various costs associated with the operation of a factory are given below:

1. Electricity used in operating machines.
2. Rent on a factory building.
3. Cloth used in drapery production.
4. Production superintendent's salary.
5. Cost of laborers assembling a product.
6. Depreciation of air purification equipment used in furniture production.
7. Janitorial salaries.
8. Peaches used in canning fruit.
9. Lubricants needed for machines.
10. Sugar used in soft-drink production.
11. Property taxes on the factory.
12. Cost of workers painting a product.
13. Depreciation on cafeteria equipment.
14. Insurance on a building used in producing TV sets.
15. Picture tubes used in TV sets.

Required Classify each cost as being either variable or fixed with respect to the number of units produced and sold. Also indicate whether each cost would typically be treated as a direct cost or an indirect cost with respect to units of product. Prepare your answer sheet as shown below:

	Cost Behavior		To Units of Product	
Cost Item	**Variable**	**Fixed**	**Direct**	**Indirect**
Example: Factory insurance		X		X

P2–13 Cost Identification The Dorilane Company specializes in producing a set of wood patio furniture consisting of a table and four chairs. The set enjoys great popularity, and the company has ample orders to keep production going at its full capacity of 2,000 sets per year. Annual cost data at full capacity follow:

Factory labor, direct	$118,000
Advertising	50,000
Factory supervision	40,000
Property taxes, factory building	3,500
Sales commissions	80,000
Insurance, factory	2,500
Depreciation, office equipment	4,000
Lease cost, factory equipment	12,000
Indirect materials, factory	6,000
Depreciation, factory building	10,000
General office supplies (billing)	3,000
General office salaries	60,000
Direct materials used (wood, bolts, etc.)	94,000
Utilities, factory	20,000

Required

1. Prepare an answer sheet with the column headings shown below. Enter each cost item on your answer sheet, placing the dollar amount under the appropriate headings. As examples, this has been done already for the first two items in the list above. Note that each cost item is classified in two ways: first, as variable or fixed, with respect to the number of units produced and sold; and second, as a selling and administrative cost or a product cost. (If the item is a product cost, it should be classified as being either direct or indirect as shown.)

	Cost Behavior		Selling or Administrative	Product Cost	
Cost Item	**Variable**	**Fixed**	**Cost**	**Direct**	**Indirect***
Factory labor, direct	$118,000			$118,000	
Advertising		$50,000	$50,000		

*To units of product.

2. Total the dollar amounts in each of the columns in (1) above. Compute the cost to produce one patio set.
3. Assume that production drops to only 1,000 sets annually. Would you expect the cost per set to increase, decrease, or remain unchanged? Explain. No computations are necessary.
4. Refer to the original data. The president's brother-in-law has considered making himself a patio set and has priced the necessary materials at a building supply store. The brother-in-law has asked the president if he could purchase a patio set from the Dorilane Company "at cost," and the president agreed to let him do so.
   a. Would you expect any disagreement between the two men over the price the brother-in-law should pay? Explain. What price does the president probably have in mind? The brother-in-law?

b. Since the company is operating at full capacity, what cost term used in the chapter might be justification for the president to charge the full, regular price to the brother-in-law and still be selling "at cost"?

P2–14 Cost Classification Listed below are a number of costs typically found in organizations.

1. Property taxes, factory.
2. Boxes used for packaging detergent.
3. Salespersons' commissions.
4. Supervisor's salary, factory.
5. Depreciation, executive automobiles.
6. Workers assembling computers.
7. Packing supplies for out-of-state shipments.
8. Insurance, finished goods warehouses.
9. Lubricants for machines.
10. Advertising costs.
11. "Chips" used in producing calculators.
12. Shipping costs on merchandise sold.
13. Magazine subscriptions, factory lunchroom.
14. Thread in a garment factory.
15. Billing costs.
16. Executive life insurance.
17. Ink used in textbook production.
18. Fringe benefits, assembly-line workers.
19. Yarn used in sweater production.
20. Receptionist, executive offices.

Required Prepare an answer sheet with column headings as shown below. For each cost item, indicate whether it would be variable or fixed with respect to the number of units produced and sold; and then whether it would be a selling cost, an administrative cost, or a manufacturing cost. If it is a manufacturing cost, indicate whether it would typically be treated as a direct cost or an indirect cost with respect to units of product. Three sample answers are provided for illustration.

				Manufacturing (product) Cost	
Cost Item	Variable or Fixed	Selling Cost	Administrative Cost	Direct	Indirect
Direct labor	V			X	
Executive salaries	F		X		
Factory rent	F				X

P2–15 Cost Identification Staci Valek began dabbling in pottery several years ago as a hobby. Her work is quite creative, and it has been so popular with friends and others that she has decided to quit her job with an aerospace firm and manufacture pottery full time. The salary from Stacy's aerospace job is $2,500 per month.

Staci will rent a small building near her home to use as a place for manufacturing the pottery. The rent will be $500 per month. She estimates that the cost of clay and glaze will be $2 for each finished piece of pottery. She will hire workers to produce the pottery at a labor rate of $8 per pot. To sell her pots, Staci feels that she must advertise heavily in the local area. An advertising agency states that it will handle all advertising for a fee of $600 per month. Staci's brother will sell the pots; he will be paid a commission of $4 for each pot sold. Equipment needed to manufacture the pots will be rented at a cost of $300 per month.

Staci has already paid the legal and filing fees associated with incorporating her business in the state. These fees amounted to $500. A small room has been located in a tourist area that Staci will use as a sales office. The rent will be $250 per month. A phone installed in the room for taking orders will cost $40 per month. In addition, a recording device will be attached to the phone for taking after-hours messages.

Staci has some money in savings that is earning interest of $1,200 per year. These savings will be withdrawn and used to get the business going. For the time being, Staci does not intend to draw any salary from the new company.

Required

1. Prepare an answer sheet with the following column headings:

Name of the Cost	Variable Cost	Fixed Cost	Product Cost			Period (selling and administrative) Cost	Opportunity Cost	Sunk Cost
			Direct Materials	Direct Labor	Manufacturing Overhead			

   List the different costs associated with the new company down the extreme left column (under Name of Cost). Then place an *X* under each heading that helps to describe the type of cost involved. There may be *X*'s under several column headings for a single cost. (That is, a cost may be a fixed cost, a period cost, and a sunk cost; you would place an *X* under each of these column headings opposite the cost.)

   Under the Variable Cost column, list only those costs that would be variable with respect to the number of units of pottery that are produced and sold.

2. All of the costs you have listed above, except one, would be differential costs between the alternatives of Staci producing pottery or staying with the aerospace firm. Which cost is *not* differential? Explain.

P2–16 Schedule of Cost of Goods Manufactured; Cost Behavior

Various cost and sales data for Meriwell Company for the just completed year follow:

Finished goods inventory, beginning	$ 20,000
Finished goods inventory, ending	40,000
Depreciation, factory	27,000
Administrative expenses	110,000
Utilities, factory	8,000
Maintenance, factory	40,000
Supplies, factory	11,000
Insurance, factory	4,000
Purchases of raw materials	125,000
Raw materials inventory, beginning	9,000
Raw materials inventory, ending	6,000
Direct labor	70,000
Indirect labor	15,000
Work in process inventory, beginning	17,000
Work in process inventory, ending	30,000
Sales	500,000
Selling expenses	80,000

Required

1. Prepare a schedule of cost of goods manufactured.
2. Prepare an income statement.
3. Assume that the company produced the equivalent of 10,000 units of product during the year just completed. What was the unit cost for direct materials? What was the unit cost for factory depreciation?
4. Assume that the company expects to produce 15,000 units of product during the coming year. What per unit cost and what total cost would you expect the company to incur for direct materials at this level of activity? For factory depreciation? (In preparing your answer, assume that direct materials is a variable cost and that depreciation is a fixed cost; also assume that depreciation is computed on a straight-line basis.)
5. As the manager responsible for production costs, explain to the president any difference in unit costs between (3) and (4) above.

P2–17 Preparing Manufacturing Statements Swift Company was organized on March 1 of the current year. After five months of start-up losses, management had expected to earn a profit during August, the most recent month. Management was disappointed, however, when the income statement for August also showed a loss. August's income statement follows:

SWIFT COMPANY
Income Statement
For the Month Ended August 31

Sales		$ 450,000
Less operating expenses:		
Indirect labor cost	$ 12,000	
Utilities	15,000	
Direct labor cost	70,000	
Depreciation, factory equipment	21,000	
Raw materials purchased	165,000	
Depreciation, sales equipment	18,000	
Insurance	4,000	
Rent on facilities	50,000	
Selling and administrative salaries	32,000	
Advertising	75,000	462,000
Net loss		$ (12,000)

After seeing the $12,000 loss for August, Swift's president stated, "I was sure we'd be profitable within six months, but our six months are up and this loss for August is even worse than July's. I think it's time to start looking for someone to buy out the company's assets—if we don't, within a few months there won't be any assets to sell. By the way, I don't see any reason to look for a new controller. We'll just limp along with Sam for the time being."

The company's controller resigned a month ago. Sam, a new assistant in the controller's office, prepared the income statement above. Sam has had little experience in manufacturing operations. Additional information about the company follows:

a. Some 60% of the utilities cost and 75% of the insurance apply to factory operations. The remaining amounts apply to selling and administrative activities.
b. Inventory balances at the beginning and end of August were:

	August 1	August 31
Raw materials	$ 8,000	$13,000
Work in process	16,000	21,000
Finished goods	40,000	60,000

c. Only 80% of the rent on facilities applies to factory operations; the remainder applies to selling and administrative activities.

The president has asked you to check over the income statement and make a recommendation as to whether the company should look for a buyer for its assets.

Required

1. As one step in gathering data for a recommendation to the president, prepare a schedule of cost of goods manufactured in good form for August.
2. As a second step, prepare a new income statement for August.
3. Based on your statements prepared in (1) and (2) above, would you recommend that the company look for a buyer?

P2–18 Schedule of Cost of Goods Manufactured; Cost Behavior Selected account balances for the year ended December 31 are provided below for Superior Company:

Selling and Administrative Salaries	$110,000
Insurance, Factory	8,000
Utilities, Factory	45,000
Purchases of Raw Materials	290,000
Indirect Labor	60,000
Direct Labor	?
Advertising Expense	80,000
Cleaning Supplies, Factory	7,000
Sales Commissions	50,000
Rent, Factory Building	120,000
Maintenance, Factory	30,000

Inventory balances at the beginning and end of the year were as follows:

	Beginning of the Year	End of the Year
Raw materials	$40,000	$10,000
Work in process	?	35,000
Finished goods	50,000	?

The total manufacturing costs for the year were $683,000; the goods available for sale totaled $740,000; and the cost of goods sold totaled $660,000.

Required

1. Prepare a schedule of cost of goods manufactured in good form and the cost of goods sold section of the company's income statement for the year.
2. Assume that the dollar amounts given above are for the equivalent of 40,000 units produced during the year. Compute the unit cost for direct materials used and the unit cost for rent on the factory building.
3. Assume that in the following year the company expects to produce 50,000 units. What per unit and total cost would you expect to be incurred for direct materials? For rent on the factory building? (In preparing your answer, you may assume that direct materials is a variable cost and that rent is a fixed cost.)
4. As the manager in charge of production costs, explain to the president the reason for any difference in unit costs between (2) and (3) above.

P2–19 Classification of Salary Cost You have just been hired by Ogden Company to fill a new position that was created in response to rapid growth in sales. It is your responsibility to coordinate shipments of finished goods from the factory to distribution warehouses located in various parts of the United States so that goods will be available as orders are received from customers.

The company is unsure how to classify your annual salary in its cost records. The company's cost analyst says that your salary should be classified as a manufacturing (product) cost; the controller says that it should be classified as a selling expense; and the president says that it doesn't matter which way your salary cost is classified.

Required

1. Which viewpoint is correct? Why?
2. From the point of view of the reported net income for the year, is the president correct in his statement that it doesn't matter which way your salary cost is classified? Explain.

P2–20 Ethics and the Manager M. K. Gallant is president of Kranbrack Corporation, a company whose stock is traded on a national exchange. In a meeting with investment analysts at the beginning of the year, Gallant had predicted that the company's earnings would grow by 20% this year. Unfortunately, sales have been less than expected for the year, and Gallant concluded within two weeks of the end of the fiscal year that it would be impossible to ultimately report an increase in earnings as large as predicted unless some drastic action was taken. Accordingly, Gallant has ordered that wherever possible, expenditures should be postponed to the new year—including canceling or postponing orders with suppliers, delaying planned maintenance and training, and cutting back on end-of-year advertising and travel. Additionally, Gallant ordered the company's controller to carefully scrutinize all costs that are currently classified as period costs and reclassify as many as possible as product costs. The company is expected to have substantial inventories of work in process and finished goods at the end of the year.

Required

1. Why would reclassifying period costs as product costs increase this period's reported earnings?
2. Do you believe Gallant's actions are ethical? Why or why not?

P2–21 Cost Behavior; Manufacturing Statement; Unit Costs Visic Company, a manufacturing firm, produces a single product. The following information has been taken from the company's production, sales, and cost records for the just completed year.

Production in units	29,000
Sales in units	?
Ending finished goods inventory in units	?
Sales in dollars	$1,300,000
Costs:	
Advertising	105,000
Entertainment and travel	40,000
Direct labor	90,000
Indirect labor	85,000
Raw materials purchased	480,000
Building rent (production uses 80% of the space; administrative and sales offices use the rest)	40,000
Utilities, factory	108,000
Royalty paid for use of production patent, $1.50 per unit produced	?
Maintenance, factory	9,000
Rent for special production equipment, $7,000 per year plus $0.30 per unit produced	?
Selling and administrative salaries	210,000
Other factory overhead costs	6,800
Other selling and administrative expenses	17,000

	Beginning of the Year	End of the Year
Inventories:		
Raw materials	$20,000	$30,000
Work in process	50,000	40,000
Finished goods	–0–	?

The finished goods inventory is being carried at the average unit production cost for the year. The selling price of the product is $50 per unit.

Required

1. Prepare a schedule of goods manufactured for the year.
2. Compute the following:
   a. The number of units in the finished goods inventory at the end of the year.
   b. The cost of the units in the finished goods inventory at the end of the year.
3. Prepare an income statement for the year.

Cases

C2–22 Missing Data; Statements; Inventory Computation "I was sure that when our battery hit the market it would be an instant success," said Roger Strong, founder and president of Solar Technology, Inc. "But just look at the gusher of red ink for the first quarter. It's obvious that we're better scientists than we are businesspeople." The data to which Roger was referring follow:

SOLAR TECHNOLOGY, INC.
Income Statement
For the Quarter Ended March 31

Sales (32,000 batteries)		$ 960,000
Less operating expenses:		
Selling and administrative salaries	$110,000	
Advertising	90,000	
Maintenance, production	43,000	
Indirect labor cost	120,000	
Cleaning supplies, production	7,000	
Purchases of raw materials	360,000	
Rental cost, facilities	75,000	
Insurance, production	8,000	
Depreciation, office equipment	27,000	
Utilities	80,000	
Depreciation, production equipment	100,000	
Direct labor cost	70,000	
Travel, salespersons	40,000	
Total operating expenses		1,130,000
Net loss		$ (170,000)

"At this rate we'll be out of business within a year," said Cindy Zhang, the company's accountant. "But I've double-checked these figures, so I know they're right."

Solar Technology was organized at the beginning of the current year to produce and market a revolutionary new solar battery. The company's accounting system was set up by Margie Wallace, an experienced accountant who recently left the company to do independent consulting work. The statement above was prepared by Zhang, her assistant.

"We may not last a year if the insurance company doesn't pay the $226,000 it owes us for the 8,000 batteries lost in the warehouse fire last week," said Roger. "The insurance adjuster says our claim is inflated, but he's just trying to pressure us into a lower figure. We have the data to back up our claim, and it will stand up in any court."

On April 3, just after the end of the first quarter, the company's finished goods storage area was swept by fire and all 8,000 unsold batteries were destroyed. (These batteries were part of the 40,000 units completed during the first quarter.) The company's insurance policy states that the company will be reimbursed for the "cost" of any finished batteries destroyed or stolen. Zhang has determined this cost as follows:

$$\frac{\text{Total costs for the quarter, \$1,130,000}}{\text{Batteries produced during the quarter, 40,000}} = \$28.25 \text{ per unit}$$

$$8{,}000 \text{ batteries} \times \$28.25 = \$226{,}000$$

The following additional information is available on the company's activities during the quarter ended March 31:

a. Inventories at the beginning and end of the quarter were as follows:

	Beginning of the Quarter	End of the Quarter
Raw materials	–0–	$10,000
Work in process	–0–	50,000
Finished goods	–0–	?

b. Eighty percent of the rental cost for facilities and 90% of the utilities cost relate to manufacturing operations. The remaining amounts relate to selling and administrative activities.

Required

1. What conceptual errors, if any, were made in preparing the income statement above?
2. Prepare a schedule of cost of goods manufactured for the first quarter.

3. Prepare a corrected income statement for the first quarter. Your statement should show in detail how the cost of goods sold is computed.
4. Do you agree that the insurance company owes Solar Technology, Inc., $226,000? Explain your answer.

C2–23 **Inventory Computations from Incomplete Data** Hector P. Wastrel, a careless employee, left some combustible materials near an open flame in Salter Company's plant. The resulting explosion and fire destroyed the entire plant and administrative offices. Justin Quick, the company's controller, and Constance Trueheart, the operations manager, were able to save only a few bits of information as they escaped from the roaring blaze.

"What a disaster," cried Justin. "And the worst part is that we have no records to use in filing an insurance claim."

"I know," replied Constance. "I was in the plant when the explosion occurred, and I managed to grab only this brief summary sheet that contains information on one or two of our costs. It says that our direct labor cost this year has totaled $180,000 and that we have purchased $290,000 in raw materials. But I'm afraid that doesn't help much; the rest of our records are just ashes."

"Well, not completely," said Justin. "I was working on the year-to-date income statement when the explosion knocked me out off my chair. I instinctively held onto the page I was working on, and from what I can make out our sales to date this year have totaled $1,200,000 and our gross margin rate has been 40% of sales. Also, I can see that our goods available for sale to customers has totaled $810,000 at cost."

"Maybe we're not so bad off after all," exclaimed Constance. "My sheet says that prime cost has totaled $410,000 so far this year and that manufacturing overhead is 70% of conversion cost. Now if we just had some information on our beginning inventories."

"Hey, look at this," cried Justin. "It's a copy of last year's annual report, and it shows what our inventories were when this year started. Let's see, raw materials was $18,000, work in process was $65,000, and finished goods was $45,000.

"Super," yelled Constance. "Let's go to work."

To file an insurance claim, the company must determine the amount of cost in its inventories as of the date of the fire. You may assume that all materials used in production during the year were direct materials.

Required Determine the amount of cost in the Raw Materials, Work in Process, and Finished Goods inventory accounts as of the date of the fire. (Hint: One way to proceed would be to reconstruct the various schedules and statements that would have been affected by the company's inventory accounts during the period.)

Group Exercises

GE2–24 **So This Is Why They're Organized This Way** Management accounting systems tend to parallel the manufacturing systems they support and control. Traditional manufacturing systems emphasized productivity (average output per hour or per employee) and cost. This was the result of a competitive philosophy that was based on mass producing a few standard products and "meeting or beating competitors on price." If a firm is going to compete on price, it had better be a low-cost producer.

Firms achieved low unit cost for a fixed set of resources by maximizing the utilization of those resources. That is, traditional production strategies were based on the economies of mass production and maximizing output for a given productive capacity. The United States has experienced over 100 years of unprecedented economic prosperity in large part because innovators like Henry Ford applied these economic principles with a vengeance.

Competitors, never being completely satisfied with their present condition, were always looking for ways to lower the cost of a product or service even further in order to gain some temporary cost advantage. Additional productivity gains were achieved by standardizing work procedures, specializing work, and using machines to enhance the productivity of individual workers.

Required

1. Henry Ford made a now-famous statement that the Model T "could be had in any color as long as it was black." Explain what he meant by this statement.
2. How would Henry Ford or any other manufacturer with a narrow product line gain even further efficiencies based on the traditional production model described above?
3. Are there any limits to lowering the cost of black Model Ts, black Bic pens, or any high-volume, commodity product? Explain.
4. Once understood, the economies of mass production were applied to most sectors of the American economy. Universities, hospitals, and airlines are prime examples. Describe how the concepts of mass production, standardization, and specialization have been applied to lower the costs of a university education. Of a stay in the hospital.
5. As you study additional chapters in this text, refer back to the basic principles described here. An understanding of these concepts will go a long way toward helping you understand why traditional management accounting systems are designed with an emphasis on cost.

GE2–25 **If Big Is Good, Bigger Must Be Better** Steel production involves a large amount of fixed costs. Since competition is defined primarily in terms of price, American steel manufacturers (and many of their manufacturing and service industry counterparts) try to gain a competitive advantage by using economies of scale and investment in technology to increase productivity and drive unit costs lower. Their substantial fixed costs are the result of their size.

Required

1. How are fixed costs and variable costs normally defined?
2. Give examples of fixed costs and variable costs for a steel company. What is the relevant measure of production activity?
3. Give examples of fixed and variable costs for a hospital, university, and auto manufacturer. What is the relevant measure of production or service activity for each of these organizations?
4. Using the examples of fixed and variable costs for steel companies from (2) above, explain the relationship between production output at a steel company and each of the following: total fixed costs, fixed cost per unit, total variable costs, variable cost per unit, total costs, and average unit cost.
5. With an *X* axis (horizontal axis) of tons produced and a *Y* axis (vertical axis) of total costs, graph total fixed costs, total variable costs, and total costs against tons produced.
6. With an *X* axis of tons produced and a *Y* axis of unit costs, graph fixed cost per unit, variable cost per unit, and total (or average) cost per unit against tons produced.
7. Explain how costs (total and per unit) behave with changes in demand once capacity has been set.

GE2–26 **Analysis of Annual Reports** Each member of your group should obtain the annual report of a company. (Your business school's library probably has a file of such annual reports.)

Required

For each company, compute the following for the two most recent years:

- Cost of sales as a percentage of sales.
- General and administrative expenses as a percentage of sales.
- Net income as a percentage of sales.

If you can, explain why there are differences in these percentages across the companies.

IE2–27 **Analysis of SEC Form 10–K** Companies whose shares are publicly traded are required to file financial documents with the Securities and Exchange Commission (SEC). One of these documents is Form 10–K, which contains the company's annual report along with other information. These and other documents can be viewed and downloaded at the SEC's web site www.sec.gov/edgarhp.htm.

Required

Financial data for Planet Hollywood International, Inc., a restaurant chain, and United Colors of Benetton, a clothing manufacturer and retailer, are discussed in Focus on Current Practice boxes in the chapter. Find Form 10–K for a different restaurant chain and a different clothing company. Compare the financial data for these two new companies with the financial data for Planet Hollywood and Benetton reported in the Focus on Current Practice boxes in the chapter. Can you explain any significant differences you observe?

Chapter Three

Systems Design: Job-Order Costing

Business Focus

Chris did not look forward to Monday morning. He had completed the company's monthly income statement on Friday, and just before leaving for the day, Chris had quietly slipped the statement into the president's inbox. Chris knew that the president would almost surely read the income statement over the weekend and would demand an explanation for the underapplied overhead on the income statement.

Chris had tried several times to explain overapplied and underapplied overhead to the president but had never really succeeded. The president was always pleased when the overhead was overapplied because it apparently increased net income, but he was in a foul mood when the overhead was underapplied because it apparently decreased net income. Chris had to find a better way to explain underapplied and overapplied overhead.

Learning Objectives

After studying Chapter 3, you should be able to:

1 Distinguish between process costing and job-order costing and identify companies that would use each costing method.

2 Identify the documents used in a job-order costing system.

3 Compute predetermined overhead rates and explain why estimated overhead costs (rather than actual overhead costs) are used in the costing process.

4 Prepare journal entries to record costs in a job-order costing system.

5 Apply overhead cost to Work in Process using a predetermined overhead rate.

6 Prepare T-accounts to show the flow of costs in a job-order costing system and prepare schedules of cost of goods manufactured and cost of goods sold.

7 Compute under- or overapplied overhead cost and prepare the journal entry to close the balance in Manufacturing Overhead to the appropriate accounts.

8 (Appendix 3A) Explain the implications of basing the predetermined overhead rate on activity at capacity rather than on estimated activity for the period.

As discussed in Chapter 2, product costing is the process of assigning costs to the products and services provided by a company. An understanding of this costing process is vital to managers, since the way in which a product or service is costed can have a substantial impact on reported net income, as well as on key management decisions.

We should keep in mind that the essential purpose of any managerial costing system should be to provide cost data to help managers plan, control, direct, and make decisions. Nevertheless, external financial reporting and tax reporting requirements often heavily influence how costs are accumulated and summarized on managerial reports. This is true of product costing.

In this chapter and in Chapter 4, we use an *absorption costing* approach to determine product costs. This was also the method that was used in Chapter 2. In **absorption costing,** *all* manufacturing costs, fixed and variable, are assigned to units of product—units are said to *fully absorb manufacturing costs.* The absorption costing approach is also known as the **full cost** approach. Later, in Chapter 8, we look at product costing from a different point of view called *variable costing,* which is often advocated as an alternative to absorption costing. Chapter 8 also discusses the strengths and weaknesses of the two approaches.

In one form or another, most countries—including the United States—require absorption costing for both external financial reporting and for tax reporting. In addition, the vast majority of companies throughout the world also use absorption costing for managerial accounting purposes. Since absorption costing is the most common approach to product costing, we discuss it first and then deal with alternatives in subsequent chapters.

Process and Job-Order Costing

objective 1

Distinguish between process costing and job-order costing and identify companies that would use each costing method.

In computing the cost of a product or a service, managers are faced with a difficult problem. Many costs (such as rent) do not change much from month to month, whereas production may change frequently, with production going up in one month and then down in another. In addition to variations in the level of production, several different products or services may be produced in a given period in the same facility. Under these conditions, how is it possible to accurately determine the cost of a product or service? In practice, assigning costs to products and services involves an averaging of some type across time periods and across products. The way in which this averaging is carried out will depend heavily on the type of production process involved. Two costing systems are commonly used in manufacturing and in many service companies; these two systems are known as *process costing* and *job-order costing.*

Process Costing

A **process costing system** is used in situations where the company produces many units of a single product (such as frozen orange juice concentrate) for long periods at a time. Examples include producing paper at Weyerhaeuser, refining aluminum ingots at Reynolds Aluminum, mixing and bottling beverages at Coca-Cola, and making wieners at Oscar Meyer. All of these industries are characterized by an essentially homogeneous product that flows evenly through the production process on a continuous basis.

The basic approach in process costing is to accumulate costs in a particular operation or department for an entire period (month, quarter, year) and then to divide this total by the number of units produced during the period. The basic formula for process costing is as follows:

$$\text{Unit cost (per gallon, pound, bottle)} = \frac{\text{Total manufacturing cost}}{\text{Total units produced (gallons, pounds, bottles)}}$$

Since one unit of product (gallon, pound, bottle) is indistinguishable from any other unit of product, each unit is assigned the same average cost as any other unit produced during the period. This costing technique results in a broad, average unit cost figure that applies to homogeneous units flowing in a continuous stream out of the production process.

Job-Order Costing

A **job-order costing system** is used in situations where many *different* products are produced each period. For example, a Levi Strauss clothing factory would typically make many different types of jeans for both men and women during a month. A particular order might consist of 1,000 stonewashed men's blue denim jeans, style number A312, with a 32-inch waist and a 30-inch inseam. This order of 1,000 jeans is called a *batch* or a *job.* In a job-order costing system, costs are traced and allocated to jobs and then the costs of the job are divided by the number of units in the job to arrive at an average cost per unit.

Other examples of situations where job-order costing would be used include large-scale construction projects managed by Bechtel International, commercial aircraft produced by Boeing, greeting cards designed and printed at Hallmark, and airline meals prepared by Marriott. All of these examples are characterized by diverse outputs. Each Bechtel project is unique and different from every other—the company may be simultaneously constructing a dam in Zaire and a bridge in Indonesia. Likewise, each airline orders a different type of meal from Marriott's catering service.

Job-order costing is also used extensively in service industries. Hospitals, law firms, movie studios, accounting firms, advertising agencies, and repair shops, for example, all use a variation of job-order costing to accumulate costs for accounting and billing purposes. Although the detailed example of job-order costing provided in the following section deals with a manufacturing firm, the same basic concepts and procedures are used by many service organizations.

The record-keeping and cost assignment problems are more complex when a company sells many different products and services than when it has only a single product. Since the products are different, the costs are typically different. Consequently, cost records must be maintained for each distinct product or job. For example, an attorney in a large criminal law practice would ordinarily keep separate records of the costs of advising and defending each of her clients. And the Levi Strauss factory mentioned above would keep separate track of the costs of filling orders for particular styles, sizes, and colors of jeans. Thus, a job-order costing system requires more effort than a process-costing system.

In this chapter, we focus on the design of a job-order costing system. In the following chapter, we focus on process costing and also look more closely at the similarities and differences between the two costing methods.

Job-Order Costing—An Overview

objective 2

Identify the documents used in a job-order costing system.

To introduce job-order costing, we will follow a specific job as it progresses through the manufacturing process. This job consists of two experimental couplings that Yost Precision Machining has agreed to produce for Loops Unlimited, a manufacturer of roller coasters. The couplings connect the cars on the roller coaster and are a critical component in the performance and safety of the ride. Before we begin our discussion, recall from Chapter 2 that companies generally classify manufacturing costs into three broad categories: (1) direct materials, (2) direct labor, and (3) manufacturing overhead. As we study the operation of a job-order costing system, we will see how each of these three types of costs is recorded and accumulated.

Managerial Accounting in Action

THE ISSUE

Yost Precision Machining is a small company in Michigan that specializes in fabricating precision metal parts that are used in a variety of applications ranging from deep-sea exploration vehicles to the inertial triggers in automobile air bags. The company's top managers gather every morning at 8:00 A.M. in the company's conference room for the daily planning meeting. Attending the meeting this morning are: Jean Yost, the company's president; David Cheung, the marketing manager; Debbie Turner, the production manager; and Marcus White, the company controller. The president opened the meeting:

Jean: The production schedule indicates we'll be starting job 2B47 today. Isn't that the special order for experimental couplings, David?
David: That's right, Jean. That's the order from Loops Unlimited for two couplings for their new roller coaster ride for Magic Mountain.
Debbie: Why only two couplings? Don't they need a coupling for every car?
David: That's right. But this is a completely new roller coaster. The cars will go faster and will be subjected to more twists, turns, drops, and loops than on any other existing roller coaster. To hold up under these stresses, Loops Unlimited's engineers had to completely redesign the cars and couplings. They want to thoroughly test the design before proceeding to large-scale production. So they want us to make just two of these new couplings for testing purposes. If the design works, then we'll have the inside track on the order to supply couplings for the whole ride.
Jean: We agreed to take on this initial order at our cost just to get our foot in the door. Marcus, will there be any problem documenting our cost so we can get paid?
Marcus: No problem. The contract with Loops stipulates that they will pay us an amount equal to our cost of goods sold. With our job-order costing system, I can tell you that number on the day the job is completed.
Jean: Good. Is there anything else we should discuss about this job at this time? No? Well then let's move on to the next item of business. ■

Measuring Direct Materials Cost

Yost Precision Machining will require four G7 Connectors and two M46 Housings to make the two experimental couplings for Loops Unlimited. If this were a standard product, there would be a *bill of materials* for the product. A **bill of materials** is a document that lists the type and quantity of each item of materials needed to complete a unit of product. In this case, there is no established bill of materials, so Yost's production staff determined the materials requirements from the blueprints submitted by the customer. Each coupling requires two connectors and one housing, so to make two couplings, four connectors and two housings are required.

Exhibit 3–1 Materials Requisition Form

Materials Requistion Number 14873 Date March 2
Job Number to Be Charged 2B47
Department Milling

Description	Quantity	Unit Cost	Total Cost
M46 Housing	2	$124	$248
G7 Connector	4	103	412
			$660

Authorized Signature *Bill White*

When an agreement has been reached with the customer concerning the quantities, prices, and shipment date for the order, a *production order* is issued. The Production Department then prepares a *materials requisition form* similar to the form in Exhibit 3–1. The **materials requisition form** is a detailed source document that (1) specifies the type and quantity of materials to be drawn from the storeroom, and (2) identifies the job to which the costs of the materials are to be charged. It serves as a means for controlling the flow of materials into production and also for making entries in the accounting records.

The Yost Precision Machining materials requisition form in Exhibit 3–1 shows that the company's Milling Department has requisitioned two M46 Housings and four G7 Connectors for job 2B47. This completed form is presented to the storeroom clerk who then issues the necessary raw materials. The storeroom clerk is not allowed to release materials without such a form bearing an authorized signature.

Job Cost Sheet

After being notified that the production order has been issued, the Accounting Department prepares a *job cost sheet* similar to the one presented in Exhibit 3–2. A **job cost sheet** is a form prepared for each separate job that records the materials, labor, and overhead costs charged to the job.

After direct materials are issued, the Accounting Department records their costs directly on the job cost sheet. Note from Exhibit 3–2, for example, that the $660 cost for direct materials shown earlier on the materials requisition form has been charged to job 2B47 on its job cost sheet. The requisition number 14873 is also recorded on the job cost sheet to make it easier to identify the source document for the direct materials charge.

In addition to serving as a means for charging costs to jobs, the job cost sheet also serves as a key part of a firm's accounting records. The job cost sheets form a subsidiary ledger to the Work in Process account. They are detailed records for the jobs in process that add up to the balance in Work in Process.

Measuring Direct Labor Cost

Direct labor cost is handled in much the same way as direct materials cost. Direct labor consists of labor charges that are easily traced to a particular job. Labor charges that cannot be easily traced directly to any job are treated as part of manufacturing overhead. As discussed in Chapter 2, this latter category of labor costs is termed *indirect labor* and includes tasks such as maintenance, supervision, and cleanup.

Exhibit 3–2 Job Cost Sheet

JOB COST SHEET

Job Number 2B47 Date Initiated March 2

Date Completed

Department Milling Units Completed

Item Special order coupling

For Stock

Direct Materials		Direct Labor			Manufacturing Overhead		
Req. No.	Amount	Ticket	Hours	Amount	Hours	Rate	Amount
14873	$660	843	5	$45			

Cost Summary		Units Shipped		
		Date	Number	Balance
Direct Materials	$			
Direct Labor	$			
Manufacturing Overhead	$			
Total Cost	$			
Unit Cost	$			

Exhibit 3–3 Employee Time Ticket

Time Ticket No. 843 Date March 3

Employee Mary Holden Station 4

Started	Ended	Time Completed	Rate	Amount	Job Number
7:00	12:00	5.0	$9	$45	2B47
12:30	2:30	2.0	9	18	2B50
2:30	3:30	1.0	9	9	Maintenance
Totals		8.0		$72	

Supervisor *R.W. Pace*

Workers use *time tickets* to record the time they spend on each job and task. A completed **time ticket** is an hour-by-hour summary of the employee's activities throughout the day. An example of an employee time ticket is shown in Exhibit 3–3. When working on a specific job, the employee enters the job number on the time ticket and notes the amount of time spent on that job. When not assigned to a particular job, the employee records the nature of the indirect labor task (such as cleanup and maintenance) and the amount of time spent on the task.

At the end of the day, the time tickets are gathered and the Accounting Department enters the direct labor-hours and costs on individual job cost sheets. (See Exhibit 3–2 for an example of how direct labor costs are entered on the job cost sheet.) The daily time tickets are source documents that are used as the basis for labor cost entries into the accounting records.

The system we have just described is a manual method for recording and posting labor costs. Many companies now rely on computerized systems and no longer record labor time by hand on sheets of paper. One computerized approach uses bar codes to enter the basic data into the computer. Each employee and each job has a unique bar code. When an employee begins work on a job, he or she scans three bar codes using a handheld device much like the bar code readers at grocery store check-out stands. The first bar code indicates that a job is being started; the second is the unique bar code on his or her identity badge; and the third is the unique bar code of the job itself. This information is fed automatically via an electronic network to a computer that notes the time and then records all of the data. When the employee completes the task, he or she scans a bar code indicating the task is complete, the bar code on his or her identity badge, and the bar code attached to the job. This information is relayed to the computer that again notes the time, and a time ticket is automatically prepared. Since all of the source data is already in computer files, the labor costs can be automatically posted to job cost sheets (or their electronic equivalents). Computers, coupled with technology such as bar codes, can eliminate much of the drudgery involved in routine bookkeeping activities while at the same time increasing timeliness and accuracy.

Focus on Current Practice

Advanced technology for recording data is even found in strawberry fields where the pay of workers is traditionally based on the amount of berries they pick. The Bob Jones Ranch in Oxnard, California, is using dime-sized metal buttons to record how many boxes of fruit each worker picks. The buttons, which are stuffed with microelectronics, are carried by the field workers. The buttons can be read in the field with a wand-like probe that immediately downloads data to a laptop computer. The information picked up by the probe includes the name of the worker; the type and quality of the crop; and the time, date, and location of the field being picked. Not only does the system supply the data needed to pay over 700 field workers but it also provides farm managers with information about which fields are most productive. Previously, two people were required every night to process the time tickets for the field workers.[1]

Application of Manufacturing Overhead

objective 3

Compute predetermined overhead rates and explain why estimated overhead costs (rather than actual overhead costs) are used in the costing process.

Manufacturing overhead must be included with direct materials and direct labor on the job cost sheet since manufacturing overhead is also a product cost. However, assigning manufacturing overhead to units of product can be a difficult task. There are three reasons for this.

1. Manufacturing overhead is an *indirect cost.* This means that it is either impossible or difficult to trace these costs to a particular product or job.
2. Manufacturing overhead consists of many different items ranging from the grease used in machines to the annual salary of the production manager.

1. Mark Boslet, "Metal Buttons Carried by Crop Pickers Serve as Mini Databases for Farmers," *The Wall Street Journal,* May 31, 1994, p. A11A.

3. Even though output may fluctuate due to seasonal or other factors, manufacturing overhead costs tend to remain relatively constant due to the presence of fixed costs.

Given these problems, about the only way to assign overhead costs to products is to use an allocation process. This allocation of overhead costs is accomplished by selecting an *allocation base* that is common to all of the company's products and services. An **allocation base** is a measure such as direct labor-hours (DLH) or machine-hours (MH) that is used to assign overhead costs to products and services.

The most widely used allocation bases are direct labor-hours and direct labor cost, with machine-hours and even units of product (where a company has only a single product) also used to some extent.

The allocation base is used to compute the **predetermined overhead rate** in the following formula:

$$\text{Predetermined overhead rate} = \frac{\text{Estimated total manufacturing overhead cost}}{\text{Estimated total units in the allocation base}}$$

Note that the predetermined overhead rate is based on *estimated* rather than actual figures. This is because the *predetermined* overhead rate is computed *before* the period begins and is used to *apply* overhead cost to jobs throughout the period. The process of assigning overhead cost to jobs is called **overhead application.** The formula for determining the amount of overhead cost to apply to a particular job is:

$$\begin{array}{c}\text{Overhead applied to}\\ \text{a particular job}\end{array} = \begin{array}{c}\text{Predetermined}\\ \text{overhead rate}\end{array} \times \begin{array}{c}\text{Amount of the allocation}\\ \text{base incurred by the job}\end{array}$$

So, for example, if the predetermined overhead rate is $8 per direct labor-hour, then $8 of overhead cost is *applied* to a job for each direct labor-hour incurred by the job. When the allocation base is direct labor-hours, the formula becomes:

$$\begin{array}{c}\text{Overhead applied to}\\ \text{a particular job}\end{array} = \begin{array}{c}\text{Predetermined}\\ \text{overhead rate}\end{array} \times \begin{array}{c}\text{Actual direct labor-hours}\\ \text{charged to the job}\end{array}$$

USING THE PREDETERMINED OVERHEAD RATE To illustrate the steps involved in computing and using a predetermined overhead rate, let's return to Yost Precision Machining. The company has estimated its total manufacturing overhead costs to be $320,000 for the year and its total direct labor-hours to be 40,000. Its predetermined overhead rate for the year would be $8 per direct labor-hour, as shown below:

$$\text{Predetermined overhead rate} = \frac{\text{Estimated total manufacturing overhead cost}}{\text{Estimated total units in the allocation base}}$$

$$\frac{\$320{,}000}{40{,}000 \text{ direct labor-hours}} = \$8 \text{ per direct labor-hour}$$

The job cost sheet in Exhibit 3–4 indicates that 27 direct labor-hours were charged to job 2B47. Therefore, a total of $216 of overhead cost would be applied to the job:

Exhibit 3–4 A Completed Job Cost Sheet

JOB COST SHEET

Job Number 2B47 — Date Initiated March 2

Date Completed March 8

Department Milling

Item Special order coupling — Units Completed 2

For Stock

Direct Materials		Direct Labor			Manufacturing Overhead		
Req. No.	Amount	Ticket	Hours	Amount	Hours	Rate	Amount
14873	$ 660	843	5	$ 45	27	$8/DLH	$216
14875	506	846	8	60			
14912	238	850	4	21			
	$1,404	851	10	54			
			27	$180			

Cost Summary	
Direct Materials	$1,404
Direct Labor	$ 180
Manufacturing Overhead	$ 216
Total Cost	$1,800
Unit Cost	$ 900*

Units Shipped		
Date	Number	Balance
March 8	—	2

*$1,800 ÷ 2 units = $900 per unit.

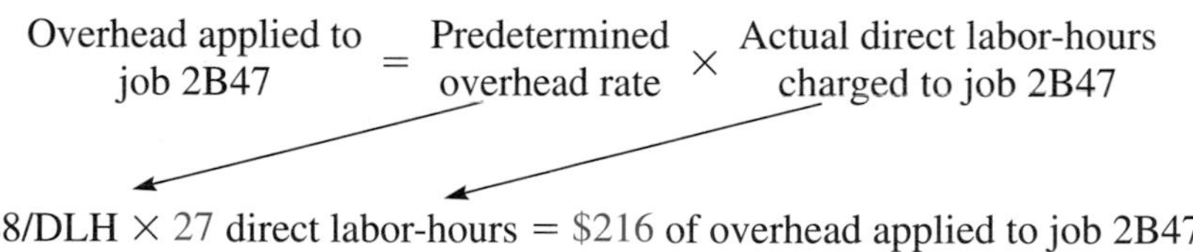

This amount of overhead has been entered on the job cost sheet in Exhibit 3–4. Note that this is *not* the actual amount of overhead caused by the job. There is no attempt to trace actual overhead costs to jobs—if that could be done, the costs would be direct costs, not overhead. The overhead assigned to the job is simply a share of the total overhead that was estimated at the beginning of the year. When a company applies overhead cost to jobs as we have done—that is, by multiplying actual activity times the predetermined overhead rate—it is called a **normal cost system.**

The overhead may be applied as direct labor-hours are charged to jobs, or all of the overhead can be applied at once when the job is completed. The choice is up to the company. If a job is not completed at year-end, however, overhead should be applied to value the work in process inventory.

THE NEED FOR A PREDETERMINED RATE Instead of using a predetermined rate, a company could wait until the end of the accounting period to compute an actual overhead rate based on the *actual* total manufacturing costs and the *actual* total units in the allocation base for the period. However, managers cite several reasons for using predetermined overhead rates instead of actual overhead rates:

1. Before the end of the accounting period, managers would like to know the accounting system's valuation of completed jobs. Suppose, for example, that Yost Precision Machining waits until the end of the year to compute its overhead rate. Then there would be no way for managers to know the cost of goods sold for job 2B47 until the close of the year, even though the job was completed and shipped to the customer in March. The seriousness of this problem can be reduced to some extent by computing the actual overhead more frequently, but that immediately leads to another problem as discussed below.
2. If actual overhead rates are computed frequently, seasonal factors in overhead costs or in the allocation base can produce fluctuations in the overhead rates. Managers generally feel that such fluctuations in overhead rates serve no useful purpose and are misleading.
3. The use of a predetermined overhead rate simplifies record keeping. To determine the overhead cost to apply to a job, the accounting staff at Yost Precision Machining simply multiplies the direct labor-hours recorded for the job by the predetermined overhead rate of $8 per direct labor-hour.

For these reasons, most companies use predetermined overhead rates rather than actual overhead rates in their cost accounting systems.

Choice of an Allocation Base for Overhead Cost

An allocation base should be used that is a *cost driver* of overhead cost. A **cost driver** is a factor, such as machine-hours, beds occupied, computer time, or flight-hours, that causes overhead costs. If a base is used to compute overhead rates that does not "drive" overhead costs, then the result will be inaccurate overhead rates and distorted product costs. For example, if direct labor-hours is used to allocate overhead, but in reality overhead has little to do with direct labor-hours, then products with high direct labor-hour requirements will shoulder an unrealistic burden of overhead and will be overcosted.

Most companies use direct labor-hours or direct labor cost as the allocation base for manufacturing overhead. However, as discussed in earlier chapters, major shifts are taking place in the structure of costs in many industries. In the past, direct labor accounted for up to 60% of the cost of many products, with overhead cost making up only a portion of the remainder. This situation has been changing—for two reasons. First, sophisticated automated equipment has taken over functions that used to be performed by direct labor workers. Since the costs of acquiring and maintaining such equipment are classified as overhead, this increases overhead while decreasing direct labor. Second, products are themselves becoming more sophisticated and complex and change more frequently. This increases the need for highly skilled indirect workers such as engineers. As a result of these two trends, direct labor is becoming less of a factor and overhead is becoming more of a factor in the cost of products in many industries.

In companies where direct labor and overhead costs have been moving in opposite directions, it would be difficult to argue that direct labor "drives" overhead costs. Accordingly, in recent years, managers in some companies have used *activity-based costing* principles to redesign their cost accounting systems. Activity-based costing is a costing technique that is designed to more accurately reflect the demands that products, customers, and other cost objects make on overhead resources. The activity-based approach is discussed in more detail in Chapter 8.

We hasten to add that although direct labor may not be an appropriate allocation basis in some industries, in others it continues to be a significant driver of manufacturing overhead.[2] The key point is that the allocation base used by the company should really drive, or cause, overhead costs, and direct labor is not always an appropriate allocation base.

Focus on Current Practice

The most recent surveys of accounting practice indicate that 62% to 74% of manufacturing companies in the United States use direct labor as the primary or secondary allocation base for overhead. Machine-hours are used by another 12% or so of manufacturers, and the remainder of the companies use a variety of different allocation bases.[3] The most recent survey in the United Kingdom reveals a very similar pattern. In the UK, direct labor is used as an allocation base by 68% to 73% of manufacturing companies.[4]

There is some evidence that the proportion of companies that use direct labor-hours as the primary or secondary allocation base has been declining in the United States.[5] Apparently managers believe that direct labor is no longer as significant a cost driver for overhead as it once was.

Focus on Current Practice

Japanese companies, like companies in the United States, most frequently use direct labor-hours as a basis for allocating manufacturing overhead. One survey of over 250 manufacturing companies in Japan found the following breakdown:[6]

Basis for Allocation of Manufacturing Overhead	Percent
Direct labor-hours only	41.7%
Machine-hours only	6.4%
Both direct labor-hours and machine-hours	43.6%
Other allocation bases	8.3%
Total	100.0%

2. George Foster and Mahendra Gupta, "Manufacturing Overhead Cost Driver Analysis," *Journal of Accounting and Economics,* January 1990, pp. 309–37.
3. Jeffrey R. Cohen and Laurence Paquette, "Management Accounting Practices: Perceptions of Controllers," *Journal of Cost Management* 5, no. 3 (Fall 1991), p. 75; and James R. Emore and Joseph A. Ness, "The Slow Pace of Meaningful Change in Cost Systems," *Journal of Cost Management* 4, no. 4 (Winter 1991).
4. Colin Drury and Mike Tayles, "Product Costing in UK Manufacturing Organizations," *The European Accounting Review* 3, no. 3 (1994), pp. 443–69.
5. A 1985 study found that nearly 94% of midwestern manufacturing companies surveyed used direct labor to some extent (either as the primary or secondary base) in overhead costing. Henry R. Schwarzbach, "The Impact of Automation on Accounting for Indirect Costs," *Management Accounting* 67, no. 3 (December 1985).
6. Michiharu Sakurai, "The Influence of Factory Automation on Management Accounting Practices," in Robert Kaplan, ed., *Measures for Manufacturing Excellence* (Cambridge, MA: Harvard Press, 1990), p. 43.

Computation of Unit Costs

With the application of Yost Precision Machining's $216 manufacturing overhead to the job cost sheet in Exhibit 3–4, the job cost sheet is almost complete. There are two final steps. First, the totals for direct materials, direct labor, and manufacturing overhead are transferred to the Cost Summary section of the job cost sheet and added together to obtain the total cost for the job. Then the total cost ($1,800) is divided by the number of units (2) to obtain the unit cost ($900). As indicated earlier, *this unit cost is an average cost and should not be interpreted as the cost that would actually be incurred if another unit were produced.* Much of the actual overhead would not change at all if another unit were produced, so the incremental cost of an additional unit is something less than the average unit cost of $900.

The completed job cost sheet is now ready to be transferred to the Finished Goods inventory account, where it will serve as the basis for valuing unsold units in ending inventory and determining cost of goods sold.

Summary of Document Flows

The sequence of events discussed above is summarized in Exhibit 3–5. A careful study of the flow of documents in this exhibit will provide a good overview of the overall operation of a job-order costing system.

Managerial Accounting in Action

THE WRAP-UP

In the 8:00 A.M. daily planning meeting on March 9, Jean Yost, the president of Yost Precision Machining, once again drew attention to job 2B47, the experimental couplings:

Jean: I see job 2B47 is completed. Let's get those couplings shipped immediately to Loops Unlimited so they can get their testing program under way. Marcus, how much are we going to bill Loops for those two units?

Marcus: Just a second, let me check the job cost sheet for that job. Here it is. We agreed to sell the experimental units at cost, so we will be charging Loops Unlimited just $900 a unit.

Jean: Fine. Let's hope the couplings work out and we make some money on the big order later.

Job-Order Costing—The Flow of Costs

objective 4

Prepare journal entries to record costs in a job-order costing system.

We are now ready to take a more detailed look at the flow of costs through the company's formal accounting system. To illustrate, we shall consider a single month's activity for Rand Company, a producer of gold and silver commemorative medallions. Rand Company has two jobs in process during April, the first month of its fiscal year. Job A, a special minting of 1,000 gold medallions commemorating the invention of motion pictures, was started during March and had $30,000 in manufacturing costs already accumulated on April 1. Job B, an order for 10,000 silver medallions commemorating the fall of the Berlin Wall, was started in April.

Exhibit 3–5 The Flow of Documents in a Job-Order Costing System

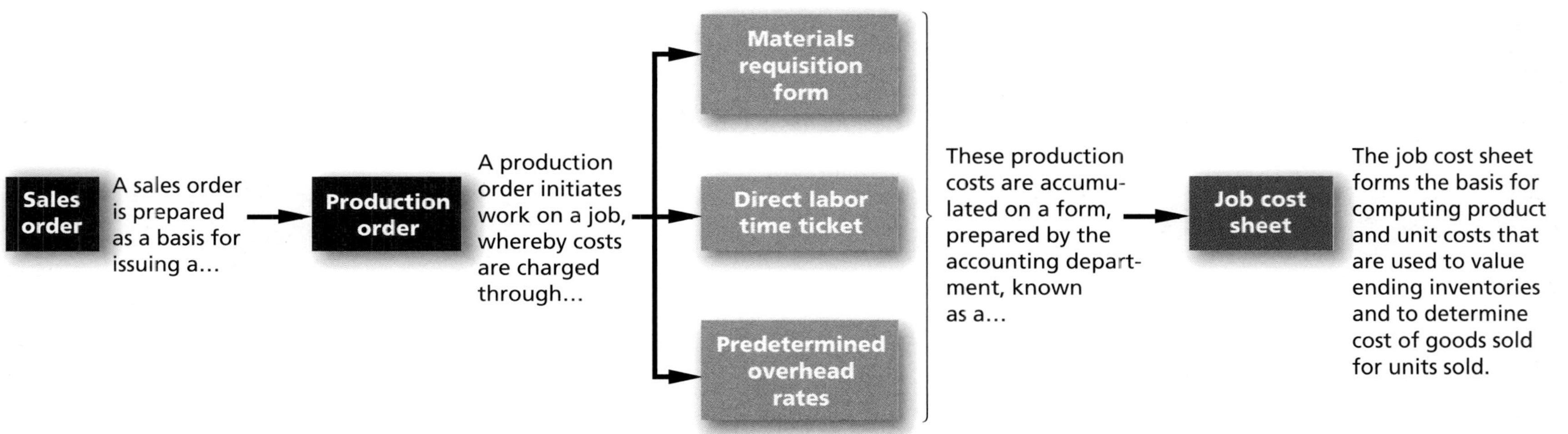

Exhibit 3–6 Raw Materials Cost Flows

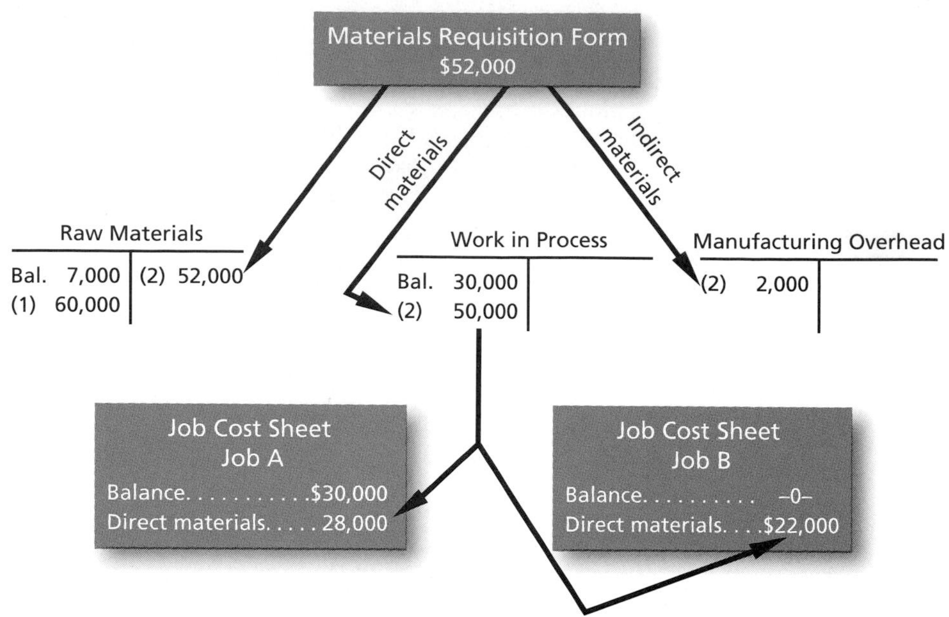

The Purchase and Issue of Materials

On April 1, Rand Company had $7,000 in raw materials on hand. During the month, the company purchased an additional $60,000 in raw materials. The purchase is recorded in journal entry (1) below:

(1)

Raw Materials	60,000	
Accounts Payable		60,000

As explained in Chapter 2, Raw Materials is an asset account. Thus, when raw materials are purchased, they are initially recorded as an asset—not as an expense.

ISSUE OF DIRECT AND INDIRECT MATERIALS During April, $52,000 in raw materials were requisitioned from the storeroom for use in production. Entry (2) records the issue of the materials to the production departments.

(2)

Work in Process	50,000	
Manufacturing Overhead	2,000	
Raw Materials		52,000

The materials charged to Work in Process represent direct materials for specific jobs. As these materials are entered into the Work in Process account, they are also recorded on the appropriate job cost sheets. This point is illustrated in Exhibit 3–6, where $28,000 of the $50,000 in direct materials is charged to job A's cost sheet and the remaining $22,000 is charged to job B's cost sheet. (In this example, all data are presented in summary form and the job cost sheet is abbreviated.)

The $2,000 charged to Manufacturing Overhead in entry (2) represents indirect materials used in production during April. Observe that the Manufacturing Overhead account is separate from the Work in Process account. The purpose of the Manufacturing Overhead account is to accumulate all manufacturing overhead costs as they are incurred during a period.

Before leaving Exhibit 3–6 we need to point out one additional thing. Notice from the exhibit that the job cost sheet for job A contains a beginning balance of

$30,000. We stated earlier that this balance represents the cost of work done during March that has been carried forward to April. Also note that the Work in Process account contains the same $30,000 balance. *The reason the $30,000 appears in both places is that the Work in Process account is a control account and the job cost sheets form a subsidiary ledger. Thus, the Work in Process account contains a summarized total of all costs appearing on the individual job cost sheets for all jobs in process at any given point in time.* (Since Rand Company had only job A in process at the beginning of April, job A's $30,000 balance on that date is equal to the balance in the Work in Process account.)

ISSUE OF DIRECT MATERIALS ONLY Sometimes the materials drawn from the Raw Materials inventory account are all direct materials. In this case, the entry to record the issue of the materials into production would be as follows:

Work in Process	XXX	
Raw Materials		XXX

Labor Cost

As work is performed in various departments of Rand Company from day to day, employee time tickets are filled out by workers, collected, and forwarded to the Accounting Department. In the Accounting Department, the tickets are costed according to the various employee wage rates, and the resulting costs are classified as either direct or indirect labor. This costing and classification for April resulted in the following summary entry:

(3)

Work in Process	60,000	
Manufacturing Overhead	15,000	
Salaries and Wages Payable		75,000

Only direct labor is added to the Work in Process account. For Rand Company, this amounted to $60,000 for April.

At the same time that direct labor costs are added to Work in Process, they are also added to the individual job cost sheets, as shown in Exhibit 3–7. During April, $40,000 of direct labor cost was charged to job A and the remaining $20,000 was charged to job B.

The labor costs charged to Manufacturing Overhead represent the indirect labor costs of the period, such as supervision, janitorial work, and maintenance.

Manufacturing Overhead Costs

Recall that all costs of operating the factory other than direct materials and direct labor are classified as manufacturing overhead costs. These costs are entered directly into the Manufacturing Overhead account as they are incurred. To illustrate, assume that Rand Company incurred the following general factory costs during April:

Utilities (heat, water, and power)	$21,000
Rent on factory equipment	16,000
Miscellaneous factory costs	3,000
Total	$40,000

The following entry records the incurrence of these costs:

(4)

Manufacturing Overhead	40,000	
Accounts Payable		40,000

Exhibit 3–7 Labor Cost Flows

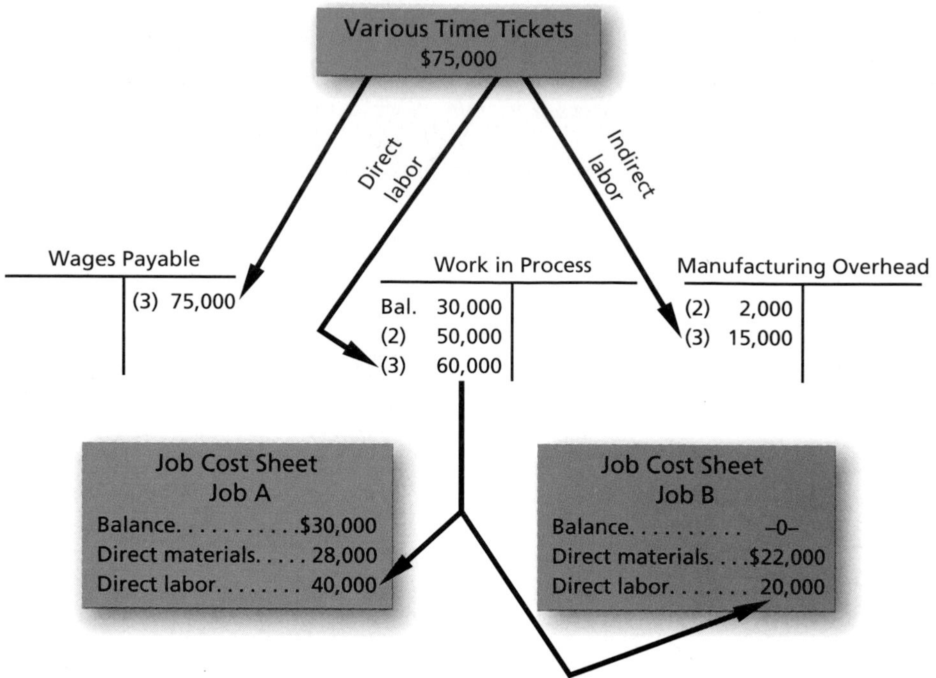

In addition, let us assume that during April, Rand Company recognized $13,000 in accrued property taxes and that $7,000 in prepaid insurance expired on factory buildings and equipment. The following entry records these items:

(5)

Manufacturing Overhead	20,000	
Property Taxes Payable		13,000
Prepaid Insurance		7,000

Finally, let us assume that the company recognized $18,000 in depreciation on factory equipment during April. The following entry records the accrual of this depreciation:

(6)

Manufacturing Overhead	18,000	
Accumulated Depreciation		18,000

In short, *all* manufacturing overhead costs are recorded directly into the Manufacturing Overhead account as they are incurred day by day throughout a period. It is important to understand that Manufacturing Overhead is a control account for many—perhaps thousands—of subsidiary accounts such as Indirect Materials, Indirect Labor, Factory Utilities, and so forth. As the Manufacturing Overhead account is debited for costs during a period, the various subsidiary accounts are also debited. In the example above and also in the assignment material for this chapter, we omit the entries to the subsidiary accounts for the sake of brevity.

objective 5

Apply overhead cost to Work in Process using a predetermined overhead rate.

The Application of Manufacturing Overhead

Since actual manufacturing costs are charged to the Manufacturing Overhead control account rather than to Work in Process, how are manufacturing overhead costs assigned to Work in Process? The answer is, by means of the predetermined overhead rate. Recall from our discussion earlier in the chapter that a predetermined overhead rate is established at the beginning of each year. The rate is calculated by dividing the

Exhibit 3–8 The Flow of Costs in Overhead Application

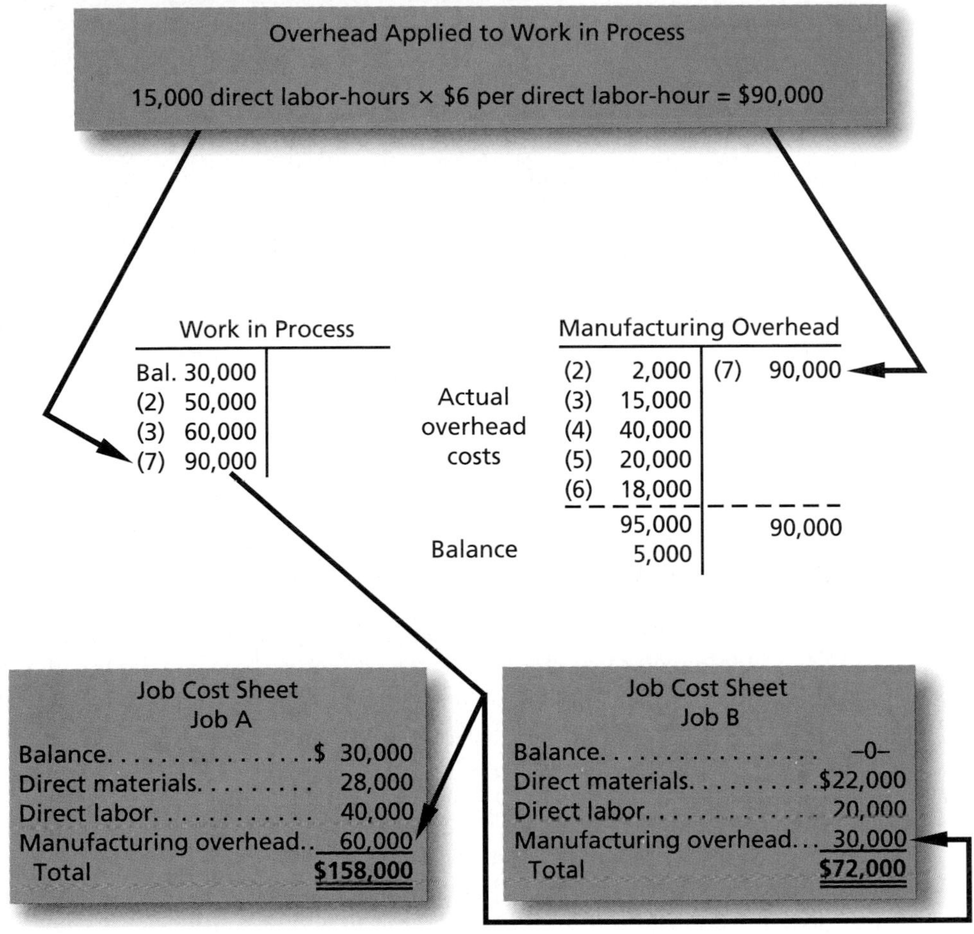

estimated total manufacturing overhead cost for the year by the estimated total units in the allocation base (measured in machine-hours, direct labor-hours, or some other base). The predetermined overhead rate is then used to apply overhead costs to jobs. For example, if direct labor-hours is the allocation base, overhead cost is applied to each job by multiplying the number of direct labor-hours charged to the job by the predetermined overhead rate.

To illustrate, assume that Rand Company has used machine-hours in computing its predetermined overhead rate and that this rate is $6 per machine-hour. Also assume that during April, 10,000 machine-hours were worked on job A and 5,000 machine-hours were worked on job B (a total of 15,000 machine-hours). Thus, $90,000 in overhead cost (15,000 machine-hours × $6 = $90,000) would be applied to Work in Process. The following entry records the application of Manufacturing Overhead to Work in Process:

(7)

Work in Process	90,000	
Manufacturing Overhead		90,000

The flow of costs through the Manufacturing Overhead account is shown in Exhibit 3–8.

The "actual overhead costs" in the Manufacturing Overhead account in Exhibit 3–8 are the costs that were added to the account in entries (2)–(6). Observe that the incurrence of these actual overhead costs [entries (2)–(6)] and the application of overhead to Work in Process [entry (7)] represent two separate and entirely distinct processes.

THE CONCEPT OF A CLEARING ACCOUNT The Manufacturing Overhead account operates as a clearing account. As we have noted, actual factory overhead costs are debited to the accounts as they are incurred day by day throughout the year. At certain intervals during the year, usually when a job is completed, overhead cost is released from the Manufacturing Overhead account and is applied to the Work in Process account by means of the predetermined overhead rate. This sequence of events is illustrated below:

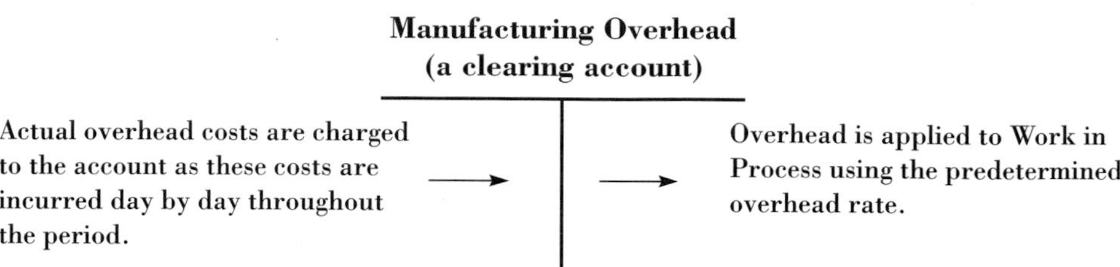

As we emphasized earlier, the predetermined overhead rate is based entirely on estimates of what overhead costs are *expected* to be, and it is established before the year begins. As a result, the overhead cost applied during a year will almost certainly turn out to be more or less than the overhead cost that is actually incurred. For example, notice from Exhibit 3–8 that Rand Company's actual overhead costs for the period are $5,000 greater than the overhead cost that has been applied to Work in Process, resulting in a $5,000 debit balance in the Manufacturing Overhead account. We will reserve discussion of what to do with this $5,000 balance until the next section, Problems of Overhead Application.

For the moment, we can conclude by noting from Exhibit 3–8 that the cost of a completed job consists of the actual materials cost of the job, the actual labor cost of the job, and the overhead cost *applied* to the job. Pay particular attention to the following subtle but important point: *Actual overhead costs are not charged to jobs; actual overhead costs do not appear on the job cost sheet nor do they appear in the Work in Process account. Only the applied overhead cost, based on the predetermined overhead rate, appears on the job cost sheet and in the Work in Process account.* Study this point carefully.

Nonmanufacturing Costs

In addition to manufacturing costs, companies also incur marketing and selling costs. As explained in Chapter 2, these costs should be treated as period expenses and charged directly to the income statement. *Nonmanufacturing costs should not go into the Manufacturing Overhead account.* To illustrate the correct treatment of nonmanufacturing costs, assume that Rand Company incurred the following selling and administrative costs during April:

Top-management salaries	$21,000
Other office salaries	9,000
Total salaries	$30,000

The following entry records these salaries:

(8)

Salaries Expense	30,000	
Salaries and Wages Payable		30,000

Assume that depreciation on office equipment during April was $7,000. The entry is as follows:

(9)

Depreciation Expense	7,000	
Accumulated Depreciation		7,000

Pay particular attention to the difference between this entry and entry (6) where we recorded depreciation on factory equipment. In journal entry (6), depreciation on factory equipment was debited to Manufacturing Overhead and is therefore a product cost. In journal entry (9) above, depreciation on office equipment was debited to Depreciation Expense. Depreciation on office equipment is considered to be a period expense rather than a product cost.

Finally, assume that advertising was $42,000 and that other selling and administrative expenses in April totaled $8,000. The following entry records these items:

(10)

Advertising Expense	42,000	
Other Selling and Administrative Expense	8,000	
Accounts Payable		50,000

Since the amounts in entries (8) through (10) all go directly into expense accounts, they will have no effect on the costing of Rand Company's production for April. The same will be true of any other selling and administrative expenses incurred during April, including sales commissions, depreciation on sales equipment, rent on office facilities, insurance on office facilities, and related costs.

Cost of Goods Manufactured

When a job has been completed, the finished output is transferred from the production departments to the finished goods warehouse. By this time, the accounting department will have charged the job with direct materials and direct labor cost, and manufacturing overhead will have been applied using the predetermined rate. A transfer of these costs must be made within the costing system that *parallels* the physical transfer of the goods to the finished goods warehouse. The costs of the completed job are transferred out of the Work in Process account and into the Finished Goods account. The sum of all amounts transferred between these two accounts represents the cost of goods manufactured for the period. (This point was illustrated earlier in Exhibit 2–6 in Chapter 2.)

In the case of Rand Company, let us assume that job A was completed during April. The following entry transfers the cost of job A from Work in Process to Finished Goods:

(11)

Finished Goods	158,000	
Work in Process		158,000

The $158,000 represents the completed cost of job A, as shown on the job cost sheet in Exhibit 3–8. Since job A was the only job completed during April, the $158,000 also represents the cost of goods manufactured for the month.

Job B was not completed by month-end, so its cost will remain in the Work in Process account and carry over to the next month. If a balance sheet is prepared at the end of April, the cost accumulated thus far on job B will appear as "Work in process inventory" in the assets section.

Cost of Goods Sold

As units in finished goods are shipped to fill customers' orders, the unit cost appearing on the job cost sheets is used as a basis for transferring the cost of the items sold from the Finished Goods account into the Cost of Goods Sold account. If a complete job is shipped, as in the case where a job has been done to a customer's specifications, then it is a simple matter to transfer the entire cost appearing on the job cost sheet into the Cost of Goods Sold account. In most cases, however, only a portion of the units involved in a particular job will be immediately sold. In these situations, the unit cost must be used to determine how much product cost should be removed from Finished Goods and charged to Cost of Goods Sold.

For Rand Company, we will assume 750 of the 1,000 gold medallions in job A were shipped to customers by the end of the month for total sales revenue of $225,000. Since 1,000 units were produced and the total cost of the job from the job cost sheet was $158,000, the unit product cost was $158. The following journal entries would record the sale (all sales are on account):

(12)

Accounts Receivable	225,000	
Sales		225,000

(13)

Cost of Goods Sold	118,500	
Finished Goods		118,500
($158 per unit × 750 units = $118,500)		

With entry (13), the flow of costs through our job-order costing system is completed.

Summary of Cost Flows

objective 6

Prepare T-accounts to show the flow of costs in a job-order costing system and prepare schedules of cost of goods manufactured and cost of goods sold.

To pull the entire Rand Company example together, journal entries (1) through (13) are summarized in Exhibit 3–9. The flow of costs through the accounts is presented in T-account form in Exhibit 3–10.

Exhibit 3–11 presents a schedule of cost of goods manufactured and a schedule of cost of goods sold for Rand Company. Note particularly from Exhibit 3–11 that the manufacturing overhead cost on the schedule of cost of goods manufactured is the overhead applied to jobs during the month—not the actual manufacturing overhead costs incurred. The reason for this can be traced back to journal entry (7) and the T-account for Work in Process that appears in Exhibit 3–10. Under a normal costing system as illustrated in this chapter, applied—not actual—overhead costs are applied to jobs and thus to Work in Process inventory. Note also the cost of goods manufactured for the month ($158,000) agrees with the amount transferred from Work in Process to Finished Goods for the month as recorded earlier in entry (11). Also note that this $158,000 figure is used in computing the cost of goods sold for the month.

An income statement for April is presented in Exhibit 3–12. Observe that the cost of goods sold figure on this statement ($123,500) is carried down from Exhibit 3–11.

Problems of Overhead Application

objective 7

Compute under- or overapplied overhead cost and prepare the journal entry to close the balance in Manufacturing Overhead to the appropriate accounts.

We need to consider two complications relating to overhead application. These are (1) the computation of underapplied and overapplied overhead and (2) the disposition of any balance remaining in the Manufacturing Overhead account at the end of a period.

Underapplied and Overapplied Overhead

Since the predetermined overhead rate is established before a period begins and is based entirely on estimated data, there generally will be a difference between the amount of overhead cost applied to Work in Process and the amount of overhead cost actually incurred during a period. In the case of Rand Company, for example, the

Exhibit 3–9 Summary of Rand Company Journal Entries

(1)		
Raw Materials	60,000	
Accounts Payable		60,000
(2)		
Work in Process	50,000	
Manufacturing Overhead	2,000	
Raw Materials		52,000
(3)		
Work in Process	60,000	
Manufacturing Overhead	15,000	
Salaries and Wages Payable		75,000
(4)		
Manufacturing Overhead	40,000	
Accounts Payable		40,000
(5)		
Manufacturing Overhead	20,000	
Property Taxes Payable		13,000
Prepaid Insurance		7,000
(6)		
Manufacturing Overhead	18,000	
Accumulated Depreciation		18,000
(7)		
Work in Process	90,000	
Manufacturing Overhead		90,000
(8)		
Salaries Expense	30,000	
Salaries and Wages Payable		30,000
(9)		
Depreciation Expense	7,000	
Accumulated Depreciation		7,000
(10)		
Advertising Expense	42,000	
Other Selling and Administrative Expense	8,000	
Accounts Payable		50,000
(11)		
Finished Goods	158,000	
Work in Process		158,000
(12)		
Accounts Receivable	225,000	
Sales		225,000
(13)		
Cost of Goods Sold	118,500	
Finished Goods		118,500

predetermined overhead rate of $6 per hour resulted in $90,000 of overhead cost being applied to Work in Process, whereas actual overhead costs for April proved to be $95,000 (see Exhibit 3–8). The difference between the overhead cost applied to Work in Process and the actual overhead costs of a period is termed either **underapplied** or **overapplied overhead.** For Rand Company, overhead was underapplied because the applied cost ($90,000) was $5,000 less than the actual cost ($95,000). If the tables had

Exhibit 3–10 Summary of Cost Flows—Rand Company

Accounts Receivable

	Debit		Credit
	XX*		
(12)	225,000		

Prepaid Insurance

	Debit		Credit
	XX		
		(5)	7,000

Raw Materials

	Debit		Credit
Bal.	7,000	(2)	52,000
(1)	60,000		
Bal.	15,000		

Work in Process

	Debit		Credit
Bal.	30,000	(11)	158,000
(2)	50,000		
(3)	60,000		
(7)	90,000		
Bal.	72,000		

Finished Goods

	Debit		Credit
Bal..	10,000	(13)	118,500
(11)	158,000		
Bal.	49,500		

Accumulated Depreciation

	Debit		Credit
			XX
		(6)	18,000
		(9)	7,000

Manufacturing Overhead

	Debit		Credit
(2)	2,000	(7)	90,000
(3)	15,000		
(4)	40,000		
(5)	20,000		
(6)	18,000		
Bal.	5,000		

Accounts Payable

	Debit		Credit
			XX
		(1)	60,000
		(4)	40,000
		(10)	50,000

Salaries and Wages Payable

	Debit		Credit
			XX
		(3)	75,000
		(8)	30,000

Property Taxes Payable

	Debit		Credit
			XX
		(5)	13,000

Capital Stock

	Debit		Credit
			XX

Retained Earnings

	Debit		Credit
			XX

Sales

	Debit		Credit
		(12)	225,000

Cost of Goods Sold

	Debit		Credit
(13)	118,500		

Salaries Expense

	Debit		Credit
(8)	30,000		

Depreciation Expense

	Debit		Credit
(9)	7,000		

Advertising Expense

	Debit		Credit
(10)	42,000		

Other Selling and Administrative Expense

	Debit		Credit
(10)	8,000		

Explanation of entries:

(1) Raw materials purchased.
(2) Direct and indirect materials issued into production.
(3) Direct and indirect factory labor cost incurred.
(4) Utilities and other factory costs incurred.
(5) Property taxes and insurance incurred on the factory.
(6) Depreciation recorded on factory assets.
(7) Overhead cost applied to Work in Process
(8) Administrative salaries expense incurred.
(9) Depreciation recorded on office equipment.
(10) Advertising and other expense incurred.
(11) Cost of goods manufactured transferred into finished goods.
(12) Sale of job A recorded.
(13) Cost of goods sold recorded for job A.

*XX = Normal balance in the account (for example, Accounts Receivable normally carries a debit balance).

Exhibit 3–11 Schedules of Cost of Goods Manufactured and Cost of Goods Sold

Cost of Goods Manufactured		
Direct materials:		
Raw materials inventory, beginning	$ 7,000	
Add: Purchases of raw materials	60,000	
Total raw materials available	67,000	
Deduct: Raw materials inventory, ending	15,000	
Raw materials used in production	52,000	
Less indirect materials included in manufacturing overhead	2,000	$ 50,000
Direct labor		60,000
Manufacturing overhead applied to work in process		90,000
Total manufacturing costs		200,000
Add: Beginning work in process inventory		30,000
		230,000
Deduct: Ending work in process inventory		72,000
Cost of goods manufactured		$158,000
Cost of Goods Sold		
Finished goods inventory, beginning		$ 10,000
Add: Cost of goods manufactured		158,000
Goods available for sale		168,000
Deduct: Finished goods inventory, ending		49,500
Unadjusted cost of goods sold		118,500
Add: Underapplied overhead		5,000
Adjusted cost of goods sold		$123,500

*Note that the underapplied overhead is added to cost of goods sold. If overhead were overapplied, it would be deducted from costs of goods sold.

Exhibit 3–12 Income Statement

RAND COMPANY
Income Statement
For the Month Ending April 30

Sales		$225,000
Less cost of goods sold ($118,500 + $5,000)		123,500
Gross margin		101,500
Less selling and administrative expenses:		
Salaries expense	$30,000	
Depreciation expense	7,000	
Advertising expense	42,000	
Other expense	8,000	87,000
Net income		$ 14,500

been reversed and the company had applied $95,000 in overhead cost to Work in Process while incurring actual overhead costs of only $90,000, then the overhead would have been overapplied.

What is the cause of underapplied or overapplied overhead? The causes can be complex, and a full explanation will have to wait for Chapters 10 and 11. Nevertheless, the basic problem is that the method of applying overhead to jobs using a predetermined overhead rate assumes that actual overhead costs will be proportional to the actual amount of the allocation base incurred during the period. If, for example, the predetermined overhead rate is $6 per machine-hour, then it is assumed that actual overhead costs incurred will be $6 for every machine-hour that is actually worked.

There are at least two reasons why this may not be true. First, much of the overhead often consists of fixed costs. Since these costs are fixed, they do not grow as the number of machine-hours incurred increases. Second, spending on overhead items may or may not be under control. If individuals who are responsible for overhead costs do a good job, those costs should be less than were expected at the beginning of the period. If they do a poor job, those costs will be more than expected. As we indicated above, however, a fuller explanation of the causes of underapplied and overapplied overhead will have to wait for later chapters.

To illustrate what can happen, suppose that two companies—Turbo Crafters and Black & Howell—have prepared the following estimated data for the coming year:

	Company	
	Turbo Crafters	**Black & Howell**
Predetermined overhead rate based on	Machine-hours	Direct materials cost
Estimated manufacturing overhead	$300,000 (a)	$120,000 (a)
Estimated machine-hours	75,000 (b)	—
Estimated direct materials cost	—	$ 80,000 (b)
Predetermined overhead rate, (a) ÷ (b)	$4 per machine-hour	150% of direct materials cost

Now assume that because of unexpected changes in overhead spending and changes in demand for the companies' products, the *actual* overhead cost and the *actual* activity recorded during the year in each company are as follows:

	Company	
	Turbo Crafters	**Black & Howell**
Actual manufacturing overhead costs	$290,000	$130,000
Actual machine-hours	68,000	—
Actual direct material costs	—	$ 90,000

For each company, note that the actual data for both cost and activity differ from the estimates used in computing the predetermined overhead rate. This results in underapplied and overapplied overhead as follows:

	Company	
	Turbo Crafters	**Black & Howell**
Actual manufacturing overhead costs	$290,000	$130,000
Manufacturing overhead cost applied to Work in Process during the year:		
68,000 *actual* machine-hours × $4	272,000	
$90,000 *actual* direct materials cost × 150% ...		135,000
Underapplied (overapplied) overhead	$ 18,000	$ (5,000)

For Turbo Crafters, notice that the amount of overhead cost that has been applied to Work in Process ($272,000) is less than the actual overhead cost for the year ($290,000). Therefore, overhead is underapplied. Also notice that the original estimate of overhead in Turbo Crafters ($300,000) is not directly involved in this computation. Its impact is felt only through the $4 predetermined overhead rate that is used.

For Black & Howell, the amount of overhead cost that has been applied to Work in Process ($135,000) is greater than the actual overhead cost for the year ($130,000), and so overhead is overapplied.

A summary of the concepts discussed above is presented in Exhibit 3–13.

Exhibit 3–13
Summary of Overhead Concepts

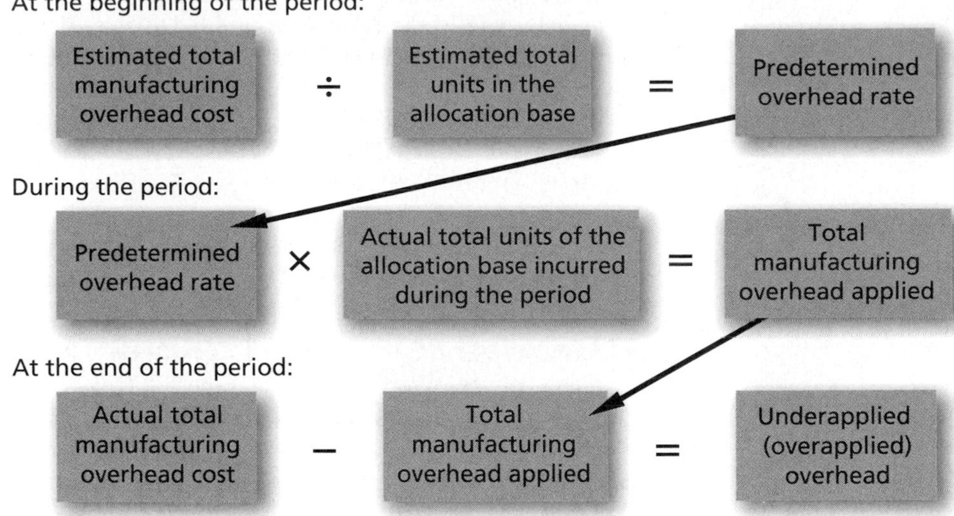

Disposition of Under- or Overapplied Overhead Balances

What disposition should be made of any under- or overapplied balance remaining in the Manufacturing Overhead account at the end of a period? Generally, any balance in the account is treated in one of two ways:

1. Closed out to Cost of Goods Sold.
2. Allocated between Work in Process, Finished Goods, and Cost of Goods Sold in proportion to the overhead applied during the current period in the ending balances of these accounts.[7]

The second method, which allocates the under- or overapplied overhead among ending inventories and Cost of Goods Sold, is equivalent to using an "actual" overhead rate and is for that reason considered by many to be more accurate than the first method. Consequently, if the amount of underapplied or overapplied overhead is material, many accountants would insist that the second method be used. In problem assignments we will always indicate which method you are to use for disposing of under- or overapplied overhead.

CLOSED OUT TO COST OF GOODS SOLD As mentioned above, closing out the balance in Manufacturing Overhead to Cost of Goods Sold is simpler than the allocation method. Returning to the example of Rand Company, the entry to close the $5,0000 of underapplied overhead to Cost of Goods Sold would be as follows:

(14)		
Cost of Goods Sold	5,000	
Manufacturing Overhead		5,000

7. Some firms prefer to make the allocation on the basis of the total cost of direct materials, direct labor, and applied manufacturing overhead in each of the accounts at the end of the period. This method is not as accurate as allocating the balance in the Manufacturing Overhead account on the basis of just the overhead applied in each of the accounts during the current period.

Note that since there is a debit balance in the Manufacturing Overhead account, Manufacturing Overhead must be credited to close out the account. This has the effect of increasing Cost of Goods Sold for April to $123,500:

Unadjusted cost of goods sold [from entry (13)]	$118,500
Add underapplied overhead [entry (14) above]	5,000
Adjusted cost of goods sold	$123,500

After this adjustment has been made, Rand Company's income statement for April will appear as was shown earlier in Exhibit 3–12.

ALLOCATED BETWEEN ACCOUNTS Allocation of under- or overapplied overhead between Work in Process, Finished Goods, and Cost of Goods Sold is more accurate than closing the entire balance into Cost of Goods Sold. The reason is that allocation assigns overhead costs to where they would have gone in the first place had it not been for the errors in the estimates going into the predetermined overhead rate.

Had Rand Company chosen to allocate the underapplied overhead among the inventory accounts and Cost of Goods Sold, it would first be necessary to determine the amount of overhead that had been applied during April in each of the accounts. The computations would have been as follows:

Overhead applied in work in process inventory, April 30	$30,000	33.33%
Overhead applied in finished goods inventory, April 30 ($60,000/1,000 units = $60 per unit) × 250 units	15,000	16.67%
Overhead applied in cost of goods sold, April ($60,000/1,000 units = $60 per unit) × 750 units	45,000	50.00%
Total overhead applied	$90,000	100.00%

Based on the above percentages, the underapplied overhead (i.e., the debit balance in Manufacturing Overhead) would be allocated as in the following journal entry:

Work in Process (33.33% × $5,000)	1,666.50	
Finished Goods (16.67% × $5,000)	833.50	
Cost of Goods Sold (50.00% × $5,000)	2,500.00	
Manufacturing Overhead		5,000.00

Note that the first step in the allocation was to determine the amount of overhead applied in each of the accounts. For Finished Goods, for example, the total amount of overhead applied to job A, $60,000, was divided by the total number of units in job A, 1,000 units, to arrive at the average overhead applied of $60 per unit. Since there were still 250 units from job A in ending finished goods inventory, the amount of overhead applied in the Finished Goods Inventory account was $60 per unit multiplied by 250 units or $15,000 in total.

If overhead had been overapplied, the entry above would have been just the reverse, since a credit balance would have existed in the Manufacturing Overhead account.

A General Model of Product Cost Flows

The flow of costs in a product costing system is presented in the form of a T-account model in Exhibit 3–14. This model applies as much to a process costing system as it does to a job-order costing system. Examination of this model can be very helpful in gaining a perspective as to how costs enter a system, flow through it, and finally end up as Cost of Goods Sold on the income statement.

Exhibit 3–14 A General Model of Cost Flows

Raw Materials	
Debited for the cost of materials purchased	Credited for direct materials added to Work in Process Credited for indirect materials added to Manufacturing Overhead

Salaries and Wages Payable	
	Credited for direct labor added to Work in Process Credited for indirect labor added to Manufacturing Overhead

Manufacturing Overhead	
Debited for actual overhead costs incurred	Credited for overhead cost applied to Work in Process
Underapplied overhead cost	Overapplied overhead cost

Work in Process	
Debited for the cost of direct materials, direct labor, and manufacturing overhead applied	Credited for the cost of goods manufactured

Finished Goods	
Debited for the cost of goods manufactured	Credited for the cost of goods sold

Cost of Goods Sold	
Debited for the cost of goods sold	

Multiple Predetermined Overhead Rates

Our discussion in this chapter has assumed that there is a single predetermined overhead rate for an entire factory called a **plantwide overhead rate.** This is, in fact, a common practice—particularly in smaller companies. But in larger companies, *multiple predetermined overhead rates* are often used. In a **multiple predetermined overhead rate** system there is usually a different overhead rate for each production department. Such a system, while more complex, is considered to be more accurate, since it can reflect differences across departments in how overhead costs are incurred. For example, overhead might be allocated based on direct labor-hours in departments that are relatively labor intensive and based on machine-hours in departments that are relatively machine intensive. When multiple predetermined overhead rates are used, overhead is applied in each department according to its own overhead rate as a job proceeds through the department.

Job-Order Costing in Service Companies

We stated earlier in the chapter that job-order costing is also used in service organizations such as law firms, movie studios, hospitals, and repair shops, as well as in manufacturing companies. In a law firm, for example, each client represents a "job," and the costs of that job are accumulated day by day on a job cost sheet as the client's case is handled by the firm. Legal forms and similar inputs represent the direct materials for the job; the time expended by attorneys represents the direct labor; and the costs of secretaries, clerks, rent, depreciation, and so forth, represent the overhead.

In a movie studio such as Columbia Pictures, each film produced by the studio is a "job," and costs for direct materials (costumes, props, film, etc.) and direct labor (actors, directors, and extras) are accounted for and charged to each film's job cost sheet. A share of the studio's overhead costs, such as utilities, depreciation of equipment, salaries of maintenance workers, and so forth, is also charged to each film. As the accompanying Focus on Current Practice box illustrates, however, there is considerable controversy about the methods used by some studios to distribute overhead costs among movies, and these controversies sometimes result in lawsuits.

In sum, the reader should be aware that job-order costing is a versatile and widely used costing method, and may be encountered in virtually any organization where there are diverse products or services.

Focus on Current Practice

"Net profit participation" contracts in which writers, actors, and directors share in the net profits of movies are common in Hollywood. For example, Winston Groom, the author of the novel *Forrest Gump,* has a contract with Paramount Pictures Corp. that calls for him to receive 3% of the net profits on the movie. However, Paramount claims that *Forrest Gump* has yet to show any profits even though it has the third-highest gross receipts of any film in history. How can this be?

Movie studios assess a variety of overhead charges including a charge of about 15% on production costs for production overhead, a charge of about 30% of gross rentals for distribution overhead, and a charge for marketing overhead that amounts to about 10% of advertising costs. After all of these overhead charges and other hotly contested accounting practices, it is a rare film that shows a profit. Fewer than 5% of released films show a profit for net profit participation purposes. Examples of "money-losing" films include *Rain Man, Batman,* and *Who Framed Roger Rabbit?* as well as *Forrest Gump.* Disgruntled writers and actors are increasingly suing studios, claiming unreasonable accounting practices that are designed to cheat them of their share of profits.[8]

Use of Bar Code Technology

Earlier in the chapter we discussed the use of bar code technology in recording labor time. Some companies are extending bar code technology to include all steps in the manufacturing process. Bar codes allow people who speak different languages to identify items, amounts, locations, work steps, and so forth, and also to communicate this information to others throughout the world. Thus, bar codes are becoming an international link that allows direct communication between a company, its customers, and its suppliers regardless of where they may be located.

---

8 Ross Engel and Bruce Ikawa, "Where's the Profit?" *Management Accounting,* January 1997, pp. 40–47.

Bar codes are often used in conjunction with electronic data interchange (EDI), which involves a network of computers linking organizations. An EDI network allows companies to electronically exchange business documents and other information that extend into all areas of business activity from ordering raw materials to shipping completed goods.

In a company with a well-developed bar code system, the manufacturing cycle begins with the receipt of a customer's order via ED. The raw materials to produce the goods come from suppliers who have bar coded the materials according to the company's preset specifications. When materials arrive at the company's plant, the bar codes are scanned to update inventory records. The bar codes are scanned again when the materials are requisitioned for use in production. The computer credits the Raw Materials inventory account for the amount and type of goods requisitioned and charges the Work in Process inventory account.

A unique bar code is assigned to each job. This bar code is scanned to update Work in Process records for labor and other costs incurred in the manufacturing process. When goods are completed, another scan is performed that transfers both the cost and quantity of goods from the Work in Process inventory account to the Finished Goods inventory account, or charges Cost of Goods Sold for goods ready to be shipped.

Goods ready to be shipped are packed into containers, which are bar coded with information that includes the customer number, the type and quantity of goods being shipped, and the order number being filled. This bar code is then used for preparing billing information and for tracking the packed goods until placed on a carrier for shipment to the customer. Some customers require that the packed goods be bar coded with point-of-sale labels that can be scanned at retail check-out counters. These scans allow the retailer to update inventory records, verify price, and generate a customer receipt.

In short, bar code technology is being integrated into all areas of business activity. It eliminates a lot of clerical drudgery and allows companies to capture more data and to analyze and report information much more quickly and completely and with less error than with manual systems.

Focus on Current Practice

Andersen Windows of Bayport, Minnesota, has developed techniques that allow it to produce just about any window configuration that a customer might order. Andersen has installed hundreds of Macintosh-based systems for designing windows at distributors and retailers around the country. Beginning with a standard design from the company's catalog, this system allows a customer to "add, change, and strip away features until they've designed a window they're pleased with . . . The computer automatically checks the window specs for structural soundness, and then generates a price quote." Once the sale is made, the retailer's computer transmits the order with all of the necessary specifications to Andersen. At Andersen, the order is assigned a unique number and is tracked "in real time, using bar code technology, from the assembly line to the warehouse. This helps ensure that what the customer orders is what gets built and ultimately what gets shipped . . . Last year the company offered a whopping 188,000 different products, yet fewer than one in 200 van loads contained an order discrepancy."[9]

9. Justin Martin, "Are You as Good as You Think You Are?" *Fortune,* September 30, 1996, pp. 94–99.

Summary

Job-order costing and process costing are widely used to track costs. Job-order costing is used in situations where the organization offers many different products or services, such as in furniture manufacturing, hospitals, and legal firms. Process costing is used where units of product are homogeneous, such as in flour milling or cement production.

Materials requisition forms and labor time tickets are used to assign direct materials and direct labor costs to jobs in a job-costing system. Manufacturing overhead costs are assigned to jobs through use of a predetermined overhead rate. The predetermined overhead rate is determined before the period begins by dividing the estimated total manufacturing cost for the period by the estimated total allocation base for the period. The most frequently used allocation bases are direct labor-hours and machine-hours. Overhead is applied to jobs by multiplying the predetermined overhead rate by the actual amount of the allocation base used by the job.

Since the predetermined overhead rate is based on estimates, the actual overhead cost incurred during a period may be more or less than the amount of overhead cost applied to production. Such a difference is referred to as under- or overapplied overhead. The under- or overapplied overhead for a period can be either (1) closed out to Cost of Goods Sold or (2) allocated between Work in Process, Finished Goods, and Cost of Goods Sold. When overhead is underapplied, manufacturing overhead costs have been understated and therefore inventories and/or expenses must be adjusted upwards. When overhead is overapplied, manufacturing overhead costs have been overstated and therefore inventories and/or expenses must be adjusted downwards.

Review Problem: Job-Order Costing

Hogle Company is a manufacturing firm that uses job-order costing. On January 1, the beginning of its fiscal year, the company's inventory balances were as follows:

Raw materials	$20,000
Work in process	15,000
Finished goods	30,000

The company applies overhead cost to jobs on the basis of machine-hours worked. For the current year, the company estimated that it would work 75,000 machine-hours and incur $450,000 in manufacturing overhead cost. The following transactions were recorded for the year:

a. Raw materials were purchased on account, $410,000.
b. Raw materials were requisitioned for use in production, $380,000 ($360,000 direct materials and $20,000 indirect materials).
c. The following costs were incurred for employee services: direct labor, $75,000; indirect labor, $110,000; sales commissions, $90,000; and administrative salaries, $200,000.
d. Sales travel costs were incurred, $17,000.
e. Utility costs were incurred in the factory, $43,000.
f. Advertising costs were incurred, $180,000.
g. Depreciation was recorded for the year, $350,000 (80% relates to factory operations, and 20% relates to selling and administrative activities).
h. Insurance expired during the year, $10,000 (70% relates to factory operations, and the remaining 30% relates to selling and administrative activities).
i. Manufacturing overhead was applied to production. Due to greater than expected demand for its products, the company worked 80,000 machine-hours during the year.
j. Goods costing $900,000 to manufacture according to their job cost sheets were completed during the year.
k. Goods were sold on account to customers during the year at a total selling price of $1,500,000. The goods cost $870,000 to manufacture according to their job cost sheets.

Required

1. Prepare journal entries to record the preceding transactions.
2. Post the entries in (1) above to T-accounts (don't forget to enter the opening balances in the inventory accounts).
3. Is Manufacturing Overhead underapplied or overapplied for the year? Prepare a journal entry to close any balance in the Manufacturing Overhead account to Cost of Goods Sold. Do not allocate the balance between ending inventories and Cost of Goods Sold.
4. Prepare an income statement for the year.

Solution to Review Problem

1.

	Debit	Credit
a. Raw Materials	410,000	
Accounts Payable		410,000
b. Work in Process	360,000	
Manufacturing Overhead	20,000	
Raw Materials		380,000
c. Work in Process	75,000	
Manufacturing Overhead	110,000	
Sales Commissions Expense	90,000	
Administrative Salaries Expense	200,000	
Salaries and Wages Payable		475,000
d. Sales Travel Expense	17,000	
Accounts Payable		17,000
e. Manufacturing Overhead	43,000	
Accounts Payable		43,000
f. Advertising Expense	180,000	
Accounts Payable		180,000
g. Manufacturing Overhead	280,000	
Depreciation Expense	70,000	
Accumulated Depreciation		350,000
h. Manufacturing Overhead	7,000	
Insurance Expense	3,000	
Prepaid Insurance		10,000

i. The predetermined overhead rate for the year would be computed as follows:

$$\frac{\text{Estimated manufacturing overhead, \$450,000}}{\text{Estimated machine-hours, 75,000}} = \text{\$6 per machine-hour}$$

Based on the 80,000 machine-hours actually worked during the year, the company would have applied $480,000 in overhead cost to production: 80,000 machine-hours × $6 = $480,000. The following entry records this application of overhead cost:

	Debit	Credit
Work in Process	480,000	
Manufacturing Overhead		480,000
j. Finished Goods	900,000	
Work in Process		900,000
k. Accounts Receivable	1,500,000	
Sales		1,500,000
Cost of Goods Sold	870,000	
Finished Goods		870,000

2.

Accounts Receivable

Debit		Credit	
(k)	1,500,000		

Manufacturing Overhead

Debit		Credit	
(b)	20,000	(i)	480,000
(c)	110,000		
(e)	43,000		
(g)	280,000		
(h)	7,000		
	460,000		480,000
		Bal.	20,000

Sales

Debit		Credit	
		(k)	1,500,000

Cost of Goods Sold

Debit		Credit	
(k)	870,000		

Prepaid Insurance

		(h)	10,000

Accumulated Depreciation

		(g)	350,000

Commissions Expense

(c)	90,000		

Administrative Salary Expense

(c)	200,000		

Raw Materials

Bal.	20,000	(b)	380,000
(a)	410,000		
Bal.	50,000		

Accounts Payable

		(a)	410,000
		(d)	17,000
		(e)	43,000
		(f)	180,000

Sales Travel Expense

(d)	17,000		

Advertising Expense

(f)	180,000		

Work in Process

Bal.	15,000	(j)	900,000
(b)	360,000		
(c)	75,000		
(i)	480,000		
Bal.	30,000		

Salaries and Wages Payable

		(c)	475,000

Depreciation Expense

(g)	70,000		

Insurance Expense

(h)	3,000		

Finished Goods

Bal.	30,000	(k)	870,000
(j)	900,000		
Bal.	60,000		

3. Manufacturing overhead is overapplied for the year. The entry to close it out to Cost of Goods Sold is as follows:

Manufacturing Overhead	20,000	
Cost of Goods Sold		20,000

4.

HOGLE COMPANY
Income Statement
For the Year Ended December 31

Sales		$1,500,000
Less cost of goods sold ($870,000 − $20,000)		850,000
Gross margin		650,000
Less selling and administrative expenses:		
Commissions expense	$ 90,000	
Administrative salaries expense	200,000	
Sales travel expense	17,000	
Advertising expense	180,000	
Depreciation expense	70,000	
Insurance expense	3,000	560,000
Net income		$ 90,000

Key Terms for Review

Absorption costing A costing method that includes all manufacturing costs—direct materials, direct labor, and both variable and fixed overhead—as part of the cost of a finished unit of product. This term is synonymous with *full cost.* (p. 86)

Allocation base A measure of activity such as direct labor-hours or machine-hours that is used to assign costs to cost objects. (p. 92)

Bill of materials A document that shows the type and quantity of each major item of materials required to make a product. (p. 88)

Cost driver A factor, such as machine-hours, beds occupied, computer time, or flight-hours, that causes overhead costs. (p. 94)

Full cost See *Absorption costing*. (p. 86)

Job cost sheet A form prepared for each job that records the materials, labor, and overhead costs charged to the job. (p. 89)

Job-order costing system A costing system used in situations where many different products, jobs, or services are produced each period. (p. 87)

Materials requisition form A detailed source document that specifies the type and quantity of materials that are to be drawn from the storeroom and identifies the job to which the costs of materials are to be charged. (p. 89)

Multiple predetermined overhead rates A costing system in which there are multiple overhead cost pools with a different predetermined rate for each cost pool, rather than a single predetermined overhead rate for the entire company. Frequently, each production department is treated as a separate overhead cost pool. (p. 111)

Normal cost system A costing system in which overhead costs are applied to jobs by multiplying a predetermined overhead rate by the actual amount of the allocation base incurred by the job. (p. 93)

Overapplied overhead A credit balance in the Manufacturing Overhead account that arises when the amount of overhead cost applied to Work in Process is greater than the amount of overhead cost actually incurred during a period. (p. 105)

Overhead application The process of charging manufacturing overhead cost to job cost sheets and to the Work in Process account. (p. 92)

Plantwide overhead rate A single predetermined overhead rate that is used throughout a plant. (p. 111)

Predetermined overhead rate A rate used to charge overhead cost to jobs in production; the rate is established in advance for each period by use of estimates of total manufacturing overhead cost and of the total allocation base for the period. (p. 92)

Process costing system A costing system used in those manufacturing situations where a single, homogeneous product (such as cement or flour) is produced for long periods of time. (p. 86)

Time ticket A detailed source document that is used to record an employee's hour-by-hour activities during a day. (p. 90)

Underapplied overhead A debit balance in the Manufacturing Overhead account that arises when the amount of overhead cost actually incurred is greater than the amount of overhead cost applied to Work in Process during a period. (p. 105)

Appendix 3A: The Predetermined Overhead Rate and Capacity

objective 8

Explain the implications of basing the predetermined overhead rate on activity at capacity rather than on estimated activity for the period.

Companies typically base their predetermined overhead rates on the estimated, or budgeted, amount of the allocation base for the upcoming period. This is the method that is used in the chapter, but it is a practice that has recently come under severe criticism.[10] An example will be very helpful in understanding why. Prahad Corporation manufactures music CDs for local recording studios. The company has a CD duplicating machine that is capable of producing a new CD every 10 seconds from a master CD. The company leases the CD duplicating machine for $3,600,000 per year, and this is the company's only manufacturing overhead. With allowances for setups and maintenance, the machine is theoretically capable of producing up to 900,000 CDs per year. However, due to weak retail sales of CDs, the company's commercial customers are unlikely to order more than 600,000 CDs next year. The company uses machine time as the allocation base for applying manufacturing overhead. These data are summarized below:

PRAHAD CORPORATION DATA

Total manufacturing overhead cost	$3,600,000 per year
Allocation base: machine time per CD	10 seconds per CD
Capacity	900,000 CDs per year
Budgeted output for next year	600,000 CDs

If Prahad follows common practice and computes its predetermined overhead rate using estimated, or budgeted, figures, then its predetermined overhead rate for next year would be $0.60 per second of machine time computed as follows:

$$\frac{\text{Estimated total manufacturing overhead cost, \$3,600,000}}{\text{Estimated total units in the allocation base, 600,000 CDs} \times \text{10 seconds per CD}} = \text{\$0.60 per second}$$

Since each CD requires 10 seconds of machine time, each CD will be charged for $6.00 of overhead cost.

Critics charge that there are two problems with this procedure. First, if predetermined overhead rates are based on budgeted activity, then the unit product costs will fluctuate depending on the budgeted level of activity for the period. For example, if the budgeted output for the year was only 450,000 CDs, the predetermined overhead rate would be $0.80 per second of machine time or $8.00 per CD rather than $6.00 per CD. In general, if budgeted output falls, the overhead cost per unit will increase; it will appear that the CDs cost more to make. Managers may then be tempted to increase prices at the worst possible time—just as demand is falling.

Second, critics charge that under the traditional approach, products are charged for resources that they don't use. When the fixed costs of capacity are spread over estimated activity, the units that are produced must shoulder the costs of unused capacity. That is why the applied overhead cost per unit increases as the level of activity falls. The critics argue that products should be charged only for the capacity that they use;

10. Institute of Management Accountants, *Measuring the Cost of Capacity: Statements on Management Accounting, Statement Number 4Y,* March 31, 1996, Montvale, NJ; Thomas Klammer, ed., *Capacity Measurement and Improvement: A Manager's Guide to Evaluating and Optimizing Capacity Productivity* (Chicago: CAM-I, Irwin Professional Publishing, 1996); and C. J. McNair, "The Hidden Costs of Capacity," *The Journal of Cost Management* (Spring 1994), pp. 12–24.

they should not be charged for the capacity they don't use. This can be accomplished by basing the predetermined overhead rate on capacity as follows:

$$\frac{\text{Total manufacturing overhead cost at capacity, \$3,600,000}}{\text{Total units in the allocation base at capacity, 900,000 CDs} \times \text{10 seconds per CD}} = \text{\$0.40 per second}$$

Since the predetermined overhead rate is $0.40 per second, the overhead cost applied to each CD would be $4.00. This charge is constant and would not be affected by the level of activity during a period. If output falls, the charge would still be $4.00 per CD.

This method will almost certainly result in underapplied overhead. If actual output at Prahad Corporation is 600,000 CDs, then only $2,400,000 of overhead cost would be applied to products ($4.00 per CD × 600,000 CDs). Since the actual overhead cost is $3,600,000, there would be underapplied overhead of $1,200,000. In another departure from tradition, the critics suggest that the underapplied overhead that results from idle capacity should be separately disclosed on the income statement as the Cost of Unused Capacity—a period expense. Disclosing this cost as a lump sum on the income statement, rather than burying it in Cost of Goods Sold or ending inventories, makes it much more visible to managers.

Official pronouncements do not prohibit basing predetermined overhead rates on capacity for external reports.[11] Nevertheless, basing the predetermined overhead rate on estimated, or budgeted, activity is a long-established practice in industry, and some managers and accountants may object to the large amounts of underapplied overhead that would often result from using capacity to determine predetermined overhead rates. And some may insist that the underapplied overhead be allocated among Cost of Goods Sold and ending inventories—which would defeat the purpose of basing the predetermined overhead rate on capacity.

Questions

3–1 Why aren't actual overhead costs traced to jobs just as direct materials and direct labor costs are traced to jobs?

3–2 When would job-order costing be used in preference to process costing?

3–3 What is the purpose of the job cost sheet in a job-order costing system?

3–4 What is a predetermined overhead rate, and how is it computed?

3–5 Explain how a sales order, a production order, a materials requisition form, and a labor time ticket are involved in producing and costing products.

3–6 Explain why some production costs must be assigned to products through an allocation process. Name several such costs. Would such costs be classified as *direct* or as *indirect* costs?

3–7 Why do firms use predetermined overhead rates rather than actual manufacturing overhead costs in applying overhead to jobs?

3–8 What factors should be considered in selecting a base to be used in computing the predetermined overhead rate?

11. Institute of Management Accountants, *Measuring the Cost of Capacity,* pp. 46–47.

3–9 If a company fully allocates all of its overhead costs to jobs, does this guarantee that a profit will be earned for the period?

3–10 What account is credited when overhead cost is applied to Work in Process? Would you expect the amount applied for a period to equal the actual overhead costs of the period? Why or why not?

3–11 What is underapplied overhead? Overapplied overhead? What disposition is made of these amounts at period end?

3–12 Enumerate two reasons why overhead might be underapplied in a given year.

3–13 What adjustment is made for underapplied overhead on the schedule of cost of goods sold? What adjustment is made for overapplied overhead?

3–14 Sigma Company applies overhead cost to jobs on the basis of direct labor cost. Job A, which was started and completed during the current period, shows charges of $5,000 for direct materials, $8,000 for direct labor, and $6,000 for overhead on its job cost sheet. Job B, which is still in process at year-end, shows charges of $2,500 for direct materials and $4,000 for direct labor. Should any overhead cost be added to job B at year-end? Explain.

3–15 A company assigns overhead cost to completed jobs on the basis of 125% of direct labor cost. The job cost sheet for job 313 shows that $10,000 in direct materials has been used on the job and that $12,000 in direct labor cost has been incurred. If 1,000 units were produced in job 313, what is the cost per unit?

3–16 What is a plantwide overhead rate? Why are multiple overhead rates, rather than a plantwide rate, used in some companies?

3–17 What happens to overhead rates based on direct labor when automated equipment replaces direct labor?

Exercises

E3–1 Which method of determining product costs, job-order costing or process costing, would be more appropriate in each of the following situations?

a. An Elmer's glue factory.
b. A textbook publisher such as McGraw-Hill.
c. An Exxon oil refinery.
d. A facility that makes Minute Maid frozen orange juice.
e. A Scott paper mill.
f. A custom home builder.
g. A shop that customizes vans.
h. A manufacturer of specialty chemicals.
i. An auto repair shop.
j. A Firestone tire manufacturing plant.
k. An advertising agency.
l. A law office.

E3–2 Kingsport Containers, Ltd, of the Bahamas experiences wide variation in demand for the 200-liter steel drums it fabricates. The leakproof, rustproof steel drums have a variety of uses from storing liquids and bulk materials to serving as makeshift musical instruments. The drums are made to order and are painted according to the customer's specifications—often in bright patterns and designs. The company is well known for the artwork that appears on its drums. Unit costs are computed on a quarterly basis by dividing each quarter's manufacturing costs (materials, labor, and overhead) by the quarter's production in units. The company's estimated costs, by quarter, for the coming year follow:

	Quarter			
	First	Second	Third	Fourth
Direct materials	$240,000	$120,000	$ 60,000	$180,000
Direct labor	128,000	64,000	32,000	96,000
Manufacturing overhead	300,000	220,000	180,000	260,000
Total manufacturing costs	$668,000	$404,000	$272,000	$536,000
Number of units to be produced	80,000	40,000	20,000	60,000
Estimated cost per unit	$8.35	$10.10	$13.60	$8.93

Management finds the variation in unit costs to be confusing and difficult to work with. It has been suggested that the problem lies with manufacturing overhead, since it is the largest element of cost. Accordingly, you have been asked to find a more appropriate way of assigning manufacturing overhead cost to units of product. After some analysis, you have determined that the company's overhead costs are mostly fixed and therefore show little sensitivity to changes in the level of production.

Required

1. The company uses a job-order costing system. How would you recommend that manufacturing overhead cost be assigned to production? Be specific, and show computations.
2. Recompute the company's unit costs in accordance with your recommendations in (1) above.

E3–3 The Polaris Company uses a job-order costing system. The following data relate to October, the first month of the company's fiscal year.

a. Raw materials purchased on account, $210,000.
b. Raw materials issued to production, $190,000 ($178,000 direct materials and $12,000 indirect materials).
c. Direct labor cost incurred, $90,000; indirect labor cost incurred, $110,000.
d. Depreciation recorded on factory equipment, $40,000.
e. Other manufacturing overhead costs incurred during October, $70,000 (credit Accounts Payable).
f. The company applies manufacturing overhead cost to production on the basis of $8 per machine-hour. There were 30,000 machine-hours recorded for October.
g. Production orders costing $520,000 according to their job cost sheets were completed during October and transferred to Finished Goods.
h. Production orders that had cost $480,000 to complete according to their job cost sheets were shipped to customers during the month. These goods were sold at 25% above cost. The goods were sold on account.

Required

1. Prepare journal entries to record the information given above.
2. Prepare T-accounts for Manufacturing Overhead and Work in Process. Post the relevant information above to each account. Compute the ending balance in each account, assuming that Work in Process has a beginning balance of $42,000.

E3–4 The following cost data relate to the manufacturing activities of Chang Company during the just completed year:

Manufacturing overhead costs incurred:	
Indirect materials	$ 15,000
Indirect labor	130,000
Property taxes, factory	8,000
Utilities, factory	70,000
Depreciation, factory	240,000
Insurance, factory	10,000
Total actual costs incurred	$473,000

Other costs incurred:	
Purchases of raw materials (both direct and indirect)	$400,000
Direct labor cost	60,000
Inventories:	
Raw materials, beginning	20,000
Raw materials, ending	30,000
Work in process, beginning	40,000
Work in process, ending	70,000

The company uses a predetermined overhead rate to apply overhead cost to production. The rate for the year was $25 per machine-hour. A total of 19,400 machine-hours was recorded for the year.

Required

1. Compute the amount of under- or overapplied overhead cost for the year.
2. Prepare a schedule of cost of goods manufactured for the year.

E3–5 The following information is taken from the accounts of Latta Company. The entries in the T-accounts are summaries of the transactions that affected those accounts during the year.

Manufacturing Overhead

	Debit		Credit
(a)	460,000	(b)	390,000
Bal.	70,000		

Work in Process

	Debit		Credit
Bal.	5,000	(c)	710,000
	260,000		
	85,000		
(b)	390,000		
Bal.	40,000		

Finished Goods

	Debit		Credit
Bal.	50,000	(d)	640,000
(c)	710,000		
Bal.	120,000		

Cost of Goods Sold

	Debit		Credit
(d)	640,000		

The overhead that had been applied to Work in Process during the year is distributed among the ending balances in the accounts as follows:

Work in Process, ending	$ 19,500
Finished Goods, ending	58,500
Cost of Goods Sold	312,000
Overhead applied	$390,000

For example, of the $40,000 ending balance in Work in Process, $19,500 was overhead that had been applied during the year.

Required

1. Identify reasons for entries (a) through (d).
2. Assume that the company closes any balance in the Manufacturing Overhead account directly to Cost of Goods Sold. Prepare the necessary journal entry.
3. Assume instead that the company allocates any balance in the Manufacturing Overhead account to the other accounts in proportion to the overhead applied in their ending balances. Prepare the necessary journal entry, with supporting computations.

E3–6 Estimated cost and operating data for three companies for the upcoming year follow:

	Company		
	X	Y	Z
Direct labor-hours	80,000	45,000	60,000
Machine-hours	30,000	70,000	21,000
Direct materials cost	$400,000	$290,000	$300,000
Manufacturing overhead cost	536,000	315,000	480,000

Predetermined overhead rates are computed using the following bases in the three companies:

Company	Overhead Rate Based on—
X	Direct labor-hours
Y	Machine-hours
Z	Direct materials cost

Required

1. Compute the predetermined overhead rate to be used in each company during the upcoming year.
2. Assume that Company X works on three jobs during the upcoming year. Direct labor-hours recorded by job are: job 418, 12,000 hours; job 419, 36,000 hours; job 420, 30,000 hours. How much overhead cost will the company apply to Work in Process for the year? If actual overhead costs total $530,000 for the year, will overhead be under- or overapplied? By how much?

E3–7 White Company has two departments, Cutting and Finishing. The company uses a job-order cost system and computes a predetermined overhead rate in each department. The Cutting Department bases its rate on machine-hours, and the Finishing Department bases its rate on direct labor cost. At the beginning of the year, the company made the following estimates:

	Department	
	Cutting	Finishing
Direct labor-hours	6,000	30,000
Machine-hours	48,000	5,000
Manufacturing overhead cost	$360,000	$486,000
Direct labor cost	50,000	270,000

Required

1. Compute the predetermined overhead rate to be used in each department.
2. Assume that the overhead rates that you computed in (1) above are in effect. The job cost sheet for job 203, which was started and completed during the year, showed the following:

	Department	
	Cutting	Finishing
Direct labor-hours	6	20
Machine-hours	80	4
Materials requisitioned	$500	$310
Direct labor cost	70	150

Compute the total overhead cost applied to job 203.

3. Would you expect substantially different amounts of overhead cost to be assigned to some jobs if the company used a plantwide overhead rate based on direct labor cost, rather than using departmental rates? Explain. No computations are necessary.

E3–8 Harwood Company is a manufacturing firm that operates a job-order costing system. Overhead costs are applied to jobs on the basis of machine-hours. At the beginning of the year, management estimated that the company would incur $192,000 in manufacturing overhead costs and work 80,000 machine-hours.

Required

1. Compute the company's predetermined overhead rate.
2. Assume that during the year the company works only 75,000 machine-hours and incurs the following costs in the Manufacturing Overhead and Work in Process accounts:

Manufacturing Overhead

Debit		Credit
(Maintenance)	21,000	?
(Indirect materials)	8,000	
(Indirect labor)	60,000	
(Utilities)	32,000	
(Insurance)	7,000	
(Depreciation)	56,000	

Work in Process

Debit		Credit
(Direct materials)	710,000	
(Direct labor)	90,000	
(Overhead)	?	

Copy the data in the T-accounts above onto your answer sheet. Compute the amount of overhead cost that would be applied to Work in Process for the year and make the entry in your T-accounts.

3. Compute the amount of under- or overapplied overhead for the year and show the balance in your Manufacturing Overhead T-account. Prepare a general journal entry to close out the balance in this account to Cost of Goods Sold.
4. Explain why the manufacturing overhead was under- or overapplied for the year.

E3–9 Dillon Products manufactures various machined parts to customer specifications. The company uses a job-order costing system and applies overhead cost to jobs on the basis of machine-hours. At the beginning of the year, it was estimated that the company would work 240,000 machine-hours and incur $4,800,000 in manufacturing overhead costs.

The company spent the entire month of January working on a large order for 16,000 custom-made machined parts. The company had no work in process at the beginning of January. Cost data relating to January follow:

a. Raw materials purchased on account, $325,000.
b. Raw materials requisitioned for production, $290,000 (80% direct materials and 20% indirect materials).
c. Labor cost incurred in the factory, $180,000 (one-third direct labor and two-thirds indirect labor).
d. Depreciation recorded on factory equipment, $75,000.
e. Other manufacturing overhead costs incurred, $62,000 (credit Accounts Payable).
f. Manufacturing overhead cost was applied to production on the basis of 15,000 machine-hours actually worked during the month.
g. The completed job was moved into the finished goods warehouse on January 31 to await delivery to the customer. (In computing the dollar amount for this entry, remember that the cost of a completed job consists of direct materials, direct labor, and *applied* overhead.)

Required

1. Prepare journal entries to record items (a) through (f) above [ignore item (g) for the moment].
2. Prepare T-accounts for Manufacturing Overhead and Work in Process. Post the relevant items from your journal entries to these T-accounts.
3. Prepare a journal entry for item (g) above.
4. Compute the unit cost that will appear on the job cost sheet.

E3–10 Leeds Architectural Consultants began operations on January 2. The following activity was recorded in the company's Work in Process account for the first month of operations:

Work in Process

Debit		Credit	
Costs of subcontracted work	230,000	To completed projects	390,000
Direct staff costs	75,000		
Studio overhead	120,000		

Leeds Architectural Consultants is a service firm, so the names of the accounts it uses are different from the names used in manufacturing firms. Costs of Subcontracted Work is basically the same thing as Direct Materials; Direct Staff Costs is the same as Direct Labor; Studio Overhead is the same as Manufacturing Overhead; and Completed Projects is the same as Finished Goods. Apart from the difference in terms, the accounting methods used by the company are identical to the methods used by manufacturing companies.

Leeds Architectural Consultants uses a job-order costing system and applies studio overhead to Work in Process on the basis of direct staff costs. At the end of January, only one job was still in process. This job (Lexington Gardens Project) had been charged with $6,500 in direct staff costs.

Required

1. Compute the predetermined overhead rate that was in use during January.
2. Complete the following job cost sheet for the partially completed Lexington Gardens Project.

Job Cost Sheet—Lexington Gardens Project
As of January 31

Costs of subcontracted work	$?
Direct staff costs	?
Studio overhead	?
Total cost to January 31	$?

E3–11 Vista Landscaping uses a job-order costing system to track the costs of its landscaping projects. The company provides garden design services as well as actually carrying out the landscaping for the client. The table below provides data concerning the three landscaping projects that were in progress during April. There was no work in process at the beginning of April.

	Project		
	Harris	Chan	James
Designer-hours	120	100	90
Direct materials cost	$4,500	$3,700	$1,400
Direct labor cost	9,600	8,000	7,200

Actual overhead costs were $30,000 for April. Overhead costs are applied to projects on the basis of designer-hours since most of the overhead is related to the costs of the garden design studio. The predetermined overhead rate is $90 per designer-hour. The Harris and Chan projects were completed in April; the James project was not completed by the end of the month.

Required

1. Compute the amount of overhead cost that would have been charged to each project during April.
2. Prepare a journal entry showing the completion of the Harris and Chan projects and the transfer of costs to the Completed Projects (i.e., Finished Goods) account.
3. What is the balance in the Work in Process account at the end of the month?
4. What is the balance in the Overhead account at the end of the month? What is this balance called?

E3–12 (Appendix 3A) Security Pension Services helps clients to set up and administer pension plans that are in compliance with tax laws and regulatory requirements. The firm uses a job-costing system in which overhead is applied to clients' accounts on the basis of professional staff hours charged to the accounts. Data concerning two recent years appear below:

	1998	1999
Estimated professional staff hours to be charged to clients' accounts	4,500	4,600
Estimated overhead cost	$310,500	$310,500
Professional staff hours available	6,000	6,000

"Professional staff hours available" is a measure of the capacity of the firm. Any hours available that are not charged to clients' accounts represent unused capacity.

Required

1. Marta Brinksi is an established client whose pension plan was set up many years ago. In both 1998 and 1999, only 2.5 hours of professional staff time were charged to Ms. Brinksi's account. If the company bases its predetermined overhead rate on the estimated overhead cost and the estimated professional staff hours to be charged to clients, how much overhead cost would have been applied to Ms. Brinksi's account in 1998? In 1999?
2. Suppose that the company bases its predetermined overhead rate on the estimated overhead cost and the estimated professional staff hours to be charged to clients as in (1) above. Also suppose that the actual professional staff hours charged to clients' accounts and the actual overhead costs turn out to be exactly as estimated in both years. By how much would the overhead be under- or overapplied in 1998? In 1999?
3. Refer back to the data concerning Ms. Brinski in (1) above. If the company bases its predetermined overhead rate on the estimated overhead cost and the *professional staff hours available,* how much overhead cost would have been applied to Ms. Brinksi's account in 1998? In 1999?
4. Suppose that the company bases its predetermined overhead rate on the estimated overhead cost and the professional staff hours available as in (3) above. Also suppose that the actual professional staff hours charged to clients' accounts and the actual overhead costs turn out to be exactly as estimated in both years. By how much would the overhead be under- or overapplied in 1998? In 1999?

Problems

P3–13 Straightforward Journal Entries; Partial T-Accounts; Income Statement Almeda Products, Inc., uses a job-order cost system. The company's inventory balances on April 1, the start of its fiscal year, were as follows:

Raw materials	$32,000
Work in process	20,000
Finished goods	48,000

During the year, the following transactions were completed:

a. Raw materials were purchased on account, $170,000.
b. Raw materials were issued from the storeroom for use in production, $180,000 (80% direct and 20% indirect).
c. Employee salaries and wages were accrued as follows: direct labor, $200,000; indirect labor, $82,000; and selling and administrative salaries, $90,000.
d. Utility costs were incurred in the factory, $65,000.
e. Advertising costs were incurred, $100,000.
f. Prepaid insurance expired during the year, $20,000 (90% related to factory operations, and 10% related to selling and administrative activities).
g. Depreciation was recorded, $180,000 (85% related to factory assets, and 15% related to selling and administrative assets).
h. Manufacturing overhead was applied to jobs at the rate of 175% of direct labor cost.
i. Goods that cost $700,000 to manufacture according to their job cost sheets were transferred to the finished goods warehouse.
j. Sales for the year totaled $1,000,000 and were all on account. The total cost to manufacture these goods according to their job cost sheets was $720,000.

Required

1. Prepare journal entries to record the transactions for the year.
2. Prepare T-accounts for Raw Materials, Work in Process, Finished Goods, Manufacturing Overhead, and Cost of Goods Sold. Post the appropriate parts of your journal entries to these T-accounts. Compute the ending balance in each account. (Don't forget to enter the beginning balances in the inventory accounts.)
3. Is Manufacturing Overhead underapplied or overapplied for the year? Prepare a journal entry to close this balance to Cost of Goods Sold.

4. Prepare an income statement for the year. (Do not prepare a schedule of cost of goods manufactured; all of the information needed for the income statement is available in the journal entries and T-accounts you have prepared.)

P3–14 Entries Directly into T-Accounts; Income Statement Hudson Company's trial balance as of January 1, the beginning of the fiscal year, is given below:

Cash	$ 7,000	
Accounts Receivable	18,000	
Raw Materials	9,000	
Work in Process	20,000	
Finished Goods	32,000	
Prepaid Insurance	4,000	
Plant and Equipment	210,000	
Accumulated Depreciation		$ 53,000
Accounts Payable		38,000
Capital Stock		160,000
Retained Earnings		49,000
Total	$300,000	$300,000

Hudson Company is a manufacturing firm and employs a job-order costing system. During the year, the following transactions took place:

a. Raw materials purchased on account, $40,000.
b. Raw materials were requisitioned for use in production, $38,000 (85% direct and 15% indirect).
c. Factory utility costs incurred, $19,100.
d. Depreciation was recorded on plant and equipment, $36,000. Three-fourths of the depreciation related to factory equipment, and the remainder related to selling and administrative equipment.
e. Advertising expense incurred, $48,000.
f. Costs for salaries and wages were incurred as follows:

Direct labor	$45,000
Indirect labor	10,000
Administrative salaries	30,000

g. Prepaid insurance expired during the year, $3,000 (80% related to factory operations, and 20% related to selling and administrative activities).
h. Miscellaneous selling and administrative expenses incurred, $9,500.
i. Manufacturing overhead was applied to production. The company applies overhead on the basis of $8 per machine-hour; 7,500 machine-hours were recorded for the year.
j. Goods that cost $140,000 to manufacture according to their job cost sheets were transferred to the finished goods warehouse.
k. Sales for the year totaled $250,000 and were all on account. The total cost to manufacture these goods according to their job cost sheets was $130,000.
l. Collections from customers during the year totaled $245,000.
m. Payments to suppliers on account during the year, $150,000; payments to employees for salaries and wages, $84,000.

Required

1. Prepare a T-account for each account in the company's trial balance and enter the opening balances shown above.
2. Record the transactions above directly into the T-accounts. Prepare new T-accounts as needed. Key your entries to the letters (a) through (m) above. Find the ending balance in each account.
3. Is manufacturing overhead underapplied or overapplied for the year? Make an entry in the T-accounts to close any balance in the Manufacturing Overhead account to Cost of Goods Sold.
4. Prepare an income statement for the year. (Do not prepare a schedule of cost of goods manufactured; all of the information needed for the income statement is available in the T-accounts.)

P3–15 Entries Directly into T-Accounts; Income Statement Supreme Videos, Inc., produces short musical videos for sale to retail outlets. The company's balance sheet accounts as of January 1, the beginning of the fiscal year, are given below.

SUPREME VIDEOS, INC.
Balance Sheet
January 1

Assets		
Current assets:		
Cash		$ 63,000
Accounts receivable		102,000
Inventories:		
Raw materials (film, costumes)	$ 30,000	
Videos in process	45,000	
Finished videos awaiting sale	81,000	156,000
Prepaid insurance		9,000
Total current assets		330,000
Studio and equipment	730,000	
Less accumulated depreciation	210,000	520,000
Total assets		$850,000
Liabilities and Stockholders' Equity		
Accounts payable		$160,000
Capital stock	$420,000	
Retained earnings	270,000	690,000
Total liabilities and stockholders' equity		$850,000

Since the videos differ in length and in complexity of production, the company uses a job-order costing system to determine the cost of each video produced. Studio (manufacturing) overhead is charged to videos on the basis of camera-hours of activity. At the beginning of the year, the company estimated that it would work 7,000 camera-hours and incur $280,000 in studio overhead cost. The following transactions were recorded for the year:

a. Film, costumes, and similar raw materials purchased on account, $185,000.
b. Film, costumes, and other raw materials issued to production, $200,000 (85% of this material was considered direct to the videos in production, and the other 15% was considered indirect).
c. Utility costs incurred in the production studio, $72,000.
d. Depreciation recorded on the studio, cameras, and other equipment, $84,000. Three-fourths of this depreciation related to actual production of the videos, and the remainder related to equipment used in marketing and administration.
e. Advertising expense incurred, $130,000.
f. Costs for salaries and wages were incurred as follows:

Direct labor (actors and directors)	$ 82,000
Indirect labor (carpenters to build sets, costume designers, and so forth)	110,000
Administrative salaries	95,000

g. Prepaid insurance expired during the year, $7,000 (80% related to production of videos, and 20% related to marketing and administrative activities).
h. Miscellaneous marketing and administrative expenses incurred, $8,600.
i. Studio (manufacturing) overhead was applied to videos in production. The company recorded 7,250 camera-hours of activity during the year.
j. Videos that cost $550,000 to produce according to their job cost sheets were transferred to the finished videos warehouse to await sale and shipment.
k. Sales for the year totaled $925,000 and were all on account. The total cost to produce these videos according to their job cost sheets was $600,000.
l. Collections from customers during the year totaled $850,000.
m. Payments to suppliers on account during the year, $500,000; payments to employees for salaries and wages, $285,000.

Required

1. Prepare a T-account for each account on the company's balance sheet and enter the opening balances.
2. Record the transactions directly into the T-accounts. Prepare new T-accounts as needed. Key your entries to the letters (a) through (m) above. Find the ending balance in each account.
3. Is the Studio (manufacturing) Overhead account underapplied or overapplied for the year? Make an entry in the T-accounts to close any balance in the Studio Overhead account to Cost of Goods Sold.
4. Prepare an income statement for the year. (Do not prepare a schedule of cost of goods manufactured; all of the information needed for the income statement is available in the T-accounts.)

P3–16 Straightfoward Journal Entries; Partial T-Accounts; Income Statement Gold Nest Company of Guandong, China, is a family-owned enterprise that makes birdcages for the South China market. A popular pastime among older Chinese men is to take their pet birds on daily excursions to teahouses and public parks where they meet with other bird owners to talk and play mahjong. A great deal of attention is lavished on these birds, and the birdcages are often elaborately constructed from exotic woods and contain porcelain feeding bowls and silver roosts. Gold Nest Company makes a broad range of birdcages that it sells through an extensive network of street vendors who receive commissions on their sales. The Chinese currency is the renminbi, which is denoted by Rmb. All of the company's transactions with customers, employees, and suppliers are conducted in cash; there is no credit.

The company uses a job-order costing system in which overhead is applied to jobs on the basis of direct labor cost. At the beginning of the year, it was estimated that the total direct labor cost for the year would be Rmb200,000 and the total manufacturing overhead cost would be Rmb330,000. At the beginning of the year, the inventory balances were as follows:

Raw materials	Rmb25,000
Work in process	10,000
Finished goods	40,000

During the year, the following transactions were completed:

a. Raw materials purchased for cash, Rmb275,000.
b. Raw materials requisitioned for use in production, Rmb280,000 (materials costing Rmb220,000 were charged directly to jobs; the remaining materials were indirect).
c. Costs for employee services were incurred as follows:

Direct labor	Rmb180,000
Indirect labor	72,000
Sales commissions	63,000
Administrative salaries	90,000

d. Rent for the year was Rmb18,000 (Rmb13,000 of this amount related to factory operations, and the remainder related to selling and administrative activities).
e. Utility costs incurred in the factory, Rmb57,000.
f. Advertising costs incurred, Rmb140,000.
g. Depreciation recorded on equipment, Rmb100,000. (Rmb88,000 of this amount was on equipment used in factory operations; the remaining Rmb12,000 was on equipment used in selling and administrative activities.)
h. Manufacturing overhead cost was applied to jobs, Rmb ___?___.
i. Goods that cost Rmb675,000 to manufacture according to their job cost sheets were completed during the year.
j. Sales for the year totaled Rmb1,250,000. The total cost to manufacture these goods according to their job cost sheets was Rmb700,000.

Required

1. Prepare journal entries to record the transactions for the year.
2. Prepare T-accounts for inventories, Manufacturing Overhead, and Cost of Goods Sold. Post relevant data from your journal entries to these T-accounts (don't forget to enter the beginning balances in your inventory accounts). Compute an ending balance in each account.

3. Is Manufacturing Overhead underapplied or overapplied for the year? Prepare a journal entry to close any balance in the Manufacturing Overhead account to Cost of Goods Sold.
4. Prepare an income statement for the year. (Do not prepare a schedule of cost of goods manufactured; all of the information needed for the income statement is available in the journal entries and T-accounts you have prepared.)

P3–17 Disposition of Under- or Overapplied Overhead Bieler & Cie of Altdorf, Switzerland, makes furniture using the latest automated technology. The company uses a job-order costing system and applies manufacturing overhead cost to products on the basis of machine-hours. The following estimates were used in preparing the predetermined overhead rate at the beginning of the year:

Machine-hours	75,000
Manufacturing overhead cost	Sfr900,000

The currency in Switzerland is the Swiss franc, which is denoted by Sfr.

During the year, a glut of furniture on the market resulted in cutting back production and a buildup of furniture in the company's warehouse. The company's cost records revealed the following actual cost and operating data for the year:

Machine-hours	60,000
Manufacturing overhead cost	Sfr850,000
Inventories at year-end:	
Raw materials	30,000
Work in process (includes overhead applied of 36,000)	100,000
Finished goods (includes overhead applied of 180,000)	500,000
Cost of goods sold (includes overhead applied of 504,000)	1,400,000

Required

1. Compute the company's predetermined overhead rate.
2. Compute the under- or overapplied overhead.
3. Assume that the company closes any under- or overapplied overhead directly to Cost of Goods Sold. Prepare the appropriate journal entry.
4. Assume that the company allocates any under- or overapplied overhead to Work in Process, Finished Goods, and Cost of Goods Sold on the basis of the amount of overhead applied in each account. Prepare the journal entry to show the allocation for the year.
5. How much higher or lower will net income be if the under- or overapplied overhead is allocated rather than closed directly to Cost of Goods Sold?

P3–18 T-Account Analysis of Cost Flows Selected ledger accounts of Moore Company are given below for the just completed year:

Raw Materials

Bal. 1/1	15,000	Credits	?
Debits	120,000		
Bal. 12/31	25,000		

Manufacturing Overhead

Debits	230,000	Credits	?

Work in Process

Bal. 1/1	20,000	Credits	470,000
Direct materials	90,000		
Direct labor	150,000		
Overhead	240,000		
Bal. 12/31	?		

Factory Wages Payable

Debits	185,000	Bal. 1/1	9,000
		Credits	180,000
		Bal. 12/31	4,000

Finished Goods			
Bal. 1/1	40,000	Credits	?
Debits	?		
Bal. 12/31	60,000		

Cost of Goods Sold		
Debits	?	

Required

1. What was the cost of raw materials put into production during the year?
2. How much of the materials in (1) above consisted of indirect materials?
3. How much of the factory labor cost for the year consisted of indirect labor?
4. What was the cost of goods manufactured for the year?
5. What was the cost of goods sold for the year (before considering under- or overapplied overhead)?
6. If overhead is applied to production on the basis of direct labor cost, what rate was in effect during the year?
7. Was manufacturing overhead under- or overapplied? By how much?
8. Compute the ending balance in the Work in Process inventory account. Assume that this balance consists entirely of goods started during the year. If $8,000 of this balance is direct labor cost, how much of it is direct materials cost? Manufacturing overhead cost?

P3–19 Multiple Departments; Overhead Rates; Costing Units of Product High Desert Potteryworks makes a variety of pottery products that it sells to retailers such as Home Depot. The company uses a job-order costing system in which predetermined overhead rates are used to apply manufacturing overhead cost to jobs. The predetermined overhead rate in the Molding Department is based on machine-hours, and the rate in the Painting Department is based on direct labor cost. At the beginning of the year, the company's management made the following estimates:

	Department	
	Molding	Painting
Direct labor-hours	12,000	60,000
Machine-hours	70,000	8,000
Direct materials cost	$510,000	$650,000
Direct labor cost	130,000	420,000
Manufacturing overhead cost	602,000	735,000

Job 205 was started on August 1 and completed on August 10. The company's cost records show the following information concerning the job:

	Department	
	Molding	Painting
Direct labor-hours	30	85
Machine-hours	110	20
Materials placed into production	$470	$332
Direct labor cost	290	680

Required

1. Compute the predetermined overhead rate used during the year in the Molding Department. Compute the rate used in the Painting Department.
2. Compute the total overhead cost applied to job 205.
3. What would be the total cost recorded for job 205? If the job contained 50 units, what would be the cost per unit?
4. At the end of the year, the records of High Desert Potteryworks revealed the following *actual* cost and operating data for all jobs worked on during the year:

	Department	
	Molding	Painting
Direct labor-hours	10,000	62,000
Machine-hours	65,000	9,000
Direct materials cost	$430,000	$680,000
Direct labor cost	108,000	436,000
Manufacturing overhead cost	570,000	750,000

What was the amount of under- or overapplied overhead in each department at the end of the year?

P3–20 Schedule of Cost of Goods Manufactured; Pricing; Work in Process Analysis Gitano Products operates a job-order cost system and applies overhead cost to jobs on the basis of direct materials *used in production* (*not* on the basis of raw materials purchased). In computing a predetermined overhead rate at the beginning of the year, the company's estimates were: manufacturing overhead cost, $800,00; and direct materials to be used in production, $500,000. The company's inventory accounts at the beginning and end of the year were:

	Beginning	Ending
Raw Materials	$ 20,000	$ 80,000
Work in Process	150,000	70,000
Finished Goods	260,000	400,000

The following actual costs were incurred during the year:

Purchase of raw materials (all direct)	$510,000
Direct labor cost	90,000
Manufacturing overhead costs:	
Indirect labor	170,000
Property taxes	48,000
Depreciation of equipment	260,000
Maintenance	95,000
Insurance	7,000
Rent, building	180,000

Required

1. a. Compute the predetermined overhead rate for the year.
   b. Compute the amount of under- or overapplied overhead for the year.
2. Prepare a schedule of cost of goods manufactured for the year.
3. Compute the Cost of Goods Sold for the year. (Do not include any under- or overapplied overhead in your Cost of Goods Sold figure.) What options are available for disposing of under- or overapplied overhead?
4. Job 215 was started and completed during the year. What price would have been charged to the customer if the job required $8,500 in direct materials and $2,700 in direct labor cost and the company priced its jobs at 25% above cost to manufacture?
5. Direct materials made up $24,000 of the $70,000 ending Work in Process inventory balance. Supply the information missing below:

Direct materials	$24,000
Direct labor	?
Manufacturing overhead	?
Work in process inventory	$70,000

P3–21 Job-Order Cost Journal Entries; Complete T-Accounts; Income Statement Film Specialties, Inc., operates a small production studio in which advertising films are made for TV and other uses. The company uses a job-order costing system to accumulate costs for each film produced. The company's trial balance as of May 1, the start of its fiscal year, is given follows:

Cash	$ 60,000	
Accounts Receivable	210,000	
Materials and Supplies	130,000	
Film in Process	75,000	
Finished Films	860,000	
Prepaid Insurance	90,000	
Studio and Equipment	5,200,000	
Accumulated Depreciation		$1,990,000
Accounts Payable		700,000
Salaries and Wages Payable		35,000
Capital Stock		2,500,000
Retained Earnings		1,400,000
Total	$6,625,000	$6,625,000

Film Specialties, Inc., uses a Production Overhead account to record all transactions relating to overhead costs and applies overhead costs to jobs on the basis of camera-hours. For the current year, the company estimated that it would incur $1,350,000 in production overhead costs, and film 15,000 camera-hours. During the year, the following transactions were completed:

a. Materials and supplies purchased on account, $690,000.
b. Materials and supplies issued from the storeroom for use in production of various films, $700,000 (80% direct to the films and 20% indirect).
c. Utility costs incurred in the production studio, $90,000.
d. Costs for employee salaries and wages were incurred as follows:

Actors, directors, and camera crew	$1,300,000
Indirect labor costs of support workers	230,000
Marketing and administrative salaries	650,000

e. Advertising costs incurred, $800,000.
f. Prepaid insurance expired during the year, $70,000. Of this amount, $60,000 related to the operation of the production studio, and the remaining $10,000 related to the company's marketing and administrative activities.
g. Depreciation recorded for the year, $650,000 (80% represented depreciation of the production studio, cameras, and other production equipment; the remaining 20% represented depreciation on facilities and equipment used in marketing and administrative activities).
h. Rental costs incurred on various facilities and equipment used in production of films, $360,000; and rental costs incurred on equipment used in marketing and administrative activities, $40,000.
i. Production overhead was applied to jobs filmed during the year. The company recorded 16,500 camera-hours.
j. Films that cost $3,400,000 to produce according to their job cost sheets were completed during the year. The films were transferred to the finished films storeroom to await delivery to customers.
k. Sales of films for the year (all on account) totaled $6,000,000. The total cost to produce these films was $4,000,000 according to their job cost sheets.
l. Collections on account from customers during the year, $5,400,000.
m. Cash payments made during the year; to creditors on account, $2,500,000; and to employees for salaries and wages, $2,200,000.

Required

1. Prepare journal entries to record the year's transactions.
2. Prepare a T-account for each account in the company's trial balance and enter the opening balances given above. Post your journal entries to the T-accounts. Prepare new T accounts as needed. Compute the ending balance in each account.
3. Is production overhead underapplied or overapplied for the year? Prepare the necessary journal entry to close the balance in Production Overhead to Cost of Films Sold.
4. Prepare an income statement for the year. (Do not prepare a schedule of cost of goods manufactured; all of the information needed for the income statement is available in the T-accounts.)

P3–22 Job Cost Sheets; Overhead Rates; Journal Entries AOZT Volzhskije Motory of St. Petersburg, Russia, makes marine motors for vessels ranging in size from harbor tugs to open-water icebreakers. (The Russian currency is the ruble, which is denoted by RUR. All currency amounts below are in thousands of RUR.)

The company uses a job-order costing system. Only three jobs—job 208, job 209, and job 210—were worked on during May and June. Job 208 was completed on June 20; the other two jobs were uncompleted on June 30. Job cost sheets on the three jobs are given below:

	Job Cost Sheet		
	Job 208	Job 209	Job 210
May costs incurred:*			
Direct materials	RUR 9,500	RUR5,100	RUR —
Direct labor	8,000	3,000	—
Manufacturing overhead	11,200	4,200	—
June costs incurred:			
Direct materials	—	6,000	7,200
Direct labor	4,000	7,500	8,500
Manufacturing overhead	?	?	?

*Jobs 208 and 209 were started during May.

The following additional information is available:

a. Manufacturing overhead is applied to jobs on the basis of direct labor cost.
b. Balances in the inventory accounts at May 31 were:

Raw Materials	RUR30,000
Work in Process	?
Finished Goods	50,000

Required

1. Prepare T-accounts for Raw Materials, Work in Process, Finished Goods, and Manufacturing Overhead. Enter the May 31 balances given above; in the case of Work in Process, compute the May 31 balance and enter it into the Work in Process T-account.
2. Prepare journal entries for *June* as follows:
   a. Prepare an entry to record the issue of materials into production and post the entry to appropriate T-accounts. (In the case of direct materials, it is not necessary to make a separate entry for each job.) Indirect materials used during June totaled RUR3,600.
   b. Prepare an entry to record the incurrence of labor cost and post the entry to appropriate T-accounts. (In the case of direct labor cost, it is not necessary to make a separate entry for each job.) Indirect labor cost totaled RUR7,000 for June.
   c. Prepare an entry to record the incurrence of RUR19,400 in various actual manufacturing overhead costs for June. (Credit Accounts Payable.) Post this entry to the appropriate T-accounts.
3. What apparent predetermined overhead rate does the company use to assign overhead cost to jobs? Using this rate, prepare a journal entry to record the application of overhead cost to jobs for June (it is not necessary to make a separate entry for each job). Post this entry to appropriate T-accounts.
4. As stated earlier, job 208 was completed during June. Prepare a journal entry to show the transfer of this job off of the production line and into the finished goods warehouse. Post the entry to appropriate T-accounts.
5. Determine the balance at June 30 in the Work in Process inventory account. How much of this balance consists of costs charged to job 209? To job 210?

P3–23 Multiple Departments; Overhead Rates Hobart, Evans, and Nix is a small law firm that contains 10 partners and 12 support persons. The firm employs a job-order costing system to accumulate costs chargeable to each client, and it is organized into two departments—the Research and Documents Department and the Litigation Department. The firm uses predetermined overhead rates to charge the costs of these departments to its clients. At the beginning of the year, the firm's management made the following estimates for the year:

	Department	
	Research and Documents	Litigation
Research-hours	24,000	—
Direct attorney-hours	9,000	18,000
Legal forms and supplies	$ 16,000	$ 5,000
Direct attorney cost	450,000	900,000
Departmental overhead cost	840,000	360,000

The predetermined overhead rate in the Research and Documents Department is based on research-hours, and the rate in the Litigation Department is based on direct attorney cost.

The costs charged to each client are made up of three elements: legal forms and supplies used, direct attorney costs incurred, and an applied amount of overhead from each department in which work is performed on the case.

Case 418-3 was initiated on February 23 and completed on May 16. During this period, the following costs and time were recorded on the case:

	Department	
	Research and Documents	Litigation
Research-hours	26	—
Direct attorney-hours	7	114
Legal forms and supplies	$ 80	$ 40
Direct attorney cost	350	5,700

Required

1. Compute the predetermined overhead rate used during the year in the Research and Documents Department. Compute the rate used in the Litigation Department.
2. Using the rates you computed in (1) above, compute the total overhead cost applied to case 418-3.
3. What would be the total cost charged to case 418-3? Show computations by department and in total for the case.
4. At the end of the year, the firm's records revealed the following *actual* cost and operating data for all cases handled during the year:

	Department	
	Research and Documents	Litigation
Research-hours	26,000	—
Direct attorney-hours	8,000	15,000
Legal forms and supplies	$ 19,000	$ 6,000
Direct attorney cost	400,000	750,000
Departmental overhead cost	870,000	315,000

Determine the amount of under- or overapplied overhead cost in each department for the year.

P3–24 Predetermined Overhead Rate and Capacity (Appendix 3A) Platinum Tracks, Inc., is a small audio recording studio located in Los Angeles. The company handles work for advertising agencies—primarily for radio ads—and has a few singers and bands as clients. Platinum Tracks handles all aspects of recording from editing to making a digital master from which CDs can be copied. The competition in the audio recording industry in Los Angeles has always been tough, but it has been getting even tougher over the last several years. The studio has been losing customers to newer studios equipped with more up-to-date equipment that are able to offer very attractive prices and excellent service. Summary data concerning the last two years of operations follow:

	1998	1999
Estimated hours of studio service	1,000	800
Estimated studio overhead cost	$160,000	$160,000
Actual hours of studio service provided	750	500
Actual studio overhead cost incurred	$160,000	$160,000
Hours of studio service at capacity	1,600	1,600

The company applies studio overhead to recording jobs on the basis of the hours of studio service provided. For example, 40 hours of studio time were required to record, edit, and master the *Verde Baja* music CD for a local Latino band. All of the studio overhead is fixed, and the actual overhead cost incurred was exactly as estimated at the beginning of the year in both 1998 and 1999.

Required

1. Platinum Tracks computes the predetermined overhead rate at the beginning of each year based on the estimated studio overhead and the estimated hours of studio service for the year. How much overhead would have been applied to the *Verde Baja* job if it had been done in 1998? In 1999? By how much would overhead have been under- or overapplied in 1998? In 1999?
2. The president of Platinum Tracks has heard that some companies in the industry have changed to a system of computing the predetermined overhead rate at the beginning of each year based on the estimated studio overhead for the year and the hours of studio service that could be provided at capacity. He would like to know what effect this method would have on job costs. How much overhead would have been applied using this method to the *Verde Baja* job if it had been done in 1998? In 1999? By how much would overhead have been under- or overapplied in 1998 using this method? In 1999?
3. How would you interpret the under- or overapplied overhead that results from using studio hours at capacity to compute the predetermined overhead rate?
4. What fundamental business problem is Platinum Tracks facing? Which method of computing the predetermined overhead rate is likely to be more helpful in facing this problem? Explain.

P3–25 Plantwide and Departmental Overhead Rates "Blast it!" said David Wilson, president of Teledex Company. "We've just lost the bid on the Koopers job by $2,000. It seems we're either too high to get the job or too low to make any money on half the jobs we bid."

Teledex Company manufactures products to customer's specifications and operates a job-order cost system. Manufacturing overhead cost is applied to jobs on the basis of direct labor cost. The following estimates were made at the beginning of the year:

	Department			
	Fabricating	Machining	Assembly	Total Plant
Direct labor	$200,000	$100,000	$300,000	$600,000
Manufacturing overhead	350,000	400,000	90,000	840,000

Jobs require varying amounts of work in the three departments. The Koopers job, for example, would have required manufacturing costs in the three departments as follows:

	Department			
	Fabricating	Machining	Assembly	Total Plant
Direct materials	$3,000	$200	$1,400	$4,600
Direct labor	2,800	500	6,200	9,500
Manufacturing overhead	?	?	?	?

The company uses a plantwide overhead rate to apply manufacturing overhead cost to jobs.

Required

1. Assuming use of a plantwide overhead rate:
   a. Compute the rate for the current year.
   b. Determine the amount of manufacturing overhead cost that would have been applied to the Koopers job.

2. Suppose that instead of using a plantwide overhead rate, the company had used a separate predetermined overhead rate in each department. Under these conditions:
   a. Compute the rate for each department for the current year.
   b. Determine the amount of manufacturing overhead cost that would have been applied to the Koopers job.
3. Explain the difference between the manufacturing overhead that would have been applied using the plantwide rate in question 1 (b) above and using the departmental rates in question 2 (b).
4. Assume that it is customary in the industry to bid jobs at 150% of total manufacturing cost (direct materials, direct labor, and applied overhead). What was the company's bid price on the Koopers job? What would the bid price have been if departmental overhead rates had been used to apply overhead cost?
5. At the end of the year, the company assembled the following *actual* cost data relating to all jobs worked on during the year.

	Department			
	Fabricating	Machining	Assembly	Total Plant
Direct materials	$190,000	$ 16,000	$114,000	$320,000
Direct labor	210,000	108,000	262,000	580,000
Manufacturing overhead	360,000	420,000	84,000	864,000

Compute the under- or overapplied overhead for the year (a) assuming that a plantwide overhead rate is used, and (b) assuming that departmental overhead rates are used.

P3–26 Comprehensive Problem: T-Accounts, Job-Order Cost Flows; Statements; Pricing Chenko Products, Inc., manufactures goods to customers' orders and uses a job-order costing system. A beginning-of-the-year trial balance for the company is given below:

Cash	$ 35,000	
Accounts Receivable	127,000	
Raw Materials	10,000	
Work in Process	44,000	
Finished Goods	75,000	
Prepaid Insurance	9,000	
Plant and Equipment	400,000	
Accumulated Depreciation		$110,000
Accounts Payable		86,000
Salaries and Wages Payable		9,000
Capital Stock		375,000
Retained Earnings		120,000
Total	$700,000	$700,000

The company applies manufacturing overhead cost to jobs on the basis of direct materials cost. The following estimates were made at the beginning of the year for purposes of computing a predetermined overhead rate: manufacturing overhead cost, $510,000; and direct materials cost, $340,000. Summarized transactions of the company for the year are given below:

a. Raw materials purchased on account, $400,000.
b. Raw materials requisitioned for use in production, $370,000 ($320,000 direct materials and $50,000 indirect materials).
c. Salary and wage costs were incurred as follows:

Direct labor	$ 76,000
Indirect labor	130,000
Selling and administrative salaries	110,000

d. Maintenance costs incurred in the factory, $81,000.
e. Travel costs incurred by salespeople, $43,000.
f. Prepaid insurance on the factory expired during the year, $7,000.

g. Utility costs incurred, $70,000 (90% related to factory operations, and 10% related to selling and administrative activities).
h. Property taxes incurred on the factory building, $9,000.
i. Advertising costs incurred, $200,000.
j. Rental cost incurred on special factory equipment, $120,000.
k. Depreciation recorded for the year, $50,000 (80% related to factory assets, and 20% related to selling and administrative assets).
l. Manufacturing overhead cost applied to jobs, $____?____.
m. Cost of goods manufactured for the year, $890,000.
n. Sales for the year totaled $1,400,000 (all on account); the cost of goods sold totaled $930,000.
o. Cash collections from customers during the year totaled $1,350,000.
p. Cash payments during the year: to employees, $300,000; on accounts payable, $970,000.

Required

1. Enter the company's transactions directly into T-accounts. (Don't forget to enter the beginning balances into the T-accounts.) Key your entries to the letters (a) through (p) above. Create new T-accounts as needed. Find the ending balance in each account.
2. Prepare a schedule of cost of goods manufactured.
3. Prepare a journal entry to close any balance in the Manufacturing Overhead account to Cost of Goods Sold. Prepare a schedule of cost of goods sold.
4. Prepare an income statement for the year.
5. Job 412 was one of the many jobs started and completed during the year. The job required $8,000 in direct materials and $1,600 in direct labor cost. If the job contained 400 units and the company billed the job at 175% of the unit cost on the job cost sheet, what price per unit would have been charged to the customer?

P3–27 Journal Entries; T-Accounts; Statements; Pricing Froya Fabrikker A/S of Bergen, Norway, is a small company that manufactures specialty heavy equipment for use in North Sea oil fields. (The Norwegian currency is the krone, which is denoted by Nkr.) The company uses a job-order costing system and applies manufacturing overhead cost to jobs on the basis of direct labor-hours. At the beginning of the year, the following estimates were made for the purpose of computing the predetermined overhead rate: manufacturing overhead cost, Nkr360,000; and direct labor-hours, 900.

The following transactions took place during the year (all purchases and services were acquired on account):

a. Raw materials were purchased for use in production, Nkr200,000.
b. Raw materials were requisitioned for use in production (all direct materials), Nkr185,000.
c. Utility bills were incurred, Nkr70,000 (90% related to factory operations, and the remainder related to selling and administrative activities).
d. Salary and wage costs were incurred:

Direct labor (975 hours)	Nkr230,000
Indirect labor	90,000
Selling and administrative salaries	110,000

e. Maintenance costs were incurred in the factory, Nkr54,000.
f. Advertising costs were incurred, Nkr136,000.
g. Depreciation was recorded for the year, Nkr95,000 (80% related to factory equipment, and the remainder related to selling and administrative equipment).
h. Rental cost incurred on buildings, Nkr120,000 (85% related to factory operations, and the remainder related to selling and administrative facilities).
i. Manufacturing overhead cost was applied to jobs, Nkr____?____.
j. Cost of goods manufactured for the year, Nkr770,000.
k. Sales for the year (all on account) totaled Nkr1,200,000. These goods cost Nkr800,000 to manufacture according to their job cost sheets.

The balances in the inventory accounts at the beginning of the year were:

Raw Materials	Nkr30,000
Work in Process	21,000
Finished Goods	60,000

Required

1. Prepare journal entries to record the preceding data.
2. Post your entries to T-accounts. (Don't forget to enter the beginning inventory balances above.) Determine the ending balances in the inventory accounts and in the Manufacturing Overhead account.
3. Prepare a schedule of cost of goods manufactured.
4. Prepare a journal entry to close any balance in the Manufacturing Overhead account to Cost of Goods Sold. Prepare a schedule of cost of goods sold.
5. Prepare an income statement for the year.
6. Job 412 was one of the many jobs started and completed during the year. The job required Nkr8,000 in direct materials and 39 hours of direct labor time at a total direct labor cost of Nkr9,200. The job contained only four units. If the company bills at a price 60% above the unit cost on the job cost sheet, what price per unit would have been charged to the customer?

Cases

C3–28 Ethics and the Manager Terri Ronsin had recently been transferred to the Home Security Systems Division of National Home Products. Shortly after taking over her new position as divisional controller, she was asked to develop the division's predetermined overhead rate for the upcoming year. The accuracy of the rate is of some importance, since it is used throughout the year and any overapplied or underapplied overhead is closed out to Cost of Goods Sold only at the end of the year. National Home Products uses direct labor-hours in all of its divisions as the allocation base for manufacturing overhead.

To compute the predetermined overhead rate, Terri divided her estimate of the total manufacturing overhead for the coming year by the production manager's estimate of the total direct labor-hours for the coming year. She took her computations to the division's general manager for approval but was quite surprised when he suggested a modification in the base. Her conversation with the general manager of the Home Security Systems Division, Harry Irving, went like this:

> **Ronsin:** Here are my calculations for next year's predetermined overhead rate. If you approve, we can enter the rate into the computer on January 1 and be up and running in the job-order costing system right away this year.
>
> **Irving:** Thanks for coming up with the calculations so quickly, and they look just fine. There is, however, one slight modification I would like to see. Your estimate of the total direct labor-hours for the year is 440,000 hours. How about cutting that to about 420,000 hours?
>
> **Ronsin:** I don't know if I can do that. The production manager says she will need about 440,000 direct labor-hours to meet the sales projections for the year. Besides, there are going to be over 430,000 direct labor-hours during the current year and sales are projected to be higher next year.
>
> **Irving:** Teri, I know all of that. I would still like to reduce the direct labor-hours in the base to something like 420,000 hours. You probably don't know that I had an agreement with your predecessor as divisional controller to shave 5% or so off the estimated direct labor-hours every year. That way, we kept a reserve that usually resulted in a big boost to net income at the end of the fiscal year in December. We called it our Christmas bonus. Corporate headquarters always seemed as pleased as punch that we could pull off such a miracle at the end of the year. This system has worked well for many years, and I don't want to change it now.

Required

1. Explain how shaving 5% off the estimated direct labor-hours in the base for the predetermined overhead rate usually results in a big boost in net income at the end of the fiscal year.
2. Should Terri Ronsin go along with the general manager's request to reduce the direct labor-hours in the predetermined overhead rate computation to 420,000 direct labor-hours?

C3–29 Incomplete Data; Review of Cost Flows In an attempt to conceal a theft of funds, Snake N. Grass, controller of Bucolic Products, Inc., placed a bomb in the company's record vault. The ensuing explosion left only fragments of the company's factory ledger, as shown below:

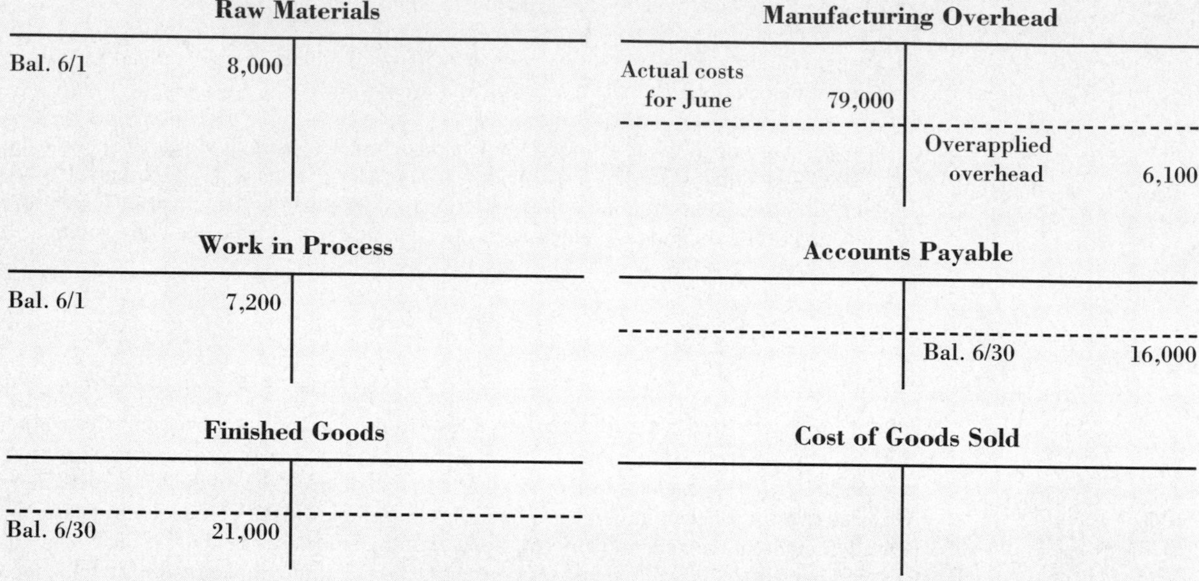

Raw Materials	
Bal. 6/1 8,000	

Manufacturing Overhead	
Actual costs for June 79,000	
	Overapplied overhead 6,100

Work in Process	
Bal. 6/1 7,200	

Accounts Payable	
	Bal. 6/30 16,000

Finished Goods	
Bal. 6/30 21,000	

Cost of Goods Sold	

To bring Mr. Grass to justice, the company must reconstruct its activities for June. You have been assigned to perform the task of reconstruction. After interviewing selected employees and sifting through charred fragments, you have determined the following additional information:

a. According to the company's treasurer, the accounts payable are for purchases of raw materials only. The company's balance sheet, dated May 31, shows that Accounts Payable had a $20,000 balance at the beginning of June. The company's bank has provided photocopies of all checks that cleared the bank during June. These photocopies show that payments to suppliers during June totaled $119,000. (All materials used during the month were direct materials.)
b. The production superintendent states that manufacturing overhead cost is applied to jobs on the basis of direct labor-hours. However, he does not remember the rate currently being used by the company.
c. Cost sheets kept in the production superintendent's office show that only one job was in process on June 30, at the time of the explosion. The job had been charged with $6,600 in materials, and 500 direct labor-hours at $8 per hour had been worked on the job.
d. A log is kept in the finished goods warehouse showing all goods transferred in from the factory. This log shows that the cost of goods transferred into the finished goods warehouse from the factory during June totaled $280,000.
e. The company's May 31 balance sheet indicates that the finished goods inventory totaled $36,000 at the beginning of June.
f. A charred piece of the payroll ledger, found after sifting through piles of smoking debris, indicates that 11,500 direct labor-hours were recorded for June. The company's Personnel Department has verified that as a result of a union contract, there are no variations in pay rates among factory employees.
g. The production superintendent states that there was no under- or overapplied overhead in the Manufacturing Overhead account at May 31.

Required Determine the following amounts:

1. Predetermined overhead rate being used by the company.
2. Raw materials purchased during June.
3. Work in process inventory, June 30.
4. Overhead applied to work in process during June.
5. Raw materials usage during June.

6. Raw materials inventory, June 30.
7. Cost of goods sold for June.

(Hint: A good way to proceed is to bring the fragmented T-accounts up to date through June 30 by posting whatever entries can be developed from the information given.)

C3–30 Critical Thinking; Interpretation of Manufacturing Overhead Rates Kelvin Aerospace, Inc., manufactures parts such as rudder hinges for the aerospace industry. The company uses a job-order costing system with a plantwide predetermined overhead rate based on direct labor-hours. On December 16, 1999, the company's controller made a preliminary estimate of the predetermined overhead rate for the year 2000. The new rate was based on the estimated total manufacturing overhead cost of $3,402,000 and the estimated 63,000 total direct labor-hours for 2000:

$$\text{Predetermined overhead rate} = \frac{\$3{,}402{,}000}{63{,}000 \text{ hours}}$$

$$= \$54 \text{ per direct labor-hour}$$

This new predetermined overhead rate was communicated to top managers in a meeting on December 19. The rate did not cause any comment because it was within a few pennies of the overhead rate that had been used during 1999. One of the subjects discussed at the meeting was a proposal by the production manager to purchase an automated milling machine built by Sunghi Industries. The president of Kelvin Aerospace, Harry Arcany, agreed to meet with the sales representative from Sunghi Industries to discuss the proposal.

On the day following the meeting, Mr. Arcany met with Jasmine Chang, Sunghi Industries' sales representative. The following discussion took place:

Arcany: Wally, our production manager, asked me to meet with you since he is interested in installing an automated milling machine. Frankly, I'm skeptical. You're going to have to show me this isn't just another expensive toy for Wally's people to play with.

Chang: This is a great machine with direct bottom-line benefits. The automated milling machine has three major advantages. First, it is much faster than the manual methods you are using. It can process about twice as many parts per hour as your present milling machines. Second, it is much more flexible. There are some up-front programming costs, but once those have been incurred, almost no setup is required to run a standard operation. You just punch in the code for the standard operation, load the machine's hopper with raw material, and the machine does the rest.

Arcany: What about cost? Having twice the capacity in the milling machine area won't do us much good. That center is idle much of the time anyway.

Chang: I was getting there. The third advantage of the automated milling machine is lower cost. Wally and I looked over your present operations, and we estimated that the automated equipment would eliminate the need for about 6,000 direct labor-hours a year. What is your direct labor cost per hour?

Arcany: The wage rate in the milling area averages about $32 per hour. Fringe benefits raise that figure to about $41 per hour.

Chang: Don't forget your overhead.

Arcany: Next year the overhead rate will be $54 per hour.

Chang: So including fringe benefits and overhead, the cost per direct labor-hour is about $95.

Arcany: That's right.

Chang: Since you can save 6,000 direct labor-hours per year, the cost savings would amount to about $570,000 a year. And our 60-month lease plan would require payments of only $348,000 per year.

Arcany: That sounds like a no-brainer. When could you install the equipment?

Shortly after this meeting, Mr. Arcany informed the company's controller of the decision to lease the new equipment, which would be installed over the Christmas vacation period. The controller realized that this decision would require a recomputation of the predetermined overhead rate for the year 2000 since the decision would affect both the manufacturing overhead and the direct labor-hours for the year. After talking with both the production manager and the sales representative from Sunghi Industries, the controller discovered that in addition to the annual lease cost of $348,000, the new machine would also require a skilled technician/programmer who would have to be hired at a cost of $50,000 per year to maintain and program the equipment. Both of these costs would be included in factory overhead. There would be no other changes in total manufacturing overhead cost, which is almost entirely fixed. The controller assumed that the new machine would result in a reduction of 6,000 direct labor-hours for the year from the levels that had initially been planned.

When the revised predetermined overhead rate for the year 2000 was circulated among the company's top managers, there was considerable dismay.

Required

1. Recompute the predetermined rate assuming that the new machine will be installed. Explain why the new predetermined overhead rate is higher (or lower) than the rate that was originally estimated for the year 2000.
2. What effect (if any) would this new rate have on the cost of jobs that do not use the new automated milling machine?
3. Why would managers be concerned about the new overhead rate?
4. After seeing the new predetermined overhead rate, the production manager admitted that he probably wouldn't be able to eliminate all of the 6,000 direct labor-hours. He had been hoping to accomplish the reduction by not replacing workers who retire or quit, but that had not been possible. As a result, the real labor savings would be only about 2,000 hours—one worker. In the light of this additional information, evaluate the original decision to acquire the automated milling machine from Sunghi Industries.

C3–31 Ethics; Predetermined Overhead Rate and Capacity (Appendix 3A) Pat Miranda, the new controller of Vault Hard Drives, Inc., has just returned from a seminar on the choice of the activity level in the predetermined overhead rate. Even though the subject did not sound exciting at first, she found that there were some important ideas presented that should get a hearing at her company. After returning from the seminar, she arranged a meeting with the production manager J. Stevens and the assistant production manager Marvin Washington.

Pat: I ran across an idea that I wanted to check out with both of you. It's about the way we compute predetermined overhead rates.
J.: We're all ears.
Pat: We compute the predetermined overhead rate by dividing the estimated total factory overhead for the coming year by the estimated total units produced for the coming year.
Marvin: We've been doing that as long as I've been with the company.
J.: And it has been done that way at every other company I've worked at, except at most places they divide by direct labor-hours.
Pat: We use units because it is simpler and we basically make one product with minor variations. But, there's another way to do it. Instead of dividing the estimated total factory overhead by the estimated total units produced for the coming year, we could divide by the total units produced at capacity.
Marvin: Oh, the Sales Department will love that. It will drop the costs on all the products. They'll go wild over there cutting prices.
Pat: That *is* a worry, but I wanted to talk to both of you first before going over to Sales.
J.: Aren't you always going to have a lot of underapplied overhead?
Pat: That's correct, but let me show you how we would handle it. Here's an example based on our budget for next year.

Budgeted (estimated) production	160,000	units
Budgeted sales	160,000	units
Capacity	200,000	units
Selling price	$60	per unit
Variable manufacturing cost	$15	per unit
Total manufacturing overhead cost (all fixed)	$4,000,000	
Administrative and selling expenses (all fixed)	$2,700,000	
Beginning inventories	–0–	

Traditional Approach to Computation of the Predetermined Overhead Rate

$$\frac{\text{Estimated total manufacturing overhead cost, \$4,000,000}}{\text{Estimated total units produced, 160,000}} = \text{\$25 per unit}$$

Budgeted Income Statement

Revenue (160,000 units × $60)		$9,600,000
Cost of goods sold:		
Variable manufacturing (160,000 units × $15)	$2,400,000	
Manufacturing overhead applied (160,000 units × $25)	4,000,000	6,400,000
Gross margin		3,200,000
Administrative and selling expenses		2,700,000
Net income		$ 500,000

New Approach to Computation of the Predetermined Overhead Rate Using Capacity in the Denominator

$$\frac{\text{Estimated total manufacturing overhead cost, \$4,000,000}}{\text{Total units at capacity, 200,000}} = \text{\$20 per unit}$$

Budgeted Income Statement

Revenue (160,000 units × $60)		$9,600,000
Cost of goods sold:		
Variable manufacturing (160,000 units × $15)	$2,400,000	
Manufacturing overhead applied (160,000 units × $20)	3,200,000	5,600,000
Gross margin		4,000,000
Cost of unused capacity [(200,000 units − 160,000 units) × $20]		800,000
Administrative and selling expenses		2,700,000
Net income		$ 500,000

J.: Whoa!! I don't think I like the looks of that "Cost of unused capacity." If that thing shows up on the income statement, someone from headquarters is likely to come down here looking for some people to lay off.
Marvin: I'm worried about something else too. What happens when sales are not up to expectations? Can we pull the "hat trick"?
Pat: I'm sorry, I don't understand.
J.: Marvin's talking about something that happens fairly regularly. When sales are down and profits look like they are going to be lower than the president told the owners they were going to be, the president comes down here and asks us to deliver some more profits.
Marvin: And we pull them out of our hat.
J.: Yeah, we just increase production until we get the profits we want.
Pat: I still don't understand. You mean you increase sales?
J.: Nope, we increase production. We're the production managers, not the sales managers.
Pat: I get it. Since you have produced more, the sales force have more units they can sell.
J.: Nope, the marketing people don't do a thing. We just build inventories and that does the trick.

Required In all of the questions below, assume that the predetermined overhead rate under the traditional method is $25 per unit and under the new method it is $20 per unit. Also assume that under the traditional method any under- or overapplied overhead is taken directly to the income statement as an adjustment to Cost of Goods Sold.

1. Suppose actual production is 160,000 units. Compute the net incomes that would be realized under the traditional and new methods if actual sales are 150,000 units and everything else turns out as expected.

2. How many units would have to be produced under each of the methods in order to realize the budgeted net income of $500,000 if actual sales are 150,000 units and everything else turns out as expected?
3. What effect does the new method based on capacity have on the volatility of net income?
4. Will the "hat trick" be easier or harder to perform if the new method based on capacity is used?
5. Do you think the "hat trick" is ethical?

Group Exercises

GE3–32 The Plant Layout Case Read the case by Wayne Morse, "Instructional Case: Rantoul Tool, Inc.," *Issues in Accounting Education,* Spring 1990, pp. 78–83. This case illustrates the impact that different manufacturing environments have on product costing procedures. The case includes a description of three manufacturing processes and diagrams of the plant layout for each process. Answer the questions in the case.

GE3–33 Talk with a Controller Look in the yellow pages or contact your local chamber of commerce or local chapter of the Institute of Certified Management Accountants to find the names of manufacturing companies in your area. Make an appointment to meet with the controller or chief financial officer of one of these companies.

Required Ask the following questions and write a brief report concerning what you found out.

1. Does the company use job-order costing, process costing, or some other method of determining product costs?
2. How is overhead assigned to products? What is the overhead rate? What is the basis of allocation? Is more than one overhead rate used?
3. Are product costs used in making any decisions? If so, what are those decisions and how are product costs used?
4. How are profits affected by changes in production volume? By changes in sales?
5. Has the company recently changed its cost system or is it considering changing its cost system? If so, why? What changes were made or what changes are being considered?

IE3–34 Job-Order versus Process Costing The chapter mentions that Bechtel International and Boeing are likely to use job-order costing in most of their lines of business. To help understand the nature of their businesses, access these companies' web sites at www.bechtel.com and www.boeing.com.

Required

1. Based on the information you found on the companies' web sites, explain why they would be more likely to use job-order costing than process costing in most of their lines of business.
2. Access the web site of TXI Riverside Cement at www.cement.com. Is this company more likely to use job-order costing or process costing for its products? Why?
3. Access the web site of Paramount Pictures at www.paramount.com. Is Paramount Pictures more likely to use job-order costing or process costing for keeping track of the costs of its movies? Why?

Chapter Four

Systems Design: Process Costing

Business Focus

Using an old family recipe, Megan started a company that produced cream soda. At first the company struggled, but as sales increased, the company expanded rapidly. Megan soon realized that to expand any further, it would be necessary to borrow money. The investment in additional equipment was too large for her to finance out of the company's current cash flows.

Megan was disappointed to find that few banks were willing to make a loan to such a small company, but she finally found a bank that would consider her loan application. However, Megan was informed that she would have to supply up-to-date financial statements with her loan application.

Megan had never bothered with financial statements before—she felt that as long as the balance in the company's checkbook kept increasing, the company was doing fine. She was puzzled how she was going to determine the value of the cream soda in the work in process and finished goods inventories. The valuation of the cream soda would affect both the cost of goods sold and the inventory balances of her company. Megan thought of perhaps using job-order costing, but her company produces only one product. Raw ingredients were continually being mixed to make more cream soda, and more bottled cream soda was always coming off the end of the bottling line. Megan didn't see how she could use a job-order costing system since the job never really ended. Perhaps there was another way to account for the costs of producing the cream soda.

Learning Objectives:

After studying Chapter 4, you should be able to:

1 Prepare journal entries to record the flow of materials, labor, and overhead through a process costing system.

2 Compute the equivalent units of production for a period by the weighted-average method.

3 Prepare a quantity schedule for a period by the weighted-average method.

4 Compute the costs per equivalent unit for a period by the weighted-average method.

5 Prepare a cost reconciliation for a period by the weighted-average method.

6 (Appendix 4A) Compute the equivalent units of production for a period by the FIFO method.

7 (Appendix 4A) Prepare a quantity schedule for a period by the FIFO method.

8 (Appendix 4A) Compute the costs per equivalent unit for a period by the FIFO method.

9 (Appendix 4A) Prepare a cost reconciliation for a period by the FIFO method.

As explained in the preceding chapter, there are two basic costing systems in use: job-order costing and process costing. A job-order costing system is used in situations where many different jobs or products are worked on each period. Examples of industries that would typically use job-order costing include furniture manufacture, special-order printing, shipbuilding, and many types of service organizations.

By contrast, **process costing** is most commonly used in industries that produce essentially homogenous (i.e., uniform) products on a continuous basis, such as bricks, corn flakes, or paper. Process costing is particularly used in companies that convert basic raw materials into homogenous products, such as Reynolds Aluminum (aluminum ingots), Scott Paper (toilet paper), General Mills (flour), Exxon (gasoline and lubricating oils), Coppertone (sunscreens), and Kellogg (breakfast cereals). In addition, process costing is often employed in companies that use a form of process costing in their assembly operations, such as Panasonic (video monitors), Compaq (personal computers), General Electric (refrigerators), Toyota (automobiles), Amana (washing machines), and Sony (CD players). A form of process costing may also be used in utilities that produce gas, water, and electricity. As suggested by the length of this list, process costing is in very wide use.

Our purpose in this chapter is to extend the discussion of product costing to include a process costing system.

Comparison of Job-Order and Process Costing

In some ways process costing is very similar to job-order costing, and in some ways it is very different. In this section, we focus on these similarities and differences in order to provide a foundation for the detailed discussion of process costing that follows.

Similarities between Job-Order and Process Costing

It is important to recognize that much of what was learned in the preceding chapter about costing and about cost flows applies equally well to process costing in this chapter. That is, we are not throwing out all that we have learned about costing and starting from "scratch" with a whole new system. The similarities that exist between job-order and process costing can be summarized as follows:

1. The same basic purposes exist in both systems, which are to assign material, labor, and overhead cost to products and to provide a mechanism for computing unit costs.
2. Both systems maintain and use the same basic manufacturing accounts, including Manufacturing Overhead, Raw Materials, Work in Process, and Finished Goods.
3. The flow of costs through the manufacturing accounts is basically the same in both systems.

As can be seen from this comparison, much of the knowledge that we have already acquired about costing is applicable to a process costing system. Our task now is simply to refine and extend this knowledge to process costing.

Exhibit 4–1
Differences between Job-Order and Process Costing

Job-Order Costing	Process Costing
1. Many different jobs are worked on during each period, with each job having different production requirements.	1. A single product is produced either on a continuous basis or for long periods of time. All units of product are identical.
2. Costs are accumulated by individual job.	2. Costs are accumulated by department.
3. The *job cost sheet* is the key document controlling the accumulation of costs by a job.	3. The *department production report* is the key document showing the accumulation and disposition of costs by a department.
4. Unit costs are computed *by job* on the job cost sheet.	4. Unit costs are computed *by department* on the department production report.

Differences between Job-Order and Process Costing

The differences between job-order and process costing arise from two factors. The first is that the flow of units in a process costing system is more or less continuous, and the second is that these units are indistinguishable from one another. Under process costing, it makes no sense to try to identify materials, labor, and overhead costs with a particular order from a customer (as we did with job-order costing), since each order is just one of many that are filled from a continuous flow of virtually identical units from the production line. Under process costing, we accumulate costs *by department,* rather than by order, and assign these costs equally to all units that pass through the department during a period.

A further difference between the two costing systems is that the job cost sheet has no use in process costing, since the focal point of that method is on departments. Instead of using job cost sheets, a document known as a **production report** is prepared for each department in which work is done on products. The production report serves several functions. It provides a summary of the number of units moving through a department during a period, and it also provides a computation of unit costs. In addition, it shows what costs were charged to the department and what disposition was made of these costs. The department production report is the key document in a process costing system.

The major differences between job-order and process costing are summarized in Exhibit 4–1.

A Perspective of Process Cost Flows

Before presenting a detailed example of process costing, it will be helpful to see how manufacturing costs flow through a process costing system.

Processing Departments

A **processing department** is any location in an organization where work is performed on a product and where materials, labor, or overhead costs are added to the product. For example, a potato chip factory operated by Nalley's might have three processing departments—one for preparing potatoes, one for cooking, and one for inspecting and packaging. A brick factory might have two processing departments—one for mixing and molding clay into brick form and one for firing the molded brick. A company can have as many or as few processing departments as are needed to complete a product or service. Some products and services may go through several processing departments,

Exhibit 4–2 Sequential Processing Departments

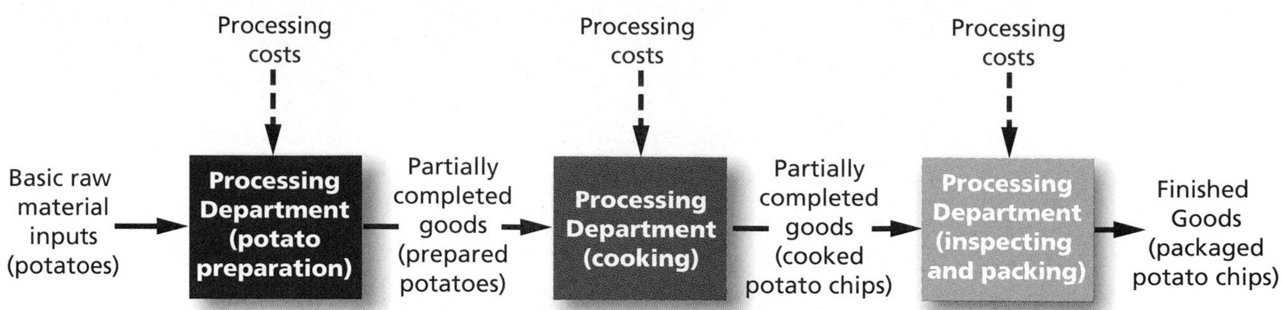

while others may go through only one or two. Regardless of the number of departments involved, all processing departments have two essential features. First, the activity performed in the processing department must be performed uniformly on all of the units passing through it. Second, the output of the processing department must be homogeneous.

The processing departments involved in making a product such as bricks would probably be organized in a *sequential* pattern. By sequential processing, we mean that units flow in sequence from one department to another. An example of processing departments arranged in a sequential pattern is given in Exhibit 4–2, which illustrates a potato chip processing plant.

A different type of processing pattern, known as *parallel processing,* is required to make some products. Parallel processing is used in those situations where after a certain point, some units may go through different processing departments than others. For example, Exxon and Shell Oil in their petroleum refining operations input crude oil into one processing department and then use the refined output for further processing into several end products. Each end product may undergo several steps of further processing after the initial refining, some of which may be shared with other end products and some of which may not.

An example of parallel processing is provided in Exhibit 4–3, which shows the process flows in a Coca-Cola™ bottling plant. In the first processing department, raw materials are mixed to make the basic concentrate. This concentrate can be used to make bottled Coke or it may be sold to restaurants and bars for use in soda fountains. Under the first option, the concentrate is sent on to the bottling department where it is mixed with carbonated water and then injected into sterile bottles and capped. In the final processing department, the bottles are inspected, labels are applied, and the bottles are packed in cartons. If the concentrate is to be sold for use in soda fountains, it is injected into large sterile metal cylinders, inspected, and packaged for shipping. This is just an example of one way in which parallel processing can be set up. The number of possible variations in parallel processing is virtually limitless.

The Flow of Materials, Labor, and Overhead Costs

Cost accumulation is simpler in a process costing system than in a job-order costing system. In a process costing system, instead of having to trace costs to hundreds of different jobs, costs are traced to only a few processing departments.

Exhibit 4–3 Parallel Processing Departments

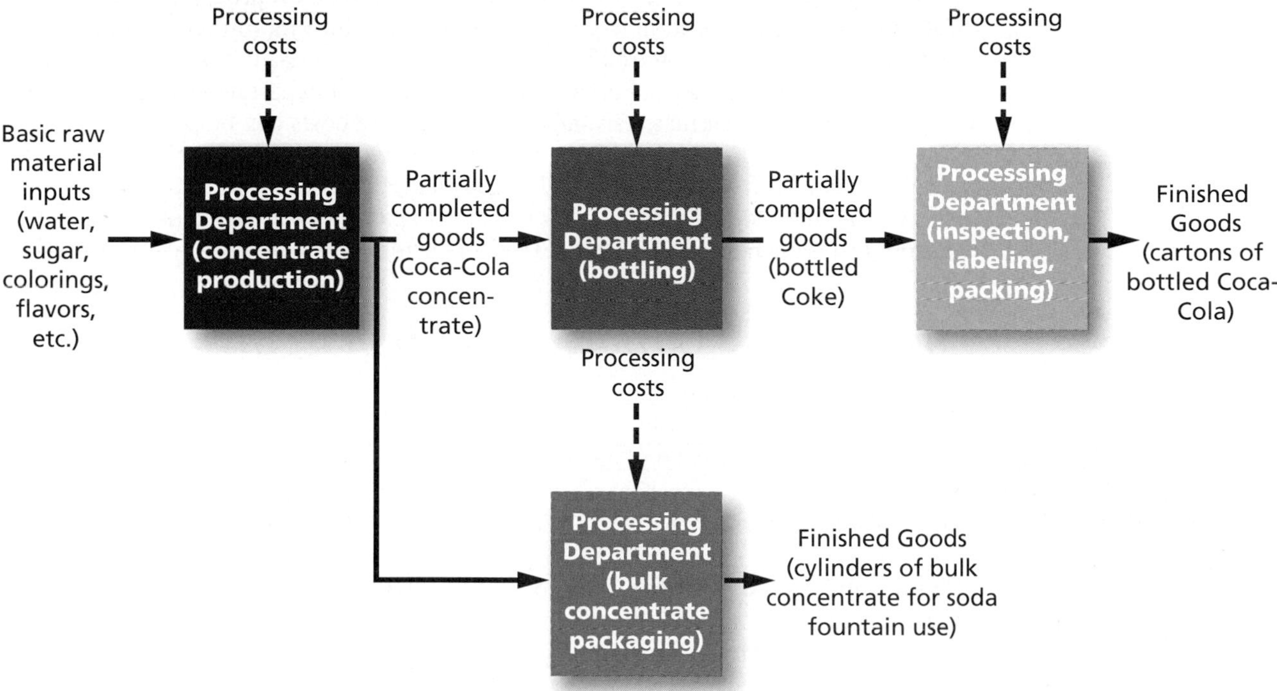

Exhibit 4–4 T-Account Model of Process Costing Flows

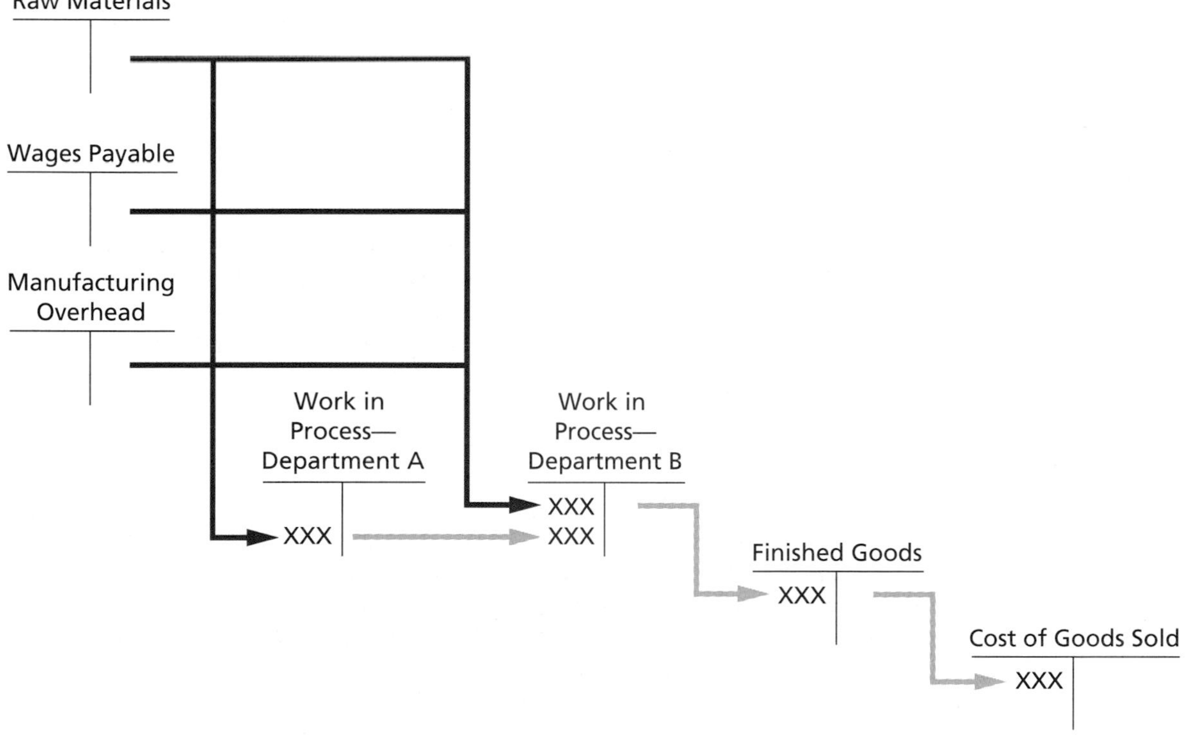

A T-account model of materials, labor, and overhead cost flows in a process costing system is given in Exhibit 4–4. Several key points should be noted from this exhibit. First, note that a separate Work in Process account is maintained for *each processing department.* In contrast, in a job-order costing system there may be only a single Work in Process account for the entire company. Second, note that the completed production of the first processing department (Department A in the exhibit) is transferred into the Work in Process account of the second processing department (Department B), where it undergoes further work. After this further work, the completed units are then transferred into Finished Goods. (In Exhibit 4–4, we show only two processing departments, but there can be many such departments in a company.)

Finally, note that materials, labor, and overhead costs can be added in *any* processing department—not just the first. Costs in Department B's Work in Process account would therefore consist of the materials, labor, and overhead costs entered directly into the account plus the costs attached to partially completed units transferred in from Department A (called **transferred-in costs**).

Materials, Labor, and Overhead Cost Entries

objective 1

Prepare journal entries to record the flow of materials, labor, and overhead through a process costing system.

To complete our discussion of cost flows in a process costing system, in the following paragraphs we show journal entries relating to materials, labor, and overhead costs and also make brief, further comments relating to each of these cost categories.

MATERIALS COSTS As in job-order costing, materials are drawn from the storeroom using a materials requisition form. As stated earlier, materials can be added in any processing department, although it is not unusual for materials to be added only in the first processing department, with subsequent departments adding only labor and overhead costs as the partially completed units move along toward completion.

Assuming that the first processing department in a company is Department A, the journal entry for placing materials into process is as follows:

Work in Process—Department A	XXX	
Raw Materials		XXX

If other materials are subsequently added in Department B, the entry is the following:

Work in Process—Department B	XXX	
Raw Materials		XXX

LABOR COSTS Since it is not necessary to identify costs with specific jobs, a time clock is generally adequate for accumulating labor costs and for allocating them to the proper department in a process costing system. Assuming again that a company has two processing departments, Department A and Department B, the following journal entry will record the labor costs for a period:

Work in Process—Department A	XXX	
Work in Process—Department B	XXX	
Salaries and Wages Payable		XXX

OVERHEAD COSTS If production is stable from period to period and if overhead costs are incurred uniformly over the year, actual overhead costs can be charged to products. However, if production levels fluctuate or if overhead costs are not incurred uniformly, charging products with actual overhead costs will result in unit product costs that vary randomly from one period to the next. In such a situation, predetermined overhead rates should be used to charge overhead cost to products, the same as in job-order costing. When predetermined overhead rates are used, each department has its own separate rate with the rates being computed in the same way as was discussed in Chapter 3. Overhead cost is then applied to units of product as the units move through the various departments. Since predetermined overhead rates are widely used in process costing, we will assume their use throughout the remainder of this chapter.

If a company has two processing departments, Department A and Department B, the following journal entry is used to apply overhead cost to products:

Work in Process—Department A	XXX	
Work in Process—Department B	XXX	
Manufacturing Overhead		XXX

COMPLETING THE COST FLOWS Once processing has been completed in a department, the units are transferred to the next department for further processing, as illustrated earlier in the T-accounts in Exhibit 4–4. The following journal entry is used to transfer the costs of partially completed units from Department A to Department B:

Work in Process—Department B	XXX	
Work in Process—Department A		XXX

After processing has been completed in Department B, the costs of the completed units are then transferred to the Finished Goods inventory account:

Finished Goods	XXX	
Work in Process—Department B		XXX

Finally, when a customer's order is filled and units are sold, the cost of the units is transferred to Cost of Goods Sold:

Cost of Goods Sold	XXX	
Finished Goods		XXX

To summarize, we stated earlier that the cost flows between accounts are basically the same in a process costing system as they are in a job-order costing system. The only noticeable difference at this point is that in a process costing system there is a separate Work in Process account for each department.

Managerial Accounting in Action

THE ISSUE

Samantha Trivers, president of Double Diamond Skis, was worried about the future of the company. After a rocky start, the company had come out with a completely redesigned ski called The Ultimate. It was made of exotic materials and featured flashy graphics. Exhibit 4–5 illustrates how this ski is manufactured. The ski was a runaway best seller—particularly among younger skiers—and had provided the company with much-needed cash for two years. However, last year a dismal snowfall in the Rocky Mountains had depressed sales, and Double Diamond was once again short of cash. Samantha was worried that another bad ski season would force Double Diamond into bankruptcy.

Just before starting production of next year's model of The Ultimate, Samantha called Jerry Madison, the company controller, into her office to discuss the reports she would need in the coming year.

Samantha: Jerry, I am going to need more frequent cost information this year. I really have to stay on top of things.
Jerry: What do you have in mind?
Samantha: I'd like reports at least once a month that detail our production costs for each department and for each pair of skis.
Jerry: That shouldn't be much of a problem. We already compile almost all of the necessary data for the annual report. The only complication is our work in process inventories. They haven't been a problem in our annual reports, since our fiscal year ends at a time when we have finished producing skis for the last model year and haven't yet started producing for the new model year. Consequently, there aren't any work in process

inventories to value for the annual report. But that won't be true for monthly reports.

Samantha: I'm not sure why that is a problem, Jerry. But I'm sure you can figure out how to solve it.

Jerry: You can count on me.

Exhibit 4–5 The Production Process at Double Diamond Skis*

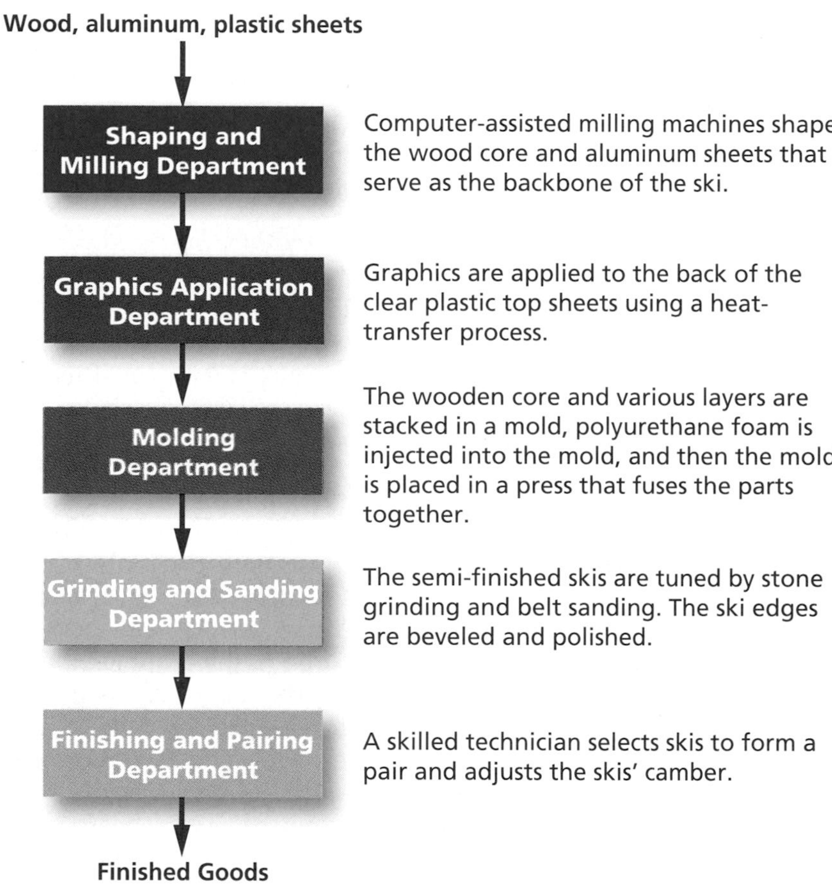

*Adapted from Bill Gout, Jesse James Doquilo, and Studio M D, "Capped Crusaders," *Skiing,* October 1993, pp. 138–44.

Equivalent Units of Production

Jerry, the controller of Double Diamond Skis, was concerned with the following problem: After materials, labor, and overhead costs have been accumulated in a department, the department's output must be determined so that unit costs can be computed. The difficulty is that a department usually has some partially completed units in its ending inventory. It does not seem reasonable to count these partially completed units as equivalent to fully completed units when counting the department's output. Therefore, Jerry will mathematically convert those partially completed units into an *equivalent* number of fully completed units. In process costing, this is done using the following formula:

Equivalent units = Number of partially completed units × Percentage completion

As the formula states, **equivalent units** is defined to be the product of the number of partially completed units and the percentage completion of those units. The equivalent units is the number of complete units that could have been obtained from the materials and effort that went into the partially complete units.

For example, suppose the Molding Department at Double Diamond has 500 units in its ending work in process inventory that are 60% complete. These 500 partially complete units are equivalent to 300 fully complete units (500 × 60% = 300). Therefore, the ending work in process inventory would be said to contain 300 equivalent units. These equivalent units would be added to any fully completed units to determine the period's output for the department—called the *equivalent units of production.*

There are two different ways of computing the equivalent units of production for a period. In this chapter, we discuss the *weighted-average method.* In Appendix 4A, the *FIFO method* is discussed. The **FIFO method** of process costing is a method in which equivalent units and unit costs relate only to work done during the current period. In contrast, the **weighted-average method** blends together units and costs from the current period with units and costs from the prior period. In the weighted-average method, the **equivalent units of production** for a department are the number of units transferred to the next department (or to finished goods) plus the equivalent units in the department's ending work in process inventory.

Weighted-Average Method

objective 2

Compute the equivalent units of production for a period by the weighted-average method.

Under the weighted-average method, a department's equivalent units are computed as described above:

Weighted-Average Method
(a separate calculation is made for each cost category in each processing department)

Equivalent units of production = Units transferred to the next department or to finished goods
+ Equivalent units in ending work in process inventory

We do not have to make an equivalent units calculation for units transferred to the next department, since we can assume that they would not have been transferred unless they were 100% complete with respect to the work performed in the transferring department.

Consider the Shaping and Milling Department at Double Diamond. This department uses computerized milling machines to precisely shape the wooden core and metal sheets that will be used to form the backbone of the ski. The following activity took place in the department in May, several months into the production of the new model of The Ultimate ski:

		Percent Completed	
	Units	**Materials**	**Conversion**
Work in process, May 1	200	50%	30%
Units started into production during May	5,000		
Units completed during May and transferred to the next department	4,800	100%*	100%*
Work in process, May 31	400	40%	25%

*It is always assumed that units transferred out of a department are 100% complete with respect to the processing done in that department.

Exhibit 4–6
Equivalent Units of Production: Weighted-Average Method

	Materials	Conversion
Units transferred to the next department	4,800	4,800
Work in process, May 31:		
400 units × 40%	160	
400 units × 25%		100
Equivalent units of production	4,960	4,900

Note the use of the term *conversion* in the table on the previous page. **Conversion cost,** as defined in Chapter 2, is direct labor cost plus manufacturing overhead cost. In process costing, conversion cost is often—but not always—treated as a single element of product cost.

Also note that the May 1 beginning work in process was 50% complete with respect to materials costs and 30% complete with respect to conversion costs. This means that 50% of the materials costs required to complete the units had already been incurred. Likewise, 30% of the conversion costs required to complete the units had already been incurred.

Since Double Diamond's work in process inventories are at different stages of completion in terms of the amounts of materials cost and conversion cost that have been added, two equivalent unit figures must be computed. The equivalent units computations are given in Exhibit 4–6.

Note from the computation in Exhibit 4–6 that units in the beginning work in process inventory are ignored. The weighted-average method is concerned only with the fact that there are 4,900 equivalent units for conversion cost in ending inventories and in units transferred to the next department—the method is not concerned with the additional fact that some of this work was accomplished in prior periods. This is a key point in the weighted-average method that is easy to overlook.

The weighted-average method blends together the work that was accomplished in prior periods with the work that was accomplished in the current period. In the FIFO method, the units and costs of prior periods are cleanly separated from the units and costs of the current period. Some managers believe the FIFO method is more accurate for this reason. However, the FIFO method is more complex than the weighted-average method and for that reason is covered in Appendix 4A.

A visual perspective of the computation of equivalent units of production is provided in Exhibit 4–7. The data are for conversion costs in the Shaping and Milling Department of Double Diamond Skis. Study this exhibit carefully before going on.

Exhibit 4–7 Visual Perspective of Equivalent Units of Production

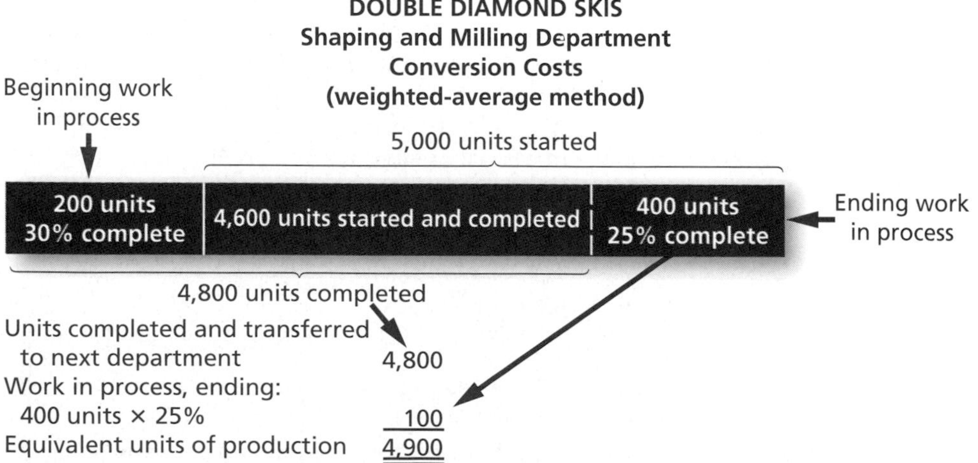

Production Report—Weighted-Average Method

The production report developed in this section contains the information requested by the president of Double Diamond Skis. The purpose of the production report is to summarize for management all of the activity that takes place in a department's Work in Process account for a period. This activity includes the units and costs that flow through the Work in Process account. As illustrated in Exhibit 4–8, a separate production report is prepared for each department.

Earlier, when we outlined the differences between job-order costing and process costing, we stated that the production report takes the place of a job cost sheet in a process costing system. The production report is a key management document and is vital to the proper operation of the system. The production report has three separate (though highly interrelated) parts:

1. A quantity schedule, which shows the flow of units through the department and a computation of equivalent units.
2. A computation of costs per equivalent unit.
3. A reconciliation of all cost flows into and out of the department during the period.

We will use the data on the next page for the May operations of the Shaping and Milling Department of Double Diamond Skis to illustrate the production report. Keep in mind that this report is only one of the five reports that would be prepared for the company since the company has five processing departments.

Exhibit 4–8 The Position of the Production Report in the Flow of Costs

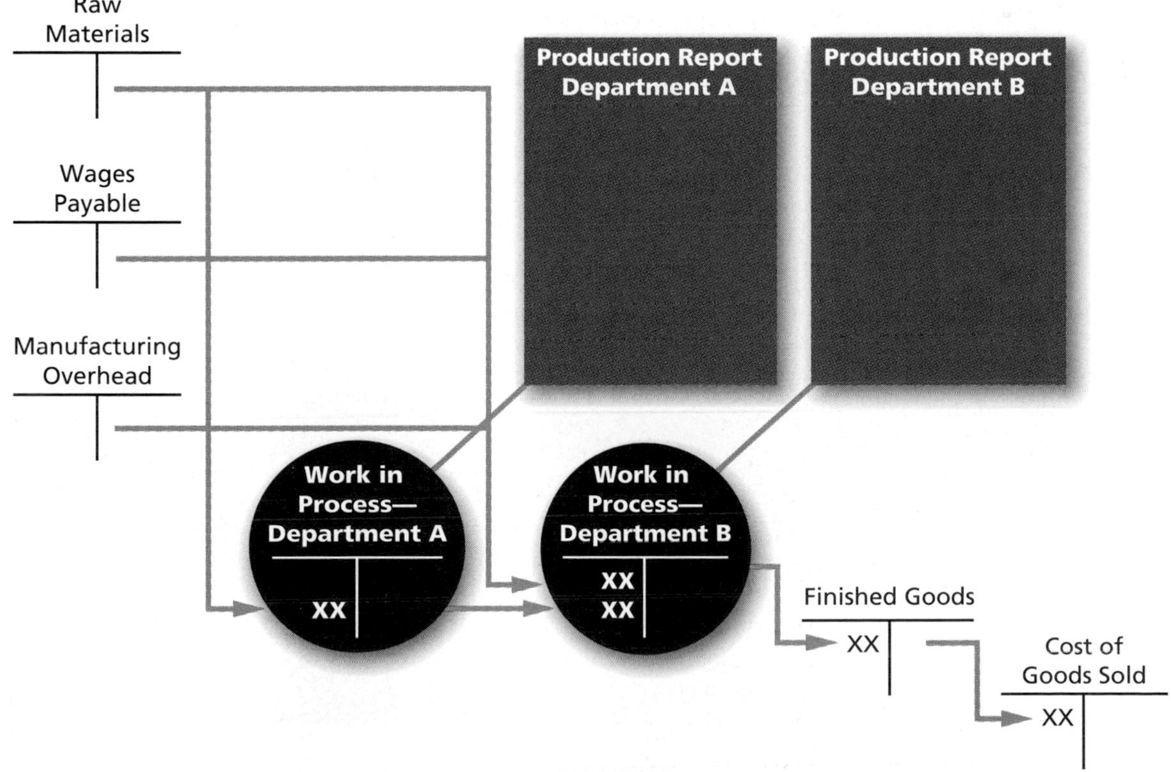

Shaping and Milling Department		
Work in process, beginning:		
Units in process		200
Stage of completion with respect to materials	50%	
Stage of completion with respect to conversion	30%	
Costs in the beginning inventory:		
Materials cost		$ 3,000
Conversion cost		1,000
Total cost in process		$ 4,000
Units started into production during May		5,000
Units completed and transferred out		4,800
Costs added to production during May:		
Materials cost		$ 74,000
Conversion cost		70,000
Total cost added in the department		$144,000
Work in process, ending:		
Units in process		400
Stage of completion with respect to materials	40%	
Stage of completion with respect to conversion	25%	

In this section, we show how a production report is prepared when the weighted-average method is used to compute equivalent units and unit costs. The preparation of a production report under the FIFO method is illustrated in Appendix 4A at the end of this chapter.

Step 1: Prepare a Quantity Schedule and Compute the Equivalent Units

objective 3

Prepare a quantity schedule for a period by the weighted-average method.

The first part of a production report consists of a **quantity schedule,** which shows the flow of units through a department and a computation of equivalent units. To illustrate, a quantity schedule combined with a computation of equivalent units is given below for the Shaping and Milling Department of Double Diamond Skis.

	Quantity Schedule	Equivalent Units	
		Materials	Conversion
Units to be accounted for:			
Work in process, May 1 (50% materials; 30% conversion added last month)	200		
Started into production	5,000		
Total units	5,200		
Units accounted for as follows:			
Transferred to the next department	4,800	4,800	4,800
Work in process, May 31 (40% materials; 25% conversion added this month)	400	160*	100†
Total units and equivalent units of production	5,200	4,960	4,900

*40% × 400 units = 160 equivalent units.
†25% × 400 units = 100 equivalent units.

The quantity schedule permits the manager to see at a glance how many units moved through the department during the period as well as to see the stage of completion of any in-process units. In addition to providing this information, the quantity schedule serves as an essential guide in preparing and tying together the remaining parts of a production report.

Step 2: Compute Costs per Equivalent Unit

objective 4

Compute the costs per equivalent unit for a period by the weighted-average method.

As stated earlier, the weighted-average method blends together the work that was accomplished in the prior period with the work that was accomplished in the current period. That is why it is called the weighted-average method; it averages together units and costs from both the prior and current periods by adding the cost in the beginning work in process inventory to the current period costs. These computations are shown below for the Shaping and Milling Department for May:

Shaping and Milling Department

	Total Cost	Materials		Conversion		Whole Unit
Cost to be accounted for:						
Work in process, May 1	$ 4,000	$ 3,000		$ 1,000		
Cost added in the Shaping and Milling Department	144,000	74,000		70,000		
Total cost (a)	$148,000	$77,000		$71,000		
Equivalent units of production (Step 1 above) (b)		4,960		4,900		
Cost per EU, (a) ÷ (b)		$15.524	+	$14.490	=	$30.014

The cost per equivalent unit (EU) that we have computed for the Shaping and Milling Department will be used to apply cost to units that are transferred to the next department, graphics application, and will also be used to compute the cost in the ending work in process inventory. For example, each unit transferred out of the Shaping and Milling Department to the Graphics Application Department will carry with it a cost of $30.014. Since the costs are passed on from department to department, the unit cost of the last department, Finishing and Pairing, will represent the final unit cost of a completed unit of product.

Step 3: Prepare a Cost Reconciliation

objective 5

Prepare a cost reconciliation for a period by the weighted-average method.

The purpose of a **cost reconciliation** is to show how the costs that have been charged to a department during a period are accounted for. Typically, the costs charged to a department will consist of the following:

1. Cost in the beginning work in process inventory.
2. Materials, labor, and overhead costs added during the period.
3. Cost (if any) transferred in from the preceding department.

In a production report, these costs are generally titled "Cost to be accounted for." They are accounted for in a production report by computing the following amounts:

1. Cost transferred out to the next department (or to Finished Goods).
2. Cost remaining in the ending work in process inventory.

Exhibit 4–9 Graphic Illustration of the Cost Reconciliation Part of a Production Report

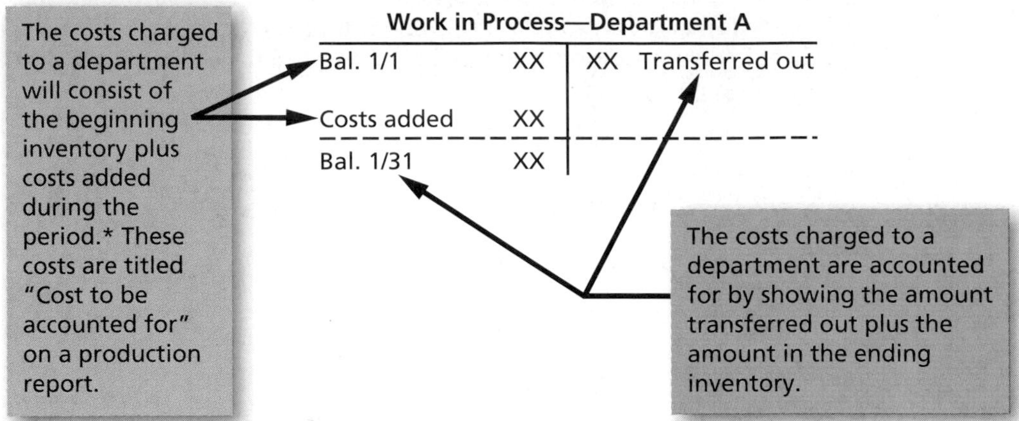

*Departments that follow Department A (Department B and so forth) will need to show the amount of cost transferred in from the preceding department.

In short, when a cost reconciliation is prepared, the "Cost to be accounted for" from step 2 is reconciled with the sum of the cost transferred out during the period plus the cost in the ending work in process inventory. This concept is shown graphically in Exhibit 4–9. Study this exhibit carefully before going on to the cost reconciliation below for the Shaping and Milling Department.

EXAMPLE OF A COST RECONCILIATION To prepare a cost reconciliation, *follow the quantity schedule line for line and show the cost associated with each group of units.* This is done in Exhibit 4–10, where we present a completed production report for the Shaping and Milling Department.

The quantity schedule in the exhibit shows that 200 units were in process on May 1 and that an additional 5,000 units were started into production during the month. Looking at the "Cost to be accounted for" in the middle part of the exhibit, notice that the units in process on May 1 had $4,000 in cost attached to them and that the Shaping and Milling Department added another $144,000 in cost to production during the month. Thus, the department has $148,000 ($4,000 + $144,000) in cost to be accounted for.

This cost is accounted for in two ways. As shown on the quantity schedule, 4,800 units were transferred to the Graphics Application Department, the next department in the production process. Another 400 units were still in process in the Shaping and Milling Department at the end of the month. Thus, part of the $148,000 "Cost to be accounted for" goes with the 4,800 units to the Graphics Application Department, and part of it remains with the 400 units in the ending work in process inventory in the Shaping and Milling Department.

Each of the 4,800 units transferred to the Graphics Application Department is assigned $30.014 in cost, for a total $144,067. The 400 units still in process at the end of the month are assigned costs according to their stage of completion. To determine the stage of completion, we refer to the equivalent units computation and bring the equivalent units figures down to the cost reconciliation part of the report. We then assign costs to these units, using the cost per equivalent unit figures already computed.

After cost has been assigned to the ending work in process inventory, the total cost that we have accounted for ($148,000) agrees with the amount that we had to account for ($148,000). Thus, the cost reconciliation is complete.

Exhibit 4–10 Production Report—Weighted-Average Method

DOUBLE DIAMOND SKIS
Shaping and Milling Department Production Report
(weighted-average method)

Quantity Schedule and Equivalent Units

	Quantity Schedule	Equivalent Units (EU) Materials	Conversion
Units to be accounted for:			
Work in process, May 1 (50% materials; 30% conversion added last month)	200		
Started into production	5,000		
Total units	5,200		
Units accounted for as follows:			
Transferred to the next department	4,800	4,800	4,800
Work in process, May 31 (40% materials; 25% conversion added this month)	400	160*	100†
Total units and equivalent units of production	5,200	4,960	4,900

Costs per Equivalent Unit

	Total Cost	Materials	Conversion	Whole Unit
Cost to be accounted for:				
Work in process, May 1	**$ 4,000**	$ 3,000	$ 1,000	
Cost added in the Shaping and Milling Department	**144,000**	74,000	70,000	
Total cost (a)	**$148,000**	$77,000	$71,000	
Equivalent units of production (above) (b)		4,960	4,900	
Cost per EU, (a) ÷ (b)		$15.524	+ $14.490	= $30.014

Cost Reconciliation

	Total Cost	Equivalent Units (above) Materials	Conversion
Cost accounted for as follows:			
Transferred to next department:			
4,800 units × **$30.014** each	**$144,067**	4,800	4,800
Work in process, May 31:			
Materials, at $15.524 per EU	2,484	160	
Conversion, at $14.490 per EU	1,449		100
Total work in process, May 31	3,933		
Total cost	$148,000		

*40% × 400 units = 160 equivalent units.
†25% × 400 units = 100 equivalent units.

EU = Equivalent unit.

Managerial Accounting in Action

THE WRAP-UP

Jerry: Here's an example of the kind of report I can put together for you every month. This particular report is for the Shaping and Milling Department. It follows a fairly standard format for industries like ours and is called a production report. I hope this is what you have in mind.
Samantha: The quantity schedule makes sense to me. I can see we had a total of 5,200 units to account for in the department, and 4,800 of those were transferred to the next department while 400 were still in process at the end of the month. What are these "equivalent units"?
Jerry: That's the problem I mentioned earlier. While there are 400 units still in process, they are far from complete. When we compute the unit costs, it wouldn't make sense to count them as whole units.
Samantha: I suppose not. I see what you are driving at. Since those 400 units are only 25% complete with respect to our conversion costs, they should only be counted as 100 units when we compute the unit costs for conversion.
Jerry: That's right. Is the rest of the report clear?
Samantha: Yes, it does seem pretty clear, although I want to work the numbers through on my own to make sure I thoroughly understand the report.
Jerry: Does this report give you the information you wanted?
Samantha: Yes, it does. I can tell how many units are in process, how complete they are, what happened to them, and their costs. While I know the unit costs are averages and are heavily influenced by our volume, they still can give me some idea of how well we are doing on the cost side. Thanks, Jerry.

A Comment about Rounding Errors

If you use a calculator or computer spreadsheet and do not round off the costs per equivalent unit, there shouldn't be any discrepancy between the "Cost to be accounted for" and the "Cost accounted for" in the cost reconciliation. However, if you round off the costs per equivalent unit, the two figures will not always exactly agree. For the report in Exhibit 4–10, the two figures do agree, but this will not always happen. In all of the homework assignments and other materials, we follow two rules: (1) all the costs per equivalent unit are rounded off to three decimal places as in Exhibit 4–10, and (2) any adjustment needed to reconcile the "Cost accounted for" with the "Cost to be accounted for" is made to the cost "transferred" amount rather than to the ending inventory.

Operation Costing

The costing systems discussed in Chapters 3 and 4 represent the two ends of a continuum. On one end we have job-order costing, which is used by companies that produce many different items—generally to customers' specifications. On the other end we have process costing, which is used by companies that produce basically homogeneous products in large quantities. Between these two extremes there are many hybrid systems that include characteristics of both job-order and process costing. One of these hybrids is called *operation costing.*

Operation costing is used in situations where products have some common characteristics and also some individual characteristics. Shoes, for example, have com-

mon characteristics in that all styles involve cutting and sewing that can be done on a repetitive basis, using the same equipment and following the same basic procedures. Shoes also have individual characteristics—some are made of expensive leathers and others may be made using inexpensive synthetic materials. In a situation such as this, where products have some common characteristics but also must be handled individually to some extent, operation costing may be used to determine product costs.

As mentioned above, operation costing is a hybrid system that employs aspects of both job-order and process costing. Products are typically handled in batches when operation costing is in use, with each batch charged for its own specific materials. In this sense, operation costing is similar to job-order costing. However, labor and overhead costs are accumulated by operation or by department, and these costs are assigned to units as in process costing. If shoes are being produced, for example, each shoe is charged the same per unit conversion cost, regardless of the style involved, but it is charged with its specific materials cost. Thus, the company is able to distinguish between styles in terms of materials, but it is able to employ the simplicity of a process costing system for labor and overhead costs.

Examples of other products for which operation costing may be used include electronic equipment (such as semiconductors), textiles, clothing, and jewelry (such as rings, bracelets, and medallions). Products of this type are typically produced in batches, but they can vary considerably from model to model or from style to style in terms of the cost of raw material inputs. Therefore, an operation costing system is well suited for providing cost data.

Summary

Process costing is used in situations where homogeneous products or services are produced on a continuous basis. Costs flow through the manufacturing accounts in basically the same way in both job-order and process costing systems. A process costing system differs from a job-order system primarily in that costs are accumulated by department (rather than by job) and the department production report replaces the job cost sheet.

To compute unit costs in a department, the department's output in terms of equivalent units must be determined. In the weighted-average method, the equivalent units for a period are the sum of the units transferred out of the department during the period and the equivalent units in ending work in process inventory at the end of the period.

The activity in a department is summarized on a production report. There are three separate (though highly interrelated) parts to a production report. The first part is a quantity schedule, which includes a computation of equivalent units and shows the flow of units through a department during a period. The second part consists of a computation of costs per equivalent unit, with unit costs being provided individually for materials, labor, and overhead as well as in total for the period. The third part consists of a cost reconciliation, which summarizes all cost flows through a department for a period.

Review Problem: Process Cost Flows and Reports

Luxguard Home Paint Company produces exterior latex paint, which it sells in one-gallon containers. The company has two processing departments—Base Fab and Finishing. White paint, which is used as a base for all the company's paints, is mixed from raw ingredients in the Base Fab Department. Pigments are added to the basic white paint, the pigmented paint is squirted under pressure into one-gallon containers, and the containers are labeled and packed for shipping in the Finishing Department. Information relating to the company's operations for April is as follows:

a. Raw materials were issued for use in production: Base Fab Department, $851,000; and Finishing Department, $629,000.
b. Direct labor costs were incurred: Base Fab Department, $330,000; and Finishing Department, $270,000.
c. Manufacturing overhead cost was applied: Base Fab Department, $665,000; and Finishing Department, $405,000.
d. Basic white paint was transferred from the Base Fab Department to the Finishing Department, $1,850,000.
e. Paint that had been prepared for shipping was transferred from the Finishing Department to Finished Goods, $3,200,000.

Required

1. Prepare journal entries to record items (a) through (e) above.
2. Post the journal entries from (1) above to T-accounts. The balance in the Base Fab Department's Work in Process account on April 1 was $150,000; the balance in the Finishing Department's Work in Process account was $70,000. After posting entries to the T-accounts, find the ending balance in each department's Work in Process account.
3. Prepare a production report for the Base Fab Department for April. The following additional information is available regarding production in the Base Fab Department during April:

Production data:	
Units (gallons) in process, April 1: 100% complete as to materials, 60% complete as to labor and overhead	30,000
Units (gallons) started into production during April	420,000
Units (gallons) completed and transferred to the Finishing Department	370,000
Units (gallons) in process, April 30: 50% complete as to materials, 25% complete as to labor and overhead	80,000
Cost data:	
Work in process inventory, April 1:	
Materials	$ 92,000
Labor	21,000
Overhead	37,000
Total cost	$150,000
Cost added during April:	
Materials	$851,000
Labor	330,000
Overhead	665,000

Solution to Review Problem

1.

		Debit	Credit
a.	Work in Process—Base Fab Department	851,000	
	Work in Process—Finishing Department	629,000	
	Raw Materials		1,480,000
b.	Work in Process—Base Fab Department	330,000	
	Work in Process—Finishing Department	270,000	
	Salaries and Wages Payable		600,000
c.	Work in Process—Base Fab Department	665,000	
	Work in Process—Finishing Department	405,000	
	Manufacturing Overhead		1,070,000
d.	Work in Process—Finishing Department	1,850,000	
	Work in Process—Base Fab Department		1,850,000
e.	Finished Goods	3,200,000	
	Work in Process—Finishing Department		3,200,000

2.

Raw Materials

Bal.	XXX	(a)	1,480,000

Salaries and Wages Payable

		(b)	600,000

Work in Process—Base Fab Department

Bal.	150,000	(d)	1,850,000
(a)	851,000		
(b)	330,000		
(c)	665,000		
Bal.	146,000		

Manufacturing Overhead

(Various actual costs)	(c)	1,070,000

Work in Process—Finishing Department

Bal.	70,000	(e)	3,200,000
(a)	629,000		
(b)	270,000		
(c)	405,000		
(d)	1,850,000		
Bal.	24,000		

Finished Goods

Bal.	XXX	
(e)	3,200,000	

LUXGUARD HOME PAINT COMPANY
Production Report—Base Fab Department
For the Month Ended April 30

Quantity Schedule and Equivalent Units

	Quantity Schedule
Units (gallons) to be accounted for:	
Work in process, April 1 (all materials, 60% labor and overhead added last month)	30,000
Started into production	420,000
Total units	450,000

		Equivalent Units (EU)		
		Materials	Labor	Overhead
Units (gallons) accounted for as follows:				
Transferred to Finishing Department	370,000	370,000	370,000	370,000
Work in process, April 30 (50% materials, 25% labor and overhead added this month)	80,000	40,000*	20,000*	20,000*
Total units and equivalent units of production	450,000	410,000	390,000	390,000

Costs per Equivalent Unit

	Total Cost	Materials	Labor	Overhead	Whole Unit
Cost to be accounted for:					
Work in process, April 1	$ 150,000	$ 92,000	$ 21,000	$ 37,000	
Cost added by the Finishing Department	1,846,000	851,000	330,000	665,000	
Total cost (a)	$1,996,000	$943,000	$351,000	$702,000	
Equivalent units of production (b)	—	410,000	390,000	390,000	
Cost per EU, (a) ÷ (b)	—	$2.30 +	$0.90 +	$1.80 =	$5.00

Cost Reconciliation

	Total Cost	Equivalent Units (above)		
		Materials	Labor	Overhead
Cost accounted for as follows:				
Transferred to Finishing Department:				
370,000 units × $5.00 each	$1,850,000	370,000	370,000	370,000
Work in process, April 30:				
Materials, at $2.30 per EU	92,000	40,000		
Labor, at $0.90 per EU	18,000		20,000	
Overhead, at $1.80 per EU	36,000			20,000
Total work in process	146,000			
Total cost	$1,996,000			

* Materials: 80,000 units × 50% = 40,000 equivalent units; labor and overhead: 80,000 units × 25% = 20,000 equivalent units.

EU = Equivalent unit.

Key Terms for Review

Conversion cost Direct labor cost plus manufacturing overhead cost. (p. 156)

Cost reconciliation The part of a production report that shows what costs a department has to account for during a period and how those costs are accounted for. (p. 159)

Equivalent units The product of the number of partially completed units and their percentage of completion with respect to a particular cost. Equivalent units are the number of complete whole units one could obtain from the materials and effort contained in partially completed units. (p. 155)

Equivalent units of production (weighted-average method) The units transferred to the next department (or to finished goods) during the period plus the equivalent units in the department's ending work in process inventory. (p. 155)

FIFO method A method of accounting for cost flows in a process costing system in which equivalent units and unit costs relate only to work done during the current period. (p. 155)

Operation costing A hybrid costing system used when products are manufactured in batches and when the products have some common characteristics and some individual characteristics. This system handles materials the same as in job-order costing and labor and overhead the same as in process costing. (p. 162)

Process costing A costing method used in situations where essentially homogeneous products are produced on a continuous basis. (p. 148)

Processing department Any location in an organization where work is performed on a product and where materials, labor, or overhead costs are added to the product. (p. 149)

Production report A report that summarizes all activity in a department's Work in Process account during a period and that contains three parts: a quantity schedule and a computation of equivalent units, a computation of total and unit costs, and a cost reconciliation. (p. 149)

Quantity schedule The part of a production report that shows the flow of units through a department during a period and a computation of equivalent units. (p. 158)

Transferred-in cost The cost attached to products that have been received from a prior processing department. (p. 152)

Weighted-average method A method of process costing that blends together units and costs from both the current and prior periods. (p. 155)

Appendix 4A: FIFO Method

The FIFO method of process costing differs from the weighted-average method in two basic ways: (1) the computation of equivalent units, and (2) the way in which costs of beginning inventory are treated in the cost reconciliation report. The FIFO method is generally considered more accurate than the weighted-average method, but it is more complex. The complexity is not a problem for computers, but the FIFO method is a little more difficult to understand and to learn than the weighted-average method.

Equivalent Units—FIFO Method

objective 6

Compute the equivalent units of production for a period by the FIFO method.

The computation of equivalent units under the FIFO method differs from the computation under the weighted-average method in two ways.

First, the "units transferred out" figure is divided into two parts. One part consists of the units from the beginning inventory that were completed and transferred out, and the other part consists of the units that were both *started* and *completed* during the current period.

Second, full consideration is given to the amount of work expended during the current period on units in the *beginning* work in process inventory as well as on units in the ending inventory. Thus, under the FIFO method, it is necessary to convert both inventories to an equivalent units basis. For the beginning inventory, the equivalent units represent the work done to *complete* the units; for the ending inventory, the equivalent units represent the work done to bring the units to a stage of partial completion at the end of the period (the same as with the weighted-average method):

The formula for computing the equivalent units of production under the FIFO method is more complex than under the weighted-average method:

FIFO Method
(a separate calculation is made for each cost category in each processing department)

Equivalent units of production = Equivalent units to complete beginning inventory*
+ Units started and completed during the period
+ Equivalent units in ending work in process inventory

Exhibit 4A–1
Equivalent Units of Production: FIFO Method

	Materials	Conversion
Work in process, May 1:		
200 units × (100% − 50%)*	100	
200 units × (100% − 30%)*		140
Units started and completed in May	4,600†	4,600†
Work in process, May 31:		
400 units × 40%	160	
400 units × 25%		100
Equivalent units of production	4,860	4,840

*This is the work needed to complete the units in beginning inventory.

†4,800 units transferred out to the next department − 200 units in beginning inventory. The FIFO method assumes that the units in beginning inventory are finished first.

$$\text{*Equivalent units to complete beginning inventory} = \text{Units in beginning inventory} \times \left(100\% - \text{Percentage completion of beginning inventory}\right)$$

Or, the equivalent units of production can also be determined as follows:

Equivalent units of production = Units transferred out
+ Equivalent units in ending work in process inventory
− Equivalent units in beginning inventory

To illustrate the FIFO method, refer again to the data for the Shaping and Milling Department at Double Diamond Skis. The department completed and transferred 4,800 units to the next department, the Graphics Application Department, during May. Since 200 of these units came from the beginning inventory, the Shaping and Milling Department must have started and completed 4,600 units during May. The 200 units in the beginning inventory were 50% complete with respect to materials and only 30% complete with respect to conversion costs when the month started. Thus, to complete these units the department must have added another 50% of materials costs and another 70% of conversion costs (100% − 30% = 70%). Following this line of reasoning, the equivalent units for the department for May would be computed as shown in Exhibit 4A–1.

Comparison of Equivalent Units of Production under the Weighted-Average and FIFO Methods

Stop at this point and compare the data in Exhibit 4A–1 with the data in Exhibit 4–6 in the chapter, which shows the computation of equivalent units under the weighted-average method. Also refer to Exhibit 4A–2, which provides a visual comparison of the two methods.

The essential difference between the two methods is that the weighted-average method blends work and costs from the prior period with work and costs in the current period, whereas the FIFO method cleanly separates the two periods. To see this more clearly, consider the following comparison of the two calculations of equivalent units:

Exhibit 4A–2 Visual Perspective of Equivalent Units of Production

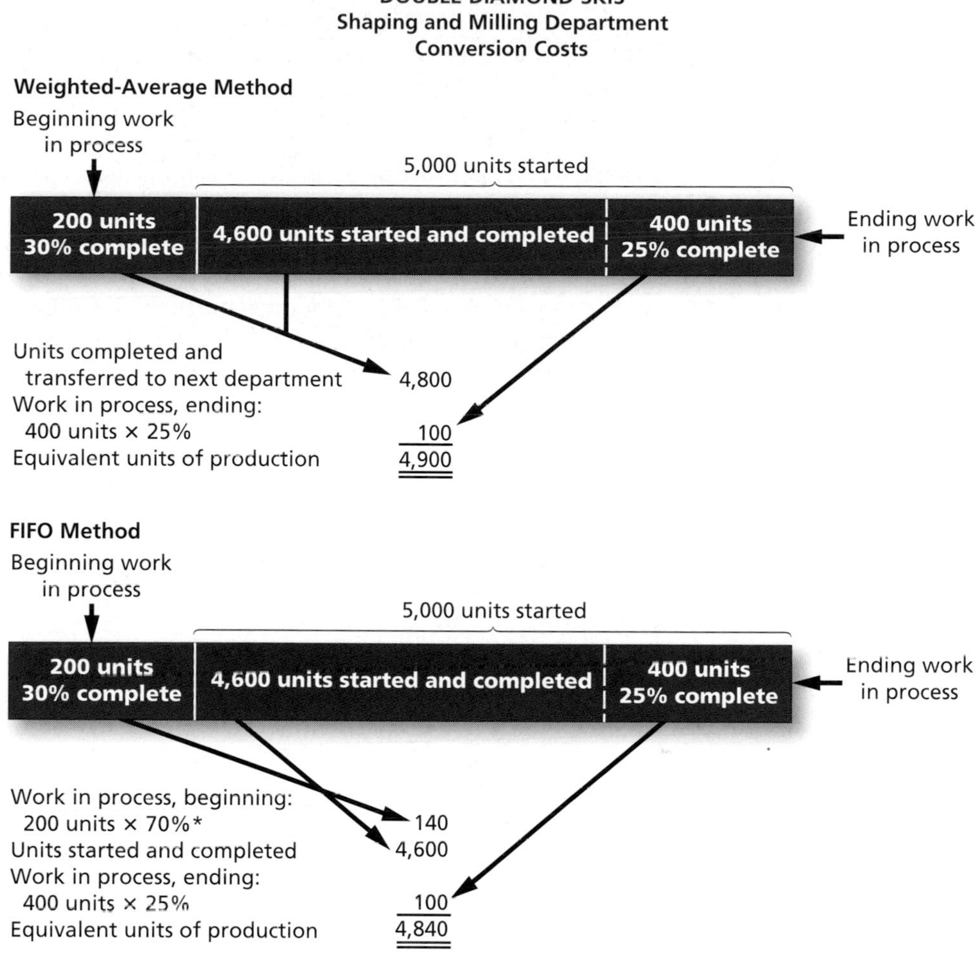

	Materials	Conversion
Equivalent units—weighted-average method	4,960	4,900
Less equivalent units in beginning inventory:		
200 units × 50%	100	
200 units × 30%		60
Equivalent units of production—FIFO method	4,860	4,840

From the above, it is evident that the FIFO method removes the equivalent units that were already in beginning inventory from the equivalent units as defined using the weighted-average method. Thus, the FIFO method isolates the equivalent units due to work performed during the current period. The weighted-average method blends together the equivalent units already in beginning inventory with the equivalent units due to work performed in the current period.

Production Report—FIFO Method

The steps followed in preparing a production report under the FIFO method are the same as those discussed earlier for the weighted-average method. However, since the FIFO method makes a distinction between units in the beginning inventory and units started during the year, the cost reconciliation portion of the report is more complex under the FIFO method than it is under the weighted-average method. To illustrate the FIFO method, we will again use the data for Double Diamond Skis on page 158.

objective 7

Prepare a quantity schedule for a period by the FIFO method.

STEP 1: PREPARE A QUANTITY SCHEDULE AND COMPUTE THE EQUIVALENT UNITS There is only one difference between a quantity schedule prepared under the FIFO method and one prepared under the weighted-average method. This difference relates to units transferred out. As explained earlier in our discussion of equivalent units, the FIFO method divides units transferred out into two parts. One part consists of the units in the beginning inventory, and the other part consists of the units started and completed during the current period. A quantity schedule showing this format for units transferred out is presented in Exhibit 4A–3, along with a computation of equivalent units for the month.

We explained earlier that in computing equivalent units under the FIFO method, we must first show the amount of work required *to complete* the units in the beginning inventory. We then show the number of units started and completed during the period, and finally we show the amount of work *completed* on the units still in process at the end of the period. Carefully trace through these computations in Exhibit 4A–3.

objective 8

Compute the costs per equivalent unit for a period by the FIFO method.

STEP 2: COMPUTE THE COSTS PER EQUIVALENT UNIT In computing unit costs under the FIFO method, we use only those costs that were incurred during the current period, and we ignore any costs in the beginning work in process inventory. Under the FIFO method, *unit costs relate only to work done during the current period.*

The costs per equivalent unit (EU) computed in Exhibit 4A–3 are used to cost units of product transferred to the next department; in addition, they are used to show the cost attached to partially completed units in the ending work in process inventory.

objective 9

Prepare a cost reconciliation report for a period by the FIFO method.

STEP 3: PREPARE A COST RECONCILIATION The purpose of cost reconciliation is to show how the costs charged to a department during a period are accounted for. With the FIFO method, two cost elements are associated with the units in the beginning work in process inventory. The first element is the cost carried over from the prior period. The second element is the cost needed *to complete* these units. For the Shaping and Milling Department, $4,000 in cost was carried over from last month. In the cost reconciliation in Exhibit 4A–3, we add to this figure the $1,523 in materials cost and $2,025 in conversion cost needed to complete these units. Note from the exhibit that these materials and conversion cost figures are computed by multiplying the costs per equivalent unit for materials and conversion times the equivalent units of work needed *to complete* the items that were in the beginning inventory. (The equivalent units figures used in this computation are brought down from the "Equivalent units" portion of the production report.)

For units started and completed during the month, we simply multiply the number of units started and completed by the total cost per unit to determine the amount transferred out. This would be $136,570 (4,600 units × $29.689 = $136,570) for the department.

Finally, the amount of cost attached to the ending work in process inventory is computed by multiplying the cost per equivalent unit figures for the month times the equivalent units for materials and conversion costs in the ending inventory. Once again, the equivalent units needed for this computation are brought down from the "Equivalent units" portion of the production report.

Exhibit 4A–4 summarizes the major similarities and differences between production reports prepared under the weighted-average and FIFO methods.

Exhibit 4A–3
Production Report—FIFO Method

DOUBLE DIAMOND SKIS
Shaping and Milling Department Production Report
(FIFO method)

Quantity Schedule and Equivalent Units

	Quantity Schedule	Equivalent Units (EU) Materials	Conversion
Units to be accounted for:			
Work in process, May 1 (50% materials; 30% conversion added last month) . .	200		
Started into production	5,000		
Total units	5,200		
Units accounted for as follows:			
Transferred to next department:			
From the beginning inventory*	200	100	140
Started and completed this month† . . .	4,600	4,600	4,600
Work in process, May 31 (40% materials; 25% conversion added this month)‡ . . .	400	160	100
Total units and equivalent units of production	5,200	4,860	4,840

Costs per Equivalent Unit

	Total Cost	Materials		Conversion		Whole Unit
Cost to be accounted for:						
Work in process, May 1	$ 4,000					
Cost added in the department (a)	144,000	$74,000		$70,000		
Total cost	$148,000					
Equivalent units of production (above) (b)		4,860		4,840		
Costs per EU, (a) ÷ (b)		$15.226	+	$14.463	=	$29.689

Cost Reconciliation

	Total Cost	Equivalent Units (above) Materials	Conversion
Cost accounted for as follows:			
Transferred to next department:			
From the beginning inventory:			
Cost in the beginning inventory	**$ 4,000**		
Cost to complete these units:			
Materials, at $15.226 per EU	**1,523**	100*	
Conversion, at $14.463 per EU	**2,025**		140*
Total cost	7,548		
Units started and completed this month, at $29.689 per unit	**136,570**	4,600†	4,600†
Total cost transferred	144,118		
Work in process, May 31:			
Materials, at $15.226 per EU	2,436	160‡	
Conversion, at $14.463 per EU	1,446		100‡
Total work in process, May 31 . . .	3,882		
Total cost	$148,000		

*Materials: 200 × (100% − 50%) = 100 equivalent units. Conversion: 200 × (100% − 30%) = 140 equivalent units.

†5,000 units started − 400 units in ending inventory = 4,600 units started and completed.

‡Materials: 400 × (40%) = 160 equivalent units. Conversion: 400 × (25%) = 100 equivalent units.

EU = Equivalent units.

Exhibit 4A–4 A Comparison of Production Report Content

Weighted-Average Method	FIFO Method
Quantity Schedule and Equivalent Units	
1. The quantity schedule includes all units transferred out in a single figure.	1. The quantity schedule divides the units transferred out into two parts. One part consists of units in the beginning inventory, and the other part consists of units started and completed during the current period.
2. In computing equivalent units, the units in the beginning inventory are treated as if they were started and completed during the current period.	2. Only work needed to *complete* units in the beginning inventory is included in the computation of equivalent units. Units started and completed during the current period are shown as a separate figure.
Total and Unit Costs	
1. The "Cost to be accounted for" part of the report is the same for both methods.	1. The "Cost to be accounted for" part of the report is the same for both methods.
2. Costs in the beginning inventory are added in with costs of the current period in computations of costs per equivalent unit.	2. Only costs of the current period are included in computations of costs per equivalent unit.
Cost Reconciliation	
1. All units transferred out are treated the same, regardless of whether they were part of the beginning inventory or started and completed during the period.	1. Units transferred out are divided into two groups: (a) units in the beginning inventory, and (b) units started and completed during the period.
2. Units in the ending inventory have cost applied to them in the same way under both methods.	2. Units in the ending inventory have cost applied to them in the same way under both methods.

A Comparison of Costing Methods

In most situations, the weighted-average and FIFO methods will produce very similar unit costs. If there never are any ending inventories, as in an ideal JIT environment, the two methods will produce identical results. The reason for this is that without any ending inventories, no costs can be carried forward into the next period and the weighted-average method will base the unit costs on just the current period's costs—just as in the FIFO method. If there *are* ending inventories, either erratic input prices or erratic production levels would also be required to generate much of a difference in unit costs under the two methods. This is because the weighted-average method will blend the unit costs from the prior period with the unit costs of the current period. Unless these unit costs differ greatly, the blending will not make much difference.

Nevertheless, from the standpoint of cost control, the FIFO method is superior to the weighted-average method. Current performance should be measured in relation to costs of the current period only, and the weighted-average method mixes costs of the current period with costs of the prior period. Thus, under the weighted-average method, the manager's apparent performance is influenced by what happened in the prior period. This problem does not arise under the FIFO method, since it makes a clear distinction between costs of prior periods and costs incurred during the current period. For the same reason, the FIFO method also provides more up-to-date cost data for decision-making purposes.

Some managers prefer the weighted-average method because they feel that the weighted-average method is simpler to apply than the FIFO method. Although this was true in the past when much accounting work was done by hand, computers can handle the additional calculations with ease once they have been appropriately programmed.

Questions

4–1 Under what conditions would it be appropriate to use a process costing system?

4–2 What similarities exist between job-order and process costing?

4–3 Costs are accumulated by job in a job-order costing system; how are costs accumulated in a process costing system?

4–4 What two essential features characterize any processing department in a process costing system?

4–5 Distinguish between departments arranged in a sequential pattern and departments arranged in a parallel pattern.

4–6 Why is cost accumulation easier under a process costing system than it is under a job-order costing system?

4–7 How many Work in Process accounts are maintained in a company using process costing?

4–8 Assume that a company has two processing departments, Mixing and Firing. Prepare a journal entry to show a transfer of partially completed units from the Mixing Department to the Firing Department.

4–9 Assume again that a company has two processing departments, Mixing and Firing. Explain what costs might be added to the Firing Department's Work in Process account during a period.

4–10 What is meant by the term *equivalent units of production* when the weighted-average method is used?

4–11 What is a quantity schedule, and what purpose does it serve?

4–12 Under process costing, it is often suggested that a product is like a rolling snowball as it moves from department to department. Why is this an apt comparison?

4–13 Watkins Trophies, Inc., produces thousands of medallions made of bronze, silver, and gold. The medallions are identical except for the materials used in their manufacture. What costing system would you advise the company to use?

4–14 Give examples of companies that might use operation costing.

4–15 (Appendix 4A) How does the computation of equivalent units under the FIFO method differ from the computation of equivalent units under the weighted-average method?

4–16 (Appendix 4A) On the cost reconciliation part of the production report, the weighted-average method treats all units transferred out in the same way. How does this differ from the FIFO method of handling units transferred out?

4–17 (Appendix 4A) From the standpoint of cost control, why is the FIFO method superior to the weighted-average method?

Exercises

E4–1 Chocolaterie de Geneve, SA, is located in a French-speaking canton in Switzerland. The company makes chocolate truffles that are sold in popular embossed tins. The company has two processing departments—Cooking and Molding. In the Cooking Department, the raw ingredients for the truffles are mixed and then cooked in special candy-making vats. In the Molding Department, the melted chocolate and other ingredients from the Cooking

Department are carefully poured into molds and decorative flourishes are applied by hand. After cooling, the truffles are packed for sale. The company uses a process costing system. The T-accounts below show the flow of costs through the two departments in April (all amounts are in Swiss francs):

Work in Process—Cooking

Bal. 4/1	8,000	Transferred out	160,000
Direct materials	42,000		
Direct labor	50,000		
Overhead	75,000		

Work in Process—Molding

Bal. 4/1	4,000	Transferred out	240,000
Transferred in	160,000		
Direct labor	36,000		
Overhead	45,000		

Required Prepare journal entries showing the flow of costs through the two processing departments during April.

E4–2 Clonex Labs, Inc., uses a process costing system. The following data are available for one department for October:

		Percent Completed	
	Units	Materials	Conversion
Work in process, October 1	30,000	65%	30%
Work in process, October 31	15,000	80%	40%

The department started 175,000 units into production during the month and transferred 190,000 completed units to the next department.

Required Compute the equivalent units of production for October assuming that the company uses the weighted-average method of accounting for units and costs.

E4–3 (Appendix 4A) Refer to the data for Clonex Labs, Inc., in E4–2.

Required Compute the equivalent units of production for October assuming that the company uses the FIFO method of accounting for units and costs.

E4–4 The Alaskan Fisheries, Inc., processes salmon for various distributors. Two departments are involved—Department 1 and Department 2. Data relating to pounds of salmon processed in Department 1 during July are presented below:

	Pounds of Salmon	Percent Completed*
Work in process, July 1	20,000	30%
Started into processing during July	380,000	—
Work in process, July 31	25,000	60%

*Labor and overhead only.

All materials are added at the beginning of processing in Department 1. Labor and overhead (conversion) costs are incurred uniformly throughout processing.

Required Prepare a quantity schedule and a computation of equivalent units for July for Department 1 assuming that the company uses the weighted-average method of accounting for units.

E4–5 (Appendix 4A) Refer to the data for The Alaskan Fisheries, Inc., in E4–4.

Required Prepare a quantity schedule and a computation of equivalent units for July for Department 1 assuming that the company uses the FIFO method of accounting for units.

E4–6 Hielta Oy, a Finnish company, processes wood pulp for various manufacturers of paper products. Data relating to tons of pulp processed during June are provided below:

		Percent Completed	
	Tons of Pulp	Materials	Labor and Overhead
Work in process, June 1	20,000	90%	80%
Work in process, June 30	30,000	60%	40%
Started into processing during June	190,000	—	—

Required
1. Compute the number of tons of pulp completed and transferred out during June.
2. Prepare a quantity schedule for June assuming that the company uses the weighted-average method.

E4–7 (Appendix 4A) Refer to the data for Hielta Oy in E4–6.

Required
1. Compute the number of tons of pulp completed and transferred out during June.
2. Prepare a quantity schedule for June assuming that the company uses the FIFO method.

E4–8 Pureform, Inc., manufactures a product that passes through two departments. Data for a recent month for the first department follow:

	Units	Materials	Labor	Overhead
Work in process, beginning	5,000	$ 4,500	$ 1,250	$ 1,875
Units started in process	45,000			
Units transferred out	42,000			
Work in process, ending	8,000			
Cost added during the month	—	52,800	21,500	32,250

The beginning work in process inventory was 80% complete as to materials and 60% complete as to processing. The ending work in process inventory was 75% complete as to materials and 50% complete as to processing.

Required
1. Assume that the company uses the weighted-average method of accounting for units and costs. Prepare a quantity schedule and a computation of equivalent units for the month.
2. Determine the costs per equivalent unit for the month.

E4–9 (Appendix 4A) Refer to the data for Pureform, Inc., in E4–8.

Required
1. Assume that the company uses the FIFO method of accounting for units and costs. Prepare a quantity schedule and a computation of equivalent units for the month.
2. Determine the costs per equivalent unit for the month.

E4–10 Helox, Inc., manufactures a product that passes through two production processes. A quantity schedule for a recent month for the first process follows:

	Quantity Schedule		
Units to be accounted for:			
Work in process, May 1 (all materials, 40% conversion cost added last month)	5,000		
Started into production	180,000		
Total units	185,000		
		Equivalent Units	
		Materials	**Conversion**
Units accounted for as follows:			
Transferred to the next process	175,000	?	?
Work in process, May 31 (all materials, 30% conversion cost added this month)	10,000	?	?
Total units	185,000	?	?

Costs in the beginning work in process inventory of the first processing department were: materials, $1,200; and conversion cost, $3,800. Costs added during the month were: materials, $54,000; and conversion cost, $352,000.

Required

1. Assume that the company uses the weighted-average method of accounting for units and costs. Determine the equivalent units for the month for the first process.
2. Compute the costs per equivalent unit for the month for the first process.

E4–11 (This exercise should be assigned only if E4–10 is also assigned.) Refer to the data for Helox, Inc., in E4–10 and to the equivalent units and costs per equivalent unit you have computed there.

Required Complete the following cost reconciliation for the first process:

Cost Reconciliation

	Total Cost	Equivalent Units	
		Materials	**Conversion**
Cost accounted for as follows:			
Transferred to the next process: (? units × $?)	$?		
Work in process, May 31:			
Materials, at _____ per EU	?	?	
Conversion, at _____ per EU	?		?
Total work in process	?		
Total cost	$?		

E4–12 (Appendix 4A) Refer to the data for Helox, Inc., in E4–10. Assume that the company uses the FIFO cost method.

Required

1. Prepare a quantity schedule and a computation of equivalent units for the month for the first process.
2. Compute the costs per equivalent unit for the month for the first process.

E4–13 (Appendix 4A) (This exercise should be assigned only if E4–12 is also assigned.) Refer to the data for Helox, Inc., in E4–10 and to the equivalent units and costs per equivalent unit that you computed in E4–12.

Required Complete the following cost reconciliation for the first process:

Cost Reconciliation

	Total Cost	Equivalent Units	
		Materials	Conversion
Cost accounted for as follows:			
Transferred to the next process:			
From the beginning inventory:			
Cost in the beginning inventory	$?		
Cost to complete these units:			
Materials, at ______ per EU	?	?	
Conversion, at ______ per EU	?		?
Total cost	?		
Units started and completed this month: ______ units × ______ each	?	?	?
Total cost transferred	?		
Work in process, May 31:			
Materials, at ______ per EU	?	?	
Conversion, at ______ per EU	?		?
Total work in process	?		
Total cost	$?		

Problems

P4–14 Weighted-Average Method; Step-by-Step Production Report

Builder Products, Inc., manufactures a caulking compound that goes through three processing stages prior to completion. Information on work in the first department, Cooking, is given below for May:

Production data:	
Units in process, May 1; 100% complete as to materials and 80% complete as to labor and overhead	10,000
Units started into production during May	100,000
Units completed and transferred out	95,000
Units in process, May 31; 60% complete as to materials and 20% complete as to labor and overhead	?
Cost data:	
Work in process inventory, May 1:	
Materials cost	$ 1,500
Labor cost	1,800
Overhead cost	5,400
Cost added during May:	
Materials cost	154,500
Labor cost	22,700
Overhead cost	68,100

Materials are added at several stages during the cooking process, whereas labor and overhead costs are incurred uniformly. The company uses the weighted-average method.

Required Prepare a production report for the Cooking Department for May. Use the following three steps in preparing your report:

1. Prepare a quantity schedule and a computation of equivalent units.
2. Compute the costs per equivalent unit for the month.
3. Using the data from (1) and (2) above, prepare a cost reconciliation.

P4–15 **Weighted-Average Method; Partial Production Report** Martin Company manufactures a single product. The company uses the weighted-average method in its process costing system. Activity for June has just been completed. An incomplete production report for the first processing department follows:

Quantity Schedule and Equivalent Units

	Quantity Schedule			
Units to be accounted for:				
Work in process, June 1 (all materials, 75% labor and overhead added last month)	8,000			
Started into production	45,000			
Total units	53,000			
		Equivalent Units (EU)		
		Materials	Labor	Overhead
Units accounted for as follows:				
Transferred to the next department	48,000	?	?	?
Work in process, June 30 (all materials, 40% labor and overhead added this month)	5,000	?	?	?
Total units	53,000	?	?	?

Costs per Equivalent Unit

	Total Cost	Materials	Labor	Overhead	Whole Unit
Cost to be accounted for:					
Work in process, June 1	$ 7,130	$ 5,150	$ 660	$ 1,320	
Cost added by the department	58,820	29,300	9,840	19,680	
Total cost (a)	$65,950	$34,450	$10,500	$21,000	
Equivalent units (b)	—	53,000	50,000	50,000	
Cost per EU, (a) ÷ (b)	—	$0.65 +	$0.21 +	$0.42 =	$1.28

Cost Reconciliation

	Total Cost
Cost accounted for as follows:	
?	?

Required

1. Prepare a schedule showing how the equivalent units were computed for the first processing department.
2. Complete the "Cost Reconciliation" part of the production report for the first processing department.

P4–16 **FIFO Method; Step-by-Step Production Report** (Appendix 4A) Selzik Company makes super-premium cake mixes that go through two processes, blending and packaging. The following activity was recorded in the Blending Department during July:

Production data:		
Units in process, July 1; 30% complete as to conversion costs		10,000
Units started into production		170,000
Units completed and transferred to Packaging		?
Units in process, July 31; 40% complete as to conversion costs		20,000
Cost data:		
Work in process inventory, July 1:		
Materials cost	$ 8,500	
Conversion cost	4,900	$ 13,400
Cost added during the month:		
Materials cost	139,400	
Conversion cost	244,200	383,600
Total cost		$397,000

All materials are added at the beginning of work in the Blending Department. Conversion costs are added uniformly during processing. The company uses the FIFO cost method.

Required Prepare a production report for the Blending Department for July. Use the following three steps as a guide in preparing your report:

1. Prepare a quantity schedule and compute the equivalent units.
2. Compute the costs per equivalent unit for the month.
3. Using the data from (1) and (2) above, prepare a cost reconciliation.

P4–17 Weighted-Average Method; Basic Production Report Sunspot Beverages, Ltd., of Fiji makes blended tropical fruit drinks in two stages. Fruit juices are extracted from fresh fruits and then blended in the Blending Department. The blended juices are then bottled and packed for shipping in the Bottling Department. The following information pertains to the operations of the Blending Department for June. (The currency in Fiji is the Fijian dollar.)

		Percent Completed	
	Units	Materials	Conversion
Work in process, beginning	20,000	100%	75%
Started into production	180,000		
Completed and transferred out	160,000		
Work in process, ending	40,000	100%	25%

Cost in the beginning work in process inventory and cost added during June were as follows for the Blending Department:

	Materials	Conversion
Work in process, beginning	$ 25,200	$ 24,800
Cost added during June	334,800	238,700

Required Prepare a production report for the Blending Department for June assuming that the company uses the weighted-average method.

P4–18 FIFO Method; Basic Production Report (Appendix 4A) Refer to the data for the Blending Department of Sunspot Beverages, Ltd., in P4–17. Assume that the company uses the FIFO method to compute unit costs rather than the weighted-average method.

Required Prepare a production report for the Blending Department for June.

P4–19 Weighted-Average Method; Interpreting a Production Report Cooperative San José of southern Sonora state in Mexico makes a unique syrup using cane sugar and local herbs. The syrup is sold in small bottles and is prized as a flavoring for drinks and for use in desserts. The bottles are sold for $12 each. (The Mexican currency is the peso and is denoted by $.) The first stage in the production process is carried out in the Mixing Department, which removes foreign matter from the raw materials and mixes them in the proper proportions in large vats. The company uses the weighted-average method in its process costing system.

A hastily prepared report for the Mixing Department for April appears below:

Quantity Schedule	
Units to be accounted for:	
Work in process, April 1 (90% materials, 80% conversion cost added last month)	30,000
Started into production	200,000
Total units	230,000
Units accounted for as follows:	
Transferred to the next department	190,000
Work in process, April 30 (75% materials, 60% conversion cost added this month	40,000
Total units	230,000
Total Cost	
Cost to be accounted for:	
Work in process, April 1	$ 98,000
Cost added during the month	827,000
Total cost	$925,000
Cost Reconciliation	
Cost accounted for as follows:	
Transferred to the next department	$805,600
Work in process, April 30	119,400
Total cost	$925,000

Cooperative San José has just been acquired by another company, and the management of the acquiring company wants some additional information about Cooperative San José's operations.

Required

1. What were the equivalent units for the month?
2. What were the costs per equivalent unit for the month? The beginning inventory consisted of the following costs: materials, $67,800; and conversion cost, $30,200. The costs added during the month consisted of: materials, $579,000; and conversion cost, $248,000.
3. How many of the units transferred to the next department were started and completed during the month?
4. The manager of the Mixing Department, anxious to make a good impression on the new owners, stated, "Materials prices jumped from about $2.50 per unit in March to $3 per unit in April, but due to good cost control I was able to hold our materials cost to less than $3 per unit for the month." Should this manager be rewarded for good cost control? Explain.

P4–20 FIFO Method; Analysis of Work in Process T-Account (Appendix 4A) Superior Brands, Inc., manufactures paint. The paint goes through three processes—cracking, mixing, and cooking. Activity in the Cracking Department during a recent month is summarized in the department's Work in Process account below:

Work in Process—Cracking Department

Inventory, April 1 (10,000 gals., 80% processed)	39,000	Completed and transferred to mixing (? gals.)	?
April costs added:			
Materials (140,000 gals.)	259,000		
Labor and overhead	312,000		
Inventory, April 30 (30,000 gals., 60% processed)	?		

The materials are entered into production at the beginning of work in the Cracking Department. Labor and overhead costs are incurred uniformly throughout the cracking process. The company uses the FIFO cost method.

Required Prepare a production report for the Cracking Department for the month.

P4–21 Weighted-Average Method; Analysis of Work in Process T-Account Weston Products manufactures an industrial cleaning compound that goes through three processing departments—Grinding, Mixing, and Cooking. All raw materials are introduced at the start of work in the Grinding Department, with conversion costs being incurred evenly throughout the grinding process. The Work in Process T-account for the Grinding Department for a recent month is given below:

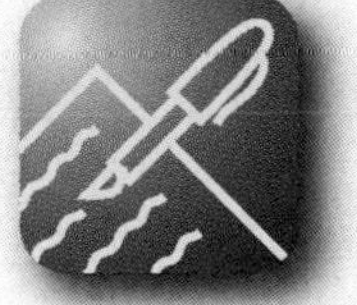

Work in Process—Grinding Department

Inventory, May 1 (18,000 lbs., 1/3 processed)	21,800	Completed and transferred to mixing (? lbs.)	?
May costs added:			
Raw materials (167,000 lbs.)	133,400		
Labor and overhead	226,800		
Inventory, May 31 (15,000 lbs., 2/3 processed)	?		

The May 1 work in process inventory consists of $14,600 in materials cost and $7,200 in labor and overhead cost. The company uses the weighted-average method to account for units and costs.

Required

1. Prepare a production report for the Grinding Department for the month.
2. What criticism can be made of the unit costs that you have computed on your production report?

P4–22 Weighted-Average Method; Journal Entries; T-Accounts; Production Report Hilox, Inc., produces an antacid product that goes through two departments—Cooking and Bottling. The company has recently hired a new assistant accountant, who has prepared the following summary of production and costs for the Cooking Department for May using the weighted-average method.

Cooking Department costs:	
Work in process inventory, May 1: 70,000 quarts, 60% complete as to materials and 30% complete as to labor and overhead	$ 61,000*
Materials added during May	570,000
Labor added during May	100,000
Overhead applied during May	235,000
Total departmental costs	$966,000

Cooking Department costs assigned to:	
Quarts completed and transferred to the Bottling Department: 400,000 quarts at _?_ per quart	$?
Work in process inventory, May 31: 50,000 quarts, 70% complete as to materials and 40% complete as to labor and overhead	?
Total departmental costs assigned	$?

*Consists of materials, $39,000; labor, $5,000; and overhead, $17,000.

The new assistant accountant has determined the cost per quart transferred to be $2.415, as follows:

$$\frac{\text{Total departmental costs, \$966,000}}{\text{Quarts completed and transferred, 400,000}} = \$2.415$$

However, the assistant accountant is unsure how to use this unit cost figure in assigning cost to the ending work in process inventory. In addition, the company's general ledger shows only $900,000 in cost transferred from the Cooking Department to the Bottling Department, which does not agree with the $966,000 figure above.

The general ledger also shows the following costs incurred in the Bottling Department during May: materials used, $130,000; direct labor cost incurred, $80,000; and overhead cost applied to products, $158,000.

Required

1. Prepare journal entries as follows to record activity in the company during May. Key your entries to the letters (a) through (g) below.
   a. Raw materials were issued to the two departments for use in production.
   b. Direct labor costs were incurred in the two departments.
   c. Manufacturing overhead costs were incurred, $400,000. (Credit Accounts Payable.) The company maintains a single Manufacturing Overhead account for the entire plant.
   d. Manufacturing overhead cost was applied to production in each department using predetermined overhead rates.
   e. Units completed as to processing in the Cooking Department were transferred to the Bottling Department, $900,000.
   f. Units completed as to processing in the Bottling Department were transferred to Finished Goods, $1,300,000.
   g. Units were sold on account, $2,000,000. The Cost of Good Sold was $1,250,000.
2. Post the journal entries from (1) above to T-accounts. Balances in selected accounts on May 1 are given below:

Raw Materials	$710,000
Work in Process—Bottling Department	85,000
Finished Goods	45,000

   After posting the entries to the T-accounts, find the ending balance in the inventory accounts and the Manufacturing Overhead accounts.
3. Prepare a production report for the Cooking Department for May.

P4–23 Weighted-Average Method; Equivalent Units; Costing of Inventories You are employed by Spirit Company, a manufacturer of digital watches. The company's chief financial officer is trying to verify the accuracy of the ending work in process and finished goods inventories prior to closing the books for the year. You have been asked to assist in this verification. The year-end balances shown on Spirit Company's books are as follows:

	Units	Costs
Work in process, December 31 (50% complete as to labor and overhead)	300,000	$ 660,960
Finished goods, December 31	200,000	1,009,800

Materials are added to production at the beginning of the manufacturing process, and overhead is applied to each product at the rate of 60% of direct labor cost. There was no finished goods inventory at the beginning of the year. A review of Spirit Company's inventory and cost records has disclosed the following data, all of which are accurate:

	Units	Costs: Materials	Costs: Labor
Work in process, January 1 (80% complete as to labor and overhead)	200,000	$ 200,000	$ 315,000
Units started into production	1,000,000		
Cost added during the year:			
Materials cost		1,300,000	
Labor cost			1,995,000
Units completed during the year	900,000		

The company uses the weighted-average cost method.

Required

1. Determine the equivalent units and costs per equivalent unit for materials, labor, and overhead for the year.
2. Determine the amount of cost that should be assigned to the ending work in process and finished goods inventories.
3. Prepare the necessary correcting journal entry to adjust the work in process and finished goods inventories to the correct balances as of December 31.
4. Determine the cost of goods sold for the year assuming there is no under- or overapplied overhead.

(CPA, adapted)

P4–24 Weighted-Average Method; Journal Entries; T-Accounts; Production Report Lubricants, Inc., produces a special kind of grease that is widely used by race car drivers. The grease is produced in two processes: refining and blending.

Raw oil products are introduced at various points in the Refining Department; labor and overhead costs are incurred evenly throughout the refining operation. The refined output is then transferred to the Blending Department.

The following incomplete Work in Process account is available for the Refining Department for March:

Work in Process—Refining Department

Debit		Credit	
March 1 inventory (20,000 gal.; 100% complete as to materials; 90% complete as to labor and overhead)	38,000	Completed and transferred to blending (? gal.)	?
March costs added:			
Raw oil materials (390,000 gal.)	495,000		
Direct labor	72,000		
Overhead	181,000		
March 31 inventory (40,000 gal.; 75% complete as to materials; 25% complete as to labor and overhead)	?		

The March 1 work in process inventory in the Refining Department consists of the following cost elements: raw materials, $25,000; direct labor, $4,000; and overhead, $9,000.

Costs incurred during March in the Blending Department were: materials used, $115,000; direct labor, $18,000; and overhead cost applied to production, $42,000. The company accounts for units and costs by the weighted-average method.

Required

1. Prepare journal entries to record the costs incurred in both the Refining Department and Blending Department during March. Key your entries to the items (a) through (g) below.
   a. Raw materials were issued for use in production.
   b. Direct labor costs were incurred.
   c. Manufacturing overhead costs for the entire factory were incurred, $225,000. (Credit Accounts Payable.)
   d. Manufacturing overhead cost was applied to production using a predetermined overhead rate.
   e. Units that were complete as to processing in the Refining Department were transferred to the Blending Department, $740,000.
   f. Units that were complete as to processing in the Blending Department were transferred to Finished Goods, $950,000.
   g. Completed units were sold on account, $1,500,000. The Cost of Goods Sold was $900,000.
2. Post the journal entries from (1) above to T-accounts. The following account balances existed at the beginning of March. (The beginning balance in the Refining Department's Work in Process account is given above.)

Raw Materials	$618,000
Work in Process—Blending Department	65,000
Finished Goods	20,000

   After posting the entries to the T-accounts, find the ending balance in the inventory accounts and the manufacturing overhead accounts.
3. Prepare a production report for the Refining Department for March.

Cases

C4–25 Ethics and the Manager Gary Stevens and Mary James are production managers in the Consumer Electronics Division of General Electronics Company, which has several dozen plants scattered in locations throughout the world. Mary manages the plant located in Des Moines, Iowa, while Gary manages the plant in El Segundo, California. Production managers are paid a salary and get an additional bonus equal to 5% of their base salary if the entire division meets or exceeds its target profits for the year. The bonus is determined in March after the company's annual report has been prepared and issued to stockholders.

Shortly after the beginning of the new year, Mary received a phone call from Gary that went like this:

Gary: How's it going, Mary?
Mary: Fine, Gary. How's it going with you?
Gary: Great! I just got the preliminary profit figures for the division for last year and we are within $200,000 of making the year's target profits. All we have to do is to pull a few strings, and we'll be over the top!
Mary: What do you mean?
Gary: Well, one thing that would be easy to change is your estimate of the percentage completion of your ending work in process inventories.
Mary: I don't know if I can do that, Gary. Those percentage completion figures are supplied by Tom Winthrop, my lead supervisor, who I have always trusted to provide us with good estimates. Besides, I have already sent the percentage completion figures to the corporate headquarters.
Gary: You can always tell them there was a mistake. Think about it, Mary. All of us managers are doing as much as we can to pull this bonus out of the hat. You may not want the bonus check, but the rest of us sure could use it.

The final processing department in Mary's production facility began the year with no work in process inventories. During the year, 210,000 units were transferred in from the prior processing department and 200,000 units were completed and sold. Costs transferred in from the prior department totaled $39,375,000. No materials are added in the final processing department. A total of $20,807,500 of conversion cost was incurred in the final processing department during the year.

Required

1. Tom Winthrop estimated that the units in ending inventory in the final processing department were 30% complete with respect to the conversion costs of the final processing department. If this estimate of the percentage completion is used, what would be the Cost of Goods Sold for the year?
2. Does Gary Stevens want the estimated percentage completion to be increased or decreased? Explain why.
3. What percentage completion would result in increasing reported net income by $200,000 over the net income that would be reported if the 30% figure were used?
4. Do you think Mary James should go along with the request to alter estimates of the percentage completion?

C4–26 Weighted-Average Method; Production Report: Second Department "I think we goofed when we hired that new assistant controller," said Ruth Scarpino, president of Provost Industries. "Just look at this production report that he prepared for last month for the Finishing Department. I can't make heads or tails out of it."

Finishing Department costs:	
Work in process inventory, April 1, 450 units; 100% complete as to materials; 60% complete as to conversion costs	$ 8,208*
Costs transferred in during the month from the preceding department, 1,950 units	17,940
Materials cost added during the month (materials are added when processing is 50% complete in the Finishing Department)	6,210
Conversion costs incurred during the month	13,920
Total departmental costs	$46,278
Finishing Department costs assigned to:	
Units completed and transferred to finished goods, 1,800 units at $25.71 per unit	$46,278
Work in process inventory, April 30, 600 units; 0% complete as to materials; 35% complete as to processing	–0–
Total departmental costs assigned	$46,278

*Consists of: cost transferred in, $4,068; materials cost, $1,980; and conversion cost, $2,160.

"He's struggling to learn our system," replied Frank Harrop, the operations manager. "The problem is that he's been away from process costing for a long time, and it's coming back slowly."

"It's not just the format of his report that I'm concerned about. Look at that $25.71 unit cost that he's come up with for April. Doesn't that seem high to you?" said Ms. Scarpino.

"Yes, it does seem high; but on the other hand, I know we had an increase in materials prices during April, and that may be the explanation," replied Mr. Harrop. "I'll get someone else to redo this report and then we may be able to see what's going on."

Provost Industries manufactures a ceramic product that goes through two processing departments—Molding and Finishing. The company uses the weighted-average method to account for units and costs.

Required

1. Prepare a revised production report for the Finishing Department.
2. Explain to the president why the unit cost on the new assistant controller's report is so high.

C4–27 FIFO Method; Production Report: Second Department (Appendix 4A) Refer to the data for Provost Industries in the preceding case. Assume that the company uses the FIFO method to account for units and costs.

Required

1. Prepare a production report for the Finishing Department for April.
2. As stated in the case, the company experienced an increase in materials prices during April. Would the effects of this price increase tend to show up more under the weighted-average method or under the FIFO method? Why?

Group Exercises

GE4–28 Operation Costing Operation costing combines characteristics of both job-order costing and process costing. It is used in those situations where the products have some common characteristics and also some individual characteristics. Examples of industries where operation costing may be appropriate include shoes, clothing, jewelry, and semiconductors.

Required Select one of the above products and research how the product is made. Construct a flowchart of the production process. Indicate which steps in the production process would use job-order costing and which steps would use process costing.

IE4–29 Choice of Costing System The web sites of a number of companies are listed below.

Required Indicate whether company would be more likely to use job-order costing or process costing. In each case explain why.

1. Stagecraft at www.stagecraft.com.
2. Biolea at www.biolea.gr.
3. Evian at www.evian.com.
4. Ircon International Limited at www.irconinternational.com.
5. Gulf Craft Inc. at www.gulfcraftinc.com.
6. Amrosi spa at www.ambrosi.it.

Chapter Five

Cost Behavior: Analysis and Use

Business Focus

Alicia was recently promoted to be the manager of Grant County Prenatal Care Clinic. Although Alicia enjoyed her work, she was frustrated by the fixed budget provided by the county. Alicia was positive that many more low-income expectant mothers could benefit from the clinic's services if a way could be found to provide additional financing.

After contacting a number of philanthropic foundations, Alicia found an interested donor. The donor expressed interest in funding some of the costs of new patients, but he did not want to pay any of the costs of existing patients whose costs were already covered by the county. Also, the donor stipulated that he would only be willing to pay the additional (i.e., variable) costs that the clinic would incur to serve new patients. He would not pay any additional fixed costs, which he also felt were the responsibility of the county. Alicia immediately agreed to this offer, but as soon as she left the donor's home, she began to wonder how she would determine the fixed and variable costs of the clinic.

Learning Objectives

After studying Chapter 5 you should be able to:

1 Explain the effect of a change in activity on both total variable costs and per unit variable costs.

2 Explain the effect of a change in activity on both total fixed costs and fixed costs expressed on a per unit basis.

3 Use a cost formula to predict costs at a new level of activity.

4 Analyze a mixed cost using the high-low method.

5 Analyze a mixed cost using the scattergraph method.

6 Explain the least-squares regression method of analyzing a mixed cost.

7 Prepare an income statement using the contribution format.

8 (Appendix 5A) Analyze a mixed cost using the least-squares regression method.

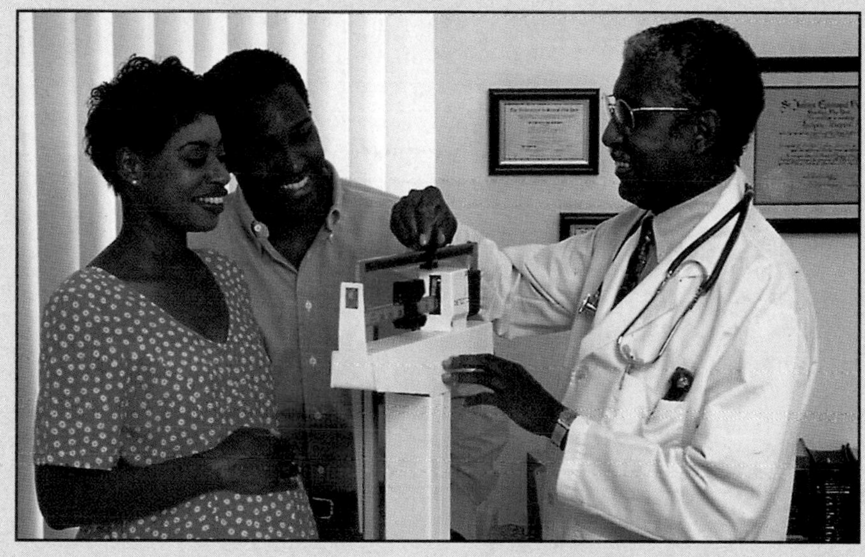

In our discussion of cost terms and concepts in Chapter 2, we stated that one way in which costs can be classified is by behavior. We defined cost behavior as meaning how a cost will react or change as changes take place in the level of business activity. An understanding of cost behavior is the key to many decisions in an organization. Managers who understand how costs behave are better able to predict what costs will be under various operating circumstances. Attempts at decision making without a thorough understanding of the costs involved—and how these costs may change with the activity level—can lead to disaster. For example, a decision to drop a particular product line might result in far less cost savings than managers had assumed—leading to a decline in profits. To avoid such problems, a manager must be able to accurately predict what costs will be at various activity levels. In this chapter, we shall find that the key to effective cost prediction lies in understanding cost behavior patterns.

We briefly review in this chapter the definitions of variable costs and fixed costs and then discuss the behavior of these costs in greater depth than we were able to do in Chapter 2. After this review and discussion, we turn our attention to the analysis of mixed costs. We conclude the chapter by introducing a new income statement format—called the contribution format—in which costs are organized by behavior rather than by the traditional functions of production, sales, and administration.

Types of Cost Behavior Patterns

In our brief discussion of cost behavior in Chapter 2, we mentioned only variable and fixed costs. There is a third behavior pattern, generally known as a *mixed* or *semivariable* cost. All three cost behavior patterns—variable, fixed, and mixed—are found in most organizations. The relative proportion of each type of cost present in a firm is known as the firm's **cost structure.** For example, a firm might have many fixed costs but few variable or mixed costs. Alternatively, it might have many variable costs but few fixed or mixed costs. A firm's cost structure can have a significant impact on decisions. We must reserve a detailed discussion of cost structure until the next chapter, however, and concentrate for the moment on gaining a fuller understanding of the behavior of each type of cost.

Variable Costs

objective 1
Explain the effect of a change in activity on both total variable costs and per unit variable costs.

We found in Chapter 2 that a variable cost is a cost whose total dollar amount varies in direct proportion to changes in the activity level. If the activity level doubles, the total dollar amount of the variable costs also doubles. If the activity level increases by only 10%, then the total dollar amount of the variable costs increases by 10% as well.

We also found in Chapter 2 that a variable cost remains constant if expressed on a *per unit* basis. To provide an example, consider Nooksack Expeditions, a small company that provides daylong whitewater rafting excursions on rivers in the North Cascade Mountains. The company provides all of the necessary equipment and experienced guides, and it serves gourmet meals to its guests. The meals are purchased from an exclusive caterer for $30 a person for a daylong excursion. If we look at the cost of the meals on a *per person* basis, the cost remains constant at $30. This $30 cost per person will not change, regardless of how many people participate in a daylong excursion. The behavior of this variable cost, on both a per unit and a total basis, is tabulated on the next page:

Number of Guests	Cost of Meals per Guest	Total Cost of Meals
250	$30	$ 7,500
500	30	15,000
750	30	22,500
1,000	30	30,000

The idea that a variable cost is constant per unit but varies in total with the activity level is crucial to an understanding of cost behavior patterns. We shall rely on this concept again and again in this chapter and in chapters ahead.

Exhibit 5–1 provides a graphic illustration of variable cost behavior. Note that the graph of the total cost of the meals slants upward to the right. This is because the total cost of the meals is directly proportional to the number of guests. In contrast, the graph of the per unit cost of meals is flat. This is because the cost of the meals per guest is constant at $30 per guest.

THE ACTIVITY BASE For a cost to be variable, it must be variable *with respect to something*. That "something" is its *activity base*. An **activity base** is a measure of whatever causes the incurrence of variable cost. In Chapter 3, we mentioned that an activity base is sometimes referred to as a *cost driver*. Some of the most common activity bases are direct labor-hours, machine-hours, units produced, and units sold. Other activity bases (cost drivers) might include the number of miles driven by salespersons, the number of pounds of laundry processed by a hotel, the number of letters typed by a secretary, and the number of occupied beds in a hospital.

To plan and control variable costs, a manager must be well acquainted with the various activity bases within the firm. People sometimes get the notion that if a cost doesn't vary with production or with sales, then it is not really a variable cost. This is not correct. As suggested by the range of bases listed above, costs are caused by many different activities within an organization. Whether a cost is considered to be variable depends on whether it is caused by the activity under consideration. For example, if a manager is analyzing the cost of service calls under a product warranty, the

Exhibit 5–1 Variable Cost Behavior

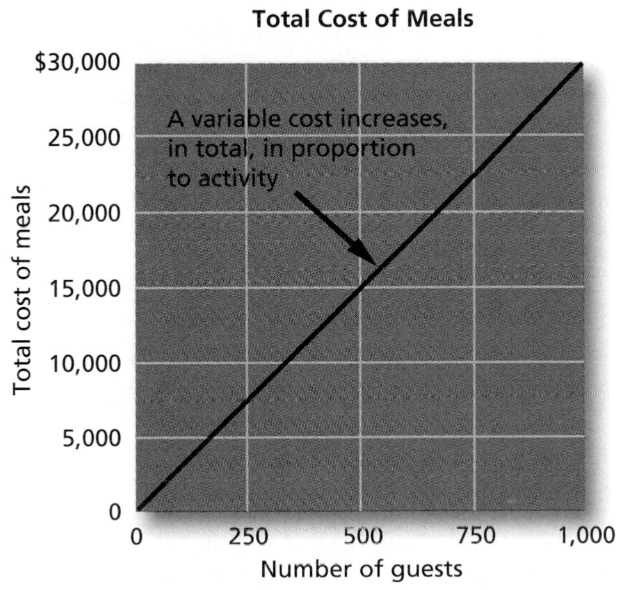

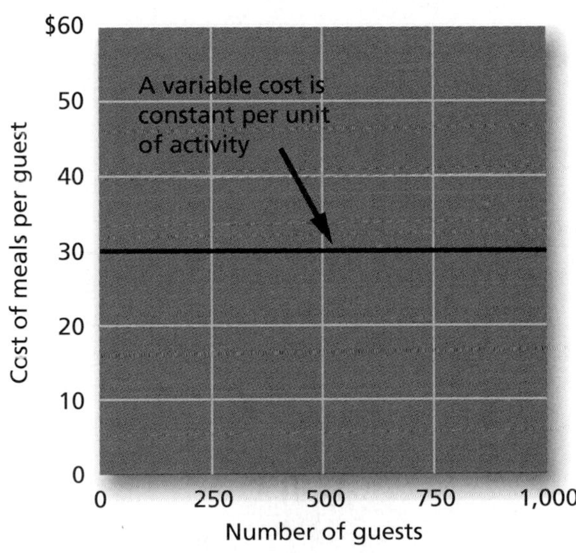

Exhibit 5–2 Examples of Variable Costs

Type of Organization	Costs that Are Normally Variable With Respect to Volume of Output
Merchandising company	Cost of goods (merchandise) sold
Manufacturing company	Manufacturing costs:
	Direct materials
	Direct labor*
	Variable portion of manufacturing overhead:
	Indirect materials
	Lubricants
	Supplies
	Power
Both merchandising and manufacturing companies	Selling, general, and administrative costs:
	Commissions
	Clerical costs, such as invoicing
	Shipping costs
Service organizations	Supplies, travel clerical

*Direct labor may or may not be variable in practice. See the discussion later in this chapter.

relevant activity measure will be the number of service calls made. Those costs that vary in total with the number of service calls made are the variable costs of making service calls.

Nevertheless, unless stated otherwise, you can assume that the activity base under consideration is the total volume of goods and services provided by the organization. So, for example, if we ask whether direct materials at Ford is a variable cost, the answer is yes, since the cost of direct materials is variable with respect to Ford's total volume of output. We will specify the activity base only when it is something other than total output.

EXTENT OF VARIABLE COSTS The number and type of variable costs present in an organization will depend in large part on the organization's structure and purpose. A public utility like Florida Power and Light, with large investments in equipment, will tend to have few variable costs. Most of the costs are associated with its plant, and these costs tend to be insensitive to changes in levels of service provided. A manufacturing company like Black and Decker, by contrast, will often have many variable costs; these costs will be associated with both the manufacture and distribution of its products to customers.

A merchandising company like Wal-Mart or J. K. Gill will usually have a high proportion of variable costs in its cost structure. In most merchandising companies, the cost of merchandise purchased for resale, a variable cost, constitutes a very large component of total cost. Service companies, by contrast, have diverse cost structures. Some service companies, such as the Skippers restaurant chain, have fairly large variable costs because of the costs of their raw materials. On the other hand, service companies involved in consulting, auditing, engineering, dental, medical, and architectural activities have very large fixed costs in the form of expensive facilities and highly trained salaried employees.

Some of the more frequently encountered variable costs are listed in Exhibit 5–2. This exhibit is not a complete listing of all costs that can be considered variable. Moreover, some of the costs listed in the exhibit may behave more like fixed than variable costs in some firms. We will see some examples of this later in the chapter. Nevertheless, Exhibit 5–2 provides a useful listing of many of the costs that normally would be considered variable with respect to the volume of output.

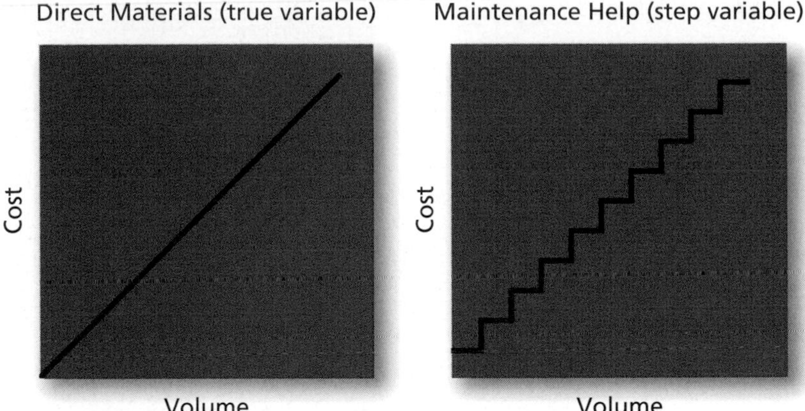

Exhibit 5–3 True Variable versus Step-Variable Costs

True Variable versus Step-Variable Costs

Not all variable costs have exactly the same behavior pattern. Some variable costs behave in a *true variable* or *proportionately variable* pattern. Other variable costs behave in a *step-variable* pattern.

TRUE VARIABLE COSTS Direct materials is a true or proportionately variable cost because the amount used during a period will vary in direct proportion to the level of production activity. Moreover, any amounts purchased but not used can be stored and carried forward to the next period as inventory.

STEP-VARIABLE COSTS The wages of maintenance workers are often considered to be a variable cost, but this labor cost doesn't behave in quite the same way as the cost of direct materials. Unlike direct materials, the time of maintenance workers is obtainable only in large chunks. Moreover, any maintenance time not utilized cannot be stored as inventory and carried forward to the next period. If the time is not used effectively, it is gone forever. Furthermore, a maintenance crew can work at a fairly leisurely pace if pressures are light but intensify its efforts if pressures build up. For this reason, somewhat small changes in the level of production may have no effect on the number of maintenance people needed to properly carry on maintenance work.

A cost that is obtainable only in large chunks (such as the labor cost of maintenance workers) and that increases or decreases only in response to fairly wide changes in the activity level is known as a **step-variable cost.** The behavior of a step-variable cost, contrasted with the behavior of a true variable cost, is illustrated in Exhibit 5–3.

Notice that the need for maintenance help changes only with fairly wide changes in volume and that when additional maintenance time is obtained, it comes in large, indivisible chunks. The strategy of management in dealing with step-variable costs must be to obtain the fullest use of services possible for each separate step. Great care must be taken in working with these kinds of costs to prevent "fat" from building up in an organization. There may be a tendency to employ additional help more quickly than needed, and there is a natural reluctance to lay people off when volume declines.

The Linearity Assumption and the Relevant Range

In dealing with variable costs, we have assumed a strictly linear relationship between cost and volume, except in the case of step-variable costs. Economists correctly point

Exhibit 5–4
Curvilinear Costs and the Relevant Range

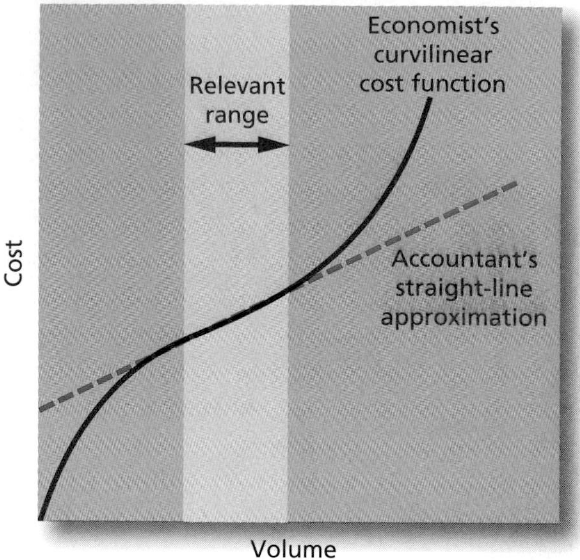

out that many costs that the accountant classifies as variable actually behave in a *curvilinear* fashion. The behavior of a **curvilinear cost** is shown in Exhibit 5–4.

Although many costs are not strictly linear when plotted as a function of volume, a curvilinear cost can be satisfactorily approximated with a straight line within a narrow band of activity known as the *relevant range.* The **relevant range** is that range of activity within which the assumptions made about cost behavior by the manager are valid. For example, note that the dashed line in Exhibit 5–4 can be used as an approximation to the curvilinear cost with very little loss of accuracy within the shaded relevant range. However, outside of the relevant range this particular straight line is a poor approximation to the curvilinear cost relationship. Managers should always keep in mind that a particular assumption made about cost behavior may be very inappropriate if activity falls outside of the relevant range.

objective 2
Explain the effect of a change in activity on both total fixed costs and fixed costs expressed on a per unit basis.

Fixed Costs

In our discussion of cost behavior patterns in Chapter 2, we stated that fixed costs remain constant in total dollar amount within the relevant range of activity. To continue the Nooksack Expeditions example, assume the company decides to rent a building for $500 per month to store its equipment. The *total* amount of rent paid is the same regardless of the number of guests the company takes on its expeditions during any given month. This cost behavior pattern is shown graphically in Exhibit 5–5.

Since fixed costs remain constant in total, the amount of fixed cost computed on a *per unit* basis becomes progressively smaller as the level of activity increases. If Nooksack Expeditions has only 250 guests in a month, the $500 fixed rental cost would amount to $2 per guest. If there are 1,000 guests, the fixed rental cost would amount to only 50 cents per guest. This aspect of the behavior of fixed costs is also displayed in Exhibit 5–5. Note that as the number of guests increases, the average unit cost drops, but it drops at a decreasing rate. The first guests have the biggest impact on unit costs.

As we noted in Chapter 2, this aspect of fixed costs can be confusing, although it is necessary in some contexts to express fixed costs on an average per unit basis. We found in Chapter 3, for example, that a broad unit cost figure containing both variable and fixed cost elements is used in *external* financial statements. For *internal* uses, however, fixed costs should not be expressed on a per unit basis because of the potential confusion. Experience has shown that for internal uses, fixed costs are most easily (and most safely) dealt with on a total basis rather than on a per unit basis.

Exhibit 5–5 Fixed Cost Behavior

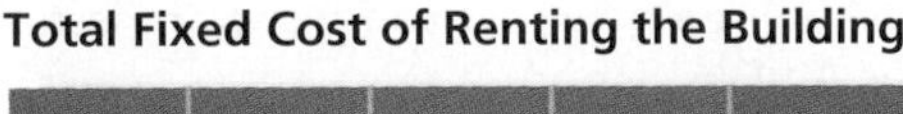

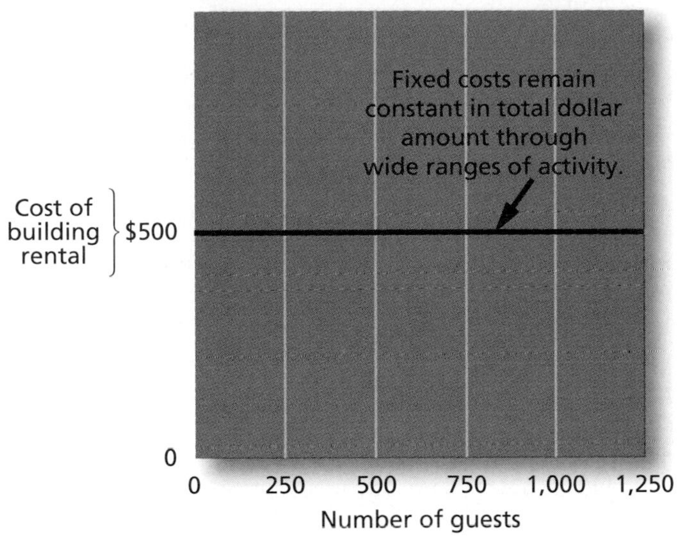

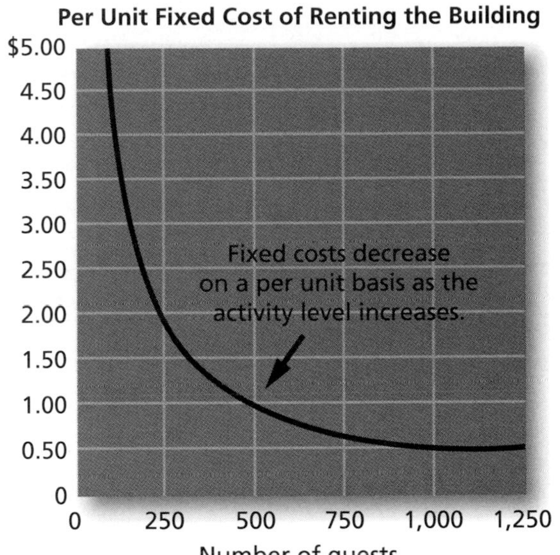

Focus on Current Practice

Airlines have long recognized that once a flight is scheduled, the variable cost of filling a seat with a passenger is very small. The costs of the cockpit flight crew, fuel, gate rentals, maintenance, aircraft depreciation, and so on, are all basically fixed with respect to the number of passengers who actually take a particular flight. The cost of the cabin flight crew is a step-variable cost—the number of flight attendants assigned to a flight will vary with the number of passengers on the flight. The only true variable costs are the costs of meals and an almost inconsequential increase in fuel consumption. Therefore, adding one passenger to a flight brings in additional revenue but has very little effect on total cost. Consequently, airlines have been stuffing more and more seats into their aircraft. Boeing 747s were configured originally with 9 seats across a row, but now they frequently have 10. One major airline has raised the number of seats in its fleet of DC-10 planes from 232 to nearly 300.[1] ■

Types of Fixed Costs

Fixed costs are sometimes referred to as a capacity costs, since they result from outlays made for buildings, equipment, skilled professional employees, and other items needed to provide the basic capacity for sustained operations. For planning purposes, fixed costs can be viewed as being either *committed* or *discretionary.*

COMMITTED FIXED COSTS **Committed fixed costs** relate to the investment in facilities, equipment, and the basic organizational structure of a firm. Examples of such costs include depreciation of buildings and equipment, taxes on real estate, insurance, and salaries of top management and operating personnel.

1. Michael J. McCarthy, "Airline Squeeze Play: More Seats, Less Legroom," *The Wall Street Journal,* April 18, 1994, pp. B1 and B6.

The two key factors about committed fixed costs are that (1) they are long term in nature, and (2) they can't be reduced to zero even for short periods of time without seriously impairing the profitability or long-run goals of the organization. Even if operations are interrupted or cut back, the committed fixed costs will still continue largely unchanged. During a recession, for example, a firm won't usually discharge key executives or sell off key facilities. The basic organizational structure and facilities ordinarily are kept intact. The costs of restoring them later are likely to be far greater than any short-run savings that might be realized.

Since it is difficult to change a committed fixed cost once the commitment has been made, management should approach these decisions with particular care. Decisions to acquire major equipment or to take on other committed fixed costs involve a long planning horizon. Management should make such commitments only after careful analysis of the available alternatives. Once a decision is made to build a certain size facility, a firm becomes locked into that decision for many years to come. Decisions relating to committed fixed costs will be examined in Chapters 14 and 15.

While not much can be done about committed fixed costs in the short run, management is generally very concerned about how these resources are *utilized*. The strategy of management must be to utilize the capacity of the organization as effectively as possible.

DISCRETIONARY FIXED COSTS **Discretionary fixed costs** (often referred to as *managed fixed costs)* usually arise from *annual* decisions by management to spend in certain fixed cost areas. Examples of discretionary fixed costs include advertising, research, public relations, management development programs, and internships for students.

Basically, two key differences exist between discretionary fixed costs and committed fixed costs. First, the planning horizon for a discretionary fixed cost is fairly short term—usually a single year. By contrast, as we indicated earlier, committed fixed costs have a planning horizon that encompasses many years. Second, discretionary fixed costs can be cut for short periods of time with minimal damage to the long-run goals of the organization. For example, a firm that has been spending $50,000 annually on management development programs may be forced because of poor economic conditions to reduce its spending in that area during a given year. Although some unfavorable consequences may result from the cutback, it is doubtful that these consequences would be as great as those that would result if the company decided to economize during the year by laying off key personnel.

Whether a particular cost is regarded as committed or discretionary may depend on management's strategy. For example, during recessions when the level of home building is down, many construction companies lay off most of their workers and virtually disband operations. Other construction companies retain large numbers of employees on the payroll, even though the workers have little or no work to do. While these latter companies may be faced with short-term cash flow problems, it will be easier for them to respond quickly when economic conditions improve. And the higher morale and loyalty of their employees may give these companies a significant competitive advantage.

The most important characteristic of discretionary fixed costs is that management is not locked into a decision regarding such costs. They can be adjusted from year to year or even perhaps during the course of a year if circumstances demand such a modification.

THE TREND TOWARD FIXED COSTS The trend in many companies is toward greater fixed costs relative to variable costs. Chores that used to be performed by hand have been taken over by machines. For example, grocery clerks at Safeway and Kroger used to key in prices by hand on cash registers. Now, most stores are equipped with barcode readers that enter price and other product information automatically. In general, competition has created pressure to give customers more value for their money—a demand that often can only be satisfied by automating business processes. For example, an H & R Block employee used to fill out tax returns for customers largely by hand and the advice given to a customer largely depended on the knowledge of that particular employee. Now, sophisticated computer software is used to complete tax returns, and the software provides the customer with tax planning and other advice tailored to the customer's needs based on the accumulated knowledge of many experts.

As machines take over more and more of the tasks that were performed by humans, the overall demand for human workers has not diminished. The demand for "knowledge" workers—those who work primarily with their minds rather than their muscles—has grown tremendously. And knowledge workers tend to be salaried, highly trained, and difficult to replace. As a consequence, the costs of compensating knowledge workers are often relatively fixed and are committed rather than discretionary costs.

IS LABOR A VARIABLE OR A FIXED COST? As the preceding discussion suggests, wages and salaries may be fixed or variable. The accompanying Focus on Current Practice boxes illustrate that the behavior of wage and salary costs will differ from one country to another, depending on labor regulations, labor contracts, and custom. In some countries, such as France, Germany, China, and Japan, management has little flexibility in adjusting the labor force to changes in business activity. In countries such as the United States and the United Kingdom, management typically has much greater latitude. However, even in these less restrictive environments, managers may choose to treat employee compensation as a fixed cost for several reasons.

First, companies have become much more reluctant to adjust the workforce in response to short-term fluctuations in sales. Most companies realize that their employees are a very valuable asset. More and more, highly skilled and trained employees are required to run a successful business, and these workers are not easy to replace. Trained workers who are laid off may never return, and layoffs undermine the morale of those workers who remain.

In addition, managers do not want to be caught with a bloated payroll in an economic downturn. Therefore, there is an increased reluctance to add workers when sales activity picks up. Many companies are turning to temporary and part-time workers to take up the slack when their permanent, full-time employees are unable to handle all of the demand for the company's products and services. In such companies, labor costs are a curious mixture of fixed and variable costs.

Many major companies have undergone waves of downsizing in recent years in which large numbers of employees—particularly middle managers—have lost their jobs. It may seem that this downsizing proves that even management salaries should be regarded as variable costs, but this would not be a valid conclusion. Downsizing has been the result of attempts to reengineer business processes and cut costs rather than a response to a decline in sales activity. This underscores an important, but subtle, point. Fixed costs can change—they just don't change in response to small changes in activity.

In sum, we cannot provide a clear-cut answer to the question "Is labor a variable or fixed cost?" It depends on how much flexibility management has and management's strategy. Nevertheless, we will assume in this text that, unless otherwise stated, direct labor is a variable cost. This assumption is more likely to be valid for companies in the United States than in countries where employment laws permit much less flexibility.

Focus on Current Practice

Reducing a company's workforce can be very expensive. In 1993, IBM decided to trim at least 25,000 people from its worldwide workforce of 300,000. To minimize the negative impact on morale of such a reduction, the company provided financial incentives to induce employees to depart voluntarily. The company offered up to half a year of salary and paid medical coverage for departing employees. The cost of the program averaged $120,000 per departing employee and totaled $3 billion.[2] ■

Focus on Current Practice

The labor laws in the country in which the company operates often affect whether employee staff costs are fixed or variable. In Europe, banks have historically had very large numbers of branches, some of which serve very small villages. These branches are expensive to staff and maintain, and banks have argued that they are a drain on profits. In Denmark and the United Kingdom, the number of branches were cut by 34% and 22%, respectively, over a span of 10 years. In both cases, this led to a 15% reduction in staff employees. In contrast, countries with more restrictive labor laws that make it difficult to lay off workers have been unable to reduce staff or the number of branches significantly. For example, in Germany the number of branches was reduced by only 2% and the number of staff by only two-tenths of a percent during the same period.[3] ■

Focus on Current Practice

Japanese law makes it difficult to lay off or fire workers or to hire away employees from competitors. Exemptions may be granted to the no-layoff rule—particularly for small companies—but this rule effectively ties an employee to a single company for life. As a result, labor is commonly regarded as a fixed cost in Japan. This reduces the ability of Japanese companies to adjust costs in response to peaks and valley in the business cycle, but there are advantages to this system. "Since Japanese workers enjoy lifetime job guarantees, they see no downside risk in helping employers improve productivity. In fact, they embrace new technology because they know it will enhance their company's future and their own jobs."[4]

There is another advantage to Japan's lifetime employment system. The really critical business assets are often people. In North America, key

2. Laurence Hooper, "IBM Will Cut Back Payments, Benefits for Voluntary Departures and Layoffs," *The Wall Street Journal,* April 5, 1993, p. A3.
3. Charles Fleming, "Kinder Cuts: Continental Banks Seek to Expand Their Way Out of Retail Trouble," *The Wall Street Journal Europe,* March 11, 1997, pp. 1 and 8.
4. Eamonn Fingleton, "Jobs for Life: Why Japan Won't Give Them Up," *Fortune,* March 20, 1995, pp.119–25.

employees can easily be hired away by a competitor—taking with them investments in training and their knowledge about the company's innovations and plans. In contrast, the difficulty of hiring a competitor's employees in Japan safeguards those assets and arguably makes Japanese companies more willing to invest in training and in research and development.

There is an important shock absorber in the Japanese employment system. As much as 40% of workers' compensation is in the form of discretionary bonuses. If a company is doing poorly, these bonuses can be reduced or omitted. ■

Fixed Costs and the Relevant Range

The concept of the relevant range, which was introduced in the discussion of variable costs, is also important in understanding fixed costs—particularly discretionary fixed costs. The levels of discretionary fixed costs are typically decided at the beginning of the year and depend on the support needs of the planned programs such as advertising and training. The scope of these programs will depend, in turn, on the overall anticipated level of activity for the year. At very high levels of activity, programs are usually broadened or expanded. For example, if the company hopes to increase sales by 25%, it would probably plan for much larger advertising costs than if no sales increase was planned. So the *planned* level of activity may affect total discretionary fixed costs. However, once the total discretionary fixed costs have been budgeted, they are unaffected by the *actual* level of activity. For example, once the advertising budget has been decided on and has been spent, it will not be affected by how many units are actually sold. Therefore, the cost is fixed with respect to the *actual* number of units sold.

Discretionary fixed costs are easier to adjust than committed fixed costs. They also tend to be less "lumpy." Committed fixed costs tend to consist of costs of buildings, equipment, and the salaries of key personnel. It is difficult to buy half a piece of equipment or to hire a quarter of a product-line manager, so the step pattern depicted in Exhibit 5–6 is typical for such costs. The relevant range of activity for a fixed cost is the range of activity over which the graph of the cost is flat as in Exhibit 5–6. As a company expands its level of activity, it may outgrow its present facilities, or the key

Exhibit 5–6 Fixed Costs and the Relevant Range

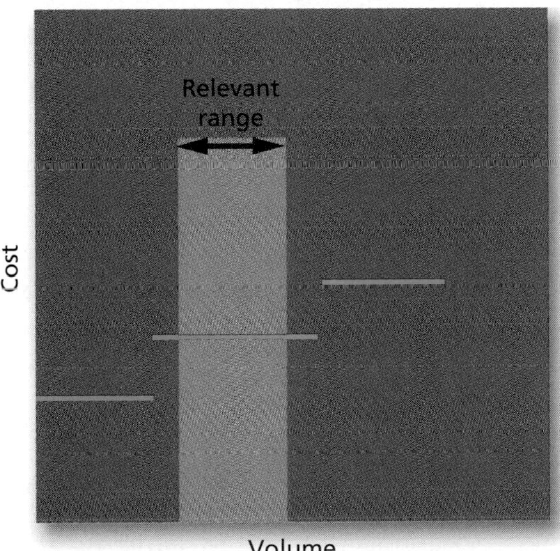

Exhibit 5–7 Mixed Cost Behavior

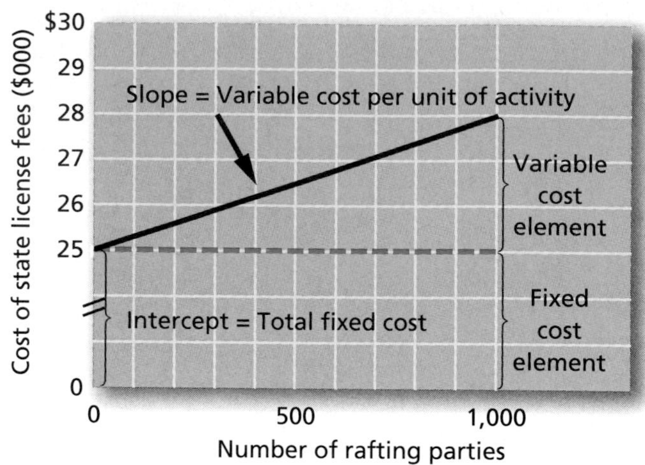

management team may need to be expanded. The result, of course, will be increased committed fixed costs as larger facilities are built and as new management positions are created.

One reaction to the step pattern depicted in Exhibit 5–6 is to say that discretionary and committed fixed costs are really just step-variable costs. To some extent this is true, since almost *all* costs can be adjusted in the long run. There are two major differences, however, between the step-variable costs depicted earlier in Exhibit 5–3 and the fixed costs depicted in Exhibit 5–6.

The first difference is that the step-variable costs can often be adjusted quickly as conditions change, whereas once fixed costs have been set, they often can't be changed easily. A step-variable cost such as maintenance labor, for example, can be adjusted upward or downward by hiring and laying off maintenance workers. By contrast, once a company has signed a lease for a building, it is locked into that level of lease cost for the life of the contract.

The second difference is that the *width of the steps* depicted for step-variable costs is much narrower than the width of the steps depicted for the fixed costs in Exhibit 5–6. The width of the steps relates to volume or level of activity. For step-variable costs, the width of a step may be 40 hours of activity or less if one is dealing, for example, with maintenance labor cost. For fixed costs, however, the width of a step may be *thousands* or even *tens of thousands* of hours of activity. In essence, the width of the steps for step-variable costs is generally so narrow that these costs can be treated essentially as variable costs for most purposes. The width of the steps for fixed costs, on the other hand, is so wide that these costs must generally be treated as being entirely fixed within the relevant range.

Mixed Costs

A **mixed cost** is one that contains both variable and fixed cost elements. Mixed costs are also known as semivariable costs. To continue the Nooksack Expeditions example, the company must pay a license fee of $25,000 per year plus $3 per rafting party to the state's Department of Natural Resources. If the company runs 1,000 rafting parties this year, then the total fees paid to the state would be $28,000, made up of $25,000 in fixed cost plus $3,000 in variable cost. The behavior of this mixed cost is shown graphically in Exhibit 5–7.

Even if Nooksack fails to attract any customers and there are no rafting parties, the company will still have to pay the license fee of $25,000. This is why the cost line in Exhibit 5–7 intersects the vertical cost axis at the $25,000 point. For each rafting party the company organizes, the total cost of the state fees will increase by $3.

Therefore, the total cost line slopes upward as the variable cost element is added to the fixed cost element.

Since the mixed cost in Exhibit 5–7 is represented by a straight line, the following equation for a straight line can be used to express the relationship between mixed cost and the level of activity:

$$Y = a + bX$$

In this equation,

Y = The total mixed cost
a = The total fixed cost (the vertical intercept of the line)
b = The variable cost per unit of activity (the slope of the line)
X = The level of activity

In the case of the state fees paid by Nooksack Expeditions, the equation is written as follows:

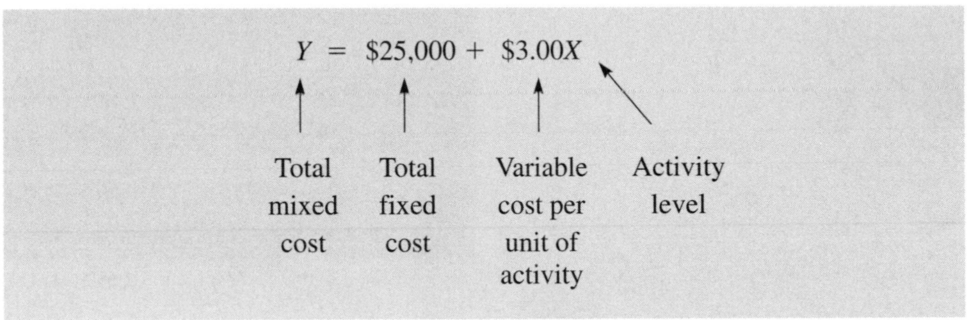

objective 3

Use a cost formula to predict costs at a new level of activity.

This equation makes it very easy to calculate what the total mixed cost would be for any level of activity within the relevant range. For example, suppose that the company expects to organize 800 rafting parties in the next year. Then the total state fees would be $27,400 calculated as follows:

$$Y = \$25{,}000 + (\$3.00 \times 800 \text{ rafting parties})$$
$$= \$27{,}400$$

Focus on Current Practice

A total of 257 American and 40 Japanese manufacturing firms responded to a questionnaire concerning their management accounting practices.[5] Among other things, the firms were asked whether they classified certain costs as variable, semivariable, or fixed. Some of the results are summarized in Exhibit 5–8. Note that firms do not all classify costs in the same way. For example, roughly 45% of the U.S. firms classify materials-handling labor costs as variable, 35% as semivariable, and 20% as fixed. Also note that the Japanese firms are much more likely than U.S. firms to classify labor costs as fixed. ■

5. NAA Tokyo Affiliate, "Management Accounting in the Advanced Management Surrounding—Comparative Study on Survey in Japan and U.S.A.," October 1988.

Exhibit 5–8
Percentages of Firms Classifying Specific Costs as Variable, Semivariable, or Fixed

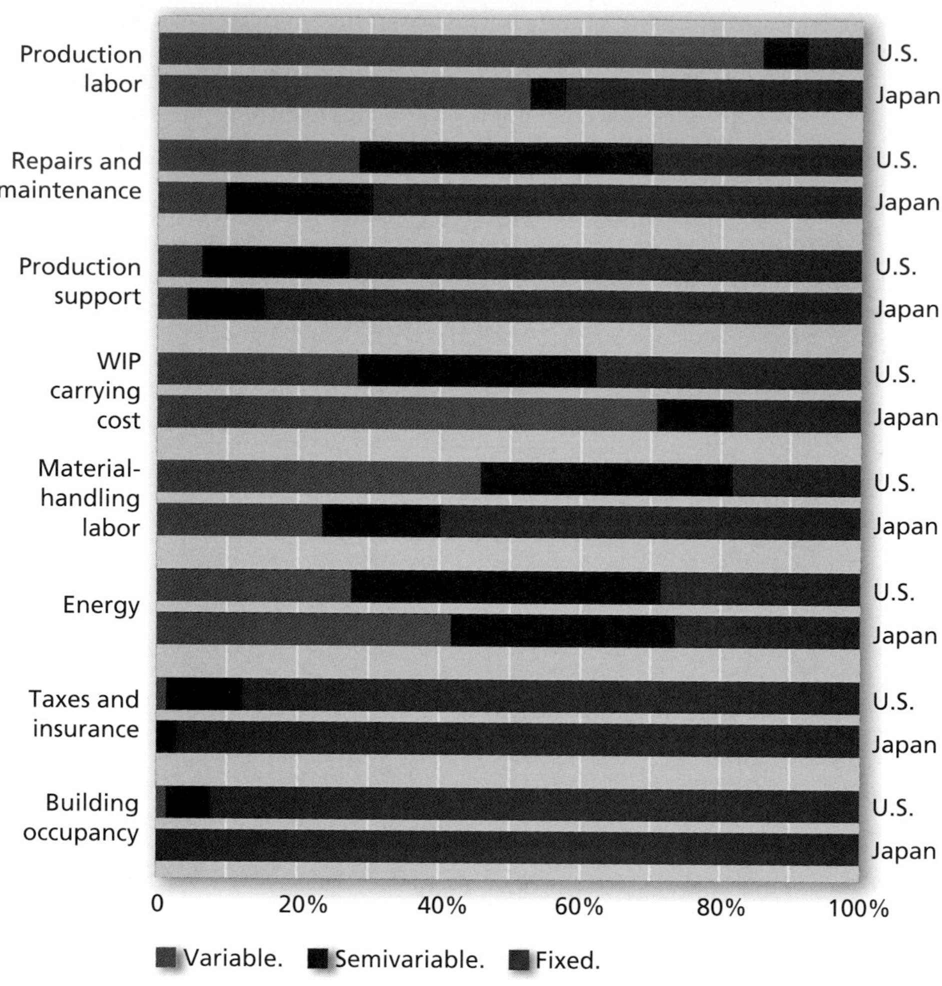

The Analysis of Mixed Costs

In practice, mixed costs are very common. For example, the cost of providing X-ray services to patients at the Harvard Medical School Hospital is a mixed cost. There are substantial fixed costs for equipment depreciation and for salaries for radiologists and technicians, but there are also variable costs for X-ray film, power, and supplies. At Southwest Airlines, maintenance costs are mixed cost. The company must incur fixed costs for renting maintenance facilities and for keeping skilled mechanics on the payroll, but the costs of replacement parts, lubricating oils, tires, and so forth, are variable with respect to how often and how far the company's aircraft are flown.

The fixed portion of a mixed cost represents the basic, minimum cost of just having a service *ready and available* for use. The variable portion represents the cost incurred for *actual consumption* of the service. The variable element varies in proportion to the amount of service that is consumed.

How does management go about actually estimating the fixed and variable components of a mixed cost? The most common methods used in practice are *account analysis* and the *engineering approach*. These methods are used most often in later chapters of this text.

In **account analysis,** each account under consideration is classified as either variable or fixed based on the analyst's prior knowledge of how the cost in the account behaves. For example, direct materials would be classified as variable and a building lease cost would be classified as fixed because of the nature of those costs. The total fixed cost is the sum of the costs for the accounts that have been classified as fixed. The variable cost per unit is estimated by dividing the sum of the costs for the accounts that have been classified as variable by the total activity.

The **engineering approach** to cost analysis involves a detailed analysis of what cost behavior should be, based on an industrial engineer's evaluation of the production methods to be used, the materials specifications, labor requirements, equipment usage, efficiency of production, power consumption, and so on. For example, Pizza Hut might use the engineering approach to estimate the cost of serving a particular take-out pizza. The cost of the pizza would be estimated by carefully costing the specific ingredients used to make the pizza, the power consumed to cook the pizza, and the cost of the container the pizza is delivered in. The engineering approach must be used in those situations where no past experience is available concerning activity and costs. In addition, it is sometimes used together with other methods to improve the accuracy of cost analysis.

Account analysis works best when analyzing costs at a fairly aggregated level, such as the cost of serving patients in the emergency room (ER) of Cook County General Hospital. The costs of drugs, supplies, forms, wages, equipment, and so on, can be roughly classified as variable or fixed and a mixed cost formula for the overall cost of the emergency room can be estimated fairly quickly. However, this method glosses over the fact that some of the accounts may have elements of both fixed and variable costs. For example, the cost of electricity for the ER is a mixed cost. Most of the electricity is used for heating and lighting and is a fixed cost. However, the consumption of electricity increases with activity in the ER since diagnostic equipment, operating theater lights, defibrillators, and so on, all consume electricity. The most effective way to estimate the fixed and variable elements of such a mixed cost may be to analyze past records of cost and activity data. These records should reveal whether electrical costs vary significantly with the number of patients and if so, by how much. The remainder of this section will be concerned with how to conduct such an analysis of past cost and activity data.

Managerial Accounting in Action

THE ISSUE

Dr. Derek Chalmers, the chief executive officer of Brentline Hospital, motioned Kinh Nguyen, the chief financial officer of the hospital, into his office.

Derek: Kinh, come on in.
Kinh: What can I do for you?
Derek: Well for one, could you get the government to rescind the bookcase full of regulations against the wall over there?
Kinh: Sorry, that's a bit beyond my authority.
Derek: Just wishing, Kinh. Actually, I wanted to talk to you about our maintenance expenses. I didn't used to have to pay attention to such things, but these expenses seem to be bouncing around a lot. Over the last half year or so they have been as low as $7,400 and as high as $9,800 per month.
Kinh: Actually, that's a pretty normal variation in those expenses.
Derek: Well, we budgeted a constant $8,400 a month. Can't we do a better job of predicting what these costs are going to be? And how do we know when we've spent too much in a month? Shouldn't there be some explanation for these variations?

Kinh: Now that you mention it, we are in the process right now of tightening up our budgeting process. Our first step is to break all of our costs down into fixed and variable components.

Derek: How will that help?

Kinh: Well, that will permit us to predict what the level of costs will be. Some costs are fixed and shouldn't change much. Other costs go up and down as our activity goes up and down. The trick is to figure out what is driving the variable component of the costs.

Derek: What about the maintenance costs?

Kinh: My guess is that the variations in maintenance costs are being driven by our overall level of activity. When we treat more patients, our equipment is used more intensively, which leads to more maintenance expense.

Derek: How would you measure the level of overall activity? Would you use patient-days?

Kinh: I think so. Each day a patient is in the hospital counts as one patient-day. The greater the number of patient-days in a month, the busier we are. Besides, our budgeting is all based on projected patient-days.

Derek: Okay, so suppose you are able to break the maintenance costs down into fixed and variable components. What will that do for us?

Kinh: Basically, I will be able to predict what maintenance costs should be as a function of the number of patient-days.

Derek: I can see where that would be useful. We could use it to predict costs for budgeting purposes.

Kinh: We could also use it as a benchmark. Based on the actual number of patient-days for a period, I can predict what the maintenance costs should have been. We can compare this to the actual spending on maintenance.

Derek: Sounds good to me. Let me know when you get the results. ■

objective 4

Analyze a mixed cost using the high-low method.

We will examine three methods that Kinh Nguyen might use to break down mixed costs into their fixed and variable elements—the *high-low method,* the *scatter-graph method,* and the *least-squares regression method.* All three methods are based on analyzing cost and activity records from a number of prior periods. In the case of Brentline Hospital, we will use the following records of maintenance costs and patient-days for the first seven months of the year to estimate the fixed and variable elements of maintenance costs:

Month	Activity Level: Patient-Days	Maintenance Cost Incurred
January	5,600	$7,900
February	7,100	8,500
March	5,000	7,400
April	6,500	8,200
May	7,300	9,100
June	8,000	9,800
July	6,200	7,800

The High-Low Method

To analyze mixed costs with the **high-low method,** you begin by identifying the period with the lowest level of activity and the period with the highest level of activity. The difference in cost observed at the two extremes is divided by the change in activity between the extremes in order to estimate the variable cost per unit of activity.

Since total maintenance cost at Brentline Hospital appears to generally increase as the activity level increases, it is likely that some variable cost element is present. Using the high-low method, we first identify the periods with the highest and lowest *activity*—in this case, June and March. We then use the activity and cost data from these two periods to estimate the variable cost component as follows:

	Patient-Days	Maintenance Cost Incurred
High activity level (June)	8,000	$9,800
Low activity level (March)	5,000	7,400
Change	3,000	$2,400

$$\text{Variable cost} = \frac{\text{Change in cost}}{\text{Change in activity}} = \frac{\$2{,}400}{3{,}000} = \$0.80 \text{ per patient-day}$$

Having determined that the variable rate for maintenance cost is 80 cents per patient-day, we can now determine the amount of fixed cost. This is done by taking total cost at *either* the high or the low activity level and deducting the variable cost element. In the computation below, total cost at the high activity level is used in computing the fixed cost element:

$$\begin{aligned}\text{Fixed cost element} &= \text{Total cost} - \text{Variable cost element}\\ &= \$9{,}800 - (\$0.80 \text{ per patient-day} \times 8{,}000 \text{ patient-days})\\ &= \$3{,}400\end{aligned}$$

Both the variable and fixed cost elements have now been isolated. The cost of maintenance can be expressed as $3,400 per month plus 80 cents per patient-day.

The cost of maintenance can also be expressed in terms of the equation for a straight line as follows:

$$Y = \$3{,}400 + \$0.80X$$

↑ Total maintenance cost (Y)   ↑ Total patient-days (X)

The data used in this illustration are shown graphically in Exhibit 5–9. Three things should be noted in relation to this exhibit:

1. Notice that cost, Y, is plotted on the vertical axis. Cost is known as the **dependent variable**, since the amount of cost incurred during a period depends on the level of activity for the period. (That is, as the level of activity increases, total cost will also increase.)
2. Notice that activity, X (patient-days in this case), is plotted on the horizontal axis. Activity is known as the **independent variable**, since it causes variations in the cost.

3. Notice that a straight line has been drawn through the points corresponding to the low and high levels of activity. In essence, that is what the high-low method does—it draws a straight line through those two points. The formula for the variable cost, $\frac{\text{Change in cost (i.e., change in } Y)}{\text{Change in activity (i.e., change in } X)}$, is basically the same as the formula for the slope of the line, $\frac{\text{Rise (i.e., change in } Y)}{\text{Run (i.e., change in } X)}$, that you are familiar with from high school algebra. This is because the slope of the line *is* the variable cost per unit. The higher the variable cost per unit, the steeper the line.

Sometimes the high and low levels of activity don't coincide with the high and low amounts of cost. For example, the period that has the highest level of activity may not have the highest amount of cost. Nevertheless, the highest and lowest levels of *activity* are always used to analyze a mixed cost under the high-low method. The reason is that the activity presumably causes costs, so the analyst would like to use data that reflects the greatest possible variation in activity.

The high-low method is very simple to apply, but it suffers from a major (and sometimes critical) defect in that it utilizes only two data points. Generally, two points are not enough to produce accurate results in cost analysis work. Additionally, periods in which the activity level is unusually low or unusually high will tend to produce inaccurate results. A cost formula that is estimated solely using data from these unusual periods may seriously misrepresent the true cost relationship that holds during normal periods. Such a distortion is evident in Exhibit 5–9. The straight line should probably be shifted down somewhat so that it is closer to more of the data points. For these reasons, other methods of cost analysis that utilize a greater number of points will generally be more accurate than the high-low method. If a manager chooses to use the high-low method, he or she should do so with a full awareness of the method's limitations.

objective 5

Analyze a mixed cost using the scattergraph method.

The Scattergraph Method

A more accurate way of analyzing mixed costs is to use the **scattergraph method,** which takes into account all of the cost data. A graph like the one that we used in Exhibit 5–9 is constructed in which cost is shown on the vertical axis and the level of activity is shown on the horizontal axis. Costs observed at various levels of activity are then plotted on the graph, and a line is fitted to the plotted points. However, rather than just fitting the line to the high and low points, all points are considered when the line is drawn. This is done through simple visual inspection of the data, with the analyst taking care that the placement of the line is representative of all points, not just the high and low ones. Typically, the line is placed so that approximately equal numbers of points fall above and below it.

A graph is this type is known as a *scattergraph,* and the line fitted to the plotted points is known as a **regression line.** The regression line, in effect, is a line of averages, with the average variable cost per unit of activity represented by the slope of the line and the average total fixed cost represented by the point where the regression line intersects the cost axis.

The scattergraph approach using the Brentline Hospital maintenance data is illustrated in Exhibit 5–10. Note that the regression line has been placed in such a way that approximately equal numbers of points fall above and below it. Also note that the line has been drawn so that it goes through one of the points. This is not absolutely necessary, but it makes subsequent calculations a little easier.

Since the regression line strikes the vertical cost axis at $3,300, that amount represents the fixed cost element. The variable cost element can be computed by subtracting the fixed cost of $3,300 from the total cost for any point lying on the

Exhibit 5–9 High-Low Method of Cost Analysis

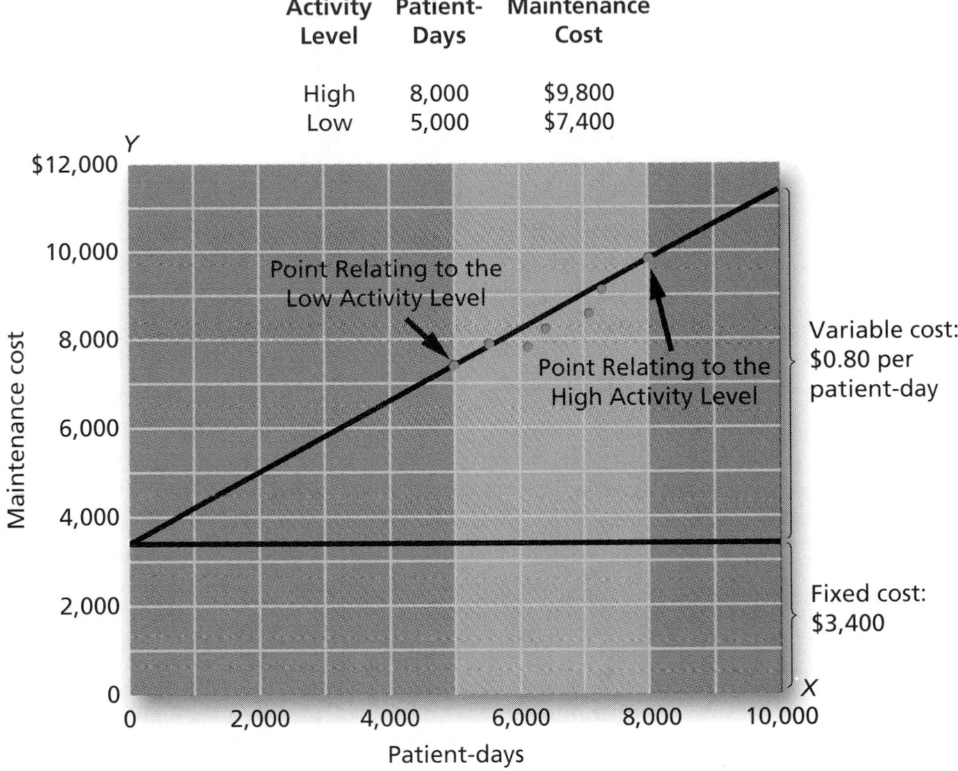

Exhibit 5–10 Scattergraph Method of Cost Analysis

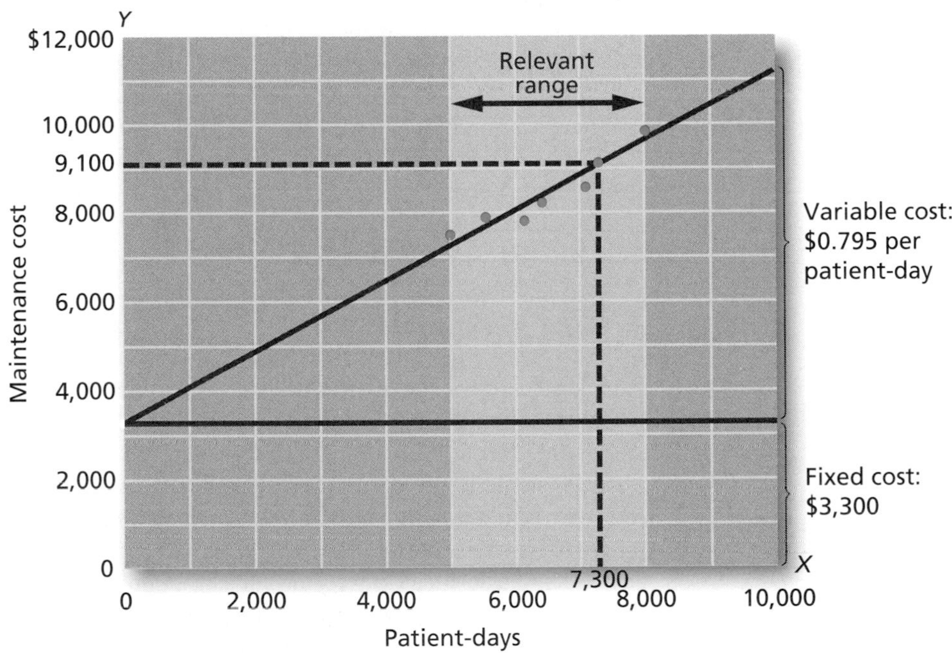

regression line. Since the point representing 7,300 patient-days lies on the regression line, we can use it. The variable cost (to the nearest tenth of a cent) would be 79.5 cents per patient-day, computed as follows:

Total cost for 7,300 patient-days (a point falling on the regression line)	$9,100
Less fixed cost element	3,300
Variable cost element	$5,800

$5,800 ÷ 7,300 patient-days = $0.795 per patient-day

Thus, the cost formula using the regression line in Exhibit 5–10 would be $3,300 per month plus 79.5 cents per patient-day.

In this example, there is not a great deal of difference between the cost formula derived using the high-low method and the cost formula derived using the scattergraph method. However, sometimes there *will* be a big difference. In those situations, more reliance should ordinarily be placed on the results of the scattergraph approach.

Also note that all of the points in Exhibit 5–10 lie reasonably close to the straight line. In other words, the estimates of the fixed and variable costs are reasonably accurate within this range of activity, so the relevant range extends at least from 5,000 to 8,000 patient-days. It may also be accurate below 5,000 patient-days and above 8,000 patient-days—we can't tell for sure without looking at more data.

A scattergraph can be an extremely useful tool in the hands of an experienced analyst. Quirks in cost behavior due to strikes, bad weather, breakdowns, and so on, become immediately apparent to the trained observer, who can make appropriate adjustments to the data when fitting the regression line. Some cost analysts would argue that a scattergraph should be the beginning point in all cost analyses, due to the benefits to be gained from having the data visually available in graph form.

There are, however, two major drawbacks to the scattergraph method. First, it is subjective. No two analysts who look at the same scattergraph are likely to draw exactly the same regression line. Second, the estimates of fixed costs are not as precise as they are with other methods, since it is difficult to precisely measure the dollar amount where the regression line intersects the vertical cost axis. Some managers are uncomfortable with these elements of subjectivity and imprecision and desire a method that will yield a precise answer that will be the same no matter who does the analysis. Fortunately, modern computer software makes it very easy to use sophisticated statistical methods, such as *least-squares regression,* that are capable of providing much more information than just the estimates of variable and fixed costs. The details of these statistical methods are beyond the scope of this text, but the basic approach is discussed below. Nevertheless, even if the least-squares regression approach is used, it is always a good idea to plot the data in a scattergraph. By simply looking at the scattergraph, you can quickly verify whether it makes sense to fit a straight line to the data using least-squares regression or some other method.

The Least-Squares Regression Method

objective 6

Explain the least-squares regression method of analyzing a mixed cost.

The **least-square regression method** is a more objective and precise approach to estimating the regression line than the scattergraph method. Rather than fitting a regression line through the scattergraph data by visual inspection, the least-squares regression method uses mathematical formulas to fit the regression line. Also, unlike the high-low method, the least-squares regression method takes all of the data into account when estimating the cost formula.

The basic idea underlying the least-squares regression method is illustrated in Exhibit 5–11 using hypothetical data points. Notice from the exhibit that the deviations from the plotted points to the regression line are measured vertically on the graph. These vertical deviations are called the regression errors and are the key to understanding what least-squares regression does. There is nothing mysterious about the least-squares regression method. It simply computes the regression line that minimizes the sum of these squared errors. The formulas that accomplish this are fairly complex and involve numerous calculations, but the principal is simple.

Fortunately, computers are adept at carrying out the computations required by the least-squares regression formulas. The data—the observed values of X and Y—are entered into the computer, and software does the rest. In the case of the Brentline Hospital maintenance cost date, we used a statistical software package on a personal

Exhibit 5–11 The Concept of Least-Squares Regression

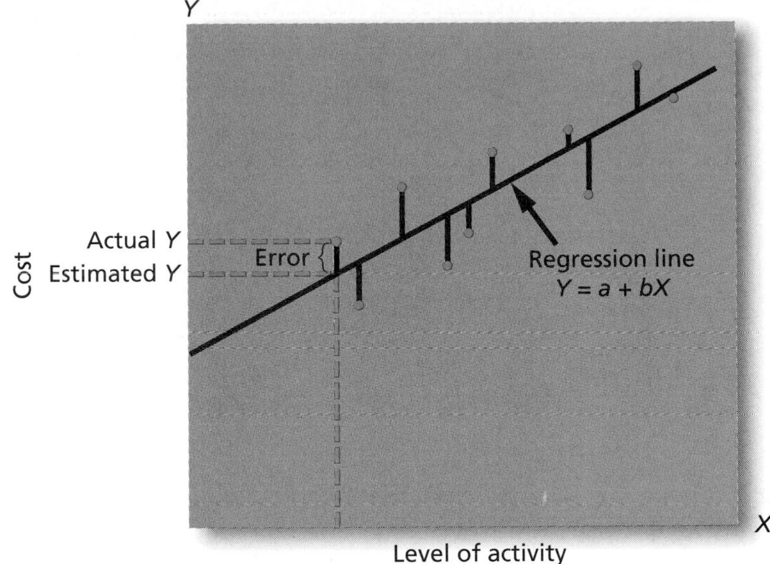

computer to calculate the following least-squares regression estimates of the total fixed cost *(a)* and the variable cost per unit of activity *(b)*:

$$a = \$3{,}431$$
$$b = \$0.759$$

Therefore, using the least-squares regression method, the fixed element of the maintenance cost is $3,431 per month and the variable portion is 75.9 cents per patient-day.

In terms of the linear equation $Y = a + bX$, the cost formula can be written as

$$Y = \$3{,}431 + \$0.759X$$

where activity *(X)* is expressed in patient-days.

While we used a personal computer to calculate the values of *a* and *b* in this example, they can also be calculated by hand. In Appendix 5A to this chapter, we can show how this can be done.

In addition to estimates of the intercept (fixed cost) and slope (variable cost per unit), least-squares regression software ordinarily provides a number of other very useful statistics. One of these statistics is the *adjusted* R^2, which is a measure of "goodness of fit." The **adjusted** $\mathbf{R^2}$ tells us the percentage of the variation in the dependent variable (cost) that is explained by variation in the independent variable (activity). The adjusted R^2 varies from 0% to 100%, and the higher the percentage, the better. In the case of the Brentline Hospital maintenance cost data, the adjusted R^2 is 88%, which indicates that 88% of the variation in maintenance costs is explained by the variation in patient-days. This is reasonably high and is an indication of a good fit. On the other hand, a low adjusted R^2 would be an indication that there is a poor fit. You should always plot the data in a scattergraph, but it is particularly important to check the data visually when there is a low adjusted R^2. A quick look at the scattergraph can reveal that there is little real relation between the cost and the activity or that the relation is something other than a simple straight line. In such cases, additional analysis would be required.

Managerial Accounting in Action

THE WRAP-UP

After completing the analysis of maintenance costs, Kinh Nguyen met with Dr. Derek Chalmers to discuss the results.

Kinh: We used least-squares regression analysis to estimate the fixed and variable components of maintenance costs. According to the results, the fixed cost per month is $3,431 and the variable cost per patient-day is 75.9 cents.

Derek: Okay, so if we plan for 7,800 patient-days next month, what is your estimate of the maintenance costs?

Kinh: That will take just a few seconds to figure out. Here it is. [And Kinh wrote the following calculations on a pad of paper.]

Fixed costs	$3,431
Variable costs:	
7,800 patient-days × $0.759 per patient-day . . .	5,920
Total expected maintenance costs	$9,351

Derek: Nine thousand three hundred and fifty *one* dollars; isn't that a bit *too* precise?

Kinh: Sure. I don't really believe the maintenance costs will be exactly this figure. However, based on the information we have, this is the best estimate we can come up with.

Derek: Don't let me give you a hard time. Even though it is an estimate, it will be a lot better than just guessing like we have done in the past. Thanks. I hope to see more of this kind of analysis. ■

Multiple Regression Analysis

In the discussion thus far, we have assumed that a single factor such as patient-days drives the variable cost component of a mixed cost. This assumption is acceptable for many mixed costs, but in some situations there may be more than one causal factor driving the variable cost element. For example, shipping costs may depend on both the number of units shipped *and* the weight of the units. In a situation such as this, *multiple regression* is necessary. **Multiple regression** is an analytical method that is used when the dependent variable (i.e., cost) is caused by more than one factor. Although adding more factors, or variables, makes the computations more complex, the principles involved are the same as in the simple least-squares regressions discussed above. Because of the complexity of the calculations, multiple regression is nearly always done with a computer.

The Contribution Format

objective 7

Prepare an income statement using the contribution format.

Once the manager has separated costs into fixed and variable elements, what is done with the data? We have already answered this question somewhat by showing how a cost formula can be used to predict costs. To answer this question more fully will require most of the remainder of this text, since much of what the manager does rests in some way on an understanding of cost behavior. One immediate and very significant application of the ideas we have developed, however, is found in a new income statement format known as the **contribution approach.** The unique thing about the contribution approach is that it provides the manager with an income statement geared directly to cost behavior.

Why a New Income Statement Format?

The *traditional approach* to the income statement, as illustrated in Chapter 2, is not organized in terms of cost behavior. Rather, it is organized in a "functional" format—emphasizing the functions of production, administration, and sales in the classification and presentation of cost data. No attempt is made to distinguish between the behavior of costs included under each functional heading. Under the heading "Administrative expense," for example, one can expect to find both variable and fixed costs lumped together.

Although an income statement prepared in the functional format may be useful for external reporting purposes, it has serious limitations when used for internal purposes. Internally, the manager needs cost data organized in a format that will facilitate planning, control, and decision-making. As we shall see in chapters ahead, these tasks are much easier when cost data are available in a fixed and variable format. The contribution approach to the income statement has been developed in response to this need.

The Contribution Approach

Exhibit 5–12 illustrates the contribution approach to the income statement with a simple example, along with the traditional approach discussed in Chapter 2.

Notice that the contribution approach separates costs into fixed and variable categories, first deducting variable expenses from sales to obtain what is known as the *contribution margin.* The **contribution margin** is the amount remaining from sales revenues after variable expenses have been deducted. This amount *contributes* toward covering fixed expenses and then toward profits for the period.

The contribution approach to the income statement is used as an internal planning and decision-making tool. Its emphasis on costs by behavior facilitates cost-volume-profit analysis, such as we shall be doing in the next chapter. The approach is also very useful in appraising management performance, in segmented reporting of profit data, and in budgeting. Moreover, the contribution approach helps managers

Exhibit 5–12 Comparison of the Contribution Income Statement with the Traditional Income Statement

Traditional Approach (costs organized by function)			Contribution Approach (costs organized by behavior)		
Sales		$12,000	Sales		$12,000
Less cost of goods sold		6,000*	Less variable expenses:		
Gross margin		6,000	Variable production	$2,000	
Less operating expenses:			Variable selling	600	
Selling	$3,100*		Variable administrative	400	3,000
Administrative	1,900*	5,000	Contribution margin		9,000
Net income		$ 1,000	Less fixed expenses:		
			Fixed production	4,000	
			Fixed selling	2,500	
			Fixed administrative	1,500	8,000
			Net income		$ 1,000

*Contains both variable and fixed expenses. This is the income statement for a manufacturing company; thus, when the income statement is placed in the contribution format, the "cost of goods sold" figure is divided between variable production costs and fixed production costs. If this were the income statement for a *merchandising* company (which simply purchases completed goods from a supplier), then the cost of goods sold would *all* be variable.

organize data pertinent to all kinds of special decisions such as product-line analysis, pricing, use of scarce resources, and make or buy analysis. All of these topics are covered in later chapters.

Summary

The ability to predict how costs will respond to changes in activity is critical for making decisions and for other major management functions. Three major classifications of costs were discussed—variable, fixed, and mixed. Mixed costs consist of a mixture of variable and fixed elements. There are three major methods of analyzing mixed costs that rely on past records of cost and activity data—the high-low method, the scattergraph approach, and lease-squares regression. The high-low method is the simplest of the three methods and can yield estimates of fixed and variable costs very quickly, but it suffers from relying on just two data points. In most situations, the least-squares regression method should be used to derive a cost formula, although the scattergraph method can also give good results. The least-squares method is objective, and a variety of useful statistics are automatically produced by most software packages along with estimates of the intercept (fixed cost) and slope (variable cost per unit). Nevertheless, even when least-squares regression is used, the data should be plotted to confirm that the relationship is really a straight line.

Managers use costs organized by behavior as a basis for many decisions. To facilitate this use, the income statement can be prepared in a contribution format. The contribution format classifies costs on the income statement by cost behavior (i.e., variable versus fixed) rather than by the functions of production, administration, and sales.

Review Problem 1: Cost Behavior

Neptune Rentals offers a boat rental service. Consider the following costs of the company over the relevant range of 5,000 to 8,000 hours of operating time for its boats:

	Hours of Operating Time			
	5,000	6,000	7,000	8,000
Total costs:				
Variable costs	$ 20,000	$?	$?	$?
Fixed costs	168,000	?	?	?
Total costs	$188,000	$?	$?	$?
Cost per hour:				
Variable cost	$?	$?	$?	$?
Fixed cost	?	?	?	?
Total cost per hour	$?	$?	$?	$?

Required Compute the missing amounts, assuming that cost behavior patterns remain unchanged within the relevant range of 5,000 to 8,000 hours.

Solution to Review Problem 1 The variable cost per hour can be computed as follows:

$$\$20{,}000 \div 5{,}000 \text{ hours} = \$4 \text{ per hour}$$

Therefore, in accordance with the behavior of variable and fixed costs, the missing amounts are as follows:

	Hours of Operating Time			
	5,000	6,000	7,000	8,000
Total costs:				
Variable costs	$ 20,000	$ 24,000	$ 28,000	$ 32,000
Fixed costs	168,000	168,000	168,000	168,000
Total costs	$188,000	$192,000	$196,000	$200,000
Cost per hour:				
Variable cost	$ 4.00	$ 4.00	$ 4.00	$ 4.00
Fixed cost	33.60	28.00	24.00	21.00
Total cost per hour	$ 37.60	$ 32.00	$ 28.00	$ 25.00

Observe that the total variable costs increase in proportion to the number of hours of operating time, but that these costs remain constant at $4 if expressed on a per hour basis.

In contrast, the total fixed costs do not change with changes in the level of activity. They remain constant at $168,000 within the relevant range. With increases in activity, however, the fixed costs decrease on a per hour basis, dropping from $33.60 per hour when the boats are operated 5,000 hours a period to only $21.00 per hour when the boats are operated 8,000 hours a period. *Because of this troublesome aspect of fixed costs, they are most easily (and most safely) dealt with on a total basis, rather than on a unit basis, in cost analysis work.*

Review Problem 2: High-Low Method

The administrator of Azalea Hills Hospital would like a cost formula linking the costs involved in admitting patients to the number of patients admitted during a month. The admitting department's costs and the number of patients admitted during the immediately preceding eight months are given in the following table:

Month	Number of Patients Admitted	Admitting Department Costs
May	1,800	$14,700
June	1,900	15,200
July	1,700	13,700
August	1,600	14,000
September	1,500	14,300
October	1,300	13,100
November	1,100	12,800
December	1,500	14,600

Required

1. Use the high-low method to establish the fixed and variable components of admitting costs.
2. Express the fixed and variable components of admitting costs as a cost formula in the linear equation form $Y = a + bX$.

Solution to Review Problem 2

1. The first step in the high-low method is to identify the periods of the lowest and highest activity. Those periods are November (1,100 patients admitted) and June (1,900 patients admitted).

   The second step is to compute the variable cost per unit using those two points:

Month	Number of Patients Admitted	Admitting Department Costs
High activity level (June)	1,900	$15,200
Low activity level (November)	1,100	12,800
Change	800	$ 2,400

$$\text{Variable cost} = \frac{\text{Change in cost}}{\text{Change in activity}} = \frac{\$2{,}400}{800} = \$3 \text{ per patient admitted}$$

The third step is to compute the fixed cost element by deducting the variable cost element from the total cost at either the high or low activity. In the computation below, the high point of activity is used:

$$\begin{aligned}\text{Fixed cost element} &= \text{Total cost} - \text{Variable cost element}\\ &= \$15{,}200 - (\$3 \times 1{,}900 \text{ patients admitted})\\ &= \$9{,}500\end{aligned}$$

2. The cost formula expressed in the linear equation form is $Y = \$9{,}500 + \$3X$.

Key Terms for Review

Account analysis A method for analyzing cost behavior in which each account under consideration is classified as either variable or fixed based on the analyst's prior knowledge of how the cost in the account behaves. (p. 202)

Activity base A measure of whatever causes the incurrence of a variable cost. For example, the total cost of X-ray film in a hospital will increase as the number of X rays taken increases. Therefore, the number of X rays is an activity base for explaining the total cost of X-ray film. (p. 191)

Adjusted R^2 A measure of goodness of fit in least-squares regression analysis. It is the percentage of the variation in the dependent variable that is explained by variation in the independent variable. (p. 209)

Committed fixed costs Those fixed costs that are difficult to adjust and that relate to the investment in facilities, equipment, and the basic organizational structure of a firm. (p. 195)

Contribution approach An income statement format that is geared to cost behavior in that costs are separated into variable and fixed categories rather than being separated according to the functions of production, sales, and administration. (p. 211)

Contribution margin The amount remaining from sales revenues after all variable expenses have been deducted. (p. 211)

Cost structure The relative proportion of fixed, variable, and mixed costs found within an organization. (p. 190)

Curvilinear costs A relationship between cost and activity that is a curve rather than a straight line. (p. 194)

Dependent variable A variable that reacts or responds to some causal factor; total cost is the dependent variable, as represented by the letter Y, in the equation $Y = a + bX$. (p. 205)

Discretionary fixed costs Those fixed costs that arise from annual decisions by management to spend in certain fixed cost areas, such as advertising and research. (p. 196)

Engineering approach A detailed analysis of cost behavior based on an industrial engineer's evaluation of the inputs that are required to carry out a particular activity and of the prices of those inputs. (p. 203)

High-low method A method of separating a mixed cost into its fixed and variable elements by analyzing the change in cost between the high and low levels of activity. (p. 205)

Independent variable A variable that acts as a causal factor; activity is the independent variable, as represented by the letter X, in the equation $Y = a + bX$. (p. 205)

Least-squares regression method A method of separating a mixed cost into its fixed and variable elements by fitting a regression line that minimizes the sum of the squared errors. (p. 208)

Mixed cost A cost that contains both variable and fixed cost elements. (p. 200)

Multiple regression An analytical method required in those situations where variations in a dependent variable are caused by more than one factor. (p. 210)

Regression line A line fitted to an array of plotted points. The slope of the line, denoted by the letter b in the linear equation $Y = a + bX$, represents the average variable cost per unit of activity. The point where the line intersects the cost axis, denoted by the letter a in the above equation, represents the average total fixed cost. (p. 206)

Relevant range The range of activity within which assumptions about variable and fixed cost behavior are valid. (p. 194)

Scattergraph method A method of separating a mixed cost into its fixed and variable elements. Under this method, a regression line is fitted to an array of plotted points by drawing a line with a straight-edge. (p. 206)

Step-variable cost A cost (such as the cost of a maintenance worker) that is obtainable only in large chunks and that increases and decreases only in response to fairly wide changes in the activity level. (p. 193)

Appendix 5A: Least-Squares Regression Calculations

objective 8

Analyze a mixed cost using the least-squares regression method.

The least-squares regression method for estimating a linear relationship is based on the equation for a straight line:

$$Y = a + bX$$

The following formulas are used to calculate the values of the vertical intercept (a) and the slope (b) that minimize the sum of the squared errors:[6]

$$b = \frac{n(\Sigma XY - (\Sigma X)(\Sigma Y)}{n(\Sigma X^2) - (\Sigma X)^2}$$

$$a = \frac{(\Sigma Y) - b(\Sigma X)}{n}$$

where:

X = The level of activity (independent variable)
Y = The total mixed cost (dependent variable)
a = The total fixed cost (the vertical intercept of the line)
b = The variable cost per unit of activity (the slope of the line)
n = Number of observations
Σ = Sum across all n observations

To illustrate how these calculations are accomplished, we will use the Brentline Hospital data from page 204.

Step 1. Compute ΣX, ΣY, ΣXY, ΣX^2, and n.

6. See calculus or statistics book for details concerning how these formulas are derived.

Month	Patient Days X	Maintenance Costs Y	XY	X^2
January	5,600	$ 7,900	$ 44,240,000	31,360,000
February	7,100	8,500	60,350,000	50,410,000
March	5,000	7,400	37,000,000	25,000,000
April	6,500	8,200	53,300,000	42,250,000
May	7,300	9,100	66,430,000	53,290,000
June	8,000	9,800	78,400,000	64,000,000
July	6,200	7,800	48,360,000	38,440,000
Total Σ	45,700	$58,700	$388,080,000	304,750,000

From this table:

$$\Sigma X = 45{,}700$$
$$\Sigma Y = \$58{,}700$$
$$\Sigma XY = \$388{,}080{,}000$$
$$\Sigma X^2 = 304{,}750{,}000$$
$$n = 7$$

Step 2. Insert the values computed in step 1 into the formula for the slope (b).

$$b = \frac{n(\Sigma YX) - (\Sigma X)(\Sigma Y)}{n(\Sigma X^2) - (\Sigma X)^2}$$

$$b = \frac{7(\$388{,}080{,}000) - (45{,}700)(\$58{,}700)}{7(304{,}750{,}000) - (45{,}700)^2}$$

$$b = \$0.759$$

Therefore, the maintenance cost is 75.9 cents per patient-day.

Step 3: Insert the values computed in step 1 and the value of b computed in step 2 into the formula for the intercept (a).

$$a = \frac{(\Sigma X) - b(\Sigma X)}{n}$$

$$a = \frac{(\$58{,}700) - \$0.759(45{,}700)}{7}$$

$$a = \$3{,}431$$

Therefore, the fixed maintenance cost is $3,431 per month. The cost formula for maintenance cost is as follows:

$$Y = a + bX$$
$$Y = \$3{,}431 + \$0.759X$$

Questions

5–1 Distinguish between (a) a variable cost, (b) a fixed cost, and (c) a mixed cost.

5–2 What effect does an increase in volume have on—

a. Unit fixed costs?
b. Unit variable costs?

c. Total fixed costs?
d. Total variable costs?

5–3 Define the following terms: (a) cost behavior, and (b) relevant range.

5–4 What is meant by an *activity base* when dealing with variable costs? Give several examples of activity bases.

5–5 Distinguish between (a) a variable cost, (b) a mixed cost, and (c) a step-variable cost. Chart the three costs on a graph, with activity plotted horizontally and cost plotted vertically.

5–6 Managers often assume a strictly linear relationship between cost and volume. How can this practice be defended in light of the fact that many costs are curvilinear?

5–7 Distinguish between discretionary fixed costs and committed fixed costs.

5–8 Classify the following fixed costs as normally being either committed or discretionary:
a. Depreciation on buildings.
b. Advertising.
c. Research.
d. Long-term equipment leases.
e. Pension payments to the firm's retirees.
f. Management development and training.

5–9 Does the concept of the relevant range apply to fixed costs? Explain.

5–10 What is the major disadvantage of the high-low method?

5–11 What methods are available for separating a mixed cost into its fixed and variable elements using past records of cost and activity data? Which method is considered to be most accurate? Why?

5–12 What is meant by a regression line? Give the general formula for a regression line. Which term represents the variable cost? The fixed cost?

5–13 Once a regression line has been drawn, how does one determine the fixed cost element? The variable cost element?

5–14 What is meant by the term *least-squares regression?*

5–15 What is the difference between ordinary least-squares regression analysis and multiple regression analysis?

5–16 What is the difference between the contribution approach to the income statement and the traditional approach to the income statement?

5–17 What is the contribution margin?

Exercises

E5–1 The Lakeshore Hotel's guest-days of occupancy and custodial supplies expense over the last seven months were:

Month	Guest-Days of Occupancy	Custodial Supplies Expense
March	4,000	$ 7,500
April	6,500	8,250
May	8,000	10,500
June	10,500	12,000
July	12,000	13,500
August	9,000	10,750
September	7,500	9,750

Guest-days is a measure of the overall activity at the hotel. For example, a guest who stays at the hotel for three days is counted as three guest-days.

Required

1. Using the high-low method, estimate a cost formula for custodial supplies expense.
2. Using the cost formula you derived above, what amount of custodial supplies expense would you expect to be incurred at an occupancy level of 11,000 guest-days?

E5–2 Refer to the data in E5–1.

Required

1. Prepare a scattergraph using the data from E5–1. Plot cost on the vertical axis and activity on the horizontal axis. Fit a regression line to your plotted points by visual inspection.
2. What is the approximate monthly fixed cost? The approximate variable cost per guest-day?
3. Scrutinize the points on your graph and explain why the high-low method would or would not yield an accurate cost formula in this situation.

E5–3 The following data relating to units shipped and total shipping expense have been assembled by Archer Company, a manufacturer of large, custom-built air-conditioning units for commercial buildings:

Month	Units Shipped	Total Shipping Expense
January	3	$1,800
February	6	2,300
March	4	1,700
April	5	2,000
May	7	2,300
June	8	2,700
July	2	1,200

Required

1. Using the high-low method, estimate a cost formula for shipping expense.
2. For the scattergraph method, do the following:
   a. Prepare a scattergraph, using the data given above. Plot cost on the vertical axis and activity on the horizontal axis. Fit a regression line to your plotted points by visual inspection.
   b. Using your scattergraph, estimate the approximate variable cost per unit shipped and the approximate fixed cost per month.
3. What factors, other than the number of units shipped, are likely to affect the company's total shipping expense? Explain.

E5–4 (Appendix 5A) Refer to the data in E5–3.

Required

1. Using the least-squares regression method, estimate a cost formula for shipping expense.
2. If you also completed E5–3, prepare a simple table comparing the variable and fixed cost elements of shipping expense as computed under the high-low method, the scattergraph method, and the least-squares regression method.

E5–5 St. Mark's Hospital contains 450 beds. The average occupancy rate is 80% per month. In other words, on average, 80% of the hospital's beds are occupied by patients. At this level of occupancy, the hospital's operating costs are $32 per occupied bed per day, assuming a 30-day month. This $32 figure contains both variable and fixed cost elements.

During June, the hospital's occupancy rate was only 60%. A total of $326,700 in operating cost was incurred during the month.

Required

1. Using the high-low method, estimate:
   a. The variable cost per occupied bed on a daily basis.
   b. The total fixed operating costs per month.
2. Assume an occupancy rate of 70% per month. What amount of total operating cost would you expect the hospital to incur?

E5–6 Hoi Chong Transport, Ltd., operates a fleet of delivery trucks in Singapore. The company has determined that if a truck is driven 105,000 kilometers during a year, the average operating cost is 11.4 cents per kilometer. If a truck is driven only 70,000 kilometers during a year, the average operating cost increases to 13.4 cents per kilometer. (The Singapore dollar is the currency used in Singapore.)

Required

1. Using the high-low method, estimate the variable and fixed cost elements of the annual cost of truck operation.
2. Express the variable and fixed costs in the form $Y = a + bX$.
3. If a truck were driven 80,000 kilometers during a year, what total cost would you expect to be incurred?

E5–7 Oki Products, Ltd., has observed the following processing costs at various levels of activity over the last 15 months:

Month	Units Produced	Processing Cost
1	4,500	$38,000
2	11,000	52,000
3	12,000	56,000
4	5,500	40,000
5	9,000	47,000
6	10,500	52,000
7	7,500	44,000
8	5,000	41,000
9	11,500	52,000
10	6,000	43,000
11	8,500	48,000
12	10,000	50,000
13	6,500	44,000
14	9,500	48,000
15	8,000	46,000

Required

1. Prepare a scattergraph by plotting the above data on a graph. Plot cost on the vertical axis and activity on the horizontal axis. Fit a line to your plotted points by visual inspection.
2. What is the approximate monthly fixed cost? The approximate variable cost per unit processed? Show your computations.

E5–8 (Appendix 5A) George Caloz & Frères, located in Grenchen, Switzerland, makes prestige high-end custom watches in small lots. The company has been in operation since 1856. One of the company's products, a platinum diving watch, goes through an etching process. The company has observed etching costs as follows over the last six weeks:

Week	Units	Total Etching Cost
1	4	SFr18
2	3	17
3	8	25
4	6	20
5	7	24
6	2	16
	30	SFr120

The Swiss currency is the Swiss Franc, which is denoted by SFr.

For planning purposes, management would like to know the amount of variable etching cost per unit and the total fixed etching cost per week.

Required

1. Using the least-squares regression method, estimate the variable and fixed elements of etching cost.
2. Express the cost data in (1) above in the form $Y = a + bX$.

3. If the company processes five units next week, what would be the expected total etching cost?

E5–9 Harris Company manufactures and sells a single product. A partially completed schedule of the company's total and per unit costs over the relevant range of 30,000 to 50,000 units produced and sold annually is given below:

	Units Produced and Sold		
	30,000	**40,000**	**50,000**
Total costs:			
Variable costs	$180,000	?	?
Fixed costs	300,000	?	?
Total costs	$480,000	?	?
Cost per unit:			
Variable cost	?	?	?
Fixed cost	?	?	?
Total cost per unit	?	?	?

Required

1. Complete the schedule of the company's total and unit costs above.
2. Assume that the company produces and sells 45,000 units during a year at a selling price of $16 per unit. Prepare an income statement in the contribution format for the year.

E5–10 The Alpine House, Inc., is a large retailer of winter sports equipment. An income statement for the company's Ski Department for a recent quarter is presented below:

THE ALPINE HOUSE, INC.
Income Statement—Ski Department
For the Quarter Ended March 31

Sales		$150,000
Less cost of goods sold		90,000
Gross margin		60,000
Less operating expenses:		
Selling expenses	$30,000	
Administrative expenses	10,000	40,000
Net income		$ 20,000

Skis sell, on the average, for $750 per pair. Variable selling expenses are $50 per pair of skis sold. The remaining selling expenses are fixed. The administrative expenses are 20% variable and 80% fixed. The company does not manufacture its own skis; it purchases them from a supplier for $450 per pair.

Required

1. Prepare an income statement for the quarter using the contribution approach.
2. For every pair of skis sold during the quarter, what was the contribution toward covering fixed expenses and toward earning profits?

Problems

P5–11 High-Low Method; Contribution Income Statement Morrisey & Brown, Ltd., of Sydney is a merchandising firm that is the sole distributor of a product that is increasing in popularity among Australian consumers. The company's income statements for the three most recent months follow:

MORRISEY & BROWN, LTD.
Income Statements
For the Three Months Ending September 30

	July	August	September
Sales in units	4,000	4,500	5,000
Sales revenue	A$400,000	A$450,000	A$500,000
Less cost of goods sold	240,000	270,000	300,000
Gross margin	160,000	180,000	200,000
Less operating expenses:			
Advertising expense	21,000	21,000	21,000
Shipping expense	34,000	36,000	38,000
Salaries and commissions	78,000	84,000	90,000
Insurance expense	6,000	6,000	6,000
Depreciation expense	15,000	15,000	15,000
Total operating expenses	154,000	162,000	170,000
Net income	A$ 6,000	A$ 18,000	A$ 30,000

(Note: Morrisey & Brown, Ltd.'s Australian-formatted income statement has been recast in the format common in the United States. The Australian dollar is denoted by A$.)

Required

1. Identify each of the company's expenses (including cost of goods sold) as being either variable, fixed, or mixed.
2. By use of the high-low method, separate each mixed expense into variable and fixed elements. State the cost formula for each mixed expense.
3. Redo the company's income statement at the 5,000-unit level of activity using the contribution format.

P5–12 Least-Squares Regression Method of Cost Analysis; Graphing (Appendix 5A) Professor John Morton has just been appointed chairperson of the Finance Department at Westland University. In reviewing the department's cost records, Professor Morton has found the following total cost associated with Finance 101 over the last several terms:

Term	Number of Sections Offered	Total Cost
Fall, last year	4	$10,000
Winter, last year	6	14,000
Summer, last year	2	7,000
Fall, this year	5	13,000
Winter, this year	3	9,500

Professor Morton knows that there are some variable costs, such as amounts paid to graduate assistants, associated with the course. He would like to have the variable and fixed costs separated for planning purposes.

Required

1. Using the least-squares regression method, estimate the variable cost per section and the total fixed cost per term for Finance 101.
2. Express the cost data derived in (1) above in the linear equation form $Y = a + bX$.
3. Assume that because of the small number of sections offered during the Winter Term this year, Professor Morton will have to offer eight sections of Finance 101 during the Fall Term. Compute the expected total cost for Finance 101. Can you see any problem with using the cost formula from (2) above to derive this total cost figure? Explain.
4. Prepare a scattergraph and fit a regression line to the plotted points using the cost formula expressed in (2) above.

P5–13 Contribution versus Traditional Income Statement Marwick's Pianos, Inc., purchases pianos from a large manufacturer and sells them at the retail level. The pianos cost, on the average, \$2,450 each from the manufacturer. Marwick's Pianos, Inc., sells the pianos to its customers at an average price of \$3,125 each. The selling and administrative costs that the company incurs in a typical month are presented below:

Costs	Cost Formula
Selling:	
Advertising	\$700 per month
Sales salaries and commissions	\$950 per month, plus 8% of sales
Delivery of pianos to customers	\$30 per piano sold
Utilities	\$350 per month
Depreciation of sales facilities	\$800 per month
Administrative:	
Executive salaries	\$2,500 per month
Insurance	\$400 per month
Clerical	\$1,000 per month, plus \$20 per piano sold
Depreciation of office equipment	\$300 per month

During August, Marwick's Pianos, Inc., sold and delivered 40 pianos.

Required

1. Prepare an income statement for Marwick's Pianos, Inc., for August. Use the traditional format, with costs organized by function.
2. Redo (1) above, this time using the contribution format, with costs organized by behavior. Show costs and revenues on both total and a per unit basis down through contribution margin.
3. Refer to the income statement you prepared in (2) above. Why might it be misleading to show the fixed costs on a per unit basis?

P5–14 Identifying Cost Behavior Patterns On the next page are a number of cost behavior patterns that might be found in a company's cost structure. The vertical axis on each graph represents total cost, and the horizontal axis on each graph represents level of activity (volume).

Required

1. For each of the following situations, identify the graph from the next page that illustrates the cost pattern involved. Any graph may be used more than once.
   a. Cost of raw materials used.
   b. Electricity bill—a flat fixed charge, plus a variable cost after a certain number of kilowatt-hours are used.
   c. City water bill, which is computed as follows:

First 1,000,000 gallons or less	\$1,000 flat fee
Next 10,000 gallons	0.003 per gallon used
Next 10,000 gallons	0.006 per gallon used
Next 10,000 gallons	0.009 per gallon used
Etc.	Etc.

   d. Depreciation of equipment, where the amount is computed by the straight-line method. When the depreciation rate was established, it was anticipated that the obsolescence factor would be greater than the wear and tear factor.
   e. Rent on a factory building donated by the city, where the agreement calls for a fixed fee payment unless 200,000 labor-hours or more are worked, in which case no rent need be paid.
   f. Salaries of maintenance workers, where one maintenance worker is needed for every 1,000 hours of machine-hours or less (that is, 0 to 1,000 hours requires one maintenance worker, 1,001 to 2,000 hours requires two maintenance workers, etc.)
   g. Cost of raw materials, where the cost decreases by 5 cents per unit for each of the first 100 units purchased, after which it remains constant at \$2.50 per unit.

h. Rent on a factory building donated by the county, where the agreement calls for rent of $100,000 less $1 for each direct labor-hour worked in excess of 200,000 hours, but a minimum rental payment of $20,000 must be paid.
i. Use of a machine under a lease, where a minimum charge of $1,000 is paid for up to 400 hours of machine time. After 400 hours of machine time, an additional charge of $2 per hour is paid up to a maximum charge of $2,000 per period.

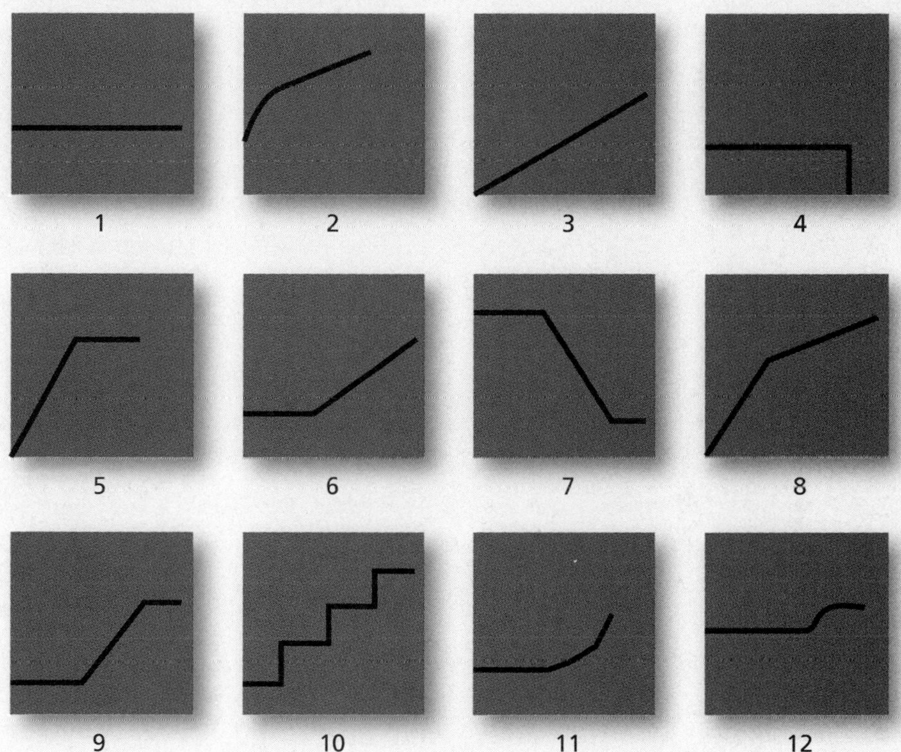

2. How would a knowledge of cost behavior patterns such as those above be of help to a manager in analyzing the cost structure of his or her firm?

(CPA, adapted)

P5–15 High-Low Method of Cost Analysis Nova Company's total overhead costs at various levels of activity are presented below:

Month	Machine-Hours	Total Overhead Costs
April	70,000	$198,000
May	60,000	174,000
June	80,000	222,000
July	90,000	246,000

Assume that the total overhead costs above consist of utilities, supervisory salaries, and maintenance. The breakdown of these costs at the 60,000 machine-hour level of activity is:

Utilities (V)	$ 48,000
Supervisory salaries (F)	21,000
Maintenance (M)	105,000
Total overhead costs	$174,000

V = variable; F = fixed; M = mixed.

Nova Company's management wants to break down the maintenance cost into its basic variable and fixed cost elements.

Required

1. As shown above, overhead costs in July amounted to $246,000. Determine how much of this consisted of maintenance cost. (Hint: to do this, it may be helpful to first determine how much of the $246,000 consisted of utilities and supervisory salaries. Think about the behavior of variable and fixed costs!)
2. By means of the high-low method, estimate a cost formula for maintenance.
3. Express the company's *total* overhead costs in the linear equation form $Y = a + bX$.
4. What *total* overhead costs would you expect to be incurred at an operating activity level of 75,000 machine-hours?

P5–16 High-Low Method of Cost Analysis Sawaya Co., Ltd., of Japan is a manufacturing company whose total factory overhead costs fluctuate considerably from year to year according to increases and decreases in the number of direct labor-hours worked in the factory. Total factory overhead costs (in Japanese yen, denoted ¥) at high and low levels of activity for recent years are given below:

	Level of Activity	
	Low	High
Direct labor-hours	50,000	75,000
Total factory overhead costs	¥14,250,000	¥17,625,000

The factory overhead costs above consist of indirect materials, rent, and maintenance. The company has analyzed these costs at the 50,000-hour level of activity as follows:

Indirect materials (V)	¥5,000,000
Rent (F)	6,000,000
Maintenance (M)	3,250,000
Total factory overhead costs	¥14,250,000

V = variable; F = fixed; M = mixed.

To have data available for planning, the company wants to break down the maintenance cost into its variable and fixed cost elements.

Required

1. Estimate how much of the ¥17,625,000 factory overhead cost at the high level of activity consists of maintenance cost. (Hint: To do this, it may be helpful to first determine how much of the ¥17,625,000 consists of indirect materials and rent. Think about the behavior of variable and fixed costs!)
2. By means of the high-low method of cost analysis, estimate a cost formula for maintenance.
3. What total factory overhead costs would you expect the company to incur at an operating level of 70,000 direct labor-hours?

P5–17 Manufacturing Statements; High-Low Method of Cost Analysis Amfac Company manufactures a single product. The company keeps careful records of manufacturing activities from which the following information has been extracted:

	Level of Activity	
	March–Low	June–High
Number of units produced	6,000	9,000
Cost of goods manufactured	$168,000	$257,000
Work in process inventory, beginning	$ 9,000	$ 32,000
Work in process inventory, ending	$ 15,000	$ 21,000
Direct materials cost per unit	$ 6	$ 6
Direct labor cost per unit	$ 10	$ 10
Manufacturing overhead cost, total	?	?

The company's manufacturing overhead cost consists of both variable and fixed cost elements. To have data available for planning, management wants to determine how much of the overhead cost is variable with units produced and how much of it is fixed per month.

Required

1. For both March and June, determine the amount of manufacturing overhead cost added to production. The company had no under- or overapplied overhead in either month. (Hint: A useful way to proceed might be to construct a schedule of cost of goods manufactured.)
2. By means of the high-low method of cost analysis, estimate a cost formula for manufacturing overhead. Express the variable portion of the formula in terms of a variable rate per unit of product.
3. If 7,000 units are produced during a month, what would be the cost of goods manufactured? (Assume that work in process inventories do not change and that there is no under- or overapplied overhead cost for the month.)

P5–18 Scattergraph Method of Cost Analysis Molina Company is a value-added computer resaler that specializes in providing services to small companies. The company owns and maintains several autos for use by the sales staff. All expenses of operating these autos have been entered into an Automobile Expense account on the company's books. Along with this record of expenses, the company has also kept a careful record of the number of miles the autos have been driven each month.

The company's records of miles driven and total auto expenses over the past 10 months are given below:

Month	Total Mileage (000)	Total Cost
January	4	$3,000
February	8	3,700
March	7	3,300
April	12	4,000
May	6	3,300
June	11	3,900
July	14	4,200
August	10	3,600
September	13	4,100
October	15	4,400

Molina Company's president wants to know the cost of operating the fleet of cars in terms of the fixed monthly cost and the variable cost per mile driven.

Required

1. Prepare a scattergraph using the data given above. Place cost on the vertical axis and activity (miles driven) on the horizontal axis. Fit a regression line to the plotted points by simple visual inspection.
2. By analyzing your scattergraph, estimate fixed cost per month and the variable cost per mile driven.

P5–19 Least-Squares Regression Method of Cost Analysis (Appendix 5A) Refer to the data for Molina Company in P5–18.

Required

1. Using the least-squares regression method, estimate the variable and fixed cost elements associated with the company's fleet of autos. (Since the Total Mileage is in thousands of miles, the variable rate you compute will also be in thousands of miles. The rate can be left in this form, or you can convert it to a per mile basis by dividing the rate you get by 1,000.)
2. From the data in (1) above, express the cost formula for auto use in the linear equation form $Y = a + bX$.

P5–20 Mixed Cost Analysis; High-Low and Scattergraph Methods Pleasant View Hospital of British Columbia has just hired a new chief administrator who is anxious to employ sound management and planning techniques in the business affairs of the hospital. Accordingly, she has directed her assistant to summarize the cost structure existing in the various departments so that data will be available for planning purposes.

The assistant is unsure how to classify the utilities costs in the Radiology Department since these costs do not exhibit either strictly variable or fixed cost behavior. Utilities costs are very high in the department due to a CAT scanner that draws a large amount of power and is kept running at all times. The scanner can't be turned off due to the long warm-up period required for its use. When the scanner is used to scan a patient, it consumes an additional burst of power. The assistant has accumulated the following data on utilities costs and use of the scanner since the first of the year.

Month	Number of Scans	Utilities Cost
January	60	$2,200
February	70	2,600
March	90	2,900
April	120	3,300
May	100	3,000
June	130	3,600
July	150	4,000
August	140	3,600
September	110	3,100
October	80	2,500

The chief administrator has informed her assistant that the utilities cost is probably a mixed cost that will have to be broken down into its variable and fixed cost elements by use of a scattergraph. The assistant feels, however, that if an analysis of this type is necessary, then the high-low method should be used, since it is easier and quicker. The controller has suggested that there may be a better approach.

Required

1. Using the high-low method, estimate a cost formula for utilities. Express the formula in the form $Y = a + bX$. (The variable rate should be stated in terms of cost per scan.)
2. Prepare a scattergraph by plotting the above data on a graph. (The number of scans should be placed on the horizontal axis, and utilities cost should be placed on the vertical axis.) Fit a regression line to the plotted points by visual inspection and estimate a cost formula for utilities.

P5–21 Least-Squares Regression Method of Cost Analysis (Appendix 5A) Refer to the data for Pleasant View Hospital in P5–20.

Required

1. Using the least-squares regression method, estimate a cost formula for utilities. (Round the variable rate to two decimal places.)
2. Refer to the graph prepared in (2) of P5–20. Explain why in this case the high-low method would be the least accurate of the three methods in deriving a cost formula.

P5–22 Least-Squares Regression Analysis; Contribution Income Statement (Appendix 5A) Milden Company has an exclusive franchise to purchase a product from the manufacturer and distribute it on the retail level. As an aid in planning, the company has decided to start using the contribution approach to the income statement internally. To have data to prepare such a statement, the company has analyzed its expenses and developed the following cost formulas:

Cost	Cost Formula
Cost of good sold	$35 per unit sold
Advertising expense	$210,000 per quarter
Sales commissions	6% of sales
Shipping expense	?
Administrative salaries	$145,000 per quarter
Insurance expense	$9,000 per quarter
Depreciation expense	$76,000 per quarter

Management has concluded that shipping expense is a mixed cost, containing both variable and fixed cost elements. Units sold and the related shipping expense over the last eight quarters follow:

Quarter	Units Sold (000)	Shipping Expense
Year 1:		
First	10	$119,000
Second	16	175,000
Third	18	190,000
Fourth	15	164,000
Year 2:		
First	11	130,000
Second	17	185,000
Third	20	210,000
Fourth	13	147,000

Milden Company's president would like a cost formula derived for shipping expense so that a budgeted income statement using the contribution approach can be prepared for the next quarter.

Required

1. Using the least-square regression method, estimate a cost formula for shipping expense. (Since the Units Sold above are in thousands of units, the variable rate you compute will also be in thousands of units. It can be left in this form, or you can convert your variable rate to a per unit basis by dividing it by 1,000.)
2. In the first quarter of Year 3, the company plans to sell 12,000 units at a selling price of $100 per unit. Prepare an income statement for the quarter using the contribution format.

Cases

C5–23 Analysis of Mixed Costs, Job-Cost System, and Activity-Based Costing Hokuriku-Seika Co., Ltd., of Yokohama, Japan, is a subcontractor to local manufacturing firms. The company specializes in precision metal cutting using focused high-pressure water jets and high-energy lasers. The company has a traditional job-cost system in which direct labor and direct materials costs are assigned directly to jobs, but factory overhead is applied using direct labor-hours as a base. Management uses this job cost data for valuing cost of goods sold and inventories for external reports. For internal decision making, management has largely ignored this cost data since direct labor costs are basically fixed and management believes overhead costs actually have little to do with direct labor-hours. Recently, management has become interested in activity-based costing (ABC) as a way of estimating job costs and other costs for decision-making purposes.

Management assembled a cross-functional team to design a prototype ABC system. Electrical costs was one of the factory overhead costs first investigated by the team. Electricity is used to provide light, to power equipment, and to heat the building in the winter and cool it in the summer. The ABC team proposed allocating electrical costs to jobs based on machine-hours since running the machines consumes significant amounts of electricity. Data assembled by the team concerning actual direct labor-hours, machine-hours, and electrical costs over a recent eight-week period appear below. (The Japanese currency is the yen, which is denoted by ¥.)

	Direct Labor-Hours	Machine-Hours	Electrical Costs
Week 1.	8,920	7,200	¥ 77,100
Week 2.	8,900	8,200	84,400
Week 3.	8,950	8,700	80,400
Week 4.	8,990	7,200	75,500
Week 5.	8,840	7,400	81,100
Week 6.	8,890	8,800	83,300
Week 7.	8,950	6,400	79,200
Week 8.	8,990	7,700	85,500
Total	71,340	61,600	¥646,500

To help assess the effect of the proposed change to machine-hours as allocation base, the eight-week totals were converted to annual figures by multiplying them by six.

	Direct Labor-Hours	Machine-Hours	Electrical Costs
Estimated annual total (eight-week total above × 6)	428,040	369,600	¥3,879,000

Required

1. Assume that the estimated annual totals from the above table are used to compute the company's predetermined overhead rate. What would be the predetermined overhead rate for electrical costs if the allocation base is direct labor-hours? Machine-hours?
2. Hokuriku-Seika Co. intends to bid on a job for a shipyard that would require 350 direct labor-hours and 270 machine-hours. How much electrical cost would be charged to this job using the predetermined overhead rate computed in (1) above if the allocation base is direct labor-hours? Machine-hours?
3. Prepare a scattergraph in which you plot direct labor-hours on the horizontal axis and electrical costs on the vertical axis. Prepare another scattergraph in which you plot machine-hours on the horizontal axis and electrical costs on the vertical axis. Do you agree with the ABC team that machine-hours is a better allocation base for electrical costs than direct labor-hours? Why?
4. Using machine-hours as the measure of activity, estimate the fixed and variable components of electrical costs using either the scattergraph (i.e., visual fit) method or least-squares regression.
5. How much electrical cost do you think would actually be caused by the shipyard job in (2) above? Explain.
6. What factors, apart from direct labor-hours and machine-hours, are likely to affect consumption of electrical power in the company?

C5–24 Mixed Cost Analysis by Three Methods (Appendix 5A) The Ramon Company manufactures a wide range of products at several plant locations. The Franklin plant, which manufactures electrical components, has been experiencing difficulties with fluctuating monthly overhead costs. The fluctuations have made it difficult to estimate the level of overhead that will be incurred for any one month.

Management wants to be able to estimate overhead costs accurately in order to better plan its operational and financial needs. A trade association publication to which Ramon Company subscribes indicates that for companies manufacturing electrical components, overhead tends to vary with direct labor-hours.

One member of the accounting staff has proposed the cost behavior pattern of the overhead costs be determined. Then overhead costs could be predicted from the budgeted direct labor-hours.

Another member of the accounting staff has suggested that a good starting place for determining the cost behavior pattern of overhead costs would be an analysis of historical data. The historical cost behavior pattern would provide a basis for estimating future overhead costs. The methods that have been proposed for determining the cost behavior pattern include high-low, scattergraph, least-squares regression, multiple regression, and exponential smoothing. Of these methods, Ramon Company has decided to employ the high-low method, the scattergraph method, and the least-squares regression method. Data on direct labor-hours and the respective overhead costs incurred have been collected for the past two years. The raw data are as follows:

	1997		1998	
Month	Direct Labor-Hours	Overhead Costs	Direct Labor-Hours	Overhead Costs
January	20,000	$84,000	21,000	$86,000
February	25,000	99,000	24,000	93,000
March	22,000	89,500	23,000	93,000
April	23,000	90,000	22,000	87,000
May	20,000	81,500	20,000	80,000
June	19,000	75,500	18,000	76,500
July	14,000	70,500	12,000	67,500
August	10,000	64,500	13,000	71,000
September	12,000	69,000	15,000	73,500
October	17,000	75,000	17,000	72,500
November	16,000	71,500	15,000	71,000
December	19,000	78,000	18,000	75,000

All equipment in the Franklin plant is leased under an arrangement calling for a flat fee up to 19,500 direct labor-hours of activity in the plant, after which lease charges are assessed on an hourly basis. Lease expense is a major item of overhead cost.

Required

1. Using the high-low method, estimate the cost formula for overhead in the Franklin plant.
2. Repeat (1) above, this time using the least-squares regression method. Your assistant has computed the following amounts, which may be helpful in your analysis.

$$\Sigma X = 435{,}000$$
$$\Sigma Y = \$1{,}894{,}000$$
$$\Sigma XY = \$35{,}170{,}500{,}000$$
$$\Sigma X^2 = 8{,}275{,}000{,}000$$

   (Round off your answers to three significant digits.)
3. Prepare a scattergraph, including on it all data for the two-year period. Fit a regression line or lines to the plotted points by visual inspection. In this part it is not necessary to compute the fixed and variable cost elements.
4. Assume that the Franklin plant works 22,500 direct labor-hours during a month. Compute the expected overhead cost for the month using the cost formulas developed above with:
   a. The high-low method.
   b. The least-squares regression method.
   c. The scattergraph method [read the expected costs directly off the graph prepared in (3) above].
5. Of the three proposed methods, which one should the Ramon Company use to estimate monthly overhead costs in the Franklin plant? Explain fully, indicating the reasons why the other methods are less desirable.
6. Would a relevant range concept probably be more or less important in the Franklin plant than in most companies?

(CMA, adapted)

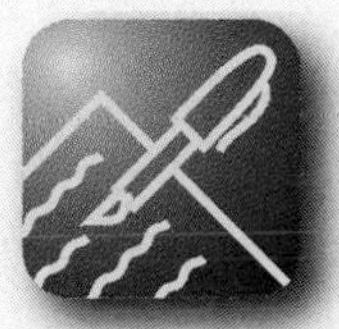

C5–25 Analysis of Mixed Costs in a Pricing Decision Maria Chavez owns a catering company that serves food and beverages at parties and business functions. Chavez's business is seasonal, with a heavy schedule during the summer months and holidays and a lighter schedule at other times.

One of the major events Chavez's customers request is a cocktail party. She offers a standard cocktail party and has estimated the cost per guest as follows:

Food and beverages	$15.00
Labor (0.5 hrs. @ $10.00/hr.)	5.00
Overhead (0.5 hrs. @ $13.98/hr.)	6.99
Total cost per guest	$26.99

The standard cocktail party lasts three hours and Chavez hires one worker for every six guests, so that works out to one-half hour of labor per guest. These workers are hired only as needed and are paid only for the hours they actually work.

When bidding on cocktail parties, Chavez adds a 15% markup to yield a price of about $31 per guest. She is confident about her estimates of the costs of food and beverages and labor but is not as comfortable with the estimate of overhead cost. The $13.98 overhead cost per labor hour was determined by dividing total overhead expenses for the last 12 months by total labor hours for the same period. Monthly data concerning overhead costs and labor-hours appear below:

Month	Labor-Hours	Overhead Expenses
January	2,500	$ 55,000
February	2,800	59,000
March	3,000	60,000
April	4,200	64,000
May	4,500	67,000
June	5,500	71,000
July	6,500	74,000
August	7,500	77,000
September	7,000	75,000
October	4,500	68,000
November	3,100	62,000
December	6,500	73,000
Total	57,600	$805,000

Chavez has received a request to bid on a 180-guest fund-raising cocktail party to be given next month by an important local charity. (The party would last the usual three hours.) She would really like to win this contract; the guest list for this charity event includes many prominent individuals she would like to land as future clients. Maria is confident that these potential customers would be favorably impressed by her company's services at the charity event.

Required

1. Estimate the contribution to profit of a standard 180-guest cocktail party if Chavez charges her usual price of $31 per guest. (In other words, by how much would her overall profit increase?)
2. How low could Chavez bid for the charity event in terms of a price per guest and still not lose money on the event itself?
3. The individual who is organizing the charity's fund-raising event has indicated that he has already received a bid under $30 from another catering company. Do you think Chavez should bid below her normal $31 per guest price for the charity event? Why or why not?

(CMA, adapted)

Group Exercises

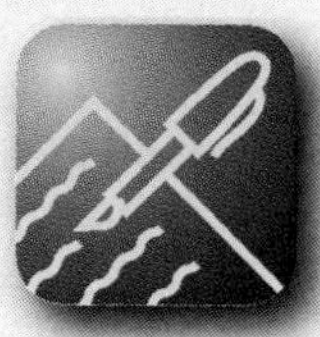

GE5–26 Economies or Diseconomies of Scale? Increased efficiency and lower costs result from economies of scale. An increase in scale or size (i.e., capacity) seldom requires a proportional increase in investment, research and development, sales and marketing, or administration. Therefore, high-volume, large-scale facilities create the potential for lower unit cost. It has been estimated that scale-related costs decrease as volume increases, usually falling by 15% to 25% per unit each time volume doubles.

Many industries including steel, autos, electric power, and universities have used scale-based economies to lower the cost of their product or service. Throughout the 1980s, U.S. steel companies invested enormous sums to modernize their plants, lower their costs, and rise from the huge losses inflicted by foreign competition. But now, "minimills," smaller, more specialized plants, are a new threat that could cause the large U.S. steel companies' profits to come crashing down if they are unable to fully realize the benefits of their size.

Required

1. Explain what impact steel company investments in modernizing their plants had on total fixed costs, fixed cost per unit, total variable costs, variable cost per unit, total costs, and average unit cost. Place this information on two graphs. On both graphs, label the *X* axis Production Volume. The *Y* axis on one graph should be labeled Total Costs, and on the other graph label the *Y* axis Unit Cost.
2. Which fixed costs are increasing rapidly, committed fixed costs (the costs related to the facilities and equipment) or discretionary fixed costs (the costs related to people who support production and sales)? Develop a specific scenario explaining how a particular fixed cost could increase over time.
3. What could cause fixed costs to increase so rapidly in your scenario?
4. Explain how gains and losses of market share can have such a huge impact on operating profits and losses of U.S. steel companies.

IE5–27 Estimating Variable and Fixed Costs Carnival Corporation owns and operates a fleet of cruise ships. The company measures its activity in terms of passenger cruise-days. For example, a family of four on a five-day cruise is counted as 20 passenger cruise-days. Many of the expenses of cruise ships—for example, the costs of food served to passengers—vary with the number of passenger cruise-days. By accessing Carnival Corporation's annual report in the Investor Relations section of their web site www.carnivalcorp.com, you can find information about their expenses and passenger cruise-days for the last three years. Operating Expenses, Selling and Administrative Expenses, and Depreciation and Amortization Expenses are listed in the company's income statement. The passenger cruise-days are listed in the section of the annual report called Management's Discussion and Analysis of Financial Condition and Results of Operations.

Required

1. For each of the three categories of expenses listed above, do the following:
   a. Plot the expense against passenger cruise-days.
   b. Using the scattergraph method, estimate the fixed and variable components of the expense. Do you have much confidence in your estimates? Why or why not?
   c. Using the high-low method, estimate the fixed and variable components of the expense. Do you have much confidence in this estimate? Why or why not?
2. Use what you believe to be the best estimates of fixed and variable costs from your analyses above to estimate how the total cost of the company varies with the number of passenger cruise-days. Express the relation in terms of the cost formula $Y = a + bX$, where *Y* is total cost and *X* is passenger cruise-days. (Ignore interest expense and income tax expense. Only include Operating Expenses, Selling and Administrative, and Depreciation and Amortization in the total cost.)

Chapter Six

Cost-Volume-Profit Relationships

Business Focus

Mike volunteered to be the director of the organization sponsoring this year's Pioneer Square Holiday Feed, an annual charitable event that provides a special holiday meal to the homeless and low-income residents of the downtown area. The event is supported by donations of cash, foodstuffs, and labor. There is a small charge for the meal, but the charge is voluntary.

Mike's organization will have to buy some groceries, including disposable tableware, and will have to hire a professional chef to make sure that health department guidelines are scrupulously followed. Mike would like to know how many meals his organization can afford to serve. This information will affect all of his planning.

Learning Objectives

After studying Chapter 6, you should be able to:

1 Explain how changes in activity affect contribution margin and net income.

2 Compute the contribution margin ratio (CM ratio) and use it to compute changes in contribution margin and net income.

3 Show the effects on contribution margin of changes in variable costs, fixed costs, selling price, and volume.

4 Compute the break-even point by both the equation method and the contribution margin method.

5 Prepare a cost-volume-profit (CVP) graph and explain the significance of each of its components.

6 Use the CVP formulas to determine the activity level needed to achieve a desired target profit.

7 Compute the margin of safety and explain its significance.

8 Compute the degree of operating leverage at a particular level of sales and explain how the degree of operating leverage can be used to predict changes in net income.

9 Compute the break-even point for a multiple product company and explain the effects of shifts in the sales mix on contribution margin and the break-even point.

Cost-volume-profit (CVP) analysis is one of the most powerful tools that managers have at their command. It helps them understand the interrelationship between cost, volume, and profit in an organization by focusing on interactions between the following five elements:

1. Prices of products.
2. Volume or level of activity.
3. Per unit variable costs.
4. Total fixed costs.
5. Mix of products sold.

Because CVP analysis helps managers understand the interrelationship between cost, volume, and profit, it is a vital tool in many business decisions. These decisions include, for example, what products to manufacture or sell, what pricing policy to follow, what marketing strategy to employ, and what type of productive facilities to acquire.

Managerial Accounting in Action

THE ISSUE

Acoustic Concepts, Inc., was founded by Prem Narayan, a graduate student in engineering, to market a radical new speaker he had designed for automobile sound systems. The speaker, called the Sonic Blaster, uses an advanced microprocessor chip to boost amplification to awesome levels. Prem contracted with a Taiwanese electronics manufacturer to produce the speaker. With seed money provided by his family, Prem placed an order with the manufacturer for completed units and ran advertisements in auto magazines.

The Sonic Blaster was an almost immediate success, and sales grew to the point that Prem moved the company's headquarters out of his apartment and into rented quarters in a neighboring industrial park. He also hired a receptionist, an accountant, a sales manager, and a small sales staff to sell the speakers to retail stores. The accountant, Bob Luchinni, had worked for several small companies where he had acted as a business advisor as well as accountant and bookkeeper. The following discussion occurred soon after Bob was hired:

Prem: Bob, I've got a lot of questions about the company's finances that I hope you can help answer.
Bob: We're in great shape. The loan from your family will be paid off within a few months.
Prem: I know, but I am worried about the risks I've taken on by expanding operations. What would happen if a competitor entered the market and our sales slipped? How far could sales drop without putting us into the red? Another question I've been trying to resolve is how much our sales would have to increase in order to justify the big marketing campaign the sales staff is pushing for.
Bob: Marketing always wants more money for advertising.
Prem: And they are always pushing me to drop the selling price on the speaker. I agree with them that a lower price will boost our volume, but I'm not sure the increased volume will offset the loss in revenue from the lower price.
Bob: It sounds like these questions all are related in some way to the relationships between our selling prices, our costs, and our volume. We shouldn't have a problem coming up with some answers. I'll need a day or two, though, to gather some data.

Prem: Why don't we set up a meeting for three days from now? That would be Thursday.
Bob: That'll be fine. I'll have some preliminary answers for you as well as a model you can use for answering similar questions in the future.
Prem: Good. I'll be looking forward to seeing what you come up with. ■

The Basics of Cost-Volume-Profit (CVP) Analysis

Bob Luchinni's preparation for the Thursday meeting begins where our study of cost behavior in the preceding chapter left off—with the contribution income statement. The contribution income statement emphasizes the behavior of costs and therefore is extremely helpful to a manager in judging the impact on profits of changes in selling price, cost, or volume. Bob will base his analysis on the following contribution income statement he prepared last month:

ACOUSTIC CONCEPTS, INC.
Contribution Income Statement
For the Month of June

	Total	Per Unit
Sales (400 speakers)	$100,000	$250
Less variable expenses	60,000	150
Contribution margin	40,000	$100
Less fixed expenses	35,000	
Net income	$ 5,000	

Notice that sales, variable expenses, and contribution margin are expressed on a per unit basis as well as in total. This is commonly done on income statements prepared for management's own use, since, as we shall see, it facilitates profitability analysis.

Contribution Margin

objective 1
Explain how changes in activity affect contribution margin and net income.

As explained in Chapter 5, contribution margin is the amount remaining from sales revenue after variable expenses have been deducted. Thus, it is the amount available to cover fixed expenses and then to provide profits for the period. Notice the sequence here—contribution margin is used *first* to cover the fixed expenses, and then whatever remains goes toward profits. If the contribution margin is not sufficient to cover the fixed expenses, then a loss occurs for the period. To illustrate with an extreme example, assume that by the middle of a particular month Acoustic Concepts has been able to sell only one speaker. At that point, the company's income statement will appear as follows:

	Total	Per Unit
Sales (1 speaker)	$ 250	$250
Less variable expenses	150	150
Contribution margin	100	$100
Less fixed expenses	35,000	
Net loss	$(34,900)	

For each additional speaker that the company is able to sell during the month, $100 more in contribution margin will become available to help cover the fixed expenses. If a second speaker is sold, for example, then the total contribution margin will increase by $100 (to a total of $200) and the company's loss will decrease by $100, to $34,800:

	Total	Per Unit
Sales (2 speakers)	$ 500	$250
Less variable expenses	300	150
Contribution margin	200	$100
Less fixed expenses	35,000	
Net loss	$(34,800)	

If enough speakers can be sold to generate $35,000 in contribution margin, then all of the fixed costs will be covered and the company will have managed to at least *break even* for the month—that is, to show neither profit nor loss but just cover all of its costs. To reach the break-even point, the company will have to sell 350 speakers in a month, since each speaker sold yields $100 in contribution margin:

	Total	Per Unit
Sales (350 speakers)	$87,500	$250
Less variable expenses	52,500	150
Contribution margin	35,000	$100
Less fixed expenses	35,000	
Net income	$ –0–	

Computation of the break-even point is discussed in detail later in the chapter; for the moment, note that the **break-even point** can be defined as the level of sales at which profit is zero.

Once the break-even point has been reached, net income will increase by the unit contribution margin for each additional unit sold. If 351 speakers are sold in a month, for example, then we can expect that the net income for the month will be $100, since the company will have sold 1 speaker more than the number needed to break even:

	Total	Per Unit
Sales (351 speakers)	$87,750	$250
Less variable expenses	52,650	150
Contribution margin	35,100	$100
Less fixed expenses	35,000	
Net income	$ 100	

If 352 speakers are sold (2 speakers above the break-even point), then we can expect that the net income for the month will be $200, and so forth. To know what the profits will be at various levels of activity, therefore, it is not necessary for a manager to prepare a whole series of income statements. The manager can simply take the number of units to be sold over the break-even point and multiply that number by the unit contribution margin. The result represents the anticipated profits for the period. Or, to estimate the effect of a planned increase in sales on profits, the manager can simply multiply the increase in units sold by the unit contribution margin. The result will be the expected increase in profits. To illustrate, if Acoustic Concepts is currently selling 400 speakers per month and plans to increase sales to 425 speakers per month, the anticipated impact on profits can be computed as follows:

Increased number of speakers to be sold	25
Contribution margin per speaker	×$100
Increase in net income	$2,500

These calculations can be verified as follows:

	Sales Volume			
	400 Speakers	425 Speakers	Difference 25 Speakers	Per Unit
Sales	$100,000	$106,250	$6,250	$250
Less variable expenses	60,000	63,750	3,750	150
Contribution margin	40,000	42,500	2,500	$100
Less fixed expenses	35,000	35,000	-0-	
Net income	$ 5,000	$ 7,500	$2,500	

To summarize the series of examples given above, if there were no sales, the company's loss would equal its fixed expenses. Each unit that is sold reduces the loss by the amount of the unit contribution margin. Once the break-even point has been reached, each additional unit sold increases the company's profit by the amount of the unit contribution margin.

Focus on Current Practice

Elgin Sweeper Company, the leading manufacturer of street sweepers in North America, manufactures five distinct sweeper models in a single facility. Historically, the company has used the traditional format for the income statement, which shows cost of goods sold, gross margin, and so forth. However, the company abandoned this format for internal use and has adopted the contribution approach. By using the contribution approach, management has discovered that key differences exist between the five sweeper models. CM ratios differ by model due to differences in variable inputs. Also, due to differences in volume, the five models differ substantially in terms of the total amount of contribution margin generated each year. Income statements in the contribution format—with breakdowns of sales, contribution margin, and CM ratios by sweeper model—now serve as the basis for internal decision making by management.[1] ■

Contribution Margin Ratio (CM Ratio)

objective 2

Compute the contribution margin ratio (CM ratio) and use it to compute changes in contribution margin and net income.

In addition to being expressed on a per unit basis, sales revenues, variable expenses, and contribution margin for Acoustic Concepts can also be expressed as a percentage of sales:

1. John P. Callan, Wesley N. Tredup, and Randy S. Wissinger, "Elgin Sweeper Company's Journey toward Cost Management," *Management Accounting* 73, no. 1 (July 1991), p. 27; and telephone interviews with management.

	Total	Per Unit	Percent of Sales
Sales (400 speakers)	$100,000	$250	100%
Less variable expenses	60,000	150	60%
Contribution margin	40,000	$100	40%
Less fixed expenses	35,000		
Net income	$ 5,000		

The contribution margin as a percentage of total sales is referred to as the **contribution margin ratio (CM ratio).** This ratio is computed as follows:

$$\text{CM ratio} = \frac{\text{Contribution margin}}{\text{Sales}}$$

For Acoustic Concepts, the computations are as follows:

$$\frac{\text{Total contribution margin, \$40,000}}{\text{Total sales, \$100,000}} = 40\% \quad \text{or} \quad \frac{\text{Per unit contribution margin, \$100}}{\text{Per unit sales, \$250}} = 40\%$$

The CM ratio is extremely useful since it shows how the contribution margin will be affected by a change in total sales. To illustrate, notice that Acoustic Concepts has a CM ratio of 40%. This means that for each dollar increase in sales, total contribution margin will increase by 40 cents ($1 sales × CM ratio of 40%). Net income will also increase by 40 cents, assuming that there are no changes in fixed costs.

As this illustration suggests, *the impact on net income of any given dollar change in total sales can be computed in seconds by simply applying the CM ratio to the dollar change.* If Acoustic Concepts plans a $30,000 increase in sales during the coming month, for example, management can expect contribution margin to increase by $12,000 ($30,000 increased sales × CM ratio of 40%). As we noted above, net income will also increase by $12,000 if fixed costs do not change.

This is verified by the following table:

	Sales Volume			
	Present	Expected	Increase	Percent of Sales
Sales	$100,000	$130,000	$30,000	100%
Less variable expenses	60,000	78,000*	18,000	60%
Contribution margin	40,000	52,000	12,000	40%
Less fixed expenses	35,000	35,000	-0-	
Net income	$ 5,000	$ 17,000	$12,000	

*$130,000 expected sales ÷ $250 per unit = 520 units. 520 units × $150 per unit = $78,000.

Some managers prefer to work with the CM ratio rather than the unit contribution margin figure. The CM ratio is particularly valuable in those situations where the manager must make trade-offs between more dollar sales of one product versus more dollar sales of another. Generally speaking, when trying to increase sales, products that yield the greatest amount of contribution margin per dollar of sales should be emphasized.

Some Applications of CVP Concepts

objective 3

Show the effects on contribution margin of changes in variable costs, fixed costs, selling price, and volume.

Bob Luchinni, the accountant at Acoustic Concepts, wanted to demonstrate to the company's president Prem Narayan how the concepts developed on the preceding pages of this text can be used in planning and decision making. Bob gathered the following basic data:

	Per Unit	Percent of Sales
Sales price	$250	100%
Less variable expenses	150	60%
Contribution margin	$100	40%

Recall that fixed expenses are $35,000 per month. Bob Luchinni will use these data to show the effects of changes in variable costs, fixed costs, sales price, and sales volume on the company's profitability.

CHANGE IN FIXED COST AND SALES VOLUME Acoustic Concepts is currently selling 400 speakers per month (monthly sales of $100,000). The sales manager feels that a $10,000 increase in the monthly advertising budget would increase monthly sales by $30,000. Should the advertising budget be increased?

The following table shows the effect of the proposed change in monthly advertising budget:

	Current Sales	Sales with Additional Advertising Budget	Difference	Percent of Sales
Sales	$100,000	$130,000	$30,000	100%
Less variable expenses	60,000	78,000	18,000	60%
Contribution margin	40,000	52,000	12,000	40%
Less fixed expenses	35,000	45,000*	10,000	
Net income	$ 5,000	$ 7,000	$ 2,000	

*$35,000 plus additional $10,000 monthly advertising budget = $45,000.

Assuming there are no other factors to be considered, the increase in the advertising budget should be approved since it would lead to an increase in net income of $2,000. There are two shorter ways to present this solution. The first alternative solution follows:

Alternative Solution 1

Expected total contribution margin:	
$130,000 × 40% CM ratio	$52,000
Present total contribution margin:	
$100,000 × 40% CM ratio	40,000
Incremental contribution margin	12,000
Change in fixed costs:	
Less incremental advertising expense	10,000
Increased net income	$ 2,000

Since in this case only the fixed costs and the sales volume change, the solution can be presented in an even shorter format, as follows:

Alternative Solution 2

Incremental contribution margin:	
$30,000 × 40% CM ratio	$12,000
Less incremental advertising expense	10,000
Increased net income	$ 2,000

Notice that this approach does not depend on a knowledge of previous sales. Also notice that it is unnecessary under either shorter approach to prepare an income statement. Both of the solutions above involve an **incremental analysis** in that they consider only those items of revenue, cost, and volume that will change if the new program is implemented. Although in each case a new income statement could have been prepared, most managers would prefer the incremental approach. The reason is that it is simpler and more direct, and it permits the decision maker to focus attention on the specific items involved in the decision.

CHANGE IN VARIABLE COSTS AND SALES VOLUME Refer to the original data. Recall that Acoustic Concepts is currently selling 400 speakers per month. Management is contemplating the use of higher-quality components, which would increase variable costs (and thereby reduce the contribution margin) by $10 per speaker. However, the sales manager predicts that the higher overall quality would increase sales to 480 speakers per month. Should the higher-quality components be used?

Solution

The $10 increase in variable costs will cause the unit contribution margin to decrease from $100 to $90.

Expected total contribution margin with higher-quality components:	
480 speakers × $90	$43,200
Present total contribution margin:	
400 speakers × $100	40,000
Increase in total contribution margin	$ 3,200

Yes, based on the information above, the higher-quality components should be used. Since fixed costs will not change, net income should increase by the $3,200 increase in contribution margin shown above.

CHANGE IN FIXED COST, SALES PRICE, AND SALES VOLUME Refer to the original data and recall again that the company is currently selling 400 speakers per month. To increase sales, the sales manager would like to cut the selling price by $20 per speaker and increase the advertising budget by $15,000 per month. The sales manager argues that if these two steps are taken, unit sales will increase by 50% to 600 speakers per month. Should the changes be made?

Solution

A decrease of $20 per speaker in the selling price will cause the unit contribution margin to decrease from $100 to $80.

Expected total contribution margin with lower selling price:	
600 speakers × $80	$48,000
Present total contribution margin:	
400 speakers × $100	40,000
Incremental contribution margin	8,000
Change in fixed costs:	
Less incremental advertising expense	15,000
Reduction in net income	$(7,000)

No, based on the information above, the changes should not be made. The same solution can be obtained by preparing comparative income statements:

	Present 400 Speakers per Month		Expected 600 Speakers per Month		
	Total	Per Unit	Total	Per Unit	Difference
Sales	$100,000	$250	$138,000	$230	$38,000
Less variable expenses	60,000	150	90,000	150	30,000
Contribution margin	40,000	$100	48,000	$ 80	8,000
Less fixed expenses	35,000		50,000*		15,000
Net income (loss)	$ 5,000		$ (2,000)		$ (7,000)

*35,000 + Additional monthly advertising budget of $15,000 = $50,000.

Notice that the effect on net income is the same as that obtained by the incremental analysis above.

CHANGE IN VARIABLE COST, FIXED COST, AND SALES VOLUME Refer to the original data. As before, the company is currently selling 400 speakers per month. The sales manager would like to place the sales staff on a commission basis of $15 per speaker sold, rather than on flat salaries that now total $6,000 per month. The sales manager is confident that the change will increase monthly sales by 15% to 460 speakers per month. Should the change be made?

Solution

Changing the sales staff from a salaried basis to a commission basis will affect both fixed and variable costs. Fixed costs will decrease by $6,000, from $35,000 to $29,000. Variable costs will increase by $15, from $150 to $165, and the unit contribution margin will decrease from $100 to $85.

Expected total contribution margin with sales staff on commissions:	
460 speakers × $85	$39,100
Present total contribution margin:	
400 speakers × $100	40,000
Decrease in total contribution margin	(900)
Change in fixed costs:	
Add salaries avoided if a commission is paid	6,000
Increase in net income	$ 5,100

Yes, based on the information above, the changes should be made. Again, the same answer can be obtained by preparing comparative income statements:

	Present 400 Speakers per Month		Expected 460 Speakers per Month		Difference: Increase or (Decrease) in Net Income
	Total	Per Unit	Total	Per Unit	
Sales	$100,000	$250	$115,000	$250	$15,000
Less variable expenses	60,000	150	75,900	165	(15,900)
Contribution margin	40,000	$100	39,100	$ 85	(900)
Less fixed expenses	35,000		29,000		6,000
Net income	$ 5,000		$ 10,100		$ 5,100

CHANGE IN REGULAR SALES PRICE Refer to the original data where Acoustic Concepts is currently selling 400 speakers per month. The company has an opportunity to make a bulk sale of 150 speakers to a wholesaler if an acceptable price can be worked out. This sale would not disturb the company's regular sales. What price per speaker should be quoted to the wholesaler if Acoustic Concepts wants to increase its monthly profits by $3,000?

Solution

Variable cost per speaker	$150
Desired profit per speaker:	
$3,000 ÷ 150 speakers	20
Quoted price per speaker	$170

Notice that no element of fixed cost is included in the computation. This is because fixed costs are not affected by the bulk sale, so all of the additional revenue that is in excess of variable costs goes to increasing the profits of the company.

Importance of the Contribution Margin

As stated in the introduction to the chapter, CVP analysis seeks the most profitable combination of variable costs, fixed costs, selling price, and sales volume. The above examples show that the effect on the contribution margin is a major consideration in deciding on the most profitable combination of these factors. We have seen that profits can sometimes be improved by reducing the contribution margin if fixed costs can be reduced by a greater amount. More commonly, however, we have seen that the way to improve profits is to increase the total contribution margin figure. Sometimes this can be done by reducing the selling price and thereby increasing volume; sometimes it can be done by increasing the fixed costs (such as advertising) and thereby increasing volume; and sometimes it can be done by trading off variable and fixed costs with appropriate changes in volume. Many other combinations of factors are possible.

The size of the unit contribution margin figure (and the size of the CM ratio) will have a heavy influence on what steps a company is willing to take to improve profits. For example, the greater the unit contribution margin for a product, the greater is the amount that a company will be willing to spend in order to increase unit sales of the product by a given percentage. This explains in part why companies with high unit contribution margins (such as auto manufacturers) advertise so heavily, while companies with low unit contribution margins (such as dishware manufacturers) tend to spend much less for advertising.

In short, the effect on the contribution margin holds the key to many decisions.

Break-Even Analysis

CVP analysis is sometimes referred to simply as break-even analysis. This is unfortunate because break-even analysis is only one element of CVP analysis—although an important element. Break-even analysis is designed to answer questions such as those asked by Prem Narayan, the president of Acoustic Concepts, concerning how far sales could drop before the company begins to lose money.

objective 4

Compute the break-even point by both the equation method and the contribution margin method.

Break-Even Computations

Earlier in the chapter we defined the break-even point to be the level of sales at which the company's profit is zero. The break-even point can be computed using either the *equation method* or the *contribution margin method*—the two methods are equivalent.

THE EQUATION METHOD The **equation method** centers on the contribution approach to the income statement illustrated earlier in the chapter. The format of this income statement can be expressed in equation form as follows:

$$\text{Profits} = \text{Sales} - (\text{Variable expenses} + \text{Fixed expenses})$$

Rearranging this equation slightly yields the following equation, which is widely used in CVP analysis:

$$\text{Sales} = \text{Variable expenses} + \text{Fixed expenses} + \text{Profits}$$

At the break-even point, profits are zero. Therefore, the break-even point can be computed by finding that point where sales just equal the total of the variable expenses plus the fixed expenses. For Acoustic Concepts, the break-even point in unit sales, Q, can be computed as follows:

$$\text{Sales} = \text{Variable expenses} + \text{Fixed expenses} + \text{Profits}$$

$$\begin{aligned} \$250Q &= \$150Q + \$35{,}000 + \$0 \\ \$100Q &= \$35{,}000 \\ Q &= \$35{,}000 \div 100 \\ Q &= 350 \text{ speakers} \end{aligned}$$

where:

$$\begin{aligned} Q &= \text{Number (quantity) of speakers sold} \\ \$250 &= \text{Unit sales price} \\ \$150 &= \text{Unit variable expenses} \\ \$35{,}000 &= \text{Total fixed expenses} \end{aligned}$$

The break-even point in sales dollars can be computed by multiplying the break-even level of unit sales by the selling price per unit:

$$350 \text{ speakers} \times \$250 = \$87{,}500$$

The break-even in total sales dollars, X, can also be directly computed as follows:

$$\text{Sales} = \text{Variable expenses 1 Fixed expenses 1 Profits}$$

$$\begin{aligned} X &= 0.60X + \$35{,}000 + \$0 \\ 0.40X &= \$35{,}000 \\ X &= \$35{,}000 \div 0.40 \\ X &= \$87{,}500 \end{aligned}$$

where:

$$\begin{aligned} X &= \text{Total salcs dollars} \\ 0.60 &= \text{Variable expenses as a percentage of sales} \\ \$35{,}000 &= \text{Total fixed expenses} \end{aligned}$$

Firms often have data available only in percentage form, and the approach we have just illustrated must then be used to find the break-even point. Notice that use of percentages in the equation yields a break-even point in sales dollars rather than in units sold. The break-even point in units sold is the following:

$$\$87{,}500 \div \$250 = 350 \text{ speakers}$$

THE CONTRIBUTION MARGIN METHOD The **contribution margin method** is actually just a shortcut version of the equation method already described. The approach centers on the idea discussed earlier that each unit sold provides a certain amount of contribution margin that goes toward covering fixed costs. To find how many units must be sold to break even, divide the total fixed costs by the unit contribution margin:

$$\text{Break-even point in units sold} = \frac{\text{Fixed expenses}}{\text{Unit contribution margin}}$$

Each speaker generates a contribution margin of \$100 (\$250 selling price, less \$150 variable expenses). Since the total fixed expenses are \$35,000, the break-even point is as follows:

$$\frac{\text{Fixed expenses}}{\text{Unit contribution margin}} = \frac{\$35{,}000}{\$100} = 350 \text{ speakers}$$

A variation of this method uses the CM ratio instead of the unit contribution margin. The result is the break-even in total sales dollars rather than in total units sold.

$$\text{Break-even point in total sales dollars} = \frac{\text{Fixed expenses}}{\text{CM ratio}}$$

In the Acoustic Concepts example, the calculations are as follows:

$$\frac{\text{Fixed expenses}}{\text{CM ratio}} = \frac{\$35{,}000}{40\%} = \$87{,}500$$

This approach, based on the CM ratio, is particularly useful in those situations where a company has multiple product lines and wishes to compute a single break-even point for the company as a whole. More is said on this point in a later section titled The Concept of Sales Mix.

Focus on Current Practice

Hesh Kestin failed in his attempt at publishing an English-language newspaper in Israel in the 1980s. His conclusion: "Never start a business with too many people or too much furniture." Kestin's newest venture is *The American,* a Sunday-only newspaper for overseas Americans. His idea is to publish *The American* on the one day of the week that the well-established *International Herald Tribune* (circulation, 190,000 copies) does not publish. But following what he learned from his first failed venture, he is doing it on a shoestring.

In contrast to the Paris-based *International Herald Tribune* with its eight-story office tower and staff of 250, Kestin has set up business in a small clapboard building on Long Island. Working at desks purchased from a thrift shop, Kestin's staff of 12 assemble the tabloid from stories pulled off wire services. The result of this frugality is that *The American*'s break-even point is only 14,000 copies. Sales topped 20,000 copies just two months after the paper's first issue.[2] ■

2. Jerry Useem, "American Hopes to Conquer the World—from Long Island," *Inc*, December 1996, p. 23.

objective 5

Prepare a cost-volume-profit (CVP) graph and explain the significance of each of its components.

CVP Relationships in Graphic Form

The relationships among revenue, cost, profit, and volume can be expressed graphically by preparing a **cost-volume-profit (CVP) graph.** A CVP graph highlights CVP relationships over wide ranges of activity and can give managers a perspective that can be obtained in no other way. To help explain his analysis to Prem Narayan, Bob Luchinni decided to prepare a CVP graph for Acoustic Concepts.

PREPARING THE CVP GRAPH Preparing a CVP graph (sometimes called a *break-even chart*) involves three steps. These steps are keyed to the graph in Exhibit 6–1:

1. Draw a line parallel to the volume axis to represent total fixed expenses. For Acoustic Concepts, total fixed expenses are $35,000.
2. Choose some volume of sales and plot the point representing total expenses (fixed and variable) at the activity level you have selected. In Exhibit 6–1, Bob Luchinni chose a volume of 600 speakers. Total expenses at that activity level would be as follows:

Fixed expenses	$ 35,000
Variable expenses (600 speakers × $150)	90,000
Total expenses	$125,000

After the point has been plotted, draw a line through it back to the point where the fixed expenses line intersects the dollars axis.

3. Again choose some volume of sales and plot the point representing total sales dollars at the activity level you have selected. In Exhibit 6–1, Bob Luchinni again chose a volume of 600 speakers. Sales at that activity level total $150,000 (600 speakers × $250). Draw a line through this point back to the origin.

The interpretation of the completed CVP graph is given in Exhibit 6–2. The anticipated profit or loss at any given level of sales is measured by the vertical distance between the total revenue line (sales) and the total expenses line (variable expenses plus fixed expenses).

The break-even point is where the total revenue and total expenses lines cross. The break-even point of 350 speakers in Exhibit 6–2 agrees with the break-even point obtained for Acoustic Concepts in earlier computations.

Exhibit 6–1 Preparing the CVP Graph

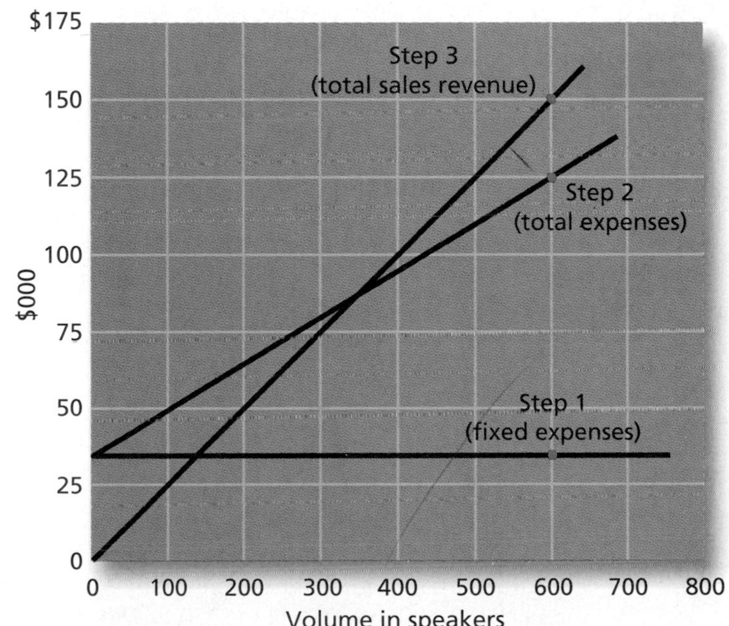

Exhibit 6–2 The Completed CVP Graph

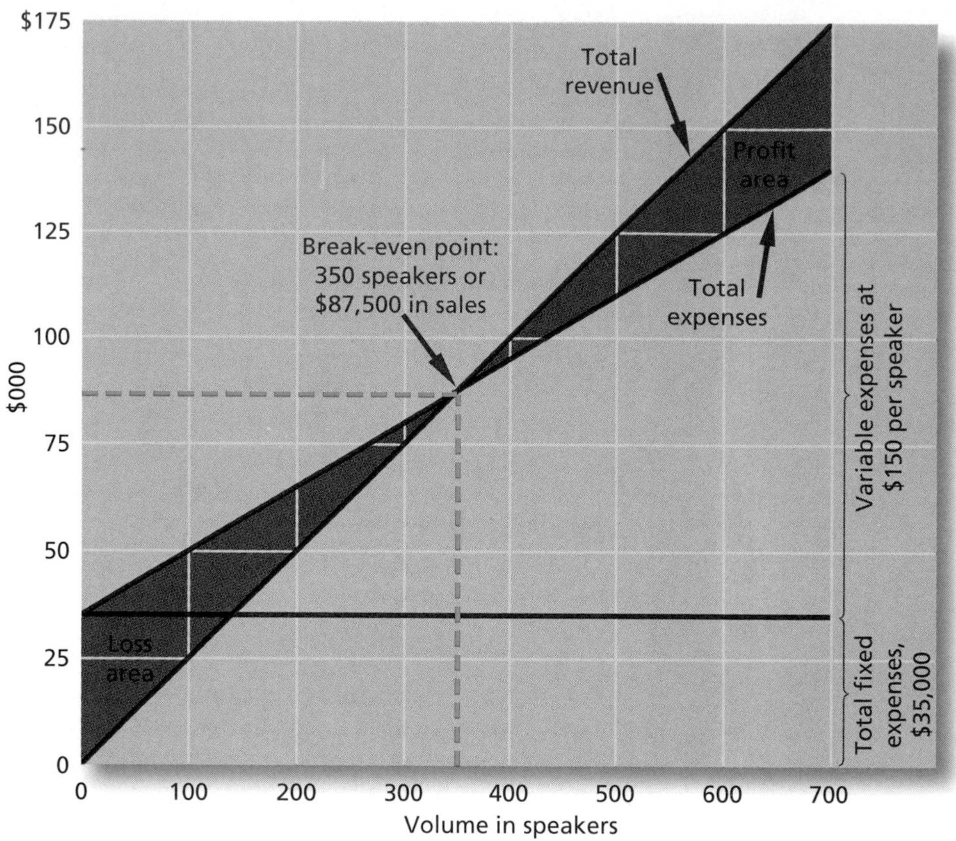

Target Profit Analysis

objective 6

Use the CVP formulas to determine the activity level needed to achieve a desired target profit.

CVP formulas can be used to determine the sales volume needed to achieve a target profit. Suppose that Prem Narayan of Acoustic Concepts would like to earn a target profit of $40,000 per month. How many speakers would have to be sold?

THE CVP EQUATION One approach is to use the equation method discussed on page 243. Instead of solving for the unit sales where profits are zero, you instead solve for the unit sales where profits are $40,000.

$$\text{Sales} = \text{Variable expenses} + \text{Fixed expenses} + \text{Profits}$$

$$\begin{aligned} \$250Q &= \$150Q + \$35{,}000 + \$40{,}000 \\ \$100Q &= \$75{,}000 \\ Q &= \$75{,}000 \div \$100 \\ Q &= 750 \text{ speakers} \end{aligned}$$

where:

$$\begin{aligned} Q &= \text{Number of speakers sold} \\ \$250 &= \text{Unit sales price} \\ \$150 &= \text{Unit variable expenses} \\ \$35{,}000 &= \text{Total fixed expenses} \\ \$40{,}000 &= \text{Target profit} \end{aligned}$$

Thus, the target profit can be achieved by selling 750 speakers per month, which represents $187,500 in total sales ($250 × 750 speakers).

THE CONTRIBUTION MARGIN APPROACH A second approach involves expanding the contribution margin formula to include the target profit:

$$\text{Units sold to attain the target profit} = \frac{\text{Fixed expenses} + \text{Target profit}}{\text{Unit contribution margin}}$$

$$\frac{\$35{,}000 \text{ fixed expenses} + \$40{,}000 \text{ target profit}}{\$100 \text{ contribution margin per speaker}} = 750 \text{ speakers}$$

This approach gives the same answer as the equation method since it is simply a shortcut version of the equation method.

The Margin of Safety

objective 7

Compute the margin of safety and explain its significance.

The **margin of safety** is the excess of budgeted (or actual) sales over the break-even volume of sales. It states the amount by which sales can drop before losses begin to be incurred. The formula for its calculation is as follows:

$$\text{Margin of safety} = \text{Total budgeted (or actual) sales} - \text{Break-even sales}$$

The margin of safety can also be expressed in percentage form. This percentage is obtained by dividing the margin of safety in dollar terms by total sales:

$$\text{Margin of safety percentage} = \frac{\text{Margin of safety in dollars}}{\text{Total budgeted (or actual) sales}}$$

The calculations for the margin of safety for Acoustic Concepts are as follows:

Sales (at the current volume of 400 speakers) (a)	$100,000
Break-even sales (at 350 speakers)	87,500
Margin of safety (in dollars) (b)	$ 12,500
Margin of safety as a percentage of sales, (b) ÷ (a)	12.5%

This margin of safety means that at the current level of sales and with the company's current prices and cost structure, a reduction in sales of $12,500, or 12.5%, would result in just breaking even.

In a single-product firm like Acoustic Concepts, the margin of safety can also be expressed in terms of the number of units sold by dividing the margin of safety in dollars by the selling price per unit. In this case, the margin of safety is 50 units ($12,500 ÷ $250 per unit = 50 units).

Focus on Current Practice

The CVP equation can also be used to infer a company's cost structure. Pak Melwani and Kumar Hathiramani, former silk merchants from Bombay, opened a soup store in Manhattan after watching a *Seinfeld* episode featuring the "soup Nazi."[3] The episode parodied a real-life soup vendor, Ali Yeganeh, whose loyal customers put up with hour-long lines and "snarling customer service." Melwani and Hathiramani approached Yeganeh about

3. Silva Sansoni, "The Starbucks of Soup?" *Forbes,* July 7, 1997, pp. 90–91.

turning his soup kitchen into a chain, but they were gruffly rebuffed. Instead of giving up, the two hired a French chef with a repertoire of 500 soups and opened a store called Soup Nutsy. For $6 per serving, Soup Nutsy daily offers 12 homemade soups, such a sherry crab bisque and Thai coconut shrimp. Melwani and Hathiramani report that in their first year of operation, they netted $210,000 on sales of $700,000. They report that it costs about $2 per serving to make the soup. So their variable expense ratio is one-third ($2 cost ÷ $6 selling price). If so, what are their fixed costs? We can answer that question using the equation approach as follows:

$$\text{Sales} = \text{Variable expenses} + \text{Fixed expenses} + \text{Profits}$$

$$\$700{,}000 = \frac{1}{3} \times \$700{,}000 + \text{Fixed expenses} + \$210{,}000$$

$$\text{Fixed expenses} = \$700{,}000 - \frac{1}{3} \times \$700{,}000 - \$210{,}000$$

$$= \$256{,}667$$

With this information, you can determine that Soup Nutsy's break-even point is about $385,000 of sales. This gives the store a comfortable margin of safety of 45% of sales. ■

Managerial Accounting in Action

THE WRAP UP

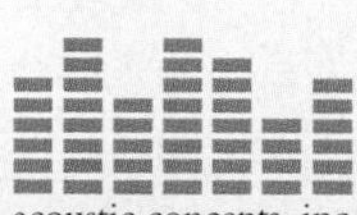

It is Thursday morning, and Prem Narayan and Bob Luchinni are discussing the results of Bob's analysis.

Prem: Bob, everything you have shown me is pretty clear. I can see what impact some of the sales manager's suggestions would have on our profits. Some of those suggestions are quite good and some are not so good. I also understand that our break-even is 350 speakers, so we have to make sure we don't slip below that level of sales. What really bothers me is that we are only selling 400 speakers a month now. What did you call the 50-speaker cushion?

Bob: That's the margin of safety.

Prem: Such a small cushion makes me very nervous. What can we do to increase the margin of safety?

Bob: We have to increase total sales or decrease the break-even point or both.

Prem: And to decrease the break-even point, we have to either decrease our fixed expenses or increase our unit contribution margin?

Bob: Exactly.

Prem: And to increase our unit contribution margin, we have to either increase our selling price or decrease the variable cost per unit?

Bob: Correct.

Prem: So what do you suggest?

Bob: Well, the analysis doesn't tell us which of these to do, but it does indicate we have a potential problem here.

Prem: If you don't have any immediate suggestions, I would like to call a general meeting next week to discuss ways we can work on increasing the margin of safety. I think everyone will be concerned about how vulnerable we are to even small downturns in sales.

Bob: I agree. This is something everyone will want to work on.

CVP Considerations in Choosing a Cost Structure

We stated in the preceding chapter that *cost structure* refers to the relative proportion of fixed and variable costs in an organization. We also stated that an organization often has some latitude in trading off between fixed and variable costs. Such a trade-off is possible, for example, by automating facilities rather than using direct labor workers.

In this section, we discuss various considerations involved in choosing a cost structure. We look first at the matter of cost structure and profit stability, and then we discuss an important concept known as *operating leverage*. Finally, we conclude the section by comparing capital-intensive (automated) and labor-intensive companies in terms of the potential risks and rewards that are inherent in the cost structures these companies have chosen.

Cost Structure and Profit Stability

When a manager has some latitude in trading off between fixed and variable costs, which cost structure is better—high variable costs and low fixed costs, or the opposite? No categorical answer to this question is possible; there may be advantages either way, depending on the specific circumstances. To show what we mean by this statement, refer to the income statements given below for two blueberry farms. Bogside Farm depends on migrant workers to pick its berries by hand, whereas Sterling Farm has invested in expensive berry-picking machines. Consequently, Bogside Farm has higher variable costs, but Sterling Farm has higher fixed costs:

	Bogside Farm		Sterling Farm	
	Amount	Percent	Amount	Percent
Sales	$100,000	100%	$100,000	100%
Less variable expenses	60,000	60%	33,000	30%
Contribution margin	40,000	40%	70,000	70%
Less fixed expenses	30,000		60,000	
Net income	$ 10,000		$ 10,000	

The question as to which farm has the better cost structure depends on many factors, including the long-run trend in sales, year-to-year fluctuations in the level of sales, and the attitude of the owners toward risk. If sales are expected to be above $100,000 in the future, then Sterling Farm probably has the better cost structure. The reason is that its CM ratio is higher, and its profits will therefore increase more rapidly as sales increase. To illustrate, assume that each farm experiences a 10% increase in sales without any increase in fixed costs. The new income statements would be as follows:

	Bogside Farm		Sterling Farm	
	Amount	Percent	Amount	Percent
Sales	$110,000	100%	$110,000	100%
Less variable expenses	66,000	60%	33,000	30%
Contribution margin	44,000	40%	77,000	70%
Less fixed expenses	30,000		60,000	
Net income	$ 14,000		$ 17,000	

Sterling Farm has experienced a greater increase in net income due to its higher CM ratio even though the increase in sales was the same for both farms.

What if sales drop below $100,000 from time to time? What are the break-even points of the two farms? What are their margins of safety? The computations needed to answer these questions are carried out below using the contribution margin method:

	Bogside Farm	Sterling Farm
Fixed expenses	$ 30,000	$ 60,000
Contribution margin ratio	÷40%	÷70%
Breakeven in total sales dollars	$ 75,000	$ 85,714
Total current sales (a)	$100,000	$100,000
Break-even sales	75,000	85,714
Margin of safety in sales dollars (b)	$ 25,000	$ 14,286
Margin of safety as a percentage of sales, (b) ÷ (a)	25.0%	14.3%

This analysis makes it clear that Bogside Farm is less vulnerable to downturns than Sterling Farm. We can identify two reasons why it is less vulnerable. First, due to its lower fixed expenses, Bogside Farm has a lower break-even point and a higher margin of safety, as shown by the computations above. Therefore, it will not incur losses as quickly as Sterling Farm in periods of sharply declining sales. Second, due to its lower CM ratio, Bogside Farm will not lose contribution margin as rapidly as Sterling Farm when sales fall off. Thus, Bogside Farm's income will be less volatile. We saw earlier that this is a drawback when sales increase, but it provides more protection when sales drop.

To summarize, without knowing the future, it is not obvious which cost structure is better. Both have advantages and disadvantages. Sterling Farm, with its higher fixed costs and lower variable costs, will experience wider swings in net income as changes take place in sales, with greater profits in good years and greater losses in bad years. Bogside Farm, with its lower fixed costs and higher variable costs, will enjoy greater stability in net income and will be more protected from losses during bad years, but at the cost of lower net income in good years.

Focus on Current Practice

In the early 1990s, after a string of very bad years, Volkswagen AG of Germany had a record year in terms of number of vehicles sold. However, instead of experiencing record profits, the company's profits plunged. The reason is that the company had allowed itself to get into a position where its break-even point was above 90% of capacity. As a result, there was a very narrow band of volume within which the company could operate profitably. The record car sales were made possible only by running its factories overtime using expensive overtime labor. In contrast, some of the stronger European auto companies have break-even points below 70% of their capacity.[4]

4. Timothy Aeppel, "VW Chief Declares a Crisis and Prescribes Bold Action," *The Wall Street Journal,* April 1, 1993, p. B4.

Operating Leverage

objective 8

Compute the degree of operating leverage at a particular level of sales and explain how the degree of operating leverage can be used to predict changes in net income.

A lever is a tool for multiplying force. Using a lever, a massive object can be moved with only a modest amount of force. In business, *operating leverage* serves a similar purpose. **Operating leverage** is a measure of how sensitive net income is to percentage changes in sales. Operating leverage acts as a multiplier. If operating leverage is high, a small percentage increase in sales can produce a much larger percentage increase in net income.

Operating leverage can be illustrated by returning to the data given above for the two blueberry farms. We previously showed that a 10% increase in sales (from \$100,000 to \$110,000 in each farm) results in a 70% increase in the net income of Sterling Farm (from \$10,000 to \$17,000) and only a 40% increase in the net income of Bogside Farm (from \$10,000 to \$14,000). Thus, for a 10% increase in sales, Sterling Farm experiences a much greater percentage increase in profits than does Bogside Farm. Therefore, Sterling Farm has greater operating leverage than Bogside Farm.

The **degree of operating leverage** at a given level of sales is computed by the following formula:

$$\text{Degree of operating leverage} = \frac{\text{Contribution margin}}{\text{Net income}}$$

The degree of operating leverage is a measure, at a given level of sales, of how a percentage change in sales volume will affect profits. To illustrate, the degree of operating leverage for the two farms at a \$100,000 sales level would be as follows:

$$\text{Bogside Farm: } \frac{\$40{,}000}{\$10{,}000} = 4$$

$$\text{Sterling Farm: } \frac{\$70{,}000}{\$10{,}000} = 7$$

Since the degree of operating leverage for Bogside Farm is 4, the farm's net income grows four times as fast as its sales. Similarly, Sterling Farm's net income grows seven times as fast as its sales. Thus, if sales increase by 10%, then we can expect the net income of Bogside Farm to increase by four times this amount, or by 40%, and the net income of Sterling Farm to increase by seven times this amount, or by 70%.

	(1) Percent Increase in Sales	(2) Degree of Operating Leverage	(3) Percent Increase in Net Income (1) × (2)
Bogside Farm	10%	4	40%
Sterling Farm	10%	7	70%

What is responsible for the higher operating leverage at Sterling Farm? The only difference between the two farms is their cost structure. If two companies have the same total revenue and same total expense but different cost structures, then the company with the higher proportion of fixed costs in its cost structure will have higher operating leverage. Referring back to the original example on page 249, when both farms have sales of \$100,000 and total expenses of \$90,000, one-third of Bogside

Farm's costs are fixed but two-thirds of Sterling Farm's costs are fixed. As a consequence, Sterling's degree of operating leverage is higher than Bogside's.[5]

The degree of operating leverage is greatest at sales levels near the break-even point and decreases as sales and profits rise. This can be seen from the tabulation below, which shows the degree of operating leverage for Bogside Farm at various sales levels. (Data used earlier for Bogside Farm are shown in color.)

Sales	$75,000	$80,000	$100,000	$150,000	$225,000
Less variable expenses	45,000	48,000	60,000	90,000	135,000
Contribution margin (a)	30,000	32,000	40,000	60,000	90,000
Less fixed expenses	30,000	30,000	30,000	30,000	30,000
Net income (b)	$ -0-	$ 2,000	$ 10,000	$ 30,000	$ 60,000
Degree of operating leverage, (a) ÷ (b)	∞	16	4	2	1.5

Thus, a 10% increase in sales would increase profits by only 15% (10% × 1.5) if the company were operating at a $225,000 sales level, as compared to the 40% increase we computed earlier at the $100,000 sales level. The degree of operating leverage will continue to decrease the farther the company moves from its break-even point. At the break-even point, the degree of operating leverage will be infinitely large ($30,000 contribution margin ÷ $0 net income = ∞).

A manager can use the degree of operating leverage to quickly estimate what impact various percentage changes in sales will have on profits, without the necessity of preparing detailed income statements. As shown by our examples, the effects of operating leverage can be dramatic. If a company is near its break-even point, then even small percentage increases in sales can yield large percentage increases in profits. *This explains why management will often work very hard for only a small increase in sales volume.* If the degree of operating leverage is 5, then a 6% increase in sales would translate into a 30% increase in profits.

Focus on Current Practice

Carnival Corporation owns and operates a fleet of cruise ships under the names Carnival Cruise Lines and Holland America Line. In an annual report, the company states that "fixed costs, including depreciation, fuel, insurance, port charges and crew costs represent more than one-third of the Company's operating expenses and do not significantly change in relation to changes in passenger loads and aggregate ticket revenue." Since the fixed costs are one-third of operating expenses, the variable expenses must be two-thirds.

Because of the company's fixed costs, increases and decreases in passenger loads have a disproportionate impact on net income. The company reported total operating expenses of $908 million and net income of $348 million on revenues of $1,557 million. Therefore, Carnival's operating leverage was about 2.73.

5. See Richard A. Lord, "Interpreting and Measuring Operating Leverage," *Issues in Accounting Education,* Fall 1995, pp. 317–29, for an extensive discussion of the impact of cost structure on the degree of operating leverage.

$$\text{Degree of operating leverage} = \frac{\text{Contribution margin}}{\text{Net income}}$$

$$= \frac{\$1{,}557 - \frac{2}{3} \times \$908}{\$348} = 2.73$$

As a result of this operating leverage, Carnival Corporation's net income grows 2.73 times as quickly as its revenue. ■

Automation: Risks and Rewards from a CVP Perspective

We have noted in preceding chapters that several factors, including the move toward flexible manufacturing systems and other uses of automation, have resulted in a shift toward greater fixed costs and less variable costs in organizations. In turn, this shift in cost structure has had an impact on the CM ratio, the break-even point, and the degree of operating leverage. Some of this impact has been favorable and some has not, as shown in Exhibit 6–3.

Many benefits can accrue from automation, but as shown in the exhibit, certain risks are introduced when a company moves toward greater amounts of fixed costs. These risks suggest that management must be careful as it automates to ensure that investment decisions are made in accordance with a carefully devised long-run strategy. This point is discussed further in Chapter 14 where we deal with investment decisions in an automated environment.

Structuring Sales Commissions

Companies generally compensate salespeople by paying them either a commission based on sales or a salary plus a sales commission. Commissions based on sales dollars can lead to lower profits in a company. To illustrate, consider Pipeline Unlimited, a producer of surfing equipment. Salespeople for the company sell the company's product to retail sporting goods stores throughout North America and the Pacific Basin. Data for two of the company's surfboards, the XR7 and Turbo models, appear below:

	Model	
	XR7	**Turbo**
Selling price	$100	$150
Less variable expenses	75	132
Contribution margin	$ 25	$ 18

Which model will salespeople push hardest if they are paid a commission of 10% of sales revenue? The answer is the Turbo, since it has the higher selling price. On the other hand, from the standpoint of the company, profits will be greater if salespeople steer customers toward the XR7 model since it has the higher contribution margin.

Exhibit 6–3 CVP Comparison of Capital-Intensive (automated) and Labor-Intensive Companies

The comparison below is between two profitable companies that have different cost structures but are otherwise identical. They sell the same products and services and have the same total sales revenues and the same total expenses. One of the companies has chosen to automate, resulting in a capital-intensive facility. The other company has chosen to rely more on human labor, resulting in a labor-intensive facility. Assuming that labor is a variable cost, the company that has automated has a higher proportion of fixed costs in its cost structure.

Item	Capital-Intensive (automated) Company	Labor-Intensive Company	Comments
The CM ratio will tend to be relatively . . .	High	Low	Variable costs in an automated company will tend to be lower than in a labor-intensive company, thereby causing the CM ratio for a given product to be higher.
Operating leverage will tend to be . . .	High	Low	Operating leverage is higher in the automated company because the companies are identical except for their cost structures and the automated company has lower variable costs and hence a larger contribution margin.
In periods of increasing sales, net income will tend to increase . . .	Rapidly	Slowly	Since both operating leverage and CM ratios tend to be high in automated companies, net income will increase more rapidly.
In periods of decreasing sales, net income will tend to decrease . . .	Rapidly	Slowly	Just as net income increases more rapidly in an automated company, so will net income decrease more rapidly as sales decrease.
The volatility of net income with changes in sales will tend to be . . .	Greater	Less	Due to its higher operating leverage, the net income in an automated company will tend to be more sensitive to changes in sales than in a labor-intensive company.
The break-even point will tend to be . . .	Higher	Lower	The break-even point in an automated company will tend to be higher because of its greater fixed costs, although this is offset to some extent by the higher CM ratio.
The margin of safety at a given level of sales will tend to be . . .	Lower	Higher	The margin of safety in an automated company will tend to be lower because of its higher break-even point.
The latitude available to management in times of economic stress will tend to be . . .	Less	Greater	With high committed fixed costs in an automated company, management is more "locked in" and has fewer options when dealing with changing economic conditions.

To eliminate such conflicts, some companies base salepersons' commissions on contribution margin rather than on sales. The reasoning goes like this: Since contribution margin represents the amount of sales revenue available to cover fixed expenses and profits, a firm's well-being will be maximized when contribution margin is maximized. By tying salesperson's commissions to contribution margin, the salespersons are automatically encouraged to concentrate on the element that is of most importance to the firm. There is no need to worry about what mix of products the salespersons sell because they will *automatically* sell the mix of products that will maximize the contribution margin. In effect, by maximizing their own well-being, they automatically maximize the well-being of the firm—assuming there is no change in fixed expenses.

Focus on Current Practice

The method of compensating salespersons must be chosen with a great deal of care. Digital Equipment Corporation's founder believed that salespersons should never sell customers something they don't need, and accordingly Digital paid them salaries rather than sales commissions. This approach worked fine for many years because "Digital's products were the hottest alternative to expensive mainframe computers, and because they were cheaper, they almost sold themselves. But when competition arrived, the Digital sales staff was hopelessly outclassed." When commissions were introduced in an attempt to stem the tide, the new system backfired. "Some salesmen sold product at little, or no profit to pump up volume—and their compensation."[6] ■

The Concept of Sales Mix

objective 9

Compute the break-even point for a multiple product company and explain the effects of shifts in the sales mix on contribution margin and the break-even point.

The preceding sections have given us some insights into the principles involved in CVP analysis, as well as some selected examples of how these principles are used by the manager. Before concluding our discussion, it will be helpful to consider one additional application of the ideas that we have developed—the use of CVP concepts in analyzing sales mix.

The Definition of Sales Mix

The term **sales mix** means the relative proportions in which a company's products are sold. Managers try to achieve the combination, or mix, that will yield the greatest amount of profits. Most companies have several products, and often these products are not equally profitable. Where this is true, profits will depend to some extent on the company's sales mix. Profits will be greater if high-margin rather than low-margin items make up a relatively large proportion of total sales.

Changes in the sales mix can cause interesting (and sometimes confusing) variations in a company's profits. A shift in the sales mix from high-margin items to low-margin items can cause total profits to decrease even though total sales may increase. Conversely, a shift in the sales mix from low-margin items to high-margin items can cause the reverse effect—total profits may increase even though total sales decrease. It is one thing to achieve a particular sales volume; it is quite a different thing to sell the most profitable mix of products.

Sales Mix and Break-Even Analysis

If a company sells more than one product, break-even analysis is somewhat more complex than discussed earlier in the chapter. The reason is that different products will have different selling prices, different costs, and different contribution margins.

6. John R. Wilke, "At Digital Equipment, a Resignation Reveals Key Problem: Selling," *The Wall Street Journal,* April 26, 1994, pp. A1, A11.

Exhibit 6–4 Multiple-Product Break-Even Analysis

SOUND UNLIMITED
Contribution Income Statement
For the Month of September

	Le Louvre CD		Le Vin CD		Total	
	Amount	Percent	Amount	Percent	Amount	Percent
Sales	$20,000	100%	$80,000	100%	$100,000	100%
Less variable expenses	15,000	75%	40,000	50%	55,000	55%
Contribution margin	$ 5,000	25%	$40,000	50%	45,000	45%
Less fixed expenses					27,000	
Net income					$ 18,000	

Computation of the break-even point:

$$\frac{\text{Fixed expenses, \$27,000}}{\text{Overall CM ratio, 45\%}} = \$60{,}000$$

Verification of the breakeven:

	Le Louvre CD		Le Vin CD		Total	
	Amount	Percent	Amount	Percent	Amount	Percent
Sales	$12,000	100%	$48,000	100%	$ 60,000	100%
Less variable expenses	9,000	75%	24,000	50%	33,000	55%
Contribution margin	$ 3,000	25%	$24,000	50%	27,000	45%
Less fixed expenses					27,000	
Net income					$ -0-	

Consequently, the break-even point will depend on the mix in which the various products are sold. To illustrate, consider Sound Unlimited, a small company that imports CD-ROMs from France for use in personal computers. At present, the company distributes the following to retail computer stores: the Le Louvre CD, a multimedia free-form tour of the famous art museum in Paris; and the Le Vin CD, which features the wines and wine-growing regions of France. Both multimedia products have sound, photos, video clips, and sophisticated software. The company's September sales, expenses, and break-even point are shown in Exhibit 6–4.

As shown in the exhibit, the break-even point is $60,000 in sales. This is computed by dividing the fixed costs by the company's *overall* CM ratio of 45%. But $60,000 in sales represents the break-even point for the company only so long as the sales mix does not change. *If the sales mix changes, then the break-even point will also change.* This is illustrated by the results for October in which the sales mix shifted away from the more profitable Le Vin CD (which has a 50% CM ratio) toward the less profitable Le Louvre CD (which has only a 25% CM ratio). These results appear in Exhibit 6–5.

Although sales have remained unchanged at $100,000, the sales mix is exactly the reverse of what it was in Exhibit 6–4, with the bulk of the sales now coming from the less profitable Le Louvre CD. Notice that this shift in the sales mix has caused both the overall CM ratio and total profits to drop sharply from the prior month—the overall CM ratio has dropped from 45% in September to only 30% in October, and net income has dropped from $18,000 to only $3,000. In addition, with the drop in the overall CM ratio, the company's break-even point is no longer $60,000 in sales. Since the company is now realizing less average contribution margin per dollar of sales, it takes more sales to cover the same amount of fixed costs. Thus, the break-even point has increased from $60,000 to $90,000 in sales per year.

Exhibit 6–5 Multiple-Product Break-Even Analysis: A Shift in Sales Mix (see Exhibit 6–4)

SOUND UNLIMITED
Contribution Income Statement
For the Month of October

	Le Louvre CD		Le Vin CD		Total	
	Amount	Percent	Amount	Percent	Amount	Percent
Sales	$80,000	100%	$20,000	100%	$100,000	100%
Less variable expenses	60,000	75%	10,000	50%	70,000	70%
Contribution margin	$20,000	25%	$10,000	50%	30,000	30%
Less fixed expenses					27,000	
Net income					$ 3,000	

Computation of the break-even point:

$$\frac{\text{Fixed expenses, \$27,000}}{\text{Overall CM ratio, 30\%}} = \$90,000$$

In preparing a break-even analysis, some assumption must be made concerning the sales mix. Usually the assumption is that it will not change. However, if the manager knows that shifts in various factors (consumer tastes, market share, and so forth) are causing shifts in the sales mix, then these factors must be explicitly considered in any CVP computations. Otherwise, the manager may make decisions on the basis of outmoded or faulty data.

Focus on Current Practice

Roger Maxwell grew up near a public golf course where he learned the game and worked as a caddie. After attending Oklahoma State on a golf scholarship, he became a golf pro and eventually rose to become vice president at Marriott, responsible for Marriott's golf courses in the United States. Sensing an opportunity to serve a niche market, Maxwell invested his life savings in opening his own golfing superstore, In Celebration of Golf (ICOG), in Scottsdale, Arizona. Maxwell says, "I'd rather sacrifice profit up front for sizzle . . . [P]eople are bored by malls. They're looking for something different." Maxwell has designed his store to be a museum-like mecca for golfing fanatics. For example, maintenance work is done in a replica of a turn-of-the-century club maker's shop.

Maxwell's approach seems to be working. In the second year of operation, Maxwell projected a profit of $81,000 on sales of $2.4 million as follows:

	Projected	Percent of Sales
Sales	$2,400,000	100%
Cost of sales	1,496,000	62⅓%
Other variable expenses	296,000	12⅓%
Contribution margin	608,000	25⅓%
Fixed expenses	527,000	
Net income	$ 81,000	

Happily for Maxwell, sales for the year were even better than expected—reaching $3.0 million. In the absence of any other changes, the net income should have been approximately $233,000, computed as follows:

	Projected	Percent of Sales
Sales	$3,000,000	100%
Cost of sales	1,870,000	62⅓%
Other variable expenses	370,000	12⅓%
Contribution margin	760,000	25⅓%
Fixed expenses	527,000	
Net income	$ 233,000	

However, net income for the year was actually $298,000—apparently because of a favorable shift in the sales mix toward higher margin items. A 25% increase in sales over the projections at the beginning of the year resulted in a 356% increase in net income. That's leverage![7] ■

Assumptions of CVP Analysis

A number of assumptions typically underlie CVP analysis:

1. Selling price is constant throughout the entire relevant range. The price of a product or service will not change as volume changes.
2. Costs are linear throughout the entire relevant range, and they can be accurately divided into variable and fixed elements. The variable element is constant per unit, and the fixed element is constant in total over the entire relevant range.
3. In multiproduct companies, the sales mix is constant.
4. In manufacturing companies, inventories do not change. The number of units produced equals the number of units sold (this assumption is considered further in the next chapter).

While some of these assumptions may be technically violated, the violations are usually not serious enough to call into question the basic validity of CVP analysis. For example, in most multiproduct companies, the sales mix is constant enough so that the results of CVP analysis are reasonably valid.

Perhaps the greatest danger lies in relying on simple CVP analysis when a manager is contemplating a large change in volume that lies outside of the relevant range. For example, a manager might contemplate increasing the level of sales far beyond what the company has ever experienced before. However, even in these situations a manager can adjust the model as we have done in this chapter to take into account anticipated changes in selling prices, fixed costs, and the sales mix that would otherwise violate the assumptions. For example, in a decision that would affect fixed costs, the change in fixed costs can be explicitly taken into account as illustrated earlier in the chapter in the Acoustic Concepts example on page 239.

7. Edward O. Welles, "Going for the Green," *Inc*, July 1996, pp. 68–75.

Summary

CVP analysis involves finding the most favorable combination of variable costs, fixed costs, selling price, sales volume, and mix of products sold. Trade-offs are possible between types of costs, as well as between costs and selling price, and between selling price and sales volume. Sometimes these trade-offs are desirable, and sometimes they are not. CVP analysis provides the manager with a powerful tool for identifying those courses of action that will improve profitability.

The concepts developed in this chapter represent a *way of thinking* rather than a mechanical set of procedures. That is, to put together the optimum combination of costs, selling price, and sales volume, the manager must be trained to think in terms of the unit contribution margin, the break-even point, the CM ratio, the sales mix, and the other concepts developed in this chapter. These concepts are dynamic in that a change in one will trigger changes in others—changes that may not be obvious on the surface.

Review Problem: CVP Relationships

Voltar Company manufactures and sells a telephone answering machine. The company's contribution format income statement for the most recent year is given below:

	Total	Per Unit	Percent of Sales
Sales (20,000 units)	$1,200,000	$60	100%
Less variable expenses	900,000	45	? %
Contribution margin	300,000	$15	? %
Less fixed expenses	240,000		
Net income	$ 60,000		

Management is anxious to improve the company's profit performance and has asked for several items of information.

Required

1. Compute the company's CM ratio and variable expense ratio.
2. Compute the company's break-even point in both units and sales dollars. Use the equation method.
3. Assume that sales increase by $400,000 next year. If cost behavior patterns remain unchanged, by how much will the company's net income increase? Use the CM ratio to determine your answer.
4. Refer to original data. Assume that next year management wants the company to earn a minimum profit of $90,000. How many units will have to be sold to meet this target profit figure?
5. Refer to the original data. Compute the company's margin of safety in both dollar and percentage form.
6. a. Compute the company's degree of operating leverage at the present level of sales.
   b. Assume that through a more intense effort by the sales staff the company's sales increase by 8% next year. By what percentage would you expect net income to increase? Use the operating leverage concept to obtain your answer.
   c. Verify your answer to (b) by preparing a new income statement showing an 8% increase in sales.
7. In an effort to increase sales and profits, management is considering the use of a higher-quality speaker. The higher-quality speaker would increase variable costs by $3 per unit, but management could eliminate one quality inspector who is paid a salary of $30,000 per year. The sales manager estimates that the higher-quality speaker would increase annual sales by at least 20%.
   a. Assuming that changes are made as described above, prepare a projected income statement for next year. Show data on a total, per unit, and percentage basis.
   b. Compute the company's new break-even point in both units and dollars of sales. Use the contribution margin method.

Solution to Review Problem

c. Would you recommend that the changes be made?

1. CM ratio:

$$\frac{\text{Contribution margin, \$15}}{\text{Selling price, \$60}} = 25\%$$

Variable expense ratio:

$$\frac{\text{Variable expense, \$45}}{\text{Selling price, \$60}} = 75\%$$

2.
$$\begin{aligned} \text{Sales} &= \text{Variable expenses} + \text{Fixed expenses} + \text{Profits} \\ \$60Q &= \$45Q + \$240{,}000 + \$0 \\ \$15Q &= \$240{,}000 \\ Q &= \$240{,}000 \div \$15 \\ Q &= 16{,}000 \text{ units; or at \$60 per unit, \$960,000} \end{aligned}$$

Alternative solution:

$$\begin{aligned} X &= 0.75X + \$240{,}000 + \$0 \\ 0.25X &= \$240{,}000 \\ X &= \$240{,}000 \div 0.25 \\ X &= \$960{,}000\text{; or at \$60 per unit, 16,000 units} \end{aligned}$$

3.

Increase in sales	$400,000
Multiply by the CM ratio	× 25%
Expected increase in contribution margin	$100,000

Since the fixed expenses are not expected to change, net income will increase by the entire $100,000 increase in contribution margin computed above.

4. Equation method:

$$\begin{aligned} \text{Sales} &= \text{Variable expenses} + \text{Fixed expenses} + \text{Profits} \\ \$60Q &= \$45Q + \$240{,}000 + \$90{,}000 \\ \$15Q &= \$330{,}000 \\ Q &= \$330{,}000 \div \$15 \\ Q &= 22{,}000 \text{ units} \end{aligned}$$

Contribution margin method:

$$\frac{\text{Fixed expenses} + \text{Target profit}}{\text{Contribution margin per unit}} = \frac{\$240{,}000 + \$90{,}000}{\$15} = 22{,}000 \text{ units}$$

5.
$$\text{Total sales} - \text{Break-even sales} = \text{Margin of safety in dollars}$$
$$\$1{,}200{,}000 - \$960{,}000 = \$240{,}000$$

$$\frac{\text{Margin of safety in dollars, \$240,000}}{\text{Total sales, \$1,200,000}} = 20\%$$

6. a.
$$\frac{\text{Contribution margin, \$300,000}}{\text{Net income, \$60,000}} = 5 \text{ (degree of operating leverage)}$$

b.

Expected increase in sales	8%
Degree of operating leverage	× 5
Expected increase in net income	40%

c. If sales increase by 8%, then 21,600 units (20,000 × 1.08 = 21,600) will be sold next year. The new income statement will be as follows:

	Total	Per Unit	Percent of Sales
Sales (21,600 units)	$1,296,000	$60	100%
Less variable expenses	972,000	45	75%
Contribution margin	324,000	$15	25%
Less fixed expenses	240,000		
Net income	$ 84,000		

Thus, the $84,000 expected net income for next year represents a 40% increase over the $60,000 net income earned during the current year:

$$\frac{\$84{,}000 - \$60{,}000 = \$24{,}000}{\$60{,}000} = 40\% \text{ increase}$$

Note from the income statement above that the increase in sales from 20,000 to 21,600 units has resulted in increases in *both* total sales and total variable expenses. It is a common error to overlook the increase in variable expenses when preparing a projected income statement.

7. a. A 20% increase in sales would result in 24,000 units being sold next year: 20,000 units × 1.20 = 24,000 units.

	Total	Per Unit	Percent of Sales
Sales (24,000 units)	$1,440,000	$60	100%
Less variable expenses . . .	1,152,000	48*	80%
Contribution margin	288,000	$12	20%
Less fixed expenses	210,000†		
Net income	$ 78,000		

*$45 + $3 = $48; $48 ÷ $60 = 80%.
†$240,000 − $30,000 = $210,000.

Note that the change in per unit variable expenses results in a change in both the per unit contribution margin and the CM ratio.

b.
$$\frac{\text{Fixed expenses, \$210,000}}{\text{Contribution margin per unit, \$12}} = 17{,}500 \text{ units}$$

$$\frac{\text{Fixed expenses, \$210,000}}{\text{CM ratio, 20\%}} = \$1{,}050{,}000 \text{ break-even sales}$$

c. Yes, based on these data the changes should be made. The changes will increase the company's net income from the present $60,000 to $78,000 per year. Although the changes will also result in a higher break-even point (17,500 units as compared to the present 16,000 units), the company's margin of safety will actually be wider than before:

Total sales − Break-even sales = Margin of safety in dollars
$1,400,000 − $1,050,000 = $390,000

As shown in (5) above, the company's present margin of safety is only $240,000. Thus, several benefits will result from the proposed changes.

Key Terms for Review

Break-even point The level of sales at which profit is zero. The break-even point can also be defined as the point where total sales equals total expenses or as the point where total contribution margin equals total fixed expenses. (p. 236)

Contribution margin method A method of computing the break-even point in which the fixed expenses are divided by the contribution margin per unit. (p. 244)

Contribution margin ratio (CM ratio) The contribution margin as a percentage of total sales. (p. 248)

Cost-volume-profit (CVP) graph The relations between revenues, costs, and level of activity in an organization presented in graphic form. (p. 245)

Degree of operating leverage A measure, at a given level of sales, of how a percentage change in sales volume will affect profits. The degree of operating leverage is computed by dividing contribution margin by net income. (p. 251)

Equation method A method of computing the break-even point that relies on the equation Sales = Variable expenses + Fixed expenses + Profits. (p. 243)

Incremental analysis An analytical approach that focuses only on those items of revenue, cost, and volume that will change as a result of a decision. (p.240)

Margin of safety The excess of budgeted (or actual) sales over the break-even volume of sales. (p. 247)

Operating leverage A measure of how sensitive net income is to a given percentage change in sales. It is computed by dividing the contribution margin by net income. (p. 251)

Sales mix The relative proportions in which a company's products are sold. Sales mix is computed by expressing the sales of each product as a percentage of total sales. (p.255)

Questions

6–1 What is meant by a product's CM ratio? How is this ratio useful in planning business operations?

6–2 Often the most direct route to a business decision is to make an incremental analysis based on the information available. What is meant by an *incremental analysis?*

6–3 Company A's cost structure includes costs that are mostly variable, whereas Company B's cost structure includes costs that are mostly fixed. In a time of increasing sales, which company will tend to realize the most rapid increase in profits? Explain.

6–4 What is meant by the term *operating leverage*?

6–5 A 10% decrease in the selling price of a product will have the same impact on net income as a 10% increase in the variable expenses. Do you agree? Why or why not?

6–6 What is meant by the term *break-even point*?

6–7 Name three approaches to break-even analysis. Briefly explain how each approach works.

6–8 In response to a request from your immediate supervisor, you have prepared a CVP graph portraying the cost and revenue characteristics of your company's product and operations. Explain how the lines on the graph and the break-even point would change if (a) the selling price per unit decreased, (b) fixed costs increased throughout the entire range of activity portrayed on the graph, and (c) variable costs per unit increased.

6–9 Al's Auto Wash charges $4 to wash a car. The variable costs of washing a car are 15% of sales. Fixed expenses total $1,700 monthly. How many cars must be washed each month for Al to break even?

6–10 What is meant by the margin of safety?

6–11 Companies X and Y are in the same industry. Company X is highly automated, whereas Company Y relies primarily on labor to make its products. If sales and total expenses in the two companies are about the same, which would you expect to have the lower margin of safety? Why?

6–12 What is meant by the term *sales mix*? What assumption is usually made concerning sales mix in CVP analysis?

6–13 Explain how a shift in the sales mix could result in both a higher break-even point and a lower net income.

Exercises

E6–1 Menlo Company manufactures and sells a single product. The company's sales and expenses for last quarter follow:

	Total	Per Unit
Sales	$450,000	$30
Less variable expenses	180,000	12
Contribution margin	270,000	$18
Less fixed expenses	216,000	
Net income	$ 54,000	

Required

1. What is the quarterly break-even point in units sold and in sales dollars?
2. Without resorting to computations, what is the total contribution margin at the break-even point?
3. How many units would have to be sold each quarter to earn a target profit of $90,000? Use the unit contribution method. Verify your answer by preparing a contribution income statement at the target level of sales.
4. Refer to the original data. Compute the company's margin of safety in both dollar and percentage terms.
5. What is the company's CM ratio? If sales increase by $50,000 per quarter and there is no change in fixed expenses, by how much would you expect quarterly net income to increase? (Do not prepare an income statement; use the CM ratio to compute your answer.)

E6–2 Lindon Company is the exclusive distributor for an automotive product. The product sells for $40 per unit and has a CM ratio of 30%. The company's fixed expenses are $180,000 per year.

Required

1. What are the variable expenses per unit?
2. Using the equation method:
   a. What is the break-even point in units and sales dollars?
   b. What sales level in units and in sales dollars is required to earn an annual profit of $60,000?
   c. Assume that by using a more efficient shipper, the company is able to reduce its variable expenses by $4 per unit. What is the company's new break-even point in units and sales dollars?
3. Repeat (2) above using the unit contribution method.

E6–3 The Hartford Symphony Guild is planning its annual dinner-dance. The dinner-dance committee has assembled the following expected costs for the event:

Dinner (per person)	$ 18
Favors and program (per person)	2
Band	2,800
Rental of ballroom	900
Professional entertainment during intermission	1,000
Tickets and advertising	1,300

The committee members would like to charge $35 per person for the evening's activities.

Required

1. Compute the break-even point for the dinner-dance (in terms of the number of persons that must attend).
2. Assume that last year only 300 persons attended the dinner-dance. If the same number attend this year, what price per ticket must be charged in order to break even?
3. Refer to the original data ($35 ticket price per person). Prepare a CVP graph for the dinner-dance from a zero level of activity up to 900 tickets sold. Number of persons should be placed on the horizontal *(X)* axis, and dollars should be placed on the vertical *(Y)* axis.

E6–4 Magic Realm, Inc., has developed a new fantasy board game. The company sold 15,000 games last year at a selling price of $20 per game. Fixed costs associated with the game total $182,000 per year, and variable costs are $6 per game. Production of the game is entrusted to a printing contractor. Variable costs consist mostly of payments to this contractor.

Required

1. Prepare an income statement for the game last year and compute the degree of operating leverage.

2. Management is confident that the company can sell 18,000 games next year (an increase of 3,000 games, or 20%, over last year). Compute:
   a. The expected percentage increase in net income for next year.
   b. The expected total dollar net income for next year. (Do not prepare an income statement; use the degree of operating leverage to compute your answer.)

E6–5 Miller Company's most recent income statement is shown below:

	Total	Per Unit
Sales (20,000 units)	$300,000	$15.00
Less variable expenses	180,000	9.00
Contribution margin	120,000	$ 6.00
Less fixed expenses	70,000	
Net income	$ 50,000	

Required Prepare a new income statement under each of the following conditions (consider each case independently):

1. The sales volume increases by 15%.
2. The selling price decreases by $1.50 per unit, and the sales volume increases by 25%.
3. The selling price increases by $1.50 per unit, fixed expenses increase by $20,000, and the sales volume decreases by 5%.
4. The selling price increases by 12%, variable expenses increase by 60 cents per unit, and the sales volume decreases by 10%.

E6–6 Fill in the missing amounts in each of the eight case situations below. Each case is independent of the others. (Hint: One way to find the missing amounts would be to prepare a contribution income statement for each case, enter the known data, and then compute the missing items.)

a. Assume that only one product is being sold in each of the four following case situations:

Case	Units Sold	Sales	Variable Expenses	Contribution Margin per Unit	Fixed Expenses	Net Income (Loss)
1	15,000	$180,000	$120,000	$?	$ 50,000	$?
2	?	100,000	?	10	32,000	8,000
3	10,000	?	70,000	13	?	12,000
4	6,000	300,000	?	?	100,000	(10,000)

b. Assume that more than one product is being sold in each of the four following case situations:

Case	Sales	Variable Expenses	Average Contribution Margin (percent)	Fixed Expenses	Net Income (Loss)
1	$500,000	$?	20	$?	$ 7,000
2	400,000	260,000	?	100,000	?
3	?	?	60	130,000	20,000
4	600,000	420,000	?	?	(5,000)

E6–7 Olongapo Sports Corporation is the distributor in the Philippines of two premium golf balls—the Flight Dynamic and the Sure Shot. Monthly sales and the contribution margin ratios for the two products follow:

	Product: Flight Dynamic	Product: Sure Shot	Total
Sales	P150,000	P250,000	P400,000
CM ratio	80%	36%	?

Fixed expenses total P183,750 per month. (The currency in the Philippines is the peso, which is denoted by P.)

Required

1. Prepare an income statement for the company as a whole. Use the format shown in Exhibit 6–4 and carry computations to one decimal place.
2. Compute the break-even point for the company based on the current sales mix.
3. If sales increase by P100,000 a month, by how much would you expect net income to increase? What are your assumptions?

E6–8 Outback Outfitters manufactures and sells recreational equipment. One of the company's products, a small camp stove, sells for $50 per unit. Variable expenses are $32 per stove, and fixed expenses associated with the stove total $108,000 per month.

Required

1. Compute the break-even point in number of stoves and in total sales dollars.
2. If the variable expenses per stove increase as a percentage of the selling price, will it result in a higher or a lower break-even point? Why? (Assume that the fixed expenses remain unchanged.)
3. At present, the company is selling 8,000 stoves per month. The sales manager is convinced that a 10% reduction in the selling price would result in a 25% increase in monthly sales of stoves. Prepare two contribution income statements, one under present operating conditions, and one as operations would appear after the proposed changes. Show both total and per unit data on your statements.
4. Refer to the data in (3) above. How many stoves would have to be sold at the new selling price to yield a minimum net income of $35,000 per month?

Problems

P6–9 Basic CVP Analysis; Graphing The Fashion Shoe Company operates a chain of women's shoe shops around the country. The shops carry many styles of shoes that are all sold at the same price. Sales personnel in the shops are paid a substantial commission on each pair of shoes sold (in addition to a small basic salary) in order to encourage them to be aggressive in their sales efforts.

The following cost and revenue data relate to Shop 48 and are typical of one of the company's many outlets:

	Per Pair of Shoes
Sales price	$ 30.00
Variable expenses:	
Invoice cost	$ 13.50
Sales commission	4.50
Total variable expenses	$ 18.00
	Annual
Fixed expenses:	
Advertising	$ 30,000
Rent	20,000
Salaries	100,000
Total fixed expenses	$150,000

Required

1. Calculate the annual break-even point in dollar sales and in unit sales for Shop 48.
2. Prepare a CVP graph showing cost and revenue data for Shop 48 from a zero level of activity up to 20,000 pairs of shoes sold each year. Clearly indicate the break-even point on the graph.
3. If 12,000 pairs of shoes are sold in a year, what would be Shop 48's net income or loss?

4. The company is considering paying the store manager of Shop 48 an incentive commission of 75 cents per pair of shoes (in addition to the salesperson's commission). If this change is made, what will be the new break-even point in dollar sales and in unit sales?
5. Refer to the original data. As an alternative to (4) above, the company is considering paying the store manager 50 cents commission on each pair of shoes sold in excess of the break-even point. If this change is made, what will be the shop's net income or loss if 15,000 pairs of shoes are sold?
6. Refer to the original data. The company is considering eliminating sales commissions entirely in its shops and increasing fixed salaries by $31,500 annually. If this change is made, what will be the new break-even point in dollar sales and in unit sales for Shop 48? Would you recommend that the change be made? Explain.

P6–10 Basics of CVP Analysis; Cost Structure Due to erratic sales of its sole product—a high-capacity battery for laptop computers—PEM, Inc., has been experiencing difficulty for some time. The company's income statement for the most recent month is given below:

Sales (19,500 units × $30)	$585,000
Less variable expenses	409,500
Contribution margin	175,500
Less fixed expenses	180,000
Net loss	$ (4,500)

Required

1. Compute the company's CM ratio and its break-even point in both units and dollars.
2. The president believes that a $16,000 increase in the monthly advertising budget, combined with an intensified effort by the sales staff, will result in an $80,000 increase in monthly sales. If the president is right, what will be the effect on the company's monthly net income or loss? (Use the incremental approach in preparing your answer.)
3. Refer to the original data. The sales manager is convinced that a 10% reduction in the selling price, combined with an increase of $60,000 in the monthly advertising budget, will cause unit sales to double. What will the new income statement look like if these changes are adopted?
4. Refer to the original data. The Marketing Department thinks that a fancy new package for the laptop computer battery would help sales. The new package would increase packaging costs by 75 cents per unit. Assuming no other changes, how many units would have to be sold each month to earn a profit of $9,750?
5. Refer to the original data. By automating certain operations, the company could reduce variable costs by $3 per unit. However, fixed costs would increase by $72,000 each month.
   a. Compute the new CM ratio and the new break-even point in both units and dollars.
   b. Assume that the company expects to sell 26,000 units next month. Prepare two income statements, one assuming that operations are not automated and one assuming that they are. (Show data on a per unit and percentage basis, as well as in total, for each alternative.)
   c. Would you recommend that the company automate its operations? Explain.

P6–11 Sales Mix Assumptions; Break-Even Analysis Gold Star Rice, Ltd., of Thailand exports Thai rice throughout Asia. The company grows three varieties of rice—Fragrant, White, and Loonzain. (The currency in Thailand is the baht, which is denoted by B.) Budgeted sales by product and in total for the coming month are shown below:

	Product							
	White		Fragrant		Loonzain		Total	
Percentage of total sales	20%		52%		28%		100%	
Sales	B150,000	100%	B390,000	100%	B210,000	100%	B750,000	100%
Less variable expenses	108,000	72%	78,000	20%	84,000	40%	270,000	36%
Contribution margin	B 42,000	28%	B312,000	80%	B126,000	60%	480,000	64%
Less fixed expenses							449,280	
Net income							B 30,720	

$$\text{Break-even sales: } \frac{\text{Fixed expenses, B449,280}}{\text{CM ratio, 0.64}} = \text{B702,000}$$

As shown by these data, net income is budgeted at B30,720 for the month and break-even sales at B702,000.

Assume that actual sales for the month total B750,000 as planned. Actual sales by product are: White, B300,000; Fragrant, B180,000; and Loonzain, B270,000.

Required

1. Prepare a contribution income statement for the month based on actual sales data. Present the income statement in the format shown above.
2. Compute the break-even sales for the month based on your actual data.
3. Considering the fact that the company met its B750,000 sales budget for the month, the president is shocked at the results shown on your income statement in (1) above. Prepare a brief memo for the president explaining why both the operating results and break-even sales are different from what was budgeted.

P6–12 Basics of CVP Analysis Feather Friends, Inc., makes a high-quality wooden birdhouse that sells for $20 per unit. Variable costs are $8 per unit, and fixed costs total $180,000 per year.

Required

Answer the following independent questions:

1. What is the product's CM ratio?
2. Use the CM ratio to determine the break-even point in sales dollars.
3. Due to an increase in demand, the company estimates that sales will increase by $75,000 during the next year. By how much should net income increase (or net loss decrease) assuming that fixed costs do not change?
4. Assume that the operating results for last year were:

Sales	$400,000
Less variable expenses	160,000
Contribution margin	240,000
Less fixed expenses	180,000
Net income	$ 60,000

   a. Compute the degree of operating leverage at the current level of sales.
   b. The president expects sales to increase by 20% next year. By what percentage should net income increase?

5. Refer to the original data. Assume that the company sold 18,000 units last year. The sales manager is convinced that a 10% reduction in the selling price, combined with a $30,000 increase in advertising, would cause annual sales in units to increase by one-third. Prepare two contribution income statements, one showing the results of last year's operations and one showing the results of operations if these changes are made. Would you recommend that the company do as the sales manager suggests?
6. Refer to the original data. Assume again that the company sold 18,000 units last year. The president does not want to change the selling price. Instead, he wants to increase the sales commission by $1 per unit. He thinks that this move, combined with some increase in advertising, would increase annual sales by 25%. By how much could advertising be increased with profits remaining unchanged? Do not prepare an income statement; use the incremental analysis approach.

P6–13 The Case of the Elusive Contribution Margin The Shirt Works sells a large variety of tee shirts and sweat shirts. Steve Hooper, the owner, is thinking of expanding his sales by hiring local high school students, on a commission basis, to sell sweat shirts bearing the name and mascot of the local high school.

These sweat shirts would have to be ordered from the manufacturer six weeks in advance, and they could not be returned because of the unique printing required. The sweat shirts would cost Mr. Hooper $8 each with a minimum order of 75 sweat shirts. Any additional sweat shirts would have to be ordered in increments of 75.

Since Mr. Hooper's plan would not require any additional facilities, the only costs associated with the project would be the costs of the sweat shirts and the costs of the sales commissions. The selling price of the sweat shirts would be $13.50 each. Mr. Hooper would pay the students a commission of $1.50 for each shirt sold.

Required

1. To make the project worthwhile, Mr. Hooper would require a $1,200 profit for the first three months of the venture. What level of sales in units and in dollars would be required to reach this target net income? Show all computations.
2. Assume that the venture is undertaken and an order is place for 75 sweat shirts. What would be Mr. Hooper's break-even point in units and in sales dollars? Show computations and explain the reasoning behind your answer.

P6–14 Interpretive Questions on the CVP Graph A CVP graph such as the one shown below is a useful technique for showing relationships between costs, volume, and profits in an organization.

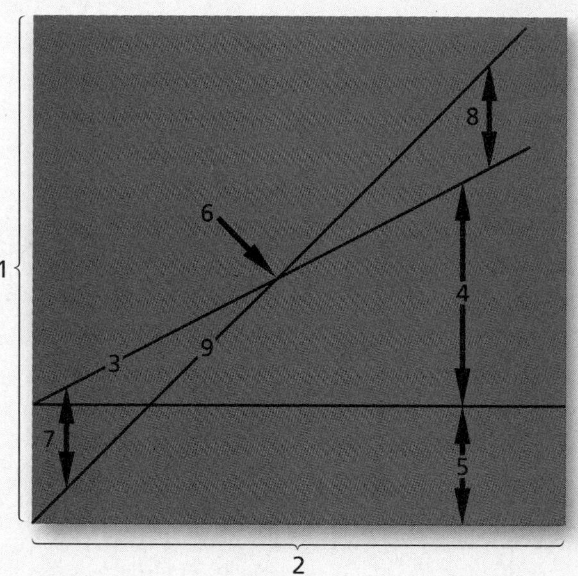

Required

1. Identify the numbered components in the CVP graph.
2. State the effect of each of the following actions on line 3, line 9, and the break-even point. For line 3 and line 9, state whether the action will cause the line to:

Remain unchanged.
Shift upward.
Shift downward.
Have a steeper slope (i.e., rotate upward).
Have a flatter slope (i.e., rotate downward).
Shift upward *and* have a steeper slope.
Shift upward *and* have a flatter slope.
Shift downward *and* have a steeper slope.
Shift downward *and* have a flatter slope.

In the case of the break-even point, state whether the action will cause the break-even point to:

Remain unchanged.
Increase.
Decrease.
Probably change, but the direction is uncertain.

Treat each case independently.

x. Example. Fixed costs are reduced by $5,000 per period.
Answer (see choices above): Line 3: Shift downward.
Line 9: Remain unchanged.
Break-even point: Decrease.

a. The unit selling price is increased from $18 to $20.
b. Unit variable costs are decreased from $12 to $10.
c. Fixed costs are increased by $3,000 per period.
d. Two thousand more units are sold during the period than were budgeted.
e. Due to paying salespersons a commission rather than a flat salary, fixed costs are reduced by $8,000 per period and unit variable costs are increased by $3.
f. Due to an increase in the cost of materials, both unit variable costs and the selling price are increased by $2.
g. Advertising costs are increased by $10,000 per period, resulting in a 10% increase in the number of units sold.
h. Due to automating an operation previously done by workers, fixed costs are increased by $12,000 per period and unit variable costs are reduced by $4.

P6–15 Sales Mix; Break-Even Analysis; Margin of Safety Island Novelties, Inc., of Palau makes two products, Hawaiian Fantasy and Tahitian Joy. Present revenue, cost, and sales data on the two products follow:

	Hawaiian Fantasy	Tahitian Joy
Selling price per unit	$15	$100
Variable expenses per unit	9	20
Number of units sold annually	20,000	5,000

Fixed expenses total $475,800 per year. The Republic of Palau uses the US dollar as its currency.

Required

1. Assuming the sales mix given above, do the following:
   a. Prepare a contribution income statement showing both dollar and percent columns for each product and for the company as a whole.
   b. Compute the break-even point in dollars for the company as a whole and the margin of safety in both dollars and percent.
2. Another product, Samoan Delight, has just come onto the market. Assume that the company could sell 10,000 units at $45 each. The variable expenses would be $36 each. The company's fixed expenses would not change.
   a. Prepare another contribution income statement, including sales of the Samoan Delight (sales of the other two products would not change). Carry percentage computations to one decimal place.
   b. Compute the company's new break-even point in dollars and the new margin of safety in both dollars and percent.
3. The president of the company examines your figures and says, "There's something strange here. Our fixed costs haven't changed and you show greater total contribution margin if we add the new product, but you also show our break-even point going up. With greater contribution margin, the break-even point should go down, not up. You've made a mistake somewhere." Explain to the president what has happened.

P6–16 Sensitivity Analysis of Net Income; Changes in Volume Minden Company introduced a new product last year for which it is trying to find an optimal selling price. Marketing studies suggest that the company can increase sales by 5,000 units for each $2 reduction in the selling price. The company's present selling price is $70 per unit, and variable expenses are $40 per unit. Fixed expenses are $540,000 per year. The present annual sales volume (at the $70 selling price) is 15,000 units.

Required

1. What is the present yearly net income or loss?
2. What is the present break-even point in units and in dollar sales?
3. Assuming that the marketing studies are correct, what is the *maximum* profit that the company can earn yearly? At how many units and at what selling price per unit would the company generate this profit?
4. What would be the break-even point in units and in dollar sales using the selling price you determined in (3) above (e.g., the selling price at the level of maximum profits)? Why is this break-even point different from the break-even point you computed in (2) above?

P6–17 Graphing; Incremental Analysis; Operating Leverage Angie Silva has recently opened The Sandal Shop in Brisbane, Australia, a store that specializes in fashionable sandals. Angie has just received a degree in business and she is anxious to apply the principles she has learned to her business. In time, she hopes to open a chain of sandal shops. As a first step, she has prepared the following analysis for her new store:

Sales price per pair of sandals	$40
Variable expenses per pair of sandals	16
Contribution margin per pair of sandals	$24
Fixed expenses per year:	
Building rental	$15,000
Equipment depreciation	7,000
Selling	20,000
Administrative	18,000
Total fixed expenses	$60,000

Required

1. How many pairs of sandals must be sold each year to break even? What does this represent in total dollar sales?
2. Prepare a CVP graph for the store from a zero level of activity up to 5,000 pairs of sandals sold each year. Indicate the break-even point on your graph.
3. Angie has decided that she must earn at least $18,000 the first year to justify her time and effort. How many pairs of sandals must be sold to reach this target profit?
4. Angie now has two salespersons working in the store—one full time and one part time. It will cost her an additional $8,000 per year to convert the part-time position to a full-time position. Angie believes that the change would bring in an additional $25,000 in sales each year. Should she convert the position? Use the incremental approach (do not prepare an income statement).
5. Refer to the original data. During the first year, the store sold only 3,000 pairs of sandals and reported the following operating results:

Sales (3,000 pair)	$120,000
Less variable expenses	48,000
Contribution margin	72,000
Less fixed expenses	60,000
Net income	$ 12,000

   a. What is the store's degree of operating leverage?
   b. Angie is confident that with a more intense sales effort and with a more creative advertising program she can increase sales by 50% next year. What would be the expected percentage increase in net income? Use the degree of operating leverage to compute your answer.

P6–18 Sales Mix; Commission Structure; Break-Even Point Carbex, Inc., produces cutlery sets out of high-quality wood and steel. The company makes a standard cutlery set and a deluxe set and sells them to retail department stores throughout the country. The standard set sells for $60, and the deluxe set sells for $75. The variable expenses associated with each set are given below (in cost per set):

	Standard	Deluxe
Production costs	$15.00	$30.00
Sales commissions (15% of sales price)	9.00	11.25

The company's fixed expenses each month are:

Advertising	$105,000
Depreciation	21,700
Administrative	63,000

Salespersons are paid on a commission basis to encourage them to be aggressive in their sales efforts. Mary Parsons, the financial vice president, watches sales commissions carefully and has noted that they have risen steadily over the last year. For this reason, she was shocked to find that even though sales have increased, profits for the current month—May—are down substantially from April. Sales, in sets, for the last two months are given below:

	Standard	Deluxe	Total
April	4,000	2,000	6,000
May	1,000	5,000	6,000

Required

1. Prepare an income statement for April and an income statement for May. Use the contribution format, with the following headings:

	Standard		Deluxe		Total	
	Amount	Percent	Amount	Percent	Amount	Percent
Sales						
Etc						

   Place the fixed expenses only in the Total column. Carry percentage computations to one decimal place. Do not show percentages for the fixed expenses.
2. Explain why there is a difference in net income between the two months, even though the same *total* number of sets was sold in each month.
3. What can be done to the sales commissions to optimize the sales mix?
4. a. Using April's figures, what was the break-even point for the month in sales dollars?
   b. Has May's break-even point gone up or down from that of April? Explain your answer without calculating the break-even point for May.

P6–19 Various CVP Questions: Break-Even Point; Cost Structure; Target Sales Northwood Company manufactures basketballs. The company has a standard ball that sells for $25. At present, the standard ball is manufactured in a small plant that relies heavily on direct labor workers. Thus, variable costs are high, totaling $15 per ball.

Last year, the company sold 30,000 standard balls, with the following results:

Sales (30,000 standard balls)	$750,000
Less variable expenses	450,000
Contribution margin	300,000
Less fixed expenses	210,000
Net income	$ 90,000

Required

1. Compute (a) the CM ratio and the break-even point in balls, and (b) the degree of operating leverage at last year's level of sales.
2. Due to an increase in labor rates, the company estimates that variable costs will increase by $3 per ball next year. If this change takes place and the selling price per ball remains constant at $25, what will be the new CM ratio and break-even point in balls?
3. Refer to the data in (2) above. If the expected change in variable costs takes place, how many balls will have to be sold next year to earn the same net income ($90,000) as last year?
4. Refer again to the data in (2) above. The president feels that the company must raise the selling price on the standard balls. If Northwood Company wants to maintain *the same CM ratio as last year,* what selling price per ball must it charge next year to cover the increased labor costs?
5. Refer to the original data. The company is discussing the construction of a new, automated plant to manufacture the standard balls. The new plant would slash variable costs per ball by 40%, but it would cause fixed costs to double in amount per year. If the new plant is built, what would be the company's new CM ratio and new break-even point in balls?
6. Refer to the data in (5) above.
   a. If the new plant is built, how many balls will have to be sold next year to earn the same net income ($90,000) as last year?

b. Assume the new plant is built and that next year the company manufactures and sells 30,000 balls (the same number as sold last year). Prepare a contribution income statement and compute the degree of operating leverage.

c. If you were a member of top management, would you have voted in favor of constructing the new plant? Explain.

P6–20 Changing Levels of Fixed and Variable Costs Neptune Company produces toys and other items for use in beach and resort areas. A small, inflatable toy has come onto the market that the company is anxious to produce and sell. Enough capacity exists in the company's plant to produce 16,000 units of the toy each month. Variable costs to manufacture and sell one unit would be $1.25, and fixed costs associated with the toy would total $35,000 per month.

The company's Marketing Department predicts that demand for the new toy will exceed the 16,000 units that the company is able to produce. Additional manufacturing space can be rented from another company at a fixed cost of $1,000 per month. Variable costs in the rented facility would total $1.40 per unit, due to somewhat less efficient operations than in the main plant. The new toy will sell for $3 per unit.

Required

1. Compute the monthly break-even point for the new toy in units and in total dollar sales. Show all computations in good form.
2. How many units must be sold each month to make a monthly profit of $12,000?
3. If the sales manager receives a bonus of 10 cents for each unit sold in excess of the break-even point, how many units must be sold each month to earn a return of 25% on the monthly investment in fixed costs?

P6–21 Changes in Cost Structure Morton Company's income statement for last month is given below:

Sales (15,000 units × $30)	$450,000
Less variable expenses	315,000
Contribution margin	135,000
Less fixed expenses	90,000
Net income	$ 45,000

The industry in which Morton Company operates is quite sensitive to cyclical movements in the economy. Thus, profits vary considerably from year to year according to general economic conditions. The company has a large amount of unused capacity and is studying ways of improving profits.

Required

1. New equipment has come onto the market that would allow Morton Company to automate a portion of its operations. Variable costs would be reduced by $9 per unit. However, fixed costs would increase to a total of $225,000 each month. Prepare two contribution-type income statements, one showing present operations and one showing how operations would appear if the new equipment is purchased. Show an Amount column, a Per Unit column, and a Percent column on each statement. Do not show percentages for the fixed costs.
2. Refer to the income statements in (1) above. For both present operations and the proposed new operations, compute (a) the degree of operating leverage, (b) the break-even point in dollars, and (c) the margin of safety in both dollar and percentage terms.
3. Refer again to the data in (1) above. As a manager, what factor would be paramount in your mind in deciding whether to purchase the new equipment? (You may assume that ample funds are available to make the purchase.)
4. Refer to the original data. Rather than purchase new equipment, the president is thinking about changing the company's marketing method. Under the new method, sales would increase by 20% each month and net income would increase by one-third. Fixed costs could be slashed to only $48,000 per month. Compute the break-even point for the company after the change in marketing method.

P6–22 Missing Data; Integration of CVP Factors You were employed just this morning by Pyrrhic Company, a prominent and rapidly growing organization. As your initial assignment, you were asked to complete an analysis of one of the company's products

for the board of directors meeting later in the day. After completing the analysis, you left your office for a few moments only to discover on returning that a broken sprinkler in the ceiling has destroyed most of your work. Only the following bits remained:

PYRRHIC COMPANY
Actual Income Statement
For the Month Ended June 30

	Total	Per Unit	Percent
Sales (? units)	$?	$?	100%
Less variable expenses	?	?	?%
Contribution margin	?	$?	?%
Less fixed expenses	?		
Net income	$?		

Break-even point:	
In units	? units
In dollars	$180,000
Margin of safety:	
In dollars	$?
In percentage	20%
Degree of operating leverage	?

The computations above are all based on actual results for June. The company's *projected* income statement for this product for July follows:

PYRRHIC COMPANY
Projected Income Statement
For the Month Ended July 31

	Total	Per Unit	Percent
Sales (33,000 units)	$?	$?	?%
Less variable expenses	?	?	?%
Contribution margin	?	$?	?%
Less fixed expenses	?		
Net income	$40,500		

To add to your woes, the company's mainframe computer is down so no data are available from that source. You do remember that sales for July are projected to increase by 10% over sales for June. You also remember that June's net income was $27,000—the same amount as your annual salary from the company. Finally, you remember that the degree of operating leverage is highly useful to the manager as a predictive tool.

Total fixed expenses, the unit selling price, and the unit variable expenses are planned to be the same in July as they were in June.

The board of directors meets in just one hour.

Required

1. For the June data, do the following:
   a. Complete the June income statement (all three columns).
   b. Compute the break-even point in units and verify the break-even point in dollars. Use the unit contribution method.
   c. Compute the margin of safety in dollars and verify the margin of safety percentage.
   d. Compute the degree of operating leverage as of June 30.
2. For the July data, do the following:
   a. Complete the July projected income statement (all three columns).
   b. Compute the margin of safety in dollars and percent and compute the degree of operating leverage. Why has the margin of safety gone up and the degree of operating leverage gone down?
3. Brimming with confidence after having completed (1) and (2) above in less than one hour, you decide to give the board of directors some added data. You know that direct labor

accounts for $1.80 of the company's per unit variable expenses. You have learned that direct labor costs may increase by one-third next year. Assuming that this cost increase takes place and that selling price and other cost factors remain unchanged, how many units will the company have to sell in a month to earn a net income equal to 20% of sales?

Cases

C6–23 Cost Structure; Break-Even; Target Profits Pittman Company is a small but growing manufacturer of telecommunications equipment. The company has no sales force of its own; rather, it relies completely on independent sales agents to market its products. These agents are paid a commission of 15% of selling price for all items sold.

Barbara Cheney, Pittman's controller, has just prepared the company's budgeted income statement for next year. The statement follows:

PITTMAN COMPANY
Budgeted Income Statement
For the Year Ended December 31

Sales		$16,000,000
Manufacturing costs:		
Variable	$7,200,000	
Fixed overhead	2,340,000	9,540,000
Gross margin		6,460,000
Selling and administrative costs:		
Commissions to agents	2,400,000	
Fixed marketing costs	120,000*	
Fixed administrative costs	1,800,000	4,320,000
Net operating income		2,140,000
Less fixed interest cost		540,000
Income before income taxes		1,600,000
Less income taxes (30%)		480,000
Net income		$ 1,120,000

* Primarily depreciation on storage facilities.

As Barbara handed the statement to Karl Vecci, Pittman's president, she commented, "I went ahead and used the agents' 15% commission rate in completing these statements, but we've just learned that they refuse to handle our products next year unless we increase the commission rate to 20%."

"That's the last straw," Karl replied angrily. "Those agents have been demanding more and more, and this time they've gone too far. How can they possibly defend a 20% commission rate?"

"They claim that after paying for advertising, travel, and the other costs of promotion, there's nothing left over for profit," replied Barbara.

"I say it's just plain robbery," retorted Karl. "And I also say it's time we dumped those guys and got our own sales force. Can you get your people to work up some cost figures for us to look at?"

"We've already worked them up," said Barbara. "Several companies we know about pay a 7.5% commission to their own salespeople, along with a small salary. Of course, we would have to handle all promotion costs, too. We figure our fixed costs would increase by $2,400,000 per year, but that would be more than offset by the $3,200,000 (20% × $16,000,000) that we would avoid on agents' commissions."

The breakdown of the $2,400,000 cost figure follows:

Salaries:	
Sales manager	$ 100,000
Salespersons	600,000
Travel and entertainment	400,000
Advertising	1,300,000
Total	$2,400,000

"Super," replied Karl. "And I note that the $2,400,000 is just what we're paying the agents under the old 15% commission rate."

"It's even better than that," explained Barbara. "We can actually save $75,000 a year because that's what we're having to pay the auditing firm now to check out the agents' reports. So our overall administrative costs would be less."

"Pull all of these number together and we'll show them to the executive committee tomorrow," said Karl. "With the approval of the committee, we can move on the matter immediately."

Required

1. Compute Pittman Company's break-even point in sales dollars for next year assuming:
   a. That the agents' commission rate remains unchanged at 15%.
   b. That the agents' commission rate is increased to 20%.
   c. That the company employs its own sales force.
2. Assume that Pittman Company decides to continue selling through agents and pays the 20% commission rate. Determine the volume of sales that would be required to generate the same net income as contained in the budgeted income statement for next year.
3. Determine the volume of sales at which net income would be equal regardless of whether Pittman Company sells through agents (at a 20% commission rate) or employs its own sales force.
4. Compute the degree of operating leverage that the company would expect to have on December 31 at the end of next year assuming:
   a. That the agents' commission rate remains unchanged at 15%.
   b. That the agents' commission rate is increased to 20%.
   c. That the company employs its own sales force.

   Use income *before* income taxes in your operating leverage computation.
5. Based on the data in (1) through (4) above, make a recommendation as to whether the company should continue to use sales agents (at a 20% commission rate) or employ its own sales force. Give reasons for your answer.

(CMA, adapted)

C6–24 Detailed Income Statement; CVP Sensitivity Analysis The most recent income statement for Whitney Company appears below:

WHITNEY COMPANY
Income Statement
For the Year Ended December 31

Sales (45,000 units at $10)			$450,000
Less cost of goods sold:			
Direct materials		$90,000	
Direct labor		78,300	
Manufacturing overhead		98,500	266,800
Gross margin			183,200
Less operating expenses:			
Selling expenses:			
Variable:			
Sales commissions	$27,000		
Shipping	5,400	32,400	
Fixed (advertising, salaries)		120,000	
Administrative:			
Variable (billing and other)		1,800	
Fixed (salaries and other)		48,000	202,200
Net loss			$(19,000)

All variable expenses in the company vary in terms of unit sold, except for sales commissions, which are based on sales dollars. Variable manufacturing overhead is 30 cents per unit. There were no beginning or ending inventories. Whitney Company's plant has a capacity of 75,000 units per year.

The company has been operating at a loss for several years. Management is studying several possible courses of action to determine what should be done to make next year profitable.

Required

1. Redo Whitney Company's income statement in the contribution format. Show both a Total column and a Per Unit column on your statement. Leave enough space to the right of your numbers to enter the solution to both parts of (2) below.
2. The president is considering two proposals prepared by members of his staff:
   a. For next year, the vice president would like to reduce the unit selling price by 20%. She is certain that this would fill the plant to capacity.
   b. For next year, the sales manager would like to increase the unit selling price by 20%, increase the sales commission to 9% of sales, and increase advertising by $100,000. Based on marketing studies, he is confident this would increase unit sales by one-third.

   Prepare two contribution income statements, one showing what profits would be under the vice president's proposal and one showing what profits would be under the sales manager's proposal. On each statement, include both Total and Per Unit columns (do not show per unit data for the fixed costs).
3. Refer to the original data. The president believes it would be a mistake to change the unit selling price. Instead, he wants to use less costly materials in manufacturing units of product, thereby reducing unit costs by 70 cents. How many units would have to be sold next year to earn a target profit of $30,200?
4. Refer to the original data. Whitney Company's board of directors believes that the company's problem lies in inadequate promotion. By how much can advertising be increased and still allow the company to earn a target return of 4.5% on sales of 60,000 units?
5. Refer to the original data. The company has been approached by an overseas distributor who wants to purchase 9,500 units on a special price basis. There would be no sales commission on these units. However, shipping costs would be increased by 50% and variable administrative costs would be reduced by 25%. In addition, a $5,700 special insurance fee would have to be paid by Whitney Company to protect the goods in transit. What unit price would have to be quoted on the 9,500 units by Whitney Company to allow the company to earn a profit of $14,250 on total operations? Regular business would not be disturbed by this special order.

C6–25 Break-Even Analysis with Step Fixed Costs Wymont Hospital operates a general hospital with separate departments such as Pediatrics, Maternity, and Surgery. Wymont Hospital charges each separate department for services to its patients such as meals and laundry and for administrative services such as billing and collections. Space and bed charges are fixed for the year.

Last year, the Pediatrics Department at Wymont Hospital charged its patients an average of $65 per day, had a capacity of 80 beds, operated 24 hours per day for 365 days, and had total revenue of $1,138,800.

Expenses charged by the hospital to the Pediatrics Department for the year were as follows:

	Basis for Allocation	
	Patient-Days (variable)	Bed Capacity (fixed)
Dietary	$ 42,952	
Janitorial		$ 12,800
Laundry	28,000	
Laboratory	47,800	
Pharmacy	33,800	
Repairs and maintenance	5,200	7,140
General administrative services		131,760
Rent		275,320
Billings and collections	87,000	
Other	18,048	25,980
	$262,800	$453,000

The only personnel directly employed by the Pediatrics Department are supervising nurses, nurses, and aides. The hospital has minimum personnel requirements for Pediatrics based on total annual patient-days in Pediatrics. Hospital requirements, beginning at the minimum expected level of operation, follow:

Annual Patient-Days	Aides	Nurses	Supervising Nurses
10,000–14,000	21	11	4
14,001–17,000	22	12	4
17,001–23,725	22	13	4
23,726–25,550	25	14	5
25,551–27,375	26	14	5
27,376–29,200	29	16	6

These staffing levels represent full-time equivalents, and it should be assumed that the Pediatrics Department always employs only the minimum number of required full-time equivalent personnel.

Annual salaries for each class of employee are: supervising nurses, $18,000; nurses, $13,000; and aides, $5,000. Salary expense for last year was $72,000, $169,000, and $110,000 for supervising nurses, nurses, and aides, respectively.

Required

1. Compute the following:
   a. The number of patient-days in the Pediatrics Department for last year. (Each day a patient is in the hospital is known as a *patient-day.*)
   b. The variable cost per patient-day for last year.
   c. The total fixed costs, including both allocated fixed costs and personnel costs, in the Pediatrics Department for each level of operation shown above (i.e., total fixed costs at the 10,000–14,000 patient-day level of operation, total fixed costs at the 14,001–17,000 patient-day level of operation, etc.).
2. Using the data computed in (1) above and any other data as needed, compute the *minimum* number of patient-days required for the Pediatrics Department to break even. You may assume that variable and fixed cost behavior and that revenue per patient-day will remain unchanged in the future.
3. Determine the minimum number of patient-days required for the Pediatrics Department to earn an annual "profit" of $200,000.

(CPA, adapted)

C6–26 Individual Product Breakevens in a Multiproduct Company

Cheryl Montoya picked up the phone and called her boss, Wes Chan, the vice president of marketing at Piedmont Fasteners Corporation: "Wes, I'm not sure how to go about answering the questions that came up at the meeting with the president yesterday."

"What's the problem?"

"The president wanted to know each product's breakeven, but I am having trouble figuring them out."

"I'm sure you can handle it, Cheryl. And, by the way, I need your analysis on my desk tomorrow morning at 8:00 sharp in time for the follow-up meeting at 9:00."

Piedmont Fasteners Corporation makes three different clothing fasteners in its manufacturing facility in North Carolina. Data concerning these products appear below:

	Velcro	Metal	Nylon
Normal annual sales volume	100,000	200,000	400,000
Unit selling price	$1.65	$1.50	$0.85
Variable cost per unit	$1.25	$0.70	$0.25

Total fixed expenses are $400,000 per year.

All three products are sold in highly competitive markets, so the company is unable to raise its prices without losing unacceptable numbers of customers.

The company has an extremely effective just-in-time manufacturing system, so there are no beginning or ending work in process or finished goods inventories.

Required

1. What is the company's over-all breakeven in total sales dollars?
2. Of the total fixed costs of $400,000, $20,000 could be avoided if the Velcro product were dropped, $80,000 if the Metal product were dropped, and $60,000 if the Nylon product were dropped. The remaining fixed costs of $240,000 consist of common fixed costs such as administrative salaries and rent on the factory building that could be avoided only by going out of business entirely.
   a. What is the break-even quantity of each product?
   b. If the company sells exactly the break-even quantity of each product, what will be the overall profit of the company?

Group Exercises

GE6–27 **CVP and Collegiate Sports** Revenue from major intercollegiate sports is an important source of funds for many colleges. Most of the costs of putting on a football or basketball game may be fixed and may increase very little as the size of the crowd increases. Thus, the revenue from every extra ticket sold may be almost pure profit.

Choose a sport played at your college or university, such as football or basketball, that generates significant revenue. Talk with the business manager of your college's sports programs before answering the following questions:

Required

1. What is the maximum seating capacity of the stadium or arena in which the sport is played? During the past year, what was the average attendance at the games? On average, what percentage of the stadium or arena capacity was filled?
2. The number of seats sold often depends on the opponent. The attendance for a game with a traditional rival (e.g., Nebraska vs. Colorado, University of Washington vs. Washington State, or Texas vs. Texas A&M) is usually substantially above the average. Also, games against conference foes may draw larger crowds than other games. As a consequence, the number of tickets sold for a game is somewhat predictable. What implications does this have for the nature of the costs of putting on a game? Are most of the costs really fixed with respect to the number of tickets sold?
3. Estimate the variable cost per ticket sold.
4. Estimate the total additional revenue that would be generated in an average game if all of the tickets were sold at their normal prices. Estimate how much profit is lost because these tickets are not sold.
5. Estimate the ancillary revenue (parking and concessions) per ticket sold. Estimate how much profit is lost in an average game from these sources of revenue as a consequence of not having a sold-out game.
6. Estimate how much additional profit would be generated for your college if every game were sold out for the entire season.

GE6–28 **Cost Structure of Airlines** The cost structure of the airline industry can serve as the basis for a discussion of a number of different cost concepts. Airlines also provide an excellent illustration of the concept of operating leverage, the sensitivity of a firm's operating profits to changes in demand, and the opportunities and risks presented by such a cost structure. Airline profits and stock prices are among some of the most volatile on Wall Street. A recent study of the U.S. airline industry disclosed the following operating cost categories and their percentage of total operating cost:*

* R. D. Banker and H. H. Johnson, "An Empirical Study of Cost Drivers in the U.S. Airline Industry," *The Accounting Review,* July 1993, pp. 576–601.

Uniform System of Accounts Required by the Department of Transportation	Mean Percentage of Operating Cost, 1981–85
Fuel and oil	24.3%
Flying operations labor (flight crews—pilots, copilots, navigators, and flight engineers)	8.6%
Passenger service labor (flight attendants)	4.6%
Aircraft traffic and servicing labor (personnel servicing aircraft and handling passengers at gates, baggage, and cargo)	8.9%
Promotions and sales labor (reservations and sales agents, advertising and publicity)	9.0%
Maintenance labor (maintenance of flight equipment and ground property and equipment)	7.0%
Maintenance materials and overhead	2.1%
Ground property and equipment (landing fees, and rental expenses and depreciation for ground property and equipment)	12.5%
Flight equipment (rental expenses and depreciation on aircraft frames and engines)	8.4%
General overhead (administrative personnel, utilities, insurance, communications, etc.)	14.6%
Total	100.0%

Required

1. What should be the objectives of airline cost accounting systems?
2. Before a flight is scheduled, what are the variable and fixed costs and their percentages?
3. Before a flight is scheduled, what are the direct and indirect costs and their percentages?
4. Once a flight is scheduled, what are the variable and fixed costs and their percentages?
5. Once a flight is scheduled, what are the direct and indirect costs and their percentages?
6. How is knowledge of variable and fixed costs useful? How is knowledge of direct and indirect costs useful?
7. Once a flight is scheduled, what is the cost of carrying extra passengers?
8. Why are profits more sensitive (more variable) to changes in demand when the cost structure contains a high proportion of fixed costs?

GE6–29 Is the Past Prologue? The "baby bust" of the 1960s and early 1970s resulted in the number of college-age 18- and 19-year-olds contracting sharply from 1980 to 1993. The number of graduating high school seniors peaked in 1979 and declined to a low of 6.9 million in 1992, a drop of nearly 40%. Throughout the eighties, tuition at private and public universities rose at an average of 9% per year, a figure far above the rise in household family incomes. Then, the demographics began to reverse themselves: the number of 18- and 19-year-olds began to increase in 1996 and will continue until they peak in 2010 at about 9.3 million for nearly a 33% increase in the college-eligible population. By 1994, tuition costs for four years at a private college had jumped to an average of $44,000 from around $13,000 in 1980. With room and board added on, the cost is at least $20,000 higher.

Required

1. If tuition increases revert to the 9% increases of the 1980s, what will four years' tuition at a private college cost by the year 2010? How affordable will a college education be at this level?
2. What scenario do you envision for college tuition costs between now and the year 2010? Why?
3. What is the cost of adding an extra student to a typical classroom? Explain this in terms of the cost structure of a university.
4. After two decades of almost uninterrupted expansion, the "baby bust" enrollment drop left many colleges with considerable underutilized capacity. What impact will increasing enrollment and economies of scale have on costs and tuition?
5. Which colleges do you expect will be helped the most by increasing enrollments—public or private?

6. Given that severe student shortages will still exist for many years to come, what strategies would you suggest to college administrators for achieving a better balance between costs and tuition revenues?

IE6–30 Estimating Breakeven By accessing Carnival Corporation's web site at www.carnival.corp, you should be able to find enough data to estimate the company's breakeven and other critical items discussed in this chapter. If you have not already done so, complete internet exercise IE5–27 before proceeding any further. The results of your analysis of IE5–27 will be used in this exercise.

The average price per passenger cruise-day for Carnival Corporation can be computed by dividing the company's total revenue for the most current year by the passenger cruise-days. Use your estimates of fixed and variable costs from IE5–27. (Ignore everything in the company's income statement below the line "Operating income before income from affiliated operations.")

Required

1. Estimate Carnival Corporation's break-even point in the number of passenger cruise-days.
2. Estimate the company's margin of safety.
3. Estimate the company's degree of operating leverage.
4. Estimate by how much the company's operating income before income from affiliated operations would increase if the passenger cruise-days increased by 2%.

Chapter Seven

Variable Costing: A Tool for Management

Business Focus

Petra is employed by a large mutual fund as an investment analyst. Her job is to closely monitor the performance of companies in the electrical equipment industry and to recommend which of these companies the mutual fund should invest in.

Before Petra joined the company, the mutual fund had invested heavily in Power Transformers, Inc. Petra knew that she should be alert for any signs of trouble at Power Transformers. She had just received the company's annual report and was puzzled by several items in the report.

First, Power Transformer's net income for the year was higher than the previous year, but not as high as many investment analysts had predicted. Second, the company's sales had actually fallen a little from the previous year. Third, the company's inventories had risen substantially. Petra wondered if these three facts might be related and if she should issue a warning about the stock to her company's investment committee.

Learning Objectives

After studying Chapter 7, you should be able to:

1 Explain how variable costing differs from absorption costing and compute the unit product cost under each method.

2 Describe how fixed manufacturing overhead costs are deferred in inventory and released from inventory under absorption costing.

3 Prepare income statements using both variable and absorption costing, and reconcile the two net income figures.

4 Explain the effect of changes in production on the net income reported under both variable and absorption costing.

5 Explain the advantages and limitations of both the variable and absorption costing methods.

6 Explain how the use of JIT reduces the difference in net income reported under the variable and absorption costing methods.

Two general approaches are used for costing products for the purposes of valuing inventories and cost of goods sold. One approach, called *absorption costing,* was discussed in Chapter 3. Absorption costing is generally used for external financial reports. The other approach, called *variable costing,* is preferred by some managers for internal decision making and must be used when an income statement is prepared in the contribution format. Ordinarily, absorption costing and variable costing produce different figures for net income, and the difference can be quite large. In addition to showing how these two methods differ, we will consider the arguments for and against each costing method and we will show how management decisions can be affected by the costing method chosen.

Overview of Absorption and Variable Costing

objective 1

Explain how variable costing differs from absorption costing and compute the unit product cost under each method.

In the last two chapters, we learned that the contribution format income statement and cost-volume-profit (CVP) analysis are valuable management tools. Both of these tools emphasize cost behavior and require that managers carefully distinguish between variable and fixed costs. Absorption costing, which was discussed in Chapters 2 and 3, assigns both variable and fixed costs to products—mingling them in a way that makes it difficult for managers to distinguish between them. This has led to the development of variable costing, which focuses on *cost behavior.* One of the strengths of variable costing is that it harmonizes fully with both the contribution approach and the CVP concepts discussed in the preceding chapter.

Absorption Costing

In Chapter 3, we learned that **absorption costing** treats *all* costs of production as product costs, regardless of whether they are variable or fixed. The cost of a unit of product under the absorption costing method therefore consists of direct materials, direct labor, and *both* variable and fixed overhead. Thus, absorption costing allocates a portion of fixed manufacturing overhead cost to each unit of product, along with the variable manufacturing costs. Because absorption costing includes all costs of production as product costs, it is frequently referred to as the **full cost** method.

Variable Costing

Under **variable costing,** only those costs of production that vary with output are treated as product costs. This would generally include direct materials, direct labor, and the variable portion of manufacturing overhead. Fixed manufacturing overhead is not treated as a product cost under this method. Rather, fixed manufacturing overhead is treated as a period cost and, like selling and administrative expenses, it is charged off in its entirety against revenue each period. Consequently, the cost of a unit of product in inventory or in cost of goods sold under the variable costing method contains no element of fixed overhead cost.

Variable costing is sometimes referred to as **direct costing** or **marginal costing.** The term *direct costing* was popular for many years, but it is slowly disappearing from day-to-day use. The term *variable costing* is more descriptive of the way in which product costs are computed when a contribution income statement is prepared.

To complete this summary comparison of absorption and variable costing, we need to consider briefly the handling of selling and administrative expenses. These expenses are never treated as product costs, regardless of the costing method in use.

Exhibit 7–1 Cost Classifications—Absorption versus Variable Costing

Absorption Costing		Variable Costing
Product costs	Direct materials	Product costs
	Direct labor	
	Variable manufacturing overhead	
	Fixed manufacturing overhead	Period costs
Period costs	Selling and administrative expenses	

Thus, under either absorption or variable costing, selling and administrative expenses are always treated as period costs and deducted from revenues as incurred.

The concepts discussed so far in this section are illustrated in Exhibit 7–1, which shows the classification of costs under both absorption and variable costing.

Unit Cost Computations

To illustrate the computation of unit costs under both absorption and variable costing, consider Boley Company, a small company that produces a single product and has the following cost structure:

Number of units produced each year		6,000
Variable costs per unit:		
Direct materials	$	2
Direct labor		4
Variable manufacturing overhead		1
Variable selling and administrative expenses		3
Fixed costs per year:		
Fixed manufacturing overhead		30,000
Fixed selling and administrative expenses		10,000

Required

1. Compute the unit product cost under absorption costing.
2. Compute the unit product cost under variable costing.

Solution

Absorption Costing	
Direct materials	$ 2
Direct labor	4
Variable manufacturing overhead	1
Total variable production cost	7
Fixed manufacturing overhead ($30,000 ÷ 6,000 units of product)	5
Unit product cost	$12

Variable Costing	
Direct materials	$ 2
Direct labor	4
Variable manufacturing overhead	1
Unit product cost	$ 7

(The $30,000 fixed manufacturing overhead will be charged off in total against income as a period expense along with the selling and administrative expenses.)

Under the absorption costing method, notice that *all* production costs, variable and fixed, are included when determining the unit product cost. Thus, if the company sells a unit of product and absorption costing is being used, then $12 (consisting of $7 variable cost and $5 fixed cost) will be deducted on the income statement as cost of goods sold. Similarly, any unsold units will be carried as inventory on the balance sheet at $12 each.

Under the variable costing method, notice that only the variable production costs are included in product costs. Thus, if the company sells a unit of product, only $7 will be deducted as cost of goods sold, and unsold units will be carried in the balance sheet inventory account at only $7 each.

Income Comparison of Absorption and Variable Costing

objective 2

Describe how fixed manufacturing overhead costs are deferred in inventory and released from inventory under absorption costing.

Income statements prepared under the absorption and variable costing approaches are shown in Exhibit 7–2. In preparing these statements, we use the date for Boley Company presented earlier, along with other information about the company as given below:

Units in beginning inventory	–0–
Units produced	6,000
Units sold	5,000
Units in ending inventory	1,000
Selling price per unit	$ 20
Selling and administrative expenses:	
Variable per unit	3
Fixed per year	10,000

	Absorption Costing	Variable Costing
Unit product cost:		
Direct materials	$ 2	$ 2
Direct labor	4	4
Variable manufacturing overhead	1	1
Fixed manufacturing overhead ($30,000 ÷ 6,000 units)	5	—
Unit product cost	$12	$ 7

Several points can be made from the financial statements in Exhibit 7–2:

1. Under the absorption costing method, if there is an increase in inventories then some of the fixed manufacturing costs of the current period will not appear on the income statement as part of cost of goods sold. Instead, these costs are deferred to a future period and are carried on the balance sheet as part of the inventory count. Such a deferral of costs is known as **fixed manufacturing overhead cost deferred in inventory.** The process involved can be explained by referring to the data for Boley Company. During the current period, Boley Company produced 6,000 units but sold only 5,000 units, thus leaving 1,000 unsold units in the ending inventory. Under the absorption costing method, each unit produced was assigned $5 in fixed overhead cost (see the unit cost computations above). Therefore, each of the 1,000 units going into inventory at the end of the period has $5 in fixed manufacturing overhead cost attached to it, or a total of $5,000 for the 1,000 units. *This fixed*

Exhibit 7–2
Comparison of Absorption and Variable Costing—Boley Company

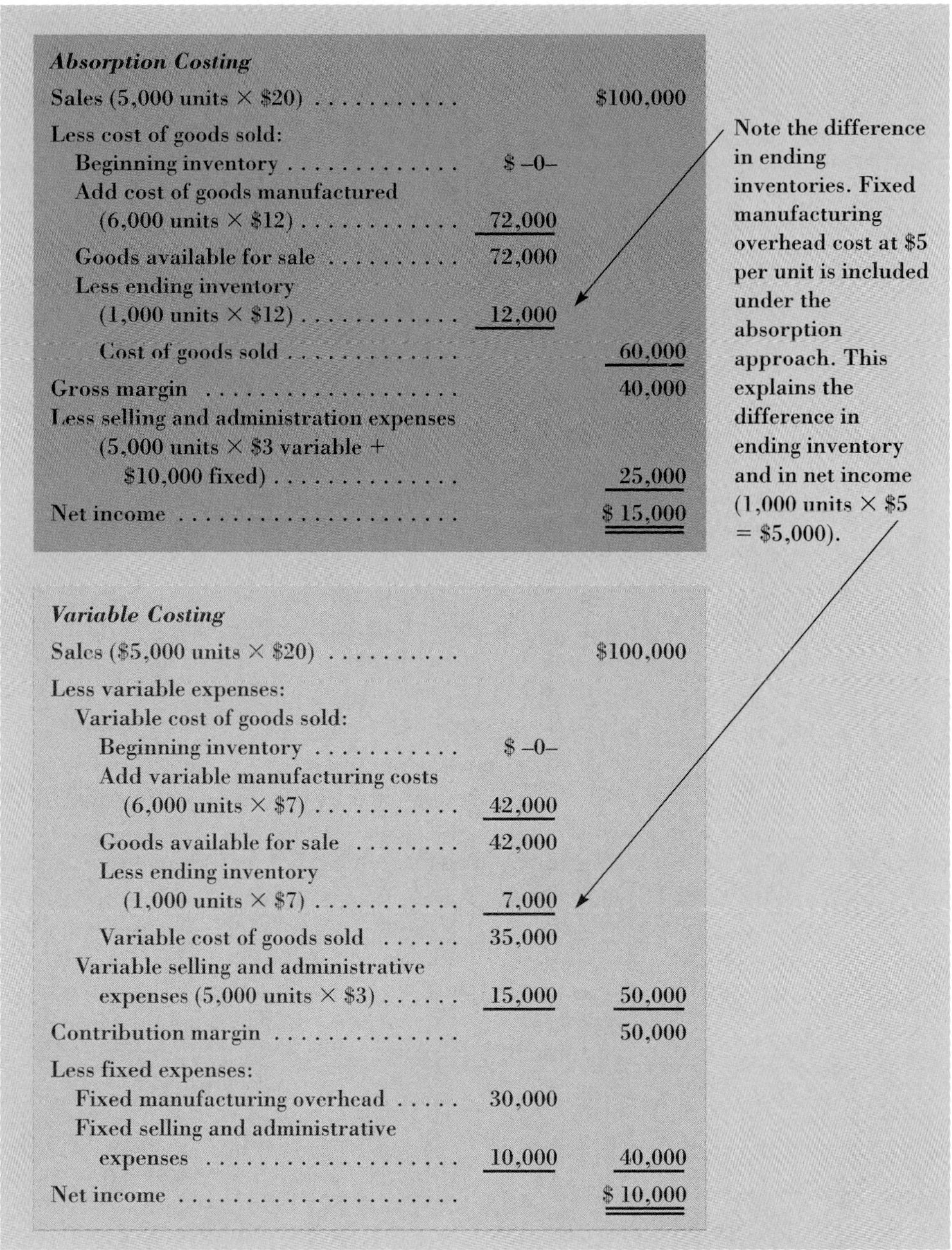

Absorption Costing		
Sales (5,000 units × $20)		$100,000
Less cost of goods sold:		
Beginning inventory	$ –0–	
Add cost of goods manufactured (6,000 units × $12)	72,000	
Goods available for sale	72,000	
Less ending inventory (1,000 units × $12)	12,000	
Cost of goods sold		60,000
Gross margin		40,000
Less selling and administration expenses (5,000 units × $3 variable + $10,000 fixed)		25,000
Net income		$ 15,000

Note the difference in ending inventories. Fixed manufacturing overhead cost at $5 per unit is included under the absorption approach. This explains the difference in ending inventory and in net income (1,000 units × $5 = $5,000).

Variable Costing		
Sales ($5,000 units × $20)		$100,000
Less variable expenses:		
Variable cost of goods sold:		
Beginning inventory	$ –0–	
Add variable manufacturing costs (6,000 units × $7)	42,000	
Goods available for sale	42,000	
Less ending inventory (1,000 units × $7)	7,000	
Variable cost of goods sold	35,000	
Variable selling and administrative expenses (5,000 units × $3)	15,000	50,000
Contribution margin		50,000
Less fixed expenses:		
Fixed manufacturing overhead	30,000	
Fixed selling and administrative expenses	10,000	40,000
Net income		$ 10,000

manufacturing overhead cost of the current period is deferred in inventory to the next period, when, hopefully, these units will be taken out of inventory and sold. The deferral of $5,000 of fixed manufacturing overhead costs can be seen clearly by analyzing the ending inventory under the absorption costing method:

Variable manufacturing costs: 1,000 units × $7	$ 7,000
Fixed manufacturing overhead costs: 1,000 units × $5	5,000
Total inventory value	$12,000

In summary, under absorption costing, of the $30,000 in fixed manufacturing overhead costs incurred during the period, only $25,000 (5,000 units sold × $5) has been included in cost of goods sold. The remaining $5,000 (1,000 units *not* sold × $5) has been deferred in inventory to the next period.

2. Under the variable costing method, the entire $30,000 in fixed manufacturing overhead costs has been treated as an expense of the current period (see the bottom portion of the variable costing income statement).
3. The ending inventory figure under the variable costing method is $5,000 lower than it is under the absorption costing method. The reason is that under variable costing, only the variable manufacturing costs are assigned to units of product and therefore included in inventory:

Variable manufacturing costs: 1,000 units × $7	$7,000

   The $5,000 difference in ending inventories explains the difference in net income reported between the two costing methods. Net income is $5,000 *higher* under absorption costing since, as explained above, $5,000 of fixed manufacturing overhead cost has been deferred in inventory to the next period under that costing method.
4. The absorption costing income statement makes no distinction between fixed and variable costs; therefore, it is not well suited for CVP computations, which are important for good planning and control. To generate data for CVP analysis, it would be necessary to spend considerable time reworking and reclassifying costs on the absorption statement.
5. The variable costing approach to costing units of product blends very well with the contribution approach to the income statement, since both concepts are based on the idea of classifying costs by behavior. The variable costing data in Exhibit 7–2 could be used immediately in CVP computations.

Essentially, the difference between the absorption costing method and the variable costing method centers on timing. Advocates of variable costing say that fixed manufacturing costs should be expensed immediately in total, whereas advocates of absorption costing say that fixed manufacturing costs should be charged against revenues bit by bit as units of product are sold. Any units of product not sold under absorption costing result in fixed costs being inventoried and carried forward *as assets* to the next period. We will defer discussing the arguments presented by each side in this dispute until after we have a better understanding of the two methods. Nevertheless, as we shall see in the following situation, the use of absorption costing can sometimes produce strange effects on income statements.

Focus On Current Practice

The Shanghai Bund Steel Works (SBSW) of the Peoples' Republic of China is a large state-owned enterprise. In recent years, state-owned companies such as SBSW have been given a great deal of autonomy, providing that they meet their financial and nonfinancial targets. However, in state-owned enterprises, management has very little freedom to adjust the workforce—eliminating jobs would create political problems. Therefore, for internal management purposes, SBSW treats labor cost as a fixed cost that is part of fixed manufacturing overhead.[1] ■

1. Yau Shiu Wing Joseph, *Management Accounting* (UK), October 1996, pp. 52–54.

Extended Comparison of Income Data

Managerial Accounting in Action

THE ISSUE

Mary O'Meara is the owner and manager of Emerald Isle Knitters, Ltd., of Galway, Republic of Ireland. The company is very small, with only 10 employees. Mary started the company three years ago with cash loaned to her by a local bank. The company manufactures a traditional wool fisherman's sweater from a pattern Mary learned from her grandmother. Like most apparel manufacturers, Emerald Isle Knitters sells its product to department stores and clothing store chains rather than to retail customers.

The sweater was an immediate success, and the company sold all of the first year's production. However, in the second year of operations, one of the company's major customers canceled its order due to bankruptcy, and the company ended the year with large stocks of unsold sweaters. The third year of operations was a great year in contrast to that disastrous second year. Sales rebounded dramatically, and all of the unsold production carried over from the second year was sold by the end of the third year.

Shortly after the close of the third year, Mary met with her accountant Sean MacLafferty to discuss the results for the year. (Note: In Ireland, the unit of currency is the punt, which is denoted by the symbol £.)

Mary: Sean, the results for this year look a lot better than for last year, but I am frankly puzzled why this year's results aren't even better than the income statement shows.
Sean: I know what you mean. The net income for this year is just £90,000. Last year it was £30,000. That is a huge improvement, but it seems that profits this year should have been even higher and profits last year should have been much less. We were in big trouble last year. I was afraid we might not even break even—yet we showed a healthy £30,000 profit. Somehow it doesn't seem quite right.
Mary: I wondered about that £30,000 profit last year, but I didn't question it since it was the only good news I had gotten for quite some time.
Sean: In case you're wondering, I didn't invent that profit last year just to make you feel better. Our auditor required that I follow certain accounting rules in preparing those reports for the bank. This may sound heretical, but we *could* use different rules for our own internal reports.
Mary: Wait a minute, rules are rules—especially in accounting.
Sean: Yes and no. For our internal reports, it might be better to use different rules than we use for the reports we send to the bank.
Mary: As I said, rules are rules. Still, I'm willing to listen if you want to show me what you have in mind.
Sean: It's a deal. ■

objective 3
Prepare income statements using both variable and absorption costing, and reconcile the two net income figures.

Immediately after the meeting with Mary, Sean put together the data and financial reports that appear in Exhibit 7–3. To make the principles clearer, Sean simplified the data so that the illustrations all use round figures.

The basic data appear at the top of Exhibit 7–3, and the absorption costing income statements as reported to the bank for last three years appear on the following page. Sean decided to try using the variable costing approach to see what effect that might have on net income. The variable costing income statements for the last three years appear on the next page.

Note that Emerald Isle Knitters maintained a steady rate of production of 25,000 sweaters per year. However, sales varied from year to year. In Year 1, production and sales were equal. In Year 2, production exceeded sales due to the canceled order. In Year 3, sales recovered and exceeded production. As a consequence, there was no change in inventories during Year 1, inventories increased during Year 2, and inventories decreased during Year 3. The change in inventories during the year is the key to understanding how absorption costing differs from variable costing. Note that when inventories increase in Year 2, absorption costing net income exceeds variable costing net income. When inventories decrease in Year 3, the opposite occurs—variable costing net income exceeds absorption costing net income. And when there is no change in inventories as in Year 1, there is no difference in net income between the two methods. Why is this? The reasons are discussed below and are briefly summarized in Exhibit 7–4.

1. When production and sales are equal, as in Year 1 for Emerald Isle Knitters, net income will generally be the same regardless of whether absorption or variable costing is used. The reason is as follows: The *only* difference that can exist between absorption and variable costing net income is the amount of fixed manufacturing overhead recognized as expense on the income statement. When everything that is produced in the year is sold, all of the fixed manufacturing overhead assigned to units of product under absorption costing become part of the year's cost of goods sold. Under variable costing, the total fixed manufacturing overhead flows directly to the income statement as an expense. So under either method, when production equals sales (and hence there is no change in inventories), all the fixed manufac-

Exhibit 7–3 Absorption and Variable Costing Statements—Emerald Isle Knitters, Ltd.

Basic Data

Selling price per unit sold	£ 20
Variable manufacturing cost per unit produced	7
Fixed manufacturing overhead costs per year	150,000
Variable selling and administrative expenses per unit sold	1
Fixed selling and administrative expenses per year	90,000

	Year 1	Year 2	Year 3	Three Years Together
Units in beginning inventory	–0–	–0–	5,000	–0–
Units produced	25,000	25,000	25,000	75,000
Units sold	25,000	20,000	30,000	75,000
Units in ending inventory	–0–	5,000	–0–	–0–

Unit Product Costs

	Year 1	Year 2	Year 3
Under variable costing (variable manufacturing costs only)	£ 7	£ 7	£ 7
Under absorption costing:			
Variable manufacturing costs	£ 7	£ 7	£ 7
Fixed manufacturing overhead costs (£150,000 spread over the number of units produced in each year)	6	6	6
Total absorption cost per unit	£13	£13	£13

(continued)

Exhibit 7–3 (concluded)

	Year 1		Year 2		Year 3		Three Years Together	
Absorption Costing								
Sales		£500,000		£400,000		£600,000		£1,500,000
Less cost of goods sold:								
Beginning inventory	£ –0–		£ –0–		£ 65,000		£ –0–	
Add cost of goods manufactured (25,000 units × £13)	325,000		325,000		325,000		975,000	
Goods available for sale	325,000		325,000		390,000		975,000	
Less ending inventory (5,000 units × £13)	–0–		65,000		–0–		–0–	
Cost of goods sold		325,000		260,000		390,000		975,000
Gross margin		175,000		140,000		210,000		525,000
Less selling and administrative expenses		115,000*		110,000*		120,000*		345,000
Net income		£ 60,000		£ 30,000		£ 90,000		£ 180,000

*The selling and administrative expenses are computed as follows:
Year 1: 25,000 units × £1 variable plus £90,000 fixed = £115,000.
Year 2: 20,000 units × £1 variable plus £90,000 fixed = £110,000.
Year 3: 30,000 units × £1 variable plus £90,000 fixed = £120,000.

	Year 1		Year 2		Year 3		Three Years Together	
Variable Costing								
Sales		£500,000		£400,000		£600,000		£1,500,000
Less variable expenses:								
Variable cost of goods sold:								
Beginning inventory	–0–		–0–		35,000		–0–	
Add variable manufacturing costs (25,000 units × £7)	175,000		175,000		175,000		525,000	
Goods available for sale	175,000		175,000		210,000		525,000	
Less ending inventory (5,000 units × £7)	–0–		35,000		–0–		–0–	
Variable costs of goods sold	175,000*		140,000*		210,000*		525,000	
Variable selling and administrative expenses (£1 per unit sold)	25,000	200,000	20,000	160,000	30,000	240,000	75,000	600,000
Contribution margin		300,000		240,000		360,000		900,000
Less fixed expenses:								
Fixed manufacturing overhead	150,000		150,000		150,000		450,000	
Fixed selling and administrative expenses	90,000	240,000	90,000	240,000	90,000	240,000	270,000	720,000
Net income		£ 60,000		£ –0–		£120,000		£ 180,000

*The variable cost of goods sold could have been computed more simply as follows:
Year 1: 25,000 units sold × £7 = £175,000.
Year 2: 20,000 units sold × £7 = £140,000.

Exhibit 7–4
Comparative Income Effects—Absorption and Variable Costing

Relation between Production and Sales for the Period	Effect on Inventories	Relation between Absorption and Variable Costing Net Incomes
Production = Sales	No change in inventories	Absorption costing net income = Variable costing net income
Production > Sales	Inventories increase	Absorption costing net income > Variable costing net income*
Production < Sales	Inventories decrease	Absorption costing net income < Variable costing net income†

*Net income is higher under absorption costing, since fixed manufacturing overhead cost is *deferred* in inventory under absorption costing as inventories increase.

†Net income is lower under absorption costing, since fixed manufacturing overhead cost is *released* from inventory under absorption costing as inventories decrease.

turing overhead incurred during the year flows through to the income statement as expense. And therefore, the net income under the two methods is the same.

2. When production exceeds sales, the net income reported under absorption costing will generally be greater than the net income reported under variable costing (see Year 2 in Exhibit 7–3). This occurs because under absorption costing, part of the fixed manufacturing overhead costs of the current period is deferred in inventory. In Year 2, for example, £30,000 of fixed manufacturing overhead costs (5,000 units × £6 per unit) has been applied to units in ending inventory. These costs are excluded from cost of goods sold.

   Under variable costing, however, *all* of the fixed manufacturing overhead costs of Year 2 have been charged immediately against income as a period cost. As a result, the net income for Year 2 under variable costing is £30,000 *lower* than it is under absorption costing. Exhibit 7–5 contains a reconciliation of the variable costing and absorption costing net income figures.
3. When production is less than sales, the net income reported under the absorption costing approach will generally be less than the net income reported under the variable costing approach (see Year 3 in Exhibit 7–3). This happens because inventories are drawn down and fixed manufacturing overhead costs that were previously deferred in inventory under absorption costing are released and charged against income (known as **fixed manufacturing overhead cost released from inventory**). In Year 3, for example, the £30,000 in fixed manufacturing overhead costs

Exhibit 7–5
Reconciliation of Variable Costing and Absorption Costing—Net Income Data from Exhibit 7–3

	Year 1	Year 2	Year 3
Variable costing net income	£60,000	£ –0–	£120,000
Add fixed manufacturing overhead costs deferred in inventory under absorption costing (5,000 units × £6 per unit)	–0–	30,000	–0–
Deduct fixed manufacturing overhead costs released from inventory under absorption costing (5,000 units × £6 per unit)	–0–	–0–	(30,000)
Absorption costing net income	£60,000	£30,000	£ 90,000

deferred in inventory under the absorption approach from Year 2 to Year 3 is released from inventory because these units were sold. As a result, the cost of goods sold for Year 3 contains not only all of the fixed manufacturing overhead costs for Year 3 (since all that was produced in Year 3 was sold in Year 3) but £30,000 of fixed manufacturing overhead costs from Year 2 as well.

By contrast, under variable costing only the fixed manufacturing overhead costs of Year 3 have been charged against Year 3. The result is that net income under variable costing is £30,000 *higher* than it is under absorption costing. Exhibit 7–5 contains a reconciliation of the variable costing and absorption costing net income figures for Year 3.

4. Over an *extended* period of time, the net income figures reported under absorption costing and variable costing will tend to be the same. The reason is that over the long run sales can't exceed production, nor can production much exceed sales. The shorter the time period, the more the net income figures will tend to differ.

Effect of Changes in Production on Net Income

objective 4

Explain the effect of changes in production on the net income reported under both variable and absorption costing.

In the Emerald Isle Knitters example in the preceding section, production was constant and sales fluctuated over the three-year period. Since sales fluctuated, the data Sean MacLafferty presented in Exhibit 7–3 allowed us to see the effect of changes in sales on net income under both variable and absorption costing.

To further investigate the differences between variable and absorption costing, Sean next put together the hypothetical example in Exhibit 7–6. In this hypothetical example, sales are constant and production fluctuates (the opposite of Exhibit 7–3). The purpose of Exhibit 7–6 is to illustrate for Mary O'Meara the effect of changes in *production* on net income under both variable and absorption costing.

Exhibit 7–6 Sensitivity of Costing Methods to Changes in Production—Hypothetical Data

Basic Data			
Selling price per unit sold			£ 25
Variable manufacturing cost per unit produced			10
Fixed manufacturing overhead costs per year			300,000
Variable selling and administrative expenses per unit sold			1
Fixed selling and administrative expenses per year			200,000
	Year 1	**Year 2**	**Year 3**
Units in beginning inventory	–0–	–0–	10,000
Units produced	40,000	50,000	30,000
Units sold	40,000	40,000	40,000
Units in ending inventory	–0–	10,000	–0–
Unit Product Costs			
Under variable costing (variable manufacturing costs only)	£10.00	£10.00	£10.00
Under absorption costing			
Variable manufacturing costs	£10.00	£10.00	£10.00
Fixed manufacturing overhead costs (£300,000 total spread over the number of units produced in each year)	7.50	6.00	10.00
Total absorption cost per unit	£17.50	£16.00	£20.00

(continued)

Exhibit 7–6 (concluded)

	Year 1		Year 2		Year 3	
Absorption Costing						
Sales (40,000 units)		£1,000,000		£1,000,000		£1,000,000
Less cost of goods sold:						
Beginning inventory	£ –0–		£ –0–		£160,000	
Add cost of goods manufactured	700,000*		800,000*		600,000*	
Goods available for sale	700,000		800,000		760,000	
Less ending inventory	–0–		160,000†		–0–	
Cost of goods sold		700,000		640,000		760,000
Gross margin		300,000		360,000		240,000
Less selling and administrative expenses (40,000 units × £1 plus £200,000)		240,000		240,000		240,000
Net income		£ 60,000		£ 120,000		£ –0–

*Cost of goods manufactured:

Year 1: 40,000 units × £17.50 = £700,000.

Year 2: 50,000 units × £16.00 = £800,000.

Year 3: 30,000 units × £20.00 = £600,000.

†Ending inventory, Year 2: 10,000 units × £16 = £160,000.

	Year 1		Year 2		Year 3	
Variable Costing						
Sales (40,000 units)		£1,000,000		£1,000,000		£1,000,000
Less variable expenses:						
Variable cost of goods sold:						
Beginning inventory	£ –0–		£ –0–		£100,000	
Add variable manufacturing costs, at £10 per unit produced	400,000		500,000		300,000	
Goods available for sale	400,000		500,000		400,000	
Less ending inventory	–0–		100,000*		–0–	
Variable cost of goods sold	400,000		400,000		400,000	
Variable selling and administrative expenses	40,000	440,000	40,000	440,000	40,000	440,000
Contribution margin		560,000		560,00		560,000
Less fixed expenses:						
Fixed manufacturing overhead	300,000		300,000		300,000	
Fixed selling and administrative expenses	200,000	500,000	200,000	500,000	200,000	500,000
Net income		£ 60,000		£ 60,000		£ 60,000

*Ending inventory, Year 2: 10,000 units × £10 = £100,000.

Variable Costing

Net income is *not* affected by changes in production under variable costing. Notice from Exhibit 7–6 that net income is the same for all three years under the variable costing approach, although production exceeds sales in one year and is less than sales in another year. In short, a change in production has no impact on net income when variable costing is in use.

Absorption Costing

Net income *is* affected by changes in production when absorption costing is in use, however. As shown in Exhibit 7–6, net income under the absorption approach goes up in Year 2, in response to the increase in production for that year, and then goes down in Year 3, in response to the drop in production for that year. Note particularly that net income goes up and down between these two years *even though the same number of units is sold in each year.* The reason for this effect can be traced to the shifting of fixed manufacturing overhead costs between periods under the absorption costing method as a result of changes in inventory.

As shown in Exhibit 7–6, production exceeds sales in Year 2, resulting in an increase of 10,000 units in inventory. Each unit produced during Year 2 has £6 in fixed manufacturing overhead costs attached to it (see the unit cost computations at the top of Exhibit 7–6). Therefore, £60,000 (10,000 units × £6) of the fixed manufacturing overhead costs of Year 2 are not charged against that year but rather are added to the inventory account (along with the variable manufacturing costs). The net income of Year 2 rises sharply, because of the deferral of these costs in inventories, even though the same number of units is sold in Year 2 as in the other years.

The reverse effect occurs in Year 3. Since sales exceed production in Year 3, that year is forced to cover all of its own fixed manufacturing overhead costs as well as the fixed manufacturing overhead costs carried forward in inventory from Year 2. A substantial drop in net income during Year 3 results from the release of fixed manufacturing overhead costs from inventories despite the fact that the same number of units is sold in that year as in the other years.

The variable costing and absorption costing net incomes are reconciled in Exhibit 7–7. This exhibit shows that the differences in net income can be traced to the effects of changes in inventories on absorption costing net income. Under absorption costing, fixed manufacturing overhead costs are deferred in inventory when inventories increase and are released from inventory when inventories decrease.

Exhibit 7–7
Reconciliation of Variable Costing and Absorption Costing—Net Income Data from Exhibit 7–6

	Year 1	Year 2	Year 3
Variable costing net income	£60,000	£ 60,000	£ 60,000
Add fixed manufacturing overhead costs deferred in inventory under absorption costing 10,000 units × £6 per unit)	–0–	60,000	–0–
Deduct fixed manufacturing overhead costs released from inventory under absorption costing (10,000 units × £6 per unit)	–0–	–0–	(60,000)
Absorption costing net income	£60,000	£120,000	£ –0–

Managerial Accounting in Action

THE WRAP-UP

After checking all of his work, Sean took the exhibits he had prepared to Mary's office where the following conversation took place:

Sean: I have some calculations I would like to show you.

Mary: Will this take long? I only have a few minutes before I have to meet with the buyer from Neiman Marcus.

Sean: Well, we can at least get started. These exhibits should help explain why our net income didn't increase this year as much as you thought it should have.

Mary: This first exhibit (i.e., Exhibit 7–3) looks like it just summarizes our income statements for the last three years.

Sean: Not exactly. There are actually two sets of income statements on this exhibit. The absorption costing income statements are the ones I originally prepared and we submitted to the bank. Below the absorption costing income statements are another set of income statements.

Mary: Those are the ones labeled variable costing.

Sean: That's right. You can see that the net incomes are the same for the two sets of income statements in our first year of operations, but they differ for the other two years.

Mary: I'll say! The variable costing statements indicate that we just broke even in the second year instead of earning a £30,000 profit. And the increase in net income between the second and third years is £120,000 instead of just £60,000. I don't know how you come up with two different net income figures, but the variable costing net income seems to be much closer to the truth. The second year was almost a disaster. We barely sold enough sweaters to cover all of our fixed costs.

Sean: You and I both know that, but the accounting rules view the situation a little differently. If we produce more than we sell, the accounting rules require that we take some of the fixed cost and assign it to the units that end up in inventories at year-end.

Mary: You mean that instead of appearing on the income statement as an expense, some of the fixed costs wind up on the balance sheet as inventories?

Sean: Precisely.

Mary: I thought accountants were conservative. Since when was it conservative to call an expense an asset?

Sean: We accountants have been debating whether fixed production costs are an asset or an expense for over 50 years.

Mary: It must have been a *fascinating* debate.

Sean: I have to admit that it ranks right up there with watching grass grow in terms of excitement level.

Mary: I don't know what the arguments are, but I can tell you for sure that we don't make any money by just producing sweaters. If I understand what you have shown me, I can increase my net income under absorption costing by simply making more sweaters—we don't have to sell them.

Sean: Correct.

Mary: So all I have to do to enjoy the lifestyle of the rich and famous is to hire every unemployed knitter in Ireland to make sweaters I can't sell.

Sean: We would have a major cash flow problem, but our net income would certainly go up.

Mary: Well, if the banks want us to use absorption costing so be it. I don't know why they would want us to report that way, but if that's what they want, that's what they'll get. Is there any reason why we can't use this

variable costing method ourselves? The statements are easier to understand, and the net income figures make more sense to me. Can't we do both?
Sean: I don't see why not. Making the adjustment from one method to the other is very simple.
Mary: Good. Let's talk about this some more after I get back from the meeting with Neiman Marcus. ■

The Impact on the Manager

Like Mary O'Meara, opponents of absorption costing argue that shifting fixed manufacturing overhead cost between periods can be confusing and can lead to misinterpretations and even to faulty decisions. Look again at the data in Exhibit 7–6; a manager might wonder why net income went up substantially in Year 2 under absorption costing when sales remained the same as in the prior year. Was it a result of lower selling costs, more efficient operations, or was some other factor involved? The manager is unable to tell, looking simply at the absorption costing income statement. Then in Year 3, net income drops sharply, even though again the same number of units is sold as in the other two years. Why would income rise in one year and then drop in the next? The figures seem erratic and contradictory and can lead to confusion and a loss of confidence in the integrity of the statement data.

By contrast, the variable costing income statements in Exhibit 7–6 are clear and easy to understand. Sales remain constant over the three-year period covered in the exhibit, so both contribution margin and net income also remain constant. The statements are consistent with what the manager would expect to happen under the circumstances, so they tend to generate confidence rather than confusion.

To avoid mistakes when absorption costing is used, readers of financial statements should be alert to changes in inventory levels. Under absorption costing, if there is an increase in inventories, fixed manufacturing overhead costs are deferred in inventories and net income is elevated. If there is a decrease in inventories, fixed manufacturing overhead costs are released from inventories and net income is depressed. Thus, fluctuations in net income can be due to changes in inventories rather than to changes in sales.

Focus on Current Practice

While managers can artificially increase net income under absorption costing by producing more than is really necessary and building up inventories, a few unscrupulous managers have stepped over the line into the area of outright fraud. By claiming inventories that don't exist, an unethical manager can produce instant profits and dress up the balance sheet. Since the value of ending inventories is subtracted from the cost of goods available for sale in order to arrive at the cost of goods sold, phantom inventories directly reduce cost of goods sold. Phantom inventories also beef up the balance sheet by increasing assets.

Auditors attempt to uncover such fraud by physically verifying the existence of inventory reported on the balance sheet. This is done by counting random samples of perhaps 5% to 10% of reported inventory items. However, this audit approach isn't always effective. For example, managers at failing Laribee Wire Manufacturing Co. attempted to keep the company afloat by creating fictitious inventories. Investigations following the company's bankruptcy revealed that managers had fraudulently overstated income by claiming inventories of over 4 million pounds of copper rod that did not exist. Such inventory fraud at Laribee turned a loss of $6.5 million into an operating profit of $5.5 million in one year alone.[2] ■

Choosing a Costing Method

objective 5

Explain the advantages and limitations of both the variable and absorption costing methods.

In choosing between variable and absorption costing, several factors should be considered by the manager. These factors are discussed in this section.

CVP Analysis and Absorption Costing

Absorption costing is widely used for both internal and external reports. Many firms use the absorption approach exclusively because of its focus on *full* costing of units of product. A weakness of the method, however, is its inability to dovetail well with CVP analysis.

To illustrate, refer again to Exhibit 7–3. Let us compute the break-even point for Emerald Isle Knitters. To obtain the break-even point, we divide total fixed costs by the contribution margin per unit:

Selling price per unit	£ 20
Variable costs per unit	8
Contribution margin per unit	£ 12

Fixed manufacturing overhead costs	£150,000
Fixed selling and administrative costs	90,000
Total fixed costs	£240,000

$$\frac{\text{Total fixed costs}}{\text{Contribution margin per unit}} = \frac{£240{,}000}{£12} = 20{,}000 \text{ units}$$

The break-even point is 20,000 units. Notice from Exhibit 7–3 that in Year 2 the firm sold exactly 20,000 units, the break-even volume. Under the contribution approach, using variable costing, the firm does break even in Year 2, showing zero net income. *Under absorption costing, however, the firm shows a positive net income of £30,000 for Year 2.* How can this be? How can absorption costing produce a positive net income when the firm sold exactly the break-even volume of units?

The answer lies in the fact that £30,000 in fixed manufacturing overhead costs were deferred in inventory during Year 2 under absorption costing and therefore did not appear as charges against income. By deferring these fixed manufacturing overhead costs in inventory, the income statement shows a profit even though the company sold exactly the break-even volume of units. Absorption costing runs into similar kinds of difficulty in other areas of CVP analysis, which assumes that variable costing is being used.

2. Lee Burton, "Convenient Fiction: Inventory Chicanery Tempts More Firms, Fools More Auditors," *The Wall Street Journal,* December 14, 1992, pp. A1, A5.

Decision Making

A basic problem with absorption costing is that fixed manufacturing overhead costs appear to be variable with respect to the number of units sold, but they are not. For example, in Exhibit 7–3, the absorption unit product cost is £13, but the variable portion of this cost is only £7. Since the product costs are stated in terms of a per unit figure, managers may mistakenly believe that if another unit is produced, it will cost the company £13.

The misperception that absorption unit product costs are variable can lead to many managerial problems, including inappropriate pricing decisions and decisions to drop products that are in fact profitable. These problems with absorption costing product costs will be discussed more fully in later chapters.

External Reporting and Income Taxes

Practically speaking, absorption costing is required for external reports in the United States. A company that attempts to use variable costing on its external financial reports runs the risk that its auditors may not accept the financial statements as conforming to generally accepted accounting principles (GAAP).[3] Tax law on this issue is clear-cut. Under the Tax Reform Act of 1986, a form of absorption costing must be used when filling out income tax forms.

Even if a company must use absorption costing for its external reports, a manager can, as Mary O'Meara suggests, use variable costing statements for internal reports. No particular accounting problems are created by using *both* costing methods—the variable costing method for internal reports and the absorption costing method for external reports. As we demonstrated earlier in Exhibits 7–5 and 7–7, the adjustment from variable costing net income to absorption costing net income is a simple one that can be easily made at year-end.

We must note, however, that using two sets of accounting data can create a problem for the top executives of publicly held corporations. The problem is that these executives are usually evaluated based on the external reports prepared for stockholders. It is difficult for managers to make decisions based on one set of accounting statements when they will be evaluated with a different set of accounting statements. Nevertheless, one study found that about half of the companies surveyed use variable costing as either the primary or as a supplementary format in reports prepared for top management.[4]

Advantages of Variable Costing and the Contribution Approach

As stated earlier, even if the absorption approach is used for external reporting purposes, variable costing, together with the contribution margin format income statement, is an appealing alternative for internal reports. The advantages of variable costing can be summarized as follows:

---

3. The situation is actually slightly ambiguous concerning whether absorption costing is strictly required. Michael Schiff, "Variable Costing: A Closer Look," *Management Accounting,* February 1987, pp. 36–39, and Eric W. Noreen and Robert M. Bowen, "Tax Incentives and the Decision to Capitalize or Expense Manufacturing Overhead," *Accounting Horizons,* March 1989, pp. 29–42, argue that official pronouncements do not actually prohibit variable costing. And both articles provide examples of companies that expense significant elements of their fixed manufacturing costs on their external reports. Nevertheless, the reality is that most accountants believe that absorption costing is required for external reporting and a manager who argues otherwise is likely to be unsuccessful.
4. William P. Cress and James B. Pettijohn, "Survey of Budget-Related Planning and Control Policies and Procedures," *Journal of Accounting Education,* Fall 1985, p. 73.

1. The data that are required for CVP analysis can be taken directly from a contribution margin format income statement. These data are not available on a conventional income statement based on absorption costing.
2. Under variable costing, the profit for a period is not affected by changes in inventories. Other things remaining equal (i.e., selling prices, costs, sales mix, etc.), profits move in the same direction as sales when variable costing is in use.
3. Managers often assume that unit product costs are variable costs. This is a problem under absorption costing, since unit product costs are a combination of both fixed and variable costs. Under variable costing, unit product costs do not contain fixed costs.
4. The impact of fixed costs on profits is emphasized under the variable costing and contribution approach. The total amount of fixed costs appears explicitly on the income statement. Under absorption costing, the fixed costs are mingled together with the variable costs and are buried in cost of goods sold and in ending inventories.
5. Variable costing data make it easier to estimate the profitability of products, customers, and other segments of the business. With absorption costing, profitability is obscured by arbitrary allocations of fixed costs. These issues will be discussed in later chapters.
6. Variable costing ties in with cost control methods such as standard costs and flexible budgets, which will be covered in later chapters.
7. Variable costing net income is closer to net cash flow than absorption costing net income. This is particularly important for companies having cash flow problems.

With all of these advantages, one might wonder why absorption costing continues to be used almost exclusively for external reporting and why it is the predominant choice for internal reports as well. This is partly due to tradition, but absorption costing is also attractive to many accountants and managers because they believe it better matches costs with revenues. Advocates of absorption costing argue that *all* manufacturing costs must be assigned to products in order to properly match the costs of producing units of product with the revenues from the units when they are sold. The fixed costs of depreciation, taxes, insurance, supervisory salaries, and so on, are just as essential to manufacturing products as are the variable costs.

Advocates of variable costing argue that fixed manufacturing costs are not really the costs of any particular unit of product. These costs are incurred in order to have the *capacity* to make products during a particular period and will be incurred even if nothing is made during the period. Moreover, whether a unit is made or not, the fixed manufacturing costs will be exactly the same. Therefore, variable costing advocates argue that fixed manufacturing costs are not part of the costs of producing a particular unit of product and thus the matching principle dictates that fixed manufacturing costs should be charged to the current period.

At any rate, absorption costing is the generally accepted method for preparing mandatory external financial reports and income tax returns. Probably because of the cost and possible confusion of maintaining two separate costing systems—one for external reporting and one for internal reporting—most companies use absorption costing for both external and internal reports.

Variable Costing and the Theory of Constraints

A form of variable costing is used in the theory of constraints (TOC), one of the management approaches that was discussed in Chapter 1. In the TOC approach, direct labor is generally considered to be a fixed cost. As discussed in earlier chapters, in many companies direct labor is not really a variable cost. Even though direct labor workers may be paid on an hourly basis, many companies have a commitment—sometimes enforced in labor contracts or by law—to guarantee workers a minimum number of paid hours. In TOC companies, there are two additional reasons to consider direct labor to be a fixed cost.

First, direct labor is not usually the constraint. In the simplest cases, the constraint is a machine. In more complex cases, the constraint is a policy (such as a poorly designed compensation scheme for salespersons) that prevents the company from using its resources more effectively. If direct labor is not the constraint, there is no reason to increase it. Hiring more direct labor would increase costs without increasing the output of salable products and services.

Second, TOC emphasizes continuous improvement to maintain competitiveness. Without committed and enthusiastic employees, sustained continuous improvement is virtually impossible. Since layoffs often have devastating effects on employee morale, managers involved in TOC are extremely reluctant to lay off employees.

For these reasons, most managers in TOC companies believe that direct labor in their companies behaves much more like a committed fixed cost than a variable cost. Hence, in the modified form of variable costing used in TOC companies, direct labor is not included as a part of product costs.

Impact of JIT Inventory Methods

objective 6

Explain how the use of JIT reduces the difference in net income reported under the variable and absorption costing methods.

As discussed in this chapter, variable and absorption costing will produce different net income figures whenever the number of units produced is different from the number of units sold—in other words, whenever there is a change in the number of units in inventory. We have also learned that the absorption costing net income figure can be erratic, sometimes moving in a direction that is opposite from the movement in sales.

When companies use just-in-time (JIT) methods, these problems are reduced. The erratic movement of net income under absorption costing and the difference in net income between absorption and variable costing occur because of changes in the number of units in inventory. Under JIT, goods are produced to customers' orders and the goal is to eliminate finished goods inventories entirely and reduce work in process inventory to almost nothing. If there is very little inventory, then changes in inventories will be very small and both variable and absorption costing will show basically the same net income figure. In that case, absorption costing net income will move in the same direction as movements in sales.

Of course, the cost of a unit of product will still be different between variable and absorption costing, as explained earlier in the chapter. But when JIT is used, the differences in net income will largely disappear.

Summary

Variable and absorption costing are alternative methods of determining unit product costs. Under variable costing, only those production costs that vary with output are treated as product costs. This includes direct materials, variable overhead, and ordinarily direct labor. Fixed manufacturing overhead is treated as a period cost and charged off against revenue as it is incurred, the same as selling and administrative expenses. By contrast, absorption costing treats fixed manufacturing overhead as a product cost, along with direct materials, direct labor, and variable overhead.

Since absorption costing treats fixed manufacturing overhead as a product cost, a portion of fixed manufacturing overhead is assigned to each unit as it is produced. If units of product are unsold at the end of a period, then the fixed manufacturing overhead cost attached to the units is carried with them into the inventory account and deferred to the next period. When these units are later sold, the fixed manufacturing overhead cost attached to them is released from the inventory account and charged against revenues as a part of cost of goods sold. Thus, under absorption costing, it is possible to defer a portion of the fixed manufacturing overhead cost of one period to the next period through the inventory account.

Unfortunately, this shifting of fixed manufacturing overhead cost between periods can cause net income to move in an erratic manner and can result in confusion and unwise decisions on the part of management. To guard against mistakes when they interpret income statement data, managers should be alert to any changes that may have taken place in inventory levels or in unit product costs during the period.

Practically speaking, variable costing can't be used externally for either financial reporting or income tax purposes. However, it may be used internally for planning purposes. The variable costing approach dovetails well with CVP concepts that are often indispensable in profit planning and decision making.

Review Problem

Dexter Company produces and sells a single product, a wooden hand loom for weaving small items such as scarves. Selected cost and operating data relating to the product for two years are given below:

Selling price per unit	$ 50
Manufacturing costs:	
Variable per unit produced:	
Direct materials	11
Direct labor	6
Variable overhead	3
Fixed per year	120,000
Selling and administrative costs:	
Variable per unit sold	5
Fixed per year	70,000

	Year 1	Year 2
Units in beginning inventory	–0–	2,000
Units produced during the year	10,000	6,000
Units sold during the year	8,000	8,000
Units in ending inventory	2,000	–0–

Required

1. Assume that the company uses absorption costing.
   a. Compute the unit product cost in each year.
   b. Prepare an income statement for each year.
2. Assume that the company uses variable costing.
   a. Compute the unit product cost in each year.
   b. Prepare an income statement for each year.
3. Reconcile the variable costing and absorption costing net income figures.

Solution to Review Problem

1. a. Under absorption costing, all manufacturing costs, variable and fixed, are included in unit product costs:

	Year 1	Year 2
Direct materials	$11	$11
Direct labor	6	6
Variable manufacturing overhead	3	3
Fixed manufacturing overhead		
($120,000 ÷ 10,000 units)	12	
($120,000 ÷ 6,000 units)		20
Unit product cost	$32	$40

b. The absorption costing income statements follow:

	Year 1		Year 2	
Sales (8,000 units × $50)		$400,000		$400,000
Less cost of goods sold:				
Beginning inventory	$ -0-		$ 64,000	
Add cost of goods manufactured				
(10,000 units × $32)	320,000			
(6,000 units × $40)			240,000	
Goods available for sale	320,000		304,000	
Less ending inventory				
(2,000 units × $32; 0 units)	64,000	256,000	-0-	304,000
Gross margin		144,000		96,000
Less selling and administrative expenses		110,000*		110,000*
Net income		$ 34,000		$ (14,000)

*Selling and administrative expenses:

Variable (8,000 units × $5)	$ 40,000
Fixed per year	70,000
Total	$110,000

2. a. Under variable costing, only the variable manufacturing costs are included in unit product costs:

	Year 1	Year 2
Direct materials	$11	$11
Direct labor	6	6
Variable manufacturing overhead . . .	3	3
Unit product cost	$20	$20

b. The variable costing income statements follow. Notice that the variable cost of goods sold is computed in a simpler, more direct manner than in the examples provided earlier. On a variable costing income statement, either approach to computing the cost of goods sold followed in this chapter is acceptable.

	Year 1		Year 2	
Sales (8,000 units × $50)		$400,000		$400,000
Less variable expenses:				
Variable cost of goods sold (8,000 units × $20)	$160,000		$160,000	
Variable selling and administrative expenses (8,000 units × $5)	40,000		40,000	
Contribution margin		200,000		200,000
Less fixed expenses:				
Fixed manufacturing overhead	120,000		120,000	
Fixed selling and administrative expenses	70,000	190,000	70,000	190,000
Net income		$ 10,000		$ 10,000)

3. The reconciliation of the variable and absorption costing net income figures follows:

	Year 1	Year 2
Variable costing net income	$10,000	$10,000
Add fixed manufacturing overhead costs deferred in inventory under absorption costing (2,000 units × $12 per unit)	24,000	
Deduct fixed manufacturing overhead costs released from inventory under absorption costing (2,000 units × $12 per unit)		24,000
Absorption costing net income	$34,000	$(14,000)

Key Terms for Review

Absorption costing A costing method that includes all manufacturing costs—direct materials, direct labor, and both variable and fixed manufacturing overhead—in the cost of a unit of product. Absorption costing is also referred to as the *full cost* method. (p. 284)

Direct costing Another term for variable costing. See *Variable costing.* (p. 284)

Fixed manufacturing overhead cost deferred in inventory The portion of the fixed manufacturing overhead cost of a period that goes into inventory under the absorption costing method as a result of production exceeding sales. (p. 286)

Fixed manufacturing overhead cost released from inventory The portion of the fixed manufacturing overhead cost of a *prior* period that becomes an expense of the current period under the absorption costing method as a result of sales exceeding production. (p. 292)

Full cost *See Absorption costing.* (p. 284)

Marginal costing Another term for variable costing. See *Variable costing.* (p. 284)

Variable costing A costing method that includes only variable manufacturing costs—direct materials, direct labor, and variable manufacturing overhead—in the cost of a unit of product. Also see *Marginal costing* or *Direct costing.* (p. 284)

Questions

7–1 What is the basic difference between absorption costing and variable costing?

7–2 Are selling and administrative expenses treated as product costs or as period costs under variable costing?

7–3 Explain how fixed manufacturing overhead costs are shifted from one period to another under absorption costing.

7–4 What arguments can be advanced in favor of treating fixed manufacturing overhead costs as product costs?

7–5 What arguments can be advanced in favor of treating fixed manufacturing overhead costs as period costs?

7–6 If production and sales are equal, which method would you expect to show the higher net income, variable costing or absorption costing? Why?

7–7 If production exceeds sales, which method would you expect to show the higher net income, variable costing or absorption costing? Why?

7–8 If fixed manufacturing overhead costs are released from inventory under absorption costing, what does this tell you about the level of production in relation to the level of sales?

7–9 Parker Company had $5,000,000 in sales and reported a $300,000 loss in its annual report to stockholders. According to a CVP analysis prepared for management's use, $5,000,000 in sales is the break-even point for the company. Did the company's inventory level increase, decrease, or remain unchanged? Explain.

7–10 Under absorption costing, how is it possible to increase net income without increasing sales?

7–11 How is the use of variable costing limited?

7–12 How does the use of JIT inventory methods reduce or eliminate the difference in reported net income between absorption and variable costing?

Exercises

E7–1 Chuck Wagon Grills, Inc., makes a single product—a handmade specialty barbecue grill that it sells for $210. Data for last year's operations follow:

Units in beginning inventory	–0–
Units produced	20,000
Units sold	19,000
Units in ending inventory	1,000
Variable costs per unit:	
Direct materials	$ 50
Direct labor	80
Variable manufacturing overhead	20
Variable selling and administrative	10
Total variable cost per unit	$ 160
Fixed costs:	
Fixed manufacturing overhead	$700,000
Fixed selling and administrative	285,000
Total fixed costs	$985,000

Required

1. Assume that the company uses variable costing. Compute the unit product cost for one barbecue grill.
2. Assume that the company uses variable costing. Prepare an income statement for the year in good form using the contribution format.
3. What is the company's break-even point in terms of the number of barbecue grills sold?

E7–2 Refer to the date in E7–1 for Chuck Wagon Grills. Assume in this exercise that the company uses absorption costing.

Required

1. Compute the unit product cost for one barbecue grill.
2. Prepare an income statement for the year in good form.

E7–3 Ida Sidha Karya Company is a family-owned company located in the village of Gianyar on the island of Bali in Indonesia. The company produces a handcrafted Balinese musical instrument called a gamelan that is similar to a xylophone. The sounding bars are cast from brass and hand-filed to attain just the right sound. The bars are then mounted on an intricately hand-carved wooden base. The gamelans are sold for 850 (thousand) rupiahs. (The currency in Indonesia is the rupiah, which is denoted by Rp.) Selected data for the company's operations last year follow (all currency values are in thousands of rupiahs):

Units in beginning inventory	–0–
Units produced	250
Units sold	225
Units in ending inventory	25
Variable costs per unit:	
Direct materials	Rp100
Direct labor	320
Variable manufacturing overhead	40
Variable selling and administrative	20
Fixed costs:	
Fixed manufacturing overhead	Rp60,000
Fixed selling and administrative	20,000

Required

1. Assume that the company uses absorption costing. Compute the unit product cost for one gamelan.
2. Assume that the company uses variable costing. Compute the unit product cost for one gamelan.

E7–4 Refer to the data in E7–3 for Ida Sidha Karya Company. An income statement prepared under the absorption costing method by the company's accountant appears below (all currency values are in thousands of rupiahs):

Sales (225 units × Rp850)		Rp191,250
Less cost of goods sold:		
Beginning inventory	Rp –0–	
Add cost of goods manufactured (250 units × Rp _?_)	175,000	
Goods available for sale	175,000	
Less ending inventory (25 units × Rp _?_)	17,500	157,500
Gross margin		33,750
Less selling and administrative expenses:		
Variable selling and administrative	4,500	
Fixed selling and administrative	20,000	24,500
Net income		Rp 9,250

Required

1. Determine how much of the ending inventory of Rp17,500 above consists of fixed manufacturing overhead cost deferred in inventory to the next period.
2. Prepare an income statement for the year using the variable costing method. Explain the difference in net income between the two costing methods.

E7–5 Sierra Company produces and sells a single product. The following costs relate to its production and sale:

Variable costs per unit:	
Direct materials	$ 9
Direct labor	10
Manufacturing overhead	5
Selling and administrative expenses	3
Fixed costs per year:	
Fixed manufacturing overhead	150,000
Fixed selling and administrative expenses	400,000

During the last year, 25,000 units were produced and 22,000 units were sold. The Finished Goods inventory account at the end of the year shows a balance of $72,000 for the 3,000 unsold units.

Required

1. Is the company using absorption costing or variable costing to cost units in the Finished Goods inventory account? Show computations to support your answer.

2. Assume that the company wishes to prepare financial statements for the year to issue to its stockholders.
   a. Is the $72,000 figure for Finished Goods inventory the correct amount to use on these statements for external reporting purposes? Explain.
   b. At what dollar amount *should* the 3,000 units be carried in the inventory for external reporting purposes?

E7–6 Lynch Company manufactures and sells a single product. The following costs were incurred during the company's first year of operations:

Variable costs per unit:	
Production:	
Direct materials	$ 6
Direct labor	9
Variable manufacturing overhead	3
Variable selling and administrative	4
Fixed costs per year:	
Fixed manufacturing overhead	300,000
Fixed selling and administrative	190,000

During the year, the company produced 25,000 units and sold 20,000 units. The selling price of the company's product is $50 per unit.

Required

1. Assume that the company uses the absorption costing method:
   a. Compute the unit product cost.
   b. Prepare an income statement for the year.
2. Assume that the company uses the variable costing method:
   a. Compute the unit product cost.
   b. Prepare an income statement for the year.

E7–7 Whitman Company has just completed its first year of operations. The company's accountant has prepared an income statement for the year, as follows (absorption costing basis):

WHITMAN COMPANY
Income Statement

Sales (35,000 units at $25)		$875,000
Less cost of goods sold:		
Beginning inventory	$ -0-	
Add cost of goods manufactured (40,000 units at $16)	640,000	
Goods available for sale	640,000	
Less ending inventory (5,000 units at $16)	80,000	560,000
Gross margin		315,000
Less selling and administrative expenses		280,000
Net income		$ 35,000

The company's selling and administrative expenses consist of $210,000 per year in fixed expenses and $2 per unit sold in variable expenses. The $16 unit product cost given above is computed as follows:

Direct materials	$ 5
Direct labor	6
Variable manufacturing overhead	1
Fixed manufacturing overhead ($160,000 ÷ 40,000 units)	4
Unit product cost	$16

Required

1. Redo the company's income statement in the contribution format using variable costing.
2. Reconcile any difference between the net income figure on your variable costing income statement and the net income figure on the absorption costing income statement above.

Problems

P7–8 Straightforward Comparison of Costing Methods High Country, Inc., produces and sells many recreational products. The company has just opened a new plant to produce a folding camp cot that will be marketed throughout the United States. The following cost and revenue data relate to May, the first month of the plant's operation:

Beginning inventory	–0–
Units produced	10,000
Units sold	8,000
Selling price per unit	$ 75
Selling and administrative expenses:	
Variable per unit	6
Fixed (total)	200,000
Manufacturing costs:	
Direct materials cost per unit	20
Direct labor cost per unit	8
Variable manufacturing overhead cost per unit	2
Fixed manufacturing overhead cost (total)	100,000

Management is anxious to see how profitable the new camp cot will be and has asked that an income statement be prepared for May.

Required

1. Assume that the company uses absorption costing.
   a. Determine the unit product cost.
   b. Prepare an income statement for May.
2. Assume that the company uses the contribution approach with variable costing.
   a. Determine the unit product cost.
   b. Prepare an income statement for May.
3. Explain the reason for any difference in the ending inventory under the two costing methods and the impact of this difference on reported net income.

P7–9 Straightforward Variable Costing Statements During Heaton Company's first two years of operations, the company reported net income as follows (absorption costing basis):

	Year 1	Year 2
Sales (@ $25)	$1,000,000	$1,250,000
Less cost of goods sold:		
Beginning inventory	–0–	90,000
Add cost of goods manufactured (@ $18)	810,000	810,000
Goods available for sale	810,000	900,000
Less ending inventory (@ $18)	90,000	–0–
Cost of goods sold	720,000	900,000
Gross margin	280,000	350,000
Less selling and administrative expenses*	210,000	230,000
Net income	$ 70,000	$ 120,000

* $2 per unit variable; $130,000 fixed each year.

The company's $18 unit product cost is computed as follows:

Direct materials	$ 4
Direct labor	7
Variable manufacturing overhead	1
Fixed manufacturing overhead ($270,000 ÷ 45,000 units)	6
Unit product cost	$18

Production and cost data for the two years are:

	Year 1	Year 2
Units produced	45,000	45,000
Units sold	40,000	50,000

Required

1. Prepare an income statement for each year in the contribution format using variable costing.
2. Reconcile the absorption costing and the variable costing net income figures for each year.

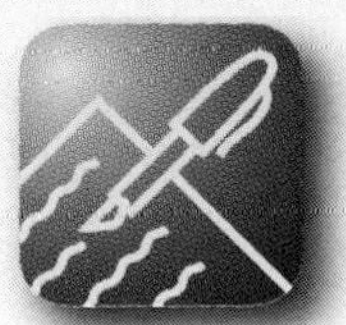

P7–10 Prepare and Reconcile Variable Costing Statements Denton Company manufactures and sells a single product. Cost data for the product are given below:

Variable costs per unit:	
Direct materials	$ 7
Direct labor	10
Variable manufacturing overhead	5
Variable selling and administrative	3
Total variable cost per unit	$ 25
Fixed costs per month:	
Fixed manufacturing overhead	$315,000
Fixed selling and administrative	245,000
Total fixed cost per month	$560,000

The product sells for $60 per unit. Production and sales data for July and August, the first two months of operations, follow:

	Units Produced	Units Sold
July	17,500	15,000
August	17,500	20,000

The company's Accounting Department has prepared income statements for both July and August. These statements, which have been prepared using absorption costing, are presented below:

	July	August
Sales	$900,000	$1,200,000
Less cost of goods sold:		
Beginning inventory	–0–	100,000
Add cost of goods manufactured	700,000	700,000
Goods available for sale	700,000	800,000
Less ending inventory	100,000	–0–
Cost of goods sold	600,000	800,000
Gross margin	300,000	400,000
Less selling and administrative expenses	290,000	305,000
Net income	$ 10,000	$ 95,000

Required

1. Determine the unit product cost under:
   a. Absorption costing.
   b. Variable costing.
2. Prepare income statements for July and August using the contribution approach, with variable costing.
3. Reconcile the variable costing and absorption costing net income figures.
4. The company's Accounting Department has determined the company's break-even point to be 16,000 units per month, computed as follows:

$$\frac{\text{Fixed cost per month, } \$560{,}000}{\text{Unit contribution margin, } \$35} = 16{,}000 \text{ units}$$

"I'm confused," said the president. "The accounting people say that our break-even point is 16,000 units per month, but we sold only 15,000 units in July, and the income statement they prepared shows a $10,000 profit for that month. Either the income statement is wrong or the break-even point is wrong." Prepare a brief memo for the president, explaining what happened on the July income statement.

S

P7–11 A Comparison of Costing Methods: Labor Fixed Far North Telecom, Ltd., of Ontario, has organized a new division to manufacture and sell cellular telephones. Monthly costs associated with the cellular phones and with the plant in which the cellular phones are manufactured are shown below:

Manufacturing costs:	
Variable costs per unit:	
Direct materials	$ 48
Variable manufacturing overhead	2
Fixed manufacturing overhead costs (total)	360,000
Selling and administrative costs:	
Variable	12% of sales
Fixed (total)	470,000

Far North Telecom regards all of its workers as full-time employees and the company has a long-standing no layoff policy. Furthermore, production is highly automated. Accordingly, the company has included in its fixed manufacturing overhead all of its labor costs. The cellular phones sell for $150 each. During September, the first month of operations, the following activity was recorded:

Units produced	12,000
Units sold	10,000

Required

1. Compute the unit product cost under:
   a. Absorption costing.
   b. Variable costing.
2. Prepare an income statement for the month using absorption costing.
3. Prepare an income statement for the month using variable costing.
4. Assume that the company must obtain additional financing in order to continue operations. As a member of top management, would you prefer to take the statement in (2) above or in (3) above with you as you meet with a group of prospective investors?
5. Reconcile the absorption costing and variable costing net income figures in (2) and (3) above for September.

P7–12 Absorption and Variable Costing; Production Constant, Sales Fluctuate Tami Tyler opened Tami's Creations, Inc., a small manufacturing company, at the beginning of the year. To get the company through its first quarter of operations, it has been necessary for Ms. Tyler to place a considerable strain on her own personal finances. The following income statement for the first quarter was prepared by a friend who has just completed a course in managerial accounting at State University.

TAMI'S CREATIONS, INC.
Income Statement
For the Quarter Ended March 31

Sales (28,000 units)		$1,120,000
Less variable expenses:		
Variable cost of goods sold*	$462,000	
Variable selling and administrative	168,000	630,000
Contribution margin		490,000
Less fixed expenses:		
Fixed manufacturing overhead	300,000	
Fixed selling and administrative	200,000	500,000
Net loss		$ (10,000)

*Consists of direct materials, direct labor, and variable manufacturing overhead.

Ms. Tyler is discouraged over the loss shown for the quarter, particularly since she had planned to use the statement as support for a bank loan. Another friend, a CPA, insists that the company should be using absorption costing rather than variable costing, and argues that if absorption costing had been used the company would probably have reported at least some profit for the quarter.

At this point, Ms. Tyler is manufacturing only one product, a swimsuit. Production and cost data relating to the swimsuit for the first quarter follow:

Units produced	30,000
Units sold	28,000
Variable costs per unit:	
Direct materials	$ 3.50
Direct labor	12.00
Variable manufacturing overhead	1.00
Variable selling and administrative	6.00

Required

1. Complete the following:
   a. Compute the unit product cost under absorption costing.
   b. Redo the company's income statement for the quarter using absorption costing.
   c. Reconcile the variable and absorption costing net income (loss) figures.
2. Was the CPA correct in suggesting that the company really earned a "profit" for the quarter? Explain.
3. During the second quarter of operations, the company again produced 30,000 units but sold 32,000 units. (Assume no change in total fixed costs.)
   a. Prepare an income statement for the quarter using variable costing.
   b. Prepare an income statement for the quarter using absorption costing.
   c. Reconcile the variable costing and absorption costing net income figures.

P7–13 Prepare and Interpret Statements; Changes in Both Sales and Production; Automation; JIT Starfax, Inc., manufactures a small part that is widely used in various electronic products such as home computers. Operating results for the first three years of activity were as follows (absorption costing basis):

	Year 1	Year 2	Year 3
Sales	$800,000	$640,000	$800,000
Cost of goods sold:			
Beginning inventory	–0–	–0–	200,000
Add cost of goods manufactured	580,000	600,000	560,000
Goods available for sale	580,000	600,000	760,000
Less ending inventory	–0–	200,000	140,000
Cost of goods sold	580,000	400,000	620,000
Gross margin	220,000	240,000	180,000
Selling and administrative expenses	190,000	180,000	190,000
Net income (loss)	$ 30,000	$ 60,000	$(10,000)

In the latter part of Year 2, a competitor went out of business and in the process dumped a large number of units on the market. As a result, Starfax's sales dropped by 20% during Year 2 even though production increased during that year. Management had expected sales to remain constant at 50,000 units; the increased production was designed to provide the company with a buffer of protection against unexpected spurts in demand. By the start of Year 3, management could see that inventory was excessive and that spurts in demand were unlikely. To work off the excessive inventories, Starfax cut back production during Year 3, as shown below:

	Year 1	Year 2	Year 3
Production in units	50,000	60,000	40,000
Sales in units	50,000	40,000	50,000

Additional information about the company follows:

a. The company's plant is highly automated. Variable manufacturing costs (direct materials, direct labor, and variable manufacturing overhead) total only $2 per unit, and fixed manufacturing costs total $480,000 per year.

b. Fixed manufacturing costs are applied to units of product on the basis of each year's production. (That is, a new fixed manufacturing overhead rate is computed each year, as in Exhibit 7–6.)

c. Variable selling and administrative expenses were $1 per unit sold in each year. Fixed selling and administrative expenses totaled $140,000 each year.

d. The company uses a FIFO inventory flow assumption.

Starfax's management can't understand why profits doubled during Year 2 when sales dropped by 20% and why a loss was incurred during Year 3 when sales recovered to previous levels.

Required

1. Prepare a new income statement for each year using the contribution approach, with variable costing.
2. Refer to the absorption costing income statements above.
   a. Compute the unit product cost in each year under absorption costing. (Show how much of this cost is variable and how much is fixed.)
   b. Reconcile the variable costing and absorption costing net income figures for each year.
3. Refer again to the absorption costing income statements. Explain why net income was higher in Year 2 than it was in Year 1 under the absorption approach, in light of the fact that fewer units were sold in Year 2 than in Year 1.
4. Refer again to the absorption costing income statements. Explain why the company suffered a loss in Year 3 but reported a profit in Year 1 although the same number of units was sold in each year.
   a. Explain how operations would have differed in Year 2 and Year 3 if the company had been using JIT inventory methods.
   b. If JIT had been in use during Year 2 and Year 3, what would the company's net income (or loss) have been in each year under absorption costing? Explain the reason for any differences between these income figures and the figures reported by the company in the statements above.

P7–14 Prepare Variable Costing Statements; Sales Constant, Production Varies; JIT Impact "This makes no sense at all," said Bill Sharp, president of Essex Company. "We sold the same number of units this year as we did last year, yet our profits have more than doubled. Who made the goof—the computer or the people who operate it?" The statements to which Mr. Sharp was referring are shown below (absorption costing basis):

	Year 1	Year 2
Sales (20,000 units each year)	$700,000	$700,000
Less cost of goods sold	460,000	400,000
Gross margin	240,000	300,000
Less selling and administrative expenses	200,000	200,000
Net income	$ 40,000	$100,000

The statements above show the results of the first two years of operation. In the first year, the company produced and sold 20,000 units; in the second year, the company again sold 20,000 units, but it increased production in order to have a stock of units on hand, as shown below:

	Year 1	Year 2
Production in units	20,000	25,000
Sales in units	20,000	20,000
Variable production cost per unit	$ 8	$ 8
Fixed manufacturing overhead costs (total)	$300,000	$300,000

Essex Company produces a single product, fixed manufacturing overhead costs are applied to the product on the basis of *each year's production.* (Thus, a new fixed manufacturing overhead rate is computed each year, as in Exhibit 7–6.) Variable selling and administrative expenses are $1 per unit sold.

Required

1. Compute the unit product cost for each year under:
   a. Absorption costing.
   b. Variable costing.
2. Prepare an income statement for each year, using the contribution approach with variable costing.
3. Reconcile the variable costing and absorption costing net income figures for each year.
4. Explain to the president why, under absorption costing, the net income for Year 2 was higher than the net income for Year 1, although the same number of units was sold in each year.
5. a. Explain how operations would have differed in Year 2 if the company had been using JIT inventory methods.
   b. If JIT has been in use during Year 2, what would the company's net income have been under absorption costing? Explain the reason for any difference between this income figure and the figure reported by the company in the statements above.

P7–15 Ethics and the Manager; Production Schedule Carlos Cavalas, the manager of Echo Products' Brazilian Division, is trying to decide what production schedule to set for the last quarter of the year. The Brazilian Division had planned to sell 3,600 units during the year, but by September 30 only the following activity had been reported:

	Units
Inventory, January 1	–0–
Production	2,400
Sales	2,000
Inventory, September 30	400

The division can rent warehouse space to store up to 1,000 units. The minimum inventory level that the division should carry is 50 units. Mr. Cavalas is aware that production must be at least 200 units per quarter in order to retain a nucleus of key employees. Maximum production is 1,500 units per quarter.

Demand has been soft, and the sales forecast for the last quarter is only 600 units. Due to the nature of the division's operations, fixed manufacturing overhead is a major element of product cost.

Required

1. Assume that the division is using variable costing. How many units should be scheduled for production during the last quarter of the year? (The basic formula for computing the required production for a period in a company is: Expected sales + Desired ending inventory − Beginning inventory = Required production.) Show computations and explain your answer. Will the number of units scheduled for production affect the division's reported income or loss for the year? Explain.
2. Assume that the division is using absorption costing and that the divisional manager is given an annual bonus based on divisional operating income. If Mr. Cavalas wants to maximize his division's operating income for the year, how many units should be scheduled for production during the last quarter? [See the formula in (1) above.] Show computations and explain your answer.
3. Identify the ethical issues involved in the decision Mr. Cavalas must make.

Cases

C7–16 Ethics and the Manager; Absorption Costing Income Statements Guochang Li was hired as chief executive officer (CEO) in late November by the board of directors of ContactGlobal, a company that produces an advanced global positioning system (GPS) device that pinpoints the user's location anywhere on earth to within a hundred meters. The previous CEO had been fired by the board of directors due to a series of shady business practices including shipping defective GPS devices to dealers.

Guochang felt that his first priority was to restore employee morale—which had suffered during the previous CEO's reign. He was particularly anxious to build a sense of trust between himself and the company's employees. His second priority was to prepare the budget for the coming year, which the board of directors wanted to review in their December 15 meeting.

After hammering out the details in meetings with key managers, Guochang was able to put together a budget that he felt the company could realistically meet during the coming year. That budget appears below:

Basic budget data	
Units in beginning inventory	–0–
Units produced	400,000
Units sold	400,000
Units in ending inventory	–0–
Variable costs per unit:	
Direct materials	$ 57.20
Direct labor	15.00
Variable manufacturing overhead	5.00
Variable selling and administrative	10.00
Total variable cost per unit	$ 87.20
Fixed costs:	
Fixed manufacturing overhead	$ 6,888,000
Fixed selling and administrative	4,560,000
Total fixed costs	$11,448,000

CONTACTGLOBAL
Budgeted Income Statement
(absorption method)

Sales (400,000 units × $120 per unit)		$48,000,000
Less cost of goods sold:		
Beginning inventory	$ –0–	
Add cost of goods manufactured (400,000 units × $94.42 per unit)	37,768,000	
Goods available for sale	37,768,000	
Less ending inventory	–0–	37,768,000
Gross margin		10,232,000
Less selling and administrative expenses:		
Variable selling and administrative (400,000 units × $10 per unit)	4,000,000	
Fixed selling and administrative	4,560,000	8,560,000
Net income		$ 1,672,000

The board of directors made it clear that this budget was not as ambitious as they had hoped. The most influential member of the board stated that "managers should have to really stretch to meet profit goals." After some discussion, the board decided to set a profit goal of $2,000,000 for the coming year. To provide strong incentives, the board agreed to pay out very substantial bonuses to top managers of $10,000 to $25,000 each if this profit goal were met. The bonus would be all-or-nothing. If actual net income turned out to be $2,000,000 or more, the bonus would be paid. Otherwise, no bonus would be paid.

Required

1. Assuming that the company does not build up its inventory (i.e., production equals sales) and its selling price and cost structure remain the same, how many units of the GPS device would have to be sold in order to meet the profit goal of $2,000,000?
2. Verify your answer to (1) above by constructing a revised budget and budgeted income statement that yields a net income of $2,000,000. Use the absorption costing method.
3. Unfortunately, by October of the next year it had become clear that the company would not be able to make the $2,000,000 target profit. In fact, it looked like the company would wind up the year as originally planned, with sales of 400,000 units, no ending inventories, and a profit of $1,672,000.

   Several managers who were reluctant to lose their year-end bonuses approached Guochang and suggested that the company could still show a profit of $2,000,000. The managers pointed out that at the present rate of sales, there was enough capacity to produce tens of thousands of additional GPS devices for the warehouse and thereby shift fixed manufacturing costs to another year. If sales are 400,000 units for the year and the selling price and cost structure remains the same, how many units would have to be produced in order to show a profit of at least $2,000,000 under absorption costing?
4. Verify your answer to (3) above by constructing an income statement. Use the absorption costing method.
5. Do you think Guochang Li should approve the plan to build ending inventories in order to attain the target profit?
6. What advice would you give to the board of directors concerning how they determine bonuses in the future?

C7–17 The Case of the Plummeting Profits; Just-in-Time (JIT) Impact

"These statements can't be right," said Ben Yoder, president of Rayco, Inc. "Our sales in the second quarter were up by 25% over the first quarter, yet these income statements show a precipitous drop in net income for the second quarter. Those accounting people have fouled something up." Mr. Yoder was referring to the following statements:

RAYCO, INC.
Income Statements
For the First Two Quarters

	First Quarter		Second Quarter	
Sales		$480,000		$600,000
Less cost of goods sold:				
Beginning inventory	$ 80,000		$140,000	
Add cost of goods manufactured	300,000		180,000	
Goods available for sale	380,000		320,000	
Less ending inventory	140,000		20,000	
Cost of goods sold	240,000		300,000	
Add underapplied overhead	—	240,000	72,000	372,000
Gross margin		240,000		228,000
Less selling and administrative expenses		200,000		215,000
Net income		$ 40,000		$ 13,000

After studying the statements briefly, Mr. Yoder called in the controller to see if the mistake in the second quarter could be located before the figures were released to the press. The controller stated, "I'm sorry to say that those figures are correct, Ben. I agree that sales went up during the second quarter, but the problem is in production. You see, we budgeted to produce 15,000 units each quarter, but a strike on the west coast among some of our suppliers forced us to cut production in the second quarter back to only 9,000 units. That's what caused the drop in net income."

Mr. Yoder was confused by the controller's explanation. He replied, "This doesn't make sense. I ask you to explain why net income dropped when sales went up and you talk about production! So what if we had to cut back production? We still were able to increase sales by 25%. If sales go up, then net income should go up. If your statements can't show a simple thing like that, then it's time for some changes in your area!"

Budgeted production and sales for the year, along with actual production and sales for the first two quarters, are given below:

	Quarter			
	First	Second	Third	Fourth
Budgeted sales (units)	12,000	15,000	15,000	18,000
Actual sales (units)	12,000	15,000	—	—
Budgeted production (units)	15,000	15,000	15,000	15,000
Actual production (units)	15,000	9,000	—	—

The company's plant is heavily automated, and fixed manufacturing overhead amounts to $180,000 each quarter. Variable manufacturing costs are $8 per unit. The fixed manufacturing overhead is applied to units of product at a rate of $12 per unit (based on the budgeted production shown above). Any under- or overapplied overhead is taken directly to cost of goods sold for the quarter. The company had 4,000 units in inventory to start the first quarter and uses the FIFO inventory flow assumption. Variable selling and administrative expenses are $5 per unit.

Required

1. What characteristic of absorption costing caused the drop in net income for the second quarter and what could the controller have said to explain the problem more fully?
2. Prepare income statements for each quarter using the contribution approach, with variable costing.
3. Reconcile the absorption costing and the variable costing net income figures for each quarter.
4. Identify and discuss the advantages and disadvantages of using the variable costing method for internal reporting purposes.

5. Assume that the company had introduced JIT inventory methods at the beginning of the second quarter. (Sales and production during the first quarter remain the same.)
   a. How many units would have been produced during the second quarter under JIT?
   b. Starting with the third quarter, would you expect any difference between the net income reported under absorption costing and under variable costing? Explain why there would or would not be any difference.

C7–18 Absorption and Variable Costing; Uneven Production; Break-Even Analysis; Just-in-Time (JIT) Impact "Now this doesn't make any sense at all," said Flora Fisher, financial vice president for Warner Company. "Our sales have been steadily rising over the last several months, but profits have been going in the opposite direction. In September we finally hit $2,000,000 in sales, but the bottom line for that month drops off to a $100,000 loss. Why aren't profits more closely correlated with sales?"

The statements to which Ms. Fisher was referring are shown below:

WARNER COMPANY
Monthly Income Statements

	July	August	September
Sales (@ $25)	$1,750,000	$1,875,000	$2,000,000
Less cost of goods sold:			
Beginning inventory	80,000	320,000	400,000
Cost applied to production:			
Variable manufacturing costs (@ $9)	765,000	720,000	540,000
Fixed manufacturing overhead	595,000	560,000	420,000
Cost of goods manufactured	1,360,000	1,280,000	960,000
Goods available for sale	1,440,000	1,600,000	1,360,000
Less ending inventory	320,000	400,000	80,000
Cost of goods sold	1,120,000	1,200,000	1,280,000
Underapplied or (overapplied) fixed overhead cost	(35,000)	—	140,000
Adjusted cost of goods sold	1,085,000	1,200,000	1,420,000
Gross margin	665,000	675,000	580,000
Less selling and administrative expenses	620,000	650,000	680,000
Net income (loss)	$ 45,000	$ 25,000	$ (100,000)

Hal Taylor, a recent graduate from State University who has just been hired by Warner Company, has stated to Ms. Fisher that the contribution approach, with variable costing, is a much better way to report profit data to management. Sales and production data for the last quarter follow:

	July	August	September
Production in units	85,000	80,000	60,000
Sales in units	70,000	75,000	80,000

Additional information about the company's operations is given below:

a. Five thousand units were in inventory on July 1.
b. Fixed manufacturing overhead costs total $1,680,000 per quarter and are incurred evenly throughout the quarter. This fixed manufacturing overhead cost is applied to units of product on the basis of a budgeted production volume of 80,000 units per month.
c. Variable selling and administrative expenses are $6 per unit sold. The remainder of the selling and administrative expenses on the statements above are fixed.
d. The company uses a FIFO inventory flow assumption. Work in process inventories are insignificant and can be ignored.

"I know production is somewhat out of step with sales," said Carla Vorhees, the company's controller. "But we had to build inventory early in the quarter in anticipation of a strike in September. Since the union settled without a strike, we then had to cut back production in September in order to work off the excess inventories. The income statements you have are completely accurate."

Required

1. Prepare an income statement for each month using the contribution approach with variable costing.
2. Compute the monthly break-even point under variable costing.
3. Explain to Ms. Fisher why profits have moved erratically over the three-month period shown in the absorption costing statements above and why profits have not been more closely related to changes in sales volume.
4. Reconcile the variable costing and absorption costing net income (loss) figures for each month. Show all computations, and show how you derive each figure used in your reconciliation.
5. Assume that the company had decided to introduce JIT inventory methods at the beginning of September. (Sales and production during July and August were as shown above.)
   a. How many units would have been produced during September under JIT?
   b. Starting with the next quarter (October, November, and December), would you expect any difference between the income reported under absorption costing and under variable costing? Explain why there would or would not be any difference.
   c. Refer to your computations in (2) above. How would JIT help break-even analysis "make sense" under absorption costing?

Group Exercises

GE7–19 One Size Fits All? Nearly 70 years ago, economist J. Maurice Clarke stated that "accountants use different costs because of their differing objectives." The business world has certainly become a lot more complicated since Professor Clarke's time. Yet people often cling to the myth of a single, unique unit cost.

Required

1. How is accounting information used? That is, for what purposes, functions, or roles is cost information used?
2. Once you've identified the uses for cost information, how would you determine the makeup of the unit cost for each use. For example, one of the uses you should have identified is the need for a unit cost to value inventory and determine incomes for external financial reporting purposes. What do generally accepted accounting principles (GAAP) have to say about what is an inventoriable product cost for financial reporting purposes?

GE7–20 Who Needs Customers? I Can Make Money without Them Tough times always seem to bring out the worst in people. When companies are desperate to stay in business or to report more favorable earnings to Wall Street, some managers just can't seem to resist the temptation to manipulate reported profits. Unfortunately, inventory is sometimes a tempting source of such manipulations. It is important to know how such earnings distortions can occur, whether they result from intentional actions or innocent miscalculations.

Required

1. What product cost concept is the basis for inventory valuation and cost of goods sold determination for external financial reporting purposes?
2. Explain the concept of "phantom" or "illusory" profits. Excluding inflation and changes in the selling prices of products, how could a firm with the same sales as last year report significantly higher profits without cutting any costs? Could a firm with sales below the break-even point report profits? Explain.
3. Are all such "fictitious" profits an attempt to distort profits and mislead investors and creditors? If not, under what economic conditions would this most likely occur?
4. Could the reverse situation occur? That is, could lower accounting profits be reported even though the firm is not economically worse off? Under what economic conditions would this most likely occur?

5. A far more serious manipulation is inventory fraud by reporting fictitious inventories. Explain how this could result in a serious overstatement of earnings and assets.

GE7–21 Changing Cost Structures and Product Costing As firms automate their operations with advanced manufacturing technology and information technology, cost structures are becoming more fixed with higher proportions of overhead.

Required

1. What implications does this trend hold for arguments favoring absorption costing? What implications does this trend hold for arguments favoring variable costing?
2. If absorption costing continues to be used for external financial reporting, what impact will inventory buildups or inventory liquidations have on future reported earnings compared with the effects they have had on past reported earnings?
3. Most firms evaluate and compensate top management, in part, on the basis of reported income. Would top management have a preference for variable costing or full absorption costing? Explain.

IE7–22 Estimating Variable Costing Net Income from an Absorption Costing Income Statement Intel Corporation is the world's largest manufacturer of computer processor chips. The company's manufacturing processes are highly automated, so most manufacturing costs are fixed. You can access the company's most recent annual report in the Investor Relations section of its web site www.intel.com. Its most recent operating income figure is on its income statement, and the values of beginning and ending inventories are on its balance sheet.

Required

Assume that Intel uses absorption costing in its annual report and that 60% of the cost of its beginning and ending inventories consists of fixed manufacturing overhead costs. Estimate the company's operating income if it had used variable costing.

Chapter Eight

Activity-Based Costing: A Tool to Aid Decision Making

Business Focus

More companies are becoming aware of the need to distinguish between their profitable and unprofitable customers. To do this, companies track how much their customers spend on their products and how much it costs to serve these customers. Profitable customers are carefully nurtured. Unprofitable customers may be let go.

For example, "Bank of America calculates its profits every month on each of its more than 75 million accounts. . . By wading through all that data . . . BofA is able to zero in on the 10% of households that are most profitable. It assigns a financial adviser to track about 300 accounts at a time. Their job: to answer questions, coordinate the bank's efforts to sell more services, and—perhaps most important—watch for warning flags that these lucrative customers may be moving their business elsewhere. . . . The heavy intervention seems to be working . . . [C]ustomer defections are down, and account balances in the top 10% have grown . . ."

Source: Paul C. Judge, "What've You Done for Us Lately?" Business Week, *September 14, 1998, pp. 137–46.*

Learning Objectives

After studying Chapter 8, you should be able to:

1 Explain the major differences between activity-based costing and a traditional costing system.

2 Distinguish between unit-level, batch-level, product-level, customer-level, and organization-sustaining activities.

3 Assign costs to cost pools using a first-stage allocation.

4 Compute activity rates for cost pools and explain how they can be used to target process improvements.

5 Assign costs to a cost object using a second-stage allocation.

6 Prepare a report showing activity-based costing product margins from an activity view.

7 Prepare an action analysis report using activity-based costing data and interpret the report.

8 Use the simplified approach to compute activity-based costs and margins.

The cost accounting systems described in Chapters 2, 3, and 4 were designed primarily to provide unit product costs for external reporting purposes. Variable costing, which was described in Chapter 7, is intended to provide managers with product cost and other information for decisions that do not affect fixed costs and capacity. Recently, there has been tremendous interest in activity-based costing. **Activity-based costing (ABC)** is a costing method that is designed to provide managers with cost information for strategic and other decisions that potentially affect capacity and therefore "fixed" costs. Activity-based costing is also used as an element of activity-based management, an approach to management that focuses on activities.

In practice, there are many "flavors" of activity-based costing. Consultants emphasize different aspects of activity-based costing, and companies interpret activity-based costing differently. Since so much variation occurs in practice, we focus our attention in this chapter on what we consider to be "the best practice"—those techniques that provide managers with the most useful information for making strategic decisions. We will assume that the ABC system is used as a supplement to, rather than as a replacement for, the company's formal cost accounting system. The cost accounting methods described in Chapters 2, 3, and 4 would continue to be used to determine product costs for external financial reports. Activity-based costing would be used to determine product and other costs for special management reports. To keep the discussion simple, we gloss over some of the relatively unimportant details that can add enormously to the complexity of activity-based costing. Even so, you are likely to find this chapter especially challenging.

objective 1

Explain the major differences between activity-based costing and a traditional costing system.

In the traditional cost accounting systems described in Chapters 2, 3, and 4, the objective is to properly value inventories and cost of goods sold for external financial reports. In activity-based costing, the objective is to understand overhead and the profitability of products and customers. As a consequence of these differences in objectives, "best practice" activity-based costing differs in a number of ways from traditional cost accounting.

In activity-based costing:

1. Nonmanufacturing as well as manufacturing costs may be assigned to products.
2. Some manufacturing costs may be excluded from product costs.
3. There are a number of overhead cost pools, each of which is allocated to products and other costing objects using its own unique measure of activity.
4. The allocation bases often differ from those used in traditional costing systems.
5. The overhead rates, or *activity rates*, may be based on the level of activity at capacity rather than on the budgeted level of activity.

As we will see later in the chapter, these differences from traditional cost accounting systems can have dramatic impacts on the apparent costs of products and the profitability of products and customers. But first, we will briefly discuss the reasons for these departures from traditional cost accounting practices.

How Costs Are Treated Under Activity-Based Costing

Nonmanufacturing Costs and Activity-Based Costing

In traditional cost accounting, only manufacturing costs are assigned to products. Selling, general, and administrative expenses are treated as period expenses and are not assigned to products. However, many of these nonmanufacturing costs are also part of the costs of producing, selling, distributing, and servicing products. For example, commissions paid to salespersons, shipping costs, and warranty repair costs can be easily traced to individual products. To determine the profitability of products and services, such nonmanufacturing costs are assigned to products in activity-based costing.

Manufacturing Costs and Activity-Based Costing

In traditional cost accounting, *all* manufacturing costs are assigned to products—even manufacturing costs that are not caused by the products. For example, a portion of the factory security guard's wages would be allocated to each product even though the guard's wages are totally unaffected by which products are made or not made during a period. In activity-based costing, a cost is assigned to a product only if there is good reason to believe that the cost would be affected by decisions concerning the product.

PLANTWIDE OVERHEAD RATE Our discussion in Chapter 3 assumed that a single overhead rate, called a *plantwide overhead rate,* was being used throughout an entire factory and that the allocation base was direct labor-hours or machine-hours. This simple approach to overhead assignment can result in distorted unit product costs when it is used for decision-making purposes.

When cost systems were developed in the 1800s, direct labor was a larger component of product costs than it is today. Data relating to direct labor were readily available and convenient to use, and managers believed there was a high positive correlation between direct labor and overhead costs. (A positive correlation between two things means that they tend to move in tandem.) Consequently, direct labor was a useful allocation base for overhead.

However, a plantwide overhead rate based on direct labor may no longer be satisfactory. First, in many companies, direct labor may no longer be highly correlated with (i.e., move in tandem with) overhead costs. Second, because of the large variety of activities encompassed in overhead, no single allocation base may be able to adequately reflect the demands that products place on overhead resources.

On an economywide basis, direct labor and overhead costs have been moving in opposite directions for a long time. As a percentage of total cost, direct labor has been declining, whereas overhead has been increasing.[1] Many tasks that used to be done by hand are now done with largely automated equipment—a component of overhead. Furthermore, product diversity has increased. Companies are creating new products and services at an ever-accelerating rate that differ in volume, batch size, and complexity. Managing and sustaining this product diversity requires many more overhead resources such as production schedulers and product design engineers, and many of these overhead resources have no obvious connection with direct labor.

Nevertheless, direct labor remains a viable base for applying overhead to products in many companies—particularly for external reports. In some companies there is still a high positive correlation between overhead costs and direct labor. And most companies throughout the world continue to base overhead allocations on direct labor or machine-hours. However, in those instances in which factorywide overhead costs do not move in tandem with factorywide direct labor, some other means of assigning costs must be found or product costs will be distorted.

---

1. Germain Böer provides some data concerning these trends in "Five Modern Management Accounting Myths," *Management Accounting,* January 1994, pp. 22–27. Data maintained by the U.S. Department of Commerce shows that since 1849, on average, material cost as a percentage of manufacturing cost has been fairly constant at 55% of sales. Labor cost has always been relatively less important and has declined steadily from 23% in 1849 to about 10% in 1987. Overhead has grown from about 18% of sales in 1947 to about 33% of sales 50 years later.

DEPARTMENTAL OVERHEAD RATES Rather than use a plantwide overhead rate, many companies use departmental overhead rates. The allocation bases used in these departmental overhead rates depend on the nature of the work performed in each department. For example, overhead costs in a machining department may be allocated on the basis of the machine-hours in that department. In contrast, the overhead costs in an assembly department may be allocated on the basis of direct labor-hours in that department.

Unfortunately, even departmental overhead rates will not correctly assign overhead costs in situations where a company has a range of products that differ in volume, batch size, or complexity of production.[2] The reason is that the departmental approach usually relies on volume as the factor in allocating overhead cost to products. For example, if the machining department's overhead is applied to products on the basis of machine-hours, it is assumed that the department's overhead costs are caused by, and are directly proportional to, machine-hours. However, the department's overhead costs are probably more complex than this and are caused by a variety of factors, including the range of products processed in the department, the number of batch setups that are required, the complexity of the products, and so on. Activity-based costing is a technique that is designed to reflect these diverse factors more accurately when costing products. It attempts to accomplish this goal by identifying the major *activities* such as batch setups, purchase order processing, and so on, that consume overhead resources. An **activity** is any event that causes the consumption of overhead resources. The costs of carrying out these activities are assigned to the products that cause the activities.

The Costs of Idle Capacity in Activity-Based Costing

In traditional cost accounting, predetermined overhead rates are computed by dividing budgeted overhead costs by a measure of budgeted activity such as budgeted direct labor-hours. This practice results in applying the costs of unused, or idle, capacity to products, and it results in unstable unit product costs as discussed in Appendix 3A. If budgeted activity falls, the overhead rate increases because the fixed components of overhead are spread over a smaller base, resulting in increased unit product costs.

In contrast to traditional cost accounting, in activity-based costing, products are charged for the costs of capacity they use—not for the costs of capacity they don't use. In other words, the costs of idle capacity are not charged to products. This results in more stable unit costs and is consistent with the objective of assigning only those costs to products that are actually caused by the products.

Designing an Activity-Based Costing (ABC) System

Experts agree on several essential characteristics of any successful implementation of activity-based costing. First, the initiative to implement activity-based costing must be strongly supported by top management. Second, the design and implementation of an ABC system should be the responsibility of a cross-functional team rather than of the accounting department. The team should include representatives from each area that will use the data provided by the ABC system. Ordinarily, this would include repre-

2. See Robin Cooper and Robert S. Kaplan, "How Cost Accounting Distorts Product Costs," *Management Accounting*, April 1988, pp. 20–27.

sentatives from marketing, production, engineering, and top management as well as technically trained accounting staff. Sometimes an outside consultant who specializes in activity-based costing acts as an advisor to the team.

The reason for insisting on strong top-management support and a multifunction team approach is rooted in the fact that it is difficult to implement changes in organizations unless those changes have the full support of those who are affected. Activity-based costing changes "the rules of the game" since it changes some of the key measures that managers use for their decision-making and for evaluating individuals' performance. Unless the managers who are directly affected by the changes in the rules have a say, there will inevitably be resistance. In addition, designing a good ABC system requires intimate knowledge of many parts of the organization's overall operations. This knowledge can only come from the people who are familiar with those operations.

Top managers must support the initiative for two reasons. First, without leadership from top management, some managers may not see any reason to change. Second, if top managers do not support the ABC system and continue to play the game by the old rules, their subordinates will quickly get the message and abandon the ABC system. Time after time, when accountants have attempted to implement an ABC system on their own without top-management support and active cooperation from other managers, the results have been ignored.

Managerial Accounting in Action

THE ISSUE

Classic Brass, Inc., makes finely machined brass fittings for a variety of applications including stanchions, cleats, and helms for luxury yachts. The president of the company, John Towers, recently attended a management conference at which activity-based costing was discussed. Following the conference, he called a meeting of the top managers in the company to discuss what he had learned. Attending the meeting were the production manager Susan Ritcher, the marketing manager Tom Olafson, and the accounting manager Mary Goodman.

John: I'm glad we could all get together this morning. The conference I just attended dealt with some issues that we have all been wondering about for some time.

Susan: Did anyone at the conference explain why my equipment always breaks down at the worst possible moment?

John: Sorry Susan, I guess it must be bad karma or something.

Tom: Did the conference tell you why we've been losing all those bids lately on our high-volume routine work?

John: Tom, you probably weren't expecting this answer, but, yes, there may be a simple reason why we've been losing those bids.

Tom: Let me guess. We've been losing the bids because we have more competition.

John: Yes, the competition has a lot to do with it. But Tom, we may have been shooting ourselves in the foot.

Tom: How so? I don't know about anyone else, but my salespeople have been hustling like crazy to get more business for the company.

Susan: Wait a minute Tom, my production people have been turning in tremendous improvements in defect rates, on-time delivery, and so on.

John: Whoa everybody. Calm down. I don't think anyone is to blame for losing the bids. Tom, when you talk with our customers, what reasons do they give for taking their business to our competitors? Is it a problem with the quality of our products or our on-time delivery?

Tom: No, they don't have any problem with our products or with our service—our customers readily admit we're among the best in the business.
Susan: Darn right!
John: Then what's the problem?
Tom: Price. The competition is undercutting our prices on the high-volume work.
John: Why are our prices too high?
Tom: Our prices aren't too high. Theirs are too low. Our competitors must be pricing below their cost.
John: Tom, why do you think that?
Tom: Well, if we charged the prices on high-volume work that our competitors are quoting, we'd be pricing below *our* cost, and I know we are just as efficient as any competitor.
Susan: Tom, why would our competitors price below their cost?
Tom: They are out to grab market share.
Susan: Does that make any sense? What good does more market share do if they are pricing below their cost?
John: I think Susan has a point Tom. Mary, you're the expert with the numbers. Can you suggest another explanation?
Mary: I was afraid you would ask that. Those unit product cost figures our department reports to you are primarily intended to be used to value inventories and determine cost of goods sold for our external financial statements. I am awfully uncomfortable about using them for bidding. In fact, I have mentioned this several times, but no one was interested.
John: Now I'm interested. Mary, are you telling us that the product cost figures we have been using for bidding are wrong? Perhaps the competition isn't pricing below our cost—we just don't know what our cost is?
Mary: Yes, that could be the problem. I just wish someone had listened earlier.
John: Does everyone agree with Mary that this is a problem we should work on?
Tom: Sure, if it means we can win more bids.
John: Okay, I want each of you to appoint one of your top people to a special team to investigate how we cost products.
Susan: Isn't this something Mary can handle with her staff?
John: Perhaps she could, but you know more about your operations than she does and besides, I want to make sure you agree with the results of the study and use them. Mary, do you agree?
Mary: Absolutely. ■

Focus on Current Practice

Diamond Courier of Philadelphia was started by Claudia Post shortly after having been fired as a salesperson for another courier service. Her downtown bicycle messenger service grew quickly—reaching $1 million in sales within 17 months. Seeing opportunities to sell other services, she added truck deliveries, airfreight services, a parts-distribution service, and a legal service that served subpoenas and prepared court filings. Within three years of beginning operations, Diamond Courier had $3.1 million in annual

sales and employed about 40 bike messengers and 25 back-office staffers in addition to providing work for about 50 independent drivers.

The company had one problem—it was losing money. Post had to sell her jewelry in order to meet the payroll and pay bills. With the help of an adviser, Post took a serious look at the profitability of each of the company's lines of business. Post had assumed that if she charged a competitive rate, kept clients happy, and increased sales, she would make money. However, an ABC analysis of her overhead costs indicated that the average cost of a bike delivery—including overhead—was $9.24, but she was charging only $4.69. "The bicycle division, which she thought of as Diamond's core business, generated just 10% of total sales and barely covered its own direct-labor and insurance costs. Worse, the division created more logistical and customer-service nightmares than any other single business, thereby generating a disproportionate share of overhead costs." Since smaller, focused competitors were charging as little as $3 per delivery, there was little alternative except to drop the bicycle messenger business and concentrate on the other, more profitable, lines of business. A similar analysis led her to also close the airfreight and parts-distribution businesses. At last report, Diamond Courier has regained a good chunk of the lost sales of $400,000 from closing these lines of business and is now operating profitably.[3] ■

After studying the existing cost accounting system at Classic Brass and reviewing articles in professional and trade journals, the special team decided to implement an activity-based costing (ABC) system. Like most other ABC implementations, the new ABC system would supplement, rather than replace, the existing cost accounting system, which would continue to be used for external financial reports. The new ABC system would be used to prepare special reports for management decisions such as bidding on new business.

The accounting manager drew the chart appearing in Exhibit 8–1 to explain the general structure of the ABC model. In activity-based costing it is assumed that cost

Exhibit 8–1 The Activity-Based Costing Model

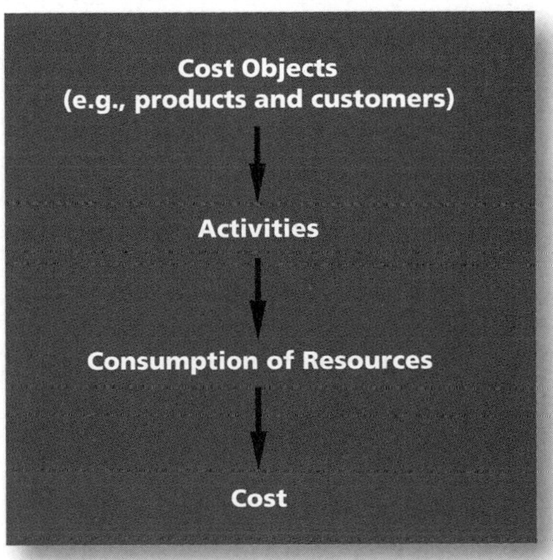

3. Susan Greco, "Are We Making Money Yet?" *Inc*, July 1996, pp. 52–61.

objects such as products generate activities. For example, a customer order for a brass spittoon generates a production order, which is an activity. It is further assumed that activities consume resources. For example, a production order uses a sheet of paper and takes time for a manager to fill out. And, it is assumed that consumption of resources leads to costs. The greater the number of sheets used to fill out production orders and the greater the amount of time devoted to filling out such orders, the greater the cost. Activity-based costing attempts to trace through these relationships to identify how products and customers affect costs.

As in most other companies, the ABC team at Classic Brass felt that the company's traditional cost accounting system adequately measures the direct material and direct labor costs of products. Therefore, the ABC study would be concerned solely with the other costs of the company—manufacturing overhead and selling, general, and administrative costs.

The team felt it was important to carefully plan how it would go about implementing the new ABC system at Classic Brass. Accordingly, the implementation process was broken down into the following six basic steps:

Steps for Implementing Activity-Based Costing:

1. Identify and define activities and activity pools.
2. Wherever possible, directly trace costs to activities and cost objects.
3. Assign costs to activity cost pools.
4. Calculate activity rates.
5. Assign costs to cost objects using the activity rates and activity measures.
6. Prepare management reports.

Identifying Activities to Include in the ABC System

objective 2

Distinguish between unit-level, batch-level, product-level, customer-level, and organization-sustaining activities.

The first major step in implementing an ABC system is to identify the activities that will form the foundation for the system. This can be difficult, time-consuming, and involves a great deal of judgment. A common procedure is for the individuals on the ABC implementation team to interview everyone—or at least all supervisors and managers—in overhead departments and ask them to describe their major activities. Ordinarily, this results in a very long list of activities.

The length of such lists of activities poses a problem. On the one hand, the greater the number of activities tracked in the ABC system, the more accurate the costs are likely to be. On the other hand, it is costly to design, implement, maintain, and use a complex system involving large numbers of activities. Consequently, the original lengthy list of activities is usually reduced to a handful by combining similar activities. For example, several actions may be involved in handling and moving raw materials—from receiving raw materials on the loading dock to sorting them into the appropriate bins in the storeroom. All of these activities might be combined into a single activity called material handling.

A useful way to think about activities and how to combine them is to organize them into five general levels: *unit-level, batch-level, product-level, customer-level,* and *organization-sustaining* activities. These levels are described as follows:[4]

1. **Unit-level activities** are performed each time a unit is produced. The costs of unit-level activities should be proportional to the number of units produced. For

4. Robin Cooper, "Cost Classification in Unit-Based and Activity-Based Manufacturing Cost Systems," *Journal of Cost Management*, Fall 1990, pp. 4–14.

example, providing power to run processing equipment would be a unit-level activity since power tends to be consumed in proportion to the number of units produced.

2. **Batch-level activities** are performed each time a batch is handled or processed, regardless of how many units are in the batch. For example, tasks such as placing purchase orders, setting up equipment, and arranging for shipments to customers are batch-level activities. They are incurred each time there is a batch (or a customer order). Costs at the batch level depend on the number of batches processed rather than on the number of units produced, the number of units sold, or other measures of volume. For example, the cost of setting up a machine for batch processing is the same regardless of whether the batch contains one or 5,000 items.
3. **Product-level activities** relate to specific products and typically must be carried out regardless of how many batches are run or units of product are produced or sold. For example, activities such as designing a product, advertising a product, and maintaining a product manager and staff are all product-level activities.
4. **Customer-level activities** relate to specific customers and include activities such as sales calls, catalog mailings, and general technical support that are not tied to any specific product.
5. **Organization-sustaining activities** are carried out regardless of which customers are served, which products are produced, how many batches are run, or how many units are made. This category includes activities such as cleaning executive offices, providing a computer network, arranging for loans, preparing annual reports to shareholders, and so on.

When combining activities in an ABC system, activities should be grouped together at the appropriate level. Batch-level activities should not be combined with unit-level activities or product-level activities with batch-level activities and so on. In general, it is best to combine only those activities that are highly correlated with each other within a level. Activities are correlated with each other if they tend to move in tandem. For example, the number of customer orders received is likely to be highly correlated with the number of completed customer orders shipped, so these two batch-level activities (receiving and shipping orders) can usually be combined with little loss of accuracy.

At Classic Brass, the ABC team, in consultation with top managers, selected the following *activity cost pools* and *activity measures*:

Activity Cost Pools at Classic Brass

Activity Cost Pool	Activity Measure
Customer orders	Number of customer orders
Product design	Number of product designs
Order size	Machine-hours
Customer relations	Number of active customers
Other	Not applicable

An **activity cost pool** is a "bucket" in which costs are accumulated that relate to a single activity in the ABC system. For example, the Customer Orders cost pool will be assigned all costs of resources that are consumed by taking and processing customer orders, including costs of processing paperwork and any costs involved in setting up machines. The measure of activity for this cost pool is simply the number of customer orders received. This is a batch-level activity, since each order generates work that occurs regardless of whether the order is for one unit or 1,000 units. The number of customer orders received is an example of an *activity measure*. An **activity measure** is an allocation base in an activity-based costing system.

The Product Design cost pool will be assigned all costs of resources consumed by designing products. The activity measure for this cost pool is the number of products designed. This is a product-level activity, since the amount of design work on a new product does not depend on the number of units ultimately ordered or batches ultimately run.

The Order Size cost pool will be assigned all costs of resources consumed as a consequence of the number of units produced, including the costs of miscellaneous factory supplies, power to run machines, and some equipment depreciation. This is a unit-level activity since each unit requires some of these resources. The activity measure for this cost pool is machine-hours.

The Customer Relations cost pool will be assigned all costs associated with maintaining relations with customers, including the costs of sales calls and the costs of entertaining customers. The activity measure for this cost pool is the number of customers the company has on its active customer list.

The Other cost pool will be assigned all overhead costs that are not associated with customer orders, product design, the size of the orders, or customer relations. These costs mainly consist of organization-sustaining costs and the costs of unused, idle capacity. These costs *will not* be assigned to products since they represent resources that are *not* consumed by products.

It is unlikely that any other company would use exactly the same activity cost pools and activities that were selected by Classic Brass. Because of the amount of judgment involved, there is considerable variation in the number and definitions of the activity cost pools and activity measures used by companies.

The Mechanics of Activity-Based Costing

After the ABC system had been designed, the team was ready to begin the process of actually computing the costs of products, customers, and other objects of interest.

Tracing Overhead Costs to Activities and Cost Objects

The second step in implementing an ABC system is to directly trace as many overhead costs as possible to the ultimate cost objects. At Classic Brass, the ultimate cost objects are products, customer orders, and customers. The company's manufacturing overhead and selling, general, and administrative costs are listed in Exhibit 8–2. In the ABC

Exhibit 8–2 Overhead Costs (both Manufacturing and Nonmanufacturing) at Classic Brass

Production Department:		
Indirect factory wages	$500,000	
Factory equipment depreciation	300,000	
Factory utilities	120,000	
Factory building lease	80,000	$1,000,000
Shipping costs *		40,000
General Administrative Department:		
Administrative wages and salaries	400,000	
Office equipment depreciation	50,000	
Administrative building lease	60,000	510,000
Marketing Department:		
Marketing wages and salaries	250,000	
Selling expenses	50,000	300,000
Total overhead costs		$1,850,000

*Shipping costs can be traced directly to customer orders.

system at Classic Brass all of these costs are considered to be "overhead" and will be assigned to cost objects as appropriate.

One of these overhead costs—shipping—can be traced directly to customer orders. Classic Brass is directly billed for each customer order it ships, so it is a simple matter to trace these costs to the customer orders. Customers do not pay these actual shipping costs; instead they pay a standard shipping charge that can differ substantially from the actual bill that Classic Brass receives from the freight company.

No other overhead costs could be directly traced to products, customer orders, or customers. Consequently, the remainder of the overhead costs would be assigned to cost objects using the ABC system.

Focus on Current Practice

Super Bakery, Inc., founded by former Pittsburgh Steelers' running back Franco Harris, supplies donuts and other baked goods to schools, hospitals, and other institutions. The company is unusual in that it is a "virtual corporation." "In a virtual corporation, only the core, strategic functions of the business are performed inside the company. The remaining support activities are outsourced to a network of external companies that specialize in each function." Super Bakery's products are sold by a network of independent brokers, and the company contracts out baking, warehousing, and shipping. What does Super Bakery itself do? The company's master baker develops products, and the company formulates and produces its own dry mixes from ingredients it has purchased. The contracted bakeries simply add water to the mix and follow the baking instructions. Super Bakery maintains four regional sales managers, and a small office staff processes orders and handles bookkeeping and accounting.

As much as possible, actual costs are traced to individual customer accounts. The remaining costs of the company are assigned to customer accounts using the following activity cost pools and activity measures:

Activity Cost Pool	Activity Measure
Advertising, trade shows, and bonds	Projected number of cases sold
Order department	Number of orders
Sales management	Time spent in each sales territory
Research and development (R&D)	Hours of R&D for each product line

Since the independent sales brokers are paid a flat 5% commission on sales, they have little incentive to make sure that the sales are actually profitable to Super Bakery. It is in the interests of the brokers to deeply discount prices if this is necessary to make a sale. Consequently, Super Bakery's regional sales managers must approve all price discounts and they use the ABC data to evaluate the profitability of the deals proposed by the brokers.[5] ■

5. Tim R. V. Davis and Bruce L. Darling, "ABC in a Virtual Corporation," *Management Accounting*, October 1996, pp. 18–26.

Assigning Costs to Activity Cost Pools

objective 3

Assign costs to cost pools using a first-stage allocation.

Most overhead costs are originally classified in the company's basic accounting system according to the departments in which they are incurred. For example, salaries, supplies, rent, and so forth, incurred by the marketing department are charged to that department. In some cases, some or all of these costs can be directly traced to one of the activity cost pools in the ABC system, which is the third step in implementing activity-based costing. For example, if the ABC system has an activity called *purchase order processing,* then all of the costs of the purchasing department could probably be traced to that activity. To the extent possible, costs should be traced directly to the activity cost pools. However, it is quite common for an overhead department to be involved in several of the activities that are tracked in the ABC system. In such situations, the costs of the department are divided among the activity cost pools via an allocation process called *first-stage allocation*. The **first-stage allocation** in an ABC system is the process by which overhead costs are assigned to activity cost pools.

The immediate problem is to figure out how to divide, for example, the $500,000 of indirect factory wages at Classic Brass shown in Exhibit 8–2 among the various activity cost pools in the ABC system. The point of activity-based costing is to determine the resources consumed by cost objects. Since indirect factory worker time is a resource, we need some way of estimating the amount of indirect factory worker time that is consumed by each activity in the ABC system. Often, the best way to get this kind of information is to ask the people who are directly involved. Members of the ABC team interview indirect factory workers (e.g., supervisors, engineers, quality inspectors, etc.) and ask them what percentage of time they spend dealing with customer orders, with product design, with processing units of product (i.e., order size), and with customer relations. These interviews are conducted with considerable care. Those who are interviewed must thoroughly understand what the activities encompass and what is expected of them in the interview. In addition, departmental managers are interviewed to determine how the nonpersonnel costs should be distributed across the activity cost pools. In each case the key question is "What percentage of the available resource is consumed by this activity?" For example, the production manager would be asked, "What percentage of the available machine capacity is consumed as a consequence of the number of units processed (i.e., size of orders)?"

The results of the interviews at Classic Brass are displayed in Exhibit 8–3. For example, factory equipment depreciation is distributed 20% to Customer Orders, 60% to Order Size, and 20% to the Other cost pool. The resource in this instance is machine time. According to the estimate made by the production manager, 60% of the total available time was used to actually process units to fill orders. Each customer order requires setting up, which also requires machine time. This activity consumes 20% of the total available machine time and is entered under the Customer Orders column. The remaining 20% of available machine time represents idle time and is entered under the Other column.

Exhibit 8–3 and many of the other exhibits in this chapter are presented in the form of Excel spreadsheets. It is often a good idea to use spreadsheet software in activity-based costing because of the large number of calculations involved. You can do all of the calculations by hand, by setting up an activity-based costing system on a spreadsheet or using other special ABC software can save a lot of work in the long run—particularly in companies that intend to periodically update their ABC systems.

We will not go into the details of how all of the percentages in Exhibit 8–3 were determined. However, note that 100% of the factory building lease has been assigned to the Other cost pool. Classic Brass has a single production facility. It has no plans to expand or to sublease any excess space. The cost of this production facility is treated as an organization-sustaining cost since there is no way to avoid even a portion of this cost if a product or customer were dropped. (Remember that organization-sustaining costs are assigned to the Other cost pool and are not allocated to products.) In contrast,

Exhibit 8–3 Results of Interviews: Distribution of Activities

	Activity Cost Pools					
	Customer Orders	Product Design	Order Size	Customer Relations	Other	Total
Production Department:						
Indirect factory wages	25%	40%	20%	10%	5%	100%
Factory equipment depreciation	20%	0%	60%	0%	20%	100%
Factory utilities	0%	10%	50%	0%	40%	100%
Factory building lease	0%	0%	0%	0%	100%	100%
Shipping costs*	NA	NA	NA	NA	NA	
General Administrative Department:						
Administrative wages and salaries	15%	5%	10%	30%	40%	100%
Office equipment depreciation	30%	0%	0%	25%	45%	100%
Administrative building lease	0%	0%	0%	0%	100%	100%
Marketing Department:						
Marketing wages and salaries	20%	10%	0%	60%	10%	100%
Selling expenses	10%	0%	0%	70%	20%	100%
Total						

*Shipping costs are not included in this and subsequent tables because they are directly traced to customer orders rather than being allocated using the ABC system.

NA = Not applicable.

Exhibit 8–4 First-Stage Allocations to Activity Cost Pools

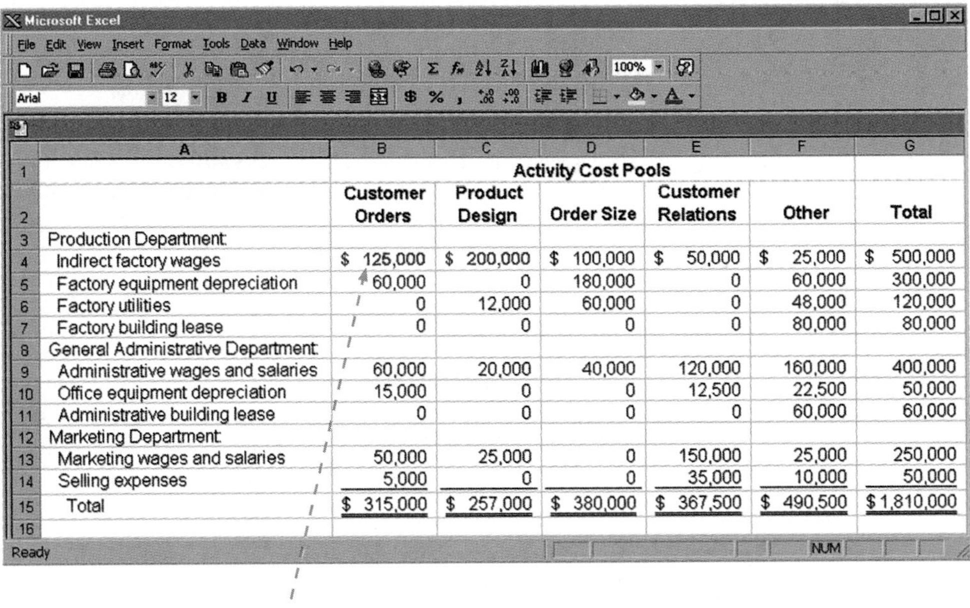

	Activity Cost Pools					
	Customer Orders	Product Design	Order Size	Customer Relations	Other	Total
Production Department:						
Indirect factory wages	$ 125,000	$ 200,000	$ 100,000	$ 50,000	$ 25,000	$ 500,000
Factory equipment depreciation	60,000	0	180,000	0	60,000	300,000
Factory utilities	0	12,000	60,000	0	48,000	120,000
Factory building lease	0	0	0	0	80,000	80,000
General Administrative Department:						
Administrative wages and salaries	60,000	20,000	40,000	120,000	160,000	400,000
Office equipment depreciation	15,000	0	0	12,500	22,500	50,000
Administrative building lease	0	0	0	0	60,000	60,000
Marketing Department:						
Marketing wages and salaries	50,000	25,000	0	150,000	25,000	250,000
Selling expenses	5,000	0	0	35,000	10,000	50,000
Total	$ 315,000	$ 257,000	$ 380,000	$ 367,500	$ 490,500	$1,810,000

Exhibit 8–3 shows that Customer Orders consume 25% of the resources represented by the $500,000 of indirect factory wages.

25% × $500,000 = $125,000

Other entries in the table are computed in a similar fashion.

some companies have separate facilities for manufacturing specific products. The costs of these separate facilities could be directly traced to the specific products.

Once the percentage distributions in Exhibit 8–3 have been established, it is a simple matter to allocate costs to the activity cost pools. The results of this first-stage allocation are displayed in Exhibit 8–4. Each cost is allocated across the activity cost pools by multiplying it by the percentages in Exhibit 8–3. For example, the indirect factory wages of $500,000 are multiplied by the 25% entry under Customer Orders in Exhibit 8–3 to arrive at the $125,000 entry under Customer Orders in Exhibit 8–4. Similarly, the indirect factory wages of $500,000 are multiplied by the 40% entry under Product Design in Exhibit 8–3 to arrive at the $200,000 entry under Product Design in Exhibit 8–4. All of the entries in Exhibit 8–4 are computed in this way.

Now that the first-stage allocations to the activity cost pools have been completed, the fourth step is to compute the activity rates.

Computation of Activity Rates

objective 4

Compute activity rates for cost pools and explain how they can be used to target process improvements.

The activity rates that will be used for assigning overhead costs to products and customers are computed by dividing the costs listed in Exhibit 8–4 by the total activity for each activity cost pool. The results of these computations are shown in Exhibit 8–5. The total activity numbers listed across the top of the table in Exhibit 8–5 were estimated by the ABC team and represent the amount of activity actually required to produce the company's present product mix and to serve its present customers. The activity at the top of each column was divided into each of the costs in the corresponding column in Exhibit 8–4 to arrive at the activity rates in Exhibit 8–5. For example, the $125,000 entry in Exhibit 8–4 for indirect factory wages under the Customer Orders column is divided by the total of 1,000 customer orders listed at the top of Exhibit 8–5 to arrive at the activity rate of $125 for indirect factory wages under the Customer Orders column in Exhibit 8–5. Similarly, the $200,000 entry in Exhibit 8–4 for indirect factory wages under the Product Design column is divided by the total number of designs (i.e., 200 product designs) to arrive at the activity rate of $1,000 per design for indirect factory wages. Note that activity rates are not computed for the Other category of costs. This is because these organization-sustaining costs and costs of idle capacity are not allocated to products and customers.

We urge you to study Exhibit 8–5 with care so that you are sure you know how each entry in the table was computed. Take each column in turn and divide each of the cost entries in Exhibit 8–4 under that column by the total activity at the top of the column in Exhibit 8–5. Once you see how the numbers were computed, it is really easy, although there are a lot of computations.

The entries at the bottom of Exhibit 8–5 indicate that on average a customer order consumes resources that cost $315; a product design consumes resources that cost $1,285; a unit of product consumes resources that cost $19 per machine-hour; and maintaining relations with a customer consumes resources that cost $3,675. Note that these are *average* figures. Some members of the ABC design team at Classic Brass argued that it would be unfair to charge all new products the same $1,285 product design cost regardless of how much design time they actually require. After discussing the pros and cons, the team concluded that it would not be worth the effort at the present time to keep track of actual design time spent on each new product. Similarly, some team members were uncomfortable assigning the same $3,675 cost to each customer. Some customers are undemanding—ordering standard products well in advance of their needs. Others are very demanding and consume large amounts of marketing and administrative staff time. These are generally customers who order customized products, who tend to order at the last minute, and who change their minds. While everyone agreed with this observation, the data that would be required to measure individual customers' demands on resources was not currently available. Rather than delay implementation of the ABC system, the team decided to defer such refinements to a later date.

Before proceeding further, it would be helpful to get a better idea of the overall process of assigning costs to products and other cost objects in an ABC system. Exhibit 8–6 provides a visual perspective of the ABC system at Classic Brass. We recommend

Exhibit 8–5
Computation of Activity Rates

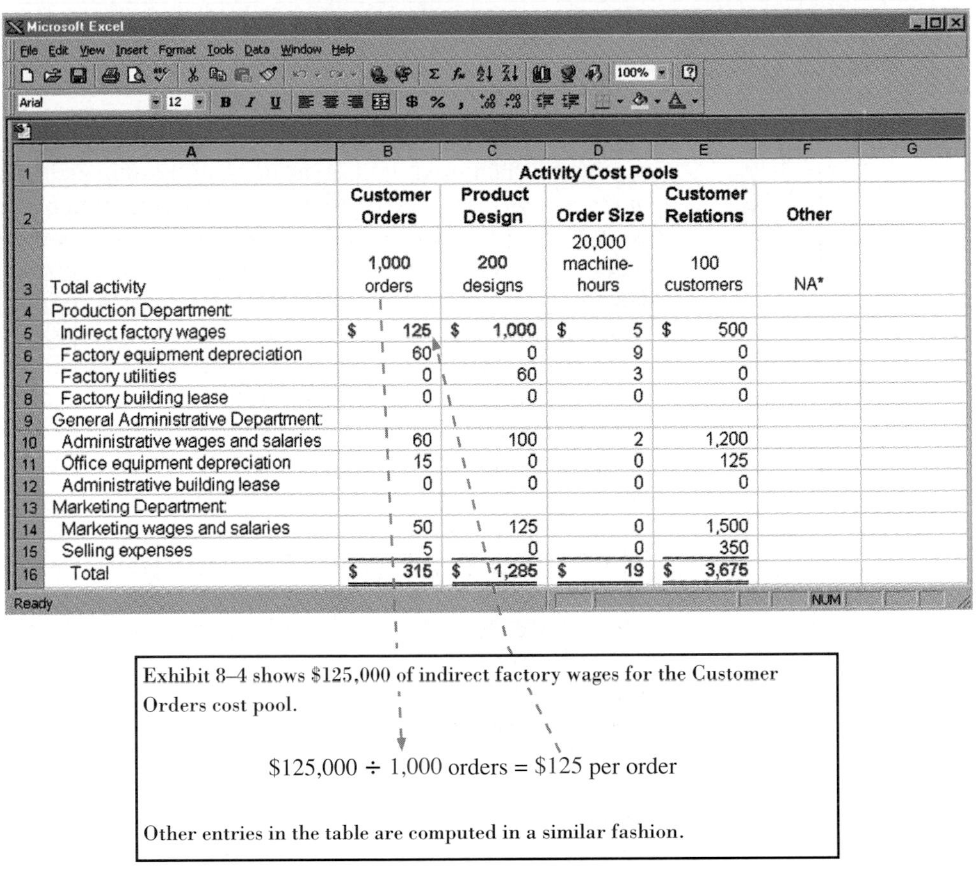

	Activity Cost Pools				
	Customer Orders	Product Design	Order Size	Customer Relations	Other
Total activity	1,000 orders	200 designs	20,000 machine-hours	100 customers	NA*
Production Department					
Indirect factory wages	$ 125	$ 1,000	$ 5	$ 500	
Factory equipment depreciation	60	0	9	0	
Factory utilities	0	60	3	0	
Factory building lease	0	0	0	0	
General Administrative Department					
Administrative wages and salaries	60	100	2	1,200	
Office equipment depreciation	15	0	0	125	
Administrative building lease	0	0	0	0	
Marketing Department					
Marketing wages and salaries	50	125	0	1,500	
Selling expenses	5	0	0	350	
Total	$ 315	$ 1,285	$ 19	$ 3,675	

*Activity rates are not computed for the Other cost pool since these costs will not be allocated further.
NA = Not applicable.

Exhibit 8–6 The Activity-Based Costing Model at Classic Brass

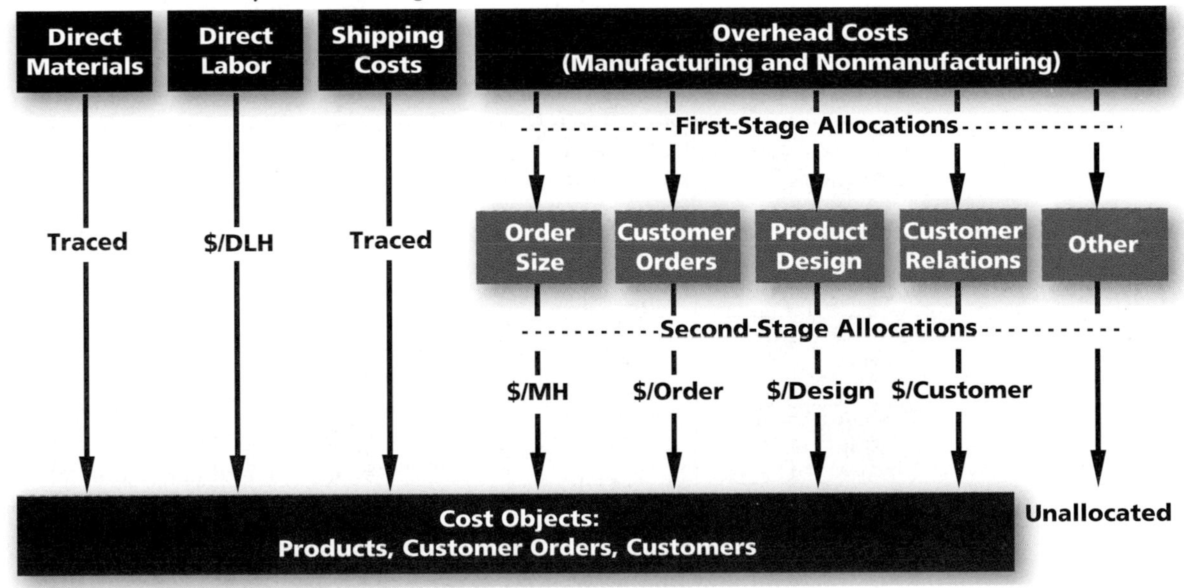

that you carefully go over this exhibit. In particular, note that the Other category, which contains organization-sustaining costs and costs of idle capacity, is not allocated to products or customers.

Targeting Process Improvements

Activity-based costing can be used to identify areas that would benefit from process improvements. Indeed, managers often cite this as the major benefit of activity-based costing.[6] When used in this way, activity-based costing is often called *activity-based management*. Basically, **activity-based management (ABM)** focuses on managing activities as a way of eliminating waste and reducing delays and defects. Activity-based management is used in organizations as diverse as manufacturing companies, hospitals, and the U.S. Marine Corps.[7] When "forty percent of the cost of running a hospital involves storing, collecting and moving information," there is obviously a great deal of room for eliminating waste and for improvement.[8]

The first step in any improvement program is to decide what to improve. The theory of constraints approach discussed in Chapter 1 is a powerful tool for targeting the area in an organization whose improvement will yield the greatest benefit. Activity-based management provides another approach. The activity rates computed in activity-based costing can provide valuable clues concerning where there is waste and scope for improvement in an organization. For example, managers at Classic Brass were surprised at the high cost of customer orders. Some customer orders are for less than $100 worth of products, and yet it costs, on average, $315 to process an order according to the activity rates calculated in Exhibit 8–5. This seemed like an awful lot of money for an activity that adds no value to the product. As a consequence, the customer order processing activity was targeted for improvement using TQM and process reengineering as discussed in Chapter 1.

Benchmarking provides a systematic approach to identifying the activities with the greatest room for improvement. For example, the Marketing Resources Group of US WEST, the telephone company, performed an ABC analysis of the activities carried out in the Accounting Department.[9] Managers computed the activity rates for the activities of the Accounting Department and then compared these rates to the costs of carrying out the same activities in other companies. Two benchmarks were used: (1) a sample of FORTUNE 100 companies, which are the largest 100 companies in the United States; and (2) a sample of "world-class" companies that had been identified by a consultant as having the best accounting practices in the world. These comparisons appear below:

Activity	Activity Measure	US WEST Cost	FORTUNE 100 Benchmark	World-Class Benchmark
Processing accounts receivable	Number of invoices processed	$3.80 per invoice	$15.00 per invoice	$4.60 per invoice
Processing accounts payable	Number of invoices processed	$8.90 per invoice	$7.00 per invoice	$1.80 per invoice
Processing payroll checks	Number of checks processed	$7.30 per check	$5.00 per check	$1.72 per check
Managing customer credit	Number of customer accounts	$12.00 per account	$16.00 per account	$5.60 per account

6. Dan Swenson, "The Benefits of Activity-Based Cost Management to the Manufacturing Industry," *Journal of Management Accounting Research*, 7 (Fall 1995), pp. 168–80.
7. Julian Freeman, "Marines Embrace Continuous Improvement: Highlight of CAM-I's Meeting," *Management Accounting*, February 1997, p. 64.
8. Kambiz Foroohar, "Rx: Software," *Forbes*, April 7, 1997, p. 114.
9. Steve Coburn, Hugh Grove, and Cynthia Fukami, "Benchmarking with ABCM," *Management Accounting*, January 1995, pp. 56–60.

It is clear from this analysis that US WEST does a good job of processing accounts receivables. Its average cost per invoice is $3.80, whereas the cost in other companies that are considered world class is even higher—$4.60 per invoice. On the other hand, the cost of processing payroll checks is significantly higher at US WEST than at benchmark companies. The cost per payroll check at US WEST is $7.30 versus $5.00 at FORTUNE 100 companies and $1.72 at world-class companies. This suggests that it may be possible to wring some waste out of this activity using TQM, process reengineering, or some other method.

Focus on Current Practice

Dayton Technologies is a business unit within Deceunich Plastic Industries, NV that produces components for vinyl window manufacturers. Like other manufacturers, the company had relied on a traditional costing system for many years. This traditional costing system had obscured the causes of overhead and opportunities for improvement. Managers at the company report that "[d]uring the [ABC] implementation process, we achieved a greater awareness of value-added versus nonvalue-added activities. Employees began to question parts of their jobs they simply performed out of habit." The high costs revealed by the ABC system of carrying out some activities "led to actions that reduced redundancies, eliminated tasks, and combined steps to simplify and reduce troubleshooting by improving training."[10] ■

Assigning Costs to Cost Objects

objective 5

Assign costs to a cost object using a second-stage allocation.

The fifth step in the implementation of activity-based costing is called *second-stage allocation*. In the **second-stage allocation**, activity rates are used to apply costs to products and customers. At Classic Brass, the ABC system might be used to apply activity costs to all of the company's products, customer orders, and customers. For purposes of illustration, we will consider only one customer—Windward Yachts. This customer ordered two different products—stanchions and a compass housing. The stanchions are a standard product that does not require any design work. In contrast, the compass housing is a custom product that required extensive designing. Data concerning these two products appear in Exhibit 8–7.

Overhead Costs Computed Using the ABC System

Direct materials and direct labor costs are the same under the old traditional cost accounting system and the new ABC system. However, the two systems handle overhead very differently.

The overhead calculations for the stanchions and compass housings are carried out in Exhibits 8–8A and 8–8B, respectively. Let's examine the ABC overhead calculations for the stanchions in Exhibit 8–8A. First note that none of the Customer

10. Neal R. Pemberton, Logan Arumugam, and Nabil Hassan, "ABM at Dayton Technologies: From Obstacles to Opportunities," *Management Accounting*, March 1996, p. 24.

Exhibit 8–7 Data concerning the Products Ordered by Windward Yachts

Standard Stanchions

1. This is a standard design that does not require any new design resources.
2. Four hundred units were ordered during the year, comprising two separate orders.
3. Each stanchion required 0.5 machine-hour, for a total of 200 machine-hours.
4. The selling price per unit was $34, for a total of $13,600.
5. Direct materials for 400 units totaled $2,110.
6. Direct labor for 400 units totaled $1,850.
7. Shipping costs for the two orders totaled $180.

Custom Compass Housing

1. This is a custom product that requires new design resources.
2. There was only one order for a single unit during the year.
3. The compass housing required 4 machine-hours.
4. The selling price was $650.
5. Direct materials was $13.
6. Direct labor was $50.
7. Shipping costs were $25.

Relations costs have been allocated to the stanchions. A customer-level cost is assigned to customers directly; it is not assigned to products. The activities required to fill the two orders for stanchions totaling 400 units are listed across the top of the exhibit. Since this is a standard product, no new designing is required and hence no design costs are allocated to the order. However, there are two orders, so each of the activity rates under the Customer Orders column in Exhibit 8–5 is multiplied by 2 to determine the Customer Orders costs for this product. For example, the activity rate for indirect factory wages for Customer Orders in Exhibit 8–5 is $125 per order. Since there are two orders, 2 × $125 = $250 is allocated to this product and appears as the first entry under the Customer Orders column in Exhibit 8–8A. Similarly, the activity rate for factory equipment depreciation for Customer Orders in Exhibit 8–5 is $60 per order. Since there are two orders, the product is charged $120. This appears as the second entry under Customer Orders in Exhibit 8–8A.

As with Exhibit 8–5, we urge you to study Exhibits 8–8A and 8–8B carefully to make sure you know how each entry in the table was computed. Take each column in turn and multiply each of the activity rates in Exhibit 8–5 under that column by the total activity at the top of the column in Exhibit 8–8A (and 8–8B). As before, once you see how the numbers are computed, it is not difficult, although there are a lot of computations.

Product Margins Computed Using the ABC System

objective 6

Prepare a report showing activity-based costing product margins from an activity view.

In Exhibit 8–9, the overhead costs computed from Exhibits 8–8A and 8–8B are combined with direct materials, direct labor, and shipping cost data. For each of the products, these combined costs are deducted from sales to arrive at product margins. Under the ABC system, the stanchions show a profit of $5,030, whereas the compass housing shows a loss of $1,114.

Note from Exhibit 8–9 that the new ABC system also includes a profitability analysis of Windward Yachts, the customer that ordered the stanchions and the custom compass housing. Such customer analyses can be easily accomplished by adding together the product margins for each of the products a customer has ordered and then subtracting the average charge of $3,675 for Customer Relations.

Exhibit 8–8A
Computation of the Overhead Cost of Two Orders for Standard Stanchions Totaling Four Hundred Units

	A	B	C	D	E	F
1		Activity Cost Pools				
2		Customer Orders	Product Design	Order Size	Customer Relations	Total (action analysis)
3	Total activity for stanchions:	2 orders	No new designing	200 machine-hours	NA	
4	Production Department:					
5	Indirect factory wages	$ 250	$ 0	$ 1,000	$ 0	$ 1,250
6	Factory equipment depreciation	120	0	1,800	0	1,920
7	Factory utilities	0	0	600	0	600
8	Factory building lease	0	0	0	0	0
9	General Administrative Department:					
10	Administrative wages and salaries	120	0	400	0	520
11	Office equipment depreciation	30	0	0	0	30
12	Administrative building lease	0	0	0	0	0
13	Marketing Department:					
14	Marketing wages and salaries	100	0	0	0	100
15	Selling expenses	10	0	0	0	10
16	Totals (activity view)	$ 630	$ 0	$ 3,800	$ 0	$ 4,430

Exhibit 8–5 shows an activity rate of $125 for indirect factory wages for the Customer Orders cost pool.

$125 per order × 2 orders = $250

Other entries in the table are computed in a similar fashion.

NA = Not applicable.

Exhibit 8–8B
Computation of the Overhead Cost of One Order for One Unit of the Custom Compass Housing

	A	B	C	D	E	F
1		Activity Cost Pools				
2		Customer Orders	Product Design	Order Size	Customer Relations	Totals (action analysis)
3	Total activity for compass housings	1 order	1 new design	4 machine-hours	NA	
4						
5	Production Department:					
6	Indirect factory wages	$ 125	$ 1,000	$ 20	$ 0	$ 1,145
7	Factory equipment depreciation	60	0	36	0	96
8	Factory utilities	0	60	12	0	72
9	Factory building lease	0	0	0	0	0
10	General Administrative Department:					
11	Administrative wages and salaries	60	100	8	0	168
12	Office equipment depreciation	15	0	0	0	15
13	Administrative building lease	0	0	0	0	0
14	Marketing Department:					
15	Marketing wages and salaries	50	125	0	0	175
16	Selling expenses	5	0	0	0	5
17	Totals (activity view)	$ 315	$ 1,285	$ 76	$ 0	$ 1,676

Exhibit 8–5 shows an activity rate of $125 for indirect factory wages for the Customer Orders cost pool.

$125 per order × 1 order = $125

Other entries in the table are computed in a similar fashion.

NA = Not applicable.

Exhibit 8–9 Product Margins—Activity-Based Costing System (Activity View)

	A	B	C
1	**Standard Stanchions**		
2	Sales (see Exhibit 8–7)		$ 13,600
3	Cost:		
4	Direct materials (see Exhibit 8–7)	$ 2,110	
5	Direct labor (see Exhibit 8–7)	1,850	
6	Shipping costs (see Exhibit 8–7)	180	
7	Customer orders (see Exhibit 8–8A)	630	
8	Product design (no new design required)	0	
9	Order size (see Exhibit 8–8A)	3,800	8,570
10	Product margin		$ 5,030
11			
12	**Custom Compass Housing**		
13	Sales (see Exhibit 8–7)		$ 650
14	Cost:		
15	Direct materials (see Exhibit 8–7)	$ 13	
16	Direct labor (see Exhibit 8–7)	50	
17	Shipping costs (see Exhibit 8–7)	25	
18	Customer orders (see Exhibit 8–8B)	315	
19	Product design (see Exhibit 8–8B)	1,285	
20	Order size (see Exhibit 8–8B)	76	1,764
21	Product margin		$ (1,114)
22			
23	**Customer Profitability Analysis—Windward Yachts**		
24	Product margins of products ordered by Windward Yachts:		
25	Standard stanchion product margin (see above)		$ 5,030
26	Custom compass housing product margin (see above)		(1,114)
27	Total product margins		3,916
28	Less: Customer relations overhead (see Exhibit 8–5)		3,675
29	Customer margin		$ 241

Comparison of Traditional and ABC Product Costs

Now that the product margins have been computed using activity-based costing, it would be interesting to compare them to the product margins computed using the company's traditional cost system.

Product Margins Computed Using the Traditional Cost System

The costs of the two products ordered by Windward Yachts are computed under the company's traditional cost accounting system in Exhibit 8–10. The company's traditional system uses a plantwide predetermined overhead rate based on machine-hours. Since the total manufacturing overhead cost is $1,000,000 (see Exhibit 8–2) and the total machine time is 20,000 machine-hours (see Exhibit 8–5), the predetermined manufacturing overhead rate for the company is $50 per machine-hour ($1,000,000 ÷ 20,000 machine-hours = $50 per machine-hour). From Exhibit 8–10, we see that when this predetermined manufacturing overhead rate is used to determine product costs, the stanchions show a loss of $360, whereas the compass housing shows a profit of $387.

The Differences between ABC and Traditional Product Costs

The costs of the products under the new ABC system are dramatically different from the costs computed using the old traditional costing system. The stanchions, which looked

Exhibit 8–10 Product Margins—Traditional Cost Accounting System

Standard Stanchions		
Margin computed using the company's old cost accounting system:		
Sales (400 units × $34)		$13,600
Cost:		
Direct materials	$ 2,110	
Direct labor	1,850	
Manufacturing overhead (400 units × 0.5 machine-hours per unit × $50 per machine-hour*)	10,000	13,960
Product margin		$ (360)
Custom Compass Housing		
Margin computed using the company's old cost accounting system:		
Sales (1 unit × $650)		$ 650
Cost:		
Direct materials	13	
Direct labor	50	
Manufacturing overhead (1 unit × 4.0 machine-hours per unit × $50 per machine-hour*)	200	263
Product margin		$ 387

* Predetermined manufacturing overhead rate:

$$\frac{\text{Total manufacturing overhead, \$1,000,000}}{\text{Total machine-hours, 20,000}} = \text{\$50 per machine-hour}$$

unprofitable under the traditional cost system, appear to be very profitable under the ABC system in Exhibit 8–9. And the compass housing, which looked profitable under the old cost system, appears to be unprofitable under the new costing system.

There are two major reasons for these changes in apparent profitability. First, under the old cost system the costs of designing products were spread across all products without regard to whether they actually required design work. Under the new ABC system, these costs are assigned only to products that actually require design work. Consequently, under the ABC system, design costs have been shifted from standard products like stanchions, which do not require any design work, to custom products like the compass housing.

Second, the Customer Orders costs, which are batch-level costs, were applied on the basis of machine-hours, a unit-level base, under the old cost system. Therefore, under the old cost system, high-volume products absorbed the bulk of these batch-level costs even though they caused no more of these costs than low-volume products that are ordered as frequently. Under the new cost system, these batch-level costs are assigned as a lump-sum to each customer order. Consequently, the new cost system shifts these costs from high-volume orders like the stanchions to low-volume orders like the compass housing.

When there are batch-level or product-level costs, activity-based costing will ordinarily shift costs from high-volume products produced in large batches to low-volume products produced in small batches. This cost shifting will usually have a greater impact on the *per unit* costs of low-volume products than on the per unit costs of high-volume products. For example, suppose that a total of $100 in batch-level cost is shifted from a high-volume, 100-unit product to a low-volume, 1-unit product. This shifting of cost will decrease the cost of the high-volume product by $1 per unit, on average, but will increase the cost of the low-volume product by $100 for the single unit. In sum, implementing activity-based costing will typically shift costs from high-volume to low-volume products, but the effects will be much more dramatic on the per unit costs of the low-volume products. The per unit costs of the low-volume products will increase far more than the per unit costs of the high-volume products will decrease.

It is important to remember another major difference between the costs of products as computed under the new ABC system at Classic Brass and product costs as computed under the old traditional cost system. Under a traditional system, only manufacturing costs are assigned to products. Under the new ABC system at Classic Brass, nonmanufacturing costs are assigned to products as well as the manufacturing costs. In addition, the organization-sustaining manufacturing costs and the costs of idle capacity are *not* assigned to products under the ABC system, whereas they *are* assigned to products under the old traditional costing system. For these reasons, the term *product cost* in this chapter has a different meaning than it had in Chapters 2, 3, and 4. In the context of an ABC system like the one implemented at Classic Brass, product costs include the costs of *all* resources consumed by the product, whether they are manufacturing costs or not.

Focus on Current Practice

The shift in overhead cost between products can be very great when activity-based costing is introduced. For many years, Hewlett-Packard assigned overhead cost to products on the basis of material cost. When the company introduced activity-based costing, one circuit board that would have been assigned about $5 in overhead cost under the old system was now assigned about $25—a 400% increase. Another circuit board that would have been assigned $123 in overhead cost under the old system was assigned only $45 under the ABC system.[11]

This shift in overhead cost between products can have a significant companywide impact. Two observers of the Hewlett-Packard experience report the following: "During a recent six-month forecast and budget cycle, the ABC system resulted in shifting millions of dollars of cost between customers and products and thus had a dramatic impact on pricing and product design decisions."[12] ■

ABC Product Costs—An Action Analysis

objective 7

Prepare an action analysis report using activity-based costing data and interpret the report.

The sixth step in implementing an ABC system is preparing management reports. The activity view of product and customer margins, as illustrated in Exhibit 8–9, may be one of those reports. However, the overhead computations in Exhibits 8–8A and 8–8B allow another view of the ABC product costs that emphasizes who in the organization is responsible for the costs and how easy it would be to actually adjust the costs in the event that the products were dropped. To help in this supplemental analysis, the ABC team applied a simple color coding scheme to the company's costs.

Ease of Adjustment Codes

The ABC team constructed Exhibit 8–11 to aid managers in the use of the ABC data. In this exhibit, each cost has been assigned an *ease of adjustment code*—Green,

11. C. Mike Merz and Arlene Hardy, "ABC Puts Accountants on Design Team at HP," *Management Accounting*, September 1993, p. 24.
12. Ibid., p. 25.

Exhibit 8–11 Ease of Adjustment Codes

Green: *Costs that adjust automatically to changes in activity without management action.*

- Direct materials
- Shipping costs

Yellow: *Costs that could, in principle, be adjusted to changes in activity, but management action would be required.*

- Direct labor
- Indirect factory wages
- Factory utilities
- Administrative wages and salaries
- Office equipment depreciation
- Marketing wages and salaries
- Selling expenses

Red: *Costs that would be very difficult to adjust to changes in activity and management action would be required.*

- Factory equipment depreciation
- Factory building lease
- Administrative building lease

Yellow, or Red. The **ease of adjustment code** reflects how easily the cost could be adjusted to changes in activity.[13] "Green" costs are those costs that would adjust more or less automatically to changes in activity without any action by managers. For example, direct materials costs would adjust to changes in orders without any action being taken by managers. If a customer does not order stanchions, the direct materials for the stanchions would not be required and would not be ordered. "Yellow" costs are those costs that could be adjusted in response to changes in activity, but such adjustments require management action; the adjustment is not automatic. The ABC team believes, for example, that direct labor costs should be included in the Yellow category. Managers must make difficult decisions and take explicit action to increase or decrease, in aggregate, direct labor costs—particularly since the company has a no layoff policy. "Red" costs are costs that could be adjusted to changes in activity only with a great deal of difficulty, and the adjustment would require management action. The building leases fall into this category, since it would be very difficult and expensive to break the leases.

The Action Analysis View of the ABC Data

Looking at Exhibit 8–8B, the totals on the right-hand side of the table indicate that the \$1,676 of overhead cost for the custom housing consists of \$1,145 of indirect factory wages, \$96 of factory equipment depreciation, and so on. These data are displayed in Exhibit 8–12, which shows an *action analysis* of the custom compass housing product. An **action analysis report** is a report showing what costs have been assigned to the cost object, such as a product or customer, and how difficult it would be to adjust the cost if there is a change in activity. Note that the Red margin at the bottom of Exhibit 8–12, (\$1,114), is exactly the same as the product margin for the custom compass housing in Exhibit 8–9.

13. The idea of using colors to code how easily costs can be adjusted was suggested to us at a seminar put on by Boeing and by an article by Alfred King, "Green Dollars and Blue Dollars: The Paradox of Cost Reduction," *Journal of Cost Management,* Fall 1993, pp. 44–52.

Exhibit 8–12 Action Analysis of Custom Compass Housing: Activity-Based Costing System

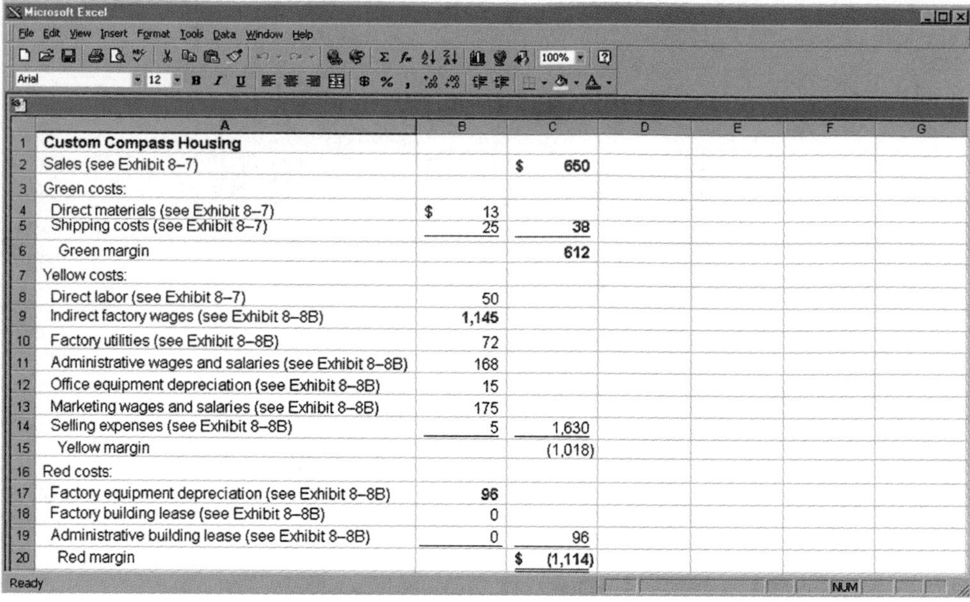

	A	B	C
1	**Custom Compass Housing**		
2	Sales (see Exhibit 8–7)		$ 650
3	Green costs:		
4	Direct materials (see Exhibit 8–7)	$ 13	
5	Shipping costs (see Exhibit 8–7)	25	38
6	Green margin		612
7	Yellow costs:		
8	Direct labor (see Exhibit 8–7)	50	
9	Indirect factory wages (see Exhibit 8–8B)	1,145	
10	Factory utilities (see Exhibit 8–8B)	72	
11	Administrative wages and salaries (see Exhibit 8–8B)	168	
12	Office equipment depreciation (see Exhibit 8–8B)	15	
13	Marketing wages and salaries (see Exhibit 8–8B)	175	
14	Selling expenses (see Exhibit 8–8B)	5	1,630
15	Yellow margin		(1,018)
16	Red costs:		
17	Factory equipment depreciation (see Exhibit 8–8B)	96	
18	Factory building lease (see Exhibit 8–8B)	0	
19	Administrative building lease (see Exhibit 8–8B)	0	96
20	Red margin		$ (1,114)

The cost data in the action analysis in Exhibit 8–12 are arranged by the color coded ease of adjustment. All of the Green costs—those that adjust more or less automatically to changes in activity—appear together at the top of the list of costs. These costs total $38 and are subtracted from the sales of $650 to yield a Green margin of $612. The same procedure is followed for the Yellow and Red costs. This action analysis indicates exactly what costs would have to be cut and how difficult it would be to cut them if the custom compass housing product were dropped. Prior to making any decision about dropping products, the managers responsible for the costs must agree to either eliminate the resources represented by those costs or to transfer the resources to an area in the organization that really needs the resources—namely, a constraint. If managers do not make such a commitment, it is likely that the costs would continue to be incurred. As a result, the company would lose the sales from the products without really saving the costs.

Managerial Accounting in Action

THE WRAP-UP

The ABC design team presented the results of its work in a meeting attended by all of the top managers of Classic Brass, including the president John Towers, the production manager Susan Richter, the marketing manager Tom Olafson, and the accounting manager Mary Goodman. The ABC team brought with them to the meeting copies of the chart showing the ABC design (Exhibit 8–6), the tables showing the product margins for the stanchions and compass housing under the company's old cost accounting system (Exhibit 8–7), the tables showing the ABC analysis of the same products (Exhibit 8–9), and the action analysis (Exhibit 8–12). After the formal presentation by the ABC team, the following discussion took place:

John: I would like to personally thank the ABC team for all of the work they have done and for an extremely interesting presentation. I am now beginning to wonder about a lot of the decisions we have made in the past using our old cost accounting system.

Mary: I hope I don't have to remind anyone that I have been warning everyone for quite some time about this problem.

John: No, you don't have to remind us Mary. I guess we just didn't understand the problem before.
John: Tom, why did we accept this order for standard stanchions in the first place if our old cost accounting system was telling us it was a big money loser?
Tom: Windward Yachts, the company that ordered the stanchions, has asked us to do a lot of custom work like the compass housing in the past. To get that work, we felt we had to accept their orders for money-losing standard products.
John: According to this ABC analysis, we had it all backwards. We are losing money on the custom products and making a fistful on the standard products.
Susan: I never did believe we were making a lot of money on the custom jobs. You ought to see all of the problems they create for us in production.
Tom: I hate to admit it, but the custom jobs always seem to give us headaches in marketing too.
John: Why don't we just stop soliciting custom work? This seems like a no-brainer to me. If we are losing money on custom jobs like the compass housing, why not suggest to our customers that they go elsewhere for that kind of work?
Tom: Wait a minute, we would lose a lot of sales.
Susan: So what, we would save a lot more costs.
Mary: Maybe yes, maybe no. Some of the costs would not disappear if we were to drop all of those products.
Tom: Like what?
Mary: Well Tom, part of your salary is included in the costs of the ABC model.
Tom: Where? I don't see anything listed that looks like my salary.
Mary: Tom, when the ABC team interviewed you they asked you what percentage of your time was spent in handling customer orders and how much was spent dealing with new product design issues. Am I correct?
Tom: Sure, but what's the point?
Mary: I believe you said that about 10% of your time is spent dealing with new products. As a consequence, 10% of your salary was allocated to the Product Design cost pool. If we were to drop all of the products requiring design work, would you be willing to take a 10% pay cut?
Tom: I trust you're joking.
Mary: Do you see the problem? Just because 10% of your time is spent on custom products doesn't mean that the company would save 10% of your salary if the custom products were dropped. Before we take a drastic action like dropping the custom products, we should identify which costs are really relevant.
John: I think I see what you are driving at. We wouldn't want to drop a lot of products just to find that our costs really haven't changed much. It is true that dropping the products would free up resources like Tom's time, but we had better be sure we have some good use for those resources *before* we take such an action.
Mary: That's why we put together the action analysis.
John: What's this red margin at the bottom of the action analysis? Isn't that a product margin?
Mary: Yes, it is. However, we call it a red margin because we should *stop* and think very, very carefully before taking any actions based on that margin.
John: Why is that?

Mary: We subtracted the costs of factory equipment depreciation to arrive at that red margin. We doubt that we could avoid any of that cost if we were to drop custom orders. We use the same machines on custom orders that we use on standard products. The factory equipment has no resale value, and it does not wear out through use.
John: What about this yellow margin?
Mary: Yellow means proceed with a great deal of caution. To get to the yellow margin we deducted from sales a lot of costs that could be adjusted only if the managers involved are willing to eliminate resources or shift them elsewhere in the organization.
John: If I understand the yellow margin correctly, the apparent loss of $1,018 on the custom stanchions is the result of the indirect factory wages of $1,145.
Susan: Right, that's basically the wages of our design engineers.
John: I wouldn't want to lay off any of our designers. Could we turn them into salespersons?
Tom: I'd love to have Shueli Park join our marketing team.
Susan: No way, she's our best designer.
John: Okay, I get the picture. We are not going to be cutting anyone's wages, we aren't going to be laying off anyone, and it looks like we may have problems getting agreement about moving people around. Where does that leave us?
Mary: What about raising prices on our custom products?
Tom: We should be able to do that. We have been undercutting the competition to make sure we got custom work. We were doing that because we thought custom work was very profitable.
John: Why don't we just charge directly for design work?
Tom: Some of our competitors already charge for design work. However, I don't think we would be able to charge enough to cover our design costs.
John: What about design work, can we do anything to make it more efficient so it costs us less? I'm not going to lay anyone off, but if we make the design process more efficient, we could lower the charge for design work and spread those costs across more customers.
Susan: That may be possible. I'll form a TQM team to look at it.
John: Let's get some benchmark data on design costs. If we set our minds to it, I'm sure we can be world class in no time.
Susan: Okay. Mary, will you help with the benchmark data?
Mary: Sure.
Tom: There is another approach we can take too. Windward Yachts probably doesn't really need a custom compass housing. One of our standard compass housings would work just fine. If we start charging for the design work, I think they will see that it would be in their own interests to use the lower-cost standard product.
John: Let's meet again in about a week to discuss our progress. Is there anything else on the agenda for today? ■

The points raised in the preceding discussion are extremely important. By measuring the resources consumed by products (and other cost objects), a "best practice" ABC system provides a much better basis for decision making than a traditional cost accounting system that spreads overhead costs around without much regard for what might be causing the overhead. A well-designed ABC system provides managers with estimates of potentially relevant costs that can be a very useful starting point for management analysis.

Activity-Based Costing and External Reports

Since activity-based costing generally provides more accurate product costs than traditional costing methods, why isn't it used for external reports? Some companies *do* use activity-based costing in their external reports, but most do not. There are a number of reasons for this. First, external reports are less detailed than internal reports prepared for decision making. On the external reports, individual product costs are not reported. Cost of goods sold and inventory valuations are disclosed, but there is no breakdown of these accounts by product. If some products are undercosted and some are overcosted, the errors tend to cancel each other when the product costs are added together.

Second, it is often very difficult to make changes in a company's accounting system. The official cost accounting systems in most large companies are usually embedded in complex computer programs that have been modified in-house over the course of many years. It is extremely difficult to make changes in such computer programs without causing numerous bugs.

Third, an ABC system such as the one described in this chapter does not conform to generally accepted accounting principles (GAAP). As discussed in Chapter 2, product costs computed for external reports must include all of the manufacturing costs and only manufacturing costs; but in an ABC system as described in this chapter, product costs exclude some manufacturing costs and include some nonmanufacturing costs. It is possible to adjust the ABC data at the end of the period to conform to GAAP, but that requires more work.

Fourth, auditors are likely to be uncomfortable with allocations that are based on interviews with the company's personnel. Such subjective data can be easily manipulated by management to make earnings and other key variables look more favorable.

For all of these reasons, most companies confine their ABC efforts to special studies for management, and they do not attempt to integrate activity-based costing into their formal cost accounting systems.

A Simplified Approach to Activity-Based Costing

objective 8

Use the simplified approach to compute activity-based costs and margins.

If an action analysis like Exhibit 8–12 is not prepared, the process of computing product margins under activity-based costing can be considerably simplified. The first-stage allocation shown in Exhibit 8–4 is still necessary, but the remainder of the computations can be streamlined.

To use the simplified approach after the first-stage allocation is completed, compute activity rates for each activity cost pool as follows:

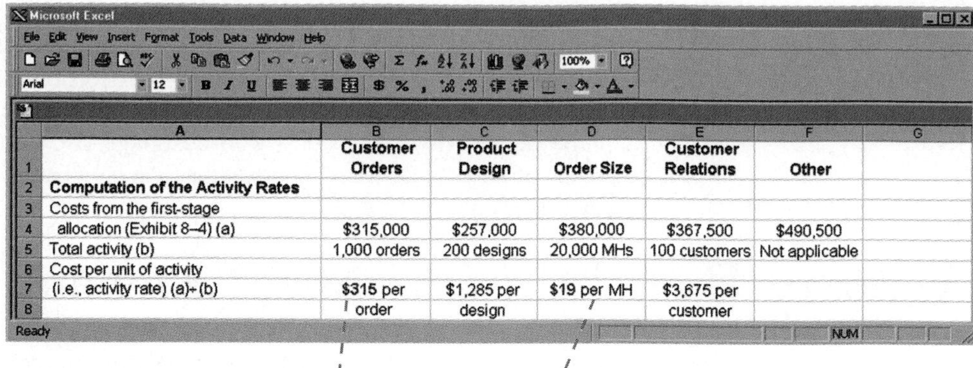

	Customer Orders	Product Design	Order Size	Customer Relations	Other
Computation of the Activity Rates					
Costs from the first-stage allocation (Exhibit 8–4) (a)	$315,000	$257,000	$380,000	$367,500	$490,500
Total activity (b)	1,000 orders	200 designs	20,000 MHs	100 customers	Not applicable
Cost per unit of activity (i.e., activity rate) (a) ÷ (b)	$315 per order	$1,285 per design	$19 per MH	$3,675 per customer	

Note that these activity rates are exactly the same as the activity rates at the bottom of Exhibit 8–5. If there is to be no activity analysis, the other numbers in Exhibit 8–5 are not needed and do not have to be computed.

Using these activity rates, the product and customer margins can be directly computed as follows:

Standard Stanchions		
Sales (see Exhibit 8–7)		$ 13,600
Cost:		
Direct materials (see Exhibit 8–7)	$ 2,110	
Direct labor (see Exhibit 8–7)	1,850	
Shipping costs (see Exhibit 8–7)	180	
Customer orders (2 orders @ $315 per order)	630	
Product design (no new design required)	0	
Order size (200 MHs @ $19 per MH)	3,800	8,570
Product margin		$ 5,030
Custom Compass Housing		
Sales (see Exhibit 8–7)		$ 650
Cost:		
Direct materials (see Exhibit 8–7)	$ 13	
Direct labor (see Exhibit 8–7)	50	
Shipping costs (see Exhibit 8–7)	25	
Customer orders (1 order @ $315 per order)	315	
Product design (1 design @ $1,285 per design)	1,285	
Order size (4 MHs @ $19 per MH)	76	1,764
Product margin		$ (1,114)

Customer Profitability Analysis—Windward Yachts	
Product margins of products ordered by Windward Yachts:	
Standard stanchion product margin (see above)	$ 5,030
Custom compass housing product margin (see above)	(1,114)
Total product margins	3,916
Less: Customer relations overhead (see above)	3,675
Customer margin	$ 241

Note that the numbers in this report match the numbers that appear in Exhibit 8–9. This simplified approach allows one to compute product and customer margins without having to do the detailed computations in all of the cells of Exhibit 8–5 and Exhibits 8–8A and 8–8B. However, this simplified approach does not provide the data that are needed to construct an action analysis.

Exhibit 8–13 How the ABC Steps Fit Together

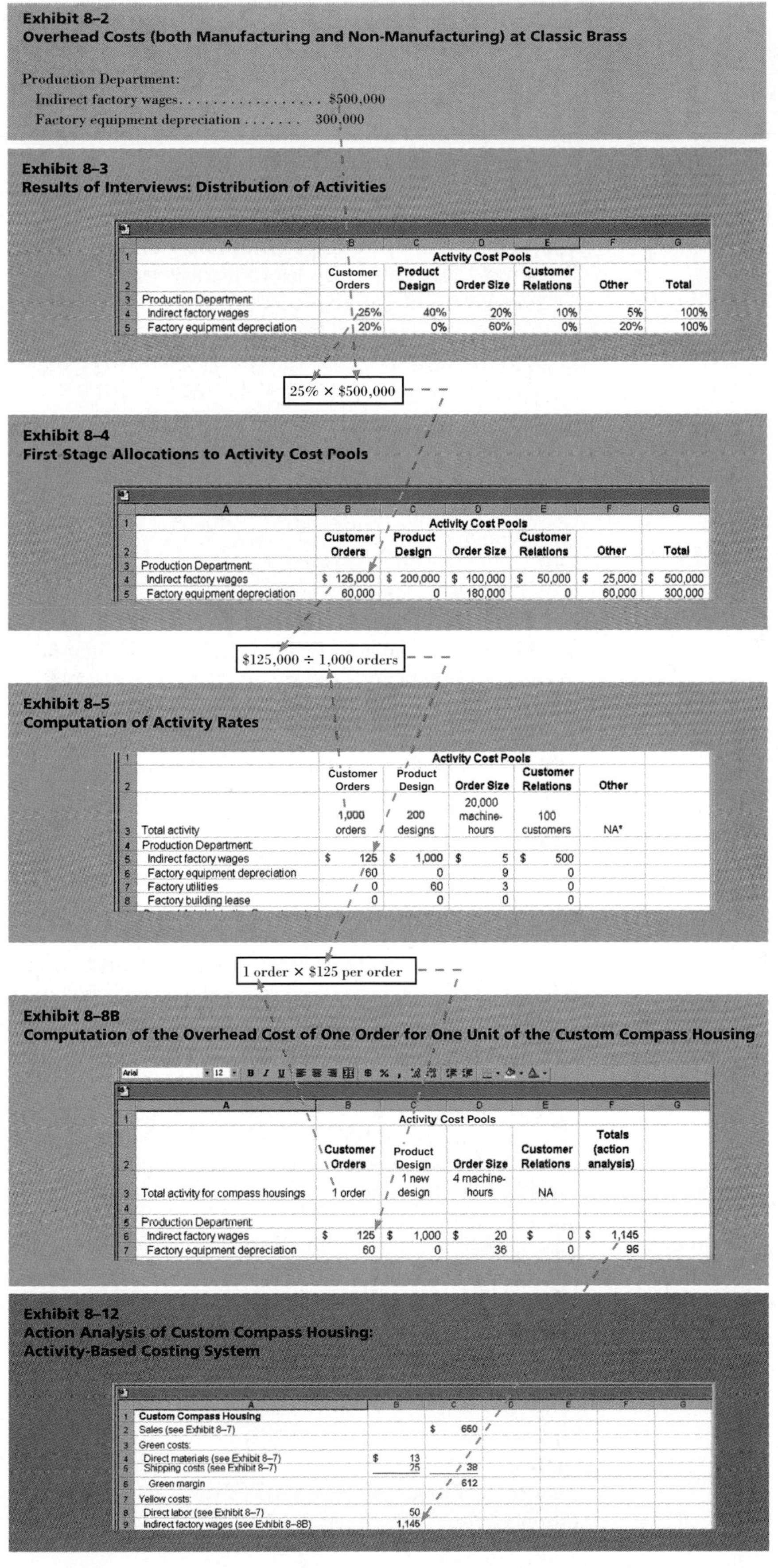

Exhibit 8–2
Overhead Costs (both Manufacturing and Non-Manufacturing) at Classic Brass

Production Department:
Indirect factory wages $500,000
Factory equipment depreciation 300,000

Exhibit 8–3
Results of Interviews: Distribution of Activities

	Activity Cost Pools					
	Customer Orders	Product Design	Order Size	Customer Relations	Other	Total
Production Department:						
Indirect factory wages	25%	40%	20%	10%	5%	100%
Factory equipment depreciation	20%	0%	60%	0%	20%	100%

25% × $500,000

Exhibit 8–4
First Stage Allocations to Activity Cost Pools

	Activity Cost Pools					
	Customer Orders	Product Design	Order Size	Customer Relations	Other	Total
Production Department:						
Indirect factory wages	$ 125,000	$ 200,000	$ 100,000	$ 50,000	$ 25,000	$ 500,000
Factory equipment depreciation	60,000	0	180,000	0	60,000	300,000

$125,000 ÷ 1,000 orders

Exhibit 8–5
Computation of Activity Rates

	Activity Cost Pools				
	Customer Orders	Product Design	Order Size	Customer Relations	Other
Total activity	1,000 orders	200 designs	20,000 machine-hours	100 customers	NA*
Production Department:					
Indirect factory wages	$ 125	$ 1,000	$ 5	$ 500	
Factory equipment depreciation	60	0	9	0	
Factory utilities	0	60	3	0	
Factory building lease	0	0	0	0	

1 order × $125 per order

Exhibit 8–8B
Computation of the Overhead Cost of One Order for One Unit of the Custom Compass Housing

	Activity Cost Pools				
	Customer Orders	Product Design	Order Size	Customer Relations	Totals (action analysis)
Total activity for compass housings	1 order	1 new design	4 machine-hours	NA	
Production Department:					
Indirect factory wages	$ 125	$ 1,000	$ 20	$ 0	$ 1,145
Factory equipment depreciation	60	0	36	0	96

Exhibit 8–12
Action Analysis of Custom Compass Housing:
Activity-Based Costing System

Custom Compass Housing		
Sales (see Exhibit 8–7)		$ 650
Green costs:		
Direct materials (see Exhibit 8–7)	$ 13	
Shipping costs (see Exhibit 8–7)	25	38
Green margin		612
Yellow costs:		
Direct labor (see Exhibit 8–7)	50	
Indirect factory wages (see Exhibit 8–8B)	1,145	

Focus on Current Practice

Bertch Cabinet Mfg., Inc., makes high-quality wooden cabinets, marble tops, and mirrors for bathrooms and kitchens. The company experimented with activity-based costing (ABC) but found that it was too difficult to set up and maintain such a complex costing system. For example, 21 separate operations are required to make a single raised panel cabinet door. The costs of keeping track of each of these operations would far exceed any conceivable benefit. Instead of building a complex ABC system, Bertch Cabinet adopted a variation of variable costing used in the Theory of Constraints. This simpler system required far less effort to build and maintain, and it was much easier to understand. In the Bertch Cabinet Mfg. variable costing system, 70% of the direct labor cost was classified as variable and the rest as fixed.[14] ■

Summary

Traditional cost accounting methods suffer from several defects that can result in distorted costs for decision-making purposes. All manufacturing costs—even those that are not caused by any specific product—are allocated to products. And nonmanufacturing costs that are caused by products are not assigned to products. Traditional methods also allocate the costs of idle capacity to products. In effect, products are charged for resources that they don't use. And finally, traditional methods tend to place too much reliance on unit-level allocation bases such as direct labor and machine-hours. This results in overcosting high-volume products and undercosting low-volume products and can lead to mistakes when making decisions.

Activity-based costing estimates the costs of the resources consumed by cost objects such as products and customers. The approach taken in activity-based costing assumes that cost objects generate activities that in turn consume costly resources. Activities form the link between costs and cost objects. Activity-based costing is concerned with overhead—both manufacturing overhead and selling, general, and administrative overhead. The accounting for direct labor and direct material is usually unaffected.

The steps that are involved in computing ABC product costs are summarized in Exhibit 8–13. Use this exhibit to trace through the key exhibits in the chapter.

To build an ABC system, companies typically choose a small set of activities that summarize much of the work performed in overhead departments. Associated with each activity is an activity cost pool. To the extent possible, overhead costs are directly traced to these activity cost pools. The remaining overhead costs are assigned to the activity cost pools in the first-stage allocation. Interviews with managers often form the basis for these allocations.

An activity rate is computed for each cost pool by dividing the costs assigned to the cost pool by the measure of activity for the cost pool. Activity rates provide useful information to managers concerning the costs of carrying out overhead activities. A particularly high cost for an activity may trigger efforts to improve the way the activity is carried out in the organization.

14. John B. MacArthur, "From Activity-Based Costing to Throughput Accounting," *Management Accounting,* April 1996, pp. 30–38.

In the second-stage allocation, the activity rates are used to apply costs to cost objects such as products and customers. The costs computed under activity-based costing are often quite different from the costs generated by a company's traditional cost accounting system. While the ABC system is almost certainly more accurate, managers should nevertheless exercise caution before making decisions based on the ABC data. A vital part of any activity-based analysis of product or customer profitability is an action analysis that identifies who is ultimately responsible for each cost and the ease with which the cost can be adjusted.

Review Problem: Activity-Based Costing

Ferris Corporation makes a single product—a fire-resistant commercial filing cabinet—that it sells to office furniture distributors. The company has a simple ABC system that it uses for internal decision making. The company has two overhead departments whose costs are listed below:

Manufacturing overhead	$500,000
Selling and administrative overhead	300,000
Total overhead costs	$800,000

The company's ABC system has the following activity cost pools and activity measures:

Activity Cost Pool	Activity Measure
Volume related	Number of units
Order related	Number of orders
Customer support	Number of customers
Other	Not applicable

Costs assigned to the "Other" activity cost pool have no activity measure; they consist of the costs of unused capacity and organization-sustaining costs—neither of which are assigned to products, orders, or customers.

Ferris Corporation distributes the costs of manufacturing overhead and of selling and administrative overhead to the activity cost pools based on employee interviews, the results of which are reported below:

Distribution of Resource Consumption Across Activities

	Volume Related	Order Related	Customer Support	Other	Total
Manufacturing overhead	50%	35%	5%	10%	100%
Selling and administrative overhead	10%	45%	25%	20%	100%
Total activity	1,000 units	250 orders	100 customers		

Required

1. Perform the first-stage allocations of overhead costs to the activity cost pools as in Exhibit 8–4.
2. Compute activity rates for the activity cost pools as in Exhibit 8–5.
3. OfficeMart is one of Ferris Corporation's customers. Last year, OfficeMart ordered filing cabinets four different times. OfficeMart ordered a total of 80 filing cabinets during the year. Construct a table as in Exhibit 8–8A showing the overhead costs of these 80 units and four orders.
4. The selling price of a filing cabinet is $595. The cost of direct materials is $180 per filing cabinet, and direct labor is $50 per filing cabinet. What is the product margin on the 80 filing cabinets ordered by OfficeMart? How profitable is OfficeMart as a customer? See Exhibit 8–9 for an example of how to complete this report.
5. Management of Ferris Corporation has assigned ease of adjustment codes to the various costs as follows:

Cost	Ease of Adjustment Code
Direct materials	Green
Direct labor	Yellow
Manufacturing overhead	Yellow
Selling and administrative overhead	Red

Prepare an activity analysis of the OfficeMart orders as in Exhibit 8–12.

Solution to Review Problem

1. The first-stage allocation of costs to the activity cost pools appears below:

	Activity Cost Pools				
	Volume Related	Order Related	Customer Support	Other	Total
Manufacturing overhead	$250,000	$175,000	$ 25,000	$ 50,000	$500,000
Selling and administrative overhead	30,000	135,000	75,000	60,000	300,000
Total cost	$280,000	$310,000	$100,000	$110,000	$800,000

2. The activity rates for the activity cost pools are:

	Volume Related	Order Related	Customer Support
Manufacturing overhead	$250	$ 700	$ 250
Selling and administrative overhead	30	540	750
Total cost	$280	$1,240	$1,000

3. The overhead cost for the four orders of a total of 80 filing cabinets would be computed as follows:

	Volume Related	Order Related	Total
Activity	80 units	4 orders	
Manufacturing overhead	$20,000	$2,800	$22,800
Selling and administrative overhead	2,400	2,160	4,560
Total cost	$22,400	$4,960	$27,360

4. The product and customer margins can be computed as follows:

Filing Cabinet Product Margin

Sales ($595 × 80)		$47,600
Cost:		
Direct materials ($180 × 80)	$14,400	
Direct labor ($50 × 80)	4,000	
Volume-related overhead (above)	22,400	
Order-related overhead (above)	4,960	45,760
Product margin		$ 1,840

Customer Profitability Analysis—OfficeMart

Product margin (above)	$ 1,840
Less: Customer support overhead (above)	1,000
Customer margin	$ 840

5. The activity analysis of the four orders for 80 filing cabinets in total is:

Action Analysis Report for Four Orders Totaling 80 Units

Sales		$47,600
Green costs:		
Direct materials	$14,400	14,400
Green margin		33,200
Yellow costs:		
Direct labor	4,000	
Manufacturing overhead	22,800	26,800
Yellow margin		6,400
Red costs:		
Selling and administrative overhead	4,560	4,560
Red margin		$ 1,840

Note: An action analysis report can also be completed for OfficeMart as a customer. The first step would be to calculate the overhead costs for OfficeMart as follows:

	Volume Related	Order Related	Customer Support	Total
Activity	80 units	4 orders	1 customer	
Manufacturing overhead	$20,000	$2,800	$ 250	$23,050
Selling and administrative overhead	2,400	2,160	750	5,310
Total cost	$22,400	$4,960	$1,000	$28,360

The action analysis report can then be easily prepared as follows:

Action Analysis Report for OfficeMart as a Customer

Sales		$47,600
Green costs:		
Direct materials	$14,400	14,400
Green margin		33,200
Yellow costs:		
Direct labor	4,000	
Manufacturing overhead	23,050	27,050
Yellow margin		6,150
Red costs:		
Selling and administrative overhead	5,310	5,310
Red margin		$ 840

Key Terms for Review

Action analysis report A report showing what costs have been assigned to a cost object, such as a product or customer, and how difficult it would be to adjust the cost if there is a change in activity. (p. 343)

Activity An event that causes the consumption of overhead resources in an organization. (p. 324)

Activity-based costing (ABC) A costing method based on activities that is designed to provide managers with cost information for strategic and other decisions that potentially affect capacity and therefore fixed costs. (p. 322)

Activity-based management (ABM) A management approach that focuses on managing activities as a way of eliminating waste and reducing delays and defects. (p. 336)

Activity cost pool A "bucket" in which costs are accumulated that relate to a single activity in the activity-based costing system. (p. 329)

Activity measure An allocation base in an activity-based costing system; ideally, a measure of the amount of activity that drives the costs in an activity cost pool. (p. 329)

Batch-level activities Activities that are performed each time a batch of goods is handled or processed, regardless of how many units are in a batch. The amount of resource consumed depends on the number of batches run rather than on the number of units in the batch. (p. 329)

Customer-level activities Activities that are carried out to support customers but that are not related to any specific product. (p. 329)

Ease of adjustment codes Costs are coded as Green, Yellow, or Red—depending on how easily the cost could be adjusted to changes in activity. "Green" costs adjust automatically to changes in activity without any action by managers. "Yellow" costs could be adjusted in response to changes in activity, but such adjustments require management action; the adjustment is not automatic. "Red" costs could be adjusted to changes in activity only with a great deal of difficulty and the adjustment would require management action. (p. 343)

First-stage allocation The process by which overhead costs are assigned to activity cost pools in an activity-based costing system. (p. 332)

Organization-sustaining activities Activities that are carried out regardless of which customers are served, which products are produced, how many batches are run, or how many units are made. (p. 329)

Product-level activities Activities that relate to specific products that must be carried out regardless of how many units are produced and sold or batches run. (p. 329)

Second-stage allocation The process by which activity rates are used to apply costs to products and customers in activity-based costing. (p. 337)

Unit-level activities Activities that arise as a result of the total volume of goods and services that are produced, and that are performed each time a unit is produced. (p. 328)

Questions

8–1 In what fundamental ways does activity-based costing differ from traditional costing methods such as those described in Chapters 2 and 3?

8–2 Why is direct labor a poor base for allocating overhead in many companies?

8–3 Why are overhead rates in activity-based costing based on the level of activity at capacity rather than on the budgeted level of activity?

8–4 Why is top management support crucial when attempting to implement an activity-based costing system?

8–5 What are unit-level, batch-level, product-level, customer-level, and organization-sustaining activities?

8–6 What types of costs should not be assigned to products in an activity-based costing system?

8–7 Why are there two stages of allocation in activity-based costing?

8–8 Why is the first stage of the allocation process in activity-based costing often based on interviews?

8–9 How can the activity rates (i.e., cost per activity) for the various activities be used to target process improvements?

8–10 When activity-based costing is used, why are manufacturing overhead costs often shifted from high-volume products to low-volume products?

8–11 Why should an activity view of product margins such as in Exhibit 8–9 be supplemented with an action analysis such as in Exhibit 8–12 when making decisions about products or customers?

8–12 Why is the activity-based costing described in this chapter probably unacceptable for external financial reports?

Exercises

E8–1 CD Express, Inc., provides CD duplicating services to software companies. The customer provides a master CD from which CD Express makes copies. An order from a customer can be for a single copy or for thousands of copies. Most jobs are broken down into batches to allow smaller jobs, with higher priorities, to have access to the machines.

Below are listed a number of activities carried out at CD Express.

a. Sales representatives' periodic visits to customers to keep them informed about the services provided by CD Express.
b. Ordering labels from the printer for a particular CD.
c. Setting up the CD duplicating machine to make copies from a particular master CD.
d. Loading the automatic labeling machine with labels for a particular CD.
e. Visually inspecting CDs and placing them by hand into protective plastic cases prior to shipping.
f. Preparation of the shipping documents for the order.
g. Periodic maintenance of equipment.
h. Lighting and heating the company's production facility.
i. Preparation of quarterly financial reports.

Required Classify each of the activities above as either a unit-level, batch-level, product-level, customer-level, or organization-sustaining activity. (An order to duplicate a particular CD is a product-level activity.) Assume the order is large enough that it must be broken down into batches.

E8–2 Listed below are a number of activities that you have observed at Ming Company, a manufacturing company. Each activity has been classified as a unit-level, batch-level, product-level, or customer-level activity.

Activity	Level of Activity	Examples of Activity Measures
a. Direct labor workers assemble a product	Unit	
b. Products are designed by engineers	Product	
c. Equipment is set up	Batch	
d. Machines are used to shape and cut materials	Unit	
e. Monthly bills are sent out to regular customers ..	Customer	
f. Materials are moved from the receiving dock to production lines	Batch	
g. All completed units are inspected for defects	Unit	

Required Complete the table by providing examples of activity measures for each activity that could be used to allocate its costs to products or customers.

E8–3 Listed below are a number of activities that you have observed at Vapo Ingman Oy, a Finnish manufacturing company. The company makes a variety of products at its plant outside Helsinki.

a. Machine settings are changed between batches of different products.
b. Parts inventories are maintained in the storeroom. (Each product requires its own unique parts.)
c. Products are milled on a milling machine.
d. New employees are hired by the personnel office.
e. New products are designed.
f. Periodic maintenance is performed on general-purpose production equipment.
g. A bill is sent to a customer who is late in making payments.
h. Yearly taxes are paid on the company's facilities.
i. Purchase orders are issued for materials to be used in production.

Required 1. Classify each of the activities above as either a unit-level, batch-level, product-level, customer-level, or organization-sustaining activity.

2. Where possible, for each activity name one or more activity measures that might be used to assign costs generated by the activity to products or customers.

E8–4 The operations vice president of Security Home Bank has been interested in investigating the efficiency of the bank's operations. She has been particularly concerned about the costs of handling routine transactions at the bank and would like to compare these costs at the bank's various branches. If the branches with the most efficient operations can be identified, their methods can be studied and then replicated elsewhere. While the bank maintains meticulous records of wages and other costs, there has been no attempt thus far to show how those costs are related to the various services provided by the bank. The operations vice president has asked your help in conducting an activity-based costing study of bank operations. In particular, she would like to know the cost of opening an account, the cost of processing deposits and withdrawals, and the cost of processing other customer transactions.

The Westfield branch of Security Home Bank has submitted the following cost data for last year:

Teller wages	$160,000
Assistant branch manager salary	75,000
Branch manager salary	80,000
Total	$315,000

Virtually all of the other costs of the branch—rent, depreciation, utilities, and so on—are organization-sustaining costs that cannot be meaningfully assigned to individual customer transactions such as depositing checks.

In addition to the cost data above, the employees of the Westfield branch have been interviewed concerning how their time was distributed last year across the activities included in the activity-based costing study. The results of those interviews appear below:

Distribution of Resource Consumption Across Activities

	Opening Accounts	Processing Deposits and Withdrawals	Processing Other Customer Transactions	Other Activities	Total
Teller wages	5%	65%	20%	10%	100%
Assistant branch manager salary	15%	5%	30%	50%	100%
Branch manager salary	5%	0%	10%	85%	100%

Required Prepare the first-stage allocation for the activity-based costing study. (See Exhibit 8–4 for an example of a first-stage allocation.)

E8–5 (This exercise is a continuation of E8–4; it should be assigned *only* if E8–4 is also assigned.) The manager of the Westfield branch of Security Home Bank has provided the following data concerning the transactions of the branch during the past year:

Activity	Total Activity at the Westfield Branch	
Opening accounts	500	new accounts opened
Processing deposits and withdrawals	100,000	deposits and withdrawals processed
Processing other customer transactions	5,000	other customer transactions processed

The lowest costs reported by other branches for these activities are displayed below:

Activity	Lowest Cost among All Security Home Bank Branches	
Opening accounts	$26.75	per new account
Processing deposits and withdrawals	$ 1.24	per deposit or withdrawal
Processing other customer transactions	$11.86	per other customer transaction

Required

1. Using the first-stage allocation from E8–4 and the above data, compute the activity rates for the activity-based costing system. (Use Exhibit 8–5 as a guide.) Round all computations to the nearest whole cent.
2. What do these results suggest to you concerning operations at the Westfield branch?

E8–6 Durban Metal Products, Ltd., of the Republic of South Africa makes specialty metal parts used in applications ranging from the cutting edges of bulldozer blades to replacement parts for Land Rovers. The company uses an activity-based costing system for internal decision-making purposes. The company has four activity cost pools as listed below:

Activity Cost Pool	Activity Measure
Order size	Number of direct labor-hours
Customer orders	Number of customer orders
Product testing	Number of testing hours
Selling	Number of sales calls

The results of the first-stage allocation of the activity-based costing system, in which the activity rates were computed, appear below:

	Order Size	Customer Orders	Product Testing	Selling
Manufacturing:				
Indirect labor	R 8.25	R180.00	R30.00	R 0.00
Factory depreciation	8.00	0.00	40.00	0.00
Factory utilities	0.10	0.00	1.00	0.00
Factory administration	0.00	48.00	18.00	30.00
General selling and administrative:				
Wages and salaries	0.50	80.00	0.00	800.00
Depreciation	0.00	12.00	0.00	40.00
Taxes and insurance	0.00	0.00	0.00	20.00
Selling expenses	0.00	0.00	0.00	200.00
Total overhead cost	R16.85	R320.00	R89.00	R1,090.00

Note: The currency in South Africa is the Rand, denoted here by R.

The managing director of the company would like information concerning the cost of a recently completed order for heavy-duty trailer axles. The order required 200 direct labor-hours, 4 hours of product testing, and 2 sales calls.

Required

1. Prepare a report showing the overhead cost of the order for heavy-duty trailer axles according to the activity-based costing system. (Use Exhibit 8–8A as a guide.) What is the total overhead cost of the order according to the activity-based costing system?
2. Explain the two different perspectives this report gives to managers concerning the nature of the overhead costs involved in the order. (Hint: Look at the row and column totals of the report you have prepared.)

E8–7 Foam Products, Inc., makes foam seat cushions for the automotive and aerospace industries. The company's activity-based costing system has four activity cost pools, which are listed below:

Activity Cost Pool	Activity Measure
Volume	Number of direct labor-hours
Batch processing	Number of batches
Order processing	Number of orders
Customer service	Number of customers

The activity rates for the cost pools have been computed as follows:

	Activity Rates			
	Volume	Batch Processing	Order Processing	Customer Service
Production overhead:				
Indirect labor	$0.60	$ 60.00	$ 20.00	$ 0.00
Factory equipment depreciation	4.00	17.00	0.00	0.00
Factory administration	0.10	7.00	25.00	150.00
General selling and administrative overhead:				
Wages and salaries	0.40	20.00	160.00	1,600.00
Depreciation	0.00	3.00	10.00	38.00
Marketing expenses	0.45	0.00	60.00	675.00
Total	$5.55	$107.00	$275.00	$2,463.00

The company just completed a single order from Interstate Trucking for 1,000 custom seat cushions. The order was produced in two batches. Each seat cushion required 0.25 direct labor-hours. The selling price was $20 per unit, the direct materials cost was $8.50 per unit, and the direct labor cost was $6.00 per unit. This was Interstate Trucking's only order during the year.

Required

1. Prepare a report showing the product margin for this order from an activity viewpoint. (Use the product report in Exhibit 8–9 as a guide.) At this point, ignore the customer service costs.
2. Prepare a report showing the customer margin on sales to Interstate Trucking from an activity viewpoint. (Use the customer profitability analysis in Exhibit 8–9 as a guide.)

E8–8 Refer to the data for Foam Products, Inc., in E8–7. In addition, management has provided their ease of adjustment codes for purposes of preparing action analyses.

	Ease of Adjustment Codes
Direct materials	Green
Direct labor	Yellow
Production overhead:	
Indirect labor	Yellow
Factory equipment depreciation	Red
Factory administration	Red
General selling and administrative:	
Wages and salaries	Red
Depreciation	Red
Marketing expenses	Yellow

Required Prepare an action analysis report on the order from Interstate Trucking. (Use the report in Exhibit 8–12 as a guide.) Ignore the customer service costs.

E8–9 Refer to the data for Foam Products, Inc., in E8–7 and E8–8. Management would like an action analysis report for the customer similar to those prepared for products, but it is unsure of how this can be done. The customer service cost of $2,463 could be deducted directly from the product margin for the order, but this would obscure how much of the customer service cost consists of Green, Yellow, and Red costs.

Required Prepare an action analysis report that shows the profitability of sales to Interstate Trucking during the year. The best way to proceed is to prepare an analysis of overhead costs as in Exhibit 8–8A but include the customer service costs in the analysis.

E8–10 Advanced Products Corporation has supplied the following data from its activity-based costing system:

Overhead Costs	
Wages and salaries	$300,000
Other overhead costs	100,000
Total overhead costs	$400,000

Activity Cost Pool	Activity Measure	Total Activity for the Year
Volume related	Number of direct labor-hours	20,000 DLHs
Order related	Number of customer orders	400 orders
Customer support	Number of customers	200 customers
Other	These costs are not allocated to products or customers	Not applicable

Distribution of Resource Consumption Across Activities

	Volume Related	Order Related	Customer Support	Other Activities	Total
Wages and salaries	40%	30%	20%	10%	100%
Other overhead costs	30%	10%	20%	40%	100%

During the year, Advanced Products completed one order for a new customer, Shenzhen Enterprises. This customer did not order any other products during the year. Data concerning that order follow:

Data concerning the Shenzhen Enterprises Order	
Units ordered	10 units
Direct labor-hours per unit	2 DLHs
Selling price	$300 per unit
Direct materials	$180 per unit
Direct labor	$ 50 per unit

Required

1. Prepare a report showing the first-stage allocations of overhead costs to the activity cost pools. (Use Exhibit 8–4 as a guide.)
2. Compute the activity rates for the activity cost pools. (Use Exhibit 8–5 as a guide.)
3. Prepare a report showing the overhead costs for the order from Shenzhen Enterprises. (Use Exhibit 8–8A as a guide. Do not include the customer support costs at this point in the analysis.)
4. Prepare a report from the activity viewpoint showing the product margin for the order and the customer margin for Shenzhen Enterprises. (Use Exhibit 8–9 as a guide.)
5. Prepare an action analysis of the order from Shenzhen Enterprises. (Use Exhibit 8–12 as a guide.) For purposes of this report, direct materials should be coded as a Green cost, direct labor and wages and salaries as Yellow costs, and other overhead costs as a Red cost.

E8–11 Hiram's Lakeside is a popular restaurant located on Lake Washington in Seattle. The owner of the restaurant has been trying to better understand costs at the restaurant and has hired a student intern to conduct an activity-based costing study. The intern, in consultation with the owner, identified the following major activities:

Activity Cost Pool	Activity Measure
Serving a party of diners	Number of parties served
Serving a diner	Number of diners served
Serving drinks	Number of drinks ordered

A group of diners who ask to sit at the same table are counted as a party. Some costs, such as the costs of cleaning linen, are the same whether one person is at a table or the table is full. Other costs, such as washing dishes, depend on the number of diners served.

Data concerning last month's operations are displayed below. The intern has already completed the first-stage allocations of costs to the activity cost pools.

	Serving a Party	Serving a Diner	Serving Drinks	Total
Total cost	$33,000	$138,000	$24,000	$195,000
Total activity	6,000 parties	15,000 diners	10,000 drinks	

The above costs include all of the costs of the restaurant except for organization-sustaining costs such as rent, property taxes, and top-management salaries.

Prior to the activity-based costing study, the owner knew very little about the costs of the restaurant. She knew that the total cost for the month (including organization-sustaining costs) was $240,000 and that 15,000 diners had been served. Therefore, the average cost per diner was $16.

Required

1. According to the activity-based costing system, what is the total cost of serving each of the following parties of diners? (You can use the simplified approach described at the end of the chapter.)
   a. A party of four diners who order three drinks in total.
   b. A party of two diners who do not order any drinks.
   c. A lone diner who orders two drinks.
2. Convert the total costs you computed in (1) above to costs per diner. In other words, what is the average cost per diner for serving each of the following parties of diners?
   a. A party of four diners who order three drinks in total.
   b. A party of two diners who do not order any drinks.
   c. A lone diner who orders two drinks.
3. Why do the costs per diner for the three different parties differ from each other and from the overall average cost of $16 per diner?

Problems

P8–12 Activity Rates and Pricing Jobs Mercer Asbestos Removal Company is in the business of removing potentially toxic asbestos insulation and related products from buildings. There has been a long-simmering dispute between the company's estimator and the work supervisors. The on-site supervisors claim that the estimators do not take enough care in distinguishing between routine work such as removal of asbestos insulation around heating pipes in older homes and nonroutine work such as removing asbestos-contaminated ceiling plaster in industrial buildings. The on-site supervisors believe that nonroutine work is far more expensive than routine work and should bear higher customer charges. The estimator sums up his position in this way: "My job is to measure the area to be cleared of asbestos. As directed by top management, I simply multiply the square footage by $2.50 to determine the bid price. Since our average cost is only $2.175 per square foot, that leaves enough cushion to take care of the additional costs of nonroutine work that shows up. Besides, it is difficult to know what is routine or not routine until you actually start tearing things apart."

Partly to shed light on this controversy, the company initiated an activity-based costing study of all of its costs. Data from the activity-based costing system follow:

Activity Cost Pool	Activity Measure
Job size	Thousands of square feet
Estimating and job setup	Number of jobs
Dealing with nonroutine jobs	Number of nonroutine jobs
Other (costs of idle capacity and organization-sustaining costs)	Not applicable; these costs are not allocated to jobs

Costs for the Year

Wages and salaries	$ 300,000
Disposal fees	700,000
Equipment depreciation	90,000
On-site supplies	50,000
Office expenses	200,000
Licensing and insurance	400,000
Total cost	$1,740,000

Distribution of Resource Consumption Across Activities

	Job Size	Estimating and Job Setup	Dealing with Nonroutine Jobs	Other	Total
Wages and salaries	50%	10%	30%	10%	100%
Disposal fees	60%	0%	40%	0%	100%
Equipment depreciation	40%	5%	20%	35%	100%
On-site supplies	60%	30%	10%	0%	100%
Office expenses	10%	35%	25%	30%	100%
Licensing and insurance	30%	0%	50%	20%	100%

Activity Cost Pool	Activity for the Year
Job size	800 thousand square feet
Estimating and job setup	500 jobs
Dealing with nonroutine jobs	100 nonroutine jobs

Note: The 100 nonroutine jobs are included in the total of 500 jobs. Both nonroutine jobs and routine jobs require estimating and setup.

Required

1. Perform the first-stage allocation of costs to the activity cost pools. (Use Exhibit 8–4 as a guide.)
2. Compute the activity rates for the activity cost pools. (Use Exhibit 8–5 as a guide or the simpler approach described at the end of the chapter.)
3. Using the activity rates you have computed, determine the total cost and the average cost per thousand square feet of each of the following jobs according to the activity-based costing system. (You will not be able to do an activity analysis because the ease of adjustment codes have not been provided.)
   a. A routine 1,000-square-foot asbestos removal job.
   b. A routine 2,000-square-foot asbestos removal job.
   c. A nonroutine 2,000-square-foot asbestos removal job.
4. Given the results you obtained in (3) above, do you agree with the estimator that the company's present policy for bidding on jobs is adequate?

P8–13 Action Analysis of a Market Pixel Studio, Inc., is a small company that creates computer-generated animations for films and television. Much of the company's work consists of short commercials for television, but the company also does realistic computer animations for special effects in movies.

The young founders of the company have become increasingly concerned with the economics of the business—particularly since many competitors have sprung up recently in the local area. To help understand the company's cost structure, an activity-based costing system has been designed. Three major activities are carried out in the company: animation concept, animation production, and contract administration. The animation concept activity is carried out at the contract proposal stage when the company bids on projects. This is an intensive activity that involves individuals from all parts of the company in creating story boards and prototype stills to be shown to the prospective client. Once a project is accepted by the client, the animation goes into production and contract administration begins. Almost all of the work involved in animation production is done by the technical staff, whereas the administrative staff is largely responsible for contract administration. The activity cost pools and their activity measures are listed below:

Activity Cost Pool	Activity Measure
Animation concept	Number of proposals
Animation production	Minutes of completed animation
Contract administration	Number of contracts

The first-stage allocation has already been completed and the activity rates have been computed. These activity rates appear below:

	Activity Rates		
	Animation Concept	Animation Production	Contract Administration
Technical staff salaries	$4,000	$ 6,000	$1,600
Animation equipment depreciation	360	1,125	–0–
Administrative wages and salaries .	1,440	150	4,800
Supplies costs	120	300	160
Facility costs	120	150	240
Total cost	$6,040	$7,725	$6,800

These activity rates include all of the costs of the company, except for the costs of idle capacity and organization-sustaining costs.

Preliminary analysis using these activity rates has indicated that the local commercial segment of the market may be unprofitable. This segment is highly competitive. Producers of local commercials may ask three or four companies like Pixel Studio to bid, which results in an unusually low ratio of accepted contracts to bids. Furthermore, the animation sequences tend to be much shorter for local commercials than for other work. Since animation work is billed at fairly standard rates according to the running time of the completed animation, this means that the revenues from these short projects tend to be below average. Data concerning activity appear below:

Activity Measure	Total Activity	Local Commercials
Number of proposals	50	25
Minutes of completed animation	80	5
Number of contracts	25	10

The total sales from the 10 contracts for local commercials was $180,000.

Required

1. Determine the cost of the local commercial market according to the activity-based costing system using Exhibit 8–8A as a guide. (Think of the local commercial market as a product.)
2. Prepare a report showing the margin from the local commercial market using the product margin report in Exhibit 8–9 as a guide. (This company has no direct materials or direct labor costs. All of the company's costs have been included in the activity-based costing system.)
3. Prepare an action analysis report concerning the local commercial market using Exhibit 8–12 as a guide. For this purpose, management has coded the various costs as follows:

	Ease of Adjustment Code
Technical staff salaries	Red
Animation equipment depreciation	Red
Administrative wages and salaries	Yellow
Supplies costs	Green
Facility costs	Red

There was some controversy in the company concerning these codes. In particular, some administrators objected to coding their own salaries Yellow, while the technical staff salaries were coded Red. However, the founders of the firm squashed these objections by pointing out that "our technical staff are our most valuable assets. Good animators are extremely difficult to find, and they would be the last to go if we had to cut back."

4. What would you recommend to management concerning the local commercial market?

P8–14 Activity-Based Costing as an Alternative to Traditional Product Costing: Simplified Method This chapter emphasizes the use of activity-based costing in internal decisions. However, a modified form of activity-based costing can also be used to develop product costs for external financial reports. For this purpose, product costs include all manufacturing overhead costs and exclude all nonmanufacturing costs. This problem illustrates such a costing system.

Ellix Company manufactures two models of ultra-high fidelity speakers, the X200 model and the X99 model. Data regarding the two products follow:

Product	Direct Labor-Hours per Unit	Annual Production	Total Direct Labor-Hours
X200	1.8	5,000 units	9,000
X99	0.9	30,000 units	27,000
			36,000

Additional information about the company follows:

a. Model X200 requires $72 in direct materials per unit, and model X99 requires $50.
b. The direct labor rate is $10 per hour.
c. The company has always used direct labor-hours as the base for applying manufacturing overhead cost to products.
d. Model X200 is more complex to manufacture than model X99 and requires the use of special equipment.
e. Because of the special work required in (d) above, the company is considering the use of activity-based costing to apply manufacturing overhead cost to products for external financial reports. Three activity cost pools have been identified as follows:

Activity Cost Pool	Activity Measure	Estimated Overhead Cost
Machine setups	Number of setups	$ 360,000
Special processing	Machine-hours	180,000
General factory	Direct labor-hours	1,260,000
		$1,800,000

Activity Measure	Expected Activity Model X200	Model X99	Total
Number of setups	50	100	150
Machine-hours	12,000	–0–	12,000
Direct labor-hours	9,000	27,000	36,000

Required

1. Assume that the company continues to use direct labor-hours as the base for applying overhead cost to products.
   a. Compute the predetermined overhead rate.
   b. Compute the unit product cost of each model.
2. Assume that the company decides to use activity-based costing to apply manufacturing overhead cost to products. (You can use the simplified approach described at the end of the chapter.)
   a. Compute the predetermined overhead rate for each activity cost pool and determine the amount of overhead cost that would be applied to each model using the activity-based costing system.
   b. Compute the unit product cost of each model.
3. Explain why manufacturing overhead cost shifted from the high-volume model to the low-volume model under activity-based costing.

P8–15 Activity Rates and Activity-Based Management Aerotraiteur SA is a French company that provides passenger and crew meals to airlines operating out of the two international airports of Paris—Orly and Charles de Gaulle (CDG). The operations at Orly and CDG are managed separately, and top management believes that there may be benefits to greater sharing of information between the two operations.

To better compare the two operations, an activity-based costing system has been designed with the active participation of the managers at both Orly and CDG. The activity-based costing system is based on the following activity cost pools and activity measures:

Activity Cost Pool	Activity Measure
Meal preparation	Number of meals
Flight-related activities	Number of flights
Customer service	Number of customers
Other (costs of idle capacity and organization-sustaining costs) . . .	Not applicable

The operation at CDG airport serves 1.5 million meals annually on 7,500 flights for 10 different airlines. (Each airline is considered one customer.) The annual cost of running the CDG airport operation, excluding only the costs of raw materials for meals, totals 29,400,000 FF.

Note: The currency in France at the time of the activity-based costing study was the franc, denoted here by FF.

Annual Cost of the CDG Operation

Cooks and delivery personnel wages . .	24,000,000 FF
Kitchen supplies	300,000
Chef salaries	1,800,000
Equipment depreciation	600,000
Administrative wages and salaries	1,500,000
Building costs	1,200,000
Total cost	29,400,000 FF

The results of employee interviews at CDG are displayed below:

Distribution of Resource Consumption Across Activities at the CDG Operation

	Meal Preparation	Flight Related	Customer Service	Other	Total
Cooks and delivery personnel wages . .	75%	20%	0%	5%	100%
Kitchen supplies	100%	0%	0%	0%	100%
Chef salaries	30%	20%	40%	10%	100%
Equipment depreciation	60%	0%	0%	40%	100%
Administrative wages and salaries . . .	0%	20%	60%	20%	100%
Building costs	0%	0%	0%	100%	100%

Required

1. Perform the first-stage allocation of costs to the activity cost pools. (Use Exhibit 8–4 as a guide.)
2. Compute the activity rates for the activity cost pools. (Use Exhibit 8–5 as a guide.)
3. The Orly operation has already concluded its activity-based costing study and has reported the following costs of carrying out activities at Orly:

	Meal Preparation	Flight Related	Customer Service
Cooks and delivery personnel wages	12.20 FF	780 FF	
Kitchen supplies	0.25		
Chef salaries	0.18	32	54,000 FF
Equipment depreciation	0.23		
Administrative wages and salaries		45	67,000
Building costs	0.00	0	0
Total cost	12.86 FF	857 FF	122,000 FF

Comparing the activity rates for the CDG operation you computed in (2) above to the activity rates for Orly, do you have any suggestions for the top management of Aerotraiteur SA?

P8–16 Activity-Based Costing as an Alternative to Traditional Product Costing: Simplified Method This chapter emphasizes the use of activity-based costing in internal decisions. However, a modified form of activity based costing can also be used to develop product costs for external financial reports. For this purpose, product costs include all manufacturing overhead costs and exclude all nonmanufacturing costs. This problem illustrates such a costing system.

Siegel Company manufactures a product that is available in both a deluxe model and a regular model. The company has manufactured the regular model for years. The deluxe model was introduced several years ago to tap a new segment of the market. Since introduction of the deluxe model, the company's profits have steadily declined and management has become increasingly concerned about the accuracy of its costing system. Sales of the deluxe model have been increasing rapidly.

Manufacturing overhead is assigned to products on the basis of direct labor-hours. For the current year, the company has estimated that it will incur $900,000 in manufacturing overhead cost and produce 5,000 units of the deluxe model and 40,000 units of the regular model. The deluxe model requires two hours of direct labor time per unit, and the regular model requires one hour. Material and labor costs per unit are as follows:

	Model	
	Deluxe	Regular
Direct materials	$40	$25
Direct labor	14	7

Required

1. Using direct labor-hours as the base for assigning overhead cost to products, compute the predetermined overhead rate. Using this rate and other data from the problem, determine the unit product cost of each model.
2. Management is considering using activity-based costing to apply manufacturing overhead cost to products for external financial reports. The activity-based costing system would have the following four activity cost centers:

Activity Cost Pool	Activity Measure	Estimated Overhead Cost
Purchasing	Purchase orders issued	$204,000
Processing	Machine-hours	182,000
Scrap/rework	Scrap/rework orders issued	379,000
Shipping	Number of shipments	135,000
		$900,000

Activity Measure	Expected Activity		
	Deluxe	Regular	Total
Purchase orders issued	200	400	600
Machine-hours	20,000	15,000	35,000
Scrap/rework orders issued	1,000	1,000	2,000
Number of shipments	250	650	900

Using the simplified approach described at the end of the chapter, determine the predetermined overhead rate for each of the four activity cost pools.

3. Using the predetermined overhead rates you computed in (2) above, do the following:
   a. Compute the total amount of manufacturing overhead cost that would be applied to each model using the activity-based costing system. After these totals have been computed, determine the amount of manufacturing overhead cost per unit of each model.
   b. Compute the unit product cost of each model.
4. From the data you have developed in (1) through (3) above, identify factors that may account for the company's declining profits.

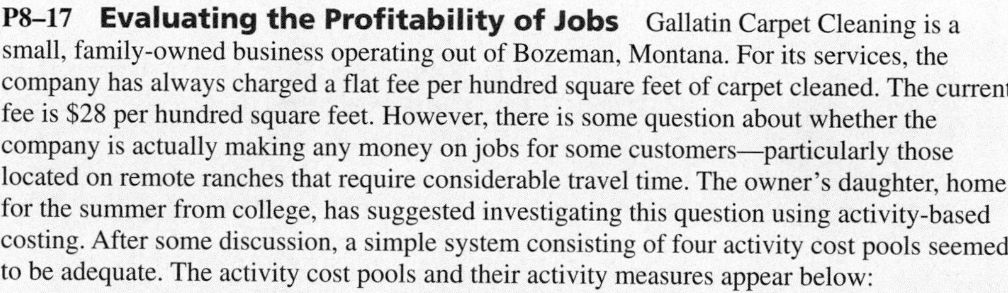

P8–17 Evaluating the Profitability of Jobs Gallatin Carpet Cleaning is a small, family-owned business operating out of Bozeman, Montana. For its services, the company has always charged a flat fee per hundred square feet of carpet cleaned. The current fee is $28 per hundred square feet. However, there is some question about whether the company is actually making any money on jobs for some customers—particularly those located on remote ranches that require considerable travel time. The owner's daughter, home for the summer from college, has suggested investigating this question using activity-based costing. After some discussion, a simple system consisting of four activity cost pools seemed to be adequate. The activity cost pools and their activity measures appear below:

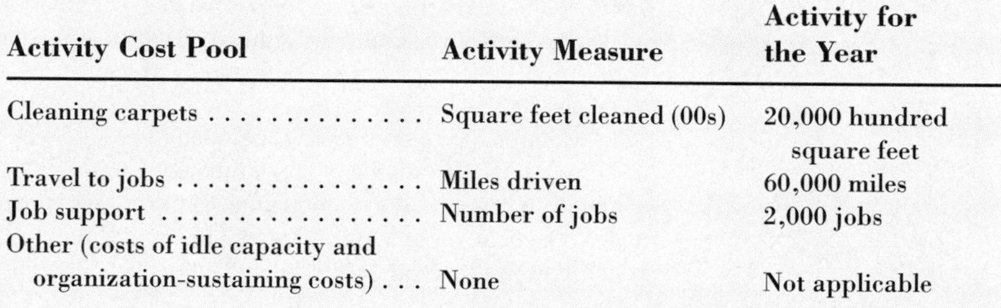

Activity Cost Pool	Activity Measure	Activity for the Year
Cleaning carpets	Square feet cleaned (00s)	20,000 hundred square feet
Travel to jobs	Miles driven	60,000 miles
Job support	Number of jobs	2,000 jobs
Other (costs of idle capacity and organization-sustaining costs)	None	Not applicable

The total cost of operating the company for the year is $430,000, which includes the following costs:

Wages	$150,000
Cleaning supplies	40,000
Cleaning equipment depreciation	20,000
Vehicle expenses	80,000
Office expenses	60,000
President's compensation	80,000
Total cost	$430,000

Resource consumption is distributed across the activities as follows:

Distribution of Resource Consumption Across Activities

	Cleaning Carpets	Travel to Jobs	Job Support	Other	Total
Wages	70%	20%	0%	10%	100%
Cleaning supplies	100%	0%	0%	0%	100%
Cleaning equipment depreciation	80%	0%	0%	20%	100%
Vehicle expenses	0%	60%	0%	40%	100%
Office expenses	0%	0%	45%	55%	100%
President's compensation	0%	0%	40%	60%	100%

Job support consists of receiving calls from potential customers at the home office, scheduling jobs, billing, resolving issues, and so on.

Required

1. Prepare the first-stage allocation of costs to the activity cost pools. (Use Exhibit 8–4 as a guide.)
2. Compute the activity rates for the activity cost pools. (Use Exhibit 8–5 as a guide.)
3. The company recently completed a 500 square foot carpet cleaning job at the Flying N ranch—a 75-mile round-trip journey from the company's offices in Bozeman. Compute the cost of this job using the activity-based costing system. (Use Exhibit 8–8A as a guide.)
4. The revenue from the Flying N ranch was $140 (5 hundred square feet @ $28 per hundred square feet). Prepare a report showing the margin from this job from an activity view. (Use Exhibit 8–9 as a guide. Think of the job as a product.)
5. Prepare an action analysis report of the Flying N ranch job. (Use Exhibit 8–12 as a guide.) The president of Gallatin Carpet Cleaning considers all of the company's costs to be Green costs except for office expenses, which is coded Yellow, and his own compensation, which is coded Red. The people who do the actual carpet cleaning are all trained part-time workers who are paid only for work actually done.
6. What do you conclude concerning the profitability of the Flying N ranch job? Explain.
7. What advice would you give the president concerning pricing jobs in the future?

P8–18 Activity-Based Costing as an Alternative to Traditional Product Costing: Simplified Method This chapter emphasizes the use of activity-based costing in internal decisions. However, a modified form of activity-based costing can also be used to develop product costs for external financial reports. For this purpose, product costs include all manufacturing overhead costs and exclude all nonmanufacturing costs. This problem illustrates such a costing system.

For many years, Zapro Company manufactured a single product called a mono-relay. Then three years ago, the company automated a portion of its plant and at the same time introduced a second product called a bi-relay which has become increasingly popular. The bi-relay is a more complex product, requiring one hour of direct labor time per unit to manufacture and extensive machining in the automated portion of the plant. The mono-relay requires only 0.75 hour of direct labor time per unit and only a small amount of machining. Manufacturing overhead costs are currently assigned to products on the basis of direct labor-hours.

Despite the growing popularity of the company's new bi-relay, profits have been declining steadily. Management is beginning to believe that there may be a problem with the company's costing system. Material and labor costs per unit are as follows:

	Mono-Relay	Bi-Relay
Direct materials	$35	$48
Direct labor (0.75 hour and 1.0 hour @ $12 per hour)	9	12

Management estimates that the company will incur $1,000,000 in manufacturing overhead costs during the current year and 40,000 units of the mono-relay and 10,000 units of the bi-relay will be produced and sold.

Required

1. Compute the predetermined manufacturing overhead rate assuming that the company continues to apply manufacturing overhead cost on the basis of direct labor-hours. Using this rate and other data from the problem, determine the unit product cost of each product.
2. Management is considering using activity-based costing to apply manufacturing overhead cost to products for external financial reports. The activity-based costing system would have the following four activity cost pools:

Activity Cost Pool	Activity Measure	Estimated Overhead Cost
Maintaining parts inventory	Number of part types	$ 180,000
Processing purchase orders	Number of purchase orders	90,000
Quality control	Number of tests run	230,000
Machine related	Machine-hours	500,000
		$1,000,000

Activity Measure	Expected Activity		
	Mono-Relay	Bi-Relay	Total
Number of part types	75	150	225
Number of purchase orders	800	200	1,000
Number of tests run	2,500	3,250	5,750
Machine-hours	4,000	6,000	10,000

Using the simplified approach described at the end of the chapter, determine the predetermined overhead rate for each of the four activity cost pools.

3. Using the predetermined manufacturing overhead rates you computed in (2) above, do the following:
   a. Compute the total amount of manufacturing overhead cost that would be applied to each product using the activity-based costing system. After these totals have been computed, determine the amount of manufacturing overhead cost per unit of each product.
   b. Compute the unit product cost of each product.
4. Look at the data you have computed in (1) through (3) above. In terms of manufacturing overhead costs, what factors make the bi-relay more costly to produce than the mono-relay? Is the bi-relay as profitable as management believes? Explain.

Cases

C8–19 Evaluating the Profitability of Customers Classic Windows is a small company that builds specialty wooden windows for local builders. For years the company has relied on a simple costing system based on direct labor-hours (DLHs) for determining the costs of its products. However, the company's president became interested in activity-based costing after reading an article about ABC in a trade journal. An activity-based costing design team was put together, and within a few months a simple system consisting of four activity cost pools had been designed. The activity cost pools and their activity measures appear below:

Activity Cost Pool	Activity Measure	Activity for the Year
Making windows	Direct labor-hours	100,000 DLHs
Processing orders	Number of orders	2,000 orders
Customer relations	Number of customers	100 customers
Other (costs of idle capacity and organization-sustaining costs)	None	Not applicable

The Processing Orders activity cost pool includes order taking, job setup, job scheduling, and so on. Direct materials and direct labor are directly assigned to jobs in both the traditional and activity-based costing systems. The total overhead cost (both nonmanufacturing and manufacturing) for the year is $1,370,000 and includes the following costs:

Manufacturing overhead costs:		
Indirect factory wages	$400,000	
Production equipment depreciation	300,000	
Other factory costs	80,000	$ 780,000
Selling and administrative expenses:		
Administrative wages and salaries	300,000	
Office expenses	40,000	
Marketing expenses	250,000	590,000
Total overhead cost		$1,370,000

Based largely on interviews with employees, the distribution of resource consumption across the activities has been estimated as follows:

Distribution of Resource Consumption Across Activities

	Making Windows	Processing Orders	Customer Relations	Other	Total
Indirect factory wages	30%	40%	10%	20%	100%
Production equipment depreciation	90%	0%	0%	10%	100%
Other factory costs	30%	0%	0%	70%	100%
Administrative wages and salaries	0%	20%	30%	50%	100%
Office expenses	0%	30%	10%	60%	100%
Marketing expenses	0%	0%	60%	40%	100%

Management of the company is particularly interested in measuring the profitability of two customers. One of the customers, Kuszik Builders, is a low-volume purchaser. The other, Western Homes, is a relatively high-volume purchaser. Details of these two customers' orders for the year appear below:

	Kuszik Builders	Western Homes
Number of orders during the year	2 orders	3 orders
Total direct labor hours	300 DLHs	2,000 DLHs
Total sales	$12,500	$68,000
Total direct materials	$ 4,200	$18,500
Total direct labor cost	$ 5,400	$36,000

Required

1. The company's traditional costing system applies manufacturing overhead to jobs strictly on the basis of direct labor-hours. Using this traditional approach, carry out the following steps:
   a. Compute the predetermined manufacturing overhead rate.
   b. Compute the total margin for all of the windows ordered by Kuszik Builders according to the traditional costing system. Do the same for Western Homes.
2. Using activity-based costing, carry out the following steps:
   a. Perform the first-stage allocation of costs to the activity cost pools. (Use Exhibit 8–4 as a guide.)
   b. Compute the activity rates for the activity cost pools. (Use Exhibit 8–5 as a guide.)
   c. Compute the overhead costs of serving each of the two customers. (You will need to construct a table like Exhibit 8–8A for each of the customers. However, unlike Exhibit 8–8A, you should fill in the column for Customer Relations as well as the other columns. Exhibit 8–8A was constructed for a product; in this case we are interested in a customer.)
   d. Prepare an action analysis report showing the margin on business with Kuszik Builders. (The ease of adjustment codes appear below.) Repeat for Western Homes.

	Ease of Adjustment Code
Direct materials	Green
Direct labor	Yellow
Indirect factory wages	Yellow
Production equipment depreciation	Yellow
Other factory costs	Yellow
Administrative wages and salaries	Red
Office expenses	Yellow
Marketing expenses	Yellow

3. Does Classic Windows appear to be losing money on either customer? Do the traditional and activity-based costing systems agree concerning the profitability of the customers? If they do not agree, which costing system do you believe? Why?

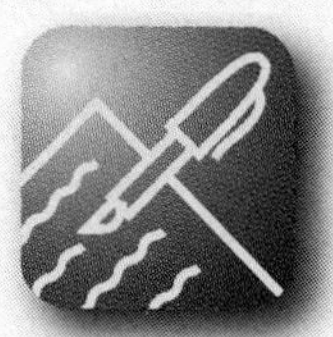

C8–20 Activity-Based Costing as an Alternative to Traditional Product Costing: Simplified Method* "A dollar of gross margin per briefcase? That's ridiculous!" roared Art Dejans, president of CarryAll, Inc. "Why do we go on producing those standard briefcases when we're able to make over $15 per unit on our specialty items? Maybe it's time to get out of the standard line and focus the whole plant on specialty work."

Mr. Dejans is referring to a summary of unit costs and revenues that he had just received from the company's Accounting Department:

	Standard Briefcases	Specialty Briefcases
Selling price per unit	$36	$40
Unit product cost	35	25
Gross margin per unit	$ 1	$15

CarryAll produces briefcases from leather, fabric, and synthetic materials in a single plant. The basic product is a standard briefcase that is made from leather lined with fabric. The standard briefcase is a high-quality item and has sold well for many years.

Last year, the company decided to expand its product line and produce specialty briefcases for special orders. These briefcases differ from the standard in that they vary in size, they contain the finest synthetic materials, and they are imprinted with the buyer's name. To reduce labor costs on the specialty briefcases, most of the cutting and stitching is done by automated machines. These machines are used to a much lesser degree in the production of standard briefcases.

"I agree that the specialty business is looking better and better," replied Sally Henrie, the company's marketing manager. "And there seems to be plenty of specialty work out there, particularly since the competition hasn't been able to touch our price. Did you know that Armor Company, our biggest competitor, charges over $50 a unit for its specialty items? Now that's what I call gouging the customer!"

A breakdown of the manufacturing cost for each of CarryAll's product lines is given below:

*Adapted from a case written by Harold P. Roth and Imogene Posey, "Management Accounting Case Study: CarryAll Company," *Management Accounting Campus Report,* Institute of Management Accountants (Fall 1991), p. 9. Used by permission.

		Standard Briefcases		Specialty Briefcases
Units produced each month		10,000		2,500
Direct materials:				
Leather	1.0 sq. yd.	$15.00	0.5 sq. yd.	$ 7.50
Fabric	1.0 sq. yd.	5.00	1.0 sq. yd.	5.00
Synthetic		—		5.00
Total materials		20.00		17.50
Direct labor	0.5 hr. @ $12	6.00	0.25 hr. @ $12	3.00
Manufacturing overhead	0.5 hr. @ $18	9.00	0.25 hr. @ $18	4.50
Unit product cost		$35.00		$25.00

Manufacturing overhead is applied to products on the basis of direct labor-hours. The rate of $18 per direct labor-hour is determined by dividing the total manufacturing overhead cost for a month by the direct labor-hours:

$$\frac{\text{Manufacturing overhead cost, \$101,250}}{\text{Direct labor-hours, 5,625}} = \text{\$18 per DLH}$$

The following additional information is available about the company and its products:

a. Standard briefcases are produced in batches of 200 units, and specialty briefcases are produced in batches of 25 units. Thus, the company does 50 setups for the standard items each month and 100 setups for the specialty items. A setup for the standard items requires one hour of time, whereas a setup for the specialty items requires two hours of time.
b. All briefcases are inspected to ensure that quality standards are met. A total of 300 hours of inspection time is spent on the standard briefcases and 500 hours of inspection time is spent on the specialty briefcases each month.
c. A standard briefcase requires 0.5 hour of machine time, and a specialty briefcase requires 2 hours of machine time.
d. The company is considering the use of activity-based costing as an alternative to its traditional costing system for computing unit product costs. Since these unit product costs will be used for external financial reporting, all manufacturing overhead costs are to be allocated to products and nonmanufacturing costs are to be excluded from product costs. The activity-based costing system has already been designed and costs allocated to the activity cost pools. The activity cost pools and activity measures are detailed below:

Activity Cost Pool	Activity Measure	Estimated Overhead Cost
Purchasing	Number of orders	$ 12,000
Material handling	Number of receipts	15,000
Production orders and setup	Setup hours	20,250
Inspection	Inspection-hours	16,000
Frame assembly	Assembly-hours	8,000
Machine related	Machine-hours	30,000
		$101,250

Activity Measure	Expected Activity		
	Standard Briefcase	Specialty Briefcase	Total
Number of orders:			
Leather	34	6	40
Fabric	48	12	60
Synthetic material	—	100	100
Number of receipts:			
Leather	52	8	60
Fabric	64	16	80
Synthetic material	—	160	160
Setup hours	?	?	?
Inspection-hours	?	?	?
Assembly-hours	800	800	1,600
Machine-hours	?	?	?

Required

1. Using activity-based costing and the simplified approach described at the end of the chapter, determine the amount of manufacturing overhead cost that would be applied to each standard briefcase and each specialty briefcase.
2. Using the data computed in (1) above and other data from the case as needed, determine the unit product cost of each product line from the perspective of the activity-based costing system.
3. Ideally, what changes should be made in CarryAll's activity-based costing system if it is to be used for making decisions about products?
4. Within the limitations of the data that have been provided, evaluate the president's concern about the profitability of the two product lines. Would you recommend that the company shift its resources entirely to production of specialty briefcases? Explain.
5. Sally Henrie stated that "the competition hasn't been able to touch our price" on specialty business. Why do you suppose the competition hasn't been able to touch CarryAll's price?

Group Exercises

GE8–21 Traditional Product Cost Systems Are Out-of-Date Many firms realize that there are fundamental problems with the methods they use to cost their products or services. But should they change from traditional product costing methods to activity-based costing (ABC) methods? It is important first of all to understand the limitations of existing product costing systems in today's competitive environment typified by a diverse product line populated by many low-volume complex products.

Required

1. What's wrong with traditional product costing systems that they no longer meet the needs of today's managers?
2. How does the cost structure of most manufacturing firms today differ from their cost structure of 20 years ago?
3. What caused this change in cost structure?
4. Why can't traditional product costing systems account for costs of product diversity? Volume diversity? Product complexity?

GE8–22 We're Doing Well but We Don't Know Why "Many U.S. companies don't know where they are making money and where they are losing (money)," says Robert S. Kaplan, a Harvard University accounting professor. Kaplan was aiming his criticism directly at traditional cost accounting systems and, in particular, at the methods used to allocate overhead costs among the many different products produced by job shops, batch manufacturers, and assemblers. Source: Ford S. Worthy, "Accounting Bores You? Wake Up," *Fortune*, October 12, 1987, pp. 43, 44, 48–50.

Part I: Standard Products Firms that sell a complete line of products usually have their bread-and-butter products. These high-volume standard or commodity products, while few in number (e.g., 20%–25% of the product line), may account for as much as 70%–80% of the business or sales volume of their firms.

Required

1. Looking at firms that manufacture a wide range of products, high-volume standard products tend to get systematically overcosted under conventional product costing systems. Describe these products along the following dimensions: competitive environment, how prices are set, stage of life cycle, market acceptance, profit margins (price less cost), general age of technology used to produce these products, degree of labor intensity in the manufacturing process, complexity of product, and batch size when manufactured.
2. Assuming the allocation of manufacturing overhead is based on direct labor cost, explain how these products get overcosted.
3. Since high-volume standard products face fierce price competition, what implications does overcosting have for reported product profitability, product emphasis, market share, future allocations of resources to support the product, and potential product discontinuance?

Part II: Specialty Products Firms that sell a complete line of products will likely have a product line dominated by a large number of low-volume specialty or custom products. While the firm may produce a large number of specialty products (e.g., 70%–80% of the product line), the cumulative sales of low-volume custom products may amount to no more than 25%–30% of sales revenues.

Required

1. Low-volume specialty or custom products tend to get systematically undercosted under conventional product costing systems. These products meet the unique needs of a particular customer and, therefore, the level of sales of any one custom product is usually relatively low when compared to the sales volume of standard products. Describe these products along the following dimensions: competitive environment, how prices are set, stage of life cycle, market acceptance, profit margins (price less cost), general age of technology used to produce these products, degree of labor intensity in the manufacturing process, complexity of product, and batch size when manufactured.
2. Assuming the allocation of manufacturing overhead is based on direct labor cost, explain how these products get undercosted.
3. As a rule, low-volume specialty products don't face the kind of direct head-to-head price competition that high-volume products confront. Instead, they compete on their unique features or performance more so than price. What implications does undercosting have for reported product profitability, product emphasis, market share, future allocations of resources to support the product, and management's perception of the future role to be played by specialty products?

GE8–23 **Impact of Changing Cost Systems on Product Costs** A manufacturing company is thinking of changing its method of computing product costs for the purposes of making decisions. Under the company's conventional direct labor-based costing system, manufacturing overhead costs are applied to products on the basis of direct labor-hours. Under the proposed activity-based costing (ABC) system, both manufacturing and nonmanufacturing overhead costs are applied to products using a variety of allocation bases at the unit, batch, and product levels.

Required

For each of the following products, indicate the impact on the product's apparent cost from switching from a conventional direct labor-based costing system to an activity-based costing system.

1. A low-volume product that is produced in small batches.
2. A high-volume product that is produced in large batches with automated equipment and that requires very few direct labor hours per unit.
3. A high-volume product that requires little machine work but a lot of direct labor.

GE8–24 **Dividing Up the Bill** You and your friends go to a restaurant as a group. At the end of the meal, the issue arises of how the bill for the group should be shared. One alternative is to figure out the cost of what each individual consumed and divide up the bill accordingly. Another alternative is to split the bill equally among the individuals.

Required Which system for dividing the bill is more equitable? Which system is easier to use? How does this issue relate to the material covered in this chapter?

IE8–25 Case Studies ABC Technologies, a consulting and software company specializing in activity-based costing and activity-based management, maintains a library of case studies written by its clients on its web site www.abctech.com. You will be asked to register to access the library, but ABC Technologies promises not to sell or give the registration information to any other person or organization. After entering the library, access the by-industry index.

Required

1. In the Health Care industry category, Issue 30 is titled "Blue Cross and Blue Shield." Access and read this case study. What specific change in processing ASO disability claims resulted from implementation of activity-based costing? Why did the activity-based costing (ABC) study trigger this change?
2. In the Construction industry category, Issue 14 is titled "ABC in the Construction Industry." Access and read this case study. Explain how a conventional costing system in the construction industry can lead to a "death spiral" and how a properly implemented ABC system eliminates this problem.
3. In the Food & Grocery industry category, Issue 5 is titled "Oregon Freeze Dry." Explain how the company's old cost system misled managers into taking inappropriate actions.

Chapter Nine
Profit Planning

Business Focus

Budgets are perhaps even more important in small service organizations than they are in large manufacturing companies. The accounting firm of Carter, Young, Wolf and Dalhauser in Nashville, Tennessee, is typical of many small firms that must keep a constant eye on their cash flows. Because of high fixed costs, small changes in revenues or a client that is delinquent in paying bills can have potentially disastrous effects on the firm's cash flows.

Lucy Carter, the managing partner of the firm, uses a formal budget for keeping cash flow on an even keel. She says, "I don't know how small CPA firms can survive without a budget in this business climate." The formal budget is based on estimated client billings (i.e., revenues) for the coming year. The annual budget is broken down into months, and each month the budget is compared to the actual financial results of the month. If the actuals fall short of the budget, adjustments may be necessary. For example, because of shortfalls in billings in one year, the firm reduced its staff by three staff accountants and added a part-time staff accountant. Because of the critical nature of client billings, Carter's staff prepares daily reports on billings that indicate how well actual billings compare to the budgeted billings on a month-to-date basis.

Source: Gene R. Barrett, "How Small CPA Firms Manage Their Cash," Journal of Accountancy, *August 1993, pp. 56–59.*

Learning Objectives

After studying Chapter 9, you should be able to:

1 Understand why organizations budget and the processes they use to create budgets.

2 Prepare a sales budget, including a schedule of expected cash receipts.

3 Prepare a production budget.

4 Prepare a direct materials budget, including a schedule of expected cash disbursements for purchases of materials.

5 Prepare a direct labor budget.

6 Prepare a manufacturing overhead budget.

7 Prepare an ending finished goods inventory budget.

8 Prepare a selling and administrative expense budget.

9 Prepare a cash budget.

10 Prepare a budgeted income statement and a budgeted balance sheet.

11 (Appendix 9A) Determine the economic order quantity (EOQ) and the reorder point.

In this chapter, we focus our attention on those steps taken by business organizations to achieve their desired levels of profits—a process that is generally called *profit planning*. We shall see that profit planning is accomplished through the preparation of a number of budgets, which, when brought together, form an integrated business plan known as the *master budget*. The master budget is an essential management tool that communicates management's plans throughout the organization, allocates resources, and coordinates activities.

The Basic Framework of Budgeting

objective 1

Understand why organizations budget and the processes they use to create budgets.

Definition of Budgeting

A **budget** is a detailed plan for the acquisition and use of financial and other resources over a specified time period. It represents a plan for the future expressed in formal quantitative terms. The act of preparing a budget is called *budgeting*. The use of budgets to control a firm's activities is known as *budgetary control*.

The **master budget** is a summary of a company's plans that sets specific targets for sales, production, distribution, and financing activities. It generally culminates in a cash budget, a budgeted income statement, and a budgeted balance sheet. In short, it represents a comprehensive expression of management's plans for the future and how these plans are to be accomplished.

Personal Budgets

Nearly everyone budgets to some extent, even though many of the people who use budgets do not recognize what they are doing as budgeting. For example, most people make estimates of their income and plan expenditures for food, clothing, housing, and so on. As a result of this planning, people restrict their spending to some predetermined, allowable amount. While they may not be conscious of the fact, these people clearly go through a budgeting process. Income is estimated, expenditures are planned, and spending is restricted in accordance with the plan. Individuals also use budgets to forecast their future financial condition for purposes such as purchasing a home, financing college education, or setting aside funds for retirement. These budgets may exist only in the mind of the individual, but they are budgets nevertheless.

The budgets of a business firm serve much the same functions as the budgets prepared informally by individuals. Business budgets tend to be more detailed and to involve more work, but they are similar to the budgets prepared by individuals in most other respects. Like personal budgets, they assist in planning and controlling expenditures; they also assist in predicting operating results and financial condition in future periods.

Difference between Planning and Control

The terms *planning* and *control* are often confused, and occasionally these terms are used in such a way as to suggest that they mean the same thing. Actually, planning and control are two quite distinct concepts. **Planning** involves developing objectives and preparing various budgets to achieve these objectives. **Control** involves the steps taken by management to increase the likelihood that the objectives set down at the planning stage are attained, and to ensure that all parts of the organization function in a manner consistent with organizational policies. To be completely effective, a good budgeting system must provide for *both* planning and control. Good planning without effective control is time wasted. On the other hand, unless plans are laid down in advance, there are no objectives toward which control can be directed.

Advantages of Budgeting

There is an old saying to the effect that "a man is usually down on what he isn't up on." Managers who have never tried budgeting are usually quick to state that budgeting is a waste of time. These managers may argue that even though budgeting may work well in *some* situations, it would never work well in their companies because operations are too complex or because there are too many uncertainties. In reality, however, managers who argue this way usually will be deeply involved in planning (albeit on an informal basis). These managers will have clearly defined thoughts about what they want to accomplish and when they want it accomplished. The difficulty is that unless they have some way of communicating their thoughts and plans to others, the only way their companies will ever attain the desired objectives will be through accident. In short, even though companies may attain a certain degree of success without budgets, they never attain the heights that could have been reached with a coordinated system of budgets.

Companies realize many benefits from a budgeting program. Among these benefits are the following:

1. Budgets provide a means of *communicating* management's plans throughout the organization.
2. Budgets force managers to *think about* and plan for the future. In the absence of the necessity to prepare a budget, too many managers would spend all of their time dealing with daily emergencies.
3. The budgeting process provides a means of *allocating resources* to those parts of the organization where they can be used most effectively.
4. The budgeting process can uncover potential *bottlenecks* before they occur.
5. Budgets *coordinate* the activities of the entire organization by *integrating* the plans of the various parts. Budgeting helps to ensure that everyone in the organization is pulling in the same direction.
6. Budgets define goals and objectives that can serve as *benchmarks* for evaluating subsequent performance.

In the past, some managers have avoided budgeting because of the time and effort involved in the budgeting process. It can be argued that budgeting is actually "free" in that the manager's time and effort are more than offset by greater profits. Moreover, with the advent of computer spreadsheet programs, *any* company—large or small—can implement and maintain a budgeting program at minimal cost. Budgeting lends itself well to readily available spreadsheet application programs.

Focus on Current Practice

Consider the following situation encountered by one of the authors at a mortgage banking firm: For years, the company operated with virtually no system of budgets whatever. Management contended that budgeting wasn't well suited to the firm's type of operation. Moreover, management pointed out that the firm was already profitable. Indeed, outwardly the company gave every appearance of being a well-managed, smoothly

operating organization. A careful look within, however, disclosed that day-to-day operations were far from smooth, and often approached chaos. The average day was nothing more than an exercise in putting out one brush fire after another. The Cash account was always at crisis levels. At the end of a day, no one ever knew whether enough cash would be available the next day to cover required loan closings. Departments were uncoordinated, and it was not uncommon to find that one department was pursuing a course that conflicted with the course pursued by another department. Employee morale was low, and turnover was high. Employees complained bitterly that when a job was well done, nobody ever knew about it.

The company was bought out by a new group of stockholders who required that an integrated budgeting system be established to control operations. Within one year's time, significant changes were evident. Brush fires were rare. Careful planning virtually eliminated the problems that had been experienced with cash, and departmental efforts were coordinated and directed toward predetermined overall company goals. Although the employees were wary of the new budgeting program initially, they became "converted" when they saw the positive effects that it brought about. The more efficient operations caused profits to jump dramatically. Communication increased throughout the organization. When a job was well done, everybody knew about it. As one employee stated, "For the first time, we know what the company expects of us." ■

Responsibility Accounting

Most of what we say in this chapter and in the next three chapters centers on the concept of *responsibility accounting*. The basic idea behind **responsibility accounting** is that a manager should be held responsible for those items—and *only* those items—that the manager can actually control to a significant extent. Each line item (i.e., revenue or cost) in the budget is made the responsibility of a manager, and that manager is held responsible for subsequent deviations between budgeted goals and actual results. In effect, responsibility accounting *personalizes* accounting information by looking at costs from a *personal control* standpoint. This concept is central to any effective profit planning and control system. Someone must be held responsible for each cost or else no one will be responsible, and the cost will inevitably grow out of control.

Being held responsible for costs does not mean that the manager is penalized if the actual results do not measure up to the budgeted goals. However, the manager should take the initiative to correct any unfavorable discrepancies, should understand the source of significant favorable or unfavorable discrepancies, and should be prepared to explain the reasons for discrepancies to higher management. The point of an effective responsibility system is to make sure that nothing "falls through the cracks," that the organization reacts quickly and appropriately to deviations from its plans, and that the organization learns from the feedback it gets by comparing budgeted goals to actual results. The point is *not* to penalize individuals for missing targets.

We will look at responsibility accounting in more detail in the next three chapters. For the moment, we can summarize the overall idea by noting that it rests on three basic premises. The first premise is that costs can be organized in terms of levels of management responsibility. The second premise is that the costs charged to a particular level are controllable at that level by its managers. And the third premise is that effective budget data can be generated as a basis for evaluating actual performance. This chapter on profit planning is concerned with the third of these premises in that the purpose of the chapter is to show the steps involved in budget preparation.

Focus on Current Practice

Budgeting plays an important role in coordinating activities in large organizations. Jerome York, the chief financial officer at IBM, discovered at one budget meeting that "the division that makes AS/400 workstations planned to churn out 10,000 more machines than the marketing division was promising to sell. He asked nicely that the two divisions agree on how many they would sell for the sake of consistency (and to cut down on the inventory problem). The rival executives said it couldn't be done. Mr. York got tougher, saying it could. Ultimately, it was."[1] ■

Choosing a Budget Period

Operating budgets are ordinarily set to cover a one-year period. The one-year period should correspond to the company's fiscal year so that the budget figures can be compared with the actual results. Many companies divide their budget year into four quarters. The first quarter is then subdivided into months, and monthly budget figures are established. These near-term figures can often be established with considerable accuracy. The last three quarters are carried in the budget at quarterly totals only. As the year progresses, the figures for the second quarter are broken down into monthly amounts, then the third-quarter figures are broken down, and so forth. This approach has the advantage of requiring periodic review and reappraisal of budget data throughout the year.

Continuous or *perpetual budgets* are used by a significant number of organizations. A **continuous** or **perpetual budget** is a 12-month budget that rolls forward one month (or quarter) as the current month (or quarter) is completed. In other words, one month (or quarter) is added to the end of the budget as each month (or quarter) comes to a close. This approach keeps managers focused on the future at least one year ahead. Advocates of continuous budgets argue that with this approach there is less danger that managers will become too focused on short-term results as the year progresses.

In this chapter, we will focus on one-year operating budgets. However, using basically the same techniques, operating budgets can be prepared for periods that extend over many years. It may be difficult to accurately forecast sales and required data much beyond a year, but even rough estimates can be invaluable in uncovering potential problems and opportunities that would otherwise be overlooked. For example, as described in the accompanying Focus on Current Practice box, as a result of preparing a five-year budget, management at The Repertory Theatre of St. Louis was able to identify an impending financial crisis.

Focus on Current Practice

The Repertory Theatre of St. Louis is a not-for-profit professional theater that is supported by contributions from donors and by ticket sales. Financially, the theater appeared to be doing well. However, a five-year budget revealed that within a few years, expenses would exceed revenues and the theater would be facing a financial crisis. Realistically, additional contributions from donors would not fill the gap. Cutting costs would not

1. Laurie Hays, "Blue Blood: IBM's Finance Chief, Ax in Hand, Scours Empire for Costs to Cut," *The Wall Street Journal,* January 26, 1994, pp. A1, A6.

work because of the theater's already lean operations; cutting costs even more would jeopardize the quality of the theater's productions. Raising ticket prices was ruled out due to competitive pressures and to the belief that this would be unpopular with many donors. The solution was to build a second mainstage performing space that would allow the theater to put on more performances and thereby sell more tickets. By developing a long-range budget, the management of The Repertory Theatre of St. Louis was able to identify in advance a looming financial crisis and to develop a solution that would avert the crisis in time.[2] ■

The Self-Imposed Budget

The success of a budget program will be determined in large part by the way in which the budget is developed. The most successful budget programs involve managers with cost control responsibilities in preparing their own budget estimates—rather than having a budget imposed from above. This approach to preparing budget data is particularly important if the budget is to be used to control and evaluate a manager's activities. If a budget is imposed on a manager from above, it will probably generate resentment and ill will rather than cooperation and increased productivity.

This budgeting approach in which managers prepare their own budget estimates—called a *self-imposed budget*—is generally considered to be the most effective method of budget preparation. A **self-imposed budget** or **participative budget** is a budget that is prepared with the full cooperation and participation of managers at all levels. Exhibit 9–1 illustrates this approach to budget preparation.

A number of advantages are commonly cited for such self-imposed budgets:

1. Individuals at all levels of the organization are recognized as members of the team whose views and judgments are valued by top management.
2. The person in direct contact with an activity is in the best position to make budget estimates. Therefore, budget estimates prepared by such persons tend to be more accurate and reliable.
3. People are more likely to work at fulfilling a budget that they have participated in setting than they are to work at fulfilling a budget that is imposed from above.
4. A self-imposed budget contains its own unique system of control in that if people are not able to meet budget specifications, they have only themselves to blame. On the other hand, if a budget is imposed from above, they can always say that the budget was unreasonable or unrealistic to start with, and therefore was impossible to meet.

Once self-imposed budgets are prepared, are they subject to any kind of review? The answer is yes. Budget estimates prepared by lower-level managers cannot necessarily be accepted without question by higher levels of management. If no system of checks and balances is present, self-imposed budgets may be too loose and allow too much "budgetary slack." The result will be inefficiency and waste. Therefore, before budgets are accepted, they must be carefully reviewed by immediate superiors. If changes from the original budget seem desirable, the items in question are discussed and modified as necessary by mutual consent.

In essence, all levels of an organization should work together to produce the budget. Since top management is generally unfamiliar with detailed, day-to-day oper-

---

2. Lawrence P. Carr, ed., "The Repertory Theatre of St. Louis (B): Strategic Budgeting," *Cases from Management Accounting Practice: Volumes 10 and 11,* Institute of Management Accountants, Montvale, NJ, 1997.

Exhibit 9–1 The Initial Flow of Budget Data in a Participative Budgeting System

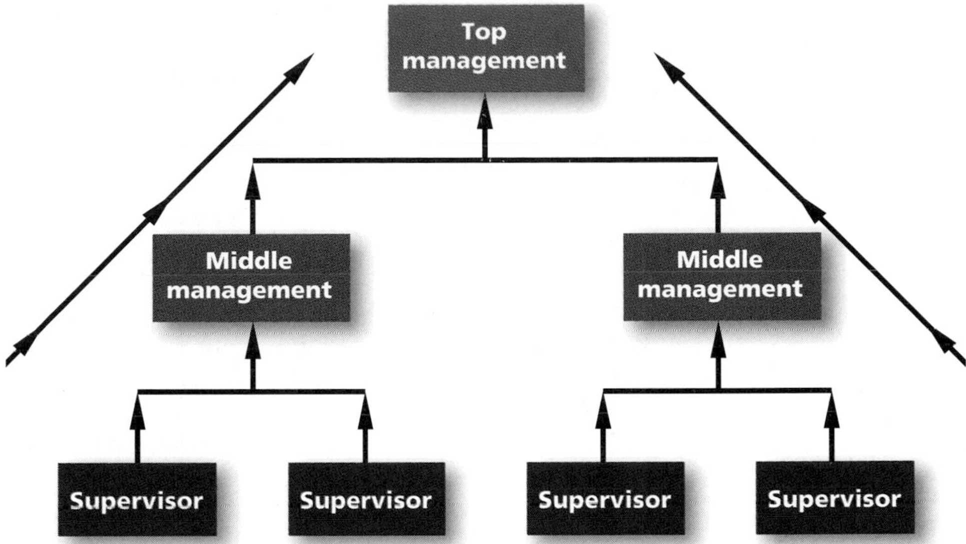

The initial flow of budget data in a participative system is from lower levels of responsibility to higher levels of responsibility. Each person with responsibility for cost control will prepare his or her own budget estimates and submit them to the next higher level of management. These estimates are reviewed and consolidated as they move upward in the organization.

ations, it should rely on subordinates to provide detailed budget information. On the other hand, top management has a perspective on the company as a whole that is vital in making broad policy decisions in budget preparation. Each level of responsibility in an organization should contribute in the way that it best can in a *cooperative* effort to develop an integrated budget document.

To be successful, a self-imposed approach to setting budgets requires that all managers understand and agree with the organization's strategy. Otherwise, the budgets proposed by the lower-level managers will lack coherent direction. We will discuss in greater detail in the following chapter how a company can go about formulating its strategy and then communicating it throughout the organization.

We have described an ideal budgetary process that involves self-imposed budgets prepared by the managers who are directly responsible for revenues and costs. Most companies deviate from this ideal. Typically, top managers initiate the budget process by issuing broad guidelines in terms of overall target profits or sales. Lower-level managers are directed to prepare budgets that meet those targets. The difficulty is that the targets set by top managers may be unrealistically high or may allow too much slack. If the targets are too high and employees know they are unrealistic, motivation will suffer. If the targets allow too much slack, waste will occur. And unfortunately top managers are often not in a position to know whether the targets they have set are appropriate. Admittedly, however, in a pure self-imposed budgeting system, lower-level managers may be tempted to build into their budgets a great deal of budgetary slack and there may be a lack of direction. Nevertheless, because of the motivational advantages of self-imposed budgets, top managers should be cautious about setting inflexible targets or otherwise imposing limits on the budgeting process.

Focus on Current Practice

Capital Cities/ABC, Inc., the former owner of the ABC television network, highlights the importance of participative budgets in the very first paragraph of its annual report to shareholders: "Decentralization is the cornerstone of our management philosophy. Our goal is to hire the best people we can find and give them the responsibility and authority they need to perform their jobs.

Decisions are made at the local level, consistent with the basic responsibilities of corporate management. Budgets, which are set yearly and reviewed quarterly, originate with the operating units that are responsible for them."[3] ■

The Matter of Human Relations

Whether or not a budget program is accepted by lower management personnel will be reflective of (1) the degree to which top management accepts the budget program as a vital part of the company's activities, and (2) the way in which top management uses budgeted data.

If a budget program is to be successful, it must have the complete acceptance and support of the persons who occupy key management positions. If lower or middle management personnel sense that top management is lukewarm about budgeting, or if they sense that top management simply tolerates budgeting as a necessary evil, then their own attitudes will reflect a similar lack of enthusiasm. Budgeting is hard work, and if top management is not enthusiastic about and committed to the budget program, then it is unlikely that anyone else in the organization will be either.

In administering the budget program, it is particularly important that top management not use the budget as a club to pressure employees or as a way to find someone to blame for a particular problem. This type of negative emphasis will simply breed hostility, tension, and mistrust rather than greater cooperation and productivity. Unfortunately, research suggests that the budget is often used as a pressure device and that great emphasis is placed on "meeting the budget" under all circumstances.[4]

Rather than being used as a pressure device, the budget should be used as a positive instrument to assist in establishing goals, in measuring operating results, and in isolating areas that are in need of extra effort or attention. Any misgivings that employees have about a budget program can be overcome by meaningful involvement at all levels and by proper use of the program over a period of time. Administration of a budget program requires a great deal of insight and sensitivity on the part of management. The ultimate object must be to develop the realization that the budget is designed to be a positive aid in achieving both individual and company goals.

Management must keep clearly in mind that the human dimension in budgeting is of key importance. It is easy for the manager to become preoccupied with the technical aspects of the budget program to the exclusion of the human aspects. Indeed, the use of budget data in a rigid and inflexible manner is the greatest single complaint of persons whose performance is being evaluated through the budget process.[5] Management should remember that the purposes of the budget are to motivate employees and to coordinate efforts. Preoccupation with the dollars and cents in the budget, or being rigid and inflexible in budget administration, can only lead to frustration of these purposes.

Focus on Current Practice

In establishing a budget, how challenging should budget targets be? In practice, companies typically set their budgets either at a "stretch" level or

3. Capital Cities/ABC, Inc., *1993 Annual Report and Form 10-K,* inside front cover.
4. Paul J. Carruth, Thurrell O. McClendon, and Milton R. Ballard, "What Supervisors Don't Like about Budget Evaluations," *Management Accounting* 64, no. 8 (February 1983), p. 42.
5. Carruth et al., "What Supervisors Don't Like . . . ," p. 91.

a "highly achievable" level. A stretch-level budget is one that has only a small chance of being met and in fact may be met less than half the time by even the most capable managers. A highly achievable budget is one that is challenging, but which can be met through hard work. Research shows that managers prefer highly achievable budgets.[6] Such budgets are generally coupled with bonuses that are given when budget targets are met, along with added bonuses when these targets are exceeded. Highly achievable budgets are believed to build a manager's confidence and to generate greater commitment to the budget program. ■

The Budget Committee

A standing **budget committee** will usually be responsible for overall policy matters relating to the budget program and for coordinating the preparation of the budget itself. This committee generally consists of the president; vice presidents in charge of various functions such as sales, production, and purchasing; and the controller. Difficulties and disputes between segments of the organization in matters relating to the budget are resolved by the budget committee. In addition, the budget committee approves the final budget and receives periodic reports on the progress of the company in attaining budgeted goals.

Disputes can (and do) erupt over budget matters. Because budgets allocate resources, the budgeting process to a large extent determines which departments get more resources and which get relatively less. Also, the budget sets the benchmarks by which managers and their departments will be at least partially evaluated. Therefore, it should not be surprising that managers take the budgeting process very seriously and invest considerable energy and even emotion in ensuring that their interests, and those of their departments, are protected. Because of this, the budgeting process can easily degenerate into an interoffice brawl in which the ultimate goal of working together toward common goals is forgotten.

Running a successful budgeting program that avoids interoffice battles requires considerable interpersonal skills in addition to purely technical skills. But even the best interpersonal skills will fail if, as discussed earlier, top management uses the budget process inappropriately as a club or as a way to find blame.

Focus on Current Practice

Budgeting is often an intensely political process in which managers jockey for resources and relaxed goals for the upcoming year. One group of consultants describes the process in this way: Annual budgets "have a particular urgency in that they provide the standard and most public framework against which managers are assessed and judged. It is, therefore, not surprising that budget-setting is taken seriously . . . Often budgets are a means for managers getting what they want. A relaxed budget will secure a relatively easy twelve months, a tight one means that their names will con-

6. See Kenneth A. Merchant, *Rewarding Results: Motivating Profit Center Managers* (Boston, MA: Harvard Business School Press, 1989). For further discussion of budget targets, see Kenneth A. Merchant, "How Challenging Should Profit Budget Targets Be?" *Management Accounting* 72, no. 5 (November 1990), pp. 46–48.

stantly be coming up in the monthly management review meeting. Far better to shift the burden of cost control and financial discipline to someone else. Budgeting is an intensely political exercise conducted with all the sharper managerial skills not taught at business school, such as lobbying and flattering superiors, forced haste, regretted delay, hidden truth, half-truths, and lies."[7] ■

The Master Budget Interrelationships

The master budget consists of a number of separate but interdependent budgets. Exhibit 9–2 provides an overview of the various parts of the master budget and how they are related.

THE SALES BUDGET A **sales budget** is a detailed schedule showing the expected sales for the budget period; typically, it is expressed in both dollars and units of product. An accurate sales budget is the key to the entire budgeting process. All of the other parts of the master budget are dependent on the sales budget in some way, as

Exhibit 9–2
The Master Budget Interrelationships

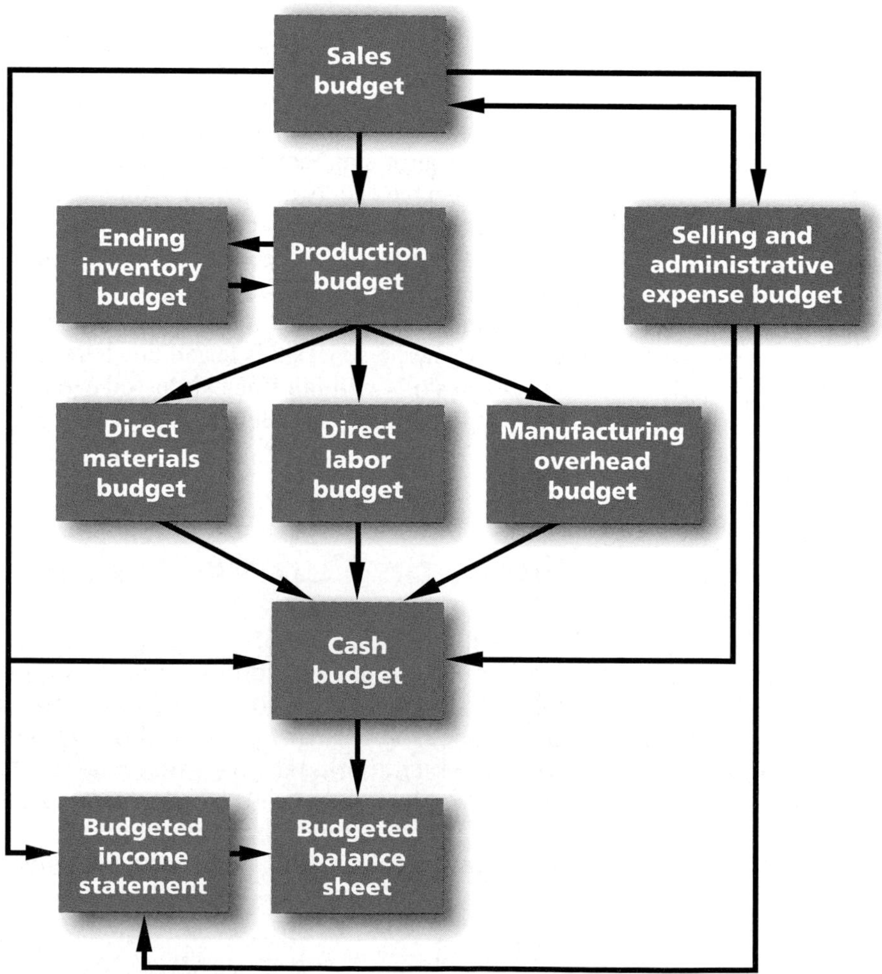

7. Michael Morrow, ed., *Activity-Based Management* (New York: Woodhead-Faulkner, 1992), p. 91.

illustrated in Exhibit 9–2. Thus, if the sales budget is sloppily done, then the rest of the budgeting process is largely a waste of time.

The sales budget will help determine how many units will have to be produced. Thus, the production budget is prepared after the sales budget. The production budget in turn is used to determine the budgets for manufacturing costs including the direct materials budget, the direct labor budget, and the manufacturing overhead budget. These budgets are then combined with data from the sales budget and the selling and administrative expense budget to determine the cash budget. In essence, the sales budget triggers a chain reaction that leads to the development of the other budgets.

As shown in Exhibit 9–2, the selling and administrative expense budget is both dependent on and a determinant of the sales budget. This reciprocal relationship arises because sales will in part be determined by the funds committed for advertising and sales promotion.

THE CASH BUDGET Once the operating budgets (sales, production, and so on) have been established, the cash budget and other financial budgets can be prepared. A **cash budget** is a detailed plan showing how cash resources will be acquired and used over some specified time period. Observe from Exhibit 9–2 that all of the operating budgets have an impact on the cash budget. In the case of the sales budget, the impact comes from the planned cash receipts to be received from sales. In the case of the other budgets, the impact comes from the planned cash expenditures within the budgets themselves.

Sales Forecasting—A Critical Step

The sales budget is usually based on the company's *sales forecast.* Sales from prior years are commonly used as a starting point in preparing the sales forecast. In addition, the manager may examine the company's unfilled back orders, the company's pricing policy and marketing plans, trends in the industry, and general economic conditions. Sophisticated statistical tools may be used to analyze the data and to build models that are helpful in predicting key factors influencing the company's sales. The accompanying Focus on Current Practice box suggests how some companies are beginning to use computer simulations to enhance their marketing strategies and sales forecasts. We will not, however, go into the details of how sales forecasts are made. This is a subject that is more appropriately covered in marketing courses.

Focus on Current Practice

Some companies are turning to elaborate computer simulations for help in forecasting sales. In one emerging approach, software designers create a "virtual economy" containing "virtual people." "These 'people,' constructed of bits of computer code, are endowed with ages, incomes, domiciles, genders and buying habits. [For example, some] buy a new music CD as soon as it hits the stores; others, only after a certain number of their neighbors own it or a certain number of radio stations have played it. All these assumptions are based on real data . . ." The computer model may contain millions of these virtual people who then react—sometimes in unpredictable ways—to advertising, sales promotions, new product offerings, and so on. Managers can use such a model to plan their marketing strategy and to forecast sales.[8] ■

8. Rita Koselka, "Playing the Game of Life," *Forbes,* April 7, 1997, pp. 100–108.

Preparing the Master Budget

Managerial Accounting in Action

THE ISSUE

Tom Wills is the majority stockholder and chief executive officer of Hampton Freeze, Inc., a company he started in 1998. The company makes premium popsicles using only natural ingredients and featuring exotic flavors such as tangy tangerine and minty mango. The company's business is highly seasonal, with most of the sales occurring in spring and summer.

In 1999, the company's second year of operations, there was a major cash crunch in the first and second quarters that almost forced the company into bankruptcy. In spite of this cash crunch, 1999 turned out to be overall a very successful year in terms of both cash flow and net income. Partly as a result of that harrowing experience, Tom decided toward the end of 1999 to hire a professional financial manager. Tom interviewed several promising candidates for the job and settled on Larry Giano, who had considerable experience in the packaged foods industry. In the job interview, Tom questioned Larry about the steps he would take to prevent a recurrence of the 1999 cash crunch:

Tom: As I mentioned earlier, we are going to wind up 1999 with a very nice profit. What you may not know is that we had some very big financial problems this year.
Larry: Let me guess. You ran out of cash sometime in the first or second quarter.
Tom: How did you know?
Larry: Most of your sales are in the second and third quarter, right?
Tom: Sure, everyone wants to buy popsicles in the spring and summer, but nobody wants them when the weather turns cold.
Larry: So you don't have many sales in the first quarter?
Tom: Right.
Larry: And in the second quarter, which is the spring, you are producing like crazy to fill orders?
Tom: Sure.
Larry: Do your customers, the grocery stores, pay you the day you make your deliveries?
Tom: Are you kidding? Of course not.
Larry: So in the first quarter, you don't have many sales. In the second quarter, you are producing like crazy, which eats up cash, but you aren't paid by your customers until long after you have paid your employees and suppliers. No wonder you had a cash problem. I see this pattern all the time in food processing because of the seasonality of the business.
Tom: So what can we do about it?
Larry: The first step is to predict the magnitude of the problem before it occurs. If we can predict early in the year what the cash shortfall is going to be, we can go to the bank and arrange for credit before we really need it. Bankers tend to be leery of panicky people who show up begging for emergency loans. They are much more likely to make the loan if you look like you know what you are doing, you have done your homework, and you are in control of the situation.
Tom: How can we predict the cash shortfall?
Larry: You can put together a cash budget. While you're at it, you might as well do a master budget. You'll find it is well worth the effort.
Tom: I don't like budgets. They are too confining. My wife budgets everything at home, and I can't spend what I want.

Larry: Can I ask a personal question?
Tom: What?
Larry: Where did you get the money to start this business?
Tom: Mainly from our family's savings. I get your point. We wouldn't have had the money to start the business if my wife hadn't been forcing us to save every month.
Larry: Exactly. I suggest you use the same discipline in your business. It is even more important here because you can't expect your employees to spend your money as carefully as you would.
Tom: I'm sold. Welcome aboard. ■

With the full backing of Tom Wills, Larry Giano set out to create a master budget for the company for the year 2000. In his planning for the budgeting process, Larry drew up the following list of documents that would be a part of the master budget:

1. A sales budget, including a schedule of expected cash collections.
2. A production budget (or merchandise purchases budget for a merchandising company).
3. A direct materials budget, including a schedule of expected cash disbursements for raw materials.
4. A direct labor budget.
5. A manufacturing overhead budget.
6. An ending finished goods inventory budget.
7. A selling and administrative expense budget.
8. A cash budget.
9. A budgeted income statement.
10. A budgeted balance sheet.

Larry felt it was important to get everyone's cooperation in the budgeting process, so he asked Tom to call a companywide meeting in which the budgeting process would be explained. At the meeting there was initially some grumbling, but Tom was able to convince nearly everyone of the necessity for planning and getting better control over spending. It helped that the cash crisis earlier in the year was still fresh in everyone's minds. As much as some people disliked the idea of budgets, they liked their jobs even more.

In the months that followed, Larry worked closely with all of the managers involved in the master budget, gathering data from them and making sure that they understood and fully supported the parts of the master budget that would affect them. In subsequent years, Larry hoped to turn the whole budgeting process over to the managers and to take a more advisory role.

The interdependent documents that Larry Giano prepared for Hampton Freeze are Schedules 1 through 10 of his company's master budget. In this section, we will study these schedules.

objective 2

Prepare a sales budget, including a schedule of expected cash receipts.

The Sales Budget

The sales budget is the starting point in preparing the master budget. As shown earlier in Exhibit 9–2, all other items in the master budget, including production, purchases, inventories, and expenses, depend on it in some way.

The sales budget is constructed by multiplying the budgeted sales in units by the selling price. Schedule 1 on the next page contains the sales budget for Hampton Freeze for the year 2000, by quarters. Notice from the schedule that the company plans to sell 100,000 cases of popsicles during the year, with sales peaking in the third quarter.

Schedule 1

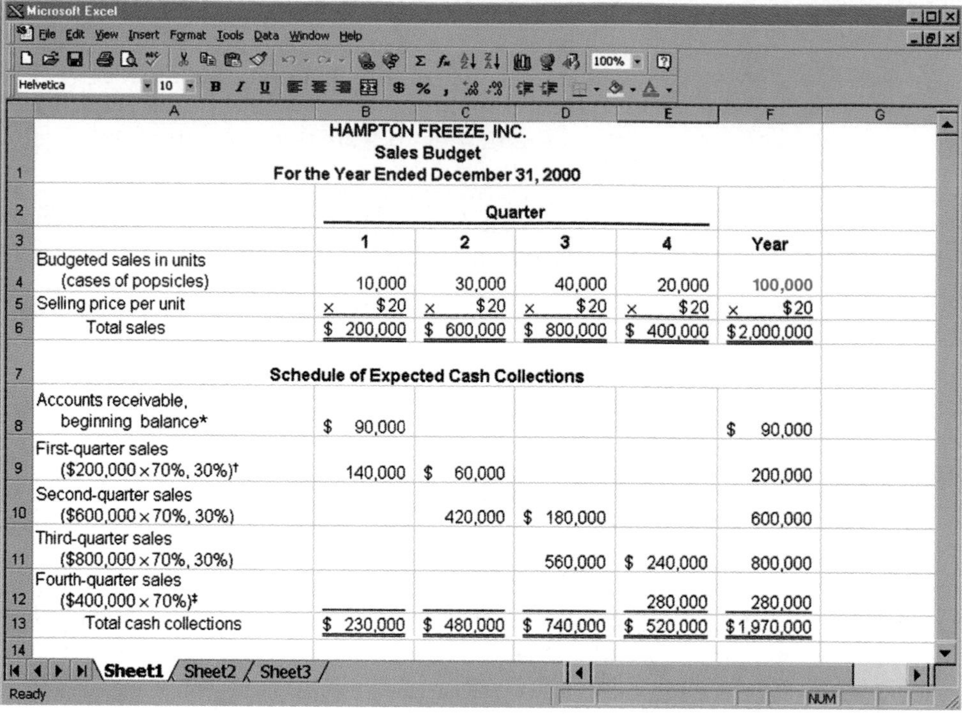

HAMPTON FREEZE, INC.
Sales Budget
For the Year Ended December 31, 2000

	Quarter 1	2	3	4	Year
Budgeted sales in units (cases of popsicles)	10,000	30,000	40,000	20,000	100,000
Selling price per unit	× $20	× $20	× $20	× $20	× $20
Total sales	$ 200,000	$ 600,000	$ 800,000	$ 400,000	$2,000,000

Schedule of Expected Cash Collections

	1	2	3	4	Year
Accounts receivable, beginning balance*	$ 90,000				$ 90,000
First-quarter sales ($200,000 × 70%, 30%)†	140,000	$ 60,000			200,000
Second-quarter sales ($600,000 × 70%, 30%)		420,000	$ 180,000		600,000
Third-quarter sales ($800,000 × 70%, 30%)			560,000	$ 240,000	800,000
Fourth-quarter sales ($400,000 × 70%)‡				280,000	280,000
Total cash collections	$ 230,000	$ 480,000	$ 740,000	$ 520,000	$1,970,000

*Cash collections from last year's fourth-quarter sales. See the beginning-of-year balance sheet on page 399.

†Cash collections from sales are as follows: 70% collected in the quarter of sale, and the remaining 30% collected in the following quarter.

‡Uncollected fourth-quarter sales appear as accounts receivable on the company's end-of-year balance sheet (see Schedule 10 on page 400).

A schedule of expected cash collections, such as the one that appears in Schedule 1 for Hampton Freeze, is prepared after the sales budget. This schedule will be needed later to prepare the cash budget. Cash collections consist of collections on sales made to customers in prior periods plus collections on sales made in the current budget period. At Hampton Freeze, experience has shown that 70% of sales are collected in the quarter in which the sale is made and the remaining 30% are collected in the following quarter. So, for example, 70% of the first quarter sales of $200,000 (or $140,000) is collected during the first quarter and 30% (or $60,000) is collected during the second quarter.

The Production Budget

objective 3

Prepare a production budget.

The production budget is prepared after the sales budget. The **production budget** lists the number of units that must be produced during each budget period to meet sales needs and to provide for the desired ending inventory. Production needs can be determined as follows:

Budgeted sales in units	XXXX
Add desired ending inventory	XXXX
Total needs	XXXX
Less beginning inventory	XXXX
Required production	XXXX

Schedule 2

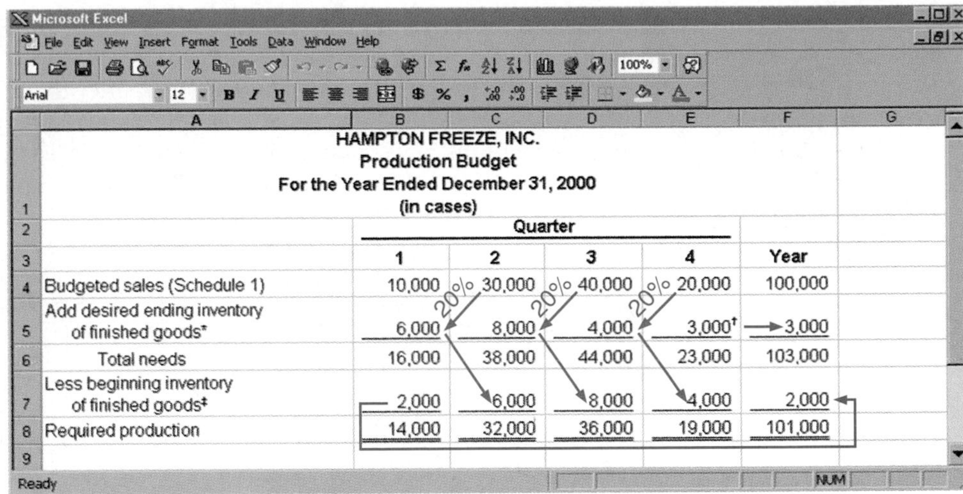

HAMPTON FREEZE, INC.
Production Budget
For the Year Ended December 31, 2000
(in cases)

	Quarter				
	1	2	3	4	Year
Budgeted sales (Schedule 1)	10,000	30,000	40,000	20,000	100,000
Add desired ending inventory of finished goods*	6,000	8,000	4,000	3,000†	3,000
Total needs	16,000	38,000	44,000	23,000	103,000
Less beginning inventory of finished goods‡	2,000	6,000	8,000	4,000	2,000
Required production	14,000	32,000	36,000	19,000	101,000

*Twenty percent of the next quarter's sales.

†Estimated.

‡The same as the prior quarter's *ending* inventory.

Schedule 2, which appears above, contains the production budget for Hampton Freeze.

Note that production requirements for a quarter are influenced by the desired level of the ending inventory. Inventories should be carefully planned. Excessive inventories tie up funds and create storage problems. Insufficient inventories can lead to lost sales or crash production efforts in the following period. At Hampton Freeze, management believes that an ending inventory equal to 20% of the next quarter's sales strikes the appropriate balance.

Inventory Purchases—Merchandising Firm

Hampton Freeze prepares a production budget, since it is a *manufacturing* firm. If it were a *merchandising* firm, then instead of a production budget it would prepare a **merchandise purchases budget** showing the amount of goods to be purchased from its suppliers during the period. The merchandise purchases budget is in the same basic format as the production budget, except that it shows goods to be purchased rather than goods to be produced, as shown below:

Budgeted cost of goods sold (in units or in dollars)	XXXXX
Add desired ending merchandise inventory	XXXXX
Total needs	XXXXX
Less beginning merchandise inventory	XXXXX
Required purchases (in units or in dollars)	XXXXX

The merchandising firm would prepare an inventory purchases budget such as the one above for each item carried in stock. Some large retail organizations make such computations on a frequent basis (particularly at peak seasons) to ensure that adequate stocks are on hand to meet customer needs.

The Direct Materials Budget

objective 4

Prepare a direct materials budget, including a schedule of expected cash disbursements for purchases of materials.

Returning to Hampton Freeze's budget data, after the production requirements have been computed, a *direct materials budget* can be prepared. The **direct materials budget** details the raw materials that must be purchased to fulfill the production budget and to provide for adequate inventories. The required purchases of raw materials are computed as follows:

Raw materials needed to meet the production schedule	XXXXX
Add desired ending inventory of raw materials	XXXXX
Total raw materials needs	XXXXX
Less beginning inventory of raw materials	XXXXX
Raw materials to be purchased	XXXXX

Preparing a budget of this kind is one step in a company's overall **material requirements planning (MRP).** MRP is an operations management tool that uses a computer to help manage materials and inventories. The objective of MRP is to ensure that the right materials are on hand, in the right quantities, and at the right time to support the production budget. The detailed operation of MRP is covered in most operations management books.

Schedule 3 contains the direct materials budget for Hampton Freeze. The only raw material included in that budget is high fructose sugar, which is the major ingredient in popsicles other than water. The remaining raw materials are relatively insignificant and are included in variable manufacturing overhead. Notice that materials requirements are first determined in units (pounds, gallons, and so on) and then translated into dollars by multiplying by the appropriate unit cost. Also note that the management of Hampton Freeze desires to maintain ending inventories of sugar equal to 10% of the following quarter's production needs.

The direct materials budget is usually accompanied by a schedule of expected cash disbursements for raw materials. This schedule is needed to prepare the overall cash budget. Disbursements for raw materials consist of payments for purchases on account in prior periods plus any payments for purchases in the current budget period. Schedule 3 contains such a schedule of cash disbursements.

The Direct Labor Budget

objective 5

Prepare a direct labor budget.

The **direct labor budget** is also developed from the production budget. Direct labor requirements must be computed so that the company will know whether sufficient labor time is available to meet production needs. By knowing in advance just what will be needed in the way of labor time throughout the budget year, the company can develop plans to adjust the labor force as the situation may require. Firms that neglect to budget run the risk of facing labor shortages or having to hire and lay off at awkward times. Erratic labor policies lead to insecurity and inefficiency on the part of employees.

To compute direct labor requirements, the number of units of finished product to be produced each period (month, quarter, and so on) is multiplied by the number of direct labor-hours required to produce a single unit. Many different types of labor may be involved. If so, then computations should be by type of labor needed. The direct labor requirements can then be translated into expected direct labor costs. How this is done will depend on the labor policy of the firm. In Schedule 4, the management of Hampton Freeze has assumed that the direct labor force will be adjusted as the work requirements change from quarter to quarter. In that case, the total direct labor cost is

Schedule 3

	HAMPTON FREEZE, INC.				
	Direct Materials Budget				
	For the Year Ended December 31, 2000				
	Quarter				
	1	**2**	**3**	**4**	**Year**
Required production (units) (Schedule 2)	14,000	32,000	36,000	19,000	101,000
Raw materials needed per unit (pounds)	× 15	× 15	× 15	× 15	× 15
Production needs (pounds)	210,000	480,000	540,000	285,000	1,515,000
Add desired ending inventory of raw materials (pounds)*	48,000	54,000	28,500	22,500	22,500
Total needs (pounds)	258,000	534,000	568,500	307,500	1,537,500
Less beginning inventory of raw materials (pounds)	21,000	48,000	54,000	28,500	21,000
Raw materials to be purchased (pounds)	237,000	486,000	514,500	279,000	1,516,500
Cost of raw materials to be purchased at $0.20 per pound	$ 47,400	$ 97,200	$ 102,900	$ 55,800	$ 303,300
Schedule of Expected Cash Disbursements for Materials					
Accounts payable, beginning balance†	$ 25,800				$ 25,800
First-quarter purchases ($47,400 × 50%, 50%)‡	23,700	$ 23,700			47,400
Second-quarter purchases ($97,200 × 50%, 50%)		48,600	$ 48,600		97,200
Third-quarter purchases ($102,900 × 50%, 50%)			51,450	$ 51,450	102,900
Fourth-quarter purchases ($55,800 × 50%)§				27,900	27,900
Total cash disbursements	$ 49,500	$ 72,300	$ 100,050	$ 79,350	$ 301,200

*Ten percent of the next quarter's production needs. For example, the second-quarter production needs are 480,000 pounds. Therefore, the desired ending inventory for the first quarter would be 10% × 480,000 pounds = 48,000 pounds. The ending inventory of 22,500 pounds for the fourth quarter is estimated.

†Cash payments for last year's fourth-quarter material purchases. See the beginning-of-year balance sheet on page 399.

‡Cash payments for purchases are as follows: 50% paid for in the quarter of purchase, and the remaining 50% paid for in the following quarter.

§Unpaid fourth-quarter purchases appear as accounts payable on the company's end-of-year balance sheet (see Schedule 10 on page 400).

computed by simply multiplying the direct labor-hour requirements by the direct labor rate per hour as was done in Schedule 4.

However, many companies have employment policies or contracts that prevent them from laying off and rehiring workers as needed. Suppose, for example, that Hampton Freeze has 50 workers who are classified as direct labor and each of them is guaranteed at least 480 hours of pay each quarter at a rate of $7.50 per hour. In that case, the minimum direct labor cost for a quarter would be as follows:

$$50 \text{ workers} \times 480 \text{ hours} \times \$7.50 = \$180{,}000$$

Note that in Schedule 4 the direct labor costs for the first and fourth quarters would have to be increased to a $180,000 level if Hampton Freeze's labor policy did not allow it to adjust the workforce at will.

Schedule 4

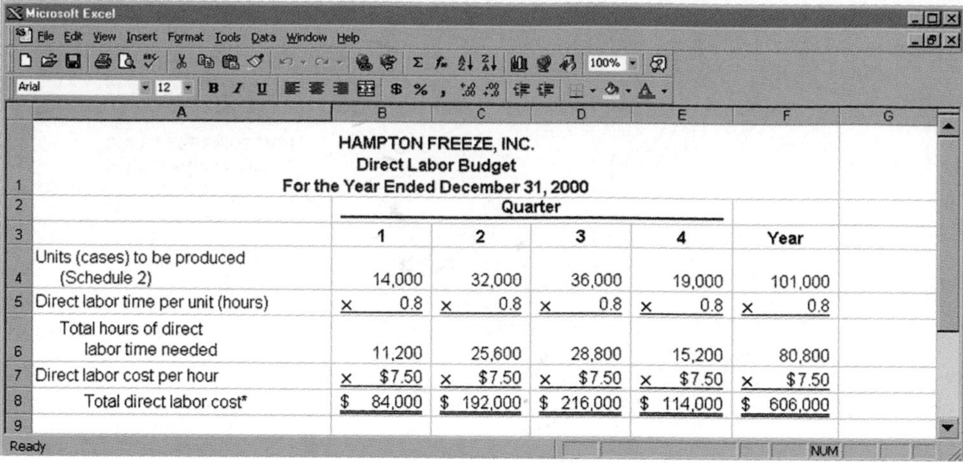

HAMPTON FREEZE, INC.					
Direct Labor Budget					
For the Year Ended December 31, 2000					
	Quarter				
	1	**2**	**3**	**4**	**Year**
Units (cases) to be produced (Schedule 2)	14,000	32,000	36,000	19,000	101,000
Direct labor time per unit (hours)	× 0.8	× 0.8	× 0.8	× 0.8	× 0.8
Total hours of direct labor time needed	11,200	25,600	28,800	15,200	80,800
Direct labor cost per hour	× $7.50	× $7.50	× $7.50	× $7.50	× $7.50
Total direct labor cost*	$ 84,000	$ 192,000	$ 216,000	$ 114,000	$ 606,000

*This schedule assumes that the direct labor workforce will be fully adjusted to the workload (i.e., "total hours of direct labor time needed") each quarter.

Schedule 5

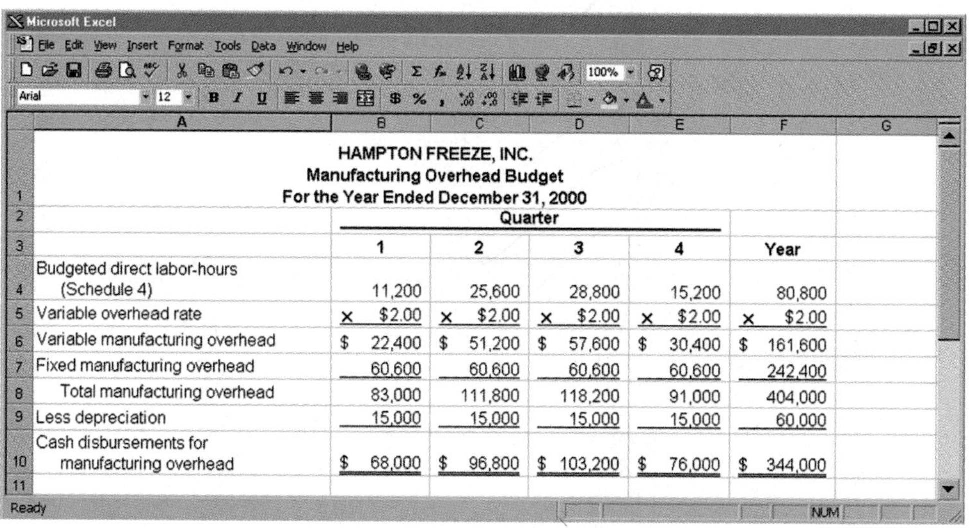

HAMPTON FREEZE, INC.					
Manufacturing Overhead Budget					
For the Year Ended December 31, 2000					
	Quarter				
	1	**2**	**3**	**4**	**Year**
Budgeted direct labor-hours (Schedule 4)	11,200	25,600	28,800	15,200	80,800
Variable overhead rate	× $2.00	× $2.00	× $2.00	× $2.00	× $2.00
Variable manufacturing overhead	$ 22,400	$ 51,200	$ 57,600	$ 30,400	$ 161,600
Fixed manufacturing overhead	60,600	60,600	60,600	60,600	242,400
Total manufacturing overhead	83,000	111,800	118,200	91,000	404,000
Less depreciation	15,000	15,000	15,000	15,000	60,000
Cash disbursements for manufacturing overhead	$ 68,000	$ 96,800	$ 103,200	$ 76,000	$ 344,000

The Manufacturing Overhead Budget

objective 6

Prepare a manufacturing overhead budget.

The **manufacturing overhead budget** provides a schedule of all costs of production other than direct materials and direct labor. Schedule 5 shows the manufacturing overhead budget for Hampton Freeze. Note how the production costs are separated into variable and fixed components. The variable component is $2 per direct labor-hour. The fixed component is $60,600 per quarter.

The last line of Schedule 5 for Hampton Freeze shows its budgeted cash disbursements for manufacturing overhead. Since some of the overhead costs are not cash outflows, the total budgeted manufacturing overhead costs must be adjusted to determine the cash disbursements for manufacturing overhead. At Hampton Freeze, the only significant noncash manufacturing overhead cost is depreciation, which is $15,000 per quarter. These noncash depreciation charges are deducted from the total budgeted manufacturing overhead to determine the expected cash disbursements. Hampton Freeze pays all overhead costs involving cash disbursements in the quarter incurred.

Schedule 6

	Item	Quantity	Cost	Total
1	**HAMPTON FREEZE, INC. Ending Finished Goods Inventory Budget (absorption costing basis) For the Year Ended December 31, 2000**			
2				
3	**Item**	**Quantity**	**Cost**	**Total**
4	Production cost per unit (case):			
5	Direct materials	15.0 pounds	$0.20 per pound	$ 3
6	Direct labor	0.8 hours	7.50 per hour	6
7	Manufacturing overhead	0.8 hours	5.00 per hour*	4
8	Unit product cost			$13
9				
10	Budgeted finished goods inventory:			
11	Ending finished goods inventory in units (Schedule 2)			3,000
12	Unit product cost (see above)			× $13
13	Ending finished goods inventory in dollars			$ 39,000
14				

*$404,000 ÷ 80,800 hours = $5.

The Ending Finished Goods Inventory Budget

objective 7

Prepare an ending finished goods inventory budget.

After completing Schedules 1–5, Larry Giano had all of the data he needed to compute unit product costs. This computation was needed for two reasons: first, to determine cost of goods sold on the budgeted income statement; and second, to know what amount to put on the balance sheet inventory account for unsold units. The carrying cost of the unsold units is computed on the **ending finished goods inventory budget.**

Larry Giano considered using variable costing in preparing Hampton Freeze's budget statements, but he decided to use absorption costing instead since the bank would very likely require that absorption costing be used. He also knew that it would be easy to convert the absorption costing financial statements to a variable costing basis later. At this point, the primary concern was to determine what financing, if any, would be required in the year 2000 and then to arrange for that financing from the bank.

The unit product cost computations are shown in Schedule 6. For Hampton Freeze, the absorption costing unit product cost is $13 per case of popsicles—consisting of $3 of direct materials, $6 of direct labor, and $4 of manufacturing overhead. For convenience, the manufacturing overhead is applied to units of product on the basis of direct labor-hours. The budgeted carrying cost of the expected ending inventory is $39,000.

The Selling and Administrative Expense Budget

objective 8

Prepare a selling and administrative expense budget.

The **selling and administrative expense budget** lists the budgeted expenses for areas other than manufacturing. In large organizations, this budget would be a compilation of many smaller, individual budgets submitted by department heads and other persons responsible for selling and administrative expenses. For example, the marketing manager in a large organization would submit a budget detailing the advertising expenses for each budget period.

Schedule 7

HAMPTON FREEZE, INC.					
Selling and Administrative Expense Budget					
For the Year Ended December 31, 2000					
	Quarter				
	1	**2**	**3**	**4**	**Year**
Budgeted sales in units (cases)	10,000	30,000	40,000	20,000	100,000
Variable selling and administrative expense per unit*	× $1.80	× $1.80	× $1.80	× $1.80	× $1.80
Variable expense	$ 18,000	$ 54,000	$ 72,000	$ 36,000	$ 180,000
Fixed selling and administrative expenses:					
Advertising	20,000	20,000	20,000	20,000	80,000
Executive salaries	55,000	55,000	55,000	55,000	220,000
Insurance		1,900	37,750		39,650
Property taxes				18,150	18,150
Depreciation	10,000	10,000	10,000	10,000	40,000
Total	85,000	86,900	122,750	103,150	397,800
Total selling and administrative expenses	103,000	140,900	194,750	139,150	577,800
Less depreciation	10,000	10,000	10,000	10,000	40,000
Cash disbursements for selling and administrative expenses	$ 93,000	$ 130,900	$ 184,750	$ 129,150	$ 537,800

*Commissions, clerical, and shipping.

Schedule 7 contains the selling and administrative expense budget for Hampton Freeze.

The Cash Budget

objective 9

Prepare a cash budget.

As illustrated in Exhibit 9–2, the cash budget pulls together much of the data developed in the preceding steps. It is a good idea to restudy Exhibit 9–2 to get the big picture firmly in mind before moving on.

The cash budget is composed of four major sections:

1. The receipts section.
2. The disbursements section
3. The cash excess or deficiency section.
4. The financing section.

The receipts section consists of a listing of all of the cash inflows, except for financing, expected during the budget period. Generally, the major source of receipts will be from sales.

The disbursements section consists of all cash payments that are planned for the budget period. These payments will include raw materials purchases, direct labor payments, manufacturing overhead costs, and so on, as contained in their respective budgets. In addition, other cash disbursements such as equipment purchases, dividends, and other cash withdrawals by owners are listed. For instance, we see in Schedule 8 that management plans to spend $130,000 during the budget period on equipment purchases and $32,000 on dividends to the owners. This is additional information that does not appear on any of the earlier schedules.

The cash excess or deficiency section is computed as follows:

Cash balance, beginning	XXXX
Add receipts	XXXX
Total cash available before financing	XXXX
Less disbursements	XXXX
Excess (deficiency) of cash available over disbursements	XXXX

If there is a cash deficiency during any budget period, the company will need to borrow funds. If there is a cash excess during any budget period, funds borrowed in previous periods can be repaid or the idle funds can be placed in short-term or other investments.

The financing section provides a detailed account of the borrowings and repayments projected to take place during the budget period. It also includes a detail of interest payments that will be due on money borrowed.[9]

Generally speaking, the cash budget should be broken down into time periods that are as short as feasible. There can be considerable fluctuations in cash balances that would be hidden by looking at a longer time period. While a monthly cash budget is most common, many firms budget cash on a weekly or even daily basis. Larry Giano has prepared a quarterly cash budget for Hampton Freeze that can be further refined as necessary. This budget appears in Schedule 8. Larry has assumed in the budget that an open line of credit can be arranged with the bank that can be used as needed to bolster the company's cash position. He has also assumed that the interest on any loans taken out with this line of credit would carry an interest rate of 10% per year. For simplicity, Larry has assumed that all borrowings and repayments are in round $1,000 amounts and that all borrowing occurs at the beginning of a quarter and all repayments are made at the end of a quarter.

In the case of Hampton Freeze, all loans have been repaid by year-end. If all loans are not repaid and a budgeted income statement or balance sheet is being prepared, then interest must be accrued on the unpaid loans. This interest will *not* appear on the cash budget (since it has not yet been paid), but it will appear as part of interest expense on the budgeted income statement and as a liability on the budgeted balance sheet.

Focus on Current Practice

Harlan Accola turned his interests in flying and photography into a business. To help pay for his pilot's license, he began selling aerial photos of farms and homes. Sales were so good that what started out as a way to finance a hobby soon became a full-scale business. He paid an outside accountant to prepare financial statements, which he admits he didn't understand. "I didn't think it was important. I thought a financial statement was just something you had to give to the bank to keep your loan OK. So I took it, looked at the bottom line, and tossed it into a desk drawer."

Accola's casual approach worked for a while. However, within a few years he had lost control of his cash flows. Unpaid creditors were hounding him, and the Internal Revenue Service was demanding overdue taxes. The bank, alarmed by the cash flow situation, demanded to be repaid the $240,000 loan it had extended to the company. Accola confesses that "I

9. The format for the statement of cash flows, which is discussed in Chapter 18, may also be used for the cash budget.

thought if I made enough sales, everything else would take care of itself. But I confused profits with cash flow." The good news is that the company recovered from its near-brush with bankruptcy, instituted formal financial planning procedures, and is now very successful.[10] ■

The Budgeted Income Statement

A budgeted income statement can be prepared from the data developed in Schedules 1–8. *The budgeted income statement is one of the key schedules in the budget process.*

Schedule 8

HAMPTON FREEZE, INC.
Cash Budget
For the Year Ended December 31, 2000

	Schedule	Quarter 1	Quarter 2	Quarter 3	Quarter 4	Year
Cash balance, beginning		$42,500	$40,000	$40,000	$40,500	$42,500
Add receipts:						
Collections from customers	1	230,000	480,000	740,000	520,000	1,970,000
Total cash available before current financing		272,500	520,000	780,000	560,500	2,012,500
Less disbursements:						
Direct materials	3	49,500	72,300	100,050	79,350	301,200
Direct labor	4	84,000	192,000	216,000	114,000	606,000
Manufacturing overhead	5	68,000	96,800	103,200	76,000	344,000
Selling and administrative	7	93,000	130,900	184,750	129,150	537,800
Equipment purchases		50,000	40,000	20,000	20,000	130,000
Dividends		8,000	8,000	8,000	8,000	32,000
Total disbursements		352,500	540,000	632,000	426,500	1,951,000
Excess (deficiency) of cash available over disbursements		(80,000)	(20,000)	148,000	134,000	61,500
Financing:						
Borrowings (at beginning)*		120,000	60,000			180,000
Repayments (at ending)				(100,000)	(80,000)	(180,000)
Interest (at 10% per year)†				(7,500)	(6,500)	(14,000)
Total financing		120,000	60,000	(107,500)	(86,500)	(14,000)
Cash balance, ending		$40,000	$40,000	$40,500	$47,500	$47,500

*The company requires a minimum cash balance of $40,000. Therefore, borrowing must be sufficient to cover the cash deficiency of $80,000 in quarter 1 and to provide for the minimum cash balance of $40,000. All borrowings and all repayments of principal are in round $1,000 amounts.

†The interest payments relate only to the principle being repaid at the time it is repaid. For example, the interest in quarter 3 relates only to the interest due on the $100,000 principal being repaid from quarter 1 borrowing: $100,000 × 10% × ¾ = $7,500. The interest paid in quarter 4 is computed as follows:

$20,000 × 10% × 1 year	$2,000
$60,000 × 10% × ¾	4,500
Total interest paid	$6,500

10. Jay Finnegan, "Everything according to Plan," *Inc.*, March 1995, pp. 78–85.

Schedule 9

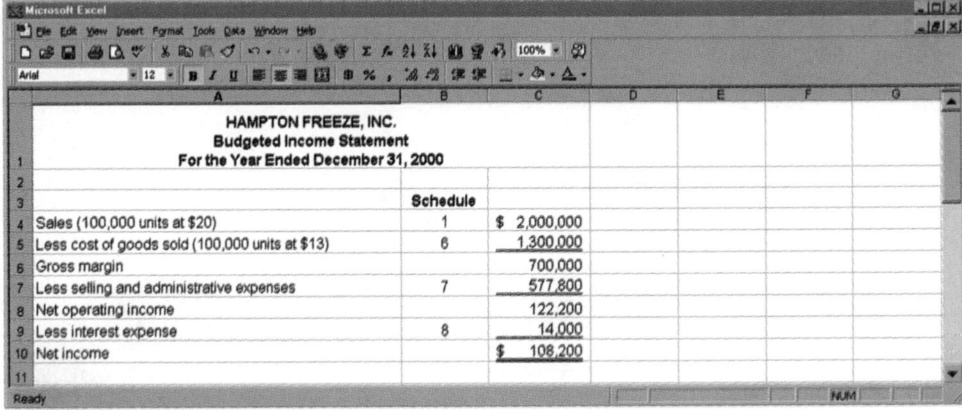

HAMPTON FREEZE, INC.
Budgeted Income Statement
For the Year Ended December 31, 2000

	Schedule	
Sales (100,000 units at $20)	1	$ 2,000,000
Less cost of goods sold (100,000 units at $13)	6	1,300,000
Gross margin		700,000
Less selling and administrative expenses	7	577,800
Net operating income		122,200
Less interest expense	8	14,000
Net income		$ 108,200

objective 10
Prepare a budgeted income statement and a budgeted balance sheet.

It shows the company's planned profit for the upcoming budget period, and it stands as a benchmark against which subsequent company performance can be measured.

Schedule 9 contains the budgeted income statement for Hampton Freeze.

The Budgeted Balance Sheet

The budgeted balance sheet is developed by beginning with the current balance sheet and adjusting it for the data contained in the other budgets. Hampton Freeze's budgeted balance sheet is presented in Schedule 10. Some of the data on the budgeted balance sheet have been taken from the company's end-of-year balance sheet for 1999 which appears below:

HAMPTON FREEZE, INC.
Balance Sheet
December 31, 1999

Assets

Current assets:		
Cash	$ 42,500	
Accounts receivable	90,000	
Raw materials inventory (21,000 pounds)	4,200	
Finished goods inventory (2,000 cases)	26,000	
Total current assets		$162,700
Plant and equipment:		
Land	80,000	
Buildings and equipment	700,000	
Accumulated depreciation	(292,000)	
Plant and equipment, net		488,000
Total assets		$650,700

Liabilities and Stockholders' Equity

Current liabilities:		
Accounts payable (raw materials)		$ 25,800
Stockholders' equity:		
Common stock, no par	$175,000	
Retained earnings	449,900	
Total stockholders' equity		624,900
Total liabilities and stockholders' equity		$650,700

Schedule 10

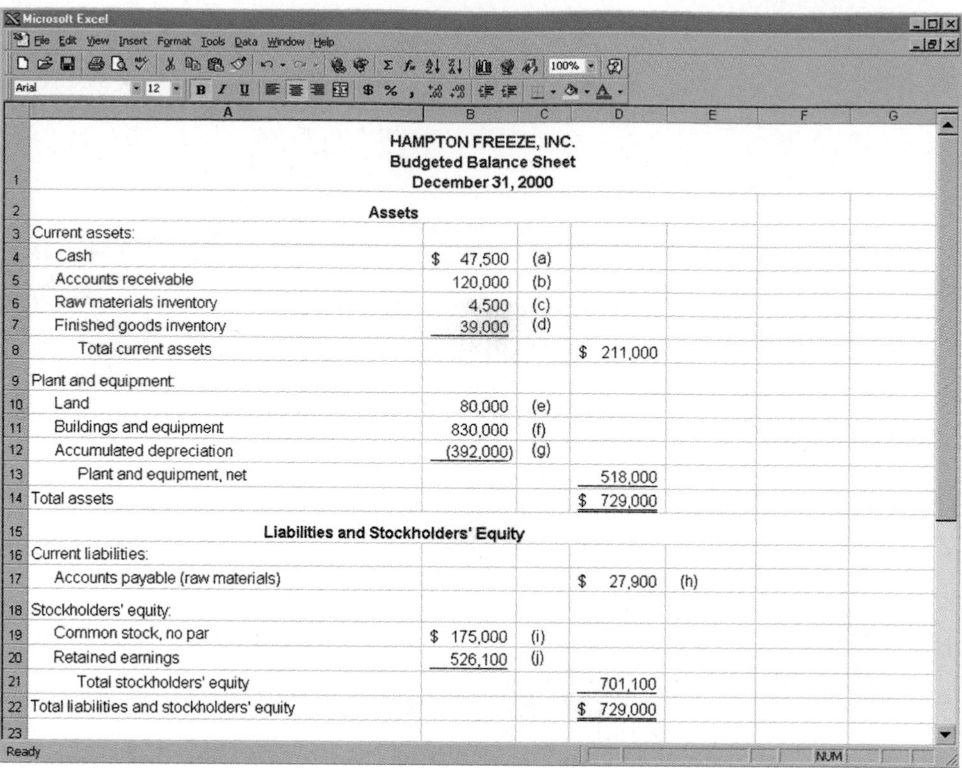

	A	B	C	D	E
1	**HAMPTON FREEZE, INC.** **Budgeted Balance Sheet** **December 31, 2000**				
2	**Assets**				
3	Current assets:				
4	Cash	$ 47,500	(a)		
5	Accounts receivable	120,000	(b)		
6	Raw materials inventory	4,500	(c)		
7	Finished goods inventory	39,000	(d)		
8	Total current assets			$ 211,000	
9	Plant and equipment:				
10	Land	80,000	(e)		
11	Buildings and equipment	830,000	(f)		
12	Accumulated depreciation	(392,000)	(g)		
13	Plant and equipment, net			518,000	
14	Total assets			$ 729,000	
15	**Liabilities and Stockholders' Equity**				
16	Current liabilities:				
17	Accounts payable (raw materials)			$ 27,900	(h)
18	Stockholders' equity:				
19	Common stock, no par	$ 175,000	(i)		
20	Retained earnings	526,100	(j)		
21	Total stockholders' equity			701,100	
22	Total liabilities and stockholders' equity			$ 729,000	

Explanation of December 31, 2000, balance sheet figures:

a. The ending cash balance, as projected by the cash budget in Schedule 8.

b. Thirty percent of fourth-quarter sales, from Schedule 1 ($400,000 × 30% = $120,000).

c. From Schedule 3, the ending raw materials inventory will be 22,500 pounds. This material costs $0.20 per pound. Therefore, the ending inventory in dollars will be 22,500 pounds × $0.20 = $4,500.

d. From Schedule 6.

e. From the December 31, 1999, balance sheet (no change).

f. The December 31, 1999, balance sheet indicated a balance of $700,000. During 2000, $130,000 additional equipment will be purchased (see Schedule 8), bringing the December 31, 2000, balance to $830,000.

g. The December 31, 1999, balance sheet indicated a balance of $292,000. During 2000, $100,000 of depreciation will be taken ($60,000 on Schedule 5 and $40,000 on Schedule 7), bringing the December 31, 2000, balance to $392,000.

h. One-half of the fourth-quarter raw materials purchases, from Schedule 3.

i. From the December 31, 1999, balance sheet (no change).

j.

December 31, 1999 balance	$449,900
Add net income, from Schedule 9	108,200
	558,100
Deduct dividends paid, from Schedule 8	32,000
December 31, 2000, balance	$526,100

Managerial Accounting in Action

THE WRAP-UP

After completing the master budget, Larry Giano took the documents to Tom Wills, chief executive officer of Hampton Freeze, for his review. The following conversation took place:

Larry: Here's the budget. Overall, the net income is excellent, and the net cash flow for the entire year is positive.

Tom: Yes, but I see on this cash budget that we have the same problem with negative cash flows in the first and second quarters that we had last year.

Larry: That's true. I don't see any way around that problem. However, there is no doubt in my mind that if you take this budget to the bank today, they'll approve an open line of credit that will allow you to borrow enough to make it through the first two quarters without any problem.

Tom: Are you sure? They didn't seem very happy to see me last year when I came in for an emergency loan.

Larry: Did you repay the loan on time?

Tom: Sure.

Larry: I don't see any problem. You won't be asking for an emergency loan this time. The bank will have plenty of warning. And with this budget, you have a solid plan that shows when and how you are going to pay off the loan. Trust me, they'll go for it.

Tom: Fantastic! It would sure make life a lot easier this year. ■

Expanding the Budgeted Income Statement

The master budget income statement in Schedule 9 focuses on a single level of activity and has been prepared using absorption costing. Some managers prefer an alternate format that focuses on a *range* of activity and that is prepared using the contribution approach. An example of a master budget income statement using this alternative is format presented in Exhibit 9–3 below:

Exhibit 9–3 Flexible Budget Income Statement

EXAMPLE COMPANY
Master Budget Income Statement

	Budget Formula (per unit)	Sales in Units		
		1,900	2,000	2,100
Sales	$ 75.00	$ 142,500	$ 150,000	$ 157,500
Less variable expenses:				
Direct materials	12.00	22,800	24,000	25,200
Direct labor	31.00	58,900	62,000	65,100
Variable manufacturing overhead	7.50	14,250	15,000	15,750
Variable selling and administrative	4.00	7,600	8,000	8,400
Total variable expenses	54.50	103,550	109,000	114,450
Contribution margin	$ 20.50	38,950	41,000	43,050
Less fixed expenses:				
Fixed manufacturing overhead		18,000	18,000	18,000
Fixed selling administrative		9,000	9,000	9,000
Total fixed expenses		27,000	27,000	27,000
Net income		$ 11,950	$ 14,000	$ 16,050

A statement such as that in Exhibit 9–3 is *flexible,* since it is geared to more than one level of activity. If, for example, the company planned to sell 2,000 units during a period but actually sold only 1,900 units, then the budget figures at the 1,900-unit level would be used to compare against actual costs and revenues. Other columns could be added to the budget as needed by simply applying the budget formulas provided.

In short, a master budget income statement in this expanded format can be very useful in planning and controlling operations. The concepts underlying a flexible approach to budgeting are discussed in later chapters.

Focus on Current Practice

Springfield Remanufacturing Corporation (SRC) rebuilds used engines. SRC was a failing division of International Harvester when it was purchased by Jack Stack and a group of employees. Mr. Stack, the CEO of the company, likens a successful business to a winning team on the playing field. He argues that in order to win:

- All team players must know the rules of the game.
- All team players must follow the action and know how to keep score.
- All team players must have a stake in the outcome.

At SRC, every employee is taught to understand the company's income statement, balance sheet, and statement of cash flows. Each Wednesday all managers attend "The Great Huddle" in which a projected income statement for the current month is filled in on a blank form. Managers report and discuss the numbers for which they are responsible. The managers then return to their departments and hold a series of "huddles" with employees in which the projected income statement is discussed and actions (called new plays) are planned. Employees are given a stake in the outcome by receiving bonuses if certain overall financial goals are met. In addition, an employee stock ownership program (ESOP) encourages employees to take a direct financial stake in the company.

The company has been very successful. Over the six years since leaving International Harvester, a share of stock in the company that was originally worth $63 has grown in value to $26,250.[11] ■

Zero-Based Budgeting

In the traditional approach to budgeting, the manager starts with last year's budget and adds to it (or subtracts from it) according to anticipated needs. This is an incremental approach to budgeting in which the previous year's budget is taken for granted as a baseline.

11. Olen L. Greer, Stevan K. Olson, and Mary Callison, "The Key to Real Teamwork: Understanding Numbers," *Management Accounting,* May 1992, pp. 39–44.

Zero-base budgeting is an alternative approach that is sometimes used—particularly in the governmental and not-for-profit sectors of the economy. Under a **zero-base budget,** managers are required to justify *all* budgeted expenditures, not just changes in the budget from the previous year. The baseline is zero rather than last year's budget.

A zero-base budget requires considerable documentation. In addition to all of the schedules in the usual master budget, the manager must prepare a series of "decision packages" in which all of the activities of the department are ranked according to their relative importance and the cost of each activity is identified. Higher-level managers can then review the decision packages and cut back in those areas that appear to be less critical or whose costs do not appear to be justified.

Nearly everyone would agree that zero-base budgeting is a good idea. The only issue is the frequency with which a zero-base review is carried out. Under zero-base budgeting, the review is performed every year. Critics of zero-base budgeting charge that properly executed zero-base budgeting is too time-consuming and too costly to justify on an annual basis. In addition, it is argued that annual reviews soon become mechanical and that the whole purpose of zero-base budgeting is then lost.

Whether or not a company should use an annual review is a matter of judgment. In some situations, annual zero-base reviews may be justified; in other situations, they may not because of the time and cost involved. However, most managers would at least agree that on occasion zero-base reviews can be very helpful.

International Aspects of Budgeting

A multinational company (MNC) faces special problems when preparing a budget. These problems arise because of fluctuations in foreign currency exchange rates, the high inflation rates found in some countries, and local economic conditions and governmental policies that affect everything from labor costs to marketing practices.

Fluctuations in foreign currency exchange rates create unique budgeting problems. Exporters may be able to predict with some accuracy their sales in the local foreign currency such as South African rands or Swiss francs. However, the amounts they eventually receive in their own currency will depend on the currency exchange rates that prevail at the time. If, for example, the currency exchange rates are less favorable than expected, the company will ultimately receive in its own currency less than it had anticipated.

Companies that are heavily involved in export operations often hedge their exposure to exchange rate fluctuations by buying and selling sophisticated financial contracts. These hedges ensure that if the company loses money in its exporting operations because of exchange rate fluctuations, it will make up that loss with gains on its financial contracts. The details of such hedging operations are covered in finance textbooks. When an MNC uses hedging operations, the costs of those activities should be budgeted along with other expenses.

Some MNCs have operations in countries with very high inflation rates—sometimes exceeding 100% a year. Such high inflation rates—called *hyperinflation*—can render a budget obsolete very quickly. A common budgeting tactic in such countries is to reduce the lead time for preparing the budget and to revise the budget frequently throughout the year in the light of the actual inflation experienced to date.

In addition to problems with exchange rates and inflation, MNCs must be sensitive to government policies in the countries in which they operate that might affect labor costs, equipment purchases, cash management, or other budget items.

Focus on Current Practice

"[In] 1985 the Toronto Blue Jays budgeted a loss for the season despite the fact that the team had the best win-loss record in the major leagues. The majority of team expenses were paid in U.S. dollars in contrast to their revenue, which was earned in Canadian dollars. To protect themselves against adverse changes in the exchange rate, the Blue Jays made forward purchases of U.S. dollars in late 1984 at 75 cents per Canadian dollar to cover a large portion of their budgeted 1985 U.S. dollar denominated expenses. In 1985, the Blue Jays profited on their hedged position when the Canadian dollar depreciated, which helped to offset losses on unhedged U.S. dollar denominated expenses during the same period."[12] ■

Summary

Our purpose has been to present an overview of the budgeting process and to show how the various operating budgets relate to each other. We have seen how the sales budget forms the foundation for profit planning. Once the sales budget has been set, the production budget and the selling and administrative budget can be prepared since they depend on how many units are to be sold. The production budget determines how many units are to be produced, so after it is prepared, the various manufacturing cost budgets can be prepared. All of these various budgets feed into the cash budget and the budgeted income statement and balance sheet. There are many connections between these various parts of the master budget. For example, the schedule of expected cash collections, which is completed in connection with the sales budget, provides data for both the cash budget and the budgeted balance sheet.

The material in this chapter is just an introduction to budgeting and profit planning. In later chapters, we will see how budgets are used to control day-to-day operations and how they are used in performance evaluation.

Review Problem: Budget Schedules

Mylar Company manufactures and sells a product that has seasonal variations in demand, with peak sales coming in the third quarter. The following information concerns operations for Year 2—the coming year—and for the first two quarters of Year 3:

a. The company's single product sells for $8 per unit. Budgeted sales in units for the next six quarters are as follows:

	Year 2 Quarter				Year 3 Quarter	
	1	2	3	4	1	2
Budgeted sales in units	40,000	60,000	100,000	50,000	70,000	80,000

b. Sales are collected in the following pattern: 75% in the quarter the sales are made, and the remaining 25% in the following quarter. On January 1, Year 2, the company's balance

12. Paul V. Mannino and Ken Milani, "Budgeting for an International Business," *Management Accounting* 73, no. 8 (February 1992), p. 37. Used by permission.

sheet showed $65,000 in accounts receivable, all of which will be collected in the first quarter of the year. Bad debts are negligible and can be ignored.

c. The company desires an ending inventory of finished units on hand at the end of each quarter equal to 30% of the budgeted sales for the next quarter. This requirement was met on December 31, Year 1, in that the company had 12,000 units on hand to start the new year.

d. Five pounds of raw materials are required to complete one unit of product. The company requires an ending inventory of raw materials on hand at the end of each quarter equal to 10% of the production needs of the following quarter. This requirement was met on December 31, Year 1, in that the company had 23,000 pounds of raw materials on hand to start the new year.

e. The raw material costs $0.80 per pound. Purchases of raw material are paid for in the following pattern: 60% paid in the quarter the purchases are made, and the remaining 40% paid in the following quarter. One January 1, Year 2, the company's balance sheet showed $81,500 in accounts payable for raw material purchases, all of which will be paid for in the first quarter of the year.

Required Prepare the following budgets and schedules for the year, showing both quarterly and total figures:

1. A sales budget and a schedule of expected cash collections.
2. A production budget.
3. A direct materials purchases budget and a schedule of expected cash payments for material purchases.

Solution to Review Problem

1. The sales budget is prepared as follows:

	Year 2 Quarter				
	1	2	3	4	Year
Budgeted sales in units . .	40,000	60,000	100,000	50,000	250,000
Selling price per unit	× $8	× $8	× $8	× $8	× $8
Total sales	$320,000	$480,000	$800,000	$400,000	$2,000,000

Based on the budgeted sales above, the schedule of expected cash collections is prepared as follows:

	Year 2 Quarter				
	1	2	3	4	Year
Accounts receivable, beginning balance	$ 65,000				$ 65,000
First-quarter sales ($320,000 × 75%, 25%)	240,000	$ 80,000			320,000
Second-quarter sales ($480,000 × 75%, 25%)		360,000	$120,000		480,000
Third-quarter sales ($800,000 × 75%, 25%)			600,000	$200,000	800,000
Fourth-quarter sales ($400,000 × 75%)				300,000	300,000
Total cash collections	$305,000	$440,000	$720,000	$500,000	$1,965,000

2. Based on the sales budget in units, the production budget is prepared as follows:

	Year 2 Quarter					Year 3 Quarter	
	1	2	3	4	Year	1	2
Budgeted sales (units)	40,000	60,000	100,000	50,000	250,000	70,000	80,000
Add desired ending inventory of finished goods*	18,000	30,000	15,000	21,000†	21,000	24,000	
Total needs	58,000	90,000	115,000	71,000	271,000	94,000	
Less beginning inventory of finished goods	12,000	18,000	30,000	15,000	12,000	21,000	
Required production	46,000	72,000	85,000	56,000	259,000	73,000	

*30% of the following quarter's budgeted sales in units.

†30% of the budgeted Year 3 first-quarter sales.

3. Based on the production budget figures, raw materials will need to be purchased as follows during the year:

	Year 2 Quarter					Year 3 Quarter
	1	2	3	4	Year 2	1
Required production (units)	46,000	72,000	85,000	56,000	259,000	73,000
Raw materials needed per unit (pounds)	× 5	× 5	× 5	× 5	× 5	× 5
Production needs (pounds)	230,000	360,000	425,000	280,000	1,295,000	365,000
Add desired ending inventory of raw materials (pounds)*	36,000	42,500	28,000	36,500†	36,500	
Total needs (pounds)	266,000	402,500	453,000	316,500	1,331,500	
Less beginning inventory of raw materials (pounds)	23,000	36,000	42,500	28,000	23,000	
Raw materials to be purchased (pounds)	243,000	366,500	410,500	288,500	1,308,500	

*Ten percent of the following quarter's production needs in pounds.

†Ten percent of the Year 3 first-quarter production needs in pounds.

Based on the raw material purchases above, expected cash payments are computed as follows:

	Year 2 Quarter				
	1	2	3	4	Year 2
Cost of raw materials to be purchased at $0.80 per pound	$194,400	$293,200	$328,400	$230,800	$1,046,800
Accounts payable, beginning balance	$ 81,500				$ 81,500
First-quarter purchases ($194,400 × 60%, 40%)	116,640	$ 77,760			194,400
Second-quarter purchases ($293,200 × 60%, 40%)		175,920	$117,280		293,200
Third-quarter purchases ($328,400 × 60%, 40%)			197,040	$131,360	328,400
Fourth-quarter purchases ($230,800 × 60%)				138,480	138,480
Total cash disbursements	$198,140	$253,680	$314,320	$269,840	$1,035,980

Key Terms for Review

Budget A detailed plan for the acquisition and use of financial and other resources over a specified time period. (p. 378)

Budget committee A group of key management persons who are responsible for overall policy matters relating to the budget program and for coordinating the preparation of the budget. (p. 385)

Cash budget A detailed plan showing how cash resources will be acquired and used over some specific time period. (p. 387)

Continuous or perpetual budget A 12-month budget that rolls forward one month as the current month is completed. (p. 381)

Control Those steps taken by management that attempt to increase the likelihood that the objectives set down at the planning stage are attained and to ensure that all parts of the organization function is a manner consistent with organizational policies. (p. 378)

Direct labor budget A detailed plan showing labor requirements over some specific time period. (p. 392)

Direct materials budget A detailed plan showing the amount of raw materials that must be purchased during a period to meet both production and inventory needs. (p. 392)

Ending finished goods inventory budget A budget showing the dollar amount of cost expected to appear on the balance sheet for unsold units at the end of a period. (p. 395)

Manufacturing overhead budget A detailed plan showing the production costs, other than direct materials and direct labor, that will be incurred over a specified time period. (p. 394)
Master budget A summary of a company's plans in which specific targets are set for sales, production, distribution, and financing activities and that generally culminates in a cash budget, budgeted income statement, and budgeted balance sheet. (p. 378)
Material requirements planning (MRP) An operations management tool that uses a computer to help manage materials and inventories. (p. 392)
Merchandise purchases budget A budget used by a merchandising company that shows the amount of goods that must be purchased from suppliers during the period. (p. 391)
Participative budget See *Self-imposed budget.* (p. 382)
Planning Developing objectives and preparing budgets to achieve these objectives. (p. 378)
Production budget A detailed plan showing the number of units that must be produced during a period in order to meet both sales and inventory needs. (p. 390)
Responsibility accounting A system of accountability in which managers are held responsible for those items of revenue and cost—and only those items—over which the manager can exert significant control. The managers are held responsible for differences between budgeted and actual results. (p. 380)
Sales budget A detailed schedule showing the expected sales for coming periods; these sales are typically expressed in both dollars and units. (p. 386)
Self-imposed budget A method of preparing budgets in which managers prepare their own budgets. These budgets are then reviewed by the manager's supervisor, and any issues are resolved by mutual agreement. (p. 382)
Selling and administrative expense budget A detailed schedule of planned expenses that will be incurred in areas other than manufacturing during a budget period. (p. 395)
Zero-based budget A method of budgeting in which managers are required to justify all costs as if the programs involved were being proposed for the first time. (p. 403)

Appendix 9A: Economic Order Quantity (EOQ) and the Reorder Point

objective 11

Determine the economic order quantity (EOQ) and the reorder point.

Inventory planning and control are an essential part of a budgeting system. Inventory levels should not be left to chance but should be carefully planned. Selecting the "right" level of inventories involves balancing three groups of costs: *inventory ordering costs, inventory carrying costs,* and the *costs of not carrying sufficient inventory.* These costs are discussed in this section.

Costs Associated with Inventory

Inventory ordering costs are incurred each time an inventory item is ordered. These costs may include clerical costs associated with ordering inventory, and some handling and transportation costs. They are triggered by the act of ordering inventory and are essentially the same whether 1 unit or 10,000 units are ordered; these costs are driven by the number of orders placed—not by the size of the orders. If inventory ordering costs are large, a manager may want to place small numbers of big orders on an infrequent basis rather than large numbers of small orders.

Inventory carrying costs are incurred to keep units in inventory. These costs include storage costs, handling costs, property taxes, insurance, and the interest on the funds invested in inventories. These costs are driven by the amount and value of inventories that are held by the company. In addition to these costs, work in process inventories create operating problems. Work in process may physically get in the way and make it difficult to keep track of operations. Moreover, work in process tends to hide problems that are not discovered until it is too late to take corrective action. This results in erratic production, inefficient operations, "lost" orders, high defect rates, and substantial risks of obsolescence. These intangible costs of work in process inventories are largely responsible for the movement to JIT. If inventory carrying costs are high, managers will want to reduce the overall level of inventories and to place frequent orders in small quantities.

The **costs of not carrying sufficient inventory** result from not having enough inventory in stock to meet customers' needs. These costs include lost sales, customer ill will, and the costs of expediting orders for goods not held in stock. If these costs are high, managers will want to hold large inventories.

Conceptually, the "right" level of inventory to carry is the level that will minimize the total of these three groups of costs. In the following pages we show how to accomplish this task. The problem is broken down into two dimensions—how much to order (or how much to produce in a single production run or batch) and how often to do it. These two decisions—how much to order and how often to order—determine the average level of inventories and the likelihood of being out of stock.

Computing the Economic Order Quantity (EOQ)

The question "How much to order?" is answered by the **economic order quantity (EOQ).** It is the order size that minimizes the sum of the costs of ordering inventory and the costs of carrying inventory. We will consider two approaches to computing the EOQ—the tabular approach and the formula approach.

THE TABULAR APPROACH Suppose that 12,000 units of a particular item are required each year. Managers could order all 12,000 units at once or they could order smaller numbers of units spread over the year—perhaps 1,000 units per month. Placing only one order would minimize the total costs of ordering inventory but would result in high inventory carrying costs, since the average inventory level would be very large. On the other hand, placing many small orders would result in high ordering costs but in low inventory carrying costs, since the average inventory level would be reduced. As stated above, the EOQ is the order size that will optimally balance these two costs—inventory ordering costs and inventory holding costs.

To show how EOQ is computed, assume that a manufacturer uses 3,000 subassemblies in the manufacturing process each year. The subassemblies are purchased from a supplier at a cost of $20 each. Other cost data are given below:

Inventory carrying costs, per unit, per year	$ 0.80
Cost of placing a purchase order	10.00

Exhibit 9A–1 contains a tabulation of the total costs associated with various order sizes for the subassemblies. Most of this table is straightforward, but the average inventory requires some explanation. If 50 units are ordered at a time and the items are ordered only when the inventory gets down to zero, then the size the of inventory will vary from 50 units to 0 units. Thus, on average, there will be 25 units in inventory. Notice that total annual cost is lowest (and is equal) at the 250- and 300-unit order sizes. The EOQ will lie somewhere between these two points. We could locate it precisely by adding more columns to the tabulation, and we would eventually zero in on 274 units as being the exact EOQ.

The cost relationships from this tabulation are shown graphically in Exhibit 9A–2. The EOQ is indicated on the graph. Notice that the EOQ minimizes the total annual costs. It also is the point where annual carrying costs and annual ordering costs are equal. At the EOQ, these two costs are exactly balanced.

Observe from the graph that total cost shows a tendency to flatten out between 200 and 400 units. Most firms look for this minimum cost range and choose an order size that falls within it, rather than choosing the exact EOQ. The primary reason is that suppliers will often ship goods only in round-lot sizes.

Exhibit 9A–1 Tabulation of Costs Associated with Various Order Sizes

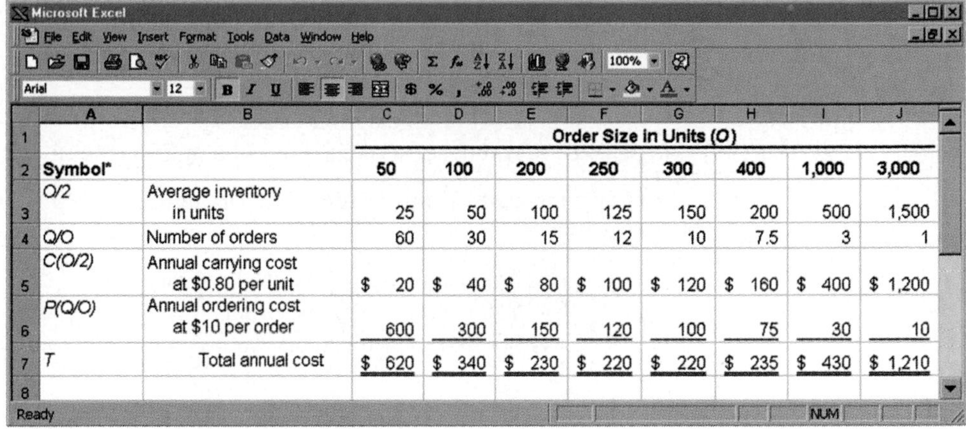

Symbol*		Order Size in Units (O)							
		50	100	200	250	300	400	1,000	3,000
O/2	Average inventory in units	25	50	100	125	150	200	500	1,500
Q/O	Number of orders	60	30	15	12	10	7.5	3	1
C(O/2)	Annual carrying cost at $0.80 per unit	$ 20	$ 40	$ 80	$ 100	$ 120	$ 160	$ 400	$ 1,200
P(Q/O)	Annual ordering cost at $10 per order	600	300	150	120	100	75	30	10
T	Total annual cost	$ 620	$ 340	$ 230	$ 220	$ 220	$ 235	$ 430	$ 1,210

Minimum total annual cost

*Symbols:

O = Order size in units (see headings above).

Q = Annual quantity used in units (3,000 in this example).

C = Annual cost of carrying one unit in stock.

P = Cost of placing one order.

T = Total annual cost.

Exhibit 9A–2 Graphic Solution to Economic Order Quantity (EOQ)

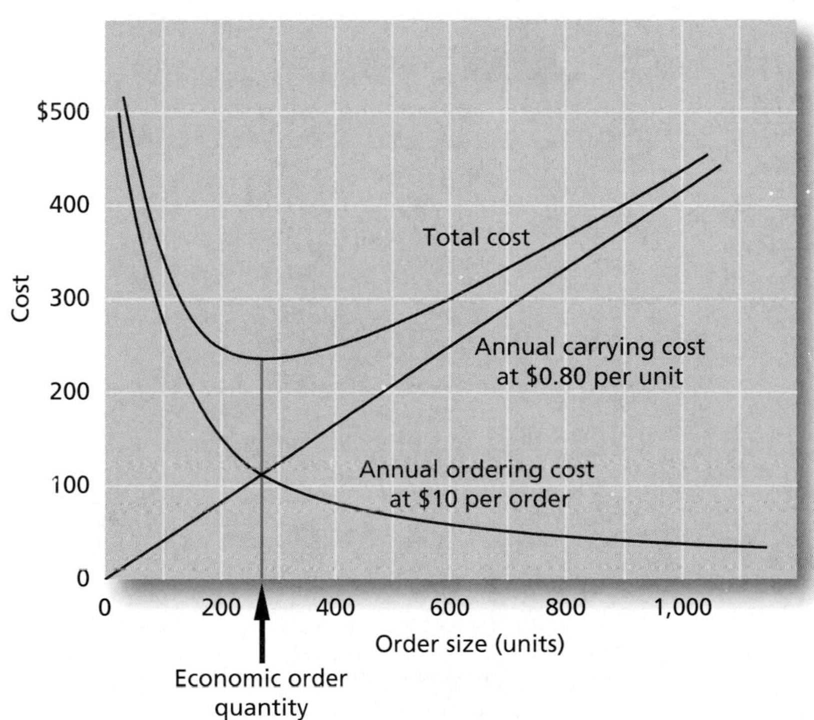

THE FORMULA APPROACH The EOQ can also be found by means of a formula that can be derived using calculus:

$$E = \sqrt{\frac{2\,QP}{C}}$$

where:

E = Economic order quantity (EOQ)
Q = Annual quantity used in units
P = Cost of placing one order
C = Annual cost of carrying one unit in stock

Using the data from the preceding example, we can directly compute the EOQ as follows:

Q = 3,000 subassemblies used per year
P = $10 cost to place one order
C = $0.80 cost to carry one subassembly in stock for one year

$$E = \sqrt{\frac{2\,QP}{C}} = \sqrt{\frac{2(3{,}000)(\$10)}{\$0.80}} = \sqrt{\frac{\$60{,}000}{\$0.80}} = \sqrt{75{,}000}$$

E = 274 units (the EOQ)

Just-in-Time (JIT) and the Economic Order Quantity (EOQ)

By examining the EOQ formula, you can see that the economic order quantity, E, will decrease if:

1. The cost of placing an order, P, decreases, or
2. The cost of carrying inventory in stock, C, increases.

Proponents of JIT argue that the cost of carrying inventory in stock is much greater than generally realized because of the waste and inefficiency that inventories create. They also argue that following JIT procedures, such as concentrating all orders on a few high-quality suppliers as discussed in Chapter 1, will dramatically reduce the cost of placing an order. As a consequence, JIT advocates argue that companies should purchase more frequently in smaller amounts. Assume, for example, that a company has used the following data to compute its EOQ:

Q = 4,800 units needed each year
P = $75 cost to place one order
C = $4.50 cost to carry one unit in stock for one year

Given these data, the EOQ would be as follows:

$$E = \sqrt{\frac{2\,QP}{C}} = \sqrt{\frac{2(4{,}800)(\$75)}{\$4.50}} = \sqrt{160{,}000}$$

E = 400 units

Now assume that as a result of JIT purchasing, the company is able to decrease the cost of placing an order to only $3. Also assume that due to the waste and inefficiency caused by inventories, the true cost of carrying a unit in stock is $8 per year. The revised EOQ would be as follows:

$$E = \sqrt{\frac{2\,QP}{C}} = \sqrt{\frac{2(4{,}800)(\$3)}{\$8}} = \sqrt{3{,}600}$$

E = 60 units

Under JIT purchasing, the company would *not* necessarily order in 60-unit lots, since purchases would be geared to current demand. Nevertheless, this example shows quite dramatically the economics behind reducing order sizes.

Production Lot Size

The EOQ concept can also be applied to the problem of determining the **economic lot size.** When companies manufacture a variety of products, they must decide how many units of one product should be manufactured before switching over to another product. The number of units in a lot, or production run, is referred to as the *lot size* or *batch size.* For example, Nintendo must decide how many units of a particular video game are to be produced in one lot before switching over to production of a different video game. This is a problem because switching from one product to another requires changing settings on machines, changing tools, and getting different materials ready for processing. Making these changes requires time and may involve substantial out-of-pocket costs. These **setup costs** are analogous to the order costs discussed above, and they can be used in the EOQ formula in place of the order costs to determine the optimal lot size.

To illustrate, Chittenden Company has determined that the following costs are associated with one of its products:

Q = 15,000 units produced each year
P = \$150 setup costs to switch production from one product to another
C = \$2 to carry one unit in stock for one year

What is the optimal production lot size for this product? It can be determined by using the EOQ formula:

$$E = \sqrt{\frac{2\,QP}{C}} = \sqrt{\frac{2(15{,}000)(\$150)}{\$2}} = \sqrt{2{,}250{,}000}$$

$$E = 1{,}500 \text{ units (economic lot size)}$$

Chittenden Company will minimize its overall costs by producing in lots of 1,500 units each.

In computing the economic lot size, note again the impact of modern manufacturing methods. First, managers now realize that the costs of holding inventory are far higher than previously assumed. Excess work in process inventories make it very difficult to operate efficiently and hence generate many unnecessary costs. Second, as discussed in Chapter 1, managers and workers are cutting setup times from many hours to a few minutes by cleverly applying techniques such as single-minute-exchange of dies. The benefit of reducing setup time is that it makes it economically feasible for the company to produce in smaller lots and to respond much more quickly to the market. Indeed, reducing setups to the barest minimum is an essential step in any successful implementation of JIT.

To illustrate how these aspects of modern manufacturing methods affect the economic lot size, consider the Chittenden Company data. Suppose that the company has been able to reduce the cost of a setup to only \$3. Further suppose that the company realizes, after more careful analysis of all of the costs of holding inventory, that the true cost of carrying a unit in stock is \$36 per year. The new economic lot size would be as follows:

$$E = \sqrt{\frac{2\,QP}{C}} = \sqrt{\frac{2(15{,}000)(\$3)}{\$36}} = \sqrt{2{,}500}$$

$$E = 50 \text{ units (economic lot size)}$$

Thus, the company's economic lot size has been reduced from 1,500 units to only 50 units—a reduction of nearly 97%.

PRODUCTION LOT SIZE AND THE THEORY OF CONSTRAINTS Managers involved in the theory of constraints would go even further in reducing lot sizes. When a particular work center is not a constraint, the only significant cost involved in setups is typically direct labor wages. However, since direct labor wages are considered to be a fixed cost rather than a variable cost in the theory of constraints, the incremental cost of setups is considered to be zero. Therefore, at work centers that are not a constraint, the economic lot size in the theory of constraints is as small as a single unit.[13]

ACTIVITY-BASED COSTING (ABC) AND THE PRODUCTION LOT SIZE Managers should be extremely cautious when applying the results of ABC analyses to computation of the economic lot size. Typically, one of the results of an ABC analysis is a dramatic increase in the apparent costs of setups. The reason for this is that under conventional costing systems, many of the costs that might be attributed to switching over from one product to another are lumped into the general manufacturing overhead cost pool and distributed to products based on direct labor-hours or some other measure of volume. When an ABC analysis is done, these costs are separately identified as setup costs. As a consequence, setup costs appear to increase, and this would seem to imply that the economic lot size should be increased. However, a close examination of the costs attributed to setups in the ABC analysis will usually reveal that most of the costs cannot actually be avoided by reducing the number of setups. For example, machinery depreciation may be included in setup costs. However, reducing the number of setups may have no impact at all on the amount of machinery depreciation actually incurred.

Reorder Point and Safety Stock

We stated that the inventory problem has two dimensions—how much to order and how often to do it. The "how often to do it" involves what are commonly termed the *reorder point* and the *safety stock.* The basic idea is to minimize the costs of holding inventory while ensuring that there will be no stockouts (i.e., situations in which there are insufficient inventories to satisfy current production requirements or customer demand). First, we will discuss the reorder point and then we will discuss the safety stock.

The **reorder point** tells the manager when to place an order or when to initiate production to replenish depleted stocks. It is dependent on three factors—the EOQ (or economic production-run size), the *lead time,* and the rate of usage during the lead time. The **lead time** can be defined as the interval between the time that an order is placed and the time when the order is finally received from the supplier or from the production line.

CONSTANT USAGE DURING THE LEAD TIME If the rate of usage during the lead time is known with certainty, the reorder point can be determined by the following formula:

$$\text{Reorder point} = \text{Lead time} \times \text{Average daily or weekly usage}$$

13. At the constraint itself, setup time is very costly, since each minute spent setting up is a minute taken away from producing output that could be sold. Therefore, setup reduction efforts should be focused on the constraint and lot sizes should be larger on the constraint than at other work centers.

To illustrate the formula's use, assume that a company's EOQ is 500 units, that the lead time is three weeks, and that the average weekly usage is 50 units.

$$\text{Reorder point} = 3 \text{ weeks} \times 50 \text{ units per week} = 150 \text{ units}$$

The reorder point would be 150 units. That is, the company will automatically place a new order for 500 units when inventory stocks drop to a level of 150 units, or three weeks' supply, left on hand

VARIABLE USAGE DURING THE LEAD TIME The previous example assumed that the 50 units per week usage rate was constant and was known with certainty. Although some firms enjoy the luxury of certainty, the more common situation is to find considerable variation in the rate of usage of inventory items from period to period. If usage varies from period to period, the firm that reorders in the way computed above may soon find itself out of stock. A sudden spurt in demand, a delay in delivery, or a snag in processing an order may cause inventory levels to be depleted before a new shipment arrives.

Companies that experience problems in demand, delivery, or processing of orders have found that they need some type of buffer to guard against stockouts. Such a buffer is called a **safety stock.** A safety stock serves as a kind of insurance against greater than usual demand and against problems in the ordering and delivery of goods. Its size is determined by deducting *average usage* from the *maximum usage* that can reasonably be expected during a period. For example, if the firm in the preceding example was faced with variable demand for its product, it would compute a safety stock as follows:

Maximum expected usage per week	65 units
Average usage per week	50 units
Excess	15 units
Lead time	× 3 weeks
Safety stock	45 units

The reorder point is then determined by *adding the safety stock to the average usage during the lead time.* In formula form, the reorder point would be as shown on the following page :

Exhibit 9A–3 Determining the Reorder Point—Variable Usage

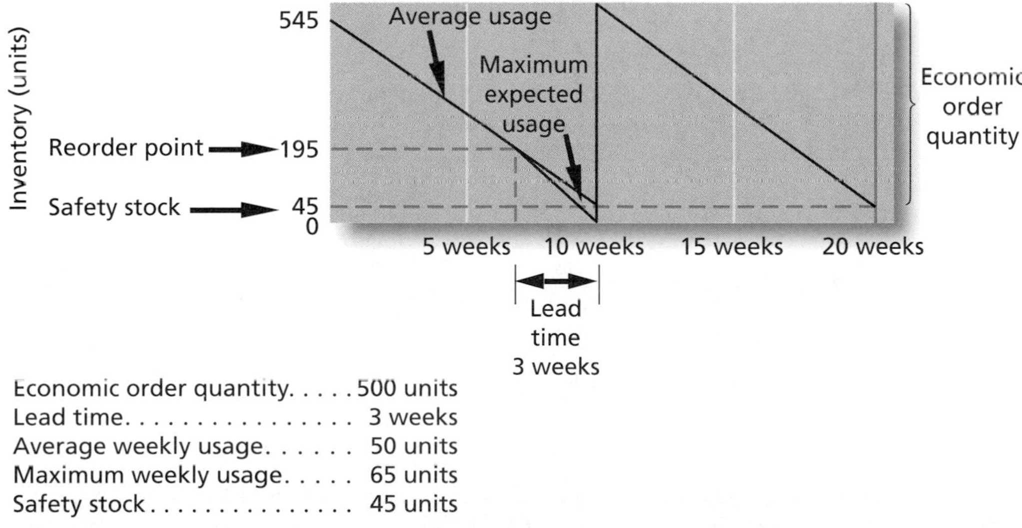

Reorder point = (3 weeks × 50 units per week) + 45 units = 195 units

Reorder point = (Lead time × Average daily or weekly usage) + Safety stock

Computation of the reorder point is shown both numerically and graphically in Exhibit 9A–3. As shown in the exhibit, the company will place a new order for 500 units when inventory stocks drop to a level of 195 units left on hand.

Key Terms for Review (Appendix 9A)

Costs of not carrying sufficient inventory Those costs that result from not having enough inventory in stock to meet customers' needs; such costs would include lost sales, customer ill will, and costs of expediting orders for items not in stock. (p. 408)

Economic lot size The number of units produced in a lot, or production run, that will result in minimizing setup costs and the costs of carrying inventory. (p. 411)

Economic order quantity (EOQ) The order size for materials that will result in minimizing the costs of ordering and carrying inventory. (p. 408)

Inventory carrying costs Those costs that result from having inventory in stock, such as rental of storage space, handling costs, property taxes, insurance, and interest on funds. These costs also should include costs of excess work in process inventories such as inefficient production, excess lead times, high defect rates, and risks of obsolence. (p. 407)

Inventory ordering costs Those costs associated with the acquisition of inventory, such as clerical costs and transportation costs. (p. 407)

Lead time The interval between the time that an order is placed and the time that the order is finally received from the supplier. (p. 412)

Reorder point The point in time when an order must be placed to replenish depleted stocks; it is determined by multiplying the lead time by the average daily or weekly usage. (p. 412)

Safety stock The difference between average usage of materials and maximum usage of materials that can reasonably be expected during the lead time. (p. 413)

Setup costs Cost involved in getting facilities ready to change over from making one product to another. (p. 411)

Questions

9–1 What is a budget? What is budgetary control?

9–2 Discuss some of the major benefits to be gained from budgeting.

9–3 What is meant by the term *responsibility accounting?*

9–4 What is a master budget? Briefly describe its contents.

9–5 Why is the sales forecast the starting point in budgeting?

9–6 "As a practical matter, planning and control mean exactly the same thing." Do you agree? Explain.

9–7 Describe the flow of budget data in an organization. Who are the participants in the budgeting process, and how do they participate?

9–8 What is a self-imposed budget? What are the major advantages of self-imposed budgets? What caution must be exercised in their use.

9–9 How can budgeting assist a firm in its employment policies?

9–10 "The principal purpose of the cash budget is to see how much cash the company will have in the bank at the end of the year." Do you agree? Explain.

9–11 How does zero-base budgeting differ from traditional budgeting?

9–12 (Appendix 9A) What three classes of costs are balanced by a company's inventory policy?

9–13 (Appendix 9A) What trade-offs in costs are involved in computing the EOQ (economic order quantity)?

9–14 (Appendix 9A) Define *lead time* and *safety stock.*

Exercises

E9–1 Silver Company makes a product that is very popular as a Mother's Day gift. Thus, peak sales occur in May of each year. These peak sales are shown in the company's sales budget for the second quarter given below:

	April	May	June	Total
Budgeted sales	$300,000	$500,000	$200,000	$1,000,000

From past experience, the company has learned that 20% of a month's sales are collected in the month of sale, that another 70% is collected in the month following sale, and that the remaining 10% is collected in the second month following sale. Bad debts are negligible and can be ignored. February sales totaled $230,000, and March sales totaled $260,000.

Required

1. Prepare a schedule of expected cash collections from sales, by month and in total, for the second quarter.
2. Assume that the company will prepare a budgeted balance sheet as of June 30. Compute the accounts receivable as of that date.

E9–2 Down Under Products, Ltd., of Australia has budgeted sales of its popular boomerang for the next four months as follows:

	Sales in Units
April	50,000
May	75,000
June	90,000
July	80,000

The company is now in the process of preparing a production budget for the second quarter. Past experience has shown that end-of-month inventory levels must equal 10% of the following month's sales. The inventory at the end of March was 5,000 units.

Required Prepare a production budget for the second quarter; in your budget, show the number of units to be produced each month and for the quarter in total.

E9–3 Three grams of musk oil are required for each bottle of Mink Caress, a very popular perfume made by a small company in western Siberia. The cost of the musk oil is 150 roubles per gram. (Siberia is located in Russia, whose currency is the rouble.) Budgeted production of Mink Caress is given below by quarters for Year 2 and for the first quarter of Year 3.

	Year 2 Quarter				Year 3 Quarter
	First	Second	Third	Fourth	First
Budgeted production, in bottles	60,000	90,000	150,000	100,000	70,000

Musk oil has become so popular as a perfume base that it has become necessary to carry large inventories as a precaution against stock-outs. For this reason, the inventory of musk oil at the end of a quarter must be equal to 20% of the following quarter's production needs. Some 36,000 grams of musk oil will be on hand to start the first quarter of Year 2.

Required Prepare a materials purchases budget for musk oil, by quarter and in total, for Year 2. At the bottom of your budget, show the amount of purchases in roubles for each quarter and for the year in total.

E9–4 You have been asked to prepare a December cash budget for Ashton Company, a distributor of exercise equipment. The following information is available about the company's operations:

a. The cash balance on December 1 will be $40,000.
b. Actual sales for October and November and expected sales for December are as follows:

	October	November	December
Cash sales	$ 65,000	$ 70,000	$ 83,000
Sales on account	400,000	525,000	600,000

Sales on account are collected over a three-month period in the following ratio: 20% collected in the month of sale, 60% collected in the month following sale, and 18% collected in the second month following sale. The remaining 2% is uncollectible.

c. Purchases of inventory will total $280,000 for December. Thirty percent of a month's inventory purchases are paid during the month of purchase. The accounts payable remaining from November's inventory purchases total $161,000, all of which will be paid in December.
d. Selling and administrative expenses are budgeted at $430,000 for December. Of this amount, $50,000 is for depreciation.
e. A new web server for the Marketing Department costing $76,000 will be purchased for cash during December, and dividends totaling $9,000 will be paid during the month.
f. The company must maintain a minimum cash balance of $20,000. An open line of credit is available from the company's bank to bolster the cash position as needed.

Required

1. Prepare a schedule of expected cash collections for December.
2. Prepare a schedule of expected cash disbursements for materials during December to suppliers for inventory purchases.
3. Prepare a cash budget for December. Indicate in the financing section any borrowing that will be needed during the month.

E9–5 A cash budget, by quarters, is given below for a retail company. Fill in the missing amounts (000 omitted). The company requires a minimum cash balance of at least $5,000 to start each quarter.

	1	2	3	4	Year
Cash balance, beginning	$ 6	$?	$?	$?	$?
Add collections from customers	?	?	96	?	323
Total cash available before current financing	71	?	?	?	?
Less disbursements:					
Purchase of inventory	35	45	?	35	?
Operating expenses	?	30	30	?	113
Equipment purchases	8	8	10	?	36
Dividends	2	2	2	2	?
Total disbursements	?	85	?	?	?
Excess (deficiency) of cash available over disbursements	(2)	?	11	?	?

Financing:					
Borrowings	?	15	—	—	?
Repayments (including interest)*	—	—	(?)	(17)	(?)
Total financing	?	?	?	?	?
Cash balance, ending	$?	$?	$?	$?	$?

*Interest will total $1,000 for the year.

E9–6 (Appendix 9A) Bedford Motor Company uses 4,500 units of Part S-10 each year. The cost of placing one order for Part S-10 is estimated to be about $20. Other costs associated with carrying Part S-10 in inventory are:

	Annual Cost per Part
Insurance	$0.20
Property taxes	0.09
Interest on funds invested	0.15
Other	0.06
Total cost	$0.50

Required

1. Compute the economic order quantity (EOQ) for Part S-10.
2. Assume that the company has been able to reduce the cost of placing an order to only $1. Also assume that when the waste and inefficiency caused by inventories is considered, the cost to carry a part in inventory jumps to $1.60 per unit. Under these conditions, what would be the EOQ?

E9–7 (Appendix 9A) Kaufheim A.G. of Dresden, Germany, distributes medical supplies throughout Germany. Selected information relating to a quick-developing X-ray film carried by the company is given below:

Economic order quantity (EOQ)	700 units
Maximum weekly usage	60 units
Lead time	4 weeks
Average weekly usage	50 units

Management is trying to determine the proper safety stock to carry on this inventory item and to determine the proper reorder point.

Required

1. Assume that no safety stock is to be carried. What is the reorder point?
2. Assume that a full safety stock is to be carried.
   a. What would be the size of the safety stock in units?
   b. What would be the reorder point?

E9–8 (Appendix 9A) Flint Company uses 9,000 units of part AK-4 each year. To get better control over its inventories, the company is anxious to determine the economic order quantity (EOQ) for this part.

Required

1. The company has determined that the cost to place an order for the part is $30, and it has determined that the cost to carry one part in inventory for one year is $1.50. Compute the EOQ for the part.
2. Assume that the cost to place an order increases from $30 to $40 per order. What will be the effect on the EOQ? Show computations.
3. Assume that the cost to carry a part in inventory increases from $1.50 to $2.00 per part. (Ordering costs remain unchanged at $30 per order.) What will be the effect on the EOQ? Show computations.
4. In (2) and (3) above, why does an increase in cost cause the EOQ to go up in one case and to go down in the other?

Problems

P9–9 Cash Budget Herbal Care Corp., a distributor of herb-based sun screens, is ready to begin its third quarter, in which peak sales occur. The company has requested a $40,000, 90-day loan from its bank to help meet cash requirements during the quarter. Since Herbal Care has experienced difficulty in paying off its loans in the past, the loan officer at the bank has asked the company to prepare a cash budget for the quarter. In response to this request, the following data have been assembled:

a. On July 1, the beginning of the third quarter, the company will have a cash balance of $44,500.
b. Actual sales for the last two months and budgeted sales for the third quarter follow:

May (actual)	$250,000
June (actual)	300,000
July (budgeted)	400,000
August (budgeted)	600,000
September (budgeted)	320,000

Past experience shows that 25% of a month's sales are collected in the month of sale, 70% in the month following sale, and 3% in the second month following sale. The remainder is uncollectible.

c. Budgeted merchandise purchases and budgeted expenses for the third quarter are given below:

	July	August	September
Merchandise purchases	$240,000	$350,000	$175,000
Salaries and wages	45,000	50,000	40,000
Advertising	130,000	145,000	80,000
Rent payments	9,000	9,000	9,000
Depreciation	10,000	10,000	10,000

Merchandise purchases are paid in full during the month following purchase. Accounts payable for merchandise purchases on June 30, which will be paid during July, total $180,000.

d. Equipment costing $10,000 will be purchased for cash during July.
e. In preparing the cash budget, assume that the $40,000 loan will be made in July and repaid in September. Interest on the loan will total $1,200.

Required

1. Prepare a schedule of expected cash collections for July, August, and September and for the quarter in total.
2. Prepare a cash budget, by month and in total, for the third quarter.
3. If the company needs a minimum cash balance of $20,000 to start each month, can the loan be repaid as planned? Explain.

P9–10 Production and Purchases Budgets Pearl Products Limited of Shenzhen, China, manufactures and distributes toys throughout South East Asia. Three cubic centimeters (cc) of solvent H300 are required to manufacture each unit of Supermix, one of the company's products. The company is now planning raw materials needs for the third quarter, the quarter in which peak sales of Supermix occur. To keep production and sales moving smoothly, the company has the following inventory requirements:

a. The finished goods inventory on hand at the end of each month must be equal to 3,000 units of Supermix plus 20% of the next month's sales. The finished goods inventory on June 30 is budgeted to be 10,000 units.
b. The raw materials inventory on hand at the end of each month must be equal to one-half of the following month's production needs for raw materials. The raw materials inventory on June 30 is budgeted to be 54,000 cc of solvent H300.
c. The company maintains no work in process inventories.

A sales budget for Supermix for the last six months of the year follows.

	Budgeted Sales in Units
July	35,000
August	40,000
September	50,000
October	30,000
November	20,000
December	10,000

Required

1. Prepare a production budget for Supermix for the months July–October.
2. Examine the production budget that you prepared in (1) above. Why will the company produce more units than it sells in July and August, and fewer units than it sells in September and October?
3. Prepare a budget showing the quantity of solvent H300 to be purchased for July, August, and September, and for the quarter in total.

P9–11 Evaluating a Company's Budget Procedures Springfield Corporation operates on a calendar-year basis. It begins the annual budgeting process in late August, when the president establishes targets for the total dollar sales and net income before taxes for the next year.

The sales target is given to the Marketing Department, where the marketing manager formulates a sales budget by product line in both units and dollars. From this budget, sales quotas by product line in units and dollars are established for each of the corporation's sales districts.

The marketing manager also estimates the cost of the marketing activities required to support the target sales volume and prepares a tentative marketing expense budget.

The executive vice president uses the sales and profit targets, the sales budget by product line, and the tentative marketing expense budget to determine the dollar amounts that can be devoted to manufacturing and corporate office expense. The executive vice president prepares the budget for corporate expenses, and then forwards to the Production Department the product-line sales budget in units and the total dollar amount that can be devoted to manufacturing.

The production manager meets with the factory managers to develop a manufacturing plan that will produce the required units when needed within the cost constraints set by the executive vice president. The budgeting process usually comes to a halt at this point because the Production Department does not consider the financial resources allocated to be adequate.

When this standstill occurs, the vice president of finance, the executive vice president, the marketing manager, and the production manager meet to determine the final budgets for each of the areas. This normally results in a modest increase in the total amount available for manufacturing costs, while the marketing expense and corporate office expense budgets are cut. The total sales and net income figures proposed by the president are seldom changed. Although the participants are seldom pleased with the compromise, these budgets are final. Each executive then develops a new detailed budget for the operations in his or her area.

None of the areas has achieved its budget in recent years. Sales often run below the target. When budgeted sales are not achieved, each area is expected to cut costs so that the president's profit target can still be met. However, the profit target is seldom met because costs are not cut enough. In fact, costs often run above the original budget in all functional areas. The president is disturbed that Springfield has not been able to meet the sales and profit targets. He hired a consultant with considerable experience with companies in Springfield's industry. The consultant reviewed the budgets for the past four years. He concluded that the product-line sales budgets were reasonable and that the cost and expense budgets were adequate for the budgeted sales and production levels.

Required

1. Discuss how the budgeting process as employed by Springfield Corporation contributes to the failure to achieve the president's sales and profit targets.
2. Suggest how Springfield Corporation's budgeting process could be revised to correct the problem.
3. Should the functional areas be expected to cut their costs when sales volume falls below budget? Explain your answer.

(CMA, adapted)

P9–12 Master Budget Preparation Minden Company is a wholesale distributor of premium European chocolates. The company's balance sheet as of April 30 is given below:

MINDEN COMPANY
Balance Sheet
April 30

Assets	
Cash	$ 9,000
Accounts receivable, customers	54,000
Inventory	30,000
Buildings and equipment, net of depreciation	207,000
Total assets	$300,000
Liabilities and Stockholders' Equity	
Accounts payable, suppliers	$ 63,000
Note payable	14,500
Capital stock, no par	180,000
Retained earnings	42,500
Total liabilities and stockholders' equity	$300,000

The company is in the process of preparing budget data for May. A number of budget items have already been prepared, as stated below:

a. Sales are budgeted at $200,000 for May. Of these sales, $60,000 will be for cash; the remainder will be credit sales. One-half of a month's credit sales are collected in the month the sales are made, and the remainder is collected in the following month. All of the April 30 receivables will be collected in May.
b. Purchases of inventory are expected to total $120,000 during May. These purchases will all be on account. Forty percent of all purchases are paid for in the month of purchase; the remainder is paid in the following month. All of the April 30 accounts payable to suppliers will be paid during May.
c. The May 31 inventory balance is budgeted at $40,000.
d. Operating expenses for May are budgeted at $72,000, exclusive of depreciation. These expenses will be paid in cash. Depreciation is budgeted at $2,000 for the month.
e. The note payable on the April 30 balance sheet will be paid during May, with $100 in interest. (All of the interest relates to May.)
f. New refrigerating equipment costing $6,500 will be purchased for cash during May.
g. During May, the company will borrow $20,000 from its bank by giving a new note payable to the bank for that amount. The new note will be due in one year.

Required

1. Prepare a cash budget for May. Support your budget with schedules showing budgeted cash receipts from sales and budgeted cash payments for inventory purchases.
2. Prepare a budgeted income statement for May. Use the traditional income statement format.
3. Prepare a budgeted balance sheet as of May 31.

P9–13 Ethics and the Manager Norton Company, a manufacturer of infant furniture and carriages, is in the initial stages of preparing the annual budget for next year. Scott Ford has recently joined Norton's accounting staff and is interested to learn as much as possible about the company's budgeting process. During a recent lunch with Marge Atkins, sales manager, and Pete Granger, production manager, Ford initiated the following conversation.

Ford: Since I'm new around here and am going to be involved with the preparation of the annual budget, I'd be interested to learn how the two of you estimate sales and production numbers.

Atkins: We start out very methodically by looking at recent history, discussing what we know about current accounts, potential customers, and the general state of consumer spending. Then, we add that usual dose of intuition to come up with the best forecast we can.

Granger: I usually take the sales projections as the basis for my projections. Of course, we have to make an estimate of what this year's ending inventories will be, which is sometimes difficult.
Ford: Why does that present a problem? There must have been an estimate of ending inventories in the budget for the current year.
Granger: Those number aren't always reliable since Marge makes some adjustments to the sales number before passing them on to me.
Ford: What kind of adjustments?
Atkins: Well, we don't want to fall short of the sales projections so we generally give ourselves a little breathing room by lowering the initial sales projection anywhere from 5% to 10%.
Granger: So, you can see why this year's budget is not a very reliable starting point. We always have to adjust the projected production rates as the year progresses and, of course, this changes the ending inventory estimates. By the way, we make similar adjustments to expenses by adding at least 10% to the estimates; I think everyone around here does the same thing.

Required

1. Marge Atkins and Pete Granger have described the use of what is sometimes called *budgetary slack.*
   a. Explain why Atkins and Granger behave in this manner and describe the benefits they expect to realize from the use of budgetary slack.
   b. Explain how the use of budgetary slack can adversely affect Atkins and Granger.
2. As a management accountant, Scott Ford believes that the behavior described by Marge Atkins and Pete Granger may be unethical. By referring to the Standards of Ethical Conduct for Practitioners of Management Accounting and Financial Management in Chapter 1, explain why the use of budgetary slack may be unethical.

(CMA, adapted)

P9–14 Tabulation Approach to Economic Order Quantity (EOQ)

(Appendix 9A) Hermanos, S.A., of Mexico City uses 15,000 ingots of a special silver alloy each year to manufacture jewelry. The ingots are purchased from a supplier in another state according to the following price schedule:

Ingots	Per Ingot
500	$30.00
1,000	29.90
1,500	29.85
2,000	29.80
2,500	29.75

The currency in Mexico is the new peso, which can be denoted by a $ sign.

Hermanos, S.A., sends its own truck to the supplier's plant to pick up the ingots. The truck's capacity is 2,500 ingots per trip. The company has been getting a full load of ingots each trip, making six trips each year. The cost of making one round trip to the supplier's plant is $500. The cost of the paperwork associated with each trip is $30.

The supplier requires that all purchases be made in round 500-ingot lots. The cost of storing one ingot for one year is $10.

Required

1. Using the tabulation approach to EOQ, compute the volume in which the company should be purchasing its ingots. Treat the savings arising from quantity discounts as a reduction in total annual trucking and storing costs.
2. Compute the annual cost savings that will be realized if the company purchases in the volume which you have determined in (1) above, as compared to its present purchase policy.

P9–15 Integration of the Sales, Production, and Purchases Budgets

Milo Company manufactures beach umbrellas. The company is now preparing detailed budgets for the third quarter and has assembled the following information to assist in the budget preparation:

a. The Marketing Department has estimated sales as follows for the remainder of the year (in units):

July	30,000	October	20,000
August	70,000	November	10,000
September	50,000	December	10,000

The selling price of the beach umbrellas is $12 per unit.

b. All sales are on account. Based on past experience, sales are collected in the following pattern:

30% in the month of sale
65% in the month following sale
5% uncollectible

Sales for June totaled $300,000.

c. The company maintains finished goods inventories equal to 15% of the following month's sales. This requirement will be met at the end of June.

d. Each beach umbrella requires 4 feet of Gilden, a material that is sometimes hard to get. Therefore, the company requires that the inventory of Gilden on hand at the end of each month be equal to 50% of the following month's production needs. The inventory of Gilden on hand at the beginning and end of the quarter will be:

June 30	72,000 feet
September 30	? feet

e. The Gilden costs $0.80 per foot. One-half of a month's purchases of Gilden is paid for in the month of purchase; the remainder is paid for in the following month. The accounts payable on July 1 for purchases of Gilden during June will be $76,000.

Required

1. Prepare a sales budget, by month and in total, for the third quarter. (Show your budget in both units and dollars.) Also prepare a schedule of expected cash collections, by month and in total, for the third quarter.
2. Prepare a production budget for each of the months July–October.
3. Prepare a materials purchases budget for Gilden, by month and in total, for the third quarter. Also prepare a schedule of expected cash payments for Gilden, by month and in total, for the third quarter.

P9–16 Cash Budget with Supporting Schedules Garden Sales, Inc., sells garden supplies. Management is planning its cash needs for the second quarter. The company usually has to borrow money during this quarter to support peak sales of lawn care equipment, which occur during May. The following information has been assembled to assist in preparing a cash budget for the quarter:

a. Budgeted monthly income statements for April–July are:

	April	May	June	July
Sales	$600,000	$900,000	$500,000	$400,000
Cost of goods sold	420,000	630,000	350,000	280,000
Gross margin	180,000	270,000	150,000	120,000
Less operating expenses:				
Selling expense	79,000	120,000	62,000	51,000
Administrative expense*	45,000	52,000	41,000	38,000
Total expenses	124,000	172,000	103,000	89,000
Net income	$ 56,000	$ 98,000	$ 47,000	$ 31,000

*Includes $20,000 depreciation each month.

b. Sales are 20% for cash and 80% on account.

c. Sales on account are collected over a three-month period in the following ratio: 10% collected in the month of sale; 70% collected in the first month following the month of sale; and the remaining 20% collected in the second month following the month of sale. February's sales totaled $200,000, and March's sales totaled $300,000.

d. Inventory purchases are paid for within 15 days. Therefore, 50% of a month's inventory purchases are paid for in the month of purchase. The remaining 50% is paid in the following month. Accounts payable at March 31 for inventory purchases during March total $126,000.
e. At the end of each month, inventory must be on hand equal to 20% of the cost of the merchandise to be sold in the following month. The merchandise inventory at March 31 is $84,000.
f. Dividends of $49,000 will be declared and paid in April.
g. Equipment costing $16,000 will be purchased for cash in May.
h. The cash balance at March 31 is $52,000; the company must maintain a cash balance of at least $40,000 at all times.
i. The company can borrow from its bank as needed to bolster the Cash account. Borrowings and repayments must be in multiples of $1,000. All borrowings take place at the beginning of a month, and all repayments are made at the end of a month. The annual interest rate is 12%. Compute interest on whole months (1/12, 2/12, and so forth).

Required

1. Prepare a schedule of expected cash collections from sales for each of the months April, May, and June, and for the quarter in total.
2. Prepare the following for merchandise inventory:
   a. An inventory purchases budget for each of the months April, May, and June.
   b. A schedule of expected cash disbursements for inventory for each of the months April, May, and June, and for the quarter in total.
3. Prepare a cash budget for the third quarter, by month as well as in total for the quarter. Show borrowings from the company's bank and repayments to the bank as needed to maintain the minimum cash balance.

P9–17 Planning Bank Financing by Means of a Cash Budget Westex Products is a wholesale distributor of industrial cleaning products. When the treasurer of Westex Products approached the company's bank in late 1999 seeking short-term financing, he was told that money was very tight and that any borrowing over the next year would have to be supported by a detailed statement of cash receipts and disbursements. The treasurer also was told that it would be very helpful to the bank if borrowers would indicate the quarters in which they would be needing funds, as well as the amounts that would be needed, and the quarters in which repayments could be made.

Since the treasurer is unsure as to the particular quarters in which the bank financing will be needed, he has assembled the following information to assist in preparing a detailed cash budget:

a. Budgeted sales and merchandise purchases for the year 2000, as well as actual sales and purchases for the last quarter of 1999, are:

	Sales	Merchandise Purchases
1999:		
Fourth quarter actual	$200,000	$126,000
2000:		
First quarter estimated	300,000	186,000
Second quarter estimated	400,000	246,000
Third quarter estimated	500,000	305,000
Fourth quarter estimated	200,000	126,000

b. The company normally collects 65% of a quarter's sales before the quarter ends and another 33% in the following quarter. The remainder is uncollectible. This pattern of collections is now being experienced in the 1999 fourth-quarter actual data.
c. Eighty percent of a quarter's merchandise purchases are paid for within the quarter. The remainder is paid in the following quarter.
d. Operating expenses for the year 2000 are budgeted quarterly at $50,000 plus 15% of sales. Of the fixed amount, $20,000 each quarter is depreciation.

e. The company will pay $10,000 in dividends each quarter.
f. Equipment purchases of $75,000 will be made in the second quarter, and purchases of $48,000 will be made in the third quarter. These purchases will be for cash.
g. The Cash account contained $10,000 at the end of 1999. The treasurer feels that this represents a minimum balance that must be maintained.
h. Any borrowing will take place at the beginning of a quarter, and any repayments will be made at the end of a quarter at an annual interest rate of 10%. Interest is paid only when principal is repaid. All borrowings and all repayments of principal must be in round $1,000 amounts. Interest payments can be in any amount. (Compute interest on whole months, e.g., 1⁄12, 2⁄12.)
i. At present, the company has no loans outstanding.

Required

1. Prepare the following by quarter and in total for the year 2000:
   a. A schedule of expected cash collections.
   b. A schedule of budgeted cash disbursements for merchandise purchases.
2. Compute the expected cash payments for operating expenses, by quarter and in total, for the year 2000.
3. Prepare a cash budget, by quarter and in total, for the year 2000. Show clearly in your budget the quarter(s) in which borrowing will be necessary and the quarter(s) in which repayments can be made, as requested by the company's bank.

P9–18 Master Budget Preparation Hillyard Company, an office supplies specialty store, prepares its master budget on a quarterly basis. The following data have been assembled to assist in preparation of the master budget for the first quarter:

a. As of December 31 (the end of the prior quarter), the company's general ledger showed the following account balances:

	Debits	Credits
Cash	$ 48,000	
Accounts Receivable	224,000	
Inventory	60,000	
Buildings and Equipment (net)	370,000	
Accounts Payable		$ 93,000
Capital Stock		500,000
Retained Earnings		109,000
	$702,000	$702,000

b. Actual sales for December and budgeted sales for the next four months are as follows:

December (actual)	$280,000
January	400,000
February	600,000
March	300,000
April	200,000

c. Sales are 20% for cash and 80% on credit. All payments on credit sales are collected in the month following sale. The accounts receivable at December 31 are a result of December credit sales.
d. The company's gross profit rate is 40% of sales.
e. Monthly expenses are budgeted as follows: salaries and wages, $27,000 per month: advertising, $70,000 per month; shipping, 5% of sales; depreciation, $14,000 per month; other expense, 3% of sales.
f. At the end of each month, inventory is to be on hand equal to 25% of the following month's sales needs, stated at cost.
g. One-half of a month's inventory purchases is paid for in the month of purchase; the other half is paid for in the following month.

h. During February, the company will purchase a new copy machine for $1,700 cash. During March, other equipment will be purchased for cash at a cost of $84,500.
i. During January, the company will declare and pay $45,000 in cash dividends.
j. The company must maintain a minimum cash balance of $30,000. An open line of credit is available at a local bank for any borrowing that may be needed during the quarter. All borrowing is done at the beginning of a month, and all repayments are made at the end of a month. Borrowings and repayments of principal must be in multiples of $1,000. Interest is paid only at the time of payment of principal. The annual interest rate is 12%. (Figure interest on whole months, e.g., 1/12, 2/12.)

Required Using the data above, complete the following statements and schedules for the first quarter:

1. Schedule of expected cash collections:

	January	February	March	Quarter
Cash sales	$ 80,000			
Credit sales	224,000			
Total cash collections	$304,000			

2. a. Inventory purchases budget:

	January	February	March	Quarter
Budgeted cost of goods sold	$240,000*	$360,000		
Add desired ending inventory	90,000†			
Total needs	330,000			
Less beginning inventory	60,000			
Required purchases	$270,000			

*For January sales: $400,000 sales × 60% cost ratio = $240,000.

†$360,000 × 25% = $90,000.

b. Schedule of cash disbursements for purchases:

	January	February	March	Quarter
December purchases	$ 93,000			$ 93,000
January purchases ($270,000)	135,000	135,000		270,000
February purchases				
March purchases				
Total cash disbursements for purchases	$228,000			

3. Schedule of cash disbursements for expenses:

	January	February	March	Quarter
Salaries and wages	$ 27,000			
Advertising	70,000			
Shipping	20,000			
Other expenses	12,000			
Total cash disbursements for operating expenses	$129,000			

4. Cash budget:

	January	February	March	Quarter
Cash balance, beginning	$ 48,000			
Add cash collections	304,000			
Total cash available	352,000			
Less disbursements:				
Purchases of inventory	228,000			
Operating expenses	129,000			
Purchases of equipment	—			
Cash dividends	45,000			
Total disbursements	402,000			
Excess (deficiency) of cash	(50,000)			
Financing:				
Etc.				

5. Prepare an income statement for the quarter ending March 31 as shown in Schedule 9 in the chapter.
6. Prepare a balance sheet as of March 31.

P9–19 Tabulation Approach; Economic Order Quantity (EOQ); Reorder Point (Appendix 9A) You have been engaged to install an inventory control system for Kiwi Electronics, Ltd., of Christchurch, New Zealand. Among the inventory control features that Kiwi Electronics desires are indicators of "how much" to order "when." The following information is furnished for one item, called a duosonic, that is carried in inventory.

a. Duosonics are sold by the gross (12 dozen) at a list price of $NZ800 per gross. (The currency in New Zealand is the New Zealand dollar, denoted here by $NZ.) Kiwi Electronics receives a 40% trade discount off list price on purchases in gross lots.
b. Freight cost is $NZ20 per gross from the shipping point to Kiwi Electronics' plant.
c. Kiwi Electronics uses about 5,000 duosonics during a 259-day production year but must purchase a total of 36 gross per year to allow for normal breakage. Minimum and maximum usages are 12 and 28 duosonics per day, respectively.
d. Normal delivery time to receive an order is 20 working days from the date that a purchase request is initiated. A stock-out (complete exhaustion of the inventory) of duosonics would stop production, and Kiwi Electronics would purchase duosonics locally at list price rather than shut down.
e. The cost of placing an order is $NZ30.
f. Space storage cost is $NZ24 per year per average gross in storage.
g. Insurance and taxes are approximately 12% of the net delivered cost of average inventory, and Kiwi Electronics expects a return of at least 8% on its average investment. (Ignore ordering costs and carrying costs in making these computations.)

Required

1. Prepare a schedule computing the total annual cost of duosonics based on uniform order lot sizes of one, two, three, four, and five gross of duosonics. (The schedule should show the total annual cost according to each lot size.) Indicate the EOQ.
2. Prepare a schedule computing the minimum stock reorder point for duosonics. This is the point below which reordering is necessary to guard against a stock-out. Factors to be considered include average lead period usage and safety stock requirements.

(CPA, adapted)

P9–20 Economic Order Quantity (EOQ); Safety Stock (Appendix 9A) Myron Metal Works, Inc., uses a small casting in one of its finished products. The castings are purchased from a foundry located in another state. In total, Myron Metal Works, Inc., purchases 54,000 castings per year at a cost of $8 per casting.

The castings are used evenly throughout the year in the production process on a 360-day-per-year basis. The company estimates that it costs $90 to place a single purchase order and about $3 to carry one casting in inventory for a year. The high carrying costs result from the need to keep the castings in carefully controlled temperature and humidity conditions, and from the high cost of insurance.

Delivery from the foundry generally takes 6 days, but it can take as much as 10 days. The days of delivery time and the percentage of their occurrence are shown in the following tabulation:

Delivery Time (days)	Percentage of Occurrence
6	75
7	10
8	5
9	5
10	5
	100

Required

1. Compute the economic order quantity (EOQ).
2. Assume that the company is willing to assume a 15% risk of being out of stock. What would be the safety stock? The reorder point?
3. Assume that the company is willing to assume only a 5% risk of being out of stock. What would be the safety stock? The reorder point?
4. Assume a 5% stock-out risk as stated in (3) above. What would be the total cost of ordering and carrying inventory for one year?
5. Refer to the original data. Assume that using process reengineering the company reduces its cost of placing a purchase order to only $6. Also, the company estimates that when the waste and inefficiency caused by inventories are considered, the true cost of carrying a unit in stock is $7.20 per year.
   a. Compute the new EOQ.
   b. How frequently would the company be placing an order, as compared to the old purchasing policy?

P9–21 Master Budget Completion Following is selected information relating to the operations of Shilow Company, a wholesale distributor:

Current assets as of March 31:	
Cash	$ 8,000
Accounts receivable	20,000
Inventory	36,000
Plant and equipment, net	120,000
Accounts payable	21,750
Capital stock	150,000
Retained earnings	12,250

a. Gross profit is 25% of sales.

b. Actual and budgeted sales data:

March (actual)	$50,000
April	60,000
May	72,000
June	90,000
July	48,000

c. Sales are 60% for cash and 40% on credit. Credit sales are collected in the month following sale. The accounts receivable at March 31 are a result of March credit sales.

d. At the end of each month, inventory is to be on hand equal to 80% of the following month's sales needs, stated at cost.

e. One-half of a month's inventory purchases is paid for in the month of purchase; the other half is paid for in the following month. The accounts payable at March 31 are a result of March purchases of inventory.

f. Monthly expenses are as follows: salaries and wages, 12% of sales; rent, $2,500 per month; other expenses (excluding depreciation), 6% of sales. Assume that these expenses are paid monthly. Depreciation is $900 per month (includes depreciation on new assets).
g. Equipment costing $1,500 will be purchased for cash in April.
h. The company must maintain a minimum cash balance of $4,000. An open line of credit is available at a local bank. All borrowing is done at the beginning of a month, and all repayments are made at the end of a month; borrowing must be in multiples of $1,000. The annual interest rate is 12%. Interest is paid only at the time of repayment of principal; figure interest on whole months (1⁄12, 2⁄12, and so forth).

Required Using the data above:

1. Complete the following schedule:

Schedule of Expected Cash Collections

	April	May	June	Quarter
Cash sales	$36,000			
Credit sales	20,000			
Total collections	$56,000			

2. Complete the following:

Inventory Purchases Budget

	April	May	June	Quarter
Budgeted cost of goods sold	$45,000*	$54,000		
Add desired ending inventory	43,200†			
Total needs	88,200			
Less beginning inventory	36,000			
Required purchases	$52,200			

*For April sales: $60,000 sales × 75% cost ratio = $45,000.
†$54,000 × 80% = $43,200

Schedule of Expected Cash Disbursements—Purchases

	April	May	June	Quarter
March purchases	$21,750			$21,750
April purchases	26,100	$26,100		52,200
May purchases				
June purchases				
Total disbursements	$47,850			

3. Complete the following:

Schedule of Expected Cash Disbursements—Operating Expenses

	April	May	June	Quarter
Salaries and wages	$ 7,200			
Rent	2,500			
Other expenses	3,600			
Total disbursements	$13,300			

4. Complete the following cash budget:

Cash Budget

	April	May	June	Quarter
Cash balance, beginning	$ 8,000			
Add cash collections	56,000			
Total cash available	64,000			
Less cash disbursements:				
For inventory	47,850			
For expenses	13,300			
For equipment	1,500			
Total cash disbursements . . .	62,650			
Excess (deficiency) of cash	1,350			
Financing:				
Etc.				

5. Prepare an income statement for the quarter ended June 30. (Use the functional format in preparing your income statement, as shown in Schedule 9 in the text.)
6. Prepare a balance sheet as of June 30)

P9–22 Integrated Operating Budgets The West Division of Vader Corporation produces an intricate component part used in Vader's major product line. The divisional manager has recently been concerned about a lack of coordination between purchasing and production personnel and believes that a monthly budgeting system would be better than the present system.

The manager of West Division has decided to develop budget information for the third quarter of the current year as a trial before the budget system is implemented for an entire fiscal year. In response to the manager's request for data that could be used to develop budget information, the controller of West Division accumulated the following data:

Sales Sales through June 30, the first six months of the current year, were 24,000 units. Actual sales in units for May and June and estimated unit sales for the next five months are detailed as follows:

May (actual)	4,000
June (actual)	4,000
July (estimated)	5,000
August (estimated)	6,000
September (estimated)	7,000
October (estimated)	7,500
November (estimated)	8,000

West Division expects to sell 65,000 units during the year ending December 31.

Direct Material Data regarding the materials used in the component are shown in the following schedule. The desired monthly ending inventory for all direct materials is to have sufficient materials on hand to provide for 50% of the next month's production needs.

Direct Material	Units of Direct Materials per Finished Component	Cost per Unit	Inventory Level June 30
No. 101	6 ounces	$2.40	35,000 ounces
No. 211	4 pounds	5.00	30,000 pounds

Direct Labor Each component must pass through three processes to be completed. Data regarding the direct labor are as follows:

Process	Direct Labor-Hours per Finished Component	Cost per Direct Labor-Hour
Forming	0.80	$8.00
Assembly	2.00	5.50
Finishing	0.25	6.00

Manufacturing Overhead West Division produced 27,000 components during the six-month period through June 30. The actual variable overhead costs incurred during this six-month period are shown below. The controller of West Division believes that the variable overhead costs will be incurred at the same rate during the last six months of the year.

Supplies	$ 59,400
Electricity	27,000
Indirect labor	54,000
Other	8,100
Total variable overhead	$148,500

The fixed manufacturing overhead costs incurred during the first six months amounted to $93,500. Fixed manufacturing overhead costs are budgeted for the full year as follows:

Supervision	$ 60,000
Taxes	7,200
Depreciation	86,400
Other	32,400
Total fixed manufacturing overhead	$186,000

Finished Goods Inventory The desired monthly ending inventory in units of completed components is 80% of the next month's estimated sales. There are 4,000 finished units in inventory on June 30.

Required

1. Prepare a production budget for the West Division for the third quarter ending September 30. Show computations by month and in total for the quarter.
2. Prepare a direct materials purchases budget in units and in dollars for each type of material for the third quarter ending September 30. Again show computations by month and in total for the quarter.
3. Prepare a direct labor budget in hours and in dollars for the third quarter ending September 30. This time it is *not* necessary to show monthly figures; show quarterly totals only. Assume that the workforce is adjusted as work requirements change.
4. Assume that the company plans to produce a total of 65,000 units for the year. Prepare a manufacturing overhead budget for the six-month period ending December 31. Again, it is *not* necessary to show monthly figures.

(CMA, adapted)

P9–23 Cash Budget for One Month Wallace Products, Ltd., is planning its cash needs for July. Since the company will be buying some new equipment during the month, the treasurer is sure that some borrowing will be needed, but he is uncertain how much. The following data have been assembled to assist the treasurer in preparing a cash budget for the month:

a. Equipment will be purchased during July for cash at a cost of $45,000.
b. Selling and administrative expenses will be:

Advertising	$110,000
Sales salaries	50,000
Administrative salaries	35,000
Shipping	2,100

c. Sales are budgeted at $800,000 for July. Customers are allowed a 2½% cash discount on accounts paid within 10 days after the end of the month of sale. Only 50% of the payments made in the month following sale fall within the discount period. (All of the company's sales are on account.)

d. On June 30, the company will have the following accounts receivable outstanding:

Month	Sales	Accounts Receivable at June 30	Percentage of Sales Uncollected at June 30	Percentage to Be Collected in July
March	$430,000	$ 6,450	1½%	?
April	590,000	35,400	6%	?
May	640,000	128,000	20%	?
June	720,000	720,000	100%	?

Bad debts are negligible. All March receivables shown above will have been collected by the end of July, and the collection pattern implicit in the schedule above will be the same in July as in previous months.

e. Production costs are budgeted as follows for July:

Prime costs:		
Raw materials to be used in production		$342,000
Direct labor		95,000
Overhead costs:		
Indirect labor	$36,000	
Utilities	1,900	
Payroll benefits	14,800	
Depreciation	28,000	
Property taxes	1,100	
Fire insurance	1,700	
Amortization of patents	3,500	
Scrapping of obsolete goods	2,600	89,600
Total production costs		$526,600

f. The raw materials inventory is budgeted to increase by $18,000 during July; other inventories will not change.

g. Half of the raw materials purchased each month is paid for in the month of purchase; the other half is paid for in the following month. Accounts payable at June 30 for raw materials purchases will be $172,000.

h. All July payroll amounts will be paid for within the month of July.

i. Utilities costs are paid for within the month.

j. The $14,800 monthly charge above for "Payroll benefits" includes the following items:

Company pension plan, including 1/12 of a $9,600 special adjustment that was paid in April	$7,000
Group insurance (payable semiannually, with the last payment having been made in January)	900
Unemployment insurance (payable monthly)	1,300
Vacation pay, which represents 1/12 of the annual cost (July's vacations will require $14,100)	5,600

k. Property taxes are paid in June of each year.

l. Fire insurance premiums were paid in January, in advance.

m. The company has an open line of credit with the Royal Calgary Bank. All borrowing from the bank must be in round $1,000 amounts.

n. The cash balance on June 30 will be $78,000; the company must maintain a cash balance of at least $75,000 at all times.

Required

1. Prepare a schedule showing expected cash collections for July.

2. Compute (a) budgeted cash disbursements for raw materials purchases, and (b) budgeted cash disbursements for overhead for July.
3. Prepare a cash budget for July in good form.
4. A member of the board of directors of Wallace Products stated, "The monthly cash budget shows the company's cash surplus or deficiency and assures us that an unexpected cash shortage will not occur." Comment on this statement.

(SMA, adapted)

Cases

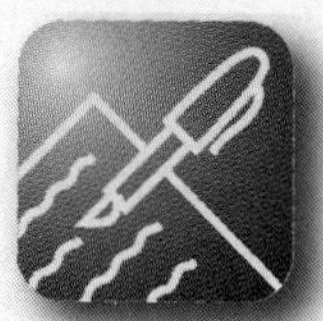

C9–24 Evaluating a Company's Budget Procedures Tom Emory and Jim Morris strolled back to their plant from the administrative offices of Ferguson & Son Mfg. Company. Tom is manager of the machine shop in the company's factory; Jim is manager of the equipment maintenance department.

The men had just attended the monthly performance evaluation meeting for plant department heads. These meetings had been held on the third Tuesday of each month since Robert Ferguson, Jr., the president's son, had become plant manager a year earlier.

As they were walking, Tom Emory spoke: "Boy, I hate those meetings! I never know whether my department's accounting reports will show good or bad performance. I'm beginning to expect the worst. If the accountants say I saved the company a dollar, I'm called 'Sir,' but if I spend even a little too much—boy, do I get in trouble. I don't know if I can hold on until I retire."

Tom had just been given the worst evaluation he had ever received in his long career with Ferguson & Son. He was the respected of the experienced machinists in the company. He had been with Ferguson & Son for many years and was promoted to supervisor of the machine shop when the company expanded and moved to its present location. The president (Robert Ferguson, Sr.) had often stated that the company's success was due to the high quality of the work of machinists like Tom. As supervisor, Tom stressed the importance of craftsmanship and told his workers that he wanted no sloppy work coming from his department.

When Robert Ferguson, Jr., became the plant manager, he directed that monthly performance comparisons be made between actual and budgeted costs for each department. The departmental budgets were intended to encourage the supervisors to reduce inefficiencies and to seek cost reduction opportunities. The company controller was instructed to have his staff "tighten" the budget slightly whenever a department attained its budget in a given month; this was done to reinforce the plant manager's desire to reduce costs. The young plant manager often stressed the importance of continued progress toward attaining the budget; he also made it know that he kept a file of these performance reports for future reference when he succeeded his father.

Tom Emory's conversation with Jim Morris continued as follows:

Emory: I really don't understand. We've worked so hard to get up to budget, and the minute we make it they tighten the budget on us. We can't work any faster and still maintain quality. I think my men are ready to quit trying. Besides, those reports don't tell the whole story. We always seem to be interrupting the big jobs for all those small rush orders. All that setup and machine adjustment time is killing us. And quite frankly, Jim, you were no help. When our hydraulic press broke down last month, your people were nowhere to be found. We had to take it apart ourselves and got stuck with all that idle time.

Morris: I'm sorry about that, Tom, but you know my department has had trouble making budget, too. We were running well behind at the time of that problem, and if we'd spent a day on that old machine, we would never have made it up. Instead we made the scheduled inspections of the forklift trucks because we knew we could do those in less than the budgeted time.

Emory: Well, Jim, at least you have some options. I'm locked into what the scheduling department assigns to me and you know they're being harassed by sales for those special orders. Incidentally, why didn't your report show all the supplies you guys wasted last month when you were working in Bill's department?

Morris: We're not out of the woods on that deal yet. We charged the maximum we could to other work and haven't even reported some of it yet.

Emory: Well, I'm glad you have a way of getting out of the pressure. The accountants seem to know everything that's happening in my department, sometimes even before I do. I thought all that budget and accounting stuff was supposed to help, but it just gets me into trouble. It's all a big pain. I'm trying to put out quality work; they're trying to save pennies.

Required

1. Identify the problems that appear to exist in Ferguson & Son Mfg. Company's budgetary control system and explain how the problems are likely to reduce the effectiveness of the system.
2. Explain how Ferguson & Son Mfg. Company's budgetary control system could be revised to improve its effectiveness.

(CMA, adapted)

C9–25 Cash Budget for a Growing Company CrossMan Corporation, a rapidly expanding crossbow distributor to retail outlets, is in the process of formulating plans for next year. Joan Caldwell, director of marketing, has completed her sales budget and is confident that sales estimates will be met or exceeded. The following budgeted sales figures show the growth expected and will provide the planning basis for other corporate departments.

	Budgeted Sales		Budgeted Sales
January	$1,800,000	July	$3,000,000
February	2,000,000	August	3,000,000
March	1,800,000	September	3,200,000
April	2,200,000	October	3,200,000
May	2,500,000	November	3,000,000
June	2,800,000	December	3,400,000

George Brownell, assistant controller, has been given the responsibility for formulating the cash budget, a critical element during a period of rapid expansion. The following information provided by operating managers will be used in preparing the cash budget.

a. CrossMan has experienced an excellent record in accounts receivable collection and expects this trend to continue. Sixty percent of billings are collected in the month after the sale and 40% in the second month after the sale. Uncollectible accounts are negligible and will not be considered in this analysis.
b. The purchase of the crossbows is CrossMan's largest expenditure; the cost of these items equals 50% of sales. Sixty percent of the crossbows are received one month prior to sale and 40% are received during the month of sale.
c. Prior experience shows that 80% of accounts payable are paid by CrossMan one month after receipt of the purchased crossbows, and the remaining 20% are paid the second month after receipt.
d. Hourly wages, including fringe benefits, depend on sales volume and are equal to 20% of the current month's sales. These wages are paid in the month incurred.
e. General and administrative expenses are budgeted to be $2,640,000 for the year. The composition of these expenses is given below. All of these expenses are incurred evenly throughout the year except the property taxes. Property taxes are paid in four equal installments in the last month of each quarter.

Salaries	$ 480,000
Promotion	660,000
Property taxes	240,000
Insurance	360,000
Utilities	300,000
Depreciation	600,000
Total	$2,640,000

f. Income tax payments are made by CrossMan in the first month of each quarter based on the income for the prior quarter. CrossMan's income tax rate is 40%. CrossMan's net income for the first quarter is projected to be $612,000.

g. Equipment and warehouse facilities are being acquired to support the company's rapidly growing sales. Purchases of equipment and facilities are budgeted at $28,000 for April and $324,000 for May.
h. CrossMan has a corporate policy of maintaining an end-of-month cash balance of $100,000. Cash is borrowed or invested monthly, as needed, to maintain this balance. Interest expense on borrowed funds is budgeted at $8,000 for the second quarter, all of which will be paid during June.
i. CrossMan uses a calendar year reporting period.

Required

1. Prepare a cash budget for CrossMan Corporation by month and in total for the second quarter. Be sure that all receipts, disbursements, and borrowing/investing amounts are shown for each month. Ignore any interest income associated with amounts invested.
2. Discuss why cash budgeting is particularly important for a rapidly expanding company such as CrossMan Corporation.

(CMA, adapted)

C9–26 Master Budget with Supporting Schedules You have just been hired as a new management trainee by Earrings Unlimited, a distributor of earrings to various retail outlets located in shopping malls across the country. In the past, the company has done very little in the way of budgeting and at certain times of the year has experienced a shortage of cash.

Since you are well trained in budgeting, you have decided to prepare comprehensive budgets for the upcoming second quarter in order to show management the benefits that can be gained from an integrated budgeting program. To this end, you have worked with accounting and other areas to gather the information assembled below.

The company sells many styles of earrings, but all are sold for the same price—$10 per pair. Actual sales of earrings for the last three months and budgeted sales for the next six months follow (in pairs of earrings):

January (actual)	20,000	June (budget)	50,000
February (actual)	26,000	July (budget)	30,000
March (actual)	40,000	August (budget)	28,000
April (budget)	65,000	September (budget)	25,000
May (budget)	100,000		

The concentration of sales before and during May is due to Mother's Day. Sufficient inventory should be on hand at the end of each month to supply 40% of the earrings sold in the following month.

Suppliers are paid $4 for a pair of earrings. One-half of a month's purchases is paid for in the month of purchase; the other half is paid for in the following month. All sales are on credit, with no discount, and payable within 15 days. The company has found, however, that only 20% of a month's sales are collected in the month of sale. An additional 70% is collected in the following month, and the remaining 10% is collected in the second month following sale. Bad debts have been negligible.

Monthly operating expenses for the company are given below:

Variable:	
Sales commissions	4% of sales
Fixed:	
Advertising	$200,000
Rent	18,000
Salaries	106,000
Utilities	7,000
Insurance expired	3,000
Depreciation	14,000

Insurance is paid on an annual basis, in November of each year.

The company plans to purchase $16,000 in new equipment during May and $40,000 in new equipment during June; both purchases will be for cash. The company declares dividends of $15,000 each quarter, payable in the first month of the following quarter.

A listing of the company's ledger accounts as of March 31 is given below:

Assets	
Cash	$ 74,000
Accounts receivable ($26,000 February sales; $320,000 March sales)	346,000
Inventory	104,000
Prepaid insurance	21,000
Property and equipment (net)	950,000
Total assets	$1,495,000

Liabilities and Stockholders' Equity	
Accounts payable	$ 100,000
Dividends payable	15,000
Capital stock	800,000
Retained earnings	580,000
Total liabilities and stockholders' equity	$1,495,000

Part of the use of the budgeting program will be to establish an ongoing line of credit at a local bank. Therefore, determine the borrowing that will be needed to maintain a minimum cash balance of $50,000. All borrowing will be done at the beginning of a month; any repayments will be made at the end of a month.

The annual interest rate will be 12%. Interest will be computed and paid at the end of each quarter on all loans outstanding during the quarter. Compute interest on whole months (1/12, 2/12, and so forth).

Required Prepare a master budget for the three-month period ending June 30. Include the following detailed budgets:

1. a. A sales budget, by month and in total.
   b. A schedule of expected cash collections from sales, by month and in total.
   c. A merchandise purchases budget in units and in dollars. Show the budget by month and in total.
   d. A schedule of expected cash disbursements for merchandise purchases, by month and in total.
2. A cash budget. Show the budget by month and in total.
3. A budgeted income statement for the three-month period ending June 30. Use the contribution approach.
4. A budgeted balance sheet as of June 30.

Group Exercises

GE9–27 Financial Pressures Hit Higher Education In the late eighties and early nineties, public universities found that they were no longer immune to the financial stress faced by their private sister institutions and the rest of Corporate America. Budget cuts were in the air across the land. When the budget ax hit, the cuts often came without warning and their size was sometimes staggering. State support for some institutions dropped by 40% or more. Most university administrators had only experienced budget increases, never budget cuts. Also, the budget setbacks usually occurred at the most inopportune time—during the school year when contractual commitments with faculty and staff had been signed, programs had been planned, and students were enrolled and taking classes.

Required

1. Should the administration be "fair" to all affected and institute a round of across-the-board cuts whenever the state announces another subsidy reduction?
2. If not across-the-board cutbacks in programs, then would you recommend more focused reductions, and if so, what priorities would you establish for bringing spending in line with revenues?

3. Since these usually are not one-time-only cutbacks, how would you manage continuous, long-term reductions in budgets extending over a period of years?
4. Should the decision-making process be top-down (centralized with top administrators) or bottom-up (participative)? Why?
5. How should issues such as protect-your-turf mentality, resistance to change, and consensus building be dealt with?
6. Since no university can afford a reputation of "going downhill," what innovative ideas or initiatives would you recommend that would return a university to a more stable, predictable environment?

Adapted from Sherry Penny, "What a University Has Learned from 4 Years of Financial Stress," *The Chronicle of Higher Education,* May 5, 1993, pp. B1–B3.

GE9–28 College Budgeting 101 Who better to tell new students about the ins and outs of budgeting for college than those who have recently lived the experience—you. Suppose you are advising incoming freshmen, or those living off campus for the first time, on money matters and how to live within a budget.

Required

1. Provide a list of typical expenses for a new college student living on campus. What is different about a student who is living off campus?
2. What advice should parents give to new students before sending them off to live on their own for the first time?
3. Which expenses should be split between parents and students? How will they be divided?
4. Which expenses can be reduced? How?
5. What role should work play?
6. What are the advantages and disadvantages of credit cards?
7. How would you suggest handling a situation where a student has spent more than his or her budget? Should parents bail the student out?
8. If the student were living off campus with several other roommates, what options do they have for handling expenses such as utilities, rent, and food? How would you advise them?
9. What should a student do if a roommate is not financially responsible and does not pay his or her share of expenses?
10. What do you do with a roommate who eats or drinks more than his or her share?

Adapted from Deborah Lohse, "Students Can Learn a Lesson on Budgeting," *The Wall Street Journal,* August 23, 1995, p. C1; and Bill Lubinger, "College Tests Your Money Handling Skills," *The Plain Dealer,* September 2, 1995, p. 3–E.

IE9–29 Talk with a Controller about Budgeting Use an on-line yellow pages directory such as www.comfind.com, home.netscape.com/netcenter/yellowpages.html?cp=ntserch, or www.athand.com to find a business or nonprofit organization in your area with a web site. Find out as much as you can about the organization's operations from its web site.

Required

Make an appointment with the controller or chief financial officer of the organization you have identified. In the meeting, find out the answers to the following questions:

1. How are the overall budget goals set?
2. What is the process used to build the budget? Who does it? How much input do operating managers have in the process? How long does it take to build the budget?
3. What are the main benefits of budgeting? How are the budgets used?

Chapter Ten

Standard Costs and the Balanced Scorecard

Business Focus

Special effects, such as the computer-generated action shots of dinosaurs in Jurassic Park, are expensive to produce. A single visual effect, lasting three to seven seconds, can cost up to $50,000. And a high-profile film may contain hundreds of these shots.

With over 30 visual-effects companies in the United States, competition is fierce. Since visual effects are produced under fixed-price contracts, visual-effects companies must carefully estimate their costs. And once a bid has been accepted, costs must be zealously monitored to make sure they do not spin out of control. Buena Vista Visual Effects, a part of Walt Disney Studios, uses a standard cost system to estimate and control costs. A "storyboard" is created for each special-effects shot; it sketches the visual effect, details the length of the shot (measured in frames—24 frames equals one second of film), and describes the work that will need to be done to create the effect. A detailed budget is then prepared using standard costs. For example, a shot may require a miniature model maker working full time for 12 weeks at a specified weekly wage. As the job progresses, this standard cost is compared to actual costs and significant cost overruns are investigated. Management attention is directed to significant variances.

Source: Ray Scalice, "Lights! Cameras! . . . Accountants?" Management Accounting, *June 1996, pp. 42–46.*

Learning Objectives

After studying Chapter 10, you should be able to:

1 Explain how direct materials standards and direct labor standards are set.

2 Compute the direct materials price and quantity variances and explain their significance.

3 Compute the direct labor rate and efficiency variances and explain their significance.

4 Compute the variable manufacturing overhead spending and efficiency variances.

5 Understand the advantages of and the potential problems with using standard costs.

6 Understand how a balanced scorecard fits together and how it supports a company's strategy.

7 Compute the delivery cycle time, the throughput time, and the manufacturing cycle efficiency (MCE).

8 (Appendix 10A) Prepare journal entries to record standard costs and variances.

In this chapter we begin our study of management control and performance measures. Quite often, these terms carry with them negative connotations—we may have a tendency to think of performance measurement as something to be feared. And indeed, performance measurements can be used in very negative ways—to cast blame and to punish. However, that is not the way they should be used. As explained in the following quotation, performance measurement serves a vital function in both personal life and in organizations:

> Imagine you want to improve your basketball shooting skill. You know that practice will help, so you [go] to the basketball court. There you start shooting toward the hoop, but as soon as the ball gets close to the rim your vision goes blurry for a second, so that you cannot observe where the ball ended up in relation to the target (left, right, in front, too far back, inside the hoop?). It would be pretty difficult to improve under those conditions. . . . (And by the way, how long would [shooting baskets] sustain your interest if you couldn't observe the outcome of your efforts?)
>
> Or imagine someone engaging in a weight loss program. A normal step in such programs is to purchase a scale to be able to track one's progress: Is this program working? Am I losing weight? A positive answer would be encouraging and would motivate me to keep up the effort, while a negative answer might lead me to reflect on the process: Am I working on the right diet and exercise program? Am I doing everything I am supposed to?, etc. Suppose you don't want to set up a sophisticated measurement system and decide to forgo the scale. You would still have some idea of how well you are doing from simple methods such as clothes feeling looser, a belt that fastens at a different hole, or simply via observation in a mirror! Now, imagine trying to sustain a weight loss program without *any* feedback on how well you are doing.
>
> In these . . . examples, availability of quantitative measures of performance can yield two types of benefits: First, performance feedback can help improve the "production process" through a better understanding of what works and what doesn't; e.g., shooting this way works better than shooting that way. Secondly, feedback on performance can sustain motivation and effort, because it is encouraging and/or because it suggests that more effort is required for the goal to be met.[1]

In the same way, performance measurement can be helpful in an organization. It can provide feedback concerning what works and what does not work, and it can help motivate people to sustain their efforts.

Our study of performance measurement begins in this chapter with the lowest levels in the organization. We work our way up the organizational ladder in subsequent chapters. In this chapter we see how various measures are used to control operations and to evaluate performance. Even though we are starting with the lowest levels in the organization, keep in mind that the performance measures used should be derived from the organization's overall strategy. For example, a company like Sony that bases its strategy on rapid introduction of innovative consumer products should use different performance measures than a company like Federal Express where on-time delivery, customer convenience, and low cost are key competitive advantages. Sony may want to keep close track of the percentage of revenues from products introduced within the last year; whereas Federal Express may want to closely monitor the percentage of packages delivered on time. Later in this chapter when we discuss the *balanced scorecard,* we will have more to say concerning the role of strategy in the selection of performance measures. But first we will see how *standard costs* are used by managers to help control costs.

Companies in highly competitive industries like Federal Express, Southwest Airlines, Dell Computer, Shell Oil, and Toyota must be able to provide high-quality goods and services at low cost. If they do not, they will perish. Stated in the starkest terms, managers must obtain inputs such as raw materials and electricity at the lowest

1. Soumitra Dutta and Jean-François Manzoni, *Process Reengineering, Organizational Change and Performance Improvement* (New York: McGraw-Hill, 1999), Chapter IV.

possible prices and must use them as effectively as possible—while maintaining or increasing the quality of the output. If inputs are purchased at prices that are too high or more input is used than is really necessary, higher costs will result.

How do managers control the prices that are paid for inputs and the quantities that are used? They could examine every transaction in detail, but this obviously would be an inefficient use of management time. For many companies, the answer to this control problem lies at least partially in standard costs.

Standard Costs—Management by Exception

A *standard* is a benchmark or "norm" for measuring performance. Standards are found everywhere. Your doctor evaluates your weight using standards that have been set for individuals of your age, height, and gender. The food we eat in restaurants must be prepared under specified standards of cleanliness. The buildings we live in must conform to standards set in building codes. Standards are also widely used in managerial accounting where they relate to the *quantity* and *cost* of inputs used in manufacturing goods or providing services.

Managers—often assisted by engineers and accountants—set quantity and cost standards for each major input such as raw materials and labor time. *Quantity standards* indicate how much of an input should be used in manufacturing a unit of product or in providing a unit of service. *Cost (price) standards* indicate what the cost, or purchase price, of the input should be. Actual quantities and actual costs of inputs are compared to these standards. If either the quantity or the cost of inputs departs significantly from the standards, managers investigate the discrepancy. The purpose is to find the cause of the problem and then eliminate it so that it does not recur. This process is called **management by exception.**

In our daily lives, we operate in a management by exception mode most of the time. Consider what happens when you sit down in the driver's seat of your car. You put the key in the ignition, you turn the key, and your car starts. Your expectation (standard) that the car will start is met; you do not have to open the car hood and check the battery, the connecting cables, the fuel lines, and so on. If you turn the key and the car does not start, then you have a discrepancy (variance). Your expectations are not met, and you need to investigate why. Note that even if the car starts after a second try, it would be wise to investigate anyway. The fact that the expectation was not met should be viewed as an opportunity to uncover the cause of the problem rather than as simply an annoyance. If the underlying cause is not discovered and corrected, the problem may recur and become much worse.

Who Uses Standard Costs?

Manufacturing, service, food, and not-for-profit organizations all make use of standards to some extent. Auto service centers like Firestone and Sears, for example, often set specific labor time standards for the completion of certain work tasks, such as installing a carburetor or doing a valve job, and then measure actual performance against these standards. Fast-food outlets such as McDonald's have exacting standards as to the quantity of meat going into a sandwich, as well as standards for the cost of the meat. Hospitals have standard costs (for food, laundry, and other items) for each occupied bed per day, as well as standard time allowances for certain routine activities, such as laboratory tests. In short, you are likely to run into standard costs in virtually any line of business that you enter.

Focus on Current Practice

A survey of manufacturing companies with annual sales in excess of $500 million found that 87% use standard costing. The survey also found that the use of standard cost systems is increasing and that standards are being applied to smaller and smaller units within the firms.[2]

Another study of 244 companies involved in traditional manufacturing, high-tech operations, and service activities found that 67% use standard cost systems. No statistically significant difference was found between companies in the use of standard costs based on either type of operation or size of company.[3] ■

Manufacturing companies often have highly developed standard costing systems in which standards relating to materials, labor, and overhead are developed in detail for each separate product. These standards are listed on a **standard cost card** that provides the manager with a great deal of information concerning the inputs that are required to produce a unit and their costs. In the following section, we provide a detailed example of the setting of standard costs and the preparation of a standard cost card.

Setting Standard Costs

Setting price and quantity standards is more an art than a science. It requires the combined expertise of all persons who have responsibility over input prices and over the effective use of inputs. In a manufacturing setting, this might include accountants, purchasing managers, engineers, production supervisors, line managers, and production workers. Past records of purchase prices and of input usage can be helpful in setting standards. However, the standards should be designed to encourage efficient *future* operations, not a repetition of *past* inefficient operations.

Ideal versus Practical Standards

Should standards be attainable all of the time, should they be attainable only part of the time, or should they be so tight that they become, in effect, "the impossible dream"? Opinions among managers vary, but standards tend to fall into one of two categories—either ideal or practical.

Ideal standards are those that can be attained only under the best circumstances. They allow for no machine breakdowns or other work interruptions, and they call for a level of effort that can be attained only by the most skilled and efficient employees working at peak effort 100% of the time. Some managers feel that such standards have a motivational value. These managers argue that even though employees know they will rarely meet the standard, it is a constant reminder of the need for ever-increasing efficiency and effort. Few firms use ideal standards. Most managers feel that ideal standards tend to discourage even the most diligent workers. Moreover, when ideal standards are used, variances from the standards have little meaning. Because of the ideal standards, large variances are normal and it is difficult to "manage by exception."

---

2. Bruce R. Gaumnitz and Felix P. Kollaritsch, "Manufacturing Cost Variances: Current Practice and Trends," *Journal of Cost Management* 5, no. 1 (Spring 1991), pp. 58–64.
3. Jeffrey R. Cohen and Laurence Paquette, "Management Accounting Practices: Perceptions of Controllers," *Journal of Cost Management* 5, no. 3 (Fall 1991), pp. 73–83.

Practical standards are defined as standards that are "tight but attainable." They allow for normal machine downtime and employee rest periods, and they can be attained through reasonable, though highly efficient, efforts by the average worker. Variances from such a standard are very useful to management in that they represent deviations that fall outside of normal operating conditions and signal a need for management attention. Furthermore, practical standards can serve multiple purposes. In addition to signaling abnormal conditions, they can also be used in forecasting cash flows and in planning inventory. By contrast, ideal standards cannot be used in forecasting and planning; they do not allow for normal inefficiencies, and therefore they result in unrealistic planning and forecasting figures.

Throughout the remainder of this chapter, we will assume the use of practical rather than ideal standards.

Managerial Accounting in Action

THE ISSUE

The Colonial Pewter Company was organized a year ago. The company's only product at present is a reproduction of an 18th century pewter bookend. The bookend is made largely by hand, using traditional metal-working tools. Consequently, the manufacturing process is labor intensive and requires a high level of skill.

Colonial Pewter has recently expanded its workforce to take advantage of unexpected demand for the bookends as gifts. The company started with a small cadre of experienced pewter workers but has had to hire less experienced workers as a result of the expansion. The president of the company, J. D. Wriston, has called a meeting to discuss production problems. Attending the meeting are Tom Kuchel, the production manager; Janet Warner, the purchasing manager; and Terry Sherman, the corporate controller.

J. D.: I've got a feeling that we aren't getting the production we should out of our new people.

Tom: Give us a chance. Some of the new people have been on board for less than a month.

Janet: Let me add that production seems to be wasting an awful lot of material—particularly pewter. That stuff is very expensive.

Tom: What about the shipment of defective pewter you bought a couple of months ago—the one with the iron contamination? That caused us major problems.

Janet: That's ancient history. How was I to know it was off-grade? Besides, it was a great deal.

J. D.: Calm down everybody. Let's get the facts before we start sinking our fangs into each other.

Tom: I agree. The more facts the better.

J. D.: Okay, Terry, it's your turn. Facts are the controller's department.

Terry: I'm afraid I can't provide the answers off the top of my head, but it won't take me too long to set up a system that can routinely answer questions relating to worker productivity, material waste, and input prices.

J. D.: How long is "not too long"?

Terry: I will need all of your cooperation, but how about a week from today?

J. D.: That's okay with me. What about everyone else?

Tom: Sure.

Janet: Fine with me.

J. D.: Let's mark it on our calendars. ■

Setting Direct Materials Standards

objective 1
Explain how direct materials standards and direct labor standards are set.

Terry Sherman's first task was to prepare price and quantity standards for the company's only significant raw material, pewter ingots. The **standard price per unit** for direct materials should reflect the final, delivered cost of the materials, net of any discounts taken. After consulting with purchasing manager Janet Warner, Terry prepared the following documentation for the standard price of a pound of pewter in ingot form:

Purchase price, top-grade pewter ingots, in 40-pound ingots . .	$ 3.60
Freight, by truck, from the supplier's warehouse	0.44
Receiving and handling	0.05
Less purchase discount	(0.09)
Standard price per pound	$ 4.00

Notice that the standard price reflects a particular grade of material (top grade), purchased in particular lot sizes (40-pound ingots), and delivered by a particular type of carrier (truck). Allowances have also been made for handling and discounts. If everything proceeds according to these expectations, the net standard price of a pound of pewter should therefore be $4.00.

The **standard quantity per unit** for direct materials should reflect the amount of material going into each unit of finished product, as well as an allowance for unavoidable waste, spoilage, and other normal inefficiencies. After consulting with the production manager, Tom Kuchel, Terry Sherman prepared the following documentation for the standard quantity of pewter going into a pair of bookends:

Material requirements as specified in the bill of materials for a pair of bookends, in pounds	2.7
Allowance for waste and spoilage, in pounds	0.2
Allowance for rejects, in pounds	0.1
Standard quantity per pair of bookends, in pounds	3.0

A **bill of materials** is a list that shows the type and quantity of each item of material going into a unit of finished product. It is a handy source for determining the basic material input per unit, but it should be adjusted for waste and other factors, as shown above, when determining the standard quantity per unit of product. "Waste and spoilage" in the table above refers to materials that are wasted as a normal part of the production process or that spoil before they are used. "Rejects" refers to the direct material contained in units that are defective and must be scrapped.

Focus on Current Practice

After many years of operating a standard cost system, a major wood products company reviewed the materials standards for its products by breaking each standard down into its basic elements. In doing so, the company discovered that there was a 20% waste factor built into the standard cost for every product. Management was dismayed to learn that the dollar amount of "allowable" waste was so large. Since the quantity standards had not been scrutinized for many years, management was unaware of the existence of this significant cost improvement potential in the company.[4] ■

4. James M. Reeve, "The Impact of Variation on Operating System Performance," *Performance Excellence* (Sarasota, FL: American Accounting Association, 1990), p. 77.

Although it is common to recognize allowances for waste, spoilage, and rejects when setting standard costs, this practice is now coming into question. Those involved in TQM (total quality management) and similar management approaches argue that no amount of waste or defects should be tolerated. If allowances for waste, spoilage, and rejects are built into the standard cost, the levels of those allowances should be periodically reviewed and reduced over time to reflect improved processes, better training, and better equipment.

Once the price and quantity standards have been set, the standard cost of material per unit of finished product can be computed as follows:

3.0 pounds per unit × \$4.00 per pound = \$12 per unit

This \$12 cost figure will appear as one item on the standard cost card of the product.

Setting Direct Labor Standards

Direct labor price and quantity standards are usually expressed in terms of a labor rate and labor-hours. The **standard rate per hour** for direct labor would include not only wages earned but also fringe benefits and other labor costs. Using last month's wage records and in consultation with the production manager, Terry determined the standard rate per hour at the Colonial Pewter Company as follows:

Basic wage rate per hour	\$10
Employment taxes at 10% of the basic rate	1
Fringe benefits at 30% of the basic rate	3
Standard rate per direct labor-hour	\$14

Many companies prepare a single standard rate for all employees in a department. This standard rate reflects the expected "mix" of workers, even though the actual wage rates may vary somewhat from individual to individual due to differing skills or seniority. A single standard rate simplifies the use of standard costs and also permits the manager to monitor the use of employees within departments. More is said on this point a little later. According to the standard computed above, the direct labor rate for Colonial Pewter should average \$14 per hour.

The standard direct labor time required to complete a unit of product (generally called the **standard hours per unit**) is perhaps the single most difficult standard to determine. One approach is to divide each operation performed on the product into elemental body movements (such as reaching, pushing, and turning over). Published tables of standard times for such movements are available. These times can be applied to the movements and then added together to determine the total standard time allowed per operation. Another approach is for an industrial engineer to do a time and motion study, actually clocking the time required for certain tasks. As stated earlier, the standard time should include allowances for coffee breaks, personal needs of employees, cleanup, and machine downtime. After consulting with the production manager, Terry prepared the following documentation for the standard hours per unit:

Basic labor time per unit, in hours	1.9
Allowance for breaks and personal needs	0.1
Allowance for cleanup and machine downtime	0.3
Allowance for rejects	0.2
Standard labor-hours per unit of product	2.5

Once the rate and time standards have been set, the standard labor cost per unit of product can be computed as follows:

2.5 hours per unit × \$14 per hour = \$35 per unit

This $35 cost figure appears along with direct materials as one item on the standard cost card of the product.

Focus on Current Practice

Industrie Natuzzi SpA, founded and run by Pasquale Natuzzi, produces handmade leather furniture for the world market in Santaeramo Del Colle in southern Italy. Natuzzi is export-oriented and has, for example, about 25% of the U.S. leather furniture market. The company's furniture is handmade by craftsmen, each of whom has a computer terminal that is linked to a sophisticated computer network. The computer terminal provides precise instructions on how to accomplish a particular task in making a piece of furniture. And the computer keeps track of how quickly the craftsman completes the task. If the craftsman beats the standard time to complete the task, the computer adds a bonus to the craftsman's pay.

The company's computers know exactly how much thread, screws, foam, leather, labor, and so on, is required for every model. "Should the price of Argentinean hides or German dyes rise one day, employees in Santaeramo enter the new prices into the computer, and the costs for all sofas with that leather and those colors are immediately recalculated. 'Everything has to be clear for me,' says Natuzzi. 'Why this penny? Where is it going?'"[5] ■

Setting Variable Manufacturing Overhead Standards

As with direct labor, the price and quantity standards for variable manufacturing overhead are generally expressed in terms of rate and hours. The rate represents *the variable portion of the predetermined overhead rate* discussed in Chapter 3; the hours represent whatever hours base is used to apply overhead to units of product (usually machine-hours or direct labor-hours, as we learned in Chapter 3). At Colonial Pewter, the variable portion of the predetermined overhead rate is $3 per direct labor-hour. Therefore, the standard variable manufacturing overhead cost per unit is computed as follows:

$$2.5 \text{ hours per unit} \times \$3 \text{ per hour} = \$7.50 \text{ per unit}$$

This $7.50 cost figure appears along with direct materials and direct labor as one item on the standard cost card in Exhibit 10–1. Observe that the **standard cost per unit** is computed by multiplying the standard quantity or hours by the standard price or rate.

Are Standards the Same as Budgets?

Standards and budgets are very similar. The major distinction between the two terms is that a standard is a *unit* amount, whereas a budget is a *total* amount. The standard cost for materials at Colonial Pewter is $12 per pair of bookends. If 1,000 pairs of bookends

5. Richard C. Morais, "A Methodical Man," *Forbes*, August 11, 1997, pp. 70–72.

Exhibit 10–1
Standard Cost Card—
Variable Production Cost

Inputs	(1) Standard Quantity or Hours	(2) Standard Price or Rate	(3) Standard Cost (1) × (2)
Direct materials	3.0 pounds	$ 4.00	$12.00
Direct labor	2.5 hours	14.00	35.00
Variable manufacturing overhead . .	2.5 hours	3.00	7.50
Total standard cost per unit			$54.50

are to be manufactured during a budgeting period, then the budgeted cost of materials would be $12,000. In effect, *a standard can be viewed as the budgeted cost for one unit of product.*

A General Model for Variance Analysis

An important reason for separating standards into two categories—price and quantity—is that different managers are usually responsible for buying and for using inputs and these two activities occur at different points in time. In the case of raw materials, for example, the purchasing manager is responsible for the price, and this responsibility is exercised at the time of purchase. In contrast, the production manager is responsible for the amount of the raw material used, and this responsibility is exercised when the materials are used in production, which may be many weeks or months after the purchase date. It is important, therefore, that we cleanly separate discrepancies due to deviations from price standards from those due to deviations from quantity standards. Differences between *standard* prices and *actual* prices and *standard* quantities and *actual* quantities are called **variances**. The act of computing and interpreting variances is called *variance analysis*.

Price and Quantity Variances

A general model for computing standard cost variances for variable costs is presented in Exhibit 10–2. This model isolates price variances from quantity variances and shows how each of these variances is computed.[6] We will be using this model throughout the chapter to compute variances for direct materials, direct labor, and variable manufacturing overhead.

Three things should be noted from Exhibit 10–2. First, note that a price variance and a quantity variance can be computed for all three variable cost elements—direct materials, direct labor, and variable manufacturing overhead—even though the variance is not called by the same name in all cases. For example, a price variance is called a *materials price variance* in the case of direct materials but a *labor rate variance* in the case of direct labor and an *overhead spending variance* in the case of variable manufacturing overhead.

Second, note that even though a price variance may be called by different names, it is computed in exactly the same way regardless of whether one is dealing with direct materials, direct labor, or variable manufacturing overhead. The same is true with the quantity variance.

6. Variance analysis of fixed costs is reserved until Chapter 11.

Exhibit 10–2 A General Model for Variance Analysis—Variable Production Costs

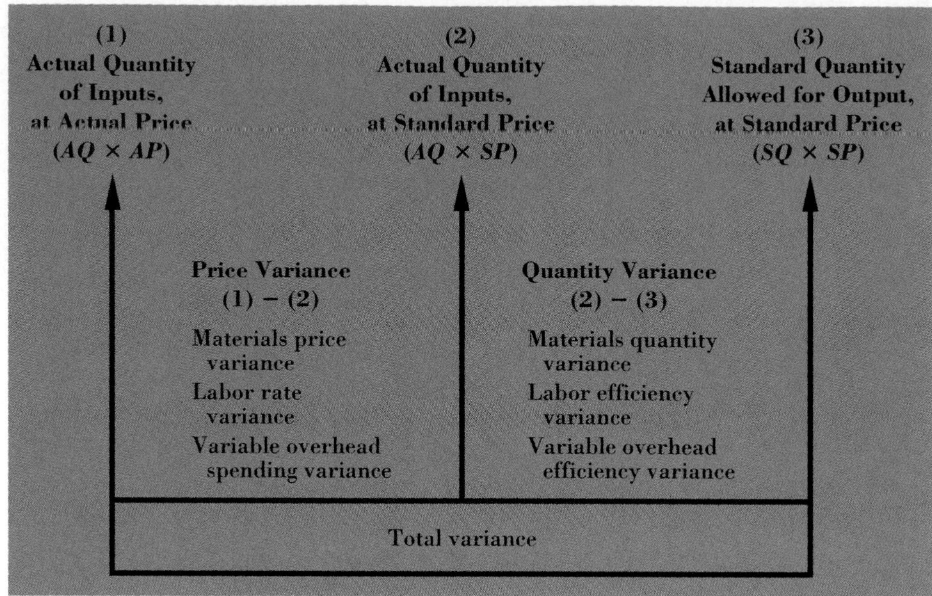

Third, note that variance analysis is actually a type of input-output analysis. The inputs represent the actual quantity of direct materials, direct labor, and variable manufacturing overhead used; the output represents the good production of the period, expressed in terms of the *standard quantity (or the standard hours) allowed for the actual output* (see column 3 in Exhibit 10–2). By **standard quantity allowed** or **standard hours allowed,** we mean the amount of direct materials, direct labor, or variable manufacturing overhead *that should have been used* to produce the actual output of the period. This could be more or could be less materials, labor, or overhead than was *actually* used, depending on the efficiency or inefficiency of operations. The standard quantity allowed is computed by multiplying the actual output in units by the standard input allowed per unit.

With this general model as a foundation, we will now examine the price and quantity variances in more detail.

Using Standard Costs—Direct Materials Variances

objective 2

Compute the direct materials price and quantity variances and explain their significance.

After determining Colonial Pewter Company's standard costs for direct materials, direct labor, and variable manufacturing overhead, Terry Sherman's next step was to compute the company's variances for June, the most recent month. As discussed in the preceding section, variances are computed by comparing standard costs to actual costs. To facilitate this comparison, Terry referred to the standard cost data contained in Exhibit 10–1. This exhibit shows that the standard cost of direct materials per unit of product is as follows:

3.0 pounds per unit × \$4.00 per pound = \$12 per unit

Colonial Pewter's purchasing records for June showed that 6,500 pounds of pewter were purchased at a cost of \$3.80 per pound. This cost figure included freight and handling and was net of the quantity discount. All of the material purchased was used during June to manufacture 2,000 pairs of pewter bookends. Using these data and the standard costs from Exhibit 10–1, Terry computed the price and quantity variances shown in Exhibit 10–3.

The three arrows in Exhibit 10–3 point to three different total cost figures. The first, \$24,700, refers to the actual total cost of the pewter that was purchased during

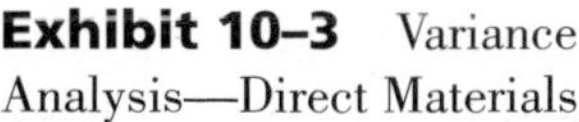

Exhibit 10–3 Variance Analysis—Direct Materials

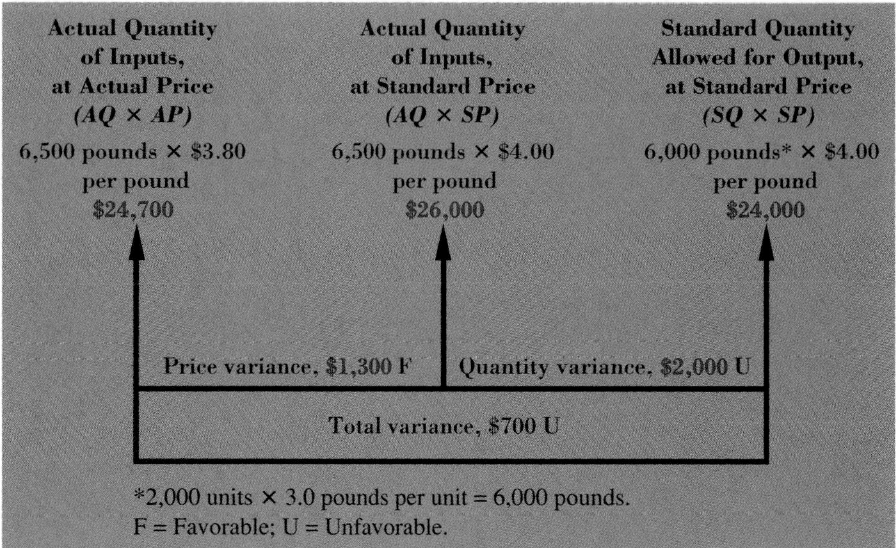

June. The second, $26,000, refers to what the pewter would have cost if it had been purchased at the standard price of $4.00 a pound rather than the actual price of $3.80 a pound. The difference between these two figures, $1,300 ($26,000 − $24,700), is the price variance. It exists because the actual purchase price was $0.20 per pound less than the standard purchase price. Since 6,500 pounds were purchased, the total amount of the variance is $1,300 ($0.20 per pound × 6,500 pounds). This variance is labeled favorable (denoted by F), since the actual purchase price was less than the standard purchase price. A price variance is labeled unfavorable (denoted by U) if the actual price exceeds the standard price.

The third arrow in Exhibit 10–3 points to $24,000—the cost that the pewter would have been had it been purchased at the standard price and only the amount allowed by the standard quantity had been used. The standards call for 3 pounds of pewter per unit. Since 2,000 units were produced, 6,000 pounds of pewter should have been used. This is referred to as the standard quantity allowed for the output. If this 6,000 pounds of pewter had been purchased at the standard price of $4.00 per pound, the company would have spent $24,000. The difference between this figure, $24,000, and the figure at the end of the middle arrow in Exhibit 10–3, $26,000, is the quantity variance of $2,000.

To understand this quantity variance, note that the actual amount of pewter used in production was 6,500 pounds. However, the standard amount of pewter allowed for the actual output is only 6,000 pounds. Therefore, a total of 500 pounds too much pewter was used to produce the actual output. To express this in dollar terms, the 500 pounds is multiplied by the standard price of $4.00 per pound to yield the quantity variance of $2,000. Why is the standard price, rather than the actual price, of the pewter used in this calculation? The production manager is ordinarily responsible for the quantity variance. If the actual price were used in the calculation of the quantity variance, the production manager would be held responsible for the efficiency or inefficiency of the purchasing manager. Apart from being unfair, fruitless arguments between the production manager and purchasing manager would occur every time the actual price of an input is above its standard price. To avoid these arguments, the standard price is used when computing the quantity variance.

The quantity variance in Exhibit 10–3 is labeled unfavorable (denoted by U). This is because more pewter was used to produce the actual output than is called for by the standard. A quantity variance is labeled unfavorable if the actual quantity exceeds the standard quantity and is labeled favorable if the actual quantity is less than the standard quantity.

The computations in Exhibit 10–3 reflect the fact that all of the material purchased during June was also used during June. How are the variances computed if a

Exhibit 10–4 Variance Analysis—Direct Materials, When the Amount Purchased Differs from the Amount Used

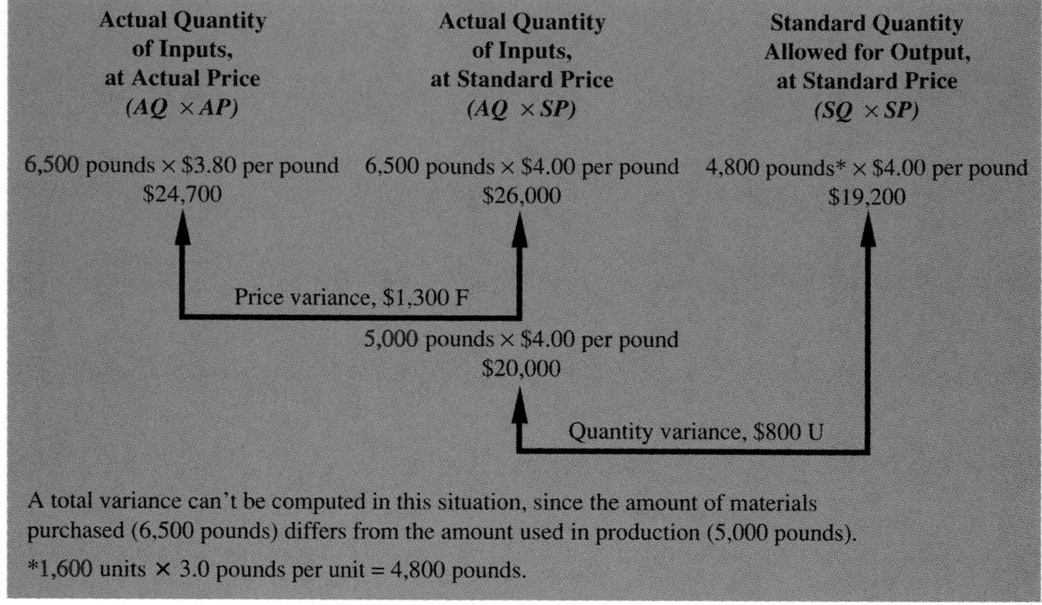

different amount of material is purchased than is used? To illustrate, assume that during June the company purchased 6,500 pounds of materials, as before, but that it used only 5,000 pounds of material during the month and produced only 1,600 units. In this case, the price variance and quantity variance would be as shown in Exhibit 10–4.

Most firms compute the materials price variance, for example, when materials *are purchased* rather than when the materials are placed into production.[7] This permits earlier isolation of the variance, since materials may remain in storage for many months before being used in production. Isolating the price variance when materials are purchased also permits the company to carry its raw materials in the inventory accounts at standard cost. This greatly simplifies assigning raw materials costs to work in process when raw materials are later placed into production.[8]

Note from the exhibit that the price variance is computed on the entire amount of material purchased (6,500 pounds), as before, whereas the quantity variance is computed only on the portion of this material used in production during the month (5,000 pounds). A quantity variance on the 1,500 pounds of material that was purchased during the month but *not* used in production (6,500 pounds purchased − 5,000 pounds used = 1,500 pounds unused) will be computed in a future period when these materials are drawn out of inventory and used in production. The situation illustrated in Exhibit 10–4 is common for companies that purchase materials well in advance of use and store the materials in warehouses while awaiting the production process.

Materials Price Variance—A Closer Look

A **materials price variance** measures the difference between what is paid for a given quantity of materials and what should have been paid according to the standard that has been set. From Exhibit 10–3, this difference can be expressed by the following formula:

7. Max Laudeman and F. W. Schaeberle, "The Cost Accounting Practices of Firms Using Standard Costs," *Cost and Management* 57, no. 4 (July–August 1983), p. 24.
8. See Appendix 10A at the end of the chapter for an illustration of journal entries in a standard cost system.

$$\text{Materials price variance} = (AQ \times AP) - (AQ \times SP)$$

Actual Quantity; Actual Price; Standard Price

The formula can be factored into simpler form as follows:

$$\text{Materials price variance} = AQ(AP - SP)$$

Some managers prefer this simpler formula, since it permits variance computations to be made very quickly. Using the data from Exhibit 10–3 in this formula, we have the following:

6,500 pounds ($3.80 per pound − $4.00 per pound) = $1,300 F

Notice that the answer is the same as that yielded in Exhibit 10–3. If the company wanted to put these data into a performance report, the data might appear as follows:

COLONIAL PEWTER COMPANY
Performance Report—Purchasing Department

Item Purchased	(1) Quantity Purchased	(2) Actual Price	(3) Standard Price	(4) Difference in Price (2) − (3)	(5) Total Price Variance (1) × (4)	Explanation
Pewter	6,500 pounds	$3.80	$4.00	$0.20	$1,300 F	Bargained for an especially favorable price.

F = Favorable; U = Unfavorable.

ISOLATION OF VARIANCES At what point should variances be isolated and brought to the attention of management? The answer is, the earlier the better. The sooner deviations from standard are brought to the attention of management, the sooner problems can be evaluated and corrected.

Once a performance report has been prepared, what does management do with the price variance data? The most significant variances should be viewed as "red flags," calling attention to the fact that an exception has occurred that will require some explanation and perhaps follow-up effort. Normally, the performance report itself will contain some explanation of the reason for the variance, as shown above. In the case of Colonial Pewter Company, the purchasing manager, Janet Warner, said that the favorable price variance resulted from bargaining for an especially favorable price.

Focus on Current Practice

The Gaumnitz and Kollaritsch study of large manufacturing companies cited earlier found that about 60% prepare variance reports on a monthly basis, another 13% prepare reports on a weekly basis, and nearly 22% prepare reports on a daily basis. The number of companies preparing daily reports has more than doubled in recent years.[9] The Cohen and Paquette study cited earlier reported essentially the same results, with only slightly fewer companies preparing monthly reports and only slightly more preparing weekly or daily reports.[10] ■

RESPONSIBILITY FOR THE VARIANCE Who is responsible for the materials price variance? Generally speaking, the purchasing manager has control over the price paid for goods and is therefore responsible for any price variances. Many factors influence the prices paid for goods, including how many units are ordered in a lot, how the order is delivered, whether the order is a rush order, and the quality of materials purchased. A deviation in any of these factors from what was assumed when the standards were set can result in a price variance. For example, purchase of second-grade materials rather than top-grade materials may result in a favorable price variance, since the lower-grade materials would generally be less costly (but perhaps less suitable for production).

There may be times, however, when someone other than the purchasing manager is responsible for a materials price variance. Production may be scheduled in such a way, for example, that the purchasing manager must request delivery by airfreight, rather than by truck. In these cases, the production manager would bear responsibility for the resulting price variances.

A word of caution is in order. Variance analysis should not be used as an excuse to conduct witch hunts or as a means of beating line managers and workers over the head. The emphasis must be on the control function in the sense of *supporting* the line managers and *assisting* them in meeting the goals that they have participated in setting for the company. In short, the emphasis should be positive rather than negative. Excessive dwelling on what has already happened, particularly in terms of trying to find someone to blame, can be destructive to the functioning of an organization.

Materials Quantity Variance—A Closer Look

The **materials quantity variance** measures the difference between the quantity of materials used in production and the quantity that should have been used according to the standard that has been set. Although the variance is concerned with the physical usage of materials, it is generally stated in dollar terms, as shown in Exhibit 10–3. The formula for the materials quantity variance is as follows:

$$\text{Materials quantity variance} = (AQ \times SP) - (SQ \times SP)$$

Actual Quantity (AQ); Standard Price (SP); Standard Quantity Allowed for Output (SQ)

9. See Gaumnitz and Kollaritsch, "Manufacturing Cost Variances: Current Practice and Trends," p. 60.
10. See Cohen and Pacquette, "Management Accounting Practices: Perceptions of Controllers," p. 77.

Again, the formula can be factored into simpler terms:

$$\text{Materials quantity variance} = SP(AQ - SQ)$$

Using the data from Exhibit 10–3 in the formula, we have the following:

$$\$4.00 \text{ per pound}(6{,}500 \text{ pounds} - 6{,}000 \text{ pounds}^*) = \$2{,}000 \text{ U}$$

*2,000 units × 3.0 pounds per unit = 6,000 pounds.

The answer, of course, is the same as that yielded in Exhibit 10–3. The data might appear as follows if a formal performance report were prepared:

COLONIAL PEWTER COMPANY
Performance Report—Production Department

Type of Materials	(1) Standard Price	(2) Actual Quantity	(3) Standard Quantity Allowed	(4) Difference in Quantity (2) − (3)	(5) Total Quantity Variance (1) × (4)	Explanation
Pewter	$4.00	6,500 pounds	6,000 pounds	500 pounds	$2,000 U	Second-grade materials unsuitable for production

F = Favorable; U = Unfavorable.

The materials quantity variance is best isolated at the time that materials are placed into production. Materials are drawn for the number of units to be produced, according to the standard bill of materials for each unit. Any additional materials are usually drawn with an excess materials requisition slip, which is different in color from the normal requisition slips. This procedure calls attention to the excessive usage of materials *while production is still in process* and provides an opportunity for early control of any developing problem.

Excessive usage of materials can result from many factors, including faulty machines, inferior quality of materials, untrained workers, and poor supervision. Generally speaking, it is the responsibility of the production department to see that material usage is kept in line with standards. There may be times, however, when the *purchasing* department may be responsible for an unfavorable materials quantity variance. If the purchasing department obtains inferior quality materials in an effort to economize on price, the materials may be unsuitable for use and may result in excessive waste. Thus, purchasing rather than production would be responsible for the quantity variance. At Colonial Pewter, the production manager, Tom Kuchel, said that second-grade materials were the cause of the unfavorable materials quantity variance for June.

Using Standard Costs—Direct Labor Variances

objective 3

Compute the direct labor rate and efficiency variances and explain their significance.

Terry's next step in determining Colonial Pewter's variances for June was to compute the direct labor variances for the month. Recall from Exhibit 10–1 that the standard direct labor cost per unit of product is $35, computed as follows:

$$2.5 \text{ hours per unit} \times \$14.00 \text{ per hour} = \$35 \text{ per unit}$$

During June, the company paid its direct labor workers $74,250, including employment taxes and fringe benefits, for 5,400 hours of work. This was an average of $13.75

Exhibit 10–5 Variance Analysis—Direct Labor

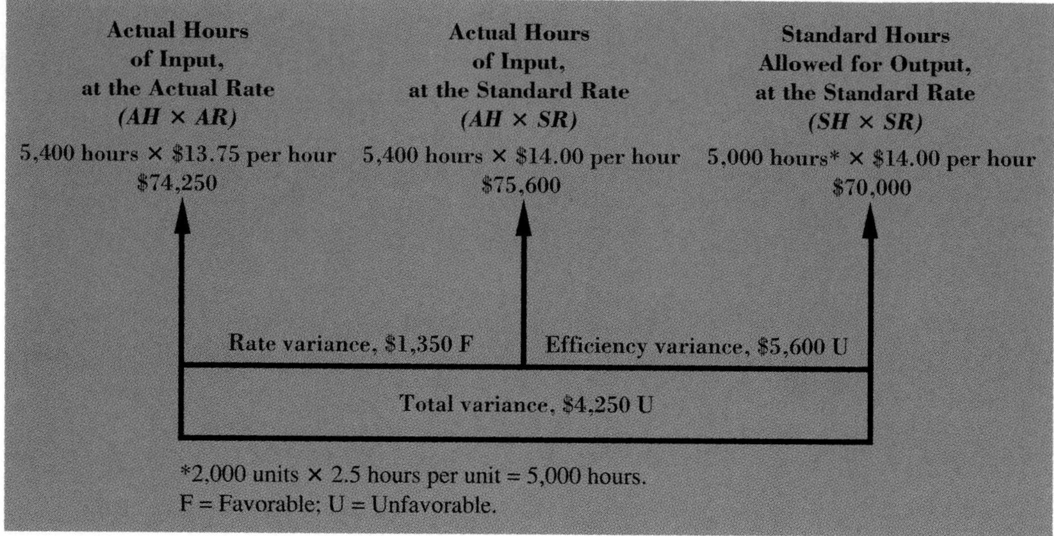

per hour. Using these data and the standard costs from Exhibit 10–1, Terry computed the direct labor rate and efficiency variances that appear in Exhibit 10–5.

Notice that the column headings in Exhibit 10–5 are the same as those used in the prior two exhibits, except that in Exhibit 10–5 the terms *hours* and *rate* are used in place of the terms *quantity* and *price.*

Labor Rate Variance—A Closer Look

As explained earlier, the price variance for direct labor is commonly termed a **labor rate variance.** This variance measures any deviation from standard in the average hourly rate paid to direct labor workers. The formula for the labor rate variance is expressed as follows:

$$\text{Labor rate variance} = (AH \times AR) - (AH \times SR)$$

Actual Hours — Actual Rate — Standard Rate

The formula can be factored into simpler form as follows:

$$\text{Labor rate variance} = AH(AR - SR)$$

Using the data from Exhibit 10–5 in the formula, we have the following:

$$5{,}400 \text{ hours } (\$13.75 \text{ per hour} - \$14.00 \text{ per hour}) = \$1{,}350 \text{ F}$$

In most firms, the rates paid to workers are quite predictable. Nevertheless, rate variances can arise through the way labor is used. Skilled workers with high hourly rates of pay may be given duties that require little skill and call for low hourly rates of pay. This will result in unfavorable labor rate variances, since the actual hourly rate of pay will exceed the standard rate specified for the particular task being performed. A reverse situation exists when unskilled or untrained workers are assigned to jobs that require some skill or training. The lower pay scale for these workers will result in favorable rate variances, although the workers may be inefficient. Finally, unfavorable rate variances can arise from overtime work at premium rates if any portion of the overtime premium is added to the direct labor account.

Who is responsible for controlling the labor rate variance? Since rate variances generally arise as a result of how labor is used, supervisors bear responsibility for seeing that labor rate variances are kept under control.

Labor Efficiency Variance—A Closer Look

The quantity variance for direct labor, more commonly called the **labor efficiency variance,** measures the productivity of labor time. No variance is more closely watched by management, since it is widely believed that increasing the productivity of direct labor time is vital to reducing costs. The formula for the labor efficiency variance is expressed as follows:

$$\text{Labor efficiency variance} = (AH \times SR) - (SH \times SR)$$

Actual Hours (AH); Standard Rate (SR); Standard Hours Allowed for Output (SH)

Factored into simpler terms, the formula is as follows:

$$\text{Labor efficiency variance} = SR(AH - SH)$$

Using the data from Exhibit 10–5 in the formula, we have the following:

$14.00 per hour(5,400 hours − 5,000 hours*) = $5,600 U

*2,000 units × 2.5 hours per unit = 5,000 hours.

Possible causes of an unfavorable labor efficiency variance include poorly trained or motivated workers; poor quality materials, requiring more labor time in processing; faulty equipment, causing breakdowns and work interruptions; poor supervision of workers; and inaccurate standards. The managers in charge of production would generally be responsible for control of the labor efficiency variance. However, the variance might be chargeable to purchasing if the acquisition of poor materials resulted in excessive labor processing time.

When the labor force is essentially fixed in the short term, another important cause of an unfavorable labor efficiency variance is insufficient demand for the output of the factory. In some firms, the actual labor-hours worked is basically fixed—particularly in the short term. Managers in these firms argue that it is difficult, and perhaps even unwise, to constantly adjust the workforce in response to changes in the workload. Therefore, the only way a work center manager can avoid an unfavorable labor efficiency variance in such firms is by keeping everyone busy all of the time. The option of reducing the number of workers on hand is not available.

Thus, if there are insufficient orders from customers to keep the workers busy, the work center manager has two options—either accept an unfavorable labor efficiency variance or build inventory.[11] A central lesson of just-in-time (JIT) is that building inventory with no immediate prospect of sale is a bad idea. Inventory—particularly work in process inventory—leads to high defect rates, obsolete goods, and generally inefficient operations. As a consequence, when the workforce is basically fixed in the short term, managers must be cautious about how labor efficiency variances are used. Some managers advocate dispensing with labor efficiency variances entirely in such situations—at least for the purposes of motivating and controlling workers on the shop floor.

Using Standard Costs—Variable Manufacturing Overhead Variances

objective 4

Compute the variable manufacturing overhead spending and efficiency variances.

The final step in Terry's analysis of Colonial Pewter's variances for June was to compute the variable manufacturing overhead variances. The variable portion of manufacturing overhead can be analyzed using the same basic formulas that are used to analyze direct materials and direct labor. Recall from Exhibit 10–1 that the standard variable manufacturing overhead is $7.50 per unit of product, computed as follows:

$$2.5 \text{ hours per unit} \times \$3.00 \text{ per hour} = \$7.50 \text{ per unit}$$

Colonial Pewter's cost records showed that the total actual variable manufacturing overhead cost for June was $15,390. Recall from the earlier discussion of the direct labor variances that 5,400 hours of direct labor time were recorded during the month and that the company produced 2,000 pairs of bookends. Terry's analysis of this overhead data appears in Exhibit 10–6.

Notice the similarities between Exhibits 10–5 and 10–6. These similarities arise from the fact that direct labor-hours are being used as a base for allocating overhead cost to units of product; thus, the same hourly figures appear in Exhibit 10–6 for variable manufacturing overhead as in Exhibit 10–5 for direct labor. The main difference between the two exhibits is in the standard hourly rate being used, which in this company is much lower for variable manufacturing overhead.

Exhibit 10–6 Variance Analysis—Variable Manufacturing Overhead

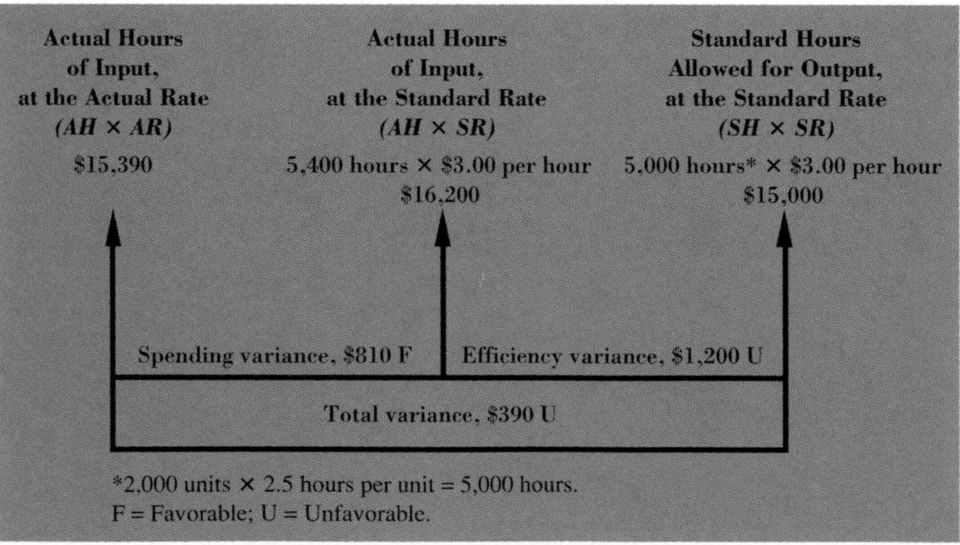

11. For further discussion, see Eliyahu M. Goldratt and Jeff Cox, *The Goal,* 2nd rev. ed. (Croton-on-Hudson, NY: North River Press, 1992).

Manufacturing Overhead Variances— A Closer Look

The formula for **variable overhead spending variance** is expressed as follows:

$$\text{Variable overhead spending variance} = (AH \times AR) - (AH \times SR)$$

Actual Hours | Actual Rate | Standard Rate

Or, factored into simpler terms:

$$\text{Variable overhead spending variance} = AH(AR - SR)$$

Using the data from Exhibit 10–6 in the formula, we have the following:

5,400 hours($2.85 per hour* − $3.00 per hour) − $810 F

*$15,390 ÷ 5,400 hours = $2.85 per hour.

The formula for the **variable overhead efficiency variance** is expressed as follows:

$$\text{Variable overhead efficiency variance} = (AH \times SR) - (SH \times SR)$$

Actual Hours | Standard Rate | Standard Hours Allowed for Output

Or, factored into simpler terms:

$$\text{Variable overhead efficiency variance} = SR(AH - SH)$$

Again using the data from Exhibit 10–6, the computation of the variance would be as follows:

$3.00 per hour(5,400 hours − 5,000 hours*) = $1,200 U

*2,000 units × 2.5 hours per unit = 5,000 hours.

We will reserve further discussion of the variable overhead spending and efficiency variances until Chapter 11, where overhead analysis is discussed in depth.

Before proceeding further, we suggest that you pause at this point and go back and review the data contained in Exhibits 10–1 through 10–6. These exhibits and the accompanying text discussion provide a comprehensive, integrated illustration of standard setting and variance analysis.

Managerial Accounting in Action

THE WRAP-UP

In preparation for the scheduled meeting to discuss Terry's analysis of Colonial Pewter's standard costs and variances, Terry distributed Exhibits 10–1 through 10–6, with supporting explanations, to the management group of Colonial Pewter. This included J. D. Wriston, the president of the company; Tom Kuchel, the production manager; and Janet Warner, the purchasing manager. J. D. Wriston opened the meeting with the following question:

J. D.: Terry, I think I understand the report you distributed, but just to make sure, would you mind summarizing the highlights of what you found?
Terry: As you can see, the biggest problems are the unfavorable materials quantity variance of $2,000 and the unfavorable labor efficiency variance of $5,600.
J. D.: Tom, you're the production boss. What do you think is responsible for the unfavorable labor efficiency variance?
Tom: It pretty much has to be the new production workers. Our experienced workers shouldn't have much problem meeting the standard of 2.5 hours per unit. We all knew that there would be some inefficiency for a while as we brought new people on board.
J. D.: No one is disputing that, Tom. However, $5,600 is a lot of money. Is this problem likely to go away very soon?
Tom: I hope so. If we were to contrast the last two weeks of June with the first two weeks, I'm sure we would see some improvement.
J. D.: I don't want to beat up on you, Tom, but this is a significant problem. Can you do something to accelerate the training process?
Tom: Sure. I could pair up each of the new guys with one of our old-timers and have them work together for a while. It would slow down our older guys a bit, but I'll bet the new workers would learn a lot.
J. D.: Let's try it. Now, what about that $2,000 unfavorable materials quantity variance?
Tom: Are you asking me?
J. D.: Well, I would like someone to explain it.
Tom: Don't look at me. It's that iron-contaminated pewter that Janet bought on her "special deal."
Janet: We got rid of that stuff months ago.
J. D.: Hold your horses. We're not trying to figure out who to blame here. I just want to understand what happened. If we can understand what happened, maybe we can fix it.
Terry: Tom, are the new workers generating a lot of scrap?
Tom: Yeah, I guess so.
J. D.: I think that could be part of the problem. Can you do anything about it?
Tom: I can watch the scrap real closely for a few days to see where it's being generated. If it is the new workers, I can have the old-timers work with them on the problem when I team them up.
J. D.: Good. Let's reconvene in a few weeks and see what has happened. Hopefully, we can get those unfavorable variances under control. ■

Structure of Performance Reports

On preceding pages we have learned that performance reports are used in a standard cost system to communicate variance data to management. Exhibit 10–7 provides an example of how these reports can be integrated in a responsibility reporting system.

Exhibit 10–7 Upward Flow of Performance Reports

President's Report
The president's performance report summarizes all company data. The president can trace the variances downward through the company as needed to determine where topmanagement time should be spent.

	Budget	Actual	Variance
Responsibility center:			
Sales manager	X	X	X
Production superintendent	$26,000	$29,000	$3,000 U
Engineering head	X	X	X
Personnel supervisor	X	X	X
Controller	X	X	X
	$54,000	$61,000	$7,000 U

Production Superintendent
The performance of each department head is summarized for the production superintendent. The totals on the superintendent's performance report are then passed upward to the next level of responsibility.

	Budget	Actual	Variance
Responsibility center:			
Cutting department	X	X	X
Machining department . . .	X	X	X
Finishing department	$11,000	$12,500	$1,500 U
Packaging department . . .	X	X	X
	$26,000	$29,000	$3,000 U

Finishing Department Head
The performance report of each supervisor is summarized on the performance report of the department head. The department totals are then passed upward to the production superintendent.

	Budget	Actual	Variance
Responsibility center:			
Sanding operation	X	X	X
Wiring operation	$ 5,000	$ 5,800	$ 800 U
Assembly operation	X	X	X
	$11,000	$12,500	$1,500 U

Wiring Operation Supervisor
The supervisor of each operation receives a performance report. The totals on these reports are then communicated upward to the next higher level of responsibility.

	Budget	Actual	Variance
Variable costs:			
Direct materials	X	X	X
Direct labor	X	X	X
Manufacturing overhead . .	X	X	X
	$ 5,000	$ 5,800	$ 800 U

Note from the exhibit that the performance reports *start at the bottom and build upward,* with managers at each level receiving information on their own performance as well as information on the performance of each manager under them in the chain of responsibility. This variance information flows upward from level to level in a pyramid fashion, with the president finally receiving a summary of all activities in the organization. If the manager at a particular level (such as the production superintendent) wants to know the reasons behind a variance, he or she can ask for the detailed performance reports prepared by the various operations or departments.

In the following section, we turn our attention to the question of how a manager can determine which variances on these reports are significant enough to warrant further attention.

Variance Analysis and Management by Exception

Variance analysis and performance reports are important elements of *management by exception*. Simply put, management by exception means that the manager's attention should be directed toward those parts of the organization where plans are not working out for one reason or another. Time and effort should not be wasted attending to those parts of the organization where things are going smoothly.

The budgets and standards discussed in this chapter and in the preceding chapter reflect management's plans. If all goes according to plan, there will be little difference between actual results and the results that would be expected according to the budgets and standards. If this happens, managers can concentrate on other issues. However, if actual results do not conform to the budget and to standards, the performance reporting system sends a signal to the manager that an "exception" has occurred. This signal is in the form of a variance from the budget or standards.

However, are all variances worth investigating? The answer is no. Differences between actual results and what was expected will almost always occur. If every variance were investigated, management would waste a great deal of time tracking down nickel-and-dime differences. Variances may occur for any of a variety of reasons—only some of which are significant and warrant management attention. For example, hotter-than-normal weather in the summer may result in higher-than-expected electrical bills for air conditioning. Or, workers may work slightly faster or slower on a particular day. Because of unpredictable random factors, one can expect that virtually every cost category will produce a variance of some kind.

How should managers decide which variances are worth investigating? One clue is the size of the variance. A variance of $5 is probably not big enough to warrant attention, whereas a variance of $5,000 might well be worth tracking down. Another clue is the size of the variance relative to the amount of spending involved. A variance that is only 0.1% of spending on an item is likely to be well within the bounds one would normally expect due to random factors. On the other hand, a variance of 10% of spending is much more likely to be a signal that something is basically wrong.

A more dependable approach is to plot variance data on a statistical control chart, such as illustrated in Exhibit 10–8. The basic idea underlying a statistical control chart is that some random fluctuations in variances from period to period are normal and to be expected even when costs are well under control. A variance should only be investigated when it is unusual relative to that normal level of random fluctuation. Typically the standard deviation of the variances is used as the measure of the normal level of fluctuations. A rule of thumb is adopted such as "investigate all variances that are more than *X* standard deviations from zero." In the control chart in Exhibit 10–8, *X* is 1.0. That is, the rule of thumb in this company is to investigate all variances that are more than one standard deviation in either direction (favorable or unfavorable) from zero. This means that the variances in weeks 7, 11, and 17 would have been investigated, but none of the others.

Exhibit 10–8 A Statistical Control Chart

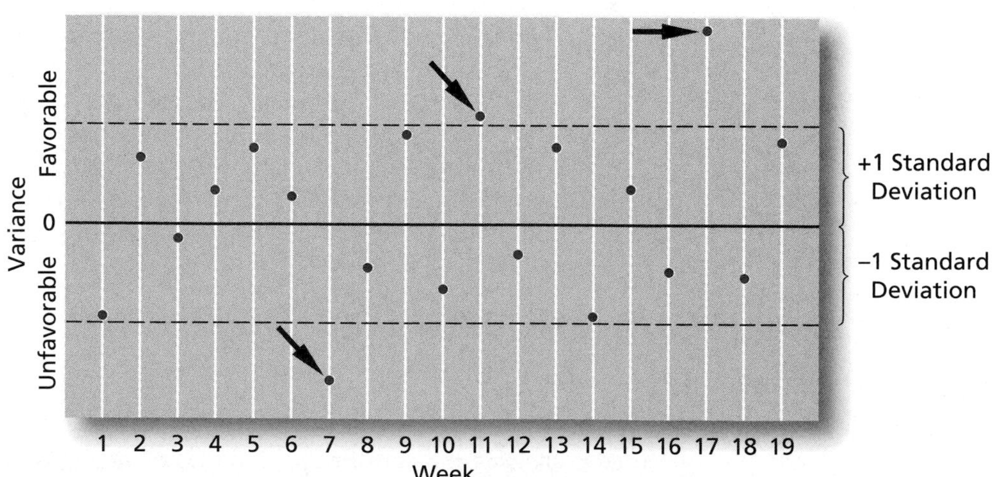

What value of *X* should be chosen? The bigger the value of *X*, the wider the band of acceptable variances that would not be investigated. Thus, the bigger the value of *X*, the less time will be spent tracking down variances, but the more likely it is that a real out-of-control situation would be overlooked. Ordinarily, if *X* is selected to be 1.0, roughly 30% of all variances will trigger an investigation even when there is no real problem. If *X* is set at 1.5, the figure drops to about 13%. If *X* is set at 2.0, the figure drops all the way to about 5%. Don't forget, however, that selecting a big value of *X* will result not only in fewer investigations but also a higher probability that a real problem will be overlooked.

In addition to watching for unusually large variances, the pattern of the variances should be monitored. For example, a run of steadily mounting variances should trigger an investigation even though none of the variances is large enough by itself to warrant investigation.

International Uses of Standard Costs

Standard costs are used by companies worldwide. A comparative study of cost accounting practices found that three-fourths of the companies surveyed in the United Kingdom, two-thirds of the companies surveyed in Canada, and 40% of the companies surveyed in Japan used standard cost systems.[12]

Standard costs were first introduced in Japan after World War II, with Nippon Electronics Company (NEC) being one of the first Japanese companies to adopt standard costs for all of its products. Many other Japanese companies followed NEC's lead after the war and developed standard cost systems. The ways in which these standard costs are used in Japan—and also in the other countries cited above—are shown in Exhibit 10–9.

Over time, the pattern of use shown in Exhibit 10–9 may change, but at present managers can expect to encounter standard costs in most industrialized nations. Moreover, the most important uses are for cost management and budgetary planning purposes.

Exhibit 10–9 Uses of Standard Costs in Four Countries

	United States	United Kingdom	Canada	Japan
Cost management	1*	2	2	1
Budgetary planning and control†	2	3	1	3
Pricing decisions	3	1	3	2
Financial statement preparation	4	4	4	4

*The numbers 1 through 4 denote importance of use, from greatest to least.

†Includes management planning.

Source: Compiled from data in a study by Shin'ichi Inoue, "Comparative Studies of Recent Development of Cost Management Problems in U.S.A., U.K., Canada, and Japan," Research Paper No. 29, Kagawa University (March 1988), p. 20.

12. Shin'ichi Inoue, "Comparative Studies of Recent Development of Cost Management Problems in U.S.A., U.K., Canada, and Japan," Research Paper No. 29, Kagawa University (March 1988), p. 17. The study included 95 United States companies, 52 United Kingdom companies, 82 Canadian companies, and 646 Japanese companies.

Evaluation of Controls Based on Standard Costs

Advantages of Standard Costs

objective 5

Understand the advantages of and potential problems with using standard costs.

Standard cost systems have a number of advantages.

1. As stated earlier, the use of standard costs is a key element in a management by exception approach. So long as costs remain within the standards, managers can focus on other issues. When costs fall significantly outside the standards, managers are alerted that there may be problems requiring attention. This approach helps managers focus on important issues.
2. So long as standards are viewed as reasonable by employees, they can promote economy and efficiency. They provide benchmarks that individuals can use to judge their own performance.
3. Standard costs can greatly simplify bookkeeping. Instead of recording actual costs for each job, the standard costs for materials, labor, and overhead can be charged to jobs.
4. Standard costs fit naturally in an integrated system of "responsibility accounting." The standards establish what costs should be, who should be responsible for them, and whether actual costs are under control.

Potential Problems with the Use of Standard Costs

The use of standard costs can present a number of potential problems. Most of these problems result from improper use of standard costs and the management by exception principle or from using standard costs in situations in which they are not appropriate.

1. Standard cost variance reports are usually prepared on a monthly basis and often are released days or even weeks after the end of the month. As a consequence, the information in the reports may be so stale that it is almost useless. Timely, frequent reports that are approximately correct are better than infrequent reports that are very precise but out of date by the time they are released. As mentioned earlier, some companies are now reporting variances and other key operating data daily or even more frequently.
2. If managers are insensitive and use variance reports as a club, morale may suffer. Employees should receive positive reinforcement for work well done. Management by exception, by its nature, tends to focus on the negative. If variances are used as a club, subordinates may be tempted to cover up unfavorable variances or take actions that are not in the best interests of the company to make sure the variances are favorable. For example, workers may put on a crash effort to increase output at the end of the month to avoid an unfavorable labor efficiency variance. In the rush to produce output, quality may suffer.
3. Labor quantity standards and efficiency variances make two important assumptions. First, they assume that the production process is labor-paced; if labor works faster, output will go up. However, output in many companies is no longer determined by how fast labor works; rather, it is determined by the processing speed of machines. Second, the computations assume that labor is a variable cost. However, as discussed in earlier chapters, in many companies, direct labor may be essentially fixed. If labor is fixed, then an undue emphasis on labor efficiency variances creates pressure to build excess work in process and finished goods inventories.

Focus on Current Practice

In an article about the big three auto makers in North America, *The Wall Street Journal* reported the following:

> General Motors is wrestling with how to change a way of life in a sprawling, hidebound bureaucracy . . . That's why GM has spent more than a year overhauling how it measures success.
>
> "Traditionally, we measured labor efficiency in the plants," Mr. Hoglund [a GM executive vice president] says, to elicit greater output per unit of labor. "Then we found out it drove all the wrong behaviors—people got rewarded for higher and higher volumes, but there was no incentive for quality." Moreover, all the comparisons were internal. Now, he says, the key measures are customer satisfaction and how various processes stack up against the best of the competition.[13] ■

4. In some cases, a "favorable" variance can be as bad or worse than an "unfavorable" variance. For example, McDonald's has a standard for the amount of hamburger meat that should be in a Big Mac. If there is a "favorable" variance, it means that less meat was used than the standard specifies. The result is a substandard Big Mac and possibly a dissatisfied customer.
5. There may be a tendency with standard cost reporting systems to emphasize meeting the standards to the exclusion of other important objectives such as maintaining and improving quality, on-time delivery, and customer satisfaction. This tendency can be reduced by using supplemental performance measures that focus on these other objectives.
6. Just meeting standards may not be sufficient; continual improvement may be necessary to survive in the current competitive environment. For this reason, some companies focus on the trends in the standard cost variances—aiming for continual improvement rather than just meeting the standards. In other companies, engineered standards are being replaced either by a rolling average of actual costs, which is expected to decline, or by very challenging target costs.

In sum, managers should exercise considerable care in their use of a standard cost system. It is particularly important that managers go out of their way to focus on the positive, rather than just on the negative, and to be aware of possible unintended consequences.

Nevertheless, standard costs are still found in the vast majority of manufacturing companies and in many service companies, although their use is changing. For evaluating performance, standard cost variances may be supplanted in the future by a particularly interesting development known as the *balanced scorecard,* which is discussed in the next section. While the balanced scorecard concept is new in most of the world, it has been eagerly embraced by a wide variety of organizations including Analog Devices, KPMG Peat Marwick, Tenneco, Allstate, AT&T, Elf Atochem, Conair-Franklin, Chemical Bank, 3COM, Rockwater, Apple Computer, Advanced Micro Devices (AMD), FMC, the Bank of Montreal, and the Massachusetts Special Olympics.

13. "Tooling Along: With Auto Profits Up, Big Three Again Get a Major Opportunity," *The Wall Street Journal,* May 4, 1994, pp. A1, A11.

Balanced Scorecard

objective 6

Understand how a balanced scorecard fits together and how it supports a company's strategy.

A **balanced scorecard** consists of an integrated set of performance measures that are derived from the company's strategy and that support the company's strategy throughout the organization.[14,15] A strategy is essentially a theory about how to achieve the organization's goals. For example, Southwest Airlines' strategy is to offer passengers low prices and fun on short-haul jet service. The low prices result from the absence of costly frills such as meals, assigned seating, and interline baggage checking. The fun is provided by flight attendants who go out of their way to entertain passengers with their antics. This is an interesting strategy. Southwest Airlines consciously hires people who have a sense of humor and who enjoy their work. Hiring and retaining such employees probably costs no more—and may cost less—than retaining grumpy flight attendants who view their jobs as a chore. Southwest Airlines' strategy is to build loyal customers through a combination of "fun"—which does not cost anything to provide—and low prices that are possible because of the lack of costly frills offered by competing airlines. The theory is that low prices and fun will lead to loyal customers, which, in combination with low costs, will lead to high profits. So far, this theory has worked.

Under the balanced scorecard approach, top management translates its strategy into performance measures that employees can understand and can do something about. For example, the amount of time passengers have to wait in line to have their baggage checked might be a performance measure for the supervisor in charge of the Southwest Airlines check-in counter at the Phoenix airport. This performance measure is easily understood by the supervisor, and can be improved by the supervisor's actions.

Common Characteristics of Balanced Scorecards

Performance measures used in the balanced scorecard approach tend to fall into the four groups illustrated in Exhibit 10–10: financial, customer, internal business processes, and learning and growth. Internal business processes are what the company does in an attempt to satisfy customers. For example, in a manufacturing company, assembling a product is an internal business process. In an airline, handling baggage is an internal business process. The basic idea is that learning is necessary to improve internal business processes; improving business processes is necessary to improve customer satisfaction; and improving customer satisfaction is necessary to improve financial results.

Note that the emphasis in Exhibit 10–10 is on *improvement*—not on just attaining some specific objective such as profits of $10 million. In the balanced scorecard approach, continual improvement is encouraged. In many industries, this is a matter of

14. The balanced scorecard concept was developed by Robert Kaplan and David Norton. For further details, see their articles "The Balanced Scorecard—Measures That Drive Performance," *Harvard Business Review*, January/February 1992, pp. 71–79; "Using the Balanced Scorecard as a Strategic Management System," *Harvard Business Review*, January/February 1996, pp. 75–85; "Why Does a Business Need a Balanced Scorecard?" *Journal of Cost Management*, May/June 1997, pp. 5–10; and their book *Translating Strategy into Action: The Balanced Scorecard* (Boston, MA: Harvard Business School Press, 1996).

15. In the 1960s, the French developed a concept similar to the balanced scorecard called Tableau de Bord or "dashboard." For details, see Michel Lebas, "Managerial Accounting in France: Overview of Past Tradition and Current Practice," *The European Accounting Review*, 1994, 3, no. 3, pp. 471–87; and Marc Epstein and Jean-François Manzoni, "The Balanced Scorecard and the Tableau de Bord: Translating Strategy into Action," *Management Accounting*, August 1997, pp. 28–36.

Exhibit 10–10 From Strategy to Performance Measures: The Balanced Scorecard

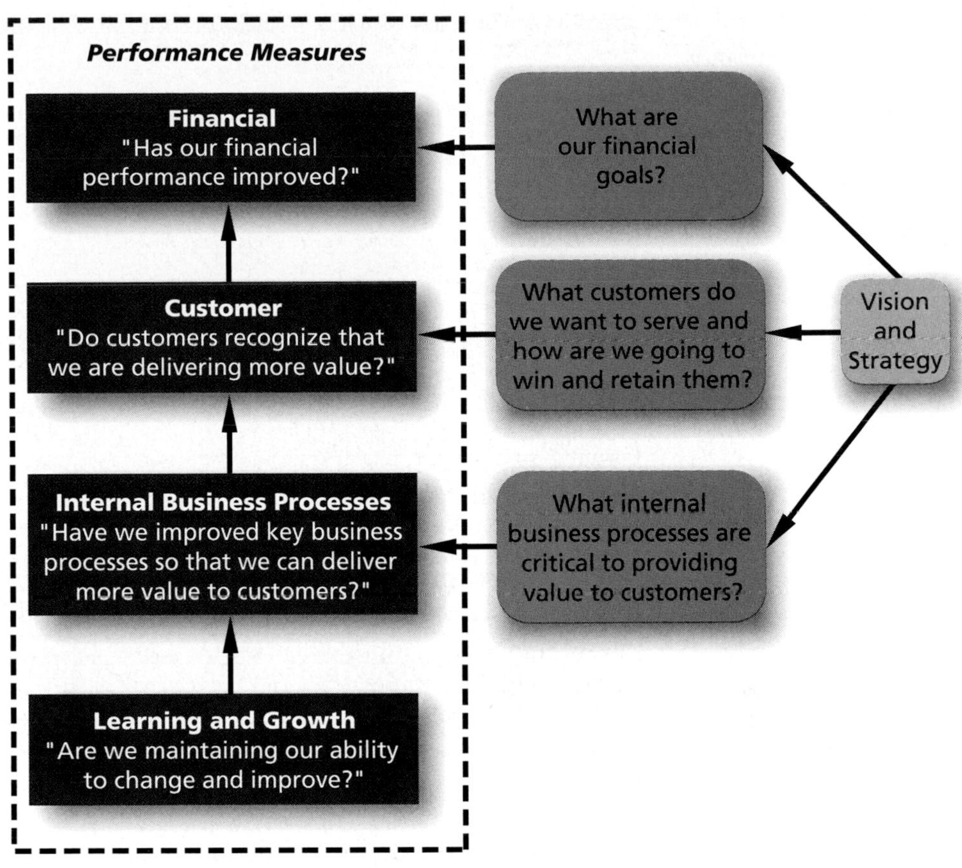

survival. If an organization does not continually improve, it will eventually lose out to competitors that do.

Financial performance measures appear at the top of Exhibit 10–10. Ultimately, most companies exist to provide financial rewards to owners. There are exceptions. Some companies—for example, The Body Shop—may have loftier goals such as providing environmentally friendly products to consumers. However, even nonprofit organizations must generate enough financial resources to stay in operation.

Ordinarily, top managers are responsible for the financial performance measures—not lower-level managers. The supervisor in charge of checking in passengers can be held responsible for how long passengers have to wait in line. However, this supervisor cannot reasonably be held responsible for the entire company's profit. That is the responsibility of the airline's top managers. We will have more to say about financial performance measures in Chapter 12.

Exhibit 10–11 lists some examples of performance measures that can be found on the balanced scorecards of companies. However, few companies, if any, would use all of these performance measures, and almost all companies would add other performance measures. Managers should carefully select the performance measures for their company's balanced scorecard, keeping the following points in mind. First and foremost, the performance measures should be consistent with, and follow from, the company's strategy. If the performance measures are not consistent with the company's strategy, people will find themselves working at cross-purposes. Second, the scorecard should not have too many performance measures. This can lead to a lack of focus and confusion.

While the entire organization will have an overall balanced scorecard, each responsible individual will have his or her own personal scorecard as well. This scorecard should consist of items the individual can personally influence that relate directly

Exhibit 10–11
Examples of Performance Measures for Balanced Scorecards

Customer Perspective	
Performance Measure	**Desired Change**
Customer satisfaction as measured by survey results	+
Number of customer complaints	–
Market share	+
Product returns as a percentage of sales	–
Percentage of customers retained from last period	+
Number of new customers	+

Internal Business Processes Perspective	
Performance Measure	**Desired Change**
Percentage of sales from new products	+
Time to introduce new products to market	–
Percentage of customer calls answered within 20 seconds	+
On-time deliveries as a percentage of all deliveries	+
Work in process inventory as a percentage of sales	–
Unfavorable standard cost variances	–
Defect-free units as a percentage of completed units	+
Delivery cycle time*	–
Throughput time*	–
Manufacturing cycle efficiency*	+
Quality costs†	–
Setup time	–
Time from call by customer to repair of product	–
Percent of customer complaints settled on first contact	+
Time to settle a customer claim	–

Learning and Growth Perspective	
Performance Measure	**Desired Change**
Suggestions per employee	+
Value-added employee‡	+
Employee turnover	–
Hours of in-house training per employee	+

*Explained later in this chapter.

†See Appendix B, Cost of Quality, at the back of the text.

‡Value-added is revenue less externally purchased materials, supplies, and services.

to the performance measures on the overall balanced scorecard. The performance measures on this personal scorecard should not be overly influenced by actions taken by others in the company or by events that are outside of the individual's control.

With those broad principles in mind, we will now take a look at how a company's strategy affects its balanced scorecard.

Focus on Current Practice

Customer satisfaction can be measured in a variety of ways. Every month Hershey Foods Corporation mails a one-page survey to a sample of its customers (i.e., food distributors, wholesalers, and grocery chains). The survey

asks customers to rate Hershey on a number of characteristics including the following:

- Courtesy, speed, and accuracy of customer service personnel.
- Quality of Hershey's carriers.
- Delivery dependability.
- Completeness of shipments.
- Condition of products when delivered.
- Speed and accuracy of Hershey's invoicing.

Customers are asked to rate Hershey in comparison with their very best suppliers, not just Hershey's direct competitors. "Whenever we see a 'poorer than' rating, the customer gets a follow-up phone call from the manager of the customer service center. This call probes for more information about the problem. Once the manager has additional information, he or she involves others in the company who can help rectify the situation. We then thank the customer for the information, explain how we will correct it, and ask them to let us know if things change."[16] ■

A Company's Strategy and the Balanced Scorecard

Returning to the performance measures in Exhibit 10–10, each company must decide which customers to target and what internal business processes are crucial to attracting and retaining those customers. Different companies, having different strategies, will target different customers with different kinds of products and services. Take the automobile industry as an example. BMW stresses engineering and handling; Volvo, safety; Jaguar, luxury detailing; Corvette, racy styling; and Toyota, reliability. Because of these differences in emphases, a one-size-fits-all approach to performance measurement won't work even within this one industry. Performance measures must be tailored to the specific strategy of each company.

Suppose, for example, that Jaguar's strategy is to offer distinctive, richly finished luxury automobiles to wealthy individuals who prize handcrafted, individualized products. Part of Jaguar's strategy might be to create such a large number of options for details, such as leather seats, interior and exterior color combinations, and wooden dashboards, that each car becomes virtually one of a kind. For example, instead of just offering tan or blue leather seats in standard cowhide, the company may offer customers the choice of an almost infinite palate of colors in any of a number of different exotic leathers. For such a system to work effectively, Jaguar would have to be able to deliver a completely customized car within a reasonable amount of time—and without incurring more cost for this customization than the customer is willing to pay. Exhibit 10–12 suggests how Jaguar might reflect this strategy in its balanced scorecard.

If the balanced scorecard is correctly constructed, the performance measures should be linked together on a cause-and-effect basis. Each link can then be read as a hypothesis in the form "If we improve this performance measure, then this other performance measure should also improve." Starting from the bottom of Exhibit 10–12, we can read the links between performance measures as follows. If employees acquire

16. Randy O. Main, "Creating Customer Satisfaction," *Sustaining Total Quality,* The Conference Board Report Number 1025 (New York, 1993), pp. 34–35.

Exhibit 10–12 A Possible Strategy at Jaguar and the Balanced Scorecard

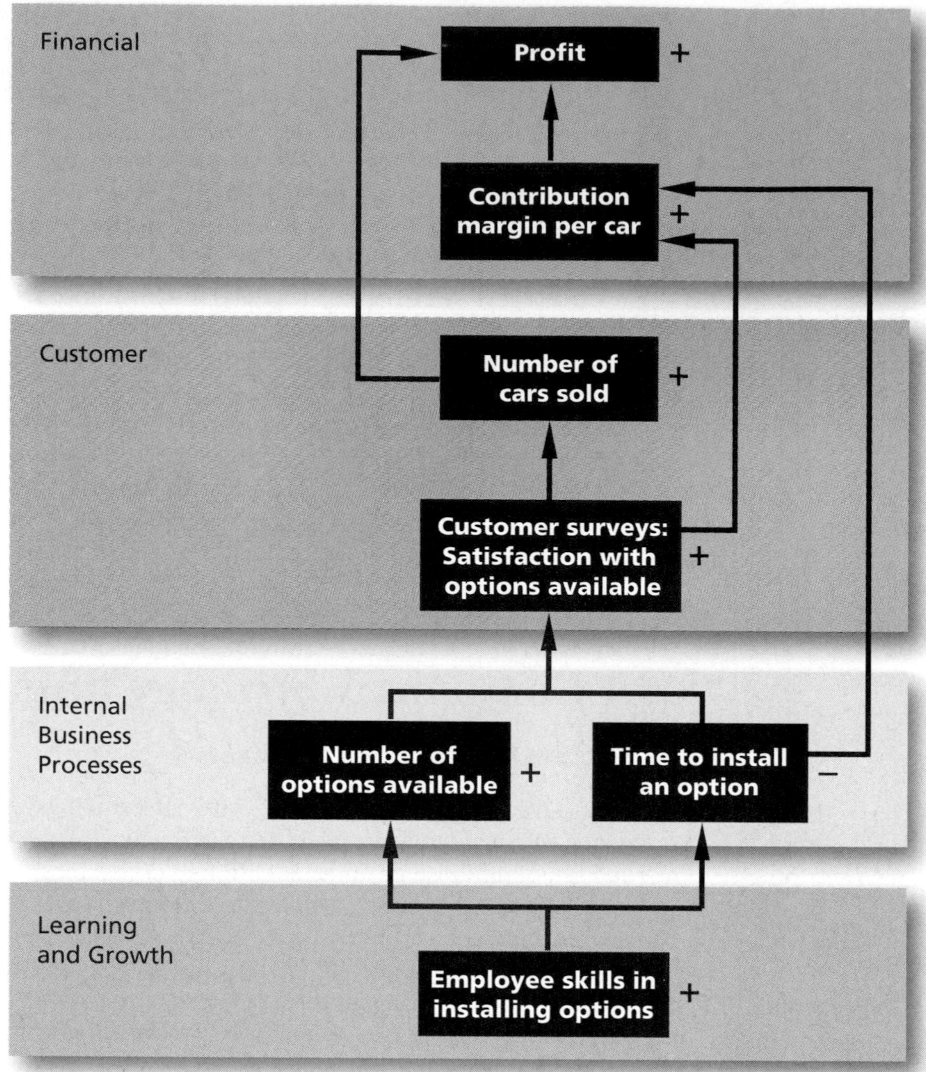

the skills to install new options more effectively, then the company can offer more options and the options can be installed in less time. If more options are available and they are installed in less time, then customer surveys should show greater satisfaction with the range of options available. If customer satisfaction improves, then the number of cars sold should increase. In addition, if customer satisfaction improves, the company should be able to maintain or increase its selling prices, and if the time to install options decreases, the costs of installing the options should decrease. Together, this should result in an increase in the contribution margin per car. If the contribution margin per car increases and more cars are sold, the result should be an increase in profits.

In essence, the balanced scorecard articulates a theory of how the company can attain its desired outcomes (financial, in this case) by taking concrete actions. While the strategy laid out in Exhibit 10–12 seems plausible, it should be regarded as only a theory that should be discarded if it proves to be invalid. For example, if the company succeeds in increasing the number of options available and in decreasing the time required to install options and yet there is no increase in customer satisfaction, the number of cars sold, the contribution margin per car, or profits, the strategy would have to be reconsidered. One of the advantages of the balanced scorecard is that it continually tests the theories underlying management's strategy. If a strategy is not working, it should become evident when some of the predicted effects (i.e., more car sales) don't occur. Without this feedback, management may drift on indefinitely with an ineffective strategy based on faulty assumptions.

Focus on Current Practice

MBNA Corporation services special customized Visa and MasterCard credit cards for over 4,000 different affinity groups such as the National Education Association, Georgetown University, and the Ringling Brothers circus. This is a desirable market niche because members of such affinity groups have significantly higher incomes and carry significantly higher credit card balances than the public at large.

To retain these profitable customers, MBNA emphasizes service—particularly speedy service. The company has set 15 different standards for service. For example, customer address changes must be processed in one day, the telephone at customer service desks must be picked up within two rings, and calls that come into the switchboard must be routed to the correct person within 21 seconds. The current goal is to meet or exceed these standards 98.5% of the time. High technology hardware and software automatically tracks each of these performance measures on a continuous basis, and the results are posted daily for all employees to see. At the end of the year, employees can earn a bonus of up to $1,000, depending on how many days the 98.5% standard has been met.[17] ■

Advantages of Timely and Graphic Feedback

Whatever performance measures are used, they should be reported on a frequent and timely basis. For example, data about defects should be reported to the responsible managers at least once a day so that action can be quickly taken if an unusual number of defects occurs. In the most advanced companies, any defect is reported *immediately*, and its cause is tracked down before any more defects can occur. Another common characteristic of the performance measures under the balanced scorecard approach is that managers focus on *trends* in the performance measures over time. The emphasis is on progress and *improvement* rather than on meeting any specific standard.

For tracking trends and improvement over time, graphic displays are often far more informative than rows or columns of numbers. Consider, for example, the problem of passengers who reserve seats but do not show up to buy their tickets. Because of these "no-show" passengers, airlines routinely overbook popular flights. The airlines gamble that there will be enough no-shows that no passenger will be bumped from the flight. Sometimes airlines lose this gamble. This results in the airline incurring substantial additional costs to either pay passengers with reservations to give them

17. Justin Martin, "Are You as Good as You Think You Are?" *Fortune*, September 30, 1996, pp. 94–99.

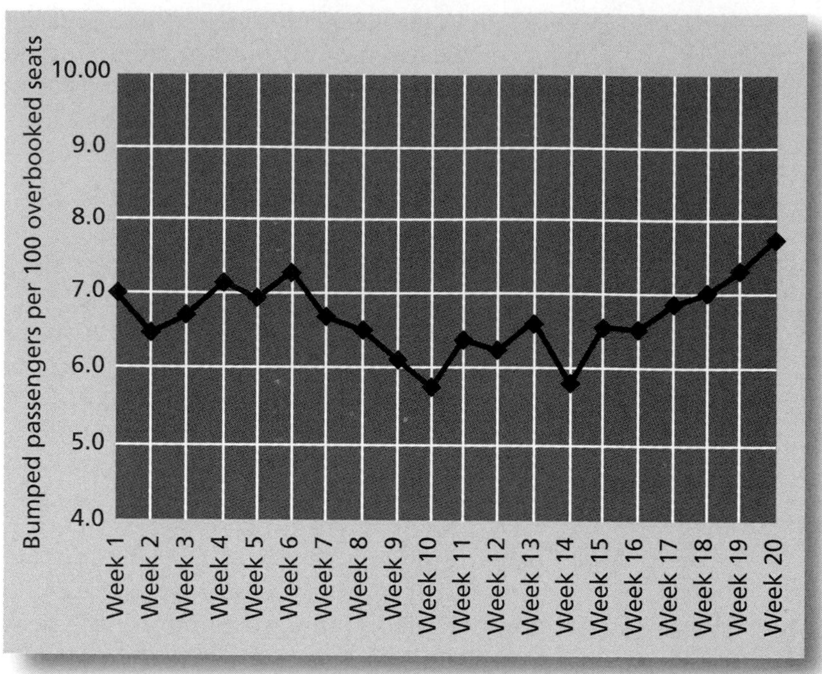

Exhibit 10-13 The Number of Passengers Bumped per Hundred Overbooked Seats

up or to house and feed excess passengers until suitable replacement flights can be found. Because of these costs (and the ill will created among passengers), airlines carefully monitor the percentage of overbooked seats that actually turn out to be a problem and result in a passenger being bumped from a flight. Suppose, for example, that an airline has recorded the following data over the last 20 weeks:

	Bumped passengers per hundred overbooked seats		Bumped passengers per hundred overbooked seats
Week 1	7.1	Week 11	6.4
Week 2	6.5	Week 12	6.3
Week 3	6.7	Week 13	6.7
Week 4	7.2	Week 14	5.8
Week 5	7.0	Week 15	6.6
Week 6	7.3	Week 16	6.6
Week 7	6.7	Week 17	6.9
Week 8	6.5	Week 18	7.1
Week 9	6.2	Week 19	7.4
Week 10	5.8	Week 20	7.8

These data are plotted in Exhibit 10–13. Note how much easier it is to spot trends and unusual points when the data are plotted than when they are displayed in the form of a table. In particular, the worrisome increase in bumped passengers over the final seven weeks is very evident in the plotted data.

Some Measures of Internal Business Process Performance

Most of the performance measures listed in Exhibit 10–11 are self-explanatory. However, three are not—*delivery cycle time*, *throughput time*, and *manufacturing cycle efficiency (MCE)*. These three important performance measures are discussed next.

Exhibit 10–14 Delivery Cycle Time and Throughput (Manufacturing Cycle) Time

Value-Added Time	Non-Value-Added Time
Process Time	Wait Time Inspection Time Move Time Queue Time

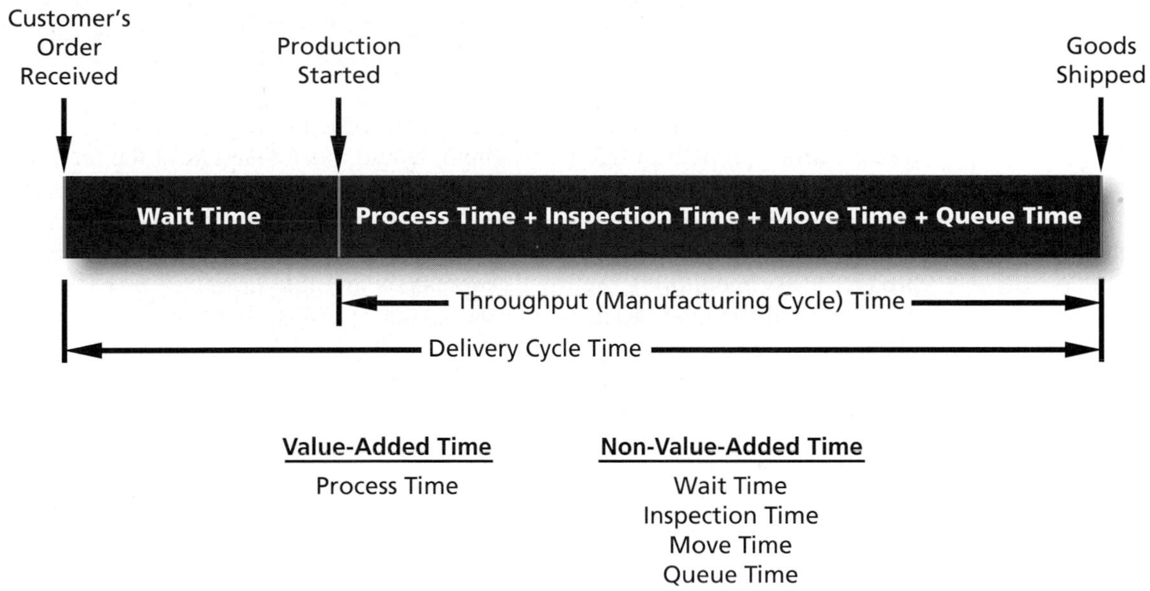

objective 7

Compute the delivery cycle time, the throughput time, and the manufacturing cycle efficiency (MCE).

DELIVERY CYCLE TIME The amount of time from when an order is received from a customer to when the completed order is shipped is called **delivery cycle time.** This time is clearly a key concern to many customers, who would like the delivery cycle time to be as short as possible. Cutting the delivery cycle time may give a company a key competitive advantage—and may be necessary for survival—and therefore many companies would include this performance measure on their balanced scorecard.

THROUGHPUT (MANUFACTURING CYCLE) TIME The amount of time required to turn raw materials into completed products is called **throughput time,** or *manufacturing cycle time*. The relationship between the delivery cycle time and the throughput (manufacturing cycle) time is illustrated in Exhibit 10–14.

Note that, as shown in Exhibit 10–14, the throughput time, or manufacturing cycle time, is made up of process time, inspection time, move time, and queue time. *Process time* is the amount of time in which work is actually done on the product. *Inspection time* is the amount of time spent ensuring that the product is not defective. *Move time* is the time required to move materials or partially completed products from workstation to workstation. *Queue time* is the amount of time a product spends waiting to be worked on, to be moved, to be inspected, or in storage waiting to be shipped.

As shown at the bottom of Exhibit 10–14, the only one of these four activities that adds value to the product is process time. The other three activities—inspecting, moving, and queueing—add no value and should be eliminated as much as possible.

MANUFACTURING CYCLE EFFICIENCY (MCE) Through concerted efforts to eliminate the *non-value-added* activities of inspecting, moving, and queueing, some companies have reduced their throughput time to only a fraction of previous levels. In turn, this has helped to reduce the delivery cycle time from months to only weeks or hours. The throughput time, which is considered to be a key measure in delivery performance, can be put into better perspective by computing the **manufacturing cycle efficiency (MCE).** The MCE is computed by relating the value-added time to the throughout time. The formula is as follows:

$$\text{MCE} = \frac{\text{Value-added time}}{\text{Throughput (manufacturing cycle) time}}$$

If the MCE is less than 1, then non-value-added time is present in the production process. An MCE of 0.5, for example, would mean that half of the total production time consisted of inspection, moving, and similar non-value-added activities. In many manufacturing companies, the MCE is less than 0.1 (10%), which means that 90% of the time a unit is in process is spent on activities that do not add value to the product.[18] By monitoring the MCE, companies are able to reduce non-value-added activities and thus get products into the hands of customers more quickly and at a lower cost.

To provide a numeric example of these measures, assume the following data for Novex Company:

Novex Company keeps careful track of the time relating to orders and their production. During the most recent quarter, the following average times were recorded for each unit or order:

	Days
Wait time	17.0
Inspection time	0.4
Process time	2.0
Move time	0.6
Queue time	5.0

Goods are shipped as soon as production is completed.

Required

1. Compute the throughput time, or velocity of production.
2. Compute the manufacturing cycle efficiency (MCE).
3. What percentage of the production time is spent in non-value-added activities?
4. Compute the delivery cycle time.

Solution

1. Throughput time = Process time + Inspection time + Move time + Queue time
   = 2.0 days + 0.4 days + 0.6 days + 5.0 days
   = 8.0 days
2. Only process time represents value-added time; therefore, the computation of the MCE would be as follows:

$$\text{MCE} = \frac{\text{Value-added time, 2.0 days}}{\text{Throughput time, 8.0 days}}$$
$$= 0.25$$

   Thus, once put into production, a typical unit is actually being worked on only 25% of the time.
3. Since the MCE is 25%, the complement of this figure, or 75% of the total production time, is spent in non-value-added activities.
4. Delivery cycle time = Wait time + Throughput time
   = 17.0 days + 8.0 days
   = 25.0 days

18. Callie Berlinger and James A. Brimson, eds., *Cost Management for Today's Advanced Manufacturing* (Boston, MA: Harvard Business School Press, 1988), p. 4.

Focus on Current Practice

Banks ordinarily require three to four weeks to approve an application for a mortgage loan on a house. The application form includes the individual's employment history, income, and financial assets and liabilities. Personnel at the bank check credit references and review the entire application before granting the loan. A manager at one bank wondered why this process takes so long and asked employees to keep track of how much time they actually worked on processing an application. He discovered that processing an application took on average 26 days, but only about 15 minutes of this time was actual work. All of the rest of the time the application was waiting in someone's in-basket. The manufacturing cycle efficiency (MCE) was therefore only 0.0004 (15 minutes/[26 days × 24 hours per day × 60 minutes per hour]). By redesigning and automating the process, the cycle time was cut down to 15 minutes and the MCE rose to 1.0. Loan applicants can now have a cup of coffee while waiting for approval.[19] ■

SOME FINAL OBSERVATIONS CONCERNING THE BALANCED SCORECARD We would like to emphasize a few points concerning the balanced scorecard. First, the balanced scorecard should be tailored to the company's strategy; each company's balanced scorecard should be unique. The examples given in this chapter are just that—examples. They should not be interpreted as general templates to be fitted to each company. Second, the balanced scorecard reflects a particular strategy, or theory, about how a company can further its objectives by taking specific actions. The theory should be viewed as tentative and subject to change if the actions do not in fact lead to attaining the company's financial and other goals. If the theory (i.e., strategy) changes, then the performance measures on the balanced scorecard should also change. The balanced scorecard should be viewed as a dynamic system that evolves as the company's strategy evolves.

Summary

A standard is a benchmark or "norm" for measuring performance. In business organizations, standards are set for both the cost and the quantity of inputs needed to manufacture goods or to provide services. Quantity standards indicate how much of a cost element, such as labor time or raw materials, should be used in manufacturing a unit of product or in providing a unit of service. Cost standards indicate what the cost of the time or the materials should be.

Standards are normally practical in nature, meaning that they can be attained by reasonable, though highly efficient, efforts. Such standards are generally felt to have a favorable motivational impact on employees.

When standards are compared to actual performance, the difference is referred to as a *variance*. Variances are computed and reported to management on a regular basis for both the price and the quantity elements of materials, labor, and overhead. Price and rate variances for inputs are computed by taking the difference between the actual and standard prices of the inputs and multiplying the result by the amount of input purchased. Quantity and efficiency variances are computed by taking the difference between the actual amount of the input used and the amount of input that is allowed for the actual output, and then multiplying the result by the standard price of the input.

19. Kaplan and Norton, *Translating Strategy into Action: The Balanced Scorecard*, pp. 118–19.

Not all variances require management time or attention. Only unusual or particularly significant variances should be investigated—otherwise a great deal of time would be spent investigating unimportant matters. Additionally, it should be emphasized that the point of the investigation should not be to find someone to blame. The point of the investigation is to pinpoint the problem so that it can be fixed and operations improved.

Traditional standard cost variance reports should often be supplemented with other performance measures. Overemphasis on standard cost variances may lead to problems in other critical areas such as product quality, inventory levels, and on-time delivery.

The balanced scorecard is a promising approach to managing organizations. A balanced scorecard consists of an integrated system of performance measures that are derived from and support the company's strategy. Different companies will have different balanced scorecards because they have different strategies. A well-constructed balanced scorecard provides a means for guiding the company and also provides feedback concerning the effectiveness of the company's strategy.

Review Problem: Standard Costs

Xavier Company produces a single product. Variable manufacturing overhead is applied to products on the basis of direct labor-hours. The standard costs for one unit of product are as follows:

Direct material: 6 ounces at $0.50 per ounce	$ 3
Direct labor: 1.8 hours at $10 per hour	18
Variable manufacturing overhead: 1.8 hours at $5 per hour	9
Total standard variable cost per unit	$30

During June, 2,000 units were produced. The costs associated with June's operations were as follows:

Material purchased: 18,000 ounces at $0.60 per ounce	$10,800
Material used in production: 14,000 ounces	—
Direct labor: 4,000 hours at $9.75 per hour	39,000
Variable manufacturing overhead costs incurred	20,800

Required Compute the materials, labor, and variable manufacturing overhead variances.

Materials Variances

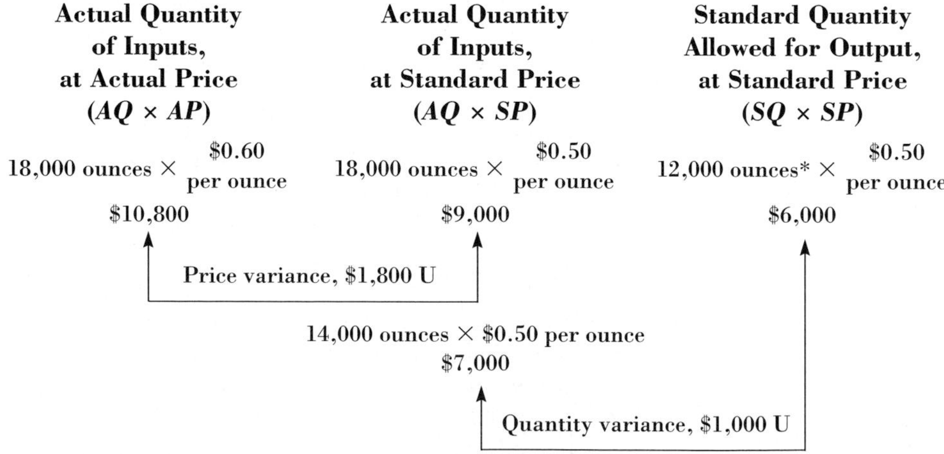

A total variance can't be computed in this situation, since the amount of materials purchased (18,000 ounces) differs from the amount of materials used in production (14,000 ounces).

*2,000 units × 6 ounces per unit = 12,000 ounces.

Using the formulas in the chapter, the same variances would be computed as:

Materials price variance = *AQ*(*AP* − *SP*)
18,000 ounces($0.60 per ounce − $0.50 per ounce) = $1,800 U
Materials quantity variance = *SP*(*AQ* − *SQ*)
$0.50 per ounce(14,000 ounces − 12,000 ounces) = $1,000 U

Labor Variances

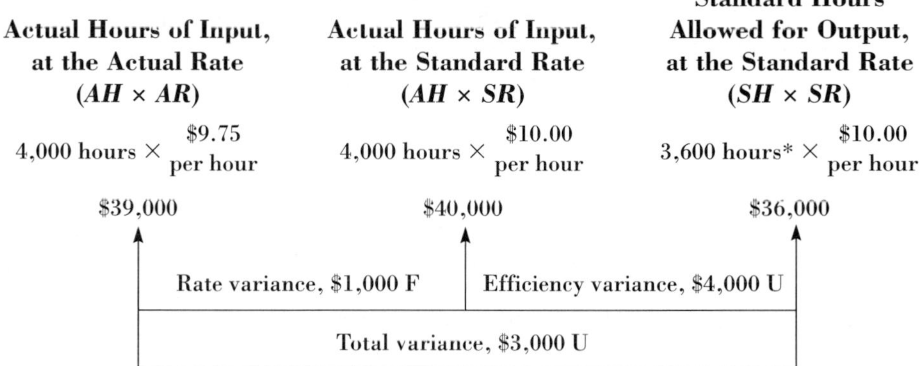

*2,000 units × 1.8 hours per unit = 3,600 hours.

Using the formulas in the chapter, the same variances would be computed as:

Labor rate variance = *AH*(*AR* − *SR*)
4,000 hours($9.75 per hour − $10.00 per hour) = $1,000 F
Labor efficiency variance = *SR*(*AH* − *SH*)
$10.00 per hour(4,000 hours − 3,600 hours) = $4,000 U

Variable Manufacturing Overhead Variances

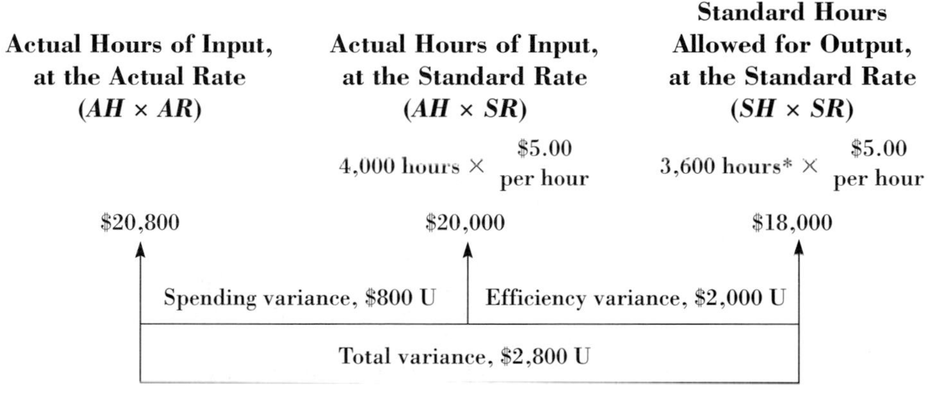

*2,000 units × 1.8 hours per unit = 3,600 hours.

Using the formulas in the chapter, the same variances would be computed as:

Variable overhead spending variance = *AH*(*AR* − *SR*)
4,000 hours($5.20 per hour* − $5.00 per hour) = $800 U

*$20,800 ÷ 4,000 hours = $5.20 per hour.

Variable overhead efficiency variance = *SR*(*AH* − *SH*)
$5.00 per hour(4,000 hours − 3,600 hours) = $2,000 U

Key Terms for Review

Balanced scorecard An integrated set of performance measures that is derived from and supports the organization's strategy. (p. 464)

Bill of materials A listing of the quantity of each type of material required to manufacture a unit of product. (p. 444)

Delivery cycle time The amount of time required from receipt of an order from a customer to shipment of the completed goods. (p. 471)

Ideal standards Standards that allow for no machine breakdowns or other work interruptions and that require peak efficiency at all times. (p. 442)

Labor efficiency variance A measure of the difference between the actual hours taken to complete a task and the standard hours allowed, multiplied by the standard hourly labor rate. (p. 455)

Labor rate variance A measure of the difference between the actual hourly labor rate and the standard rate, multiplied by the number of hours worked during the period. (p. 454)

Management by exception A system of management in which standards are set for various operating activities, with actual results then compared to these standards. Any differences that are deemed significant are brought to the attention of management as "exceptions." (p. 441)

Manufacturing cycle efficiency (MCE) Process (value-added) time as a percentage of throughput time. (p. 471)

Materials price variance A measure of the difference between the actual unit price paid for an item and the standard price, multiplied by the quantity purchased. (p. 450)

Materials quantity variance A measure of the difference between the actual quantity of materials used in production and the standard quantity allowed, multiplied by the standard price per unit of materials. (p. 452)

Practical standards Standards that allow for normal machine downtime and other work interruptions and that can be attained through reasonable, though highly efficient, efforts by the average worker. (p. 443)

Standard cost card A detailed listing of the standard amounts of materials, labor, and overhead that should go into a unit of product, multiplied by the standard price or rate that has been set for each cost element. (p. 442)

Standard cost per unit The standard cost of a unit of product as shown on the standard cost card; it is computed by multiplying the standard quantity or hours by the standard price or rate for each cost element. (p. 446)

Standard hours allowed The time that should have been taken to complete the period's output as computed by multiplying the actual number of units produced by the standard hours per unit. (p. 448)

Standard hours per unit The amount of labor time that should be required to complete a single unit of product, including allowances for breaks, machine downtime, cleanup, rejects, and other normal inefficiencies. (p. 445)

Standard price per unit The price that should be paid for a single unit of materials, including allowances for quality, quantity purchased, shipping, receiving, and other such costs, net of any discounts allowed. (p. 444)

Standard quantity allowed The amount of materials that should have been used to complete the period's output as computed by multiplying the actual number of units produced by the standard quantity per unit. (p. 448)

Standard quantity per unit The amount of materials that should be required to complete a single unit of product, including allowances for normal waste, spoilage, rejects, and similar inefficiencies. (p. 444)

Standard rate per hour The labor rate that should be incurred per hour of labor time, including employment taxes, fringe benefits, and other such labor costs. (p. 445)

Throughput time The amount of time required to turn raw materials into completed products. (p. 471)

Variable overhead efficiency variance The difference between the actual activity (direct labor-hours, machine-hours, or some other base) of a period and the standard activity allowed, multiplied by the variable part of the predetermined overhead rate. (p. 457)

Variable overhead spending variance The difference between the actual variable overhead cost incurred during a period and the standard cost that should have been incurred based on the actual activity of the period. (p. 457)

Variance The difference between standard prices and quantities on the one hand and actual prices and quantities on the other hand. (p. 447)

Appendix 10A: General Ledger Entries to Record Variances

objective 8

Prepare journal entries to record standard costs and variances.

Although standard costs and variances can be computed and used by management without being formally entered into the accounting records, most organizations prefer to make formal entries. Formal entry tends to give variances a greater emphasis than informal, off-the-record computations. This emphasis gives a clear signal of management's desire to keep costs within the limits that have been set. In addition, formal use of standard costs simplifies the bookkeeping process enormously. Inventories and cost of goods sold can be valued at their standard costs—eliminating the need to keep track of the actual cost of each unit.

Direct Materials Variances

To illustrate the general ledger entries needed to record standard cost variances, we will return to the data contained in the review problem at the end of the chapter. The entry to record the purchase of direct materials would be as follows:

Raw Materials (18,000 ounces at $0.50 per ounce)	9,000	
Materials Price Variance (18,000 ounces at $0.10 per ounce U)	1,800	
Accounts Payable (18,000 ounces at $0.60 per ounce)		10,800

Notice that the price variance is recognized when purchases are made, rather than when materials are actually used in production. This permits the price variance to be isolated early, and it also permits the materials to be carried in the inventory account at standard cost. As direct materials are later drawn from inventory and used in production, the quantity variance is isolated as follows:

Work in Process (12,000 ounces at $0.50 per ounce)	6,000	
Materials Quantity Variance (2,000 ounces U at $0.50 per ounce) . . .	1,000	
Raw Materials (14,000 ounces at $0.50 per ounce)		7,000

Thus, direct materials enter into the Work in Process account at standard cost, in terms of both price and quantity.

Notice that both the price variance and the quantity variance above are unfavorable and are debit entries. If these variances had been favorable, they would have appeared as credit entries, as in the case of the direct labor rate variance below.

Direct Labor Variances

Referring again to the cost data in the review problem at the end of the chapter, the general ledger entry to record the incurrence of direct labor cost would be:

Work in Process (3,600 hours at $10.00 per hour)	36,000	
Labor Efficiency Variance (400 hours U at $10.00 per hour)	4,000	
Labor Rate Variance (4,000 hours at $0.25 per hour F)		1,000
Wages Payable (4,000 hours at $9.75 per hour)		39,000

Thus, as with direct materials, direct labor costs enter into the Work in Process account at standard, both in terms of the rate and in terms of the hours allowed for the actual production of the period.

Variable Manufacturing Overhead Variances

Variable manufacturing overhead variances generally are not recorded in the accounts separately but rather are determined as part of the general analysis of overhead, which is discussed in Chapter 11.

Cost Flows in a Standard Cost System

The flows of costs through the company's accounts are illustrated in Exhibit 10A–1. Note that entries into the various inventory accounts are made at standard cost—not actual cost. The differences between actual and standard costs are entered into special accounts that accumulate the various standard cost variances. Ordinarily, these standard cost variance accounts are closed out to Cost of Goods Sold at the end of the period. Unfavorable variances increase Cost of Goods Sold, and favorable variances decrease Cost of Goods Sold.

Exhibit 10A–1 Cost Flows in a Standard Cost System*

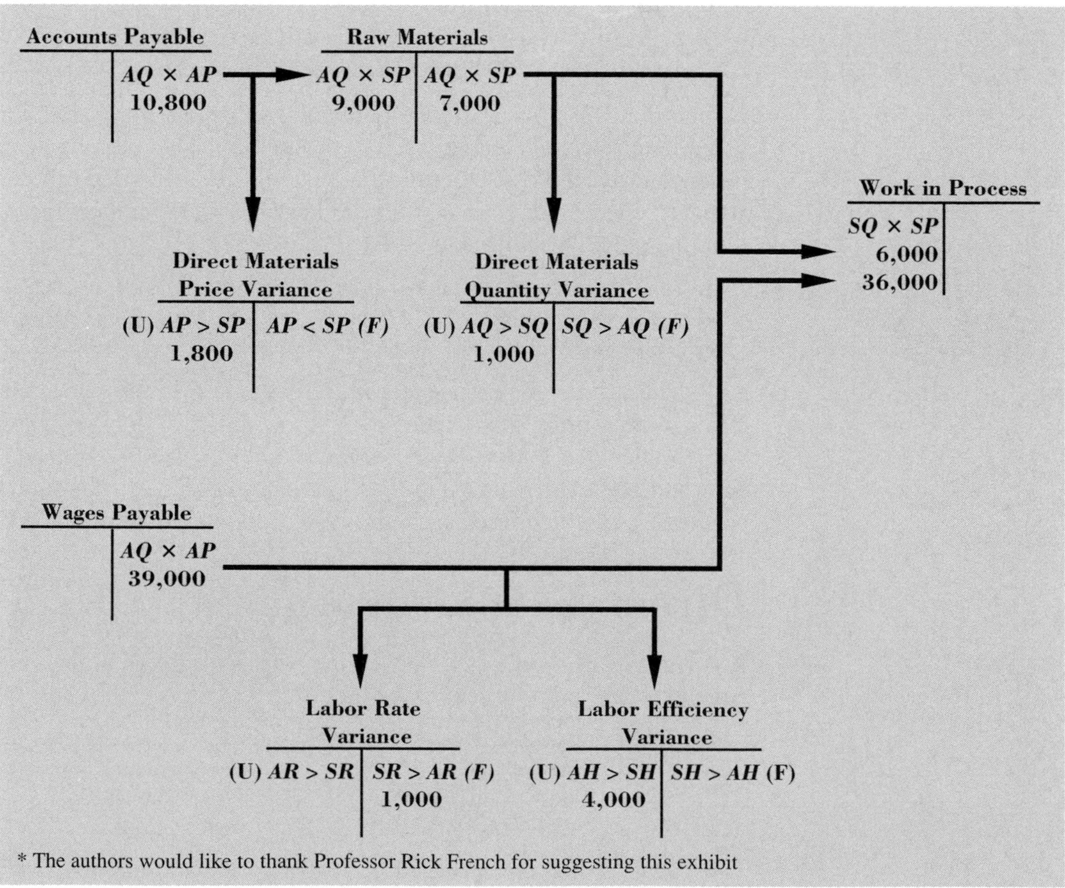

* The authors would like to thank Professor Rick French for suggesting this exhibit

Questions

10–1 What is a quantity standard? What is a price standard?

10–2 Distinguish between ideal and practical standards.

10–3 If employees are chronically unable to meet a standard, what effect would you expect this to have on their productivity?

10–4 What is the difference between a standard and a budget?

10–5 What is meant by the term *variance*?

10–6 What is meant by the term *management by exception*?

10–7 Why are variances generally segregated in terms of a price variance and a quantity variance?

10–8 Who is generally responsible for the materials price variance? The materials quantity variance? The labor efficiency variance?

10–9 The materials price variance can be computed at what two different points in time? Which point is better? Why?

10–10 An examination of the cost records of the Chittenden Furniture Company reveals that the materials price variance is favorable but that the materials quantity variance is unfavorable by a substantial amount. What might this indicate?

10–11 What dangers lie in using standards as punitive tools?

10–12 "Our workers are all under labor contracts; therefore, our labor rate variance is bound to be zero." Discuss.

10–13 What effect, if any, would you expect poor quality materials to have on direct labor variances?

10–14 If variable manufacturing overhead is applied to production on the basis of direct labor-hours and the direct labor efficiency variance is unfavorable, will the variable overhead efficiency variance be favorable or unfavorable, or could it be either? Explain.

10–15 What is a statistical control chart, and how is it used?

10–16 Why can undue emphasis on labor efficiency variances lead to excess work in process inventories?

10–17 Why does the balanced scorecard differ from company to company?

10–18 Why does the balanced scorecard include financial performance measures as well as measures of how well internal business processes are doing?

10–19 What is the difference between the delivery cycle time and the throughput time? What four elements make up the throughput time? Into what two classes can these four elements be placed?

10–20 If a company has a manufacturing cycle efficiency (MCE) of less than 1, what does it mean? How would you interpret an MCE of 0.40?

10–21 (Appendix 10A) What are the advantages of making formal journal entries in the accounting records for variances?

Exercises

E10–1 Martin Company manufactures a powerful cleaning solvent. The main ingredient in the solvent is a raw material called Echol. Information on the purchase and use of Echol follows:

Purchase of Echol Echol is purchased in 15-gallon containers at a cost of $115 per container. A discount of 2% is offered by the supplier for payment within 10 days, and Martin Company takes all discounts. Shipping costs, which Martin Company must pay, amount to $130 for an average shipment of 100 15-gallon containers of Echol.

Use of Echol The bill of materials calls for 7.6 quarts of Echol per bottle of cleaning solvent. (There are four quarts in a gallon.) About 5% of all Echol used is lost through spillage or evaporation (the 7.6 quarts above is the *actual* content per bottle). In addition, statistical analysis has shown that every 41st bottle is rejected at final inspection because of contamination.

Required

1. Compute the standard purchase price for one quart of Echol.
2. Compute the standard quantity of Echol (in quarts) per salable bottle of cleaning solvent.
3. Using the data from (1) and (2) above, prepare a standard cost card showing the standard cost of Echol per bottle of cleaning solvent.

E10–2 Bandar Industries Berhad of Malaysia manufactures sporting equipment. One of the company's products, a football helmet for the North American market, requires a special plastic. During the quarter ending June 30, the company manufactured 35,000 helmets, using 22,500 kilograms of plastic in the process. The plastic cost the company RM 171,000. (The currency in Malaysia is the ringgit, which is denoted here by RM.)

According to the standard cost card, each helmet should require 0.6 kilograms of plastic, at a cost of RM 8 per kilogram.

Required

1. What cost for plastic should have been incurred in the manufacture of the 35,000 helmets? How much greater or less is this than the cost that was incurred?
2. Break down the difference computed in (1) above in terms of a materials price variance and a materials quantity variance.

E10–3 Huron Company produces a commercial cleaning compound known as Zoom. The direct materials and direct labor standards for one unit of Zoom are given below:

	Standard Quantity or Hours	Standard Price or Rate	Standard Cost
Direct materials	4.6 pounds	$ 2.50 per pound	$11.50
Direct labor	0.2 hours	12.00 per hour	2.40

During the most recent month, the following activity was recorded:

a. Twenty thousand pounds of material were purchased at a cost of $2.35 per pound.
b. All of the material purchased was used to produce 4,000 units of Zoom.
c. A total of 750 hours of direct labor time was recorded at a total labor cost of $10,425.

Required

1. Compute the direct materials price and quantity variances for the month.
2. Compute the direct labor rate and efficiency variances for the month.

E10–4 Refer to the data in E10–3. Assume that instead of producing 4,000 units during the month, the company produced only 3,000 units, using 14,750 pounds of material in the production process. (The rest of the material purchased remained in inventory.)

Required Compute the direct materials price and quantity variances for the month.

E10–5 Erie Company manufactures a small cassette player called the Jogging Mate. The company uses standards to control its costs. The labor standards that have been set for one Jogging Mate cassette player are as follows:

Standard Hours	Standard Rate per Hour	Standard Cost
18 minutes	$12.00	$3.60

During August, 5,750 hours of direct labor time were recorded in the manufacture of 20,000 units of the Jogging Mate. The direct labor cost totaled $73,600 for the month.

Required

1. What direct labor cost should have been incurred in the manufacture of the 20,000 units of the Jogging Mate? By how much does this differ from the cost that was incurred?
2. Break down the difference in cost from (1) above into a labor rate variance and a labor efficiency variance.
3. The budgeted variable manufacturing overhead rate is $4 per direct labor-hour. During August, the company incurred $21,850 in variable manufacturing overhead cost. Compute the variable overhead spending and efficiency variances for the month.

E10–6 Dawson Toys, Ltd., produces a toy called the Maze. The company has recently established a standard cost system to help control costs and has established the following standards for the Maze toy:

Direct materials: 6 microns per toy at $0.50 per micron
Direct labor: 1.3 hours per toy at $8 per hour

During July, the company produced 3,000 Maze toys. Production data for the month on the toy follow:

Direct materials: 25,000 microns were purchased for use in production at a cost of $0.48 per micron. Some 5,000 of these microns were still in inventory at the end of the month.
Direct labor: 4,000 direct labor-hours were worked at a cost of $36,000.

Required

1. Compute the following variances for July:
   a. Direct materials price and quantity variances.
   b. Direct labor rate and efficiency variances.
2. Prepare a brief explanation of the significance and possible causes of each variance.

E10–7 The auto repair shop of Quality Motor Company uses standards to control the labor time and labor cost in the shop. The standard labor cost for a motor tune-up is given below:

Job	Standard Hours	Standard Rate	Standard Cost
Motor tune-up	2.5	$9	$22.50

The record showing the time spent in the shop last week on motor tune-ups has been misplaced. However, the shop supervisor recalls that 50 tune-ups were completed during the week, and the controller recalls the following variance data relating to tune-ups:

Labor rate variance	$87 F
Total labor variance	93 U

Required

1. Determine the number of actual labor-hours spent on tune-ups during the week.
2. Determine the actual hourly rate of pay for tune-ups last week.

(Hint: A useful way to proceed would be to work from known to unknown data either by using the variance formulas or by using the columnar format shown in Exhibit 10–5.)

E10–8 Management of Mittel Rhein AG of Köln, Germany, would like to reduce the amount of time between when a customer places an order and when the order is shipped. For the first quarter of operations during the current year the following data were reported:

	Days
Inspection time	0.3
Wait time (from order to start of production)	14.0
Process time	2.7
Move time	1.0
Queue time	5.0

Required

1. Compute the throughput time, or velocity of production.
2. Compute the manufacturing cycle efficiency (MCE) for the quarter.
3. What percentage of the throughput time was spent in non-value-added activities?
4. Compute the delivery cycle time.
5. If by use of just-in-time (JIT) all queue time during production is eliminated, what will be the new MCE?

E10–9 (Appendix 10A) Genola Fashions began production of a new product on June 1. The company uses a standard cost system and has established the following standards for one unit of the new product:

	Standard Quantity or Hours	Standard Price or Rate	Standard Cost
Direct materials	2.5 yards	$14 per yard	$35.00
Direct labor	1.6 hours	8 per hour	12.80

During June, the following activity was recorded relative to the new product:

a. Purchasing acquired 10,000 yards of material at a cost of $13.80 per yard.
b. Production used 8,000 yards of the material to manufacture 3,000 units of the new product.
c. Production reported 5,000 hours of labor time worked directly on the new product; the cost of this labor time was $43,000.

Required

1. For materials:
   a. Compute the direct materials price and quantity variances.
   b. Prepare journal entries to record the purchase of materials and the use of materials in production.
2. For direct labor:
   a. Compute the direct labor rate and efficiency variances.
   b. Prepare a journal entry to record the incurrence of direct labor cost for the month.
3. Post the entries you have prepared to the following T-accounts:

Raw Materials

	Debit	Credit
	?	?
Bal.	?	

Accounts Payable

Debit	Credit
	138,000

Materials Price Variance

Debit	Credit

Wages Payable

Debit	Credit
	43,000

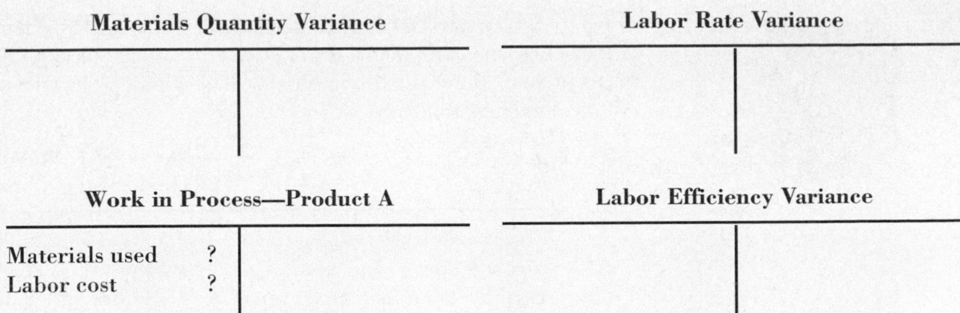

Problems

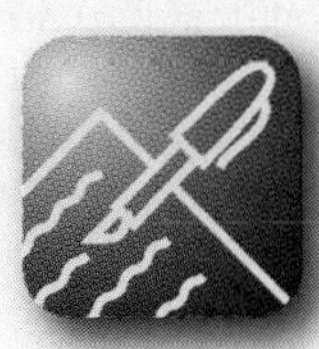

P10–10 Hospital; Basic Variance Analysis John Fleming, chief administrator for Valley View Hospital, is concerned about costs for tests in the hospital's lab. Charges for lab tests are consistently higher at Valley View than at other hospitals and have resulted in many complaints. Also, because of strict regulations on amounts reimbursed for lab tests, payments received from insurance companies and governmental units have not been high enough to provide an acceptable level of profit for the lab.

Mr. Fleming has asked you to evaluate costs in the hospital's lab for the past month. The following information is available:

a. Basically, two types of tests are performed in the lab—blood tests and smears. During the past month, 1,800 blood tests and 2,400 smears were performed in the lab.
b. Small glass plates are used in both types of tests. During the past month, the hospital purchased 12,000 plates at a cost of $28,200. This cost is net of a 6% quantity discount. Some 1,500 of these plates were still on hand unused at the end of the month; there were no plates on hand at the beginning of the month.
c. During the past month, 1,150 hours of labor time were recorded in the lab. The cost of this labor time was $13,800.
d. Variable overhead cost last month in the lab for utilities and supplies totaled $7,820.

Valley View Hospital has never used standard costs. By searching industry literature, however, you have determined the following nationwide averages for hospital labs:

Plates: Two plates are required per lab test. These plates cost $2.50 each and are disposed of after the test is completed.

Labor: Each blood test should require 0.3 hours to complete, and each smear should require 0.15 hours to complete. The average cost of this lab time is $14 per hour.

Overhead: Overhead cost is based on direct labor-hours. The average rate for variable overhead is $6 per hour.

Mr. Fleming would like a complete analysis of the cost of plates, labor, and overhead in the lab for the last month so that he can get to the root of the lab's cost problem.

Required

1. Compute a materials price variance for the plates purchased last month and a materials quantity variance for the plates used last month.
2. For labor cost in the lab:
   a. Compute a labor rate variance and a labor efficiency variance.
   b. In most hospitals, one-half of the workers in the lab are senior technicians and one-half are assistants. In an effort to reduce costs, Valley View Hospital employs only one-fourth senior technicians and three-fourths assistants. Would you recommend that this policy be continued? Explain.
3. Compute the variable overhead spending and efficiency variances. Is there any relationship between the variable overhead efficiency variance and the labor efficiency variance? Explain.

P10–11 Straightforward Variance Analysis Becton Labs, Inc., produces various chemical compounds for industrial use. One compound, called Fludex, is prepared by means of an elaborate distilling process. The company has developed standard costs for one unit of Fludex, as follows:

	Standard Quantity	Standard Price or Rate	Standard Cost
Direct materials	2.5 ounces	$20.00 per ounce	$50.00
Direct labor	1.4 hours	12.50 per hour	17.50
Variable manufacturing overhead	1.4 hours	3.50 per hour	4.90
			$72.40

During November, the following activity was recorded by the company relative to production of Fludex:

a. Materials purchased, 12,000 ounces at a cost of $225,000.
b. There was no beginning inventory of materials on hand to start the month; at the end of the month, 2,500 ounces of material remained in the warehouse unused.
c. The company employs 35 lab technicians to work on the production of Fludex. During November, each worked an average of 160 hours at an average rate of $12 per hour.
d. Variable manufacturing overhead is assigned to Fludex on the basis of direct labor-hours. Variable manufacturing overhead costs during November totaled $18,200.
e. During November, 3,750 good units of Fludex were produced.

The company's management is anxious to determine the efficiency of the activities surrounding the production of Fludex.

Required

1. For materials used in the production of Fludex:
   a. Compute the price and quantity variances.
   b. The materials were purchased from a new supplier who is anxious to enter into a long-term purchase contract. Would you recommend that the company sign the contract? Explain.
2. For direct labor employed in the production of Fludex:
   a. Compute the rate and efficiency variances.
   b. In the past, the 35 technicians employed in the production of Fludex consisted of 20 senior technicians and 15 assistants. During November, the company experimented with only 15 senior technicians and 20 assistants in order to save costs. Would you recommend that the new labor mix be continued? Explain.
3. Compute the variable overhead spending and efficiency variances. What relationship can you see between this efficiency variance and the labor efficiency variance?

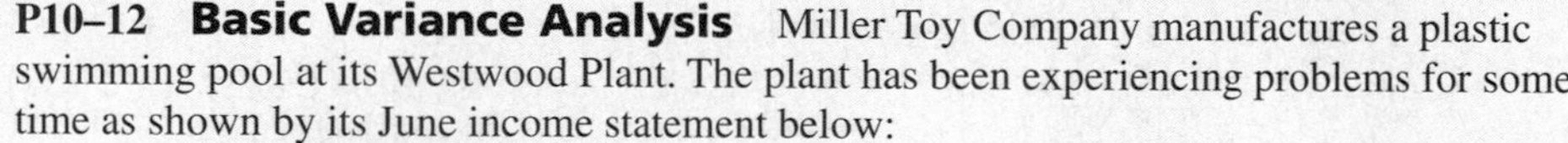

P10–12 Basic Variance Analysis Miller Toy Company manufactures a plastic swimming pool at its Westwood Plant. The plant has been experiencing problems for some time as shown by its June income statement below:

	Budgeted	Actual
Sales (15,000 pools)	$450,000	$450,000
Less variable expenses:		
Variable cost of goods sold*	180,000	196,290
Variable selling expenses	20,000	20,000
Total variable expenses	200,000	216,290
Contribution margin	250,000	233,710
Less fixed expenses:		
Manufacturing overhead	130,000	130,000
Selling and administrative	84,000	84,000
Total fixed expenses	214,000	214,000
Net income	$ 36,000	$ 19,710

*Contains direct materials, direct labor, and variable manufacturing overhead.

Janet Dunn, who has just been appointed general manager of the Westwood Plant, has been given instructions to "get things under control." Upon reviewing the plant's income statement, Ms. Dunn has concluded that the major problem lies in the variable cost of goods sold. She has been provided with the following standard cost per swimming pool:

	Standard Quantity or Hours	Standard Price or Rate	Standard Cost
Direct materials	3.0 pounds	$2.00 per pound	$ 6.00
Direct labor	0.8 hours	6.00 per hour	4.80
Variable manufacturing overhead . . .	0.4 hours*	3.00 per hour	1.20
Total standard cost			$12.00

*Based on machine-hours.

Ms. Dunn has determined that during June the plant produced 15,000 pools and incurred the following costs:

a. Purchased 60,000 pounds of materials at a cost of $1.95 per pound.
b. Used 49,200 pounds of materials in production. (Finished goods and work in process inventories are insignificant and can be ignored.)
c. Worked 11,800 direct labor-hours at a cost of $7.00 per hour.
d. Incurred variable manufacturing overhead cost totaling $18,290 for the month. A total of 5,900 machine-hours was recorded.

It is the company's policy to close all variances to cost of goods sold on a monthly basis.

Required

1. Compute the following variances for June:
   a. Direct materials price and quantity variances.
   b. Direct labor rate and efficiency variances.
   c. Variable overhead spending and efficiency variances.
2. Summarize the variances that you computed in (1) above by showing the net overall favorable or unfavorable variance for the month. What impact did this figure have on the company's income statement? Show computations.
3. Pick out the two most significant variances that you computed in (1) above. Explain to Ms. Dunn possible causes of these variances.

P10–13 Variances; Unit Costs; Journal Entries (Appendix 10A) Trueform Products, Inc., produces a broad line of sports equipment and uses a standard cost system for control purposes. Last year the company produced 8,000 of its varsity footballs. The standard costs associated with this football, along with the actual costs incurred last year, are given below (per football):

	Standard Cost	Actual Cost
Direct materials:		
Standard: 3.7 feet at $5.00 per foot	$18.50	
Actual: 4.0 feet at $4.80 per foot		$19.20
Direct labor:		
Standard: 0.9 hours at $7.50 per hour	6.75	
Actual: 0.8 hours at $8.00 per hour		6.40
Variable manufacturing overhead:		
Standard: 0.9 hours at $2.50 per hour	2.25	
Actual: 0.8 hours at $2.75 per hour		2.20
Total cost per football	$27.50	$27.80

The president was elated when he saw that actual costs exceeded standard costs by only $0.30 per football. He stated, "I was afraid that our unit cost might get out of hand when we gave out those raises last year in order to stimulate output. But it's obvious our costs are well under control."

There was no inventory of materials on hand to start the year. During the year, 32,000 feet of materials were purchased and used in production.

Required

1. For direct materials:
   a. Compute the price and quantity variances for the year.
   b. Prepare journal entries to record all activity relating to direct materials for the year.
2. For direct labor:
   a. Compute the rate and efficiency variances.
   b. Prepare a journal entry to record the incurrence of direct labor cost for the year.
3. Compute the variable overhead spending and efficiency variances.
4. Was the president correct in his statement that "our costs are well under control"? Explain.
5. State possible causes of each variance that you have computed.

P10–14 Internal Business Process Performance Measures DataSpan, Inc., automated its plant at the start of the current year and installed a flexible manufacturing system. The company is also evaluating its suppliers and moving toward a just-in-time (JIT) inventory system. Many adjustment problems have been encountered, among which are problems relating to performance measurement. After much study, the company has decided to use the performance measures below as part of its balanced scorecard, and it has gathered data relating to these measures for the first four months of operations.

	Month			
	1	2	3	4
Throughput time (days)	?	?	?	?
Delivery cycle time (days)	?	?	?	?
Manufacturing cycle efficiency (MCE)	?	?	?	?
Percentage of on-time deliveries	91%	86%	83%	79%
Total throughput (units)	3,210	3,072	2,915	2,806

Management has asked for your help in computing throughput time, delivery cycle time, and MCE. The following average times have been logged over the last four months:

	Average per Month (in days)			
	1	2	3	4
Move time per unit	0.4	0.3	0.4	0.4
Process time per unit	2.1	2.0	1.9	1.8
Wait time per order before start of production	16.0	17.5	19.0	20.5
Queue time per unit	4.3	5.0	5.8	6.7
Inspection time per unit	0.6	0.7	0.7	0.6

Required

1. For each month, compute the following operating performance measures:
   a. The throughput time, or velocity of production.
   b. The MCE.
   c. The delivery cycle time.
2. Evaluate the company's performance over the last four months
3. Refer to the move time, process time, and so forth, given above for month 4.
   a. Assume that in month 5 the move time, process time, and so forth, are the same as in month 4, except that through the use of JIT inventory methods the company is able to completely eliminate the queue time during production. Compute the new throughput time and MCE.
   b. Assume in month 6 that the move time, process time, and so forth, are again the same as in month 4, except that the company is able to completely eliminate both the queue time during production and the inspection time. Compute the new throughput time and MCE.

P10–15 Developing Standard Costs Danson Company is a chemical manufacturer that supplies various products to industrial users. The company plans to introduce a new chemical solution, called Nysap, for which it needs to develop a standard product cost. The following information is available on the production of Nysap:

a. Nysap is made by combining a chemical compound (nyclyn) and a solution (salex), and boiling the mixture. A 20% loss in volume occurs for both the salex and the nyclyn during boiling. After boiling, the mixture consists of 9.6 liters of salex and 12 kilograms of nyclyn per 10-liter batch of Nysap.
b. After the boiling process is complete, the solution is cooled slightly before 5 kilograms of protet are added per 10-liter batch of Nysap. The addition of the protet does not affect the total liquid volume. The resulting solution is then bottled in 10-liter containers.
c. The finished product is highly unstable, and one 10-liter batch out of six is rejected at final inspection. Rejected batches have no commercial value and are thrown out.
d. It takes a worker 35 minutes to process one 10-liter batch of Nysap. Employees work an eight-hour day, including one hour per day for rest breaks and cleanup.

Required

1. Determine the standard quantity for each of the raw materials needed to produce an acceptable 10-liter batch of Nysap.
2. Determine the standard labor time to produce an acceptable 10-liter batch of Nysap.
3. Assuming the following purchase prices and costs, prepare a standard cost card for materials and labor for one acceptable 10-liter batch of Nysap:

Salex	$1.50 per liter
Nyclyn	2.80 per kilogram
Protet	3.00 per kilogram
Direct labor cost	9.00 per hour

(CMA, adapted)

P10–16 Standards and Variances from Incomplete Data Highland Company produces a lightweight backpack that is popular with college students. Standard variable costs relating to a single backpack are given below:

	Standard Quantity or Hours	Standard Price or Rate	Standard Cost
Direct materials	?	$6 per yard	$?
Direct labor	?	?	?
Variable manufacturing overhead	?	$3 per hour	?
Total standard cost			$?

During March, 1,000 backpacks were manufactured and sold. Selected information relating to the month's production is given below:

	Materials Used	Direct Labor	Variable Manufacturing Overhead
Total standard cost allowed*	$16,800	$10,500	$4,200
Actual costs incurred	15,000	?	3,600
Materials price variance	?		
Materials quantity variance	1,200 U		
Labor rate variance		?	
Labor efficiency variance		?	
Variable overhead spending variance			?
Variable overhead efficiency variance			?

*For the month's production.

The following additional information is available for March's production:

Actual direct labor-hours	1,500
Standard overhead rate per hour	$3.00
Standard price of one yard of materials	6.00
Difference between standard and actual cost per backpack produced during March	0.15 F

Overhead is applied to production on the basis of direct labor-hours.

Required

1. What is the standard cost of a single backpack?
2. What was the actual cost per backpack produced during March?
3. How many yards of material are required at standard per backpack?
4. What was the materials price variance for March?
5. What is the standard direct labor rate per hour?
6. What was the labor rate variance for March? The labor efficiency variance?
7. What was the variable overhead spending variance for March? The variable overhead efficiency variance?
8. Prepare a standard cost card for one backpack.

P10–17 Computations from Incomplete Data Sharp Company manufactures a product for which the following standards have been set:

	Standard Quantity or Hours	Standard Price or Rate	Standard Cost
Direct materials	3 feet	$5 per foot	$15
Direct labor	? hours	? per hour	?

During March, the company purchased direct materials at a cost of $55,650, all of which were used in the production of 3,200 units of product. In addition, 4,900 hours of direct labor time were worked on the product during the month. The cost of this labor time was $36,750. The following variances have been computed for the month:

Materials quantity variance	$4,500 U
Total labor variance	1,650 F
Labor efficiency variance	800 U

Required

1. For direct materials:
   a. Compute the actual cost per foot for materials for March.
   b. Compute the materials price variance and a total variance for materials.
2. For direct labor:
   a. Compute the standard direct labor rate per hour.
   b. Compute the standard hours allowed for the month's production.
   c. Compute the standard hours allowed per unit of product.

(Hint: In completing the problem, it may be helpful to move from known to unknown data either by using the columnar format shown in Exhibits 10–3 and 10–5 or by using the variance formulas.)

P10–18 Variance Analysis with Multiple Lots Hillcrest Leisure Wear, Inc., manufactures men's clothing. The company has a single line of slacks that is produced in lots, with each lot representing an order from a customer. As a lot is completed, the customer's store label is attached to the slacks before shipment.

Hillcrest has a standard cost system and has established the following standards for a dozen slacks:

	Standard Quantity or Hours	Standard Price or Rate	Standard Cost
Direct materials	32 yards	$2.40 per yard	$76.80
Direct labor	6 hours	7.50 per hour	45.00

During October, Hillcrest worked on three orders for slacks. The company's job cost records for the month reveal the following:

Lot	Units in Lot (dozens)	Materials Used (yards)	Hours Worked
48	1,500	48,300	8,900
49	950	30,140	6,130
50	2,100	67,250	10,270

The following additional information is available:

a. Hillcrest purchased 180,000 yards of material during October at a cost of $424,800.
b. Direct labor cost incurred during the month for production of slacks amounted to $192,280.
c. There was no work in process inventory on October 1. During October, lots 48 and 49 were completed, and lot 50 was 100% complete as to materials and 80% complete as to labor.

Required

1. Compute the materials price variance for the materials purchased during October.
2. Determine the materials quantity variance for October in both yards and dollars:
   a. For each lot worked on during the month.
   b. For the company as a whole.
3. Compute the labor rate variance for October.
4. Determine the labor efficiency variance for the month in both hours and dollars:
   a. For each lot worked on during the month.
   b. For the company as a whole.
5. In what situations might it be better to express variances in units (hours, yards, and so on) rather than in dollars? In dollars rather than in units?

(CPA, adapted)

P10–19 Variance Analysis; Incomplete Data; Journal Entries (Appendix 10A) Maple Products, Ltd., manufactures a hockey stick that is used worldwide. The standard cost of one hockey stick is:

	Standard Quantity or Hours	Standard Price or Rate	Standard Cost
Direct materials	? feet	$3.00 per foot	$?
Direct labor	2 hours	? per hour	?
Variable manufacturing overhead	? hours	1.30 per hour	?
Total standard cost			$27.00

Last year, 8,000 hockey sticks were produced and sold. Selected cost data relating to last year's operations follow:

	Dr.	Cr.
Direct materials purchased (60,000 feet) . .	$174,000	
Wages payable (? hours)		$79,200*
Work in process—direct materials	115,200	
Direct labor rate variance		3,300
Variable overhead efficiency variance	650	

*Relates to the actual direct labor cost for the year.

The following additional information is available for last year's operations:

a. No materials were on hand at the start of last year. Some of the materials purchased during the year were still on hand in the warehouse at the end of the year.
b. The variable manufacturing overhead rate is based on direct labor-hours. Total actual variable manufacturing overhead cost for last year was $19,800.
c. Actual direct materials usage for last year exceeded the standard by 0.2 feet per stick.

Required

1. For direct materials:
   a. Compute the price and quantity variances for last year.
   b. Prepare journal entries to record all activities relating to direct materials for last year.
2. For direct labor:
   a. Verify the rate variance given above and compute the efficiency variance for last year.
   b. Prepare a journal entry to record activity relating to direct labor for last year.
3. Compute the variable overhead spending variance for last year and verify the variable overhead efficiency variance given above.
4. State possible causes of each variance that you have computed.
5. Prepare a completed standard cost card for one hockey stick.

P10–20 Perverse Effects of Some Performance Measures There is often more than one way to improve a performance measure. Unfortunately, some of the actions taken by managers to make their performance look better may actually harm the organization. For example, suppose the marketing department is held responsible only for increasing the performance measure "total revenues." Increases in total revenues may be achieved by working harder and smarter, but they can also usually be achieved by simply cutting prices. The increase in volume from cutting prices almost always results in greater total revenues; however, it does not always lead to greater total profits. Those who design performance measurement systems need to keep in mind that managers who are under pressure to perform may take actions to improve performance measures that have negative consequences elsewhere.

Required

For each of the following situations, describe actions that managers might take to show improvement in the performance measure but which do not actually lead to improvement in the organization's overall performance.

1. Concerned with the slow rate at which new products are brought to market, top management of a consumer electronics company introduces a new performance measure—speed-to-market. The research and development department is given responsibility for this performance measure, which measures the average amount of time a product is in development before it is released to the market for sale.
2. The CEO of a telephone company has been under public pressure from city officials to fix the large number of public pay phones that do not work. The company's repair people complain that the problem is vandalism and damage caused by theft of coins from coin boxes—particularly in high-crime areas in the city. The CEO says she wants the problem solved and has pledged to city officials that there will be substantial improvement by the end of the year. To ensure that this is done, she makes the managers in charge of installing and maintaining pay phones responsible for increasing the percentage of public pay phones that are fully functional.
3. A manufacturing company has been plagued by the chronic failure to ship orders to customers by the promised date. To solve this problem, the production manager has been given the responsibility of increasing the percentage of orders shipped on time. When a customer calls in an order, the production manager and the customer agree to a delivery date. If the order is not completed by that date, it is counted as a late shipment.
4. Concerned with the productivity of employees, the board of directors of a large multinational corporation has dictated that the manager of each subsidiary will be held responsible for increasing the revenue per employee of his or her subsidiary.

P10–21 Internal Business Process Performance Measures Tombro Industries is in the process of automating one of its plants and developing a flexible manufacturing system. The company is finding it necessary to make many changes in operating procedures. Progress has been slow, particularly in trying to develop new performance measures for the factory.

In an effort to evaluate performance and determine where improvements can be made, management has gathered the following data relating to activities over the last four months:

	Month			
	1	2	3	4
Quality control measures:				
Number of defects	185	163	124	91
Number of warranty claims	46	39	30	27
Number of customer complaints	102	96	79	58
Material control measures:				
Purchase order lead time	8 days	7 days	5 days	4 days
Scrap as a percent of total cost	1%	1%	2%	3%
Machine performance measures:				
Percentage of machine downtime	3%	4%	4%	6%
Use as a percentage of availability	95%	92%	89%	85%
Setup time (hours)	8	10	11	12
Delivery performance measures:				
Throughput time, or velocity	?	?	?	?
Manufacturing cycle efficiency (MCE)	?	?	?	?
Delivery cycle time	?	?	?	?
Percentage of on-time deliveries	96%	95%	92%	89%

The president has read in industry journals that the throughput time, the MCE, and the delivery cycle time are important measures of performance, but no one is sure how they are computed. You have been asked to assist the company, and you have gathered the following data relating to these measures:

	Average per Month (in days)			
	1	2	3	4
Wait time per order before start of production	9.0	11.5	12.0	14.0
Inspection time per unit	0.8	0.7	0.7	0.7
Process time per unit	2.1	2.0	1.9	1.8
Queue time per unit	2.8	4.4	6.0	7.0
Move time per unit	0.3	0.4	0.4	0.5

As part of its modernization process, the company is also moving toward a just-in-time (JIT) inventory system. Over the next year, the company hopes to have the bulk of its raw materials and parts on a JIT basis.

Required

1. For each month, compute the following performance measures:
   a. The throughput time, or velocity of production.
   b. The MCE.
   c. The delivery cycle time.
2. Using the performance measures given in the main body of the problem and the performance measures computed in (1) above, do the following:
   a. Identify the areas where the company seems to be improving.
   b. Identify the areas where the company seems to be deteriorating.
3. Refer to the inspection time, process time, and so forth, given above for month 4.
   a. Assume that in month 5 the inspection time, process time, and so forth, are the same as for month 4, except that the company is able to completely eliminate the queue time during production. Compute the new throughput time and MCE.
   b. Assume that in month 6 the inspection time, process time, and so forth, are the same as in month 4, except that the company is able to eliminate both the queue time during production and the inspection time. Compute the new throughput time and MCE.

P10–22 Internal Business Process Performance Measures and Standard Costs "I've never seen such awful results," roared Ben Carrick, manufacturing vice president of Vorelli Industries. "I thought JIT and automation were supposed to make us more efficient, but just look at last month's efficiency report on Zets, our major product in this plant. The labor efficiency variance was $120,000 *unfavorable*. That's four times higher than it's ever been before. If you add on the $102,000 unfavorable material price variance on Zets, that's over $220,000 down the drain in a single month on just one product. Have you people in purchasing and production lost control over everything?"

"Now take it easy, Ben," replied Sandi Shipp, the company's purchasing agent. "We knew when we adopted JIT that our material costs would go up somewhat. But we're locking onto the very best suppliers, and they're making deliveries three times a day for our Zets product. In a few months, we'll be able to offset most of our higher purchasing costs by completely vacating three rented warehouses."

"And I know our labor efficiency variance looks bad," responded Raul Duvall, the company's production superintendent, "but it doesn't tell the whole story. With JIT flow lines and our new equipment, we've never been more efficient in the plant."

"How can you say you're efficient when you took 90,000 direct labor-hours to produce just 30,000 Zets last month?" asked Ben Carrick. "That works out to be 3 hours per unit, but according to the standard cost card you should be able to produce a Zet in just 2.5 hours. Do you call that efficient?"

"The problem is that the president wants us to use JIT on the finished goods side of the plant as well as on the raw materials side," explained Raul. "So we're trying to gear production to demand, but at the moment we have to cut production back somewhat in order to work off our finished goods inventory of Zets. This will go on for several more months before we'll be able to get production completely in balance with current demand. And don't forget that our line people aren't just standing around when their machines are idle. Under the new system, they're doing their own inspections and they do maintenance on their own equipment."

"It had better *not* go on for several more months," roared Ben Carrick, "at least not if you people down in production want any bonuses this year. I've been looking at these reports for 30 years, and I know inefficiency when I see it. Let's get things back under control."

After leaving Ben Carrick's office, Raul Duvall has approached you for help in developing some performance measures that will show the actual efficiency of the company's production process. Working with Raul, you have gathered the following information:

a. The company manufactures several products in this plant. A standard cost card for Zets is given below:

	Standard Quantity or Hours	Standard Price or Rate	Standard Cost
Direct materials	18 feet	$3.00 per foot	$54.00
Direct labor	2.5 hours	8.00 per hour	20.00
Variable manufacturing overhead	2.5 hours	2.80 per hour	7.00
Total standard cost			$81.00

b. During June, the most recent month, the company purchased 510,000 feet of material for production of Zets at a cost of $3.20 per foot. All of this material was used in the production of 30,000 units during the month. A large part of the production process is now automated, and the company is experiencing less waste each month.

c. The company maintains a stable workforce to produce Zets. Persons who previously were inspectors and on the maintenance crew have been reassigned as direct labor workers. During June, 90,000 hours were logged by direct labor workers on the Zets flow lines. The average pay rate was $7.85 per hour.

d. Variable manufacturing overhead cost is assigned to products on the basis of direct labor-hours. During June, the company incurred $207,000 in variable manufacturing overhead costs associated with the manufacture of Zets.

e. Demand for Zets is increasing over time, and top management is discussing the possibility of constructing additional production facilities.

f. The following information has been gathered from computers located on the production line. This information is expressed in hours per unit of the Zets product.

Processing: As workers have become more familiar with the new equipment and procedures, average processing time per unit has declined over the last three months, from 2.6 hours in April, to 2.5 hours in May, to 2.4 hours in June.

Inspection: Workers are now directly responsible for quality control, which accounts for the following changes in inspection time per unit over the last three months: April, 1.3 hours; May, 0.9 hours; and June, 0.1 hours.

Movement of goods: With the change to JIT flow lines, goods now move shorter distances between machines. Move time per unit over the past three months has been: April, 1.9 hours; May, 1.4 hours; and June, 0.6 hours.

Queue time in cells: Better coordination of production with demand has resulted in less queue time as goods move along the production line. The data for the last three months are: April, 8.2 hours; May, 5.2 hours; and June, 1.9 hours.

Required

1. Compute the materials price and quantity variances using traditional variance analysis. Is the decrease in waste apparent in this computation? Explain. If the company wants to compute the materials price variance, what should be done to make this computation more appropriate?
2. Compute the direct labor rate and efficiency variances using traditional variance analysis. Do you agree with Ben Carrick that the efficiency variance is still appropriate as a measure of performance for the company? Explain why you do or do not agree.
3. Compute the variable manufacturing overhead spending and efficiency variances using traditional variance analysis. Would you expect that a correlation still exists between direct labor and the incurrence of variable manufacturing overhead cost in the company? Explain, using data from your variance computations to support your position.
4. Compute the following for April, May, and June for Zets:
   a. The throughput time per unit.
   b. The manufacturing cycle efficiency (MCE).
5. Which performance measures do you think are more appropriate in this situation—the labor efficiency variance or throughput time per unit and manufacturing cycle efficiency?

P10–23 Developing Standard Costs ColdKing Company is a small producer of fruit-flavored frozen desserts. For many years, ColdKing's products have had strong regional sales on the basis of brand recognition; however, other companies have begun marketing similar products in the area, and price competition has become increasingly important. John Wakefield, the company's controller, is planning to implement a standard cost system for ColdKing and has gathered considerable information from his co-workers on production and material requirements for ColdKing's products. Wakefield believes that the use of standard costing will allow ColdKing to improve cost control and make better pricing decisions.

ColdKing's most popular product is raspberry sherbet. The sherbet is produced in 10-gallon batches, and each batch requires 6 quarts of good raspberries. The fresh raspberries are sorted by hand before they enter the production process. Because of imperfections in the raspberries and normal spoilage, 1 quart of berries is discarded for every 4 quarts of acceptable berries. Three minutes is the standard direct labor time for the sorting that is required to obtain 1 quart of acceptable raspberries. The acceptable raspberries are then blended with the other ingredients; blending requires 12 minutes of direct labor time per batch. After blending, the sherbet is packaged in quart containers. Wakefield has gathered the following pricing information:

a. ColdKing purchases raspberries at a cost of $0.80 per quart. All other ingredients cost a total of $0.45 per gallon.
b. Direct labor is paid at the rate of $9.00 per hour.
c. The total cost of material and labor required to package the sherbet is $0.38 per quart.

Required

1. Develop the standard cost for the direct cost components (materials, labor, and packaging) of a 10-gallon batch of raspberry sherbet. The standard cost should identify the standard quantity, standard rate, and standard cost per batch for each direct cost component of a batch of raspberry sherbet.
2. As part of the implementation of a standard cost system at ColdKing, John Wakefied plans to train those responsible for maintaining the standards on how to use variance analysis. Wakefield is particularly concerned with the causes of unfavorable variances.
   a. Discuss possible causes of unfavorable materials price variances and identify the individual(s) who should be held responsible for these variances.
   b. Discuss possible causes of unfavorable labor efficiency variances and identify the individual(s) who should be held responsible for these variances.

(CMA, adapted)

P10–24 Standard Costs and Variance Analysis Marvel Parts, Inc., manufactures auto accessories. One of the company's products is a set of seat covers that can be adjusted to fit nearly any small car. The company has a standard cost system in use for all of its products. According to the standards that have been set for the seat covers, the factory should work 2,850 hours each month to produce 1,900 sets of covers. The standard costs associated with this level of production activity are:

	Total	Per Set of Covers
Direct materials	$42,560	$22.40
Direct labor	17,100	9.00
Variable manufacturing overhead (based on direct labor-hours)	6,840	3.60
		$35.00

During August, the factory worked only 2,800 direct labor-hours and produced 2,000 sets of covers. The following actual costs were recorded during the month:

	Total	Per Set of Covers
Direct materials (12,000 yards)	$45,600	$22.80
Direct labor	18,200	9.10
Variable manufacturing overhead	7,000	3.50
		$35.40

At standard, each set of covers should require 5.6 yards of material. All of the materials purchased during the month were used in production.

Required Compute the following variances for August:

1. The materials price and quantity variances.
2. The labor rate and efficiency variances.
3. The variable overhead spending and efficiency variances.

Cases

C10–25 Ethics and the Manager Stacy Cummins, the newly hired controller at Merced Home Products, Inc., was disturbed by what she had discovered about the standard costs at the Home Security Division. In looking over the past several years of quarterly earnings reports at the Home Security Division, she noticed that the first-quarter earnings were always poor, the second-quarter earnings were slightly better, the third-quarter earnings were again slightly better, and then the fourth quarter and the year always ended with a spectacular performance in which the Home Security Division always managed to meet or exceed its target profit for the year. She also was concerned to find letters from the company's external auditors to top management warning about an unusual use of standard costs at the Home Security Division.

When Ms. Cummins ran across these letters, she asked the assistant controller, Gary Farber, if he knew what was going on at the Home Security Division. Gary said that it was common knowledge in the company that the vice president in charge of the Home Security Division, Preston Lansing, had rigged the standards at the Home Security Division in order to produce the same quarterly earnings pattern every year. According to company policy, variances are taken directly to the income statement as an adjustment to cost of goods sold.

Favorable variances have the effect of increasing net income, and unfavorable variances have the effect of decreasing net income. Lansing had rigged the standards so that there were always large favorable variances. Company policy was a little vague about when these variances have to be reported on the divisional income statements. While the intent was clearly to recognize variances on the income statement in the period in which they arise, nothing in the company's accounting manuals actually explicitly required this. So for many years Lansing had followed a practice of saving up the favorable variances and using them to create a nice smooth pattern of earnings growth in the first three quarters, followed by a big "Christmas present" of an extremely good fourth quarter. (Financial reporting regulations forbid carrying variances forward from one year to the next on the annual audited financial statements, so all of the variances must appear on the divisional income statement by the end of the year.)

Ms. Cummins was concerned about these revelations and attempted to bring up the subject with the president of Merced Home Products but was told that "we all know what Lansing's doing, but as long as he continues to turn in such good reports, don't bother him." When Ms. Cummins asked if the board of directors was aware of the situation, the president somewhat testily replied, "Of course they are aware."

Required

1. How did Preston Lansing probably "rig" the standard costs—are the standards set too high or too low? Explain.
2. Should Preston Lansing be permitted to continue his practice of managing reported earnings?
3. What should Stacy Cummins do in this situation?

C10–26 Behavioral Impact of Standard Costs and Variances Terry Travers is the manufacturing supervisor of Aurora Manufacturing Company, which produces a variety of plastic products. Some of these products are standard items that are listed in the company's catalog, while others are made to customer specifications. Each month, Travers receives a performance report showing the budget for the month, the actual activity, and the variance between budget and actual. Part of Travers' annual performance evaluation is based on his department's performance against budget. Aurora's purchasing manager, Sally Christensen, also receives monthly performance reports and she, too, is evaluated in part on the basis of these reports.

The monthly reports for June had just been distributed when Travers met Christensen in the hallway outside their offices. Scowling, Travers began the conversation, "I see we have another set of monthly performance reports hand-delivered by that not very nice junior employee in the budget office. He seemed pleased to tell me that I'm in trouble with my performance again."

Christensen: I got the same treatment. All I ever hear about are the things I haven't done right. Now I'll have to spend a lot of time reviewing the report and preparing explanations. The worst part is that it's now the 21st of July so the information is almost a month old, and we have to spend all this time on history.

Travers: My biggest gripe is that our production activity varies a lot from month to month, but we're given an annual budget that's written in stone. Last month we were shut down for three days when a strike delayed delivery of the basic ingredient used in our plastic formulation, and we had already exhausted our inventory. You know about that problem, though, because we asked you to call all over the country to find an alternate source of supply. When we got what we needed on a rush basis, we had to pay more than we normally do.

Christensen: I expect problems like that to pop up from time to time—that's part of my job—but now we'll both have to take a careful look at our reports to see where the charges are reflected for that rush order. Every month I spend more time making sure I should be charged for each item reported than I do making plans for my department's daily work. It's really frustrating to see charges for things I have no control over.

Travers: The way we get information doesn't help, either. I don't get copies of the reports you get, yet a lot of what I do is affected by your department, and by most of the other departments we have. Why do the budget and accounting people assume that I should only be told about my operations even though the president regularly gives us pep talks about how we all need to work together as a team?

Christensen: I seem to get more reports than I need, and I am never asked to comment on them until top management calls me on the carpet about my department's shortcomings. Do you ever hear comments when your department shines?

Travers: I guess they don't have time to review the good news. One of my problems is that all the reports are in dollars and cents. I work with people, machines, and materials. I need information to help me *this* month to solve *this* month's problems—not another report of the dollars expended *last* month or the month before.

Required

1. Based on the conversation between Terry Travers and Sally Christensen, describe the likely motivation and behavior of these two employees resulting from Aurora Manufacturing Company's standard cost and variance reporting system.
2. When properly implemented, both employees and companies should benefit from a system involving standard costs and variances.
   a. Describe the benefits that can be realized from a standard cost system.
   b. Based on the situation presented above, recommend ways for Aurora Manufacturing Company to improve its standard cost and variance reporting system so as to increase employee motivation.

(CMA, adapted)

C10–27 **Unit Costs, Variances, and Journal Entries from Incomplete Data** (Appendix 10A) You are employed by Olster Company, which manufactures products for the senior citizen market. As a rising young executive in the company, you are scheduled to make a presentation in a few hours to your superior. This presentation relates to last week's production of Maxitol, a popular health tonic that is manufactured by Olster Company. Unfortunately, while studying ledger sheets and variance summaries by poolside in the company's fitness area, you were bumped and dropped the papers into the pool. In desperation, you fished the papers from the water, but you have discovered that only the following fragments are readable:

Maxitol—Standard Cost Card

	Standard Quantity or Hours	Standard Price or Rate	Standard Cost
Material A	6 gallons	$8 per gall	$
Material B		per pou	
Direct labor		per ho	0
Standard cost per batc			$99.50

Maxitol—General Ledger Accounts

Raw Materials—A

Debit		Credit
Bal. 3/1	0	
Bal. 3/7	2,000	

Work in Process

Debit		Credit
Bal. 3/1	0	
Material A	5,760	
Bal. 3/7	0	

Material A—Price Variance

Debit	Credit
	300

Wages Payable

Debit	Credit
	4,100

Raw Materials—B

Debit		Credit
Bal. 3/1	700	2,500
Bal. 3/7	1,400	

Labor Rate Variance

Debit	Credit
500	

Material B—Quantity Variance

Debit	Credit
100	

Accounts Payable

Debit	Credit
	11,460

You remember that the accounts payable are for purchases of both material A and material B. You also remember that only 10 direct labor workers are involved in the production of Maxitol and that each worked 40 hours last week. The wages payable above are for wages earned by these workers.

You realize that to be ready for your presentation, you must reconstruct all data relating to Maxitol very quickly. As a start, you have called purchasing and found that 1,000 gallons of material A and 800 pounds of material B were purchased last week.

Required

1. How many batches of Maxitol were produced last week? (This is a key figure; be sure it's right before going on.)
2. For material A:
   a. What was the cost of material A purchased last week?
   b. How many gallons were used in production last week?
   c. What was the quantity variance?
   d. Prepare journal entries to record all activity relating to material A for last week.
3. For material B:
   a. What is the standard cost per pound for material B?
   b. How many pounds of material B were used in production last week? How many pounds should have been used at standard?
   c. What is the standard quantity of material B per batch?
   d. What was the price variance for material B last week?
   e. Prepare journal entries to record all activity relating to material B for last week.
4. For direct labor:
   a. What is the standard rate per direct labor-hour?
   b. What are the standard hours per batch?
   c. What were the standard hours allowed for last week's production?
   d. What was the labor efficiency variance for last week?
   e. Prepare a journal entry to record all activity relating to direct labor for last week.
5. Complete the standard cost card shown above for one batch of Maxitol.

C10–28 Balanced Scorecard Weierman Department Store is located in the downtown area of a medium-sized city in the American Midwest. While the store had been profitable for many years, it is facing increasing competition from large national chains that have set up stores in the city's suburbs. Recently the downtown area has been undergoing revitalization, and the owners of Weierman Department Store are somewhat optimistic that profitability can be restored.

In an attempt to accelerate the return to profitability, the management of Weierman Department Store is in the process of designing a balanced scorecard for the company. Management believes the company should focus on two key problems. First, customers are taking longer and longer to pay the bills they incur on the department store's charge card and they have far more bad debts than are normal for the industry. If this problem were solved, the company would have far more cash to make much needed renovations. Investigation has revealed that much of the problem with late payments and unpaid bills is apparently due to disputed bills that are the result of incorrect charges on the customer bills. These incorrect charges usually occur because salesclerks enter data incorrectly on the charge account slip. Second, the company has been incurring large losses on unsold seasonal apparel. Such items are ordinarily resold at a loss to discount stores that specialize in such distress items.

The meeting in which the balanced scorecard approach was discussed was disorganized and ineffectively led—possibly because no one other than one of the vice presidents had read anything about how to put a balanced scorecard together. Nevertheless, a number of potential performance measures were suggested by various managers. These potential performance measures are listed below:

Performance measures suggested by various managers:

- Total sales revenue.
- Percentage of salesclerks trained to correctly enter data on charge account slips.
- Customer satisfaction with accuracy of charge account bills from monthly customer survey.
- Sales per employee.
- Travel expenses for buyers for trips to fashion shows.

- Average age of accounts receivables.
- Courtesy shown by junior staff members to senior staff members based on surveys of senior staff.
- Unsold inventory at the end of the season as a percentage of total cost of sales.
- Sales per square foot of floor space.
- Percentage of suppliers making just-in-time deliveries.
- Quality of food in the staff cafeteria based on staff surveys.
- Written-off accounts receivables (bad debts) as a percentage of sales.
- Percentage of charge account bills containing errors.
- Percentage of employees who have attended the city's cultural diversity workshop.
- Total profit.
- Profit per employee.

Required

1. As someone with more knowledge of the balanced scorecard than almost anyone else in the company, you have been asked to build an integrated balanced scorecard. In your scorecard, use only performance measures suggested by the managers above. You do not have to use all of the performance measures suggested by the managers, but you should build a balanced scorecard that reveals a strategy for dealing with the problems with accounts receivable and with unsold merchandise. Construct the balanced scorecard following the format used in Exhibit 10–12. Do not be particularly concerned with whether a specific performance measure falls within the learning and growth, internal business process, customer, or financial perspective. However, clearly show the causal links between the performance measures with arrows and whether the performance measures should show increases or decreases.
2. Assume that the company adopts your balanced scorecard. After operating for a year, there are improvements in some performance measures but not in others. What should management do next?
3. a. Suppose that customers express greater satisfaction with the accuracy of their charge account bills but the performance measures for the average age of receivables and for bad debts do not improve. Explain why this might happen.
   b. Suppose that the performance measures for the average age of accounts receivable, bad debts, and unsold inventory improve, but total profits do not. Explain why this might happen. Assume in your answer that the explanation lies within the company.

Group Exercises

GE10–29 Conventional Production Practices Traditional U.S. manufacturing systems were based on the economies of mass production and, therefore, focused primarily on productivity (average output per employee) and unit cost. Work processes were standardized, and production volume was maximized by increasing investments in economies of scale. Historically, direct labor costs amounted to approximately 30% to 40% of total manufacturing costs. To control high labor costs, American plant managers were constantly exhorted to increase output, produce at or below standard unit costs, and minimize unfavorable cost variances.

Required

1. Can you cite service industries that have used the same mass production and economies of scale philosophy to prosper?
2. Describe the traditional manufacturing environment and how American companies manage costs by maximizing production volume.
3. Traditionally, what performance measures were used to measure and evaluate the performance of direct labor and shop floor personnel?
4. Given that everyone from the plant manager on down wants to perform well, what incentives did these performance measures provide factory workers and shop floor supervisors?
5. What potential results did these performance incentives have?
6. Cycle time or throughput time, the time it takes to complete a job once it is started, is very important to customers. What impact did the combination of production factors—the factory layout, increasing volume, and decreasing unit cost—have on cycle times?

7. Today, production management is not only under pressure to contain (if not reduce) costs but customers are also demanding (and getting) increasing quality and a wider choice of products and services. How would production managers likely respond to demands for higher quality parts and a wider variety of finished products while still functioning under traditional mass-production systems?

GE10–30 Lean (i.e., JIT) Production Systems Lean production systems are one of the most important business innovations of this century. Toyota Motor Company deserves much credit for developing many of the key features of modern-day lean production systems. Lean production is delivering materials to the shop floor just in time for use and producing just in time to meet present demand. Successful implementations of lean production techniques eliminate a lot of the waste, excess, delay, and uncertainty associated with traditional manufacturing systems.

Required

1. What is lean (i.e., JIT) production?
2. Describe the JIT manufacturing environment and how American companies manage costs by producing just in time.
3. If properly implemented, how does lean production benefit the firm? How does JIT manufacturing affect traditional performance measures such as direct labor efficiency, direct labor utilization, and machine utilization? What sort of performance measures must be implemented to achieve rather than defeat the objectives of JIT manufacturing?
4. How does the performance measurement system differ under JIT production from that under traditional production systems? Give specific examples of JIT performance measures.
5. How is the cost accounting system affected by a change to lean production?
6. Today, production managers are not only under pressure to reduce costs but to increase quality and shorten lead times. How do lean production systems manage to improve these three seemingly conflicting demands?

GE10–31 Standards in an Auto Repair Shop Make an appointment to meet with the manager of an auto repair shop that uses standards. In most cases, this would be an auto repair shop that is affiliated with a national chain such as Firestone or Sears or the service department of a new-car dealer.

Required At the scheduled meeting, find out the answers to the following questions:

1. How are standards set?
2. Are standards practical or ideal?
3. How are the standards used?
4. Is the actual time taken to complete a task compared to the standard time?
5. What are the consequences of unfavorable variances? Of favorable variances?
6. Do the standards and variances create any potential problems?

GE10–32 Standards in Practice Identify a company in your local area that is likely to use standards such as a commercial bakery, commercial printer, chain restaurant, or manufacturer. After verifying that the company uses standards, make an appointment to meet with the manager, controller, or chief financial officer of the organization.

Required At the scheduled meeting, find out the answers to the following questions:

1. How are standards set?
2. Are standards practical or ideal?
3. How are the standards used?
4. What are the consequences of unfavorable variances? Of favorable variances?
5. Do the standards and variances create any potential problems?

IE10–33 Interpreting the Scores on the Balanced Scorecard A balanced scorecard involves many different measures of performance ranging from the company's net income to the amount of time a customer must wait in line. How does a manager looking at a balanced scorecard know whether a particular score is good or bad? If a customer waits on

average 30 seconds, is that good or bad? Is a net income of $10 million good or bad? CorVu Corporation is one of a number of companies that have developed balanced scorecard software. The company discusses the problem of interpreting performance measures on its web site www.corvu.com/papers/bsc.htm. Another software developer, Ergometrics, shows how balanced scorecard data can be visually displayed in the form of gauges on its web site www.ergometrics.com.

Required

1. Explain how CorVu Corporation computes its normalized scores.
2. Indicate how each of the Key Performance Indicators (KPIs) in CorVu Corporation's example could be displayed as gauges.
3. Suggest alternative methods for normalizing scores that might be useful to managers. Your alternatives should allow managers to tell at a glance whether performance is good or bad and improving or deteriorating.

Chapter Eleven

Flexible Budgets and Overhead Analysis

Business Focus

Dr. Salinas had just been unexpectedly appointed director of Providence Medical Center. The previous director, who had instituted tight budgetary controls, was extremely unpopular with the hospital's staff. This had led to his sacking by the hospital's board of directors. Dr. Salinas suspected that he had been chosen for the job because of his popularity rather than any innate management ability. He thought of himself as a physician rather than as a manager.

Shortly after taking over as director, the hospital's lab supervisor came storming into Dr. Salinas's office, threw a computer-generated report on Dr. Salinas's desk, and angrily stated: "Here, look at this report. It says we spent too much money in the Lab Department. We spent 5% more than had been authorized in the annual budget. Well, of course we did! Practically every department in the hospital asked for more tests that they had predicted at budget time! What are we supposed to do, refuse to run tests once we ran over budget?" Dr . Salinas responded: "Of course not. You have to run the tests. However, we also have to keep some control over our spending. On the other hand, I agree it isn't fair to hold you to the original budget. I don't see the solution right now, but I will work on it."

Learning Objectives

After studying Chapter 11, you should be able to:

1 Prepare a flexible budget and explain the advantages of the flexible budget approach over the static budget approach.

2 Prepare a performance report for both variable and fixed overhead costs using the flexible budget approach.

3 Use the flexible budget to prepare a variable overhead performance report containing only a spending variance.

4 Use the flexible budget to prepare a variable overhead performance report containing both a spending and an efficiency variance.

5 Explain the significance of the denominator activity figure in determining the standard cost of a unit of product.

6 Apply overhead cost to units of product in a standard cost system.

7 Compute and interpret the fixed overhead budget and volume variances.

Controlling overhead costs is a major preoccupation of managers in business, in government, and in not-for-profit organizations. Overhead is a major cost, if not *the* major cost, in most large organizations. It costs Microsoft very little to download copies of its software onto hard disks and to provide purchasers with software manuals; almost all of Microsoft's costs are in research and development and marketing—elements of overhead. Or consider Disney World. The only direct cost of serving a particular guest is the cost of the food the guest consumes at the park; virtually all of the other costs of running the amusement park are overhead. At Boeing, there are far more direct costs, but there are still huge amounts of overhead in the form of engineering salaries, buildings, insurance, administrative salaries, and marketing costs.

Control of overhead costs poses special problems. Costs like direct materials and direct labor are often easier to understand, and therefore to control, than overhead, which can include everything from the disposable coffee cup in the visitor's waiting area to the president's salary. Overhead is usually made up of many separate costs—many of which may be small. This makes it impractical to control them in the same way that costs such as direct materials and direct labor are controlled. And some overhead costs are variable, some are fixed, and some are a mixture of fixed and variable. These particular problems can be largely overcome by the use of flexible budgets—a topic that was briefly discussed in Chapter 9. In this chapter, we study flexible budgets in greater detail and learn how they can be used to control costs. We also expand the study of overhead variances that we started in Chapter 10.

Flexible Budgets

Characteristics of a Flexible Budget

objective 1

Prepare a flexible budget and explain the advantages of the flexible budget approach over the static budget approach.

The budgets that we studied in Chapter 9 were *static budgets.* A **static budget** is prepared for only the planned level of activity. This approach is suitable for planning purposes, but it is inadequate for evaluating how well costs are controlled. If the actual activity during a period differs from what was planned, it would be misleading to simply compare actual costs to the static budget. If activity is higher than expected, the variable costs should be higher than expected; and if activity is lower than expected, the variable costs should be lower than expected.

Flexible budgets take into account changes in costs that should occur as a consequence of changes in activity. A **flexible budget** provides estimates of what cost should be for any level of activity within a specified range. When a flexible budget is used in performance evaluation, actual costs are compared to what the *costs should have been for the actual level of activity during the period* rather than to the budgeted costs from the original budget. This is a very important distinction—particularly for variable costs. If adjustments for the level of activity are not made, it is very difficult to interpret discrepancies between budgeted and actual costs.

Deficiencies of the Static Budget

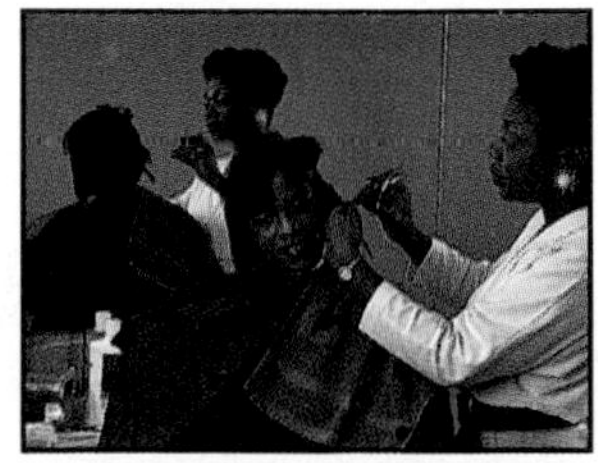

To illustrate the difference between a static budget and a flexible budget, we will consider the case of Rick's Hairstyling, a tony hairstyling salon located in Beverly Hills that is owned and managed by Rick Manzi. The salon has very loyal customers—many of whom are associated with the film industry. Despite the glamour associated with his salon, Rick is a very shrewd businessman. Recently he has been attempting to get better control over his overhead, and at the urging of his accounting and business adviser Victoria Kho, he has begun to prepare monthly budgets. Victoria Kho is a certified

Exhibit 11–1

RICK'S HAIRSTYLING
Static Budget
For the Month Ended March 31

Budgeted number of client-visits	5,000
Budget variable overhead costs:	
Hairstyling supplies	$ 6,000
Client gratuities	20,000
Electricity	1,000
Total variable overhead cost	27,000
Budgeted fixed overhead costs:	
Support staff wages and salaries	8,000
Rent	12,000
Insurance	1,000
Utilities other than electricity	500
Total fixed overhead cost	21,500
Total budgeted overhead cost	$48,500

public accountant and certified management accountant in independent practice who specializes in small service-oriented businesses like Rick's Hairstyling.

At the end of February, Rick carefully prepared the March budget for overhead items that appears in Exhibit 11–1. Rick believes that the number of customers served in a month is the best way to measure the overall level of activity in his salon. Rick refers to these visits as client-visits. A customer who comes into the salon and has his or her hair styled is counted as one client-visit. After some discussion with Victoria Kho, Rick identified three major categories of variable overhead costs—hairstyling supplies, client gratuities, and electricity—and four major categories of fixed costs support staff wages and salaries, rent, insurance, and utilities other than electricity. Client gratuities consist of flowers, candies, and glasses of champagne that Rick gives to his customers while they are in the salon. Rick considers electricity to be a variable cost, since almost all of the electricity in the salon is consumed in running blow-dryers, curling irons, and other hairstyling equipment.

To develop the budget for variable overhead, Rick estimated that the average cost per client-visit should be $1.20 for hairstyling supplies, $4.00 for client gratuities, and $0.20 for electricity. Based on his estimate of 5,000 client-visits in March, Rick budgeted for $6,000 ($1.20 per client-visit × 5,000 client-visits) in hairstyling supplies, $20,000 ($4.00 per client-visit × 5,000 client-visits) in client gratuities, and $1,000 ($0.20 per client-visit × 5,000 client-visits) in electricity.

The budget for fixed overhead items was based on Rick's records of how much he had spent on these items in the past. The budget included $8,000 for support staff wages and salaries, $12,000 for rent, $1,000 for insurance, and $500 for utilities other than electricity.

At the end of March, Rick prepared a report comparing actual to budgeted costs. That report appears in Exhibit 11–2. The problem with that report, as Rick immediately realized, is that it compares costs at one level of activity (5,200 client-visits) to costs at a different level of activity (5,000 client-visits). Since Rick had 200 more client-visits than expected, his variable costs *should* be higher than budgeted. The static budget performance report confuses control over activity and control over costs. From Rick's standpoint, the increase in activity was good and should be counted as a favorable variance, but the increase in activity has an apparently negative impact on the costs in the report. Rick knew that something would have to be done to make the report more meaningful, but he was unsure of what to do. So he made an appointment to meet with Victoria Kho to discuss the next step.

Exhibit 11–2

RICK'S HAIRSTYLING
Static Budget Performance Report
For the Month Ended March 31

	Actual	Budgeted	Variance
Client-visits	5,200	5,000	200 F
Variable overhead costs:			
Hairstyling supplies	$ 6,400	$ 6,000	$ 400 U*
Client gratuities	22,300	20,000	2,300 U*
Electricity	1,020	1,000	20 U*
Total variable overhead cost	29,720	27,000	2,720 U*
Fixed overhead costs:			
Support staff wages and salaries	8,100	8,000	100 U
Rent	12,000	12,000	–0–
Insurance	1,000	1,000	–0–
Utilites other than electricity	470	500	30 F
Total fixed overhead cost	21,570	21,500	70 U
Total overhead cost	$51,290	$48,500	$2,790 U*

*The cost variances for variable costs and for total overhead are useless for evaluating how well costs were controlled since they have been derived by comparing actual costs at one level of activity to budgeted costs at a different level of activity.

Managerial Accounting in Action

THE ISSUE

Victoria: How is the budgeting going?
Rick: Pretty well. I didn't have any trouble putting together the overhead budget for March. I also made out a report comparing the actual costs for March to the budgeted costs, but that report isn't giving me what I really want to know.
Victoria: Because your actual level of activity didn't match your budgeted activity?
Rick: Right. I know that shouldn't affect my fixed costs, but we had a lot more client-visits than I had expected and that had to affect my variable costs.
Victoria: So you want to know whether the actual costs are justified by the actual level of activity you had in March?
Rick: Precisely.
Victoria: If you leave your reports and data with me, I can work on it later today, and by tomorrow I'll have a report to show to you. Actually, I have a styling appointment for later this week. Why don't I move my appointment up to tomorrow, and I will bring along the analysis so we can discuss it.
Rick: That's great. ■

How a Flexible Budget Works

objective 2

Prepare a performance report for both fixed and variable overhead costs using the flexible budget approach.

The basic idea of the flexible budget approach is that a budget does not have to be static. Depending on the actual level of activity, a budget can be adjusted to show what costs *should be* for that specific level of activity. To illustrate how flexible budgets work, Victoria wrote a report for Rick that is simple to prepare (Exhibit 11–3). It shows how overhead costs can be expected to change, depending on the monthly level of activity. Within the activity range of 4,900 to 5,200 client-visits, the fixed costs are expected to remain the same. For the variable overhead costs, Victoria multiplied Rick's per client costs ($1.20 for hairstyling supplies, $4.00 for client gratuities, and $0.20 for electricity) by the appropriate number of client-visits in each column. For example, the $1.20 cost of hairstyling supplies was multiplied by 4,900 client-visits to give the total cost of $5,880 for hairstyling supplies at that level of activity.

Using Flexible Budgeting Concept in Performance Evaluation

To get a better idea of how well Rick's variable overhead costs were controlled in March, Victoria applied the flexible budgeting concept to create a new performance report. (Exhibit 11–4). Using the flexible budget approach, Victoria constructed a budget based on the *actual* number of client-visits for the month. The budget is prepared by multiplying the actual level of activity by the cost formula for each of the variable cost categories. For example, using the $1.20 per client-visit for hairstyling supplies, the total cost for this item *should be* $6,240 for 5,200 client-visits ($1.20 × 5,200). Since the actual cost for hairstyling supplies was $6,400, the unfavorable variance was $160.

Contrast the performance report in Exhibit 11–4 with the static budget approach in Exhibit 11–2. The variance for hairstyling supplies was $400 unfavorable using the

Exhibit 11–3 Illustration of the Flexible Budgeting Concept

RICK'S HAIRSTYLING
Flexible Budget
For the Month Ended March 31

Budgeted number of client-visits 5,000

Overhead Costs	Cost Formula (per client-visit)	Activity (in client-visits)			
		4,900	5,000	5,100	5,200
Variable overhead costs:					
Hairstyling supplies	$1.20	$ 5,880	$ 6,000	$ 6,120	$ 6,240
Client gratuities	4.00	19,600	20,000	20,400	20,800
Electricity (variable)	0.20	980	1,000	1,020	1,040
Total variable overhead cost	$5.40	26,460	27,000	27,540	28,080
Fixed overhead costs:					
Support staff wages and salaries		8,000	8,000	8,000	8,000
Rent		12,000	12,000	12,000	12,000
Insurance		1,000	1,000	1,000	1,000
Utilities other than electricity		500	500	500	500
Total fixed overhead cost		21,500	21,500	21,500	21,500
Total overhead cost		$47,960	$48,500	$49,040	$49,580

Exhibit 11-4

RICK'S HAIRSTYLING
Flexible Budget Performance Report
For the Month Ended March 31

Budgeted number of client-visits	5,000			
Actual number of client-visits	5,200			

Overhead Costs	Cost Formula (per client-visit)	Actual Costs Incurred for 5,200 Client-Visits	Budget Based on 5,200 Client-Visits	Variance
Variable overhead costs:				
Hairstyling supplies	$1.20	$ 6,400	$ 6,240	$ 160 U
Client gratuities	4.00	22,300	20,800	1,500 U
Electricity (variable)	0.20	1,020	1,040	20 F
Total variable overhead cost	$5.40	29,720	28,080	1,640 U
Fixed overhead costs:				
Support staff wages and salaries		8,100	8,000	100 U
Rent		12,000	12,000	-0-
Insurance		1,000	1,000	-0-
Utilities other than electricity		470	500	30 F
Total fixed overhead cost		21,570	21,500	70 U
Total overhead cost		$51,290	$49,580	$1,710 U

static budget approach. In that exhibit, apples were being compared to oranges in the case of the variable cost items. Actual costs at one level of activity were being compared to budgeted costs at a different level of activity. Because actual activity was higher by 200 client-visits than budgeted activity, the total cost of hairstyling supplies *should* have been $240 ($1.20 per client-visit × 200 client-visits) higher than budgeted. As a result, $240 of the $400 "unfavorable" variance in the static budget performance report in Exhibit 11–2 was spurious.

In contrast, the flexible budget performance report in Exhibit 11–4 provides a more valid assessment of performance. Apples are compared to apples. Actual costs are compared to what costs should have been at the actual level of activity. When this is done, we see that the variance is $160 unfavorable rather than $400 unfavorable as it was in the original static budget performance report. In some cases, as with electricity in Rick's report, an unfavorable variance may be transformed into a favorable variance when an increase in activity is properly taken into account in a performance report.

Managerial Accounting in Action

THE WRAP-UP

The following discussion took place the next day at Rick's salon.

Victoria: Let me show you what I've got. [Victoria shows the report contained in Exhibit 11–4.] All I did was multiply the costs per client-visit by the number of client-visits you actually had in March for the variable costs. That allowed me to come up with a better benchmark for what the variable costs should have been.

Rick: That's what you labeled the "budget based on 5,200 client-visits"?

Victoria: That's right. Your original budget was based on 5,000 client-visits, so it understated what the variable overhead costs should be when you actually serve 5,200 customers.
Rick: That's clear enough. These variances aren't quite as shocking as the variances on my first report.
Victoria: Yes, but you still have an unfavorable variance of $1,500 for client gratuities.
Rick: I know how that happened. In March there was a big Democratic Party fund-raising dinner that I forgot about when I prepared the March budget. Everyone in the film industry was there.
Victoria: Even Arnold Schwarzeneger?
Rick: Well, all the Democrats were there. At any rate, to fit all of our regular clients in, we had to push them through here pretty fast. Everyone still got top-rate service, but I felt pretty bad about not being able to spend as much time with each customer. I wanted to give my customers a little extra something to compensate them for the less personal service, so I ordered a lot of flowers which I gave away by the bunch.
Victoria: With the prices you charge, Rick, I am sure the gesture was appreciated.
Rick: One thing bothers me about the report. Why are some of my actual fixed costs different from what I budgeted? Doesn't fixed mean that they are not supposed to change?
Victoria: We call these costs *fixed* because they shouldn't be affected by *changes in the level of activity.* However, that doesn't mean that they can't change for other reasons. For example, your utilities bill, which includes natural gas for heating, varies with the weather.
Rick: I can see that. March was warmer than normal, so my utilities bill was lower than I had expected.
Victoria: The use of the term *fixed* also suggests to people that the cost can't be controlled, but that isn't true. It is often easier to control fixed costs than variable costs. For example, it would be fairly easy for you to change your insurance bill by adjusting the amount of insurance you carry. It would be much more difficult for you to have much of an impact on the variable electric bill, which is a necessary part of serving customers.
Rick: I think I understand, but it *is* confusing.
Victoria: Just remember that a cost is called variable if it is proportional to activity; it is called fixed if it does not depend on the level of activity. However, fixed costs can change for reasons having nothing to do with changes in the level of activity. And controllability has little to do with whether a cost is variable or fixed. Fixed costs are often more controllable than variable costs. ■

Using the flexible budget approach, Rick Manzi now has a much better way of assessing whether overhead costs are under control. The analysis is not so simple, however, in companies that provide a variety of products and services. The number of units produced or customers served may not be an adequate measure of overall activity. For example, does it make sense to count a Sony floppy diskette, worth only a few dollars, as equivalent to a large-screen Sony TV? If the number of units produced is used as a measure of overall activity, then the floppy diskette and the large-screen TV would be counted as equivalent. Clearly, the number of units produced (or customers served) may not be appropriate as an overall measure of activity when the organization has a variety of products or services; a common denominator may be needed.

The Measure of Activity—A Critical Choice

What should be used as the measure of activity when the company produces a variety of products and services? At least three factors are important in selecting an activity base for an overhead flexible budget:

1. There should be a causal relationship between the activity base and variable overhead costs. Changes in the activity base should cause, or at least be highly correlated with, changes in the variable overhead costs in the flexible budget. Ideally, the variable overhead costs in the flexible budget should vary in direct proportion to changes in the activity base. For example, in a carpentry shop specializing in handmade wood furniture, the costs of miscellaneous supplies such as glue, wooden dowels, and sandpaper can be expected to vary with the number of direct labor-hours. Direct labor-hours would therefore be a good measure of activity to use in a flexible budget for the costs of such supplies.
2. The activity base should not be expressed in dollars or other currency. For example, direct labor cost is usually a poor choice for an activity base in flexible budgets. Changes in wage rates affect the activity base but do not usually result in a proportionate change in overhead. For example, we would not ordinarily expect to see a 5% increase in the consumption of glue in a carpentry shop if the workers receive a 5% increase in pay. Therefore, it is normally best to use physical rather than financial measures of activity in flexible budgets.
3. The activity base should be simple and easily understood. A base that is not easily understood will probably result in confusion and misunderstanding. It is difficult to control costs if people don't understand the reports or do not accept them as valid.

Variable Overhead Variances—A Closer Look

A special problem arises when the flexible budget is based on *hours* of activity (such as direct labor-hours) rather than on units of product or number of customers served. The problem relates to whether actual hours or standard hours should be used to develop the flexible budget on the performance report.

The Problem of Actual versus Standard Hours

The nature of the problem can best be seen through a specific example. MicroDrive Corporation is an automated manufacturer of precision personal computer disk-drive motors. Data concerning the company's variable manufacturing overhead costs are shown in Exhibit 11–5.

MicroDrive Corporation uses machine-hours as the activity base in its flexible budget. Based on the budgeted production of 25,000 motors and the standard of 2 machine-hours per motor, the budgeted level of activity was 50,000 machine-hours. However, actual production for the year was only 20,000 motors, and 42,000 hours of machine time were used to produce these motors. According to the standard, only

Exhibit 11–5
MicroDrive Corporation Data

Budgeted production	25,000	motors
Actual production	20,000	motors
Standard machine-hours per motor	2	machine-hours per motor
Budgeted machine-hours (2 3 25,000)	50,000	machine-hours
Standard machine-hours allowed for the actual production (2 3 20,000)	40,000	machine-hours
Actual machine-hours	42,000	machine-hours
Variable overhead costs per machine-hour:		
Indirect labor	$0.80	per machine-hour
Lubricants	0.30	per machine-hour
Power	0.40	per machine-hour
Actual total variable overhead costs:		
Indirect labor	$36,600	
Lubricants	11,000	
Power	24,000	
Total actual variable overhead cost	$71,000	

40,000 hours of machine time should have been used (40,000 hours = 2 hours per motor × 20,000 motors).

In preparing an overhead performance report for the year, MicroDrive could use the 42,000 machine-hours actually worked during the year *or* the 40,000 machine-hours that should have been worked according to the standard. If the actual hours are used, only a spending variance will be computed. If the standard hours are used, both a spending *and* an efficiency variance will be computed. Both of these approaches are illustrated in the following sections.

Spending Variance Alone

objective 3
Use the flexible budget to prepare a variable overhead performance report containing only a spending variance.

If MicroDrive Corporation bases its overhead performance report on the 42,000 machine-hours actually worked during the year, then the performance report will show only a spending variance for variable overhead. A performance report prepared in this way is shown in Exhibit 11–6.

The formula for the spending variance was introduced in the preceding chapter. That formula is:

$$\text{Variable overhead spending variance} = (AH \times AR) - (AH \times SR)$$

Actual Hours — Actual Rate — Standard Rate

Or, in factored form:

$$\text{Variable overhead spending variance} = AH\,(AR - SR)$$

Exhibit 11-6

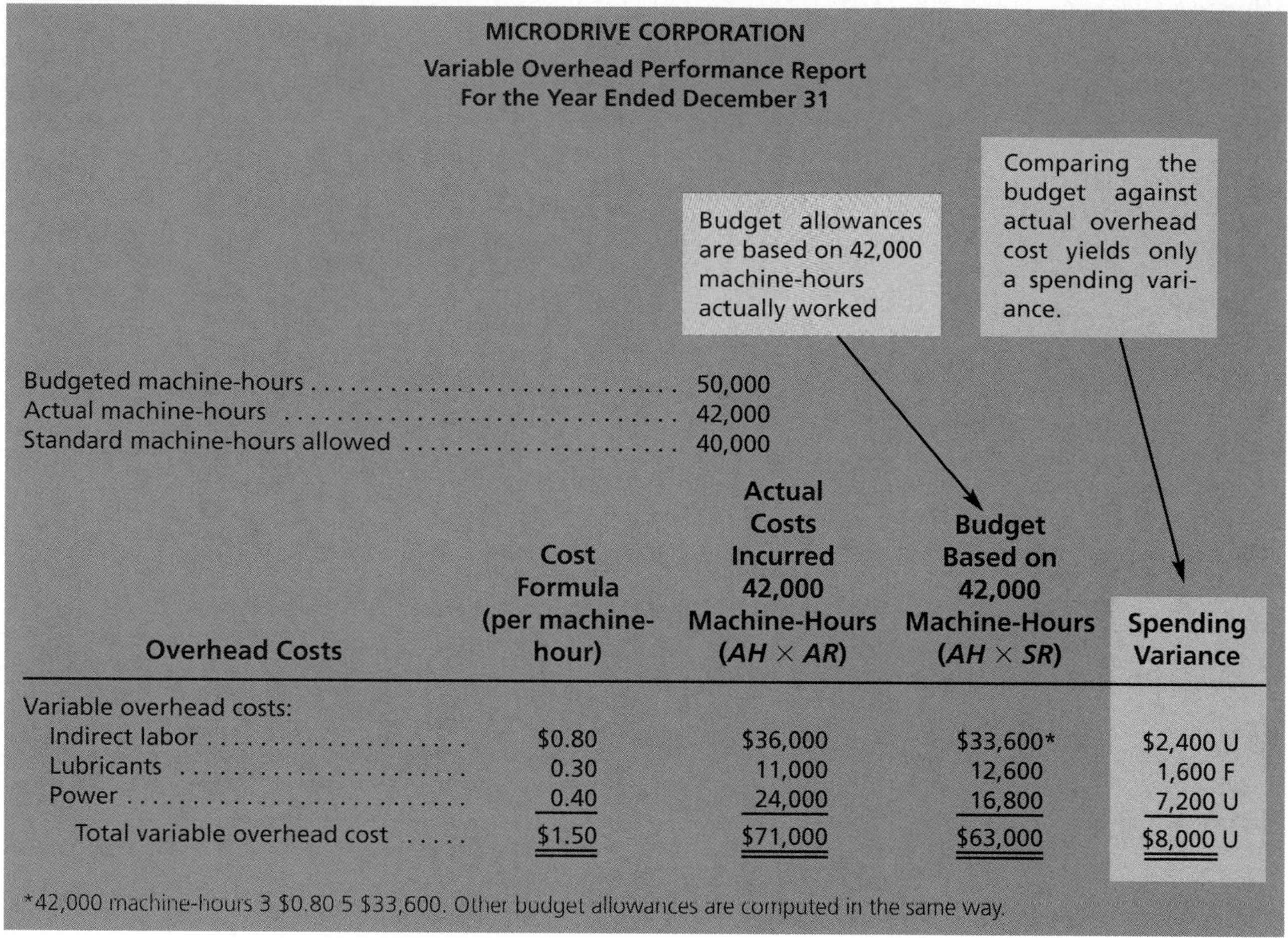

MICRODRIVE CORPORATION
Variable Overhead Performance Report
For the Year Ended December 31

Budget allowances are based on 42,000 machine-hours actually worked

Comparing the budget against actual overhead cost yields only a spending variance.

Budgeted machine-hours	50,000
Actual machine-hours	42,000
Standard machine-hours allowed	40,000

Overhead Costs	Cost Formula (per machine-hour)	Actual Costs Incurred 42,000 Machine-Hours (*AH* × *AR*)	Budget Based on 42,000 Machine-Hours (*AH* × *SR*)	Spending Variance
Variable overhead costs:				
Indirect labor	$0.80	$36,000	$33,600*	$2,400 U
Lubricants	0.30	11,000	12,600	1,600 F
Power	0.40	24,000	16,800	7,200 U
Total variable overhead cost	$1.50	$71,000	$63,000	$8,000 U

*42,000 machine-hours 3 $0.80 5 $33,600. Other budget allowances are computed in the same way.

The report in Exhibit 11–6 is structured around the first, or unfactored, format.

INTERPRETING THE SPENDING VARIANCE The variable overhead spending variance is useful only if the cost driver for variable overhead really is the actual hours worked. Then the flexible budget based on the actual hours worked is a valid benchmark that tells us how much *should* have been spent in total on variable overhead items during the period. The actual overhead costs would be larger than this benchmark, resulting in an unfavorable variance, if either (1) the variable overhead items cost more to purchase than the standards allow or (2) more variable overhead items were used than the standards allow. So the spending variance includes both price and quantity variances. In principle, these variances could be separately reported, but this is seldom done. Ordinarily, the price element in this variance will be small, so the variance will mainly be influenced by how efficiently variable overhead resources such as production supplies are used.

objective 4

Use the flexible budget to prepare a variable overhead performance report containing both a spending and an efficiency variance.

Both Spending and Efficiency Variances

If management of MicroDrive Corporation wants both a spending and an efficiency variance for variable overhead, then it should compute budget allowances for *both* the 40,000 machine-hour and the 42,000 machine-hour levels of activity. A performance report prepared in this way is shown in Exhibit 11–7.

Note from Exhibit 11–7 that the spending variance is the same as the spending variance shown in Exhibit 11–6. The performance report in Exhibit 11–7 has simply

Exhibit 11-7

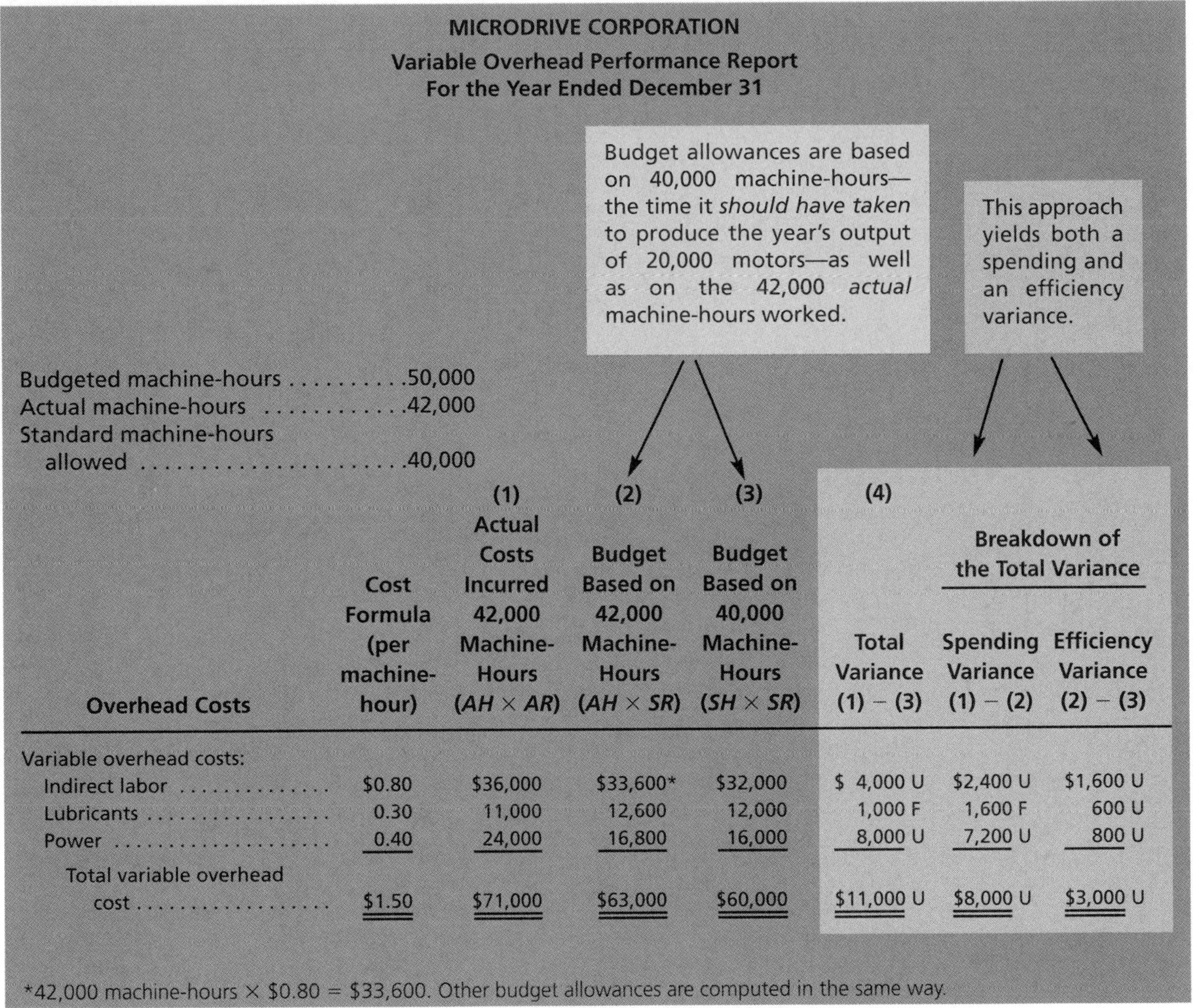

MICRODRIVE CORPORATION
Variable Overhead Performance Report
For the Year Ended December 31

Budget allowances are based on 40,000 machine-hours—the time it *should have taken* to produce the year's output of 20,000 motors—as well as on the 42,000 *actual* machine-hours worked.

This approach yields both a spending and an efficiency variance.

Budgeted machine-hours 50,000
Actual machine-hours 42,000
Standard machine-hours allowed .40,000

Overhead Costs	Cost Formula (per machine-hour)	(1) Actual Costs Incurred 42,000 Machine-Hours (*AH* × *AR*)	(2) Budget Based on 42,000 Machine-Hours (*AH* × *SR*)	(3) Budget Based on 40,000 Machine-Hours (*SH* × *SR*)	(4) Breakdown of the Total Variance: Total Variance (1) − (3)	Spending Variance (1) − (2)	Efficiency Variance (2) − (3)
Variable overhead costs:							
Indirect labor	$0.80	$36,000	$33,600*	$32,000	$ 4,000 U	$2,400 U	$1,600 U
Lubricants	0.30	11,000	12,600	12,000	1,000 F	1,600 F	600 U
Power	0.40	24,000	16,800	16,000	8,000 U	7,200 U	800 U
Total variable overhead cost	$1.50	$71,000	$63,000	$60,000	$11,000 U	$8,000 U	$3,000 U

*42,000 machine-hours × $0.80 = $33,600. Other budget allowances are computed in the same way.

been expanded to include an efficiency variance as well. Together, the spending and efficiency variances make up the total variance.

INTERPRETING THE EFFICIENCY VARIANCE Like the variable overhead spending, the variable overhead efficiency variance is useful only if the cost driver for variable overhead really is the actual hours worked. Then any increase in hours actually worked should result in additional variable overhead costs. Consequently, if too many hours were used to create the actual output, this is likely to result in an increase in variable overhead. The variable overhead efficiency variance is an estimate of the effect on variable overhead costs of inefficiency in the use of the base (i.e., hours). In a sense, the term *variable overhead efficiency variance* is a misnomer. It seems to suggest that it measures the efficiency with which variable overhead resources were used. It does not. It is an estimate of the indirect effect on variable overhead costs of inefficiency in the use of the activity base.

Recall from the preceding chapter that the variable overhead efficiency variance is a function of the difference between the actual hours incurred and the hours that should have been used to produce the period's output:

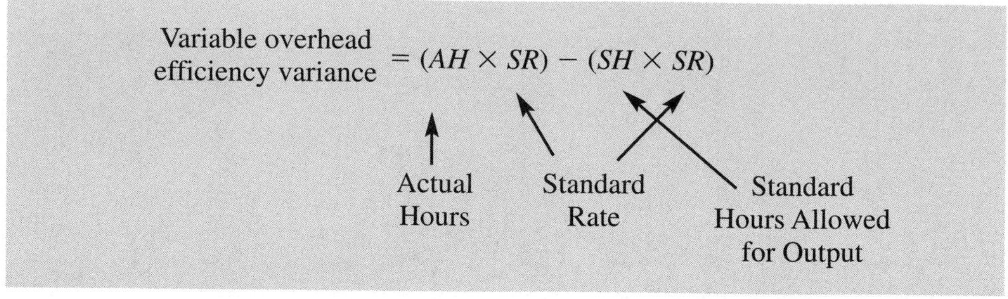

Or, in factored form:

$$\text{Variable overhead efficiency variance} = SR(AH - SH)$$

If more hours are worked than are allowed at standard, then the overhead efficiency variance will be unfavorable. However, as discussed above, the inefficiency is not in the use of overhead *but rather in the use of the base itself.*

This point can be illustrated by looking again at Exhibit 11–7. Two thousand more machine-hours were used during the period than should have been used to produce the period's output. Each of these hours presumably required the incurrence of $1.50 of variable overhead cost, resulting in an unfavorable variance of $3,000 (2,000 hours × $1.50 = $3,000). Although this $3,000 variance is called an overhead efficiency variance, it could better be called a machine-hours efficiency variance, since it results from using too many machine-hours rather than from inefficient use of overhead resources. However, the term *overhead efficiency variance* is so firmly ingrained in day-to-day use that a change is unlikely. Even so, be careful to interpret the variance with a clear understanding of what it really measures.

CONTROL OF THE EFFICIENCY VARIANCE Who is responsible for control of the overhead efficiency variance? Since the variance really reflects efficiency in the utilization of the base underlying the flexible budget, whoever is responsible for control of this base is responsible for control of the variance. If the base is direct labor-hours, then the supervisor responsible for the use of labor time will be responsible for any overhead efficiency variance.

Activity-Based Costing and the Flexible Budget

It is unlikely that all of the variable overhead in a complex organization is driven by a single factor such as the number of units produced or the number of labor-hours or machine-hours. Activity-based costing provides a way of recognizing a variety of overhead cost drivers and thereby increasing the accuracy of the costing system. In activity-based costing, each overhead cost pool has its own measure of activity. The actual spending in each overhead cost pool can be independently evaluated using the techniques discussed in this chapter. The only difference is that the cost formulas for variable overhead costs will be stated in terms of different kinds of activities instead of all being stated in terms of units or a common measure of activity such as direct labor-hours or machine-hours. If done properly, activity-based costing can greatly enhance the usefulness of overhead performance reports by recognizing multiple causes of overhead costs. But the usefulness of overhead performance reports depends on how carefully the reports are done. In particular, managers must take care to separate the variable from the fixed costs in the flexible budgets.[1]

Focus on Current Practice

Caterpillar, Inc., a manufacturer of heavy equipment and a pioneering company in the development and use of activity-based costing, divides its overhead costs into three large pools—the logistics cost pool, the manufacturing cost pool, and the general cost pool. In turn, these three cost pools are subdivided into scores of activity centers, with each center having its own flexible budget from which variable and fixed overhead rates are developed. In an article describing the company's cost system, the systems manager stated that "the many manufacturing cost center rates are the unique elements that set Caterpillar's system apart from simple cost systems."[2] ■

Overhead Rates and Fixed Overhead Analysis

The detailed analysis of fixed overhead differs considerably from the analysis of variable overhead, simply because of the difference in the nature of the costs involved. To provide a background for our discussion, we will first review briefly the need for, and computation of, predetermined overhead rates. This review will be helpful, since the predetermined overhead rate plays a major role in fixed overhead analysis. We will then show how fixed overhead variances are computed and make some observations as to their usefulness to managers.

Flexible Budgets and Overhead Rates

objective 5

Explain the significance of the denominator activity figure in determining the standard cost of a unit of product.

Fixed costs come in large, indivisible pieces that by definition do not change with changes in the level of activity within the relevant range. As we learned in Chapter 3, this creates a problem in product costing, since a given level of fixed overhead cost spread over a small number of units will result in a higher cost per unit than if the same amount of cost is spread over a large number of units. Consider the data in the following table:

Month	(1) Fixed Overhead Cost	(2) Number of Units Produced	(3) Unit Cost (1)÷(2)
January	$6,000	1,000	$6.00
February	6,000	1,500	4.00
March	6,000	800	7.50

1. See Mak and Roush, "Managing Activity Costs with Flexible Budgeting and Variance Analysis," *Accounting Horizons*, September 1996, pp. 141–46, for an insightful discussion of activity-based costing and overhead variance analysis.
2. Lou F. Jones, "Product Costing at Caterpillar," *Management Accounting* 72, no. 8 (February 1991), p. 39.

Notice that the large number of units produced in February results in a low unit cost ($4.00), whereas the small number of units produced in March results in a high unit cost ($7.50). This problem arises only in connection with the fixed portion of overhead, since by definition the variable portion of overhead remains constant on a per unit basis, rising and falling in total proportionately with changes in the activity level. Most managers feel that the fixed portion of unit cost should be stabilized so that a single unit cost figure can be used throughout the year. As we learned in Chapter 3, this stability can be accomplished through use of the predetermined overhead rate.

Throughout the remainder of this chapter, we will be analyzing the fixed overhead costs of MicroDrive Corporation. To assist us in that task, the flexible budget of the company—including fixed costs—is displayed in Exhibit 11–8. Note that the total fixed overhead costs amount to $300,000 within the range of activity in the flexible budget.

DENOMINATOR ACTIVITY The formula that we used in Chapter 3 to compute the predetermined overhead rate is given below

$$\text{Predetermined overhead rate} = \frac{\text{Estimated total manufacturing overhead cost}}{\text{Estimated total units in the base (MH, DLH, etc.)}}$$

The estimated total units in the base in the formula for the predetermined overhead rate is called the **denominator activity.** Recall from our discussion in Chapter 3 that once an estimated activity level (denominator activity) has been chosen, it remains unchanged throughout the year, even if the actual activity turns out to be different from what was estimated. The reason for not changing the denominator is to maintain stability in the amount of overhead applied to each unit of product regardless of when it is produced during the year.

COMPUTING THE OVERHEAD RATE When we discussed predetermined overhead rates in Chapter 3, we didn't explain how the estimated total manufacturing cost was determined. This figure can be derived from the flexible budget. Once the

Exhibit 11–8

MICRODRIVE CORPORATION
Flexible Budgets at Various Levels of Activity

Overhead Costs	Cost Formula (per machine-hour)	Activity (in machine-hours) 40,000	45,000	50,000	55,000
Variable overhead costs:					
Indirect labor	$0.80	$ 32,000	$ 36,000	$ 40,000	$ 44,000
Lubricants	0.30	12,000	13,500	15,000	16,500
Power	0.40	16,000	18,000	20,000	22,000
Total variable overhead cost	$1.50	60,000	67,500	75,000	82,500
Fixed overhead costs:					
Depreciation		100,000	100,000	100,000	100,000
Supervisory salaries		160,000	160,000	160,000	160,000
Insurance		40,000	40,000	40,000	40,000
Total fixed overhead cost		300,000	300,000	300,000	300,000
Total overhead cost		$360,000	$367,500	$375,000	$382,500

denominator level of activity has been chosen, the flexible budget can be used to determine the total amount of overhead cost that should be incurred at that level of activity. The predetermined overhead rate can then be computed using the following variation on the basic formula for the predetermined overhead rate:

$$\text{Predetermined overhead rate} = \frac{\text{Overhead from the flexible budget at the denominator level of activity}}{\text{Denominator level of activity}}$$

To illustrate, refer to MicroDrive Corporation's flexible budget for manufacturing overhead in Exhibit 11–8. Suppose that the budgeted activity level for the year is 50,000 machine-hours and that this will be used as the denominator activity in the formula for the predetermined overhead rate. The numerator in the formula is the estimated total overhead cost of \$375,000 when the activity is 50,000 machine-hours. This figure is taken from the flexible budget in Exhibit 11–8. In sum, the predetermined overhead rate for MicroDrive Corporation will be computed as follows:

$$\frac{\$375{,}000}{50{,}000\text{ MH}} = \$7.50 \text{ per machine-hour}$$

Or the company can break its predetermined overhead rate down into variable and fixed elements rather than using a single combined figure:

$$\text{Variable element: } \frac{\$75{,}000}{50{,}000\text{ MH}} = \$1.50 \text{ per machine-hour (MH)}$$

$$\text{Fixed element: } \frac{\$300{,}000}{50{,}000\text{ MH}} = \$6 \text{ per machine-hour (MH)}$$

For every standard machine-hour of operation, work in process will be charged with \$7.50 of overhead, of which \$1.50 will be variable overhead and \$6.00 will be fixed overhead. If a disk-drive motor should take two machine-hours to complete, then its cost will include \$3 variable overhead and \$12 fixed overhead, as shown on the following standard cost card:

Standard Cost Card—Per Motor

Direct materials (assumed)	\$14
Direct labor (assumed)	6
Variable overhead (2 machine-hours at \$1.50)	3
Fixed overhead (2 machine-hours at \$6)	12
Total standard cost per motor	\$35

In sum, the flexible budget provides the estimated overhead cost needed to compute the predetermined overhead rate. Thus, the flexible budget plays a key role in determining the amount of fixed and variable overhead cost that will be charged to units of product.

Overhead Application in a Standard Cost System

objective 6

Apply overhead cost to units of product in a standard cost system.

To understand the fixed overhead variances, it is necessary first to understand how overhead is applied to work in process in a standard cost system. In Chapter 3, recall that we applied overhead to work in process on the basis of actual hours of activity (multiplied by the predetermined overhead rate). This procedure was correct, since at

Exhibit 11–9 Applied Overhead Costs: Normal Cost System versus Standard Cost System

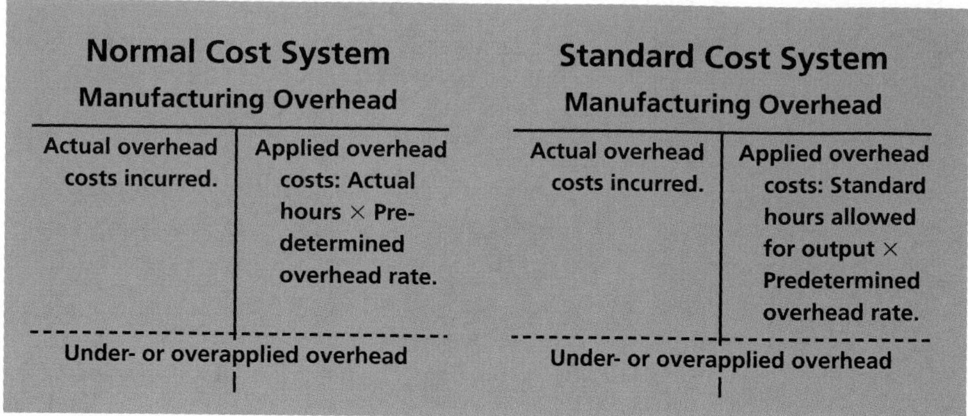

the time we were dealing with a normal cost system.[3] However, we are now dealing with a standard cost system. In such a system, overhead is applied to work in process on the basis of the *standard hours allowed for the output of the period* rather than on the basis of the actual number of hours worked. This point is illustrated in Exhibit 11–9. In a standard cost system, every unit of product moving along the production line bears the same amount of overhead cost, regardless of any variations in efficiency that may have been involved in its production.

The Fixed Overhead Variances

objective 7

Compute and interpret the fixed overhead budget and volume variances.

To illustrate the computation of fixed overhead variances, we will refer again to the data for MicroDrive Corporation.

Denominator activity in machine-hours	50,000
Budgeted fixed overhead costs	$300,000
Fixed portion of the predetermined overhead rate (computed earlier)	$6

Let us assume that the following actual operating results were recorded for the year:

Actual machine-hours	42,000
Standard machine-hours allowed*	40,000
Actual fixed overhead costs:	
Depreciation	$100,000
Supervisory salaries	172,000
Insurance	36,000
Total actual cost	$308,000

*For the actual production of the year.

From these data, two variances can be computed for fixed overhead—a *budget variance* and a *volume variance.* The variances are shown in Exhibit 11–10.

Notice from the exhibit that overhead has been applied to work in process on the basis of 40,000 standard hours allowed for the output of the year rather than on the basis of 42,000 actual hours worked. As stated earlier, this keeps unit costs from being affected by any variations in efficiency.

3. Normal cost systems are discussed on page 92 in Chapter 3.

The Budget Variance—A Closer Look

The **budget variance** is the difference between the actual fixed overhead costs incurred during the period and the budgeted fixed overhead costs as contained in the flexible budget. It can be computed as shown in Exhibit 11–10 or by using the following formula:

$$\text{Budget variance} = \text{Actual fixed overhead cost} - \text{Flexible budget fixed overhead cost}$$

Applying this formula to MicroDrive Corporation, the budget variance would be as follows:

$$\$308{,}000 - \$300{,}000 = \$8{,}000\ \text{U}$$

The variances computed for the fixed costs at Rick's Hairstyling in Exhibit 11–4 are all budget variances, since they represent the difference between the actual fixed overhead cost and the budgeted fixed overhead cost from the flexible budget.

An expanded overhead performance report for MicroDrive Corporation appears in Exhibit 11–11. This report now includes the budget variances for fixed overhead as well as the spending variances for variable overhead that were in Exhibit 11–6.

The budget variances for fixed overhead can be very useful, since they represent the difference between how much *should* have been spent (according to the flexible budget) and how much was actually spent. For example, supervisory salaries has a $12,000 unfavorable variance. There should be some explanation for this large variance. Was it due to an increase in salaries? Was it due to overtime? Was another supervisor hired? If so, why was another supervisor hired—this was not included in the budget when activity for the year was planned.

The Volume Variance—A Closer Look

The **volume variance** is a measure of utilization of plant facilities. The variance arises whenever the standard hours allowed for the output of a period are different from the

Exhibit 11–10
Computation of the Fixed Overhead Variances

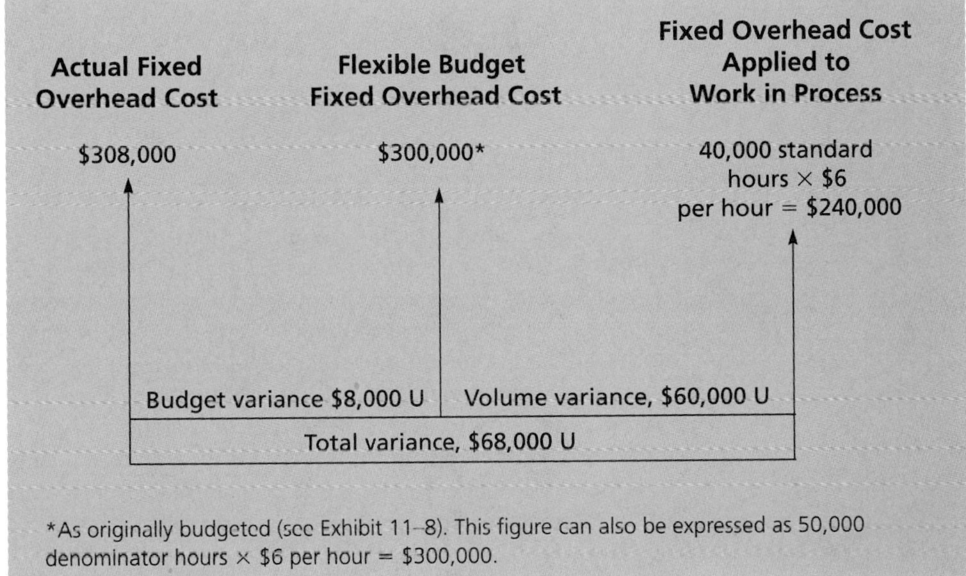

Exhibit 11–11 Fixed Overhead Costs on the Overhead Performance Report

MICRODRIVE CORPORATION
Overhead Performance Report
For the Year Ended December 31

Budgeted machine-hours 50,000
Actual machine-hours 42,000
Standard machine-hours allowed 40,000

Overhead Costs	Cost Formula (per machine-hour)	Actual Costs 42,000 Machine-Hours	Budget Based on 42,000 Machine-Hours	Spending or Budget Variance
Variable overhead costs:				
Indirect labor	$0.80	$ 36,000	$ 33,600	$ 2,400 U
Lubricants	0.30	11,000	12,600	1,600 F
Power	0.40	24,000	16,800	7,200 U
Total variable overhead cost	$1.50	71,000	63,000	8,000 U
Fixed overhead costs:				
Depreciation		100,000	100,000	—
Supervisory salaries		172,000	160,000	12,000 U
Insurance		36,000	40,000	4,000 F
Total fixed overhead cost		308,000	300,000	8,000 U
Total overhead cost		$379,000	$363,000	$16,000 U

denominator activity level that was planned when the period began. It can be computed as shown in Exhibit 11–10 or by means of the following formula:

$$\text{Volume variance} = \begin{array}{c}\text{Fixed portion of}\\ \text{the predetermined}\\ \text{overhead rate}\end{array} \times \left(\begin{array}{c}\text{Denominator}\\ \text{hours}\end{array} - \begin{array}{c}\text{Standard hours}\\ \text{allowed}\end{array}\right)$$

Applying this formula to MicroDrive Corporation, the volume variance would be computed as follows:

$$\$6 \text{ per MH } (50{,}000 \text{ MH} - 40{,}000 \text{ MH}) = \$60{,}000 \text{ U}$$

Note that this computation agrees with the volume variance as shown in Exhibit 11–10. As stated earlier, the volume variance is a measure of utilization of available plant facilities. An unfavorable variance, as above, means that the company operated at an activity level *below* that planned for the period. A favorable variance would mean that the company operated at an activity level *greater* than that planned for the period.

It is important to note that the volume variance does not measure over- or under-spending. A company normally would incur the same dollar amount of fixed overhead cost regardless of whether the period's activity was above or below the planned (denominator) level. In short, the volume variance is an activity-related variance. It is explainable only by activity and is controllable only through activity.

To summarize:

1. If the denominator activity and the standard hours allowed for the output of the period are the same, then there is no volume variance.

2. If the denominator activity is greater than the standard hours allowed for the output of the period, then the volume variance is unfavorable, signifying an underutilization of available facilities.
3. If the denominator activity is less than the standard hours allowed for the output of the period, then the volume variance is favorable, signifying a higher utilization of available facilities than was planned.

Graphic Analysis of Fixed Overhead Variances

Some insights into the budget and volume variances can be gained through graphic analysis. A graph containing these variances is presented in Exhibit 11–12.

As shown in the graph, fixed overhead cost is applied to work in process at the predetermined rate of $6 for each standard hour of activity. (The applied-cost line is the upward-sloping line on the graph.) Since a denominator level of 50,000 machine-hours was used in computing the $6 rate, the applied-cost line crosses the budget-cost line at exactly the 50,000 machine-hour point. Thus, if the denominator hours and the standard hours allowed for the output are the same, there can be no volume variance, since the applied-cost line and the budget-cost line will exactly meet on the graph. It is only when the standard hours differ from the denominator hours that a volume variance can arise.

In the case at hand, the standard hours allowed for the actual output (40,000 hours) are less than the denominator hours (50,000 hours); the result is an unfavorable volume variance, since less cost was applied to production than was originally budgeted. If the situation had been reversed and the standard hours allowed for the actual output had exceeded the denominator hours, then the volume variance on the graph would have been favorable.

Exhibit 11–12
Graphic Analysis of Fixed Overhead Variances

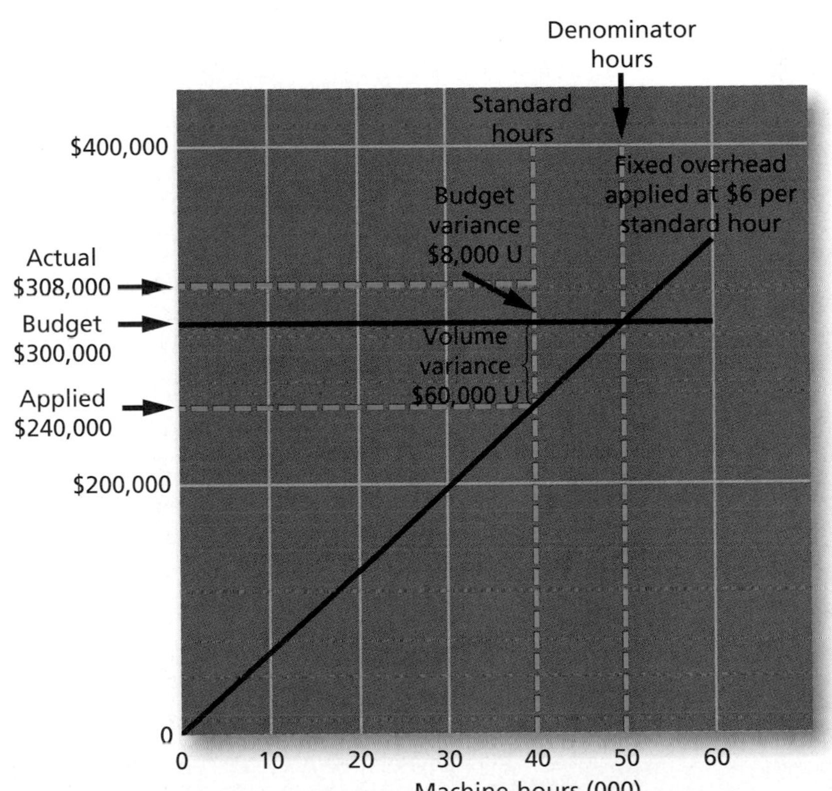

Cautions in Fixed Overhead Analysis

The reason we get a volume variance for fixed overhead is that the total fixed cost does not depend on activity; yet when applying the costs to work in process, we act *as if* the fixed costs were variable and depended on activity. This point can be seen from the graph in Exhibit 11–12. Notice from the graph that the fixed overhead costs are applied to work in process at a rate of $6 per hour *as if* they were variable. Treating these costs as if they were variable is necessary for product costing purposes, but there are some real dangers here. The manager can easily become misled and start thinking of the fixed costs as if they were *in fact* variable.

The manager must keep clearly in mind that fixed overhead costs come in large, indivisible pieces. Expressing fixed costs on a unit or per hour basis, though necessary for product costing for external reports, is artificial. Increases or decreases in activity in fact have no effect on total fixed costs within the relevant range of activity. Even though fixed costs are expressed on a unit or per hour basis, they are *not* proportional to activity. In a sense, the volume variance is the error that occurs as a result of treating fixed costs as variable costs in the costing system.

Because of the confusion that can arise concerning the interpretation of the volume variance, some companies present the volume variance in physical units (hours) rather than in dollars. These companies feel that stating the variance in physical units gives management a clearer signal concerning the cause of the variance.

Overhead Variances and Under- or Overapplied Overhead Cost

Four variances relating to overhead cost have been computed for MicroDrive Corporation in this chapter. These four variances are as follows:

Variable overhead spending variance (p. 512) . .	$ 8,000 U
Variable overhead efficiency variance (p. 512) . .	3,000 U
Fixed overhead budget variance (p. 519)	8,000 U
Fixed overhead volume variance (p. 519)	60,000 U
Total overhead variance	$79,000 U

Recall from Chapter 3 that under- or overapplied overhead is the difference between the amount of overhead applied to products and the actual overhead costs incurred during a period. Basically, the overhead variances we have computed in this chapter break the under- or overapplied overhead down into variances that can be used by managers for control purposes. Consequently, *the sum of the overhead variances equals the under- or overapplied overhead cost for a period.*

Furthermore, in a standard cost system, unfavorable variances are equivalent to underapplied overhead and favorable variances are equivalent to overapplied overhead. Unfavorable variances occur because more was spent on overhead than the standards allow. Underapplied overhead occurs when more was spent on overhead than was applied to products during the period. But in a standard costing system, the standard amount of overhead allowed is exactly the same amount of overhead applied to products. Therefore, in a standard costing system, unfavorable variances and underapplied overhead are the same thing, as are favorable variances and overapplied overhead.

For MicroDrive Corporation, the total overhead variance was $79,000 unfavorable. Therefore, its overhead cost was underapplied by $79,000 for the year. To solidify this point in your mind, *carefully study the review problem at the end of the chapter!* This review problem provides a comprehensive summary of overhead analysis, including the computation of under- or overapplied overhead cost in a standard cost system.

Review Problem: Overhead Analysis

(This problem provides a comprehensive review of Chapter 11, including the computation of under- or overapplied overhead and its breakdown into the four overhead variances.)

Data for the manufacturing overhead of Aspen Company are given below:

Overhead Costs	Cost Formula (per machine-hour)	Machine-Hours 5,000	6,000	7,000
Variable overhead costs:				
Supplies	$0.20	$ 1,000	$ 1,200	$ 1,400
Indirect labor	0.30	1,500	1,800	2,100
Total variable overhead cost	$0.50	2,500	3,000	3,500
Fixed overhead costs:				
Depreciation		4,000	4,000	4,000
Supervision		5,000	5,000	5,000
Total fixed overhead cost		9,000	9,000	9,000
Total overhead cost		$11,500	$12,000	$12,500

Five hours of machine time are required per unit of product. The company has set denominator activity for the coming period at 6,000 machine-hours (or 1,200 units). The computation of the predetermined overhead rate would be as follows:

$$\text{Total: } \frac{\$12,000}{6,000 \text{ MH}} = \$2,00 \text{ per machine-hour}$$

$$\text{Variable element: } \frac{\$3,000}{6,000 \text{ MH}} = \$0.50 \text{ per machine-hour}$$

$$\text{Fixed element: } \frac{\$9,000}{6,000 \text{ MH}} = \$1.50 \text{ per machine-hour}$$

Assume the following *actual* results for the period:

Number of units produced	1,300 units
Actual machine-hours	6,800 machine-hours
Standard machine-hours allowed*	6,500 machine-hours
Actual variable overhead cost	$4,200
Actual fixed overhead cost	9,400

*1,300 units × 5 machine-hours per unit.

Therefore, the company's Manufacturing Overhead account would appear as follows at the end of the period:

Manufacturing Overhead

	Debit	Credit	
Actual overhead costs	13,600*	13,000†	Applied overhead costs
Underapplied overhead	600		

* $4,200 variable + $9,400 fixed = $13,600

† 6,500 standard hours × $2 per machine hour = $13,000. In a standard cost system, overhead is applied on the basis of standard hours, not actual hours.

Required Analyze the $600 underapplied overhead in terms of:

1. A variable overhead spending variance.
2. A variable overhead efficiency variance.
3. A fixed overhead budget variance.
4. A fixed overhead volume variance.

Variable Overhead Variances

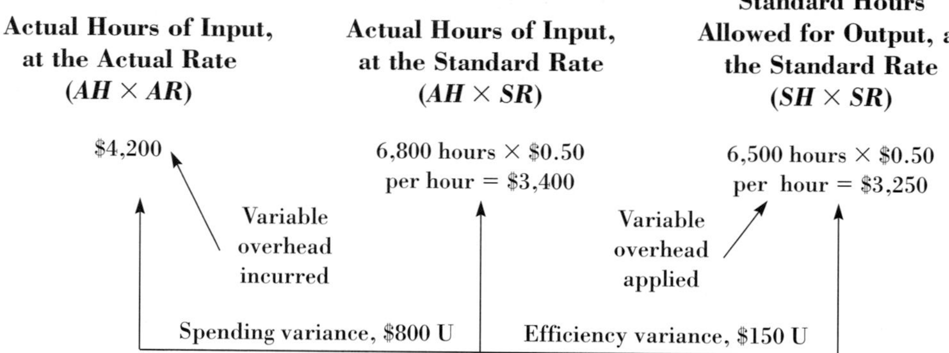

These same variances in the alternative format would be as follows:

Variable overhead spending variance:

$$\text{Spending variance} = (AH \times AR) - (AH \times SR)$$

$$(\$4{,}200^*) - (6{,}800 \text{ hours} \times \$0.50 \text{ per hour}) = \$800 \text{ U}$$

$^*AH \times AR$ equals the total actual cost for the period.

Variable overhead efficiency variance:

$$\text{Efficiency variance} = SR(AH - SH)$$

$$\$0.50 \text{ per hour } (6{,}800 \text{ hours} - 6{,}500 \text{ hours}) = \$150 \text{ U}$$

Fixed Overhead Variances

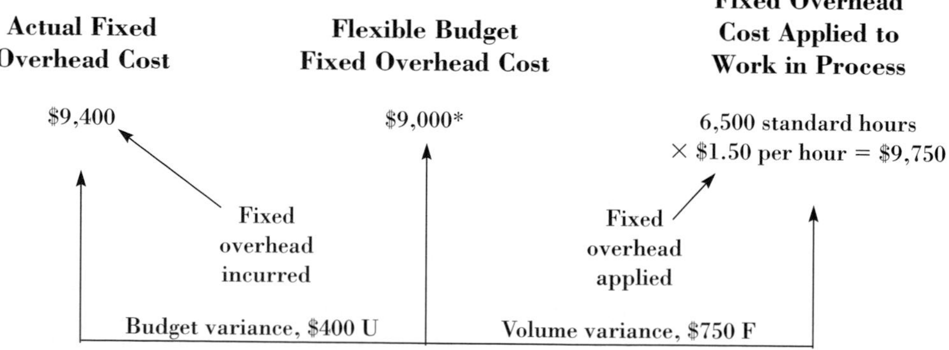

*Can be expressed as: 6,000 denominator hours × $1.50 per hour = $9,000.

These same variances in the alternative format would be as follows:

Fixed overhead budget variance:

$$\text{Budget variance} = \text{Actual fixed overhead cost} - \text{Flexible budget fixed overhead cost}$$

$$\$9{,}400 - \$9{,}000 = \$400 \text{ U}$$

Fixed overhead volume variance:

$$\text{Volume variance} = \begin{matrix}\text{Fixed portion}\\ \text{of the predetermined}\\ \text{overhead rate}\end{matrix} \times \begin{matrix}\text{(Denominator hours} - \\ \text{Standard hours)}\end{matrix}$$

$$\$1.50 \text{ per hour } (6{,}000 \text{ hours} - 6{,}500 \text{ hours}) = \$750 \text{ F}$$

Summary of Variances

A summary of the four overhead variances is given below:

Variable overhead:	
Spending variance	$800 U
Efficiency variance	150 U
Fixed overhead:	
Budget variance	400 U
Volume variance	750 F
Underapplied overhead	$600

Notice that the $600 summary variance figure agrees with the underapplied balance in the company's Manufacturing Overhead account. This agreement verifies the accuracy of our variance analysis.

Key Terms for Review

Budget variance A measure of the difference between the actual fixed overhead costs incurred during the period and budgeted fixed overhead costs as contained in the flexible budget. (p. 519)

Denominator activity The activity figure used to compute the predetermined overhead rate. (p. 516)

Flexible budget A budget that is designed to cover a range of activity and that can be used to develop budgeted costs at any point within that range to compare to actual costs incurred. (p. 504)

Static budget A budget designed for only one level of activity. (p. 504)

Volume variance The variance that arises whenever the standard hours allowed for the output of a period are different from the denominator activity level that was used to compute the predetermined overhead rate. (p. 519)

Questions

11–1 What is a static budget?

11–2 What is a flexible budget and how does it differ from a static budget?

11–3 Name three criteria that should be considered in choosing an activity base on which to construct a flexible budget.

11–4 In comparing budgeted data with actual data in a performance report for variable overhead, what variance(s) will be produced if the budgeted data are based on actual hours worked? On both actual hours worked and standard hours allowed?

11–5 What is meant by the term *standard hours allowed?*

11–6 How does the variable manufacturing overhead spending variance differ from the materials price variance?

11–7 Why is the term *overhead efficiency variance* a misnomer?

11–8 In what way is the flexible budget involved in product costing?

11–9 What is meant by the term *denominator level of activity?*

11–10 Why do we apply overhead to work in process on the basis of standard hours allowed in Chapter 11 when we applied it on the basis of actual hours in Chapter 3? What is the difference in costing systems between the two chapters?

11–11 In a standard cost system, what two variances are computed for fixed manufacturing overhead?

11–12 What does the fixed overhead budget variance measure?

11–13 Under what circumstances would you expect the volume variance to be favorable? Unfavorable? Does the variance measure deviations in spending for fixed overhead items? Explain.

11–14 How might the volume variance be measured, other than in dollars?

11–15 What dangers are there in expressing fixed costs on a per unit basis?

11–16 In Chapter 3, you became acquainted with the concept of under- or overapplied overhead. The under- or overapplied overhead can be broken down into what four variances?

11–17 If factory overhead is overapplied for August, would you expect the total of the overhead variances to be favorable or unfavorable?

Exercises

E11–1 An incomplete flexible budget is given below for Lavage Rapide, a Swiss company that owns and operates a large automatic carwash facility near Geneva. The Swiss currency is the Swiss franc, which is denoted by SFr.

LAVAGE RAPIDE
Flexible Budget
For the Month Ended August 31

Overhead Costs	Cost Formula (per car)	Activity(cars) 8,000	9,000	10,000
Variable overhead costs:				
Cleaning supplies	?	?	7,200 SFr	?
Electricity	?	?	2,700	?
Maintenance	?	?	1,800	?
Total variable overhead cost	?	?	?	?
Fixed overhead costs:				
Operator wages		?	9,000	?
Depreciation		?	6,000	?
Rent		?	8,000	?
Total fixed overhead cost		?	?	?
Total overhead cost		?	?	?

Required Fill in the missing data.

E11–2 Refer to the data in Exercise 11–1. Lavage Rapide's owner-manager would like to prepare a budget for August assuming an activity level of 8,800 cars.

Required Prepare a static budget for August. Use Exhibit 11–1 in the chapter as your guide.

E11–3 Refer to the data in Exercise 11–1. Lavage Rapide's actual level of activity during August was 8,900 cars, although the owner had constructed his static budget for the month assuming the level of activity would be 8,800 cars. The actual overhead costs incurred during August are given below:

	Actual Costs Incurred for 8,900 Cars
Variable overhead costs:	
Cleaning supplies	7,080 SFr
Electricity	2,460
Maintenance	1,550
Fixed overhead costs:	
Operator wages	9,100
Depreciation	7,000
Rent	8,000

Required Prepare a flexible budget performance report for both the variable and fixed overhead costs for August. Use Exhibit 11–4 in the chapter as your guide.

E11–4 The cost formulas for Emory Company's manufacturing overhead costs are given below. These cost formulas cover a relevant range of 15,000 to 25,000 machine-hours each year.

Overhead Costs	Cost Formula
Utilities	\$0.30 per machine-hour
Indirect labor	\$52,000 plus \$1.40 per machine-hour
Supplies	\$0.20 per machine-hour
Maintenance	\$18,000 plus \$0.10 per machine-hour
Depreciation	\$90,000

Required Prepare a flexible budget in increments of 5,000 machine-hours. Include all costs in your budget.

E11–5 The variable portion of Murray Company's flexible budget for manufacturing overhead is given below:

Variable Overhead Costs	Cost Formula (per machine-hour)	Machine-Hours		
		10,000	12,000	14,000
Supplies	\$0.20	\$ 2,000	\$ 2,400	\$ 2,800
Maintenance	0.80	8,000	9,600	11,200
Utilities	0.10	1,000	1,200	1,400
Rework time	0.40	4,000	4,800	5,600
Total variable overhead cost	\$1.50	\$15,000	\$18,000	\$21,000

During a recent period, the company recorded 11,500 machine-hours of activity. The variable overhead costs incurred were:

Supplies	\$2,400
Maintenance	8,000
Utilities	1,100
Rework time	5,300

The budgeted activity for the period had been 12,000 machine-hours.

Required

1. Prepare a variable overhead performance report for the period. Indicate whether variances are favorable (F) or unfavorable (U). Show only a spending variance on your report.
2. Discuss the significance of the variances. Might some variances be the result of others? Explain.

E11–6 The check-clearing office of Columbia National Bank is responsible for processing all checks that come to the bank for payment. Managers at the bank believe that variable overhead costs are essentially proportional to the number of labor-hours worked in the office, so labor-hours is used as the activity base for budgeting and for performance reports for variable overhead costs in the department. Data for September, the most recent month, appear below:

Budgeted labor-hours	3,080
Actual labor-hours	3,100
Standard labor-hours allowed for the actual number of checks processed	3,200

	Cost Formula (per labor-hour)	Actual Costs Incurred in September
Variable overhead costs:		
Office supplies	$0.10	$ 365
Staff coffee lounge	0.20	520
Indirect labor	0.90	2,710
Total variable overhead cost	$1.20	$3,595

Required

Prepare a variable overhead performance report for September for the check-clearing office that includes both spending and efficiency variances. Use Exhibit 11–7 as a guide.

E11–7 Operating at a normal level of 30,000 direct labor-hours, Lasser Company produces 10,000 units of product each period. The direct labor wage rate is $6 per hour. Two and one-half yards of direct materials go into each unit of product; the material costs $8.60 per yard. The flexible budget used to plan and control manufacturing overhead costs is given below (in condensed form):

Overhead Costs	Cost Formula (per direct labor-hour	Direct Labor-Hours 20,000	30,000	40,000
Variable costs	$1.90	$ 38,000	$ 57,000	$ 76,000
Fixed costs		168,000	168,000	168,000
Total overhead cost		$206,000	$225,000	$244,000

Required

1. Using 30,000 direct labor-hours as the denominator activity, compute the predetermined overhead rate and break it down into variable and fixed elements.
2. Complete the standard cost card below for one unit of product:

Direct materials, 2.5 yards at $8.60	$21.50
Direct labor, ?	?
Variable overhead, ?	?
Fixed overhead, ?	?
Total standard cost per unit	$?

E11–8 Norwall Company's flexible budget for manufacturing overhead (in condensed form) is given below:

Overhead Costs	Cost Formula (per machine-hour)	Machine-Hours		
		50,000	60,000	70,000
Variable costs	$3	$150,000	$180,000	$210,000
Fixed costs		300,000	300,000	300,000
Total overhead cost		$450,000	$480,000	$510,000

The following information is available for a recent period:

a. A denominator activity of 60,000 machine-hours is used to compute the predetermined overhead rate.
b. At the 60,000 standard machine-hours level of activity, the company should produce 40,000 units of product.
c. The company's actual operating results were:

Number of units produced	42,000
Actual machine-hours	64,000
Actual variable overhead costs	$185,000
Actual fixed overhead costs	302,400

Required

1. Compute the predetermined overhead rate and break it down into variable and fixed cost elements.
2. Compute the standard hours allowed for the actual production.
3. Compute the variable overhead spending and efficiency variances and the fixed overhead budget and volume variances.

E11–9 Selected operating information on three different companies for a recent year is given below:

	Company		
	A	B	C
Full-capacity machine-hours	10,000	18,000	20,000
Budgeted machine-hours*	9,000	17,000	20,000
Actual machine-hours	9,000	17,800	19,000
Standard machine-hours allowed for actual production	9,500	16,000	20,000

*Denominator activity for computing the predetermined overhead rate.

Required For each company, state whether the company would have a favorable or unfavorable volume variance and why.

E11–10 The standard cost card for the single product manufactured by Cutter, Inc., is given below:

Standard Cost Care—per Unit	
Direct materials, 3 yards at $6	$18
Direct labor, 4 hours at $7.75	31
Variable overhead, 4 hours at $1.50	6
Fixed overhead, 4 hours at $5	20
Total standard cost per unit	$75

Manufacturing overhead is applied to production on the basis of direct labor-hours. During the year, the company worked 37,000 hours and manufactured 9,500 units of product. Selected data relating to the company's fixed manufacturing overhead cost for the year are shown below:

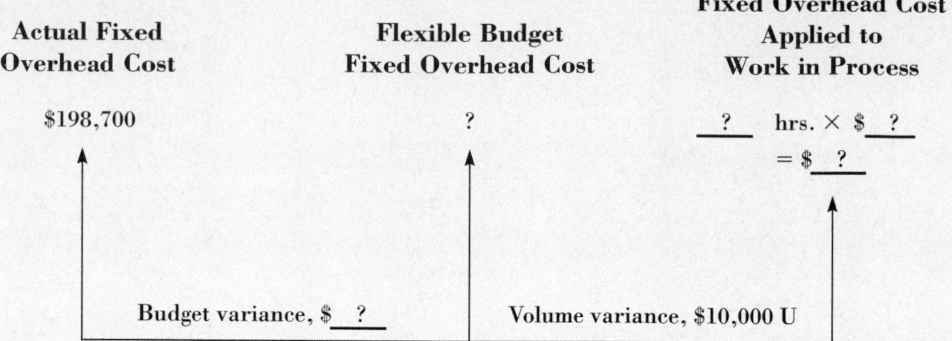

Required

1. What were the standard hours allowed for the year's production?
2. What was the amount of fixed overhead cost contained in the flexible budget for the year?
3. What was the fixed overhead budget variance for the year?
4. What denominator activity level did the company use in setting the predetermined overhead rate for the year?

E11–11 Selected information relating to Yost Company's operations for the most recent year is given below:

Activity:	
Denominator activity (machine-hours) .	45,000
Standard hours allowed per unit	3
Number of units produced	14,000
Costs:	
Actual fixed overhead costs incurred . .	$267,000
Fixed overhead budget variance	3,000 F

The company applies overhead cost to products on the basis of machine-hours.

Required

1. What were the standard hours allowed for the actual production?
2. What was the fixed portion of the predetermined overhead rate?
3. What was the volume variance?

Problems

P11–12 Preparing a Revised Performance Report Several years ago, Westmont Company developed a comprehensive budgeting system for profit planning and control purposes. The line supervisors have been very happy with the system and with the reports being prepared on their performance, but both middle and upper management have expressed considerable dissatisfaction with the information being generated by the system. A typical manufacturing overhead performance report for a recent period is shown below:

WESTMONT COMPANY
Overhead Performance Report—Assembly Department
For the Quarter Ended March 31

	Actual	Budget	Variance
Machine-hours	35,000	40,000	
Variable overhead costs:			
Indirect materials	$ 29,700	$ 32,000	$2,300 F
Rework time	7,900	8,000	100 F
Utilities	51,800	56,000	4,200 F
Machine setup	11,600	12,000	400 F
Total variable overhead cost	101,000	108,000	7,000 F
Fixed overhead costs:			
Maintenance	79,200	80,000	800 F
Inspection	60,000	60,000	—
Total fixed overhead cost	139,200	140,000	800 F
Total overhead cost	$240,200	$248,000	$7,800 F

After receiving a copy of this overhead performance report, the supervisor of the Assembly Department stated, "These reports are super. It makes me feel really good to see how well things are going in my department. I can't understand why those people upstairs complain so much."

The budget data above are for the original planned level of activity for the quarter.

Required

1. The company's vice president is uneasy about the performance reports being prepared and would like you to evaluate their usefulness to the company.
2. What changes, if any, would you recommend be made in the overhead performance report above in order to give better insight into how well the supervisor is controlling costs?
3. Prepare a new overhead performance report for the quarter, incorporating any changes you suggested in (2) above. (Include both the variable and the fixed costs in your report.)

P11–13 Applying the Flexible Budget Approach The St. Lucia Blood Bank, a private charity partly supported by government grants, is located on the Caribbean island of St. Lucia. The Blood Bank has just finished its operations for September, which was a particularly busy month due to a powerful hurricane that hit neighboring islands causing many injuries. The hurricane largely bypassed St. Lucia, but residents of St. Lucia willingly donated their blood to help people on other islands. As a consequence, the blood bank collected and processed over 20% more blood than had been originally planned for the month.

A report prepared by a government official comparing actual costs to budgeted costs for the Blood Bank appears below. (The currency on St. Lucia is the East Caribbean dollar.) Continued support from the government depends on the Blood Bank's ability to demonstrate control over their costs.

ST. LUCIA BLOOD BANK
Cost Control Report
For the Month Ended September 30

	Actual	Budget	Variance
Liters of blood collected	620	500	120 F
Variable costs:			
Medical supplies	$ 9,350	$ 7,500	$1,850 U
Lab tests	6,180	6,000	180 U
Refreshments for donors	1,340	1,000	340 U
Administrative supplies	400	250	150 U
Total variable cost	17,270	14,750	2,520 U
Fixed costs:			
Staff salaries	10,000	10,000	—
Equipment depreciation	2,800	2,500	300 U
Rent	1,000	1,000	—
Utilities	570	500	70 U
Total fixed cost	14,370	14,000	370 U
Total cost	$31,640	$28,750	$2,890 U

The managing director of the Blood Bank was very unhappy with this report, claiming that his costs were higher than expected due to the emergency on the neighboring islands. He also pointed out that the additional costs had been fully covered by payments from grateful recipients on the other islands. The government official who prepared the report countered that all of the figures had been submitted by the Blood Bank to the government; he was just pointing out that actual costs were a lot higher than promised in the budget.

Required

1. Prepare a new performance report for September using the flexible budget approach. (Note: Even though some of these costs might be classified as direct costs rather than as overhead, the flexible budget approach can still be used to prepare a flexible budget performance report.)
2. Do you think any of the variances in the report you prepared should be investigated? Why?

S

P11–14 Standard Cost Card: Materials, Labor, and All Overhead Variances Flandro Company uses a standard cost system and sets predetermined overhead rates on the basis of direct labor-hours. The following data are taken from the company's budget for the current year:

Denominator activity (direct labor-hours)	10,000
Variable manufacturing overhead cost	$25,000
Fixed manufacturing overhead cost	59,000

The standard cost card for the company's only product is given below:

Direct materials, 3 yards at $4.40	$13.20
Direct labor, 2 hours at $6	12.00
Manufacturing overhead, 140% of direct labor cost	16.80
Standard cost per unit	$42.00

During the year, the company produced 6,000 units of product and incurred the following costs:

Materials purchased, 24,000 yards at $4.80	$115,200
Materials used in production (in yards)	18,500
Direct labor cost incurred, 11,600 hours at $6.50	$ 75,400
Variable manufacturing overhead cost incurred	29,580
Fixed manufacturing overhead cost incurred	60,400

Required

1. Redo the standard cost card in a clearer, more usable format by detailing the variable and fixed overhead cost elements.
2. Prepare an analysis of the variances for materials and labor for the year.
3. Prepare an analysis of the variances for variable and fixed overhead for the year.
4. What effect, if any, does the choice of a denominator activity level have on unit standard costs? Is the volume variance a controllable variance from a spending point of view? Explain.

P11–15 Basic Overhead Analysis Chilczuk, S.A., of Gdansk, Poland, is a major producer of classic Polish sausage. The company uses a standard cost system to help in the control of costs. Overhead is applied to production on the basis of labor-hours. According to the company's flexible budget, the following manufacturing overhead costs should be incurred at an activity level of 35,000 labor-hours (the denominator activity level):

Variable overhead costs	PZ 87,500
Fixed overhead costs	210,000
Total overhead cost	PZ297,500

The currency in Poland is the zloty, which is denoted here by PZ.

During the most recent year, the following operating results were recorded:

Activity:	
Actual labor-hours worked	30,000
Standard labor-hours allowed for output	32,000
Cost:	
Actual variable overhead cost incurred	PZ 78,000
Actual fixed overhead cost incurred	209,400

At the end of the year, the company's Manufacturing Overhead account contained the following data:

Manufacturing Overhead

Actual	287,400	Applied	272,000
	15,400		

Management would like to determine the cause of the PZ15,400 underapplied overhead.

Required

1. Compute the predetermined overhead rate. Break the rate down into variable and fixed cost elements.
2. Show how the PZ272,000 Applied figure in the Manufacturing Overhead account was computed.
3. Analyze the PZ15,400 underapplied overhead figure in terms of the variable overhead spending and efficiency variances and the fixed overhead budget and volume variances.
4. Explain the meaning of each variance that you computed in (3) above.

P11–16 Integration of Materials, Labor, and Overhead Variances "Wonderful! Not only did our salespeople do a good job in meeting the sales budget this year, but our production people did a good job in controlling costs as well," said Kim Clark, president of Martell Company. "Our $18,000 overall manufacturing cost variance is only 1.5% of the $1,200,000 standard cost of products sold during the year. That's well within the 3% parameter set by management for acceptable variances. It looks like everyone will be in line for a bonus this year."

The company produces and sells a single product. A standard cost card for the product follows:

Standard Cost Card—per Unit of Product	
Direct materials, 2 feet at $8.45	$16.90
Direct labor, 1.4 hours at $8	11.20
Variable overhead, 1.4 hours at $2.50	3.50
Fixed overhead, 1.4 hours at $6	8.40
Standard cost per unit	$40.00

The following additional information is available for the year just completed:

a. The company manufactured 30,000 units of product during the year.
b. A total of 64,000 feet of material was purchased during the year at a cost of $8.55 per foot. All of this material was used to manufacture the 30,000 units. There were no beginning or ending inventories for the year.
c. The company worked 45,000 direct labor-hours during the year at a cost of $7.80 per hour.
d. Overhead is applied to products on the basis of direct labor-hours. Data relating to manufacturing overhead costs follow:

Denominator activity level (direct labor-hours)	35,000
Budgeted fixed overhead costs (from the overhead flexible budget)	$210,000
Actual variable overhead costs incurred	108,000
Actual fixed overhead costs incurred	211,800

Required

1. Compute the direct materials price and quantity variances for the year.
2. Compute the direct labor rate and efficiency variances for the year.
3. For manufacturing overhead compute:
   a. The variable overhead spending and efficiency variances for the year.
   b. The fixed overhead budget and volume variances for the year.
4. Total the variances you have computed, and compare the net amount with the $18,000 mentioned by the president. Do you agree that bonuses should be given to everyone for good cost control during the year? Explain.

P11–17 Flexible Budget and Overhead Performance Report You have just been hired by FAB Company, the manufacturer of a revolutionary new garage door opening device. John Foster, the president, has asked that you review the company's costing system and "do what you can to help us get better control of our manufacturing overhead costs." You find that the company has never used a flexible budget, and you suggest that preparing such a budget would be an excellent first step in overhead planning and control.

After much effort and analysis, you are able to determine the following cost formulas for the company's normal operating range of 20,000 to 30,000 machine-hours each month:

Overhead Costs	Cost Formula
Utilities	$0.90 per machine-hour
Maintenance	$1.60 per machine-hour plus $40,000 per month
Machine setup	$0.30 per machine-hour
Indirect labor	$0.70 per machine-hour plus $130,000 per month
Depreciation	$70,000 per month

To show the president how the flexible budget concept works, you have gathered the following actual cost data for the most recent month, March, in which the company worked 26,000 machine-hours and produced 15,000 units:

Utilities	$ 24,200
Maintenance	78,100
Machine setup	8,400
Indirect labor	149,600
Depreciation	71,500
Total cost	$331,800

The only variance in the fixed costs for the month was with depreciation, which was increased as a result of a purchase of new equipment.

The company had originally planned to work 30,000 machine-hours during March.

Required

1. Prepare a flexible budget for the company in increments of 5,000 hours.
2. Prepare an overhead performance report for the company for March. (Use the format illustrated in Exhibit 11–11.)
3. What additional information would you need to compute an overhead efficiency variance for the company?

P11–18 Spending and Efficiency Variances; Evaluating an Overhead Performance Report Frank Western, supervisor of the Machining Department for Freemont Company, was visibly upset after being reprimanded for his department's poor performance over the prior month. The department's performance report is given below:

FREEMONT COMPANY
Performance Report—Machining Department

	Cost Formula (per machine-hour)	Actual	Budget	Variance
Machine-hours		38,000	35,000	
Variable overhead costs:				
Utilities	$0.40	$ 15,700	$ 14,000	$ 1,700 U
Indirect labor	2.30	86,500	80,500	6,000 U
Supplies	0.60	26,000	21,000	5,000 U
Maintenance	1.20	44,900	42,000	2,900 U
Total variable overhead cost	$4.50	173,100	157,500	15,600 U
Fixed overhead costs:				
Supervision		38,000	38,000	—
Maintenance		92,400	92,000	400 U
Depreciation		80,000	80,000	—
Total fixed overhead cost		210,400	210,000	400 U
Total overhead cost		$383,500	$367,500	$16,000 U

"I just can't understand all the red ink," said Western to Sarah Mason, supervisor of another department. "When the boss called me in, I thought he was going to give me a pat on the back because I know for a fact that my department worked more efficiently last month than it has ever worked before. Instead, he tore me apart. I thought for a minute that it might be over the supplies that were stolen out of our warehouse last month. But they only amounted to a couple of thousand dollars, and just look at this report. *Everything* is unfavorable, and I don't even know why."

The budget for the Machining Department had called for production of 14,000 units last month, which is equal to a budgeted activity level of 35,000 machine-hours (at a standard time of 2.5 hours per unit). Actual production in the Machining Department for the month was 16,000 units.

Required

1. Evaluate the overhead performance report given above and explain why the variances are all unfavorable.
2. Prepare a new overhead performance report that will help Mr. Western's superiors assess efficiency and cost control in the Machining Department. (Hint: Exhibit 11–7 may be helpful in structuring your report; however, the report you prepare should include both variable and fixed costs.)

3. Would the supplies stolen out of the warehouse be included as part of the variable overhead spending variance or as part of the variable overhead efficiency variance for the month? Explain.

P11–19 Detailed Performance Report The cost formulas for variable overhead costs in a machining operation are given below:

Variable Overhead Costs	Cost Formula (per machine-hour)
Power	$0.30
Setup time	0.20
Polishing wheels	0.16
Maintenance	0.18
Total variable overhead cost	$0.84

During August, the machining operation was scheduled to work 11,250 machine-hours and to produce 4,500 units of product. The standard machine time per unit of product is 2.5 hours. A strike near the end of the month forced a cutback in production. Actual results for the month were:

Actual machine-hours worked . . .	9,250
Actual number of units produced .	3,600

Actual costs for the month were:

Variable Overhead Costs	Total Actual Costs	Per Machine-Hour
Power	$2,405	$0.26
Setup time	2,035	0.22
Polishing wheels	1,110	0.12
Maintenance	925	0.10
Total variable overhead cost	$6,475	$0.70

Required Prepare an overhead performance report for the machining operation for August. Use column headings in your report as shown below:

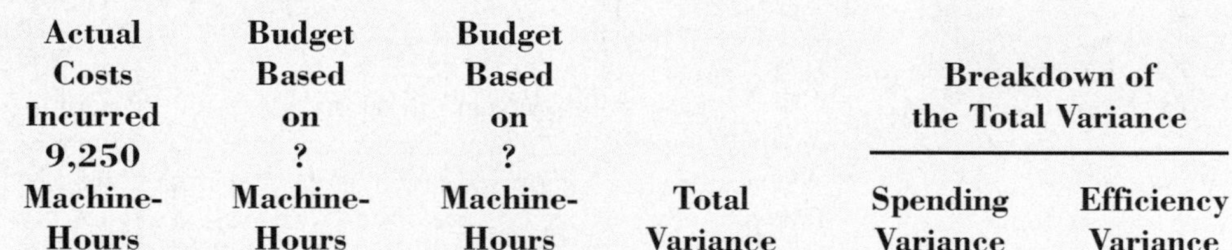

Overhead Costs	Cost Formula (per machine-hour)	Actual Costs Incurred 9,250 Machine-Hours	Budget Based on ? Machine-Hours	Budget Based on ? Machine-Hours	Total Variance	Breakdown of the Total Variance: Spending Variance	Breakdown of the Total Variance: Efficiency Variance

P11–20 Standard Cost Card and Overhead Analysis Lane Company manufactures a single product that requires a great deal of hand labor. Overhead cost is applied on the basis of direct labor-hours. The company's condensed flexible budget for manufacturing overhead is given below:

Overhead Costs	Cost Formula (per direct labor-hour)	Direct Labor-Hours 45,000	60,000	75,000
Variable costs	$2	$ 90,000	$120,000	$150,000
Fixed costs		480,000	480,000	480,000
Total overhead cost . . .		$570,000	$600,000	$630,000

The company's product requires 3 pounds of material that has a standard cost of $7 per pound and 1.5 hours of direct labor time that has a standard rate of $6 per hour.

The company planned to operate at a denominator activity level of 60,000 direct labor-hours and to produce 40,000 units of product during the most recent year. Actual activity and costs for the year were as follows:

Number of units produced	42,000
Actual direct labor-hours worked	65,000
Actual variable overhead cost incurred	$123,500
Actual fixed overhead cost incurred	483,000

Required

1. Compute the predetermined overhead rate for the year. Break the rate down into variable and fixed elements.
2. Prepare a standard cost card for the company's product; show the details for all manufacturing costs on your standard cost card.
3. Do the following:
   a. Compute the standard hours allowed for the year's production.
   b. Complete the following Manufacturing Overhead T-account for the year:

Manufacturing Overhead

?	?
?	?

4. Determine the reason for any under- or overapplied overhead for the year by computing the variable overhead spending and efficiency variances and the fixed overhead budget and volume variances.
5. Suppose the company had chosen 65,000 direct labor-hours as the denominator activity rather than 60,000 hours. State which, if any, of the variances computed in (4) above would have changed, and explain how the variance(s) would have changed. No computations are necessary.

P11–21 Standard Cost Card; Fixed Overhead Analysis; Graphing When planning operations for the year, Southbrook Company chose a denominator activity of 40,000 direct labor-hours. According to the company's flexible budget, the following manufacturing overhead costs should be incurred at this activity level:

Variable overhead costs	$ 72,000
Fixed overhead costs	360,000

The company produces a single product that requires 2.5 hours to complete. The direct labor rate is $6 per hour. Eight yards of material are needed to complete one unit of product; the material has a standard cost of $4.50 per yard. Overhead is applied to production on the basis of direct labor-hours.

Required

1. Compute the predetermined overhead rate. Break the rate down into variable and fixed cost elements.
2. Prepare a standard cost card for one unit of product using the following format:

Direct materials, 8 yards at $4.50	$36
Direct labor, ?	?
Variable overhead, ?	?
Fixed overhead, ?	?
Standard cost per unit	$?

3. Prepare a graph with cost on the vertical (*Y*) axis and direct labor-hours on the horizontal (*X*) axis. Plot a line on your graph from a zero level of activity to 60,000 direct labor-hours for each of the following costs:
   a. Budgeted fixed overhead (in total).
   b. Applied fixed overhead [applied at the hourly rate computed in (1) above].
4. Assume that during the year actual activity is as follows:

Number of units produced	14,000
Actual direct labor-hours worked	33,000
Actual fixed overhead cost incurred	$361,800

a. Compute the fixed overhead budget and volume variances for the year.
b. Show the volume variance on the graph you prepared in (3) above.

5. Disregard the data in (4) above. Assume instead that actual activity during the year is as follows:

Number of units produced	20,000
Actual direct labor-hours worked	52,000
Actual fixed overhead costs incurred	$361,800

a. Compute the fixed overhead budget and volume variances for the year.
b. Show the volume variance on the graph you prepared in (3) above.

P11–22 Flexible Budget and Overhead Analysis Harper Company assembles all of its products in the Assembly Department. Budgeted costs for the operation of this department for year have been set as follows:

Variable overhead costs:	
Direct materials	$ 900,000
Direct labor	675,000
Utilities	45,000
Indirect labor	67,500
Supplies	22,500
Total variable overhead cost	1,710,000
Fixed overhead costs:	
Insurance	8,000
Supervisory salaries	90,000
Depreciation	160,000
Equipment rental	42,000
Total fixed overhead cost	300,000
Total budgeted overhead cost	$2,010,000
Budgeted direct labor-hours	75,000

Since the assembly work is done mostly by hand, operating activity in this department is best measured by direct labor-hours. The cost formulas used to develop the budgeted costs above are valid over a relevant range of 60,000 to 90,000 direct labor-hours per year.

Required

1. Prepare a manufacturing overhead flexible budget in good form for the Assembly Department. Make your budget in increments of 15,000 direct labor-hours. (The company does not include direct materials and direct labor costs in the flexible budget.)
2. Assume that the company computes predetermined overhead rates by department. Compute the rates that will be used by the Assembly Department to apply overhead costs to production. Break this rate down into variable and fixed cost elements.
3. Suppose that during the year the following actual activity and costs are recorded by the Assembly Department:

Actual direct labor-hours worked	73,000
Standard direct labor-hours allowed for the output of the year	70,000
Actual variable overhead cost incurred	$124,100
Actual fixed overhead cost incurred	301,600

Complete the following:

a. A T-account for manufacturing overhead costs in the Assembly Department for the year is given below. Determine the amount of applied overhead cost for the year, and compute the under- or overapplied overhead.

Manufacturing Overhead

Actual cost 425,700	

b. Analyze the under- or overapplied overhead figure in terms of the variable overhead spending and efficiency variances and the fixed overhead budget and volume variances.

P11–23 Flexible Budget; Overhead Performance Report Gant Products, Inc., has recently introduced budgeting as an integral part of its corporate planning process. The company's first effort at constructing a flexible budget for manufacturing overhead is shown below:

Percentage of capacity	80%	100%
Machine-hours	4,800	6,000
Maintenance	$1,480	$ 1,600
Supplies	1,920	2,400
Utilities	1,940	2,300
Supervision	3,000	3,000
Machine setup	960	1,200
Total overhead cost	$9,300	$10,500

The budgets above are for costs over a relevant range of 80% to 100% of capacity on a monthly basis. The managers who will be working under these budgets have control over both fixed and variable costs.

Required

1. Redo the company's flexible budget, presenting it in better format. Show the budget at 80%, 90%, and 100% levels of capacity. (Use the high-low method to separate fixed and variable costs.)
2. Express the budget prepared in (1) above in cost formula form using a single cost formula to express all overhead costs.
3. The company operated at 95% of capacity during April in terms of actual hours of machine time recorded in the factory. Five thousand six hundred standard machine-hours were allowed for the output of the month. Actual overhead costs incurred were:

Maintenance	$ 2,083
Supplies	3,420
Utilities	2,666
Supervision	3,000
Machine setup	855
Total overhead cost	$12,024

   The fixed costs had no variances. Prepare an overhead performance report for April. Structure your report so that it shows only a spending variance for overhead. You may assume that the master budget for April called for an activity level during the month of 6,000 machine-hours.
4. Upon receiving the performance report you have prepared, the production manager commented, "I have two observations to make. First, I think there's an error on your report. You show an unfavorable spending variance for supplies, yet I know that we paid exactly the budgeted price for all the supplies we used last month. Pat Stevens, the purchasing agent, made a comment to me that our supplies prices haven't changed in over a year. Second, I wish you would modify your report to include an efficiency variance for overhead. The reason is that waste has been a problem in the factory for years and the efficiency variance would help us get overhead waste under control."
   a. Explain the probable cause of the unfavorable spending variance for supplies.
   b. Compute an efficiency variance for *total* variable overhead and explain to the production manager why it would or would not contain elements of overhead waste.

P11–24 Activity-Based Costing and the Flexible Budget Approach The Little Theatre is a nonprofit organization devoted to staging theater productions of plays for children in Manchester, England. The theater has a very small full-time professional administrative staff. Through a special arrangement with the actors' union, actors and directors rehearse without pay and are paid only for actual performances.

The costs of 1998's operations appear below. (The currency in England was the pound, denoted £.) During 1998, The Little Theatre had six different productions—each of which was performed 18 times. For example, one of the productions was Peter the Rabbit, which had the usual six-week run with three performances on each weekend.

THE LITTLE THEATRE
Cost Report
For the Year Ended 31 December 1998

Number of productions	6
Number of performance of each production	18
Total number of performances	108
Actual costs incurred:	
Actors' and directors' wages	£216,000
Stagehands' wages	32,400
Ticket booth personnel and ushers' wages	16,200
Scenery, costumes, and props	108,000
Theater hall rent	54,000
Printed programs	27,000
Publicity	12,000
Administrative expenses	43,200
Total cost	£508,800

Some of the costs vary with the number of productions, some with the number of performances, and some are relatively fixed and depend on neither the number of productions nor the number of performances. The costs of scenery, costumes, and props and of publicity vary with the number of productions. It doesn't make any difference how many times Peter the Rabbit is performed, the cost of the scenery is the same. Likewise, the cost of publicizing a play with posters and radio commercials is the same whether there are 10, 20, or 30 performances of the play. On the other hand, the wages of the actors, directors, stagehands, ticket booth personnel, and ushers vary with the number of performances. The greater the number of performances, the higher the wage costs will be. Similarly, the costs of renting the hall and printing the programs will vary with the number of performances. Administrative expenses are more difficult to pin down, but the best estimate is that approximately 75% of these costs are fixed, 15% depend on the number of productions staged, and the remaining 10% depend on the number of performances.

At the end of 1998, the board of directors of the theater authorized expanding the theater's program in 1999 to seven productions, with 24 performances each. Not surprisingly, actual costs for 1999 were considerably higher than the costs for 1998. (Grants from donors and ticket sales were also correspondingly higher.) Data concerning 1999's operations appear below:

THE LITTLE THEATRE
Cost Report
For the Year Ended 31 December 1999

Number of productions	7
Number of performances of each production	24
Total number of performances	168
Actual costs incurred:	
Actors' and directors' wages	£341,800
Stagehands' wages	49,700
Ticket booth personnel and ushers' wages	25,900
Scenery, costumes, and props	130,600
Theater hall rent	78,000
Printed programs	38,300
Publicity	15,100
Administrative expenses	47,500
Total cost	£726,900

Even though many of the costs above may be considered direct costs rather than overhead, the flexible budget approach covered in the chapter can still be used to evaluate how well these costs are controlled. The principles are the same whether a cost is a direct cost or is overhead.

Required

1. Use the actual results from 1998 to estimate the cost formulas for the flexible budget for The Little Theatre. Keep in mind that the theater has two measures of activity—the number of productions and the number of performances.
2. Prepare a performance report for 1999 using the flexible budget approach and both measures of activity. Assume there was no inflation. (Note: To evaluate administrative expenses, first determine the flexible budget amounts for the three elements of administrative expenses. Then compare the total of the three elements to the actual administrative expense of £47,500.)
3. If you were on the board of directors of the theater, would you be pleased with how well costs were controlled during 1999? Why or why not?
4. The cost formulas provide figures for the average cost per production and average cost per performance. How accurate do you think these figures would be for predicting the cost of a new production or of an additional performance of a particular production?

P11–25 Selection of a Denominator; Overhead Analysis Morton Company's condensed flexible budget for manufacturing overhead is given below:

Overhead Costs	Cost Formula (per direct labor-hour)	Direct Labor-Hours 20,000	30,000	45,000
Variable costs	$4.50	$ 90,000	$135,000	$180,000
Fixed costs		270,000	270,000	270,000
Total overhead cost		$360,000	$405,000	$450,000

The company manufactures a single product that requires two direct labor-hours to complete. The direct labor wage rate is $5 per hour. Four feet of raw material are required for each unit of product; the standard cost of the material is $8.75 per foot.

Although long-run normal activity is 30,000 direct labor-hours each year, the company expects to operate at a 40,000-hour level of activity this year.

Required

1. Assume that the company chooses 30,000 direct labor-hours as the denominator level of activity. Compute the predetermined overhead rate, breaking it down into variable and fixed cost elements.
2. Assume that the company chooses 40,000 direct labor-hours as the denominator level of activity. Repeat the computations in (1) above.
3. Complete two standard cost cards as outlined below. Each card should relate to a single unit of product.

Denominator Activity: 30,000 Direct Labor-Hours

Direct materials, 4 feet at $8.75	$35.00
Direct labor, ?	?
Variable overhead, ?	?
Fixed overhead, ?	?
Standard cost per unit	$?

Denominator Activity: 40,000 Direct Labor-Hours

Direct materials, $4 feet at $8.75	$35.00
Direct labor, ?	?
Variable overhead, ?	?
Fixed overhead, ?	?
Standard cost per unit	$?

4. Assume that the company produces 18,000 units and works 38,000 actual direct labor-hours during the year. Actual manufacturing overhead costs for the year are:

Variable costs	$174,800
Fixed costs	271,600
Total overhead cost	$446,400

Do the following:

a. Compute the standard hours allowed for this year's production.

b. Complete the Manufacturing Overhead account below. Assume that the company uses 30,000 direct labor-hours (long-run normal activity) as the denominator activity figure in computing predetermined overhead rates, as you have done in (1) above.

Manufacturing Overhead

Debit		Credit
Actual costs	446,400	?
?		?

c. Determine the cause of the under- or overapplied overhead for the year by computing the variable overhead spending and efficiency variances and the fixed overhead budget and volume variances.

5. Looking at the variances you have computed, what appears to be the major disadvantage of using long-run normal activity rather than expected actual activity as a denominator in computing the predetermined overhead rate? What advantages can you see to offset this disadvantage?

Cases

C11–26 Ethics and the Manager Tom Kemper is the controller of the Wichita manufacturing facility of Prudhom Enterprises, Incorporated. Among the many reports that must be filed with corporate headquarters is the annual overhead performance report. The report covers an entire fiscal year, which ends on December 31, and is due at corporate headquarters shortly after the beginning of the New Year. Kemper does not like putting work off to the last minute, so just before Christmas he put together a preliminary draft of the overhead performance report. Some adjustments would be required for transactions that occur between Christmas and New Year's Day, but there are generally very few of these. A copy of the preliminary draft report, which Kemper completed on December 21, follows:

WICHITA MANUFACTURING FACILITY
Overhead Performance Report
December 21 Preliminary Draft

Budgeted machine-hours 200,000
Actual machine-hours 180,000

Overhead Costs	Cost Formula (per machine-hour)	Actual Costs 180,000 Machine-Hours	Budget Based on 180,000 Machine-Hours	Spending or Budget Variance
Variable overhead costs:				
Power	$0.10	$ 19,750	$ 18,000	$ 1,750 U
Supplies	0.25	47,000	45,000	2,000 U
Abrasives	0.30	58,000	54,000	4,000 U
Total variable overhead cost	$0.65	124,750	117,000	7,750 U
Fixed overhead costs:				
Depreciation		345,000	332,000	13,000 U
Supervisory salaries		273,000	275,000	2,000 F
Insurance		37,000	37,000	—
Industrial engineering		189,000	210,000	21,000 F
Factory building lease		60,000	60,000	—
Total fixed overhead cost		904,000	914,000	10,000 F
Total overhead cost		$1,028,750	$1,031,000	$ 2,250 F

Melissa Ilianovitch, the general manager at the Wichita facility, asked to see a copy of the preliminary draft report at 4:45 P.M. on December 23. Kemper carried a copy of the report to her office where the following discussion took place:

Ilianovitch: Ouch! Almost all of the variances on the report are unfavorable. The only thing that looks good at all are the favorable variances for supervisory salaries and for industrial engineering. How did we have an unfavorable variance for depreciation?

Kemper: Do you remember that milling machine that broke down because the wrong lubricant was used by the machine operator?

Ilianovitch: Only vaguely.

Kemper: It turned out we couldn't fix it. We had to scrap the machine and buy a new one.

Ilianovitch: This report doesn't look good. I was raked over the coals last year when we had just a few unfavorable variances.

Kemper: I'm afraid the final report is going to look even worse.

Ilianovitch: Oh?

Kemper: The line item for industrial engineering on the report is for work we hired Ferguson Engineering to do for us on a contract basis. The original contract was for $210,000, but we asked them to do some additional work that was not in the contract. Under the terms of the contract, we have to reimburse Ferguson Engineering for the costs of the additional work. The $189,000 in actual costs that appear on the preliminary draft report reflects only their billings up through December 21. The last bill they had sent us was on November 28, and they completed the project just last week. Yesterday I got a call from Laura Sunder over at Ferguson and she said they would be sending us a final bill for the project before the end of the year. The total bill, including the reimbursements for the additional work, is going to be . . .

Ilianovitch: I am not sure I want to hear this.

Kemper: $225,000
Ilianovitch: Ouch! Ouch! Ouch!
Kemper: The additional work we asked them to do added $15,000 to the cost of the project.
Ilianovitch: No way can I turn in a performance report with an overall unfavorable variance. They'll kill me at corporate headquarters. Call up Laura at Ferguson and ask her not to send the bill until after the first of the year. We have to have that $21,000 favorable variance for industrial engineering on the performance report.

Required What should Tom Kemper do? Explain.

C11–27 **Incomplete Data** Each of the cases below is independent. You may assume that each company uses a standard cost system and that each company's flexible budget for manufacturing overhead is based on standard machine-hours.

Item	Company A	Company B
1. Denominator activity in hours	?	40,000
2. Standard hours allowed for units produced	32,000	?
3. Actual hours worked	30,000	?
4. Flexible budget variable overhead per machine-hour	$?	$ 2.80
5. Flexible budget fixed overhead (total)	?	?
6. Actual variable overhead cost incurred	54,000	117,000
7. Actual fixed overhead cost incurred	209,400	302,100
8. Variable overhead cost applied to production*	?	117,600
9. Fixed overhead cost applied to production*	192,000	?
10. Variable overhead spending variance	?	?
11. Variable overhead efficiency variance	3,500 F	8,400 U
12. Fixed overhead budget variance	?	2,100 U
13. Fixed overhead volume variance	18,000 U	?
14. Variable portion of the predetermined overhead rate	?	?
15. Fixed portion of the predetermined overhead rate	?	?
16. Underapplied (or overapplied) overhead	?	?

*Based on standard hours allowed for units produced

Required Compute the unknown amounts. (Hint: One way to proceed would be to use the format for variance analysis found in Exhibit 10–6 for variable overhead and in Exhibit 11–10 for fixed overhead.)

C11–28 **Working Backwards from Variance Data** You have recently graduated from State University and have accepted a position with Vitex, Inc., the manufacturer of a popular consumer product. During your first week on the job, the vice president has been favorably impressed with your work. She has been so impressed, in fact, that yesterday she called you into her office and asked you to attend the executive committee meeting this morning for the purpose of leading a discussion on the variances reported for last period. Anxious to favorably impress the executive committee, you took the variances and supporting data home last night to study.

On your way to work this morning, the papers were laying on the seat of your new, red convertible. As you were crossing a bridge on the highway, a sudden gust of wind caught the papers and blew them over the edge of the bridge and into the stream below. You managed to retrieve only one page, which contains the following information:

Standard Cost Card

Direct materials, 6 pounds at $3	$18.00
Direct labor, 0.8 hours at $5	4.00
Variable overhead, 0.8 hours at $3	2.40
Fixed overhead, 0.8 hours at $7	5.60
Standard cost per unit	$30.00

	Total Standard Cost*	Variances Reported: Price or Rate	Spending or Budget	Quantity or Efficiency	Volume
Direct materials	$405,000	$6,900 F		$9,000 U	
Direct labor	90,000	4,850 U		7,000 U	
Variable overhead	54,000		$1,300 F	?† U	
Fixed overhead	126,000		500 F		$14,000 U

* Applied to Work in Process during the period.

† Figure obliterated.

You recall that manufacturing overhead cost is applied to production on the basis of direct labor-hours and that all of the materials purchased during the period were used in production. Since the company uses JIT to control work flows, work in process inventories are insignificant and can be ignored.

It is now 8:30 A.M. The executive committee meeting starts in just one hour; you realize that to avoid looking like a bungling fool you must somehow generate the necessary "backup" data for the variances before the meeting begins. Without backup data it will be impossible to lead the discussion or answer any questions.

Required

1. How many units were produced last period? (Think hard about this one!)
2. How many pounds of direct material were purchased and used in production?
3. What was the actual cost per pound of material?
4. How many actual direct labor-hours were worked during the period?
5. What was the actual rate paid per direct labor-hour?
6. How much actual variable manufacturing overhead cost was incurred during the period?
7. What is the total fixed manufacturing overhead cost in the company's flexible budget?
8. What were the denominator hours for last period?

C11–29 Preparing a Performance Report Using Activity-Based Costing Boyne University offers an extensive continuing education program in many cities throughout the state. For the convenience of its faculty and administrative staff and to save costs, the university employs a supervisor to operate a motor pool. The motor pool operated with 20 vehicles until February, when an additional automobile was acquired. The motor pool furnishes gasoline, oil, and other supplies for its automobiles. A mechanic does routine maintenance and minor repairs. Major repairs are done at a nearby commercial garage.

Each year, the supervisor prepares an operating budget that informs the university administration of the funds needed for operating the motor pool. Depreciation (straight line) on the automobiles is recorded in the budget in order to determine the cost per mile of operating the vehicles.

The following schedule presents the operating budget for the current year, which has been approved by the university. The schedule also shows actual operating costs for March of the current year compared to one-twelfth of the annual operating budget.

UNIVERSITY MOTOR POOL

Budget Report for March

	Annual Operating Budget	Monthly Budget*	March Actual	(Over) Under Budget
Gasoline	$ 42,000	$ 3,500	$ 4,300	$(800)
Oil, minor repairs, parts	3,600	300	380	(80)
Outside repairs	2,700	225	50	175
Insurance	6,000	500	525	(25)
Salaries and benefits	30,000	2,500	2,500	—
Depreciation of vehicles	26,400	2,200	2,310	(110)
Total costs	$110,700	$ 9,225	$10,065	$(840)
Total miles	600,000	50,000	63,000	
Cost per mile	$ 0.1845	$0.1845	$0.1598	
Number of automobiles in use	20	20	21	

* Annual operating budget ÷ 12 months.

The annual operating budget was constructed on the following assumptions:

a. Twenty automobiles in the motor pool.
b. Thirty thousand miles driven per year per automobile.
c. Fifteen miles per gallon per automobile.
d. $1.05 per gallon of gasoline.
e. $0.006 cost per mile for oil, minor repairs, and parts.
f. $135 cost per automobile per year for outside repairs.
g. $300 cost per automobile per year for insurance.

The supervisor of the motor pool is unhappy with the monthly report comparing budget and actual costs for March, claiming it presents an unfair picture of performance. A previous employer used flexible budgeting to compare actual costs to budgeted amounts.

Required

1. Prepare a new performance report for March showing budgeted costs, actual costs, and variances. In preparing your report, use flexible budgeting techniques to compute the monthly budget figures.
2. What are the deficiencies in the performance report presented above? How does the report that you prepared in (1) above overcome these deficiencies?

(CMA, adapted)

Group Exercises

GE11–30 Overhead Control For years, U.S. manufacturers followed a strategy of low-cost mass production to gain competitive advantage by pursuing economics of scale—maximizing production of a single product in a single facility. In order to leverage economies of scale into further reductions in unit cost, firms built bigger factories and filled those plants with bigger, faster, and more specialized machines. With total overhead costs increasing, plant managers ran larger lots and pushed costs lower by maximizing the volume of throughput in each department and at each workstation.

Of necessity, the variety of products made had to increase in order to gain the volume necessary to fully utilize the ever-larger and more costly facilities and machinery. As the variety of parts and products produced in any single plant increased, the need for support staff to manage and control production through the plant increased. In time, overhead costs had increased to 30%–40% of total manufacturing costs, while direct labor decreased to 10%–15% of total manufacturing costs and is still dropping.

Required

1. How did plant management control machine-related costs? Traditionally, what performance measures were used to measure and evaluate the performance of machinery?
2. What incentives did these machine-based performance measures provide plant management and shop floor supervisors? What potential results did these performance incentives have?
3. What is production support? Describe how and why production support increased over time.
4. How did plant management attempt to control this increasing category of production support overhead?
5. What is the overhead absorption variance? How was underapplied overhead interpreted?
6. Because of the increasing complexity of the plant, quality problems became an ever-present problem in the operations of a factory. How did plant management view quality in this environment, and what role did quality play in the day-to-day operations of the factory? What is the concept of an acceptable quality level (AQL)?
7. How did cost accounting account for scrap, spoilage, and rework?
8. Who was responsible for quality? How was their performance measured? What implications did this have for understanding and controlling the costs of poor quality?
9. Traditional cost accounting systems encourage some highly questionable behavior. Can you identify any other questionable actions not already identified above?

GE11–31 **Cost Control and Company Size** Suppose two factories are located side by side. One plant is extremely large and complex with more than 4,000 employees, 40 production departments, 25 production support departments (e.g., production scheduling), three eight-hour shifts, and an annual budget in excess of $250 million. This plant, one of 20 National Motors assembly plants, makes NM's Great Iroquois sport-utility vehicle.

The other factory is much smaller and is managed by its owner. This plant employs 105 workers, has two 10-hour shifts, and has a budget of $4.5 million annually. Although machines of a similar type are grouped together in the plant, the facility is not large enough to be divided into different production departments. In addition to the owner, there is an engineer who designs the products on a computer-aided design system, an accountant, a secretary, and two shift foremen. This job shop makes molds that are used to produce a variety of products. For example, one recent job was for a mold that would produce the front panel of the disk drive on an MBI Activa personal computer.

Required

1. What are the primary concerns or issues for each plant?
2. What should the objectives of each plant's cost system be?
3. Given these objectives, what kind of accounting reports and performance measures would be appropriate for managing each factory? Be sure to explain your reasoning for using the reports and performance measures that you recommend.
4. To report timely and relevant information, how often would you issue such reports and measures of performance?

GE11–32 **Choice of Denominator Activity Level** American Widget, Inc., makes a number of high-volume standard products that are sold in highly competitive markets. As a result, its cost system stresses cost control. American uses a standard cost system and updates standards on a regular and timely basis. Until recently, expected annual capacity was the basis for determining predetermined factory overhead rates. This rate was used for internal planning and reporting and performance evaluation purposes, as well as for inventory valuation.

Recently, John Phillips, controller, has proposed changing the basis for internal planning and reporting from expected annual capacity to practical capacity. Since practical capacity remains relatively constant unless there is a plant expansion or purchase of new manufacturing machinery, Phillips believes this change would facilitate planning and budgeting.

Phillips has held one meeting with department managers and presented them with their new annual budgets prepared on the basis of the new, proposed practical capacity standard. There was little discussion. Later, a member of the cost accounting staff pointed out that the new standard for determining predetermined overhead rates would be tighter than the old standard.

Required

1. If the new annual budgets for American Widget reflect the implementation of tighter standards based on practical capacity:
   a. What negative behavioral implications for employees and department managers could occur as a result of this change?
   b. What could American Widget management do to mitigate the negative behavioral effects?
2. Explain how tight cost standards within an organization could have positive behavioral effects.
3. Identify the individuals who should participate in setting standards and describe the benefits to an organization of their participation in the standard setting process.

(CMA, adapted)

GE11–33 **Analyzing Your College's Budget** Obtain a copy of your college or university's budget and actual results for the most recently completed year.

Required

1. Determine the major assumptions used in the last budget (e.g., number of students; tuition per student; number of employees; increases in wages, salaries, benefits; changes in occupancy costs; etc.).
2. Compare the budgeted revenue amounts with the actual results. Try to determine the reasons for any differences.
3. Compare budgeted expenses with the actual results. Try to determine the reasons for any differences.

IE11–34 **Talk with a Controller about Overhead Analysis** Use an online yellow pages directory such as www.comfind.com, www.athand.com, or home.netscape.com/netcenter/yellowpages.html?cp=ntserch to find a business or nonprofit organization in your area with a web site. Find out as much as you can about the organization's operations from its web site.

Required

Make an appointment with the controller or chief financial officer of the organization you have identified. In the meeting, find out the answers to the following questions:

1. Are actual overhead costs compared to a static budget, to a flexible budget, or to something else?
2. Does the organization distinguish between variable and fixed overhead costs in its performance reports?
3. What are the consequences of an unfavorable variance? Of a favorable variance?

Chapter Twelve
Segment Reporting and Decentralization

Business Focus

E & A Company (the name has been changed to conceal the company's true identity) provides a wide range of engineering and architectural consulting services to both government and industry. For many years, the company pooled all operating costs and allocated them to its three branch offices on the basis of labor cost. When it abandoned this practice and started tracing costs such as rent directly to the offices, while at the same time assigning other costs on a more appropriate basis, the reported profits of one branch office doubled, the reported profits of another branch office changed from a loss to a profit, and the reported profits of the third branch office changed from a profit to a loss.

Source: Beth M. Chaffman and John Talbott, "Activity-Based Costing in a Service Organization," CMA *64, no. 10 (December/January 1991), p. 18.*

Learning Objectives

After studying Chapter 12, you should be able to:

1 Differentiate between cost centers, profit centers, and investment centers, and explain how performance is measured in each.

2 Prepare a segmented income statement using the contribution format, and explain the difference between traceable fixed costs and common fixed costs.

3 Identify three business practices that hinder proper cost assignment.

4 Compute the return on investment (ROI).

5 Show how changes in sales, expenses, and assets affect an organization's ROI.

6 Compute residual income and understand the strengths and weaknesses of this method of measuring performance.

7 (Appendix 12A) Determine the range, if any, within which a negotiated transfer price should fall.

Once an organization grows beyond a few people, it becomes impossible for the top manager to make decisions about everything. For example, the CEO of the Hyatt Hotel chain cannot be expected to decide whether a particular hotel guest at the Hyatt Hotel on Maui should be allowed to check out later than the normal checkout time. To some degree, managers have to delegate decisions to those who are at lower levels in the organization. However, the degree to which decisions are delegated varies from organization to organization.

Decentralization in Organizations

A **decentralized organization** is one in which decision making is not confined to a few top executives but rather is spread throughout the organization, with managers at various levels making key operating decisions relating to their sphere of responsibility. Decentralization is a matter of degree, since all organizations are decentralized to some extent out of necessity. At one extreme, a strongly decentralized organization is one in which there are few, if any, constraints on the freedom of even the lowest-level managers and employees to make decisions. At the other extreme, in a strongly centralized organization, lower-level managers have little freedom to make a decision. Although most organizations fall somewhere between these two extremes, there is a pronounced trend toward more and more decentralization.

Advantages and Disadvantages of Decentralization

Decentralization has many benefits, including:

1. Top management is relieved of much day-to-day problem solving and is left free to concentrate on strategy, on higher-level decision making, and on coordinating activities.
2. Decentralization provides lower-level managers with vital experience in making decisions. Without such experience, they would be ill-prepared to make decisions when they are promoted into higher-level positions.
3. Added responsibility and decision-making authority often result in increased job satisfaction. It makes the job more interesting and provides greater incentives for people to put out their best efforts.
4. Lower-level managers generally have more detailed and up-to-date information about conditions in their own area of responsibility than top managers. Therefore, the decisions of lower-level managers are often based on better information.
5. It is difficult to evaluate a manager's performance if the manager is not given much latitude in what he or she can do.

Decentralization has four major disadvantages:

1. Lower-level managers may make decisions without fully understanding the "big picture." While top-level managers typically have less detailed information about operations than the lower-level managers, they usually have more information about the company as a whole and may have a better understanding of the company's strategy. This situation can be avoided to some extent with the use of modern management information systems that can, in principle, give every manager at every level the same information that goes to the CEO and other top-level managers.

2. In a truly decentralized organization, there may be a lack of coordination among autonomous managers. This problem can be reduced by clearly defining the company's strategy and communicating it effectively throughout the organization.
3. Lower-level managers may have objectives that are different from the objectives of the entire organization. For example, some managers may be more interested in increasing the sizes of their departments than in increasing the profits of the company.[1] To some degree, this problem can be overcome by designing performance evaluation systems that motivate managers to make decisions that are in the best interests of the company.
4. In a strongly decentralized organization, it may be more difficult to effectively spread innovative ideas. Someone in one part of the organization may have a terrific idea that would benefit other parts of the organization, but without strong central direction the idea may not be shared with and adopted by other parts of the organization.

Decentralization and Segment Reporting

Effective decentralization requires *segmental reporting.* In addition to the company-wide income statement, reports are needed for individual segments of the organization. A **segment** is a part or activity of an organization about which managers would like cost, revenue, or profit data. Examples of segments include divisions of a company, sales territories, individual stores, service centers, manufacturing plants, marketing departments, individual customers, and product lines. As we shall see, a company's operations can be segmented in many ways. For example, a grocery store chain like Safeway or Kroger's can segment their businesses by geographic region, by individual store, by the nature of the merchandise (i.e., green groceries, canned goods, paper goods), by brand name, and so on. In this chapter, we learn how to construct income statements for such business segments. These segmented income statements are useful in analyzing the profitability of segments and in measuring the performance of segment managers.

Cost, Profit, and Investment Centers

objective 1

Differentiate between cost centers, profit centers, and investment centers, and explain how performance is measured in each.

Decentralized companies typically categorize their business segments into cost centers, profit centers, and investment centers—depending on the responsibilities of the managers of the segments.[2]

COST CENTER A **cost center** is a business segment whose manager has control over costs but not over revenue or investment funds. Service departments such as

1. There is a similar problem with top-level managers as well. The shareholders of the company have, in effect, decentralized by delegating their decision-making authority to the top managers. Unfortunately, top managers may abuse that trust by spending too much company money on palatial offices, rewarding themselves and their friends too generously, and so on. The issue of how to ensure that top managers act in the best interests of the owners of the company continues to puzzle experts. To a large extent, the owners rely on performance evaluation using return on investment and residual income measures as discussed later in the chapter and on bonuses and stock options. The stock market is also an important disciplining mechanism. If top managers squander the company's resources, the price of the company's stock will almost surely fall—resulting in a loss of prestige, bonuses, and possibly a job.
2. Some companies classify business segments that are responsible mainly for generating revenue, such as an insurance sales office, as *revenue centers.* Other companies would consider this to be just another type of profit center, since costs of some kind (salaries, rent, utilities) are usually deducted from the revenues in the segment's income statement.

accounting, finance, general administration, legal, personnel, and so on, are usually considered to be cost centers. In addition, manufacturing facilities are often considered to be cost centers. The managers of cost centers are expected to minimize cost while providing the level of services or the amount of products demanded by the other parts of the organization. For example, the manager of a production facility would be evaluated at least in part by comparing actual costs to how much the costs should have been for the actual number of units produced during the period.

PROFIT CENTER In contrast to a cost center, a **profit center** is any business segment whose manager has control over both cost and revenue. Like a cost center, however, a profit center generally does not have control over investment funds. For example, the manager in charge of one of the Six Flags amusement parks would be responsible for both the revenues and costs, and hence the profits, of the amusement park but may not have control over major investments in the park. Profit center managers are often evaluated by comparing actual profit to targeted or budgeted profit.

INVESTMENT CENTER An **investment center** is any segment of an organization whose manager has control over cost, revenue, and investments in operating assets. For example, the vice president of the Truck Division at General Motors would have a great deal of discretion over investments in the division. The vice president of the Truck Division would be responsible for initiating investment proposals, such as funding research into more fuel-efficient engines for sport-utility vehicles. Once the proposal has been approved by the top level of managers at General Motors and the board of directors, the vice president of the Truck Division would then be responsible for making sure that the investment pays off. Investment center managers are usually evaluated using return on investment or residual income measures as discussed later in the chapter.

Responsibility Centers

Responsibility center is broadly defined as any part of an organization whose manager has control over cost, revenue, or investment funds. Cost centers, profit centers, and investment centers are *all* known as responsibility centers.

objective 2

Prepare a segmented income statement using the contribution format, and explain the difference between traceable fixed costs and common fixed costs.

A partial organization chart for Universal Foods Corporation, a company in the snack food and beverage industry, appears in Exhibit 12–1. This partial organization chart indicates how the various business segments of the company are classified in terms of responsibility. Note that the cost centers are the departments and work centers that do not generate significant revenues by themselves. These are staff departments such as finance, legal, and personnel, and operating units such as the bottling plant, warehouse, and beverage distribution center. The profit centers are business segments that generate revenues and include the beverage, salty snacks, and confections product segments. The vice president of operations oversees allocation of investment funds across the product segments and is responsible for revenues and costs and so is treated as an investment center. And finally, corporate headquarters is an investment center, since it is responsible for all revenues, costs, and investments.

Segment Reporting and Profitability Analysis

As previously discussed, a different kind of income statement is required for evaluating the performance of business segments—an income statement that emphasizes segments rather than the performance of the company as a whole. This point is illustrated in the following discussion.

Exhibit 12–1 Business Segments Classified as Cost, Profit, and Investment Centers

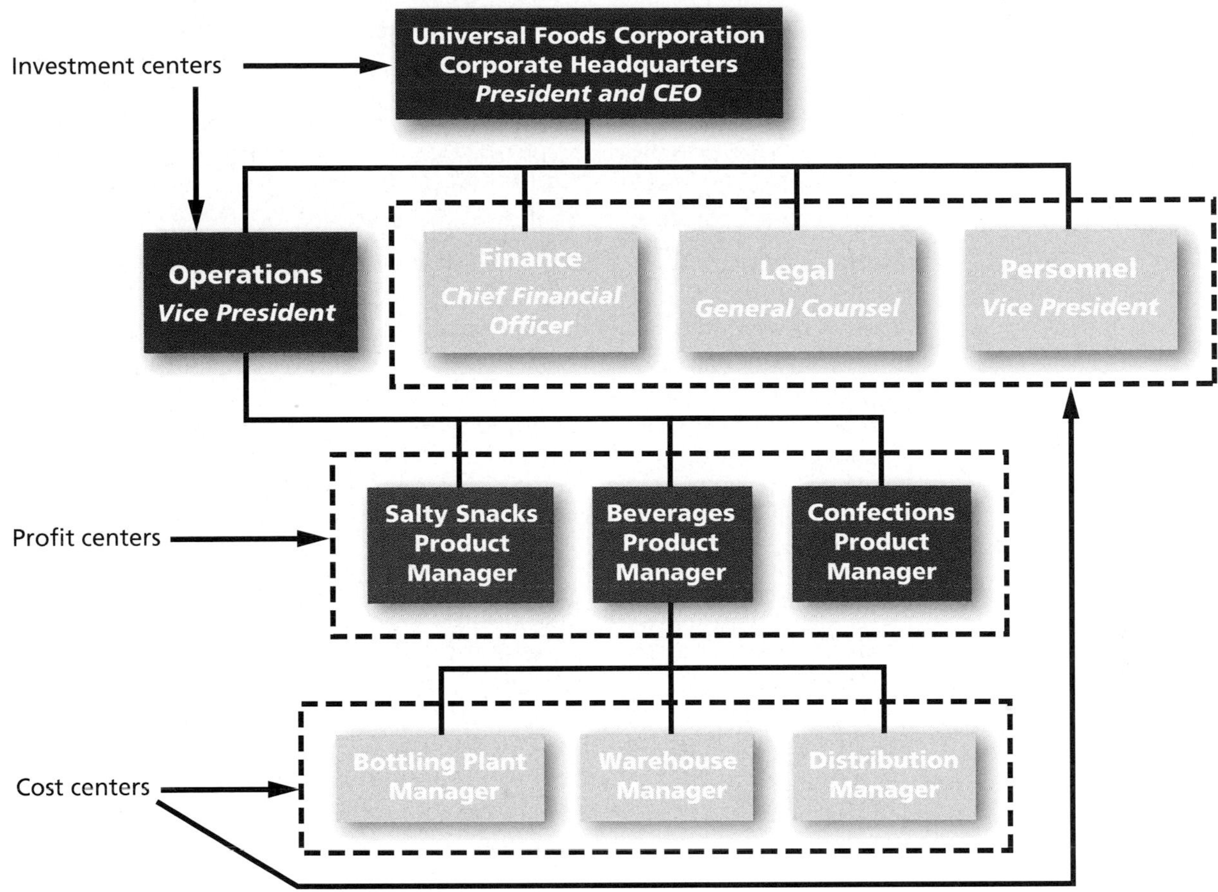

Managerial Accounting in Action

THE ISSUE

softsolutionsinc.

SoftSolutions, Inc., is a rapidly growing computer software company founded by Lori Saffer, who had previously worked in a large software company, and Marjorie Matsuo, who had previously worked in the hotel industry as a general manager. They formed the company to develop and market user-friendly accounting and operations software designed specifically for hotels. They quit their jobs, pooled their savings, hired several programmers, and got down to work.

The first sale was by far the most difficult. No hotel wanted to be the first to use an untested product from an unknown company. After overcoming this obstacle with persistence, good luck, dedication to customer service, and a very low introductory price, the company's sales burgeoned.

The company quickly developed similar business software for other specialized markets and then branched out into clip art and computer games. Within four years of its founding, the organization had grown to the point where Saffer and Matsuo were no longer able to personally direct all of the company's activities. Decentralization had become a necessity.

Accordingly, the company was split into two divisions—Business Products and Consumer Products. By mutual consent, Matsuo took the title president and Saffer took the title vice president of the Business Products

Division. Chris Worden, a programmer who had spearheaded the drive into the clip art and computer games markets, was designated vice president of the Consumer Products Division.

Almost immediately, the issue arose of how best to evaluate the performance of the divisions. Matsuo called a meeting to consider this issue and asked Saffer, Worden, and the controller, Bill Carson, to attend. The following discussion took place at that meeting:

Marjorie Matsuo: We need to find a better way to measure the performance of the divisions.
Chris Worden: I agree. Consumer Products has been setting the pace in this company for the last two years, and we should be getting more recognition.
Lori Saffer: Chris, we are delighted with the success of the Consumer Products Division.
Chris Worden: I know. But it is hard to figure out just how successful we are with the present accounting reports. All we have are sales and cost of goods sold figures for the division.
Bill Carson: What's the matter with those figures? They are prepared using generally accepted accounting principles.
Chris Worden: The sales figures are fine. However, cost of goods sold includes some costs that really aren't the costs of our division, and it excludes some costs that are. Let's take a simple example. Everything we sell in the Consumer Products Division has to pass through the automatic bar-coding machine, which applies a unique bar code to the product.
Lori Saffer: We know. Every item we ship must have a unique identifying bar code. That's true for items from the Business Products Division as well as for items from the Consumer Products Division.
Chris Worden: That's precisely the point. Whether an item comes from the Business Products Division or the Consumer Products Division, it must pass through the automatic bar-coding machine after the software has been packaged. How much of the cost of the automatic bar coder would be saved if we didn't have any consumer products?
Marjorie Matsuo: Since we have only one automatic bar coder and we would need it anyway to code the business products, I guess none of the cost would be saved.
Chris Worden: That's right. And since none of the cost could be saved even if the entire Consumer Products Division were eliminated, how can we logically say that some of the cost of the automatic bar coder is a cost of the Consumer Products Division?
Lori Saffer: Just a minute, Chris, are you saying that my Business Products Division should be charged with the entire cost of the automatic bar coder?
Chris Worden: No, that's not what I am saying.
Marjorie Matsuo: But Chris, I don't see how we can have sensible performance reports without making someone responsible for costs like the cost of the automatic bar coder. Bill, as our accounting expert, what do you think?
Bill Carson: I have some ideas for handling issues like the automatic bar coder. The best approach would probably be for me to put together a draft performance report. We can discuss it at the next meeting when everyone has something concrete to look at.
Marjorie Matsuo: Okay, let's see what you come up with. ■

Bill Carson, the controller of SoftSolutions, realized that segmented income statements would be required to more appropriately evaluate the performance of the two divisions. To construct the segmented reports, he would have to carefully segregate costs that are attributable to the two divisions from costs that are not. Since most of the disputes over costs would be about fixed costs such as the automatic bar-coding machine, he knew he would also have to separate fixed from variable costs. Under the conventional absorption costing income statement prepared for the entire company, variable and fixed production costs were being commingled in the cost of goods sold.

Largely for these reasons, Bill Carson decided to use the contribution format income statement discussed in earlier chapters. Recall that when the contribution format is used: (1) the cost of goods sold consists only of the variable manufacturing costs; (2) the variable and fixed costs are listed in separate sections; and (3) a contribution margin is computed. When such a statement is segmented as in this chapter, fixed costs are broken down further into what are called traceable and common costs as discussed later. This breakdown allows a *segment margin* to be computed for each segment of the company. The segment margin is a valuable tool for assessing the long-run profitability of a segment and is also a much better tool for evaluating performance than the usual absorption costing reports.

Levels of Segmented Statements

A portion of the segmented report Bill Carson prepared is shown in Exhibit 12–2. The contribution format income statement for the entire company appears at the very top of the exhibit under the column labeled Total Company. Immediately to the right of this column are two columns—one for each of the two divisions. We can see that the divisional segment margin is $60,000 for the Business Products Division and $40,000 for the Consumer Products Division. This is the portion of the report that was specifically requested by the company's divisional managers. They wanted to know how much each of their divisions was contributing to the company's profits.

However, segmented income statements can be prepared for activities at many levels in a company. To provide more information to the company's divisional managers, Bill Carson has further segmented the divisions according to their major product lines. In the case of the Consumer Products Division, the product lines are clip art and computer games. Going even further, Bill Carson has segmented each of the product lines according to how they are sold—in retail computer stores or by catalog sales. In Exhibit 12–2, this further segmentation is illustrated for the computer games product line. Notice that as we go from one segmented statement to another, we look at smaller and smaller pieces of the company. While not shown in Exhibit 12–2, Bill Carson also prepared segmented income statements for the major product lines in the Business Products Division.

Substantial benefits are received from a series of statements such as those contained in Exhibit 12–2. By carefully examining trends and results in each segment, a manager is able to gain considerable insight into the company's operations viewed from many different angles. And advanced computer-based information systems are making it easier and easier to construct such statements and to keep them continuously current.

Sales and Contribution Margin

To prepare an income statement for a particular segment, variable expenses are deducted from the sales to yield the contribution margin for the segment. It is important to keep in mind that the contribution margin tells us what happens to profits as volume changes—holding a segment's capacity and fixed costs constant. The contribution margin is especially useful in decisions involving temporary uses of capacity such as special orders.

Exhibit 12–2
SoftSolutions, Inc.—Segmented Income Statements in the Contribution Format

Segments Defined as Divisions

	Total Company	Divisions: Business Products Division	Divisions: Consumer Products Division
Sales	$500,000	$300,000	$200,000
Less variable expenses:			
Variable cost of goods sold	180,000	120,000	60,000
Other variable expenses	50,000	30,000	20,000
Total variable expenses	230,000	150,000	80,000
Contribution margin	270,000	150,000	120,000
Less traceable fixed expenses	170,000	90,000	80,000*
Divisional segment margin	100,000	$ 60,000	$ 40,000
Less common fixed expenses not traceable to the individual divisions	85,000		
Net income	$ 15,000		

Segments Defined as Product Lines of the Consumer Products Division

	Consumer Products Division	Product Line: Clip Art	Product Line: Computer Games
Sales	$200,000	$ 75,000	$125,000
Less variable expenses:			
Variable cost of goods sold	60,000	20,000	40,000
Other variable expenses	20,000	5,000	15,000
Total variable expenses	80,000	25,000	55,000
Contribution margin	120,000	50,000	70,000
Less traceable fixed expenses	70,000	30,000	40,000
Product-line segment margin	50,000	$ 20,000	$ 30,000
Less common fixed expenses not traceable to the individual product lines	10,000		
Divisional segment margin	$ 40,000		

Segments Defined as Sales Channels for One Product Line, Computer Games, of the Consumer Products Division

	Computer Games	Sales Channels: Retail Stores	Sales Channels: Catalog Sales
Sales	$125,000	$100,000	$ 25,000
Less variable expenses:			
Variable cost of goods sold	40,000	32,000	8,000
Other variable expenses	15,000	5,000	10,000
Total variable expenses	55,000	37,000	18,000
Contribution margin	70,000	63,000	7,000
Less traceable fixed expenses	25,000	15,000	10,000
Sales-channel segment margin	45,000	$ 48,000	$ (3,000)
Less common fixed expenses not traceable to the individual sales channels	15,000		
Product-line segment margin	$ 30,000		

*Notice that this $80,000 in traceable fixed expense is divided into two parts—$70,000 traceable and $10,000 common—when the Consumer Products Division is broken down into product lines. The reasons for this are discussed later under Traceable Costs Can Become Common Costs.

Decisions concerning the most effective uses of existing capacity often involve only variable costs and revenues, which of course are the very elements involved in contribution margin. Such decisions will be discussed in detail in Chapter 13.

Traceable and Common Fixed Costs

The most puzzling aspect of Exhibit 12–2 is probably the treatment of fixed costs. The report has two kinds of fixed costs—traceable and common. Only the *traceable fixed costs* are charged to the segments in the segmented income statements in the report. If a cost is not traceable to a segment, then it is not assigned to the segment.

A **traceable fixed cost** of a segment is a fixed cost that is incurred because of the existence of the segment—if the segment had never existed, the fixed cost would not have been incurred; and/or if the segment were eliminated, the fixed cost would disappear. Examples of traceable fixed costs include the following:

- The salary of the Fritos product manager at PepsiCo is a *traceable* fixed cost of the Fritos business segment of PepsiCo.
- The maintenance cost for the building in which Boeing 747s are assembled is a *traceable* fixed cost of the 747 business segment of Boeing.
- The liability insurance at Disney World is a *traceable* fixed cost of the Disney World business segment of the Disney Corporation.

A **common fixed cost** is a fixed cost that supports the operations of more than one segment but is not traceable in whole or in part to any one segment. Even if a segment were entirely eliminated, there would be no change in a true common fixed cost. Note the following:

- The salary of the CEO of General Motors is a *common* fixed cost of the various divisions of General Motors.
- The cost of the automatic bar-coding machine at SoftSolutions is a *common* fixed cost of the Consumer Products Division and of the Business Products Division.
- The cost of the receptionist's salary at an office shared by a number of doctors is a *common* fixed cost of the doctors. The cost is traceable to the office, but not to any one of the doctors individually.

IDENTIFYING TRACEABLE FIXED COSTS The distinction between traceable and common fixed costs is crucial in segment reporting, since traceable fixed costs are charged to the segments, whereas common fixed costs are not. In an actual situation, it is sometimes hard to determine whether a cost should be classified as traceable or common.

The general guideline is to treat as traceable costs *only those costs that would disappear over time if the segment itself disappeared.* For example, if the Consumer Products Division were sold or discontinued, it would no longer be necessary to pay the division manager's salary. Therefore the division manager's salary should be classified as a traceable fixed cost of the division. On the other hand, the president of the company undoubtedly would continue to be paid even if the Consumer Products Division were dropped. In fact, he or she might even be paid more if dropping the division was a good idea. Therefore, the president's salary is common to both divisions. The same idea can be expressed in another way: *treat as traceable costs only those costs that are added as a result of the creation of a segment.*

ACTIVITY-BASED COSTING Some costs are easy to identify as traceable costs. For example, the costs of advertising Crest toothpaste on television are clearly traceable to Crest. A more difficult situation arises when a building, machine, or other resource is shared by two or more segments. For example, assume that a multiproduct company leases warehouse space that is used for storing the full range of its products. Would the lease cost of the warehouse be a traceable or a common cost of the products? Managers familiar with activity-based costing might argue that the lease cost is traceable and should be assigned to the products according to how much space the products use in the warehouse. In like manner, these managers would argue that order processing costs, sales support costs, and other selling, general, and administrative (SG&A) expenses should also be charged to segments according to the segments' consumption of SG&A resources.

To illustrate, consider Holt Corporation, a company that manufactures concrete pipe for industrial uses. The company has three products—9-inch pipe, 12-inch pipe, and 18-inch pipe. Space is leased in a large warehouse on a yearly basis as needed. The lease cost of this space is $4 per square foot per year. The 9-inch pipe occupies 1,000 square feet of space, 12-inch pipe occupies 4,000 square feet, and 18-inch pipe occupies 5,000 square feet. The company also has an order processing department that incurred $150,000 in order processing costs last year. Management believes that order processing costs are driven by the number of orders placed by customers in a year. Last year 2,500 orders were placed, of which 1,200 were for 9-inch pipe, 800 were for 12-inch pipe, and 500 were for 18-inch pipe. Given these data, the following costs would be assigned to each product using the activity-based costing approach:

Warehouse space cost:	
9-inch pipe: $4 × 1,000 square feet	$ 4,000
12-inch pipe: $4 × 4,000 square feet	16,000
18-inch pipe: $4 × 5,000 square feet	20,000
Total cost assigned	$ 40,000
Order processing costs:	
$150,000 ÷ 2,500 orders = $60 per order	
9-inch pipe: $60 × 1,200 orders	$ 72,000
12-inch pipe: $60 × 800 orders	48,000
18-inch pipe: $60 × 500 orders	30,000
Total cost assigned	$150,000

This method of assigning costs combines the strength of activity-based costing with the power of the contribution approach and greatly enhances the manager's ability to measure the profitability and performance of segments. However, managers must still ask themselves if the costs would in fact disappear over time if the segment itself disappeared. In the case of Holt Corporation, it is clear that the $20,000 in warehousing costs for the 18-inch pipe would be eliminated if 18-inch pipes were no longer being produced. The company would simply rent less warehouse space the following year. However, suppose the company owns the warehouse. Then it is not so clear that $20,000 of the cost of the warehouse would really disappear if the 18-inch pipes were discontinued as a product. The company might be able to sublease the space, or use it for other products, but then again the space might simply be empty while the costs of the warehouse continue to be incurred.

In assigning costs to segments, the key point is to resist the temptation to allocate costs (such as depreciation of corporate facilities) that are clearly common in nature and that would continue regardless of whether the segment exists or not. *Any allocation of common costs to segments will reduce the value of the segment margin as a guide to long-run segment profitability and segment performance.* This point will be discussed at length later in the chapter.

Traceable Costs Can Become Common Costs

Fixed costs that are traceable to one segment may be a common cost of another segment. For example, an airline might want a segmented income statement that shows the segment margin for a particular flight from Los Angeles to Paris, further broken

Exhibit 12–3
Reclassification of Traceable Fixed Expenses from Exhibit 12–2.

	Total Company	Segment: Business Products Division	Segment: Consumer Products Division
Contribution margin	$270,000	$150,000	$120,000
Less traceable fixed expenses	170,000	90,000	80,000

	Consumer Products Division	Segment: Clip Art	Segment: Computer Games
Contribution margin	$120,000	$50,000	$70,000
Less traceable fixed expenses	70,000	30,000	40,000
Product-line segment margin	50,000	$20,000	$30,000
Less common fixed expenses	10,000		
Divisional segment margin	$ 40,000		

down into first-class, business-class, and economy-class segment margins. The airline must pay a substantial landing fee at Charles DeGaulle airport in Paris. This fixed landing fee is a traceable cost of the flight, but it is a common cost of the first-class, business-class, and economy-class segments. Even if the first-class cabin is empty, the entire landing fee must be paid. So the landing fee is not a traceable cost of the first-class cabin. But on the other hand, paying the fee is necessary in order to have any first-class, business-class, or economy-class passengers. So the landing fee is a common cost of these three classes.

The dual nature of some of the fixed costs can be seen from the diagram in Exhibit 12–3. Notice from the diagram that when segments are defined as divisions, the Consumer Products Division has $80,000 in traceable fixed expenses. Only $70,000 of this amount remains traceable, however, when we narrow the definition of a segment from divisions to product lines. Notice that the other $10,000 then becomes a common cost of the two product lines of the Consumer Products Division.

Why would $10,000 of traceable fixed cost become a common cost when the division is divided into product lines? The $10,000 is the monthly salary of the manager of the Consumer Products Division. This salary is a traceable cost of the division as a whole, but it is a common cost of the division's product lines. The manager's salary is a necessary cost of having the two product lines, but even if one of the product lines were discontinued entirely, the manager's salary would probably not be cut. Therefore, none of the manager's salary can be really traced to the individual products.

The $70,000 traceable fixed cost of the product lines consists of the costs of product-specific advertising. A total of $30,000 was spent on advertising clip art and $40,000 was spent on advertising computer games. These costs can clearly be traced to the individual product lines.

Segment Margin

Observe from Exhibit 12–2 that the **segment margin** is obtained by deducting the traceable fixed costs of a segment from the segment's contribution margin. It represents the margin available after a segment has covered all of its own costs. *The* *segment margin is the best gauge of the long-run profitability of a segment,* since it includes only those costs that are caused by the segment. If a segment can't cover its own costs, then that segment probably should not be retained (unless it has important side effects on other segments). Notice from Exhibit 12–2, for example, that Catalog Sales has a negative segment margin. This means that the segment is not covering its own costs; it is generating more costs than it collects in revenue.[3]

From a decision-making point of view, the segment margin is most useful in major decisions that affect capacity such as dropping a segment. By contrast, as we noted earlier, the contribution margin is most useful in decisions relating to short-run changes in volume, such as pricing special orders that involve utilization of existing capacity.

Managerial Accounting in Action

THE WRAP-UP

softsolutionsinc.

Shortly after Bill Carson, the SoftSolutions, Inc., controller, completed the draft segmented income statement, he sent copies to the other managers and scheduled a meeting in which the report could be explained. The meeting was held on the Monday following the first meeting; and Marjorie Matsuo, Lori Saffer, and Chris Worden were all in attendance.

Lori Saffer: I think these segmented income statements are fairly self-explanatory. However, there is one thing I wonder about.

Bill Carson: What's that?

Lori Saffer: What is this common fixed expense of $85,000 listed under the total company? And who is going to be responsible for it if neither Chris nor I have responsibility?

Bill Carson: The $85,000 of common fixed expenses represents expenses like general administrative salaries and the costs of common production equipment such as the automatic bar-coding machine. Marjorie, do you want to respond to the question about responsibility for these expenses?

Marjorie Matsuo: Sure. Since I'm the president of the company, I'm responsible for those costs. Some things can be delegated, others cannot be. It wouldn't make any sense for either you or Chris to make decisions about the bar coder, since it affects both of you. That's an important part of my job—making decisions about resources that affect all parts of the organization. This report makes it much clearer who is responsible for what. I like it.

Chris Worden: So do I—my division's segment margin is higher than the net income for the entire company.

Marjorie Matsuo: Don't get carried away, Chris. Let's not misinterpret what this report means. The segment margins *have* to be big to cover the common costs of the company. We can't let the big segment margins lull us into a sense of complacency. If we use these reports, we all have to agree that our objective is to increase all of the segment margins over time.

Lori Saffer: I'm willing to give it a try.

Chris Worden: The reports make sense to me.

Marjorie Matsuo: So be it. Then the first item of business would appear to be a review of catalog sales of computer games, where we appear to be losing money. Chris, could you brief us on this at our next meeting?

Chris Worden: I'd be happy to. I have been suspecting for some time that our catalog sales strategy could be improved.

Marjorie Matsuo: We look forward to hearing your analysis. Meeting's adjourned. ■

---

3. Retention or elimination of product lines and other segments is covered in more depth in Chapter 13.

There Is More Than One Way to Segment a Company

SoftSolutions segmented its sales by division, by product line within each division, and by sales channel. An organization can be segmented in many ways. For example, two different ways of segmenting the sales of the General Electric Company are displayed in Exhibit 12–4. In the first diagram, the company's sales are segmented by geographic region. In the second diagram, they are segmented by products. Note that each of the diagrams could be continued, providing progressively more detailed segment data. For example, the sales in France could be broken down by major product line, then by product. Similar breakdowns could be done of General Electric's costs and segment margins, although that would require substantial additional analytical work to identify the segments to which various costs should be assigned.

Segment breakdowns such as those shown in Exhibit 12–4 give a company's managers the ability to look at the company from many different directions. With the

Exhibit 12–4
General Electric Company's Revenues Segmented by Geographic Region and Products

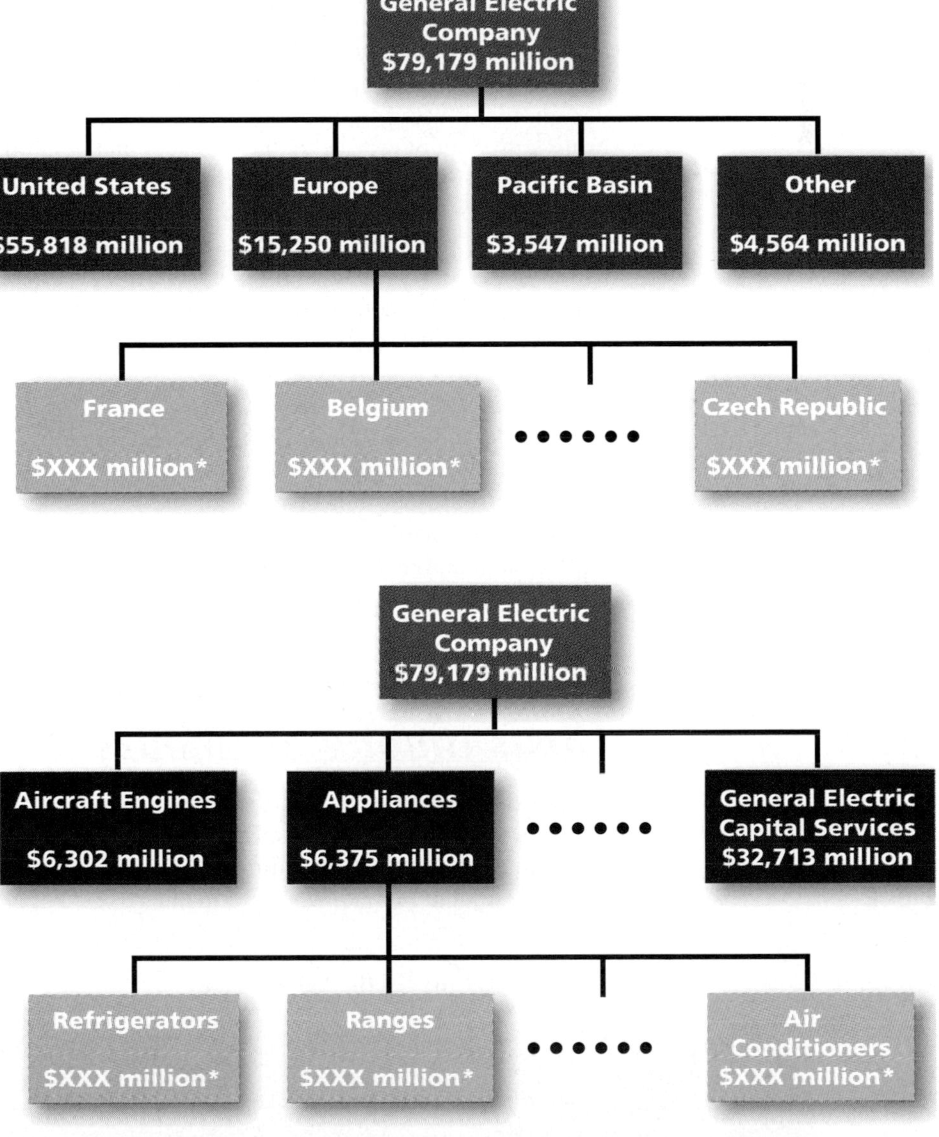

*These sales figures are not publicly disclosed by GE, but they are readily available within the company to managers.

increasing availability of companywide databases and sophisticated management information system software, detailed segmental reports of revenues, costs, and margins are becoming much easier to do.

Hindrances to Proper Cost Assignment

objective 3

Identify three business practices that hinder proper cost assignment.

For segment reporting to accomplish its intended purposes, costs must be properly assigned to segments. If the purpose is to determine the profits being generated by a particular division, then all of the costs attributable to that division—and only those costs—should be assigned to it. Unfortunately, three business practices greatly hinder proper cost assignment: (1) omission of some costs in the assignment process, (2) the use of inappropriate methods for allocating costs among segments of a company, and (3) assignment to segments of costs that are really common costs.

Omission of Costs

The costs assigned to a segment should include all costs attributable to that segment from the company's entire *value chain.* The **value chain,** which is illustrated in Exhibit 12–5, consists of the major business functions that add value to a company's products and services. All of these functions, from research and development, through product design, manufacturing, marketing, distribution, and customer service, are required to bring a product or service to the customer and generate revenues.

However, as discussed in Chapters 2, 3, and 7, only manufacturing costs are included in product costs for financial reporting purposes. Consequently, when trying to determine product profitability for internal decision-making purposes, some companies deduct only manufacturing costs from product revenues. As a result, such companies omit from their profitability analysis part or all of the "upstream" costs in the value chain, which consist of research and development and product design, and the "downstream" costs, which consist of marketing, distribution, and customer service. Yet these nonmanufacturing costs are just as essential in determining product profitability as are the manufacturing costs. These upstream and downstream costs, which are usually titled *Selling, General, and Administrative (SG&A)* on the income statement, can represent half or more of the total costs of an organization. If either the upstream or downstream costs are omitted in profitability analysis, then the product is undercosted and management may unwittingly develop and maintain products that in the long run result in losses rather than profits for the company.

Inappropriate Methods for Allocating Costs among Segments

Cross-subsidization, or cost distortion, occurs when costs are improperly assigned among a company's segments. Cross-subsidization can occur in two ways; first, when companies fail to trace costs directly to segments in those situations where it is feasible to do so; and second, when companies use inappropriate bases to allocate costs.

Exhibit 12–5 Business Functions Making Up the Value Chain

Research and Development	Product Design	Manufacturing	Marketing	Distribution	Customer Service

FAILURE TO TRACE COSTS DIRECTLY Costs that can be traced directly to a specific segment of a company should not be allocated to other segments. Rather, such costs should be charged directly to the responsible segment. For example, the rent for a branch office of an insurance company should be charged directly against the branch to which it relates rather than included in a companywide overhead pool and then spread throughout the company.

INAPPROPRIATE ALLOCATION BASE Some companies allocate costs to segments using arbitrary bases such as sales dollars or cost of goods sold. For example, under the sales dollars approach, costs are allocated to the various segments according to the percentage of company sales generated by each segment. Thus, if a segment generates 20% of total company sales, it would be allocated 20% of the company's SG&A expenses as its "fair share." This same basic procedure is followed if costs of goods sold or some other measure is used as the allocation base.

For this approach to be valid, the allocation base must actually drive the overhead cost. (Or at least the allocation base should be highly correlated with the cost driver of the overhead cost.) For example, when sales dollars is used as the allocation base for SG&A expenses, it is implicitly assumed that SG&A expenses change in proportion to changes in total sales. If that is not true, the SG&A expenses allocated to segments will be misleading.

Arbitrarily Dividing Common Costs among Segments

The third business practice that leads to distorted segment costs is the practice of assigning nontraceable costs to segments. For example, some companies allocate the costs of the corporate headquarters building to products on segment reports. However, in a multiproduct company, no single product is likely to be responsible for any significant amount of this cost. Even if a product were eliminated entirely, there would usually be no significant effect on any of the costs of the corporate headquarters building. In short, there is no cause-and-effect relation between the cost of the corporate headquarters building and the existence of any one product. As a consequence, any allocation of the cost of the corporate headquarters building to the products must be arbitrary.

Common costs like the costs of the corporate headquarters building are necessary, of course, to have a functioning organization. The common practice of arbitrarily allocating these costs to segments is often justified on the grounds that "someone" has to "cover the common costs." While it is undeniably true that the common costs must be covered, arbitrarily allocating common costs to segments does not ensure that this will happen. In fact, adding a share of common costs to the real costs of a segment may make an otherwise profitable segment appear to be unprofitable. If a manager erroneously eliminates the segment, the revenues will be lost, the real costs of the segment will be saved, but the common costs will still be there. The net effect will be to reduce the profits of the company as a whole and make it even more difficult to "cover the common costs."

In sum, the way many companies handle segment reporting results in cost distortion. This distortion results from three practices—the failure to trace costs directly to a specific segment when it is feasible to do so, the use of inappropriate bases for allocating costs, and the allocation of common costs to segments. These practices are widespread. One study found that 60% of the companies surveyed made no attempt to assign SG&A costs to segments on a cause-and-effect basis.[4]

4. James R. Emore and Joseph A. Ness, "The Slow Pace of Meaningful Change in Cost Systems," *Journal of Cost Management* 4, no. 4 (Winter 1991), p. 39.

Focus on Current Practice

Segment profits can be seriously distorted by arbitrary allocations of common fixed costs. Steven Spielberg, the legendary movie producer and director, learned this lesson early in his career. Spielberg's contract with Columbia Pictures for *Close Encounters of the Third Kind* stipulated that he would receive 17.5% of the profits from the film. But even though the film grossed over $300 million at the box office, he ended up with only about $5 million. "Spielberg was discovering the first rule of Hollywood accounting: Even the biggest hits show very little 'profit' after overhead, interest and distribution fees are generously factored in . . . So he went to Universal and to Warner Bros. and negotiated the basic deal that he still uses today: a cut of the revenues so that he makes out even if the film doesn't make any money or if the studio inflates the costs; some control over the accounting so profits show up as profits; and half the earnings." With such a deal, Spielberg is believed to have made over $250 million from *Jurassic Park*.[5] ■

Rate of Return for Measuring Managerial Performance

objective 4

Compute the return on investment (ROI).

When a company is truly decentralized, segment managers are given a great deal of autonomy. So great is this autonomy that the various profit and investment centers are often viewed as being virtually independent businesses, with their managers having about the same control over decisions as if they were in fact running their own independent firms. With this autonomy, fierce competition often develops among managers, with each striving to make his or her segment the "best" in the company.

Competition between investment centers is particularly keen for investment funds. How do top managers in corporate headquarters go about deciding who gets new investment funds as they become available, and how do these managers decide which investment centers are most profitably using the funds that have already been entrusted to their care? One of the most popular ways of making these judgments is to measure the rate of return that investment center managers are able to generate on their assets. This rate of return is called the *return on investment (ROI).*

The Return on Investment (ROI) Formula

The **return on investment (ROI)** is defined as net operating income divided by average operating assets:

$$\text{ROI} = \frac{\text{Net operating income}}{\text{Average operating assets}}$$

5. Randall Lane, "I Want Gross," *Forbes,* September 26, 1994, pp. 104–8.

There are some issues about how to measure net operating income and average operating assets, but this formula seems clear enough. The higher the return on investment (ROI) of a business segment, the greater the profit generated per dollar invested in the segment's operating assets.

Net Operating Income and Operating Assets Defined

Note that *net operating income,* rather than net income, is used in the ROI formula. **Net operating income** is income before interest and taxes and is sometimes referred to as EBIT (earnings before interest and taxes). The reason for using net operating income in the formula is that the income figure used should be consistent with the base to which it is applied. Notice that the base (i.e., denominator) consists of *operating assets.* Thus, to be consistent we use net operating income in the numerator.

Operating assets include cash, accounts receivable, inventory, plant and equipment, and all other assets held for productive use in the organization. Examples of assets that would not be included in the operating assets category, (i.e., examples of nonoperating assets) would include land held for future use, an investment in another company, or a factory building rented to someone else. The operating assets base used in the formula is typically computed as the average of the operating assets between the beginning and the end of the year.

Plant and Equipment: Net Book Value or Gross Cost?

A major issue in ROI computations is the dollar amount of plant and equipment that should be included in the operating assets base. To illustrate the problem involved, assume that a company reports the following amounts for plant and equipment on its balance sheet:

Plant and equipment	$3,000,000
Less accumulated depreciation	900,000
Net book value	$2,100,000

What dollar amount of plant and equipment should the company include with its operating assets in computing ROI? One widely used approach is to include only the plant and equipment's *net book value*—that is, the plant's original cost less accumulated depreciation ($2,100,000 in the example above). A second approach is to ignore depreciation and include the plant's entire *gross cost* in the operating assets base ($3,000,000 in the example above). Both of these approaches are used in actual practice, even though they will obviously yield very different operating asset and ROI figures.

The following arguments can be raised for using net book value to measure operating assets and for using gross cost to measure operating assets in ROI computation:

Arguments for Using Net Book Value to Measure Operating Assets in ROI Computations:

1. The net book value method is consistent with how plant and equipment are reported on the balance sheet (i.e., cost less accumulated depreciation to date).
2. The net book value method is consistent with the computation of operating income, which includes depreciation as an operating expense.

Arguments for Using Gross Cost to Measure Operating Assets in ROI Computations:

1. The gross cost method eliminates both the age of equipment and the method of depreciation as factors in ROI computations. (Under the net book value method, ROI will tend to increase over time as net book value declines due to depreciation.)
2. The gross cost method does not discourage replacement of old, worn-out equipment. (Under the net book value method, replacing fully depreciated equipment with new equipment can have a dramatic, adverse effect on ROI.)

Managers generally view consistency as the most important of the considerations above. As a result, a majority of companies use the net book value approach in ROI computations. In this text, we will also use the net book value approach unless a specific exercise or problem directs otherwise.

Controlling the Rate of Return

objective 5

Show how changes in sales, expenses, and assets affect an organization's ROI.

When we first defined the return on investment, we used the following formula:

$$\text{ROI} = \frac{\text{Net operating income}}{\text{Average operating assets}}$$

We can modify this formula slightly by introducing sales as follows:

$$\text{ROI} = \frac{\text{Net operating income}}{\text{Sales}} \times \frac{\text{Sales}}{\text{Average operating assets}}$$

The first term on the right-hand side of the equation is the *margin,* which is defined as follows:

$$\text{Margin} = \frac{\text{Net operating income}}{\text{Sales}}$$

The **margin** is a measure of management's ability to control operating expenses in relation to sales. The lower the operating expenses per dollar of sales, the higher the margin earned.

The second term on the right-hand side of the preceding equation is *turnover* which is defined as follows:

$$\text{Turnover} = \frac{\text{Sales}}{\text{Average operating assets}}$$

Turnover is a measure of the sales that are generated for each dollar invested in operating assets.

The following alternative form of the ROI formula, which we will use most frequently, combines margin and turnover:

$$\text{ROI} = \text{Margin} \times \text{Turnover}$$

Exhibit 12–6 Elements of Return on Investment (ROI)

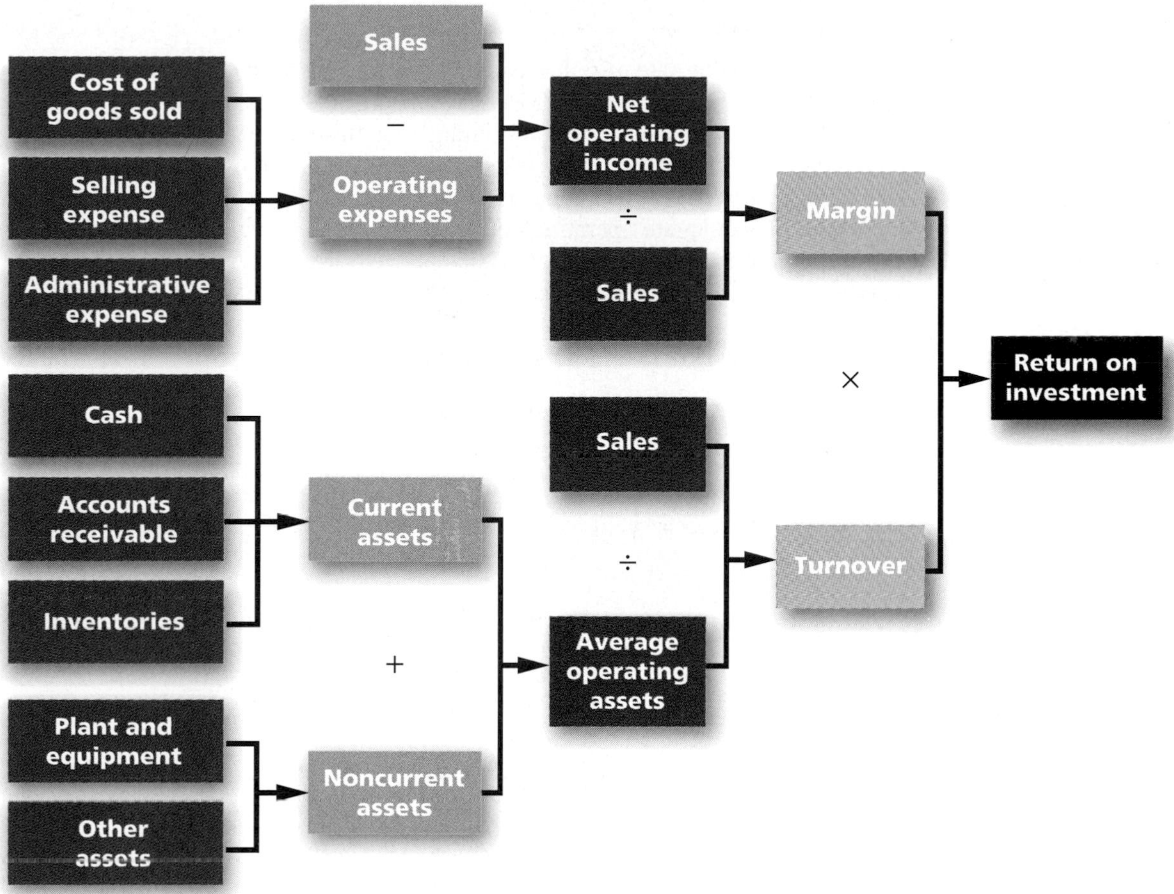

Which formula for ROI should be used—the original one stated in terms of net operating income and average operating assets or this one stated in terms of margin and turnover? Either can be used—they will always give the same answer. However, the margin and turnover formulation provides some additional insights.

Some managers tend to focus too much on margin and ignore turnover. To some degree at least, the margin can be a valuable indicator of a manager's performance. Standing alone, however, it overlooks one very crucial area of a manager's responsibility—the investment in operating assets. Excessive funds tied up in operating assets, which depresses turnover, can be just as much of a drag on profitability as excessive operating expenses, which depresses margin. One of the advantages of ROI as a performance measure is that it forces the manager to control the investment in operating assets as well as to control expenses and the margin.

Du Pont pioneered the ROI concept and recognized the importance of looking at both margin and turnover in assessing the performance of a manager. The ROI formula is now widely used as the key measure of the performance of an investment center. The ROI formula blends together many aspects of the manager's responsibilities into a single figure that can be compared to the returns of competing investment centers, the returns of other firms in the industry, and to the past returns of the investment center itself.

Du Pont also developed the diagram that appears in Exhibit 12–6. This exhibit helps managers understand how they can control ROI. An investment center manager can increase ROI in basically three ways:

1. Increase sales.
2. Reduce expenses.
3. Reduce assets.

To illustrate how the rate of return can be improved by each of these three actions, consider how the manager of the Monthaven Burger Grill is evaluated. Burger Grill is a small chain of upscale casual restaurants that has been rapidly adding outlets via franchising. The Monthaven franchise is owned by a group of local surgeons who have little time to devote to management and little expertise in business matters. Therefore, they delegate operating decisions—including decisions concerning investment in operating assets such as inventories—to a professional manager they have hired. The manager is evaluated largely based on the ROI the franchise generates.

The following data represent the results of operations for the most recent month:

Net operating income	\$ 10,000
Sales	100,000
Average operating assets	50,000

The rate of return generated by the Monthaven Burger Grill investment center is as follows:

$$\text{ROI} = \text{Margin} \times \text{Turnover}$$

$$\frac{\text{Net operating income}}{\text{Sales}} \times \frac{\text{Sales}}{\text{Average operating assets}}$$

$$\frac{\$10{,}000}{\$100{,}000} \times \frac{\$100{,}000}{\$50{,}000}$$

$$10\% \times 2 = 20\%$$

As we stated above, to improve the ROI figure, the manager can (1) increase sales, (2) reduce expenses, or (3) reduce the operating assets.

APPROACH 1: INCREASE SALES Assume that the manager of the Monthaven Burger Grill is able to increase sales from \$100,000 to \$110,000. Assume further that either because of good cost control or because some costs in the company are fixed, the net operating income increases even more rapidly, going from \$10,000 to \$12,000 per period. The operating assets remain constant.

$$\text{ROI} = \frac{\$12{,}000}{\$110{,}000} \times \frac{\$110{,}000}{\$50{,}000}$$

$$10.91\% \times 2.2 = 24\% \text{ (as compared to 20\% above)}$$

APPROACH 2: REDUCE EXPENSES Assume that the manager of the Monthaven Burger Grill is able to reduce expenses by \$1,000 so that net operating income increases from \$10,000 to \$11,000. Both sales and operating assets remain constant.

$$\text{ROI} = \frac{\$11{,}000}{\$100{,}000} \times \frac{\$100{,}000}{\$50{,}000}$$

$$11\% \times 2 = 22\% \text{ (as compared to 20\% above)}$$

APPROACH 3: REDUCE ASSETS Assume that the manager of the Monthaven Burger Grill is able to reduce operating assets from \$50,000 to \$40,000. Sales and net operating income remain unchanged.

$$\text{ROI} = \frac{\$10{,}000}{\$100{,}000} \times \frac{\$100{,}000}{\$40{,}000}$$

$$10\% \quad \times \quad 2.5 \quad = 25\% \text{ (as compared to 20\% above)}$$

A clear understanding of these three approaches to improving the ROI figure is critical to the effective management of an investment center. We will now look at each approach in more detail.

Increase Sales

In first looking at the ROI formula, one is inclined to think that the sales figure is neutral, since it appears as the denominator in the margin computation and as the numerator in the turnover computation. We *could* cancel out the sales figure, but we don't do so for two reasons. First, this would tend to draw attention away from the fact that the rate of return is a function of *two* variables, margin and turnover. And second, it would tend to conceal the fact that a change in sales can affect both the margin and the turnover in an organization. To explain, a change in sales can affect the *margin* if expenses increase or decrease at a different rate than sales. For example, a company may be able to keep a tight control on its costs as its sales go up, with the result that net operating income increases more rapidly than sales and increases the margin. Or a company may have fixed expenses that remain constant as sales go up, resulting in an increase in the net operating income and in the margin. Either (or both) of these factors could have been responsible for the increase in the margin percentage from 10% to 10.91% illustrated in approach 1 above.

Further, a change in sales can affect the *turnover* if sales either increase or decrease without a proportionate increase or decrease in the operating assets. In the first approach above, for example, sales increased from $100,000 to $110,000, but the operating assets remained unchanged. As a result, the turnover increased from 2 to 2.2 for the period.

Reduce Expenses

Often the easiest route to increased profitability and to a stronger ROI figure is to simply cut the "fat" out of an organization through a concerted effort to control expenses. When margins begin to be squeezed, this is generally the first line of attack by a manager. Discretionary fixed costs usually come under scrutiny first, and various programs are either curtailed or eliminated in an effort to cut costs. Managers must be careful, however, not to cut out muscle and bone along with the fat. Also, they must remember that frequent cost-cutting binges can destroy morale. Most managers now agree that it is best to stay "lean and mean" all of the time.

Reduce Operating Assets

Managers have always been sensitive to the need to control sales, operating expenses, and operating margins. However, they have not always been equally sensitive to the need to control investment in operating assets. Firms that have adopted the ROI approach to measuring managerial performance report that one of the first reactions of investment center managers is to trim their investment in operating assets. The reason, of course, is that these managers soon realize that an excessive investment in operating assets reduces turnover and hurts the ROI. As these managers reduce their investment in operating assets, funds are released that can be used elsewhere in the organization.

How can an investment center manager control the investment in operating assets? One approach is to eliminate unneeded inventory. JIT purchasing and JIT manufacturing have been extremely helpful in reducing inventories of all types, with the result that ROI figures have improved dramatically in some companies. Another approach is to devise various methods of speeding up the collection of receivables. For example, many firms now employ the lockbox technique by which customers in distant states send their payments directly to post office boxes in their area. The funds are received and deposited by a local bank on behalf of the payee firm. This speeds up the collection process, since the payments are not delayed in the postal system. As a result of the speedup in collection, the accounts receivable balance is reduced and the asset turnover is increased.

ROI and the Balanced Scorecard

Simply exhorting managers to increase ROI is not sufficient. Managers who are told to increase ROI will naturally wonder how this is to be accomplished. The Du Pont scheme, which is illustrated in Exhibit 12–6, provides managers with *some* guidance. Generally speaking, ROI can be increased by increasing sales, decreasing costs, and/or decreasing investments in operating assets. However, it may not be obvious to managers *how* they are supposed to increase sales, decrease costs, and decrease investments in a way that is consistent with the company's strategy. For example, a manager who is given inadequate guidance may cut back on investments that are critical to implementing the company's strategy.

For that reason, as discussed in Chapter 10, when managers are evaluated based on ROI, a balanced scorecard approach is advised. And indeed, ROI, or residual income (discussed below), is typically included as one of the financial performance measures on a company's balanced scorecard. As we discussed in Chapter 10, the balanced scorecard provides a way of communicating a company's strategy to managers throughout the organization. The scorecard indicates *how* the company intends to improve its financial performance. A well-constructed balanced scorecard should answer questions like: "What internal business processes should be improved?" and "Which customer should be targeted and how will they be attracted and retained at a profit?" In short, a well-constructed balanced scorecard can provide managers with a road map that indicates how the company intends to increase its ROI. In the absence of such a road map of the company's strategy, managers may have difficulty understanding what they are supposed to do to increase ROI and they may work at cross-purposes rather than in harmony with the overall strategy of the company.

Criticisms of ROI

Although ROI is widely used in evaluating performance, it is not a perfect tool. The method is subject to the following criticisms:

1. Just telling managers to increase ROI may not be enough. Managers may not know how to increase ROI; they may increase ROI in a way that is inconsistent with the company's strategy; or they may take actions that increase ROI in the short run but harm the company in the long run (such as cutting back on research and development). This is why ROI is best used as part of a balanced scorecard as discussed above. A balanced scorecard can provide concrete guidance to managers, make it more likely that actions taken are consistent with the company's strategy, and reduce the likelihood that short-run performance will be enhanced at the expense of long-term performance.

2. A manager who takes over a business segment typically inherits many committed costs over which the manager has no control. These committed costs may be relevant in assessing the performance of the business segment as an investment but make it difficult to fairly assess the performance of the manager relative to other managers.
3. As discussed in the next section, a manager who is evaluated based on ROI may reject profitable investment opportunities.

Residual Income—Another Measure of Performance

objective 6

Compute residual income and understand the strengths and weaknesses of this method of measuring performance.

Another approach to measuring an investment center's performance focuses on a concept known as *residual income.* **Residual income** is the net operating income that an investment center earns above the minimum required return on its operating assets. **Economic value added (EVA)** is a similar concept that differs in some details from residual income.[6] For example, under the economic value added concept, funds used for research and development are treated as investments rather than as expenses.[7] However, for our purposes, we will not draw any distinction between residual income and economic value added.

When residual income or economic value added is used to measure performance, the purpose is to maximize the total amount of residual income or economic value added, not to maximize overall ROI. Organizations as diverse as Coca-Cola, Quaker Oats, the United States Postal Service, Varity Corporation, and Husky Injection Molding have embraced some version of residual income in recent years.

For purposes of illustration, consider the following data for an investment center—the Ketchican Division of Alaskan Marine Services Corporation.

ALASKAN MARINE SERVICES CORPORATION
Ketchican Division
Basic Data for Performance Evaluation

Average operating assets	$100,000
Net operating income	$ 20,000
Minimum required rate of return	15%

Alaskan Marine Services Corporation has long had a policy of evaluating investment center managers based on ROI, but it is considering a switch to residual income. The controller of the company, who is in favor of the change to residual income, has provided the following table that shows how the performance of the division would be evaluated under each of the two methods:

6. The basic idea underlying residual income and economic value added has been around for over 100 years. In recent years, economic value added has been popularized and trademarked by the consulting firm Stern, Stewart & Co.
7. Over 100 different adjustments could be made for deferred taxes, LIFO reserves, provisions for future liabilities, mergers and acquisitions, gains or losses due to changes in accounting rules, operating leases, and other accounts, but most companies make only a few. For further details, see S. David Young, *Economic Value Added,* INSEAD working paper 02/97–4667, INSEAD, 77305 Fontainebleau, France.

ALASKAN MARINE SERVICES CORPORATION
Ketchican Division

	Alternative Performance Measures	
	ROI	**Residual Income**
Average operating assets	$100,000 (a)	$100,000
Net operating income	$ 20,000 (b)	$ 20,000
ROI, (b) ÷ (a)	20%	
Minimum required return (15% × $100,000)		15,000
Residual income		$ 5,000

The reasoning underlying the residual income calculation is straightforward. The company is able to earn a rate of return of at least 15% on its investments. Since the company has invested $100,000 in the Ketchican Division in the form of operating assets, the company should be able to earn at least $15,000 (15% × $100,000) on this investment. Since the Ketchican Division's net operating income is $20,000, the residual income above and beyond the minimum required return is $5,000. If residual income is adopted as the performance measure to replace ROI, the manager of the Ketchican Division would be evaluated based on the growth from year to year in residual income.

Focus on Current Practice

According to *Fortune* magazine, "Managers who run their businesses according to the precepts of EVA have hugely increased the value of their companies. Investors who know about EVA, and know which companies are employing it, have grown rich. Little wonder that highly regarded major corporations—Coca-Cola, AT&T, Quaker Oats, Briggs & Stratton, CSX, and many others—are flocking to the concept . . . Here's how Coca-Cola CEO Roberto Goizueta, a champion wealth creator, explained it: 'We raise capital to make concentrate, and sell it at an operating profit. Then we pay the cost of capital. Shareholders pocket the difference.' "[8] ■

Motivation and Residual Income

One of the primary reasons why the controller of Alaskan Marine Services Corporation would like to switch from ROI to residual income has to do with how managers view new investments under the two performance measurement schemes. The residual income approach encourages managers to make investments that are profitable for the entire company but that would be rejected by managers who are evaluated by the ROI formula.

To illustrate this problem, suppose that the manager of the Ketchican Division is considering purchasing a computerized diagnostic machine to aid in servicing marine diesel engines. The machine would cost $25,000 and is expected to generate additional operating income of $4,500 a year. From the standpoint of the company, this would be

8. Shawn Tully, "The Real Key to Creating Wealth," *Fortune,* September 20, 1993, pp. 38–50. Copyright © 1993 Time Inc. All rights reserved.

a good investment since it promises a rate of return of 18% ($4,500 ÷ $25,000), which is in excess of the company's minimum required rate of return of 15%.

If the manager of the Ketchican Division is evaluated based on residual income, she would be in favor of the investment in the diagnostic machine as shown below:

ALASKAN MARINE SERVICES CORPORATION
Ketchican Division
Performance Evaluated Using Residual Income

	Present	New Project	Overall
Average operating assets	$100,000	$25,000	$125,000
Net operating income	$ 20,000	$ 4,500	$ 24,500
Minimum required return	15,000	3,750*	18,750
Residual income	$ 5,000	$ 750	$ 5,750

*$25,000 × 15% = $3,750.

Since the project would increase the residual income of the Ketchican Division, the manager would want to invest in the new diagnostic machine.

Now suppose that the manager of the Ketchican Division is evaluated based on ROI. The effect of the diagnostic machine on the division's ROI is computed below:

ALASKAN MARINE SERVICES CORPORATION
Ketchican Division
Performance Evaluated Using ROI

	Present	New Project	Overall
Average operating assets (a)	$100,000	$25,000	$125,000
Net operating income (b)	$ 20,000	$ 4,500†	$ 24,500
ROI, (b) ÷ (a)	20%	18%	19.6%

†$25,000 × 18%= $4,500.

The new project reduces the division's ROI from 20% to 19.6%. This happens because the 18% rate of return on the new diagnostic machine, while above the company's 15% minimum rate of return, is below the division's present ROI of 20%. Therefore, the new diagnostic machine would drag the division's ROI down even though it would be a good investment from the standpoint of the company as a whole. If the manager of the division is evaluated based on ROI, she will be reluctant to even propose such an investment.

Basically, a manager who is evaluated based on ROI will reject any project whose rate of return is below the division's current ROI even if the rate of return on the project is above the minimum required rate of return for the entire company. In contrast, any project whose rate of return is above the minimum required rate of return for the company will result in an increase in residual income. Since it is in the best interests of the company as a whole to accept any project whose rate of return is above the minimum required rate of return, managers who are evaluated based on residual income will tend to make better decisions concerning investment projects than managers who are evaluated based on ROI.

Focus on Current Practice

Quaker Oats provides an example of how use of EVA can change the way a company operates. "Until Quaker adopted the concept [of EVA] in 1991, its businesses had one overriding goal—increasing quarterly earnings. To do it, they guzzled capital. They offered sharp price discounts at the end of each

quarter, so plants ran overtime turning out huge shipments of Gatorade, Rice-A-Roni, 100% Natural Cereal, and other products. Managers led the late rush, since their bonuses depended on raising operating profits each quarter . . . Pumping up sales requires many warehouses (capital) to hold vast temporary inventories (more capital). But who cared? Quaker's operating businesses paid no charge for capital in internal accounting, so they barely noticed. It took EVA to spotlight the problem . . . One plant has trimmed inventories from $15 million to $9 million, even though it is producing much more, and Quaker has closed five of 15 warehouses, saving $6 million a year in salaries and capital costs."[9] ■

Divisional Comparison and Residual Income

The residual income approach has one major disadvantage. It can't be used to compare the performance of divisions of different sizes. You would expect larger divisions to have more residual income than smaller divisions, not necessarily because they are better managed but simply because of the bigger numbers involved.

As an example, consider the following residual income computations for Division X and Division Y:

	Division	
	X	Y
Average operating assets (a)	$1,000,000	$250,000
Net operating income	$ 120,000	$ 40,000
Minimum required return: 10% × (a)	100,000	25,000
Residual income	$ 20,000	$ 15,000

Observe that Division X has slightly more residual income than Division Y, but that Division X has $1,000,000 in operating assets as compared to only $250,000 in operating assets for Division Y. Thus, Division X's greater residual income is probably more a result of its size than the quality of its management. In fact, it appears that the smaller division is better managed, since it has been able to generate nearly as much residual income with only one-fourth as much in operating assets to work with. This problem can be reduced to some degree by focusing on the percentage change in residual income from year to year rather than on the absolute amount of the residual income.

Summary

Segment reports can provide information for evaluating the profitability and performance of divisions, product lines, sales territories, and other segments of a company. Under the contribution approach to segment reporting, only those costs that are traceable are assigned to a segment. Fixed common costs and other nontraceable costs are not allocated to a segment. A cost is considered to be traceable to a segment only if the

9. Shawn Tully, "The Real Key to Creating Wealth," *Fortune,* September 20, 1993, pp. 38–50.

cost is caused by the segment and eliminating the segment would result in avoiding the cost.

Costs that are traceable to a segment are further classified as either variable or fixed. The contribution margin is sales less variable costs. The segment margin is the contribution margin less the traceable fixed costs of the segment.

For purposes of evaluating the performance of managers, there are at least three kinds of business segments—cost centers, profit centers, and investment centers. Return on investment (ROI) is widely used to evaluate investment center performance. However, there is a trend toward using residual income or economic value added instead of ROI. The residual income and economic value added approaches encourage profitable investments in many situations where the ROI approach would discourage investment.

Review Problem 1: Segmented Statements

The business staff of the legal firm Frampton, Davis & Smythe has constructed the following report which breaks down the firm's overall results for last month in terms of its two main business segments—family law and commercial law:

	Total	Family Law	Commercial Law
Revenues from clients	$1,000,000	$400,000	$600,000
Less variable expenses	220,000	100,000	120,000
Contribution margin	780,000	300,000	480,000
Less traceable fixed expenses	670,000	280,000	390,000
Segment margin	110,000	20,000	90,000
Less common fixed expenses	60,000	24,000	36,000
Net income	$ 50,000	$ (4,000)	$ 54,000

However, this report is not quite correct. The common fixed expenses such as the managing partner's salary, general administrative expenses, and general firm advertising have been allocated to the two segments based on revenues from clients.

Required

1. Redo the segment report, eliminating the allocation of common fixed expenses. Show both Amount and Percent columns for the firm as a whole and for each of the segments. Would the firm be better off financially if the family law segment were dropped? (Note: Many of the firm's commercial law clients also use the firm for their family law requirements such as drawing up wills.)
2. The firm's advertising agency has proposed an ad campaign targeted at boosting the revenues of the family law segment. The ad campaign would cost $20,000, and the advertising agency claims that it would increase family law revenues by $100,000. The managing partner of Frampton, Davis & Smythe believes this increase in business could be accommodated without any increase in fixed expenses. What effect would this ad campaign have on the family law segment margin and on overall net income of the firm?

Solution to Review Problem 1

1. The corrected segmented income statement appears below:

	Total		Family Law		Commercial Law	
	Amount	Percent	Amount	Percent	Amount	Percent
Revenues from clients	$1,000,000	100%	$400,000	100%	$600,000	100%
Less variable expenses	220,000	22%	100,000	25%	120,000	20%
Contribution margin	780,000	78%	300,000	75%	480,000	80%
Less traceable fixed expenses	670,000	67%	280,000	70%	390,000	65%
Segment margin	110,000	11%	$ 20,000	5%	$ 90,000	15%
Less common fixed expenses	60,000	6%				
Net income	$ 50,000	5%				

No, the firm would not be financially better off if the family law practice were dropped. The family law segment is covering all of its own costs and is contributing $20,000 per month to covering the common fixed expenses of the firm. While the segment margin as a percent of sales is much lower for family law than for commercial law, it is still profitable; and it is likely that family law is a service that the firm must provide to its commercial clients in order to remain competitive.

2. The ad campaign would be expected to add $55,000 to the family law segment as follows:

Increased revenues from clients	$100,000
Family law contribution margin ratio	×75%
Incremental contribution margin	75,000
Less cost of the ad campaign	20,000
Increased segment margin	$ 55,000

Since there would be no increase in fixed expenses (including common fixed expenses), the increase in overall net income should also be $55,000.

Review Problem 2: Return on Investment (ROI) and Residual Income

The Magnetic Imaging Division of Medical Diagnostics, Inc., has reported the following results for last year's operations:

Sales	$25 million
Net operating income	3 million
Average operating assets	10 million

Required

1. Compute the margin, turnover, and ROI for the Magnetic Imaging Division.
2. Top management of Medical Diagnostics, Inc., has set a minimum required rate of return on average operating assets of 25%. What is the Magnetic Imaging Division's residual income for the year?

Solution to Review Problem 2

1. The required calculations appear below:

$$\text{Margin} = \frac{\text{Net operating income, \$3,000,000}}{\text{Sales, \$25,000,000}}$$
$$= 12\%$$

$$\text{Turnover} = \frac{\text{Sales, \$25,000,000}}{\text{Average operating assets, \$10,000,000}}$$
$$= 2.5$$

$$\text{ROI} = \text{Margin} \times \text{Turnover}$$
$$= 12\% \times 2.5$$
$$= 30\%$$

2. The residual income for the Magnetic Imaging Division is computed as follows:

Average operating assets	$10,000,000
Net operating income	$ 3,000,000
Minimum required return (25% × $10,000,000)	2,500,000
Residual income	$ 500,000

Key Terms for Review

Common fixed cost A fixed cost that supports more than one business segment, but is not traceable in whole or in part to any one of the business segments. (p. 559)

Cost center A business segment whose manager has control over cost but has no control over revenue or the use of investment funds. (p. 553)

Decentralized organization An organization in which decision making is not confined to a few top executives but rather is spread throughout the organization. (p. 552)

Economic value added (EVA) A concept similar to residual income. (p. 573)

Investment center A business segment whose manager has control over cost and over revenue and that also has control over the use of investment funds. (p. 554)

Margin Net operating income divided by sales. (p. 568)

Net operating income Income before interest and income taxes have been deducted. (p. 567)

Operating assets Cash, accounts receivable, inventory, plant and equipment, and all other assets held for productive use in an organization. (p. 567)

Profit center A business segment whose manager has control over cost and revenue but has no control over the use of investment funds. (p. 554)

Residual income The net operating income that an investment center earns above the required return on its operating assets. (p. 573)

Responsibility center Any business segment whose manager has control over cost, revenue, or the use of investment funds. (p. 554)

Return on investment (ROI) Net operating income divided by average operating assets. It also equals margin multiplied by turnover. (p. 566)

Segment Any part or activity of an organization about which the manager seeks cost, revenue, or profit data. (p. 553)

Segment margin The amount computed by deducting the traceable fixed costs of a segment from the segment's contribution margin. It represents the margin available after a segment has covered all of its own costs. (p. 561)

Traceable fixed cost A fixed cost that is incurred because of the existence of a particular business segment. (p. 559)

Turnover The amount of sales generated in an investment center for each dollar invested in operating assets. It is computed by dividing sales by the average operating assets figure. (p. 568)

Value chain The major business functions that add value to a company's products and services. These functions consist of research and development, product design, manufacturing, marketing, distribution, and customer service. (p. 564)

Appendix 12A: Transfer Pricing

There are special problems in evaluating the performance of business segments when goods or services are transferred from one division to another. The problems revolve around the question of what *transfer price* to charge between the segments. A **transfer price** is the price charged when one segment of a company provides goods or services to another segment of the company. For example, most companies in the oil industry, such as Exxon, Shell, and Texaco, have petroleum refining and retail sales divisions that are evaluated on the basis of ROI or residual income. The petroleum refining division processes crude oil into gasoline, kerosene, lubricants, and other end products. The retail sales division takes gasoline and other products from the refining division and sells them through the company's chain of service stations. Each product has a price for transfers within the company. Suppose the transfer price for gasoline is $0.80 a gallon. Then the refining division gets credit for $0.80 a gallon of revenue on its segment report and the retailing division must deduct $0.80 a gallon as an expense on its segment report. Clearly, the refining division would like the transfer price to be as high as possible, whereas the retailing division would like the transfer price to be as low as possible. However, the transaction has no direct effect on the entire company's reported profit. It is like taking money out of one pocket and putting it into the other.

Managers are intensely interested in how transfer prices are set, since they can have a dramatic effect on the apparent profitability of a division. Three common approaches are used to set transfer prices:

1. Allow the managers involved in the transfer to negotiate their own transfer price.
2. Set transfer prices at cost using:
   a. Variable cost.
   b. Full (absorption) cost.
3. Set transfer prices at the market price.

We will consider each of these transfer pricing methods in turn, beginning with negotiated transfer prices. Throughout the discussion we should keep in mind that *the fundamental objective in setting transfer prices is to motivate the managers to act in the best interests of the overall company.* In contrast, **suboptimization** occurs when managers do not act in the best interests of the overall company or even in the best interests of their own segment.

Negotiated Transfer Prices

objective 7

Determine the range, if any, within which a negotiated transfer price should fall.

A **negotiated transfer price** is a transfer price that is agreed on between the selling and purchasing divisions. Negotiated transfer prices have several important advantages. First, this approach preserves the autonomy of the divisions and is consistent with the spirit of decentralization. Second, the managers of the divisions are likely to have much better information about the potential costs and benefits of the transfer than others in the company.

When negotiated transfer prices are used, the managers who are involved in a proposed transfer within the company meet to discuss the terms and conditions of the transfer. They may decide not to go through with the transfer, but if they do, they must agree to a transfer price. Generally speaking, we cannot predict the exact transfer price they will agree to. However, we can confidently predict two things: (1) the selling division will agree to the transfer only if the profits of the selling division increase as a result of the transfer, and (2) the purchasing division will agree to the transfer only if the profits of the purchasing division also increase as a result of the transfer. This may seem obvious, but it is an important point.

Clearly, if the transfer price is below the selling division's cost, a loss will occur on the transaction and the selling division will refuse to agree to the transfer. Likewise, if the transfer price is set too high, it will be impossible for the purchasing division to make any profit on the transferred item. For any given proposed transfer, the transfer price has both a lower limit (determined by the situation of the selling division) and an upper limit (determined by the situation of the purchasing division). The actual transfer price agreed to by the two division managers can fall anywhere between those two limits. These limits determine the **range of acceptable transfer prices**—the range of transfer prices within which the profits of both divisions participating in a transfer would increase.

An example will help us to understand negotiated transfer prices. Harris & Louder, Ltd. owns fast-food restaurants and snack food and beverage manufacturers in the United Kingdom. One of the restaurants, Pizza Maven, serves a variety of beverages along with pizzas. One of the beverages is ginger beer, which is served on tap. Harris & Louder has just purchased a new division, Imperial Beverages, that produces ginger beer. The managing director of Imperial Beverages has approached the managing director of Pizza Maven about purchasing Imperial Beverage ginger beer for sale at Pizza Maven restaurants rather than its usual brand of ginger beer. Managers at Pizza Maven agree that the quality of Imperial Beverages' ginger beer is comparable to the quality of their regular brand. It is just a question of price. The basic facts are listed below:

Imperial Beverage:		
Ginger beer production capacity per month	10,000	barrels
Variable cost per barrel of ginger beer	£8	per barrel
Fixed costs per month	£70,000	
Selling price of Imperial Beverage ginger beer on the outside market	£20	per barrel
Pizza Maven:		
Purchase price of regular brand of ginger beer	£18	per barrel
Monthly consumption of ginger beer	2,000	barrels

THE SELLING DIVISION'S LOWEST ACCEPTABLE TRANSFER PRICE The selling division, Imperial Beverage will be interested in a proposed transfer only if its profit increases. Clearly, the transfer price must not fall below the variable cost per barrel of £8. In addition, if Imperial Beverage has insufficient capacity to fill the Pizza Maven order, then it would have to give up some of its regular sales. Imperial Beverages would expect to be compensated for the contribution margin on these lost sales. In sum, if the transfer has no effect on fixed costs, then from the selling division's standpoint, the transfer price must cover both the variable costs of producing the transferred units and any opportunity costs from lost sales.

Seller's perspective:

$$\text{Transfer price} \geq \begin{array}{c}\text{Variable cost}\\ \text{per unit}\end{array} + \frac{\text{Total contribution margin on lost sales}}{\text{Number of units transferred}}$$

THE PURCHASING DIVISION'S HIGHEST ACCEPTABLE TRANSFER PRICE The purchasing division, Pizza Maven, will be interested in the proposal only if its profit increases. In cases like this where a purchasing division has an outside supplier, the purchasing division's decision is simple. Buy from the inside supplier if the price is less than the price offered by the outside supplier.

Purchaser's perspective:

$$\text{Transfer price} \leq \text{Cost of buying from outside supplier}$$

We will consider several different hypothetical situations and see what the range of acceptable transfer prices would be in each situation.

SELLING DIVISION WITH IDLE CAPACITY Suppose that Imperial Beverages has sufficient idle capacity to satisfy the demand for ginger beer from Pizza Maven without cutting into sales of ginger beer to its regular customers. To be specific, let's suppose that Imperial Beverages is selling only 7,000 barrels of ginger beer a month on the outside market. That leaves unused capacity of 3,000 barrels a month—more than enough to satisfy Pizza Maven's requirement of 2,000 barrels a month. What range of transfer prices, if any, would make both divisions better off with the transfer of 2,000 barrels a month?

1. The selling division, Imperial Beverage, will be interested in the proposal only if:

$$\text{Transfer price} \geq \begin{array}{c}\text{Variable cost}\\\text{per unit}\end{array} + \frac{\text{Total contribution margin on lost sales}}{\text{Number of units transferred}}$$

   Since Imperial Beverage has ample idle capacity, there are no lost outside sales. And since the variable cost per unit is £8, the lowest acceptable transfer price as far as the selling division is concerned is also £8.

$$\text{Transfer price} \geq £8 + \frac{£0}{2{,}000} = £8$$

2. The purchasing division, Pizza Maven, can buy similar ginger beer from an outside vendor for £18. Therefore, Pizza Maven would be unwilling to pay more than £18 per barrel for Imperial Beverage's ginger beer.

$$\text{Transfer price} \leq \text{Cost of buying from outside supplier} = £18$$

3. Combining the requirements of both the selling division and the purchasing division, the acceptable range of transfer prices in this situation is:

$$£8 \leq \text{Transfer price} \leq £18$$

   Assuming that the managers understand their own businesses and that they are cooperative, they should be able to agree on a transfer price within this range.

Focus on Current Practice

Teva Pharmaceutical Industries Ltd. of Israel rejected the negotiated transfer price approach because senior executives believed that this approach would lead to endless, nonproductive arguments. Instead, the company uses activity-based costing to set its transfer prices. Marketing divisions are charged for unit-level costs based on the actual quantities of each product they acquire. In addition, they are charged batch-level costs based on the actual number of batches their orders require. Product-level and facility-level costs are charged to the marketing divisions annually in lump sums—the details will be covered in Chapter 16. Essentially, Teva Pharmaceutical Industries sets its transfer prices at carefully computed variable costs. As long as Teva Pharmaceutical Industries has unused capacity, this system sends the marketing managers the correct signals about how much it really costs the company to produce each product. With this information, the marketing managers are much better equipped to make pricing and other decisions regarding the products.[10] ■

SELLING DIVISION WITH NO IDLE CAPACITY Suppose that Imperial Beverages has *no* idle capacity; it is selling 10,000 barrels of ginger beer a month on the outside market at £20 per barrel. To fill the order from Pizza Maven, Imperial Beverages would have to divert 2,000 barrels from its regular customers. What range of transfer prices, if any, would make both divisions better off transferring the 2,000 barrels within the company?

1. The selling division, Imperial Beverage, will be interested in the proposal only if:

$$\text{Transfer price} \geq \frac{\text{Variable cost}}{\text{per unit}} + \frac{\text{Total contribution margin on lost sales}}{\text{Number of units transferred}}$$

   Since Imperial Beverage has no idle capacity, there *are* lost outside sales. The contribution margin per barrel on these outside sales is £12 (£20 − £8).

$$\text{Transfer price} \geq £8 + \frac{(£20 - £8) \times 2{,}000}{2{,}000} = £8 + (£20 - £8) = £20$$

   Thus, as far as the selling division is concerned, the transfer price must at least cover the revenue on the lost sales, which is £20 per barrel. This makes sense since the cost of producing the 2,000 barrels is the same whether they are sold on the inside market or on the outside. The only difference is that the selling division loses the revenue of £20 per barrel if it transfers the barrels to Pizza Maven.

2. As before, the purchasing division, Pizza Maven, would be unwilling to pay more than the £18 per barrel it is already paying for similar ginger beer from its regular supplier.

$$\text{Transfer price} \leq \text{Cost of buying from outside supplier} = £18$$

3. Therefore, the selling division would insist on a transfer price of at least £20. But the purchasing division would refuse any transfer price above £18. It is impossible to satisfy both division managers simultaneously; there can be no agreement on a transfer price and no transfer will take place. Is this good? The answer is yes. From the standpoint of the entire company, the transfer doesn't make sense. Why give up sales of £20 to save £18?

   Basically, the transfer price is a mechanism for dividing between the two divisions any profit the entire company earns as a result of the transfer. If the company loses money on the transfer, there will be no profit to divide up, and it will be impossible for the two divisions to come to an agreement. On the other

10. Robert S. Kaplan, Dan Weiss, and Eyal Desheh, "Transfer Pricing with ABC," *Management Accounting,* May 1997, pp. 20–28.

hand, if the company makes money on the transfer, there will be a potential profit to share, and it will always be possible for the two divisions to find a mutually agreeable transfer price that increases the profits of both divisions. If the pie is bigger, it is always possible to divide it up in such a way that everyone has a bigger piece.

SELLING DIVISION HAS SOME IDLE CAPACITY Suppose now that Imperial Beverages is selling 9,000 barrels of ginger beer a month on the outside market. Pizza Maven can only sell one kind of ginger beer on tap. They cannot buy 1,000 barrels from Imperial Beverages and 1,000 barrels from their regular supplier; they must buy all of their ginger beer from one source.

To fill the entire 2,000-barrel a month order from Pizza Maven, Imperial Beverages would have to divert 1,000 barrels from its regular customers who are paying £20 per barrel. The other 1,000 barrels can be made using idle capacity. What range of transfer prices, if any, would make both divisions better off transferring the 2,000 barrels within the company?

1. As before, the selling division, Imperial Beverage, will insist on a transfer price that at least covers their variable cost and opportunity cost:

$$\text{Transfer price} \geq \frac{\text{Variable cost}}{\text{per unit}} + \frac{\text{Total contribution margin on lost sales}}{\text{Number of units transferred}}$$

   Since Imperial Beverage does not have enough idle capacity to fill the entire order for 2,000 barrels, there *are* lost outside sales. The contribution margin per barrel on the 1,000 barrels of lost outside sales is £12 (£20 − £8).

$$\text{Transfer price} \geq £8 + \frac{(£20 - £8) \times 1{,}000}{2{,}000} = £8 + £6 = £14$$

   Thus, as far as the selling division is concerned, the transfer price must cover the variable cost of £8 plus the average opportunity cost of lost sales of £6.

2. As before, the purchasing division, Pizza Maven, would be unwilling to pay more than the £18 per barrel it pays its regular supplier.

$$\text{Transfer price} \leq \text{Cost of buying from outside suppliers} = £18$$

3. Combining the requirements for both the selling and purchasing divisions, the range of acceptable transfer prices is:

$$£14 \leq \text{Transfer price} \leq £18$$

   Again, assuming that the managers understand their own businesses and that they are cooperative, they should be able to agree on a transfer price within this range.

NO OUTSIDE SUPPLIER If Pizza Maven has no outside supplier for the ginger beer, the highest price the purchasing division would be willing to pay depends on how much the purchasing division expects to make on the transferred units—excluding the transfer price. If, for example, Pizza Maven expects to earn £30 per barrel of ginger beer after paying its own expenses, then it should be willing to pay up to £30 per barrel to Imperial Beverages. Remember, however, that this assumes Pizza Maven cannot buy ginger beer from other sources.

EVALUATION OF NEGOTIATED TRANSFER PRICES As discussed earlier, if a transfer within the company would result in higher overall profits for the company, there is always a range of transfer prices within which both the selling and purchasing division would also have higher profits if they agree to the transfer. Therefore, if the managers understand their own businesses and are cooperative, then they should always be able to agree on a transfer price if it is in the best interests of the company that they do so.

The difficulty is that not all managers understand their own businesses and not all managers are cooperative. As a result, negotiations often break down even when it would be in the managers' own best interests to come to an agreement. Sometimes that is the fault of the way managers are evaluated. If managers are pitted against each other rather than against their own past performance or reasonable benchmarks, a non-cooperative atmosphere is almost guaranteed. Nevertheless, it must be admitted that even with the best performance evaluation system, some people by nature are not cooperative.

Possibly because of the fruitless and protracted bickering that often accompanies disputes over transfer prices, most companies rely on some other means of setting transfer prices. Unfortunately, as we will see below, all of the alternatives to negotiated transfer prices have their own serious drawbacks.

Transfers at the Cost to the Selling Division

Many companies set transfer prices at either the variable cost or full (absorption) cost incurred by the selling division. Although the cost approach to setting transfer prices is relatively simple to apply, it has some major defects.

First, the use of cost—particularly full cost—as a transfer price can lead to bad decisions and thus suboptimization. Return to the example involving the ginger beer. The full cost of ginger beer can never be less than £15 per barrel (£8 per barrel variable cost + £7 per barrel fixed cost at capacity). What if the cost of buying the ginger beer from an outside supplier is less than £15—for example, £14 per barrel? If the transfer price were bureaucratically set at full cost, then Pizza Maven would never want to buy ginger beer from Imperial Beverage, since it could buy its ginger beer from the outside supplier at less cost. However, from the standpoint of the company as a whole, ginger beer should be transferred from Imperial Beverage to Pizza Maven whenever Imperial Beverage has idle capacity. Why? Because when Imperial Beverage has idle capacity, it only costs the company £8 in variable cost to produce a barrel of ginger beer, but it costs £14 per barrel to buy from outside suppliers.

Second, if cost is used as the transfer price, the selling division will never show a profit on any internal transfer. The only division that shows a profit is the division that makes the final sale to an outside party.

A third problem with cost-based prices is that they do not provide incentives to control costs. If the costs of one division are simply passed on to the next, then there is little incentive for anyone to work to reduce costs. This problem can be overcome to some extent by using standard costs rather than actual costs for transfer prices.

Despite these shortcomings, cost-based transfer prices are commonly used in practice. Advocates argue that they are easily understood and convenient to use.

Transfers at Market Price

Some form of competitive **market price** (i.e., the price charged for an item on the open market) is often regarded as the best approach to the transfer pricing problem—particularly if transfer price negotiations routinely become bogged down.

The market price approach is designed for situations in which there is an *intermediate market* for the transferred product or service. By **intermediate market,** we mean a market in which the product or service is sold in its present form to outside customers. If the selling division has no idle capacity, the market price in the intermediate market is the perfect choice for the transfer price. The reason for this is that if the selling division can sell a transferred item on the outside market instead, then the real cost of the transfer as far as the company is concerned is the opportunity cost of the lost revenue on the outside sale. Whether the item is transferred internally or sold on the outside intermediate market, the production costs are exactly the same. If the market price is used as the transfer price, the selling division manager will not lose anything by making the transfer, and the purchasing division manager will get the correct signal about how much it really costs the company for the transfer to take place.

While the market price works beautifully when there is no idle capacity, difficulties occur when the selling division has idle capacity. Recalling once again the ginger beer example, the outside market price for the ginger beer produced by Imperial Beverage is £20 per barrel. However, Pizza Maven can purchase all of the ginger beer it wants from outside suppliers for £18 per barrel. Why would Pizza Maven ever buy from Imperial Beverage if Pizza Maven is forced to pay Imperial Beverage's market price? In some market price-based transfer pricing schemes, the transfer price would be lowered to £18, the outside vendor's market price, and Pizza Maven would be directed to buy from Imperial Beverage as long as Imperial Beverage is willing to sell. This scheme can work reasonably well, but a drawback is that managers at Pizza Maven will regard the cost of ginger beer as £18 rather than the £8, which is the real cost to the company when the selling division has idle capacity. Consequently, the managers of Pizza Maven will make pricing and other decisions based on an incorrect cost.

Unfortunately, none of the possible solutions to the transfer pricing problem are perfect—not even market-based transfer prices.

Divisional Autonomy and Suboptimization

A question often arises as to how much autonomy should be granted to divisions in setting their own transfer prices and in making decisions concerning whether to sell internally or to sell outside. Should the divisional heads have complete authority to make these decisions, or should top corporate management step in if it appears that a decision is about to be made that would result in suboptimization? For example, if the selling division has idle capacity and divisional managers are unable to agree on a transfer price, should top corporate management step in and *force* a settlement?

Efforts should always be made, of course, to bring disputing managers together. But the almost unanimous feeling among top corporate executives is that divisional heads should not be forced into an agreement over a transfer price. That is, if a manager flatly refuses to change his or her position in a dispute, *then this decision should be respected* even if it results in suboptimization. This is simply the price that is paid for divisional autonomy. If top corporate management steps in and forces the decisions in difficult situations, then the purposes of decentralization are defeated and the company simply becomes a centralized operation with decentralization of only minor decisions and responsibilities. In short, if a division is to be viewed as an autonomous unit with independent profit responsibility, then it must have control over its own destiny—even to the extent of having the right to make bad decisions.

We should note, however, that if a division consistently makes bad decisions, the results will sooner or later reduce its profit and rate of return, and the divisional manager may find that he or she has to defend the division's performance. Even so, the manager's right to get into an embarrassing situation must be respected if decentralization is to operate successfully. Divisional autonomy and independent profit responsibility generally lead to much greater success and profitability than do closely controlled, centrally administered operations. Part of the price of this success is occasional suboptimization due to pettiness, bickering, or just plain stubbornness.

Furthermore, one of the major reasons for decentralizing is that top managers cannot know enough about every detail of operations to make every decision themselves. To impose the correct transfer price, top managers would have to know details about the intermediate market, variable costs, and capacity utilization. If top managers have all of this information, it is not clear why they decentralized in the first place.

Exhibit 12A–2
Domestic and International Transfer Pricing Objectives

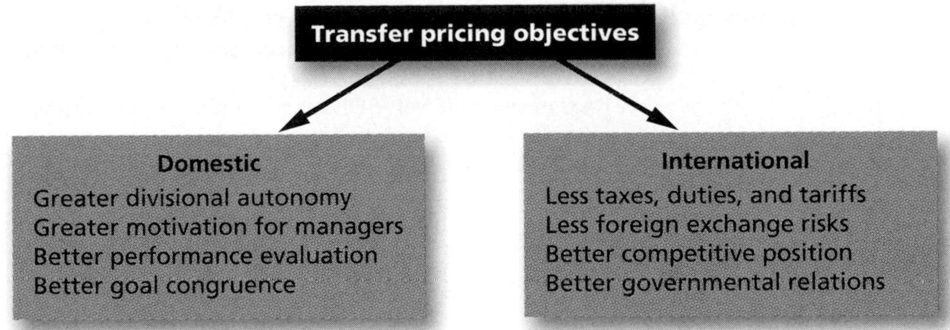

International Aspects of Transfer Pricing

The objectives of transfer pricing change when a multinational corporation (MNC) is involved and the goods and services being transferred cross international borders. The objectives of international transfer pricing, as compared to domestic transfer pricing, are summarized in Exhibit 12A–1.[11]

As shown in the exhibit, the objectives of international transfer pricing focus on minimizing taxes, duties, and foreign exchange risks, along with enhancing a company's competitive position and improving its relations with foreign governments. Although domestic objectives such as managerial motivation and divisional autonomy are always important, they often become secondary when international transfers are involved. Companies will focus instead on charging a transfer price that will slash its total tax bill or that will strengthen a foreign subsidiary.

For example, charging a low transfer price for parts shipped to a foreign subsidiary may reduce customs duty payments as the parts cross international borders, or it may help the subsidiary to compete in foreign markets by keeping the subsidiary's costs low. On the other hand, charging a high transfer price may help an MNC draw profits out of a country that has stringent controls on foreign remittances, or it may allow an MNC to shift income from a country that has high income tax rates to a country that has low rates.

Review Problem 3: Transfer Pricing

Situation A

Collyer Products, Inc., has a Valve Division that manufactures and sells a standard valve as follows:

Capacity in units	100,000
Selling price to outside customers on the intermediate market	$30
Variable costs per unit	16
Fixed costs per unit (based on capacity)	9

The company has a Pump Division that could use this valve in the manufacture of one of its pumps. The Pump Division is currently purchasing 10,000 valves per year from an overseas supplier at a cost of $29 per valve.

11. The exhibit is adapted from Wagdy M. Abdallah, "Guidelines for CEOs in Transfer Pricing Policies," *Management Accounting* 70, no. 3 (September 1988), p. 61.

Required

1. Assume that the Valve Division has ample idle capacity to handle all of the Pump Division's needs. What is the acceptable range, if any, for the transfer price between the two divisions?
2. Assume that the Valve Division is selling all that it can produce to outside customers on the intermediate market. What is the acceptable range, if any, for the transfer price between the two divisions?
3. Assume again that the Valve Division is selling all that it can produce to outside customers on the intermediate market. Also assume that \$3 in variable expenses can be avoided on transfers within the company, due to reduced selling costs. What is the acceptable range, if any, for the transfer price between the two divisions?

Solution to Situation A

1. Since the Valve Division has idle capacity, it does not have to give up any outside sales to take on the Pump Division's business. Applying the formula for the lowest acceptable transfer price from the viewpoint of the selling division, we get:

$$\text{Transfer price} \geq \begin{matrix}\text{Variable cost}\\ \text{per unit}\end{matrix} + \frac{\text{Total contribution margin on lost sales}}{\text{Number of units transferred}}$$

$$\text{Transfer price} \geq \$16 + \frac{\$0}{10{,}000} = \$16$$

The Pump Division would be unwilling to pay more that \$29, the price it is currently paying an outside supplier for its valves. Therefore, the transfer price must fall within the range:

$$\$16 \leq \text{Transfer price} \leq \$29$$

2. Since the Valve Division is selling all that it can produce on the intermediate market, it would have to give up some of these outside sales to take on the Pump Division's business. Thus, the Valve Division has an opportunity cost that is the total contribution margin on lost sales:

$$\text{Transfer price} \geq \begin{matrix}\text{Variable cost}\\ \text{per unit}\end{matrix} + \frac{\text{Total contribution margin on lost sales}}{\text{Number of units transferred}}$$

$$\text{Transfer price} \geq \$16 + \frac{(\$30 - \$16) \times 10{,}000}{10{,}000} = \$16 + \$14 = \$30$$

Since the Pump Division can purchase valves from an outside supplier at only \$29 per unit, no transfers will be made between the two divisions.

3. Applying the formula for the lowest acceptable price from the viewpoint of the selling division, we get:

$$\text{Transfer price} \geq \begin{matrix}\text{Variable cost}\\ \text{per unit}\end{matrix} + \frac{\text{Total contribution margin on lost sales}}{\text{Number of units transferred}}$$

$$\text{Transfer price} \geq (\$16 - \$3) + \frac{(\$30 - \$16) \times 10{,}000}{10{,}000} = \$13 + \$14 = \$27$$

In this case, the transfer price must fall within the range:

$$\$27 \leq \text{Transfer price} \leq \$29$$

Situation B

Refer to the original data in situation A above. Assume that the Pump Division needs 20,000 special high-pressure valves per year. The Valve Division's variable costs to manufacture and ship the special valve would be \$20 per unit. To produce these special valves, the Valve Division would have to reduce its production and sales of regular valves from 100,000 units per year to 70,000 units per year.

Required As far as the Valve Division is concerned, what is the lowest acceptable transfer price?

Solution to Situation B To produce the 20,000 special valves, the Valve Division will have to give up sales of 30,000 regular valves to outside customers. Applying the formula for the lowest acceptable price from the viewpoint of the selling division, we get:

$$\text{Transfer price} \geq \begin{matrix}\text{Variable cost}\\ \text{per unit}\end{matrix} + \frac{\text{Total contribution margin on lost sales}}{\text{Number of units transferred}}$$

$$\text{Transfer price} \geq \$20 + \frac{(\$30 - \$16) \times 30{,}000}{20{,}000} = \$20 + \$21 = \$41$$

Key Terms for Review (Appendix 12A)

Intermediate market A market in which a transferred product or service is sold in its present form to outside customers. (p. 585)

Market price The price being charged for an item on the open (intermediate) market. (p. 585)

Negotiated transfer price A transfer price agreed on between buying and selling divisions. (p. 580)

Range of acceptable transfer prices The range of transfer prices within which the profits of both the selling division and the purchasing division would increase as a result of a transfer. (p. 581)

Suboptimization An overall level of profitability that is less than a segment or a company is capable of earning. (p. 580)

Transfer price The price charged when one division or segment provides goods or services to another division or segment of an organization. (p. 580)

Questions

12–1 What is meant by the term *decentralization?*

12–2 What benefits result from decentralization?

12–3 Distinguish between a cost center, a profit center, and an investment center.

12–4 Define a segment of an organization. Give several examples of segments.

12–5 How does the contribution approach assign costs to segments of an organization?

12–6 Distinguish between a traceable cost and a common cost. Give several examples of each.

12–7 Explain how the segment margin differs from the contribution margin.

12–8 Why aren't common costs allocated to segments under the contribution approach?

12–9 How is it possible for a cost that is traceable to a segment to become a common cost if the segment is divided into further segments?

12–10 What is meant by the terms *margin* and *turnover?*

12–11 What are the three basic approaches to improving return on investment (ROI)?

12–12 What is meant by residual income?

12–13 In what way can the use of ROI as a performance measure for investment centers lead to bad decisions? How does the residual income approach overcome this problem?

12–14 (Appendix 12A) What is meant by the term *transfer price,* and why are transfer prices needed?

12–15 (Appendix 12A) From the standpoint of a selling division that has idle capacity, what is the minimum acceptable transfer price for an item?

12–16 (Appendix 12A) From the standpoint of a selling division that has *no* idle capacity, what is the minimum acceptable transfer price for an item?

12–17 (Appendix 12A) What are the advantages and disadvantages of cost-based transfer prices?

12–18 (Appendix 12A) If a market price for a product can be determined, why isn't it always the best transfer price?

Exercises

E12–1 Royal Lawncare Company produces and sells two packaged products, Weedban and Greengrow. Revenue and cost information relating to the products follow:

	Product	
	Weedban	Greengrow
Selling price per unit	$ 6.00	$ 7.50
Variable expenses per unit	2.40	5.25
Traceable fixed expenses per year	45,000	21,000

Common fixed expenses in the company total $33,000 annually. Last year the company produced and sold 15,000 units of Weedban and 28,000 units of Greengrow.

Required Prepare an income statement segmented by product lines. Show both Amount and Percent columns for the company as a whole and for each of the products.

E12–2 Raner, Harris, & Chan is a consulting firm that specializes in information systems for medical and dental clinics. The firm has two offices—one in Chicago and one in Minneapolis. The firm classifies the direct costs of consulting jobs as variable costs. A segmented income statement for the company's most recent year is given below:

	Total Company		Segment			
			Chicago		Minneapolis	
Sales	$450,000	100%	$150,000	100%	$300,000	100%
Less variable expenses	225,000	50%	45,000	30%	180,000	60%
Contribution margin	225,000	50%	105,000	70%	120,000	40%
Less traceable fixed expenses	126,000	28%	78,000	52%	48,000	16%
Office segment margin	99,000	22%	$ 27,000	18%	$ 72,000	24%
Less common fixed expenses not traceable to segments	63,000	14%				
Net income	$ 36,000	8%				

Required

1. By how much would the company's net income increase if Minneapolis increased its sales by $75,000 per year? Assume no change in cost behavior patterns.
2. Refer to the original data. Assume that sales in Chicago increase by $50,000 next year and that sales in Minneapolis remain unchanged. Assume no change in fixed costs.
   a. Prepare a new segmented income statement for the company using the format above. Show both amounts and percentages.
   b. Observe from the income statement you have prepared that the contribution margin ratio for Chicago has remained unchanged at 70% (the same as in the data above) but that the segment margin ratio has changed. How do you explain the change in the segment margin ratio?

E12–3 Refer to the data in E12–2. Assume that Minneapolis' sales by major market are:

	Minneapolis		Segment: Medical		Segment: Dental	
Sales	$300,000	100%	$200,000	100%	$100,000	100%
Less variable expenses	180,000	60%	128,000	64%	52,000	52%
Contribution margin	120,000	40%	72,000	36%	48,000	48%
Less traceable fixed expenses	33,000	11%	12,000	6%	21,000	21%
Product-line segment margin	87,000	29%	$ 60,000	30%	$ 27,000	27%
Less common fixed expenses not traceable to markets	15,000	5%				
Divisional segment margin	$ 72,000	24%				

The company would like to initiate an intensive advertising campaign in one of the two market segments during the next month. The campaign would cost $5,000. Marketing studies indicate that such a campaign would increase sales in the Medical market by $40,000 or increase sales in the Dental market by $35,000.

Required

1. In which of the markets would you recommend that the company focus its advertising campaign? Show computations to support your answer.
2. In E12–2, Minneapolis shows $48,000 in traceable fixed expenses. What happened to the $48,000 in this exercise?

E12–4 Wingate Company, a wholesale distributor of videotapes, has been experiencing losses for some time, as shown by its most recent monthly income statement below:

Sales	$1,000,000
Less variable expenses	390,000
Contribution margin	610,000
Less fixed expenses	625,000
Net income (loss)	$ (15,000)

In an effort to isolate the problem, the president has asked for an income statement segmented by division. Accordingly, the Accounting Department has developed the following information:

	Division: East	Division: Central	Division: West
Sales	$250,000	$400,000	$350,000
Variable expenses as a percentage of sales	52%	30%	40%
Traceable fixed expenses	$160,000	$200,000	$175,000

Required

1. Prepare an income statement segmented by divisions, as desired by the president. Show both Amount and Percent columns for the company as a whole and for each division.

2. As a result of a marketing study, the president believes that sales in the West Division could be increased by 20% if advertising in that division were increased by $15,000 each month. Would you recommend the increased advertising? Show computations.

E12–5 You have a client who operates a large upscale grocery store that has a full range of departments. The management has encountered difficulty in using accounting data as a basis for decisions as to possible changes in departments operated, products, marketing methods, and so forth. List several overhead costs, or costs not applicable to a particular department, and explain how the existence of such costs (sometimes called *common costs*) complicates and limits the use of accounting data in making decisions in such a store.

(CPA, adapted)

E12–6 Selected operating data for two divisions of Outback Brewing, Ltd., of Australia are given below:

	Division	
	Queensland	**New South Wales**
Sales	$4,000,000	$7,000,000
Average operating assets	2,000,000	2,000,000
Net operating income	360,000	420,000
Property, plant, and equipment (net)	950,000	800,000

Required

1. Compute the rate of return for each division using the return on investment (ROI) formula stated in terms of margin and turnover.
2. So far as you can tell from the data, which divisional manager seems to be doing the better job? Why?

E12–7 Provide the missing data in the following tabulation:

	Division		
	Alpha	**Bravo**	**Charlie**
Sales	$?	$11,500,000	$?
Net operating income	?	920,000	210,000
Average operating assets	800,000	?	?
Margin	4%	?	7%
Turnover	5	?	?
Return on investment (ROI)	?	20%	14%

E12–8 Meiji Isetan Corp. of Japan has two regional divisions with headquarters in Osaka and Yokohama. Selected data on the two divisions follow (in millions of yen, denoted by ¥):

	Division	
	Osaka	**Yokohama**
Sales	¥3,000,000	¥9,000,000
Net operating income	210,000	720,000
Average operating assets	1,000,000	4,000,000

Required

1. For each division, compute the return on investment (ROI) in terms of margin and turnover. Where necessary, carry computations to two decimal places.
2. Assume that the company evaluates performance by use of residual income and that the minimum required return for any division is 15%. Compute the residual income for each division.
3. Is Yokohama's greater amount of residual income an indication that it is better managed? Explain.

E12–9 Selected sales and operating data for three divisions of a multinational structural engineering firm are given below:

	Division		
	Asia	Europe	North America
Sales	$12,000,000	$14,000,000	$25,000,000
Average operating assets	3,000,000	7,000,000	5,000,000
Net operating income	600,000	560,000	800,000
Minimum required rate of return	14%	10%	16%

Required

1. Compute the return on investment (ROI) for each division using the formula stated in terms of margin and turnover.
2. Compute the residual income for each division.
3. Assume that each division is presented with an investment opportunity that would yield a 15% rate of return.
   a. If performance is being measured by ROI, which division or divisions will probably accept the opportunity? Reject? Why?
   b. If performance is being measured by residual income, which division or divisions will probably accept the opportunity? Reject? Why?

E12–10 A family friend has asked your help in analyzing the operations of three anonymous companies. Supply the missing data in the tabulation below:

	Company		
	A	B	C
Sales	$9,000,000	$7,000,000	$4,500,000
Net operating income	?	280,000	?
Average operating assets	3,000,000	?	1,800,000
Return on investment (ROI)	18%	14%	?
Minimum required rate of return:			
Percentage	16%	?	15%
Dollar amount	?	320,000	?
Residual income	?	?	90,000

E12–11 (Appendix 12A) Sako Company's Audio Division produces a speaker that is widely used by manufacturers of various audio products. Sales and cost data on the speaker follow:

Selling price per unit on the intermediate market	$60
Variable costs per unit	42
Fixed costs per unit (based on capacity)	8
Capacity in units	25,000

Sako Company has just organized a Hi-Fi Division that could use this speaker in one of its products. The Hi-Fi Division will need 5,000 speakers per year. It has received a quote of $57 per speaker from another manufacturer. Sako Company evaluates divisional managers on the basis of divisional profits.

Required

1. Assume that the Audio Division is now selling only 20,000 speakers per year to outside customers on the intermediate market.
   a. From the standpoint of the Audio Division, what is the lowest acceptable transfer price for speakers sold to the Hi-Fi Division?
   b. From the standpoint of the Hi-Fi Division, what is the highest acceptable transfer price for speakers purchased from the Audio Division?
   c. If left free to negotiate without interference, would you expect the division managers to voluntarily agree to the transfer of 5,000 speakers from the Audio Division to the Hi-Fi Division? Why or why not?
   d. From the standpoint of the entire company, should the transfer take place? Why or why not?
2. Assume that the Audio Division is selling all of the speakers it can produce to outside customers on the intermediate market.

a. From the standpoint of the Audio Division, what is the lowest acceptable transfer price for speakers sold to the Hi-Fi Division?
b. From the standpoint of the Hi-Fi Division, what is the highest acceptable transfer price for speakers purchased from the Audio Division?
c. If left free to negotiate without interference, would you expect the division managers to voluntarily agree to the transfer of 5,000 speakers from the Audio Division to the Hi-Fi Division? Why or why not?
d. From the standpoint of the entire company, should the transfer take place? Why or why not?

E12–12 (Appendix 12A) In each of the cases below, assume that Division X has a product that can be sold either to outside customers on an intermediate market or to Division Y of the same company for use in its production process. The managers of the divisions are evaluated based on their divisional profits.

	Case	
	A	**B**
Division X:		
Capacity in units	200,000	200,000
Number of units being sold on the intermediate market	200,000	160,000
Selling price per unit on the intermediate market	$90	$75
Variable costs per unit	70	60
Fixed costs per unit (based on capacity)	13	8
Division Y:		
Number of units needed for production	40,000	40,000
Purchase price per unit now being paid to an outside supplier	$86	$74

Required

1. Refer to the data in case A above. Assume in this case that $3 per unit in variable costs can be avoided on intracompany sales. If the managers are free to negotiate and make decisions on their own, will a transfer take place? If so, within what range will the transfer price fall? Explain.
2. Refer to the data in case B above. In this case there will be no savings in variable costs on intracompany sales. If the managers are free to negotiate and make decisions on their own, will a transfer take place? If so, within what range will the transfer price fall? Explain.

E12–13 (Appendix 12A) Division A manufactures electronic circuit boards. The boards can be sold either to Division B of the same company or to outside customers. Last year, the following activity occurred in Division A:

Selling price per circuit board	$125
Production cost per circuit board	90
Number of circuit boards:	
Produced during the year	20,000
Sold to outside customers	16,000
Sold to Division B	4,000

Sales to Division B were at the same price as sales to outside customers. The circuit boards purchased by Division B were used in an electronic instrument manufactured by that division (one board per instrument). Division B incurred $100 in additional cost per instrument and then sold the instruments for $300 each.

Required

1. Prepare income statements for Division A, Division B, and the company as a whole.
2. Assume that Division A's manufacturing capacity is 20,000 circuit boards. Next year, Division B wants to purchase 5,000 circuit boards from Division A rather than 4,000. (Circuit boards of this type are not available from outside sources.) From the standpoint of the company as a whole, should Division A sell the 1,000 additional circuit boards to Division B or continue to sell them to outside customers? Explain.

Problems

P12–14 Restructuring a Segmented Statement Losses have been incurred in Millard Company for some time. In an effort to isolate the problem and improve the company's performance, management has requested that the monthly income statement be segmented by sales region. The company's first effort at preparing a segmented statement is given below. This statement is for May, the most recent month of activity.

	Sales Region		
	West	**Central**	**East**
Sales	$450,000	$800,000	$ 750,000
Less regional expenses (traceable):			
Cost of goods sold	162,900	280,000	376,500
Advertising	108,000	200,000	210,000
Salaries	90,000	88,000	135,000
Utilities	13,500	12,000	15,000
Depreciation	27,000	28,000	30,000
Shipping expense	17,100	32,000	28,500
Total regional expenses	418,500	640,000	795,000
Regional income (loss) before corporate expenses	31,500	160,000	(45,000)
Less corporate expenses:			
Advertising (general)	18,000	32,000	30,000
General administrative expense	50,000	50,000	50,000
Total corporate expenses	68,000	82,000	80,000
Net income (loss)	$ (36,500)	$ 78,000	$(125,000)

Cost of goods sold and shipping expense are both variable; other costs are all fixed.

Millard Company is a wholesale distributor of office products. It purchases office products from manufacturers and distributes them in the three regions given above. The three regions are about the same size, and each has its own manager and sales staff. The products that the company distributes vary widely in profitability.

Required

1. List any disadvantages or weaknesses that you see to the statement format illustrated above.
2. Explain the basis that is apparently being used to allocate the corporate expenses to the regions. Do you agree with these allocations? Explain.
3. Prepare a new segmented income statement for May using the contribution approach. Show a Total column as well as data for each region. Include percentages on your statement for all columns.
4. Analyze the statement that you prepared in (3) above. What points that might help to improve the company's performance would you be particularly anxious to bring to the attention of management?

P12–15 Segment Reporting Vulcan Company's income statement for last month is given below:

VULCAN COMPANY
Income Statement
For the Month Ended June 30

Sales	$750,000
Less variable expenses	336,000
Contribution margin	414,000
Less fixed expenses	378,000
Net income	$ 36,000

Management is disappointed with the company's performance and is wondering what can be done to improve profits. By examining sales and cost records, you have determined the following:

a. The company is divided into two sales territories—Northern and Southern. The Northern territory recorded $300,000 in sales and $156,000 in variable expenses during June; the remaining sales and variable expenses were recorded in the Southern territory. Fixed expenses of $120,000 and $108,000 are traceable to the Northern and Southern territories, respectively. The rest of the fixed expenses are common to the two territories.

b. The company sells two products—Paks and Tibs. Sales of Paks and Tibs totaled $50,000 and $250,000, respectively, in the Northern territory during June. Variable expenses are 22% of the selling price for Paks and 58% for Tibs. Cost records show that $30,000 of the Northern territory's fixed expenses are traceable to Paks and $40,000 to Tibs, with the remainder common to the two products.

Required

1. Prepare segmented income statements first showing the total company broken down between sales territories and then showing the Northern territory broken down by product line. Show both Amount and Percent columns for the company in total and for each segment.
2. Look at the statement you have prepared showing the total company segmented by sales territory. What points revealed by this statement should be brought to the attention of management?
3. Look at the statement you have prepared showing the Northern territory segmented by product lines. What points revealed by this statement should be brought to the attention of management?

P12–16 Segment Reporting; Activity-Based Cost Assignment

Diversified Products, Inc., has recently acquired a small publishing company that Diversified Products intends to operate as one of its investment centers. The newly acquired company has three books that it offers for sale—a cookbook, a travel guide, and a handy speller. Each book sells for $10. The publishing company's most recent monthly income statement is given below:

	Total Company		Product Line: Cookbook	Travel Guide	Handy Speller
Sales	$300,000	100%	$90,000	$150,000	$60,000
Less expenses:					
Printing costs	102,000	34%	27,000	63,000	12,000
Advertising	36,000	12%	13,500	19,500	3,000
General sales	18,000	6%	5,400	9,000	3,600
Salaries	33,000	11%	18,000	9,000	6,000
Equipment depreciation	9,000	3%	3,000	3,000	3,000
Sales commissions	30,000	10%	9,000	15,000	6,000
General administration	42,000	14%	14,000	14,000	14,000
Warehouse rent	12,000	4%	3,600	6,000	2,400
Depreciation—office facilities	3,000	1%	1,000	1,000	1,000
Total expenses	285,000	95%	94,500	139,500	51,000
Net income (loss)	$ 15,000	5%	$(4,500)	$ 10,500	$ 9,000

The following additional information is available about the company:

a. Only printing costs and sales commissions are variable; all other costs are fixed. The printing costs (which include materials, labor, and variable overhead) are traceable to the three product lines as shown in the statement above. Sales commissions are 10% of sales for any product.

b. The same equipment is used to produce all three books, so the equipment depreciation cost has been allocated equally among the three product lines. An analysis of the company's activities indicates that the equipment is used 30% of the time to produce cookbooks, 50% of the time to produce travel guides, and 20% of the time to produce handy spellers.

c. The warehouse is used to store finished units of product, so the rental cost has been allocated to the product lines on the basis of sales dollars. The warehouse rental cost is $3 per square foot per year. The warehouse contains 48,000 square feet of space, of which 7,200 square feet is used by the cookbook line, 24,000 square feet by the travel guide line, and 16,800 square feet by the handy speller line.

d. The general sales cost above includes the salary of the sales manager and other sales costs not traceable to any specific product line. This cost has been allocated to the product lines on the basis of sales dollars.

e. The general administration cost and depreciation of office facilities both relate to overall administration of the company as a whole. These costs have been allocated equally to the three product lines.

f. All other costs are traceable to the three product lines in the amounts shown on the statement above.

The management of Diversified Products, Inc., is anxious to improve the new investment center's 5% return on sales.

Required

1. Prepare a new segmented income statement for the month using the contribution approach. Show both an Amount column and a Percent column for the company as a whole and for each product line. Adjust allocations of equipment depreciation and of warehouse rent as indicated by the additional information provided.
2. After seeing the income statement in the main body of the problem, management has decided to eliminate the cookbook, since it is not returning a profit, and to focus all available resources on promoting the travel guide.
   a. Based on the statement you have prepared, do you agree with the decision to eliminate the cookbook? Explain.
   b. Based on the statement you have prepared, do you agree with the decision to focus all available resources on promoting the travel guide? Explain. (You may assume that an ample market is available for all three product lines.)
3. What additional points would you bring to the attention of management that might help to improve profits?

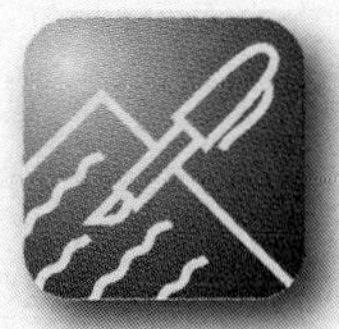

P12–17 Return on Investment (ROI); Comparison of Company Performance Comparative data on three companies in the same industry are given below:

	Company		
	A	B	C
Sales	$600,000	$500,000	$?
Net operating income	84,000	70,000	?
Average operating assets	300,000	?	1,000,000
Margin	?	?	3.5%
Turnover	?	?	2
ROI	?	7%	?

Required

1. What advantages can you see in breaking down the ROI computation into two separate elements, margin and turnover?
2. Fill in the missing information above, and comment on the relative performance of the three companies in as much detail as the data permit. Make *specific recommendations* on steps to be taken to improve the return on investment, where needed.

(Adapted from National Association of Accountants, *Research Report No.35,* p. 34)

P12–18 Return on Investment (ROI) and Residual Income Financial data for Joel de Paris, Inc., for last year follow:

JOEL DE PARIS, INC.
Balance Sheet

	Ending Balance	Beginning Balance
Assets		
Cash	$ 120,000	$ 140,000
Accounts receivable	530,000	450,000
Inventory	380,000	320,000
Plant and equipment, net	620,000	680,000
Investment in Buisson, S.A.	280,000	250,000
Land (undeveloped)	170,000	180,000
Total assets	$2,100,000	$2,020,000
Liabilities and Stockholders' Equity		
Accounts payable	$ 310,000	$ 360,000
Long-term debt	1,500,000	1,500,000
Stockholders' equity	290,000	160,000
Total liabilities and stockholders' equity	$2,100,000	$2,020,000

JOEL DE PARIS, INC.
Income Statement

Sales		$4,050,000
Less operating expenses		3,645,000
Net operating income		405,000
Less interest and taxes:		
Interest expense	$ 150,000	
Tax expense	110,000	260,000
Net income		$ 145,000

The company paid dividends of $15,000 last year. The "Investment in Buisson, S.A.," on the balance sheet represents an investment in the stock of another company.

Required

1. Compute the company's margin, turnover, and ROI for last year.
2. The board of directors of Joel de Paris, Inc., has set a minimum required return of 15%. What was the company's residual income last year?

P12–19 Return on Investment (ROI) and Residual Income "I know headquarters wants us to add on that new product line," said Dell Havasi, manager of Billings Company's Office Products Division. "But I want to see the numbers before I make any move. Our division has led the company for three years, and I don't want any letdown."

Billings Company is a decentralized organization with five autonomous divisions. The divisions are evaluated on the basis of the return that they are able to generate on invested assets, with year-end bonuses given to the divisional managers who have the highest ROI figures. Operating results for the company's Office Products Division for the most recent year are given below:

Sales	$10,000,000
Less variable expenses	6,000,000
Contribution margin	4,000,000
Less fixed expenses	3,200,000
Net operating income	$ 800,000
Divisional operating assets	$ 4,000,000

The company had an overall ROI of 15% last year (considering all divisions). The Office Products Division has an opportunity to add a new product line that would require an additional investment in operating assets of $1,000,000. The cost and revenue characteristics of the new product line per year would be:

Sales	$2,000,000
Variable expenses	60% of sales
Fixed expenses	$640,000

Required

1. Compute the Office Products Division's ROI for the most recent year; also compute the ROI as it will appear if the new product line is added.
2. If you were in Dell Havasi's position, would you be inclined to accept or reject the new product line? Explain.
3. Why do you suppose headquarters is anxious for the Office Products Division to add the new product line?
4. Suppose that the company views a return of 12% on invested assets as being the minimum that any division should earn and that performance is evaluated by the residual income approach.
   a. Compute the Office Products Division's residual income for the most recent year; also compute the residual income as it will appear if the new product line is added.
   b. Under these circumstances, if you were in Dell Havasi's position, would you accept or reject the new product line? Explain.

P12–20 (Appendix 12A) Transfer Price; Well-Defined Intermediate Market Hrubec Products, Inc., operates a Pulp Division that manufactures wood pulp for use in the production of various paper goods. Revenue and costs associated with a ton of pulp follow:

Selling price		$70
Less expenses:		
Variable	$42	
Fixed (based on a capacity of 50,000 tons per year)	18	60
Net income		$10

Hrubec Products has just acquired a small company that manufactures paper cartons. This company will be treated as a division of Hrubec with full profit responsibility. The newly formed Carton Division is currently purchasing 5,000 tons of pulp per year from a supplier at a cost of $70 per ton, less a 10% quantity discount. Hrubec's president is anxious for the Carton Division to begin purchasing its pulp from the Pulp Division if an acceptable transfer price can be worked out.

Required

For (1) and (2) below, assume that the Pulp Division can sell all of its pulp to outside customers at the normal $70 price.

1. Are the managers of the Carton and Pulp Divisions likely to agree to a transfer price for 5,000 tons of pulp next year? Why or why not?
2. If the Pulp Division meets the price that the Carton Division is currently paying to its supplier and sells 5,000 tons of pulp to the Carton Division each year, what will be the effect on the profits of the Pulp Division, the Carton Division, and the company as a whole?

For (3)–(6) below, assume that the Pulp Division is currently selling only 30,000 tons of pulp each year to outside customers at the stated $70 price.

3. Are the managers of the Carton and Pulp Divisions likely to agree to a transfer price for 5,000 tons of pulp next year? Why or why not?
4. Suppose that the Carton Divisions outside supplier drops its price (net of the quantity discount) to only $59 per ton. Should the Pulp Division meet this price? Explain. If the Pulp Division does *not* meet the $59 price, what will be the effect on the profits of the company as a whole?
5. Refer to (4) above. If the Pulp Division refuses to meet the $59 price, should the Carton Division be required to purchase from the Pulp Division at a higher price for the good of the company as a whole?

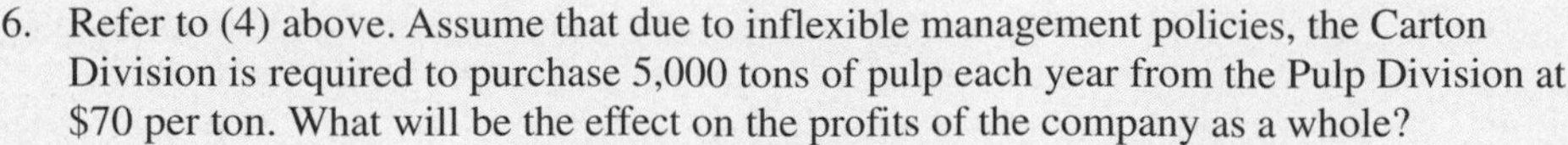

6. Refer to (4) above. Assume that due to inflexible management policies, the Carton Division is required to purchase 5,000 tons of pulp each year from the Pulp Division at $70 per ton. What will be the effect on the profits of the company as a whole?

P12–21 (Appendix 12A) Basic Transfer Pricing Alpha and Beta are divisions within the same company. The managers of both divisions are evaluated based on their own division's return on investment (ROI). Assume the following information relative to the two divisions:

	Case			
	1	2	3	4
Alpha Division:				
Capacity in units	80,000	400,000	150,000	300,000
Number of units now being sold to outside customers on the intermediate market	80,000	400,000	100,000	300,000
Selling price per unit on the intermediate market	$30	$90	$75	$50
Variable costs per unit	18	65	40	26
Fixed costs per unit (based on capacity)	6	15	20	9
Beta Division:				
Number of units needed annually	5,000	30,000	20,000	120,000
Purchase price now being paid to an outside supplier	$27	$89	$75*	—

*Before any quantity discount.

Managers are free to decide if they will participate in any internal transfers. All transfer prices are negotiated.

Required

1. Refer to case 1 above. Alpha Division can avoid $2 per unit in commissions on any sales to Beta Division. Will the managers agree to a transfer and if so, within what range will the transfer price be? Explain.
2. Refer to case 2 above. A study indicates that Alpha Division can avoid $5 per unit in shipping costs on any sales to Beta Division.
   a. Would you expect any disagreement between the two divisional managers over what the transfer price should be? Explain.
   b. Assume that Alpha Division offers to sell 30,000 units to Beta Division for $88 per unit and that Beta Division refuses this price. What will be the loss in potential profits for the company as a whole?
3. Refer to case 3 above. Assume that Beta Division is now receiving an 8% quantity discount from the outside supplier.
   a. Will the managers agree to a transfer? If so, what is the range within which the transfer price would be?
   b. Assume that Beta Division offers to purchase 20,000 units from Alpha Division at $60 per unit. If Alpha Division accepts this price, would you expect its ROI to increase, decrease, or remain unchanged? Why?
4. Refer to case 4 above. Assume that Beta Division wants Alpha Division to provide it with 120,000 units of a *different* product from the one that Alpha Division is now producing. The new product would require $21 per unit in variable costs and would require that Alpha Division cut back production of its present product by 45,000 units annually. What is the lowest acceptable transfer price from Alpha Division's perspective?

P12–22 Activity-Based Segment Reporting "That commercial market has been dragging us down for years," complained Shanna Reynolds, president of Morley Products. "Just look at that anemic income figure for the commercial market. That market had three million dollars more in sales than the home market, but only a few thousand dollars more in profits. What a loser it is!"

The income statement to which Ms. Reynolds was referring follows:

	Total Company		Commercial Market	Home Market	School Market
Sales	$20,000,000	100.0%	$8,000,000	$5,000,000	$7,000,000
Less expenses:					
Cost of goods sold	9,500,000	47.5%	3,900,000	2,400,000	3,200,000
Sales support	3,600,000	18.0%	1,440,000	900,000	1,260,000
Order processing	1,720,000	8.6%	688,000	430,000	602,000
Warehousing	940,000	4.7%	376,000	235,000	329,000
Packing and shipping	520,000	2.6%	208,000	130,000	182,000
Advertising	1,690,000	8.5%	676,000	422,500	591,500
General management	1,310,000	6.6%	524,000	327,500	458,500
Total expenses	19,280,000	96.4%	7,812,000	4,845,000	6,623,000
Net income	$ 720,000	3.6%	$ 188,000	$ 155,000	$ 377,000

"I agree," said Walt Divot, the company's vice president. "We need to focus more of our attention on the school market, since it's our best segment. Maybe that will bolster profits and get the stockholders off our backs."

The following additional information is available about the company:

a. Morley Products is a wholesale distributor of various goods; the cost of goods sold figures above are traceable to the markets in the amounts shown.
b. Sales support, order processing, and packing and shipping are considered by management to be variable costs. Warehousing, general management, and advertising are fixed costs. These costs have all been allocated to the markets on the basis of sales dollars—a practice that the company has followed for years.
c. You have compiled the following data.

Cost Pool and Allocation Base	Total Cost	Amount of Activity: Total	Commercial Market	Home Market	School Market
Sales support (number of calls)	$3,600,000	24,000	8,000	5,000	11,000
Order processing (number of orders)	1,720,000	8,600	1,750	5,200	1,650
Warehousing (square feet of space)	940,000	117,500	35,000	65,000	17,500
Packing and shipping (pounds shipped)	520,000	104,000	24,000	16,000	64,000

d. You have determined the following breakdown of the company's advertising expense and general management expense:

	Total	Market: Commercial	Home	School
Advertising:				
Traceable	$1,460,000	$700,000	$180,000	$580,000
Common	230,000			
General management:				
Traceable—salaries	410,000	150,000	120,000	140,000
Common	900,000			

The company is searching for ways to improve profit, and you have suggested that a segmented statement in which costs are assigned on the basis of activities might provide some useful insights for management.

Required

1. Refer to the data in (c) above. Determine a rate for each cost pool. Then, using this rate, compute the amount of cost assignable to each market.

2. Using the data from (1) above and other data from the problem, prepare a revised segmented statement for the company. Use the contribution format. Show an Amount column and a Percent column for the company as a whole and for each market segment. Carry percentage figures to one decimal place. (Remember to include warehousing among the fixed expenses.)
3. What, if anything, in your segmented statement should be brought to the attention of management? Explain.

P12–23 Multiple Segmented Income Statements Companhia Bradesco, S.A., of Brazil has two divisions. The company's income statement segmented by divisions for last year is given below (the currency in Brazil is the real, denoted here by R):

	Total Company	Division: Plastics	Division: Glass
Sales	R1,500,000	R900,000	R600,000
Less variable expenses	700,000	400,000	300,000
Contribution margin	800,000	500,000	300,000
Less traceable fixed expenses:			
Advertising	300,000	180,000	120,000
Depreciation	140,000	92,000	48,000
Administration	220,000	118,000	102,000
Total	660,000	390,000	270,000
Divisional segment margin	140,000	R110,000	R 30,000
Less common fixed expenses	100,000		
Net income	R 40,000		

Top management doesn't understand why the Glass Division has such a low segment margin when its sales are only one-third less than sales in the Plastics Division. Accordingly, management has directed that the Glass Division be further segmented into product lines. The following information is available on the product lines in the Glass Division:

	Glass Division Product Lines: Flat Glass	Auto Glass	Specialty Glass
Sales	R200,000	R300,000	R100,000
Traceable fixed expenses:			
Advertising	30,000	42,000	48,000
Depreciation	10,000	24,000	14,000
Administration	14,000	21,000	7,000
Variable expenses as a percentage of sales	65%	40%	50%

Analysis shows that R60,000 of the Glass Division's administration expenses are common to the product lines.

Required

1. Prepare a segmented income statement for the Glass Division with segments defined as product lines. Use the contribution approach. Show both an Amount column and a Percent column for the division in total and for each product line.
2. Management is surprised by Specialty Glass's poor showing and would like to have the product line segmented by market. The following information is available about the two markets in which Specialty Glass is sold:

	Specialty Glass Markets	
	Domestic	Foreign
Sales	R60,000	R40,000
Traceable fixed expenses:		
Advertising	18,000	30,000
Variable expenses as a percentage of sales	50%	50%

All of Specialty Glass's depreciation and administration expenses are common to the markets in which the product is sold. Prepare a segmented income statement for Specialty Glass with segments defined as markets. Again use the contribution approach and show both Amount and Percent columns.

3. Refer to the statement prepared in (1) above. The sales manager wants to run a special promotional campaign on one of the products over the next month. A market study indicates that such a campaign would increase sales of Flat Glass by R40,000 or sales of Auto Glass by R30,000. The campaign would cost R8,000. Show computations to determine which product line should be chosen.

P12–24 Return on Investment (ROI) Analysis The income statement for Huerra Company for last year is given below:

	Total	Unit
Sales	$4,000,000	$80.00
Less variable expenses	2,800,000	56.00
Contribution margin	1,200,000	24.00
Less fixed expenses	840,000	16.80
Net operating income	360,000	7.20
Less income taxes (30%)	108,000	2.16
Net income	$ 252,000	$ 5.04

The company had average operating assets of $2,000,000 during the year.

Required

1. Compute the company's ROI for the period using the ROI formula stated in terms of margin and turnover.

   For each of the following questions, indicate whether the margin and turnover will increase, decrease, or remain unchanged as a result of the events described, and then compute the new ROI figure. Consider each question separately, starting in each case from the data used to compute the original ROI in (1) above.
2. By use of just-in-time (JIT), the company is able to reduce the average level of inventory by $400,000. (The released funds are used to pay off short-term creditors.)
3. The company achieves a cost savings of $32,000 per year by using less costly materials.
4. The company issues bonds and uses the proceeds to purchase $500,000 in machinery and equipment. Interest on the bonds is $60,000 per year. Sales remain unchanged. The new, more efficient equipment reduces production costs by $20,000 per year.
5. As a result of a more intense effort by salespeople, sales are increased by 20%; operating assets remain unchanged.
6. Obsolete items of inventory carried on the records at a cost of $40,000 are scrapped and written off as a loss since they are unsalable.
7. The company uses $200,000 of cash (received on accounts receivable) to repurchase and retire some of its common stock.

P12–25 Return on Investment (ROI) and Residual Income Raddington Industries produces tool and die machinery for manufacturers. The company expanded vertically several years ago by acquiring Reigis Steel Company, one of its suppliers of alloy steel plates. Raddington decided to maintain Reigis' separate identity and therefore established the Reigis Steel Division as one of its investment centers.

Raddington evaluates its divisions on the basis of ROI. Management bonuses are also based on ROI. All investments in operating assets are expected to earn a minimum rate of return of 11%.

Reigis' ROI has ranged from 14% to 17% since it was acquired by Raddington. During the past year, Reigis had an investment opportunity that would yield an estimated rate of return of 13%. Reigis' management decided against the investment because it believed the investment would decrease the division's overall ROI.

Last year's income statement for Reigis Steel Division is given below. The division's operating assets employed were $12,960,000 at the end of the year, which represents an 8% increase over the previous year-end balance.

REIGIS STEEL DIVISION
Divisional Income Statement
For the Year Ended December 31

Sales		$31,200,000
Cost of goods sold		16,500,000
Gross margin		14,700,000
Less operating expenses:		
Selling expenses	$5,620,000	
Administrative expenses	7,208,000	12,828,000
Net operating income		$ 1,872,000

Required

1. Compute the following performance measures for the Reigis Steel Division:
   a. ROI. (Remember, ROI is based on the *average* operating assets, computed from the beginning-of-year and end-of-year balances.) State ROI in terms of margin and turnover.
   b. Residual income.
2. Would the management of Reigis Steel Division have been more likely to accept the investment opportunity it had last year if residual income were used as a performance measure instead of ROI? Explain.
3. The Reigis Steel Division is a separate investment center within Raddington Industries. Identify the items Reigis must be free to control if it is to be evaluated fairly by either the ROI or residual income performance measures.

(CMA, adapted)

P12–26 **Cost-Volume-Profit Analysis; Return on Investment (ROI); Transfer Pricing** The Valve Division of Bendix, Inc., produces a small valve that is used by various companies as a component part in their products. Bendix, Inc., operates its divisions as autonomous units, giving its divisional managers great discretion in pricing and other decisions. Each division is expected to generate a rate of return of at least 14% on its operating assets. The Valve Division has average operating assets of $700,000. The valves are sold for $5 each. Variable costs are $3 per valve, and fixed costs total $462,000 per year. The division has a capacity of 300,000 valves each year.

Required

1. How many valves must the Valve Division sell each year to generate the desired rate of return on its assets?
   a. What is the margin earned at this level of sales?
   b. What is the turnover at this level of sales?
2. Assume that the Valve Division's current ROI is just equal to the minimum required 14%. In order to increase the division's ROI, the divisional manager wants to increase the selling price per valve by 4%. Market studies indicate that an increase in the selling price would cause sales to drop by 20,000 units each year. However, operating assets could be reduced by $50,000 due to decreased needs for accounts receivable and inventory. Compute the margin, turnover, and ROI if these changes are made.
3. Refer to the original data. Assume again that the Valve Division's current ROI is just equal to the minimum required 14%. Rather than increase the selling price, the sales manager wants to reduce the selling price per valve by 4%. Market studies indicate that this would fill the plant to capacity. In order to carry the greater level of sales, however, operating

assets would increase by $50,000. Compute the margin, turnover, and ROI if these changes are made.

4. Refer to the original data. Assume that the normal volume of sales is 280,000 valves each year at a price of $5 per valve. Another division of the company is currently purchasing 20,000 valves each year from an overseas supplier, at a price of $4.25 per valve. The manager of the Valve Division has adamantly refused to meet this price, pointing out that it would result in a loss for his division:

Selling price per valve		$ 4.25
Cost per valve:		
Variable	$3.00	
Fixed ($462,000 ÷ 300,000 valves)	1.54	4.54
Net loss per valve		$(0.29)

The manager of the Valve Division also points out that the normal $5 selling price barely allows his division the required 14% rate of return. "If we take on some business at only $4.25 per unit, then our ROI is obviously going to suffer," he reasons, "and maintaining that ROI figure is the key to my future. Besides, taking on these extra units would require us to increase our operating assets by at least $50,000 due to the larger inventories and receivables we would be carrying." Would you recommend that the Valve Division sell to the other division at $4.25? Show ROI computations to support your answer.

P12–27 (Appendix 12A) Market-Based Transfer Price Stavos Company's Cabinet Division manufactures a standard cabinet for television sets. The cost per cabinet is:

Variable cost per cabinet	$ 70
Fixed cost per cabinet	30*
Total cost per cabinet	$100

*Based on a capacity of 10,000 cabinets per year.

Part of the Cabinet Division's output is sold to outside manufacturers of television sets and part is sold to Stavos Company's Quark Division, which produces a TV set under its own name. The Cabinet Division charges $140 per cabinet for all sales.

The costs, revenue, and net income associated with the Quark Division's TV set is given below:

Selling price per TV set		$480
Less variable cost per TV set:		
Cost of the cabinet	$140	
Variable cost of electronic parts	210	
Total variable cost		350
Contribution margin		130
Less fixed costs per TV set		80*
Net income per TV set		$ 50

*Based on a capacity of 3,000 sets per year.

The Quark Division has an order from an overseas source for 1,000 TV sets. The overseas source wants to pay only $340 per set.

Required

1. Assume that the Quark Division has enough idle capacity to fill the 1,000-set order. Is the division likely to accept the $340 price or to reject it? Explain.
2. Assume that both the Cabinet Division and the Quark Division have idle capacity. Under these conditions, would it be an advantage or a disadvantage to the company as a whole for the Quark Division to reject the $340 price? Show computations to support your answer.
3. Assume that the Quark Division has idle capacity but that the Cabinet Division is operating at capacity and could sell all of its cabinets to outside manufacturers. Compute

the dollar advantage or disadvantage of the Quark Division accepting the 1,000-set order at the $340 unit price.

4. What conclusions do you draw concerning the use of market price as a transfer price in intracompany transactions?

P12–28 (Appendix 12A) Negotiated Transfer Price Ditka Industries has several independent divisions. The company's Tube Division manufactures a picture tube used in television sets. The Tube Division's income statement for last year, in which 8,000 tubes were sold, is given below:

	Total	Unit
Sales	$1,360,000	$170.00
Less cost of goods sold	840,000	105.00
Gross margin	520,000	65.00
Less selling and administrative expenses	390,000	48.75
Divisional net income	$ 130,000	$ 16.25

As shown above, it costs the Tube Division $105 to produce a single tube. This figure consists of the following costs:

Direct materials	$ 38
Direct labor	27
Manufacturing overhead (75% fixed)	40
Total cost per tube	$105

The Tube Division has fixed selling and administrative expenses of $350,000 per year.

Ditka Industries has just formed a new division, called the TV Division, that will produce a television set that requires a high-resolution picture tube. The Tube Division has been asked to manufacture 2,500 of these tubes each year and sell them to the TV Division. As one step in determining the price that should be charged to the TV Division, the Tube Division has estimated the following cost for each of the new high-resolution tubes:

Direct materials	$ 60
Direct labor	49
Manufacturing overhead (⅔ fixed)	54
Total cost per tube	$163

To manufacture the new tubes, the Tube Division would have to reduce production of its regular tubes by 3,000 units per year. There would be no variable selling and administrative expenses on the intracompany business, and total fixed overhead costs would not change. Assume direct labor is a variable cost.

Required

1. Determine the lowest acceptable transfer price from the perspective of the Tube Division for each of the new high-resolution tubes.
2. Assume that the TV Division has found an outside supplier that will provide the new tubes for only $200 each. If the Tube Division meets this price, what will be the effect on the profits of the company as a whole?

P12–29 Segmented Statements; Product-Line Analysis "At last, I can see some light at the end of the tunnel," said Steve Adams, president of Jelco Products. "Our losses have shrunk from over $75,000 a month at the beginning of the year to only $26,000 for August. If we can just isolate the remaining problems with products A and C, we'll be in the black by the first of next year."

The company's income statement for the latest month (August) is presented below (absorption costing basis):

JELCO PRODUCTS
Income Statement
For August

	Total Company	Product A	Product B	Product C
Sales	$1,500,000	$600,000	$400,000	$500,000
Less cost of goods sold	922,000	372,000	220,000	330,000
Gross margins	578,000	228,000	180,000	170,000
Less operating expenses:				
Selling	424,000	162,000	112,000	150,000
Administrative	180,000	72,000	48,000	60,000
Total operating expenses	604,000	234,000	160,000	210,000
Net income (loss)	$ (26,000)	$ (6,000)	$ 20,000	$(40,000)

"What recommendations did that business consultant make?" asked Mr. Adams. "We paid the guy $100 an hour; surely he found something wrong." "He says our problems are concealed by the way we make up our statements," replied Sally Warren, the executive vice president. "He left us some data on what he calls 'traceable' and 'common' costs that he says we should be isolating in our reports." The data to which Ms. Warren was referring are shown below:

	Total Company	Product A	Product B	Product C
Variable costs:*				
Production (materials, labor, and variable overhead)	—	18%	32%	20%
Selling	—	10%	8%	10%
Traceable fixed costs:				
Production	$376,000	$180,000	$36,000	$160,000
Selling	282,000	102,000	80,000	100,000
Common fixed costs:				
Production	210,000	—	—	—
Administrative	180,000	—	—	—

*As a percentage of sales.

"I don't see anything wrong with our statements," said Mr. Adams. "Bill, our chief accountant, says that he has been using this format for over 30 years. He's also very careful to allocate all of our costs to the products."

"I'll admit that Bill always seems to be on top of things," replied Ms. Warren. "By the way, purchasing says that the X7 chips we use in products A and B are on back order and won't be available for several weeks. From the looks of August's income statement, we had better concentrate our remaining inventory of X7 chips on product B." (Two X7 chips are used in both product A and product B.)

The following additional information is available on the company:

a. Work in process and finished goods inventories are negligible and can be ignored.
b. Products A and B each sell for $250 per unit, and product C sells for $125 per unit. Strong market demand exists for all three products.

Required

1. Prepare a new income statement for August, segmented by product and using the contribution approach. Show both Amount and Percent columns for the company in total and for each product.

2. Assume that Mr. Adams is considering the elimination of product C due to the losses it is incurring. Based on the statement you prepared in (1) above, what points would you make for or against elimination of product C?
3. Do you agree with the company's decision to concentrate the remaining inventory of X7 chips on product B? Why or why not?
4. Product C is sold in both a vending and a home market with sales and cost data as follows:

	Total	Market: Vending	Market: Home
Sales	$500,000	$50,000	$450,000
Variable costs:*			
Production	—	20%	20%
Selling	—	28%	8%
Traceable fixed costs:			
Selling	$ 75,000	$45,000	$ 30,000

*As a percentage of sales.

The remainder of product C's fixed selling costs and all of product C's fixed production costs are common to the markets in which product C is sold.

a. Prepare an income statement showing product C segmented by market. Use the contribution approach and show both Amount and Percent columns for the product in total and for each market.
b. What points revealed by this statement would you be particularly anxious to bring to the attention of management?

P12–30 (Appendix 12A) Transfer Pricing with and without Idle Capacity The Electronics Division of Far North Telecom, Ltd., of Canada manufactures an electrical switching unit that can be sold either to outside customers or to the Fiber Optics Division of Far North Telecom. Selected operating data on the two divisions are given below:

Electronics Division:	
Unit selling price to outside customers	$ 80
Variable production cost per unit	52
Variable selling and administrative expense per unit	9
Fixed production cost in total	300,000*
Fiber Optics Division:	
Outside purchase price per unit (before any quantity discount)	80

*Capacity 25,000 units per year.

The Fiber Optics Division now purchases the switch from an outside supplier at the regular $80 intermediate price less a 5% quantity discount. Since the switch manufactured by the Electronics Division is of the same quality and type used by the Fiber Optics Division, consideration is being given to buying internally rather than from the outside supplier. As the company's president stated, "It's just plain smart to buy and sell within the corporate family."

A study has determined that the variable selling and administrative expenses of the Electronics Division would be cut by one-third for any sales to the Fiber Optics Division. Top management wants to treat each division as an autonomous unit with independent profit responsibility.

Required

1. Assume that the Electronics Division is currently selling only 20,000 units per year to outside customers and that the Fiber Optics Division needs 5,000 units per year.
   a. What is the lowest acceptable transfer price from the perspective of the Electronics Division? Explain.
   b. What is the highest acceptable transfer price from the perspective of the Fiber Optics Division? Explain.
   c. Assume that the Fiber Optics Division finds an outside supplier that will sell the electrical unit for only $65 per unit. Should the Electronics Division be required to meet this price? Explain.

d. Refer to the original data. Assume that the Electronics Division decides to raise its price to $85 per unit. If the Fiber Optics Division is forced to pay this price and to start purchasing from the Electronics Division, will this result in greater or less total corporate profits? How much per unit?
e. Under the circumstances posed in (d) above, should the Fiber Optics Division be forced to purchase from the Electronics Division? Explain.

2. Assume that the Electronics Division can sell all that it produces to outside customers. Repeat (a) through (e) above.

Cases

C12–31 Service Organization; Segment Reporting Music Teachers, Inc., is an educational association for music teachers that has 20,000 members. The association operates from a central headquarters but has local membership chapters throughout the United States. Monthly meetings are held by the local chapters to discuss recent developments on topics of interest to music teachers. The association's journal, *Teachers' Forum,* is issued monthly with features about recent developments in the field. The association publishes books and reports and also sponsors professional courses that qualify for continuing professional education credit. The association's statement of revenues and expenses for the current year is presented below.

MUSIC TEACHERS, INC.
Statement of Revenues and Expenses
For the Year Ended November 30

Revenues	$3,275,000
Less expenses:	
Salaries	920,000
Personnel costs	230,000
Occupancy costs	280,000
Reimbursement of member costs to local chapters	600,000
Other membership services	500,000
Printing and paper	320,000
Postage and shipping	176,000
Instructors' fees	80,000
General and administrative	38,000
Total expenses	3,144,000
Excess of revenues over expenses	$ 131,000

The board of directors of Music Teachers, Inc., has requested that a segmented statement of operations be prepared showing the contribution of each profit center to the association. The association has four profit centers: Membership Division, Magazine Subscriptions Division, Books and Reports Division, and Continuing Education Division. Mike Doyle has been assigned responsibility for preparing the segmented statement, and he has gathered the following data prior to its preparation.

a. Membership dues are $100 per year, of which $20 is considered to cover a one-year subscription to the association's journal. Other benefits include membership in the association and chapter affiliation. The portion of the dues covering the magazine subscription ($20) should be assigned to the Magazine Subscription Division.
b. One-year subscriptions to *Teachers' Forum* were sold to nonmembers and libraries at $30 per subscription. A total of 2,500 of these subscriptions were sold last year. In addition to subscriptions, the magazine generated $100,000 in advertising revenues. The costs per magazine subscription were $7 for printing and paper and $4 for postage and shipping.
c. A total of 28,000 technical reports and professional texts were sold by the Books and Reports Division at an average unit selling price of $25. Average costs per publication were $4 for printing and paper and $2 for postage and shipping.
d. The association offers a variety of continuing education courses to both members and nonmembers. The one-day courses had a tuition cost of $75 each and were attended by

2,400 students. A total of 1,760 students took two-day courses at a tuition cost of $125 for each student. Outside instructors were paid to teach some courses.

e. Salary costs and space occupied by division follow:

	Salaries	Space Occupied (square feet)
Membership	$210,000	2,000
Magazine Subscriptions	150,000	2,000
Books and Reports	300,000	3,000
Continuing Education	180,000	2,000
Corporate staff	80,000	1,000
Total	$920,000	10,000

Personnel costs are 25% of salaries in the separate divisions as well as for the corporate staff. The $280,000 in occupancy costs includes $50,000 in rental cost for a warehouse used by the Books and Reports Division for storage purposes.

f. Printing and paper costs other than for magazine subscriptions and for books and reports relate to the Continuing Education Division.

g. General and administrative expenses include costs relating to overall administration of the association as a whole. The company's corporate staff does some mailing of materials for general administrative purposes.

The expenses that can be traced or assigned to the corporate staff, as well as any other expenses that are not traceable to the profit centers, will be treated as common costs. It is not necessary to distinguish between variable and fixed costs.

Required

1. Prepare a segmented statement of revenues and expenses for Music Teachers, Inc. This statement should show the segment margin for each division as well as results for the association as a whole.
2. Give arguments for and against allocating *all* costs of the association to the four divisions.

(CMA, adapted)

C12–32 (Appendix 12A) Transfer Pricing; Divisional Performance
Weller Industries is a decentralized organization with six divisions. The company's Electrical Division produces a variety of electrical items, including an X52 electrical fitting. The Electrical Division (which is operating at capacity) sells this fitting to its regular customers for $7.50 each; the fitting has a variable manufacturing cost of $4.25.

The company's Brake Division has asked the Electrical Division to supply it with a large quantity of X52 fittings for only $5 each. The Brake Division, which is operating at 50% of capacity, will put the fitting into a brake unit that it will produce and sell to a large commercial airline manufacturer. The cost of the brake unit being built by the Brake Division follows:

Purchased parts (from outside vendors)	$22.50
Electrical fitting X52	5.00
Other variable costs	14.00
Fixed overhead and administration	8.00
Total cost per brake unit	$49.50

Although the $5 price for the X52 fitting represents a substantial discount from the regular $7.50 price, the manager of the Brake Division believes that the price concession is necessary if his division is to get the contract for the airplane brake units. He has heard "through the grapevine" that the airplane manufacturer plans to reject his bid if it is more than $50 per brake unit. Thus, if the Brake Division is forced to pay the regular $7.50 price for the X52 fitting, it will either not get the contract or it will suffer a substantial loss at a time when it is already operating at only 50% of capacity. The manager of the Brake Division argues that the price concession is imperative to the well-being of both his division and the company as a whole.

Weller Industries uses return on investment (ROI) and dollar profits in measuring divisional performance.

Required

1. Assume that you are the manager of the Electrical Division. Would you recommend that your division supply the X52 fitting to the Brake Division for $5 each as requested? Why or why not? Show all computations.
2. Would it be to the economic advantage of the company as a whole for the Electrical Division to supply the fittings to the Brake Division if the airplane brakes can be sold for $50? Show all computations, and explain your answer.
3. In principle, should it be possible for the two managers to agree to a transfer price in this particular situation? If so, within what range would that transfer price lie?
4. Discuss the organizational and manager behavior problems, if any, inherent in this situation. What would you advise the company's president to do in this situation?

(CMA, adapted)

Group Exercises

GE12–33 Performance Measurement at a Service Firm How do service-oriented firms' performance measurement and compensation systems compare with those of manufacturing firms? To study one well-run service business, ask the manager of your local McDonald's if he or she could spend some time discussing what performance measures McDonald's uses to evaluate store managers and how these performance measures tie in with the compensation of the store managers.

Required

Organize your analysis into the following areas:

1. What are McDonald's goals, that is, the broad, long-range plans of the company (e.g., to increase market share)?
2. What are the critical success factors (CSF), that is, the key areas in which things must go right if the company is to be successful (e.g., low selling prices based on low production costs)?
3. What are the performance measures that help to motivate and monitor progress toward achieving each CSF (e.g., continuous reduction in cost of quality)?
4. Are performance measures consistent with the store manager's compensation plan?

GE12–34 Evaluating Innovative and Standard Products Some firms choose a strategy that involves competing in established markets by selling high-volume standard products that have wide acceptance. Other firms choose a strategy that emphasizes competing in niche markets by selling low-volume innovative products that have a more narrow application.

Required

1. What criteria do customers use when choosing to purchase each type of product?
2. What measures should plant managers use to control and evaluate the financial performance of each product?
3. From your reading of Chapters 9–12, how do you think plant managers would control and evaluate the financial performance of each product?

GE12–35 How Do Capital Markets Evaluate Performance? Internally, companies usually use accounting measures to motivate and evaluate the performance of managers of corporate groups, divisions, product lines, and departments. How do investors use accounting information in determining whether to buy, sell, or hold onto a stock?

Most companies pay their top managers a salary and a bonus. The bonus part of their compensation is usually based on how well the executive performs against some accounting-based performance target. For example, some percentage of the CEO's bonus may be earned when he or she achieves a certain increase in earnings per share or, in the case of a division manager, when he or she exceeds a certain percentage increase in operating profits. Yet, there are numerous examples of CEOs and other top officers who have met their performance targets, but the stock price of the company lags or flounders for years on end. Top management prospers but stockholders may not.

Required

1. If a company consistently earns a profit year-in and year-out, do stockholders and prospective stockholders have a right to expect anything more than that from corporate management?
2. Is there any cost to holding large stocks of inventory? Is there any cost associated with the fixed assets—property, plant, and equipment—of capital-intensive businesses? Is there any cost of having idle assets or underutilized assets like buildings and equipment?
3. Is there any internal accounting charge for the money invested in working capital and fixed assets?
4. What is the cost of debt? Is there a similar cost associated with stockholders' equity? Explain.
5. Based on the discussion in (2) through (4) above, how does management create value (increase the stock price)? Under what conditions would the stock price languish or even decrease?
6. How would knowledge of this information influence how top management allocates the company's scarce cash resources within the firm?
7. Design a performance measurement system for senior-level officers and for divisional managers that is more consistent with enhancing a company's market value.
8. Do general economic conditions have any impact on a company's market value? How would you change the design of the performance measurement and compensation system to control for the fortune (or misfortune) of managing a company or division when general economic conditions were improving (or deteriorating)?

GE12–36 **College Segment Reports** Obtain a copy of your college or university's most recent financial report prepared for internal use.

Required

1. Does the financial report break down the results into major segments such as schools, academic departments, intercollegiate sports, and so on? Can you determine the financial contribution (i.e., revenues less expenses) of each segment from the report?
2. If the report attempts to show the financial contribution of each major segment, does the report follow the principles for segment reporting in this chapter? If not, what principles are violated and what harm, if any, can occur as a result from violating those principles?

IE12–37 **Return on Investment (ROI) Analysis** ROI is the product of a company's margin and turnover. In this exercise you will be computing margin, turnover, and ROI using data from the annual reports of several companies. Before starting on this exercise, you should know that in some cases it won't be completely clear which assets should be considered operating assets. Don't worry about this. Do the best you can and just be consistent from year to year within the same company.

Required

On the web site of each company below, you should be able to find directions to the company's annual report (sometimes referred to as Form 10-K). Using data from the company's two most recent annual reports, compute the company's margin, turnover, and ROI for the two most recent years. Using these ratios, briefly discuss the company's performance.

1. Apple Computer, www.apple.com.
2. Campbell Soup. www.campbellsoup.com.
3. Hershey Foods, www.hersheys,com.
4. Sprint, www.sprint.com.

Chapter Thirteen

Relevant Costs for Decision Making

Business Focus

A failure to recognize the existence of sunk costs can lead to bad business decisions. As evidence, consider the following incident related by a business consultant after encountering a frustrated and angry fellow traveler ("Mr. Smith") whose flight home faced a lengthy delay:

Mr. Smith had recently flown into St. Louis on a commercial airline for a two-day business trip. While there, he learned that his company's private airplane had flown in the day before and would leave on the same day that he was scheduled to leave. Mr. Smith immediately cashed in his $200 commercial airline ticket and made arrangements to fly back on the company plane. He flew home feeling pretty good about saving his company the $200 fare and being able to depart on schedule.

About two weeks later, however, Mr. Smith's boss asked him why the department had been cross-charged $400 for his return trip when the commercial airfare was only $200. Mr. Smith explained that "the company plane was flying back regardless, and there were a number of empty seats."

How could Mr. Smith's attempt to save his company $200 end up "costing" his department $400? The problem is that Mr. Smith recognized something that his company's cost allocation system did not: namely, that the vast majority of the costs associated with flying the plane home were already sunk and, thus, unavoidable at the time he made the decision to fly home. By failing to distinguish between sunk (i.e., unavoidable) and avoidable costs, the cost allocation system was causing the firm and its managers to make uneconomic business decisions.

It is now clear why Mr. Smith was so frustrated the day I ran into him in St. Louis. His company's plane was sitting on the runway with a number of empty seats and ready to take off for the very

Learning Objectives

After studying Chapter 13, you should be able to:

1 Distinguish between relevant and irrelevant costs in decisions.

2 Prepare an analysis showing whether to keep or replace old equipment.

3 Prepare an analysis showing whether a product line or other organizational segment should be dropped or retained.

4 Prepare a well-organized make or buy analysis.

5 Prepare an analysis showing whether a special order should be accepted.

6 Determine the most profitable use of a constrained resource.

7 Prepare an analysis showing whether joint products should be sold at the split-off point or processed further.

same destination. Yet there was no way Mr. Smith was going to fly on that plane even though doing so was the "best business decision."

Source: Dennis L. Weisman, "How Cost Allocation Systems Can Lead Managers Astray," Journal of Cost Management *5, no. 1 (Spring 1991), p. 4. Used by permission.*

Making decisions is one of the basic functions of a manager. Managers are constantly faced with problems of deciding what products to sell, what production methods to use, whether to make or buy component parts, what prices to charge, what channels of distribution to use, whether to accept special orders at special prices, and so forth. Decision making is often a difficult task that is complicated by the existence of numerous alternatives and massive amounts of data, only some of which may be relevant.

Every decision involves choosing from among at least two alternatives. In making a decision, the costs and benefits of one alternative must be compared to the costs and benefits of other alternatives. Costs that differ between alternatives are called **relevant costs.** Distinguishing between relevant and irrelevant cost and benefit data is critical for two reasons. First, irrelevant data can be ignored and need not be analyzed. This can save decision makers tremendous amounts of time and effort. Second, bad decisions can easily result from erroneously including irrelevant cost and benefit data when analyzing alternatives. To be successful in decision making, managers must be able to tell the difference between relevant and irrelevant data and must be able to correctly use the relevant data in analyzing alternatives. The purpose of this chapter is to develop these skills by illustrating their use in a wide range of decision-making situations. We hasten to add that these decision-making skills are as important in your personal life as they are to managers. After completing your study of the material in this chapter, you should be able to think more clearly about decisions in all facets of your life.

Cost Concepts for Decision Making

Four cost terms discussed in Chapter 2 are particularly applicable to this chapter. These terms are *differential costs, incremental costs, opportunity costs,* and *sunk costs.* You may find it helpful to turn back to Chapter 2 and refresh your memory concerning these terms before reading on.

Identifying Relevant Costs and Benefits

objective 1
Distinguish between relevant and irrelevant costs in decisions.

Only those costs and benefits that differ in total between alternatives are relevant in a decision. If a cost will be the same regardless of the alternative selected, then the decision has no effect on the cost and it can be ignored. For example, if you are trying to decide whether to go to a movie or to rent a videotape for the evening, the rent on your apartment is irrelevant. Whether you go to a movie or rent a videotape, the rent on your apartment will be exactly the same and is therefore irrelevant in the decision. On the other hand, the cost of the movie ticket and the cost of renting the videotape would be relevant in the decision since they are *avoidable costs.*

An **avoidable cost** is a cost that can be eliminated in whole or in part by choosing one alternative over another. By choosing the alternative of going to the movie, the cost of renting the videotape can be avoided. By choosing the alternative of renting the videotape, the cost of the movie ticket can be avoided. Therefore, the cost of the movie ticket and the cost of renting the videotape are both avoidable costs. On the other hand, the rent on the apartment is not an avoidable cost of either alternative. You would continue to rent your apartment under either alternative. Avoidable costs are relevant costs. Unavoidable costs are irrelevant costs.

Two broad categories of costs are never relevant in decisions. These irrelevant costs are:

1. Sunk costs.
2. Future costs that do not differ between the alternatives.

As we learned in Chapter 2, a **sunk cost** is a cost that has already been incurred and that cannot be avoided regardless of what a manager decides to do. Sunk costs are always the same, no matter what alternatives are being considered, and they are therefore always irrelevant and should be ignored. On the other hand, future costs that do differ between alternatives *are* relevant. For example, when deciding whether to go to a movie or rent a videotape, the cost of buying a movie ticket and the cost of renting a videotape have not yet been incurred. These are future costs that differ between alternatives when the decision is being made and therefore are relevant.

Along with sunk cost, the term **differential cost** was introduced in Chapter 2. In managerial accounting, the terms *avoidable cost, differential cost, incremental cost,* and *relevant cost* are often used interchangeably. To identify the costs that are avoidable (differential) in a particular decision situation and are therefore relevant, these steps can be followed:

1. Eliminate costs and benefits that do not differ between alternatives. These irrelevant costs consist of (a) sunk costs and (b) future costs that do not differ between alternatives.
2. Use the remaining costs and benefits that do differ between alternatives in making the decision. The costs that remain are the differential, or avoidable, costs.

Different Costs for Different Purposes

We need to recognize from the outset of our discussion that costs that are relevant in one decision situation are not necessarily relevant in another. Simply put, this means that *the manager needs different costs for different purposes.* For one purpose, a particular group of costs may be relevant; for another purpose, an entirely different group of costs may be relevant. Thus, in *each* decision situation the manager must examine the data at hand and isolate the relevant costs. Otherwise, the manager runs the risk of being misled by irrelevant data.

The concept of "different costs for different purposes" is basic to managerial accounting; we shall see its application frequently in the pages that follow.

Sunk Costs Are Not Relevant Costs

One of the most difficult conceptual lessons that managers have to learn is that sunk costs are never relevant in decisions. The temptation to include sunk costs in the analysis is especially strong in the case of book value of old equipment. We focus on book value of old equipment below, and then we consider other kinds of sunk costs in other parts of the chapter. We shall see that regardless of the kind of sunk cost involved, the conclusion is always the same—sunk costs are not avoidable, and therefore they should be ignored in decisions.

Managerial Accounting in Action

THE ISSUE

SoaringWings, Inc., is a small manufacturer of high-quality hang gliders. The most critical component of a hang glider is its metal frame, which must be very strong and yet very light. The frames are made by brazing together tubes of high-strength, but lightweight, metal alloys. Most of the brazing must be done by hand, but some can be done in an automated process by machine. Pete Kronski, the production manager of SoaringWings, Inc., has been trying to convince J. J. Marker, the company's president, to purchase a new brazing machine from Furimoro Industries. This machine would replace an old brazing machine from Bryston, Inc., that generates a large amount of scrap and waste.

On a recent blustery morning, Pete and J. J. happened to drive into the company's parking lot at the same time. The following conversation occurred as they walked together into the building.

Pete: Morning, J. J. Have you had a chance to look at the specifications on the new brazing machine from Furimoro Industries that I gave you last week?

J. J.: Are you still bugging me about the brazing machine?

Pete: You know it's almost impossible to keep that old Bryston brazing machine working within tolerances.

J. J.: I know, I know. But we're carrying the Bryston machine on the books for $140,000.

Pete: That's right. But I've done some investigating, and we could sell it for $90,000 to a plumbing company in town that doesn't require as tight tolerances as we do.

J. J.: Pete, that's just brilliant! You want me to sell a $140,000 machine for $90,000 and take a loss of $50,000. Do you have any other great ideas this morning?

Pete: J. J., I know it sounds far-fetched, but we would actually save money buying the new machine.

J. J.: I'm skeptical. However, if you can show me the hard facts, I'll listen.

Pete: Fair enough. I'll do it. ■

Book Value of Old Equipment

objective 2

Prepare an analysis showing whether to keep or replace old equipment.

Pete first gathered the following data concerning the old machine and the proposed new machine:

Old Machine	
Original cost	$175,000
Remaining book value	140,000
Remaining life	4 years
Disposal value now	$ 90,000
Disposal value in four years	–0–
Annual variable expenses to operate	345,000
Annual revenue from sales	500,000

Proposed New Machine	
List price new	$200,000
Expected life	4 years
Disposal value in four years	$ –0–
Annual variable expenses to operate	300,000
Annual revenue from sales	500,000

Should the old machine be disposed of and the new machine purchased? The first reaction of SoaringWings' president was to say no, since disposal of the old machine would result in a "loss" of $50,000:

Old Machine	
Remaining book value	$140,000
Disposal value now	90,000
Loss if disposed of now	$ 50,000

Given this potential loss if the old machine is sold, a manager may reason, "We've already made an investment in the old machine, so now we have no choice but to use it until our investment has been fully recovered." A manager may tend to think this way even though the new machine is clearly more efficient than the old machine. An error made in the past cannot be corrected by simply *using* the machine. The investment that has been made in the old machine is a sunk cost. The portion of this investment that remains on the company's books (the book value of $140,000) should not be considered in a decision about whether to buy the new machine. Pete Kronski verified the irrelevance of the book value of the old machine by the following analysis:[1]

	Total Cost and Revenues—Four Years		
	Keep Old Machine	Purchase New Machine	Differential Costs and Benefits
Sales	$ 2,000,000	$ 2,000,000	$ –0–
Variable expenses	(1,380,000)	(1,200,000)	180,000
Cost (depreciation) of the new machine	—	(200,000)	(200,000)
Depreciation of the old machine or book value write-off	(140,000)	(140,000)*	–0–
Disposal value of the old machine	—	90,000*	90,000
Total net operating income over the four years	$ 480,000	$ 550,000	$ 70,000

*For external reporting purposes, the $140,000 remaining book value of the old machine and the $90,000 disposal value would be netted together and deducted as a single $50,000 "loss" figure.

Looking at all four years together, notice that the firm will be $70,000 better off by purchasing the new machine. Also notice that the $140,000 book value of the old machine had *no effect* on the outcome of the analysis. Since this book value is a sunk cost, it must be absorbed by the firm regardless of whether the old machine is kept and used or whether it is sold. If the old machine is kept and used, then the $140,000 book value is deducted in the form of depreciation. If the old machine is sold, then the $140,000 book value is deducted in the form of a lump-sum write-off. Either way, the company bears the same $140,000 cost and the differential cost is zero.

FOCUSING ON RELEVANT COSTS What costs in the example above are relevant in the decision concerning the new machine? Looking at the original cost data, we should eliminate (1) the sunk costs and (2) the future costs and benefits that do not differ between the alternatives at hand.

1. The sunk costs:
   a. The remaining book value of the old machine ($140,000).
2. The future costs and benefits that do not differ:
   a. The sales revenue ($500,00 per year).
   b. The variable expenses (to the extent of $300,000 per year).

1. The computations involved in this example are taken one step further in Chapters 14 and 15 where we discuss the time value of money and the use of present value in decision making.

The costs and benefits that remain will form the basis for a decision. The analysis is as follows:

	Differential Costs and Benefits— Four Years
Reduction in variable expense promised by the new machine ($45,000* per year × 4 years)	$ 180,000
Cost of the new machine	(200,000)
Disposal value of the old machine	90,000
Net advantage of the new machine	$ 70,000

*$345,000 − $300,000 = $45,000.

Note that the items above are the same as those in the last column of the earlier analysis and represent those costs and benefits that differ between the two alternatives. Armed with this analysis, Pete felt confident that he would be able to explain the financial advantages of the new machine to the president of the company.

Managerial Accounting in Action

THE WRAP-UP

Pete Kronski took his analysis to the office of J. J. Marker, the president of SoaringWings, where the following conversation took place.

Pete: J. J., do you remember that discussion we had about the proposed new brazing machine?

J. J.: Sure I remember. Did you find out that I'm right?

Pete: Not exactly. Here's the analysis where I compare the profit with the old machine over the next four years to the profit with the new machine.

J. J.: I see you're claiming the profit is $70,000 higher with the new machine. Are you assuming higher sales with the new machine?

Pete: No, I have assumed total sales of $2,000,000 over the four years in either situation. The real advantage comes with the reduction in variable expenses of $180,000.

J. J.: Where are those reductions going to come from?

Pete: The new brazing machine should cut our scrap and rework rate at least in half. That results in substantial savings in materials and labor costs.

J. J.: What about the $50,000 loss on the old machine?

Pete: What really matters is the $200,000 cost of the new machine and the $90,000 salvage value of the old machine. The book value of the old machine is irrelevant. No matter what we do, that cost will eventually flow through the income statement as a charge in one form or another.

J. J.: I find that hard to accept, but it is difficult to argue with your analysis.

Pete: The analysis actually understates the advantages of the new machine. We don't catch all of the defects caused by the old machine, and defective products are sometimes sold to customers. With the new machine, I expect our warranty costs to decrease and our repeat sales to increase. And I would hate to be held responsible for any accidents caused by defective brazing by our old machine.

Pete: Okay, I'm convinced. Put together a formal proposal, and we'll present it at the next meeting of the board of directors. ■

Future Costs That Do Not Differ Are Not Relevant Costs

We stated above that people often have difficulty accepting the idea that sunk costs are never relevant in a decision. Some people also have difficulty accepting the principle that future costs that do not differ between alternatives are never relevant in a decision. An example will help illustrate how future costs *should* be handled in a decision.

Focus on Current Practice

In the early 1990s, General Motors Corp. laid off tens of thousands of its hourly workers who would nevertheless continue to receive full pay under union contracts. GM entered into an agreement with one of its suppliers, Android Industries, Inc., to use laid-off GM workers. GM agreed to pay the wages of the workers who would be supervised by Android Industries. In return, Android subtracted the wages from the bills it submitted to GM under their current contract. This reduction in contract price is pure profit to GM, since GM would have had to pay the laid-off workers in any case.[2] ■

An Example of Irrelevant Future Costs

A company is contemplating the purchase of a new labor-saving machine that will cost $30,000 and have a 10-year useful life. Data concerning the company's annual sales and costs with and without the new machine are shown below:

	Current Situation	Situation with the New Machine
Units produced and sold	5,000	5,000
Selling price per unit	$ 40	$ 40
Direct materials cost per unit	14	14
Direct labor cost per unit	8	5
Variable overhead cost per unit	2	2
Fixed costs, other	62,000	62,000
Fixed costs, new machine	—	3,000

The new machine promises a saving of $3 per unit in direct labor costs ($8 − $5 = $3), but it will increase fixed costs by $3,000 per year. All other costs, as well as the total number of units produced and sold, will remain the same. Following the steps outlined earlier, the analysis is as follows:

1. Eliminate the sunk costs. (No sunk costs are included in this example.)
2. Eliminate the future costs and benefits that do not differ between the alternatives.

2. "GM Agrees to Allow a Parts Supplier to Use Some of Its Idled Employees," *The Wall Street Journal,* November 30, 1992, p. B3.

Exhibit 13–1
Differential Cost Analysis

	5,000 Units Produced and Sold		
	Present Method	New Machine	Differential Costs and Benefits
Sales	$200,000	$200,000	$ -0-
Variable expenses:			
Direct materials	70,000	70,000	-0-
Direct labor	40,000	25,000	15,000
Variable overhead	10,000	10,000	-0-
Total variable expenses	120,000	105,000	
Contribution margin	80,000	95,000	
Less fixed expenses:			
Other	62,000	62,000	-0-
New machine	-0-	3,000	(3,000)
Total fixed expenses	62,000	65,000	
Net operating income	$ 18,000	$ 30,000	$12,000

a. The selling price per unit and the number of units sold do not differ between the alternatives. (Therefore, total future sales revenues will not differ.)
b. The direct materials cost per unit, the variable overhead cost per unit, and the number of units produced do not differ between the alternatives. (Therefore, total future direct materials costs and variable overhead costs will not differ.)
c. The "Fixed costs, other" do not differ between the alternatives.

The remaining costs—direct labor costs and the fixed costs associated with the new machine—are the only relevant costs.

Savings in direct labor costs ($5,000 units at a cost saving of $3 per unit)	$15,000
Less increase in fixed costs	3,000
Net annual cost savings promised by the new machine	$12,000

This solution can be verified by looking at *all* of the cost data (both those that are relevant and those that are not) under the two alternatives. This is done in Exhibit 13–1. Notice from the exhibit that the net advantage in favor of buying the machine is $12,000—the same answer we obtained by focusing on just the relevant costs. Thus, we can see that future costs that do not differ between alternatives are indeed irrelevant in the decision-making process and can be safely eliminated from the analysis.

Why Isolate Relevant Costs?

In the preceding example, we used two different approaches to analyze the alternatives. First, we considered only the relevant costs; and second, we considered all costs, both those that were relevant and those that were not. We obtained the same answer under both approaches. It would be natural to ask, "Why bother to isolate relevant costs when total costs will do the job just as well?" Isolating relevant costs is desirable for at least two reasons.

First, only rarely will enough information be available to prepare a detailed income statement for both alternatives such as we have done in the preceding examples. Assume, for example, that you are called on to make a decision relating to a *single operation* of a multidepartmental, multiproduct firm. Under these circumstances, it would be virtually impossible to prepare an income statement of any type. You would have to rely on your ability to recognize which costs are relevant and which are not in order to assemble that data necessary to make a decision.

Second, mingling irrelevant costs with relevant costs may cause confusion and distract attention from the matters that are really critical. Furthermore, the danger always exists that an irrelevant piece of data may be used improperly, resulting in an incorrect decision. The best approach is to ignore irrelevant data and base the decision entirely on the relevant data.

Relevant cost analysis, combined with the contribution approach to the income statement, provides a powerful tool for making decisions. We will investigate various uses of this tool in the remaining sections of this chapter.

Focus on Current Practice

A decision analysis can be flawed by incorrectly including irrelevant costs such as sunk costs and future costs that do not differ between alternatives. It can also be flawed by omitting future costs that *do* differ between alternatives. This is particularly a problem with environmental costs that have dramatically increased in recent years and about which many managers have little knowledge.

Consider the environmental complications posed by a decision of whether to install a solvent-based or powder-based system for spray-painting parts. In a solvent painting system, parts are sprayed as they move along a conveyor. The paint that misses the part is swept away by a wall of water, called a water curtain. The excess paint accumulates in a pit as sludge that must be removed each month. Environmental regulations classify this sludge as hazardous waste. As a result, the company must obtain a permit to produce the waste and must maintain meticulous records of how the waste is transported, stored, and disposed of. The annual costs of complying with these regulations can easily exceed $140,000 in total for a painting facility that initially costs only $400,000 to build. The costs of complying with environmental regulations include the following:

- The waste sludge must be hauled to a special disposal site. The typical disposal fee is about $300 per barrel or $55,000 per year for a modest solvent-based painting system.
- Workers must be specially trained to handle the paint sludge.
- The company must carry special insurance.
- The company must pay substantial fees to the state for releasing pollutants (i.e., the solvent) into the air.
- The water in the water curtain must be specially treated to remove contaminants. This cost can run into the tens of thousands of dollars per year.

In contrast, a powder-based painting system avoids almost all of these environmental costs. Excess powder used in the painting process can be recovered and reused without creating a hazardous waste. Additionally, the powder-based system does not release contaminants into the atmosphere. Therefore, even though the cost of building a powder-based system may be higher than the cost of building a solvent-based system, over the long run the costs of the powder-based system may be far lower due to the high environmental costs of a solvent-based system. Managers need to be aware of such environmental costs and take them fully into account when making decisions.[3] ■

Adding and Dropping Product Lines and Other Segments

objective 3

Prepare an analysis showing whether a product line or other organizational segment should be dropped or retained.

Decisions relating to whether old product lines or other segments of a company should be dropped and new ones added are among the most difficult that a manager has to make. In such decisions, many qualitative and quantitative factors must be considered. Ultimately, however, any final decision to drop an old segment or to add a new one is going to hinge primarily on the impact the decision will have on net operating income. To assess this impact, it is necessary to make a careful analysis of the costs involved.

An Illustration of Cost Analysis

Consider the three major product lines of the Discount Drug Company—drugs, cosmetics, and housewares. Sales and cost information for the preceding month for each separate product line and for the store in total are given in Exhibit 13–2.

What can be done to improve the company's overall performance? One product line—housewares—shows a net operating loss for the month. Perhaps dropping this

Exhibit 13–2
Discount Drug Company Product Lines

		Product Line		
	Total	Drugs	Cosmetics	Housewares
Sales	$250,000	$125,000	$75,000	$50,000
Less variable expenses	105,000	50,000	25,000	30,000
Contribution margin	145,000	75,000	50,000	20,000
Less fixed expenses:				
Salaries	50,000	29,500	12,500	8,000
Advertising	15,000	1,000	7,500	6,500
Utilities	2,000	500	500	1,000
Depreciation—fixtures	5,000	1,000	2,000	2,000
Rent	20,000	10,000	6,000	4,000
Insurance	3,000	2,000	500	500
General administrative	30,000	15,000	9,000	6,000
Total fixed expenses	125,000	59,000	38,000	28,000
Net operating income (loss)	$ 20,000	$ 16,000	$12,000	$ (8,000)

3. Germain Böer, Margaret Curtin, and Louis Hoyt, "Environmental Cost Management," *Management Accounting,* September 1998, pp. 28–38.

line would cause profits in the company as a whole to improve. In deciding whether the line should be dropped, management should reason as follows:

If the housewares line is dropped, then the company will lose $20,000 per month in contribution margin. By dropping the line, however, it may be possible to avoid some fixed costs. It may be possible, for example, to discharge certain employees, or it may be possible to reduce advertising costs. If by dropping the housewares line the company is able to avoid more in fixed costs than it loses in contribution margin, then it will be better off if the line is eliminated, since overall net income should improve. On the other hand, if the company is not able to avoid as much in fixed costs as it loses in contribution margin, then the housewares line should be retained. In short, the manager should ask, "What costs can I avoid if I drop this product line?"

As we have seen from our earlier discussion, not all costs are avoidable. For example, some of the costs associated with a product line may be sunk costs. Other costs may be allocated common costs that will not differ in total regardless of whether the product line is dropped or retained. As discussed in Chapter 8, an activity-based costing analysis may be used to help identify the relevant costs.

To show how the manager should proceed in a product-line analysis, suppose that the management of the Discount Drug Company has analyzed the costs being charged to the three product lines and has determined the following:

1. The salaries expense represents salaries paid to employees working directly in each product-line area. All of the employees working in housewares would be discharged if the line is dropped.
2. The advertising expense represents direct advertising of each product line and is avoidable if the line is dropped.
3. The utilities expense represents utilities costs for the entire company. The amount charged to each product line is an allocation based on space occupied and is not avoidable if the product line is dropped.
4. The depreciation expense represents depreciation on fixtures used for display of the various product lines. Although the fixtures are nearly new, they are custom-built and will have little resale value if the housewares line is dropped.
5. The rent expense represents rent on the entire building housing the company; it is allocated to the product lines on the basis of sales dollars. The monthly rent of $20,000 is fixed under a long-term lease agreement.
6. The insurance expense represents insurance carried on inventories within each of the three product-line areas.
7. The general administrative expense represents the costs of accounting, purchasing, and general management, which are allocated to the product lines on the basis of sales dollars. Total administrative costs will not change if the housewares line is dropped.

With this information, management can identify costs that can and cannot be avoided if the product line is dropped:

	Total Cost	Not Avoidable*	Avoidable
Salaries	$ 8,000		$ 8,000
Advertising	6,500		6,500
Utilities	1,000	$ 1,000	
Depreciation—fixtures	2,000	2,000	
Rent	4,000	4,000	
Insurance	500		500
General administrative	6,000	6,000	
Total fixed expenses	$28,000	$13,000	$15,000

*These costs represent either (1) sunk costs or (2) future costs that will not change if the housewares line is retained or discontinued.

Exhibit 13–3
A Comparative Format for Product-Line Analysis

	Keep Housewares	Drop Housewares	Difference: Net Income Increase or (Decrease)
Sales	$50,000	$ -0-	$(50,000)
Less variable expenses	30,000	-0-	30,000
Contribution margin	20,000	-0-	(20,000)
Less fixed expenses:			
Salaries	8,000	-0-	8,000
Advertising	6,500	-0-	6,500
Utilities	1,000	1,000	-0-
Depreciation—fixtures	2,000	2,000	-0-
Rent	4,000	4,000	-0-
Insurance	500	-0-	500
General administrative	6,000	6,000	-0-
Total fixed expenses	28,000	13,000	15,000
Net operating income (loss)	$ (8,000)	$(13,000)	$ (5,000)

To determine how dropping the line will affect the overall profits of the company, we can compare the contribution margin that will be lost to the costs that can be avoided if the line is dropped:

Contribution margin lost if the housewares line is discontinued (see Exhibit 13–2)	$(20,000)
Less fixed costs that can be avoided if the housewares line is discontinued (see above)	15,000
Decrease in overall company net operating income	$ (5,000)

In this case, the fixed costs that can be avoided by dropping the product line are less than the contribution margin that will be lost. Therefore, based on the data given, the housewares line should not be discontinued unless a more profitable use can be found for the floor and counter space that it is occupying.

A Comparative Format

Some managers prefer to approach decisions of this type by preparing comparative income statements showing the effects on the company as a whole of either keeping or dropping the product line in question. A comparative analysis of this type for the Discount Drug Company is shown in Exhibit 13–3.

As shown by column 3 in the exhibit, overall company net operating income will decrease by $5,000 each period if the housewares line is dropped. This is the same answer, of course, as we obtained in our earlier analysis.

Beware of Allocated Fixed Costs

Our conclusion that the housewares line should not be dropped seems to conflict with the data shown earlier in Exhibit 13–2. Recall from the exhibit that the housewares line is showing a loss rather than a profit. Why keep a line that is showing a loss? The explanation for this apparent inconsistency lies at least in part with the common fixed costs that are being allocated to the product lines. As we observed in Chapter 12, one of the great dangers in allocating common fixed costs is that such allocations can make a product line (or other segment of a business) *look* less profitable than it really is. By allocating the common fixed costs among all product lines, the housewares line has

Exhibit 13–4
Discount Drug Company Product Lines—Recast in Contribution Format (from Exhibit 13–2)

	Total	Product Line: Drugs	Product Line: Cosmetics	Product Line: House-wares
Sales	$250,000	$125,000	$75,000	$50,000
Less variable expenses	105,000	50,000	25,000	30,000
Contribution margin	145,000	75,000	50,000	20,000
Less traceable fixed expenses:				
Salaries	50,000	29,500	12,500	8,000
Advertising	15,000	1,000	7,500	6,500
Depreciation—fixtures	5,000	1,000	2,000	2,000
Insurance	3,000	2,000	500	500
Total	73,000	33,500	22,500	17,000
Product-line segment margin	72,000	$ 41,500	$27,500	$ 3,000*
Less common fixed expenses:				
Utilities	2,000			
Rent	20,000			
General administrative	30,000			
Total	52,000			
Net operating income	$ 20,000			

*If the housewares line is dropped, this $3,000 in segment margin will be lost to the company. In addition, we have seen that the $2,000 depreciation on the fixtures is a sunk cost that cannot be avoided. The sum of these two figures ($3,000 + $2,000 = $5,000) would be the decrease in the company's overall profits if the housewares line were discontinued.

been made to *look* as if it were unprofitable, whereas, in fact, dropping the line would result in a decrease in overall company net operating income. This point can be seen clearly if we recast the data in Exhibit 13–2 and eliminate the allocation of the common fixed costs. This recasting of data—using the segmented approach from Chapter 12—is shown in Exhibit 13–4.

Exhibit 13–4 gives us a much different perspective of the housewares line than does Exhibit 13–2. As shown in Exhibit 13–4, the housewares line is covering all of its own traceable fixed costs and is generating a $3,000 segment margin toward covering the common fixed costs of the company. Unless another product line can be found that will generate a greater segment margin than this, the company would be better off keeping the housewares line. By keeping the line, the company's overall net operating income will be higher than if the product line were dropped.

Additionally, we should note that managers may choose to retain an unprofitable product line if the line is necessary to the sale of other products or if it serves as a "magnet" to attract customers. Bread, for example, is not an especially profitable line in food stores, but customers expect it to be available, and many would undoubtedly shift their buying elsewhere if a particular store decided to stop carrying it.

Focus on Current Practice

A bakery distributed its products through route salespersons, each of whom loaded a truck with an assortment of products in the morning and spent the day calling on customers in an assigned territory. Believing that some items were more profitable than others, management asked for an analysis

of product costs and sales. The accountants to whom the task was assigned allocated all manufacturing and marketing costs to products to obtain a net profit for each product. The resulting figures indicated that some of the products were being sold at a loss, and management discontinued these products. However, when this change was put into effect, the company's overall profit declined. It was then seen that by dropping some products, sales revenues had been reduced without commensurate reduction in costs because the common manufacturing costs and route sales costs had to be continued in order to make and sell the remaining products. ■

The Make or Buy Decision

objective 4

Prepare a well-organized make or buy analysis.

Many steps may be involved in getting a finished product into the hands of a consumer. First, raw materials may have to be obtained through mining, drilling, growing crops, raising animals, and so forth. Second, these raw materials may have to be processed to remove impurities and to extract the desirable and usable materials. Third, the usable materials may have to undergo some preliminary fabrication so as to be usable in final products. For example, cotton must be made into thread and textiles before being made into clothing. Fourth, the actual manufacturing of the finished product must take place. And finally, the finished product must be distributed to the ultimate consumer. All of these steps taken together are called a *value chain.*

Separate companies may carry out each of the steps in the value chain or a single company may carry out several of the steps. When a company is involved in more than one of these steps in the entire value chain, it is following a policy of **vertical integration.** Vertical integration is very common. Some firms control *all* of the activities in the value chain from producing basic raw materials right up to the final distribution of finished goods. Other firms are content to integrate on a smaller scale by purchasing many of the parts and materials that go into their finished products.

A decision to produce a fabricated part internally, rather than to buy the part externally from a supplier, is called a **make or buy decision.** Actually, any decision relating to vertical integration is a make or buy decision, since the company is deciding whether to meet its own needs internally or to buy externally.

Focus on Current Practice

Sometimes, qualitative factors dictate that a company buy rather than make certain parts. Cummins Engine Company, a manufacturer of diesel engines, recently faced the problem of developing much more advanced piston designs in order to meet mandated emissions standards. Pistons are the "guts" of the engine, so management was reluctant to outsource these parts. However, advanced pistons could already be acquired from several outside suppliers whose cumulative volumes of piston production were many times larger than that of Cummins. This volume had allowed the suppliers to invest 20 times as much as Cummins in research and development and to build advanced manufacturing processes. Consequently, the suppliers were far ahead of Cummins and were likely to remain so without substantial investments that would be difficult to justify. Therefore, management decided to outsource the production of pistons.[4] ■

4. Ravi Venkatesan, "Strategic Sourcing: to Make or Not to Make," *Harvard Business Review*, November–December 1992, p. 104.

Strategic Aspects of the Make or Buy Decision

Integration provides certain advantages. An integrated firm is less dependent on its suppliers and may be able to ensure a smoother flow of parts and materials for production than a nonintegrated firm. For example, a strike against a major parts supplier can interrupt the operations of a nonintegrated firm for many months, whereas an integrated firm that is producing its own parts might be able to continue operations. Also, many firms feel that they can control quality better by producing their own parts and materials, rather than by relying on the quality control standards of outside suppliers. In addition, the integrated firm realizes profits from the parts and materials that it is "making" rather than "buying," as well as profits from its regular operations.

The advantages of integration are counterbalanced by some advantages of using external suppliers. By pooling demand from a number of firms, a supplier may be able to enjoy economies of scale in research and development and in manufacturing. These economies of scale can result in higher quality and lower costs than would be possible if the firm were to attempt to make the parts on its own. A company must be careful, however, to retain control over activities that are essential to maintaining its competitive position. For example, Hewlett-Packard controls the software for a laser printer it makes in cooperation with Canon Inc. of Japan to prevent Canon from coming out with a competing product. The present trend appears to be toward less vertical integration, with some companies like Sun Microsystems concentrating on hardware and software design and relying on outside supplies for almost everything else in the value chain.[5] These factors suggest that the make or buy decision should be weighed very carefully.

An Example of Make or Buy

To provide an illustration of a make or buy decision, consider Mountain Goat Cycles. The company is now producing the heavy-duty gear shifters used in its most popular line of mountain bikes. The company's Accounting Department reports the following costs of producing the shifter internally:

	Per Unit	8,000 Units
Direct materials	$ 6	$ 48,000
Direct labor	4	32,000
Variable overhead	1	8,000
Supervisor's salary	3	24,000
Depreciation of special equipment	2	16,000
Allocated general overhead	5	40,000
Total cost	$21	$168,000

An outside supplier has offered to sell Mountain Goat Cycles 8,000 shifters a year at a price of only $19 each. Should the company stop producing the shifters internally and start purchasing them from the outside supplier? To approach the decision from a financial point of view, the manager should again focus on the differential costs. As we have seen, the differential costs can be obtained by eliminating those costs that are not avoidable—that is, by eliminating (1) the sunk costs and (2) the future costs that will continue regardless of whether the shifters are produced internally or purchased outside. The costs that remain after making these eliminations are the costs that

5. Ralph E. Drtina, "The Outsourcing Decision," *Management Accounting,* March 1994, pp. 56–62.

Exhibit 13–5 Mountain Goat Cycles Make or Buy Analysis

	Production "Cost" per Unit	Per Unit Differential Costs		Total Differential Costs—8,000 Units	
		Make	Buy	Make	Buy
Direct materials	$ 6	$ 6		$ 48,000	
Direct labor	4	4		32,000	
Variable overhead	1	1		8,000	
Supervisor's salary	3	3		24,000	
Depreciation of special equipment	2	—		—	
Allocated general overhead	5	—		—	
Outside purchase price			$19		$152,000
Total cost	$21	$14	$19	$112,000	$152,000
Difference in favor of continuing to make		$5		$40,000	

are avoidable to the company by purchasing outside. If these avoidable costs are less than the outside purchase price, then the company should continue to manufacture its own shifters and reject the outside supplier's offer. That is, the company should purchase outside only if the outside purchase price is less than the costs that can be avoided internally as a result of stopping production of the shifters.

Looking at the data on the previous page, note first that depreciation of special equipment is listed as one of the costs of producing the shifters internally. Since the equipment has already been purchased, this depreciation is a sunk cost and is therefore irrelevant. If the equipment could be sold, its salvage value would be relevant. Or if the machine could be used to make other products, this could be relevant as well. However, we will assume that the equipment has no salvage value and that it has no other use except making the heavy-duty gear shifters.

Also note that the company is allocating a portion of its general overhead costs to the shifters. Any portion of this general overhead cost that would actually be eliminated if the gear shifters were purchased rather than made would be relevant in the analysis. However, it is likely that the general overhead costs allocated to the gear shifters are in fact common to all items produced in the factory and would continue unchanged even if the shifters are purchased from the outside. Such allocated common costs are not differential costs (since they do not differ between the make or buy alternatives) and should be eliminated from the analysis along with the sunk costs.

The variable costs of producing the shifters (materials, labor, and variable overhead) are differential costs, since they can be avoided by buying the shifters from the outside supplier. If the supervisor can be discharged and his or her salary avoided by buying the shifters, then it too will be a differential cost and relevant to the decision. Assuming that both the variable costs and the supervisor's salary can be avoided by buying from the outside supplier, then the analysis takes the form shown in Exhibit 13–5.

Since it costs $5 less per unit to continue to make the shifters, Mountain Goat Cycles should reject the outside supplier's offer. However, there is one additional factor that the company may wish to consider before coming to a final decision. This factor is the opportunity cost of the space now being used to produce the shifters.

The Matter of Opportunity Cost

If the space now being used to produce the shifters *would otherwise be idle,* then Mountain Goat Cycles should continue to produce its own shifters and the supplier's offer should be rejected, as stated above. Idle space that has no alternative use has an opportunity cost of zero.

But what if the space now being used to produce shifters could be used for some other purpose? In that case, the space would have an opportunity cost that would have to be considered in assessing the desirability of the supplier's offer. What would this opportunity cost be? It would be the segment margin that could be derived from the best alternative use of the space.

To illustrate, assume that the space now being used to produce shifters could be used to produce a new cross-country bike that would generate a segment margin of $60,000 per year. Under these conditions, Mountain Goat Cycles would be better off to accept the supplier's offer and to use the available space to produce the new product line:

	Make	Buy
Differential cost per unit (see prior example)	$ 14	$ 19
Number of units needed annually	× 8,000	× 8,000
Total annual cost	112,000	152,000
Opportunity cost—segment margin forgone on a potential new product line	60,000	
Total cost	$172,000	$152,000
Difference in favor of purchasing from the outside supplier	$ 20,000	

Opportunity costs are not recorded in accounts of an organization. They do not represent actual dollar outlays. Rather, they represent economic benefits that are *forgone* as a result of pursuing some course of action. The opportunity costs of Mountain Goat Cycles are sufficiently large in this case to make continued production of the shifters very costly from an economic point of view.

Special Orders

objective 5

Prepare an analysis showing whether a special order should be accepted.

Managers often must evaluate whether a *special order* should be accepted, and if the order is accepted, the price that should be charged. A **special order** is a one-time order that is not considered part of the company's normal ongoing business. To illustrate, Mountain Goat Cycles has just received a request from the Seattle Police Department to produce 100 specially modified mountain bikes at a price of $179 each. The bikes would be used to patrol some of the more densely populated residential sections of the city. Mountain Goat Cycles can easily modify its City Cruiser model to fit the specifications of the Seattle Police. The normal selling price of the City Cruiser bike is $249, and its unit product cost is $182 as shown below:

Direct materials	$ 86
Direct labor	45
Manufacturing overhead	51
Unit product cost	$182

The variable portion of the above manufacturing overhead is $6 per unit. The order would have no effect on the company's total fixed manufacturing overhead costs.

The modifications to the bikes consist of welded brackets to hold radios, nightsticks, and other gear. These modifications would require $17 in incremental variable costs. In addition, the company would have to pay a graphics design studio $1,200 to design and cut stencils that would be used for spray painting the Seattle Police Department's logo and other identifying marks on the bikes.

This order should have no effect on the company's other sales. The production manager says that she can handle the special order without disrupting any of the regular scheduled production.

What effect would accepting this order have on the company's net operating income?

Only the incremental costs and benefits are relevant. Since the existing fixed manufacturing overhead costs would not be affected by the order, they are not incremental costs and are therefore not relevant. The incremental net operating income can be computed as follows:

	Per Unit	Total 100 Bikes
Incremental revenue	$179	$17,900
Incremental costs:		
Variable costs:		
Direct materials	86	8,600
Direct labor	45	4,500
Variable manufacturing overhead	6	600
Special modifications	17	1,700
Total variable cost	$154	15,400
Fixed cost:		
Purchase of stencils		1,200
Total incremental cost		16,600
Incremental net operating income		$ 1,300

Therefore, even though the price on the special order ($179) is below the normal unit product cost ($182) and the order would require incurring additional costs, the order would result in an increase in net operating income. In general, a special order is profitable as long as the incremental revenue from the special order exceeds the incremental costs of the order. We must note, however, that it is important to make sure that there is indeed idle capacity and that the special order does not cut into normal sales. For example, if the company was operating at capacity, opportunity costs would have to be taken into account as well as the incremental costs that have already been detailed above.

Utilization of a Constrained Resource

objective 6

Determine the most profitable use of a constrained resource.

Managers are routinely faced with the problem of deciding how constrained resources are going to be utilized. A department store, for example, has a limited amount of floor space and therefore cannot stock every product that may be available. A manufacturing firm has a limited number of machine-hours and a limited number of direct labor-hours at its disposal. When a limited resource of some type restricts the company's ability to satisfy demand, the company is said to have a **constraint.** Because of the constrained resource, the company cannot fully satisfy demand, so the manager must decide how the constrained resource should be used. Fixed costs are usually unaffected by such choices, so the manager should select the course of action that will maximize the firm's *total* contribution margin.

Contribution in Relation to a Constrained Resource

To maximize total contribution margin, a firm should not necessarily promote those products that have the highest *unit* contribution margins. Rather, total contribution margin will be maximized by promoting those products or accepting those orders that provide the highest unit contribution margin *in relation to the constrained resource.* To illustrate, Mountain Goat Cycles makes a line of paniers—a saddlebag for bicycles. There are two models of paniers—a touring model and a mountain model. Cost and revenue data for the two models of paniers are given below:

	Model	
	Mountain Panier	Touring Panier
Selling price per unit	$25	$30
Variable cost per unit	10	18
Contribution margin per unit	$15	$12
Contribution margin (CM) ratio	60%	40%

The mountain panier appears to be much more profitable than the touring panier. It has a $15 per unit contribution margin as compared to only $12 per unit for the touring model, and it has a 60% CM ratio as compared to only 40% for the touring model.

But now let us add one more piece of information—the plant that makes the paniers is operating at capacity. Ordinarily this does not mean that every machine and every person in the plant is working at the maximum possible rate. Because machines have different capacities, some machines will be operating at less than 100% of capacity. However, if the plant as a whole cannot produce any more units, some machine or process must be operating at capacity. The machine or process that is limiting overall output is called the **bottleneck**—it is the constraint.

At Mountain Goat Cycles, the bottleneck is a particular stitching machine. The mountain panier requires 2 minutes of stitching time, and each unit of the touring panier requires 1 minute of stitching time. Since this stitching machine already has more work than it can handle, something will have to be cut back. In this situation, which product is more profitable? To answer this question, the manager should look at the *contribution margin per unit of the constrained resource.* This figure is computed by dividing the contribution margin by the amount of the constrained resource a unit of product requires. These calculations are carried out below for the mountain and touring paniers.

	Model	
	Mountain Panier	Touring Panier
Contribution margin per unit (above) (a)	$15.00	$12.00
Time on the stitching machine required to produce one unit (b)	2 min.	1 min.
Contribution margin per unit of the constrained resource, (a) ÷ (b)	$7.50/min.	$12.00/min.

It is now easy to decide which product is less profitable and should be de-emphasized. Each minute of processing time on the stitching machine that is devoted to the touring panier results in an increase of $12 in contribution margin and profits.

The comparable figure for the mountain panier is only $7.50 per minute. Therefore, the touring model should be emphasized. Even though the mountain model has the larger per unit contribution margin and the larger CM ratio, the touring model provides the larger contribution margin in relation to the constrained resource.

To verify that the touring model is indeed the more profitable product, suppose an hour of additional stitching time is available and that there are unfilled orders for both products. The additional hour on the stitching machine could be used to make either 30 mountain paniers (60 minutes ÷ 2 minutes) or 60 touring paniers (60 minutes ÷ 1 minute), with the following consequences:

	Model	
	Mountain Panier	Touring Panier
Contribution margin per unit (above) (a)	$ 15	$ 12
Additional units that can be processed in one hour	× 30	× 60
Additional contribution margin	$450	$720

This example clearly shows that looking at unit contribution margins alone is not enough; the contribution margin must be viewed in relation to the amount of the constrained resource each product requires.

Focus on Current Practice

The bottleneck at Southwestern Ohio Steel is the blanking line. On the blanking line, large rolls of steel up to 60 inches wide are cut into flat sheets. Setting up the blanking line between jobs takes an average of 2.5 hours, and during this time, the blanking line is shut down.

Management estimates the opportunity cost of lost sales at $225 per hour, which is the contribution margin per hour of the blanking line for a typical order. Under these circumstances, a new loading device with an annual fixed cost of $36,000 that would save 720 setup hours per year looked like an excellent investment. The new loading device would have an average cost of only $50 per hour ($36,000 ÷ 720 hours = $50) compared to the $225 per hour the company would generate in added contribution margin.[6] ■

Managing Constraints

Profits can be increased by effectively managing the organization's constraints. One aspect of managing constraints is to decide how to best utilize them. As discussed above, if the constraint is a bottleneck in the production process, the manager should

6. Robert J. Campbell, "Steeling Time with ABC or TOC," *Management Accounting,* January 1995, pp. 31–36.

select the product mix that maximizes the total contribution margin. In addition, the manager should take an active role in managing the constraint itself. Management should focus efforts on increasing the efficiency of the bottleneck operation and on increasing its capacity. Such efforts directly increase the output of finished goods and will often pay off in an almost immediate increase in profits.

It is often possible for a manager to effectively increase the capacity of the bottleneck, which is called **relaxing (or elevating) the constraint.** For example, the stitching machine operator could be asked to work overtime. This would result in more available stitching time and hence more finished goods that can be sold. The benefits from relaxing the constraint in such a manner are often enormous and can be easily quantified. The manager should first ask, "What would I do with additional capacity at the bottleneck if it were available?" In the example, if there are unfilled orders for both the touring and mountain paniers, the additional capacity would be used to process more touring paniers, since that would be a better use of the additional capacity. In that situation, the additional capacity would be worth $12 per minute or $720 per hour. This is because adding an hour of capacity would generate an additional $720 of contribution margin if it would be used solely to process more touring paniers. Since overtime pay for the operator is likely to be much less than $720 per hour, running the stitching machine on overtime would be an excellent way to increase the profits of the company while at the same time satisfying customers.

To reinforce this concept, suppose that making touring paniers has already been given top priority and consequently there are only unfilled orders for the mountain panier. How much would it be worth to the company to run the stitching machine overtime in this situation? Since the additional capacity would be used to make the mountain panier, the value of that additional capacity would drop to $7.50 per minute or $450 per hour. Nevertheless, the value of relaxing the constraint would still be quite high.

These calculations indicate that managers should pay great attention to bottleneck operations. If a bottleneck machine breaks down or is ineffectively utilized, the losses to the company can be quite large. In our example, for every minute the stitching machine is down due to breakdowns or setups, the company loses between $7.50 and $12.00. The losses on an hourly basis are between $450 and $720! In contrast, there is no such loss of contribution margin if time is lost on a machine that is not a bottleneck—such machines have excess capacity anyway.

The implications are clear. Managers should focus much of their attention on managing bottlenecks. As we have discussed, managers should emphasize products that most profitably utilize the constrained resource. They should also make sure that products are processed smoothly through the bottlenecks, with minimal lost time due to breakdowns and setups. And they should try to find ways to increase the capacity at the bottlenecks.

The capacity of a bottleneck can be effectively increased in a number of ways, including:

- Working overtime on the bottleneck.
- Subcontracting some of the processing that would be done at the bottleneck.
- Investing in additional machines at the bottleneck.
- Shifting workers from processes that are not bottlenecks to the process that *is* a bottleneck.
- Focusing business process improvement efforts such as TQM and Business Process Re-engineering on the bottleneck.
- Reducing defective units. Each defective unit that is processed through the bottleneck and subsequently scrapped takes the place of a good unit that could be sold.

The last three methods of increasing the capacity of the bottleneck are particularly attractive, since they are essentially free and may even yield additional cost savings.

Focus on Current Practice

It is often possible to elevate the constraint at very low cost. Western Textile Products makes pockets, waistbands, and other clothing components. The constraint at the company's plant in Greenville, South Carolina, was the slitting machines. These large machines slit huge rolls of textiles into appropriate widths for use on other machines. Management was contemplating adding a second shift to elevate the constraint. However, investigation revealed that the slitting machines were actually being run only one hour in a nine-hour shift. "The other eight hours were required to get materials, load and unload the machine, and do setups. Instead of adding a second shift, a second person was assigned to each machine to fetch materials and do as much of the setting up as possible off-line while the machine was running." This approach resulted in increasing the run time to four hours. If another shift had been added without any improvement in how the machines were being used, the cost would have been much higher and there would have been only a one-hour increase in run time.[7]

The Problem of Multiple Constraints

What does a firm do if it has more than one potential constraint? For example, a firm may have limited raw materials, limited direct labor-hours available, limited floor space, and limited advertising dollars to spend on product promotion. How would it proceed to find the right combination of products to produce? The proper combination or "mix" of products can be found by use of a quantitative method known as *linear programming,* which is covered in quantitative methods and operations management courses.

Joint Product Costs and the Contribution Approach

objective 7

Prepare an analysis showing whether joint products should be sold at the split-off point or processed further.

In some industries, a number of end products are produced from a single raw material input. A grisly, but apt, example is provided by the meat-packing industry. A great variety of end products—bacon, ham, spareribs, pork roasts, and so on—are produced from a single pig. Firms that produce several end products from a common input (e.g., a pig) are faced with the problem of deciding how the cost of that input is going to be divided among the end products. Before we address this problem, it will be helpful to define three terms—joint products, joint product costs, and split-off point.

Two or more products that are produced form a common input are known as **joint products.** The term **joint product costs** is used to describe those manufacturing costs that are incurred in producing joint products up to the split-off point. The **split-off point** is that point in the manufacturing process at which the joint products (bacon, ham, spareribs, and so on) can be recognized as separate products. At that point, some of the joint products will be in final form, ready to be marketed to the consumer. Others

7. Eric Noreen, Debra Smith, and James T. Mackey, *The Theory of Constraints and Its Implications for Management Accounting* (Croton-on-Hudson, NY: The North River Press, 1995), pp. 84–85.

Exhibit 13–6
Joint Products

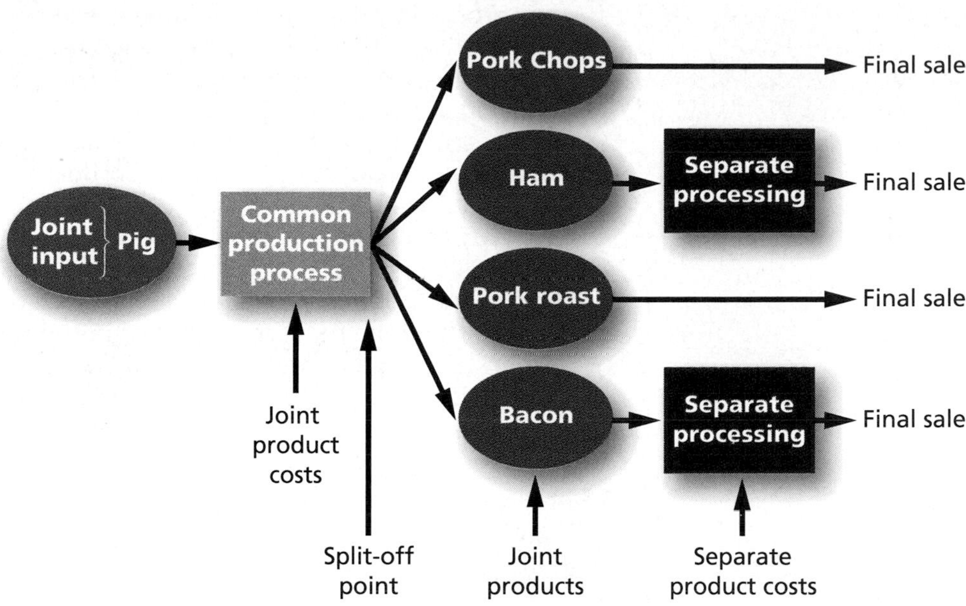

will still need further processing on their own before they are in marketable form. These concepts are presented graphically in Exhibit 13–6.

The Pitfalls of Allocation

Joint product costs are really common costs incurred to simultaneously produce a variety of end products. Traditional cost accounting books contain various approaches to allocating these common costs among the different products at the split-off point. A typical approach is to allocate the joint product costs according to the relative sales value of the end products.

Although allocation of joint product costs is needed for some purposes, such as balance sheet inventory valuation, allocations of this kind should be viewed with great caution *internally* in the decision-making process. Unless a manager proceeds with care, he or she may be led into incorrect decisions as a result of relying on allocated common costs. The Focus on Current Practice box below discusses an actual business situation illustrating an incorrect decision that resulted from using allocated costs.

Focus on Current Practice

A company located on the Gulf of Mexico is a producer of soap products. Its six main soap product lines are produced from common inputs. Joint product costs up to the split-off point constitute the bulk of the production costs for all six product lines. These joint product costs are allocated to the six product lines on the basis of the relative sales value of each line at the split-off point.

The company has a waste product that results from the production of the six main product lines. Until a few years ago, the company loaded the waste onto barges and dumped it into the Gulf of Mexico, since the waste was thought to have no commercial value. The dumping was stopped, however, when the company's research division discovered that with some

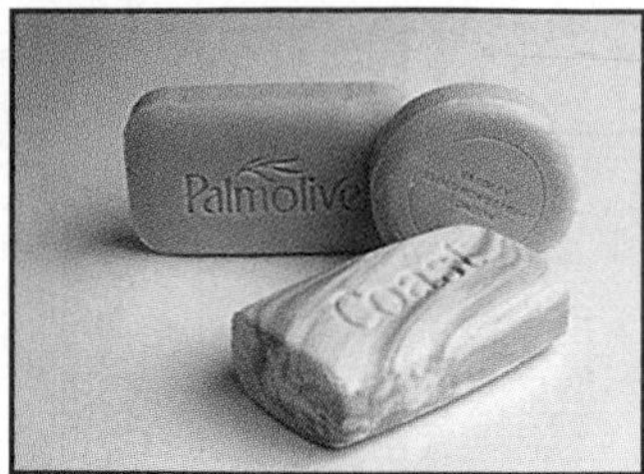

further processing the waste could be made commercially salable as a fertilizer ingredient. The further processing was initiated at a cost of $175,000 per year. The waste was then sold to fertilizer manufacturers at a total price of $300,000 per year.

The accountants responsible for allocating manufacturing costs included the sales value of the waste product along with the sales value of the six main product lines in their allocation of the joint product costs at the split-off point. This allocation resulted in the waste product being allocated $150,000 in joint product cost. This $150,000 allocation, when added to the further processing costs of $175,000 for the waste, caused the waste product to show the net loss computed in the table below.

When presented with this analysis, the company's management decided that further processing of the waste was not desirable after all. The company went back to dumping the waste in the Gulf. In addition to being unwise from an economic viewpoint, this dumping also raises questions regarding the company's social responsibility and the environmental impact of its actions.

Sales value of the waste product after further processing	$ 300,000
Less costs assignable to the waste product	325,000
Net loss	$ (25,000)

Sell or Process Further Decisions

Joint product costs are irrelevant in decisions regarding what to do with a product from the split-off point forward. The reason is that by the time one arrives at the split-off point, the joint product costs have already been incurred and therefore are sunk costs. In the case of the soap company (see the accompanying Focus on Current Practice box), the $150,000 in allocated joint costs should not have been permitted to influence what was done with the waste product from the split-off point forward. The analysis should have been as follows:

	Dump in Gulf	Process Further
Sales value	–0–	$300,000
Additional processing costs	–0–	175,000
Contribution margin	–0–	$125,000
Advantage of processing further	$125,000	

Decisions of this type are known as **sell or process further decisions.** It will always be profitable to continue processing a joint product after the split-off point *so long as the incremental revenue from such processing exceeds the incremental processing cost incurred after the split-off point.* Joint product costs that have already been incurred up to the split-off point are sunk costs, which are always irrelevant in decisions concerning what to do from the split-off point forward.

To provide a detailed example of a sell or process further decision, assume that three products are derived from a single raw material input. Cost and revenue data relating to the products are presented in Exhibit 13–7 along with an analysis of which products should be sold at the split-off point and which should be processed further. As shown in the exhibit, products B and C should both be processed further; product A should be sold at the split-off point.

Exhibit 13–7 Sell or Process Further Decision

	Product		
	A	B	C
Sales value at the split-off point	$120,000	$150,000	$60,000
Sales value after further processing	160,000	240,000	90,000
Allocated joint product costs	80,000	100,000	40,000
Cost of further processing	50,000	60,000	10,000
Analysis of sell or process further:			
Sales value after further processing	$160,000	$240,000	$90,000
Sales value at the split-off point	120,000	150,000	60,000
Incremental revenue from further processing	40,000	90,000	30,000
Cost of further processing	50,000	60,000	10,000
Profit (loss) from further processing	$(10,000)	$ 30,000	$20,000

Activity-Based Costing and Relevant Costs

As discussed in Chapter 8, activity-based costing can be used to help identify potentially relevant costs for decision-making purposes. Activity-based costing improves the traceability of costs by focusing on the activities caused by a product or other segment. Managers should exercise caution against reading more into this "traceability" than really exists. People have a tendency to assume that if a cost is traceable to a segment, then the cost is automatically an avoidable cost. That is not true. As emphasized in Chapter 8, the costs provided by a well-designed activity-based costing system are only *potentially* relevant. Before making a decision, managers must still decide which of the potentially relevant costs are actually avoidable. Only those costs that are avoidable are relevant and the others should be ignored.

To illustrate, refer again to the data relating to the housewares line in Exhibit 13–4 on page 627. The $2,000 depreciation on fixtures is a traceable cost of the houseware lines because it relates to activities in that department. We found, however, that the $2,000 is not avoidable if the housewares line is dropped. The key lesson here is that the method used to assign a cost to a product or other segment does not change the basic nature of the cost. A sunk cost such as depreciation of old equipment is still a sunk cost regardless of whether it is traced directly to a particular segment on an activity basis, allocated to all segments on the basis of labor-hours, or treated in some other way in the costing process. Regardless of the method used to assign costs to products or other segments, the manager still must apply the principles discussed in this chapter to determine the costs that are avoidable in each situation.[8]

Summary

All of the material in this chapter consists of applications of one simple but powerful idea. Only those costs and benefits that differ between alternatives are relevant in a decision. All other costs and benefits are irrelevant and can and should be ignored. In particular, sunk costs are irrelevant as are future costs that do not differ between alternatives.

8. For further discussion, see Douglas Sharp and Linda P. Christensen, "A New View of Activity-Based Costing," *Management Accounting* 73, no.7 (September 1991), pp. 32–34; and Maurice L. Hirsch, Jr., and Michael C. Nibbelin, "Incremental, Separable, Sunk, and Common Costs in Activity-Based Costing," *Journal of Cost Management* 6, no. 1 (Spring 1992), pp. 39–47.

This simple idea was applied in a variety of situations including decisions that involve replacing equipment, making or buying a component, adding or dropping a product line, processing a joint product further, and using a constrained resource. This list includes only a tiny sample of the possible applications of the relevant cost concept. Indeed, *any* decision involving costs hinges on the proper identification and analysis of the costs that are relevant. We will continue to focus on the concept of relevant costs in the following two chapters where long-run investment decisions are considered.

Review Problem: Relevant Costs

Charter Sports Equipment manufactures round, rectangular, and octagonal trampolines. Data on sales expenses for the past month follow:

		Trampoline		
	Total	Round	Rectangular	Octagonal
Sales	$1,000,000	$ 140,000	$500,000	$360,000
Less variable expenses	410,000	60,000	200,000	150,000
Contribution margin	590,000	80,000	300,000	210,000
Less fixed expenses:				
Advertising—traceable	216,000	41,000	110,000	65,000
Depreciation of special equipment	95,000	20,000	40,000	35,000
Line supervisors' salaries	19,000	6,000	7,000	6,000
General factory overhead*	200,000	28,000	100,000	72,000
Total fixed expenses	530,000	95,000	257,000	178,000
Net operating income (loss)	$ 60,000	$(15,000)	$ 43,000	$ 32,000

*A common cost that is allocated on the basis of sales dollars.

Management is concerned about the continued losses shown by the round trampolines and wants a recommendation as to whether or not the line should be discontinued. The special equipment used to produce the trampolines has no resale value. If the round trampoline model is dropped, the two line supervisors assigned to the model would be discharged.

Required

1. Should production and sale of the round trampolines be discontinued? You may assume that the company has no other use for the capacity now being used to produce the round trampolines. Show computations to support your answer.
2. Recast the above data in a format that would be more usable to management in assessing the long-run profitability of the various product lines.

Solution to Review Problem

1. No, production and sale of the round trampolines should not be discontinued. Computations to support this answer follow:

Contribution margin lost if the round trampolines are discontinued		$(80,000)
Less fixed costs that can be avoided:		
Advertising—traceable	$41,000	
Line supervisors' salaries	6,000	47,000
Decrease in net operating income for the company as a whole		$(33,000)

The depreciation of the special equipment represents a sunk cost, and therefore it is not relevant to the decision. The general factory overhead is allocated and will presumably continue regardless of whether or not the round trampolines are discontinued; thus, it also is not relevant to the decision.

Alternative Solution to Question 1

	Keep Round Tramps	Drop Round Tramps	Difference: Net Income Increase or (Decrease)
Sales	$140,000	$ –0–	$(140,000)
Less variable expenses	60,000	–0–	60,000
Contribution margin	80,000	–0–	(80,000)
Less fixed expenses:			
Advertising—traceable	41,000	–0–	41,000
Depreciation of special equipment	20,000	20,000	–0–
Line supervisors' salaries	6,000	–0–	6,000
General factory overhead	28,000	28,000	–0–
Total fixed expenses	95,000	48,000	47,000
Net operating income (loss)	$(15,000)	$(48,000)	$ (33,000)

2. If management wants a clear picture of the profitability of the segments, the general factory overhead should not be allocated. It is a common cost and therefore should be deducted from the total product-line segment margin, as shown in Chapter 12. A more useful income statement format would be as follows:

		Trampoline		
	Total	Round	Rectangular	Octagonal
Sales	$1,000,000	$140,000	$500,000	$360,000
Less variable expenses	410,000	60,000	200,000	150,000
Contribution margin	590,000	80,000	300,000	210,000
Less traceable fixed expenses:				
Advertising—traceable	216,000	41,000	110,000	65,000
Depreciation of special equipment	95,000	20,000	40,000	35,000
Line supervisors' salaries	19,000	6,000	7,000	6,000
Total traceable fixed expenses	330,000	67,000	157,000	106,000
Product-line segment margin	260,000	$ 13,000	$143,000	$104,000
Less common fixed expenses	200,000			
Net operating income (loss)	$ 60,000			

Key Terms for Review

Avoidable cost Any cost that can be eliminated (in whole or in part) by choosing one alternative over another in a decision-making situation. In managerial accounting, this term is synonymous with *relevant cost* and *differential cost.* (p. 616)

Bottleneck A machine or process that limits total output because it is operating at capacity. (p. 633)

Constraint A limitation under which a company must operate, such as limited machine time available or limited raw materials available that restricts the company's ability to satisfy demand. (p. 632)

Differential cost Any cost that differs between alternatives in a decision-making situation. In managerial accounting, this term is synonymous with *avoidable cost* and *relevant cost.* (p. 617)

Joint product costs Costs that are incurred up to the split-off point in producing joint products. (p. 636)

Joint products Two or more items that are produced from a common input. (p. 636)

Make or buy decision A decision as to whether an item should be produced internally or purchased from an outside supplier. (p. 628)

Relaxing (or elevating) the constraint An action that increases the capacity of a bottleneck. (p. 635)

Relevant cost A cost that differs between alternatives in a particular decision. In managerial accounting, this term is synonymous with *avoidable cost* and *differential cost.* (p. 616)

Sell or process further decision A decision as to whether a joint product should be sold at the split-off point or processed further and sold at a later time in a different form. (p. 638)

Special order A one-time order that is not considered part of the company's normal on-going business. (p. 631)

Split-off point That point in the manufacturing process where some or all of the joint products can be recognized as individual products. (p. 636)

Sunk cost Any cost that has already been incurred and that cannot be changed by any decision made now or in the future. (p. 616)

Vertical integration The involvement by a company in more than one of the steps from production of basic raw materials to the manufacture and distribution of a finished product. (p. 628)

Questions

13–1 What is a *relevant cost?*

13–2 Define the following terms: *incremental cost, opportunity cost,* and *sunk cost.*

13–3 Are variable costs always relevant costs? Explain.

13–4 The book value of a machine (as shown on the balance sheet) is an asset to a company, but this same book value is irrelevant in decision making. Explain why this is so.

13–5 "Sunk costs are easy to spot—they're simply the fixed costs associated with a decision." Do you agree? Explain.

13–6 "Variable costs and differential costs mean the same thing." Do you agree? Explain.

13–7 "All future costs are relevant in decision making." Do you agree? Why?

13–8 Prentice Company is considering dropping one of its product lines. What costs of the product line would be relevant to this decision? Irrelevant?

13–9 "If a product line is generating a loss, then that's pretty good evidence that the product line should be discontinued." Do you agree? Explain.

13–10 What is the danger in allocating common fixed costs among product lines or other segments of an organization?

13–11 How does opportunity cost enter into the make or buy decision?

13–12 Give four examples of possible constraints.

13–13 How will relating product contribution margins to the constrained resource they require help a company ensure that profits will be maximized?

13–14 Define the following terms: *joint products, joint product costs,* and *split-off point.*

13–15 From a decision-making point of view, what pitfalls are there in allocating common costs among joint products?

13–16 What guideline can be used in determining whether a joint product should be sold at the split-off point or processed further?

13–17 Airlines sometimes offer reduced rates during certain times of the week to members of a businessperson's family if they accompany him or her on trips. How does the concept of relevant costs enter into the decision to offer reduced rates of this type?

Exercises

E13–1 Listed below are a number of costs that may be relevant in decisions faced by the management of Svahn, AB, a Swedish manufacturer of sailing yachts:

	Case 1		Case 2	
Item	**Relevant**	**Not Relevant**	**Relevant**	**Not Relevant**
a. Sales revenue				
b. Direct materials				
c. Direct labor				
d. Variable manufacturing overhead				
e. Depreciation—Model B100 machine				
f. Book value—Model B100 machine				
g. Disposal value—Model B100 machine				
h. Market value—Model B300 machine (cost)				
i. Depreciation—Model B300 machine				
j. Fixed manufacturing overhead (general)				
k. Variable selling expense				
l. Fixed selling expense				
m. General administrative overhead				

Required Copy the information above onto your answer sheet and place an X in the appropriate column to indicate whether each item is relevant or not relevant in the following situations (requirement 1 relates to Case 1 above, and requirement 2 relates to Case 2):

1. Management is considering purchasing a Model B300 machine to use in addition to the company's present Model B100 machine. This will increase the company's production and sales. The increase in volume will be large enough to require increases in fixed selling expenses and in general administrative overhead, but not in the fixed manufacturing overhead.
2. Management is instead considering replacing its present Model B100 machine with a new Model B300 machine. The Model B100 machine would be sold. This change will have no effect on production or sales, other than some savings in direct materials costs due to less waste.

E13–2 Bill has just returned from a duck hunting trip. He has brought home eight ducks. Bill's friend, John, disapproves of duck hunting, and to discourage Bill from further hunting, John has presented him with the following cost estimate per duck:

Camper and equipment:	
Cost, $12,000; usable for eight seasons; 10 hunting trips per season	$150
Travel expense (pickup truck):	
100 miles at $0.12 per mile (gas, oil, and tires—$0.07 per mile: depreciation and insurance—$0.05 per mile)	12
Shotgun shells (two boxes)	20
Boat:	
Cost, $2,320, usable for eight seasons; 10 hunting trips per season	29
Hunting license:	
Cost, $30 for the season; 10 hunting trips per season	3
Money lost playing poker:	
Loss, $18 (Bill plays poker every weekend)	18
A fifth of Old Grandad:	
Cost, $8 (used to ward off the cold)	8
Total cost	$240
Cost per duck ($240 ÷ 8 ducks)	$ 30

Required

1. Assuming that the duck hunting trip Bill has just completed is typical, what costs are relevant to a decision as to whether Bill should go duck hunting again this season?
2. Suppose that Bill gets lucky on his next hunting trip and shoots 10 ducks in the amount of time it took him to shoot 8 ducks on his last trip. How much would it have cost him to shoot the last two ducks?
3. Which costs are relevant in a decision of whether Bill should give up hunting? Explain.

E13–3 Thalassines Kataskeves, S.A., of Greece makes marine equipment. The company has been experiencing losses on its bilge pump product line for several years. The most recent quarterly income statement for the bilge pump product line is given below:

THALASSINES KATASKEVES, S.A.
Income Statement—Bilge Pump
For the Quarter Ended March 31

Sales		DR850,000
Less variable expenses:		
Variable manufacturing expenses	DR330,000	
Sales commissions	42,000	
Shipping	18,000	
Total variable expenses		390,000
Contribution margin		460,000
Less fixed expenses:		
Advertising	270,000	
Depreciation of equipment (no resale value)	80,000	
General factory overhead	105,000*	
Salary of product-line manager	32,000	
Insurance on inventories	8,000	
Purchasing department expenses	45,000†	
Total fixed expenses		540,000
Net loss		DR(80,000)

*Common costs allocated on the basis of machine-hours.
†Common costs allocated on the basis of sales dollars.

The currency in Greece is the drachma, denoted here by DR. The discontinuance of the bilge pump product line would not affect sales of other product lines and would have no noticeable effect on the company's total general factory overhead or total Purchasing Department expenses.

Required

Would you recommend that the bilge pump product line be discontinued? Support your answer with appropriate computations.

E13–4 Hollings Company sells office furniture in the Rocky Mountain area. As part of its service, it delivers furniture to customers.

The costs associated with the acquisition and annual operation of a delivery truck are given below:

Insurance	$1,600
Licenses	250
Taxes (vehicle)	150
Garage rent for parking (per truck)	1,200
Depreciation ($9,000 ÷ 5 years)	1,800*
Gasoline, oil, tires, and repairs	0.07 per mile

*Based on obsolescence rather than on wear and tear.

Required

1. Assume that Hollings Company has purchased one truck and that the truck has been driven 50,000 miles during the first year. Compute the average cost per mile of owning and operating the truck.

2. At the beginning of the second year, Hollings Company is unsure whether to use the truck or leave it parked in the garage and have all hauling done commercially. (The state requires the payment of vehicle taxes even if the vehicle isn't used.) What costs from the previous list are relevant to this decision? Explain.
3. Assume that the company decides to use the truck during the second year. Near year-end an order is received from a customer over 1,000 miles away. What costs from the previous list are relevant in a decision between using the truck to make the delivery and having the delivery done commercially? Explain.
4. Occasionally, the company could use two trucks at the same time. For this reason, some thought is being given to purchasing a second truck. The total miles driven would be the same as if only one truck were owned. What costs from the previous list are relevant to a decision over whether to purchase the second truck? Explain.

E13–5 Barlow Company manufactures three products: A, B, and C. The selling price, variable costs, and contribution margin for one unit of each product follow:

	Product		
	A	B	C
Selling price	$180	$270	$240
Less variable expenses:			
Direct materials	24	72	32
Other variable expenses	102	90	148
Total variable expenses	126	162	180
Contribution margin	$ 54	$108	$ 60
Contribution margin ratio	30%	40%	25%

The same raw material is used in all three products. Barlow Company has only 5,000 pounds of material on hand and will not be able to obtain any more material for several weeks due to a strike in its supplier's plant. Management is trying to decide which product(s) to concentrate on next week in filling its backlog of orders. The material costs $8 per pound.

Required

1. Compute the amount of contribution margin that will be obtained per pound of material used in each product.
2. Which orders would you recommend that the company work on next week—the orders for product A, product B, or product C? Show computations.
3. A foreign supplier could furnish Barlow with additional stocks of the raw material at a substantial premium over the usual price. If there is unfilled demand for all three products, what is the highest price that Barlow Company should be willing to pay for an additional pound of materials?

E13–6 Troy Engines, Ltd., manufactures a variety of engines for use in heavy equipment. The company has always produced all of the necessary parts for its engines, including all of the carburetors. An outside supplier has offered to produce and sell one type of carburetor to Troy Engines, Ltd., for a cost of $35 per unit. To evaluate this offer, Troy Engines, Ltd., has gathered the following information relating to its own cost of producing the carburetor internally:

	Per Unit	15,000 Units per Year
Direct materials	$14	$210,000
Direct labor	10	150,000
Variable manufacturing overhead	3	45,000
Fixed manufacturing overhead, traceable	6*	90,000
Fixed manufacturing overhead, allocated	9	135,000
Total cost	$42	$630,000

*One-third supervisory salaries; two-thirds depreciation of special equipment (no resale value).

Required

1. Assuming that the company has no alternative use for the facilities that are now being used to produce the carburetors, should the outside supplier's offer be accepted? Show all computations.
2. Suppose that if the carburetors were purchased, Troy Engines, Ltd., could use the freed capacity to launch a new product. The segment margin of the new product would be $150,000 per year. Should Troy Engines, Ltd., accept the offer to buy the carburetors for $35 per unit? Show all computations.

E13–7 Waukee Railroad is considering the purchase of a powerful, high-speed wheel grinder to replace a standard wheel grinder that is now in use. Selected information on the two machines is given below:

	Standard Wheel Grinder	High-Speed Wheel Grinder
Original cost new	$20,000	$30,000
Accumulated depreciation to date.	6,000	—
Current salvage value	9,000	—
Estimated cost per year to operate	15,000	7,000
Remaining years of useful life.	5 years	5 years

Required

Prepare a computation covering the five-year period that will show the net advantage or disadvantage of purchasing the high-speed wheel grinder. Use only relevant costs in your analysis.

E13–8 The Regal Cycle Company manufactures three types of bicycles—a dirt bike, a mountain bike, and a racing bike. Data on sales and expenses for the past quarter follow:

	Total	Dirt Bikes	Mountain Bikes	Racing Bikes
Sales	$300,000	$90,000	$150,000	$60,000
Less variable manufacturing and selling expenses	120,000	27,000	60,000	33,000
Contribution margin	180,000	63,000	90,000	27,000
Less fixed expenses:				
Advertising, traceable	30,000	10,000	14,000	6,000
Depreciation of special equipment	23,000	6,000	9,000	8,000
Salaries of product-line managers	35,000	12,000	13,000	10,000
Common allocated costs*	60,000	18,000	30,000	12,000
Total fixed expenses	148,000	46,000	66,000	36,000
Net operating income (loss)	$ 32,000	$17,000	$ 24,000	$ (9,000)

*Allocated on the basis of sales dollars.

Management is concerned about the continued losses shown by the racing bikes and wants a recommendation as to whether or not the line should be discontinued. The special equipment used to produce racing bikes has no resale value and does not wear out.

Required

1. Should production and sale of the racing bikes be discontinued? Show computations to support your answer.
2. Recast the above data in a format that would be more usable to management in assessing the long-run profitability of the various product lines.

E13–9 Han Products manufactures 30,000 units of part S-6 each year for use on its production line. At this level of activity, the cost per unit for part S-6 is as follows:

Direct materials	$ 3.60
Direct labor	10.00
Variable overhead	2.40
Fixed overhead	9.00
Total cost per part	$25.00

An outside supplier has offered to sell 30,000 units of part S-6 each year to Han Products for $21 per part. If Han Products accepts this offer, the facilities now being used to manufacture part S-6 could be rented to another company at an annual rental of $80,000. However, Han Products has determined that two-thirds of the fixed overhead being applied to part S-6 would continue even if part S-6 were purchased from the outside supplier.

Required Prepare computations to show the net dollar advantage or disadvantage of accepting the outside supplier's offer.

E13–10 Dorsey Company manufacturers three products from a common input in a joint processing operation. Joint processing costs up to the split-off point total $350,000 per quarter. The company allocates these costs to the joint products on the basis of their total sales value at the split-off point. Unit selling prices and total output at the split-off point are as follows:

Product	Selling Price	Quarterly Output
A	$16 per pound	15,000 pounds
B	8 per pound	20,000 pounds
C	25 per gallon	4,000 gallons

Each product can be processed further after the split-off point. Additional processing requires no special facilities. The additional processing costs (per quarter) and unit selling prices after further processing are given below:

Product	Additional Processing Costs	Selling Price
A	$63,000	$20 per pound
B	80,000	13 per pound
C	36,000	32 per gallon

Required Which product or products should be sold at the split-off point and which product or products should be processed further? Show computations.

Problems

P13–11 Relevant Cost Analysis; Book Value Murl Plastics, Inc., purchased a new machine one year ago at a cost of $60,000. Although the machine operates well, the president of Murl Plastics is wondering if the company should replace it with a new electronically operated machine that has just come on the market. The new machine would slash annual operating costs by two-thirds, as shown in the comparative data below:

	Present Machine	Proposed New Machine
Purchase cost new	$60,000	$90,000
Estimated useful life new	6 years	5 years
Annual operating costs	$42,000	$14,000
Annual straight-line depreciation	10,000	18,000
Remaining book value	50,000	—
Salvage value now	10,000	—
Salvage value in 5 years	-0-	-0-

In trying to decide whether to purchase the new machine, the president has prepared the following analysis:

Book value of the old machine	$50,000
Less salvage value	10,000
Net loss from disposal	$40,000

"Even though the new machine looks good," said the president, "we can't get rid of that old machine if it means taking a huge loss on it. We'll have to use the old machine for at least a few more years."

Sales are expected to be $200,000 per year, and selling and administrative expenses are expected to be $126,000 per year, regardless of which machine is used.

Required

1. Prepare a summary income statement covering the next five years, assuming:
   a. That the new machine is not purchased.
   b. That the new machine is purchased.
2. Determine the desirability of purchasing the new machine using only relevant costs in your analysis.

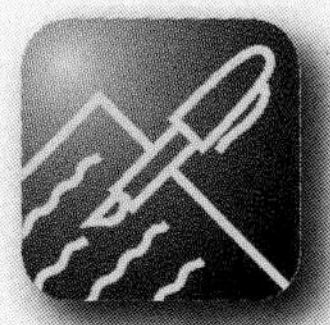

P13–12 Dropping a Flight; Analysis of Operating Policy Profits have been decreasing for several years at Pegasus Airlines. In an effort to improve the company's performance, consideration is being given to dropping several flights that appear to be unprofitable.

A typical income statement for one such flight (flight 482) is given below (per flight):

Ticket revenue (175 seats × 40% occupancy × $200 ticket price)	$14,000	100.0%
Less variable expenses ($15 per person)	1,050	7.5
Contribution margin	12,950	92.5%
Less flight expenses:		
Salaries, flight crew	1,800	
Flight promotion	750	
Depreciation of aircraft	1,550	
Fuel for aircraft	6,800	
Liability insurance	4,200	
Salaries, flight assistants	500	
Baggage loading and flight preparation	1,700	
Overnight costs for flight crew and assistants at destination	300	
Total flight expenses	17,600	
Net operating loss	$ (4,650)	

The following additional information is available about flight 482:

a. Members of the flight crew are paid fixed annual salaries, whereas the flight assistants are paid by the flight.
b. One-third of the liability insurance is a special charge assessed against flight 482 because in the opinion of the insurance company, the destination of the flight is in a "high-risk" area. The remaining two-thirds would be unaffected by a decision to drop flight 482.
c. The baggage loading and flight preparation expense is an allocation of ground crews' salaries and depreciation of ground equipment. Dropping flight 482 would have no effect on the company's total baggage loading and flight preparation expenses.
d. If flight 482 is dropped, Pegasus Airlines has no authorization at present to replace it with another flight.
e. Depreciation of aircraft is due entirely to obsolescence. Depreciation due to wear and tear is negligible.
f. Dropping flight 482 would not allow Pegasus Airlines to reduce the number of aircraft in its fleet or the number of flight crew on its payroll.

Required

1. Prepare an analysis showing what impact dropping flight 482 would have on the airline's profits.
2. The airline's scheduling officer has been criticized because only about 50% of the seats on Pegasus' flights are being filled compared to an average of 60% for the industry. The scheduling officer has explained that Pegusus' average seat occupancy could be improved considerably by eliminating about 10% of the flights, but that doing so would reduce profits. Explain how this could happen.

P13–13 Relevant Cost Potpourri Unless otherwise indicated, each of the following parts is independent. In all cases, show computations to support your answer.

1. A merchandising company has two departments, A and B. A recent monthly income statement for the company follows:

		Department	
	Total	A	B
Sales	$4,000,000	$3,000,000	$1,000,000
Less variable expenses	1,300,000	900,000	400,000
Contribution margin	2,700,000	2,100,000	600,000
Less fixed expenses	2,200,000	1,400,000	800,000
Net operating income (loss)	$ 500,000	$ 700,000	$ (200,000)

   A study indicates that $340,000 of the fixed expenses being charged to Department B are sunk costs or allocated costs that will continue even if B is dropped. In addition, the elimination of Department B will result in a 10% decrease in the sales of Department A. If Department B is dropped, what will be the effect on the net operating income of the company as a whole?

2. For many years Futura Company has purchased the starters that it installs in its standard line of farm tractors. Due to a reduction in output of certain of its products, the company has idle capacity that could be used to produce the starters. The chief engineer has recommended against this move, however, pointing out that the cost to produce the starters would be greater than the current $8.40 per unit purchase price:

	Per Unit	Total
Direct materials	$3.10	
Direct labor	2.70	
Supervision	1.50	$60,000
Depreciation	1.00	40,000
Variable manufacturing overhead	0.60	
Rent	0.30	12,000
Total production cost	$9.20	

   A supervisor would have to be hired to oversee production of the starters. However, the company has sufficient idle tools and machinery that no new equipment would have to be purchased. The rent charge above is based on space utilized in the plant. The total rent on the plant is $80,000 per period. Depreciation is due to obsolescence rather than wear and tear. Prepare computations to show the dollar advantage or disadvantage per period of making the starters.

3. Wexpro, Inc., produces several products from processing of 1 ton of clypton, a rare mineral. Material and processing costs total $60,000 per ton, one-fourth of which is allocated to product X. Seven thousand units of product X are produced from each ton of clypton. The units can either be sold at the split-off point for $9 each, or processed further at a total cost of $9,500 and then sold for $12 each. Should product X be processed further or sold at the split-off point?

4. Benoit Company produces three products, A, B, and C. Data concerning the three products follows (per unit):

	Product		
	A	B	C
Selling price	$80	$56	$70
Less variable expenses:			
Direct materials	24	15	9
Other variable expenses	24	27	40
Total variable expenses	48	42	49
Contribution margin	$32	$14	$21
Contribution margin ratio	40%	25%	30%

Demand for the company's products is very strong, with far more orders each month than the company has raw materials available to produce. The same material is used in each product. The material costs $3 per pound with a maximum of 5,000 pounds available each month. Which orders would you advise the company to accept first, those for A, for B, or for C? Which orders second? Third?

5. Delta Company produces a single product. The cost of producing and selling a single unit of this product at the company's normal activity level of 60,000 units per year is:

Direct materials	$5.10
Direct labor	3.80
Variable manufacturing overhead	1.00
Fixed manufacturing overhead	4.20
Variable selling and administrative expense	1.50
Fixed selling and administrative expense	2.40

The normal selling price is $21 per unit. The company's capacity is 75,000 units per year. An order has been received from a mail-order house for 15,000 units at a special price of $14 per unit. This order would not affect regular sales. If the order is accepted, by how much will annual profits be increased or decreased? (The order will not change the company's total fixed costs.)

6. Refer to the data in (5) above. Assume the company has 1,000 units of this product left over from last year that are vastly inferior to the current model. The units must be sold through regular channels at reduced prices. What unit cost figure is relevant for establishing a minimum selling price for these units? Explain.

P13–14 Sell or Process Further Decision (Prepared from a situation suggested by Professor John W. Hardy.) Lone Star Meat Packers is a major processor of beef and other meat products. The company has a large amount of T-bone steak on hand, and it is trying to decide whether to sell the T-bone steaks as they are initially cut or to process them further into filet mignon and the New York cut.

If the T-bone steaks are sold as initially cut, the company figures that a 1-pound T-bone steak would yield the following profit:

Selling price ($2.25 per pound)	$2.25
Less joint product cost	1.80
Profit per pound	$0.45

Instead of being sold an initially cut, the T-bone steaks could be further processed into filet mignon and New York cut steaks. Cutting one side of a T-bone steak provides the filet mignon, and cutting the other side provides the New York cut. One 16-ounce T-bone steak thus cut will yield one 6-ounce filet mignon and one 8-ounce New York cut; the remaining ounces are waste. The cost of processing the T-bone steaks into these cuts is $0.25 per pound. The filet mignon can be sold for $4.00 per pound, and the New York cut can be sold for $2.80 per pound.

Required

1. Determine the profit per pound from further processing the T-bone steaks.
2. Would you recommend that the T-bone steaks be sold as initially cut or processed further? Why?

P13–15 Make or Buy Analysis "In my opinion, we ought to stop making our own drums and accept that outside supplier's offer," said Wim Niewindt, managing director of Antilles Refining, N.V., of Aruba. "At a price of 18 florins per drum, we would be paying 5 florins less than it costs us to manufacture the drums in our own plant. (The currency in Aruba is the florin, denoted below by fl.) Since we use 60,000 drums a year, that would be an annual cost savings of 300,000 florins." Antilles Refining's present cost to manufacture one drum is given below (based on 60,000 drums per year):

Direct material	fl10.35
Direct labor	6.00
Variable overhead	1.50
Fixed overhead (fl2.80 general company overhead, fl1.60 depreciation and, fl0.75 supervision)	5.15
Total cost per drum	fl23.00

A decision about whether to make or buy the drums is especially important at this time since the equipment being used to make the drums is completely worn out and must be replaced. The choices facing the company are:

Alternative 1: Purchase new equipment and continue to make the drums. The equipment would cost fl810,000; it would have a six-year useful life and no salvage value. The company uses straight-line depreciation.

Alternative 2: Purchase the drums from an outside supplier at fl18 per drum under a six-year contract.

The new equipment would be more efficient than the equipment that Antilles Refining has been using and, according to the manufacturer, would reduce direct labor and variable overhead costs by 30%. The old equipment has no resale value. Supervision cost (fl45,000 per year) and direct materials cost per drum would not be affected by the new equipment. The new equipment's capacity would be 90,000 drums per year. The company has no other use for the space being used to produce the drums.

The company's total general company overhead would be unaffected by this decision.

Required

1. To assist the managing director in making a decision, prepare an analysis showing what the total cost and the cost per drum would be under each of the two alternatives given above. Assume that 60,000 drums are needed each year. Which course of action would you recommend to the managing director?
2. Would your recommendation in (1) above be the same if the company's needs were: (a) 75,000 drums per year or (b) 90,000 drums per year? Show computations to support your answer, with costs presented on both a total and a per unit basis.
3. What other factors would you recommend that the company consider before making a decision?

P13–16 Selected Relevant Cost Questions Andretti Company has a single product called a Dak. The company normally produces and sells 60,000 Daks each year at a selling price of $32 per unit. The company's unit costs at this level of activity are given below:

Direct materials	$10.00	
Direct labor	4.50	
Variable manufacturing overhead	2.30	
Fixed manufacturing overhead	5.00	($300,000 total)
Variable selling expenses	1.20	
Fixed selling expenses	3.50	($210,000 total)
Total cost per unit	$26.50	

A number of questions relating to the production and sale of Daks follow. Each question is independent.

Required

1. Assume that Andretti Company has sufficient capacity to produce 90,000 Daks each year without any increase in fixed manufacturing overhead costs. The company could increase

its sales by 25% above the present 60,000 units each year if it were willing to increase the fixed selling expenses by $80,000. Would the increase fixed expenses be justified?

2. Assume again that Andretti Company has sufficient capacity to produce 90,000 Daks each year. A customer in a foreign market wants to purchase 20,000 Daks. Import duties on the Daks would be $1.70 per unit, and costs for permits and licenses would be $9,000. The only selling costs that would be associated with the order would be $3.20 per unit shipping cost. You have been asked by the president to compute the per unit break-even price on this order.
3. The company has 1,000 Daks on hand that have some irregularities and are therefore considered to be "seconds." Due to the irregularities, it will be impossible to sell these units at the normal price through regular distribution channels. What unit cost figure is relevant for setting a minimum selling price?
4. Due to a strike in its supplier's plant, Andretti Company is unable to purchase more material for the production of Daks. The strike is expected to last for two months. Andretti Company has enough material on hand to continue to operate at 30% of normal levels for the two-month period. As an alternative, Andretti could close its plant down entirely for the two months. If the plant were closed, fixed overhead costs would continue at 60% of their normal level during the two-month period; the fixed selling costs would be reduced by 20% while the plant was closed. What would be the dollar advantage or disadvantage of closing the plant for the two-month period?
5. An outside manufacturer has offered to produce Daks for Andretti Company and to ship them directly to Andretti's customers. If Andretti Company accepts this offer, the facilities that it uses to produce Daks would be idle; however, fixed overhead costs would be reduced by 75% of their present level. Since the outside manufacturer would pay for all the costs of shipping, the variable selling costs would be only two-thirds of their present amount. Compute the unit cost figure that is relevant for comparison to whatever quoted price is received from the outside manufacturer.

P13–17 Discontinuance of a Store Superior Markets, Inc., operates three stores in a large metropolitan area. A segmented income statement for the company for the last quarter is given below:

SUPERIOR MARKETS, INC.
Income Statement
For the Quarter Ended September 30

	Total	North Store	South Store	East Store
Sales	$3,000,000	$720,000	$1,200,000	$1,080,000
Cost of goods sold	1,657,200	403,200	660,000	594,000
Gross margin	1,342,800	316,800	540,000	486,000
Operating expenses:				
Selling expenses	817,000	231,400	315,000	270,600
Administrative expenses	383,000	106,000	150,900	126,100
Total expenses	1,200,000	337,400	465,900	396,700
Net operating income (loss)	$ 142,800	$(20,600)	$ 74,100	$ 89,300

The North Store has consistently shown losses over the past two years. For this reason, management is giving consideration to closing the store. The company has retained you to make a recommendation as to whether the store should be closed or kept open. The following additional information is available for your use:

a. The breakdown of the selling and administrative expenses is as follows:

	Total	North Store	South Store	East Store
Selling expenses:				
Sales salaries	$239,000	$ 70,000	$ 89,000	$ 80,000
Direct advertising	187,000	51,000	72,000	64,000
General advertising*	45,000	10,800	18,000	16,200
Store rent	300,000	85,000	120,000	95,000
Depreciation of store fixtures	16,000	4,600	6,000	5,400
Delivery salaries	21,000	7,000	7,000	7,000
Depreciation of delivery equipment	9,000	3,000	3,000	3,000
Total selling expenses	$817,000	$231,400	$315,000	$270,600

*Allocated on the basis of sales dollars.

	Total	North Store	South Store	East Store
Administrative expenses:				
Store management salaries	$ 70,000	$ 21,000	$ 30,000	$ 19,000
General office salaries*	50,000	12,000	20,000	18,000
Insurance on fixtures and inventory	25,000	7,500	9,000	8,500
Utilities	106,000	31,000	40,000	35,000
Employment taxes	57,000	16,500	21,900	18,600
General office—other*	75,000	18,000	30,000	27,000
Total administrative expenses	$383,000	$106,000	$150,900	$126,100

*Allocated on the basis of sales dollars.

b. The lease on the building housing the North Store can be broken with no penalty.
c. The fixtures being used in the North Store would be transferred to the other two stores if the North Store were closed.
d. The general manager of the North Store would be retained and transferred to another position in the company if the North Store were closed. She would be filling a position that would otherwise be filled by hiring a new employee at a salary of $11,000 per quarter. The general manager of the North Store would be retained at her normal salary of $12,000 per quarter. All other employees in the store would be discharged.
e. The company has one delivery crew that serves all three stores. One delivery person could be discharged if the North Store were closed. This person's salary is $4,000 per quarter. The delivery equipment would be distributed to the other stores. The equipment does not wear out through use, but does eventually become obsolete.
f. The company's employment taxes are 15% of salaries.
g. One-third of the insurance in the North Store is on the store's fixtures.
h. The "General office salaries" and "General office—other" relate to the overall management of Superior Markets, Inc. If the North Store were closed, one person in the general office could be discharged because of the decrease in overall workload. This person's salary is $6,000 per quarter.

Required

1. Prepare a schedule showing the change in revenues and expenses and the impact on the company's overall net income that would result if the North Store were closed.
2. Assuming that the store space can't be subleased, what recommendation would you make to the management of Superior Markets, Inc.?

3. Assume that if the North Store were closed, at least one-fourth of its sales would transfer to the East Store, due to strong customer loyalty to Superior Markets. The East Store has ample capacity to handle the increased sales. You may assume that the increased sales in the East Store would yield the same gross margin rate as present sales in that store. What effect would these factors have on your recommendation concerning the North Store? Show all computations to support your answer.

P13–18 Shutdown versus Continue-to-Operate Decision (Note: This type of decision is similar to that of dropping a product line.)

Birch Company normally produces and sells 30,000 units of RG-6 each month. RG-6 is a small electrical relay used in the automotive industry as a component part in various products. The selling price is $22 per unit, variable costs are $14 per unit, fixed manufacturing overhead costs total $150,000 per month, and fixed selling costs total $30,000 per month.

Employment-contract strikes in the companies that purchase the bulk of the RG-6 units have caused Birch Company's sales to temporarily drop to only 8,000 units per month. Birch Company estimates that the strikes will last for about two months, after which time sales of RG-6 should return to normal. Due to the current low level of sales, however, Birch Company is thinking about closing down its own plant during the two months that the strikes are on. If Birch Company does close down its plant, it is estimated that fixed manufacturing overhead costs can be reduced to $105,000 per month and that fixed selling costs can be reduced by 10%. Start-up costs at the end of the shutdown period would total $8,000. Since Birch Company uses just-in-time (JIT) production methods, no inventories are on hand.

Required

1. Assuming that the strikes continue for two months, as estimated, would you recommend that Birch Company close its own plant? Show computations in good form.
2. At what level of sales (in units) for the two-months period should Birch Company be indifferent between closing the plant or keeping it open? Show computations. (Hint: This is a type of break-even analysis, except that the fixed cost portion of your break-even computation should include only those fixed costs that are relevant [i.e., avoidable] over the two-month period.)

P13–19 Make or Buy Decision Silven Industries, which manufacturers and sells a highly successful line of summer lotions and insect repellents, has decided to diversify in order to stabilize sales throughout the year. A natural area for the company to consider is the production of winter lotions and creams to prevent dry and chapped skin.

After considerable research, a winter products line has been developed. However, Silven's president has decided to introduce only one of the new products for this coming winter. If the product is a success, further expansion in future years will be initiated.

The product selected (called Chap-Off) is a lip balm that will be sold in a lipstick-type tube. The product will be sold to wholesalers in boxes of 24 tubes for $8 per box. Because of excess capacity, no additional fixed overhead costs will be incurred to produce the product. However, a $90,000 charge for fixed overhead will be absorbed by the product under the company's absorption costing system.

Using the estimated sales and production of 100,000 boxes of Chap-Off, the Accounting Department has developed the following cost per box:

Direct material	$3.60
Direct labor	2.00
Manufacturing overhead	1.40
Total cost	$7.00

The costs above include costs for producing both the lip balm and the tube into which the lip balm is to be placed. As an alternative to making the tubes, Silven has approached a supplier to discuss the possibility of purchasing the tubes for Chap-Off. The purchase price of the empty tubes from the supplier would be $1.35 per box of 24 tubes. If Silven Industries accepts the purchase proposal, it is predicted that direct labor and variable manufacturing overhead costs per box of Chap-Off would be reduced by 10% and that direct materials costs would be reduced by 25%.

Required

1. Should Silven Industries make or buy the tubes? Show calculations to support your answer.

2. What would be the maximum purchase price acceptable to Silven Industries? Support your answer with an appropriate explanation.
3. Instead of sales of 100,000 boxes, revised estimates show sales volume at 120,000 boxes. At this new volume, additional equipment at an annual rental of $40,000 must be acquired to manufacture the tubes. Assuming that the outside supplier will not accept an order for less than 100,000 boxes, should Silven Industries make or buy the tubes? Show computations to support your answer.
4. Refer to the data in (3) above. Assume that the outside supplier will accept an order of any size for the tubes at $1.35 per box. How, if at all, would this change your answer? Show computations.
5. What qualitative factors should Silven Industries consider in determining whether they should make or buy the tubes?

(CMA, heavily adapted)

P13–20 Accept or Reject Special Orders Polaski Company manufactures and sells a single product called a Ret. Operating at capacity, the company can produce and sell 30,000 Rets per year. Costs associated with this level of production and sales are given below:

	Unit	Total
Direct materials	$15	$ 450,000
Direct labor	8	240,000
Variable manufacturing overhead	3	90,000
Fixed manufacturing overhead	9	270,000
Variable selling expense	4	120,000
Fixed selling expense	6	180,000
Total cost	$45	$1,350,000

The Rets normally sell for $50 each. Fixed manufacturing overhead is constant at $270,000 per year within the range of 25,000 through 30,000 Rets per year.

Required

1. Assume that due to a recession, Polaski Company expects to sell only 25,000 Rets through regular channels next year. A large retail chain has offered to purchase 5,000 Rets if Polaski is willing to accept a 16% discount off the regular price. There would be no sales commissions on this order; thus, variable selling expenses would be slashed by 75%. However, Polaski Company would have to purchase a special machine to engrave the retail chain's name on the 5,000 units. This machine would cost $10,000. Polaski Company has no assurance that the retail chain will purchase additional units any time in the future. Determine the impact on profits next year if this special order is accepted.
2. Refer to the original data. Assume again that Polaski Company expects to sell only 25,000 Rets through regular channels next year. The U.S. Army would like to make a one-time-only purchase of 5,000 Rets. The Army would pay a fixed fee of $1.80 per Ret, and in addition it would reimburse Polaski Company for all costs of production (variable and fixed) associated with the units. Since the army would pick up the Rets with its own trucks, there would be no variable selling expenses of any type associated with this order. If Polaski Company accepts the order, by how much will profits be increased or decreased for the year?
3. Assume the same situation as that described in (2) above, except that the company expects to sell 30,000 Rets through regular channels next year. Thus, accepting the U.S. Army's order would require giving up regular sales of 5,000 Rets. If the Army's order is accepted, by how much will profits be increased or decreased from what they would be if the 5,000 Rets were sold through regular channels?

P13–21 Utilization of a Constrained Resource The Walton Toy Company manufactures a line of dolls and a doll dress sewing kit. Demand for the dolls is increasing, and management requests assistance from you in determining an economical sales and production mix for the coming year. The company's Sales Department provides the following information:

Product	Estimated Demand Next Year (units)	Selling Price per Unit
Debbie	50,000	$13.50
Trish	42,000	5.50
Sarah	35,000	21.00
Mike	40,000	10.00
Sewing kit	325,000	8.00

The standard costs for direct materials and direct labor per unit are as follows:

Product	Direct Materials	Direct Labor
Debbie	$4.30	$3.20
Trish	1.10	2.00
Sarah	6.44	5.60
Mike	2.00	4.00
Sewing kit	3.20	1.60

The following additional information is available:

a. The company's plant has a capacity of 130,000 direct labor-hours per year on a single-shift basis. The company's present employees and equipment can produce all five products.
b. The direct labor rate is $8 per hour; this rate is expected to remain unchanged during the coming year.
c. Fixed costs total $520,000 per year. Variable overhead costs are $2 per direct labor-hour.
d. All of the company's nonmanufacturing costs are fixed.
e. The company's present inventory of finished products is negligible and can be ignored.

Required

1. Determine the contribution margin per direct labor-hour expended on each product.
2. Prepare a schedule showing the total direct labor-hours that will be required to produce the units estimated to be sold during the coming year.
3. Examine the data you have computed in (1) and (2) above. Indicate how much of each product should be made so that total production time is equal to the 130,000 hours available.
4. What is the highest price, in terms of a rate per hour, that Walton Toy Company would be willing to pay for additional capacity (that is, for added direct labor time)?
5. Assume again that the company does not want to reduce sales of any product. Identify ways in which the company could obtain the additional output.

(CPA, heavily adapted)

P13–22 Evaluating the Profitability of a Product; Break Even Tracey Douglas is the owner and managing director of Heritage Garden Furniture, Ltd., a South African company that makes museum-quality reproductions of antique outdoor furniture. Ms. Douglas would like advice concerning the advisability of eliminating the model C3 lawnchair. These lawnchairs have been among the company's best-selling products, but they seem to be unprofitable.

A condensed statement of operating income for the company and for the model C3 lawnchair for the quarter ended June 30 follows:

	All Products	Model C3 Lawnchair
Sales	R2,900,000	R300,000
Cost of sales:		
Direct materials	759,000	122,000
Direct labor	680,000	72,000
Fringe benefits (20% of direct labor)	136,000	14,400
Variable manufacturing overhead	28,000	3,600
Building rent and maintenance	30,000	4,000
Depreciation	75,000	19,100
Total cost of sales	1,708,000	235,100
Gross margin	1,192,000	64,900
Selling and administrative expenses:		
Product managers' salaries	75,000	10,000
Sales commissions (5% of sales)	145,000	15,000
Fringe benefits (20% of salaries and commissions)	44,000	5,000
Shipping	120,000	10,000
General administrative expenses	464,000	48,000
Total selling and administrative expenses	848,000	88,000
Net operating income (loss)	R 344,000	R (23,100)

The currency in South Africa is the rand, denoted here by R.

The following additional data have been supplied by the company:

a. Direct labor is a variable cost at Heritage Garden Furniture.
b. All of the company's products are manufactured in the same facility and use the same equipment. Building rent and maintenance and depreciation are allocated to products using various bases. The equipment does not wear out through use; it eventually becomes obsolete.
c. There is ample capacity to fill all orders.
d. Dropping the model C3 lawnchair would have no effect on sales of other product lines.
e. Inventories of work in process or finished goods are insignificant.
f. Shipping costs are traced directly to products.
g. General administrative expenses are allocated to products on the basis of sales dollars. There would be no effect on the total general administrative expenses if the model C3 lawnchair were dropped.
h. If the model C3 lawnchair were dropped, the product manager would be laid off.

Required

1. Given the current level of sales, would you recommend that the model C3 lawnchair be dropped? Prepare appropriate computations to support your answer.
2. What would sales of the model C3 lawnchair have to be, at minimum, in order to justify retaining the product? (Hint: Set this up as a break-even problem but include only the relevant costs from (1) above.)

P13–23 Sell or Process Further Decision Cum-Clean Corporation produces a variety of cleaning compounds and solutions for both industrial and household use. While most of its products are processed independently, a few are related, such as the company's Grit 337 and its Sparkle silver polish.

Grit 337 is a coarse cleaning powder with many industrial uses. It costs $1.60 a pound to make, and it has a selling price of $2.00 a pound. A small portion of the annual production of Grit 337 is retained in the factory for further processing. It is combined with several other ingredients to form a paste that is marketed as Sparkle silver polish. The silver polish sells for $4.00 per jar.

This further processing requires one-fourth pound of Grit 337 per jar of silver polish. The additional direct costs involved in the processing of a jar of silver polish are:

Other ingredients	$0.65
Direct labor	1.48
Total direct cost	$2.13

Overhead costs associated with the processing of the silver polish are:

Variable manufacturing overhead cost	25% of direct labor cost
Fixed manufacturing overhead cost (per month):	
Production supervisor	$1,600
Depreciation of mixing equipment	1,400

The production supervisor has no duties other than to oversee production of the silver polish. The mixing equipment is special-purpose equipment acquired specifically to produce the silver polish. It has only negligible resale value.

Direct labor is a variable cost at Cum-Clean Corporation.

Advertising costs for the silver polish total $4,000 per month. Variable selling costs associated with the silver polish are 7.5% of sales.

Due to a recent decline in the demand for silver polish, the company is wondering whether its continued production is advisable. The sales manager feels that it would be more profitable to just sell all of the Grit 337 as a cleaning powder.

Required

1. What is the incremental contribution margin per jar from further processing of Grit 337 into silver polish?
2. What is the minimum number of jars of silver polish that must be sold each month to justify the continued processing of Grit 337 into silver polish? Show all computations in good form.

(CMA, heavily adapted)

Cases

C13–24 Ethics and the Manager; Shut Down or Continue Operations

Haley Romeros had just been appointed vice president of the Rocky Mountain Region of the Bank Services Corporation (BSC). The company provides check processing services for small banks. The banks send checks presented for deposit or payment to BSC, which records the data on each check in a computerized database. BSC then sends the data electronically to the nearest Federal Reserve Bank check-clearing center where the appropriate transfers of funds are made between banks. The Rocky Mountain Region has three check processing centers, which are located in Billings, Montana; Great Falls, Montana; and Clayton, Idaho. Prior to her promotion to vice president, Ms. Romeros had been the manager of a check processing center in New Jersey.

Immediately upon assuming her new position, Ms. Romeros requested a complete financial report for the just-ended fiscal year from the region's controller, John Littlebear. Ms. Romeros specified that the financial report should follow the standardized format required by corporate headquarters for all regional performance reports. That report follows:

BANK SERVICES CORPORATION (BSC)
Rocky Mountain Region
Financial Performance

		Check Processing Centers		
	Total	**Billings**	**Great Falls**	**Clayton**
Sales	$50,000,000	$20,000,000	$18,000,000	$12,000,000
Operating expenses:				
Direct labor	32,000,000	12,500,000	11,000,000	8,500,000
Variable overhead	850,000	350,000	310,000	190,000
Equipment depreciation	3,900,000	1,300,000	1,400,000	1,200,000
Facility expense	2,800,000	900,000	800,000	1,100,000
Local administrative expense*	450,000	140,000	160,000	150,000
Regional administrative expense†	1,500,000	600,000	540,000	360,000
Corporate administrative expense‡	4,750,000	1,900,000	1,710,000	1,140,000
Total operating expense	46,250,000	17,690,000	15,920,000	12,640,000
Net operating income	$ 3,750,000	$ 2,310,000	$ 2,080,000	$ (640,000)

*Local administrative expenses are the administrative expenses incurred at the check processing centers.

†Regional administrative expenses are allocated to the check processing centers based on sales.

‡Corporate administrative expenses are charged to segments of the company such as the Rocky Mountain Region and the check processing centers at the rate of 9.5% of their sales.

Upon seeing this report, Ms. Romeros summoned John Littlebear for an explanation.

Romeros: What's the story on Clayton? It didn't have a loss the previous year did it?
Littlebear: No, the Clayton facility has had a nice profit every year since it was opened six years ago, but Clayton lost a big contract this year.
Romeros: Why?
Littlebear: One of our national competitors entered the local market and bid very aggressively on the contract. We couldn't afford to meet the bid. Clayton's costs—particularly their facility expenses—are just too high. When Clayton lost the contract, we had to lay off a lot of employees, but we could not reduce the fixed costs of the Clayton facility.
Romeros: Why is Clayton's facility expense so high? It's a smaller facility than either Billings and Great Falls and yet its facility expense is higher.
Littlebear: The problem is that we are able to rent suitable facilities very cheaply at Billings and Great Falls. No such facilities were available at Clayton, we had them built. Unfortunately, there were big cost overruns. The contractor we hired was inexperienced at this kind of work and in fact went bankrupt before the project was completed. After hiring another contractor to finish the work, we were way over budget. The large depreciation charges on the facility didn't matter at first because we didn't have much competition at the time and could charge premium prices.
Romeros: Well we can't do that anymore. The Clayton facility will obviously have to be shut down. Its business can be shifted to the other two check processing centers in the region.
Littlebear: I would advise against that. The $1,200,000 in depreciation at the Clayton facility is misleading. That facility should last indefinitely with proper maintenance. And it has no resale value; there is no other commercial activity around Clayton.
Romeros: What about the other costs at Clayton?
Littlebear: If we shifted Clayton's business over to the other two processing centers in the region, we wouldn't save anything on direct labor or variable overhead costs. We might save $90,000 or so in local administrative expense, but we would not save any regional administrative expense and corporate headquarters would still charge us 9.5% of our sales as corporate administrative expense.

In addition, we would have to rent more space in Billings and Great Falls in order to handle the work transferred from Clayton; that would probably cost us at least $600,000 a year. And don't forget that it will cost us something to move the equipment from Clayton to Billings and Great Falls. And the move will disrupt service to customers.

Romeros: I understand all of that, but a money-losing processing center on my performance report is completely unacceptable.

Littlebear: And if you shut down Clayton, you are going to throw some loyal employees out of work.

Romeros: That's unfortunate, but we have to face hard business realities.

Littlebear: And you would have to write off the investment in the facilities at Clayton.

Romeros: I can explain a write-off to corporate headquarters; hiring an inexperienced contractor to build the Clayton facility was my predecessor's mistake. But they'll have my head at headquarters if I show operating losses every year at one of my processing centers. Clayton has to go. At the next corporate board meeting, I am going to recommend that the Clayton facility be closed.

Required

1. From the standpoint of the company as a whole, should the Clayton processing center be shut down and its work redistributed to other processing centers in the region? Explain.
2. Do you think Haley Romeros's decision to shut down the Clayton facility is ethical? Explain.
3. What influence should the depreciation on the facilities at Clayton have on prices charged by Clayton for its services?

C13–25 Sell or Process Further Decision The Scottie Sweater Company produces sweaters under the "Scottie" label. The company buys raw wool on the market and processes it into wool yarn from which the sweaters are woven. One spindle of wool yarn is required to produce one sweater. The costs and revenues associated with the sweaters are given below:

		Per Sweater
Selling price		$ 30.00
Cost to manufacture:		
Raw materials:		
Buttons, thread, lining	$ 2.00	
Wool yarn	16.00	
Total raw materials	18.00	
Direct labor	5.80	
Manufacturing overhead	8.70	32.50
Manufacturing profit (loss)		$ (2.50)

Originally, all of the wool yarn was used to produce sweaters, but in recent years a market has developed for the wool yarn itself. The yarn is purchased by other companies for use in production of wool blankets and other wool products. Since the development of the market for the wool yarn, a continuing dispute has existed in the Scottie Sweater Company as to whether the yarn should be sold simply as yarn or processed into sweaters. Current cost and revenue data on the yarn are given below:

		Per Spindle of Yarn
Selling price		$20.00
Cost to manufacture:		
Raw materials (raw wool)	$7.00	
Direct labor	3.60	
Manufacturing overhead	5.40	16.00
Manufacturing profit		$ 4.00

The market for sweaters is temporarily depressed, due to unusually warm weather in the western states where the sweaters are sold. This has made it necessary for the company to discount the selling price of the sweaters to $30 from the normal $40 price. Since the market for wool yarn has remained strong, the dispute has again surfaced over whether the yarn should be sold outright rather than processed into sweaters. The sales manager thinks that the production of sweaters should be discontinued; she is upset about having to sell sweaters at a

$2.50 loss when the yarn could be sold for a $4.00 profit. However, the production superintendent is equally upset at the suggestion that he close down a large portion of the factory. He argues that the company is in the sweater business, not the yarn business, and that the company should focus on its core strength.

Due to the nature of the production process, virtually all of the manufacturing overhead costs are fixed and would not be affected even if sweaters were discontinued. Manufacturing overhead is assigned to products on the basis of 150% of direct labor cost.

Required

1. Would you recommend that the wool yarn be sold outright or processed into sweaters? Show computations in good form to support your answer and explain your reasoning.
2. What is the lowest price that the company should accept for a sweater? Show computations in good form to support your answer and explain your reasoning.

C13–26 Make or Buy; Optimal Use of a Constrained Resource

Sportway, Inc., is a wholesale distributor supplying a wide range of moderately priced sporting equipment to large chain stores. About 60% of Sportway's products are purchased from other companies while the remainder of the products are manufactured by Sportway. The company has a Plastics Department that is currently manufacturing molded fishing tackle boxes. Sportway is able to manufacture and sell 8,000 tackle boxes annually, making full use of its direct labor capacity at available workstations. Presented below are the selling price and costs associated with Sportway's tackle boxes.

Selling price per box		$86.00
Cost per box:		
Molded plastic	$ 8.00	
Hinges, latches, handle	9.00	
Direct labor ($15 per hour)	18.75	
Manufacturing overhead	12.50	
Selling and administrative cost	17.00	65.25
Net operating income per box		$20.75

Because Sportway believes it could sell 12,000 tackle boxes if it had sufficient manufacturing capacity, the company has looked into the possibility of purchasing the tackle boxes for distribution. Maple Products, a steady supplier of quality products, would be able to provide up to 9,000 tackle boxes per year at a price of $68 per box delivered to Sportway's facility.

Traci Kader, Sportway's production manager, has suggested that the company could make better use of its Plastics Department by manufacturing skateboards. To support her position, Traci has a market study that indicates an expanding market for skateboards. Traci believes that Sportway could expect to sell 17,500 skateboards annually at a price of $45 per skateboard. Traci's estimate of the costs to manufacture the skateboards is presented below.

Selling price per skateboard		$45.00
Cost per skateboard:		
Molded plastic	$5.50	
Wheels, hardware	7.00	
Direct labor ($15 per hour)	7.50	
Manufacturing overhead	5.00	
Selling and administrative cost	9.00	34.00
Net operating income per skateboard		$11.00

In the Plastics Department, Sportway uses direct labor-hours as the application base for manufacturing overhead. Included in the manufacturing overhead for the current year is $50,000 of fixed overhead costs, of which 40% is traceable to the Plastics Department and 60% is allocated factorywide manufacturing overhead cost. The remaining manufacturing overhead cost is variable with respect to direct labor-hours. The skateboards could be produced with existing equipment and personnel in the Plastics Department.

For each unit of product that Sportway sells, regardless of whether the product has been purchased or is manufactured by Sportway, there is an allocated $6 fixed cost per unit for distribution. This $6 per unit is included in the selling and administrative cost for all products.

The remaining amount of selling and administrative cost for all products—purchased or manufactured—is variable. The total selling and administrative cost figure for the purchased tackle boxes would be $10 per unit.

Required

1. Determine the number of direct labor-hours per year being used to manufacture tackle boxes.
2. Compute the contribution margin per unit for:
   a. Purchased tackle boxes.
   b. Manufactured tackle boxes.
   c. Manufactured skateboards.
3. Determine the number of tackle boxes (if any) that Sportway should purchase and the number of tackle boxes and/or skateboards that it should manufacture, and compute the improvement in net income that will result from this product mix over current operations.

(CMA, adapted)

C13–27 Plant Closing Decision GianAuto Corporation manufactures automobiles, vans, and trucks. Among the various GianAuto plants around the United States is the Denver Cover Plant. Coverings made primarily of vinyl and upholstery fabric are sewn at the Denver Cover Plant and used to cover interior seating and other surfaces of GianAuto products.

Ted Vosilo is the plant manager for Denver Cover. The Denver Cover Plant was the first GianAuto plant in the region. As other area plants were opened, Vosilo, in recognition of his management ability, was given responsibility for managing them. Vosilo functions as a regional manager, although the budget for him and his staff is charged to the Denver Cover Plant.

Vosilo has just received a report indicating that GianAuto could purchase the entire annual output of Denver Cover from outside suppliers for $35 million. Vosilo was astonished at the low outside price because the budget for Denver Cover's operating costs for the coming year was set at $52 million. Vosilo believes that GianAuto will have to close down operations at Denver Cover in order to realize the $22 million in annual cost savings.

The budget for Denver Cover's operating costs for the coming year is presented below. Additional facts regarding the plant's operations are as follows:

a. Due to Denver Cover's commitment to use high-quality fabrics in all its products, the Purchasing Department was instructed to place blanket purchase orders with major suppliers to ensure the receipt of sufficient materials for the coming year. If these orders are canceled as a consequence of the plant closing, termination charges would amount to 20% of the cost of direct materials.
b. Approximately 800 plant employees will lose their jobs if the plant is closed. This includes all of the direct laborers and supervisors as well as the plumbers, electricians, and other skilled workers classified as indirect plant workers. Some would be able to find new jobs while many others would have difficulty. All employees would have difficulty matching Denver Cover's base pay of $9.40 per hour, which is the highest in the area. A clause in Denver Cover's contract with the union may help some employees; the company must provide employment assistance to its former employees for 12 months after a plant closing. The estimated cost to administer this service would be $1.5 million for the year.
c. Some employees would probably choose early retirement because GianAuto has an excellent pension plan. In fact, $3 million of the annual pension expense would continue whether Denver Cover is open or not.
d. Vosilo and his staff would not be affected by the closing of Denver Cover. They would still be responsible for administering three other area plants.
e. Denver Cover considers equipment depreciation to be a variable cost and uses the units-of-production method to depreciate its equipment; Denver Cover is the only GianAuto plant to use this depreciation method. However, Denver Cover uses the customary straight-line method to depreciate its building.

DENVER COVER PLANT
Annual Budget for Operating Costs

Materials		$14,000,000
Labor:		
Direct	$13,100,000	
Supervision	900,000	
Indirect plant	4,000,000	18,000,000
Overhead:		
Depreciation—equipment	3,200,000	
Depreciation—building	7,000,000	
Pension expense	5,000,000	
Plant manager and staff	800,000	
Corporate allocation	4,000,000	20,000,000
Total budgeted costs		$52,000,000

Required

1. Without regard to costs, identify the advantages to GianAuto Corporation of continuing to obtain covers from its own Denver Cover Plant.
2. GianAuto Corporation plans to prepare a financial analysis that will be used in deciding whether or not to close the Denver Cover Plant. Management has asked you to identify:
   a. The annual budgeted costs that are relevant to the decision regarding closing the plant (show the dollar amounts).
   b. The annual budgeted costs that are *not* relevant to the decision regarding closing the plant, and explain why they are not relevant (again show the dollar amounts).
   c. Any nonrecurring costs that would arise due to the closing of the plant, and explain how they would affect the decision (again show any dollar amounts).
3. Looking at the data you have prepared in (2) above, should the plant be closed? Show computations and explain your answer.
4. Identify any revenues or costs not specifically mentioned in the problem that GianAuto should consider before making a decision.

(CMA, adapted)

Group Exercises

GE13–28 What's the Cost? Nearly 70 years ago, eminent economist J. Maurice Clarke stated that "accountants use different costs because of their differing objectives." The business world has certainly become a lot more complicated since Professor Clarke's insightful comment. Management accountants today are expected to be a lot more conversant and knowledgeable about business operations. They are expected to add value to their company by their ability to bring the right information to bear on a decision. To do that, management accountants must be able to identify, analyze, and help solve problems. They have to operationalize Professor Clarke's statement.

Required

1. What are the different uses for accounting information? That is, for what purposes or functions is cost information used? Try to identify as many uses as you can and then try to group similar or related uses under some common heading, for example, external reporting.
2. Define each of the following cost or revenue concepts and give examples of decisions or situations where the concept would be used.
   a. Sunk cost.
   b. Avoidable cost.
   c. Opportunity cost.
   d. Joint cost.
   e. Contribution margin per unit of constrained resource.

GE13–29 Outsourcing May Be Hazardous to Your Health Outsourcing, when a company contracts with third parties to produce some of its parts or products, has become commonplace among U.S. manufacturers. Thirty years ago, when factories were a lot less complex, factory burden rates of 50% or less of direct labor cost were deemed reasonable. But today, overhead burden rates of 500% of direct labor are common and rates of 1,000% or more are not unusual. As a result, outsourcing has gained widespread acceptance over the past 15 years. Products with high direct labor content are especially susceptible to being outsourced to parts of the world where labor rates are a lot less than they are in the United States.

Required

1. What is the meaning of manufacturing overhead rates of 500% or more of direct labor?
2. What implications do such high burden rates hold for products high in direct labor content?
3. If products with a high direct labor content are outsourced to low-wage areas of the United States or to less-developed, low-wage foreign countries, what impact will that have on the cost structure of the company? Cite specific categories of costs affected by the outsourcing strategy.
4. What happens to the costs of the remaining products when a product is outsourced?
5. Can you think of any drawbacks to outsourcing in a less-developed foreign land or any limitations to a strategy dependent on labor cost savings?
6. Continuing with the line of thinking developed in (1)–(3) above, what happens next?

IE13–30 Altering the Product Mix Maxager Technology, Inc., provides manufacturers with software that calculates minute by minute how much more profit could be made by adjusting their product mix and by solving specific production problems. Access the company's web site at www.maxager.com and read about Cast Alloys's experience with the software in the section on Successes.

Required

1. Why would a company change its product mix rather than just produce and sell more of everything?
2. How does the Maxager Technology's software probably determine how to change the product mix to generate more profits?
3. How does the software probably determine how much profit could be made by solving specific production problems?

Chapter Fourteen

Capital Budgeting Decisions

Business Focus

When Steven Burd became the CEO of Safeway, he slashed annual capital spending from $550 million to $290 million. Burd gave the following reason: "We had projects that were not returning the cost of money. So we cut spending back, which made the very best projects come to the surface."

Safeway set a minimum 22.5% pretax return on investment in all new store and remodeling projects. With that discipline in place, Safeway again increased capital spending. Recently it spent about $1 billion in a single year, adding 40 to 45 new stores and remodeling more than 200. Burd says he has emphasized expanding existing stores because the older stores generally have excellent real estate locations and the added size brings strong increases in sales.

Source: Adapted from Robert Berner, "Safeway's Resurgence Is Built on Attention to Detail," The Wall Street Journal, *October 2, 1998, p. B4.*

Learning Objectives

After studying Chapter Fourteen you should be able to:

1 Determine the acceptability of an investment project using the net present value method.

2 Determine the acceptability of an investment project using the internal rate of return method (with interpolation, if needed).

3 Explain how the cost of capital is used as a screening tool.

4 Prepare a net present value analysis of two competing investment projects using either the incremental-cost approach or the total-cost approach.

5 Make a capital budgeting analysis involving automated equipment.

6 Rank investment projects in order of preference using (1) the internal rate of return method and (2) the net present value method with the profitability index.

7 Determine the payback period for an investment.

8 Compute the simple rate of return for an investment.

9 (Appendix 14A) Explain the concept of present value and make present value computations with and without the present value tables.

The term **capital budgeting** is used to describe how managers plan significant outlays on projects that have long-term implications such as the purchase of new equipment and the introduction of new products. Most companies have many more potential projects than can actually be funded. Hence, managers must carefully select those projects that promise the greatest future return. How well managers make these capital budgeting decisions is a critical factor in the long-run profitability of the company.

Capital budgeting involves *investment*—a company must commit funds now in order to receive a return in the future. Investments are not limited to stocks and bonds. Purchase of inventory or equipment is also an investment. For example, PepsiCo makes an investment when it opens a new Pizza Hut restaurant. L. L. Bean makes an investment when it installs a new computer to handle customer billing. DaimlerChrysler makes an investment when it redesigns a product such as the Jeep Eagle and must retool its production lines. Merck & Co. invests in medical research. All of these investments are characterized by a commitment of funds today in the expectation of receiving a return in the future in the form of additional cash inflows or reduced cash outflows.

Capital Budgeting—Planning Investments

Typical Capital Budgeting Decisions

What types of business decisions require capital budgeting analysis? Virtually any decision that involves an outlay now in order to obtain some return (increase in revenue or reduction in costs) in the future. Typical capital budgeting decisions include:

1. Cost reduction decisions. Should new equipment be purchased to reduce costs?
2. Expansion decisions. Should a new plant, warehouse, or other facility be acquired to increase capacity and sales?
3. Equipment selection decisions. Which of several available machines would be the most cost effective to purchase?
4. Lease or buy decisions. Should new equipment be leased or purchased?
5. Equipment replacement decisions. Should old equipment be replaced now or later?

Capital budgeting decisions tend to fall into two broad categories—*screening decisions* and *preference decisions.* **Screening decisions** are those relating to whether a proposed project meets some preset standard of acceptance. For example, a firm may have a policy of accepting projects only if they promise a return of, say, 20% on the investment. The required rate of return is the minimum rate of return a project must yield to be acceptable.

Preference decisions, by contrast, relate to selecting from among several *competing* courses of action. To illustrate, a firm may be considering five different machines to replace an existing machine on the assembly line. The choice of which machine to purchase is a *preference* decision.

In this chapter, we initially discuss ways of making screening decisions. Preference decisions are discussed toward the end of the chapter.

INSTRUCTOR'S NOTE

Ask students if they would prefer to receive $100 today or a year from now. Almost everyone will prefer the $100 today. Ask why. Some will say that the value of the dollar could decline due to inflation. Others will say they would like to spend the money now. Tell them to assume there is no inflation and they can't spend the money until a year from now. Then repeat the question. Some students should respond that the $100 could be put in a bank and be worth more in a year. Therefore, the money should be taken now. This is the reasoning underlying present value: a dollar today is worth more than a dollar in the future, since a dollar today can be invested.

The Time Value of Money

As stated earlier, business investments commonly promise returns that extend over fairly long periods of time. Therefore, in approaching capital budgeting decisions, it is necessary to employ techniques that recognize *the time value of money.* A dollar today is worth more than a dollar a year from now. The same concept applies in choosing between investment projects. Those projects that promise returns earlier in time are preferable to those that promise returns later in time.

The capital budgeting techniques that recognize the above two characteristics of business investments most fully are those that involve *discounted cash flows.* We will spend most of this chapter illustrating the use of discounted cash flow methods in making capital budgeting decisions. If you are not already familiar with discounting and the use of present value tables, you should read Appendix 14A, The Concept of Present Value, at the end of this chapter before proceeding any further.

Discounted Cash Flows—The Net Present Value Method

There are two approaches to making capital budgeting decisions by means of discounted cash flows. One is the *net present value method,* and the other is the *internal rate of return method* (sometimes called the *time-adjusted rate of return method*). The net present value method is discussed in this section; the internal rate of return method is discussed in the next section.

objective 1

Determine the acceptability of an investment project using the net present value method.

The Net Present Value Method Illustrated

Under the net present value method, the present value of all cash inflows is compared to the present value of all cash outflows that are associated with an investment project. The difference between the present value of these cash flows, called the **net present value,** determines whether or not the project is an acceptable investment. To illustrate, let us assume the following data:

Example A

Harper Company is contemplating the purchase of a machine capable of performing certain operations that are now performed manually. The machine will cost $5,000, and it will last for five years. At the end of the five-year period, the machine will have a zero scrap value. Use of the machine will reduce labor costs by $1,800 per year. Harper Company requires a minimum return of 20% before taxes on all investment projects.[1]

Should the machine be purchased? Harper Company must determine whether a cash investment now of $5,000 can be justified if it will result in an $1,800 reduction in cost each year over the next five years. It may appear that the answer is obvious since the total cost savings is $9,000 (5 × $1,800). However, the company can earn a 20% return by investing its money elsewhere. It is not enough that the cost reductions cover just the original cost of the machine; they must also yield at least a 20% return or the company would be better off investing the money elsewhere.

To determine whether the investment is desirable, it is necessary to discount the stream of annual $1,800 cost savings to its present value and then to compare this discounted present value with the cost of the new machine. Since Harper Company requires a minimum return of 20% on all investment projects, this rate is used in the discounting process. Exhibit 14–1 shows how this analysis is done.

According to the analysis, Harper Company should purchase the new machine. The present value of the cost savings is $5,384, as compared to a present value of only $5,000 for the investment required (cost of the machine). Deducting the present value

1. For simplicity, we assume in this chapter and in the next chapter that there is no inflation. The impact of inflation on discounted cash flow analysis is discussed in Appendix 14B to this chapter. Also, in this chapter we ignore income taxes. The impact of income taxes on capital budgeting decisions will be covered in the next chapter.

Exhibit 14–1
Net Present Value Analysis of a Proposed Project

Initial cost		$5,000
Life of the project (years)		5
Annual cost savings		$1,800
Salvage value		-0-
Required rate of return		20%

Item	Year(s)	Amount of Cash Flow	20% Factor	Present Value of Cash Flows
Annual cost savings	1–5	$ 1,800	2.991*	$ 5,384
Initial investment	Now	(5,000)	1.000	(5,000)
Net present value				$ 384

*From Table 14C–4 in Appendix 14C at the end of this chapter.

of the investment required from the present value of the cost savings gives a *net present value* of $384. Whenever the net present value is zero or greater, as in our example, an investment project is acceptable. Whenever the net present value is negative (the present value of the cash outflows exceeds the present value of the cash inflows), an investment project is not acceptable. In sum:

If the Net Present Value Is . . .	Then the Project Is . . .
Positive	Acceptable, since it promises a return greater than the required rate of return.
Zero	Acceptable, since it promises a return equal to the required rate of return.
Negative	Not acceptable, since it promises a return less than the required rate of return.

A full interpretation of the solution would be as follows: The new machine promises more than the required 20% rate of return. This is evident from the positive net present value of $384. Harper Company could spend up to $5,384 for the new machine and still obtain the minimum required 20% rate of return. The net present value of $384, therefore, shows the amount of "cushion" or "margin of error." One way to look at this is that the company could underestimate the cost of the new machine by up to $384, or overestimate the net present value of the future cash savings by up to $384, and the project would still be financially attractive.

Emphasis on Cash Flows

In capital budgeting decisions, the focus is on cash flows and not on accounting net income. The reason is that accounting net income is based on accrual concepts that ignore the timing of cash flows into and out of an organization. From a capital budgeting standpoint the timing of cash flows is important, since a dollar received today is more valuable than a dollar received in the future. Therefore, even though the accounting net income figure is useful for many things, it is not used in discounted cash flow analysis. Instead of determining accounting net income, the manager must concentrate on identifying the specific cash flows associated with an investment project.

What kinds of cash flows should the manager look for? Although the specific cash flows will vary from project to project, certain types of cash flows tend to recur as explained in the following paragraphs.

TYPICAL CASH OUTFLOWS Most projects will have an immediate cash outflow in the form of an initial investment in equipment or other assets. Any salvage value realized from the sale of old equipment can be recognized as a cash inflow or as a reduction in the required investment. In addition, some projects require that a company expand its working capital. **Working capital** is current assets (cash, accounts receivable, and inventory) less current liabilities. When a company takes on a new project, the balances in the current asset accounts will often increase. For example, opening a new Nordstrom's department store would require additional cash in sales registers, increased accounts receivable for new customers, and more inventory to stock the shelves. These additional working capital needs should be treated as part of the initial investment in a project. Also, many projects require periodic outlays for repairs and maintenance and for additional operating costs. These should all be treated as cash outflows for capital budgeting purposes.

TYPICAL CASH INFLOWS On the cash inflow side, a project will normally either increase revenues or reduce costs. Either way, the amount involved should be treated as a cash inflow for capital budgeting purposes. (In regard to this point, notice that so far as cash flows are concerned, a *reduction in costs is equivalent to an increase in revenues.*) Cash inflows are also frequently realized from salvage of equipment when a project is terminated. In addition, upon termination of a project, any working capital that was tied up in the project can be released for use elsewhere and should be treated as a cash inflow. Working capital is released, for example, when a company sells off its inventory or collects its receivables. (If the released working capital is not shown as a cash inflow at the termination of a project, then the project will go on being charged for the use of the funds forever!)

In summary, the following types of cash flows are common in business investment projects:

Cash outflows:
- Initial investment (including installation costs).
- Increased working capital needs.
- Repairs and maintenance.
- Incremental operating costs.

Cash inflows:
- Incremental revenues.
- Reduction in costs.
- Salvage value.
- Release of working capital.

Recovery of the Original Investment

When computing the present value of a project, depreciation is not deducted for two reasons.

First, depreciation is not a current cash outflow.[2] As discussed above, discounted cash flow methods of making capital budgeting decisions focus on *cash flows.* Although depreciation is a vital concept in computing net income for financial statements, it is not relevant in an analytical framework that focuses on cash flows.

A second reason for not deducting depreciation is that discounted cash flow methods *automatically* provide for return of the original investment, thereby making a deduction for depreciation unnecessary. To demonstrate this point, let us assume the following data:

Example B

Carver Hospital is considering the purchase of an attachment for its X-ray machine that will cost $3,170. The attachment will be usable for four years, after which time it will have no salvage value.

---

2. Although depreciation itself is not a cash outflow, it does have an effect on cash outflows for income taxes. We shall take a look at this effect in the following chapter when we discuss the impact of income taxes on capital budgeting.

Exhibit 14–2
Carver Hospital—Net Present Value Analysis of X-Ray Attachment

Initial cost	$3,170
Life of the project (years)	4
Annual net cash inflow	$1,000
Salvage value	-0-
Required rate of return	10%

Item	Year(s)	Amount of Cash Flow	10% Factor	Present Value of Cash Flows
Annual net cash inflow	1–4	$ 1,000	3.170*	$ 3,170
Initial investment	Now	(3,170)	1.000	(3,170)
Net present value				$ -0-

*From Table 14C–4 in Appendix 14C.

Exhibit 14–3 Carver Hospital—Breakdown of Annual Cash Inflows

Year	(1) Investment Outstanding during the Year	(2) Cash Inflow	(3) Return on Investment (1) × 10%	(4) Recovery of Investment during the Year (2) — (3)	(5) Unrecovered Investment at the End of the Year (1) — (4)
1	$3,170	$1,000	$317	$ 683	$2,487
2	2,487	1,000	249	751	1,736
3	1,736	1,000	173	827	909
4	909	1,000	91	909	-0-
Total investment recovered				$3,170	

It will increase net cash inflows by $1,000 per year in the X-ray department. The hospital's board of directors has instructed that no investments are to be made unless they have an annual return of at least 10%.

A present value analysis of the desirability of purchasing the X-ray attachment is presented in Exhibit 14–2. Notice that the attachment promises exactly a 10% return on the original investment, since the net present value is zero at a 10% discount rate.

Each annual $1,000 cash inflow arising from use of the attachment is made up of two parts. One part represents a recovery of a portion of the original $3,170 paid for the attachment, and the other part represents a return *on* this investment. The breakdown of each year's $1,000 cash inflow between recover *of* investment and return *on* investment is shown in Exhibit 14–3.

The first year's $1,000 cash inflow consists of a $317 interest return (10%) *on* the $3,170 original investment, plus a $683 return *of* that investment. Since the amount of the unrecovered investment decreases over the four years, the dollar amount of the interest return also decreases. By the end of the fourth year, all $3,170 of the original investment has been recovered.

Simplifying Assumptions

In working with discounted cash flows, at least two simplifying assumptions are usually made.

The first assumption is that all cash flows other than the initial investment occur at the end of a period. This is somewhat unrealistic in that cash flows typically occur somewhat uniformly *throughout* a period. The purpose of this assumption is just to simplify computations.

The second assumption is that all cash flows generated by an investment project are immediately reinvested. It is further assumed that the reinvested funds will yield a rate of return equal to the discount rate. Unless these conditions are met, the return computed for the project will not be accurate. To illustrate, we used a discount rate of 10% for the Carver Hospital in Exhibit 14–2. Unless the funds released each period are immediately reinvested at a 10% return, the net present value computed for the X-ray attachment will be misstated.

Choosing a Discount Rate

To use the net present value method, we must choose some rate of return for discounting cash flows to their present value. In Example A we used a 20% rate of return, and in Example B we used a 10% rate of return. These rates were chosen somewhat arbitrarily simply for the sake of illustration.

The firm's *cost of capital* is usually regarded as the most appropriate choice for the discount rate. The **cost of capital** is the average rate of return the company must pay to its long-term creditors and shareholders for the use of their funds. The mechanics involved in cost of capital computations are covered in finance texts and will not be considered here.

An Extended Example of the Net Present Value Method

To conclude our discussion of the net present value method, we present below an extended example of how it is used in analyzing an investment proposal. This example will also help to tie together (and to reinforce) many of the ideas developed thus far.

Example C

Under a special licensing arrangement, Swinyard Company has an opportunity to market a new product in the western United States for a five-year period. The product would be purchased from the manufacturer, with Swinyard Company responsible for all costs of promotion and distribution. The licensing arrangement could be renewed at the end of the five-year period at the option of the manufacturer. After careful study, Swinyard Company has estimated that the following costs and revenues would be associated with the new product:

Cost of equipment needed	$ 60,000
Working capital needed	100,000
Overhaul of the equipment in four years	5,000
Salvage value of the equipment in five years	10,000
Annual revenues and costs:	
Sales revenues	200,000
Cost of goods sold	125,000
Out-of-pocket operating costs (for salaries, advertising, and other direct costs)	35,000

At the end of the five-year period, the working capital would be released for investment elsewhere if the manufacturer decided not to renew the licensing arrangement. Swinyard Company's discount rate and cost of capital is 20%. Would you recommend that the new product be introduced?

This example involves a variety of cash inflows and cash outflows. The solution is given in Exhibit 14–4.

Notice particularly how the working capital is handled in this exhibit. It is counted as a cash outflow at the beginning of the project and as a cash inflow when it is released at the end of the project. Also notice how the sales revenues, cost of goods sold, and out-of-pocket costs are handled. **Out-of-pocket costs** are actual cash outlays

Exhibit 14–4 The Net Present Value Method—An Extended Example

Sales revenues	$200,000
Less cost of goods sold	125,000
Less out-of-pocket costs for salaries, advertising, etc.	35,000
Annual net cash inflows	$ 40,000

Item	Year(s)	Amount of Cash Flows	20% Factor	Present Value of Cash Flows
Purchase of equipment	Now	$ (60,000)	1.000	$ (60,000)
Working capital needed	Now	(100,000)	1.000	(100,000)
Overhaul of equipment	4	(5,000)	0.482*	(2,410)
Annual net cash inflows from sales of the product line	1–5	40,000	2.991†	119,640
Salvage value of the equipment	5	10,000	0.402*	4,020
Working capital released	5	100,000	0.402*	40,200
Net present value				$ 1,450

*From Table 14C–3 in Appendix 14C.

†From Table 14C–4 in Appendix 14C.

for salaries, advertising, and other operating expenses. Depreciation would not be an out-of-pocket cost, since it involves no current cash outlay.

Since the overall net present value is positive, the new product should be added assuming the company has no better use for the investment funds.

Discounted Cash Flows—The Internal Rate of Return Method

objective 2

Determine the acceptability of an investment project using the internal rate of return method (with interpolation, if needed).

The **internal rate of return** (or **time-adjusted rate of return**) can be defined as the interest yield promised by an investment project over its useful life. It is sometimes referred to simply as the **yield** on a project. The internal rate of return is computed by finding the discount rate that equates the present value of a project's cash outflows with the present value of its cash inflows. In other words, the internal rate of return is that discount rate that will cause the net present value of a project to be equal to zero.

The Internal Rate of Return Method Illustrated

To illustrate the internal rate of return method, let us assume the following data:

Example D

Glendale School District is considering the purchase of a large tractor-pulled lawn mower. At present, the lawn is mowed using a small hand-pushed gas mower. The large, tractor-pulled mower will cost $16,950 and will have a useful life of 10 years. It will have only a negligible scrap value, which can be ignored. The tractor-pulled mower would do the job much more quickly than the old mower and would result in a labor savings of $3,000 per year.

To compute the internal rate of return promised by the new mower, we must find the discount rate that will cause the net present value of the project to be zero. How do we do this? The simplest and most direct approach *when the net cash inflow is the same every year* is to divide the investment in the project by the expected net annual

Exhibit 14–5
Evaluation of the Mower Purchase Using a 12% Discount Rate

Initial cost	$16,950
Life of the project (years)	10
Annual cost savings	$ 3,000
Salvage value	-0-

Item	Year(s)	Amount of Cash Flow	12% Factor	Present Value of Cash Flows
Annual cost savings	1–10	$ 3,000	5.650*	$ 16,950
Initial investment	Now	(16,950)	1.000	(16,950)
Net present value				$ -0-

*From Table 14C–4 in Appendix 14C.

cash inflow. This computation will yield a factor from which the internal rate of return can be determined. The formula is as follows:

$$\text{Factor of the internal rate of return} = \frac{\text{Investment required}}{\text{Net annual cash inflow}} \qquad (1)$$

The factor derived from formula (1) is then located in the present value tables to see what rate of return it represents. Using formula (1) and the data for Glendale School District's proposed project, we get:

$$\frac{\text{Investment required}}{\text{Net annual cash inflow}} = \frac{\$16{,}950}{\$3{,}000} = 5.650$$

Thus, the discount factor that will equate a series of $3,000 cash inflows with a present investment of $16,950 is 5.650. Now we need to find this factor in Table 14C–4 in Appendix 14C to see what rate of return it represents. We should use the 10-period line in Table 14C–4 since the cash flows for the project continue for 10 years. If we scan along the 10-period line, we find that a factor of 5.650 represents a 12% rate of return. Therefore, the internal rate of return promised by the mower project is 12%. We can verify this by computing the project's net present value using a 12% discount rate. This computation is made in Exhibit 14–5.

Notice from Exhibit 14–5 that using a 12% discount rate equates the present value of the annual cash inflows with the present value of the investment required in the project, leaving a zero net present value. The 12% rate therefore represents the internal rate of return promised by the project.

Salvage Value and Other Cash Flows

The technique just demonstrated works very well if a project's cash flows are identical every year. But what if they are not? For example, what if a project will have some salvage value at the end of its life in addition to the annual cash inflows? Under these circumstances, a trial-and-error process is necessary to find the rate of return that will equate the cash inflows with the cash outflows. The trial-and-error process can be carried out by hand, or it can be carried out by means of computer software programs such as spreadsheets that perform the necessary computations in seconds. In short, erratic or uneven cash flows should not prevent a manager from determining a project's internal rate of return.

The Process of Interpolation

Interpolation is used to find rates of return that do not appear in published interest tables. Interest tables are usually printed in terms of whole percentages (10%, 12%, and so forth), whereas projects often have fractional rates of return. To illustrate the process of interpolation, assume the following data:

Investment required	$6,000
Annual cost savings	1,500
Life of the project	10 years

What is the internal rate of return promised by this project? Using formula (1), the appropriate factor is 4.000:

$$\frac{\text{Investment required}}{\text{Net annual cash inflow}} = \frac{\$6{,}000}{\$1{,}500} = 4.000$$

Looking at Table 14C–4 in Appendix 14C and scanning along the 10-period line, we find that a factor of 4.000 represents a rate of return somewhere between 20% and 22%. To find the rate we are after, we must interpolate, as follows:

	Present Value Factors	
20% factor	4.192	4.192
True factor	4.000	
22% factor		3.923
Difference	0.192	0.269

$$\text{Internal rate of return} = 20\% + \left(\frac{0.192}{0.269} \times 2\%\right)$$

$$\text{Internal rate of return} = 21.4\%$$

Using the Internal Rate of Return

Once the internal rate of return has been computed, what does the manager do with the information? The internal rate of return is compared to the company's *required rate of return.* The required rate of return is the minimum rate of return that an investment project must yield to be acceptable. If the internal rate of return is *equal* to or *greater* than the required rate of return, then the project is acceptable. If it is *less* than the required rate of return, then the project is rejected. Quite often, the company's cost of capital is used as the required rate of return. The reasoning is that if a project can't provide a rate of return at least as great as the cost of the funds invested in it, then it is not profitable.

In the case of the Glendale School District example used earlier, let us assume that the district has set a minimum required rate of return of 15% on all projects. Since the large mower promises a rate of return of only 12%, it does not clear this hurdle and would therefore be rejected as a project.

The Cost of Capital as a Screening Tool

objective 3

Explain how the cost of capital is used as a screening tool.

As we have seen in preceding examples, the cost of capital often operates as a *screening* device, helping the manager screen out undesirable investment projects. This screening is accomplished in different ways, depending on whether the company is using the internal rate of return method or the net present value method in its capital budgeting analysis.

Exhibit 14–6
Capital Budgeting Screening Decisions

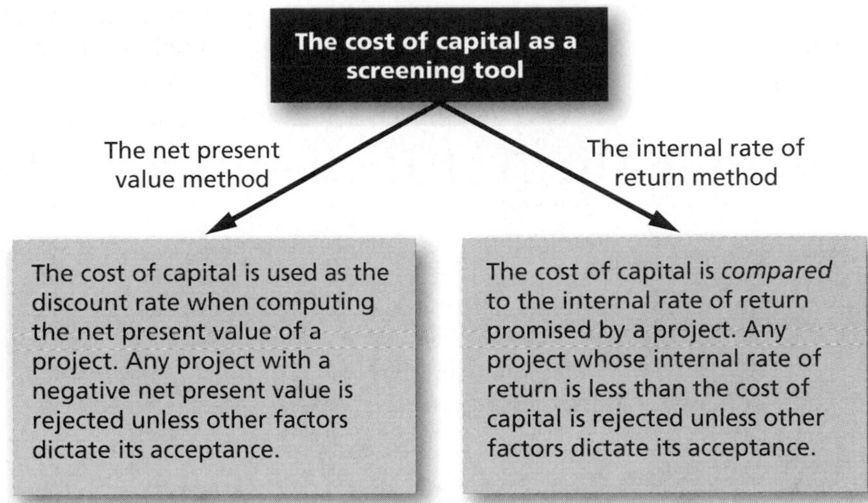

When the internal rate of return method is used, the cost of capital is used as the *hurdle rate* that a project must clear for acceptance. If the internal rate of return of a project is not great enough to clear the cost of capital hurdle, then the project is ordinarily rejected. We saw the application of this idea in the Glendale School District example, where the hurdle rate was set at 15%.

When the net present value method is used, the cost of capital is the *discount rate* used to compute the net present value of a proposed project. Any project yielding a negative net present value is rejected unless other factors are significant enough to require its acceptance. (This point is discussed further in a following section, Investments in Automated Equipment.)

The use of the cost of capital as a screening tool is summarized in Exhibit 14–6.

Comparison of the Net Present Value and the Internal Rate of Return Methods

The net present value method has several important advantages over the internal rate of return method.

First, the net present value method is often simpler to use. As mentioned earlier, the internal rate of return method may require hunting for the discount rate that results in a net present value of zero. This can be a very laborious trial-and-error process, although it can be automated to some degree using a computer spreadsheet.

Second, a key assumption made by the internal rate of return method is questionable. Both methods assume that cash flows generated by a project during its useful life are immediately reinvested elsewhere. However, the two methods make different assumptions concerning the rate of return that is earned on those cash flows. The net present value method assumes the rate of return is the discount rate, whereas the internal rate of return method assumes the rate of return is the internal rate of return on the project. Specifically, if the internal rate of return of the project is high, this assumption may not be realistic. It is generally more realistic to assume that cash inflows can be reinvested at a rate of return equal to the discount rate—particularly if the discount rate is the company's cost of capital or an opportunity rate of return. For example, if the discount rate is the company's cost of capital, this rate of return can be actually realized by paying off the company's creditors and buying back the company's stock with cash flows from the project. In short, when the net present value method and the internal rate of return method do not agree concerning the attractiveness of a project, it is best to go with the net present value method. Of the two methods, it makes the more realistic assumption about the rate of return that can be earned on cash flows from the project.

Expanding the Net Present Value Method

objective 4

Prepare a net present value analysis of two competing investment projects using either the incremental-cost approach or the total-cost approach.

So far all of our examples have involved only a single investment alternative. We will now expand the net present value method to include two alternatives. In addition, we will integrate the concept of relevant costs into the discounted cash flow analysis.

The net present value method can be used to compare competing investment projects in two ways. One is the *total-cost approach,* and the other is the *incremental-cost approach.* Each approach is illustrated below.

The Total-Cost Approach

The total-cost approach is the most flexible method of making a net present value analysis of competing projects. To illustrate the mechanics of the approach, let us assume the following data:

Example E

Harper Ferry Company provides a ferry service across the Mississippi River. One of its ferryboats is in poor condition. This ferry can be renovated at an immediate cost of $20,000. Further repairs and an overhaul of the motor will be needed five years from now at a cost of $8,000. In all, the ferry will be usable for 10 years if this work is done. At the end of 10 years, the ferry will have to be scrapped at a salvage value of approximately $6,000. The scrap value of the ferry right now is $7,000. It will cost $30,000 each year to operate the ferry, and revenues will total $40,000 annually.

As an alternative, Harper Ferry Company can purchase a new ferryboat at a cost of $36,000. The new ferry will have a life of 10 years, but it will require some repairs at the end of 5 years. It is estimated that these repairs will amount to $3,000. At the end of 10 years, it is estimated that the ferry will have a scrap value of $6,000. It will cost $21,000 each year to operate the ferry, and revenues will total $40,000 annually.

Harper Ferry Company requires a return of at least 18% before taxes on all investment projects.

Should the company purchase the new ferry or renovate the old ferry? Exhibit 14–7 gives the solution using the total-cost approach.

Two points should be noted from the exhibit. First, observe that *all* cash inflows and *all* cash outflows are included in the solution under each alternative. No effort has been made to isolate those cash flows that are relevant to the decision and those that are not relevant. The inclusion of all cash flows associated with each alternative gives the approach its name—the *total-cost* approach.

Second, notice that a net present value figure is computed for each of the two alternatives. This is a distinct advantage of the total-cost approach in that an unlimited number of alternatives can be compared side by side to determine the best action. For example, another alternative for Harper Ferry Company would be to get out of the ferry business entirely. If management desired, the net present value of this alternative could be computed to compare with the alternatives shown in Exhibit 14–7. Still other alternatives might be open to the company. Once management has determined the net present value of each alternative that it wishes to consider, it can select the course of action that promises to be the most profitable. In the case at hand, given only the two alternatives, the data indicate that the most profitable course is to purchase the new ferry.[3]

3. The alternative with the highest net present value is not always the best choice, although it is the best choice in this case. For further discussion, see the section Preference Decisions—The Ranking of Investment Projects.

Exhibit 14–7 The Total-Cost Approach to Project Selection

	New Ferry	Old Ferry
Annual revenues	$40,000	$40,000
Annual cash operating costs	21,000	30,000
Net annual cash inflows	$19,000	$10,000

Item	Year(s)	Amount of Cash Flows	18% Factor*	Present Value of Cash Flows
Buy the new ferry:				
Initial investment	Now	$(36,000)	1.000	$(36,000)
Repairs in five years	5	(3,000)	0.437	(1,311)
Net annual cash inflows	1–10	19,000	4.494	85,386
Salvage of the old ferry	Now	7,000	1.000	7,000
Salvage of the new ferry	10	6,000	0.191	1,146
Net present value				56,221
Keep the old ferry:				
Initial repairs	Now	$(20,000)	1.000	(20,000)
Repairs in five years	5	(8,000)	0.437	(3,496)
Net annual cash inflows	1–10	10,000	4.494	44,940
Salvage of the old ferry	10	6,000	0.191	1,146
Net present value				22,590
Net present value in favor of buying the new ferry				$ 33,631

*All factors are from Tables 14C–3 and 14C–4 in Appendix 14C.

The Incremental-Cost Approach

When only two alternatives are being considered, the incremental-cost approach offers a simpler and more direct route to a decision. Unlike the total-cost approach, it focuses only on differential costs.[4] The procedure is to include in the discounted cash flow analysis only those costs and revenues that *differ* between the two alternatives being considered. To illustrate, refer again to the data in Example E relating to Harper Ferry Company. The solution using only differential costs is presented in Exhibit 14–8.

Two things should be noted from the data in this exhibit. First, notice that the net present value of $33,631 shown in Exhibit 14–8 agrees with the net present value shown under the total-cost approach in Exhibit 14–7. This agreement should be expected, since the two approaches are just different roads to the same destination.

Second, notice that the costs used in Exhibit 14–8 are just mathematical differences between the costs shown for the two alternatives in the prior exhibit. For example, the $16,000 incremental investment required to purchase the new ferry in Exhibit 14–8 is the difference between the $36,000 cost of the new ferry and the $20,000 cost required to renovate the old ferry from Exhibit 14–7. The other figures in Exhibit 14–8 have been computed in the same way.

4. Technically, the incremental-cost approach is misnamed, since it focuses on differential costs (that is, on both cost increases and decreases) rather than just on incremental costs. As used here, the term *incremental costs* should be interpreted broadly to include both cost increases and cost decreases.

Exhibit 14–8 The Incremental-Cost Approach to Project Selection

Item	Year(s)	Amount of Cash Flows	18% Factor*	Present Value of Cash Flows
Incremental investment required to purchase the new ferry	Now	$(16,000)	1.000	$(16,000)
Repairs in five years avoided	5	5,000	0.437	2,185
Increased net annual cash inflows	1–10	9,000	4.494	40,446
Salvage of the old ferry	Now	7,000	1.000	7,000
Difference in salvage value in 10 years	10	-0-	—	-0-
Net present value in favor of buying the new ferry				$ 33,631

*All factors are from Tables 14C–3 and 14C–4 in Appendix 14C.

Least-Cost Decisions

Revenues are not directly involved in some decisions. For example, a company that does not charge for delivery service may need to replace an old delivery truck, or a company may be trying to decide whether to lease or to buy its fleet of executive cars. In situations such as these, where no revenues are involved, the most desirable alternative will be the one that promises the *least total cost* from the present value perspective. Hence, these are known as least-cost decisions. To illustrate a least-cost decision, assume the following data:

Example F

Val-Tek Company is considering the replacement of an old threading machine. A new threading machine is available that could substantially reduce annual operating costs. Selected data relating to the old and the new machines are presented below:

	Old Machine	New Machine
Purchase cost when new	$20,000	$25,000
Salvage value now	3,000	—
Annual cash operating costs	15,000	9,000
Overhaul needed immediately	4,000	—
Salvage value in six years	-0-	5,000
Remaining life	6 years	6 years

Val-Tek Company's cost of capital is 10%.

Exhibit 14–9 provides an analysis of the alternatives using the total-cost approach.

As shown in the exhibit, the new machine has the lowest total cost when the present value of the net cash outflows is considered. An analysis of the two alternatives using the incremental-cost approach is presented in Exhibit 14–10. As before, the data in this exhibit represent the differences between the alternatives as shown under the total-cost approach.

Capital Budgeting and Nonprofit Organizations

Capital budgeting concepts can be applied in all types of organizations. Note, for example, the different types of organizations used in the examples in this chapter. These organizations include a hospital, a company working under a licensing agreement, a school district, a company operating a ferryboat service, and a manufacturing company. The diversity of these examples shows the range and power of discounted cash flow methods.

Exhibit 14–9 The Total-Cost Approach (Least-Cost Decision)

Item	Year(s)	Amount of Cash Flows	10% Factor*	Present Value of Cash Flows
Buy the new machine:				
Initial investment	Now	$(25,000)	1.000	$(25,000)†
Salvage of the old machine	Now	3,000	1.000	3,000†
Annual cash operating costs	1–6	(9,000)	4.355	(39,195)
Salvage of the new machine	6	5,000	0.564	2,820
Present value of net cash outflows				(58,375)
Keep the old machine:				
Overhaul needed now	Now	$ (4,000)	1.000	$ (4,000)
Annual cash operating costs	1–6	(15,000)	4.355	(65,325)
Present value of net cash outflows				(69,325)
Net present value in favor of buying the new machine				$ 10,950

*All factors are from Tables 14C–3 and 14C–4 in Appendix 14C.
†These two items could be netted into a single $22,500 incremental-cost figure ($25,000 − $3,000 = $22,000).

Exhibit 14–10 The Incremental-Cost Approach (Least-Cost Decision)

Item	Year(s)	Amount of Cash Flows	10% Factor*	Present Value of Cash Flows
Incremental investment required to purchase the new machine	Now	$(21,000)	1.000	$(21,000)†
Salvage of the old machine	Now	3,000	1.000	3,000†
Savings in annual cash operating costs	1–6	6,000	4.355	26,130
Difference in salvage value in six years	6	5,000	0.564	2,820
Net present value in favor of buying the new machine				$ 10,950

*All factors are from Tables 14C–3 and 14C–4 in Appendix 14C.
†These two items could be netted into a single $18,000 incremental-cost figure ($21,000 − $3,000 = $18,000).

One problem faced by *nonprofit* organizations in capital budgeting is determining the proper discount rate. Some nonprofit organizations use the rate of interest paid on special bond issues (such as an issue for street improvements or an issue to build a school) as their discount rate; others use the rate of interest that could be earned by placing money in an endowment fund rather than spending it on capital improvements; and still others use discount rates that are set somewhat arbitrarily by governing boards.

The greatest danger lies in using a discount rate that is too low. Most government agencies, for example, at one time used the interest rate on government bonds as their discount rate. It is now recognized that this rate is too low and has resulted in the acceptance of many projects that should not have been undertaken.[5] To resolve this

5. See *Federal Capital Budgeting: A Collection of Haphazard Practices,* GAO, P.O. Box 6015, Gaithersburg, MD., PAD-81-19, February 26, 1981.

problem, the Office of Management and Budget has specified that federal government units must use a discount rate of at least 10% on all projects.[6] For nonprofit units such as schools and hospitals, it is generally recommended that the discount rate should "approximate the average rate of return on private sector investments."[7]

Investments in Automated Equipment

objective 5

Make a capital budgeting analysis involving automated equipment.

Future cash flows are often uncertain or difficult to estimate. Investments in automated equipment provide a good example. They tend to be large, and their benefits are often indirect and intangible and therefore hard to quantify.

The cost involved in automating a process is much greater than the cost of purchasing conventional equipment. Single pieces of automated equipment, such as a robot or computerized numerically controlled machine, can cost $1 million or more. A flexible manufacturing system, involving one or more cells, can cost up to $50 million. Even more important, the front-end investment in machinery often constitutes less than half the total cost of automating. The nonhardware costs such as engineering, software development, and implementation of the system can equal or exceed the cost of the equipment itself. Clearly, it is important to realistically estimate such costs before embarking on an automation project.

Focus on Current Practice

Rockwell International Corp.'s Herman M. Reininga wanted to buy an $80,000 laser to etch contract numbers on communications systems sold to the Pentagon. But the division's financial staff laughed him out of the meeting (in which he recommended the purchase). The laser would save only $4,000 in direct labor each year. At that rate, it would take 20 years to recover the cost.

Three years later, Reininga got his laser. He presented data showing that finished radios sat around for two weeks waiting for an antique etching operation to finish identity plates. The laser would do the job in 10 minutes, moving shipments out faster—and saving the company $200,000 a year in inventory-holding costs.[8] ■

Benefits from Automation

The benefits of automation roughly fall into two classes—tangible benefits and intangible benefits.

The tangible benefits are much easier to identify and measure than the intangible benefits. The tangible benefits of automation usually include decreased labor costs and

6. Office of Management and Budget Circular No. A-94, March 1972. The U.S. Postal Service is exempted from the 10% rate as are all water resource projects and all lease or buy decisions.
7. Robert N. Anthony and David W. Young, *Management Control in Nonprofit Organizations,* 5th ed. (Homewood, Ill.: Richard D. Irwin, Inc., 1994), p. 445.
8. Reprinted from "The Productivity Paradox," *Business Week,* No. 3055 (June 6, 1988), p. 104, by special permission.

a reduction in defective output. The reduction in defective output results in fewer inspections, and less scrap, waste, and rework. It can also result in less warranty work. General Electric reports, for example, that automating its dishwasher manufacturing plant resulted in a 50% reduction in its service call rate.

The intangible benefits of automated systems generally result from their greater speed, consistency, reliability, and flexibility. These factors permit greater throughput and a greater variety of products, and they enhance product quality. In turn, the greater throughput, variety of products, and higher quality should lead to greater sales and profits, although the precise amount of the increase is very difficult to forecast. Automated processes also allow a company to reduce its inventories, since the company can more quickly respond to shifts in customer demand.

Finally, some managers argue that automation is necessary as a matter of self-preservation. When a company's competition is automating, the company faces the prospect of a loss in market share from attempting to make do with technologically obsolete products and operations. And if a company does not maintain its technical edge, it will lose the ability to catch up with the competition later on. Companies that hold back and do not automate may lose their ability to recognize and then implement the key elements of new technology that provide competitive advantage.

Note that the tangible benefits above represent potential *cost savings,* whereas the intangible benefits represent potential *revenue enhancements.* Generally, it's easier to measure the amount of cost savings associated with an investment project, and that's why items such as reduced direct labor cost always show up in a capital budgeting analysis. But it is harder to measure the impact of a potential revenue enhancement such as greater flexibility or faster market response. As a result, managers may overlook such items when evaluating the benefits from automated equipment. The intangible benefits must be explicitly considered, however, or faulty decisions will follow.

Focus on Current Practice

The effects of incorporating lost sales in automation decisions can be dramatic. United Architects, a midsized architectural firm located in Southern California, was considering an investment in a computer-aided design and drafting (CADD) system that would produce appealing three-dimensional perspectives to show to clients. The CADD system the firm was considering cost nearly $600,000 and had annual operating costs in the neighborhood of $100,000. When only the cost savings over the existing means of producing such drawings were considered, the CADD system appeared to be financially unattractive. It had a negative net present value of several hundred thousand dollars. However, professionals at the firm pointed out that several key contracts had been recently lost because competitors had CADD equipment. The drawings produced on competitors' CADD systems looked much more impressive and professional to clients than the drawings produced with United Architects' old equipment. When the estimated lost contribution margins on such projects were included in the cash flow analysis, the project showed a positive net present value in excess of $600,000. Management decided to make the investment.[9] ■

9. John Y. Lee, "The Service Sector: Investing in New Technology to Stay Alive," *Management Accounting,* June 1991, pp. 45–48.

Decision Framework for Intangible Benefits

A fairly simple procedure can be followed when the intangible benefits are uncertain and significant. Suppose, for example, that a company with a 16% cost of capital is considering purchasing automated equipment that would have a 15-year useful life. Also suppose that a discounted cash flow analysis of just the tangible costs and benefits shows a negative net present value of $223,000. Clearly, if the intangible benefits are large enough, they could turn this negative net present value into a positive net present value. In this case, the amount of additional cash flow per year from the intangible benefits that would be needed to make the project financially attractive can be computed as follows:

Net present value (negative)	$(223,000)
Factor for an annuity of 16% for 15 periods (from Table 14C–4 in Appendix 14C)	5.575

$$\frac{\text{Net present value, \$(223,000)}}{\text{Present value factor, 5.575}} = \$40{,}000$$

Thus, if intangible benefits such as greater flexibility, higher quality of output, and avoidance of capital decay are worth at least $40,000 a year to the company, then the automated equipment should be purchased. If, in the judgment of management, these intangible benefits are *not* worth $40,000 a year, then no purchase should be made.[10]

This technique can be used in other situations in which the future benefits of a current investment are uncertain or intangible. For example, this technique can be used to assess an investment in research on a new type of drug whose market potential is highly uncertain.

Preference Decisions—The Ranking of Investment Projects

objective 6

Rank investment projects in order of preference using (1) the internal rate of return method and (2) the net present value method with the profitability index.

Recall that when considering investment opportunities, managers must make two types of decisions—screening decisions and preference decisions. Screening decisions pertain to whether or not some proposed investment is acceptable. Preference decisions come *after* screening decisions and attempt to answer the following question: "How do the remaining investment proposals, all of which have been screened and provide an acceptable rate of return, rank in terms of preference? That is, which one(s) would be *best* for the firm to accept?"

Preference decisions are more difficult to make than screening decisions because investment funds are usually limited. This often requires that some (perhaps many) otherwise very profitable investment opportunities must be passed up.

Sometimes preference decisions are called ranking decisions, or rationing decisions, because they ration limited investment funds among many competing alternatives, or there may be many alternatives that must be ranked. Either the internal rate of return method or the net present value method can be used in making preference decisions. However, as discussed earlier, if the two methods are in conflict, it is best to use the net present value method, which is more reliable.

10. Robert E. Bennett and James A. Hendricks suggest such a procedure in "Justifying the Acquisition of Automated Equipment," *Management Accounting* 69 (July 1987), p. 46.

Internal Rate of Return Method

When using the internal rate of return method to rank competing investment projects, the preference rule is: *The higher the internal rate of return, the more desirable the project.* An investment project with an internal rate of return of 18% is preferable to another project that promises a return of only 15%. Internal rate of return is widely used to rank projects.

Net Present Value Method

If the net present value method is used to rank projects, the net present value of one project cannot be compared directly to the net present value of another project unless the investments in the projects are of equal size. For example, assume that a company is considering two competing investments, as shown below:

	Investment	
	A	B
Investment required	$(80,000)	$(5,000)
Present value of cash inflows	81,000	6,000
Net present value	$ 1,000	$ 1,000

Each project has a net present value of $1,000, but the projects are not equally desirable. The project requiring an investment of only $5,000 is much more desirable when funds are limited than the project requiring an investment of $80,000. To compare the two projects on a valid basis, the present value of the cash inflows should be divided by the investment required. The result is called the **profitability index**. The formula for the profitability index follows:

$$\text{Profitability index} = \frac{\text{Present value of cash inflows}}{\text{Investment required}} \qquad (2)$$

The profitability indexes for the two investments above would be computed as follows:

	Investment	
	A	B
Present value of cash inflows (a)	$81,000	$6,000
Investment required (b)	$80,000	$5,000
Profitability index, (a) ÷ (b)	1.01	1.20

When using the profitability index to rank competing investments projects, the preference rule is: *The higher the profitability index, the more desirable the project.* Applying this rule to the two investments above, investment B should be chosen over investment A.

The profitability index is an application of the techniques for utilizing scarce resources discussed in Chapter 13. In this case, the scarce resource is the limited funds available for investment, and the profitability index is similar to the contribution margin per unit of the scarce resource.

A few details should be clarified with respect to the computation of the profitability index. The "Investment required" refers to any cash outflows that occur at the beginning of the project, reduced by any salvage value recovered from the sale of old equipment. The "Investment required" also includes any investment in working capital that the project may need. Finally, we should note that the "Present value of cash inflows" is net of all *out*flows that occur after the project starts.

Focus on Current Practice

Several different techniques can be used to take into account uncertainties about future cash flows in capital budgeting. The uncertainties are particularly apparent in the drug business where it costs an average of $359 million and 10 years to bring a new drug through the governmental approval process and to market. And once on the market, 7 out of 10 products fail to return the company's cost of capital.

Merck & Co. manages the financial risks and uncertainties of drug research using a Research Planning Model they have developed. The model, which produces net present value estimates and other key statistics, is based on a wide range of scientific and financial variables—most of which are uncertain. For example, the future selling price of any drug resulting from current research is usually highly uncertain, but managers at Merck & Co. can at least specify a range within which the selling price is likely to fall. The computer is used to draw a value at random, within the permissible range, for each of the variables in the model. The model then computes a net present value. This process is repeated many times, and each time a new value of each of the variables is drawn at random. In this way, Merck is able to produce a probability distribution for the net present value. This can be used, for example, to estimate the probability that the project's net present value will exceed a certain level. "What are the payoffs of all this sophistication? In short, better decisions."[11] ■

Other Approaches to Capital Budgeting Decisions

Discounted cash flow methods have gained widespread acceptance as decision-making tools. Other methods of making capital budgeting decisions are also used, however, and are preferred by some managers. In this section, we discuss two such methods known as *payback* and *simple rate of return.* Both methods have been in use for a hundred years or more, but they are now declining in popularity as primary tools for project evaluation.

objective 7
Determine the payback period for an investment.

The Payback Method

The payback method centers on a span of time known as the *payback period.* The **payback period** can be defined as the length of time that it takes for a project to recoup its initial cost out of the cash receipts that it generates. This period is sometimes referred to as "the time that it takes for an investment to pay for itself." The basic premise of

11. Nancy A. Nichols, "Scientific Management at Merck: An Interview with CFO Judy Lewent," *Harvard Business Review,* January–February 1994, pp. 89–99.

the payback method is that the more quickly the cost of an investment can be recovered, the more desirable is the investment.

The payback period is expressed in years. *When the net annual cash inflow is the same every year,* the following formula can be used to compute the payback period:

$$\text{Payback period} = \frac{\text{Investment required}}{\text{Net annual cash inflow*}} \qquad (3)$$

*If new equipment is replacing old equipment, this becomes incremental net annual cash inflow.

To illustrate the payback method, assume the following data:

Example G

York Company needs a new milling machine. The company is considering two machines: machine A and machine B. Machine A costs $15,000 and will reduce operating costs by $5,000 per year. Machine B costs only $12,000 but will also reduce operating costs by $5,000 per year.

Required Which machine should be purchased according to the payback method?

$$\text{Machine A payback period} = \frac{\$15{,}000}{\$5{,}000} = 3.0 \text{ years}$$

$$\text{Machine B payback period} = \frac{\$12{,}000}{\$5{,}000} = 2.4 \text{ years}$$

According to the payback calculations, York Company should purchase machine B, since it has a shorter payback period than machine A.

Evaluation of the Payback Method

The payback method is not a true measure of the profitability of an investment. Rather, it simply tells the manager how many years will be required to recover the original investment. Unfortunately, a shorter payback period does not always mean that one investment is more desirable than another.

To illustrate, consider again the two machines used in the example above. Since machine B has a shorter payback period than machine A, it *appears* that machine B is more desirable than machine A. But if we add one more piece of data, this illusion quickly disappears. Machine A has a projected 10-year life, and machine B has a projected 5-year life. It would take two purchases of machine B to provide the same length of service as would be provided by a single purchase of machine A. Under these circumstances, machine A would be a much better investment than machine B, even though machine B has a shorter payback period. Unfortunately, the payback method has no inherent mechanism for highlighting differences in useful life between investments. Such differences can be very important, and relying on payback alone may result in incorrect decisions.

A further criticism of the payback method is that it does not consider the time value of money. A cash inflow to be received several years in the future is weighed equally with a cash inflow to be received right now. To illustrate, assume that for an investment of $8,000 you can purchase either of the two following streams of cash inflows:

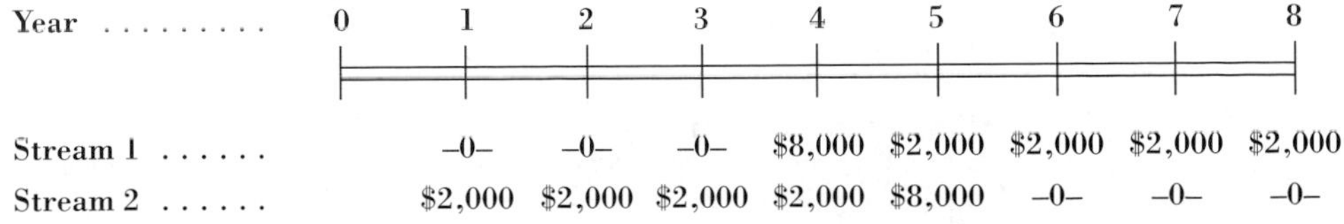

Year	0	1	2	3	4	5	6	7	8
Stream 1		–0–	–0–	–0–	$8,000	$2,000	$2,000	$2,000	$2,000
Stream 2		$2,000	$2,000	$2,000	$2,000	$8,000	–0–	–0–	–0–

Which stream of cash inflows would you prefer to receive in return for your $8,000 investment? Each stream has a payback period of 4.0 years. Therefore, if payback alone were relied on in making the decision, you would be forced to say that the streams are equally desirable. However, from the point of view of the time value of money, stream 2 is much more desirable than stream 1.

On the other hand, under certain conditions the payback method can be very useful. For one thing, it can help identify which investment proposals are in the "ballpark." That is, it can be used as a screening tool to help answer the question, "Should I consider this proposal further?" If a proposal doesn't provide a payback within some specified period, then there may be no need to consider it further. In addition, the payback period is often of great importance to new firms that are "cash poor." When a firm is cash poor, a project with a short payback period but a low rate of return might be preferred over another project with a high rate of return but a long payback period. The reason is that the company may simply need a faster return of its cash investment. And finally, the payback method is sometimes used in industries where products become obsolete very rapidly—such as consumer electronics. Since products may last only a year or two, the payback period on investments must be very short.

Focus on Current Practice

Capital budgeting techniques are widely used in large nonprofit organizations. A survey of universities in the United Kingdom revealed that 41% use the net present value method, 23% use the internal rate of return method, 29% use the payback method, and 11% use the accounting rate of return method. (Some universities use more than one method.) Furthermore, the central Funding Council of the United Kingdom requires that the net present value method be used for projects whose lifespans exceed 20 years.[12] ■

An Extended Example of Payback

As shown by formula (3) given earlier, the payback period is computed by dividing the investment in a project by the net annual cash inflows that the project will generate. If new equipment is replacing old equipment, then any salvage to be received on disposal of the old equipment should be deducted from the cost of the new equipment, and only the *incremental* investment should be used in the payback computation. In addition, any depreciation deducted in arriving at the project's net income must be added back to obtain the project's expected net annual cash inflow. To illustrate, assume the following data:

Example H

Goodtime Fun Centers, Inc., operates many outlets in the eastern states. Some of the vending machines in one of its outlets provide very little revenue, so the company is considering removing the machines and installing equipment to dispense soft ice cream. The equipment would cost $80,000 and have an eight-year useful life. Incremental annual revenues and costs associated with the sale of ice cream would be as follows:

12. Paul Cooper, "Management Accounting Practices in Universities," *Management Accounting (U.K.)*, February 1996, pp. 28–30.

Exhibit 14–11
Computation of the Payback Period

Step 1: *Compute the net annual cash inflow.* Since the net annual cash inflow is not given, it must be computed before the payback period can be determined:

Net income (given above)	$20,000
Add: Noncash deduction for depreciation	10,000
Net annual cash inflow	$30,000

Step 2: *Compute the payback period.* Using the net annual cash inflow figure from above, the payback period can be determined as follows:

Cost of the new equipment	$80,000
Less salvage value of old equipment	5,000
Investment required	$75,000

$$\text{Payback period} = \frac{\text{Investment required}}{\text{Net annual cash inflow}}$$

$$= \frac{\$75{,}000}{\$30{,}000} = 2.5 \text{ years}$$

Sales	$150,000
Less cost of ingredients	90,000
Contribution margin	60,000
Less fixed expenses:	
Salaries	27,000
Maintenance	3,000
Depreciation	10,000
Total fixed expenses	40,000
Net income	$ 20,000

The vending machines can be sold for a $5,000 scrap value. The company will not purchase equipment unless it has a payback of three years or less. Should the equipment to dispense ice cream be purchased?

An analysis as to whether the proposed equipment meets the company's payback requirements is given in Exhibit 14–11. Several things should be noted from the data in this exhibit. First, notice that depreciation is added back to net income to obtain the net annual cash inflow from the new equipment. As stated earlier in the chapter, depreciation is not a cash outlay; thus, it must be added back to net income in order to adjust net income to a cash basis. Second, notice in the payback computation that the salvage value from the old machines has been deducted from the cost of the new equipment, and that only the incremental investment has been used in computing the payback period.

Since the proposed equipment has a payback period of less than three years, the company's payback requirement has been met.

Focus on Current Practice

Intel Corporation invests a billion to a billion and a half dollars in plants to fabricate computer processor chips such as the Pentium III. But the fab plants can only be used to make state-of-the-art chips for about two years. By that time, the equipment is obsolete and the plant must be converted to making less complicated chips. Under such conditions of rapid obsolescence, the payback method may be the most appropriate way to evaluate investments. If the project does not pay back within a few years, it may never pay back its initial investment.[13] ■

Payback and Uneven Cash Flows

When the cash flows associated with an investment project change from year to year, the simple payback formula that we outlined earlier is no longer usable, and the computations involved in deriving the payback period can be fairly complex. Consider the following data:

Year	Investment	Cash Inflow
1	$4,000	$1,000
2		–0–
3		2,000
4	2,000	1,000
5		500
6		3,000
7		2,000
8		2,000

What is the payback period on this investment? The answer is 5.5 years, but to obtain this figure it is necessary to track the unrecovered investment year by year. The steps involved in this process are shown in Exhibit 14–12. By the middle of the sixth year, sufficient cash inflows will have been realized to recover the entire investment of $6,000 ($4,000 + $2,000).

objective 8

Compute the simple rate of return for an investment.

The Simple Rate of Return Method

The **simple rate of return** method is another capital budgeting technique that does not involve discounted cash flows. The method is also known as the accounting rate of return, the unadjusted rate of return, and the financial statement method.

Exhibit 14–12 Payback and Uneven Cash Flows

Year	(1) Beginning Unrecovered Investment	(2) Additional Investment	(3) Total Unrecovered Investment (1) + (2)	(4) Cash Inflow	(5) Ending Unrecovered Investment (3) – (4)
1	$4,000		$4,000	$1,000	$3,000
2	3,000		3,000	–0–	3,000
3	3,000		3,000	2,000	1,000
4	1,000	$2,000	3,000	1,000	2,000
5	2,000		2,000	500	1,500
6	1,500		1,500	3,000	–0–
7	–0–		–0–	2,000	–0–
8	–0–		–0–	2,000	–0–

13. "Pentium at a Glance," *Forbes ASAP,* February 26, 1996, p. 66.

Unlike the other capital budgeting methods that we have discussed, the simple rate of return method does not focus on cash flows. Rather, it focuses on accounting net income. The approach is to estimate the revenues that will be generated by a proposed investment and then to deduct from these revenues all of the projected operating expenses associated with the project. This net income figure is then related to the initial investment in the project, as shown in the following formula:

$$\text{Simple rate of return} = \frac{\text{Incremental revenues} - \text{Incremental expenses, including depreciation} = \text{Incremental net income}}{\text{Initial investment*}} \qquad (4)$$

*The investment should be reduced by any salvage from the sale of old equipment.

Or, if a cost reduction project is involved, formula (4) becomes:

$$\text{Simple rate of return} = \frac{\text{Cost savings} - \text{Depreciation on new equipment}}{\text{Initial investment*}} \qquad (5)$$

*The investment should be reduced by any salvage from the sale of old equipment.

Example I

Brigham Tea, Inc., is a processor of a nontannic acid tea. The company is contemplating purchasing equipment for an additional processing line. The additional processing line would increase revenues by $90,000 per year. Incremental cash operating expenses would be $40,000 per year. The equipment would cost $180,000 and have a nine-year life. No salvage value is projected.

Required

1. Compute the simple rate of return.
2. Compute the internal rate of return and compare it to the simple rate of return.

Solution

1. By applying the formula for the simple rate of return found in equation (4), we can compute the simple rate of return:

$$\text{Simple rate of return} = \frac{\begin{bmatrix}\$90{,}000 \\ \text{Incremental} \\ \text{revenues}\end{bmatrix} - \begin{bmatrix}\$40{,}000 \text{ Cash operating expenses} \\ + \$20{,}000 \text{ Depreciation}\end{bmatrix}}{\$180{,}000 \text{ Initial investment}}$$

$$= \frac{\$30{,}000}{\$180{,}000}$$

$$- 16.7\%$$

2. The rate computed in (1) above, however, is far below the internal rate of return of approximately 24%:

$$\text{Factor of the internal rate of return} = \frac{\$180{,}000}{\$50{,}000^*} = 3.600$$

*$30,000 net income + $20,000 depreciation = $50,000; or the annual cash inflow can be computed as $90,000 increased revenues − $40,000 cash expenses = $50,000.

By scanning across the nine-year line in Table 14C–4 in Appendix 14C, we can see that the internal rate of return is approximately 24%.

Example J

Midwest Farms, Inc., hires people on a part-time basis to sort eggs. The cost of this hand-sorting process is $30,000 per year. The company is investigating the purchase of an egg-sorting machine that would cost $90,000 and have a 15-year useful life. The machine would have negligible salvage value, and it would cost $10,000 per year to operate and maintain. The egg-sorting equipment currently being used could be sold now for a scrap value of $2,500.

Required Compute the simple rate of return on the new egg-sorting machine.

Solution A cost reduction project is involved in this situation. By applying the formula for the simple rate of return found in equation (5), we can compute the simple rate of return as follows:

$$\text{Simple rate of return} = \frac{\$20{,}000^{*}\text{ Cost savings} - \$6{,}000^{\dagger}\text{ Depreciation on new equipment}}{\$90{,}000 - \$2{,}500}$$

$$= 16.0\%$$

*$30,000 − $10,000 = $20,000 cost savings.
†$90,000 ÷ 15 years = $6,000 depreciation.

Criticisms of the Simple Rate of Return

The most damaging criticism of the simple rate of return method is that it does not consider the time value of money. A dollar received 10 years from now is viewed as being just as valuable as a dollar received today. Thus, the manager can be misled if the alternatives being considered have different cash flow patterns. For example, assume that project A has a high simple rate of return but yields the bulk of its cash flows many years from now. Another project, B, has a somewhat lower simple rate of return but yields the bulk of its cash flows over the next few years. Project A has a higher simple rate of return than project B; however, project B might in fact be a much better investment if the time value of money were considered.

Postaudit of Investment Projects

A **postaudit** of an investment project involves a follow-up after the project has been approved to see whether or not expected results are actually realized. This is a key part of the capital budgeting process in that it provides management with an opportunity, over time, to see if realistic data are being submitted to support capital budgeting proposals. It also provides an opportunity to reinforce successful projects as needed, to strengthen or perhaps salvage projects that are encountering difficulty, to terminate unsuccessful projects before losses become too great, and to improve the overall quality of future investment proposals.

In performing a postaudit, the same technique should be used as was used in the original approval process. That is, if a project was approved on the basis of a net present value analysis, then the same procedure should be used in performing the postaudit. However, the data used in the postaudit analysis should be *actual observed data* rather than estimated data. This affords management with an opportunity to make a side-by-side comparison to see how well the project has worked out. It also helps assure that estimated data received on future proposals will be carefully prepared, since the persons submitting the data will know that their estimates will be given careful scrutiny in the postaudit process. Actual results that are far out of line with original estimates should be carefully reviewed by management, and corrective action taken as necessary. Those managers responsible for the original estimates should be required to provide a full explanation of any major differences between estimated and actual results.[14]

14. For further discussion, see Lawrence A. Gordon and Mary D. Myers, "Postauditing Capital Projects," *Management Accounting* 72, no. 7 (January 1991), pp. 39–42. This study of 282 large U.S. companies states that "an increasing number of firms are recognizing the importance of the postaudit stage" (p. 41).

Summary

Investment decisions should take into account the time value of money since a dollar today is more valuable than a dollar received in the future. The net present value and internal rate of return methods both reflect this fact. In the net present value method, future cash flows are discounted to their present value so that they can be compared on a valid basis with current cash outlays. The difference between the present value of the cash inflows and the present value of the cash outflows is called the project's net present value. If the net present value of the project is negative, the project is rejected. The discount rate in the net present value method is usually a minimum required rate of return such as the company's cost of capital.

The internal rate of return is the rate of return that equates the present value of the cash inflows and the present value of the cash outflows, resulting in a zero net present value. If the internal rate of return is less than the company's minimum required rate of return, the project is rejected.

After rejecting projects whose net present values are negative or whose internal rates of return are less than the minimum required rate of return, the company may still have more projects than can be supported with available funds. The remaining projects can be ranked using either the profitability index or their internal rates of return. The profitability index is computed by dividing the present value of the project's future net cash inflows by the required initial investment.

Some companies prefer to use either payback or the simple rate of return to evaluate investment proposals. The payback period is the number of periods that are required to recover the initial investment in the project. The simple rate of return is determined by dividing a project's accounting net income by the initial investment in the project.

Review Problem 1: Basic Present Value Computations

Each of the following situations is independent. Work out your own solution to each situation, and then check it against the solution provided.

1. John has just reached age 58. In 12 years, he plans to retire. Upon retiring, he would like to take an extended vacation, which he expects will cost at least $4,000. What lump-sum amount must he invest now to have the needed $4,000 at the end of 12 years if the rate of return is:
   a. Eight percent?
   b. Twelve percent?
2. The Morgans would like to send their daughter to an expensive music camp at the end of each of the next five years. The camp costs $1,000 a year. What lump-sum amount would have to be invested now to have the $1,000 at the end of each year if the rate of return is:
   a. Eight percent?
   b. Twelve percent?
3. You have just received an inheritance from a relative. You can invest the money and either receive a $20,000 lump-sum amount at the end of 10 years or receive $1,400 at the end of each year for the next 10 years. If your minimum desired rate of return is 12%, which alternative would you prefer?

Solution to Review Problem 1

1. a. The amount that must be invested now would be the present value of the $4,000, using a discount rate of 8%. From Table 14C–3 in Appendix 14C, the factor for a discount rate of 8% for 12 periods is 0.397. Multiplying this discount factor by the $4,000 needed in 12 years will give the amount of the present investment required: $4,000 × 0.397 = $1,588.
   b. We will proceed as we did in (a) above, but this time we will use a discount rate of 12%. From Table 14C–3 in Appendix 14C, the factor for a discount rate of 12% for 12 periods is 0.257. Multiplying this discount factor by the $4,000 needed in 12 years will give the amount of the present investment required: $4,000 × 0.257 = $1,028.

Notice that as the discount rate (desired rate of return) increases, the present value decreases.

2. This part differs from (1) above in that we are now dealing with an annuity rather than with a single future sum. The amount that must be invested now will be the present value of the $1,000 needed at the end of each year for five years. Since we are dealing with an annuity, or a series of annual cash flows, we must refer to Table 14C–4 in Appendix 14C for the appropriate discount factor.
   a. From Table 14C–4 in Appendix 14C, the discount factor for 8% for five periods is 3.993. Therefore, the amount that must be invested now to have $1,000 available at the end of each year for five years is $1,000 × 3.993 = $3,993.
   b. From Table 14C–4 in Appendix 14C, the discount factor for 12% for five periods is 3.605. Therefore, the amount that must be invested now to have $1,000 available at the end of each year for five years is $1,000 × 3.605 = $3,605.

   Again, notice that as the discount rate (desired rate of return) increases, the present value decreases. At a higher rate of return we can invest less than would have been needed if a lower rate of return were being earned.
3. For this part we will need to refer to both Tables 14C–3 and 14C–4 in Appendix 14C. From Table 14C–3, we will need to find the discount factor for 12% for 10 periods, then apply it to the $20,000 lump sum to be received in 10 years. From Table 14C–4, we will need to find the discount factor for 12% for 10 periods, then apply it to the series of $1,400 payments to be received over the 10-year period. Whichever alternative has the higher present value is the one that should be selected.

$20,000 × 0.322 = $6,440
$1,400 × 5.650 = $7,910

Thus, you would prefer to receive the $1,400 per year for 10 years rather than the $20,000 lump sum.

Review Problem 2: Comparison of Capital Budgeting Methods

Lamar Company is studying a project that would have an eight-year life and require a $1,600,000 investment in equipment. At the end of eight years, the project would terminate and the equipment would have no salvage value. The project would provide net income each year as follows:

Sales		$3,000,000
Less variable expenses		1,800,000
Contribution margin		1,200,000
Less fixed expenses:		
Advertising, salaries, and other fixed out-of-pocket costs	$700,000	
Depreciation	200,000	
Total fixed expenses		900,000
Net income		$ 300,000

The company's discount rate is 18%.

Required

1. Compute the net annual cash inflow from the project.
2. Compute the project's net present value. Is the project acceptable?
3. Compute the project's internal rate of return. Interpolate to one decimal place.
4. Compute the project's payback period. If the company requires a maximum payback of three years, is the project acceptable?
5. Compute the project's simple rate of return.

Solution to Review Problem 2

1. The net annual cash inflow can be computed by deducting the cash expenses from sales:

Sales	$3,000,000
Less variable expenses	1,800,000
Contribution margin	1,200,000
Less advertising, salaries, and other fixed out-of-pocket costs	700,000
Net annual cash inflow	$ 500,000

Or it can be computed by adding depreciation back to net income:

Net income	$300,000
Add: Noncash deduction for depreciation	200,000
Net annual cash inflow	$500,000

2. The net present value can be computed as follows:

Item	Year(s)	Amount of Cash Flows	18% Factor	Present Value of Cash Flows
Cost of new equipment	Now	$(1,600,000)	1.000	$(1,600,000)
Net annual cash inflow	1–8	500,000	4.078	2,039,000
Net present value				$ 439,000

Yes, the project is acceptable since it has a positive net present value.

3. The formula for computing the factor of the internal rate of return is:

$$\text{Factor of the internal rate of return} = \frac{\text{Investment required}}{\text{Net annual cash inflow}}$$

$$= \frac{\$1{,}600{,}000}{\$500{,}000} = 3.200$$

Looking in Table 14C–4 in Appendix 14C at the end of the chapter and scanning along the 8-period line, we find that a factor of 3.200 represents a rate of return somewhere between 26% and 28%. To find the rate we are after, we must interpolate as follows:

26% factor	3.241	3.241
True factor	3.200	
28% factor		3.076
Difference	0.041	0.165

$$\text{Internal rate of return} = 26\% + \left(\frac{0.041}{0.165} \times 2\%\right)$$

$$= 26.5\%$$

4. The formula for the payback period is:

$$\text{Payback period} = \frac{\text{Investment required}}{\text{Net annual cash inflow}}$$

$$= \frac{\$1{,}600{,}000}{\$500{,}000}$$

$$= 3.2 \text{ years}$$

No, the project is not acceptable when measured by the payback method. The 3.2 years payback period is greater than the maximum 3 years set by the company.

5. The formula for the simple rate of return is:

$$\text{Simple rate of return} = \frac{\text{Incremental revenues} - \text{Incremental expenses, including depreciation} = \text{Net income}}{\text{Initial investment}}$$

$$= \frac{\$300{,}000}{\$1{,}600{,}000}$$

$$= 18.75\%$$

Key Terms for Review

Capital budgeting The process of planning significant outlays on projects that have long-term implications such as the purchase of new equipment or the introduction of a new product. (p. 668)

Cost of capital The overall cost to an organization of obtaining investment funds, including the cost of both debt sources and equity sources. (p. 673)

Internal rate of return The discount rate at which the net present value of an investment project is zero; thus, the internal rate of return represents the interest yield promised by a project over its useful life. This term is synonymous with *time-adjusted rate of return.* (p. 674)

Net present value The difference between the present value of the cash inflows and the present value of the cash outflows associated with an investment project. (p. 669)

Out-of-pocket costs Actual cash outlays for salaries, advertising, repairs, and similar costs. (p. 673)

Payback period The length of time that it takes for a project to recover its initial cost out of the cash receipts that it generates. (p. 686)

Postaudit The follow-up after a project has been approved and implemented to determine whether expected results are actually realized. (p. 692)

Preference decision A decision as to which of several competing acceptable investment proposals is best. (p. 668)

Profitability index The ratio of the present value of a project's cash inflows to the investment required. (p. 685)

Required rate of return The minimum rate of return that an investment project must yield to be acceptable. (p. 676)

Screening decision A decision as to whether a proposed investment meets some preset standard of acceptance. (p. 668)

Simple rate of return The rate of return computed by dividing a project's annual accounting net income by the initial investment required. (p. 690)

Time-adjusted rate of return This term is synonymous with *internal rate of return.* (p. 674)

Working capital The excess of current assets over current liabilities. (p. 671)

Yield A term synonymous with *internal rate of return* and *time-adjusted rate of return.* (p. 674)

Appendix 14A: The Concept of Present Value

objective 9

Explain the concept of present value and make present value computations with and without present value tables.

A dollar received today is more valuable than a dollar received a year from now for the simple reason that if you have a dollar today, you can put it in the bank and have more than a dollar a year from now. Since dollars today are worth more than dollars in the future, we need some means of weighting cash flows that are received at different times so that they can be compared. The theory of interest provides us with the means of making such comparisons. With a few simple calculations, we can adjust the value of a dollar received any number of years from now so that it can be compared with the value of a dollar in hand today.

The Theory of Interest

If a bank pays 5% interest, then a deposit of \$100 today will be worth \$105 one year from now. This can be expressed in mathematical terms by means of the following equation:

$$F_1 = P(1 + r) \tag{6}$$

where F_1 = the amount to be received in one period, P = the amount invested now, and r = the rate of interest per period.

If the investment made now is $100 deposited in a bank savings account that is to earn interest at 5%, then P = $100 and r = 0.05. Under these conditions, F_1 = $105, the amount to be received in one year.

The $100 present outlay is called the **present value** of the $105 amount to be received in one year. It is also known as the *discounted value* of the future $105 receipt. The $100 figure represents the value in present terms of $105 to be received a year from now when the interest rate is 5%.

COMPOUND INTEREST What if the investor leaves his or her money in the bank for a second year? In that case, by the end of the second year the original $100 deposit will have grown to $110.25:

Original deposit	$100.00
Interest for the first year:	
$100 × 0.05	5.00
Amount at the end of the first year	105.00
Interest for the second year:	
$105 × 0.05	5.25
Amount at the end of the second year	$110.25

Notice that the interest for the second year is $5.25, as compared to only $5 for the first year. The reason for the greater interest earned during the second year is that during the second year, interest is being paid *on interest.* That is, the $5 interest earned during the first year has been left in the account and has been added to the original $100 deposit when computing interest for the second year. This is known as **compound interest.** The compounding we have done is annual compounding. Interest can be compounded on a semiannual, quarterly, or even more frequent basis. Many savings institutions are now compounding interest on a daily basis. The more frequently compounding is done, the more rapidly the balance will grow.

We can determine the balance in an account after n periods using the following equation:

$$F_n = P(1 + r)^n \tag{7}$$

where n = the number of periods.

If n = 2 years and the interest rate is 5% per year, then our computation of the value of F in two years will be as follows:

$$F_2 = \$100(1 + 0.05)^2$$
$$F_2 = \$110.25$$

PRESENT VALUE AND FUTURE VALUE Exhibit 14A–1 shows the relationship between present value and future value as expressed in the theory of interest equations. As shown in the exhibit, if $100 is deposited in a bank at 5% interest, it will grow to $127.63 by the end of five years if interest is compounded annually.

Computation of Present Value

An investment can be viewed in two ways. It can be viewed either in terms of its future value or in terms of its present value. We have seen from our computations above that if we know the present value of a sum (such as our $100 deposit), it is a relatively simple

Exhibit 14A–1
The Relationship between Present Value and Future Value

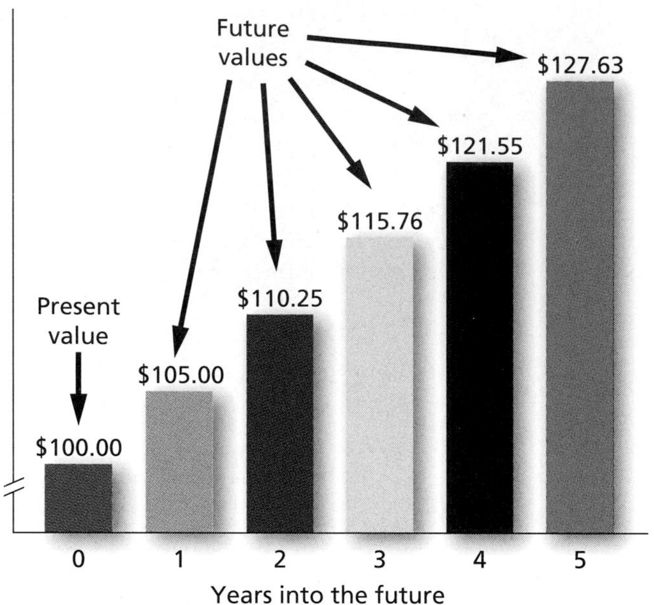

task to compute the sum's future value in n years by using equation (7). But what if the tables are reversed and we know the *future* value of some amount but we do not know its present value?

For example, assume that you are to receive $200 two years from now. You know that the future value of this sum is $200, since this is the amount that you will be receiving in two years. But what is the sum's present value—what is it worth *right now?* The present value of any sum to be received in the future can be computed by turning equation (7) around and solving for P:

$$P = \frac{F_n}{(1 + r)^n} \tag{8}$$

In our example, F = $200 (the amount to be received in the future), $r = 0.05$ (the rate of interest), and $n = 2$ (the number of years in the future that the amount is to be received).

$$P = \frac{\$200}{(1 + 0.05)^2}$$

$$P = \frac{\$200}{1.1025}$$

$$P = \$181.40$$

As shown by the computation above, the present value of a $200 amount to be received two years from now is $181.40 if the interest rate is 5%. In effect, $181.40 received *right now* is equivalent to $200 received two years from now if the rate of return is 5%. The $181.40 and the $200 are just two ways of looking at the same thing.

The process of finding the present value of a future cash flow, which we have just completed, is called **discounting.** We have *discounted* the $200 to its present value of $181.40. The 5% interest figure that we have used to find this present value is called the **discount rate.** Discounting future sums to their present value is a common practice in business, particularly in capital budgeting decisions.

If you have a power key (y^x) on your calculator, the above calculations are fairly easy. However, some of the present value formulas we will be using are more complex and difficult to use. Fortunately, tables are available in which many of the calculations have already been done for you. For example, Table 14C–3 in Appendix 14C shows the discounted present value of $1 to be received at various periods in the future at various interest rates. The table indicates that the present value of $1 to be received two periods from now at 5% is 0.907. Since in our example we want to know the present value of $200 rather than just $1, we need to multiply the factor in the table by $200:

$$\$200 \times 0.907 = \$181.40$$

This answer is the same as we obtained earlier using the formula in equation (8).

Present Value of a Series of Cash Flows

Although some investments involve a single sum to be received (or paid) at a single point in the future, other investments involve a *series* of cash flows. A series (or stream) of identical cash flows is known as an **annuity.** To provide an example, assume that a firm has just purchased some government bonds in order to temporarily invest funds that are being held for future plant expansion. The bonds will yield interest of $15,000 each year and will be held for five years. What is the present value of the stream of interest receipts from the bonds? As shown in Exhibit 14A–2, the present value of this stream is $54,075 if we assume a discount rate of 12% compounded annually. The discount factors used in this exhibit were taken from Table 14C–3 in Appendix 14C.

Two points are important in connection with Exhibit 14A–2. First, notice that the farther we go forward in time, the smaller is the present value of the $15,000 interest receipt. The present value of $15,000 received a year from now is $13,395, as compared to only $8,505 for the $15,000 interest payment to be received five years from now. This point simply underscores the fact that money has a time value.

The second point is that the computations involved in Exhibit 14A–2 involved unnecessary work. The same present value of $54,075 could have been obtained more easily by referring to Table 14C–4 in Appendix 14C. Table 14C–4 contains the present value of $1 to be received each year over a *series* of years at various interest rates. Table 14C–4 has been derived by simply adding together the factors from Table 14C–3. To illustrate, we used the factors on the next page from Table 14C–3 in the computations in Exhibit 14A–2:

Exhibit 14A–2
Present Value of a Series of Cash Receipts

Year	Factor at 12% (Table 14C–3)	Interest Received	Present Value
1	0.893	$15,000	$13,395
2	0.797	15,000	11,955
3	0.712	15,000	10,680
4	0.636	15,000	9,540
5	0.567	15,000	8,505
			$54,075

Year	Table 14C–3 Factors at 12%
1	0.893
2	0.797
3	0.712
4	0.636
5	0.567
	3.605

The sum of the five factors above is 3.605. Notice from Table 14C–4 that the factor for $1 to be received each year for five years at 12% is also 3.605. If we use this factor and multiply it by the $15,000 annual cash inflow, then we get the same $54,075 present value that we obtained earlier in Exhibit 14A–2.

$$\$15{,}000 \times 3.605 = \$54{,}075$$

Therefore, when computing the present value of a series (or stream) of cash flows, Table 14C–4 should be used.

To summarize, the present value tables in Appendix 14C should be used as follows:

Table 14C–3: This table should be used to find the present value of a single cash flow (such as a single payment or receipt) occurring in the future.
Table 14C–4: This table should be used to find the present value of a series (or stream) of identical cash flows beginning at the end of the current year and continuing into the future.

The use of both of these tables is illustrated in various exhibits in the main body of the chapter. *When a present value factor appears in an exhibit, you should take the time to trace it back into either Table 14C–3 or Table 14C–4 to get acquainted with the tables and how they work.* (Review Problem 1 at the end of the chapter is designed for those who would like some practice in present value analysis before attempting the homework exercises and problems.)

Key Terms for Review (Appendix 14A)

Annuity A series, or stream of identical cash flows. (p. 699)
Compound interest The process of paying interest on interest in an investment. (p. 698)
Discount rate The rate of return that is used to find the present value of a future cash flow. (p. 699)
Discounting The process of finding the percent value of a future cash flow. (p. 698)
Present value The value now of an amount that will be received in some future period. (p. 697)

Appendix 14B: Inflation and Capital Budgeting

Doesn't inflation have an impact in a capital budgeting analysis? The answer is a qualified yes in that inflation does have an impact on the *numbers* that are used in a capital budgeting analysis, but it does not have an impact on the *results* of the analysis if certain conditions are satisfied. To show what we mean by this statement, we will use the following data:

Example K

Martin Company wants to purchase a new machine that costs $36,000. The machine would provide annual cost savings of $20,000, and it would have a three-year life with no salvage value. For each of the next three years, the company expects a 10% inflation rate in the cash flows associated with the new machine. If the company's cost of capital is 23.2%, should the new machine be purchased?

To answer this question, it is important to know how the cost of capital was derived. Ordinarily, it is based on the market rates of return on the company's various sources of financing—both debt and equity. This market rate of return includes expected inflation; the higher the expected rate of inflation, the higher the market rate of return on debt and equity. When the inflationary effect is removed from the market rate of return, the result is called a real rate of return. For example, if the inflation rate of 10% is removed from Martin's cost of capital of 23.2%, the "real cost of capital" is only 12%, as shown in Exhibit 14B–1. (You can't simply subtract the inflation rate from the market cost of capital to obtain the real cost of capital. The computations are a bit more complex than that.)

When performing a net present value analysis, one must be consistent. The market-based cost of capital reflects inflation. Therefore, if a market-based cost of capital is used to discount cash flows, then the cash flows should be adjusted upwards to reflect the effects of inflation in forthcoming periods. Computations for Martin Company under this approach are given in solution B in Exhibit 14B–1.

On the other hand, there is no need to adjust the cash flows upward if the "real cost of capital" is used in the analysis (since the inflationary effects have been taken

Exhibit 14B–1 Capital Budgeting and Inflation

Reconciliation of the Market-Based and Real Costs of Capital

The real cost of capital	12.0%
The inflation factor	10.0%
The combined effect (12% × 10% = 1.2%)	1.2%
The market-based cost of capital	23.2%

Solution A: Inflation Not Considered

Item	Year(s)	Amount of Cash Flows	12% Factor	Present Value of Cash Flows
Initial investment	Now	$(36,000)	1.000	$(36,000)
Annual cost savings	1–3	20,000	2.402	48,040
Net present value				$ 12,040‡

Solution B: Inflation Considered

Item	Year(s)	Amount of Cash Flows	Price Index Number*	Price-Adjusted Cash Flows	23.2% Factor†	Present Value of Cash Flows
Initial investment	Now	$(36,000)	1.000	$(36,000)	1.000	$(36,000)
Annual cost savings . . .	1	20,000	1.100	22,000	0.812	17,864
	2	20,000	1.210	24,200	0.659	15,948
	3	20,000	1.331	26,620	0.535	14,242
Net present value						$ 12,054‡

*Computation of the price-index numbers, assuming a 10% inflation rate each year: Year 1, $(1.10)^1 = 1.10$; Year 2, $(1.10)^2 = 1.21$; and Year 3, $(1.10)^3 = 1.331$.

†Discount formulas are computed using the formula $1/(1 + r)^n$, where r is the discount factor and n is the number of years. The computations are $1/1.232 = 0.812$ for Year 1; $1/(1.232)^2 = 0.659$ for Year 2; and $1/(1.232)^3 = 0.535$ for Year 3.

‡These amounts are different only because of rounding error.

out of the discount rate). Computations for Martin Company under this approach are given in solution A in Exhibit 14B–1. Note that under solutions A and B that the answer will be the same (within rounding error) regardless of which approach is used, so long as one is consistent and all of the cash flows associated with the project are affected in the same way by inflation.

Several points should be noted about solution B, where the effects of inflation are explicitly taken into account. First, note that the annual cost savings are adjusted for the effects of inflation by multiplying each year's cash savings by a price-index number that reflects a 10% inflation rate. (Observe from the footnotes to the exhibit how the index number is computed for each year.) Second, note that the net present value obtained in solution B, where inflation is explicitly taken into account, is the same, within rounding error, to that obtained in solution A, where the inflation effects are ignored. This result may seem surprising, but it is logical. The reason is that we have adjusted both the cash flows and the discount rate so that they are consistent, and these adjustments cancel each other out across the two solutions.

Throughout the chapter we assume for simplicity that there is no inflation. In that case, the market-based and real costs of capital are the same, and there is no reason to adjust the cash flows for inflation since there is none. When there is inflation, the unadjusted cash flows can be used in the analysis if all of the cash flows are affected identically by inflation and the real cost of capital is used to discount the cash flows. Otherwise, the cash flows should be adjusted for inflation and the market-based cost of capital should be used in the analysis.

Appendix 14C: Future Value and Present Value Tables

Exhibit 14C–1
Future Value of $1;
$F_n = P(1 + r)^n$

Periods	4%	6%	8%	10%	12%	14%	20%
1	1.040	1.060	1.080	1.100	1.120	1.140	1.200
2	1.082	1.124	1.166	1.210	1.254	1.300	1.440
3	1.125	1.191	1.260	1.331	1.405	1.482	1.728
4	1.170	1.263	1.361	1.464	1.574	1.689	2.074
5	1.217	1.338	1.469	1.611	1.762	1.925	2.488
6	1.265	1.419	1.587	1.772	1.974	2.195	2.986
7	1.316	1.504	1.714	1.949	2.211	2.502	3.583
8	1.369	1.594	1.851	2.144	2.476	2.853	4.300
9	1.423	1.690	1.999	2.359	2.773	3.252	5.160
10	1.480	1.791	2.159	2.594	3.106	3.707	6.192
11	1.540	1.898	2.332	2.853	3.479	4.226	7.430
12	1.601	2.012	2.518	3.139	3.896	4.818	8.916
13	1.665	2.133	2.720	3.452	4.364	5.492	10.699
14	1.732	2.261	2.937	3.798	4.887	6.261	12.839
15	1.801	2.397	3.172	4.177	5.474	7.138	15.407
20	2.191	3.207	4.661	6.728	9.646	13.743	38.338
30	3.243	5.744	10.063	17.450	29.960	50.950	237.380
40	4.801	10.286	21.725	45.260	93.051	188.880	1469.800

Exhibit 14C–2
Future Value of an Annuity of \$1 in Arrears; $F_n = \frac{(1 + r)^n - 1}{r}$

Periods	4%	6%	8%	10%	12%	14%	20%
1	1.000	1.000	1.000	1.000	1.000	1.000	1.000
2	2.040	2.060	2.080	2.100	2.120	2.140	2.220
3	3.122	3.184	3.246	3.310	3.374	3.440	3.640
4	4.247	4.375	4.506	4.641	4.779	4.921	5.368
5	5.416	5.637	5.867	6.105	6.353	6.610	7.442
6	6.633	6.975	7.336	7.716	8.115	8.536	9.930
7	7.898	8.394	8.923	9.487	10.089	10.730	12.916
8	9.214	9.898	10.637	11.436	12.300	13.233	16.499
9	10.583	11.491	12.488	13.580	14.776	16.085	20.799
10	12.006	13.181	14.487	15.938	17.549	19.337	25.959
11	13.486	14.972	16.646	18.531	20.655	23.045	32.150
12	15.026	16.870	18.977	21.385	24.133	27.271	39.580
13	16.627	18.882	21.495	24.523	28.029	32.089	48.497
14	18.292	21.015	24.215	27.976	32.393	37.581	59.196
15	20.024	23.276	27.152	31.773	37.280	43.842	72.035
20	29.778	36.778	45.762	57.276	75.052	91.025	186.690
30	56.085	79.058	113.283	164.496	241.330	356.790	1181.900
40	95.026	154.762	259.057	442.597	767.090	1342.000	7343.900

Exhibit 14C–3 Present Value of \$1; $P = \frac{F_n}{(1 + r)^n}$

Period	4%	5%	6%	8%	10%	12%	14%	16%	18%	20%	22%	24%	26%	28%	30%	40%
1	0.962	0.952	0.943	0.926	0.909	0.893	0.877	0.862	0.847	0.833	0.820	0.806	0.794	0.781	0.769	0.714
2	0.925	0.907	0.890	0.857	0.826	0.797	0.769	0.743	0.718	0.694	0.672	0.650	0.630	0.610	0.592	0.510
3	0.889	0.864	0.840	0.794	0.751	0.712	0.675	0.641	0.609	0.579	0.551	0.524	0.500	0.477	0.455	0.364
4	0.855	0.823	0.792	0.735	0.683	0.636	0.592	0.552	0.516	0.482	0.451	0.423	0.397	0.373	0.350	0.260
5	0.822	0.784	0.747	0.681	0.621	0.567	0.519	0.476	0.437	0.402	0.370	0.341	0.315	0.291	0.269	0.186
6	0.790	0.746	0.705	0.630	0.564	0.507	0.456	0.410	0.370	0.335	0.303	0.275	0.250	0.227	0.207	0.133
7	0.760	0.711	0.665	0.583	0.513	0.452	0.400	0.354	0.314	0.279	0.249	0.222	0.198	0.178	0.159	0.095
8	0.731	0.677	0.627	0.540	0.467	0.404	0.351	0.305	0.266	0.233	0.204	0.179	0.157	0.139	0.123	0.068
9	0.703	0.645	0.592	0.500	0.424	0.361	0.308	0.263	0.225	0.194	0.167	0.144	0.125	0.108	0.094	0.048
10	0.676	0.614	0.558	0.463	0.386	0.322	0.270	0.227	0.191	0.162	0.137	0.116	0.099	0.085	0.073	0.035
11	0.650	0.585	0.527	0.429	0.350	0.287	0.237	0.195	0.162	0.135	0.112	0.094	0.079	0.066	0.056	0.025
12	0.625	0.557	0.497	0.397	0.319	0.257	0.208	0.168	0.137	0.112	0.092	0.076	0.062	0.052	0.043	0.018
13	0.601	0.530	0.469	0.368	0.290	0.229	0.182	0.145	0.116	0.093	0.075	0.061	0.050	0.040	0.033	0.013
14	0.577	0.505	0.442	0.340	0.263	0.205	0.160	0.125	0.099	0.078	0.062	0.049	0.039	0.032	0.025	0.009
15	0.555	0.481	0.417	0.315	0.239	0.183	0.140	0.108	0.084	0.065	0.051	0.040	0.031	0.025	0.020	0.006
16	0.534	0.458	0.394	0.292	0.218	0.163	0.123	0.093	0.071	0.054	0.042	0.032	0.025	0.019	0.015	0.005
17	0.513	0.436	0.371	0.270	0.198	0.146	0.108	0.080	0.060	0.045	0.034	0.026	0.020	0.015	0.012	0.003
18	0.494	0.416	0.350	0.250	0.180	0.130	0.095	0.069	0.051	0.038	0.028	0.021	0.016	0.012	0.009	0.002
19	0.475	0.396	0.331	0.232	0.164	0.116	0.083	0.060	0.043	0.031	0.023	0.017	0.012	0.009	0.007	0.002
20	0.456	0.377	0.312	0.215	0.149	0.104	0.073	0.051	0.037	0.026	0.019	0.014	0.010	0.007	0.005	0.001
21	0.439	0.359	0.294	0.199	0.135	0.093	0.064	0.044	0.031	0.022	0.015	0.011	0.008	0.006	0.004	0.001
22	0.422	0.342	0.278	0.184	0.123	0.083	0.056	0.038	0.026	0.018	0.013	0.009	0.006	0.004	0.003	0.001
23	0.406	0.326	0.262	0.170	0.112	0.074	0.049	0.033	0.022	0.015	0.010	0.007	0.005	0.003	0.002	
24	0.390	0.310	0.247	0.158	0.102	0.066	0.043	0.028	0.019	0.013	0.008	0.006	0.004	0.003	0.002	
25	0.375	0.295	0.233	0.146	0.092	0.059	0.038	0.024	0.016	0.010	0.007	0.005	0.003	0.002	0.001	
26	0.361	0.281	0.220	0.135	0.084	0.053	0.033	0.021	0.014	0.009	0.006	0.004	0.002	0.002	0.001	
27	0.347	0.268	0.207	0.125	0.076	0.047	0.029	0.018	0.011	0.007	0.005	0.003	0.002	0.001	0.001	
28	0.333	0.255	0.196	0.116	0.069	0.042	0.026	0.016	0.010	0.006	0.004	0.002	0.002	0.001	0.001	
29	0.321	0.243	0.185	0.107	0.063	0.037	0.022	0.014	0.008	0.005	0.003	0.002	0.001	0.001	0.001	
30	0.308	0.231	0.174	0.099	0.057	0.033	0.020	0.012	0.007	0.004	0.003	0.002	0.001	0.001		
40	0.208	0.142	0.097	0.046	0.022	0.011	0.005	0.003	0.001	0.001						

Exhibit 14C–4 Present Value of an Annuity of $1 in Arrears; $P_n = \frac{1}{r}\left[1 - \frac{1}{(1 + r)^n}\right]$

Period	4%	5%	6%	8%	10%	12%	14%	16%	18%	20%	22%	24%	26%	28%	30%	40%
1	0.962	0.952	0.943	0.926	0.909	0.893	0.877	0.862	0.847	0.833	0.820	0.806	0.794	0.781	0.769	0.714
2	1.886	1.859	1.833	1.783	1.736	1.690	1.647	1.605	1.566	1.528	1.492	1.457	1.424	1.392	1.361	1.224
3	2.775	2.723	2.673	2.577	2.487	2.402	2.322	2.246	2.174	2.106	2.042	1.981	1.923	1.868	1.816	1.589
4	3.630	3.546	3.465	3.312	3.170	3.037	2.914	2.798	2.690	2.589	2.494	2.404	2.320	2.241	2.166	1.879
5	4.452	4.330	4.212	3.993	3.791	3.605	3.433	3.274	3.127	2.991	2.864	2.745	2.635	2.532	2.436	2.035
6	5.242	5.076	4.917	4.623	4.355	4.111	3.889	3.685	3.498	3.326	3.167	3.020	2.885	2.759	2.643	2.168
7	6.002	5.786	5.582	5.206	4.868	4.564	4.288	4.039	3.812	3.605	3.416	3.242	3.083	2.937	2.802	2.263
8	6.733	6.463	6.210	5.747	5.335	4.968	4.639	4.344	4.078	3.837	3.619	3.421	3.241	3.076	2.925	2.331
9	7.435	7.108	6.802	6.247	5.759	5.328	4.946	4.607	4.303	4.031	3.786	3.566	3.366	3.184	3.019	2.379
10	8.111	7.722	7.360	6.710	6.145	5.650	5.216	4.833	4.494	4.192	3.923	3.682	3.465	3.269	3.092	2.414
11	8.760	8.306	7.887	7.139	6.495	5.988	5.453	5.029	4.656	4.327	4.035	3.776	3.544	3.335	3.147	2.438
12	9.385	8.863	8.384	7.536	6.814	6.194	5.660	5.197	4.793	4.439	4.127	3.851	3.606	3.387	3.190	2.456
13	9.986	9.394	8.853	7.904	7.103	6.424	5.842	5.342	4.910	4.533	4.203	3.912	3.656	3.427	3.223	2.468
14	10.563	9.899	9.295	8.244	7.367	6.628	6.002	5.468	5.008	4.611	4.265	3.962	3.695	3.459	3.249	2.477
15	11.118	10.380	9.712	8.559	7.606	6.811	6.142	5.575	5.092	4.675	4.315	4.001	3.726	3.483	3.268	2.484
16	11.652	10.838	10.106	8.851	7.824	6.974	6.265	5.669	5.162	4.730	4.357	4.033	3.751	3.503	3.283	2.489
17	12.166	11.274	10.477	9.122	8.022	7.120	6.373	5.749	5.222	4.775	4.391	4.059	3.771	3.518	3.295	2.492
18	12.659	11.690	10.828	9.372	8.201	7.250	6.467	5.818	5.273	4.812	4.419	4.080	3.786	3.529	3.304	2.494
19	13.134	12.085	11.158	9.604	8.365	7.366	6.550	5.877	5.316	4.844	4.442	4.097	3.799	3.539	3.311	2.496
20	13.590	12.462	11.470	9.818	8.514	7.469	6.623	5.929	5.353	4.870	4.460	4.110	3.808	3.546	3.316	2.497
21	14.029	12.821	11.764	10.017	8.649	7.562	6.687	5.973	5.384	4.891	4.476	4.121	3.816	3.551	3.320	2.498
22	14.451	13.163	12.042	10.201	8.772	7.645	6.743	6.011	5.410	4.909	4.488	4.130	3.822	3.556	3.323	2.498
23	14.857	13.489	12.303	10.371	8.883	7.718	6.792	6.044	5.432	4.925	4.499	4.137	3.827	3.559	3.325	2.499
24	15.247	13.799	12.550	10.529	8.985	7.784	6.835	6.073	5.451	4.937	4.507	4.143	3.831	3.562	3.327	2.499
25	15.622	14.094	12.783	10.675	9.077	7.843	6.873	6.097	5.467	4.948	4.514	4.147	3.834	3.564	3.329	2.499
26	15.983	14.375	13.003	10.810	9.161	7.896	6.906	6.118	5.480	4.956	4.520	4.151	3.837	3.566	3.330	2.500
27	16.330	14.643	13.211	10.935	9.237	7.943	6.935	6.136	5.492	4.964	4.525	4.154	3.839	3.567	3.331	2.500
28	16.663	14.898	13.406	11.051	9.307	7.984	6.961	6.152	5.502	4.970	4.528	4.157	3.840	3.568	3.331	2.500
29	16.984	15.141	13.591	11.158	9.370	8.022	6.983	6.166	5.510	4.975	4.531	4.159	3.841	3.569	3.332	2.500
30	17.292	15.373	13.765	11.258	9.427	8.055	7.003	6.177	5.517	4.979	4.534	4.160	3.842	3.569	3.332	2.500
40	19.793	17.159	15.046	11.925	9.779	8.244	7.105	6.234	5.548	4.997	4.544	4.166	3.846	3.571	3.333	2.500

Questions

14–1 What is the difference between capital budgeting screening decisions and capital budgeting preference decisions?

14–2 What is meant by the term *time value of money?*

14–3 What is meant by the term *discounting?*

14–4 Why can't accounting net income figures be used in the net present value and internal rate of return methods of making capital budgeting decisions?

14–5 Why are discounted cash flow methods of making capital budgeting decisions superior to other methods?

14–6 What is net present value? Can it ever be negative? Explain.

14–7 Identify two simplifying assumptions associated with discounted cash flow methods of making capital budgeting decisions.

14–8 If a firm has to pay interest of 14% on long-term debt, then its cost of capital is 14%. Do you agree? Explain.

14–9 What is meant by an investment project's internal rate of return? How is the internal rate of return computed?

14–10 Explain how the cost of capital serves as a screening tool when dealing with (a) the net present value method and (b) the internal rate of return method.

14–11 As the discount rate increases, the present value of a given future cash flow also increases. Do you agree? Explain.

14–12 Refer to Exhibit 14–4. Is the return on this investment proposal exactly 20%, slightly more than 20%, or slightly less than 20%? Explain.

14–13 Frontier Company is investigating the purchase of a piece of automated equipment, but after considering the savings in labor costs the machine has a negative net present value. If no other cost savings can be identified, should the company reject the equipment? Explain.

14–14 Why are preference decisions sometimes called *rationing* decisions?

14–15 How is the profitability index computed, and what does it measure?

14–16 What is the preference rule for ranking investment projects under the net present value method?

14–17 Can an investment with a profitability index of less than 1.00 be an acceptable investment? Explain.

14–18 What is the preference rule for ranking investment projects using the internal rate of return?

14–19 What is meant by the term *payback period?* How is the payback period determined?

14–20 How can the payback method be useful to the manager?

14–21 What is the major criticism of the payback and simple rate of return methods of making capital budgeting decisions?

Exercises

E14–1 Consider each of the following situations independently. (Ignore income taxes.)

1. In three years, when he is discharged from the Air Force, Steve wants to buy a power boat that will cost $8,000. What lump-sum amount must he invest now to have the $8,000 at the end of three years if he can invest money at:
   a. Ten percent?
   b. Fourteen percent?
2. Annual cash inflows that will arise from two competing investment projects are given below:

Year	Investment A	Investment B
1	$ 3,000	$12,000
2	6,000	9,000
3	9,000	6,000
4	12,000	3,000
	$30,000	$30,000

   Each investment project will require the same investment outlay. You can invest money at an 18% rate of return. Compute the present value of the cash inflows for each investment.

3. Julie has just retired. Her company's retirement program has two options as to how retirement benefits can be received. Under the first option, Julie would receive a lump sum of $150,000 immediately as her full retirement benefit. Under the second option, she would receive $14,000 each year for 20 years plus a lump-sum payment of $60,000 at the end of the 20-year period. If she can invest money at 12%, which option would you recommend that she accept? Use present value analysis.

E14–2 Each of the following parts is independent. (Ignore income taxes.)

1. The Atlantic Medical Clinic can purchase a new computer system that will save $7,000 annually in billing costs. The computer system will last for eight years and have no salvage value. What is the maximum purchase price that the Atlantic Medical Clinic should be willing to pay for the new computer system if the clinic's required rate of return is:
   a. Sixteen percent?
   b. Twenty percent?
2. The Caldwell *Herald* newspaper reported the following story:

   Frank Ormsby of Caldwell is the state's newest millionaire. By choosing the six winning numbers on last week's state lottery, Mr. Ormsby has won the week's grand prize totaling $1.6 million. The State Lottery Commission has indicated that Mr. Ormsby will receive his prize in 20 annual installments of $80,000 each.

   a. If Mr. Ormsby can invest money at a 12% rate of return, what is the present value of his winnings?
   b. Is it correct to say that Mr. Ormsby is the "state's newest millionaire"? Explain your answer.
3. Fraser Company will need a new warehouse in five years. The warehouse will cost $500,000 to build. What lump-sum amount should the company invest now to have the $500,000 available at the end of the five-year period? Assume that the company can invest money at:
   a. Ten percent.
   b. Fourteen percent.

E14–3 Kathy Myers frequently purchases stocks and bonds, but she is uncertain how to determine the rate of return that she is earning. For example, three years ago she paid $13,000 for 200 shares of the common stock of Malti Company. She received a $420 cash dividend on the stock at the end of each year for three years. At the end of three years, she sold the stock for $16,000. Kathy would like to earn a return of at least 14% on all of her investments. She is not sure whether the Malti Company stock provided a 14% return and would like some help with the necessary computations.

Required (ignore income taxes) Using the net present value method, determine whether or not the Malti Company stock provided a 14% return. Use the general format illustrated in Exhibit 14–4 and round all computations to the nearest whole dollar.

E14–4 Labeau Products, Ltd., of Perth, Australia, has $35,000 to invest. The company is trying to decide between two alternative uses for the funds. The alternatives are:

	Invest in Project X	Invest in Project Y
Investment required	$35,000	$35,000
Annual cash inflows	9,000	—
Single cash inflow at the end of 10 years	—	150,000
Life of the project	10 years	10 years

The company's discount rate is 18%.

Required (ignore income taxes) Which alternative would you recommend that the company accept? Show all computations using the net present value approach. Prepare a separate computation for each project.

E14–5 Perot Industries has $100,000 to invest. The company is trying to decide between two alternative uses of the funds. The alternatives are:

	Project A	Project B
Cost of equipment required	$100,000	—
Working capital investment required	—	$100,000
Annual cash inflows	21,000	16,000
Salvage value of equipment in six years	8,000	—
Life of the project	6 years	6 years

The working capital needed for project B will be released at the end of six years for investment elsewhere. Perot Industries' discount rate is 14%.

Required (ignore income taxes)

Which investment alternative (if either) would you recommend that the company accept? Show all computations using the net present value format. Prepare a separate computation for each project.

E14–6 Complete the following cases (ignore income taxes):

1. Preston Company requires a minimum return of 14% on all investments. The company can purchase a new machine at a cost of $84,900. The new machine would generate cash inflows of $15,000 per year and have a 12-year useful life with no salvage value. Compute the machine's net present value. (Use the format shown in Exhibit 14–1.) Is the machine an acceptable investment? Explain.
2. The Walton *Daily News* is investigating the purchase of a new auxiliary press that has a projected life of 18 years. It is estimated that the new press will save $30,000 per year in cash operating costs. If the new press costs $217,500, what is its internal rate of return? Is the press an acceptable investment if the company's required rate of return is 16%? Explain.
3. Refer to the data above for the Walton *Daily News.* How much would the annual cash inflows (cost savings) have to be for the new press to provide the required 16% rate of return? Round your answer to the nearest whole dollar.

E14–7 Wendell's Donut Shoppe is investigating the purchase of a new donut-making machine. The new machine would permit the company to reduce the amount of part-time help needed, at a cost savings of $3,800 per year. In addition, the new machine would allow the company to produce one new style of donut, resulting in the sale of at least 1,000 dozen more donuts each year. The company realizes a contribution margin of $1.20 per dozen donuts sold. The new machine would cost $18,600 and have a six-year useful life.

Required (ignore income taxes)

1. What would be the total annual cash inflows associated with the new machine for capital budgeting purposes?
2. Compute the internal rate of return promised by the new machine. Interpolate, and round your final answer to the nearest tenth of a percent.
3. In addition to the data given above, assume that the machine will have a $9,125 salvage value at the end of six years. Under these conditions, compute the internal rate of return to the nearest *whole* percent. (Hint: You may find it helpful to use the net present value approach; find the discount rate that will cause the net present value to be closest to zero. Use the format shown in Exhibit 14–4.)

E14–8 Henrie's Drapery Service is investigating the purchase of a new machine for cleaning and blocking drapes. The machine would cost $130,400, including freight and installation. Henrie's has estimated that the new machine would increase the company's cash inflows, net of expenses, by $25,000 per year. The machine would have a 10-year useful life and no salvage value.

Required (ignore income taxes)

1. Compute the machine's internal rate of return.
2. Compute the machine's net present value. Use a discount rate of 14% and the format shown in Exhibit 14–5. Why do you have a zero net present value? If the company's cost of capital is 10%, is this an acceptable investment? Explain.

3. Suppose that the new machine would increase the company's annual cash inflows, net of expenses, by only $22,500 per year. Under these conditions, compute the internal rate of return. Interpolate as needed and round your final answer to the nearest tenth of a percent.

E14–9 Solve the three following present value exercises:

Required (ignore income taxes)

1. The Cambro Foundation, a nonprofit organization, is planning to invest $104,950 in a project that will last for three years. The project will provide cash inflows as follows:

Year 1	$30,000
Year 2	40,000
Year 3	?

   Assuming that the project will yield exactly a 12% rate of return, what is the expected cash inflow for Year 3?
2. Lukow Products is investigating the purchase of a piece of automated equipment that will save $400,000 each year in direct labor and inventory carrying costs. This equipment costs $2,500,000 and is expected to have a 15-year useful life with no salvage value. The company requires a minimum 20% return on all equipment purchases. Management anticipates that this equipment will provide intangible benefits such as greater flexibility, higher quality of output, and experience in automation. What dollar value per year would management have to attach to these intangible benefits to make the equipment an acceptable investment?
3. The Matchless Dating Service has made an investment in video and recording equipment that costs $106,700. The equipment is expected to generate cash inflows of $20,000 per year. How many years will the equipment have to be used to provide the company with a 10% rate of return on its investment?

E14–10 Information on four investment proposals is given below:

	Investment Proposal			
	A	B	C	D
Investment required	$(90,000)	$(100,000)	$(70,000)	$(120,000)
Present value of cash inflows	126,000	90,000	105,000	160,000
Net present value	$ 36,000	$ (10,000)	$ 35,000	$ 40,000
Life of the project	5 years	7 years	6 years	6 years

Required

1. Compute the profitability index for each investment proposal.
2. Rank the proposals in terms of preference.

E14–11 A piece of laborsaving equipment has just come onto the market that Mitsui Electronics, Ltd., could use to reduce costs in one of its plants in Japan. Relevant data relating to the equipment follow (currency is in thousands of yen, denoted by ¥):

Purchase cost of the equipment . .	¥432,000
Annual cost savings that will be provided by the equipment	¥90,000
Life of the equipment	12 years

Required (ignore income taxes)

1. Compute the payback period for the equipment. If the company requires a payback period of four years or less, would the equipment be purchased?
2. Compute the simple rate of return on the equipment. Use straight-line depreciation based on the equipment's useful life. Would the equipment be purchased if the company requires a rate of return of at least 14%?

E14–12 Nick's Novelties, Inc., is considering the purchase of electronic pinball machines to place in amusement houses. The machines would cost a total of $300,000, have an eight-year useful life, and have a total salvage value of $20,000. Based on experience with other equipment, the company estimates that annual revenues and expenses associated with the machines would be as follows:

Revenues from use		$200,000
Less operating expenses:		
Commissions to amusement houses	$100,000	
Insurance	7,000	
Depreciation	35,000	
Maintenance	18,000	160,000
Net income		$ 40,000

Required (ignore income taxes)

1. Assume that Nick's Novelties, Inc., will not purchase new equipment unless it provides a payback period of four years or less. Would the company purchase the pinball machines?
2. Compute the simple rate of return promised by the pinball machines. If the company requires a simple rate of return of at least 12%, will the pinball machines be purchased?

Problems

P14–13 Basic Net Present Value Analysis Windhoek Mines, Ltd., of Namibia, is contemplating the purchase of equipment to exploit a mineral deposit that is located on land to which the company has mineral rights. An engineering and cost analysis has been made, and it is expected that the following cash flows would be associated with opening and operating a mine in the area:

Cost of new equipment and timbers	R275,000
Working capital required	100,000
Net annual cash receipts	120,000*
Cost to construct new roads in three years	40,000
Salvage value of equipment in four years	65,000

*Receipts from sales of ore, less out-of-pocket costs for salaries, utilities, insurance, and so forth.

The currency in Namibia is the rand, here denoted by R.

It is estimated that the mineral deposit would be exhausted after four years of mining. At that point, the working capital would be released for reinvestment elsewhere. The company's discount rate is 20%.

Required (ignore income taxes)

Determine the net present value of the proposed mining project. Should the project be accepted? Explain.

P14–14 Basic Net Present Value Analysis The Sweetwater Candy Company would like to buy a new machine that would automatically "dip" chocolates. The dipping operation is currently done largely by hand. The machine the company is considering costs $120,000. The manufacturer estimates that the machine would be usable for 12 years but would require the replacement of several key parts at the end of the sixth year. These parts would cost $9,000, including installation. After 12 years, the machine could be sold for about $7,500.

The company estimates that the cost to operate the machine will be only $7,000 per year. The present method of dipping chocolates costs $30,000 per year. In addition to reducing costs, the new machine will increase production by 6,000 boxes of chocolates per year. The company realizes a contribution margin of $1.50 per box. A 20% rate of return is required on all investments.

Required (ignore income taxes)

1. What are the net annual cash inflows that will be provided by the new dipping machine?
2. Computer the new machine's net present value. Use the incremental cost approach and round all dollar amounts to the nearest whole dollar.

P14–15 Net Present Value Analysis; Automation Decision "I'm not sure we should lay out $500,000 for that automated welding machine," said Jim Alder, president of the Superior Equipment Company. "That' s a lot of money, and it would cost us $80,000 for software and installation, and another $3,000 every month just to maintain the thing. In addition, the manufacturer admits that it would cost $45,000 more at the end of seven years to replace worn-out parts."

"I admit it's a lot of money," said Franci Rogers, the controller. "But you know the turnover problem we've had with the welding crew. This machine would replace six welders at a cost savings of $108,000 per year. And we would save another $6,500 per year in reduced material waste. When you figure that the automated welder would last for 12 years, that adds up to a pile of savings. I'm sure the return would be greater than our 16% required rate of return."

"I'm still not convinced," countered Mr. Alder. "We can only get $12,000 scrap value out of our old welding equipment if we sell it now, and all that new machine will be worth in 12 years is $20,000 for parts. But have your people work up the figures and we'll talk about them at the executive committee meeting tomorrow."

Required (ignore income taxes)

1. Compute the net annual cost savings promised by the automated welding machine.
2. Using the data from (1) above and other data from the problem, compute the automated welding machine's net present value. (Use the incremental-cost approach.) Would you recommend purchase? Explain.
3. Assume that management can identify several intangible benefits associated with the automated welding machine, including greater flexibility in shifting from one type of product to another, improved quality of output, and faster delivery as a result of reduced throughput time. What dollar value per year would management have to attach to these intangible benefits in order to make the new welding machine an acceptable investment?

P14–16 Preference Ranking of Investment Projects The management of Revco Products is exploring five different investment opportunities. Information on the five projects under study is given below:

	Project Number				
	1	2	3	4	5
Investment required	$(270,000)	$(450,000)	$(400,000)	$(360,000)	$(480,000)
Present value of cash inflows at a 10% discount rate	336,140	522,970	379,760	433,400	567,270
Net present value	$ 66,140	$ 72,970	$ (20,240)	$ 73,400	$ 87,270
Life of the project	6 years	3 years	5 years	12 years	6 years
Internal rate of return	18%	19%	8%	14%	16%

The company's required rate of return is 10%; thus, a 10% discount rate has been used in the present value computations above. Limited funds are available for investment, so the company can't accept all of the available projects.

Required

1. Compute the profitability index for each investment project.
2. Rank the five projects according to preference, in terms of:
   a. Net present value.
   b. Profitability index.
   c. Internal rate of return.
3. Which ranking do you prefer? Why?

P14–17 Simple Rate of Return; Payback Paul Swanson has an opportunity to acquire a franchise from The Yogurt Place, Inc., to dispense frozen yogurt products under The Yogurt Place name. Mr. Swanson has assembled the following information relating to the franchise:

a. A suitable location in a large shopping mall can be rented for $3,500 per month.
b. Remodeling and necessary equipment would cost $270,000. The equipment would have an estimated 15-year life and an estimated $18,000 salvage value. Straight-line depreciation would be used, and the salvage value would be considered in computing depreciation deductions.
c. Based on similar outlets elsewhere, Mr. Swanson estimates that sales would total $300,000 per year. Ingredients would cost 20% of sales.
d. Operating costs would include $70,000 per year for salaries, $3,500 per year for insurance, and $27,000 per year for utilities. In addition, Mr. Swanson would have to pay a commission to The Yogurt Place, Inc., of 12.5% of sales.

Rather than obtain the franchise, Mr. Swanson could invest his funds in long-term corporate bonds that would yield a 12% annual return.

Required (ignore income taxes)

1. Prepare an income statement that shows the expected net income each year from the franchise outlet. Use the contribution format.
2. Compute the simple rate of return promised by the outlet. If Mr. Swanson requires a simple rate of return of at least 12%, should he obtain the franchise?
3. Compute the payback period on the outlet. If Mr. Swanson wants a payback of four years or less, should the outlet be opened?

P14–18 Net Present Value Analysis of Securities Linda Clark received $175,000 from her mother's estate. She placed the funds into the hands of a broker, who purchased the following securities on Linda's behalf:

a. Common stock was purchased at a cost of $95,000. The stock paid no dividends, but it was sold for $160,000 at the end of three years.
b. Preferred stock was purchased at its par value of $30,000. The stock paid a 6% dividend (based on par value) each year for three years. At the end of three years, the stock was sold for $27,000.
c. Bonds were purchased at a cost of $50,000. The bonds paid $3,000 in interest every six months. After three years, the bonds were sold for $52,700. (Note: In discounting a cash flow that occurs semiannually, the procedure is to halve the discount rate and double the number of periods. Use the same procedure in discounting the proceeds from the sale.)

The securities were all sold at the end of three years so that Linda would have funds available to open a new business venture. The broker stated that the investments had earned more than a 16% return, and he gave Linda the following computation to support his statement:

Common stock:	
Gain on sale ($160,000 − $95,000)	$65,000
Preferred stock:	
Dividends paid (6% × $30,000 × 3 years)	5,400
Loss on sale ($27,000 − $30,000)	(3,000)
Bonds:	
Interest paid ($3,000 × 6 periods)	18,000
Gain on sale ($52,700 − $50,000)	2,700
Net gain on all investments	$88,100

$$\frac{\$88{,}100 \div 3 \text{ years}}{\$175{,}000} = 16.8\%$$

Required (ignore income taxes)

1. Using a 16% discount rate, compute the net present value of *each* of the three investments. On which investment(s) did Linda earn a 16% rate of return? (Round computations to the nearest whole dollar.)
2. Considering all three investments together, did Linda earn a 16% rate of return? Explain.
3. Linda wants to use the $239,700 proceeds ($160,000 + $27,000 + $52,700 = $239,700) from sale of the securities to open a retail store under a 12-year franchise contract. What

net annual cash inflow must the store generate for Linda to earn a 14% return over the 12-year period? Round computations to the nearest whole dollar.

P14–19 Net Present Value Analysis of a New Product Matheson Electronics has just developed a new electronic device which, when mounted on an automobile, will tell the driver how many miles the automobile is traveling per gallon of gasoline.

The company is anxious to begin production of the new device. To this end, marketing and cost studies have been made to determine probable costs and market potential. These studies have provided the following information:

a. New equipment would have to be acquired to produce the device. The equipment would cost $315,000 and have a 12-year useful life. After 12 years, it would have a salvage value of about $15,000.
b. Sales in units over the next 12 years are projected to be as follows:

Year	Sales in Units
1	6,000
2	12,000
3	15,000
4–12	18,000

c. Production and sales of the device would require working capital of $60,000 to finance accounts receivable, inventories, and day-to-day cash needs. This working capital would be released at the end of the project's life.
d. The devices would sell for $35 each; variable costs for production, administration, and sales would be $15 per unit.
e. Fixed costs for salaries, maintenance, property taxes, insurance, and straight-line depreciation on the equipment would total $135,000 per year. (Depreciation is based on cost less salvage value.)
f. To gain rapid entry into the market, the company would have to advertise heavily. The advertising program would be:

Year	Amount of Yearly Advertising
1–2	$180,000
3	150,000
4–12	120,000

g. Matheson Electronics' board of directors has specified that all new products must have a return of at least 14% to be acceptable.

Required
(ignore income taxes)

1. Compute the net cash inflow (cash receipts less yearly cash operating expenses) anticipated from sale of the device for each year over the next 12 years.
2. Using the data computed in (1) above and other data provided in the problem, determine the net present value of the proposed investment. Would you recommend that Matheson accept the device as a new product?

P14–20 Opening a Small Business; Net Present Value In eight years, Kent Duncan will retire. He has $150,000 to invest, and he is exploring the possibility of opening a self-service auto wash. The auto wash could be managed in the free time he has available from his regular occupation, and it could be closed easily when he retires. After careful study, Mr. Duncan has determined the following:

a. A building in which an auto wash could be installed is available under an eight-year lease at a cost of $1,700 per month.
b. Purchase and installation costs of equipment would total $150,000. In eight years the equipment could be sold for about 10% of its original cost.
c. An investment of an additional $2,000 would be required to cover working capital needs for cleaning supplies, change funds, and so forth. After eight years, this working capital would be released for investment elsewhere.

d. Both an auto wash and a vacuum service would be offered with a wash costing $1.50 and the vacuum costing 25 cents per use.
e. The only variable costs associated with the operation would be 23 cents per wash for water and 10 cents per use of the vacuum for electricity.
f. In addition to rent, monthly costs of operation would be: cleaning, $450; insurance, $75; and maintenance, $500.
g. Gross receipts from the auto wash would be about $1,350 per week. According to the experience of other auto washes, 70% of the customers using the wash would also use the vacuum.

Mr. Duncan will not open the auto wash unless it provides at least a 10% return, since this is the amount that could be earned by simply placing the $150,000 in a high-grade securities.

Required (ignore income taxes)

1. Assuming that the auto wash will be open 52 weeks a year, compute the expected net annual cash receipts (gross cash receipts less cash disbursements) from its operation. (Do not include the cost of the equipment, the working capital, or the salvage value in these computations.)
2. Would you advise Mr. Duncan to open the car wash? Show computations using the net present value method of investment analysis. Round all dollar figures to the nearest whole dollar.

P14–21 Replacement Decision Bilboa Freightlines, S.A., of Panama, has a small truck that it uses for intracity deliveries. The truck is in bad repair and must be either overhauled or replaced with a new truck. The company has assembled the following information. (Panama uses the U.S. dollar as its currency):

	Present Truck	New Truck
Purchase cost new	$21,000	$30,000
Remaining book value	11,500	—
Overhaul needed now	7,000	—
Annual cash operating costs	10,000	6,500
Salvage value—now	9,000	—
Salvage value—eight years from now	1,000	4,000

If the company keeps and overhauls its present delivery truck, then the truck will be usable for eight more years. If a new truck is purchased, it will be used for eight years, after which it will be traded in on another truck. The new truck would be diesel-operated, resulting in a substantial reduction in annual operating costs, as shown above.

The company computes depreciation on a straight-line basis. All investment projects are evaluated using a 16% discount rate.

Required (ignore income taxes)

1. Should Bilboa Freightlines keep the old truck or purchase the new one? Use the total-cost approach to net present value in making your decision. Round to the nearest whole dollar.
2. Redo (1) above, this time using the incremental-cost approach.

P14–22 Net Present Value; Automated Equipment; Postaudit Saxon Products, Inc., is investigating the purchase of a robot for use on the company's assembly line. Selected data relating to the robot are provided below:

Cost of the robot	$1,800,000
Installation and software	900,000
Annual savings in labor costs	?
Annual savings in inventory carrying costs	210,000
Monthly increase in power and maintenance costs	2,500
Salvage value in 10 years	70,000
Useful life	10 years

Engineering studies suggest that use of the robot will result in a savings of 50,000 direct labor-hours each year. The labor rate is $8 per hour. Also, the smoother work flow made possible by the use of automation will allow the company to reduce the amount of inventory on hand by $400,000. This inventory reduction will take place at the end of the first year of operation; the released funds will be available for use elsewhere in the company. Saxon Products requires a 20% return on all purchases of equipment.

Shelly Martins, the controller, has noted that all of Saxon's competitors are automating their plants. She is pessimistic, however, about whether Saxon's management will allow it to automate. In preparing the proposal for the robot, she stated to a colleague, "Let's just hope that reduced labor and inventory costs can justify the purchase of this automated equipment. Otherwise, we'll never get it. You know how the president feels about equipment paying for itself out of reduced costs."

Required (ignore income taxes)

1. Determine the net *annual* cost savings if the robot is purchased. (Do not include the $400,000 inventory reduction or the salvage value in this computation.)
2. Compute the net present value of the proposed investment in the robot. Based on these data, would you recommend that the robot be purchased? Explain.
3. Assume that the robot is purchased. At the end of the first year, Shelly Martins has found that some items didn't work out as planned. Due to unforeseen problems, software and installation costs were $75,000 more than estimated and direct labor has been reduced by only 45,000 hours per year, rather than by 50,000 hours. Assuming that all other cost data were accurate, does it appear that the company made a wise investment? Show computations using the net present value format as in (2) above. (Hint: It might be helpful to place yourself back at the beginning of the first year with the new data.)
4. Upon seeing your analysis in (3) above, Saxon's president stated, "That robot is the worst investment we've ever made. And now we'll be stuck with it for years."
   a. Explain to the president what benefits other than cost savings might accrue from use of the new automated equipment.
   b. Compute for the president the dollar amount of cash inflow that would be needed each year from the benefits in (a) above for the automated equipment to yield a 20% rate of return.

P14–23 Rental Property Decision Raul Martinas, professor of languages at Eastern University, owns a small office building adjacent to the university campus. He acquired the property 10 years ago at a total cost of $530,000—$50,000 for the land and $480,00 for the building. He has just received an offer from a realty company that wants to purchase the property; however, the property has been a good source of income over the years, so Professor Martinas is unsure whether he should keep it or sell it. His alternatives are:

Keep the property. Professor Martinas' accountant has kept careful records of the income realized from the property over the past 10 years. These records indicate the following annual revenues and expenses:

Rental receipts		$140,000
Less building expenses:		
Utilities	$25,000	
Depreciation of building	16,000	
Property taxes and insurance	18,000	
Repairs and maintenance	9,000	
Custodial help and supplies	40,000	108,000
Net income		$ 32,000

Professor Martinas makes a $12,000 mortgage payment each year on the property. The mortgage will be paid off in eight more years. He has been depreciating the building by the straight-line method, assuming a salvage value of $80,000 for the building which he still thinks is an appropriate figure. He feels sure that the building can be rented for another 15 years. He also feels sure that 15 years from now the land will be worth three times what he paid for it.

Sell the property. A realty company has offered to purchase the property by paying $175,000 immediately and $26,500 per year for the next 15 years. Control of the property would go to the realty company immediately. To sell the property, Professor

Martinas would need to pay the mortgage off, which could be done by making a lump-sum payment of $90,000.

Required (ignore income taxes)

Assume that Professor Martinas requires a 12% rate of return. Would you recommend he keep or sell the property? Show computations using the net present value method and the total-cost approach.

P14–24 Lease or Buy Decision The Riteway Ad Agency provides cars for its sales staff. In the past, the company has always purchased its cars outright from a dealer and then sold the cars after three years' use. The company's present fleet of cars is three years old and will be sold very shortly. To provide a replacement fleet, the company is considering two alternatives:

Alternative 1: The company can purchase the cars outright, as in the past, and sell the cars after three years' use. Ten cars will be needed, which can be purchased at a discounted price of $17,000 each. If this alternative is accepted, the following costs will be incurred on the fleet as a whole:

Annual cost of servicing, taxes, and licensing	$3,000
Repairs, first year	1,500
Repairs, second year	4,000
Repairs, third year	6,000

At the end of three years, the fleet could be sold for one-half of the original purchase price.

Alternative 2: The company can lease the cars under a three-year lease contract. The lease cost would be $55,000 per year (the first payment due at the end of Year 1). As part of this lease cost, the owner would provide all servicing and repairs, license the cars, and pay all the taxes. Riteway would be required to make a $10,000 security deposit at the beginning of the lease period, which would be refunded when the cars were returned to the owner at the end of the lease contract.

Required (ignore income taxes)

1. Riteway Ad Agency has an 18% cost of capital. Use the total-cost approach to determine the present value of the cash flows associated with each alternative. Round all dollar amounts to the nearest whole dollar. Which alternative should the company accept?
2. Using the data in (1) above and other data as needed, explain why it is often less costly for a company to lease equipment and facilities rather than to buy them.

P14–25 Internal Rate of Return; Sensitivity Analysis "In my opinion, a tanning salon would be a natural addition to our spa and very popular with our customers," said Stacey Winder, manager of the Lifeline Spa. "Our figures show that we could remodel the building next door to our spa and install all of the necessary equipment for $330,000. I have contacted tanning salons in other areas, and I am told that the tanning beds will be usable for about nine years. I am also told that a four-bed salon such as we are planning would generate a cash inflow of about $80,000 per year after all expenses."

"It does sound very appealing," replied Kevin Leblanc, the spa's accountant. "Let me push the numbers around a bit and see what kind of a return the salon would generate."

Required (ignore income taxes)

1. Compute the internal rate of return promised by the tanning salon. Interpolate to the nearest tenth of a percent.
2. Assume that Ms. Winder will not open the salon unless it promises a return of at least 14%. Compute the amount of annual cash inflow that would provide this return on the $330,000 investment.
3. Although nine years is the average life of tanning salon equipment, Ms. Winder has found that this life can vary substantially. Compute the internal rate of return if the life were (a) 6 years and (b) 12 years rather than 9 years. Interpolate to the nearest tenth of a percent. Is there any information provided by these computations that you would be particularly anxious to show Ms. Winder?
4. Ms. Winder has also found that although $80,000 is an average cash inflow from a four-bed salon, some salons vary as much as 20% from this figure. Compute the internal rate of

return if the annual cash inflows were (a) 20% less and (b) 20% greater than $80,000. Interpolate to the nearest tenth of a percent.

5. Assume that the $330,000 investment is made and that the salon is opened as planned. Because of concerns about the effects of excessive tanning, however, the salon is not able to attract as many customers as planned. Cash inflows are only $50,000 per year, and after eight years the salon equipment is sold to a competitor for $135,440. Compute the internal rate of return (to the nearest whole percent) earned on the investment over the eight-year period. (Hint: A useful way to proceed is to find the discount rate that will cause the net present value to be equal to, or near, zero.)

P14–26 Preference Ranking of Investment Projects Oxford Company has limited funds available for investment and must ration the funds among five competing projects. Selected information on the five projects follows:

Project	Investment Required	Net Present Value	Life of the Project (years)	Internal Rate of Return (percent)
A	$160,000	$44,323	7	18%
B	135,000	42,000	12	16%
C	100,000	35,035	7	20%
D	175,000	38,136	3	22%
E	150,000	(8,696)	6	8%

The net present values above have been computed using a 10% discount rate. The company wants your assistance in determining which project to accept first, which to accept second, and so forth.

Required

1. Compute the profitability index for each project.
2. In order of preference, rank the five projects in terms of:
   a. Net present value.
   b. Profitability index.
   c. Internal rate of return.
3. Which ranking do you prefer? Why?

P14–27 Simple Rate of Return; Payback Sharkey's Fun Center contains a number of electronic games as well as a miniature golf course and various rides located outside the building. Paul Sharkey, the owner, would like to construct a water slide on one portion of his property. Mr. Sharkey has gathered the following information about the slide:

a. Water slide equipment could be purchased and installed at a cost of $330,000. According to the manufacturer, the slide would be usable for 12 years after which it would have no salvage value.
b. Mr. Sharkey would use straight-line depreciation on the slide equipment.
c. To make room for the water slide, several rides would be dismantled and sold. These rides are fully depreciated, but they could be sold for $60,000 to an amusement park in a nearby city.
d. Mr. Sharkey has concluded that about 50,000 more people would use the water slide each year than have been using the rides. The admission price would be $3.60 per person (the same price that the Fun Center has been charging for the rides).
e. Based on experience at other water slides, Mr. Sharkey estimates that incremental operating expenses each year for the slide would be: salaries, $85,000; insurance, $4,200; utilities, $13,000; and maintenance, $9,800.

Required (ignore income taxes)

1. Prepare an income statement showing the expected net income each year from the water slide.
2. Compute the simple rate of return expected from the water slide. Based on this computation, would the water slide be constructed if Mr. Sharkey requires a simple rate of return of at least 14% on all investments?

3. Compute the payback period for the water slide. If Mr. Sharkey requires a payback period of five years or less, would the water slide be constructed?

P14–28 Simple Rate of Return; Payback; Internal Rate of Return Honest John's Used Cars, Inc., has always hired students from the local university to wash the cars on the lot. Honest John is considering the purchase of an automatic car wash that would be used in place of the students. The following information has been gathered by Honest John's accountant to help Honest John make a decision on the purchase:

a. Payments to students for washing cars total $15,000 per year at present.
b. The car wash would cost $21,000 installed, and it would have a 10-year useful life. Honest John uses straight-line depreciation on all assets. The car wash would have a negligible salvage value in 10 years.
c. Annual out-of-pocket costs associated with the car wash would be: wages of students to operate the wash, keep the soap bin full, and so forth, $6,300; utilities, $1,800; and insurance and maintenance, $900.
d. Honest John now earns a return of 20% on the funds invested in his inventory of used cars. He feels that he would have to earn an equivalent rate on the car wash for the purchase to be attractive.

Required
(ignore income taxes)

1. Determine the annual savings that would be realized in cash operating costs if the car wash were purchased.
2. Compute the simple rate of return promised by the car wash. (Hint: Note that this is a cost reduction project.) Will Honest John accept this project if he expects a 20% return?
3. Compute the payback period on the car wash. Honest John (who has a reputation for being somewhat of a nickel-nurser) will not purchase any equipment unless it has a payback of four years or less. Will he purchase the car wash equipment?
4. Compute (to the nearest whole percent) the internal rate of return promised by the car wash. Based on this computation, does it appear that the simple rate of return would normally be an accurate guide in investment decisions?

P14–29 Simple Rate of Return; Payback Westwood Furniture Company is considering the purchase of two different items of equipment, as described below:

Machine A. A compacting machine has just come onto the market that would permit Westwood Furniture Company to compress sawdust into various shelving products. At present the sawdust is disposed of as a waste product. The following information is available on the machine:

a. The machine would cost $420,000 and would have a 10% salvage value at the end of its 12-year useful life. The company uses straight-line depreciation and considers salvage value in computing depreciation deductions.
b. The shelving products manufactured from use of the machine would generate revenues of $300,000 per year. Variable manufacturing costs would be 20% of sales.
c. Fixed expenses associated with the new shelving products would be (per year): advertising, $40,000: salaries, $110,000; utilities, $5,200; and insurance, $800.

Machine B. A second machine has come onto the market that would allow Westwood Furniture Company to automate a sanding process that is now done largely by hand. The following information is available:

a. The new sanding machine would cost $234,000 and would have no salvage value at the end of its 13-year useful life. The company would use straight-line depreciation on the new machine.
b. Several old pieces of sanding equipment that are fully depreciated would be disposed of at a scrap value of $9,000.
c. The new sanding machine would provide substantial annual savings in cash operating costs. It would require an operator at an annual salary of $16,350 and $5,400 in annual maintenance costs. The current, hand-operated sanding procedure costs the company $78,000 per year in total.

Westwood Furniture Company requires a simple rate of return of 15% on all equipment purchases. Also, the company will not purchase equipment unless the equipment has a payback period of 4.0 years or less.

Required (ignore income taxes)

1. For machine A:
   a. Prepare an income statement showing the expected net income each year from the new shelving products. Use the contribution format.
   b. Compute the simple rate of return.
   c. Compute the payback period.
2. For machine B:
   a. Compute the simple rate of return.
   b. Compute the payback period.
3. According to the company's criteria, which machine, if either, should the company purchase?

P14–30 Simple Rate of Return; Payback; Internal Rate of Return The Elberta Fruit Farm of Ontario has always hired transient workers to pick its annual cherry crop. Francie Wright, the farm manager, has just received information on a cherry picking machine that is being purchased by many fruit farms. The machine is a motorized device that shakes the cherry tree, causing the cherries to fall onto plastic tarps that funnel the cherries into bins. Ms. Wright has gathered the following information to decide whether a cherry picker would be a profitable investment for the Elberta Fruit Farm:

a. At present, the farm is paying an average of $40,000 per year to transient workers to pick the cherries.
b. The cherry picker would cost $94,500, and it would have an estimated 12-year useful life. The farm uses straight-line depreciation on all assets and considers salvage value in computing depreciation deductions. The estimated salvage value of the cherry picker is $4,500.
c. Annual out-of-pocket costs associated with the cherry picker would be: cost of an operator and an assistant, $14,000; insurance, $200; fuel, $1,800; and a maintenance contract, $3,000.

Required (ignore income taxes)

1. Determine the annual savings in cash operating costs that would be realized if the cherry picker were purchased.
2. Compute the simple rate of return expected from the cherry picker. (Hint: Note that this is a cost reduction project.) Would the cherry picker be purchased if Elberta Fruit Farm requires a return of 16%?
3. Compute the payback period on the cherry picker. The Elberta Fruit Farm will not purchase equipment unless it has a payback period of five years or less. Would the cherry picker be purchased?
4. Compute (to the nearest whole percent) the internal rate of return promised by the cherry picker. Based on this computation, does it appear that the simple rate of return would normally be an accurate guide in investment decisions?

Cases

C14–31 Lease or Buy Decision Top-Quality Stores, Inc., owns a nationwide chain of supermarkets. The company is going to open another store soon, and a suitable building site has been located in an attractive and rapidly growing area. In discussing how the company can acquire the desired building and other facilities needed to open the new store, Sam Watkins, the company's vice president in charge of sales, stated, "I know most of our competitors are starting to lease facilities rather than buy, but I just can't see the economics of it. Our development people tell me that we can buy the building site, put a building on it, and get all the store fixtures we need for just $850,000. They also say that property taxes, insurance, and repairs would run $20,000 a year. When you figure that we plan to keep a site for 18 years, that's a total cost of $1,210,000. But then when you realize that the property will be worth at least a half million in 18 years, that's a net cost to us of only $710,000. What would it cost to lease the property?"

"I understand that Beneficial Insurance Company is willing to purchase the building site, construct a building and install fixtures to our specifications, and then lease the facility to us for 18 years at an annual lease payment of $120,000," replied Lisa Coleman, the company's executive vice president.

"That's just my point," said Sam. "At $120,000 a year, it would cost us a cool $2,160,000 over the 18 years. That's three times what it would cost to buy, and what would we have left at the end? Nothing! The building would belong to the insurance company!"

"You're overlooking a few things," replied Lisa. "For one thing, the treasurer's office says that we could only afford to put $350,000 down if we buy the property, and then we would have to pay the other $500,000 off over four years at $175,000 a year. So there would be some interest involved on the purchase side that you haven't figured in."

"But that little bit of interest is nothing compared to over 2 million bucks for leasing," said Sam. "Also, if we lease I understand we would have to put up an $8,000 security deposit that we wouldn't get back until the end. And besides that, we would still have to pay all the yearly repairs and maintenance costs just like we owned the property. No wonder those insurance companies are so rich if they can swing deals like this."

"Well, I'll admit that I don't have all the figures sorted out yet," replied Lisa. "But I do have the operating cost breakdown for the building, which includes $7,500 annually for property taxes, $8,000 for insurance, and $4,500 for repairs and maintenance. If we lease, Beneficial will handle its own insurance costs and of course the owner will have to pay the property taxes. I'll put all this together and see if leasing makes any sense with our required rate of return of 16%. The president wants a presentation and recommendation in the executive committee meeting tomorrow. Let's see, development said the first lease payment would be due now and the remaining ones due in years 1–17. Development also said that this store should generate a net cash inflow that's well above the average for our stores."

Required (ignore income taxes)

1. Using the net present value approach, determine whether Top-Quality Stores, Inc., should lease or buy the new facility. Assume that you will be making your presentation before the company's executive committee, and remember that the president detests sloppy, disorganized reports.
2. What reply will you make in the meeting if Sam Watkins brings up the issue of the building's future sales value?

C14–32 Equipment Acquisition: Uneven Cash Flows Kingsley Products, Ltd., is using a model 400 shaping machine to make one of its products. The company is expecting to have a large increase in demand for the product and is anxious to expand its productive capacity. Two possibilities are under consideration:

Alternative 1. Purchase another model 400 shaping machine to operate along with the currently owned model 400 machine.

Alternative 2. Purchase a model 800 shaping machine and use the currently owned model 400 machine as standby equipment. The model 800 machine is a high-speed unit with double the capacity of the model 400 machine.

The following additional information is available on the two alternatives:

a. Both the model 400 machine and the model 800 machine have a 10-year life from the time they are first used in production. The scrap value of both machines is negligible and can be ignored. Straight-line depreciation is used.
b. The cost of a new model 800 machine is $300,000.
c. The model 400 machine now in use cost $160,000 three years ago. Its present book value is $112,000, and its present market value is $90,000.
d. A new model 400 machine costs $170,000 now. If the company decides not to buy the model 800 machine, then the currently owned model 400 machine will have to be replaced in seven years at a cost of $200,000. The replacement machine will be sold at the end of tenth year for $140,000.
e. Production over the next 10 years is expected to be:

Year	Production in Units
1	40,000
2	60,000
3	80,000
4–10	90,000

f. The two models of machines are not equally efficient. Comparative variable costs per unit are:

	Model	
	400	800
Materials per unit	$0.25	$0.40
Direct labor per unit	0.49	0.16
Supplies and lubricants per unit	0.06	0.04
Total variable cost per unit	$0.80	$0.60

g. The model 400 machine is less costly to maintain than the model 800 machine. Annual repairs and maintenance costs on a model 400 machine are $2,500.

h. Repairs and maintenance costs on a model 800 machine, with a model 400 machine used as standby, would total $3,800 per year.

i. No other factory costs will change as a result of the decision between the two machines.

j. Kingsley Products requires a 20% rate of return on all investments.

Required (ignore income taxes)

1. Which alternative should the company choose? Use the net present value approach.
2. Suppose that the cost of labor increases by 10%. Would this make the model 800 machine more or less desirable? Explain. No computations are needed.
3. Suppose that the cost of materials doubles. Would this make the model 800 machine more or less desirable? Explain. No computations are needed.

C14–33 Expansion Decision; Net Present Value; Postaudit of a Project

Romano's Pizzas, Inc., operates pizza shops in several states. One of the company's most profitable shops is located adjacent to the campus of a large university. A small bakery next to the shop has just gone out of business, and Romano's Pizzas has an opportunity to lease the vacated space for $18,000 per year under a 15-year lease. Romano's management is considering two ways in which the available space might be used.

Alternative 1. The pizza shop in this location is currently selling 40,000 pizzas per year. Management is confident that sales could be increased by 75% by taking out the wall between the pizza shop and the vacant space and expanding the pizza outlet. Costs for remodeling and for new equipment would be $550,000. Management estimates that 20% of the new sales would be small pizzas, 50% would be medium pizzas, and 30% would be large pizzas. Selling prices and costs for ingredients for the three sizes of pizzas follow (per pizza):

	Selling Price	Cost of Ingredients
Small	$ 6.70	$1.30
Medium	8.90	2.40
Large	11.00	3.10

An additional $7,500 of working capital would be needed to carry the larger volume of business. This working capital would be released at the end of the lease term. The equipment would have a salvage value of $30,000 in 15 years, when the lease ends.

Alternative 2. Romano's sales manager feels that the company needs to diversify its operations. He has suggested that an opening be cut in the wall between the pizza shop and the vacant space and that video games be placed in the space, along with a small snack bar. Costs for remodeling and for the snack bar facilities would be $290,000. The games would be leased from a large distributor of such equipment. The distributor has stated that based on the use of game centers elsewhere, Romano's could expect about 26,000 people to use the center each year and to spend an average of $5 each on the machines. In addition, it is estimated that the snack bar would provide a net cash inflow of $15,000 per year. An investment of $4,000 in working capital would be needed. This working capital investment would be released at the end of the lease term. The snack bar equipment would have a salvage value of about $12,000 in 15 years.

Romano's management is unsure which alternative to select and has asked you to help in making the decision. You have gathered the following information relating to added costs that would be incurred each year under the two alternatives:

	Expand the Pizza Shop	Install the Game Center
Rent—building space	$18,000	$18,000
Rent—video games	—	30,000
Salaries	54,000	17,000
Utilities	13,200	5,400
Insurance and other	7,800	9,600

Required (ignore income taxes)

1. Compute the expected net *annual* cash inflow from each alternative (cash receipts from sales and games less related cash expenses). Do *not* include present sales from the pizza shop in the computation.
2. The company requires a rate of return on all of its investments of at least 16%. Compute the net present value of each alternative. Use the total-cost approach and round all dollar amounts to the nearest whole dollar. Which alternative would you recommend?
3. Assume that the company decides to accept alternative 2. At the end of the first year, the company finds that only 21,000 people used the game center during the year (each person spent $5 on games). Also the snack bar provided a net cash inflow of only $13,000. In light of this information, does it appear that the game center will provide the company's 16% required rate of return? Show computations to support your answer. (Hint: It might be useful to go back to the beginning of the first year under alternative 2 with the new information.)
4. The sales manager has suggested that an advertising program be initiated to draw another 5,000 people into the game center each year. Assuming that another 5,000 people can be attracted into the center and that the snack bar receipts increase to the level originally estimated, how much can be spent on advertising each year and still allow the game center to provide a 16% rate of return?

Group Exercises

GE14–34 **Capital Budgets in Colleges** In recent years, your college or university has probably undertaken a capital budgeting project such as building or renovating a facility. Investigate one of these capital budgeting projects. You will probably need the help of your university's or college's accounting or finance office.

Required

1. Determine the total cost of the project and the source of the funds for the project. Did the money come from state funds, gifts, grants, endowments, or the school's general fund?
2. Did the costs of the project stay within budget?
3. What financial criteria were used to evaluate the project?
4. If the net present value method or internal rate of return method was used, review the calculations. Do you agree with the calculations and methods used?
5. If the net present value method was not used to evaluate the project, estimate the project's net present value. If all of the required data are not available, make reasonable estimates for the missing data. What discount rate did you use? Why?
6. Evaluate the capital budgeting procedures that were actually used by your college or university.

GE14–35 Performance Measurement, Capital Budgeting, and Management Compensation Nearly every major decentralized American business uses some measure of profitability or return on investment (ROI) to assess the performance of their divisional managers. Most companies evaluate managers over the short term (quarterly and annually) and tie their bonus compensation to exceeding a target level of profit or ROI for their business unit. This provides top management with a consistent basis for evaluating business unit managers.

It is assumed that there is a high correlation between ROI and the market value of the firm. That is, the underlying assumption is that a high and growing ROI will result in an increase in the common stock price and market value of the firm. This is a very important issue since the evaluation and compensation of most managers is determined by using accounting-based measures of performance.

Required

1. Are short-term accounting measures of performance consistent with the long-term interests of customers, employees, and shareholders? Explain and give examples.
2. This chapter indicated that discounted cash flow (DCF) models were best for determining the long-run impact of capital projects on the market value of the firm. The previous chapter indicated that most firms use quarterly and annual accounting measures of performance, like ROI, to evaluate the performance of managers once those assets have been acquired. Discuss the conflicts between short-term accounting-based measures of performance and the DCF models.
3. In an attempt to alleviate some of these conflicts, corporations could evaluate and compensate performance based on improvement in long-term (three to five years) accounting measures of performance like ROI. Evaluate this idea.
4. Historically, companies have used stock options (the right to buy stock at a certain price in the future, usually the price on the date the option was issued) to motivate management to take a long-term viewpoint. What are the advantages and disadvantages of this form of performance evaluation and compensation?
5. U.S. businesses have typically rewarded individual accomplishment rather than broader performance measures that reward team-based results. Evaluate each of these options.

GE14–36 Advanced Manufacturing Technologies and DCF In the 1980s, the use of discounted cash flow (DCF) methods of analysis came under increasing criticism. In particular, DCF methods were found to be deficient when used to evaluate investments in new computer-integrated manufacturing (CIM) technologies. Critics claimed that DCF methods of analysis were biased against investments in CIM technology because DCF analysis did not consider the full range of benefits provided by CIM technology. Kaplan responded to this criticism in Robert Kaplan, "Must CIM Be Justified by Faith Alone," *Harvard Business Review,* March–April 1986, pp. 87–95.

Required

1. Briefly discuss the major technical issues that have led to the misapplication of the DCF analysis.
2. Discuss the more obvious or tangible benefits related to investments in CIM technology.
3. Discuss the less obvious or intangible benefits related to investments in CIM technology.
4. Briefly explain how a capital budgeting analyst might approach quantifying the difficult-to-quantify intangible benefits.

GE14–37 Investing in Wind Power Besides being an environmentally appealing alternative to other methods of generating electrical power, wind turbines can be profitable. The Danish Wind Turbine Manufacturers Association maintains a web site at www.windpower.dk/tour/econ/econ.htm that allows you to compute the net present value of investments in wind-powered turbines.

Required

1. Verify the net present value calculation for the default data that already appear on the screen.
2. Change the real interest rate (i.e., discount rate) to 12%. What happens to the net present value of the wind turbine? What happens to the real rate of return (i.e., the internal rate of return)?
3. Keep the real interest rate set at 12%. How high would the price per kWh (i.e., kilowatt-hour) for electricity have to be to make this an attractive investment?

Chapter Fifteen

Income Taxes in Capital Budgeting Decisions

Business Focus

The costs of complying with the income tax regulations is illustrated by the resources that DaimlerChrysler devotes to the task. As explained in *Fortune* magazine, "Chrysler's chief tax counsel, John Lofredo, has a team of 30 tax pros at his Highland Park, Michigan, headquarters and another 25 at two subsidiaries—typical staffing for a major U.S. corporation . . . He also has two offices full of IRS agents—nine on any given day—camped out at Chrysler, haggling over past and present audits and appeals. Says Lofredo: 'They could end the income tax system today, and I'd still have ten years of work to do just settling up past disputes.' "

Source: Rob Norton, "Our Screwed-Up Tax Code," Fortune, *September 6, 1993, p. 34.*

Learning Objectives

After studying Chapter 15, you should be able to:

1 Compute the after-tax cost of a tax-deductible cash expense and the after-tax benefit from a taxable cash receipt.

2 Explain how depreciation deductions are computed under the Modified Accelerated Cost Recovery System (MACRS).

3 Compute the tax savings arising from the depreciation tax shield using both the MACRS tables and the optional straight-line method.

4 Compute the after-tax net present value of an investment proposal.

In our discussion of capital budgeting in the preceding chapter, we ignored income taxes for two reasons. First, many organizations do not pay income taxes. Not-for-profit organizations, such as hospitals and charitable foundations, and governmental agencies are exempt from income taxes. Second, capital budgeting is complex and is best absorbed in small doses. Now that we have a solid groundwork in the concepts of present value and discounting, we can explore the effects of income taxes on capital budgeting decisions.

The U.S. tax code is enormously complex. We only scratch the surface in this text. To keep the subject within reasonable bounds, we have made many simplifying assumptions about the tax code throughout the chapter. The most important of these assumptions are that (1) with the exception of depreciation calculations, taxable income equals net income as computed for financial reports; and (2) the tax rate is a flat percentage of taxable income.[1] The actual tax code is far more complex than this. However, these and the other simplifications that we make throughout the chapter allow us to cover the most important implications of income taxes for capital budgeting, while suppressing details that are relatively unimportant in understanding the big picture.

Focus on Current Practice

The U.S. income tax code is mind numbingly complex. As stated in *Fortune* magazine, "No tax lawyer knows it all, few know much of it, and it may have become, in effect, unknowable." Says Sandy Navin, director of taxes at General Mills: "There are areas of the tax code where you have no way of telling whether you're coming up with the right answer, because of the complexity. You wait until the audit and hope you can come to an understanding with the government."[2] ■

The Concept of After-Tax Cost

objective 1

Compute the after-tax cost of a tax-deductible cash expense and the after-tax benefit from a taxable cash receipt.

Businesses, like individuals, must pay income taxes. In the case of businesses, the amount of income tax that must be paid is determined by the company's net taxable income. Tax deductible expenses (tax deductions) decrease the company's net taxable income and hence reduce the taxes the company must pay. For this reason, expenses are often stated on an *after-tax* basis. For example, if a company pays rent of $10 million a year but this expense results in a reduction in income taxes of $3 million, the after-tax cost of the rent is $7 million. An expenditure net of its tax effect is known as **after-tax cost.**

1. Under current tax law in the United States, corporate income tax rates are to some degree progressive. The income tax rate for corporations varies between 15% and 39% of taxable income—depending on the level of taxable income. When state and foreign income taxes are included in the tax computations, the total tax bill can exceed 40%. In this text we make the simplifying assumption that the corporate tax rate is either a flat 30% or 40% of taxable income.
2. Rob Norton, "Our Screwed-Up Tax Code," *Fortune,* September 6, 1993, p. 34.

Exhibit 15–1
The Computation of After-Tax Cost

	Without Training Program	With Training Program
Sales	$850,000	$850,000
Less tax deductible expenses:		
Salaries, insurance, and other	700,000	700,000
New training program		60,000
Total expenses	700,000	760,000
Taxable income	$150,000	$ 90,000
Income taxes (30%)	$ 45,000	$ 27,000

Cost of new training program	$60,000
Less: Reduction in income taxes ($45,000 − $27,000)	18,000
After-tax cost of the new training program	$42,000

To illustrate, assume that a company with a tax rate of 30% is contemplating a training program that costs $60,000. What impact will this have on the company's taxes? To keep matters simple, let's suppose the training program has no immediate effect on sales. How much does the company actually pay for the training program after taking into account the impact of this expense on taxes? The answer is $42,000 as shown in Exhibit 15–1. While the training program costs $60,000 before taxes, it would reduce the company's taxes by $18,000, so its *after-tax* cost would be only $42,000.

The after-tax cost of any tax-deductible cash expense can be determined using the following formula:[3]

$$\begin{array}{c}\text{After-tax cost}\\ \text{(net cash outflow)}\end{array} = (1 - \text{Tax rate}) \times \text{Tax-deductible cash expense} \qquad (1)$$

We can verify the accuracy of this formula by applying it to the $60,000 training program expenditure:

$$(1 - 0.30) \times \$60{,}000 = \$42{,}000 \text{ after-tax cost of the training program}$$

This formula is very useful since it provides the actual amount of cash a company must pay after taking into consideration tax effects. It is this actual, after-tax, cash outflow that should be used in capital budgeting decisions.

Similar reasoning applies to revenues and other *taxable* cash inflows. Since these cash receipts are taxable, the company must pay out a portion of them in taxes. The **after-tax benefit,** or net cash inflow, realized from a particular cash receipt can be obtained by applying a simple variation of the cash expenditure formula used above:

$$\begin{array}{c}\text{After-tax benefit}\\ \text{(net cash inflow)}\end{array} = (1 - \text{Tax rate}) \times \text{Taxable cash receipt} \qquad (2)$$

3. This formula assumes that a company is operating at a profit; if it is operating at a loss, the tax situation can be very complex. For simplicity, we assume in all examples, exercises, and problems that the company is operating at a profit.

We emphasize the term *taxable cash receipts* because not all cash inflows are taxable. For example, the release of working capital at the termination of an investment project would not be a taxable cash inflow, since it simply represents a return of original investment.

Focus on Current Practice

Simply filling out tax returns involves tremendous efforts and costs taxpayers billions of dollars each year. "For 90% of U.S. corporations (those with less than $1 million in assets), the total cost of complying with the . . . federal income tax code exceeded their income tax liability by 390%. In layman's terms, this means that for every $100 in taxes paid by America's small businesses, $390 was paid by these businesses to comply with the taxes."[4] ■

Depreciation Tax Shield

Depreciation is not a cash flow. For this reason, depreciation was ignored in Chapter 14 in all discounted cash flow computations. However, depreciation does affect the taxes that must be paid and therefore has an indirect effect on the company's cash flows.

To illustrate the effect of depreciation deductions on tax payments, consider a company with annual cash sales of $500,000 and cash operating expenses of $310,000. In addition, the company has a depreciable asset on which the depreciation deduction is $90,000 per year. The tax rate is 30%. As shown in Exhibit 15–2, the depreciation deduction reduces the company's taxes by $27,000. In effect, the depreciation deduction of $90,000 *shields* $90,000 in revenues from taxation and thereby *reduces* the amount of taxes that the company must pay. Because depreciation deductions shield revenues from taxation, they are generally referred to as a **depreciation tax shield.**[5] The reduction in tax payments made possible by the depreciation tax shield is equal to the amount of the depreciation deduction, multiplied by the tax rate as follows:

$$\text{Tax savings from the depreciation tax shield} = \text{Tax rate} \times \text{Depreciation deduction} \qquad (3)$$

We can verify this formula by applying it to the $90,000 depreciation deduction in our example:

$$0.30 \times \$90{,}000 = \$27{,}000 \text{ reduction in tax payments}$$

In this chapter, when we estimate after-tax cash flows for capital budgeting decisions, we will include the tax savings provided by the depreciation tax shield.

A summary of the concepts we have introduced so far is given in Exhibit 15–3.

4. Arthur P. Hall, "Accounting Costs, Another Tax," *The Wall Street Journal,* December 9, 1993, p. A18.
5. The term *depreciation tax shield* may convey the impression that there is something underhanded about depreciation deductions—that companies are getting some sort of a special tax break. However, to use the depreciation deduction, a company must have already acquired a depreciable asset—which typically requires a cash outflow. Essentially, the tax code requires companies to delay recognizing the cash outflow as an expense until depreciation charges are recorded.

Exhibit 15–2
The Impact of Depreciation Deductions on Tax Payments

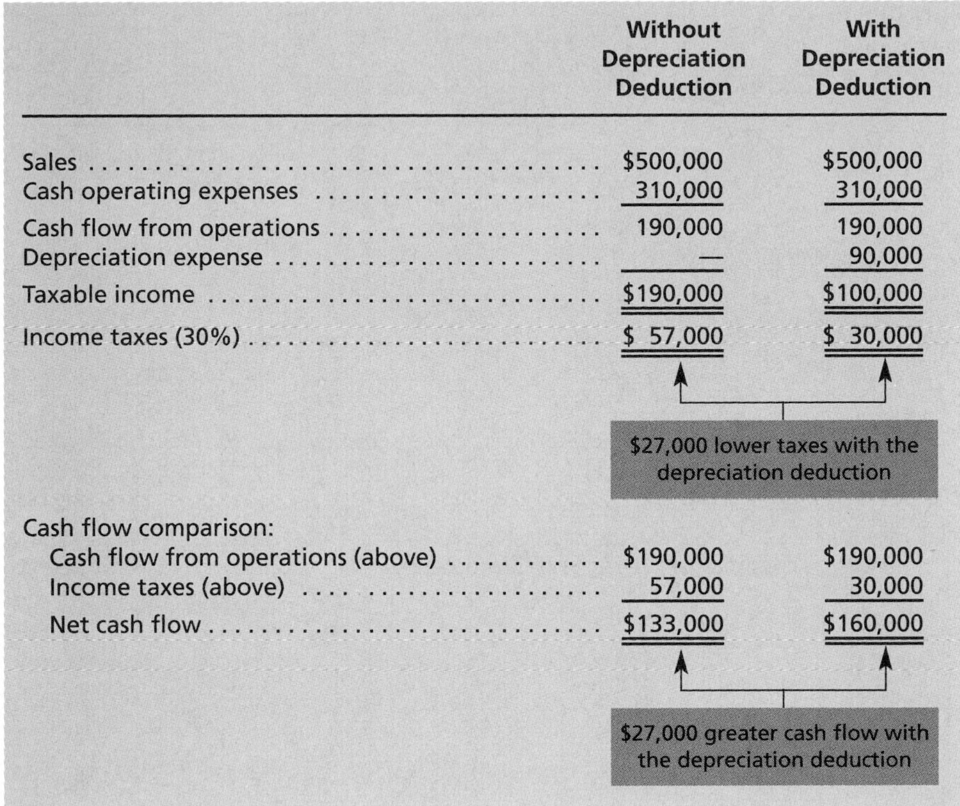

	Without Depreciation Deduction	With Depreciation Deduction
Sales	$500,000	$500,000
Cash operating expenses	310,000	310,000
Cash flow from operations	190,000	190,000
Depreciation expense	—	90,000
Taxable income	$190,000	$100,000
Income taxes (30%)	$ 57,000	$ 30,000

	Without Depreciation Deduction	With Depreciation Deduction
Cash flow comparison:		
Cash flow from operations (above)	$190,000	$190,000
Income taxes (above)	57,000	30,000
Net cash flow	$133,000	$160,000

Exhibit 15–3
Tax Adjustments Required in a Capital Budgeting Analysis

Item	Treatment
Tax-deductible cash expense*	Multiply by (1 − Tax rate) to get after-tax cost.
Taxable cash receipt*	Multiply by (1 − Tax rate) to get after-tax cash inflow.
Depreciation deduction	Multiply by the tax rate to get the tax savings from the depreciation tax shield.

*Cash expenses can be deducted from the cash receipts and the difference multiplied by (1 − Tax rate). See the example at the top of Exhibit 15–7.

Modified Accelerated Cost Recovery System

objective 2
Explain how depreciation deductions are computed under the Modified Accelerated Cost Recovery System (MACRS).

In the past, depreciation deductions for tax purposes were closely tied to the useful life of an asset, with year-by-year depreciation deductions typically computed by the straight-line method, the sum-of-the-years'-digits method, or the double-declining-balance method. Also, in computing depreciation deductions, companies generally deducted the salvage value from the asset's cost and depreciated only the remainder. These approaches can still be used for computing depreciation deductions on financial statements. However, the U.S. Congress in 1981 and in 1986 made sweeping changes in the way that depreciation deductions are computed for tax purposes.

This new approach to depreciation deductions is now known as the **Modified Accelerated Cost Recovery System (MACRS).** MACRS accelerates depreciation by placing all depreciable assets into one of nine property classes. The various property classes under the MACRS rules are presented in Exhibit 15–4.

Exhibit 15–4
MACRS Property Classes

MACRS Property Class and Depreciation Method	Examples of Assets Included in This Class
3-year property 200% declining balance	Most small tools are included; the law specifically *excludes* autos and light trucks from this property class.
5-year property 200% declining balance	Autos and trucks, computers, typewriters, copiers, duplicating equipment, and research and experimentation equipment are included.
7-year property 200% declining balance	Office furniture and fixtures, and most items of machinery and equipment used in production are included.
10-year property 200% declining balance	Various machinery and equipment, such as that used in petroleum distilling and refining and in the milling of grain, are included.
15-year property 150% declining balance	Sewage treatment plants, telephone and electrical distribution facilities, and land improvements are included.
20-year property 150% declining balance	Service stations and other real property with a useful life of less than 27.5 years are included.
27.5-year property Straight line	All residential rental property is included.
31.5-year property Straight line	Nonresidential real property placed in service before May 13, 1993.
39-year property Straight line	Nonresidential real property placed in service after May 13, 1993.

Two key points should be noted about the data in Exhibit 15–4. First, each MACRS property class has a prescribed life. This is the life that must be used to depreciate any asset within that property class, regardless of the asset's actual useful life. Thus, an asset in the seven-year property class would be depreciated over seven years regardless of its actual useful life. These property classes make it possible to depreciate assets over quite short periods of time. Office equipment, for example, may have a useful life of 10 years or more, but it is in the MACRS 7-year property class. Therefore, the MACRS rules permit office equipment to be depreciated more quickly than would be indicated by its actual useful life.

Second, note from Exhibit 15–4 that the MACRS property classes utilize various depreciation methods and rates. To simplify depreciation computations, preset tables are available that show allowable depreciation deductions by year for each of the MACRS property classes. Six of these tables are presented in Exhibit 15–5. The percentage figures used in the tables are based on the declining-balance method of depreciation. A 200% rate was used to develop the figures dealing with the 3-, 5-, 7-, and 10-year property classes; and a 150% rate was used to develop the figures dealing with the 15- and 20-year property classes. In all cases, the tables automatically switch to straight-line depreciation at the point where depreciation deductions would be greater under that method. The tables in Exhibit 15–5 apply to both new and used property.

Special MACRS Rules

When computing depreciation deductions under the MACRS approach for the first six property classes (3-year property through 20-year property), taxpayers are permitted to take only a half year's depreciation in the first year and the last year of an asset's life. This is known as the **half-year convention.** In effect, the half-year convention adds a

Exhibit 15–5
MACRS Depreciation Tables by Property Class—Half-Year Convention*

Year	3-Year	5-Year	7-Year	10-Year	15-Year	20-Year
	Property Class					
1	33.3%	20.0%	14.3%	10.0%	5.0%	3.8%
2	44.5	32.0	24.5	18.0	9.5	7.2
3	14.8†	19.2	17.5	14.4	8.6	6.7
4	7.4	11.5†	12.5	11.5	7.7	6.2
5		11.5	8.9†	9.2	6.9	5.7
6		5.8	8.9	7.4	6.2	5.3
7			8.9	6.6†	5.9†	4.9
8			4.5	6.6	5.9	4.5†
9				6.5	5.9	4.5
10				6.5	5.9	4.5
11				3.3	5.9	4.5
12					5.9	4.5
13					5.9	4.5
14					5.9	4.5
15					5.9	4.5
16					3.0	4.4
17						4.4
18						4.4
19						4.4
20						4.4
21						2.2
Total	100.0%	100.0%	100.0%	100.0%	100.0%	100.0%

*For ease of computations, percentage figures in the tables have been rounded to three decimal places (e.g., 33.3 percent for three-year property would be 0.333 in decimal form). Tables prepared by the Internal Revenue Service carry these computations to either four or five decimal places, depending on the property class. In preparing tax returns and other data for the Internal Revenue Service, the IRS tables should be used.

†Denotes the year of changeover to straight-line depreciation.

full year onto the recovery period for an asset, as shown in the tables in Exhibit 15–5. (The half-year convention is built into the figures in the tables.) Note from the exhibit, for example, that assets in the three-year property class are depreciated over *four* years with only a half year's depreciation being allowed in the first and fourth years. In like manner, assets in the five-year property class are depreciated over *six* years, with the same pattern holding true for the other property classes. The half-year convention is followed regardless of the time of year in which an asset is purchased or the time of year in which it is sold.[6]

Another special MACRS rule is that salvage value is not considered in computing depreciation deductions. Thus, depreciation deductions are computed on a basis of the full, original cost of an asset without any offset for the asset's expected salvage value. This is actually a benefit to the taxpayer, since it allows the entire cost of an asset to be written off as depreciation expense. However, since the entire cost of an asset is written off, any salvage value realized from sale of the asset at the end of its useful life is fully taxable as income.

Using the MACRS Tables

To illustrate how the tables in Exhibit 15–5 are used to compute depreciation deductions, assume that Wendover Company purchased an industrial robot on January 2. Cost and other data relating to the equipment follow:

6. Under some circumstances, a midquarter convention can also be used for some property, but it will not be discussed further in this text.

Cost of the equipment	$200,000
Salvage value	3,000
Useful life	14 years

Even though the equipment has a useful life of 14 years, it will be in the MACRS 7-year property class since it is production equipment (see Exhibit 15–4). Under MACRS, salvage value is ignored; therefore, Wendover Company's depreciation deductions for tax purposes will be computed on the robot's full $200,000 original cost, as follows:

Year	Cost of the Robot	MACRS Percentage*	Depreciation Deduction
1	$200,000	14.3%	$ 28,600
2	200,000	24.5%	49,000
3	200,000	17.5%	35,000
4	200,000	12.5%	25,000
5	200,000	8.9%	17,800
6	200,000	8.9%	17,800
7	200,000	8.9%	17,800
8	200,000	4.5%	9,000
		100.0%	$200,000

*From the table for the seven-year property class in Exhibit 15–5.

Note that depreciation is taken over eight years since the tables provide for only a half-year's depreciation in the first and last years.

Optional Straight-Line Method

Under MACRS, a company can elect (i.e., choose) to compute depreciation deductions by the **optional straight-line method.** Under the optional straight-line method, a company is permitted to ignore the MACRS tables and to spread its depreciation deductions somewhat evenly over an asset's property class life.

To provide an example, assume that Emerson Company purchased a high-capacity photocopier at a cost of $10,000 on April 1. The equipment has a $600 salvage value, and it is in the MACRS five-year property class. If the company elects to use the optional straight-line method, it can deduct $1,000 depreciation in the first year:

$$\$10{,}000 \div 5 \text{ years} = \$2{,}000 \text{ per year; } \$2{,}000 \times 1/2 = \$1{,}000$$

For the next four years the company can deduct $2,000 depreciation each year, and in the final year it can deduct the remaining $1,000 as shown below:

Year	Depreciation Deduction
1 (half year's depreciation)	$1,000
2	2,000
3	2,000
4	2,000
5	2,000
6 (half year's depreciation)	1,000

Note that the half-year convention is followed when using the optional straight-line method, the same as with the MACRS tables. Also note that in accordance with the MACRS rules, the asset's salvage value was not considered in computing the depreciation deductions.

The option of being able to use the straight-line method in lieu of the percentages in the MACRS tables may be of value to new firms and to firms experiencing economic difficulties. The reason is that such firms often have little or no current taxable income and thus may prefer to stretch out depreciation deductions rather than to accelerate them.

Managerial Accounting in Action

THE ISSUE

Eagle Peak is a major Rocky Mountain destination ski resort managed by Chuck Redding. The company is considering the purchase of three 12-passenger Helimann SnoCats that would provide skier access to areas on the back of the mountain that are not served by ski lifts. The demand for such a service is very high—expert skiers are willing to pay over $200 a day for access to untracked powder snow. While Redding is familiar with net present value analysis, he is uncertain about the tax implications of the proposed purchases and has asked for advice from Marcia Sykes, a local CPA and enthusiastic skier who provides accounting and business consulting services. The following discussion took place in Redding's office:

Chuck: It's good to see you, Marcia. I'm glad you could drop by.
Marcia: No problem. My skis are in the locker, and I'll hit the slope after we talk.
Chuck: You may have heard that we are thinking about buying some SnoCats to provide service to the back side of the mountain.
Marcia: From all the talk in town, I don't think you are going to have any trouble selling tickets.
Chuck: I know. Some of the local powder snow freaks have been trying to get us to sell them advance tickets.
Marcia: Does the economics of the SnoCats make sense?
Chuck: I'm not sure. I figured out the present value of all of the cash flows except for one thing and that's the depreciation.
Marcia: Depreciation isn't a cash flow.

(continued)

Chuck: You're right. What I meant was that I haven't figured out what impact the depreciation would have on our taxes.
Marcia: If you give me all of your data, I should have an answer for you within a day or two.
Chuck: Great. ■

The Choice of a Depreciation Method

objective 3

Compute the tax savings arising from the depreciation tax shield using both the MACRS tables and the optional straight-line method.

As stated earlier, companies can use any depreciation method they want on financial statements, but they must use the MACRS rules for tax purposes. And in fact, most companies do use different depreciation methods on their financial reports than on their tax reports. For capital budgeting purposes, the MACRS tax rules should be used for computing depreciation since the purpose of the calculations is to estimate the impact the depreciation deductions will have on the taxes the company must pay.

In preparing data for the Eagle Peak ski resort, Marcia Sykes decided to provide information comparing the MACRS optional straight-line method to the MACRS tables. She knew that most companies choose to use the MACRS tables, since the accelerated methods of depreciation built into the tables are advantageous from a present value point of view. Nevertheless, for purposes of comparison, she wanted to also illustrate the tax savings from depreciation using the optional straight-line method. The SnoCat is in the five-year MACRS property class. The calculations that appear in Exhibit 15–6 confirmed that depreciating the SnoCats using the MACRS tables would provide a greater tax savings in present value terms than using the optional straight-line method. Note that the tax savings in Exhibit 15–6 are computed by multiplying the depreciation deduction in each year by the tax rate as we have already seen in equation (3). Also note that the discount rate is the company's *after-tax* cost of capital. We won't go into the details of how this is computed, but you should be aware that both cash flows and the discount rate are affected by income taxes.

After completing her analysis, Marcia took her work to Eagle Peak to show to Redding.

Managerial Accounting in Action

WRAP-UP

Marcia: Here's the analysis you asked for. The present value of the tax savings from the depreciation deductions is $63,476.
Chuck: I see two totals in this analysis, one for $57,987 and one for $63,476. And what is this MACRS thing?
Marcia: MACRS stands for Maddening, Archaic, and Confusing Regulations.
Chuck: Really?
Marcia: No, just teasing. It's an acronym the IRS uses to refer to its method for accelerated depreciation.
Chuck: This MACRS thing *does* look confusing. Isn't there a simpler way?
Marcia: Sure, you could use the optional straight-line method. But simplicity has a cost. In fact, the cost would be about fifty-five hundred dollars in additional taxes.
Chuck: On second thought, I think I'll forget about simplicity.
Marcia: For profitable companies like Eagle Peak, the MACRS tables always provide a better tax deal than the optional straight-line method.

You get more of the tax benefit earlier and can put the tax savings to work for you.
Chuck: With those tax savings and the rest of the cash flows, this investment looks like a winner. Would you like to be the first passenger on our new SnoCat service?
Marcia: Absolutely! ■

Example of Income Taxes and Capital Budgeting

Armed with an understanding of the MACRS depreciation rules and the concepts of after-tax cost, after-tax revenue, and depreciation tax shield, we are now prepared to examine a comprehensive example of income taxes and capital budgeting. The data for the example are on the next page.

Exhibit 15–6
Tax Shield Effects of Depreciation

Cost of the SnoCats	$300,000
Useful life	9 years
Property class life	5 years
Salvage value	–0–
After-tax cost of capital	14%
Income tax rate	30%

Year	Depreciation Deduction	Tax Shield: Income Tax Savings at 30%	14% Factor	Present Value of Tax Savings
Straight-Line Depreciation with Half-Year Convention:				
1	$30,000	$ 9,000	0.877	$ 7,893
2	60,000	18,000	0.769	13,842
3	60,000	18,000	0.675	12,150
4	60,000	18,000	0.592	10,656
5	60,000	18,000	0.519	9,342
6	30,000	9,000	0.456	4,104
				$57,987

MACRS Tables—Five-Year Property Class with Half-Year Convention:

Year	Cost	MACRS Percentage	Depreciation Deduction	Tax Shield: Income Tax Savings at 30%	14% Factor	Present Value of Tax Savings
1	$300,000	20.0%	$60,000	$18,000	0.877	$15,786
2	300,000	32.0%	96,000	28,800	0.769	22,147
3	300,000	19.2%	57,600	17,280	0.675	11,664
4	300,000	11.5%	34,500	10,350	0.592	6,127
5	300,000	11.5%	34,500	10,350	0.519	5,372
6	300,000	5.8%	17,400	5,220	0.456	2,380
						$63,476

objective 4

Compute the after-tax net present value of an investment proposal.

Holland Company owns the mineral rights to land that has a deposit of ore. The company is uncertain as to whether it should purchase equipment and open a mine on the property. After careful study, the following data have been assembled by the company:

Cost of equipment needed	$300,000
Working capital needed	75,000
Estimated annual cash receipts from sales of ore	250,000
Estimated annual cash expenses for salaries, insurance, utilities, and other cash expenses of mining the ore	170,000
Cost of road repairs needed in 6 years	40,000
Salvage value of the equipment in 10 years	100,000
MACRS property class	7-year property class

The ore in the mine would be exhausted after 10 years of mining activity, at which time the mine would be closed. The equipment would then be sold for its salvage value. Holland Company uses the MACRS tables in computing depreciation deductions. The company's after-tax cost of capital is 12% and its tax rate is 30%.

Should Holland Company purchase the equipment and open a mine on the property? The solution to the problem is given in Exhibit 15–7. We suggest that you go through this solution item by item and note the following points:

Cost of new equipment. The initial investment of $300,000 in the new equipment is included in full with no reductions for taxes. This represents an *investment,* not an expense, so no tax adjustment is needed. (Only revenues and expenses are adjusted for the effects of taxes.) However, this investment does affect taxes through the depreciation deductions that are considered below.

Working capital. Observe that the working capital needed for the project is included in full with no reductions for taxes. Like the cost of new equipment, working capital is an investment and not an expense so it needs no tax adjustment. Also observe that no tax adjustment is made when the working capital is released at the end of the project's life. The release of working capital is not a taxable cash flow, since it merely represents a return of investment funds back to the company.

Net annual cash receipts. The net annual cash receipts from sales of ore are adjusted for the effects of income taxes, as discussed earlier in the chapter. Note at the top of Exhibit 15–7 that the annual cash expenses are deducted from the annual cash receipts to obtain a net cash receipts figure. This just simplifies computations. (Many of the exercises and problems that follow already provide a net annual cash receipts figure, thereby eliminating the need to make this computation.)

Road repairs. Since the road repairs occur just once (in the sixth year), they are treated separately from other expenses. Road repairs would be a tax-deductible cash expense, and therefore they are adjusted for the effects of income taxes, as discussed earlier in the chapter.

Depreciation deductions. The equipment is in the MACRS seven-year property class. The tax savings provided by depreciation deductions under the MACRS rules are included in the present value computations in the same way as was illustrated earlier in the chapter (see Exhibit 15–6). Note that depreciation deductions are kept separate from cash expenses. These are unlike items, and they should be treated separately in a capital budgeting analysis.

Salvage value of equipment. Since under the MACRS rules a company does not consider salvage value in computing depreciation deductions, book value will be zero at the end of the life of an asset. Thus, any salvage value received is fully taxable as income to the company. The after-tax benefit is determined by multiplying the salvage value by (12Tax rate), as discussed earlier.

Exhibit 15–7 Example of Income Taxes and Capital Budgeting

	Per Year
Cash receipts from sales of ore	$250,000
Less payments for salaries, insurance, utilities, and other cash expenses	170,000
Net cash receipts	$ 80,000

Items and Computations	Year(s)	(1) Amount	(2) Tax Effect*	After-Tax Cash Flows (1) × (2)	12% Factor	Present Value of Cash Flows
Cost of new equipment	Now	$(300,000)	—	$(300,000)	1.000	$(300,000)
Working capital needed	Now	(75,000)	—	(75,000)	1.000	(75,000)
Net annual cash receipts (above)	1–10	80,000	1 − 0.30	56,000	5.650	316,400
Road repairs	6	(40,000)	1 − 0.30	(28,000)	0.507	(14,196)
Depreciation deductions:						
Year / Cost / MACRS Percentage / Depreciation Deduction						
1 . . . $300,000 14.3% $42,900	1	42,900	0.30	12,870	0.893	11,493
2 . . . 300,000 24.5% 73,500	2	73,500	0.30	22,050	0.797	17,574
3 . . . 300,000 17.5% 52,500	3	52,500	0.30	15,750	0.712	11,214
4 . . . 300,000 12.5% 37,500	4	37,500	0.30	11,250	0.636	7,155
5 . . . 300,000 8.9% 26,700	5	26,700	0.30	8,010	0.567	4,542
6 . . . 300,000 8.9% 26,700	6	26,700	0.30	8,010	0.507	4,061
7 . . . 300,000 8.9% 26,700	7	26,700	0.30	8,010	0.452	3,621
8 . . . 300,000 4.5% 13,500	8	13,500	0.30	4,050	0.404	1,636
Salvage value of equipment	10	100,000	1 − 0.30	70,000	0.322	22,540
Release of working capital	10	75,000	—	75,000	0.322	24,150
Net present value						$ 35,190

*Taxable cash receipts and tax-deductible cash expenses are multiplied by (1−Tax rate) to determine the after-tax cash flow. Depreciation deductions are multiplied by the tax rate itself to determine the after-tax cash flow figure (i.e., tax savings from the depreciation tax shield).

Since the net present value of the proposed mining project is positive, the equipment should be purchased and the mine opened. Study Exhibit 15–7 thoroughly. *Exhibit 15–7 is a key exhibit in the chapter!*

The Total-Cost Approach and Income Taxes

As stated in the preceding chapter, the total-cost approach is used to compare two or more competing investment proposals. To provide an example of this approach when income taxes are involved, assume the following data:

> The *Daily Globe* has an auxiliary press that was purchased two years ago. The newspaper is thinking about replacing this press with a newer, faster model. The alternatives are as follows:
>
> *Buy a new press* A new press could be purchased for $150,000. It would have a useful life of eight years, after which time it would be sold for $10,000. The old press could be sold now for $40,000. (The book value of the old press is $63,000.) If the new press is purchased, it would be depreciated using the MACRS tables and would be in the five-year property class. The new press would cost $60,000 each year to operate.

Exhibit 15–8 Income Taxes and Capital Budgeting: Total-Cost Approach

Items and Computations	Year(s)	(1) Amount	(2) Tax Effect	After-Tax Cash Flows (1) × (2)	10% Factor	Present Value of Cash Flows
Buy the new press:						
Cost of the new press	Now	$(150,000)	—	$(150,000)	1.000	$(150,000)
Annual cash operating costs	1–8	(60,000)	1 − 0.30	(42,000)	5.335	(224,070)
Depreciation deductions:						
Year — Cost — MACRS Percentage — Depreciation Deduction						
1 . . . . $150,000 — 20.0% — $30,000	1	30,000	0.30	9,000	0.909	8,181
2 . . . . 150,000 — 32.0% — 48,000	2	48,000	0.30	14,400	0.826	11,894
3 . . . . 150,000 — 19.2% — 28,800	3	28,800	0.30	8,640	0.751	6,489
4 . . . . 150,000 — 11.5% — 17,250	4	17,250	0.30	5,175	0.683	3,535
5 . . . . 150,000 — 11.5% — 17,250	5	17,250	0.30	5,175	0.621	3,214
6 . . . . 150,000 — 5.8% — 8,700	6	8,700	0.30	2,610	0.564	1,472
Cash flow from sale of the old press:						
Cash received from the sale	Now	40,000	—	40,000	1.000	40,000
Tax savings from the loss on sale:						
Present book value $63,000						
Sale price (above) 40,000						
Loss on the sale $23,000	1	23,000	0.30	6,900	0.909	6,272
Salvage value of the new press	8	10,000	1 − 0.30	7,000	0.467	3,269
Present value of cash flows						$(289,744)
Keep the old press:						
Annual cash operating costs	1–8	$(85,000)	1 − 0.30	$(59,500)	5.335	$(317,433)
Overhaul needed	5	(20,000)	1 − 0.30	(14,000)	0.621	(8,694)
Depreciation deductions:						
Year — Cost — Depreciation Deduction						
1 . . . . $90,000 — $18,000*	1	18,000	0.30	5,400	0.909	4,909
2 . . . . 90,000 — 18,000	2	18,000	0.30	5,400	0.826	4,460
3 . . . . 90,000 — 18,000	3	18,000	0.30	5,400	0.751	4,055
4 . . . . 90,000 — 9,000	4	9,000	0.30	2,700	0.683	1,844
Salvage value of the old press	8	5,000	1 − 0.30	3,500	0.467	1,635
Present value of cash flows						$(309,224)
Net present value in favor of purchasing the new press						$ 19,480

*$90,000 ÷ 5 years = $18,000 per year. Two years' depreciation has already been taken on the old press.

Keep the old press. The old press was purchased two years ago at a cost of $90,000. The press is in the MACRS five-year property class and is being depreciated by the optional straight-line method. The old press will last for eight more years, but it will need an overhaul in five years that will cost $20,000. Cash operating costs of the old press are $85,000 each year. The old press will have a salvage value of $5,000 at the end of eight more years.

The tax rate is 30%. The *Daily Globe* requires an after-tax return of 10% on all investments in equipment.

Should the *Daily Globe* keep its old press or buy the new press? The solution using the total-cost approach is presented in Exhibit 15–8. Most of the items in this exhibit have already been discussed in connection with Exhibit 15–7. Only a couple of points need elaboration:

Exhibit 15–9 Income Taxes and Capital Budgeting: Incremental-Cost Approach

Items and Computations	Year(s)	(1) Amount	(2) Tax Effect	After-Tax Cash Flows (1) × (2)	10% Factor	Present Value of Cash Flows
Cost of the new press	Now	$(150,000)	—	$(150,000)	1.000	$(150,000)
Savings in annual cash operating costs	1–8	25,000	1 − 0.30	17,500	5.335	93,363
Overhaul avoided	5	20,000	1 − 0.30	14,000	0.621	8,694
Difference in depreciation:						
Year / Depreciation Deduction: New Press / Old Press / Difference						
1 ..... $30,000 / $18,000 / $12,000	1	12,000	0.30	3,600	0.909	3,272
2 ..... 48,000 / 18,000 / 30,000	2	30,000	0.30	9,000	0.826	7,434
3 ..... 28,800 / 18,000 / 10,800	3	10,800	0.30	3,240	0.751	2,433
4 ..... 17,250 / 9,000 / 8,250	4	8,250	0.30	2,475	0.683	1,690
5 ..... 17,250 / — / 17,250	5	17,250	0.30	5,175	0.621	3,214
6 ..... 8,700 / — / 8,700	6	8,700	0.30	2,610	0.564	1,472
Cash flow from sale of the old press:						
Cash received from the sale	Now	40,000	—	40,000	1.000	40,000
Tax savings from the loss on sale (see Exhibit 15–8)	1	23,000	0.30	6,900	0.909	6,272
Difference in salvage value in eight years:						
Salvage from the new press ... $10,000						
Salvage from the old press 5,000						
Difference ... 5,000	8	5,000	1 − 0.30	3,500	0.467	1,635
Net present value in favor of purchasing the new press						$19,480

Note: The figures in this exhibit are derived from the *differences* between the two alternatives given in Exhibit 15–8.

Annual cash operating costs. Since no revenues are identified with the project, we simply place the cash operating costs on an after-tax basis and discount them as we did in Chapter 14.

Sale of the old press. The computation of the cash inflow from sale of the old press is more involved than the other items in Exhibit 15–8. Note that *two* cash inflows are connected with this sale. The first is a $40,000 cash inflow in the form of the sale price. The second is a $6,900 cash inflow in the form of a reduction in income taxes, resulting from the tax shield provided by the loss sustained on the sale. This tax shield functions in the same way as the tax shield provided by depreciation deductions. That is, the $23,000 loss shown in the exhibit on sale of the old press (the difference between the sale price of $40,000 and the book value of $63,000) is fully deductible from income in the year the loss is sustained. This loss shields income from taxation, thereby causing a reduction in the income taxes that would otherwise be payable. The tax savings resulting from the loss tax shield are computed by multiplying the loss by the tax rate (the same procedure as for depreciation deductions): $23,000 × 0.30 = $6,900.

A second solution to this problem is presented in Exhibit 15–9, where the incremental-cost approach is used. Notice both from this exhibit and from Exhibit 15–8 that the net present value is $19,480 in favor of buying the new press.

This concludes our study of capital budgeting.

Summary

Unless a company is a tax-exempt organization, such as a not-for-profit school or a governmental unit, income taxes should be considered in making capital budgeting decisions. Tax-deductible cash expenditures and taxable cash receipts are placed on an after-tax basis by multiplying them by (1 − Tax rate). Only the after-tax amount should be used in determining the desirability of an investment proposal.

Although depreciation is not a cash outflow, it is a valid deduction for tax purposes and as such affects income tax payments. The depreciation tax shield—computed by multiplying the depreciation deduction by the tax rate itself—also results in savings in income taxes. Since accelerated methods of depreciation provide the bulk of their tax shield early in the life of an asset, they are advantageous from a present value point of view.

Review Problem: Capital Budgeting and Taxes

Leisure Tours, Inc., is considering two investment projects—one of which involves purchasing a bus. Relevant cost and cash inflow information on each project is given below:

	Project A	Project B
Investment in passenger bus	$70,000	
Investment in working capital		$70,000
Net annual cash inflows	13,500	13,500
Life of the project	8 years	8 years

The bus will have a $5,000 salvage value in eight years. The bus is in the MACRS five-year property class, and it will be depreciated by the MACRS optional straight-line method. At the end of eight years, the working capital in project B will be released for use elsewhere.

The company requires an after-tax return of 10% on all investments. The tax rate is 30%.

Required Compute the net present value of each investment project.

Solution to Review Problem

Items and Computations			Year(s)	(1) Amount	(2) Tax Effect	(1) × (2) After-Tax Cash Flows	10% Factor	Present Value of Cash Flows
Project A:								
Investment in passenger bus			Now	$(70,000)	—	$(70,000)	1.000	$(70,000)
Net annual cash inflows			1–8	13,500	1 − 0.30	9,450	5.335	50,416
Depreciation deductions:								
Year	**Cost**	**Depreciation Deduction**						
1	$70,000	$ 7,000*	1	7,000	0.30	2,100	0.909	1,909
2	70,000	14,000	2	14,000	0.30	4,200	0.826	3,469
3	70,000	14,000	3	14,000	0.30	4,200	0.751	3,154
4	70,000	14,000	4	14,000	0.30	4,200	0.683	2,869
5	70,000	14,000	5	14,000	0.30	4,200	0.621	2,608
6	70,000	7,000*	6	7,000	0.30	2,100	0.564	1,184
Salvage value of the bus			8	5,000	1 − 0.30	3,500	0.467	1,635
Net present value								$ (2,756)

(continued)

Items and Computations	Year(s)	(1) Amount	(2) Tax Effect	(1) × (2) After-Tax Cash Flows	10% Factor	Present Value of Cash Flows
Project B						
Investment in working capital	Now	$(70,000)	—	$(70,000)	1.000	$(70,000)
Net annual cash inflows	1–8	13,500	1 − 0.30	9,450	5.335	50,416
Release of working capital	8	70,000	—	70,000	0.467	32,690
Net present value						$ 13,106

*$70,000 ÷ 5 years ÷ $14,000; $14,000 × 1/2 ÷ $7,000. The half-year convention is followed when computing depreciation for the first and last years.

Key Terms for Review

After-tax benefit The amount of net cash inflow realized from a taxable cash receipt after income tax effects have been considered. The amount is determined by multiplying the taxable cash receipt by (1 − Tax rate). (p. 727)

After-tax cost The amount of net cash outflow resulting from a tax-deductible cash expense after income tax effects have been considered. The amount is determined by multiplying the tax-deductible cash expense by (1 − Tax rate). (p. 726)

Depreciation tax shield A reduction in tax that results from depreciation deductions. The reduction in tax is computed by multiplying the depreciation deduction by the tax rate. (p. 728)

Half-year convention A requirement under the Modified Accelerated Cost Recovery System (MACRS) that allows a company to take only a half year's depreciation in the first and last years of an asset's depreciation period. (p. 730)

Modified Accelerated Cost Recovery System (MACRS) A method of depreciation required for income tax purposes that depends on which of nine property classes an asset belongs to. (p. 729)

Optional straight-line method A method of computing depreciation deductions under MACRS that can be used instead of the MACRS tables. (p. 732)

Questions

15–1 What is meant by after-tax cost and how is the concept used in capital budgeting decisions?

15–2 What is a depreciation tax shield and how does it affect capital budgeting decisions?

15–3 The three most widely used depreciation methods are straight line, sum-of-the-years' digits, and double-declining balance. Explain why a company might use one or more of these methods to compute depreciation expense in its published financial statements instead of the Modified Accelerated Cost Recovery System (MACRS).

15–4 Why do companies generally prefer accelerated methods of depreciation to the straight-line method of depreciation for income tax reporting?

15–5 Ludlow Company is considering the introduction of a new product line. Would an increase in the income tax rate tend to make the new investment more or less attractive? Explain.

15–6 Assume that an old piece of equipment is sold at a loss. From a capital budgeting point of view, what two cash inflows will be associated with the sale?

15–7 Assume that a new piece of equipment costs $40,000 and that the tax rate is 30%. Should the new piece of equipment be shown in the capital budgeting analysis as a cash outflow of $40,000, or should it be shown as a cash outflow of $28,000 [$40,000 × (1 − 0.30)]? Explain.

15–8 Assume that a company has cash operating expenses of $15,000 and a depreciation expense of $10,000. Can these two items be added together and treated as one in a capital budgeting analysis, or should they be kept separate? Explain.

Exercises

E15–1 a. Neal Company would like to initiate a management development program for its executives. The program would cost $100,000 per year to operate. What would be the after-tax cost of the program if the company's income tax rate is 30%?

b. Smerk's Department Store has rearranged the merchandise display cases on the first floor of its building, placing fast turnover items near the front door. This rearrangement has caused the company's contribution margin (and taxable income) to increase by $40,000 per month. If the company's income tax rate is 30%, what is the after-tax benefit from this rearrangement of facilities?

c. Perfect Press, Inc., has just purchased a new binding machine at a cost of $210,000. The machine falls in the MACRS seven-year property class and has a $14,000 salvage value. Using the MACRS optional straight-line method, determine the yearly tax savings from the depreciation tax shield. Assume that the income tax rate is 30%.

d. Repeat (c) above, this time using the MACRS tables in Exhibit 15–5.

E15–2 Morgan Industries has an opportunity to penetrate a new market by making some modifications to one of its existing products. These modifications would require the purchase of various tools and small items of equipment that would cost $80,000 and have a four-year useful life. The equipment would have a $7,500 salvage value and would be depreciated using the MACRS tables for the three-year property class.

The modified product would generate before-tax net cash receipts of $35,000 per year. It is estimated that the equipment would require repairs in the third year that would cost $14,000. The company's tax rate is 30%, and its after-tax cost of capital is 12%.

Required

1. Compute the net present value of the proposed investment in tools and equipment.
2. Would you recommend that the tools and equipment be purchased? Explain.

E15–3 Dwyer Company is considering two investment projects. Relevant cost and cash flow information on the two projects is given below:

	Project A	Project B
Investment in heavy trucks	$130,000	
Investment in working capital		$130,000
Net annual cash inflows	25,000	25,000
Life of the project	9 years*	9 years

*Useful life of the trucks

The trucks will have a $15,000 salvage value in nine years, and they will be depreciated using the optional straight-line method. At the end of nine years, the working capital will be released for use elsewhere. The company requires an after-tax return of 12% on all investments. The tax rate is 30%. The trucks are in the MACRS five-year property class.

Required Compute the net present value of each investment project. Round all dollar amounts to the nearest whole dollar.

E15–4 The Midtown Cafeteria employs five people to operate antiquated dishwashing equipment. The cost of wages for these people and for maintenance of the equipment is $85,000 per year. Management is considering the purchase of a single, highly automated dishwashing machine that would cost $160,000 and have a useful life of 12 years. This machine would require the services of only three people to operate at a cost of $48,000 per year. A maintenance contract on the machine would cost an additional $2,000 per year. New water jets would be needed on the machine in six years at a total cost of $15,000.

The old equipment is fully depreciated and has no resale value. The new machine will have a salvage value of $9,000 at the end of its 12-year useful life. The Midtown Cafeteria uses the MACRS tables for depreciation purposes. The new equipment would be in the MACRS seven-year property class. Management requires a 14% after-tax return on all equipment purchases. The company's tax rate is 30%.

Required

1. Determine the before-tax net annual cost savings that the new dishwashing machine will provide.
2. Using the data from (1) above and other data from the exercise, compute the new dishwashing machine's net present value. Round all dollar amounts to the nearest whole dollar. Would you recommend that it be purchased?

Problems

P15–5 Basic Net Present Value Analysis The Diamond Freight Company has been offered a seven-year contract to haul munitions for the government. Since this contract would represent new business, the company would have to purchase several new heavy-duty trucks at a cost of $350,000 if the contract were accepted. Other data relating to the contract follow:

Net annual cash receipts (before taxes) from the contract	$105,000
Cost of replacing the motors in the trucks in four years	45,000
Salvage value of the trucks at termination of the contract	18,000

With the motors being replaced after four years, the trucks will have a useful life of seven years. To raise money to assist in the purchase of the new trucks, the company will sell several old, fully depreciated trucks for a total selling price of $16,000. The company uses the MACRS tables to compute depreciation for tax purposes and requires a 16% after-tax return on all equipment purchases. The tax rate is 30%. The trucks would be in the MACRS five-year property class.

Required Compute the net present value of this investment opportunity. Round all dollar amounts to the nearest whole dollar. Would you recommend that the contract be accepted?

P15–6 Straightforward Net Present Value Analysis The Four-Seasons Timber Company estimates that the following costs would be associated with the cutting and sale of timber on land to which it has cutting rights:

Investment in equipment needed for cutting and removing the timber	$400,000
Working capital investment needed	75,000
Annual cash receipts, from sale of timber, net of related cash operating costs (before taxes)	88,000
Cost of reseeding the land	60,000

The timber would be exhausted after 10 years of cutting and sales; all reseeding would be done in the 10th year. The equipment would have a useful life of 15 years, but it would be sold for an estimated 20% of its original cost when cutting was completed. The company uses the MACRS tables in computing depreciation deductions for tax purposes. The equipment is in the MACRS seven-year property class. The tax rate is 30% and Four-Seasons' after-tax cost of captial is 12%. The working capital would be released for use elsewhere at the completion of the project.

Since the timber is difficult to get to and of marginal quality, management is uncertain as to whether it should proceed with the project.

Required

1. Compute the net present value of this investment project. Round all dollar amounts to the nearest whole dollar.
2. Would you recommend that the investment project be undertaken? Explain.

P15–7 Various Depreciation Methods; Net Present Value Fencik Laboratories has been offered an eight-year contract to provide materials relating to the government's space exploration program. Management has determined that the following costs and revenues would be associated with the contract:

Cost of special equipment	$600,000
Working capital needed	115,000
Annual revenues from the contract	450,000
Annual out-of-pocket costs for materials, salaries, and so forth	280,000
Salvage value of the equipment in eight years	9,000

Although the equipment would have a useful life of nine years, it would have little salvage value remaining at the end of the contract period, as shown above. Fencik's after-tax cost of capital is 14%; its tax rate is 30%. At the end of the contract period, the working capital will be released for use elsewhere. The equipment is in the MACRS five-year property class.

Required

1. Assume that Fencik Laboratories uses the MACRS optional straight-line depreciation method for tax purposes. Determine the net present value of the proposed contract. Round all dollar amounts to the nearest whole dollar.
2. Assume that Fencik Laboratories uses the MACRS tables to compute depreciation deductions. Determine the net present value of the proposed contract. Round all dollar amounts to the nearest whole dollar.
3. How do you explain the difference in rate of return between (1) and (2) above?

P15–8 Net Present Value Analysis The Island Travel Service (ITS) operates out of Kuna, Hawaii. ITS has an opportunity to purchase several small charter boats that were recently repossessed by a local bank. Although the boats cost $700,000 new and are only three years old, they can be purchased by ITS for the "bargain basement" price of $430,000, payable $250,000 down and $60,000 each year for three years, without interest.

After some study, ITS's manager, Biff Coletti, has determined that the boats could be operated an average of 250 days per year. Records kept by the previous owner (now in the hands of the bank) indicate that the boats carried an average of 70 tourists per day. Mr. Coletti is confident that this could be increased to at least 140 tourists per day by dropping the tour price from $18 to $10 per person. The local bank has estimated the following annual expenses associated with the boats:

Salaries for a manager and for boat operators	$160,000
Insurance	9,000
Fuel	72,000
Bank payments*	60,000
Promotion	18,000
Maintenance	4,200
Rent for docking space	10,000
Fees and maritime taxes	6,800
Depreciation	27,333†
Total expenses	$367,333

*For the first three years only.

†$430,000 cost − $20,000 estimated salvage value = $410,000 depreciable cost; $410,000 ÷ 15 years = $27,333 per year.

To cover possible damage from docking, ITS would have to make an immediate deposit of $1,800 to the harbor authorities; this deposit would be refundable at the end of the boat's 15-year remaining useful life. In nine years, the boat hulls would require major scraping and resealing at a cost of $35,000.

If the boats are purchased, ITS will use the MACRS tables to compute depreciation for tax purposes. The boats are in the MACRS 10-year property class. ITS's after-tax cost of capital is 10% and the tax rate is 30%.

Required

1. Compute the net cash receipts (before income taxes) each year from operating the boats.
2. Using net present value analysis, determine whether the boats should be purchased. Round all dollar amounts to the nearest whole dollar.

P15–9 Uneven Cash Flows; Net Present Value "All of the engineering studies say that tar sand is excellent for use in road construction," said Holly Edwards, chief engineer for Dieter Mining Company. "With road construction projected to be at peak levels over the next 10 years, now is the time for us to extract and sell the tar sand off of tract 370 in the southern part of the state."

"I'm not so sure," replied Tom Collins, the vice president. "Prices are really soft for tar sand. The best we can hope to get is $7 a ton, and the accounting people say it will cost us at least $3 a ton for utilities, supplies, and selling expenses. That doesn't leave much in the way of contribution margin."

"I know we won't get much per ton," replied Holly, "but our studies show that we have 1,735,000 tons of tar sand in the area. I figure we can extract 90,000, 145,000, and 240,000 tons the first three years, respectively, and then the remainder evenly over the next seven years. Even at only $7 a ton, that'll bring a lot of cash flow into the company."

"But you're forgetting that we have other costs, too," said Tom. "Fixed costs for salaries, insurance, and so forth, directly associated with the tar sand project would be $450,000 a year. Besides that, we would have to pay out an additional $250,000 at the end of the project for filling and leveling the land. You know how tough those environmental people can get if things don't look right. And all of this doesn't even consider the $800,000 cost of special equipment that we would need or the $75,000 we would have to put up for working capital to carry inventories and accounts receivable. I'm uneasy about the whole idea."

"You've got to look at the big picture, Tom. You'll get the working capital back in 10 years when the project is completed. In addition, we can depreciate that equipment and save a bundle in taxes at our 30% tax rate. Besides that, since the equipment would have a 12-year useful life, it would still have some use left when the project was completed. I'm sure we could sell it to someone for at least 5% of its original cost."

"All of that sounds fine, Holly, but I'll still bet the project won't provide the 18% after-tax return we require. Let's give all this to accounting and have them do a present value analysis for us."

Required

1. Compute the before-tax net cash receipts each year from the extraction and sale of the tar sand. (Do not include the cost of filling and leveling the land in this computation.)
2. Using the data from (1) above and other data from the problem as needed, prepare a net present value analysis to determine whether the company should purchase the equipment and extract the tar sand. Round all dollar amounts to the nearest whole dollar. You may assume that the company *as a whole* will have a positive taxable income in every year so that a tax benefit would be realized from any operating losses associated with the tar sand project. Also assume that the special equipment belongs in the MACRS seven-year property class.

P15–10 Various Depreciation Methods; Net Present Value Walter Miller, manufacturing vice president of Atlantic Industries, has been anxious for some time to purchase a piece of high-pressure equipment for use in the company's coal liquefaction research project. The equipment would cost $720,000 and would have an eight-year useful life. It would have a salvage value equal to about 5% of its original cost. In addition to the cost of the equipment, the company would have to increase its working capital by $10,000 to handle the more rapid processing of material by the new equipment.

An analysis that Mr. Miller has just received from his staff indicates that the equipment will not provide the 16% after-tax return required by Atlantic Industries. In making this analysis, Mr. Miller's staff estimated that the equipment would save the company $200,000 per year in its research program as a result of speeding up several key processes. The only significant maintenance work required on the equipment would be the installation of new pressure seals in five years at a cost of $80,000. In doing the analysis, Mr. Miller had instructed his staff to depreciate the equipment by the MACRS optional straight-line method, since the company always uses straight-line depreciation for accounting purposes. The company's tax rate is 30%. The equipment is in the MACRS five-year property class.

Upon seeing the analysis done by Mr. Miller's staff, the company's controller has suggested that the analysis be redone using the MACRS tables rather than the optional straight-line method. Somewhat irritated by this suggestion, Mr. Miller replied, "You accountants and your fancy bookkeeping methods! What difference does it make what depreciation method we use—we have the same investment, the same cost savings, and the same total depreciation either way. That equipment just doesn't measure up to our rate of return requirements. How you make the bookkeeping entries for depreciation won't change that fact."

Required

1. Compute the net present value of the equipment using the optional straight-line method for computing depreciation as instructed by Mr. Miller.
2. Compute the net present value of the equipment using the MACRS tables as suggested by the controller. Round all dollar amounts to the nearest whole dollar.
3. Explain to Mr. Miller how the depreciation method used can affect the rate of return generated by an investment project.

P15–11 A Comparison of Investment Alternatives; Total-Cost Approach Julia Vanfleet is professor of mathematics at a western university. She has received a $225,000 inheritance from her father's estate, and she is anxious to invest it between now and the time she retires in 12 years. Professor Vanfleet's position with the university pays a salary of $60,000 per year. Her tax rate is 20%. Since the state in which the university is located is experiencing extreme budgetary problems, this salary is expected to remain unchanged in the foreseeable future. Professor Vanfleet is considering two alternatives for investing her inheritance.

Alternative 1. Corporate bonds can be purchased that mature in 12 years and that bear interest at 10%. This interest would be taxable and paid annually. Alternative 1 would permit Professor Vanfleet to stay with the university.

Alternative 2. A small retail business is available for sale that can be purchased for $225,000. The following information relates to this alternative:

a. Of the purchase price, $80,000 would be for fixtures and other depreciable items. The remainder would be for the company's working capital (inventory, accounts receivable, and cash). The fixtures and other depreciable items would have a remaining useful life of at least 12 years and would be in the MACRS 7-year property class. At the end of 12 years these depreciable items would have a negligible salvage value; however, the working capital would be recovered (either through sale or liquidation of the business) for reinvestment elsewhere.
b. The store building would be leased. At the end of 12 years, if Professor Vanfleet could not find someone to buy the business, it would be necessary to pay $2,000 to the owner of the building to break the lease.
c. The MACRS tables would be used for depreciation purposes.
d. Store records indicate that sales have averaged $850,000 per year and out-of-pocket costs (including rent on the building) have averaged $760,000 per year (*not* including income taxes).
e. Since Professor Vanfleet would operate the store herself, it would be necessary for her to leave the university if this alternative were selected.

Required

Advise Professor Vanfleet as to which alternative should be selected. Use the total-cost approach to net present value in your analysis, and a discount rate of 8%. Round all dollar amounts to the nearest whole dollar.

P15–12 Equipment Replacement; Incremental Cost Approach "That new RAM 8000 is the most sophisticated piece of duplicating equipment available," said Monte Salazar, purchasing agent for Blinko's Copy Service. "The copier it would replace is putting out 5,600,000 pages a year, but the RAM would increase that output by 20%."

"I agree it's a powerful machine," replied Angie Carlson, the operations manager. "But we can only get $110,000 for the copier it would replace and that copier cost us $260,000 just two years ago. I don't think we can justify taking a huge loss on our old equipment every time something new hits the market. Besides, do you realize that the RAM 8000 costs $375,000?"

"Yes, and it's worth every dollar," said Monte. "To prove it, let's have accounting work up an analysis to see if the RAM 8000 meets the 14% after-tax rate of return that we require on new equipment."

In response to Monte's request, accounting has gathered the following information:

a. Both the old copier and the RAM 8000 are in the MACRS five-year property class.
b. The old copier is being depreciated by the optional straight-line method. Two years' depreciation has been taken; thus, the copier's book value is $182,000. Depreciation over the next four years will be: Years 1–3, $52,000 per year; and Year 4, $26,000.
c. The RAM 8000 would be depreciated using the MCARS tables. The manufacturer estimates that it would have a $15,000 salvage value at the end of its eight-year useful life. The old copier will be worth nothing in eight years.
d. Blinko's Copy Service pays 1.5 cents per page for paper; the company's customers pay an average of 9 cents per page for copy work.
e. To keep the RAM 8000 operating at peak efficiency, the company would purchase a maintenance contract that would cost $4,000 more per year than its present maintenance contract.
f. The RAM 8000 would need to have the drum and photo plates replaced in five years; the cost would be $30,000.
g. Blinko's Copy Service has a tax rate of 30%.

Required

1. Compute the incremental net annual cash receipts (before taxes) expected from the RAM 8000. (Do not include the cost of the drum and photo plates in this computation.)
2. Use net present value analysis to determine whether the RAM 8000 will provide the company's required rate of return. Use the incremental-cost approach. Round all dollar amounts to the nearest whole dollar.

P15–13 Comparison of Total-Cost and Incremental-Cost Approaches Reliable Waste Systems provides a solid waste collection service in a large metropolitan area. The company is considering the purchase of several new trucks to replace an equal number of old trucks now in use. The new trucks would cost $650,000, but they would require only one operator per truck (compared to two operators for the trucks now being used), as well as provide other cost savings. A comparision of total annual cash operating costs between the old trucks that would be replaced and the new trucks is provided below:

	Old Trucks	New Trucks
Salaries—operators	$170,000	$ 85,000
Fuel	14,000	9,000
Insurance	6,000	11,000
Maintenance	10,000	5,000
Total annual cash operating costs	$200,000	$110,000

If the new trucks are purchased, the old trucks will be sold to a company in a nearby city for $85,000. These trucks cost $400,000 when they were new, have a current book value of $120,000, and have been used for four years. They are in the MACRS five-year property class; the optional straight-line method is being used to depreciate these trucks for tax purposes.

If the new trucks are not purchased, the old trucks will be used for seven more years and then sold for an estimated $15,000 scrap value. However, to keep the old trucks operating, extensive repairs will be needed in one year that will cost $170,000. These repairs will be expensed for tax purposes in the year incurred.

The new trucks would have a useful life of seven years and would be depreciated using the MACRS tables. They would have an estimated $60,000 salvage value at the end of their useful life. The company's tax rate is 30%, and its after-tax cost of capital is 12%. The trucks are in the MACRS five-year property class.

Required

1. Use the total-cost approach to net present value analysis to determine whether the new trucks should be purchased. Round all dollar amounts to the nearest whole dollar.

2. Repeat the computations in (1) above, this time using the incremental-cost approach to net present value analysis.

P15–14 Ethics and the Manager The Fore Corporation is an integrated food processing company that has operations in over two dozen countries. Fore's corporate headquarters is in Chicago, and the company's executives frequently travel to visit Fore's foreign and domestic facilities.

Fore has a fleet of aircraft that consists of two business jets with international range and six smaller turboprop aircraft that are used on shorter flights. Company policy is to assign aircraft to trips on the basis of minimizing cost, but the practice is to assign the aircraft based on the organizational rank of the traveler. Fore offers its aircraft for short-term lease or for charter by other organizations whenever Fore itself does not plan to use the aircraft. Fore surveys the market often in order to keep its lease and charter rates competitive.

William Earle, Fore's vice president of finance, has claimed that a third business jet can be justified financially. However, some people in the controller's office have surmised that the real reason for a third business jet was to upgrade the aircraft used by Earle. Presently, the people outranking Earle keep the two business jets busy with the result that Earle usually files in smaller turboprop aircraft.

The third business jet would cost $11 million. A capital expenditure of this magnitude requires a formal proposal with projected cash flows and net present value computations using Fore's minimum required rate of return. If Fore's president and the finance committee of the board of directors approve the proposal, it will be submitted to the full board of directors. The board has final approval on capital expenditures exceeding $5 million and has established a firm policy of rejecting any discretionary proposal that has a negative net present value.

Earle asked Rachel Arnett, assistant corporate controller, to prepare a proposal on a third business jet. Arnett gathered the following data:

- Acquisition cost of the aircraft, including instrumentation and interior furnishing.
- Operating cost of the aircraft for company use.
- Projected avoidable commercial airfare and other avoidable costs from company use of the plane.
- Projected value of executive time saved by using the third business jet.
- Projected contribution margin from incremental lease and charger activity.
- Estimated resale value of the aircraft.
- Estimated income tax effects of the proposal.

When Earle reviewed Arnett's completed proposal and saw the large negative net present value figure, he returned the proposal to Arnett. With a glare, Earle commented, "You must have made an error. The proposal should look better than that."

Feeling some pressure, Arnett went back and checked her computations; she found no errors. However, Earle's message was clear. Arnett discarded her projections and estimates that she believed were reasonable and replaced them with figures that had a remote chance of actually occurring but were more favorable to the proposal. For example, she used first-class airfares to refigure the avoidable commercial airfare costs, even though company policy was to fly coach. She found revising the proposal to be distressing.

The revised proposal still had a negative net present value. Earle's anger was evident as he told Arnett to revise the proposal again, and to start with a $100,000 positive net present value and work backwards to compute supporting estimates and projections.

Required

1. Explain whether Rachel Arnett's revision of the proposal was in violation of the Standards of Ethical Conduct for Practitioners of Management Accounting and Financial Management.
2. Was William Earle in violation of the Standards of Ethical Conduct for Practitioners of Management Accounting and Financial Management by telling Arnett specifically how to revise the proposal? Explain your answer.
3. Identify specific internal controls that Fore Corporation could implement to prevent unethical behavior on the part of the vice president of finance.

(CMA, adapted)

Cases

C15–15 Make or Buy Decision; Total-Cost Approach Jonfran Company manufactures three different models of paper shredders, including the waste container which serves as the base. While the shredder heads are different for all three models, the waste container is the same. The number of waste containers that Jonfran will need during the next five years is estimated as follows:

Year 1	50,000	Year 4	55,000
Year 2	50,000	Year 5	55,000
Year 3	52,000		

The equipment used to manufacture the waste containers must be replaced because it has broken and can't be repaired. The new equipment has a list price of $945,000 but will be purchased at a 2% discount. The freight on the equipment would be $11,000, and installation costs would total $22,900. The equipment would be purchased and placed into service in January of Year 1. It would have a five-year useful life and would be in the MACRS three-year property class. (The company uses the MACRS tables for tax purposes.) The equipment would have a salvage value of $15,000 at the end of its useful life.

The new equipment would be more efficient than the old equipment and it would slash both direct labor and variable overhead costs in half. However, the new equipment would require the use of a slightly heavier gauge of metal, which would increase direct material costs by 30%. The company uses JIT inventory methods, but the heavier gauge metal is sometimes hard to get so the company would have to keep a small quantity on hand, which would increase working capital needs by $20,000.

The old equipment is fully depreciated and is not included in the fixed overhead. The old equipment can be sold now for $1,500; Jonfran has no alternative use for the manufacturing space at this time, so if the new equipment is not purchased, the old equipment will be left in place.

Rather than replace the old equipment, one of Jonfran's production managers has suggested that the waste containers be purchased. One supplier has quoted a price of $28 per container. This price is $7 less than Jonfran's current manufacturing cost, which is presented below:

Direct materials		$10
Direct labor		8
Variable overhead		6
Fixed overhead:		
Supervision	$2	
Facilities	5	
General	4	11
Total cost per unit		$35

Jonfran uses a plantwide predetermined fixed overhead rate. If the waste containers are purchased outside, the salary and benefits of one supervisor, included in the fixed overhead at $45,000, would be eliminated. No other changes would be made in the other cash and noncash items included in fixed overhead except depreciation on the new equipment.

Jonfran is subject to a 30% tax rate and requires a 14% after-tax return on all equipment purchases.

Required Using net present value analysis, determine whether the company should purchase the new equipment and make the waste containers or purchase the containers from the outside supplier. Use the total-cost approach and round all dollar amounts to the nearest whole dollar.

(CMA, adapted)

C15–16 Replacement of Riding Horses; Incremental-Cost Approach

The High-Step Riding Stables, Inc., operates a number of exclusive riding stables in the western United States. The company's Northmount Stable is not doing well even though it was provided with 60 new riding horses just two years ago. Evan Black, marketing vice president, wants to sell these horses and purchase 60 Appaloosa riding horses to use in their place. He feels certain that these beautiful animals would enhance the image of the stable and greatly increase revenues. In fact, he has asked the company's Accounting Department to develop a projected income statement for the coming year assuming use of both the present horses and the Appaloosa horses.

	Present Horses	Appaloosa Horses
Revenues from patrons	$275,000	$320,000
Less operating expenses:		
Salaries—manager and handlers	90,000	90,000
Feed	32,000	41,000
Insurance on the horses	8,000	12,500
Depreciation, stables and equipment	108,000	108,000
Depreciation horses*	10,000	28,500
Total operating expenses	208,000	231,000
Income before income taxes	27,000	40,000
Less income taxes (30%)	8,100	12,000
Net income	$ 18,900	$ 28,000

*Present horses: $90,000 cost ÷ 9 years = $10,000. Appaloosa horses: $210,000 cost − (60 horses × $175 sale value = $10,500) = $199,500; $199,500 ÷ 7 years = $28,500

Shauna Brosnan, operations vice president, is less enthused about the purchase. She stated, "I agree that the Appaloosas are beautiful, but look at what they would cost us. There are many other ways we could use that $210,000 in the company, and according to my computations all of these other ways would yield a return well over our 10% after-tax cost of capital."

"That's the best part of this whole deal," replied Evan. "The Appaloosas would provide a fantastic rate of return. Just look at these figures I've worked up:"

$$\text{Simple rate of return} = \frac{\text{Net income}}{\text{Initial investment} - \text{Sale of the old horses}}$$

$$= \frac{\$28{,}000}{\$210{,}000 - \$55{,}000} = 18.1\%$$

"Do you have any investments that will beat 18%?"

"No, I'll admit I don't," replied Shauna, "and your figures are impressive; but I'm still uneasy about the whole thing. Give me time to look at these figures a little more closely, and then I'll get back with you later."

After some effort, Shauna accumulated the following additional information:

a. Assume that horses are in the MACRS five-year property class. For tax purposes, the company is using the optional straight-line method to compute depreciation on the 60 horses now owned by Northmount Stable.
b. If the Appaloosa horses are purchased, they will be depreciated using the MACRS tables. These horses have a remaining useful life of seven years.
c. The 60 horses now owned by Northmount Stable will have no resale value at the end of their useful life to the stable.
d. The Appaloosa horses would be registered; to maintain this registration, the company would have to pay a renewal fee of $80 per horse four years from now.

e. To maintain a high sheen on their coats, the Appaloosa would have a special grain mixture added to their diets. Carrying a supply of the grain mixture on hand would require a $3,000 increase in the working capital requirements for the stable.

Required

1. Using net present value analysis, determine whether the Appaloosa horses should be purchased. Use the incremental-cost approach, and round all dollar amounts to the nearest whole dollar.
2. Do you agree with the way Evan has computed the simple rate of return on the horses? Explain your answer.

C15–17 **Make or Buy Decision; Incremental-Cost Approach** Lamb Company manufactures several products, including all of the component parts that go into these products. One unique part, a valve stem, requires specialized tools that are worn out and need to be replaced. Management has decided that the only alternative to replacing these tools is to acquire the valve stem from an outside source. A supplier is willing to provide the valve stem at a unit sales price of $20 if at least 70,000 units are ordered each year.

Lamb Company's average production of valve stems over the past three years has been 80,000 units each year. Expectations are that this volume will remain constant over the next four years. Cost records indicate that unit product costs for the valve stem over the last several years have been as follows:

Direct materials	$ 3.60
Direct labor	3.90
Variable manufacturing overhead	1.50
Fixed manufacturing overhead*	9.00
Unit product cost	$18.00

*Depreciation of tools (that must now be replaced) accounts for one-third of the fixed overhead. The balance is for other fixed overhead costs of the factory that require cash expenditures.

If the specialized tools are purchased, they will cost $2,500,000 and will have a disposal value of $100,000 at the end of their four-year useful life. Straight-line depreciation would be used for financial reporting purposes, but the MACRS tables would be used for tax purposes. The tools would be in the MACRS three-year property class. Lamb Company has a 30% tax rate, and management requires a 12% after-tax return on investment.

The sales representative for the manufacturer of the specialized tools has stated, "The new tools will allow direct labor and variable overhead to be reduced by $1.60 per unit." Data from another company using identical tools and experiencing similar operating conditions, except that annual production generally averages 100,000 units, confirms the direct labor and variable overhead cost savings. However, the other company indicates that it experienced an increase in raw material cost due to the higher quality of material that had to be used with the new tools. The other company indicates that its unit product costs have been as follows:

Direct materials	$ 4.50
Direct labor	3.00
Variable manufacturing overhead	0.80
Fixed manufacturing overhead	10.80
Unit product cost	$19.10

Referring to the figures above, Eric Madsen, Lamb's production manager, stated, "These numbers look great until you consider the difference in volume. Even with the reduction in labor and variable overhead cost, I'll bet our total unit cost figure would increase to over $20 with the new tools."

Although the old tools being used by Lamb Company are now fully depreciated, they have a salvage value of $45,000. These tools will be sold if the new tools are purchased; however, if the new tools are not purchased, then the old tools will be retained as standby equipment. Lamb Company's Accounting Department has confirmed that total fixed manufacturing overhead costs, other than depreciation, will not change regardless of the decision made concerning the valve stems. However, Accounting has estimated that working capital needs will increase by $60,000 if the new tools are purchased due to the higher quality of material required in the manufacture of the valve stems.

Required

1. Prepare a net present value analysis that will help Lamb Company's management decide whether the new tools should be purchased. Use the incremental-cost approach and round all dollar amounts to the nearest whole dollar.
2. Identify additional factors that Lamb Company's management should consider before a decision is made about whether to manufacture or buy the valve stems.

(CMA, adapted)

Group Exercises

IE15–18 The Complexity of U.S. Income Taxes U.S. federal income tax rules are mind-numbingly complex. For example, find Publication 946, How to Depreciate Property, on the Internal Revenue Service's web side www.irs.ustreas.gov. Find the chapter of Publication 946 dealing with the Modified Accelerated Cost Recovery System (MACRS) and the section in that chapter titled "How to Figure the Deduction Using the Tax Tables."

Required

1. Service stations and other real property are usually included in the 20-year property class. However, gas station convenience stores are treated differently. Which property class do they belong to? Does this special rule favor or penalize gas station convenience stores? Do you have any guess as to why gas station convenience stores are treated differently from other real property?
2. Property in the 10-year property class is usually depreciated over 10 years. However, if the property is on an Indian reservation, the rule is different. Over how many years is property located on an Indian reservation depreciated if it is in the 10-year property class? Does this special rule favor or penalize property located on Indian reservations? Do you have any guess as to why property located on Indian reservations is treated differently than other property?

IE15–19 An Alternative Approach to Determining After-Tax Cash Flows The General Services Administration, an agency of the federal government, has prepared a document titled "An Analytical Framework for Capital Planning and Investment Control for Information Technology." This document explains capital budgeting and it can be viewed on the Web at http://www.itpolicy.gsa.gov/mke/caplan1.htm. Find Exhibit 3 that shows the annual cash flows for Hypothetical Corporation.

Required

1. How does the method for computing the annual net cash flows on this web page differ from the method used in this text?
2. Using the basic data for Hypothetical Corporation, compute the annual net cash flows using the method from the text. Does there appear to be a mistake in the way the working capital has been treated in Exhibit 3 on the web site?

Chapter Sixteen

Service Department Costing: An Activity Approach

Business Focus

Bellcore (Bell Communications Research) has 25 service centers that provide support to the company's operating units. Several years ago the company discovered that some service center rates had increased to intolerable levels because of an antiquated costing system.

For example, at one point the company's word processing service center was charging $50 per typed page. This very high charge forced engineers, researchers, and other highly paid people to type their own documents. The exorbitant rates forced other users to go outside the company for typing, graphics, and related services. After a major restructuring of the cost allocation system, including better tracing of costs to the service centers, rates in word processing, graphics, and other service centers were brought into line with competing rates elsewhere.

Source: Edward J. Kovac and Henry P. Troy, "Getting Transfer Prices Right: What Bellcore Did," Harvard Business Review *89, no. 5 (September–October 1989).*

Learning Objectives

After studying Chapter 16, you should be able to:

1 Allocate service department costs to other departments using the direct method.

2 Allocate service department costs to other departments using the step method.

3 Allocate variable and fixed service department costs separately at the beginning of a period and at the end of the period.

Departments within an organization can be divided into two broad classes: (1) operating departments and (2) service departments. **Operating departments** include those departments or units where the central purposes of the organization are carried out. Examples of such departments or units would include the Surgery Department at Mt. Sinai Hospital; the undergraduate and graduate programs at UCLA; and producing departments such as Milling, Assembly, and Painting in a manufacturing company such as John Deere.

Service departments, by contrast, do not engage directly in operating activities. Rather, they provide services or assistance to the operating departments. Examples of service departments include Cafeteria, Internal Auditing, Personnel, Cost Accounting, and Purchasing. Although service departments do not engage directly in the operating activities of an organization, the costs that they incur are generally viewed as being part of the cost of the final product or service, the same as are materials, labor, and overhead in a manufacturing company or medications in a hospital.

Chapter 1 stated that most organizations have one or more service departments that provide services for the entire organization. In this chapter, we look more closely at service departments and consider how their costs are allocated to the units they serve for planning, costing, and other purposes. The major question we consider is: How much of a service department's cost is to be allocated to each of the units that it serves? This is an important question, since the amount of service department cost allocated to a particular unit can have a significant impact on the computed cost of the goods or services that the unit is providing and can affect an operating unit's performance evaluation.

Allocations Using the Direct and Step Methods

Allocating service department costs begins with selecting the proper allocation base—the first topic in this section. After completing this discussion, we will move on to consider how to account for services that service departments provide to each other.

Selecting Allocation Bases

Many companies use a two-stage costing process. In the first stage, costs are assigned to the operating departments; in the second stage, costs are assigned from the operating departments to products and services. We focused on the second stage of this allocation process in Chapter 3 and reserved discussion of first-stage costing procedures to this chapter. On the following pages we discuss the assignment of costs from service departments to operating departments, *which represents the first stage of the two-stage costing process.*

Costs are usually assigned from a service department to other departments using an allocation base, which is some measure of activity. The costs being allocated should be "driven" by the allocation base. Ideally, the total cost of the service department should be proportional to the size of the allocation base. Managers also often argue that the allocation base should reflect as accurately as possible the benefits that the various departments receive from the services that are being provided. For example, most managers would argue that the square feet of building space occupied by each operating department should be used as the allocation base for janitorial services since both the benefits and costs of janitorial services tend to be proportional to the amount of space occupied by a department. Examples of allocation bases for some service departments are listed in Exhibit 16–1. A given service department's costs may be allocated using more than one base. For example, data processing costs may be allocated on the basis of CPU minutes for mainframe computers *and* on the basis of the number of personal computers used in each operating department.

Exhibit 16–1
Examples of Bases Used in Allocating Service Department Costs

Service Department	Bases (cost drivers) Involved
Laundry	Pounds of laundry
Airport Ground Services	Number of flights
Cafeteria	Number of employees; number of meals
Medical Facilities	Cases handled; number of employees; hours worked
Materials Handling	Hours of service; volume handled
Data Processing	CPU minutes; lines printed; disk storage used; number of personal computers
Custodial Services (building and grounds)	Square footage occupied
Cost Accounting	Labor-hours; clients or patients serviced
Power	KWh used; capacity of machines
Human Resources	Number of employees; employee turnover; training hours
Receiving, Shipping, and Stores	Units handled; number of requisitions; space occupied
Factory Administration	Total labor-hours
Maintenance	Machine-hours

Although the previous paragraph explains how to select an allocation base, another critical factor should not be overlooked. The allocations should be clear and straightforward and easily understood by the managers to whom the costs are being allocated.

Focus on Current Practice

For many years, Hughes Aircraft allocated service department costs to operating departments using head count as the primary base because of its simplicity. Recently, the company has adopted an activity-based approach as it has taken dramatic steps to improve its costing system. Selected examples of service department allocations now made by the company are shown in the table below.

In describing the improved system, two Hughes managers stated, "For the first time operating units understand, and therefore can control, their level of cost absorption through an evaluation of their own activities. In addition, the metrics derived for each allocation serve as budgeting tools, [as] a method of communication between the providers and absorbers of an activity, and [as] a method for performance measurement in an era of continuous measurable improvement."[1] ■

Service Department	Allocation Bases	Metrics
Human Resources	Head count	$/head
	Hires	$/hire
	Union employees	$/head
	Training hours	$/training hour
Security	Square footage	$/square foot
Data Processing	Lines printed	$/line
	CPU minutes	$/CPU minute
	Storage	$/storage unit

1. Jack Haedicke and David Feil, "Hughes Aircraft Sets the Standard for ABC," *Management Accounting* 72, no. 8 (February 1991), pp. 31–32.

Interdepartmental Services

Many service departments provide services for each other, as well as for operating departments. The Cafeteria Department, for example, provides food for all employees, including those assigned to other service departments. In turn, the Cafeteria Department may receive services from other service departments, such as from Custodial Services or from Personnel. Services provided between service departments are known as **interdepartmental** or **reciprocal services.**

Three approaches are used to allocate the costs of service departments to other departments. These are known as the *direct method,* the *step method,* and the *reciprocal method.* All three methods are discussed in the following paragraphs.

objective 1

Allocate service department costs to other departments using the direct method.

DIRECT METHOD The **direct method** is the simplest of the three cost allocation methods. It ignores the services provided by a service department to other service departments and allocates all costs directly to operating departments. Even if a service department (such as Personnel) provides a large amount of service to another service department (such as the cafeteria), no allocations are made between the two departments. Rather, all costs are allocated *directly* to the operating departments. Hence the term *direct method.*

Focus on Current Practice

At Georgia Tech, service department costs are allocated to intercollegiate sports programs using the direct method.[2] For example, the costs of the Sports Medicine Department are allocated on the basis of the number of student athletes in each intercollegiate sport. The results of these allocations appear below:

	Total	Football	Basketball	Baseball	Track	Other
Revenue	$11,434,461	$5,278,970	$4,070,519	$ 526,858	$ 254,940	$1,303,174
Direct costs	7,878,954	4,111,908	1,800,892	426,662	317,854	1,221,636
Pre-allocation margin	3,555,507	1,167,062	2,269,627	100,196	(62,914)	81,538
Allocated costs	3,886,525	1,975,390	723,915	241,522	163,224	782,474
Surplus (deficit)	$ (331,018)	$ (808,328)	$1,545,712	$(141,326)	$(226,138)	$ (700,938)

The direct costs are those costs that are identifiable with a specific sport, such as a sport's operating budget, recruiting costs, scholarships, and salaries. The indirect costs, which are allocated, include Sports Medicine, Facilities, Sports Information, Academic Center, Student-Athlete Program, Office Supplies, Legal and Audit, Accounting Office, Marketing, and Administrative. Allocations of these indirect costs to the sports programs can make a big difference in their apparent profitability. For example, the football program shows a margin of $1,167,062 based on just its direct costs, but a loss of over $800,000 when indirect costs are allocated to the program. ■

---

2. C. David Strupeck, Ken Milani, and James E. Murphy III, "Financial Management at Georgia Tech," *Management Accounting,* February 1993, pp. 58–63. Reprinted from *Management Accounting.* Copyright © by Institute of Management Accountants, Montvale, NJ, February 1993.

Exhibit 16–2 Direct Method of Allocation

	Service Department		Operating Department		
	Hospital Administration	Custodial Services	Laboratory	Daily Patient Care	Total
Departmental costs before allocation	$ 360,000	$ 90,000	$261,000	$689,000	$1,400,000
Allocation:					
Hospital Administration costs (18⁄48, 30⁄48)*	(360,000)		135,000	225,000	
Custodial Services costs (5⁄50, 45⁄50)†		(90,000)	9,000	81,000	
Total costs after allocation	$ -0-	$ -0-	$405,000	$995,000	$1,400,000

*Based on the employee-hours in the two operating departments, which are 18,000 hours + 30,000 hours = 48,000 hours.

†Based on the space occupied by the two operating departments, which is 5,000 square feet + 45,000 square feet = 50,000 square feet.

To provide an example of the direct method, assume that Mountain View Hospital has two service departments and two operating departments as shown below:

	Service Department		Operating Department		
	Hospital Administration	Custodial Services	Laboratory	Daily Patient Care	Total
Departmental costs before allocation	$360,000	$90,000	$261,000	$689,000	$1,400,000
Employee hours	12,000	6,000	18,000	30,000	66,000
Space occupied—square feet	10,000	200	5,000	45,000	60,200

In the allocations that follow, Hospital Administration costs will be allocated on the basis of employee-hours and Custodial Services costs will be allocated on the basis of square feet occupied.

The direct method of allocating the hospital's service department costs to the operating departments is shown in Exhibit 16–2. Several things should be carefully noted in this exhibit. First, even though there are employee-hours in both the Hospital Administration Department itself and in the Custodial Services Department, these employee-hours are ignored when allocating service department costs using the direct method. *Under the direct method, any of the allocation base attributable to the service departments themselves is ignored; only the amount of the allocation base attributable to the operating departments is used in the allocation.* Note that the same rule is used when allocating the costs of the Custodial Services Department. Even though the Hospital Administration and Custodial Services departments occupy some space, this is ignored when the Custodial Services costs are allocated. Finally, note that after all allocations have been completed, all of the departmental costs are contained in the two operating departments. These costs will form the basis for preparing overhead rates for purposes of costing products and services produced in the operating departments.

Although the direct method is simple, it is less accurate than the other methods since it ignores interdepartmental services. This can lead to distorted product and service costs. Even so, many organizations use the direct method because of its simplicity.

Exhibit 16–3
Graphic Illustration—Step Method

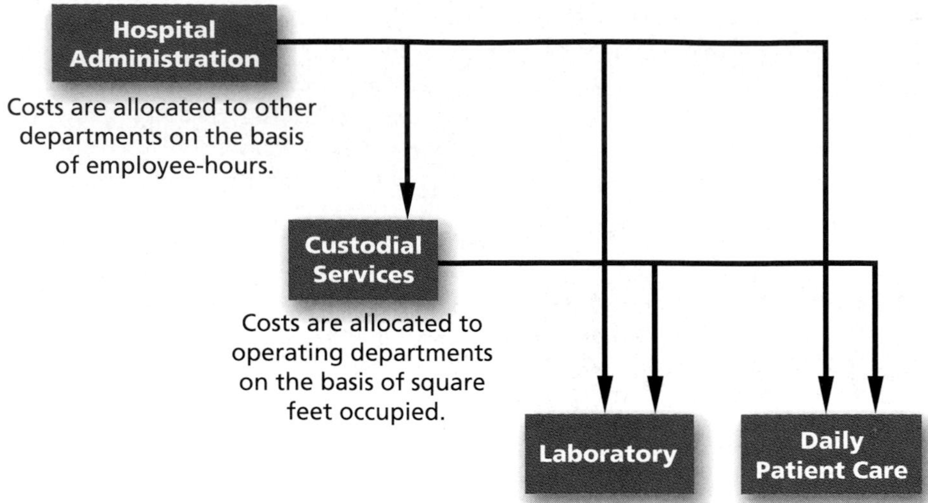

objective 2

Allocate service department costs to other departments using the step method.

STEP METHOD Unlike the direct method, the **step method** provides for allocation of a service department's costs to other service departments, as well as to operating departments. The step method is sequential. The sequence typically begins with the department that provides the greatest amount of service to other service departments. After its costs have been allocated, the process continues, step by step, ending with the department that provides the least amount of services to other service departments. This step procedure is illustrated in graphic form in Exhibit 16–3, assuming that the Hospital Administration costs are allocated first at Mountain View Hospital.

Exhibit 16–4 uses the allocations of the Mountain View Hospital to show the details of the step method. Note the following three key points about these allocations. First, under the Allocation heading in Exhibit 16–4, you see two allocations, or steps. In the step method, the first step allocates the costs of Hospital Administration to another service department (Custodial Services) as well as to the operating departments. The allocation base for Hospital Administration costs now includes the employee-hours for Custodial Services as well as for the operating departments. However, the allocation base still excludes the employee-hours for Hospital Administration itself. *In both the direct and step methods, any amount of the allocation base attributable to the service department whose cost is being allocated is always ignored.* Second, looking again at Exhibit 16–4, note that in the second step under the Allocation heading, the cost of Custodial Services is allocated to the two operating departments, and none of the cost is allocated to Hospital Administration even though Hospital Administration occupies space in the building. *In the step method, any amount of the allocation base that is attributable to a service department whose cost has already been allocated is ignored.* After a service department's costs have been allocated, costs of other service departments are not reallocated back to it. Third, note that the cost of Custodial Services allocated to other departments in the second step ($130,000) in Exhibit 16–4 includes the costs of Hospital Administration that were allocated to Custodial Services in the first step in Exhibit 16–4.

Focus on Current Practice

Group Health Cooperative of Puget Sound is a large health maintenance organization with 500 service departments that account for 30% of Group Health's total costs. The step method is used to allocate these costs to patient care departments and then to patients. These allocations are done so that costs can be summarized in a variety of ways including "by consumers, by diagnostic groupings, by employer groups, and by specific populations, such as Medicare, Medicaid, AIDS, Heart Care, and so on."[3] ■

RECIPROCAL METHOD The **reciprocal method** gives full recognition to interdepartmental services. Under the step method discussed above only partial recognition of interdepartmental services is possible, since the step method always allocates costs forward—never backward. The reciprocal method, by contrast, allocates service department costs in *both* directions. Thus, since Custodial Services in the prior example provides service for Hospital Administration, part of Custodial Services' costs will be allocated *back* to Hospital Administration if the reciprocal method is used. At the same time, part of Hospital Administration's costs will be allocated *forward* to Custodial Services. This type of reciprocal allocation requires the use of simultaneous linear equations. These equations can be complex and will not be illustrated here. Examples of the reciprocal method can be found in more advanced cost accounting texts.

The reciprocal method is rarely used in practice for two reasons. First, the computations are relatively complex. Although the complexity issue could be overcome by use of computers, there is no evidence that computers have made the reciprocal method more popular. Second, the step method usually provides results that are a reasonable approximation of the results that the reciprocal method would provide. Thus, companies have little motivation to use the more complex reciprocal method.

REVENUE PRODUCING DEPARTMENTS To conclude our discussion of allocation methods, it is important to note that even though most service departments are cost centers and therefore generate no revenues, a few service departments such as the cafeteria may charge for the services they perform. If a service department generates revenues, these revenues should be offset against the department's costs, and only

Exhibit 16–4 Step Method of Allocation

	Service Department		Operating Department		
	Hospital Administration	Custodial Services	Laboratory	Daily Patient Care	Total
Departmental costs before allocation	$ 360,000	$ 90,000	$261,000	$ 689,000	$1,400,000
Allocation:					
Hospital Administration costs (6/54, 18/54, 30/54)*	(360,000)	40,000	120,000	200,000	
Custodial Services costs (5/50, 45/50)†		(130,000)	13,000	117,000	
Total costs after allocation	$ -0-	$ -0-	$394,000	$1,006,000	$1,400,000

*Based on the employee-hours in Custodial Services and the two operating departments, which are 6,000 hours + 18,000 hours + 30,000 hours = 54,000 hours.

†As in Exhibit 16–2, this allocation is based on the space occupied by the two operating departments.

3. John Y. Lee and Pauline Nefcy, "The Anatomy of an Effective HMO Cost Management System," *Management Accounting,* January 1997, p. 52.

the net amount of cost remaining after this offset should be allocated to other departments within the organization. In this manner, the other departments will not be required to bear costs for which the service department has already been reimbursed.

Allocating Costs by Behavior

Whenever possible, service department costs should be separated into variable and fixed classifications and allocated separately. This approach is necessary to avoid possible inequities in allocation, as well as to provide more useful data for planning and control of departmental operations.

Variable Costs

Variable costs are out-of-pocket costs of providing services that vary in total in proporation to fluctuations in the level of service provided. Food cost in a cafeteria would be a variable cost, for example, and one would expect this cost to vary proportionately with the number of persons using the cafeteria.

As a general rule, variable costs should be charged to consuming departments according to whatever activity causes the incurrence of the costs involved. If, for example, the variable costs of a service department such as maintenance are caused by the number of machine-hours worked in the producing departments, then variable maintenance costs should be allocated to the producing deparments using machine-hours as the allocation basis. By this means, the departments directly responsible for the incurrence of servicing costs are required to bear them in proportion to their actual usage of the service.

Technically, the assigning of variable servicing costs to consuming departments can more accurately be termed *charges* than allocations, since the service department is actually charging the consuming departments at some fixed rate per unit of service provided. In effect, the service department is saying, "I'll charge you *X* dollars for every unit of my service that you consume. You can consume as much or as little as you desire; the total charge you bear will vary proportionately."

Fixed Costs

The fixed costs of service departments represent the costs of making capacity available for use. These costs should be allocated to consuming departments in *predetermined lump-sum amounts.* By predetermined lump-sum amounts we mean that the total amount charged to each consuming department is determined in advance and, once determined, does not change from period to period. The lump-sum amount charged to a department can be based either on the department's peak-period or long-run average servicing needs. The logic behind lump-sum allocations of this type is as follows:

When a service department is first established, its capacity will be determined by the needs of the departments that it will service. This capacity may reflect the peak-period needs of the other departments, or it may reflect their long-run average or "normal" servicing needs. Depending on how much servicing capacity is provided for, it will be necessary to make a commitment of resources to the servicing unit, which will be reflected in its fixed costs. These fixed costs should be borne by the consuming departments in proportion to the amount of capacity each consuming department requires. That is, if available capacity in the service department has been provided to meet the peak-period needs of consuming departments, then the fixed costs of the service department should be allocated in predetermined lump-sum amounts to consuming departments on this basis. If available capacity has been provided only to meet "normal" or long-run average needs, then the fixed costs should be allocated on this basis.

Once set, allocations should not vary from period to period, since they represent the cost of having a certain level of service capacity available and on line for each consuming department. The fact that a consuming department does not need a peak level or even a "normal" level of servicing every period is immaterial; if it requires such servicing at certain times, then the capacity to deliver it must be available. It is the responsibility of the consuming departments to bear the cost of that availability.

To illustrate this idea, assume that Novak Company has just organized a Maintenance Department to service all machines in the Cutting, Assembly, and Finishing Departments. In determining the capacity of the newly organized Maintenance Department, the various producing departments estimated that they would have the following peak-period needs for maintenance:

Department	Peak-Period Maintenance Needs in Terms of Number of Hours of Maintenance Work Required	Percent of Total Hours
Cutting	900	30%
Assembly	1,800	60%
Finishing	300	10%
	3,000	100%

Therefore, in allocating the Maintenance Department fixed costs to the producing departments, 30% (i.e., 900/3,000 = 30%) should be allocated to the Cutting Department, 60% to the Assembly Department, and 10% to the Finishing Department. These lump-sum allocations *will not change* from period to period unless there is some shift in peak-period servicing needs.

Should Actual or Budgeted Costs Be Allocated?

Should the *actual* or *budgeted* costs of a service department be allocated to operating departments? The answer is that budgeted costs should be allocated. What's wrong with allocating actual costs? Allocating actual costs burdens the operating departments with any inefficiencies in the service department. If actual costs are allocated, then any lack of cost control on the part of the service department is simply buried in a routine allocation to other departments.

Any variance over budgeted costs should be retained in the service department and closed out at year-end against the company's revenues or against cost of goods sold, along with other variances. Operating department managers justifiably complain bitterly if they are forced to absorb service department inefficiencies.

A Summary of Cost Allocation Guidelines

To summarize the material covered in preceding sections, we can note the following three guidelines to remenber about allocating service department costs:

1. If possible, the distinction between variable and fixed costs in service departments should be maintained.
2. Variable costs should be allocated at the budgeted rate, according to whatever activity (miles driven, direct labor-hours, number of employees) causes the incurrence of the cost.

a. If the allocations are being made at the beginning of the year, they should be based on the budgeted activity level planned for the consuming departments. The allocation formula would be:

$$\text{Variable cost allocated at the beginning of the period} = \text{Budgeted rate} \times \text{Budgeted activity}$$

b. If the allocations are being made at the end of the year, they should be based on the actual activity level that has occurred during the year. The allocation formula would be:

$$\text{Variable cost allocated at the end of the period} = \text{Budgeted rate} \times \text{Actual activity}$$

Allocations made at the beginning of the year would be to provide data for computing overhead rates for costing of products and billing of services in the operating departments. Allocations made at the end of the year would be to provide data for comparing actual performance to planned performance.

3. Fixed costs represent the costs of having service capacity available. Where feasible, these costs should be allocated in predetermined lump-sum amounts. The lump-sum amount going to each department should be in proportion to the servicing needs that gave rise to the investment in the service department in the first place. (This might be either peak-period needs for servicing or long-run average needs.) Budgeted fixed costs, rather than actual fixed costs, should always be allocated.

Implementing the Allocation Guidelines

objective 3

Allocate variable and fixed service department costs separately at the beginning of a period and at the end of the period.

We will now use specific examples to show how to implement the three guidelines given above. First, we focus on the allocation of costs for a single department, and then we will develop a more extended example involving multiple departments.

BASIC ALLOCATION TECHNIQUES Seaboard Airlines is divided into a Freight Division and a Passenger Division. The company has a single aircraft Maintenance Department that provides servicing to both divisions. Variable servicing costs are budgeted at $10 per flight-hour. The fixed costs of the Maintenance Department are budgeted based on the peak-period demand, which occurs during the Thanksgiving to New Year's holiday period. The airline wants to make sure that none of its aircraft are grounded during this key period due to unavailability of maintenance facilities. Approximately 40% of the maintenance during this period is performed on the Freight Division's equipment, and 60% is performed on the Passenger Division's equipment. These figures and the budgeted flight-hours for the coming year appear below:

	Percent of Peak Period Capacity Required	Budgeted Flight-Hours
Freight Division	40%	9,000
Passenger Division . . .	60%	15,000
Total	100%	24,000

Given these data, the amount of cost that would be allocated to each division from the aircraft Maintenance Department at the beginning of the coming year would be as follows:

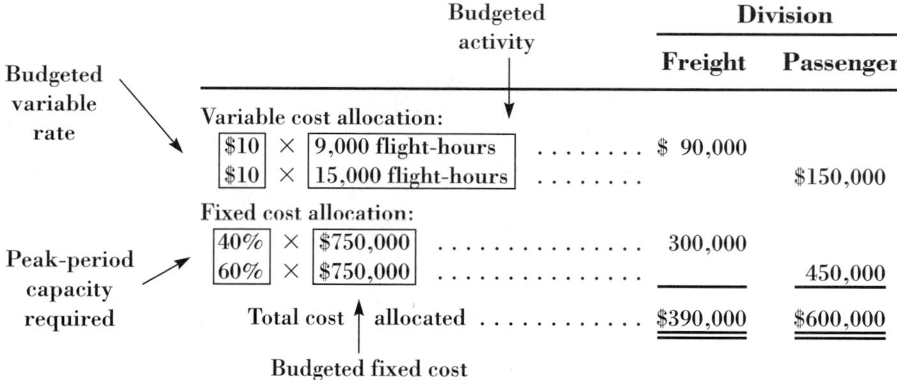

	Freight	Passenger
Variable cost allocation:		
\$10 × 9,000 flight-hours	\$ 90,000	
\$10 × 15,000 flight-hours		\$150,000
Fixed cost allocation:		
40% × \$750,000	300,000	
60% × \$750,000		450,000
Total cost allocated	\$390,000	\$600,000

As explained earlier, these allocated costs would be included in the flexible budgets of the respective divisions and included in the computation of divisional overhead rates.

At the end of the year, Seaboard Airlines' management may want to make a second allocation, this time based on actual activity, in order to compare actual performance for the year against planned performance. To illustrate, year-end records show that actual costs in the aircraft Maintenance Department for the year were variable costs, \$260,000; and fixed costs, \$780,000. One division logged more flight-hours during the year than planned, and the other division logged fewer flight-hours than planned, as shown below:

	Flight-Hours	
	Budgeted (see above)	**Actual**
Freight Division	9,000	8,000
Passenger Division	15,000	17,000
Total flight-hours	24,000	25,000

The amount of actual service department cost charged to each division for the year would be as follows:

		Division	
	Actual activity	**Freight**	**Passenger**
Variable cost allocation:			
Budgeted variable rate → \$10 × 8,000 flight-hours		\$ 80,000	
\$10 × 17,000 flight-hours			\$170,000
Fixed cost allocation:			
Peak-period capacity required → 40% × \$750,000		300,000	
60% × \$750,000			450,000
Total cost allocated		\$380,000	\$620,000

Budgeted fixed cost

Notice that variable servicing cost is charged to the operating divisions based on the budgeted rate (\$10 per hour) and the *actual activity* for the year. In contrast, the charges for fixed costs are exactly the same as they were at the beginning of the year. Also note that the two operating divisions are *not* charged for the actual costs of the service department, which may be influenced by inefficiency in the service department

Exhibit 16–5 Effect of Allocations on Products and Services

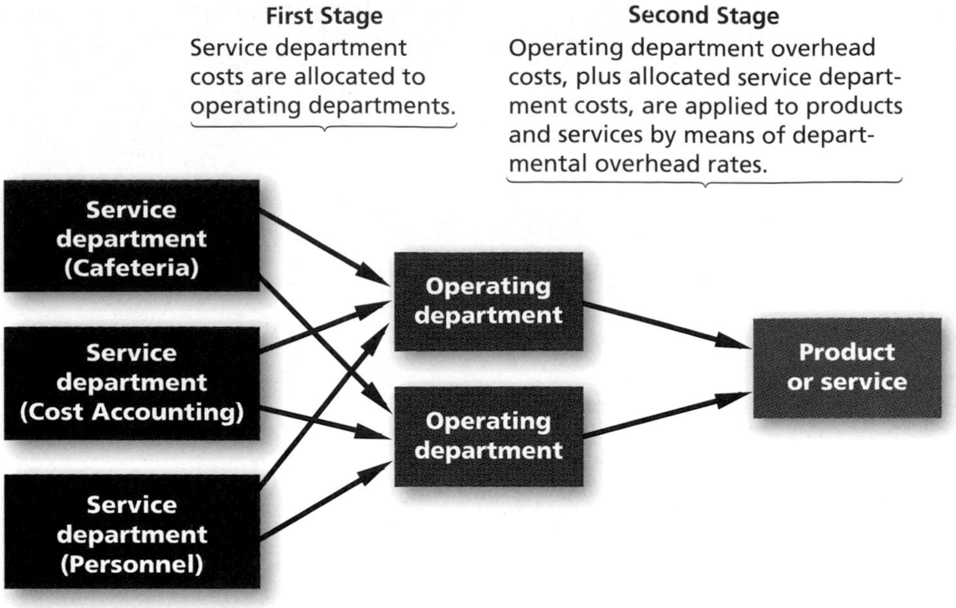

and be beyond the control of the managers of the operating divisions. Instead, the service department is held responsible for the unallocated actual costs as shown below:

	Variable	Fixed
Total actual costs incurred	$260,000	$780,000
Costs allocated (above)	250,000*	750,000
Spending variance—not allocated . . .	$ 10,000	$ 30,000

*$10 per flight-hour × 25,000 actual flight-hours = $250,000

These variances will be closed out against the company's overall revenues for the year, along with any other variances that may occur.

Effect of Allocations on Operating Departments

Once allocations have been completed, what do the operating departments do with the allocated service department costs? The allocations are typically included in performance evaluations of the operating departments and also included in determining their profitability.

In addition, if the operating departments are responsible for developing overhead rates for costing of products or services, then the allocated costs are combined with the other costs of the operating departments, and the total is used as a basis for rate computations. This rate development process is illustrated in Exhibit 16–5.

The flexible budget serves as the means for combining allocated service department costs with operating department costs and for computing overhead rates. An example is presented in Exhibit 16–6. Note from the exhibit that both variable and fixed service department costs have been allocated to Superior Company's Milling Department and are included on the latter's flexible budget. Since allocated service department costs become an integral part of the flexible budget, they are automatically included in overhead rate computations, as shown at the bottom of the exhibit.

Exhibit 16–6
Flexible Budget Containing Allocated Service Department Costs

SUPERIOR COMPANY
Flexible Budget—Milling Department

Budgeted direct labor-hours 50,000

Overhead Costs	Cost Formula (per direct labor-hour)	Direct Labor-Hours 40,000	50,000	60,000
Variable overhead costs:				
Indirect labor	$1.45	$ 58,000	$ 72,500	$ 87,000
Indirect material	0.90	36,000	45,000	54,000
Utilities	0.10	4,000	5,000	6,000
Allocation—Cafeteria	0.15	6,000	7,500	9,000
Total variable overhead cost . . .	$2.60	104,000	130,000	156,000
Fixed overhead costs:				
Depreciation		85,000	85,000	85,000
Supervisory salaries		110,000	110,000	110,000
Property taxes		9,000	9,000	9,000
Allocation—Cafeteria		**21,000**	**21,000**	**21,000**
Allocation—Human Resources		**45,000**	**45,000**	**45,000**
Total fixed overhead cost		270,000	270,000	270,000
Total overhead cost		$374,000	$400,000	$426,000

$$\text{Predetermined overhead rate} = \frac{\$400,000}{50,000 \text{ DLH}} = \$8 \text{ per direct labor-hour}$$

An Extended Example

Proctor Company has three service departments—Building Maintenance, Cafeteria, and Inspection. The company also has two operating departments—Shaping and Assembly. The service departments provide services to each other, as well as to the operating departments. Types of costs in the service departments and bases for allocation are given below:

Department	Type of Cost	Base for Allocation
Building Maintenance	Fixed costs	Square footage occupied
Cafeteria	Variable costs	Number of employees
	Fixed costs	10% to Inspection, 40% to Shaping, and 50% to Assembly
Inspection	Variable costs	Direct labor-hours
	Fixed costs	70% to Shaping and 30% to Assembly

Proctor Company allocates service department costs by the step method in the following order:

1. Building Maintenance.
2. Cafeteria.
3. Inspection.

Assume the following budgeted cost and operating data for the year:

Department	Variable Cost	Fixed Cost
Building Maintenance	—	$130,000
Cafeteria	$200 per employee	250,000
Inspection	$0.06 per direct labor-hour	548,000

Department	Number of Employees	Direct Labor-Hours	Square Footage of Space Occupied (square feet)
Building Maintenance	6*	—	3,000
Cafeteria	9*	—	4,000
Inspection	30	—	1,000
Shaping	190	300,000	8,000
Assembly	250	500,000	13,000
Total	485	800,000	29,000

*Although there are employees in both of these service departments, under the step method, costs are only allocated *forward*—never backward. For this reason, the costs of the Cafeteria Department will be allocated *forward* on the basis of the number of employees in the Inspection, Shaping, and Assembly departments.

In addition to the service department costs listed above, the company's Shaping Department has budgeted $1,340,000 in overhead costs, and its Assembly Department has budgeted $1,846,000 in overhead costs.

Cost allocations from the service departments to the operating departments are as shown in Exhibit 16–7. In the first panel of Exhibit 16–7, the variable costs of the service department are allocated to the various departments using the step method and budgeted rates and budgeted activity. For example, the variable cost of the Cafeteria Department is $200 per employee, so the Inspection Department, with 30 employees, is allocated $6,000 of this variable cost. In the second panel of Exhibit 16–7, the fixed costs of the service departments are allocated. Building Maintenance is allocated first using square feet occupied by each of the other departments as the allocation base. Then the fixed costs of the Cafeteria and Inspection departments are allocated based on the given percentages. After both the variable and fixed service department costs have been allocated, the predetermined overhead rates for the two operating departments are computed toward the bottom of the exhibit.

Some Cautions in Allocating Service Department Costs

Pitfalls in Allocating Fixed Costs

Rather than allocate fixed costs in predetermined lump-sum amounts, some firms allocate them by use of a *variable* allocation base that fluctuates from period to period. This practice can distort decisions and create serious inequities between departments. The inequities will arise from the fact that the fixed costs allocated to one department will be heavily influenced by what happens in *other* departments or segments of the organization.

To illustrate, assume that Kolby Products has an auto service center that provides maintenance work on the fleet of autos used in the company's two sales territories. The auto service center costs are all fixed. Contrary to good practice, the company allocates these fixed costs to the sales territories on the basis of actual miles driven (a variable base). Selected cost data for the last two years follow:

Exhibit 16–7

THE PROCTOR COMPANY
Beginning-of-Year Cost Allocations for Purposes of
Preparing Predetermined Overhead Rates

	Building Maintenance	Cafeteria	Inspection	Shaping	Assembly
Variable costs to be allocated	$ -0-	$ 94,000	$ 42,000	$ —	$ —
Cafeteria allocation at $200 per employee:					
30 employees × $200	—	(6,000)	6,000	—	—
190 employees × $200	—	(38,000)	—	38,000	—
250 employees × $200	—	(50,000)	—	—	50,000
Inspection allocation at $0.06 per direct labor-hour:					
300,000 DLH × $0.06	—	—	(18,000)	18,000	—
500,000 DLH × $0.06	—	—	(30,000)	—	30,000
Total	-0-	-0-	-0-	56,000	80,000
Fixed costs to be allocated	130,000	250,000	548,000		
Building Maintenance allocation at $5 per square foot:*					
4,000 square feet × $5	(20,000)	20,000	—	—	—
1,000 square feel × $5	(5,000)	—	5,000	—	—
8,000 square feet × $5	(40,000)	—	—	40,000	—
13,000 square feet × $5	(65,000)	—	—	—	65,000
Cafeteria allocation:†					
10% × $270,000	—	(27,000)	27,000	—	—
40% × $270,000	—	(108,000)	—	108,000	—
50% × $270,000	—	(135,000)	—	—	135,000
Inspection allocation: ‡					
70% × $580,000	—	—	(406,000)	406,000	—
30% × $580,000	—	—	(174,000)	—	174,000
Total	-0-	-0-	-0-	554,000	374,000
Total allocated costs	$ -0-	$ -0-	$ -0-	610,000	454,000
Other flexible budget costs at the planned activity level				1,340,000	1,846,000
Total overhead costs				$1,950,000	$2,300,000(a)
Budgeted direct labor hours				300,000	500,000(b)
Predetermined overhead rate, (a) ÷ (b)				$ 6.50	$ 4.50

*Square footage of space	29,000 square feet
Less Building Maintenance space	3,000 square feet
Net space for allocation	26,000 square feet

$$\frac{\text{Building Maintenance fixed costs, \$130,000}}{\text{Net space for allocation, 26,000 square feet}} = \text{\$5 per square foot}$$

†Cafeteria fixed costs	$250,000
Allocated from Building Maintenance	20,000
Total cost to be allocated	$270,000

Allocation percentages are given in the problem.

‡Inspection fixed costs	$548,000
Allocated from Building Maintenance	5,000
Allocated from Cafeteria	27,000
Total cost to be allocated	$580,000

Allocation percentages are given in the problem

	Year 1	Year 2
Auto service center costs (all fixed)	$120,000 (a)	$120,000 (a)
Western sales territory—miles driven	1,500,000	1,500,000
Eastern sales territory—miles driven	1,500,000	900,000
Total miles driven	3,000,000 (b)	2,400,000 (b)
Allocation rate per mile, (a) ÷ (b)	$0.04	$0.05

Notice that the Western sales territory maintained an activity level of 1,500,000 miles driven in both years. On the other hand, the Eastern sales territory allowed its activity to drop off from 1,500,000 miles in Year 1 to only 900,000 miles in Year 2. The auto service center costs that would have been allocated to the two sales territories over the two-year span using actual miles driven as the allocation base are as follows:

Year 1:	
Western sales territory: 1,500,000 miles at $0.04	$ 60,000
Eastern sales territory: 1,500,000 miles at $0.04	60,000
Total cost allocated	$120,000
Year 2:	
Western sales territory: 1,500,000 miles at $0.05	$ 75,000
Eastern sales territory: 900,000 miles at $0.05	45,000
Total cost allocated	$120,000

In Year 1, the two sales territories share the service department costs equally. In Year 2, however, the bulk of the service department costs are allocated to the Western sales territory. This is not because of any increase in activity in the Western sales territory; rather, it is because of the *decrease* in activity in the Eastern sales territory. Even though the Western sales territory maintained the same level of activity in both years, the use of a variable allocation base has caused it to be penalized with a heavier cost allocation in Year 2 because of what has happened in *another* part of the company.

This kind of inequity is almost inevitable when a variable allocation base is used to allocate fixed costs. The manager of the Western sales territory undoubtedly will be upset about the inequity forced on his territory, but he will feel powerless to do anything about it. The result will be a loss of confidence in the system and considerable ill feeling.

Beware of Sales Dollars as an Allocation Base

Over the years, sales dollars have been a favorite allocation base for service department costs. One reason is that a sales dollars base is simple, straightforward, and easy to work with. Another reason is that people tend to view sales dollars as a measure of well-being, or "ability to pay," and, hence, as a measure of how readily costs can be absorbed from other parts of the organization.

Unfortunately, sales dollars are often a very poor allocation base, for the reason that sales dollars vary from period to period, whereas the costs being allocated are often largely *fixed* in nature. As discussed earlier, if a variable base is used to allocate fixed costs, inequities can result between departments, since the costs being allocated to one department will depend in large part on what happens in *other* departments. For example, a letup in sales effort in one department will shift allocated costs off that department and onto other, more productive departments. In effect, the departments putting forth the best sales efforts are penalized in the form of higher allocations, simply because of inefficiencies elsewhere that are beyond their control. The result is often bitterness and resentment on the part of the managers of the better departments.

Consider the following situation encountered by one of the authors:

A large men's clothing store has one service department and three sales departments—Suits, Shoes, and Accessories. The Service Department's costs total $60,000 per period and are allocated to the three sales departments acording to sales dollars. A recent period showed the following allocation:

	Department			
	Suits	**Shoes**	**Accessories**	**Total**
Sales by department	$260,000	$40,000	$100,000	$400,000
Percentage of total sales	65%	10%	25%	100%
Allocation of service department costs, based on percentage of total sales	$ 39,000	$ 6,000	$ 15,000	$ 60,000

In a following period, the manager of the Suits Department launched a very successful program to expand sales by $100,000 in his department. Sales in the other two departments remained unchanged. Total service department costs also remained unchanged, but the allocation of these costs changed substantially, as shown below:

	Department			
	Suits	**Shoes**	**Accessories**	**Total**
Sales by department	$360,000	$40,000	$100,000	$500,000
Percentage of total sales	72%	8%	20%	100%
Allocation of service department costs, based on percentage of total sales	$ 43,200	$ 4,800	$ 12,000	$ 60,000
Increase (or decrease) from prior allocation	4,200	(1,200)	(3,000)	—

The manager of the Suits Department complained that as a result of his successful effort to expand sales in his department, he was being forced to carry a larger share of the service department costs. On the other hand, the managers of the departments that showed no improvement in sales were relieved of a portion of the costs that they had been carrying. Yet there had been no change in the amount of services provided for any department.

The manager of the Suits Department viewed the increased service department cost allocation to his department as a penalty for his outstanding performance, and he wondered whether his efforts had really been worthwhile after all in the eyes of top management.

Sales dollars should be used as an allocation base only in those cases where there is a direct causal relationship between sales dollars and the service department costs being allocated. In those situations where service department costs are fixed, they should be allocated according to the three guidelines discussed earlier in the chapter.

No Distinction Made between Fixed and Variable Costs

Unfortunately, many companies do not distinguish between fixed and variable costs in their service department allocations. An example of such an allocation was given earlier in Exhibit 16–4, where we first illustrated the step method.

Should All Costs Be Allocated?

As a general rule, any service department costs that are incurred as a result of specific services provided to operating departments should be allocated back to these departments and used to compute overhead rates and to measure performance and profitability. The only time when this general rule is not followed is in those situations where, in the view of the management, allocation would result in an undesirable behavioral response from people in the operating departments. This is particularly a problem when, in violation of the principles stated earlier, fixed costs are allocated to operating units on the basis of their actual usage of a service. For example, in periods when departments are under pressure to cut costs, they may be reluctant to use the services of systems design analysts and internal consultants because of the charges that would be involved.

To avoid discouraging use of a service that is beneficial to the entire organization, some firms do not charge for the service at all. These managers feel that by making such services a free commodity, departments will be more inclined to take full advantage of their benefits.

Other firms take a somewhat different approach. They agree that charging according to usage may discourage utilization of such services as systems design, but they argue that such services should not be free. Instead of providing free services, these firms take what is sometimes called a **retainer fee approach.** This is essentially the predetermined lump-sum approach discussed above for fixed costs. Each department is charged a flat amount each year, regardless of how much or how little of the service it utilizes. If a department knows it is going to be charged a certain amount for systems design services, *regardless of usage,* then it is more likely to use the service.

Focus on Current Practice

It can be unwise for a service department to offer free services to other departments, as shown by the following experience:

> [A hospital] established a policy of allowing its employees to eat all they wanted in the cafeteria, free of charge. The administration believed that the hospital's cost of providing this employee benefit would be low because the kitchen facilities were a fixed cost.
>
> However, the hospital's food services costs shot up. An investigation revealed that the employees were wasting large amounts of food. Some were taking several entrees, tasting them, and throwing the rest away.
>
> When the policy was changed and the employees were charged a token amount—about a third of a comparable meal elsewhere—the wasting of food declined dramatically. In fact, the decrease in the Food Service Department's costs were greater than the revenue generated by the nominal charge.[4] ■

Summary

Service departments are organized to provide some needed service in a single, centralized place, rather than to have all units within the organization provide the service for themselves. Although service departments do not engage directly in production or other operating activities, the costs that they incur are vital to the overall success of an

4. Leon B. Hoshower and Robert P. Crum, "Controlling Service Center Costs," *Management Accounting* 69, no. 5 (November 1987), p. 44. Used by permission.

organization and therefore are properly included as part of the cost of its products and services.

Service department costs are charged to operating departments by an allocation process. In turn, the operating departments include the allocated costs within their flexible budgets, from which overhead rates are computed for purposes of costing of products or services.

Variable and fixed service department costs should be allocated separately. The variable costs should be allocated according to whatever activity causes their incurrence. The fixed costs should be allocated in predetermined lump-sum amounts according to either the peak-period or the long-run average servicing needs of the consuming departments. Budgeted costs, rather than actual costs, should always be allocated to avoid the passing on of inefficiency between departments. Any variances between budgeted and actual service department costs should be kept within the service departments for analysis purposes, then written off against revenues or against cost of goods sold, along with other variances.

Review Problem: Direct and Step Methods

Kovac Printing Company has three service departments and two operating departments. Selected data for the five departments relating to the most recent period follow:

	Service Department			Operating Department		
	Training	Janitorial	Maintenance	Offset Printing	Lithography	Total
Overhead costs	$360,000	$210,000	$96,000	$400,000	$534,000	$1,600,000
Number of employees	120	70	280	630	420	1,520
Square feet of space occupied	10,000	20,000	40,000	80,000	200,000	350,000
Hours of press time	—	—	—	30,000	60,000	90,000

The company allocates service department costs in the following order and using the bases indicated: Training (number of employees), Janitorial (space occupied), and Maintenance (hours of press time). The company makes no distinction between variable and fixed service department costs.

Required

1. Use the direct method to allocate service department costs to the operating departments.
2. Use the step method to allocate service department costs to the operating departments.

Solution to Review Problem

1. Under the direct method, service department costs are allocated directly to the operating departments. Supporting computations for these allocations follow:

	Allocation Bases					
	Training		Janitorial		Maintenance	
Offset Printing data	630 employees	3/5	80,000 square feet	2/7	30,000 hours	1/3
Lithography data	420 employees	2/5	200,000 square feet	5/7	60,000 hours	2/3
Total	1,050 employees	5/5	280,000 square feet	7/7	90,000 hours	3/3

Given these allocation rates, the allocations to the operating departments would be as follows:

	Service Department			Operating Department		
	Training	Janitorial	Maintenance	Offset Printing	Lithography	Total
Overhead costs	$ 360,000	$ 210,000	$ 96,000	$400,000	$534,000	$1,600,000
Allocation:						
Training (3/5; 2/5)	(360,000)			216,000	144,000	
Janitorial (2/7; 5/7)		(210,000)		60,000	150,000	
Maintenance (1/3; 2/3)			(96,000)	32,000	64,000	
Total overhead cost after allocations	$ –0–	$ –0–	$ –0–	$708,000	$892,000	$1,600,000

2. Under the step method, services rendered between service departments are recognized when costs are allocated to other departments. Starting with the training service department, supporting computations for these allocations follow:

	Allocation Bases					
	Training		Janitorial		Maintenance	
Janitorial data	70 employees	5%	—		—	
Maintenance data	280 employees	20%	40,000 square feet	1/8	—	
Offset Printing data	630 employees	45%	80,000 square feet	2/8	30,000 hours	1/3
Lithography data	420 employees	30%	200,000 square feet	5/8	60,000 hours	2/3
Total	1,400 employees	100%	320,000 square feet	8/8	90,000 hours	3/3

Given these allocation rates, the allocations to the various departments would be as follows:

	Service Department			Operating Department		
	Training	Janitorial	Maintenance	Offset Printing	Lithography	Total
Overhead costs	$ 360,000	$ 210,000	$ 96,000	$400,000	$534,000	$1,600,000
Allocation:						
Training (5%; 20%; 45%; 30%)*	(360,000)	18,000	72,000	162,000	108,000	
Janitorial (1/8; 2/8; 5/8)		(228,000)	28,500	57,000	142,500	
Maintenance (1/3; 2/3)			(196,500)	65,500	131,000	
Total overhead cost after allocations	$ –0–	$ –0–	$ –0–	$684,500	$915,500	$1,600,000

*Allocation rates can be shown either in percentages, in fractions, or as a dollar rate per unit of activity. Both percentages and fractions are shown in this problem for sake of illustration. *It is better to use fractions if percentages would result in odd decimals.*

Key Terms for Review

Direct method The allocation of all of a service department's costs directly to operating departments without recognizing services provided to other service departments. (p. 758)

Interdepartmental services Services provided between service departments. Also see *Reciprocal services.* (p. 758)

Operating department A department or similar unit in an organization within which the central purposes of the organization are carried out. (p. 756)

Reciprocal method A method of allocating service department costs that gives full recognition to interdepartmental services. (p. 761)

Reciprocal services Services provided between service departments. Also see *Interdepartmental services.* (p. 758)

Retainer fee approach A method of allocating service department costs in which other departments are charged a flat amount each period regardless of usage of the service involved. (p. 772)

Service department A department that provides support or assistance to operating departments and that does not engage directly in production or in other operating activities of an organization. (p. 756)

Step method The allocation of a service department's costs to other service departments, as well as to operating departments, in a sequential manner. The sequence starts with the service department that provides the greatest amount of service to other departments. (p. 760)

Questions

16–1 What is the difference between a service department and an operating department? Give several examples of service departments.

16–2 How are service department costs assigned to products and services?

16–3 What are interdepartmental service costs? How are such costs allocated to other departments under the step method?

16–4 How are service department costs allocated to other departments under the direct method?

16–5 If a service department generates revenues, how do these revenues enter into the allocation of the department's costs to other departments?

16–6 What guidelines should govern the allocation of fixed service department costs to other departments? The allocation of variable service department costs?

16–7 "A variable base should never be used in allocating fixed service department costs to operating departments." Explain.

16–8 Why might it be desirable not to allocate some service department costs to operating departments?

Exercises

E16–1 The Ferre Publishing Company has three service departments and two operating departments. Selected data from a recent period on the five departments follow:

	Service Department			Operating Department		
	A	B	C	1	2	Total
Overhead costs	$140,000	$105,000	$48,000	$275,000	$430,000	$998,000
Number of employees	60	35	140	315	210	760
Square feet of space occupied	15,000	10,000	20,000	40,000	100,000	185,000
Hours of press time	—	—	—	30,000	60,000	90,000

The company allocates service department costs by the step method in the following order: A (number of employees), B (space occupied), and C (hours of press time). The company makes no distinction between variable and fixed service department costs.

Required Using the step method, allocate the service department costs to the operating departments.

E16–2 Refer to the data for the Ferre Publishing Company in E16–1. Assume that the company allocates service department costs by the direct method, rather than by the step method.

Required Assuming that the company uses the direct method, how much overhead cost would be allocated to each operating department?

E16–3 Hannibal Steel Company has a Transport Services Department that provides trucks to haul ore from the company's mine to its two steel mills—the Northern Plant and the Southern Plant. Budgeted costs for the Transport Services Department total $350,000 per year, consisting of $0.25 per ton variable cost and $300,000 fixed cost. The level of fixed cost is determined by peak-period requirements. During the peak period, the Northern Plant requires 70% of the Transport Services Department's capacity and the Southern Plant requires 30%.

During the coming year, 120,000 tons of ore are budgeted to be hauled for the Northern Plant and 60,000 tons of ore for the Southern Plant.

Required Compute the amount of Transport Services Department cost that should be allocated to each plant at the beginning of the year for purposes of computing predetermined overhead rates. (The company allocates variable and fixed costs separately.)

E16–4 Refer to the data in E16–3. Assume that it is now the end of the year. During the year, the Transport Services Department actually hauled the following amounts of ore for the two plants: Northern Plant, 130,000 tons; Southern Plant, 50,000 tons. The Transport Services Department incurred $364,000 in cost during the year, of which $54,000 was variable cost and $310,000 was fixed cost.

Management wants end-of-year service department cost allocations in order to compare actual performance to planned performance.

Required

1. Determine how much of the $54,000 in variable cost should be allocated to each plant.
2. Determine how much of the $310,000 in fixed cost should be allocated to each plant.
3. Should any of the $364,000 in the Transport Services Department cost not be allocated to the plants? Explain.

E16–5 Konig Enterprises, Ltd., owns and operates three restaurants in Vancouver, B.C. The company allocates its fixed administrative expenses to the three restaurants on the basis of sales dollars. During 1998, the fixed administrative expenses totaled $2,000,000. These expenses were allocated as follows:

	Restaurant			
	Rick's Harborside	Imperial Garden	Ginger Wok	Total
Total sales—1998	$16,000,000	$15,000,000	$9,000,000	$40,000,000
Percentage of total sales	40%	37.5%	22.5%	100%
Allocation (based on the above percentages)	$ 800,000	$ 750,000	$ 450,000	$ 2,000,000

During 1999, the following year, the Imperial Garden restaurant increased its sales by two-thirds. The sales levels in the other two restaurants remained unchanged. As a result of the Imperial Garden's sales increase, the company's 1999 sales data were as follows:

	Restaurant			
	Rick's Harborside	Imperial Garden	Ginger Wok	Total
Total sales—1999	$16,000,000	$25,000,000	$9,000,000	$50,000,000
Percentage of total sales	32%	50%	18%	100%

Fixed administrative expenses remained unchanged at $2,000,000 during 1999.

Required

1. Using sales dollars as an allocation base, show the allocation of the fixed administrative expenses among the three restaurants for 1999.
2. Compare your allocation from (1) above to the allocation for 1998. As the manager of the Imperial Garden, how would you feel about the allocation that has been charged to you for 1999?
3. Comment on the usefulness of sales dollars as an allocation base.

E16–6 Westlake Hospital has a Radiology Department that provides X-ray services to the hospital's three operating departments. The variable costs of the Radiology Department are allocated to the operating departments on the basis of the number of X-rays provided for each department. Budgeted and actual data relating to the cost of X-rays taken last year are given below:

	Variable Costs	
	Budgeted	Actual
Radiology Department	$18 per X-ray	$20 per X-ray

The budgeted and actual number of X-rays provided for each operating department last year follow:

	Pediatrics	OB Care	General Hospital
Budgeted number of X-rays	7,000	4,500	12,000
Actual number of X-rays taken	6,000	3,000	15,000

Required Determine the amount of Radiology Department variable cost that should have been allocated to each of the three operating departments at the end of last year for purposes of comparing actual performance to planned performance.

E16–7 Refer to Westlake Hospital in E16–6. In addition to the Radiology Department, the hospital also has a Janitorial Services Department that provides services to all other departments in the hospital. The fixed costs of the two service departments are allocated on the following bases:

Department	Basis for Allocation	
Janitorial Services	Square footage of space occupied:	
	Radiology Department	6,000 square feet
	Pediatrics	30,000 square feet
	OB Care	24,000 square feet
	General Hosptial	90,000 square feet
Radiology	Long-run average X-ray needs per year:	
	Pediatrics	9,000 X-rays
	OB Care	6,000 X-rays
	General Hospital	15,000 X-rays

Budgeted and actual fixed costs in the two service departments for the year follow:

	Janitorial Services	Radiology
Budgeted fixed costs	$375,000	$590,000
Actual fixed costs	381,000	600,000

Required

1. Show the allocation of the fixed costs of the two service departments at the beginning of the year for purposes of computing overhead rates in the operating departments. The hospital uses the step method of allocation.
2. Show the allocation of the fixed costs of the two service departments at the end of the year for purposes of comparing actual performance to planned performance.

Problems

P16–8 Cost Allocation: Step Method versus Direct Method The Sendai Co., Ltd., of Japan has budgeted costs in its various departments as follows for the coming year:

Factory Administration	¥270,000,000
Custodial Services	68,760,000
Personnel	28,840,000
Maintenance	45,200,000
Machining—overhead	376,300,000
Assembly—overhead	175,900,000
Total cost	¥965,000,000

The Japanese currency is the yen, denoted by ¥. The company allocates service department costs to other departments in the order listed below.

Department	Number of Employees	Total Labor-Hours	Square Feet of Space Occupied	Direct Labor-Hours	Machine-hours
Factory Administration	12	—	5,000	—	—
Custodial Services	4	3,000	2,000	—	—
Personnel	5	5,000	3,000	—	—
Maintenance	25	22,000	10,000	—	—
Machining	40	30,000	70,000	20,000	70,000
Assembly	60	90,000	20,000	80,000	10,000
	146	150,000	110,000	100,000	80,000

Machining and Assembly are operating departments; the other departments all act in a service capacity. The company does not make a distinction between fixed and variable service department costs. Factory Administration is allocated on the basis of labor-hours; Custodial Services on the basis of square feet occupied; Personnel on the basis of number of employees; and Maintenance on the basis of machine-hours.

Required

1. Allocate service department costs to using departments by the step method. Then compute predetermined overhead rates in the operating departments using a machine-hours basis in Machining and a direct labor-hours basis in Assembly.
2. Repeat (1) above, this time using the direct method. Again compute predetermined overhead rates in Machining and Assembly.
3. Assume that the company doesn't want to bother with allocating service department costs but simply wants to compute a single plantwide overhead rate based on total overhead costs (both service department and operating department) divided by total direct labor-hours. Compute the overhead rate.
4. Suppose a job requires machine and labor time as follows:

	Machine-Hours	Direct Labor-Hours
Machining Department	190	25
Assembly Department	10	75
Total hours	200	100

Using the overhead rates computed in (1), (2), and (3) above, compute the amount of overhead cost that would be assigned to the job if the overhead rates were developed using the step method, the direct method, and the plantwide method.

P16–9 Various Allocation Methods Sharp Motor Company has an Auto Division and a Truck Division. The company has a cafeteria that serves the employees of both divisions. The costs of operating the cafeteria are budgeted at $40,000 per month plus $3 per meal served. The company pays all the cost of the meals.

The fixed costs of the cafeteria are determined by peak-period requirements. The Auto Division is responsible for 65% of the peak-period requirements, and the Truck Division is responsible for the other 35%.

For June, the Auto Division has estimated that it will need 35,000 meals served, and the Truck Division has estimated that it will need 20,000 meals served.

Required

1. At the beginning of June, how much cafeteria cost should be allocated to each division for flexible budget planning purposes?
2. Assume that it is now the end of June. Cost records in the cafeteria show that actual fixed costs for the month totaled $42,000 and that actual meal costs totaled $128,000. Due to unexpected layoffs of employees during the month. only 20,000 meals were served to the Auto Division. Another 20,000 meals were served to the Truck Division, as planned. How much of the actual cafeteria costs for the month should be allocated to each division? (Management uses these end-of-month allocations to compare actual performance with planned performance.)
3. Refer to the data in (2) above. Assume that the company folllows the practice of allocating *all* cafeteria costs to the divisions in proportion to the number of meals served to each division during the month. On this basis, how much cost would be allocated to each division for June?
4. What criticisms can you make of the allocation method used in (3) above?
5. If managers of operating departments know that fixed service costs are going to be allocated on the basis of peak-period requirements, what will be their probable strategy as they report their estimate of peak-period requirements to the company's budget committee? As a member of top management, what would you do to neutralize any such strategies?

P16–10 Cost Allocation in a Hospital; Step Method Woodbury Hospital has three service departments and three operating departments. Estimated cost and operating data for all departments in the hospital for the forthcoming quarter are presented in the table below:

	Service Department			Operating Department			
	Housekeeping Services	Food Services	Admin. Services	Labor-atory	Radiology	General Hospital	Total
Variable costs	$ —	$193,860	$158,840	$243,600	$304,800	$ 74,500	$ 975,600
Fixed costs	87,000	107,200	90,180	162,300	215,700	401,300	1,063,680
Total cost	$87,000	$301,060	$249,020	$405,900	$520,500	$475,800	$2,039,280
Meals served	—	—	800	2,000	1,000	68,000	71,800
Percentage of peak-period needs—Food Services	—	—	0.8%	2.4%	1.6%	95.2%	100%
Square feet of space	5,000	13,000	6,500	10,000	7,500	108,000	150,000
Files processed	—	—	—	14,000	7,000	25,000	46,000
Percentage of peak-period needs—Admin. Services	—	—	—	30%	20%	50%	100%

The costs of the service department are allocated by the step method using the bases and in the order shown in the following table:

Service Department	Costs Incurred	Bases for Allocation
Housekeeping Services	Fixed	Square feet of space
Food Services	Variable	Meals served
	Fixed	Peak-period needs—Food Services
Administrative Services	Variable	Files processed
	Fixed	Peak-period needs—Admin. Services

All billing in the hospital is done through Laboratory, Radiology, or General Hospital. The hospital's administrator wants the costs of the three service departments allocated to these three billing centers.

Required Prepare the cost allocation desired by the hospital administrator. (Use the step method.) Include under each billing center the direct costs of the center, as well as the costs allocated from the service departments.

P16–11 Beginning- and End-of-Year Allocations Tasman Products, Ltd., of Australia has a Maintenance Department that services the equipment in the company's Forming Department and Assembly Department. The cost of this servicing is allocated to the operating departments on the basis of machine-hours. Cost and other data relating to the Maintenance Department and to the other two departments for the most recent year are presented below. (The currency in Australia is the Australian dollar.)

Data for the Maintenance Department follow:

	Budget	Actual
Variable costs for lubricants	$ 96,000*	$110,000
Fixed costs for salaries and other	150,000	153,000

*Budgeted at $0.40 per machine-hour.

Data for the Forming and Assembly departments follow:

	Percentage of Peak-Period Capacity Required	Machine-Hours Budget	Machine-Hours Actual
Forming Department	70%	160,000	190,000
Assembly Department	30%	80,000	70,000
Total	100%	240,000	260,000

The company allocates variable and fixed costs separately. The level of fixed costs in the Maintenance Department is determined by peak-period requirements.

Required

1. Assume that it is the beginning of the year. An allocation of Maintenance Department cost must be made to the operating departments to assist in computing predetermined overhead rates. How much of the budgeted Maintenance Department cost above would be allocated to each department?
2. Assume that it is now the end of the year. Management would like data to assist in comparing actual performance against planned performance in the Maintenance Department and in the other departments.
   a. How much of the actual Maintenance Department costs above should be allocated to the Forming Department and to the Assembly Department? Show all computations.
   b. Is there any portion of the actual Maintenance Department costs that should not be allocated to the other departments? If all costs would be allocated, explain why; if a portion would not be allocated, compute the amount and explain why it would not be allocated.

P16–12 Equity in Allocations; Computer Center "These allocations don't make any sense at all," said Bob Cosic, manager of National Airlines' Freight Division. "We used the computer less during the second quarter than we did during the first quarter, yet we were allocated more cost. Is that fair? In fact, we picked up the lion's share of the computer's cost during the second quarter, even though we're a lot smaller than the Domestic Passenger Division."

National Airlines established a Computer Center to service its three operating divisions. The company allocates the cost of the center to the divisions on the basis of the number of pages of printout for invoices, tickets, and so forth, provided each quarter. Allocations for the first two quarters to which Mr. Cosic was referring are given below:

		Division		
			Passenger	
	Total	Freight	Domestic	Overseas
First quarter actual results:				
Pages of printout	300,000	90,000	180,000	30,000
Percentage of total	100%	30%	60%	10%
Computer cost allocated	$172,000	$51,600	$103,200	$17,200
Second quarter actual results:				
Pages of printout	200,000	80,000	70,000	50,000
Percentage of total	100%	40%	35%	25%
Computer cost allocated	$168,000	$67,200	$ 58,800	$42,000

"Now don't get upset, Bob," replied Colleen Rogers, the controller. "Those allocations are fair. As you can see, your division received the largest share of the computer's output during the second quarter and therefore it has been allocated the largest share of cost. Although use of the Computer Center was off somewhat during the second quarter, keep in mind that most of the center's costs are fixed and therefore continue regardless of how much the computer is used. Also, remember that we built enough capacity into the Computer Center to handle the divisions' peak-period needs, and that cost has to be absorbed by someone. The fairest way to handle it is to charge according to usage from quarter to quarter. When you use the computer more, you get charged more; it's as simple as that."

"That's just the point," replied Cosic. "I didn't use the computer more, I used it less. So why am I charged more?"

The Freight Division requires 30% of the Computer Center's capacity during peak periods; the Domestic Passenger Division, 50%; and the Overseas Passenger Division, 20%. The peak period occurs in the fourth quarter of the year.

Required

1. Is there any merit to Mr. Cosic's complaint? Explain.
2. Using the high-low method, determine the cost formula for the Computer Center in terms of a variable rate per page and total fixed cost each quarter.
3. Reallocate the Computer Center costs for the first and second quarters in accordance with the cost allocation principles discussed in the chapter. Allocate the variable and fixed costs separately.

P16–13 Multiple Departments; Step Method; Predetermined Overhead Rates Bombay Castings, Ltd., has two producing departments, Fabrication and Finishing, and three service departments. The service departments and the bases on which their costs are allocated to using departments are listed below:

Department	Cost	Allocation Bases
Building and Grounds	Fixed	Square footage occupied
Administration	Variable	Number of employees
	Fixed	Employees at full capacity
Equipment Maintenance	Variable	Machine-hours
	Fixed	40% to Fabrication
		60% to Finishing

Indian currency is denominated in rupees, denoted here by R.

Service department costs are allocated to using departments by the step method in the order shown. The company has developed the cost and operating data given in the following table for purposes of preparing overhead rates in the two producing departments:

	Building and Grounds	Adminis-tration	Equip-ment Mainte-nance	Fabrication	Finishing	Total
Variable costs	R –0–	R22,200	R16,900	R146,000	R320,000	R 505,100
Fixed costs	88,200	60,000	24,000	420,000	490,000	1,082,200
Total cost	R88,200	R82,200	R40,900	R566,000	R810,000	R1,587,300
Budgeted employees	6	4	30	450	630	1,120
Employees at full capacity	8	4	45	570	885	1,512
Square footage of space occupied	600	500	1,400	12,000	15,500	30,000
Budgeted machine-hours	—	—	—	70,000	105,000	175,000

Required

1. Show the allocation of service department costs to producing departments for purposes of preparing overhead rates in Fabrication and Finishing.
2. Assuming that overhead rates are set on the basis of machine-hours, compute the overhead rate for each producing department.
3. Assume the following *actual* data for the year for the Administration Department:

Actual variable costs	R23,800
Actual employees for the year:	
Building and Grounds	6
Administration	4
Equipment Maintenance	32
Fabrication	460
Finishing	625
	1,127

Compute the amount of end-of-year Administration Department variable cost that should be allocated to each department. (Management uses these end-of-year allocations to compare actual performance to planned performance.)

P16–14 Cost Allocation in a Resort; Step Method The Bayview Resort has three operating units—the Convention Center, Food Services, and Guest Lodging—through which all billing is done. These three operating units are supported by three service units—General Administration, Cost Accounting, and Laundry. The costs of the service units are allocated by the step method using the bases and in the order shown below:

General Administration:

Fixed costs—allocated 10% to Cost Accounting, 4% to the Laundry, 30% to the Convention Center, 16% to Food Services, and 40% to Guest Lodging.

Cost Accounting:

Variable costs—allocated on the basis of the number of items processed each period.

Fixed costs—allocated on the basis of peak-period requirements.

Laundry:

Variable costs—allocated on the basis of the number of pounds of laundry processed each period.

Fixed costs—allocated on the basis of peak-period requirements.

Cost and operating data for all units in the resort for a recent quarter are given in the following table:

	Service Unit			Operating Unit			
	General Adminis-tration	Cost Ac-counting	Laundry	Conven-tion Center	Food Services	Guest Lodging	Total
Variable costs	$ -0-	$ 70,000	$143,000	$ -0-	$ 52,000	$ 24,000	$ 289,000
Fixed costs	200,000	110,000	65,900	95,000	375,000	486,000	1,331,900
Total overhead cost	$200,000	$180,000	$208,900	$95,000	$427,000	$510,000	$1,620,900
Pounds of laundry processed	—	—	—	20,000	15,000	210,000	245,000
Percentage of peak-period requirements—Laundry	—	—	—	10%	6%	84%	100%
Number of items processed	1,000	—	800	1,200	3,000	9,000	15,000
Percentage of peak-period requirements—Cost Accounting	—*	—	7%	13%	20%	60%	100%

*General administration is excluded from the computation of peak-period requirements due to the order in which the service unit costs are allocated.

Since all billing is done through the Convention Center, Food Services, and Guest Lodging, the resort's general manager wants the costs of the three service units allocated to these three billing centers.

Required Prepare the cost allocation desired by the resort's general manager. Include under each billing center the direct costs of the center, as well as the costs allocated from the service units.

Cases

C16–15 Direct Method; Plantwide versus Departmental Overhead Rates Hobart Products manufactures a complete line of fiberglass attaché cases and suitcases. Hobart has three manufacturing departments—Molding, Component, and Assembly—and two service departments—Power and Maintenance.

The sides of the cases are manufactured in the Molding Department. The frames, hinges, locks, and so forth, are manufactured in the Component Department. The cases are completed in the Assembly Department. Varying amounts of materials, time, and effort are required for each of the various cases. The Power Department and Maintenance Department provide services to the manufacturing departments.

Hobart has always used a plantwide overhead rate. Direct labor-hours are used to assign the overhead to products. The overhead rate is computed by dividing the company's total estimated overhead cost by the total estimated direct labor-hours to be worked in the three manufacturing departments.

Whit Portlock, manager of Cost Accounting, has recommended that the company use departmental overhead rates rather than a single, plantwide rate. Planned operating costs and expected levels of activity for the coming year have been developed by Mr. Portlock and are presented below:

	Service Department	
	Power	Maintenance
Departmental activity measures:		
Estimated usage in the coming year	80,000 KWh	12,500 hours*
Departmental costs:		
Materials and supplies	$ 500,000	$ 25,000
Variable labor	140,000	-0-
Fixed overhead	1,200,000	375,000
Total service department cost	$1,840,000	$400,000

*Hours of maintenance time.

	Manufacturing Department		
	Molding	**Component**	**Assembly**
Departmental activity measures:			
Direct labor-hours	50,000	200,000	150,000
Machine-hours	87,500	12,500	–0–
Departmental costs:			
Raw materials	$1,630,000	$3,000,000	$ 25,000
Direct labor	350,000	2,000,000	1,300,000
Variable overhead	210,500	1,000,000	1,650,000
Fixed overhead	1,750,000	620,000	749,500
Total departmental cost	$3,940,500	$6,620,000	$3,824,500

	Manufacturing Department		
	Molding	**Component**	**Assembly**
Use of service departments:			
Maintenance:			
Estimated usage in hours of maintenance time for the coming year	9,000	2,500	1,000
Percentage of peak-period Maintenance Department capacity required	70%	20%	10%
Power:			
Estimated usage in kilowatt-hours for the coming year	36,000	32,000	12,000
Percentage of peak-period Power Department capacity required	50%	35%	15%

Required

1. Assume that the company will use a single, plantwide overhead rate for the coming year, the same as in the past. Compute the plantwide rate that would be used.
2. Assume that Whit Portlock has been asked to develop departmental overhead rates for the three manufacturing departments for comparison with the plantwide rate. In order to develop these rates, do the following:
   a. Using the direct method, allocate the service department costs to the manufacturing departments. In each case, allocate the variable and fixed costs separately.
   b. Compute overhead rates for the three manufactuing departments for the coming year. In computing the rates, use a machine-hours basis in the Molding Department and a direct labor-hours basis in the other two departments.
3. Assume that Hobart Products has one small attaché case that has the following annual requirements for machine time and direct labor time in the various departments:

	Machine-Hours	Direct Labor-Hours
Molding Department	3,000	1,000
Component Department	800	2,500
Assembly Department	—	4,000
Total hours	3,800	7,500

   a. Compute the amount of overhead cost that would be allocated to this attaché case if a plantwide overhead rate is used. Repeat the computation, this time assuming that departmental overhead rates are used.
   b. Hobart Products bases its selling prices on its computed costs—adding a percentage markup. Management is concerned because this attaché case is priced well below competing products of competitors. On the other hand, certain other of Hobart's

products are priced well above the prices of competitors with the result that profits in the company are deteriorating because of declining sales. Looking at the computations in (a) above, what effect is the use of a plantwide rate having on the costing of products and therefore on selling prices?

4. What additional steps could Hobart Products take to improve its overhead costing?

(CMA, adapted)

C16–16 Step Method versus Direct Method "This is really an odd situation," said Jim Carter, general manager of Highland Publishing Company. "We get most of the jobs we bid on that require a lot of press time in the Printing Department, yet profits on those jobs are never as high as they ought to be. On the other hand, we lose most of the jobs we bid on that require a lot of time in the Binding Department. I would be inclined to think that the problem is with our overhead rates, but we're already computing separate overhead rates for each department like the trade journals advise. So what else could be wrong?"

Highland Publishing Company is a large organization that offers a variety of printing and binding work. The Printing and Binding departments are supported by three service departments. The costs of these service departments are allocated to other departments in the order listed below. (For each service department, use the allocation base that provides the best measure of service provided, as discussed in the chapter.)

Department	Total Labor-Hours	Square Feet of Space Occupied	Number of Employees	Machine-Hours	Direct Labor-Hours
Personnel	20,000	4,000	10	—	—
Custodial Services	30,000	6,000	15	—	—
Maintenance	50,000	20,000	25	—	—
Printing	90,000	80,000	40	150,000	60,000
Binding	260,000	40,000	120	30,000	175,000
	450,000	150,000	210	180,000	235,000

Budgeted overhead costs in each department for the current year are shown below (no distinction is made between variable and fixed costs):

Personnel	$ 360,000
Custodial Services	141,000
Maintenance	201,000
Printing	525,000
Binding	373,500
Total budgeted cost	$1,600,500

Because of its simplicity, the company has always used the direct method to allocate service department costs to the two operating departments.

Required

1. Using the step method, allocate the service department costs to the other departments. Then compute predetermined overhead rates for the current year using a machine-hours basis in the Printing Department and a direct labor-hours basis in the Binding Department.
2. Repeat (1) above, this time using the direct method. Again compute predetermined overhead rates in the Printing and Binding departments.
3. Assume that during the current year the company bids on a job that requires machine and labor time as follows:

	Machine-Hours	Direct Labor-Hours
Printing Department	15,400	900
Binding Department	800	2,000
Total hours	16,200	2,900

a. Determine the amount of overhead cost that would be assigned to the job if the company used the overhead rates developed in (1) above. Then determine the amount of overhead cost that would be assigned to the job if the company used the overhead rates developed in (2) above.

b. Explain to Mr. Carter, the general manager, why the step method would provide a better basis for computing predetermined overhead rates than the direct method.

Group Exercises

GE16–17 Understanding the Cost of Complexity Service departments (or production support departments in the case of a manufacturer) make up a large and growing part of the cost structure of most businesses. This is as true in hospitals, financial institutions, universities, and other service industries as it is in manufacturing. The overall costs of service departments are high and rising. In many manufacturing firms, production support department costs can average 40% or more of total manufacturing costs. Yet, in reality, very little is known about the source or behavior of these discretionary fixed costs. If you don't know where these costs came from and you don't have a good understanding of how the costs behave, it is going to be very difficult to control and reduce these costs.

In an effort to reduce costs, many companies think all they have to do is reduce head count, a demoralizing and debilitating experience not only for those who lose their jobs, but also for those who remain employed. One sure sign of problems with this head-count-reduction approach is that more than half of firms refill these positions within a year after eliminating them.

Required

1. Choose an industry with which you are somewhat familiar (or know someone who is familiar with the industry) and list seven or eight major production support or service departments in the factory or other facility in this industry. What is the output of each of these support or service departments?
2. Assume a relatively uncomplicated factory (facility) where just a single, standard product (or service) is mass produced. Describe the activity or work being done in each of the service areas of this focused firm.
3. Now assume a more complicated operation for another factory located close by where a wide range of products are made or services are offered—some are standard products/services while others are made to order, some are high-volume products/services while others are low volume, and some are fairly complex products/services while others are relatively simple. Describe the activity or work being done in the various service functions for this full-service firm.
4. Which factory or facility has higher production support costs? Why?
5. Explain the relationship between the range of products produced and the size of the support departments. When does the output of each of these support departments increase? When does the cost of each of these support departments increase?
6. Most firms are under increasing pressure to reduce costs. How would you go about bringing the overall level of service department costs down?

GE16–18 Complexity and Cost Drivers in the Purchasing Function Have several different groups contact the purchasing departments of a number of local manufacturers (one per group), a chain of grocery or retail stores, and at least one large hospital (or, if you can find a purchasing manager willing to speak to your class, that could be almost as effective). Indicate that your management accounting class is studying the purchasing function and would like to interview someone who has an in-depth knowlege of all the department's activities. The interviews should be designed to help you understand how complex purchasing has become—how many employees work in purchasing, what are their major activities, how many different parts (or items) does the company purchase, how many purchase orders are prepared during a year, how many vendors does the company deal with, how many shipments are received, what is the average size of a purchase order, how many purchase orders are for less than $500, and so forth. Once the interview is completed, organize the information in a form that can be reported to the rest of the class in an understandable fashion.

The purchasing representative may not know all of this information, especially if his or her company has not undergone a study in preparation for reducing the cost of the procurement process. That's OK. The objective here is to gain an understanding of all the complexities involved and their impact on cost.

GE16–19 Reengineering Purchasing Each group should take the information developed from GE16–18 above and begin to consider how to reduce the cost of the purchasing function while maintaining (or even improving) the quality and service level of the various activities performed. It may be helpful to speak with someone who has either reengineered his or her company's purchasing function or is applying continuous improvement techniques to reduce the time spent on low-value activities.

It would be even better if one of these individuals could speak to the class about his or her experiences in redesigning the purchasing function. (Note to the Instructor: Be sure that students complete their assignments before they hear the experiences of the speaker.)

Required

1. Who are the customers of purchasing and accounts payable and what are their requirements?
2. With the help of your instructor and starting with the preparation of a materials requisition, map out or document the process flow. Identify as many steps or tasks in the entire procurement/accounts payable process as you can.
3. Prepare a process flowchart or workflow diagram (with boxes and circles) for each step in the process. This provides a good visual reference of the order as it moves through the entire procurement cycle.
4. Determine whether each step or task is value-added (VA) or non-value-added (NVA). To determine whether a step is VA or NVA, ask if eliminating that step or task would in any way cause customer satisfaction to decline.

GE16–20 Necessity Is the Mother of Invention In an effort to reduce spending in areas where the value added is low, many companies are attempting to reduce or eliminate the "paper chase" so endemic to the purchasing and accounts payable process. Corporate management is putting pressure on purchasing and finance to cut costs of processing transactions by anywhere from 35% to 90%.

Many companies have found that purchases of less than $2,500 make up the majority of purchase orders. On average, more than half of all purchases are for less than $500. A phenomenon often observed in business—called Pareto's Law—holds forth here too: 80% of the purchases account for only 20% of the dollar volume. Most of these are for so-called MRO purchases (maintenance, repairs, and operations) for things like office supplies, replacement machine parts, machine lubrication, and other relatively low-cost items incidental to production. It can cost a company anywhere from $15 to $150 to process a purchase order (PO) and another $100 to manage the purchase. No company can afford to spend this much to process a PO of $500 or less. By some estimates, the cost to process a PO is far more costly than this once you consider the requestor's time, purchasing's time, receiving's time, accounts payable's time, and the treasury office's time, not to mention the supplier's time.

Required

If you have answered (4) of GE16–19 above, you have completed all the steps preliminary to improving or reengineering the purchasing of MRO items. How could you significantly reduce the cost of processing MRO items? Think boldly and identify all activities that can be either reduced or eliminated altogether.

IE16–21 Interpreting the Results of a Step Method Allocation Service department costs can be allocated to revenue-producing departments using the step method approach. However, how relevant are these costs for decision-making purposes? A short report concerning the costs of the University of Florida Health Science Center's Emergency Department is given on the web site gema.library.ucsf.edu:8081/Originals/SAEMabs/SA38.html.

Required

1. What is the average cost of a patient-visit at the Emergency Department (ED) according to the step method allocation?
2. How much cost could actually be saved at the Emergency Department by diverting a patient to a lower-cost facility?

IE16–22 Charging for Use of a Motor Pool The U.S. Department of Health and Human Services handles numerous grants and disbursements to government and other organizations. The department has developed guidelines for accounting for service department costs for organizations that are seeking funds. These guidelines are described on the web site www.dhhs.gov/progorg/grantsnet/state/pt4.html in the document titled "Attachment C—Requirements For Cost Allocation Plans." Find Illustration 4–5 that describes how the costs of a motor pool should be charged to user departments. For example, the Public Health Department of the county might use one of the county's motor pool cars to transport a group of public health nurses to a training session in a nearby city.

Required

1. According to the Sample Central Service Cost Allocation Plan, how should user departments be charged for the use of vehicles? How does this method differ from the method described in this text?
2. Are there any disadvantages to the method for charging for the use of motor pool vehicles that is recommended by the Department of Health and Human Services?

Chapter Seventeen

"How Well Am I Doing?" Statement of Cash Flows

Business Focus

One veteran entrepreneur describes the importance of cash flow in the following terms: "There's a hard lesson we all have to learn when we go into business. The lesson is that you live or die on cash flow. Sales are nice. Profits are even nicer. But it's cash flow that determines whether or not you survive. Where most first-time entrepreneurs trip up is in failing to understand that more sales almost always mean less cash flow—and less cash flow means trouble."

Source: Norm Brodsky, "Paying for Growth," Inc., *October 1996, p. 29.*

2 State the general rules for determining whether transactions should be classified as operating activities, investing activities, or financing activities.

3 Prepare a statement of cash flows using the indirect method to determine the "Net cash provided by operating activities."

Three major financial statements are ordinarily required for external reports—an income statement, a balance sheet, and a statement of cash flows. The purpose of the **statement of cash flows** is to highlight the major activities that directly and indirectly impact cash flows and hence affect the overall cash balance. Managers focus on cash for a very good reason—without sufficient cash at the right times, a company may miss golden opportunities or may even fall into bankruptcy.

The statement of cash flows answers questions that cannot be answered by the income statement and balance sheet. For example, the statement of cash flows can be used to answer questions like the following: Where did Delta Airlines get the cash to pay a dividend of nearly $140 million in a year in which, according to its income statement, it lost more than $1 billion? How was The Walt Disney Company able to invest nearly $800 million in expansion of its theme parks, including a major renovation of Epcot Center, despite a loss of more than $500 million on its investment in EuroDisney? Where did Wendy's International, Inc., get $125 million to expand its chain of fast-food restaurants in a year in which its net income was only $79 million and it did not raise any new debt? To answer such questions, familiarity with the statement of cash flows is required.

The statement of cash flows is a valuable analytical tool for managers as well as for investors and creditors, although managers tend to be more concerned with *prospective* statements of cash flows that are prepared as part of the budgeting process. The statement of cash flows can be used to answer crucial questions such as the following:

1. Is the company generating sufficient positive cash flows from its ongoing operations to remain viable?
2. Will the company be able to repay its debts?
3. Will the company be able to pay its usual dividend?
4. Why is there a difference between net income and net cash flow for the year?
5. To what extend will the company have to borrow money in order to make needed investments?

In this chapter, our focus is on the development of the statement of cash flows and on its use as a tool for assessing the well-being of a company.

The Basic Approach to a Statement of Cash Flows

objective 1

Know how to classify changes in noncash balance sheet accounts as sources or uses of cash.

For the statement of cash flows to be useful to managers and others, it is important that companies employ a common definition of cash. It is also important that the statement be constructed using consistent guidelines for identifying activities that are *sources* of cash and *uses* of cash. The proper definition of cash and the guidelines to use in identifying sources and uses of cash are discussed in this section.

Definition of Cash

In preparing a statement of cash flows, the term *cash* is broadly defined to include both cash and cash equivalents. **Cash equivalents** consist of short-term, highly liquid investments such as Treasury bills, commercial paper, and money market funds. Such investments are made solely for the purpose of generating a return on funds that are temporarily idle. Instead of simply holding cash, most companies invest their excess cash reserves in these types of interest-bearing assets that can be easily converted into cash. These short-term, liquid assets are usually included in *marketable securities* on the balance sheet. Since such assets are equivalent to cash, they are included with cash in preparing a statement of cash flows.

Constructing the Statement of Cash Flows Using Changes in Noncash Balance Sheet Accounts

While not the recommended procedure, a type of statement of cash flows could be constructed by simply summarizing all of the debits and credits to the Cash and Cash Equivalents accounts during a period. However, this approach would overlook all of the transactions in which there is an implicit exchange of cash. For example, when a company purchases inventory on credit, there is an implicit exchange of cash. In essence, the supplier loans the company cash, which the company then uses to acquire inventory from the supplier. Rather than just looking at the transactions that explicitly involve cash, financial statement users are interested in all of the transactions that implicitly or explicitly involve cash. When inventory is purchased on credit, the Inventory account increases, which is an implicit *use* of cash. At the same time, Accounts Payable increases, which is an implicit *source* of cash. In general, increases in the Inventory account can be classified as uses of cash and increases in the Accounts Payable account can be classified as sources of cash. This suggests that analyzing changes in balance sheet accounts, such as Inventory and Accounts Payable, will uncover both the explicit and implicit sources and uses of cash. And this is indeed the basic approach taken in the statement of cash flows. The logic underlying this approach is demonstrated in Exhibit 17–1.

Exhibit 17–1 requires some explanation. The exhibit shows how net cash flow can be explained in terms of net income, dividends, and changes in balance sheet accounts. The first line in the exhibit consists of the balance sheet equation: Assets = Liabilities + Stockholders' Equity. The first step is to recognize that assets consist of cash and noncash assets. This is shown in the second line of the exhibit. The third line in the exhibit recognizes that if the account balances are always equal, then the changes in the account balances must be equal too. The next step is simply to note that the change in cash for a period is by definition the company's net cash flow, which

Exhibit 17–1 Explaining Net Cash Flow by Analysis of the Noncash Balance Sheet Accounts

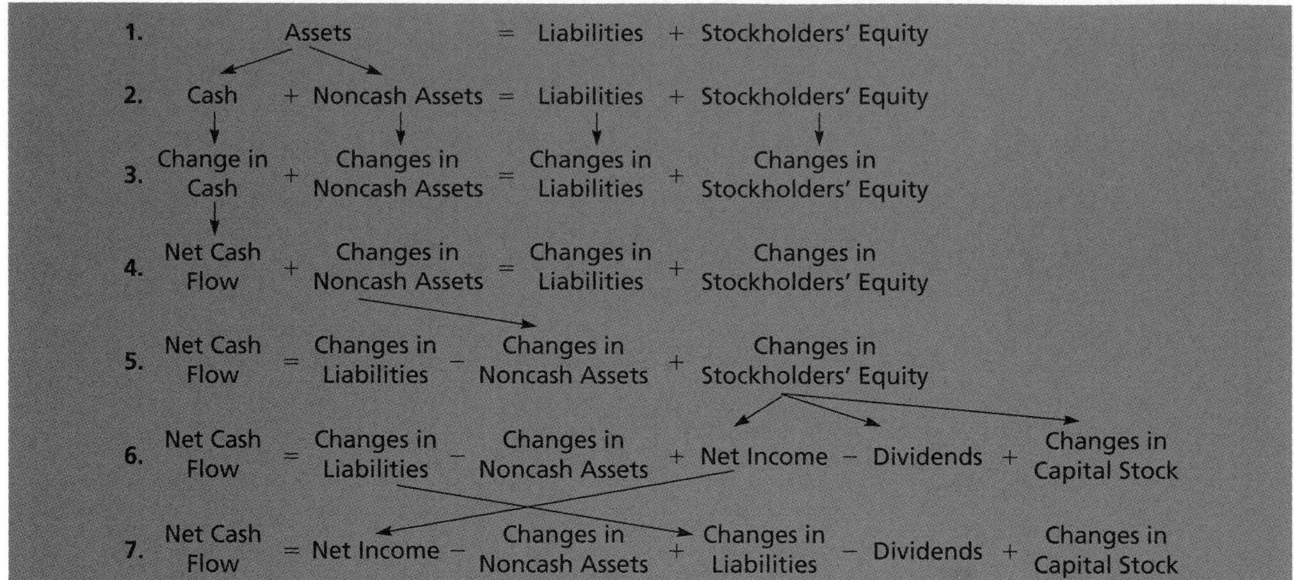

Exhibit 17–2
Classifications of Sources and Uses of Cash

	Sources (i.e., credits)	Uses (i.e., debits)
Net income	Always	
Net loss		Always
Changes in noncash assets	Decreases	Increases
Changes in liabilities*	Increases	Decreases
Changes in capital stock accounts .	Increases	Decreases
Dividends paid to stockholders		Always
	Total sources −	Total uses = Net cash flow

*Contra asset accounts, such as the Accumulated Depreciation and Amortization account, follow the rules for liabilities.

yields line 4 in the exhibit. The only difference between line 4 and line 5 is that the changes in noncash assets is moved from the left-hand side of the equation to the right-hand side. This is done because we are attempting to explain net cash flow, so it should be by itself on the left-hand side of the equation. To get from line 5 to line 6, we need to remember that stockholders' equity is affected by net income, dividends, and changes in capital stock. Net income increases stockholders' equity, while dividends reduce stockholders' equity. To get from line 6 of the exhibit to line 7, a few terms on the right-hand side of the equation are rearranged.

According to equation 7 in Exhibit 17–1, the net cash flow for a period can be determined by starting with net income, then deducting changes in noncash assets, adding changes in liabilities, deducting dividends paid to stockholders, and finally adding changes in capital stock. It is important to realize that changes in accounts can be either increases (positive) or decreases (negative), and this affects how we should interpret equation 7 in Exhibit 17–1. For example, increases in liabilities are added back to net income, whereas decreases in liabilities are deducted from net income to arrive at the net cash flow. On the other hand, increases in noncash assets are deducted from net income while decreases in noncash assets are added back to net income. Exhibit 17–2 summarizes the appropriate classifications—in terms of sources and uses—of net income, dividends, and changes in the noncash balance sheet accounts.

The classifications in Exhibit 17–2 seem to make sense. Positive net income generates cash, whereas a net loss consumes cash. Decreases in noncash assets, such as sale of inventories or property, are a source of cash. Increases in noncash assets, such as purchase of inventories or property, are a use of cash. Increases in liabilities, such as taking out a loan, are a source of cash. Decreases in liabilities, such as paying off a loan, are a use of cash. Increases in capital stock accounts, such as sale of common stock, are a source of cash. And payments of dividends to stockholders use cash.

Constructing a simple statement of cash flows is a straightforward process. Begin with net income (or net loss) and then add to it everything listed as sources in Exhibit 17–2 and subtract from it everything listed as uses. This will be illustrated with an example in the next section.

An Example of a Simplified Statement of Cash Flows

To illustrate the ideas introduced in the preceding section, we construct in this section a *simplified* statement of cash flows for Nordstrom, Inc., one of the leading fashion retailers in the United States. This simplified statement does not follow the format required by the FASB for external financial reports, but it shows where the numbers come from in a statement of cash flows and how they fit together. In later sections, we will show how the same basic data can be used to construct a full-fledged statement of cash flows that would be acceptable for external reports.

Constructing a Simplified Statement of Cash Flows

According to Exhibit 17–2, to construct a statement of cash flows we need the company's net income or loss, the changes in each of its balance sheet accounts, and the dividends paid to stockholders for the year. We can obtain this information from the Nordstrom financial statements that appear in Exhibits 17–3, 17–4, and 17–5. In a few

Exhibit 17–3

NORDSTROM, INC.*
Income Statement
(dollars in millions)

Net sales	$3,638
Less cost of sales	2,469
Gross margin	1,169
Less operating expenses	941
Net operating income	228
Nonoperating items:	
Gain on sale of store	3
Income before taxes	231
Less income taxes	91
Net income	$ 140

*This statement is loosely based on an actual income statement published by Nordstrom. Among other differences, there was no "Gain on sale of store" in the original statement. This "gain" has been included here to illustrate how to handle gains and losses on a statement of cash flows.

Exhibit 17–4

NORDSTROM, INC.*
Comparative Balance Sheet
(dollars in millions)

	Ending Balance	Beginning Balance	Change	Source or Use?
Assets				
Current assets:				
Cash and cash equivalents	$ 91	$ 29	**$ +62**	
Accounts receivable	637	654	−17	Source
Merchandise inventory	586	537	+49	Use
Total current assets	1,314	1,220		
Property, buildings, and equipment	1,517	1,394	+123	Use
Less accumulated depreciation and amortization	654	561	+93	Source
Net property, buildings, and equipment	863	833		
Total assets	$2,177	$2,053		
Liabilities and Stockholders' Equity				
Current liabilities:				
Accounts payable	$ 264	$ 220	+44	Source
Accrued wages and salaries payable	193	190	+3	Source
Accrued income taxes payable	28	22	+6	Source
Notes payable	40	38	+2	Source
Total current liabilities	525	470		
Long-term debt	439	482	−43	Use
Deferred income taxes	47	49	−2	Use
Total liabilities	1,011	1,001		
Stockholders' equity:				
Common stock	157	155	+2	Source
Retained earnings	1,009	897	+112	†
Total stockholders' equity	1,166	1,052		
Total liabilities and stockholders' equity	$2,177	$2,053		

*This statement differs from the actual statement published by Nordstrom.

†The change in retained earnings of $112 million equals the net income of $140 million less the cash dividends paid to stockholders of $28 million. Net income is classified as a source and dividends as a use.

Exhibit 17–5

NORDSTROM, INC.*
Statement of Retained Earnings
(dollars in millions)

Retained earnings, beginning balance	$ 897
Add: Net income	140
	1,037
Deduct: Dividends paid	28
Retained earnings, ending balance	$1,009

*This statement differs in a few details from the actual statement published by Nordstrom.

Exhibit 17–6

NORDSTROM, INC.
Simplified Statement of Cash Flows
(dollars in millions)

Note: This simplified statement is for illustration purposes only. It should *not* be used to complete end-of-chapter homework assignments or for preparing an actual statement of cash flows. See Exhibit 17–12 for the proper format for a statement of cash flows.

Sources		
Net income	$140	
Decreases in noncash assets:		
Decrease in accounts receivable	17	
Increases in liabilities (and contra asset accounts):		
Increase in accumulated depreciation and amortization	93	
Increase in accounts payable	44	
Increase in accrued wages and salaries	3	
Increase in accrued income taxes	6	
Increase in notes payable	2	
Increases in capital stock accounts:		
Increase in common stock	2	
Total sources		$307
Uses		
Increases in noncash assets:		
Increase in merchandise inventory	49	
Increase in property, buildings, and equipment	123	
Decreases in liabilities:		
Decrease in long-term debt	43	
Decrease in deferred income taxes	2	
Dividends	28	
Total uses		245
Net cash flow		$ 62

instances, the actual statements have been simplified for ease of computation and discussion.

Note that changes between the beginning and ending balances have been computed for each of the balance sheet accounts in Exhibit 17–4, and each change has been classified as a source or use of cash. For example, accounts receivable decreased by $17 million. And, according to Exhibit 17–2, a decrease in such an asset account is classified as a source of cash.

A *simplified* statement of cash flows appears in Exhibit 17–6. This statement was constructed by gathering together all of the entries listed as sources in Exhibit 17–4 and all of the entries listed as uses. The sources exceeded the uses by $62 million. This is the net cash flow for the year and is also, by definition, the change in cash and cash equivalents for the year. (Trace this $62 million figure back to Exhibit 17–4.)

The Need for a More Detailed Statement

While the simplified statement of cash flows in Exhibit 17–6 is not difficult to construct, it is not acceptable for external financial reports and is not as useful as it could be for internal reports. The FASB requires that the statement of cash flows follow a different format and that a few of the entries be modified. Nevertheless, almost all of the entries on a full-fledged statement of cash flows are the same as the entries on the simplified statement of cash flows—they are just in a different order.

In the following sections, we will discuss the modifications to the simplified statement that are necessary to conform to external reporting requirements.

Organization of the Full-Fledged Statement of Cash Flows

objective 2

State the general rules for determining whether transactions should be classified as operating activities, investing activities, or financing activities.

To make it easier to compare statements of cash flows from different companies, the Financial Accounting Standards Board (FASB) requires that companies follow prescribed rules for preparing the statement of cash flows. Most companies follow these rules for internal reports as well as for external financial statements.

One of the FASB requirements is that the statement of cash flows be divided into three sections: *operating activities, investing activities,* and *financing activities.* The guidelines to be followed in classifying transactions under these three heads are summarized in Exhibit 17–7 and discussed below.

Operating Activities

Generally, **operating activities** are those activities that enter into the determination of net income. Technically, however, the FASB defines operating activities as all the transactions that are not classified as investing or financing activities. Generally speaking, this includes all transactions affecting current assets. It also includes all transactions affecting current liabilities except for issuing and repaying a note payable. Operating activities also include changes in noncurrent balance sheet accounts that directly affect net income such as the Accumulated Depreciation and Amortization account.

Investing Activities

Generally speaking, transactions that involve acquiring or disposing of noncurrent assets are classified as **investing activities.** These transactions include acquiring or selling property, plant, and equipment; acquiring or selling securities held for long-term investment, such as bonds and stocks of other companies; and lending money to another entity (such as a subsidiary) and the subsequent collection of the loan. However, as previously discussed, changes in noncurrent assets that directly affect net income such as depreciation and amortization charges are classified as operating activities.

Exhibit 17–7
Guidelines for Classifying Transactions as Operating, Investing, and Financing Activities

- Operating activities
  - Net income
  - Changes in current assets
  - Changes in noncurrent assets that affect net income (e.g., depreciation)
  - Changes in current liabilities (except for debts to lenders and dividends payable)
  - Changes in noncurrent liabilities that affect net income
- Investing activities
  - Changes in noncurrent assets that are not included in net income
- Financing activities:
  - Changes in the current liabilities that are debts to lenders rather than obligations to suppliers, employees, or the government
  - Changes in noncurrent liabilities that are not included in net income
  - Changes in capital stock accounts
  - Dividends

Financing Activities

As a general rule, borrowing from creditors or repaying creditors as well as transactions with the company's owners are classified as **financing activities.** For example, when a company borrows money by issuing a bond, the transaction is classified as a financing activity. However, transactions with creditors that affect net income are classified as operating activities. For example, interest on the company's debt is included in operating activities rather than financing activities because interest is deducted as an expense in computing net income. In contrast, dividend payments to owners do not affect net income and therefore are classified as financing rather than operating activities.

Most changes in current liabilities are considered to be operating activities unless the transaction involves borrowing money directly from a lender, as with a note payable, or repaying such a debt. Transactions involving accounts payable, wages payable, and taxes payable are included in operating activities rather than financing activities, since these transactions occur on a routine basis and involve the company's suppliers, employees, and the government rather than lenders.

Other Issues in Preparing the Statement of Cash Flows

We must consider several other issues before we can illustrate the preparation of a statement of cash flows that would be acceptable for external financial reports. These issues are (1) whether amounts on the statement should be presented gross or net, (2) whether operating activities should be presented using the direct or indirect method, and (3) whether direct exchanges should be reported on the statement.

Cash Flows: Gross or Net?

For both financing and investing activities, items on the statement of cash flows should be presented in gross amounts rather than in net amounts. To illustrate, suppose that Macy's Department Stores purchases $50 million in property during the year and sells other property for $30 million. Instead of showing the net change of $20 million, the company must show the gross amounts of both the purchases and the sales. The purchases would be recorded as a use of cash, and the sales would be recorded as a source of cash. In like manner, if Alcoa receives $80 million from the issue of long-term bonds and then pays out $30 million to retire other bonds, the two transactions must be reported separately on the statement of cash flows rather than being netted against each other.

The gross method of reporting does *not* extend to operating activities, where debits and credits to an account are ordinarily netted against each other on the statement of cash flows. For example, if Sears adds $600 million to its accounts receivable as a result of sales during the year and $520 million of receivables is collected, only the net increase of $80 million would be reported on the statement of cash flows.

Operating Activities: Direct or Indirect Method?

The net result of the cash inflows and outflows arising from operating activities is known formally as the **"Net cash provided by operating activities."** This figure can be computed by either the direct or the indirect method.

Under the **direct method,** the income statement is reconstructed on a cash basis from top to bottom. For example, in the direct method, cash collected from customers is used instead of revenue, and payments to suppliers is used instead of cost of sales. In essence, cash receipts are counted as revenues and cash disbursements are counted as expenses. The difference between the cash receipts and cash disbursements is the net cash provided by operating activities for the period.

Under the **indirect method,** the operating activities section of the statement of cash flows is constructed by starting with net income and adjusting it to a cash basis. That is, rather than directly computing cash sales, cash expenses, and so forth, these amounts are arrived at *indirectly* by removing from net income any items that do not affect cash flows. The indirect method has an advantage over the direct method in that it shows the reasons for any differences between net income and the net cash provided by operating activities. The indirect method is also known as the **reconciliation method.**

Which method should be used for constructing the operating activities section of the statement of cash flows—the direct method or the indirect method? Both methods will result in exactly the same figure for the net cash provided by operating activities. However, for external reporting purposes, the FASB *recommends* and *encourages* the use of the direct method. But there is a catch. If the direct method is used, there must be a supplementary reconciliation of net income with operating cash flows. In essence, if a company chooses to use the direct method, it must also go to the trouble to construct a statement in which a form of the indirect method is used. However, if a company chooses to use the indirect method for determining the net cash flows from operating activities, there is no requirement that it also report the results of using the direct method.

Not surprisingly, a recent survey of 600 companies revealed that only 11, or 1.8%, use the direct method to construct the statement of cash flows for external reports.[1] The remaining 98.2% probably use the indirect method because it is simply less work. While there are some good reasons for using the direct method, we use the indirect method in this chapter. The direct method is discussed and illustrated in Appendix 17A at the end of the chapter.

Direct Exchange Transactions

Companies sometimes enter into **direct exchange transactions** in which noncurrent balance sheet items are swapped. For example, a company might issue common stock that is directly exchanged for property. Or a company might induce its creditors to swap their long-term debt for common stock of the company. Or a company might acquire equipment under a long-term lease contract offered by the seller.

Direct exchange transactions are not reported on the statement of cash flows. However, such direct exchanges are disclosed in a separate schedule that accompanies the statement.

An Example of a Full-Fledged Statement of Cash Flows

In this section, we apply the FASB rules to construct a statement of cash flows for Nordstrom that would be acceptable for external reporting. The approach we take is based on an analysis of changes in balance sheet accounts, as in our earlier discussion of the simplified statement of cash flows. Indeed, as you will see, the full-fledged state-

1. American Institute of Certified Public Accountants, *Accounting Trends and Techniques: 1996* (Jersey City, NJ, 1997), p. 495.

objective 3

Prepare a statement of cash flows using the indirect method to determine the "Net cash provided by operating activities."

ment of cash flows is for the most part just a reorganized form of the simplified statement that appears in Exhibit 17–6.

The format for the operating activities part of the statement of cash flows is shown in Exhibit 17–8. For example, consider the effect of an increase in the Accounts Receivable account on the net cash provided by operating activities. Since the Accounts Receivable account is a noncash asset, we know from Exhibit 17–2 that increases in this account are treated as *uses* of cash. In other words, increases in Accounts Receivable are deducted when determining net cash flows. Intuitive explanations for this and other adjustments are sometimes slippery, but commonly given explanations are listed in Exhibit 17–9 for some of these adjustments. For example, Exhibit 17–9 suggests that an increase in Accounts Receivable is deducted from net income because sales have been recorded for which no cash has been collected. Therefore, to adjust net income to a cash basis, the increase in the Accounts Receivable account must be deducted from net income to show that cash-basis sales are less than reported sales. However, we can more simply state that an increase in Accounts Receivable is deducted when computing net cash flows because, according to the logic of Exhibits 17–1 and 17–2, increases in all noncash assets must be deducted.

Eight Basic Steps to Preparing the Statement of Cash Flows

We recommend that you use a worksheet such as the one in Exhibit 17–10 on page 804 to prepare the statement of cash flows. Preparing a statement of cash flows can be confusing, and important details can be easily overlooked without such an aid. The work-

Exhibit 17–8 General Model: Indirect Method of Determining the "Net Cash Provided by Operating Activities"

	Add (+) or Deduct (−) to Adjust Net Income
Net income	$XXX
Adjustments needed to convert net income to a cash basis:	
Depreciation, depletion, and amortization charges	+
Add (deduct) changes in current asset accounts affecting revenue or expense:*	
Increase in the account	−
Decrease in the account	+
Add (deduct) changes in current liability accounts affecting revenue or expense:†	
Increase in the account	+
Decrease in the account	−
Add (deduct) gains or losses on sales of assets:	
Gain on sales of assets	−
Loss on sales of assets	+
Add (deduct) changes in the Deferred Income Taxes account:	
Increase in the account	+
Decrease in the account	−
Net cash provided by operating activities	$XXX

*Examples include accounts receivable, accrued receivables, inventory, and prepaid expenses.

†Examples include accounts payable, accrued liabilities, and taxes payable.

Exhibit 17–9 Explanation of Adjustments for Changes in Current Asset and Current Liability Accounts (see Exhibit 17–8)

	Change in the Account	This Change Means That . . .	Therefore, to Adjust to a Cash Basis under the Indirect Method, We Must . . .
Accounts Receivable and Accrued Receivables	Increase	Sales (revenues) have been reported for which no cash has been collected.	Deduct the amount from net income to show that cash-basis sales are less than reported sales (revenues).
	Decrease	Cash has been collected for which no sales (revenues) have been reported for the current period.	Add the amount to net income to show that cash-basis sales are greater than reported sales (revenues).
Inventory	Increase	Goods have been purchased that are not included in cost of goods sold (COGS).	Deduct the amount from net income to show that cash-basis COGS is greater than reported COGS.
	Decrease	Goods have been included in COGS that were purchased in a prior period.	Add the amount to net income to show that cash-basis COGS is less than reported COGS.
Prepaid Expenses	Increase	More cash has been paid out for services than has been reported as expense.	Deduct the amount from net income to show that cash-basis expenses are greater than reported expenses.
	Decrease	More has been reported as expense for services than has been paid out in cash.	Add the amount to net income to show that cash-basis expenses are less than reported expenses.
Accounts Payable and Accrued Liabilities	Increase	More has been reported as expense for goods and services than has been paid out in cash.	Add the amount to net income to show that cash-basis expenses for goods and services are less than reported expenses.
	Decrease	More cash has been paid out for goods and services than has been reported as expense.	Deduct the amount from net income to show that cash-basis expenses for goods and services are greater than reported expenses.
Taxes Payable	Increase	More income tax expense has been reported than has been paid out in cash.	Add the amount to net income to show that cash-basis expenses are less than reported expenses.
	Decrease	More cash has been paid to the tax authorities than has been reported as income tax expense.	Deduct the amount from net income to show that cash-basis expenses are greater than reported expenses.

sheet in Exhibit 17–10 and statement of cash flows can be prepared using the eight steps that follow. This brief summary of the steps will be followed by more detailed explanations later.

1. Copy onto the worksheet the title of each account appearing on the comparative balance sheet except for cash and cash equivalents and retained earnings. To avoid confusion, contra asset accounts such as the Accumulated Depreciation and Amortization account should be listed with the liabilities. Contra asset accounts are treated the same way as liabilities on the statement of cash flows.
2. Compute the change from the beginning balance to the ending balance in each balance sheet account. Break the change in retained earnings down into net income and dividends paid to stockholders.
3. Using Exhibit 17–2 as a guide, code each entry on the worksheet as a source or a use.

4. Under the Cash Flow Effect column, write sources as positive numbers and uses as negative numbers.
5. Make any necessary adjustments to reflect gross, rather than net, amounts involved in transactions—including adjustments for gains and losses. Some of these adjustments may require adding new entries to the bottom of the worksheet. The net effect of all such adjusting entries must be zero.
6. Classify each entry on the worksheet as an operating activity, investing activity, or financing activity according to the FASB's criteria, as given in Exhibit 17–7.
7. Copy the data from the worksheet to the statement of cash flows section by section, starting with the operating activities section.
8. At the bottom of the statement of cash flows prepare a reconciliation of the beginning and ending balances of cash and cash equivalents. The net change in cash and cash equivalents shown at the bottom of this statement should equal the change in the Cash and Cash Equivalents accounts during the year.

On the following pages we will apply these eight steps to the data contained in the comparative balance sheet for Nordstrom, Inc., found in Exhibit 17–4 on page 796. *As we discuss each step, refer to Exhibit 17–4 and trace the data from this exhibit into the worksheet in Exhibit 17–10.*

Setting Up the Worksheet (Steps 1–4)

As indicated above, step 1 in preparing the worksheet is to simply list all of the relevant account titles from the company's balance sheet. Note that we have done this for Nordstrom, Inc., on the worksheet in Exhibit 17–10. (The titles of Nordstrom's accounts have been taken from the company's comparative balance sheet, which is found in Exhibit 17–4 on page 796.) The only significant differences between Nordstrom's balance sheet accounts and the worksheet listing are that (1) the Accumulated Depreciation and Amortization account has been moved down with the liabilities on the worksheet, (2) the Cash and Cash Equivalents accounts have been omitted, and (3) the change in retained earnings has been broken down into net income and dividends.

As stated in step 2, the change in each account's balance during the year is listed in the first column of the worksheet. We have entered these changes for Nordstrom's accounts onto the worksheet in Exhibit 17–10. (Refer to Nordstrom's comparative balance sheet in Exhibit 17–4 to see how these changes were computed.)

Then, as indicated in step 3, each change on the worksheet is classified as either a source or a use of cash. Whether a change is a source or a use can be determined by referring back to Exhibit 17–2 on page 794, where we first discussed these classifications. For example, Nordstrom's Merchandise Inventory account increased by $49 million during the year. According to Exhibit 17–2, increases in noncash asset accounts are classified as uses of cash, so an entry has been made to that effect in the second column of the worksheet for the Merchandise Inventory account.

So far, nothing is new. All of this was done already in Exhibit 17–4 in preparation for constructing the simplified statement of cash flows. Step 4 is mechanical, but it helps prevent careless errors. Sources are coded as positive changes and uses as negative changes in the Cash Flow Effect column on the worksheet.

Adjustments to Reflect Gross, Rather than Net, Amounts (Step 5)

As discussed earlier, the FASB requires that gross, rather than net, amounts be disclosed in the investing and financing sections. This rule requires special treatment of gains and losses. To illustrate, suppose that Nordstrom decided to sell an old store and

Exhibit 17–10

NORDSTROM, INC.
Statement of Cash Flows Worksheet
(dollars in millions)

	(1) Change	(2) Source or Use?	(3) Cash Flow Effect	(4) Adjustments	(5) Adjusted Effect (3)+(4)	(6) Classification*
Assets (except cash and cash equivalents)						
Current assets:						
Accounts receivable	$ −17	Source	$ +17		$ +17	Operating
Merchandise inventory	**+49**	Use	−49		−49	Operating
Noncurrent assets:						
Property, buildings, and equipment	+123	Use	−123	$−15	**−138**	Investing
Contra Assets, Liabilities, and Stockholders' Equity						
Contra assets:						
Accumulated depreciation and amortization	+93	Source	+93	+10	**+103**	Operating
Current liabilities:						
Accounts payable	+44	Source	+44		+44	Operating
Accrued wages and salaries payable	+3	Source	+3		+3	Operating
Accrued income taxes payable	+6	Source	+6		+6	Operating
Notes payable	+2	Source	+2		+2	Financing
Noncurrent liabilities:						
Long-term debt	−43	Use	−43		−43	Financing
Deferred income taxes		Use	−2		−2	Operating
Stockholders' equity:						
Common stock	+2	Source	+2		+2	Financing
Retained earnings:						
Net income	+140	Source	+140		+140	Operating
Dividends	−28	Use	−28		−28	Financing
Additional Entries						
Proceeds from sale of store				+8	**+8**	Investing
Gain on sale of store				−3	−3	Operating
Total (net cash flow)			$ +62	$ 0	$ +62	

*See Exhibit 17–11 (page 806) for the reasons for these classifications.

move its retail operations to a new location. Assume that the original cost of the old store was $15 million, its accumulated depreciation was $10 million, and that it was sold for $8 million in cash. The journal entry to record this transaction appears below:

Cash	8,000,000	
Accumulated Depreciation and Amortization	10,000,000	
Property, Buildings, and Equipment		15,000,000
Gain on Sale		3,000,000

The $3 million gain is reflected in the income statement in Exhibit 17–3 on page 795.

We can reconstruct the gross additions to the Property, Buildings, and Equipment account and the gross charges to the Accumulated Depreciation and Amortization account with the help of T-accounts:

Property, Buildings, and Equipment				**Accumulated Depreciation and Amortization**			
Bal.	1,394					561	Bal.
Additions (plug*)	138	15	Disposal of store	Disposal of store	10	103	Depreciation charges (plug)
Bal.	1,517					654	Bal.

*By *plug* we mean the balancing figure in the account.

According to the FASB rules, the gross additions of $138 million to the Property, Buildings, and Equipment account should be disclosed on the statement of cash flows rather than the net change in the account of $123 million ($1,517 million − $1,394 million = $123 million). Likewise, the gross depreciation charges of $103 million should be disclosed rather than the net change in the Accumulated Depreciation and Amortization account of $93 million ($654 million − $561 million = $93 million). And the cash proceeds of $8 million from sale of the building should also be disclosed on the statement of cash flows. All of this is accomplished, while preserving the correct overall net cash flows on the statement, by using the above journal entry to make adjusting entries on the worksheet. As indicated in Exhibit 17–2, the debits are recorded as positive adjustments, and the credits are recorded as negative adjustments. These adjusting entries are recorded under the Adjustments column in Exhibit 17–10.

It may not be clear why the gain on the sale is *deducted* in the operating activities section of the statement of cash flows. The company's $140 million net income, which is part of the operating activities section, includes the $3 million gain on the sale of the store. But this $3 million gain must be reported in the *investing* activities section of the statement of cash flows as part of the $8 million proceeds from the sale transaction. Therefore, to avoid double counting, the $3 million gain is deducted from net income in the operating activities section of the statement. The adjustments we have made on the worksheet accomplish this. The $3 million gain will be deducted in the operating activities section, and all $8 million of the sale proceeds will be shown as an investing item. As a result, all of the gain will be included in the investing section of the statement of cash flows and none of it will be in the operating activities section. There will be no double-counting of the gain.

In the case of a loss on the sale of an asset, we do the opposite. The loss is added back to the net income figure in the operating activities section of the statement of cash flows. Whatever cash proceeds are received from the sale of the asset are reported in the investing activities section.

Before turning to step 6 in the process of building the statement of cash flows, one small step is required. Add the Adjustments in column (4) to the Cash Flow Effect in column (3) to arrive at the Adjusted Effect in column (5).

Classifying Entries as Operating, Investing, or Financing Activities (Step 6)

In step 6, each entry on the worksheet is classified as an operating, investing, or financing activity using the guidelines in Exhibit 17–7 on page 798. These classifications are entered directly on the worksheet in Exhibit 17–10 and are explained in Exhibit 17–11. Most of these classifications are straightforward, but the classification of the change in the Deferred Income Taxes account may require some additional explanation. Because of the way income tax expense is determined for financial reporting purposes, the expense that appears on the income statement often differs from the taxes that are actually owed to the government. Usually, the income tax expense overstates the

Exhibit 17–11 Classifications of Entries on Nordstrom's Statement of Cash Flows

Entry	Classification	Reason
• Changes in Accounts Receivable and Merchandise Inventory	Operating activity	Changes in current assets are included in operating activities.
• Change in Property, Buildings, and Equipment	Investing activity	Changes in noncurrent assets that do not directly affect net income are included in investing activities.
• Change in Accumulated Depreciation and Amortization	Operating activity	Depreciation and amortization directly affect net income and are therefore included in operating activities.
• Changes in Accounts Payable, Accrued Wages and Salaries Payable, and Accrued Income Taxes Payable	Operating activity	Changes in current liabilities (except for notes payable) are included in operating activities.
• Change in Notes Payable	Financing activity	Issuing or repaying notes payable is classified as a financing activity.
• Change in Long-Term Debt	Financing activity	Changes in noncurrent liabilities that do not directly affect net income are included in financing activities.
• Change in Deferred Income Taxes	Operating activity	Deferred income taxes result from income tax expense that directly affects net income. Therefore, this entry is included in operating activities.
• Change in Common Stock	Financing activity	Changes in capital stock accounts are always included in financing activities.
• Net income	Operating activity	Net income is always included in operating activities.
• Dividends	Financing activity	Dividends paid to stockholders are always included in financing activities.
• Proceeds from sale of store	Investing activity	The gross amounts received on disposal of noncurrent assets are included in investing activities.
• Gains from sale of store	Operating activity	Gains and losses directly affect net income and are therefore included in operating activities.

company's actual income tax liability for the year. When this happens, the journal entry to record income taxes includes a credit to Deferred Income Taxes:

Income Tax Expense	XXX	
Income Taxes Payable		XXX
Deferred Income Taxes (plug)		XXX

Since deferred income taxes arise directly from the computation of an expense, the changes in the Deferred Income Taxes account is included in the operating activities section of the statement of cash flows.

In the case of Nordstrom, the Deferred Income Taxes account decreased during the year, so income tax expense was apparently less than the company's income tax liability for the year by $2 million. In other words, for some reason Nordstrom had to pay the government $2 million more than the income tax expense recorded on the income statement, and therefore this additional cash outflow must be deducted to convert net income to a cash basis. Or, looking back again to Exhibit 17–2, Deferred Income Taxes is a liability account. Since this liability account decreased during the year, the change is counted as a use of cash and is deducted in determining net cash flow for the year.

The Completed Statement of Cash Flows (Steps 7 and 8)

Once the worksheet is completed, it is easy to complete step 7 by constructing an actual statement of cash flows. Nordstrom's statement of cash flows appears in Exhibit 17–12. Trace each item from the worksheet into this statement.

The operating activities section of the statement follows the format laid out in Exhibit 17–8, beginning with net income. The other entries in the operating activities section are considered to be adjustments required to convert net income to a cash basis. The sum of all of the entries under the operating activities section is called the "Net cash provided by operating activities."

The investing activities section comes next on the statement of cash flows. The worksheet entries that have been classified as investing activities are recorded in this section in any order. The sum of all the entries in this section is called the "Net cash used for investing activities."

The financing activities section of the statement follows the investing activities section. The worksheet entries that have been classified as financing activities are recorded in this section in any order. The sum of all of the entries in this section is called the "Net cash provided by financing activities."

Finally, for step 8, the bottom of the statement of cash flows contains a reconciliation of the beginning and ending balances of cash and cash equivalents.

Exhibit 17–12

NORDSTROM, INC.*
Statement of Cash Flows—Indirect Method
(dollars in millions)

Operating Activities	
Net income	$ 140
Adjustments to convert net income to a cash basis:	
Depreciation and amortization charges	103
Decrease in accounts receivable	17
Increase in merchandise inventory	(49)
Increase in accounts payable	44
Increase in accrued wages and salaries payable	3
Increase in accrued income taxes payable	6
Decrease in deferred income taxes	(2)
Gain on sale of store	(3)
Net cash provided by operating activities	259
Investing Activities	
Additions to property, buildings, and equipment	(138)
Proceeds from sale of store	8
Net cash used in investing activities	(130)
Financing Activities	
Increase in notes payable	2
Decrease in long-term debt	(43)
Increase in common stock	2
Cash dividends paid	(28)
Net cash used in financing activities	(67)
Net increase in cash and cash equivalents	62
Cash and cash equivalents at beginning of year	29
Cash and cash equivalents at end of year	$ 91

Reconciliation of the beginning and ending cash balances

*This statement differs from the actual statement published by Nordstrom.

Interpretation of the Statement of Cash Flows

The completed statement of cash flows in Exhibit 17–12 provides a very favorable picture of Nordstrom's cash flows. The net cash flow from operations is a healthy $259 million. This positive cash flow permitted the company to make substantial additions to its property, buildings, and equipment and to pay off a substantial portion of its long-term debt. If similar conditions prevail in the future, the company can continue to finance substantial growth from its own cash flows without the necessity of raising debt or selling stock.

When interpreting a statement of cash flows, it is particularly important to scrutinize the net cash provided by operating activities. This figure provides a measure of how successful the company is in generating cash on a continuing basis. A negative cash flow from operations would usually be a sign of fundamental difficulties. A positive cash flow from operations is necessary to avoid liquidating assets or borrowing money just to sustain day-to-day operations.

Depreciation, Depletion, and Amortization

There are a few pitfalls that the unwary can fall into when reading a statement of cash flows. Perhaps the most common is to misinterpret the nature of the depreciation charges on the statement of cash flows. Since depreciation is added back to net income, there is a tendency to think that all you have to do to increase net cash flow is to increase depreciation charges. This is false. In a merchandising company like Nordstrom, increasing the depreciation charge by X dollars would decrease net income by X dollars because of the added expense taken. Adding back the depreciation charge to net income on the statement of cash flows simply cancels out the reduction in net income caused by the depreciation charge. Referring back to Exhibit 17–2 on page 794, depreciation, depletion, and amortization charges are added back to net income on the statement of cash flows because they are a decrease in an asset (or, an increase in a contra asset)—not because they generate cash.

Summary

The statement of cash flows is one of the three major financial statements prepared by organizations. It explains how cash was generated and how it was used during a period. The statement of cash flows is widely used as a tool for assessing the financial health of organizations.

In general, sources of cash include net income, decreases in assets, increases in liabilities, and increases in stockholders' capital accounts. Uses of cash include increases in assets, decreases in liabilities, decreases in stockholders' capital accounts, and dividends. A simplified form of the statement of cash flows can be easily constructed using just these definitions and a comparative balance sheet.

For external reporting purposes, the statement of cash flows must be organized in terms of operating, investing, and financing activities. While there are some exceptions, changes in noncurrent assets are generally included in investing activities and changes in noncurrent liabilities are generally included in financing activities. And, with a few exceptions, operating activities include net income and changes in current assets and current liabilities.

An analyst should pay particularly close attention to the net cash provided by operating activities, since this provides a measure of how successful the company is in generating cash on a continuing basis.

Review Problem

Rockford Company's comparative balance sheet for 1999 and the company's income statement for the year follow:

ROCKFORD COMPANY
Comparative Balance Sheet
December 31, 1999, and 1998
(dollars in millions)

	1999	1998
Assets		
Cash	$ 26	$ 10
Accounts receivable	180	270
Inventory	205	160
Prepaid expenses	17	20
Plant and equipment	430	309
Less accumulated depreciation	(218)	(194)
Long-term investments	60	75
Total assets	$ 700	$ 650
Liabilities and Stockholders' Equity		
Accounts payable	$ 230	$ 310
Accrued liabilities	70	60
Bonds payable	135	40
Deferred income taxes	15	8
Common stock	140	140
Retained earnings	110	92
Total liabilities and stockholders' equity	$ 700	$ 650

ROCKFORD COMPANY
Income Statement
For the Year Ended December 31, 1999
(dollars in millions)

Sales	$1,000
Less cost of sales	530
Gross margin	470
Less operating expenses	352
Net operating income	118
Nonoperating items:	
Loss on sale of equipment	(4)
Income before taxes	114
Less income taxes	48
Net income	$ 66

Notes: Dividends of $48 million were paid in 1999. The loss on sale of equipment of $4 million reflects a transaction in which equipment with an original cost of $12 million and accumulated depreciation of $5 million was sold for $3 million in cash.

Required Using the indirect method, determine the net cash provided by operating activities for 1999 and construct a statement of cash flows for the year.

Solution to Review Problem

A worksheet for Rockford Company appears below. Using the worksheet, it is a simple matter to construct the statement of cash flows, including the net cash provided by operating activities.

ROCKFORD COMPANY
Statement of Cash Flows Worksheet
For the Year Ended December 31, 1999
(dollars in millions)

	(1) Change	(2) Source or Use?	(3) Cash Flow Effect	(4) Adjust-ments	(5) Adjusted Effect (3)+(4)	(6) Classi-fication
Assets (except cash and cash equivalents)						
Current assets:						
Accounts receivable	$ −90	Source	$ +90		$ +90	Operating
Inventory	+45	Use	−45		−45	Operating
Prepaid expenses	−3	Source	+3		+3	Operating
Noncurrent assets:						
Property, buildings, and equipment	+121	Use	−121	$−12	−133	Investing
Long-term investments	−15	Source	+15		+15	Investing
Contra Assets, Liabilities, and Stockholders' Equity						
Contra assets:						
Accumulated depreciation	+24	Source	+24	+5	+29	Operating
Current liabilities:						
Accounts payable	−80	Use	−80		−80	Operating
Accrued liabilities	+10	Source	+10		+10	Operating
Noncurrent liabilities:						
Bonds payable	+95	Source	+95		+95	Financing
Deferred income taxes	+7	Source	+7		+7	Operating
Stockholders' equity:						
Common stock	+0	—	+0		+0	Financing
Retained earnings:						
Net income	+66	Source	+66		+66	Operating
Dividends	−48	Use	−48		−48	Financing
Additional Entries						
Proceeds from sale of equipment				+3	+3	Investing
Loss on sale of equipment				+4	+4	Operating
Total (net cash flow)			$ +16	$ 0	$ +16	

ROCKFORD COMPANY
Statement of Cash Flows—Indirect Method
For the Year Ended December 31, 1999
(dollars in millions)

Operating Activities	
Net income	$ 66
Adjustments to convert net income to a cash basis:	
Depreciation and amorization charges	29
Decrease in accounts receivable	90
Increase in inventory	(45)
Decrease in prepaid expenses	3
Decrease in accounts payable	(80)
Increase in accrued liabilities	10
Increase in deferred income taxes	7
Loss on sale of equipment	4
Net cash provided by operating activities	84

continued

Investing Activities:	
Additions to property, buildings, and equipment	(133)
Decrease in long-term investments	15
Proceeds from sale of equipment	3
Net cash used in investing activities	(115)
Financing Activities:	
Increase in bonds payable	95
Cash dividends paid	(48)
Net cash used in financing activities	47
Net increase in cash and cash equivalents	16
Cash and cash equivalents at beginning of year	10
Cash and cash equivalents at end of year	$ 26

Note that the $16 increase in cash and cash equivalents agrees with the $16 increase in the company's Cash account shown in the balance sheet on page 809, and it agrees with the total in column (5) on page 810.

Key Terms for Review

Cash equivalents Short-term, highly liquid investments such as Treasury bills, commercial paper, and money market funds that are made solely for the purpose of generating a return on funds that are temporarily idle. (p. 793)

Direct exchange transactions Transactions involving only noncurrent balance sheet accounts. For example, a company might issue common stock that is directly exchanged for property. (p. 800)

Direct method A method of computing the cash provided by operating activities in which the income statement is reconstructed on a cash basis from top to bottom. (p. 800)

Financing activities All transactions (other than payment of interest) involving borrowing from creditors or repaying creditors as well as transactions with the company's owners (except stock dividends and stock splits). (p. 799)

Indirect method A method of computing the cash provided by operating activities that starts with net income and adjusts it to a cash basis. It is also known as the *reconciliation method.* (p. 800)

Investing activities Transactions that involve acquiring or disposing of noncurrent assets. (p. 798)

Net cash provided by operating activities The net result of the cash inflows and outflows arising from day-to-day operations. (p. 799)

Operating activities Transactions that enter into the determination of net income. (p. 798)

Reconciliation method See *Indirect method.* (p. 800)

Statement of cash flows A financial statement that highlights the major activities that directly and indirectly impact cash flows and hence affect the overall cash balance. (p. 792)

Appendix 17A: The Direct Method of Determining the "Net Cash Provided by Operating Activities"

objective 4

Use the direct method to determine the "Net cash provided by operating activities."

As stated in the main body of the chapter, to compute the "Net cash provided by operating activities" under the direct method, we must reconstruct the income statement on a cash basis from top to bottom. A model is presented in Exhibit 17A–1 that shows the adjustments that must be made to adjust sales, expenses, and so forth, to a cash basis. To illustrate, we have included in the exhibit the Nordstrom data from the chapter.

Exhibit 17A–1
General Model: Direct Method of Determining the "Net Cash Provided by Operating Activities"

Revenue or Expense Item	Add (+) or Deduct (−) to Adjust to a Cash Basis	Illustration—Nordstrom (in millions)	
Sales revenue (as reported)		$3,638	
Adjustments to a cash basis:			
1. Increase in accounts payable	−		
2. Decrease in accounts receivable	+	+17	
Total			$3,655
Cost of goods sold (as reported)		2,469	
Adjustments to a cash basis:			
3. Increase in merchandise inventory	+	+49	
4. Decrease in merchandise inventory	−		
5. Increase in accounts payable	−	−44	
6. Decrease in accounts payable	+		
Total			2,474
Operating expenses (as reported)		941	
Adjustments to a cash basis:			
7. Increase in prepaid expenses	+		
8. Decrease in prepaid expenses	−		
9. Increase in accrued liabilities	−	−3	
10. Decrease in accrued liabilities	+		
11. Period's depreciation, depletion, and amortization charges	−	−103	
Total			835
Income tax expense (as reported)		91	
Adjustments to a cash basis:			
12. Increase in accrued taxes payable	−	−6	
13. Decrease in accrued taxes payable	+		
14. Increase in deferred income taxes	−		
15. Decrease in deferred income taxes	+	+2	
Total			87
Net cash provided by operating activities			$ 259

Note that the "Net cash provided by operating activities" figure ($259 million) agrees with the amount computed in the chapter by the indirect method. The two amounts agree, since the direct and indirect methods are just different roads to the same destination. The investing and financing activities sections of the statement will be exactly the same as shown for the indirect method in Exhibit 17–12. The only difference between the indirect and direct methods is in the operating activities section.

Similarities and Differences in the Handling of Data

Although we arrive at the same destination under either the direct or the indirect methods, not all data are handled in the same way in the adjustment process. Stop for a moment, flip back to the general model for the indirect method in Exhibit 17–8 on page 801 and compare the adjustments made in that exhibit to the adjustments made for the direct method in Exhibit 17A–1. The adjustments for accounts that affect revenue are the same in the two methods. In either case, increases in the account are deducted and decreases in the accounts are added. The adjustments for accounts that affect expenses, however, are handled in *opposite* ways in the indirect and direct methods. This is because under the indirect method the adjustments are made to *net income,* whereas under the direct method the adjustments are made to the *expense accounts* themselves.

To illustrate this difference, note the handling of prepaid expenses and depreciation in the indirect and direct methods. Under the indirect method (Exhibit 17–8), an increase in the Prepaid Expenses account is *deducted* from net income in computing the amount of cash provided by operations. Under the direct method (Exhibit 17A–1), an increase in Prepaid Expenses is *added* to operating expenses. The reason for the difference can be explained as follows: An increase in Prepaid Expenses means that more cash has been paid out for items such as insurance than has been included as expense for the period. Therefore, to adjust net income to a cash basis, we must either deduct this increase from net income (indirect method) or we must add this increase to operating expenses (direct method). Either way, we will end up with the same figure for cash provided by operations. In like manner, depreciation is added to net income under the indirect method to cancel out its effect (Exhibit 17–8), whereas it is deducted from operating expenses under the direct method to cancel out its effect (Exhibit 17A–1). These differences in the handling of data are true for all other expense items in the two methods.

In the matter of gains and losses on sales of assets, no adjustments are needed at all under the direct method. These gains and losses are simply ignored, since they are not part of sales, cost of goods sold, operating expenses, or income taxes. Observe that in Exhibit 17A–1, Nordstrom's $3 million gain on the sale of the store is not listed as an adjustment in the operating activities section.

Special Rules—Direct and Indirect Methods

As stated earlier, when the direct method is used, the FASB requires a reconciliation between net income and the net cash provided by operating activities, as determined by the indirect method. Thus, *when a company elects to use the direct method, it must also present the indirect method* in a separate schedule accompanying the statement of cash flows.

On the other hand, if a company elects to use the indirect method to compute the net cash provided by operating activities, then it must also provide a special breakdown of data. The company must provide a separate disclosure of the amount of interest and the amount of income taxes paid during the year. The FASB requires this separate disclosure so that users can take the data provided by the indirect method and make estimates of what the amounts for sales, income taxes, and so forth, would have been if the direct method had been used instead.

Questions

17–1 What is the purpose of a statement of cash flows?

17–2 What are *cash equivalents,* and why are they included with cash on a statement of cash flows?

17–3 What are the three major sections on a statement of cash flows, and what are the general rules that determine the transactions that should be included in each section?

17–4 Why is interest paid on amounts borrowed from banks and other lenders considered to be an operating activity when the amounts borrowed are financing activities?

17–5 If an asset is sold at a gain, why is the gain deducted from net income when computing the cash provided by operating activities under the indirect method?

17–6 Why aren't transactions involving accounts payable considered to be financing activities?

17–7 Give an example of a direct exchange and explain how such exchanges are handled when preparing a statement of cash flows.

17–8 Assume that a company repays a $300,000 loan from its bank and then later in the same year borrows $500,000. What amount(s) would appear on the statement of cash flows?

17–9 How do the direct and the indirect methods differ in their approach to computing the cash provided by operating activities?

17–10 A business executive once stated, "Depreciation is one of our biggest sources of cash." Do you agree that depreciation is a source of cash? Explain.

17–11 If the balance in Accounts Receivable increases during a period, how will this increase be handled under the indirect method when computing the cash provided by operating activities?

17–12 If the balance in Accounts Payable decreases during a period, how will this decrease be handled under the direct method in computing the cash provided by operating activities?

17–13 During the current year, a company declared and paid a $60,000 cash dividend and a 10% stock dividend. How will these two items be treated on the current year's statement of cash flows?

17–14 Would a sale of equipment for cash be considered a financing activity or an investment activity? Why?

17–15 (Appendix 17A) A merchandising company showed $250,000 in cost of goods sold on its income statement. The company's beginning inventory was $75,000, and its ending inventory was $60,000. The accounts payable balance was $50,000 at the beginning of the year and $40,000 at the end of the year. Using the direct method, adjust the company's cost of goods sold to a cash basis.

Exercises

E17–1 For the just completed year, Hanna Company reported a net income of $35,000. Balances in the company's current asset and current liability accounts at the beginning and end of the year were:

	End of Year	Beginning of Year
Current assets:		
Cash	$ 30,000	$ 40,000
Accounts receivable	125,000	106,000
Inventory	213,000	180,000
Prepaid expenses	6,000	7,000
Current liabilities:		
Accounts payable	210,000	195,000
Accrued liabilities	4,000	6,000

The Deferred Income Taxes account on the balance sheet increased by $4,000 during the year, and depreciation charges were $20,000.

Required Using the indirect method, determine the cash provided by operating activities for the year.

E17–2 (Appendix 17A) Refer to the data for Hanna Company in E17–1. The company's income statement for the year appears below:

Sales	$350,000
Less cost of goods sold	140,000
Gross margin	210,000
Less operating expenses	160,000
Income before taxes	50,000
Less income taxes (30%)	15,000
Net income	$ 35,000

Required Using the direct method (and the data from E17–1), convert the company's income statement to a cash basis.

E17–3 Below are transactions that took place in Placid Company during the past year:

a. Equipment was purchased.
b. A cash dividend was declared and paid.
c. Accounts receivable decreased.
d. Short-term investments were purchased.
e. Equipment was sold.
f. Preferred stock was sold to investors.
g. A stock dividend was declared and issued.
h. Interest was paid to long-term creditors.
i. Salaries and wages payable decreased.
j. Stock of another company was purchased.
k. Bonds were issued that will be due in 10 years.
l. Rent was received from subleasing of space, reducing rents receivable.
m. Common stock was repurchased and retired.

Required Prepare an answer sheet with the following headings:

	Activity			Not		
Transaction	**Operating**	**Investing**	**Financing**	**Reported**	**Source**	**Use**
a.						
b.						
etc.						

Enter the transactions above on your answer sheet and indicate how the effects of each transaction would be classified on a statement of cash flows. Place an *X* in the Operating, Investing, or Financing column and an *X* in the Source or Use column as appropriate.

E17–4 Changes in various accounts and gains and losses on sales of assets during the year for Argon Company are given below:

Item	Amount
Accounts Receivable	$ 90,000 decrease
Accrued Interest Receivable	4,000 increase
Inventory	120,000 increase
Prepaid Expenses	3,000 decrease
Accounts Payable	65,000 decrease
Accrued Liabilities	8,000 increase
Deferred Income Taxes	12,000 increase
Sale of equipment	7,000 gain
Sale of long-term investments	10,000 loss

Required Prepare an answer sheet using the following column headings:

Item	Amount	Add	Deduct

On your answer sheet, enter the items and amounts on page 815. For each item, place an *X* in the Add or Deduct column to indicate whether the dollar amount should be added to or deducted from net income under the indirect method when computing the cash provided by operating activities for the year.

E17–5 Comparative financial statement data for Carmono Company follow:

	1999	1998
Cash	$ 3	$ 6
Accounts receivable	22	24
Inventory	50	40
Plant and Equipment	240	200
Less accumulated depreciation	(65)	(50)
Total assets	$250	$220
Accounts payable	$ 40	$ 36
Common stock	150	145
Retained earnings	60	39
Total liabilities and stockholders' equity	$250	$220

For 1999, the company reported net income as follows:

Sales	$275
Cost of goods sold	150
Gross margin	125
Operating expenses	90
Net income	$ 35

Dividends of $14 were declared and paid during 1999.

Required Using the indirect method, prepare a statement of cash flows for 1999.

E17–6 (Appendix 17A) Refer to the data for Carmono Company in E17–5.

Required Using the direct method, convert the company's income statement to a cash basis.

E17–7 The following changes took place during the year in Pavolik Company's balance sheet accounts:

Cash	$ 5 D	Accounts Payable	$ 35 I
Accounts Receivable	110 I	Accrued Liabilities	4 D
Inventory	70 D	Bonds Payable	150 I
Prepaid Expenses	9 I	Deferred Income Taxes	8 I
Long-Term Investments	6 D	Common Stock	80 D
Plant and Equipment	200 I	Retained Earnings	54 I
Accumulated Depreciation	(60) I		
Land	15 D		

D = Decrease; I = Increase.

Long-term investments that had cost the company $6 were sold during the year for $16, and land that had cost $15 was sold for $9. In addition, the company declared and paid $30 in cash dividends during the year. No sales or retirements of plant and equipment took place during the year.

The company's income statement for the year follows:

Sales		$700
Less cost of goods sold		400
Gross margin		300
Less operating expenses		184
Net operating income		116
Nonoperating items:		
Gain on sale of investments	$10	
Loss on sale of land	6	4
Income before taxes		120
Less income taxes		36
Net income		$ 84

The company's beginning cash balance was $90, and its ending balance was $85.

Required

1. Use the indirect method to determine the cash provided by operating activities for the year.
2. Prepare a statement of cash flows for the year.

E17–8 (Appendix 17A) Refer to the data for Pavolik Company in E17–7.

Required Use the direct method to convert the company's income statement to a cash basis.

Problems

P17–9 Classifying Transactions on a Statement of Cash Flows Below are a number of transactions that took place in Seneca Company during the past year:

a. Common stock was sold for cash.
b. Interest was paid on a note, decreasing Interest Payable.
c. Bonds were retired.
d. A long-term loan was made to a subsidiary.
e. Interest was received on the loan in (d) above, reducing Interest Receivable.
f. A stock dividend was declared and issued on common stock.
g. A building was acquired by issuing shares of common stock.
h. Equipment was sold for cash.
i. Short-term investments were sold.
j. Cash dividends were declared and paid.
k. Preferred stock was converted into common stock.
l. Deferred Income Taxes, a long-term liability, was reduced.
m. Dividends were received on stock of another company held as an investment.
n. Equipment was purchased by giving a long-term note to the seller.

Required Prepare an answer sheet with the following column headings:

Transaction	Source, Use, or Neither	Activity			Reported in a Separate Schedule	Not on the Statement
		Operating	Investing	Financing		

Enter the letter of the transaction in the left column and indicate whether the transaction would be a source, use, or neither. Then place an *X* in the appropriate column to show the proper classification of the transaction on the statement of cash flows, or to show if it would not appear on the statement at all.

P17–10 Indirect Method; Statement of Cash Flows Balance sheet accounts for Joyner Company contained the following amounts at the end of Years 1 and 2:

	Year 2	Year 1
Debit Balance Accounts		
Cash	$ 4,000	$ 21,000
Accounts Receivable	250,000	170,000
Inventory	310,000	260,000
Prepaid Expenses	7,000	14,000
Loan to Hymas Company	40,000	—
Plant and Equipment	510,000	400,000
Total	$1,121,000	$865,000
Credit Balance Accounts		
Accumulated Depreciation	$ 132,000	$120,000
Accounts Payable	310,000	250,000
Accrued Liabilities	20,000	30,000
Bonds Payable	190,000	70,000
Deferred Income Taxes	45,000	42,000
Common Stock	300,000	270,000
Retained Earnings	124,000	83,000
Total	$1,121,000	$865,000

The company's income statement for Year 2 follows:

Sales	$900,000
Less cost of goods sold	500,000
Gross margin	400,000
Less operating expenses	328,000
Net operating income	72,000
Gain on sale of equipment	8,000
Income before taxes	80,000
Less income taxes	24,000
Net income	$ 56,000

Equipment that had cost $40,000 and on which there was accumulated depreciation of $30,000 was sold during Year 2 for $18,000. Cash dividends totaling $15,000 were declared and paid during Year 2.

Required

1. Using the indirect method, compute the cash provided by operating activities for Year 2.
2. Prepare a statement of cash flows for Year 2.
3. Prepare a brief explanation as to why cash declined so sharply during the year.

P17–11 Direct Method; Statement of Cash Flows (Appendix 17A) Refer to the financial statement data for Joyner Company in P17–10. Sam Conway, president of the company, considers $15,000 to be a minimum cash balance for operating purposes. As can be seen from the balance sheet data, only $4,000 in cash was available at the end of the current year. The sharp decline is puzzling to Mr. Conway, particularly since sales and profits are at a record high.

Required

1. Using the direct method, adjust the company's income statement to a cash basis for Year 2.
2. Using the data from (1) above and other data from the problem as needed, prepare a statement of cash flows for Year 2.
3. Explain to Mr. Conway why cash declined so sharply during the year.

P17–12 Indirect Method; Statement of Cash Flows Comparative financial statements for Weaver Company follow:

WEAVER COMPANY
Comparative Balance Sheet
December 31, 1999, and 1998

	1999	1998
Assets		
Cash	$ 9	$ 15
Accounts receivable	340	240
Inventory	125	175
Prepaid expenses	10	6
Plant and equipment	610	470
Less accumulated depreciation	(93)	(85)
Long-term investments	16	19
Total assets	$1,017	$840
Liabilities and Stockholders' Equity		
Accounts payable	$ 310	$230
Accrued liabilities	60	72
Bonds payable	290	180
Deferred income taxes	40	34
Common stock	210	250
Retained earnings	107	74
Total liabilities and stockholders' equity	$1,017	$840

WEAVER COMPANY
Income Statement
For the Year Ended December 31, 1999

Sales		$800
Less cost of goods sold		500
Gross margin		300
Less operating expenses		213
Net operating income		87
Nonoperating items:		
Gain on sale of investments	$7	
Loss on sale of equipment	4	3
Income before taxes		90
Less income taxes		27
Net income		$ 63

During 1999, the company sold some equipment for $20 that had cost $40 and on which there was accumulated depreciation of $16. In addition, the company sold long-term investments for $10 that had cost $3 when purchased several years ago. Cash dividends totaling $30 were paid during 1999.

Required

1. Using the indirect method, determine the cash provided by operating activities for 1999.
2. Use the information in (1) above, along with an analysis of the remaining balance sheet accounts, and prepare a statement of cash flows for 1999.

P17–13 Direct Method; Statement of Cash Flows (Appendix 17A) Refer to the financial statement data for Weaver Company in P17–12.

Required

1. Using the direct method, adjust the company's income statement for 1999 to a cash basis.
2. Use the information obtained in (1) above, along with an analysis of the remaining balance sheet accounts, and prepare a statement of cash flows for 1999.

P17–14 Indirect Method; Statement of Cash Flows Mary Walker, president of Rusco Products, considers $14,000 to be the minimum cash balance for operating purposes. As can be seen from the statements below, only $8,000 in cash was available at the end of 1999. Since the company reported a large net income for the year, and also issued both bonds and common stock, the sharp decline in cash is puzzling to Ms. Walker.

RUSCO PRODUCTS
Comparative Balance Sheet
July 31, 1999, and 1998

	1999	1998
Assets		
Current assets:		
Cash	$ 8,000	$ 21,000
Accounts receivable	120,000	80,000
Inventory	140,000	90,000
Prepaid expenses	5,000	9,000
Total current assets	273,000	200,000
Long-term investments	50,000	70,000
Plant and equipment	430,000	300,000
Less accumulated depreciation	60,000	50,000
Net plant and equipment	370,000	250,000
Total assets	$693,000	$520,000
Liabilities and Stockholders' Equity		
Current liabilities:		
Accounts payable	$123,000	$ 60,000
Accrued liabilities	8,000	17,000
Total current liabilities	131,000	77,000
Bonds payable	70,000	
Deferred income taxes	20,000	12,000
Stockholders' equity:		
Preferred stock	80,000	96,000
Common stock	286,000	250,000
Retained earnings	106,000	85,000
Total stockholders' equity	472,000	431,000
Total liabilities and stockholders' equity	$693,000	$520,000

RUSCO PRODUCTS
Income Statement
For the Year Ended July 31, 1999

Sales		$500,000
Less cost of goods sold		300,000
Gross margin		200,000
Less operating expenses		158,000
Net operating income		42,000
Nonoperating items:		
Gain on sale of investments	$ 10,000	
Loss on sale of equipment	2,000	8,000
Income before taxes		50,000
Less income taxes		20,000
Net income		$ 30,000

The following additional information is available for the year 1999.

a. Dividends totaling $9,000 were declared and paid in cash.
b. Equipment was sold during the year for $8,000. The equipment had originally cost $20,000 and had accumulated depreciation of $10,000.
c. The decrease in the Preferred Stock account is the result of a conversion of preferred stock into an equal dollar amount of common stock.
d. Long-term investments that had cost $20,000 were sold during the year for $30,000.

Required

1. Using the indirect method, compute the cash provided by operating activities for 1999.
2. Using the data from (1) above, and other data from the problem as needed, prepare a statement of cash flows for 1999.
3. Explain to the president the major reasons for the decline in the company's cash position.

P17–15 Direct Method; Statement of Cash Flows (Appendix 17A) Refer to the financial statements for Rusco Products in P17–14. Since the Cash account decreased so dramatically during 1999, the company's executive committee is anxious to see how the income statement would appear on a cash basis.

Required

1. Using the direct method, adjust the company's income statement for 1999 to a cash basis.
2. Using the data from (1) above, and other data from the problem as needed, prepare a statement of cash flows for 1999.
3. Prepare a brief explanation for the executive committee setting forth the major reasons for the sharp decline in cash during the year.

P17–16 Indirect Method; Statement of Cash Flows; Worksheet "See, I told you things would work out," said Barry Kresmier, president of Lomax Company. "We expanded sales from $1.6 million to $2.0 million in 1999, nearly doubled our warehouse space, and ended the year with more cash in the bank than we started with. A few more years of expansion like this and we'll be the industry leaders."

"Yes, I'll admit our statements look pretty good," replied Sheri Colson, the company's vice president. "But we're doing business with a lot of companies we don't know much about and that worries me. I'll admit, though, that we're certainly moving a lot of merchandise; our inventory is actually down from last year."

A comparative balance sheet for Lomax Company containing data for the last two years follows:

LOMAX COMPANY
Comparative Balance Sheet
December 31, 1999, and 1998

	1999	1998
Assets		
Current assets:		
Cash	$ 42,000	$ 27,000
Marketable securities	19,000	13,000
Accounts receivable	710,000	530,000
Inventory	848,000	860,000
Prepaid expenses	10,000	5,000
Total current assets	1,629,000	1,435,000
Long-term investments	60,000	110,000
Loans to subsidiaries	130,000	80,000
Plant and equipment	3,170,000	2,600,000
Less accumulated depreciation	810,000	755,000
Net plant and equipment	2,360,000	1,845,000
Goodwill	84,000	90,000
Total assets	$4,263,000	$3,560,000
Liabilities and Stockholders' Equity		
Current liabilities:		
Accounts payable	$ 970,000	$ 670,000
Accrued liabilities	65,000	82,000
Total current liabilities	1,035,000	752,000
Long-term notes	820,000	600,000
Deferred income taxes	95,000	80,000
Total liabilities	1,950,000	1,432,000
Stockholders' equity:		
Common stock	1,740,000	1,650,000
Retained earnings	573,000	478,000
Total stockholders' equity	2,313,000	2,128,000
Total liabilities and stockholders' equity	$4,263,000	$3,560,000

The following additional information is available about the company's activities during 1999:

a. Cash dividends declared and paid to the common stockholders totaled $75,000.
b. Long-term notes with a value of $380,000 were repaid during the year.
c. Equipment was sold during the year for $70,000. The equipment had cost $130,000 and had $40,000 in accumulated depreciation on the date of sale.
d. Long-term investments were sold during the year for $110,000. These investments had cost $50,000 when purchased several years ago.
e. The company's income statement for 1999 follows:

Sales		$2,000,000
Less cost of goods sold		1,300,000
Gross margin		700,000
Less operating expenses		490,000
Net operating income		210,000
Nonoperating items:		
Gain on sale of investments	$60,000	
Loss on sale of equipment	20,000	40,000
Income before taxes		250,000
Less income taxes		80,000
Net income		$ 170,000

Required

1. Prepare a worksheet like Exhibit 17–10 for Lomax Company.
2. Using the indirect method, prepare a statement of cash flows for the year 1999.
3. What problems relating to the company's activities are revealed by the statement of cash flows that you have prepared?

P17–17 Direct Method; Adjusting the Income Statement to a Cash Basis (Appendix 17A) Refer to the data for the Lomax Company in P17–16. All of the long-term notes issued during 1999 are being held by Lomax's bank. The bank's management wants the income statement adjusted to a cash basis so that it can compare the cash basis statement to the accrual basis statement.

Required Use the direct method to convert Lomax Company's 1999 income statement to a cash basis.

P17–18 Missing Data; Indirect Method; Statement of Cash Flows Below are listed the *changes* in Yoric Company's balance sheet accounts for the past year:

	Debits	Credits
Cash	$ 17,000	
Accounts Receivable	110,000	
Inventory		$ 65,000
Prepaid Expenses		8,000
Long-Term Loans to Subsidiaries		30,000
Long-Term Investments	80,000	
Plant and Equipment	220,000	
Accumulated Depreciation		5,000
Accounts Payable		32,000
Accrued Liabilities	9,000	
Bonds Payable		400,000
Deferred Income Taxes		16,000
Common Stock	170,000	
Retained Earnings		50,000
	$606,000	$606,000

The following additional information is available about last year's activities:

a. Net income for the year was $____?____.
b. The company sold equipment during the year for $15,000. The equipment had cost the company $50,000 when purchased and it had $37,000 in accumulated depreciation at the time of sale.
c. Cash dividends were declared and paid during the year, $20,000.
d. Depreciation charges for the year were $____?____.
e. The opening and closing balances in the Plant and Equipment and Accumulated Depreciation accounts are given below:

	Opening	Closing
Plant and Equipment	$1,580,000	$1,800,000
Accumulated Depreciation	675,000	680,000

f. The balance in the Cash account at the beginning of the year was $23,000; the balance at the end of the year was $____?____.
g. If data are not given explaining the change in an account, make the most reasonable assumption as to the cause of the change.

Required Using the indirect method, prepare a statement of cash flows for the year.

P17–19 Missing Data; Indirect Method; Statement of Cash Flows Oxident Products is the manufacturer of a vitamin supplement. The *changes* that have taken place in the company's balance sheet accounts as a result of the past year's activities follow:

Debit Balance Accounts	Net Increase (Decrease)
Cash	$ (10,000)
Accounts Receivable	(81,000)
Inventory	230,000
Prepaid Expenses	(6,000)
Long-Term Loans to Subsidiaries	100,000
Long-Term Investments	(120,000)
Plant and Equipment	500,000
Net increase	$ 613,000

Credit Balance Accounts	
Accumulated Depreciation	$ 90,000
Accounts Payable	(70,000)
Accrued Liabilities	35,000
Bonds Payable	400,000
Deferred Income Taxes	8,000
Preferred Stock	(180,000)
Common Stock	270,000
Retained Earnings	60,000
Net increase	$ 613,000

The following additional information is available about last year's activities:

a. The company sold equipment during the year for $40,000. The equipment had cost the company $100,000 when purchased and it had $70,000 in accumulated depreciation at the time of sale.
b. Net income for the year was $____?____.
c. The balance in the Cash account at the beginning of the year was $52,000; the balance at the end of the year was $____?____.
d. The company declared and paid $30,000 in cash dividends during the year.
e. Long-term investments that had cost $120,000 were sold during the year for $80,000.
f. The balances in the Plant and Equipment and Accumulated Depreciation accounts for tthe past year are given below:

	Ending	Beginning
Plant and Equipment	$3,200,000	$2,700,000
Accumulated Depreciation	1,500,000	1,410,000

g. If data are not given explaining the change in an account, make the most reasonable assumption as to the cause of the change.

Required Using the indirect method, prepare a statement of cash flows for the past year. Show all computations for items that appear on your statement.

Group Exercises

GE17–20 This Is a Problem? We Should Be So Lucky With the economy in expansion, profits at America's large corporations are high, and cash flowing in is at record levels. Management at these firms must decide what to do with the growing pool of cash. Should they plow it back into the business? Should they try to please stockholders by buying back stock? Or should they pay down debt, some of it accumulated when the firms acquired other businesses? And as growth in the economy slows, cash flow will remain high, and management will feel even more pressure to make a decision.

Required

1. Discuss the advantages and disadvantages (risks) of each alternative.
2. What kind of return on investment (ROI) would a firm earn from each alternative?
3. Are there other options that haven't been considered? If so, what risks are involved? What kind of a ROI could you expect?

GE17–21 **What's Wrong with This Picture?** Suppose a new company with a "hot" new product is very profitable but the company goes out of business. How could that happen? Explain.

IE17–22 **Reconciling the Statement of Cash Flows with the Balance Sheet** As shown in the chapter, it should be possible to reconcile the statement of cash flows with the changes in noncash balance sheet accounts. In practice, this is often difficult because the net change in a balance sheet account may have been decomposed into increases and decreases in the account or it may be netted against some other change in a balance sheet account when shown on the statement of cash flows. Find Nike's most recent annual report by accessing its home page at www.nike.com.

Required

As far as you can, trace the changes in Nike's noncash balance sheet accounts to the statement of cash flows.

IE17–23 **Interpreting Financial Statements** Find ATT Corporation's latest annual report at its web site at www.att.com and General Electric Corporation's (GE) annual report at its web site at www.ge.com.

Required

1. Do ATT and GE use the direct or indirect method of presenting operating activities on their statements of cash flow?
2. The statement of cash flow should list data for three years. Determine if there was a major change in the overall cash flow or in any of the three activities (operating, investing, and financing) for either corporation in any of the last two years. If so, is there any clear reason for the major change?
3. Is there a major difference between the net cash flow and the net income for either corporation in any of the last two years? If so, explain why.

Chapter Eighteen

"How Well Am I Doing?" Financial Statement Analysis

Business Focus

Rick Burrock, the managing director of an accounting firm based in Minneapolis, advises his small business clients to keep a tight rein on credit extended to customers. "You need to convey to your customers, right from the beginning, that you will work very hard to satisfy them and that in return, you expect to be paid on time. Start by investigating all new customers. A credit report helps, but with a business customer you can find out even more by requesting financial statements . . . Using the balance sheet, divide current assets by current liabilities to calculate the current ratio. If a company's current ratio is below 1.00, it will be paying out more than it expects to collect; you may want to reconsider doing business with that company or insist on stricter credit terms."

Source: Jill Andresky Fraser, "Hands on Collections: Get Paid Promptly," Inc., *November 1996, p. 87.*

1 Explain the need for and limitations of financial statement analysis.

2 Prepare financial statements in comparative form and explain how such statements are used.

3 Place the balance sheet and the income statement in common-size form and properly interpret the results.

4 Identify the ratios used to measure the well-being of the common stockholder and state each ratio's formula and interpretation.

5 Explain what is meant by the term *financial leverage* and show how financial leverage is measured.

6 Identify the ratios used to measure the well-being of the short-term creditor and state each ratio's formula and interpretation.

7 Identify the ratios used to measure the well-being of the long-term creditor and state each ratio's formula and interpretation.

All financial statements are essentially historical documents. They tell what *has happened* during a particular period of time. However, most users of financial statements are concerned about what *will happen* in the future. Stockholders are concerned with future earnings and dividends. Creditors are concerned with the company's future ability to repay its debts. Managers are concerned with the company's ability to finance future expansion. Despite the fact that financial statements are historical documents, they can still provide valuable information bearing on all of these concerns.

Financial statement analysis involves careful selection of data from financial statements for the primary purpose of forecasting the financial health of the company. This is accomplished by examining trends in key financial data, comparing financial data across companies, and analyzing key financial ratios. In this chapter, we consider some of the more important ratios and other analytical tools that analysts use in attempting to predict the future course of events in business organizations.

Managers are also vitally concerned with the financial ratios discussed in this chapter. First, the ratios provide indicators of how well the company and its business units are performing. Some of these ratios would ordinarily be used in a balanced scorecard approach as discussed in Chapter 10. The specific ratios selected depend on the company's strategy. For example, a company that wants to emphasize responsiveness to customers may closely monitor the inventory turnover ratio discussed later in this chapter. Second, since managers must report to shareholders and may wish to raise funds from external sources, managers must pay attention to the financial ratios used by external investors to evaluate the company's investment potential and creditworthiness.

Limitations of Financial Statement Analysis

objective 1

Explain the need for and limitations of financial statement analysis.

Although financial statement analysis is a highly useful tool, it has two limitations that we must mention before proceeding any further. These two limitations involve the comparability of financial data between companies and the need to look beyond ratios.

Comparison of Financial Data

Comparisons of one company with another can provide valuable clues about the financial health of an organization. Unfortunately, differences in accounting methods between companies sometimes make it difficult to compare the companies' financial data. For example, if one firm values its inventories by the LIFO method and another firm by the average cost method, then direct comparisons of financial data such as inventory valuations and cost of goods sold between the two firms may be misleading. Sometimes enough data is presented in footnotes to the financial statements to restate data to a comparable basis. Otherwise, the analyst should keep in mind the lack of comparability of the data before drawing any definite conclusions. Nevertheless, even with this limitation in mind, comparisons of key ratios with other companies and with industry averages often suggest avenues for further investigation.

The Need to Look beyond Ratios

An inexperienced analyst may assume that ratios are sufficient in themselves as a basis for judgments about the future. Nothing could be further from the truth. Conclusions based on ratio analysis must be regarded as tentative in nature. Ratios should not be viewed as an end, but rather they should be viewed as a *starting point,* as indicators of what to pursue in greater depth. They raise many questions, but they rarely answer any questions by themselves.

In addition to ratios, other sources of data should be analyzed in order to make judgments about the future of an organization. The analyst should look, for example, at industry trends, technological changes, changes in consumer tastes, changes in broad economic factors, and changes within the firm itself. A recent change in a key management position, for example, might provide a basis for optimism about the future, even though the past performance of the firm (as shown by its ratios) may have been mediocre.

Statements in Comparative and Common-Size Form

Few figures appearing on financial statements have much significance standing by themselves. It is the relationship of one figure to another and the amount and direction of change over time that are important in financial statement analysis. How does the analyst key in on significant relationships? How does the analyst dig out the important trends and changes in a company? Three analytical techniques are widely used:

1. Dollar and percentage changes on statements.
2. Common-size statements.
3. Ratios.

The first and second techniques are discussed in this section; the third technique is discussed in the next section. To illustrate these analytical techniques, we analyze the financial statements of Brickey Electronics, a producer of computer and television components.

Dollar and Percentage Changes on Statements

objective 2
Prepare financial statements in comparative form and explain how such statements are used.

A good place to begin in financial statement analysis is to put statements in comparative form. This consists of little more than putting two or more years' data side by side. Statements cast in comparative form underscore movements and trends and may give the analyst valuable clues as to what to expect.

Exhibit 18–1

BRICKEY ELECTRONICS
Comparative Balance Sheet
December 31, 1999, and 1998
(dollars in thousands)

	1999	1998	Increase (Decrease) Amount	Increase (Decrease) Percent
Assets				
Current assets:				
Cash	$ 1,200	$ 2,350	$(1,150)	(48.9)%*
Accounts receivable, net	6,000	4,000	2,000	50.0%
Inventory	8,000	10,000	(2,000)	(20.0)%
Prepaid expenses	300	120	180	150.0%
Total current assets	15,500	16,470	(970)	(5.9)%
Property and equipment:				
Land	4,000	4,000	-0-	-0-%
Buildings and equipment, net	12,000	8,500	3,500	41.2%
Total property and equipment	16,000	12,500	3,500	28.0%
Total assets	$31,500	$28,970	$ 2,530	8.7%
Liabilities and Stockholders' Equity				
Current liabilities:				
Accounts payable	$ 5,800	$ 4,000	$ 1,800	45.0%
Accrued payables	900	400	500	125.0%
Notes payable, short term	300	600	(300)	(50.0)%
Total current liabilities	7,000	5,000	2,000	40.0%
Long-term liabilities:				
Bonds payable, 8%	7,500	8,000	(500)	(6.3)%
Total liabilities	14,500	13,000	1,500	11.5%
Stockholders' equity:				
Preferred stock, $100 par, 6%, $100 liquidation value	2,000	2,000	-0-	-0-%
Common stock, $12 par	6,000	6,000	-0-	-0-%
Additional paid-in capital	1,000	1,000	-0-	-0-%
Total paid-in capital	9,000	9,000	-0-	-0-%
Retained earnings	8,000	6,970	1,030	14.8%
Total stockholders' equity	17,000	15,970	1,030	6.4%
Total liabilities and stockholders' equity	$31,500	$28,970	$ 2,530	8.7%

*Since we are measuring the amount of change between 1998 and 1999, the dollar amounts for 1998 become the base figures for expressing these changes in percentage form. For example, Cash decreased by $1,150 between 1998 and 1999. This decrease expressed in percentage form is computed as follows: $1,150 ÷ $2,350 = 48.9%. Other percentage figures in this exhibit and Exhibit 18–2 are computed in the same way.

Examples of financial statements placed in comparative form are given in Exhibits 18–1 and 18–2. These statements of Brickey Electronics reveal the firm has been experiencing substantial growth. The data on these statements are used as a basis for discussion throughout the remainder of the chapter.

HORIZONTAL ANALYSIS Comparison of two or more years' financial data is known as **horizontal analysis** or **trend analysis.** Horizontal analysis is facilitated by

Exhibit 18–2

BRICKEY ELECTRONICS
Comparative Income Statement and Reconciliation of Retained Earnings
For the Years Ended December 31, 1999, and 1998
(dollars in thousands)

	1999	1998	Increase (Decrease) Amount	Increase (Decrease) Percent
Sales	**$52,000**	$48,000	**$4,000**	8.3%
Cost of goods sold	**36,000**	31,500	**4,500**	14.3%
Gross margin	16,000	16,500	(500)	(3.0)%
Operating expenses:				
Selling expenses	7,000	6,500	500	7.7%
Administrative expenses	5,860	6,100	(240)	(3.9)%
Total operating expenses	12,860	12,600	260	2.1%
Net operating income	**3,140**	3,900	(760)	(19.5)%
Interest expense	**640**	700	(60)	(8.6)%
Net income before taxes	2,500	3,200	(700)	(21.9)%
Less income taxes (**30%**)	750	960	(210)	(21.9)%
Net income	**1,750**	2,240	$ (490)	(21.9)%
Dividends to preferred stockholders, $6 per share (see Exhibit 18–1)	**120**	120		
Net income remaining for common stockholders	1,630	2,120		
Dividends to common stockholders, **$1.20** per share	600	600		
Net income added to retained earnings	1,030	1,520		
Retained earnings, beginning of year	6,970	5,450		
Retained earnings, end of year	$ 8,000	$ 6,970		

showing changes between years in both dollar *and* percentage form, as has been done in Exhibits 18–1 and 18–2. Showing changes in dollar form helps the analyst focus on key factors that have affected profitability or financial position. For example, observe in Exhibit 18–2 that sales for 1999 were up $4 million over 1998, but that this increase in sales was more than negated by a $4.5 million increase in cost of goods sold.

Showing changes between years in percentage form helps the analyst to gain *perspective* and to gain a feel for the *significance* of the changes that are taking place. A $1 million increase in sales is much more significant if the prior year's sales were $2 million than if the prior year's sales were $20 million. In the first situation, the increase would be 50%—undoubtedly a significant increase for any firm. In the second situation, the increase would be only 5%—perhaps just a reflection of normal growth.

TREND PERCENTAGES Horizontal analysis of financial statements can also be carried out by computing *trend percentages.* **Trend percentages** state several years' financial data in terms of a base year. The base year equals 100%, with all other years stated as some percentage of this base. To illustrate, consider Compaq Computer Corporation which vies with IBM and Dell Computer for the number one position in personal computer sales. Compaq enjoyed tremendous growth in the early to mid-1990s, as evidenced by the following data:

	1996	1995	1994	1993	1992	1991	1990	1989
Sales (millions) . .	$18,109	$14,775	$10,866	$7,191	$4,000	$3,271	$3,599	$2,876
Net income (millions)	1,313	789	867	462	213	131	455	333

By simply looking at these data, one can see that sales increased in nearly every year since 1989. But how rapidly have sales been increasing and have the increases in net income kept pace with the increases in sales? By looking at the raw data alone, it is difficult to answer these questions. The increases in sales and the increases in net income can be put into better perspective by stating them in terms of trend percentages, with 1989 as the base year. These percentages (all rounded) are given below:

	1996	1995	1994	1993	1992	1991	1990	1989
Sales (millions)*	630%	513%	378%	250%	139%	114%	125%	100%
Net income (millions)	394%	237%	260%	139%	64%	39%	137%	100%

*For 1990, $3,599 ÷ $2,876 = 125%; for 1991, $3,271 ÷ $2,876 = 114%; and so forth.

The trend analysis is particularly striking when the data are plotted as in Exhibit 18–3. Compaq's sales growth has been impressive and even spectacular since 1992, but the growth in net income has been more sporadic. The roller-coaster-like performance of net income is likely due to a combination of intense competitive pressures, rapid technological change in the personal computer industry, general trends in the economy, and strategic decisions made by management. As explained in *The Wall Street Journal:*

> [In 1992], Compaq jettisoned its strategy of charging premium prices, after experiencing slumping sales and plummeting earnings in 1991. Under its new chief executive officer . . . the company initiated a price war, slashed its costs to offset plunging margins and broadened its product line. Sales have been surging ever since.[1]

Exhibit 18–3
COMPAQ COMPUTER CORPORATION
Trend Analysis of Sales and Net Income

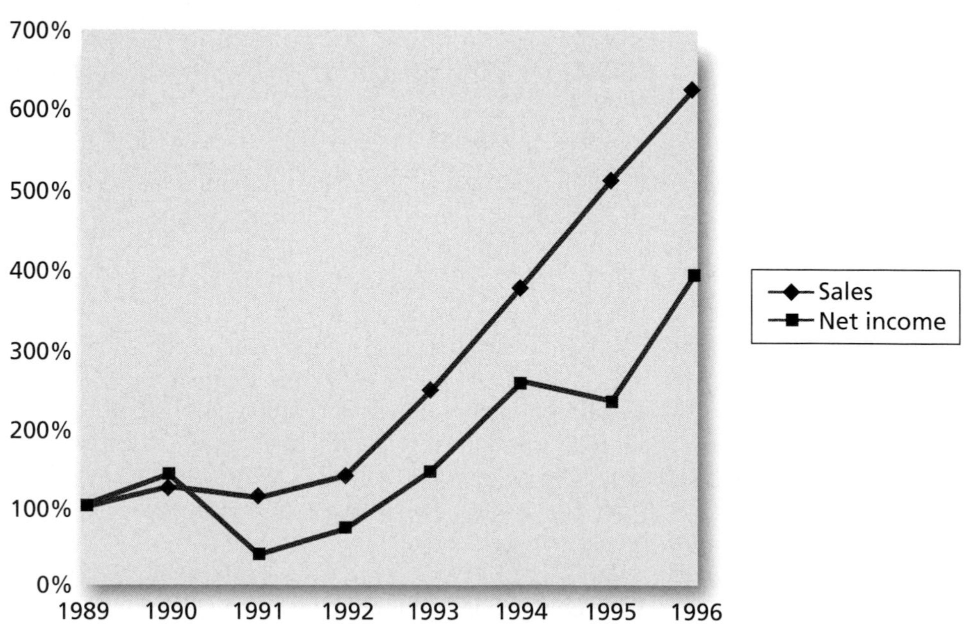

1. Jim Carlton, "Compaq PCs Outsold IBM and Apple World-Wide during the First Quarter," *The Wall Street Journal,* Wednesday, May 25, 1994, p. A3.

Common-Size Statements

objective 3

Place the balance sheet and the income statement in common-size form and properly interpret the results.

Key changes and trends can also be highlighted by the use of *common-size statements.* A **common-size statement** is one that shows the items appearing on it in percentage form as well as in dollar form. Each item is stated as a percentage of some total of which that item is a part. The preparation of common-size statements is known as **vertical analysis.**

Common-size statements are particularly useful when comparing data from different companies. For example, in a recent year, Wendy's net income was about $110 million, whereas McDonald's was $1,427 million. This comparison is somewhat misleading because of the dramatically different sizes of the two companies. To put this in better perspective, the net income figures can be expressed as a percentage of the sales revenues of each company. Since Wendy's sales revenues were $1,746 million and McDonald's were $9,794 million, Wendy's net income as a percentage of sales was about 6.3% and McDonald's was about 14.6%. While the comparison still favors McDonald's, the contrast between the two companies has been placed on a more comparable basis.

THE BALANCE SHEET One application of the vertical analysis idea is to state the separate assets of a company as percentages of total assets. A common-size statement of this type is shown in Exhibit 18–4 for Brickey Electronics.

Notice from Exhibit 18–4 that placing all assets in common-size form clearly shows the relative importance of the current assets as compared to the noncurrent assets. It also shows that significant changes have taken place in the *composition* of the current assets over the last year. Notice, for example, that the receivables have increased in relative importance and that both cash and inventory have declined in relative importance. Judging from the sharp increase in receivables, the deterioration in the cash position may be a result of inability to collect from customers.

THE INCOME STATEMENT Another application of the vertical analysis idea is to place all items on the income statement in percentage form in terms of sales. A common-size statement of this type is shown in Exhibit 18–5.

By placing all items on the income statement in common size in terms of sales, it is possible to see at a glance how each dollar of sales is distributed among the various costs, expenses, and profits. And by placing successive years' statements side by side, it is easy to spot interesting trends. For example, as shown in Exhibit 18–5, the cost of goods sold as a percentage of sales increased from 65.7% in 1998 to 69.2% in 1999. Or looking at this from a different viewpoint, the *gross margin percentage* declined from 34.3% in 1998 to 30.8% in 1999. Managers and investment analysts often pay close attention to the gross margin percentage since it is considered a broad gauge of profitability. The **gross margin percentage** is computed as follows:

$$\text{Gross margin percentage} = \frac{\text{Gross margin}}{\text{Sales}}$$

The gross margin percentage tends to be more stable for retailing companies than for other service companies and for manufacturers since the cost of goods sold in retailing excludes fixed costs. When fixed costs are included in the cost of goods sold figure, the gross margin percentage tends to increase and decrease with sales volume. With increases in sales volume, the fixed costs are spread across more units and the gross margin percentage improves.

While a higher gross margin percentage is generally considered to be better than a lower gross margin percentage, there are exceptions. Some companies purposely choose a strategy emphasizing low prices (and hence low gross margins). An increasing

Exhibit 18–4

BRICKEY ELECTRONICS
Common-Size Comparative Balance Sheet
December 31, 1999, and 1998
(dollars in thousands)

			Common-Size Percentages	
	1999	1998	1999	1998
Assets				
Current assets:				
Cash	$ 1,200	$ 2,350	3.8%*	8.1%
Accounts receivable, net	6,000	4,000	19.0%	13.8%
Inventory	8,000	10,000	25.4%	34.5%
Prepaid expenses	300	120	1.0%	0.4%
Total current assets	15,500	16,470	49.2%	56.9%
Property and equipment:				
Land	4,000	4,000	12.7%	13.8%
Buildings and equipment, net	12,000	8,500	38.1%	29.3%
Total property and equipment	16,000	12,500	50.8%	43.1%
Total assets	$31,500	$28,970	100.0%	100.0%
Liabilities and Stockholders' Equity				
Current liabilities:				
Accounts payable	$ 5,800	$ 4,000	18.4%	13.8%
Accrued payables	900	400	2.8%	1.4%
Notes payable, short term	300	600	1.0%	2.1%
Total current liabilities	7,000	5,000	22.2%	17.3%
Long-term liabilities:				
Bonds payable, 8%	7,500	8,000	23.8%	27.6%
Total liabilities	14,500	13,000	46.0%	44.9%
Stockholders' equity:				
Preferred stock, $100, 6%, $100 liquidation value	2,000	2,000	6.4%	6.9%
Common stock, $12 par	6,000	6,000	19.0%	20.7%
Additional paid-in capital	1,000	1,000	3.2%	3.5%
Total paid-in capital	9,000	9,000	28.6%	31.1%
Retained earnings	8,000	6,970	25.4%	24.0%
Total stockholders' equity	17,000	15,970	54.0%	55.1%
Total liabilities and stockholders' equity	$31,500	$28,970	100.0%	100.0%

*Each asset account on a common-size statement is expressed in terms of total assets, and each liability and equity account is expressed in terms of total liabilities and stockholders' equity. For example, the percentage figure above for Cash in 1999 is computed as follows: $1,200 ÷ $31,500 = 3.8%.

gross margin in such a company might be a sign that the company's strategy is not being effectively implemented.

Common-size statements are also very helpful in pointing out efficiencies and inefficiencies that might otherwise go unnoticed. To illustrate, in 1999, Brickey Electronics' selling expenses increased by $500,000 over 1998. A glance at the common-size income statement shows, however, that on a relative basis, selling expenses were no higher in 1999 than in 1998. In each year they represented 13.5% of sales.

Exhibit 18–5

BRICKEY ELECTRONICS
Common-Size Comparative Income Statement
For the Years Ended December 31, 1999, and 1998
(dollars in thousands)

			Common-Size Percentages	
	1999	1998	1999	1998
Sales	$52,000	$48,000	100.0%	100.0%
Cost of goods sold	36,000	31,500	69.2%	65.6%
Gross margin	16,000	16,500	30.8%	34.4%
Operating expenses:				
Selling expenses	7,000	6,500	13.5%	13.5%
Administrative expenses	5,860	6,100	11.3%	12.7%
Total operating expenses	12,860	12,600	24.7%	26.2%
Net operating income	3,140	3,900	6.0%	8.1%
Interest expense	640	700	1.2%	1.5%
Net income before taxes	2,500	3,200	4.8%	6.7%
Income taxes (30%)	750	960	1.4%	2.0%
Net income	$ 1,750	$ 2,240	3.4%	4.7%

*Note that the percentage figures for each year are expressed in terms of total sales for the year. For example, the percentage figure for cost of goods sold in 1999 is computed as follows:

$36,000 ÷ $52,000 = 69.2%

Ratio Analysis—The Common Stockholder

objective 4

Identify the ratios used to measure the well-being of the common stockholder and state each ratio's formula and interpretation.

A number of financial ratios are used to assess how well the company is doing from the standpoint of the stockholders. These ratios naturally focus on net income, dividends, and stockholders' equities.

Earnings per Share

An investor buys a share of stock in the hope of realizing a return in the form of either dividends or future increases in the value of the stock. Since earnings form the basis for dividend payments, as well as the basis for future increases in the value of shares, investors are always interested in a company's reported *earnings per share.* Probably no single statistic is more widely quoted or relied on by investors than earnings per share, although it has some inherent limitations, as discussed below.

Earnings per share is computed by dividing net income available for common stockholders by the average number of common shares outstanding during the year. "Net income available for common stockholders" is net income less dividends paid to the owners of the company's preferred stock.[2]

2. Another complication can arise when a company has issued securities such as executive stock options or warrants that can be converted into shares of common stock. If these conversions were to take place, the same earnings would have to be distributed among a greater number of common shares. Therefore, a supplemental earnings per share figure, called diluted earnings per share, may have to be computed. Refer to a current intermediate financial accounting text for details.

$$\text{Earnings per share} = \frac{\text{Net income} - \text{Preferred dividends}}{\text{Average number of common shares outstanding}}$$

Using the data in Exhibits 18–1 and 18–2, we see that the earnings per share for Brickey Electronics for 1999 would be computed as follows:

$$\frac{\$1{,}750{,}000 - \$120{,}000}{(500{,}000 \text{ shares}^* + 500{,}000 \text{ shares})/2} = \$3.26$$

*$6,000,000 ÷ 12 = 500,000 shares

Price-Earnings Ratio

The relationship between the market price of a share of stock and the stock's current earnings per share is often quoted in terms of a **price-earnings ratio.** If we assume that the current market price for Brickey Electronics' stock is $40 per share, the company's price-earnings ratio would be computed as follows:

$$\text{Price-earnings ratio} = \frac{\text{Market price per share}}{\text{Earnings per share}}$$

$$\frac{\$40}{\$3.26} = 12.3$$

The price-earnings ratio is 12.3; that is, the stock is selling for about 12.3 times its current earnings per share.

The price-earnings ratio is widely used by investors as a general guideline in gauging stock values. A high price-earnings ratio means that investors are willing to pay a premium for the company's stock—presumably because the company is expected to have higher than average future earnings growth. Conversely, if investors believe a company's future earnings growth prospects are limited, the company's price-earnings ratio would be relatively low.

Dividend Payout and Yield Ratios

Investors hold shares in a company because they anticipate an attractive return. The return sought isn't always dividends. Many investors prefer not to receive dividends. Instead, they prefer to have the company retain all earnings and reinvest them internally in order to support growth. The stocks of companies that adopt this approach, loosely termed *growth stocks,* often enjoy rapid upward movement in market price. Other investors prefer to have a dependable, current source of income through regular dividend payments. Such investors seek out stocks with consistent dividend records and payout ratios.

THE DIVIDEND PAYOUT RATIO The **dividend payout ratio** gauges the portion of current earnings being paid out in dividends. Investors who seek growth in market price would like this ratio to be small, whereas investors who seek dividends prefer it to be large. This ratio is computed by relating dividends per share to earnings per share for common stock:

$$\text{Dividend payout ratio} = \frac{\text{Dividends per share}}{\text{Earnings per share}}$$

For Brickey Electronics, the dividend payout ratio for 1999 is computed as follows:

$$\frac{\$1.20 \text{ (see Exhibit 18–2)}}{\$3.26} = 36.8\%$$

There is no such thing as a "right" payout ratio, even though it should be noted that the ratio tends to be similar for companies within a particular industry. Industries with ample opportunities for growth at high rates of return on assets tend to have low payout ratios, whereas payout ratios tend to be high in industries with limited reinvestment opportunities.

THE DIVIDEND YIELD RATIO The **dividend yield ratio** is obtained by dividing the current dividends per share by the current market price per share:

$$\text{Dividend yield ratio} = \frac{\text{Dividends per share}}{\text{Market price per share}}$$

The market price for Brickey Electronics' stock is $40 per share so the dividend yield is computed as follows:

$$\frac{\$1.20}{\$40} = 3.0\%$$

The dividend yield ratio measures the rate of return (in the form of cash dividends only) that would be earned by an investor who buys the common stock at the current market price. A low dividend yield ratio is neither bad nor good by itself. As discussed above, a company may pay out very little dividends because it has ample opportunities for reinvesting funds within the company at high rates of return.

Return on Total Assets

Managers have both *financing* and *operating* responsibilities. Financing responsibilities relate to how one *obtains* the funds needed to provide for the assets in an organization. Operating responsibilities relate to how one *uses* the assets once they have been obtained. Both are vital to a well-managed firm. However, care must be taken not to confuse or mix the two when assessing the performance of a manager. That is, whether funds have been obtained from creditors or from stockholders should not be allowed to influence one's assessment of *how well* the assets have been employed since being received by the firm.

The **return on total assets** is a measure of operating performance that shows how well assets have been employed. It is defined as follows:

$$\text{Return on total assets} = \frac{\text{Net income} + [\text{Interest expense} \times (1 - \text{Tax Rate})]}{\text{Average total assets}}$$

Adding interest expense back to net income results in an adjusted earnings figure that shows what earnings would have been if the assets had been acquired solely by selling shares of stock. With this adjustment, the return on total assets can be compared for companies with differing amounts of debt or over time for a single company that has changed its mix of debt and equity. Thus, the measurement of how well the assets have been employed is not influenced by how the assets were financed. Notice that the interest expense is placed on an after-tax basis by multiplying it by the factor (1 − Tax rate).

The return on total assets for Brickey Electronics for 1999 would be computed as follows (from Exhibits 18–1 and 18–2):

Net income	$ 1,750,000	
Add back interest expense: $640,000 × (1 − 0.30)	448,000	
Total	$ 2,198,000	(a)
Assets, beginning of year	$28,970,000	
Assets, end of year	31,500,000	
Total	$60,470,000	
Average total assets: $60,470,000 ÷ 2	$30,235,000	(b)
Return on total assets, (a) ÷ (b)	7.3%	

Brickey Electronics has earned a return of 7.3% on average assets employed over the last year.

Return on Common Stockholders' Equity

One of the primary reasons for operating a corporation is to generate income for the benefit of the common stockholders. One measure of a company's success in this regards is the **return on common stockholders' equity,** which divides the net income remaining for common stockholders by the average common stockholders' equity for the year. The formula is as follows:

$$\text{Return on common stockholders' equity} = \frac{\text{Net income} - \text{Preferred dividends}}{\text{Average common stockholders' equity}}$$

where

$$\text{Average common stockholders' equity} = \text{Average total stockholders' equity} - \text{Average preferred stock}$$

For Brickey Electronics, the return on common stockholders' equity is 11.3% for 1999 as shown below:

Net income	$ 1,750,000	
Deduct preferred dividends	120,000	
Net income remaining for common stockholders	$ 1,630,000	(a)
Average stockholders' equity	$16,485,000*	
Deduct average preferred stock	2,000,000†	
Average common stockholders' equity	$14,485,000	(b)
Return on common stockholders' equity, (a) ÷ (b)	11.3%	

*$15,970,000 + $17,000,000 = $32,970,000; $32,970,000 ÷ 2 = $16,485,000.

†$2,000,000 + $2,000,000 = $4,000,000; $4,000,000 ÷ 2 = $2,000,000.

Compare the return on common stockholders' equity above (11.3%) with the return on total assets computed in the preceding section (7.3%). Why is the return on common stockholders' equity so much higher? The answer lies in the principle of *financial leverage.* Financial leverage is discussed in the following paragraphs.

Financial Leverage

objective 5

Explain what is meant by the term *financial leverage* and show how financial leverage is measured.

Financial leverage (often called *leverage* for short) involves acquiring assets with funds that have been obtained from creditors or from preferred stockholders at a fixed rate of return. If the assets in which the funds are invested are able to earn a rate of return *greater* than the fixed rate of return required by the funds' suppliers, then we have **positive financial leverage** and the common stockholders benefit.

For example, suppose that CBS is able to earn an after-tax return of 12% on its broadcasting assets. If the company can borrow from creditors at a 10% interest rate in order to expand its assets, then the common stockholders can benefit from positive leverage. The borrowed funds invested in the business will earn an after-tax return of 12%, but the after-tax interest cost of the borrowed funds will be only 7% [10% interest rate × (1 − 0.30) = 7%]. The difference will go to the common stockholders.

We can see this concept in operation in the case of Brickey Electronics. Notice from Exhibit 18–1 that the company's bonds payable bear a fixed interest rate of 8%. The after-tax interest cost of these bonds is only 5.6% [8% interest rate × (1 − 0.30) = 5.6%]. The company's assets are generating an after-tax return of 7.3%, as we computed earlier. Since this return on assets is greater than the after-tax interest cost of the bonds, leverage is positive, and the difference accrues to the benefit of the common stockholders. This explains in part why the return on common stockholders' equity (11.3%) is greater than the return on total assets (7.3%).

Unfortunately, leverage is a two-edged sword. If assets are unable to earn a high enough rate to cover the interest costs of debt, or to cover the preferred dividend due to the preferred stockholders, *then the common stockholder suffers.* Under these circumstances, we have **negative financial leverage.**

THE IMPACT OF INCOME TAXES Debt and preferred stock are not equally efficient in generating positive leverage. The reason is that interest on debt is tax deductible, whereas preferred dividends are not. This usually makes debt a much more effective source of positive leverage than preferred stock.

To illustrate this point, suppose that the Hospital Corporation of America is considering three ways of financing a $100 million expansion of its chain of hospitals:

1. $100 million from an issue of common stock.
2. $50 million from an issue of common stock, and $50 million from an issue of preferred stock bearing a dividend rate of 8%.
3. $50 million from an issue of common stock, and $50 million from an issue of bonds bearing an interest rate of 8%.

Assuming that the Hospital Corporation of America can earn an additional $15 million each year before interest and taxes as a result of the expansion, the operating results under each of the three alternatives are shown in Exhibit 18–6.

If the entire $100 million is raised from an issue of common stock, then the return to the common stockholders will be only 10.5%, as shown under alternative 1 in the exhibit. If half of the funds are raised from an issue of preferred stock, then the return to the common stockholders increases to 13%, due to the positive effects of leverage. However, if half of the funds are raised from an issue of bonds, then the return to the common stockholders jumps to 15.4%, as shown under alternative 3. Thus, long-term debt is much more efficient in generating positive leverage than is preferred stock. The reason is that the interest expense on long-term debt is tax deductible, whereas the dividends on preferred stock are not.

THE DESIRABILITY OF LEVERAGE Because of leverage, having some debt in the capital structure can substantially benefit the common stockholder. For this reason, most companies today try to maintain a level of debt that is considered to be normal within the industry. Many companies, such as commercial banks and other

Exhibit 18–6 Leverage from Preferred Stock and Long-Term Debt

	Alternatives: $100,000,000 Issue of Securities		
	Alternative 1: $100,000,000 Common Stock	Alternative 2: $50,000,000 Common Stock; $50,000,000 Preferred Stock	Alternative 3: $50,000,000 Common Stock; $50,000,000 Bonds
Earnings before interest and taxes	$ 15,000,000	$15,000,000	$15,000,000
Deduct interest expense (8% × $50,000,000)	—	—	4,000,000
Net income before taxes	15,000,000	15,000,000	11,000,000
Deduct income taxes (30%)	4,500,000	4,500,000	3,300,000
Net income	10,500,000	10,500,000	7,700,000
Deduct preferred dividends (8% × $50,000,000)	—	4,000,000	—
Net income remaining for common (a)	$ 10,500,000	$ 6,500,000	$ 7,700,000
Common stockholders' equity (b)	$100,000,000	$50,000,000	$50,000,000
Return on common stockholders' equity (a) ÷ (b)	10.5%	13.0%	15.4%

financial institutions, rely heavily on leverage to provide an attractive return on their common shares.

Book Value per Share

Another statistic frequently used in attempting to assess the well-being of the common stockholder is book value per share. The **book value per share** measures the amount that would be distributed to holders of each share of common stock if all assets were sold at their balance sheet carrying amounts (i.e., book values) and if all creditors were paid off. Thus, book value per share is based entirely on historical costs. The formula for computing it is as follows:

$$\text{Book value per share} = \frac{\text{Common stockholders' equity (Total stockholders' equity} - \text{Preferred stock)}}{\text{Number of common shares outstanding}}$$

Total stockholders' equity (see Exhibit 18–1)	$17,000,000
Deduct preferred stock (see Exhibit 18–1)	2,000,000
Common stockholders' equity	$15,000,000

The book value per share of Brickey Electronics' common stock is computed as follows:

$$\frac{\$15{,}000{,}000}{500{,}000 \text{ shares}} = \$30$$

If this book value is compared with the $40 market value of Brickey Electronics stock, then the stock appears to be somewhat overpriced. However, as we discussed earlier, market prices reflect expectations about future earnings and dividends, whereas book value largely reflects the results of events that occurred in the past. Ordinarily, the market value of a stock exceeds its book value. For example, in a recent year, Microsoft's common stock often traded at over 4 times its book value, and Coca-Cola's market value was over 17 times its book value.

Focus on Current Practice

McDonald's Corporation provides an interesting illustration of the use of financial ratios. Data for a recent year appear below:

Net income	$1,427 million
Interest expense	$340 million
Tax rate	34.2%
Average total assets	$14,503 million
Preferred stock dividends	$40 million
Average common stockholders' equity	$6,857 million
Common stock dividends per share	$0.26
Earnings per share	$1.97
Market price per share—end of year	$42.125
Book value per share	$10.73

Some key financial ratios are computed below:

$$\text{Return on total assets} = \frac{\$1{,}427 + [\$340 \times (1 - 0.342)]}{\$14{,}503} = 11.4\%$$

$$\text{Return on common stockholders' equity} = \frac{\$1{,}427 - \$40}{\$6{,}857} = 20.2\%$$

$$\text{Dividend payout ratio} = \frac{\$0.26}{\$1.97} = 13.2\%$$

$$\text{Dividend yield ratio} = \frac{\$0.26}{\$42.125} = 0.62\%$$

The return on common stockholders' equity of 20.2% is higher than the return on total assets of 11.4%, and therefore the company has positive financial leverage. (About half of the company's financing is provided by creditors; the rest is provided by common and preferred stockholders.) According to the company's annual report, "Given McDonald's high return on equity and assets, management believes it is prudent to reinvest a significant portion of earnings back into the business. Accordingly, the common stock [dividend] yield is relatively modest." Indeed, only 13.2% of earnings are paid out in dividends. In relation to the stock price, this is a dividend yield of less than 1%. Finally, note that the market value per share is over four times as large as the book value per share. This premium over book value reflects the market's perception that McDonald's earnings will continue to grow in the future. ■

Ratio Analysis—The Short-Term Creditor

objective 6

Identify the ratios used to measure the well-being of the short-term creditor and state each ratio's formula and interpretation.

Short-term creditors, such as suppliers, want to be repaid on time. Therefore, they focus on the company's cash flows and on its working capital since these are the company's primary sources of cash in the short run.

Working Capital

The excess of current assets over current liabilities is known as **working capital.** The working capital for Brickey Electronics is computed below:

Working capital = Current assets − Current liabilities

	1999	1998
Current assets	$15,500,000	$16,470,000
Current liabilities	7,000,000	5,000,000
Working capital	$ 8,500,000	$11,470,000

The amount of working capital available to a firm is of considerable interest to short-term creditors, *since it represents assets financed from long-term capital sources that do not require near-term repayment.* Therefore, the greater the working capital, the greater is the cushion of protection available to short-term creditors and the greater is the assurance that short-term debts will be paid when due.

Although it is always comforting to short-term creditors to see a large working capital balance, a large balance by itself is no assurance that debts will be paid when due. Rather than being a sign of strength, a large working capital balance may simply mean that obsolete inventory is being accumulated. Therefore, to put the working capital figure into proper perspective, it must be supplemented with other analytical work. The following four ratios (the current ratio, the acid-test ratio, the accounts receivable turnover, and the inventory turnover) should all be used in connection with an analysis of working capital.

Current Ratio

The elements involved in the computation of working capital are frequently expressed in ratio form. A company's current assets divided by its current liabilities is known as the **current ratio:**

$$\text{Current ratio} = \frac{\text{Current assets}}{\text{Current liabilities}}$$

For Brickey Electronics, the current ratios for 1998 and 1999 would be computed as follows:

1999	1998
$\frac{\$15,500,000}{\$7,000,000} = 2.21$ to 1	$\frac{\$16,470,000}{\$5,000,000} = 3.29$ to 1

Although widely regarded as a measure of short-term debt-paying ability, the current ratio must be interpreted with great care. A *declining* ratio, as above, might be a sign of a deteriorating financial condition. On the other hand, it might be the result of eliminating obsolete inventories or other stagnant current assets. An *improving* ratio might be the result of an unwise stockpiling of inventory, or it might indicate an improving financial situation. In short, the current ratio is useful, but tricky to interpret. To avoid a blunder, the analyst must take a hard look at the individual assets and liabilities involved.

The general rule of thumb calls for a current ratio of 2 to 1. This rule is subject to many exceptions, depending on the industry and the firm involved. Some industries can operate quite successfully on a current ratio of slightly over 1 to 1. The adequacy of a current ratio depends heavily on the *composition* of the assets involved. For example, as we see in the table below, both Worthington Corporation and Greystone, Inc., have current ratios of 2 to 1. However, they are not in comparable financial condition. Greystone is likely to have difficulty meeting its current financial obligations, since almost all of its current assets consist of inventory rather than more liquid assets such as cash and accounts receivable.

	Worthington Corporation	Greystone, Inc.
Current assets:		
Cash	$ 25,000	$ 2,000
Accounts receivable, net	60,000	8,000
Inventory	85,000	160,000
Prepaid expenses	5,000	5,000
Total current assets	$175,000	$175,000 (a)
Current liabilities	$ 87,500	$ 87,500 (b)
Current ratio, (a) ÷ (b)	2 to 1	2 to 1

Acid-Test (Quick) Ratio

The **acid-test (quick) ratio** is a much more rigorous test of a company's ability to meet its short-term debts. Inventories and prepaid expenses are excluded from total current assets, leaving only the more liquid (or "quick") assets to be divided by current liabilities.

$$\text{Acid-test ratio} = \frac{\text{Cash} + \text{Marketable securities} + \text{Current receivables*}}{\text{Current liabilities}}$$

*Current receivables include both accounts receivable and any short-term notes receivable.

The acid-test ratio is designed to measure how well a company can meet its obligations without having to liquidate or depend too heavily on its inventory. Since inventory may be difficult to sell in times of economic stress, it is generally felt that to be properly protected, each dollar of liabilities should be backed by at least $1 of quick assets. Thus, an acid-test ratio of 1 to 1 is broadly viewed as being adequate in many firms.

The acid-test ratios for Brickey Electronics for 1998 and 1999 are computed below:

	1999	1998
Cash (see Exhibit 18–1)	$1,200,000	$2,350,000
Accounts receivable (see Exhibit 18–1)	6,000,000	4,000,000
Total quick assets	$7,200,000	$6,350,000 (a)
Current liabilities (see Exhibit 18–1)	$7,000,000	$5,000,000 (b)
Acid-test ratio, (a) ÷ (b)	1.03 to 1	1.27 to 1

Although Brickey Electronics has an acid-test ratio for 1999 that is within the acceptable range, an analyst might be concerned about several disquieting trends revealed in the company's balance sheet. Notice in Exhibit 18–1 that short-term debts are rising, while the cash position seems to be deteriorating. Perhaps the weakened cash position is a result of the greatly expanded volume of accounts receivable. One wonders why the accounts receivable have been allowed to increase so rapidly in so brief a time.

In short, as with the current ratio, the acid-test ratio should be interpreted with one eye on its basic components.

Accounts Receivable Turnover

The **accounts receivable turnover** is a rough measure of how many times a company's accounts receivable have been turned into cash during the year. It is frequently used in conjunction with an analysis of working capital, since a smooth flow from accounts receivable into cash is an important indicator of the "quality" of a company's working capital and is critical to its ability to operate. The accounts receivable turnover is computed by dividing sales on account (i.e., credit sales) by the average accounts receivable balance for the year.

$$\text{Accounts receivable turnover} = \frac{\text{Sales on account}}{\text{Average accounts receivable balance}}$$

Assuming that all sales for the year were on account, the accounts receivable turnover for Brickey Electronics for 1999 would be computed as follows:

$$\frac{\text{Sales on account}}{\text{Average accounts receivable balance}} = \frac{\$52{,}000{,}000}{\$5{,}000{,}000^*} = 10.4 \text{ times}$$

*$4,000,000 + $6,000,000 = $10,000,000; $10,000,000 ÷ 2 = $5,000,000 average.

The turnover figure can then be divided into 365 to determine the average number of days being taken to collect an account (known as the **average collection period**).

$$\text{Average collection period} = \frac{\text{365 days}}{\text{Accounts receivable turnover}}$$

The average collection period for Brickey Electronics for 1999 is computed as follows:

$$\frac{365}{10.4 \text{ times}} = 35 \text{ days}$$

This simply means that on average it takes 35 days to collect on a credit sale. Whether the average of 35 days taken to collect an account is good or bad depends on the credit terms Brickey Electronics is offering its customers. If the credit terms are 30 days, than a 35-day average collection period would usually be viewed as very good. Most customers will tend to withhold payment for as long as the credit terms will allow and may even go over a few days. This factor, added to ever-present problems with a few slow-paying customers, can cause the average collection period to exceed normal credit terms by a week or so and should not cause great alarm.

On the other hand, if the company's credit terms are 10 days, then a 35-day average collection period is worrisome. The long collection period may result from many old unpaid accounts of doubtful collectability, or it may be a result of poor day-to-day credit management. The firm may be making sales with inadequate credit checks on customers, or perhaps no follow-ups are being made on slow accounts.

Inventory Turnover

The **inventory turnover ratio** measures how many times a company's inventory has been sold and replaced during the year. It is computed by dividing the cost of goods sold by the average level of inventory on hand:

$$\text{Inventory turnover} = \frac{\text{Cost of goods sold}}{\text{Average inventory balance}}$$

The average inventory figure is the average of the beginning and ending inventory figures. Since Brickey Electronics has a beginning inventory of $10,000,000 and an ending inventory of $8,000,000, its average inventory for the year would be $9,000,000. The company's inventory turnover for 1999 would be computed as follows:

$$\frac{\text{Cost of goods sold}}{\text{Average inventory balance}} = \frac{\$36{,}000{,}000}{\$9{,}000{,}000} = 4 \text{ times}$$

The number of days being taken to sell the entire inventory one time (called the **average sale period**) can be computed by dividing 365 by the inventory turnover figure:

$$\text{Average sale period} = \frac{365 \text{ days}}{\text{Inventory turnover}}$$

$$\frac{365}{4 \text{ times}} = 91\tfrac{1}{4} \text{ days}$$

The average sale period varies from industry to industry. Grocery stores tend to turn their inventory over very quickly, perhaps as often as every 12 to 15 days. On the other hand, jewelry stores tend to turn their inventory over very slowly, perhaps only a couple of times each year.

If a firm has a turnover that is much slower than the average for its industry, then it may have obsolete goods on hand, or its inventory stocks may be needlessly high. Excessive inventories tie up funds that could be used elsewhere in operations. Managers sometimes argue that they must buy in very large quantities to take advantage of the best discounts being offered. But these discounts must be carefully weighed against the added costs of insurance, taxes, financing, and risks of obsolescence and deterioration that result from carrying added inventories.

Inventory turnover has been increasing in recent years as companies have adopted just-in-time (JIT) methods. Under JIT, inventories are purposely kept low, and thus a company utilizing JIT methods may have a very high inventory turnover as compared to other companies. Indeed, one of the goals of JIT is to increase inventory turnover by systematically reducing the amount of inventory on hand.

Ratio Analysis—The Long-Term Creditor

objective 7

Identify the ratios used to measure the well-being of the long-term creditor and state each ratio's formula and interpretation.

The position of long-term creditors differs from that of short-term creditors in that they are concerned with both the near-term *and* the long-term ability of a firm to meet its commitments. They are concerned with the near term since the interest they are entitled to is normally paid on a current basis. They are concerned with the long term since they want to be fully repaid on schedule.

Since the long-term creditor is usually faced with greater risks than the short-term creditor, firms are often required to agree to various restrictive covenants, or rules, for the long-term creditor's protection. Examples of such restrictive covenants include the maintenance of minimum working capital levels and restrictions on payment of dividends to common stockholders. Although these restrictive covenants are in widespread use, they must be viewed as a poor second to adequate future *earnings* from the point of view of assessing protection and safety. Creditors do not want to go to court to collect their claims; they would much prefer staking the safety of their claims for interest and eventual repayment of principal on an orderly and consistent flow of funds from operations.

Times Interest Earned Ratio

The most common measure of the ability of a firm's operations to provide protection to the long-term creditor is the **times interest earned ratio.** It is computed by dividing earnings *before* interest expense and income taxes (i.e., net operating income) by the yearly interest charges that must be met:

$$\text{Times interest earned} = \frac{\text{Earnings before interest expense and income taxes}}{\text{Interest expense}}$$

For Brickey Electronics, the times interest earned ratio for 1999 would be computed as follows:

$$\frac{\$3{,}140{,}000}{\$640{,}000} = 4.9 \text{ times}$$

Earnings before income taxes must be used in the computation, since interest expense deductions come *before* income taxes are computed. Creditors have first claim on earnings. Only those earnings remaining after all interest charges have been provided for are subject to income taxes.

Generally, earnings are viewed as adequate to protect long-term creditors if the times interest earned ratio is 2 or more. Before making a final judgment, however, it would be necessary to look at a firm's long-run *trend* of earnings and evaluate how vulnerable the firm is to cyclical changes in the economy.

Debt-to-Equity Ratio

Long-term creditors are also concerned with keeping a reasonable balance between the portion of assets provided by creditors and the portion of assets provided by the stockholders of a firm. This balance is measured by the **debt-to-equity ratio:**

$$\text{Debt-to-equity ratio} = \frac{\text{Total liabilities}}{\text{Stockholders' equity}}$$

	1999	1998
Total liabilities	$14,500,000	$13,000,000 (a)
Stockholders' equity	17,000,000	15,970,000 (b)
Debt-to-equity ratio, (a) ÷ (b)	0.85 to 1	0.81 to 1

The debt-to-equity ratio indicates the amount of assets being provided by creditors for each dollar of assets being provided by the owners of a company. In 1998, creditors of Brickey Electronics were providing 81 cents of assets for each $1 of assets being provided by stockholders; the figure increased only slightly to 85 cents by 1999.

Creditors would like the debt-to-equity ratio to be relatively low. The lower the ratio, the greater the amount of assets being provided by the owners of a company and the greater is the buffer of protection to creditors. By contrast, common stockholders would like the ratio to be relatively high, since through leverage, common stockholders can benefit from the assets being provided by creditors.

In most industries, norms have developed over the years that serve as guides to firms in their decisions as to the "right" amount of debt to include in the capital structure. Different industries face different risks. For this reason, the level of debt that is appropriate for firms in one industry is not necessarily a guide to the level of debt that is appropriate for firms in a different industry.

Focus on Current Practice

Emmanuel Kampouris, the Egyptian-born CEO of American Standard, has transformed the manufacturer of bathroom fixtures, coolers, and truck parts into a lean competitor. The key to this transformation has been "demand flow technology"—a sort of just-in-time (JIT) on steroids. In addition to cutting inventories, the aim is to slash manufacturing time. The end result is the capability to respond to the customer faster, at lower cost, and with greater variety than before. At Home Depot, Standard's plumbing, heating, and air-conditioning goods now arrive within days—not months—of being ordered. Overall, the company has reduced its inventories by more than 50%—hundreds of millions of dollars of savings. Inventory turnover has improved from less than 5 times to over 11 times, and working capital has declined from 8.6% of sales to 4.9%. The interest savings alone on the reduced inventories are over $60 million per year. Kampouris has also slashed the company's debt by nearly $1 billion—dropping the company's debt-to-equity ratio from 87.5% down to about 39%.[3] ■

Summary of Ratios and Sources of Comparative Ratio Data

Exhibit 18–7 contains a summary of the ratios discussed in this chapter. The formula for each ratio and a summary comment on each ratio's significance are included in the exhibit.

3. "American Standard Wises Up," *Business Week,* November 18, 1996, p. 50; Shawn Tully, "American Standard: Prophet of Zero Working Capital," *Fortune,* June 13, 1994, pp. 113–14.

Exhibit 18–7 Summary of Ratios

Ratio	Formula	Significance
Gross margin percentage	Gross margin ÷ Sales	A broad measure of profitability
Earnings per share (of common stock)	(Net income − Preferred dividends) ÷ Average number of common shares outstanding	Tends to have an effect on the market price per share, as reflected in the price-earnings ratio
Price-earnings ratio	Market price per share ÷ Earnings per share	An index of whether a stock is relatively cheap or relatively expensive in relation to current earnings
Dividend payout ratio	Dividends per share ÷ Earnings per share	An index showing whether a company pays out most of its earnings in dividends or reinvests the earnings internally
Dividend yield ratio	Dividends per share ÷ Market price per share	Shows the return in terms of cash dividends being provided by a stock
Return on total assets	{Net income + [Interest expense × (1 − Tax rate)]} ÷ Average total assets	Measure of how well assets have been employed by management
Return on common stockholders' equity	(Net income − Preferred dividends) ÷ Average common stockholders' equity (Average total stockholders' equity − Average preferred stock)	When compared to the return on total assets, measures the extent to which financial leverage is working for or against common stockholders
Book value per share	Common stockholders' equity (Total stockholders' equity − Preferred stock) ÷ Number of common shares outstanding	Measures the amount that would be distributed to holders of common stock if all assets were sold at their balance sheet carrying amounts and if all creditors were paid off
Working capital	Current assets − Current liabilities	Measures the company's ability to repay current liabilities using only current assets.
Current ratio	Current assets ÷ Current liabilities	Test of short-term debt-paying ability
Acid-test (quick) ratio	(Cash + Marketable securities + Current receivables) ÷ Current liabilities	Test of short-term debt-paying ability without having to rely on inventory
Accounts receivable turnover	Sales on account ÷ Average accounts receivable balance	A rough measure of how many times a company's accounts receivable have been turned into cash during the year
Average collection period (age of receivables)	365 days ÷ Accounts receivable turnover	Measure of the average number of days taken to collect an account receivable
Inventory turnover	Cost of goods sold ÷ Average inventory balance	Measure of how many times a company's inventory has been sold during the year
Average sale period (turnover in days)	365 days ÷ Inventory turnover	Measure of the average number of days taken to sell the inventory one time
Times interest earned	Earnings before interest expense and income taxes ÷ Interest expense	Measure of the company's ability to make interest payments
Debt-to-equity ratio	Total liabilities ÷ Stockholders' equity	Measure of the amount of assets being provided by creditors for each dollar of assets being provided by the stockholders

Exhibit 18–8
Published Sources of Financial Ratios

Source	Content
EDGAR, Securities and Exchange Commission. Web site that is updated continuously. http://www.sec.gov/edaux/formlynx.htm	An exhaustive database accessible on the World Wide Web that contains reports filed by companies with the SEC. These reports can be downloaded.
Almanac of Business and Industrial Financial Ratios. Prentice-Hall. Published annually.	An exhaustive source that contains common-size income statements and financial ratios by industry and by size of companies within each industry.
Annual Statement Studies. Robert Morris Associates. Published annually.	A widely used publication that contains common-size statements and financial ratios on individual companies. The companies are arranged by industry.
Moody's Industrial Manual and *Moody's Bank and Finance Manual.* Dun & Bradstreet. Published annually.	An exhaustive source that contains financial ratios on all companies listed on the New York Stock Exchange, the American Stock Exchange, and regional American exchanges.
Key Business Ratios. Dun & Bradstreet. Published annually.	Fourteen commonly used financial ratios are computed for over 800 major industry groupings.
Standard & Poor's Industry Survey. Standard & Poor's. Published annually.	Various statistics, including some financial ratios, are provided by industry and on leading companies within each industry grouping.

Exhibit 18–8 contains a listing of published sources that provide comparative ratio data organized by industry. These sources are used extensively by managers, investors, and analysts in doing comparative analyses and in attempting to assess the well-being of companies. The World Wide Web also contains a wealth of financial and other data. A search engine such as Alta Vista, Yahoo, or Excite can be used to track down information on individual companies. Many companies have their own web sites on which they post their latest financial reports and news of interest to potential investors. The *EDGAR* database listed in Exhibit 18–8 is a particularly rich source of data. It contains copies of all reports filed by companies with the SEC since about 1995—including annual reports filed as form 10-K.

Summary

The data contained in financial statements represent a quantitative summary of a firm's operations and activities. Someone who is skillful at analyzing these statements can learn much about a company's strengths, weaknesses, emerging problems, operating efficiency, profitability, and so forth.

Many techniques are available to analyze financial statements and to assess the direction and importance of trends and changes. In this chapter, we have discussed three such analytical techniques—dollar and percentage changes in statements, common-size statements, and ratio analysis. Refer to Exhibit 18–7 for a detailed listing of the ratios. This listing also contains a brief statement as to the significance of each ratio.

Review Problem: Selected Ratios and Financial Leverage

Starbucks Coffee Company is the leading retailer and roaster of specialty coffee in North America with over 1,000 stores offering freshly brewed coffee, pastries, and coffee beans. Data from recent financial statements are given below:

STARBUCKS COFFEE COMPANY
Comparative Balance Sheet
(dollars in thousands)

	End of Year	Beginning of Year
Assets		
Current assets:		
Cash	$126,215	$ 20,944
Marketable securities	103,221	41,507
Accounts receivable	17,621	9,852
Inventories	83,370	123,657
Other current assets	9,114	9,390
Total current assets	339,541	205,350
Property and equipment, net	369,477	244,728
Other assets	17,595	18,100
Total assets	$726,613	$468,178
Liabilities and Stockholders' Equity		
Current liabilities:		
Accounts payable	$ 38,034	$ 28,668
Short-term bank loans	16,241	13,138
Accrued payables	18,005	13,436
Other current liabilities	28,881	15,804
Total current liabilities	101,091	71,046
Long-term liabilities:		
Bonds payable	165,020	80,398
Other long-term liabilities	8,842	4,503
Total liabilities	274,953	155,947
Stockholders' equity:		
Preferred stock	–0–	–0–
Common stock and additional paid-in capital	361,309	265,679
Retained earnings	90,315	46,552
Total stockholders' equity	451,660	312,231
Total liabilities and stockholders' equity	$726,613	$468,178

Note: The effective interest rate on the bonds payable was about 5%.

STARBUCKS COFFEE COMPANY
Comparative Income Statement
(dollars in thousands)

	Current Year	Prior Year
Revenue	$696,481	$465,213
Cost of goods sold	335,800	211,279
Gross margin	360,681	253,934

Operating expenses:		
Store operating expenses	$210,693	$148,757
Other operating expenses	19,787	13,932
Depreciation and amortization	35,950	22,486
General and administrative expenses	37,258	28,643
Total operating expenses	303,688	213,818
Net operating income	56,993	40,116
Gain on sale of investment	9,218	–0–
Plus interest income	11,029	6,792
Less interest expense	8,739	3,765
Net income before taxes	68,501	43,143
Less income taxes (about 38.5%)	26,373	17,041
Net income	$ 42,128	$ 26,102

Required For the current year:

1. Compute the return on total assets.
2. Compute the return on common stockholders' equity.
3. Is Starbucks' financial leverage positive or negative? Explain.
4. Compute the current ratio.
5. Compute the acid-test (quick) ratio.
6. Compute the inventory turnover.
7. Compute the average sale period.
8. Compute the debt-to-equity ratio.

Solution to Review Problem

1. Return on total assets:

$$\text{Return on total assets} = \frac{\text{Net income} + [\text{Interest expense} \times (1 - \text{Tax rate})]}{\text{Average total assets}}$$

$$\frac{\$42{,}128 + [\$8{,}739 \times (1 - 0.385)]}{(\$726{,}613 + \$468{,}178)/2} = 8.0\% \text{ (rounded)}$$

2. Return on common stockholders' equity:

$$\text{Return on common stockholders' equity} = \frac{\text{Net income} - \text{Preferred dividends}}{\text{Average common stockholders' equity}}$$

$$\frac{\$42{,}128 - \$0}{(\$451{,}660 + \$312{,}231)/2} = 11.0\% \text{ (rounded)}$$

3. The company has positive financial leverage, since the return on common stockholders' equity (11%) is greater than the return on total assets (8%). The positive financial leverage was obtained from current liabilities and the bonds payable. The interest rate on the bonds is substantially less than the return on total assets.
4. Current ratio:

$$\text{Current ratio} = \frac{\text{Current assets}}{\text{Current liabilities}}$$

$$\frac{\$339{,}541}{\$101{,}091} = 3.36 \text{ (rounded)}$$

5. Acid-test (quick) ratio:

$$\text{Acid-test ratio} = \frac{\text{Cash} + \text{Marketable securities} + \text{Current receivables}}{\text{Current liabilities}}$$

$$\frac{\$126{,}215 + \$103{,}221 + \$17{,}261}{\$101{,}091} = 2.44 \text{ (rounded)}$$

This acid-test ratio is quite high and provides Starbucks with the ability to fund rapid expansion.

6. Inventory turnover:

$$\text{Inventory turnover} = \frac{\text{Cost of goods sold}}{\text{Average inventory balance}}$$

$$\frac{\$335{,}800}{(\$83{,}370 + \$123{,}657)/2} = 3.24 \text{ (rounded)}$$

7. Average sale period:

$$\text{Average sale period} = \frac{\text{365 days}}{\text{Inventory turnover}}$$

$$\frac{\text{365 days}}{3.24} = \text{113 days (rounded)}$$

8. Debt-to-equity ratio:

$$\text{Debt-to-equity ratio} = \frac{\text{Total liabilities}}{\text{Stockholders' equity}}$$

$$\frac{\$274{,}953}{\$451{,}660} = 0.61 \text{ (rounded)}$$

Key Terms for Review

(Note: Definitions and formulas for all financial ratios are shown in Exhibit 18–7. These definitions and formulas are not repeated here.)

Common-size statements A statement that shows the items appearing on it in percentage form as well as in dollar form. On the income statement, the percentages are based on total sales revenue; on the balance sheet, the percentages are based on total assets. (p. 833)

Financial leverage Acquiring assets with funds that have been obtained from creditors or from preferred stockholders at a fixed rate of return. (p. 839)

Horizontal analysis A side-by-side comparison of two or more years' financial statements. (p. 830)

Negative financial leverage A situation in which the fixed return to a company's creditors and preferred stockholders is greater than the return on total assets. In this situation, the return on common stockholders' equity will be *less* than the return on total assets. (p. 839)

Positive financial leverage A situation in which the fixed return to a company's creditors and preferred stockholders is less than the return on total assets. In this situation, the return on common stockholders' equity will be *greater* than the return on total assets. (p. 839)

Trend analysis See *Horizontal analysis.* (p. 830)

Trend percentages The expression of several years' financial data in percentage form in terms of a base year. (p. 831)

Vertical analysis The presentation of a company's financial statements in common-size form. (p. 833)

Questions

18–1 What three basic analytical techniques are used in financial statement analysis?

18–2 Distinguish between horizontal and vertical analysis of financial statement data.

18–3 What is the basic purpose for examining trends in a company's financial ratios and other data? What other kinds of comparisons might an analyst make?

18–4 Why does the financial analyst compute financial ratios rather than simply studying raw financial data? What dangers are there in the use of ratios?

18–5 Assume that two companies in the same industry have equal earnings. Why might these companies have different price-earnings ratios? If a company has a price-earnings ratio of 20 and reports earnings per share for the current year of $4, at what price would you expect to find the stock selling on the market?

18–6 Armcor, Inc., is in a rapidly growing technological industry. Would you expect the company to have a high or low dividend payout ratio?

18–7 Distinguish between a manager's *financing* and *operating* responsibilities. Which of these responsibilities is the return on total assets ratio designed to measure?

18–8 What is meant by the dividend yield on a common stock investment?

18–9 What is meant by the term *financial leverage?*

18–10 The president of a medium-size plastics company was recently quoted in a business journal as stating, "We haven't had a dollar of interest-paying debt in over 10 years. Not many companies can say that." As a stockholder in this firm, how would you feel about its policy of not taking on interest-paying debt?

18–11 Why is it more difficult to obtain positive financial leverage from preferred stock than from long-term debt?

18–12 If a stock's market value exceeds its book value, then the stock is overpriced. Do you agree? Explain.

18–13 Weaver Company experiences a great deal of seasonal variation in its business activities. The company's high point in business activity is in June; its low point is in January. During which month would you expect the current ratio to be highest?

18–14 A company seeking a line of credit at a bank was turned down. Among other things, the bank stated that the company's 2 to 1 current ratio was not adequate. Give reasons why a 2 to 1 current ratio might not be adequate.

18–15 If you were a long-term creditor of a firm, would you be more interested in the firm's long-term or short-term debt-paying ability? Why?

18–16 A young college student once complained to one of the authors, "The reason that corporations are such big spenders is that Uncle Sam always picks up part of the tab." What did he mean by this statement?

Exercises

E18–1 Rotorua Products, Ltd., of New Zealand markets agricultural products for the burgeoning Asian consumer market. The company's current assets, current liabilities, and sales have been reported as follows over the last five years (Year 5 is the most recent year):

	Year 5	Year 4	Year 3	Year 2	Year 1
Sales	$NZ2,250,000	$NZ2,160,000	$NZ2,070,000	$NZ1,980,000	$NZ1,800,000
Cash	$NZ 30,000	$NZ 40,000	$NZ 48,000	$NZ 65,000	$NZ 50,000
Accounts receivable, net	570,000	510,000	405,000	345,000	300,000
Inventory	750,000	720,000	690,000	660,000	600,000
Total current assets	$NZ1,350,000	$NZ1,270,000	$NZ1,143,000	$NZ1,070,000	$NZ 950,000
Current liabilities	$NZ 640,000	$NZ 580,000	$NZ 520,000	$NZ 440,000	$NZ 400,000

$NZ stands for New Zealand dollars.

Required

1. Express all of the asset, liability, and sales data in trend percentages. (Show percentages for each item.) Use Year 1 as the base year and carry computations to one decimal place.
2. Comment on the results of your analysis.

E18–2 A comparative income statement is given below for McKenzie Sales, Ltd., of Toronto:

MCKENZIE SALES, LTD.
Comparative Income Statement
For the Years Ended June 30, 1999, and 1998

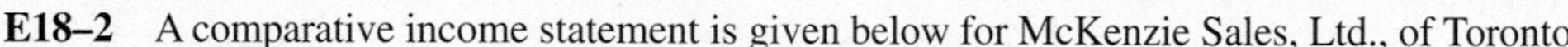

	1999	1998
Sales	$8,000,000	$6,000,000
Less cost of goods sold	4,984,000	3,516,000
Gross margin	3,016,000	2,484,000
Less operating expenses:		
Selling expenses	1,480,000	1,092,000
Administrative expenses	712,000	618,000
Total expenses	2,192,000	1,710,000
Net operating income	824,000	774,000
Less interest expense	96,000	84,000
Net income before taxes	$ 728,000	$ 690,000

Members of the company's board of directors are surprised to see that net income increased by only $38,000 when sales increased by two million dollars.

Required

1. Express each year's income statement in common-size percentages. Carry computations to one decimal place.
2. Comment briefly on the changes between the two years.

E18–3 The financial statements for Castile Products, Inc., are given below:

CASTILE PRODUCTS, INC.
Balance Sheet
December 31

Assets

Current assets:	
Cash	$ 6,500
Accounts receivable, net	35,000
Merchandise inventory	70,000
Prepaid expenses	3,500
Total current assets	115,000
Property and equipment, net	185,000
Total assets	$300,000

Liabilities and Stockholders' Equity		
Liabilities:		
Current liabilities		$ 50,000
Bonds payable, 10%		80,000
Total liabilities		130,000
Stockholders' equity:		
Common stock, $5 per value	$ 30,000	
Retained earnings	140,000	
Total stockholders' equity		170,000
Total liabilities and equity		$300,000

CASTILE PRODUCTS, INC.
Income Statement
For the Year Ended December 31

Sales	$420,000
Less cost of goods sold	292,500
Gross margin	127,500
Less operating expenses	89,500
Net operating income	38,000
Interest expense	8,000
Net income before taxes	30,000
Income taxes (30%)	9,000
Net income	$ 21,000

Account balances at the beginning of the year were: accounts receivable, $25,000; and inventory, $60,000. All sales were on account.

Required Compute financial ratios as follows:

1. Gross margin percentage.
2. Current ratio. (Industry average: 2.5 to 1.)
3. Acid-test (quick) ratio. (Industry average: 1.3 to 1.)
4. Debt-to-equity ratio.
5. Accounts receivable turnover in days. (Terms: 2/10, n/30.)
6. Inventory turnover in days. (Industry average: 64 days.)
7. Times interest earned.
8. Book value per share. (Market price: $42.)

E18–4 Refer to the financial statements for Castile Products, Inc., in E18–3. In addition to the data in these statements, assume that Castile Products, Inc., paid dividends of $2.10 per share during the year. Also assume that the company's common stock had a market price of $42 at the end of the year and there was no change in the number of outstanding shares of common stock during the year.

Required Compute financial ratios as follows:

1. Earnings per share.
2. Dividend payout ratio.
3. Dividend yield ratio.
4. Price-earnings ratio. (Industry average: 10.)

E18–5 Refer to the financial statements for Castile Products, Inc., in E18–3. Assets at the beginning of the year totaled $280,000, and the stockholders' equity totaled $161,600.

Required Compute the following:

1. Return on total assets.
2. Return on common stockholders' equity.
3. Was financial leverage positive or negative for the year? Explain.

E18–6 Selected financial data from the June 30 year-end statements of Safford Company are given below:

Total assets	$3,600,000
Long-term debt (12% interest rate)	500,000
Preferred stock, $100 par, 8%	900,000
Total stockholders' equity	2,400,000
Interest paid on long-term debt	60,000
Net income	280,000

Total assets at the beginning of the year were $3,000,000; total stockholders' equity was $2,200,000. There has been no change in the preferred stock during the year. The company's tax rate is 30%.

Required

1. Compute the return on total assets.
2. Compute the return on common stockholders' equity.
3. Is financial leverage positive or negative? Explain.

E18–7 Norsk Optronics, ALS, of Bergen, Norway, had a current ratio of 2.5 to 1 on June 30 of the current year. On that date, the company's assets were:

Cash		Kr 90,000
Accounts receivable	Kr300,000	
Less allowance for doubtful accounts	40,000	260,000
Inventory		490,000
Prepaid expenses		10,000
Plant and equipment, net		800,000
Total assets		Kr1,650,000

The Norwegian currency is the krone, denoted here by the symbol Kr.

Required

1. What was the company's working capital on June 30?
2. What was the company's acid-test (quick) ratio on June 30?
3. The company paid an account payable of Kr40,000 immediately after June 30.
   a. What effect did this transaction have on working capital? Show computations.
   b. What effect did this transaction have on the current ratio? Show computations.

Problems

P18–8 Effect of Leverage on the Return on Common Equity Several investors are in the process of organizing a new company. The investors believe that $1,000,000 will be needed to finance the new company's operations, and they are considering three methods of raising this amount of money.

Method A: All $1,000,000 can be obtained through issue of common stock.
Method B: $500,000 can be obtained through issue of common stock and the other $500,000 can be obtained through issue of $100 par value, 8% preferred stock.
Method C: $500,000 can be obtained through issue of common stock, and the other $500,000 can be obtained through issue of bonds carrying an interest rate of 8%.

The investors organizing the new company are confident that it can earn $170,000 each year before interest and taxes. The tax rate will be 30%.

Required

1. Assuming that the investors are correct in their earnings estimate, compute the net income that would go to the common stockholders under each of the three financing methods listed above.
2. Using the income data computed in (1) above, compute the return on common equity under each of the three methods.
3. Why do methods B and C provide a greater return on common equity than does method A? Why does method C provide a greater return on common equity than method B?

P18–9 Effects of Transactions on Working Capital, Current Ratio, and Acid-Test (Quick) Ratio Denna Company's working capital accounts at the beginning of the year are given below:

Cash	$ 50,000
Marketable Securities	30,000
Accounts Receivable, net	200,000
Inventory	210,000
Prepaid Expenses	10,000
Accounts Payable	150,000
Notes Due within One Year	30,000
Accrued Liabilities	20,000

During the year, Denna Company completed the following transactions:

x. Paid a cash dividend previously declared, $12,000.
a. Issued additional shares of capital stock for cash, $100,000.
b. Sold inventory costing $50,000 for $80,000, on account.
c. Wrote off uncollectible accounts in the amount of $10,000. The company uses the allowance method of accounting for bad debts.
d. Declared a cash dividend, $15,000.
e. Paid accounts payable, $50,000.
f. Borrowed cash on a short-term note with the bank, $35,000.
g. Sold inventory costing $15,000 for $10,000 cash.
h. Purchased inventory on account, $60,000.
i. Paid off all short-term notes due, $30,000.
j. Purchased equipment for cash, $15,000.
k. Sold marketable securities costing $18,000 for cash, $15,000.
l. Collected cash on accounts receivable, $80,000.

Required

1. Compute the following amounts and ratios as of the beginning of the year:
   a. Working capital.
   b. Current ratio.
   c. Acid-test (quick) ratio.
2. Indicate the effect of each of the transactions given above on working capital, the current ratio, and the acid-test (quick) ratio. Give the effect in terms of increase, decrease, or none. Item (x) is given below as an example of the format to use:

	The Effect on		
Transaction	Working Capital	Current Ratio	Acid-Test Ratio
(x) Paid a cash dividend previously declared	None	Increase	Increase

P18–10 Ratio Analysis and Common-Size Statements Paul Sabin organized Sabin Electronics 10 years ago in order to produce and sell several electronic devices on which he had secured patents. Although the company has been fairly profitable, it is now experiencing a severe cash shortage. For this reason, it is requesting a $500,000 long-term loan from Gulfport State Bank, $100,000 of which will be used to bolster the Cash account and $400,000 of which will be used to modernize certain key items of equipment. The company's financial statements for the two most recent years follow:

SABIN ELECTRONICS
Comparative Balance Sheet

	This Year	Last Year
Assets		
Current assets:		
Cash	$ 70,000	$ 150,000
Marketable securities	—	18,000
Accounts receivable, net	480,000	300,000
Inventory	950,000	600,000
Prepaid expenses	20,000	22,000
Total current assets	1,520,000	1,090,000
Plant and equipment, net	1,480,000	1,370,000
Total assets	$3,000,000	$2,460,000
Liabilities and Stockholders' Equity		
Liabilities:		
Current liabilities	$ 800,000	$ 430,000
Bonds payable, 12%	600,000	600,000
Total liabilities	1,400,000	1,030,000
Stockholders' equity:		
Preferred stock, $25 par, 8%	250,000	250,000
Common stock, $10 par	500,000	500,000
Retained earnings	850,000	680,000
Total stockholders' equity	1,600,000	1,430,000
Total liabilities and equity	$3,000,000	$2,460,000

SABIN ELECTRONICS
Comparative Income Statement

	This Year	Last Year
Sales	$5,000,000	$4,350,000
Less cost of goods sold	3,875,000	3,450,000
Gross margin	1,125,000	900,000
Less operating expenses	653,000	548,000
Net operating income	472,000	352,000
Less interest expense	72,000	72,000
Net income before taxes	400,000	280,000
Less income taxes (30%)	120,000	84,000
Net income	280,000	196,000
Dividends paid:		
Preferred dividends	20,000	20,000
Common dividends	90,000	75,000
Total dividends paid	110,000	95,000
Net income retained	170,000	101,000
Retained earnings, beginning of year	680,000	579,000
Retained earnings, end of year	$ 850,000	$ 680,000

During the past year, the company introduced several new product lines and raised the selling prices on a number of old product lines in order to improve its profit margin. The company also hired a new sales manager, who has expanded sales into several new territories. Sales terms are 2/10, n/30. All sales are on account. Assume that the following ratios are typical of firms in the electronics industry:

Current ratio	2.5 to 1
Acid-test (quick) ratio	1.3 to 1
Average age of receivables	18 days
Inventory turnover in days	60 days
Debt-to-equity ratio	0.90 to 1
Times interest earned	6.0 times
Return on total assets	13%
Price-earnings ratio	12

Required

1. To assist the Gulfport State Bank in making a decision about the loan, compute the following ratios for both this year and last year:
   a. The amount of working capital.
   b. The current ratio.
   c. The acid-test (quick) ratio.
   d. The average age of receivables. (The accounts receivable at the beginning of last year totaled $250,000.)
   e. The inventory turnover in days. (The inventory at the beginning of last year totaled $500,000.)
   f. The debt-to-equity ratio.
   g. The number of times interest was earned.
2. For both this year and last year:
   a. Present the balance sheet in common-size format.
   b. Present the income statement in common-size format down through net income.
3. Comment on the results of your analysis in (1) and (2) above and make a recommendation as to whether or not the loan should be approved.

P18–11 Investor Ratios; Recommendation on Stock Purchase Refer to the financial statements and other data in P18–10. Assume that you are an account executive for a large brokerage house and that one of your clients has asked for a recommendation about the possible purchase of Sabin Electronics' stock. You are not acquainted with the stock and for this reason wish to do certain analytical work before making a recommendation.

Required

1. You decide first to assess the well-being of the common stockholders. For both this year and last year, compute:
   a. The earnings per share. There has been no change in preferred or common stock over the last two years.
   b. The dividend yield ratio for common. The company's stock is currently selling for $40 per share; last year it sold for $36 per share.
   c. The dividend payout ratio for common.
   d. The price-earnings ratio. How do investors regard Sabin Electronics as compared to other firms in the industry? Explain.
   e. The book value per share of common. Does the difference between market value and book value suggest that the stock is overpriced? Explain.
2. You decide next to assess the company's rate of return. Compute the following for both this year and last year:
   a. The return on total assets. (Total assets at the beginning of last year were $2,300,000.)
   b. The return on common equity. (Stockholders' equity at the beginning of last year was $1,329,000.)
   c. Is the company's financial leverage positive or negative? Explain.
3. Would you recommend that your client purchase shares of Sabin Electronics' stock? Explain.

P18–12 Comprehensive Problem on Ratio Analysis You have just been hired as a loan officer at Slippery Rock State Bank. Your supervisor has given you a file containing a request from Lydex Company, a manufacturer of safety helmets, for a $3,000,000, five-year loan. Financial statement data on the company for the last two years follow:

LYDEX COMPANY
Comparative Balance Sheet

	This Year	Last Year
Assets		
Current assets:		
Cash	$ 960,000	$ 1,260,000
Marketable securities	–0–	300,000
Accounts receivable, net	2,700,000	1,800,000
Inventory	3,900,000	2,400,000
Prepaid expenses	240,000	180,000
Total current assets	7,800,000	5,940,000
Plant and equipment, net	9,300,000	8,940,000
Total assets	$17,100,000	$14,880,000
Liabilities and Stockholders' Equity		
Liabilities:		
Current liabilities	$ 3,900,000	$ 2,760,000
Note payable, 10%	3,600,000	3,000,000
Total liabilities	7,500,000	5,760,000
Stockholders' equity:		
Preferred stock, 8%, $30 par value	1,800,000	1,800,000
Common stock, $80 par value	6,000,000	6,000,000
Retained earnings	1,800,000	1,320,000
Total stockholders' equity	9,600,000	9,120,000
Total liabilities and stockholders' equity	$17,100,000	$14,880,000

LYDEX COMPANY
Comparative Income Statement

	This Year	Last Year
Sales (all on account)	$15,750,000	$12,480,000
Less cost of goods sold	12,600,000	9,900,000
Gross margin	3,150,000	2,580,000
Less operating expenses	1,590,000	1,560,000
Net operating income	1,560,000	1,020,000
Less interest expense	360,000	300,000
Net income before taxes	1,200,000	720,000
Less income taxes (30%)	360,000	216,000
Net income	840,000	504,000
Dividends paid:		
Preferred dividends	144,000	144,000
Common dividends	216,000	108,000
Total dividends paid	360,000	252,000
Net income retained	480,000	252,000
Retained earnings, beginning of year	1,320,000	1,068,000
Retained earnings, end of year	$ 1,800,000	$ 1,320,000

Helen McGuire, who just a year ago was appointed president of Lydex Company, argues that although the company has had a "spotty" record in the past, it has "turned the corner," as evidenced by a 25% jump in sales and by a greatly improved earnings picture between last year and this year. McGuire also points out that investors generally have recognized the improving situation at Lydex, as shown by the increase in market value of the company's common stock, which is currently selling for $72 per share (up from $40 per share last year). McGuire feels that with her leadership and with the modernized equipment that the $3,000,000 loan will permit the company to buy, profits will be even stronger in the future. McGuire has a reputation in the industry for being a good manager who runs a "tight" ship.

Not wanting to botch your first assignment, you decide to generate all the information that you can about the company. You determine that the following ratios are typical of firms in Lydex Company's industry:

Current ratio	2.3 to 1
Acid-test (quick) ratio	1.2 to 1
Average age of receivables	30 days
Inventory turnover	60 days
Return on assets	9.5%
Debt-to-equity ratio	0.65 to 1
Times interest earned	5.7
Price-earnings ratio	10

Required

1. You decide first to assess the rate of return that the company is generating. Compute the following for both this year and last year:
   a. The return on total assets. (Total assets at the beginning of last year were $12,960,000.)
   b. The return on common equity. (Stockholders' equity at the beginning of last year totaled $9,048,000. There has been no change in preferred or common stock over the last two years.)
   c. Is the company's financial leverage positive or negative? Explain.
2. You decide next to assess the well-being of the common stockholders. For both this year and last year, compute:
   a. The earnings per share.
   b. The dividend yield ratio for common.
   c. The dividend payout ratio for common.
   d. The price-earnings ratio. How do investors regard Lydex Company as compared to other firms in the industry? Explain.
   e. The book value per share of common. Does the difference between market value per share and book value per share suggest that the stock at its current price is a bargain? Explain.
   f. The gross margin percentage.
3. You decide, finally, to assess creditor ratios to determine both short-term and long-term debt-paying ability. For both this year and last year, compute:
   a. Working capital.
   b. The current ratio.
   c. The acid-test ratio.
   d. The average age of receivables. (The accounts receivable at the beginning of last year totaled $1,560,000.)
   e. The inventory turnover. (The inventory at the beginning of last year totaled $1,920,000.) Also compute the number of days required to turn the inventory one time (use a 365-day year).
   f. The debt-to-equity ratio.
   g. The number of times interest was earned.
4. Evaluate the data computed in (1) to (3) above, and using any additional data provided in the problem, make a recommendation to your supervisor as to whether the loan should be approved.

P18–13 Common-Size Financial Statements Refer to the financial statement data for Lydex Company given in P18–12.

Required

For both this year and last year:

1. Present the balance sheet in common-size format.
2. Present the income statement in common-size format down through net income.
3. Comment on the results of your analysis.

P18–14 Interpretation of Completed Ratios Paul Ward is interested in the stock of Pecunious Products, Inc. Before purchasing the stock, Mr. Ward would like to learn as much as possible about the company. However, all he has to go on is the current year's (Year 3) annual report, which contains no comparative data other than the summary of ratios given below:

	Year 3	Year 2	Year 1
Sales trend	128.0	115.0	100.0
Current ratio	2.5:1	2.3:1	2.2:1
Acid-test (quick) ratio	0.8:1	0.9:1	1.1:1
Accounts receivable turnover	9.4 times	10.6 times	12.5 times
Inventory turnover	6.5 times	7.2 times	8.0 times
Dividend yield	7.1%	6.5%	5.8%
Dividend payout ratio	40%	50%	60%
Return on total assets	12.5%	11.0%	9.5%
Return on common equity	14.0%	10.0%	7.8%
Dividends paid per share*	$1.50	$1.50	$1.50

*There have been no changes in common stock outstanding over the three-year period.

Mr. Ward would like answers to a number of questions about the trend of events in Pecunious Products, Inc., over the last three years. His questions are:

a. Is it becoming easier for the company to pay its bills as they come due?
b. Are customers paying their accounts at least as fast now as they were in Year 1?
c. Is the total of the accounts receivable increasing, decreasing, or remaining constant?
d. Is the level of inventory increasing, decreasing, or remaining constant?
e. Is the market price of the company's stock going up or down?
f. Is the amount of the earnings per share increasing or decreasing?
g. Is the price-earning ratio going up or down?
h. Is the company employing financial leverage to the advantage of the common stockholders?

Required Answer each of Mr. Ward's questions using the data given above. In each case, explain how you arrived at your answer.

P18–15 Effects of Transactions on Various Financial Ratios In the right-hand column below, certain financial ratios are listed. To the left of each ratio is a business transaction or event relating to the operating activities of Delta Company.

Business Transaction or Event	Ratio
1. The company declared a cash dividend.	Current ratio
2. The company sold inventory on account at cost.	Acid-test (quick) ratio
3. The company issued bonds with an interest rate of 8%. The company's return on assets is 10%.	Return on common stockholders' equity
4. The company's net income decreased by 10% between last year and this year. Long-term debt remained unchanged.	Times interest earned
5. A previously declared cash dividend was paid.	Current ratio
6. The market price of the company's common stock dropped from 24½ to 20. The dividend paid per share remained unchanged.	Dividend payout ratio
7. Obsolete inventory totaling $100,000 was written off as a loss.	Inventory turnover ratio
8. The company sold inventory for cash at a profit.	Debt-to-equity ratio
9. Changed customer credit terms from 2/10, n/30 to 2/15, n/30 to comply with a change in industry practice.	Accounts receivable turnover ratio
10. Issued a common stock dividend on common stock.	Book value per share

11.	The market price of the company's common stock increased from 24½ to 30.	Book value per share
12.	The company paid $40,000 on accounts payable.	Working capital
13.	Issued a common stock dividend to common stockholders.	Earnings per share
14.	Paid accounts payable	Debt-to-equity ratio
15.	Purchased inventory on open account.	Acid-test (quick) ratio
16.	Wrote off an uncollectible account against the Allowance for Bad Debts.	Current ratio
17.	The market price of the company's common stock increased from 24½ to 30. Earnings per share remained unchanged.	Price-earnings ratio
18.	The market price of the company's common stock increased from 24½ to 30. The dividend paid per share remained unchanged.	Dividend yield ratio

Required Indicate the effect that each business transaction or event would have on the ratio listed opposite to it. State the effect in terms of increase, decrease, or no effect on the ratio involved, and give the reason for your choice of answer. In all cases, assume that the current assets exceed the current liabilities both before and after the event or transaction. Use the following format for your answers:

	Effect on Ratio	Reason for Increase, Decrease, or No Effect
1.		
Etc.		

P18–16 Comprehensive Problem Part 1 Investor Ratios (P18–17 and P18–18 delve more deeply into the data presented below. Each problem is independent.) Empire Labs, Inc., was organized several years ago to produce and market several new "miracle drugs." The company is small but growing, and you are considering the purchase of some of its common stock as an investment. The following data on the company are available for the past two years:

EMPIRE LABS, INC.
Comparative Income Statement
For the Years Ended December 31

	This Year	Last Year
Sales	$20,000,000	$15,000,000
Less cost of goods sold	13,000,000	9,000,000
Gross margin	7,000,000	6,000,000
Less operating expenses	5,260,000	4,560,000
Net operating income	1,740,000	1,440,000
Less interest expense	240,000	240,000
Net income before taxes	1,500,000	1,200,000
Less income taxes (30%)	450,000	360,000
Net income	$ 1,050,000	$ 840,000

EMPIRE LABS, INC.
Comparative Retained Earnings Statement
For the Years Ended December 31

	This Year	Last Year
Retained earnings, January 1	$2,400,000	$1,960,000
Add net income (above)	1,050,000	840,000
Total	3,450,000	2,800,000

	This Year	Last Year
Deduct cash dividends paid:		
Preferred dividends	120,000	120,000
Common dividends	360,000	280,000
Total dividends paid	480,000	400,000
Retained earnings, December 31	$2,970,000	$2,400,000

EMPIRE LABS, INC.
Comparative Balance Sheet
December 31

	This Year	Last Year
Assets		
Current assets:		
Cash	$ 200,000	$ 400,000
Accounts receivable, net	1,500,000	800,000
Inventory	3,000,000	1,200,000
Prepaid expenses	100,000	100,000
Total current assets	4,800,000	2,500,000
Plant and equipment, net	5,170,000	5,400,000
Total assets	$9,970,000	$7,900,000
Liabilities and Stockholders' Equity		
Liabilities:		
Current liabilities	$2,500,000	$1,000,000
Bonds payable, 12%	2,000,000	2,000,000
Total liabilities	4,500,000	3,000,000
Stockholders' equity:		
Preferred stock, 8%, $10 par	1,500,000	1,500,000
Common stock, $5 par	1,000,000	1,000,000
Retained earnings	2,970,000	2,400,000
Total stockholders' equity	5,470,000	4,900,000
Total liabilities and stockholders' equity	$9,970,000	$7,900,000

After some research, you have determined that the following ratios are typical of firms in the pharmaceutical industry:

Dividend yield ratio	3%
Dividend payout ratio	40%
Price-earnings ratio	16
Return on total assets	13.5%
Return on common equity	20%

The company's common stock is currently selling for $60 per share. Last year the stock sold for $45 per share.

There has been no change in the preferred or common stock outstanding over the last three years.

Required

1. In analyzing the company, you decide first to compute the earnings per share and related ratios. For both last year and this year, compute:
   a. The earnings per share.
   b. The dividend yield ratio.
   c. The dividend payout ratio.
   d. The price-earnings ratio.
   e. The book value per share of common stock.
   f. The gross margin percentage.

2. You decide next to determine the rate of return that the company is generating. For both last year and this year, compute:
   a. The return on total assets. (Total assets were $6,500,000 at the beginning of last year.)
   b. The return on common stockholders' equity. (Common stockholders' equity was $2,900,000 at the beginning of last year.)
   c. Is financial leverage positive or negative? Explain.
3. Based on your work in (1) and (2) above, does the company's common stock seem to be an attractive investment? Explain.

P18–17 Comprehensive Problem Part 2 Creditor Ratios Refer to the data in P18–16. Although Empire Labs, Inc., has been very profitable since it was organized several years ago, the company is beginning to experience some difficulty in paying its bills as they come due. Management has approached Security National Bank requesting a two-year, $500,000 loan to bolster the cash account.

Security National Bank has assigned you to evaluate the loan request. You have gathered the following data relating to firms in the pharmaceutical industry:

Current ratio	2.4 to 1
Acid-test (quick) ratio	1.2 to 1
Average age of receivables	16 days
Inventory turnover in days	40 days
Time interest earned	7 times
Debt-to-equity ratio	0.70 to 1

The following additional information is available on Empire Labs, Inc.:

a. All sales are on account.
b. At the beginning of last year, the accounts receivable balance was $600,000 and the inventory balance was $1,000,000.

Required

1. Compute the following amounts and ratios for both last year and this year:
   a. The working capital.
   b. The current ratio.
   c. The acid-test ratio.
   d. The accounts receivable turnover in days.
   e. The inventory turnover in days.
   f. The times interest earned.
   g. The debt-to-equity ratio.
2. Comment on the results of your analysis in (1) above.
3. Would you recommend that the loan be approved? Explain.

P18–18 Comprehensive Problem Part 3 Common-Size Statements Refer to the data in P18–16. The president of Empire Labs, Inc., is deeply concerned. Sales increased by $5 million from last year to this year, yet the company's net income increased by only a small amount. Also, the company's operating expenses went up this year, even though a major effort was launched during the year to cut costs.

Required

1. For both last year and this year, prepare the income statement and the balance sheet in common-size format. Round computations to one decimal place.
2. From your work in (1) above, explain to the president why the increase in profits was so small this year. Were any benefits realized from the company's cost-cutting efforts? Explain.

P18–19 Incomplete Statements; Analysis of Ratios Incomplete financial statements for Pepper Industries follow:

PEPPER INDUSTRIES
Balance Sheet
March 31

Current assets:	
Cash	$?
Accounts receivable, net	?
Inventory	?
Total current assets	?
Plant and equipment, net	?
Total assets	$?
Liabilities:	
Current liabilities	$ 320,000
Bonds payable, 10%	?
Total liabilities	?
Stockholders' equity:	
Common stock, $5 par value	?
Retained earnings	?
Total stockholders' equity	?
Total liabilities and stockholders equity	$?

PEPPER INDUSTRIES
Income Statement
For the Year Ended March 31

Sales	$4,200,000
Less cost of goods sold	?
Gross margin	?
Less operating expenses	?
Net operating income	?
Less interest expense	80,000
Net income before taxes	?
Less income taxes (30%)	?
Net income	$?

The following additional information is available about the company:

a. All sales during the year were on account.
b. There was no change in the number of shares of common stock outstanding during the year.
c. The interest expense on the income statement relates to the bonds payable; the amount of bonds outstanding did not change during the year.
d. Selected balances at the *beginning* of the current fiscal year were:

Accounts receivable	$ 270,000
Inventory	360,000
Total assets	1,800,000

e. Selected financial ratios computed from the statements above for the current year are:

Earnings per share	$2.30
Debt-to-equity ratio	0.875 to 1
Accounts receivable turnover	14.0 times
Current ratio	2.75 to 1
Return on total assets	18.0%
Times interest earned	6.75 times
Acid-test (quick) ratio	1.25 to 1
Inventory turnover	6.5 times

Required Compute the missing amounts on the company's financial statements. (Hint: What's the difference between the acid-test ratio and the current ratio?)

P18–20 Ethics and the Manager Venice InLine, Inc., was founded by Russ Perez to produce a specialized in-line skate he had designed for doing aerial tricks. Up to this point, Russ has financed the company from his own savings and from retained profits. However, Russ now faces a cash crisis. In the year just ended, an acute shortage of high-impact roller bearings had developed just as the company was beginning production for the Christmas season. Russ had been assured by the suppliers that the roller bearings would be delivered in time to make Christmas shipments, but the suppliers had been unable to fully deliver on this promise. As a consequence, Venice InLine had large stocks of unfinished skates at the end of the year and had been unable to fill all of the orders that had come in from retailers for the Christmas season. Consequently, sales were below expectations for the year, and Russ does not have enough cash to pay his creditors.

Well before the accounts payable were to become due, Russ visited a local bank and inquired about obtaining a loan. The loan officer at the bank assured Russ that there should not be any problem getting a loan to pay off his accounts payable—providing that on his most recent financial statements the current ratio was above 2.0, the acid-test ratio was above 1.0, and net operating income was at least four times the interest on the proposed loan. Russ promised to return later with a copy of his financial statements.

Russ would like to apply for a $80,000 six-month loan bearing an interest rate of 10% per year.

The unaudited financial reports of the company appear below:

VENICE INLINE, INC.
Comparative Balance Sheet
As of December 31
(dollars in thousands)

	This Year	Last Year
Assets		
Current assets:		
Cash	$ 70	$150
Accounts receivable, net	50	40
Inventory	160	100
Prepaid expenses	10	12
Total current assets	290	302
Property and equipment	270	180
Total assets	$560	$482
Liabilities and Stockholders' Equity		
Current liabilities:		
Accounts payable	$154	$ 90
Accrued payables	10	10
Total current liabilities	164	100
Long-term liabilities	—	—
Total liabilities	164	100
Stockholders' equity:		
Common stock and additional paid-in capital	100	100
Retained earnings	296	282
Total stockholders' equity	396	382
Total liabilities and stockholders' equity	$560	$482

VENICE INLINE, INC.
Income Statement
For the Year Ended December 31
(dollars in thousands)

	This Year
Sales (all on account)	$420
Cost of goods sold	290
Gross margin	130
Operating expenses:	
Selling expenses	42
Administrative expenses	68
Total operating expenses	110
Net operating income	20
Interest expense	—
Net income before taxes	20
Less income taxes (30%)	6
Net income	$ 14

Required

1. Based on the above unaudited financial statements and the statement made by the loan officer, would the company qualify for the loan?
2. Last year Russ purchased and installed new, more efficient equipment to replace an older plastic injection molding machine. Russ had originally planned to sell the old machine but found that it is still needed whenever the plastic injection molding process is a bottleneck. When Russ discussed his cash flow problems with his brother-in-law, he suggested to Russ that the old machine be sold or at least reclassified as inventory on the balance sheet since it could be readily sold. At present, the machine is carried in the Property and Equipment account and could be sold for its net book value of $45,000. The bank does not require audited financial statements. What advice would you give to Russ concerning the machine?

Group Exercises

GE18–21 What Information Do the Experts Use? Who better to consult than the experienced professionals whose job it is to ferret out information about a company's value or creditworthiness?

Required

1. Have students volunteer to contact an experienced securities analyst from a local brokerage firm and a credit analyst from a local financial institution and invite them to speak to the class about what sources of information they use and how they use that information in making informed decisions about companies. It would be helpful if the class prepared a set of questions far enough in advance of their scheduled presentation that the guest speakers had time to think about the questions and prepare any relevant materials.
2. Capital markets appear to adjust very rapidly to new information about a company, an industry, or general economic conditions—both domestic and international. For this to happen, there must be nearly continuous communication and exchange of information between financial analysts, companies, and investors/credit grantors. Ask the guest analysts to explain this information exchange process and the flow of information between the different groups.
3. As sophisticated as this information system is, sometimes professional analysts and investors get "fooled." How does this happen? What can be done to minimize this problem?

GE18–22 Striving for Quality on the Earnings Statement How successful a company has been over a period of time usually involves some assessment of the firm's earnings. When evaluating profits, investors should consider the quality and sources of the company's earnings as well as their amount. In other words, the source of earnings is as important a consideration as the size of earnings.

For this series of questions, students will need the financial statements of a firm. The financial statements of Coca-Cola, Johnson & Johnson, AT&T, Procter & Gamble, Quaker Oats, Briggs & Stratton, CSX, and American Airlines are just a few that might prove helpful for answering the following questions:

Required

1. What products or services is this business selling? With this in mind, discuss the differences between operating profits and the bottom line—profits after all revenues and expenses.
2. Do you think a dollar of earnings coming from operations is any more or less valuable than a dollar of earnings generated from some other source below operating profits (e.g., one-time gains from selling assets or one-time write-offs for charges related to closing a plant)? Explain.
3. What is the concept of operating leverage and operating risk? What is the relationship between operating leverage, operating risk, and operating profits, and return on assets?
4. What is the concept of financial leverage and financial risk? What is the relationship between financial leverage, financial risk, profits, and return on common stock equity?
5. Looking through the eyes of an investor, how would the above factors influence the stock price of a firm over an entire economic cycle?

GE18–23 Has GE Conquered the Business Cycle? *The Wall Street Journal* alleges that General Electric, the industrial and financial-services conglomerate, manages its earnings to smooth out the high earnings years and to fill in the low earnings years. The end result of this smoothing is that the company is able to report steady earnings growth year after year.

Practitioners of earnings management can use a variety of maneuvers to show a steady upward trend in earnings. These maneuvers include timing gains and losses to smooth out earnings and timing the acquisitions of other companies so as to use their earnings to cover blips in the acquiring company's own earnings. Source: Randall Smith, Steven Lipin, and Amal Kumar Naj, "How General Electric Damps Fluctuations in Its Annual Earnings," *The Wall Street Journal,* November 3, 1994, pp. A1, A11.

Required

1. Why would companies "manage earnings"?
2. Are there any risks of having business decisions (e.g., the acquisition of another business) influenced by the decision's impact on the reported profits of the company?
3. Do you see any ethical issues involved in managing earnings? Explain.
4. How would investors and financial analysts view the financial statements of companies that are known to manage earnings?

IE18–24 Computing Financial Ratios Toys "R" Us is a worldwide toy retailer whose web home page is located at www.tru.com. Like must companies, its most recent annual report can be accessed from its home page.

Required Compute the following financial ratios for Toys "R" Us for the most recent year:

1. Return on total assets.
2. Current ratio.
3. Acid-test (quick) ratio.
4. Inventory turnover.
5. Average sale period.
6. Times interest earned.
7. Debt-to-equity ratio.

IE18–25 Comparing Financial Ratios Sears, Roebuck and Co. has its web home page at www.sears.com. The company's recent annual reports can be accessed from this web site.

Required

1. Compute the following financial ratios for Sears for the two most recent years and indicate whether each ratio has improved or deteriorated.
   a. Return on total assets.
   b. Current ratio.
   c. Acid-test (quick) ratio.
   d. Inventory turnover.
   e. Average sale period.
   f. Times interest earned.
   g. Debt-to-equity ratio.
2. Based on your analysis above, can you conclude anything about the performance of Sears over the past year?

Appendix A

Pricing Products and Services

Learning Objectives

After studying this appendix, you should be able to:

1. Compute the profit-maximizing price of a product or service using the price elasticity of demand and variable cost.
2. Compute the selling price of a product using the absorption costing approach.
3. Compute the markup percentage under the absorption costing approach.
4. Compute the target cost for a new product or service.
5. Compute and use the billing rates used in time and material pricing.

Introduction

Some businesses have no pricing problems. They make a product that is in competition with other, identical products for which a market price already exists. Customers will not pay more than this price, and there is no reason for any company to charge less. Under these circumstances, the company simply charges the prevailing market price. Markets for basic raw materials such as farm products and minerals follow this pattern.

In this appendix, we are concerned with the more common situation in which a company is faced with the problem of setting its own prices. Clearly, the pricing decision can be critical. If the price is set too high, customers will avoid purchasing the company's products. If the price is set too low, the company's costs may not be covered.

The usual approach in pricing is to *mark up* cost.[1] A product's **markup** is the difference between its selling price and its cost. The markup is usually expressed as a percentage of cost. This approach is called **cost-plus pricing** because the predetermined markup percentage is applied to the cost base to determine a target selling price.

Selling price = Cost + (Markup percentage × Cost)

For example, if a company uses a markup of 50%, it adds 50% to the costs of its products to determine the selling price. If a product costs $10, then it would charge $15 for the product.

1. There are some legal restrictions on prices. Antitrust laws prohibit "predatory" prices, which are generally interpreted by the courts to mean a price below average variable cost. "Price discrimination" — charging different prices to customers in the same market for the same product or service —is also prohibited by the law.

There are two key issues when the cost-plus approach to pricing is used. First, what cost should be used? Second, how should the markup be determined? Several alternative approaches are considered in this appendix, starting with the approach generally favored by economists.

The Economists' Approach to Pricing

objective 1

Compute the profit-maximizing price of a product or service using the price elasticity of demand and variable cost.

If a company raises the price of a product, unit sales ordinarily fall. Because of this, pricing is a delicate balancing act in which the benefits of higher revenues per unit are traded off against the lower volume that results from charging higher prices. The sensitivity of unit sales to changes in price is called the *price elasticity of demand.*

Elasticity of Demand

A product's price elasticity should be a key element in setting its price. The **price elasticity of demand** measures the degree to which the volume of unit sales for a product or service is affected by a change in price. Demand for a product is said to be *inelastic* if a change in price has little effect on the number of units sold. The demand for designer perfumes sold by trained personnel at cosmetic counters in department stores is relatively inelastic. Lowering prices on these luxury goods has little effect on sales volume; factors other than price are more important in generating sales. On the other hand, demand for a product is said to be *elastic* if a change in price has a substantial effect on the volume of units sold. An example of a product whose demand is elastic is gasoline. If a gas station raises its price for gasoline, there will usually be a substantial drop in volume as customers seek lower prices elsewhere.

Price elasticity is very important in determining prices. Managers should set higher markups over cost when customers are relatively insensitive to price (i.e., demand is inelastic) and lower markups when customers are relatively sensitive to price (i.e., demand is elastic). This principle is followed in department stores. Merchandise sold in the bargain basement has a much lower markup than merchandise sold elsewhere in the store because customers who shop in the bargain basement are much more sensitive to price (i.e., demand is elastic).

The price elasticity of demand for a product or service, ϵ_d, can be estimated using the following formula.[2,3]

$$\epsilon_d = \frac{\ln(1 + \%\text{ change in quantity sold})}{\ln(1 + \%\text{ change in price})}$$

For example, suppose that the managers of Nature's Garden believe that every 10% increase in the selling price of their apple-almond shampoo would result in a 15% decrease in the number of bottles of shampoo sold.[4] The price elasticity of demand for this product would be computed as follows:

$$\epsilon_d = \frac{\ln(1 + (-0.15))}{\ln(1 + (0.10))} = \frac{\ln(0.85)}{\ln(1.10)} = -1.71$$

2. The term "ln( )" is the natural log function. You can compute the natural log of any number using the LN or ln$x$ key on your calculator. For example, $\ln(0.85) = -0.1625$.
3. This formula assumes that the price elasticity of demand is constant. This occurs when the relation between the selling price, p, and the unit sales, q, can be expressed in the following form: $\ln(q) = a + \epsilon_d \ln(p)$. Even if this is not precisely true, the formula provides a useful way to estimate a product's real price elasticity.
4. The estimated change in unit sales should take into account competitors' responses to a price change.

For comparison purposes, the managers of Nature's Garden believe that another product, strawberry glycerin soap, would experience a 20% drop in unit sales if its price were increased by 10%. (Purchasers of this product are more sensitive to price than the purchasers of the apple-almond shampoo.) The price elasticity of demand for the strawberry glycerin soap is:

$$\epsilon_d = \frac{\ln(1 + (-0.20))}{\ln(1 + (0.10))} = \frac{\ln(0.80)}{\ln(1.10)} = -2.34$$

Both of these products, like other normal products, have a price elasticity that is less than -1. Note also that the price elasticity of demand for the strawberry glycerin soap is larger (in absolute value) than the price elasticity of demand for the apple-almond shampoo. The more sensitive customers are to price, the larger (in absolute value) is the price elasticity of demand. In other words, a larger (in absolute value) price elasticity of demand indicates a product whose demand is more elastic.

In the next subsection, the price elasticity of demand will be used to compute the selling price that maximizes the profits of the company.

The Profit-Maximizing Price

Under certain conditions, it can be shown that the profit-maximizing price can be determined by marking up *variable cost* using the following formula:[5]

$$\text{Profit-maximizing markup on variable cost} = \left(\frac{\epsilon_d}{1+\epsilon_d}\right) - 1$$

Using the above markup is equivalent to setting the selling price using the this formula:

$$\text{Profit-maximizing price} = \left(\frac{\epsilon_d}{1+\epsilon_d}\right) \text{Variable cost per unit}$$

The profit-maximizing prices for the two Nature's Garden products are computed below using these formulas:

	Apple-Almond Shampoo	Strawberry Glycerin Soap
Price elasticity of demand (ϵ_d)	-1.71	-2.34
Profit-maximizing markup on variable cost (a)	$\left(\frac{-1.71}{-1.71+1}\right) - 1$	$\left(\frac{-2.34}{-2.34+1}\right) - 1$
	$= 2.41 - 1 = 1.41$ or 141%	$= 1.75 - 1 = 0.75$ or 75%
Variable cost per unit—given (b)	$2.00	$0.40
Markup, (a) × (b)	2.82	0.30
Profit-maximizing price	$4.82	$0.70

5. The formula assumes that (a) the price elasticity of demand is constant; (b) Total cost = Total fixed cost + Variable cost per unit × q; and (c) the price of the product has no effect on the sales or costs of any other product. The formula can be derived using calculus.

Exhibit A-1 The Optimal Markup on Variable Cost as a Function of the Sensitivity of Unit Sales to Price

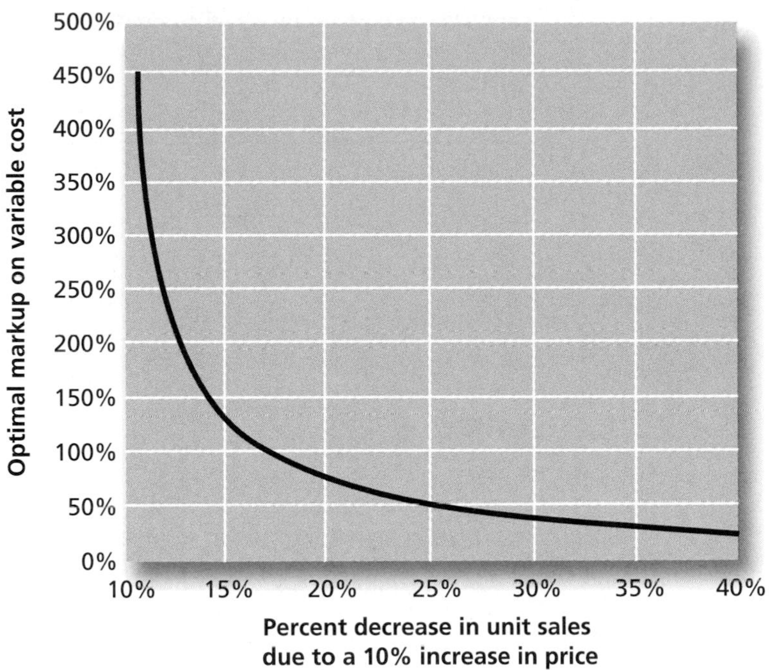

Note that the 75% markup for the strawberry glycerin soap is lower than the 141% markup for the apple-almond shampoo. The reason for this is that purchasers of strawberry glycerin soap are more sensitive to price than the purchasers of apple-almond shampoo. This could be because strawberry glycerin soap is a relatively common product with close substitutes available in nearly every grocery store.

Exhibit A–1 shows how the profit-maximizing markup is affected by how sensitive unit sales are to price. For example, if a 10% increase in price leads to a 20% decrease in unit sales, then the optimal markup on variable cost according to the exhibit is 75%—the figure computed above for the strawberry glycerin soap. Note that the optimal markup drops as unit sales become more sensitive to price.

Caution is advised when using these formulas to establish a selling price. The assumptions underlying the formulas are probably not completely true, and the estimate of the percentage change in unit sales that would result from a given percentage change in price is likely to be inexact. Nevertheless, the formulas can provide valuable clues regarding whether prices should be increased or decreased. Suppose, for example, that the strawberry glycerin soap is currently being sold for $0.60 per bar. The formula indicates that the profit-maximizing price is $0.70 per bar. Rather than increasing the price by $0.10, it would be prudent to increase the price by a more modest amount to observe what happens to unit sales and to profits.

The formula for the profit-maximizing price also conveys a very important lesson. The optimal selling price should depend on two factors—the variable cost per unit and how sensitive unit sales are to changes in price. In particular, fixed costs play no role in setting the optimal price. If the total fixed costs are the same whether the company charges $0.60 or $0.70, they cannot be relevant in the decision of which price to charge for the soap. Fixed costs are relevant when deciding whether to offer a product but are not relevant when deciding how much to charge for the product.

Incidentally, we can directly verify that an increase in selling price for the strawberry glycerin soap from the current price of $0.60 per bar is warranted, based just on the forecast that a 10% increase in selling price would lead to a 20% decrease in unit sales. Suppose, for example, that Nature's Garden is currently selling 200,000 bars of the soap per year at the price of $0.60 a bar. If the change in price has no effect on the company's fixed costs or on other products, the effect on profits of increasing the price by 10% can be computed as follows:

	Present Price	Higher Price
Selling price	$0.60	$0.60 + (0.10 × $0.60) = $0.66
Unit sales	200,000	200,000 − (0.20 × 200,000) = 160,000
Sales	$120,000	$105,600
Variable cost	80,000	64,000
Contribution margin	$ 40,000	$ 41,600

Despite the apparent optimality of prices based on marking up variable costs according to the price elasticity of demand, surveys consistently reveal that most managers approach the pricing problem from a completely different perspective.[6] They prefer to mark up some version of full, not variable, costs, and the markup is based on desired profits rather than on factors related to demand.

The Absorption Costing Approach to Cost-Plus Pricing

objective 2

Compute the selling price of a product using the absorption costing approach.

The absorption costing approach to cost-plus pricing differs from the economists' approach both in what costs are marked up and in how the markup is determined. Under the absorption approach to cost-plus pricing, the cost base is the absorption costing unit product cost as defined in Chapters 2, 3, and 4 rather than variable cost.

Setting a Target Selling Price Using the Absorption Costing Approach

To illustrate, let us assume that the management of Ritter Company wants to set the selling price on a product that has just undergone some design modifications. The Accounting Department has provided cost estimates for the redesigned product as shown below:

	Per Unit	Total
Direct materials	$6	
Direct labor	4	
Variable manufacturing overhead	3	
Fixed manufacturing overhead	—	$70,000
Variable selling, general, and administrative expenses	2	
Fixed selling, general, and administrative expenses	—	60,000

6. One study found that 83% of the 504 large manufacturing companies surveyed used some form of full cost (either absorption cost or absorption cost plus selling, general, and administrative expenses) as a basis for pricing. The remaining 17% used only variable costs as a basis for pricing decisions. See V. Govindarajan and Robert N. Anthony, "How Firms Use Cost Data in Pricing Decisions," *Management Accounting* July 1983x, pp. 30–36. A more recent, but less extensive, survey by Eunsup Shim and Ephraim F. Sudit, "How Manufacturers Price Products," *Management Accounting,* February 1995, pp. 37–39, found similar results.

On the other hand, a survey of small-company executives summarized in *Inc.*, November 1996, p. 84, revealed that only 41% set prices based on cost. The others charge what they think customers are willing to pay or what the market demands.

Exhibit A–2
Price Quotation Sheet—Absorption Basis (10,000 Units)

Direct materials	$ 6
Direct labor	4
Variable manufacturing overhead	3
Fixed manufacturing overhead (based on 10,000 units)	7
Unit product cost	20
Markup to cover selling, general, and administrative expenses and desired profit—50% of unit manufacturing cost	10
Target selling price	$30

The first step in the absorption costing approach to cost-plus pricing is to compute the unit product cost. For Ritter Company, this amounts to $20 per unit at a volume of 10,000 units, as computed below:

Direct materials	$ 6
Direct labor	4
Variable manufacturing overhead	3
Fixed manufacturing overhead ($70,000 ÷ 10,000 units)	7
Unit product cost	$20

Ritter Company has a general policy of marking up unit product costs by 50%. A price quotation sheet for the company prepared using the absorption approach is presented in Exhibit A-2. Note that selling, general, and administrative (SG&A) costs are not included in the cost base. Instead, the markup is supposed to cover these expenses. Let us see how some companies compute these markup percentages.

Determining the Markup Percentage

objective 3
Compute the markup percentage under the absorption costing approach.

How did Ritter Company arrive at its markup percentage of 50%? This figure could be a widely used rule of thumb in the industry or just a company tradition that seems to work. The markup percentage may also be the result of an explicit computation. As we have discussed, the markup over cost ideally should be largely determined by market conditions. However, a popular approach is to at least start with a markup based on cost and desired profit. The reasoning goes like this. The markup must be large enough to cover SG&A expenses and provide an adequate return on investment (ROI). Given the forecasted unit sales, the markup can be computed as follows:

$$\text{Markup percentage on absorption cost} = \frac{\begin{pmatrix}\text{Required ROI}\\ \times\ \text{Investment}\end{pmatrix} + \text{SG\&A expenses}}{\text{Unit sales} \times \text{Unit product cost}}$$

To show how the formula above is applied, assume Ritter Company must invest $100,000 to produce and market 10,000 units of the product each year. The $100,000 investment covers purchase of equipment and funds needed to carry inventories and accounts receivable. If Ritter Company requires a 20% ROI, then the markup for the product would be determined as follows:

$$\text{Markup percentage on absorption cost} = \frac{(20\% \times \$100{,}000) + (\$2 \times 10{,}000 + \$60{,}000)}{10{,}000 \times \$20}$$

$$\text{Markup percentage on absorption cost} = \frac{(\$20{,}000) + (\$80{,}000)}{\$200{,}000} = 50\%$$

Exhibit A–3 Income Statement and ROI Analysis—Ritter Company Actual Unit Sales = 10,000 Units; Selling Price = $30

Direct materials	$ 6
Direct labor	4
Variable manufacturing overhead	3
Fixed manufacturing overhead ($70,000 ÷ 10,000 units)	7
Unit product cost	$20

RITTER COMPANY
Absorption Costing Income Statement

Sales ($30 × 10,000 units)	$300,000
Less cost of goods sold ($20 × 10,000 units)	200,000
Gross margin	100,000
Less selling, general, and administration expenses ($2 × 10,000 units +$60,000)	80,000
Net operating income	$ 20,000

ROI

$$\text{ROI} = \frac{\text{Net operating income}}{\text{Average operating assets}} = \frac{\$20{,}000}{\$100{,}000} = 20\%$$

As shown earlier, this markup of 50% leads to a target selling price of $30 for Ritter Company. As shown in Exhibit A–3, *if the company actually sells 10,000 units* of the product at this price, the company's ROI on this product will indeed be 20%. If it turns out that more than 10,000 units are sold at this price, the ROI will be greater than 20%. If less than 10,000 units are sold, the ROI will be less than 20%. *The required ROI will be attained only if the forecasted unit sales volume is attained.*

Problems with the Absorption Costing Approach

Using the absorption costing approach, the pricing problem looks deceptively simple. All you have to do is compute your unit product cost, decide how much profit you want, and then set your price. It appears that you can ignore demand and arrive at a price that will safely yield whatever profit you want. However, as noted above, the absorption costing approach relies on a forecast of unit sales. Neither the markup nor the unit product cost can be computed without such a forecast.

The absorption costing approach essentially assumes that customers *need* the forecasted unit sales and will pay whatever price the company decides to charge. However, customers have a choice. If the price is too high, they can buy from a competitor or they may choose not to buy at all. Suppose, for example, that when Ritter Company sets its price at $30, it sells only 7,000 units rather than the 10,000 units forecasted. As shown in Exhibit A–4, the company would then have a loss of $25,000 on the product instead of a profit of $20,000.[7] Some managers believe that the absorption

7. When there is only one product and it is inherently profitable, it is always possible to at least break even using the absorption costing approach. This is not true when there is more than one product and the company has common fixed costs. It may be *impossible* to break even using an absorption costing approach when there is more than one product—even when it would be possible to make substantial profits using the economists' approach to pricing. For details, see Eric Noreen and David Burgstahler, "Full Cost Pricing and the Illusion of Satisficing," *Journal of Management Accounting Research*, 9 (1997).

Exhibit A–4 Income Statement and ROI Analysis—Ritter Company Actual Unit Sales = 7,000 Units; Selling Price = $30

Direct materials	$ 6
Direct labor	4
Variable manufacturing overhead	3
Fixed manufacturing overhead ($70,000 ÷ 7,000 units)	10
Unit product cost	$23

RITTER COMPANY
Absorption Costing Income Statement

Sales ($30 × 7,000 units)	$210,000
Less cost of goods sold ($23 × 7,000 units)	161,000
Gross margin	49,000
Less selling, general, and administration expenses ($2 × 7,000 units + $60,000)	74,000
Net operating income	$ (25,000)

ROI

$$\text{ROI} = \frac{\text{Net operating income}}{\text{Average operating assets}}$$

$$= \frac{-\$25,000}{}$$

$$= -25\%$$

costing approach to pricing is safe. This is an illusion. The absorption costing approach is safe only as long as customers choose to buy at least as many units as managers forecasted they would buy.

Focus On Current Practice

Rather than focusing on costs—which can be dangerous if forecasted unit volume does not materialize—many managers focus on customer value when making pricing decisions.

The ticket-services manager of the Washington Opera Company, Jimmy Legarreta, faced a difficult decision. After a financially unsuccessful season, he knew he had to do something about the opera company's pricing policy. Friday and Saturday performances were routinely sold out, and demand for the best seats far exceeded supply. Meanwhile, tickets for midweek performances were often left unsold. "Legarreta also knew that not all seats were equal, even in the sought-after orchestra section. So the ticket manager and his staff sat in every one of the opera house's 2,200 seats and gave each a value according to the view and the acoustics. . . . In the end, the opera raised prices for its most coveted seats by as much as 50% but also dropped the prices of some 600 seats. The gamble paid off in a 9% revenue increase during the next season."[8] ■

8. Susan Greco, "Are Your Prices Right?" *Inc.*, January 1997, p. 88.

Target Costing

objective 4

Compute the target cost for a new product or service.

Our discussion thus far has presumed that a product has already been developed, has been costed, and is ready to be marketed as soon as a price is set. In many cases, the sequence of events is just the reverse. That is, the company will already *know* what price should be charged, and the problem will be to *develop* a product that can be marketed profitably at the desired price. Even in this situation, where the normal sequence of events is reversed, cost is still a crucial factor. The company's approach will be to employ *target costing*. **Target costing** is the process of determining the maximum allowable cost for a new product and then developing a prototype that can be profitably made for that maximum target cost figure. Many companies use target costing, including Compaq, Culp, Cummins Engine, Daihatsu Motors, DaimlerChrysler, Ford, Isuzu Motors, ITT Automotive, Komatsu, Matsushita Electric, Mitsubishi Kasei, NEC, Nippodenso, Nissan, Olympus, Sharp, Texas Instruments, and Toyota.

The target cost for a product is computed by starting with the product's anticipated selling price and then deducting the desired profit, as follows:

Target cost = Anticipated selling price − Desired profit

The product development team is given the responsibility of designing the product so that it can be made for no more than the target cost.

Focus on Current Practice

Target costing is widely used in Japan. In the automobile industry, the target cost for a new model is decomposed into target costs for each of the elements of the car—down to a target cost for each of the individual parts. The designers draft a trial blueprint, and a check is made to see if the estimated cost of the car is within reasonable distance of the target cost. If not, design changes are made, and a new trial blueprint is drawn up. This process continues until there is sufficient confidence in the design to make a prototype car according to the trial blueprint. If there is still a gap between the target cost and estimated cost, the design of the car will be further modified.

After repeating this process a number of times, the final blueprint is drawn up and turned over to the production department. In the first several months of production, the target costs will ordinarily not be achieved due to problems in getting a new model into production. However, after that initial period, target costs are compared to actual costs and discrepancies between the two are investigated with the aim of eliminating the discrepancies and achieving target costs.[9] ■

Reasons for Using Target Costing

The target costing approach was developed in recognition of two important characteristics of markets and costs. The first is that many companies have less control over price

9. Yasuhiro Monden and Kazuki Hamada, "Target Costing and Kaizen Costing in Japanese Automobile Companies," *Journal of Management Accounting Research* 3 (Fall 1991), pp. 16–34.

than they would like to think. The market (i.e., supply and demand) really determines prices, and a company that attempts to ignore this does so at its peril. Therefore, the anticipated market price is taken as a given in target costing. The second observation is that most of the cost of a product is determined in the design stage. Once a product has been designed and has gone into production, not much can be done to significantly reduce its cost. Most of the opportunities to reduce cost come from designing the product so that it is simple to make, uses inexpensive parts, and is robust and reliable. If the company has little control over market price and little control over cost once the product has gone into production, then it follows that the major opportunities for affecting profit come in the design stage where valuable features that customers are willing to pay for can be added and where most of the costs are really determined. So that is where the effort is concentrated—in designing and developing the product. The difference between target costing and other approaches to product development is profound. Instead of designing the product and then finding out how much it costs, the target cost is set first and then the product is designed so that the target cost is attained.

Focus on Current Practice

Nicolas G. Hayek, the head of the Swiss Corporation for Microelectronics and Watchmaking, has led the remarkable resurgence of the Swiss watch industry. The company makes watches spanning the market from the low-end fashion Swatch to the high-end prestigious Omega. Hayek explains the company's manufacturing strategy as follows:

> We must build where we live . . . We have to change . . . the instinctive reaction that if a company has a mass-market consumer product, the only place to build it is Asia or Mexico. CEOs must say to their people: "We will build this product in our country at a lower cost and with higher quality than anywhere else in the world." Then we have to figure out how to do it.
>
> We do this all the time. We agree on the performance specifications of a new product—a watch, a pager, a telephone. Then we assemble a project team. We present the team with some target economics: this is how much the product can sell for, not one penny more; this is the margin we need to support advertising, promotion, and so on. Thus these are the costs we can afford. Now go design a product and a production system that allows us to build it at those costs—in Switzerland.
>
> That means focusing on labor. If we can design a manufacturing process in which direct labor accounts for less than 10% of total costs, there is nothing to stop us from building a product in Switzerland, the most expensive country in the world. Nothing.[10]

An Example of Target Costing

To provide a simple numerical example of target costing, assume the following situation: Handy Appliance Company feels that there is a market niche for a hand mixer with certain new features. Surveying the features and prices of hand mixers already on the market, the Marketing Department believes that a price of $30 would be about right for the new mixer. At that price, Marketing estimates that 40,000 of the new mixers could be sold annually. To design, develop, and produce these new mixers, an investment of $2,000,000 would be required. The company desires a 15% ROI. Given these

10. Reprinted by permission of *Harvard Business Review.* Excerpt from William Taylor, "Message and Muscle: An Interview with Swatch Titan Nicolas Hayek," *Harvard Business Review,* March–April 1993. Copyright © 1993 by the President and Fellows of Harvard College. All rights reserved.

data, the target cost to manufacture, sell, distribute, and service one mixer is $22.50 as shown below.

Projected sales (50,000 mixers × $30)	$1,200,000
Less desired profit (15% × $2,000,000)	300,000
Target cost for 40,000 mixers	$ 900,000
Target cost per mixer ($900,000 ÷ 40,000 mixers)	$22.50

This $22.50 target cost would be broken down into target costs for the various functions: manufacturing, marketing, distribution, after-sales service, and so on. Each functional area would be responsible for keeping its actual costs within target.

Focus on Current Practice

Boeing has set a goal of reducing the costs of its new aircraft by 25% to 30%.[11] This is not an arbitrary goal. Boeing views its major competitor to be the existing fleet of aircraft already owned by airlines rather than Airbus. As long as airlines believe it is cheaper to keep old aircraft in service rather than to replace them with new aircraft, Boeing's sales will suffer. By cutting its costs 25% to 30% and passing on the savings to its customers in the form of lower selling prices, Boeing expects to generate more demand for replacement aircraft. "Boeing's 25% to 30% cost-reduction target isn't guesswork. It's the precise saving needed to drive out the old planes." Kenneth Raff of American Airlines says: "If Boeing can cut its costs 25%, a lot of old planes will turn into beer cans." ■

Service Companies—Time and Material Pricing

objective 5

Compute and use the billing rates used in time and material pricing.

Some companies—particularly in service industries—use a variation on cost-plus pricing called **time and material pricing.** Under this method, two pricing rates are established—one based on direct labor time and the other based on the cost of direct material used. This pricing method is widely used in repair shops, in printing shops, and by many professionals such as physicians and dentists. The time and material rates are usually market-determined. In other words, the rates are determined by the interplay of supply and demand and by competitive conditions in the industry. However, some companies set the rates using a process similar to the process followed in the absorption costing approach to cost-plus pricing. In this case, the rates include allowances for selling, general, and administrative expenses; for other direct and indirect costs; and for a desired profit. This section will show how the rates might be set using the cost-plus approach.

Time Component

The time component is typically expressed as a rate per hour of labor. The rate is computed by adding together three elements: (1) the direct costs of the employee, including salary and fringe benefits; (2) a pro rata allowance for selling, general, and

11. Shawn Tully, "Can Boeing Reinvent Itself?" *Fortune,* March 8, 1993, pp. 66–73.

administrative expenses of the organization; and (3) an allowance for a desired profit per hour of employee time. In some organizations (such as a repair shop), the same hourly rate will be charged regardless of which employee actually works on the job; in other organizations, the rate may vary by employee. For example, in a public accounting firm, the rate charged for a new assistant accountant's time will generally be less than the rate charged for an experienced senior accountant or for a partner.

Material Component

The material component is determined by adding a **material loading charge** to the invoice price of any materials used on the job. The material loading charge is designed to cover the costs of ordering, handling, and carrying materials in stock, plus a profit margin on the materials themselves.

An Example of Time and Material Pricing

To provide a numerical example of time and material pricing, assume the following data:

The Quality Auto Shop uses time and material pricing for all of its repair work. The following costs have been budgeted for the coming year:

	Repairs	Parts
Mechanics' wages	$300,000	$ —
Service manager—salary	40,000	—
Parts manager—salary	—	36,000
Clerical assistant—salary	18,000	15,000
Retirement and insurance—16% of salaries and wages	57,280	8,160
Supplies	720	540
Utilities	36,000	20,800
Property taxes	8,400	1,900
Depreciation	91,600	37,600
Invoice cost of parts used	—	400,000
Total budgeted cost	$552,000	$520,000

The company expects to bill customers for 24,000 hours of repair time. A profit o $7 per hour of repair time is considered to be feasible, given the competitive conditions in the market. For parts, the competitive markup on the invoice cost of parts used is 15%.

Exhibit A–5 shows the computation of the billing rate and the material loading charge to be used over the next year. Note that the billing rate, or time component, is $30 per hour of repair time and the material loading charge is 45% of the invoice cost of parts used. Using these rates, a repair job that requires 4.5 hours of mechanics time and $200 in parts would be billed as follows:

Labor time: 4.5 hours × $30		$135
Parts used:		
Invoice cost	$200	
Material loading charge: 45% × $200	90	290
Total price of the job		$425

Rather than using labor-hours as the basis for computing the time rate, a machine shop, a printing shop, or a similar organization might use machine-hours.

This method of setting prices is a variation of the absorption costing approach. As such, it is not surprising that it suffers from the same problem. Customers may not be willing to pay the rates that have been computed. If actual business is less than the

Exhibit A–5 Time and Material Pricing

	Time Component: Repairs		Parts: Material Loading Charge	
	Total	Per Hour*	Total	Percent†
Cost of mechanics' time:				
Mechanics' wages	$300,000			
Retirement and insurance (16% of wages)	48,000			
Total cost	348,000	$14.50		
For repairs—other cost of repair service. For parts—costs of ordering, handling, and storing parts:				
Repairs service manager—salary	40,000		$ —	
Parts manager—salary	—		36,000	
Clerical assistant—salary	18,000		15,000	
Retirement and insurance (16% of salaries)	9,280		8,160	
Supplies	720		540	
Utilities	36,000		20,800	
Property taxes	8,400		1,900	
Depreciation	91,600		37,600	
Total cost	204,000	8.50	120,000	30%
Desired profit:				
24,000 hours × $7	168,000	7.00	—	
15% × $400,000	—		60,000	15%
Total amount to be billed	$720,000	$30.00	$180,000	45%

*Based on 24,000 hours.

†Based on $400,000 invoice cost of parts. The charge for ordering, handling, and storing parts, for example, is computed as follows: $120,000 cost ÷ $400,000 invoice cost = 30%.

forecasted 24,000 hours and $400,000 worth of parts, the profit objectives will not be met and the company may not even break even.

Summary

Pricing involves a delicate balancing act. Higher prices result in more revenue per unit sold but drive down unit sales. Exactly where to set prices to maximize profit is a difficult problem, but, in general, the markup over cost should be highest for those products where customers are least sensitive to price. The demand for such products is said to be price inelastic.

Managers often rely on cost-plus formulas to set target prices. In the absorption costing approach, the cost base is absorption costing unit product cost and the markup is computed to cover both nonmanufacturing costs and to provide an adequate return on investment. However, costs will not be covered and there will not be an adequate return on investment unless the unit sales forecast used in the cost-plus formula is accurate. If applying the cost-plus formula results in a price that is too high, the unit sales forecast will not be attained.

Some companies take a different approach to pricing. Instead of starting with costs and then determining prices, they start with prices and then determine allowable costs. Companies that use target costing estimate what a new product's market price is likely to be based on its anticipated features and prices of products already on the market. They subtract desired profit from the estimated market price to arrive at the product's target cost. The design and development team is then given the responsibility of ensuring that the actual cost of the new product does not exceed the target cost.

Key Terms for Review

Cost-plus pricing A pricing method in which a predetermined markup is applied to a cost base to determine the target selling price. (p. 872)

Markup The difference between the selling price of a product or service and its cost. The markup is usually expressed as a percentage of cost. (p. 872)

Material loading charge A markup applied to the cost of materials that is designed to cover the costs of ordering, handling, and carrying materials in stock and to provide for some profit. (p. 883)

Price elasticity of demand A measure of the degree to which the volume of unit sales for a product or service is affected by a change in price. (p. 873)

Target costing The process of determining the maximum allowable cost for a new product and then developing a prototype that can be profitably manufactured and distributed for that maximum target cost figure. (p. 880)

Time and material pricing A pricing method, often used in service firms, in which two pricing rates are established—one based on direct labor time and the other based on direct materials used. (p. 882)

Questions

A–1 What is meant by cost-plus pricing?

A–2 What does the price elasticity of demand measure? What is meant by inelastic demand? What is meant by elastic demand?

A–3 According to the economists' approach to setting prices, the profit-maximizing price should depend on what two factors?

A–4 Which product should have a larger markup over variable cost, a product whose demand is elastic or a product whose demand is inelastic?

A–5 When the absorption costing approach to cost-plus pricing is used, what is the markup supposed to cover?

A–6 What assumption does the absorption costing approach make about how consumers react to prices?

A–7 Discuss the following statement: "Full cost can be viewed as a floor of protection. If a firm always sets its prices above full cost, it will never have to worry about operating at a loss."

A–8 What is target costing? How do target costs enter into the pricing decision?

A–9 What is time and material pricing?

Exercises

EA–1 Maria Lorenzi owns an ice cream stand that she operates during the summer months in West Yellowstone, Montana. Her store caters primarily to tourists passing through town on their way to Yellowstone National Park.

Maria is unsure of how she should price her ice cream cones and has experimented with two prices in successive weeks during the busy August season. The number of people who entered the store was roughly the same in the two weeks. During the first week, she priced the cones at \$1.89 and 1,500 cones were sold. During the second week, she priced the cones at \$1.49 and 2,340 cones were sold. The variable cost of a cone is \$0.43 and consists solely of the costs of the ice cream and of the cone itself. The fixed expenses of the ice cream stand are $675 per week.

Required

1. Did Maria make more money selling the cones for $1.89 or for $1.49?
2. Estimate the price elasticity of demand for the ice cream cones.
3. Estimate the profit-maximizing price for ice cream cones.

EA–2 Martin Company is considering the introduction of a new product. To determine a target selling price, the company has gathered the following information:

Number of units to be produced and sold each year	14,000
Unit product cost	$ 25
Projected annual selling, general, and administrative expenses	50,000
Estimated investment required by the company	750,000
Desired return on investment (ROI)	12%

Required The company uses the absorption costing approach to cost-plus pricing.

1. Compute the markup the company will have to use to achieve the desired ROI.
2. Compute the target selling price per unit.

EA–3 Shimada Products Corporation of Japan is anxious to enter the electronic calculator market. Management believes that in order to be competitive in world markets, the electronic calculator that the company is developing can't be priced at more than $15. Shimada requires a minimum return of 12% on all investments. An investment of $5,000,000 would be required to acquire the equipment needed to produce the 300,000 calculators that management believes can be sold each year at the $15 price.

Required Compute the target cost of one calculator.

EA–4 The Reliable TV Repair Shop had budgeted the following costs for next year:

Repair technicians:	
Wages	$120,000
Fringe benefits	30,000
Selling, administrative, and other costs of the repairs operation per year	90,000
Materials:	
Costs of ordering, handling, and storing parts	20% of invoice cost

In total, the company expects 10,000 hours of repair time it can bill to customers. According to competitive conditions, the company believes it should aim for a profit of $6 per hour of repair time. The competitive markup on materials is 40% of invoice cost. The company uses time and material pricing.

Required

1. Compute the time rate and the material loading charge that would be used to bill jobs.
2. One of the company's repair technicians has just completed a repair job that required 2.5 hours of time and $80 in parts (invoice cost). Compute the amount that would be billed for the job.

Problems

PA–5 Economists' Approach to Pricing The postal service of St. Vincent, an island in the West Indies, obtains a significant portion of its revenues from sales of special souvenir sheets to stamp collectors. The souvenir sheets usually contain several high-value St. Vincent stamps depicting a common theme, such as the life of Princess Diana. The souvenir sheets are designed and printed for the postal service by Imperial Printing, a stamp agency service company in the United Kingdom. The souvenir sheets cost the postal service $0.80 each. (The currency in St. Vincent is the East Caribbean dollar.) St. Vincent has been selling these souvenir sheets for $7.00 each and ordinarily sells about 100,000 units. To test the market, the postal service recently priced a new souvenir sheet at $8.00 and sales dropped to 85,000 units.

Required

1. Does the postal service of St. Vincent make more money selling souvenir sheets for $7.00 each or $8.00 each?
2. Estimate the price elasticity of demand for the souvenir sheets.
3. Estimate the profit-maximizing price for souvenir sheets.
4. If Imperial Printing increases the price it charges to the St. Vincent postal service for souvenir sheets to $1.00 each, how much should the St. Vincent postal service charge its customers for the souvenir sheets?

PA–6 Standard Costs; Markup Computations; Pricing Decisions Wilderness Products, Inc., has designed a self-inflating sleeping pad for use by backpackers and campers. The following information is available about the new product:

a. An investment of $1,350,000 will be necessary to carry inventories and accounts receivable and to purchase some new equipment needed in the manufacturing process. The company requires a 24% return on investment for new products.
b. A standard cost card has been prepared for the sleeping pad, as shown below:

	Standard Quantity or Hours	Standard Price or Rate	Standard Cost
Direct materials	4.0 yards	$ 2.70 per yard	$10.80
Direct labor	2.4 hours	8.00 per hour	19.20
Manufacturing overhead (1/5 variable)	2.4 hours	12.50 per hour	30.0
Total standard cost per pad			$60.00

c. The only variable selling, general, and administrative expenses on the pads will be $9 per pad sales commission. Fixed selling, general, and administrative expenses will be (per year):

Salaries	$ 82,000
Warehouse rent	50,000
Advertising and other	600,000
Total	$732,000

d. Since the company manufactures many products, it is felt that no more than 38,400 hours of direct labor time per year can be devoted to production of the new sleeping pads.
e. Manufacturing overhead costs are allocated to products on the basis of direct labor-hours.

Required

1. Assume that the company uses the absorption approach to cost-plus pricing.
   a. Compute the markup that the company needs on the pads to achieve a 24% return on investment (ROI) if it sells all of the pads it can produce.
   b. Using the markup you have computed, prepare a price quotation sheet for a single sleeping pad.
   c. Assume that the company is able to sell all of the pads that it can produce. Prepare an income statement for the first year of activity and compute the company's ROI for the year on the pads.
2. After marketing the sleeping pads for several years, the company is experiencing a falloff in demand due to an economic recession. A large retail outlet will make a bulk purchase of pads if its label is sewn in and if an acceptable price can be worked out. What is the absolute minimum price that would be acceptable for this special order?

PA–7 Target Costing National Restaurant Supply, Inc., sells restaurant equipment and supplies throughout most of the United States. Management of the company is considering adding a machine that makes sorbet to its line of ice cream making machines. Management is preparing to enter into negotiations with the Swedish manufacturer of the sorbet machine concerning the price at which the machine would be sold to National Restaurant Supply.

Management of National Restaurant Supply believes the sorbet machine can be sold to its customers in the United States for $4,950. At that price, annual sales of the sorbet machine should be 100 units. If the sorbet machine is added to National Restaurant Supply's product lines, the company will have to invest $600,000 in inventories and special warehouse fixtures. The variable cost of selling the sorbet machines would be $650 per machine.

Required

1. If National Restaurant Supply requires a 15% return on investment (ROI), what is the maximum amount the company would be willing to pay the Swedish manufacturer for the sorbet machines?
2. The manager who is flying to Sweden to negotiate the purchase price of the machines would like to know how the purchase price of the machines would affect National Restaurant Supply's ROI. Construct a chart that shows National Restaurant Supply's ROI as a function of the purchase price of the sorbet machine. Put the purchase price on the *X*-axis and the resulting ROI on the *Y*-axis. Plot the ROI for purchase prices between $3,000 and $4,000 per machine.
3. After many hours of negotiations, management has concluded that the Swedish manufacturer is unwilling to sell the sorbet machine at a low enough price so that National Restaurant Supply is able to earn its 15% required ROI. Apart from simply giving up on the idea of adding the sorbet machine to National Restaurant Supply's product lines, what could management do?

PA–8 **Time and Material Pricing** City Appliance, Inc., operates an appliance service business with a fleet of trucks dispatched by radio in response to calls from customers. The company's profit margin has dropped steadily over the last two years, and management is concerned that pricing rates for time and material may be out of date. According to industry trade magazines, the company should be earning $8.50 per hour of repair service time, and a profit of 10% of the invoice cost of parts used. The company maintains a large parts inventory in order to give prompt repair service to customers.

Costs associated with repair work and with the parts inventory over the past year are provided below:

	Repairs	Parts
Repair service manager—salary	$ 25,000	$ —
Parts manager—salary	—	20,000
Repair technicians—wages	180,000	—
Office assistant—salary	9,000	3,000
Depreciation—trucks and equipment	15,400	—
Depreciation—buildings and fixtures	6,000	17,500
Retirement benefits (15% of salaries and wages)	32,100	3,450
Health insurance (5% of salaries and wages)	10,700	1,150
Utilities	2,600	12,000
Truck operating costs	36,000	—
Property taxes	900	3,400
Liability and fire insurance	1,500	1,900
Supplies	800	600
Invoice cost of parts used	—	210,000
Total cost	$320,000	$273,000

During the past year, customers were billed for 20,000 hours of repair time.

Required

1. Using the data above, compute the following:
   a. The rate that would be charged per hour of repair service time using time and material pricing.
   b. The material loading charge that would be used in billing jobs. The material loading charge should be expressed as a percentage of the invoice cost of parts.
2. Assume that the company adopts the rates that you have computed in (1) above. What would be the total price charged on a repair that requires 1½ hours of service time and $108 in parts?
3. During the past year, the company billed repair service time at $20 per hour and added a material loading charge of 35% to parts. If the company adopts the rates that you have computed in (1) above, would you expect the company's profits to improve? Explain.

PA–9 Missing Data; Markup Computations: Return on Investment (ROI); Pricing South Seas Products, Inc., has designed a new surfboard to replace its old surfboard line. Because of the unique design of the new surfboard, the company anticipates that it will be able to sell all the boards that it can produce. On this basis, the following incomplete budgeted income statement for the first year of activity is available:

Sales (? boards at ? per board)	$?
Less cost of goods sold (? boards at ? per board)	1,600,000
Gross margin	?
Less selling, general, and administrative expenses	1,130,000
Net income	$?

Additional information on the new surfboard is given below:

a. An investment of $1,500,000 will be necessary to carry inventories and accounts receivable and to purchase some new equipment needed in the manufacturing process. The company requires an 18% return on investment for all products.

b. A partially completed standard cost card for the new surfboard follows:

	Standard Quantity or Hours	Standard Price or Rate	Standard Cost
Direct materials	6 feet	$4.50 per foot	$27
Direct labor	2 hours	? per hour	?
Manufacturing overhead	?	? per hour	?
Total standard cost per surfboard			$?

c. The company will employ 20 workers in the manufacture of the new surfboards. Each will work a 40-hour week, 50 weeks a year.

d. Other information relating to production and costs follows:

Variable manufacturing overhead cost (per board)	$ 5
Variable selling cost (per board)	10
Fixed manufacturing overhead cost (total)	600,000
Fixed selling, general, and administrative cost (total)	?
Number of boards produced and sold (per year)	?

e. Overhead costs are allocated to production on the basis of direct labor-hours.

Required

1. Complete the standard cost card for a single surfboard.
2. Assume that the company uses the absorption costing approach to cost-plus pricing.
   a. Compute the markup that the company needs on the surfboards to achieve an 18% ROI.
   b. Using the markup you have computed, prepare a price quotation sheet for a single surfboard.
   c. Assume, as stated, that the company is able to sell all of the surfboards that it can produce. Complete the income statement for the first year of activity, and then compute the company's ROI for the year.
3. Assuming that direct labor is a variable cost, how many units would the company have to sell at the price you computed in (2) above to achieve the 18% ROI? How many units would have to be sold to just break even without achieving the 18% ROI?

PA–10 Economists' Approach to Pricing; Absorption Costing Approach to Cost-Plus Pricing Software Solutions, Inc., was started by two young software engineers to market SpamBlocker, a software application they had written that screens incoming e-mail messages and eliminates unsolicited mass mailings. Sales of the software have been good at 50,000 units a month, but the company has been losing money as shown on next page:

Sales (50,000 units × $25 per unit)	$1,250,000
Variable cost (50,000 units × $6 per unit)	300,000
Contribution margin	950,000
Fixed expenses	960,000
Net operating income (loss)	$ (10,000)

The company's only variable cost is the $6 fee it pays to another company to reproduce the software on floppy diskettes, print manuals, and package the result in an attractive box for sale to consumers. Monthly fixed selling, general, and administrative expenses total $960,000

The company's marketing manager has been arguing for some time that the software is priced too high. She estimates that every 5% decrease in price will yield an 8% increase in unit sales. The marketing manager would like your help in preparing a presentation to the company's owners concerning the pricing issue.

Required

1. To help the marketing manager prepare for her presentation, she has asked you to fill in the blanks in the following table. The selling prices in the table were computed by successively decreasing the selling price by 5%. The estimated unit sales were computed by successively increasing the unit sales by 8%. For example, $23.75 is 5% less than $25.00 and 54,000 units is 8% more than 50,000 units.

Selling Price	Estimated Unit Sales	Sales	Variable Cost	Fixed Expenses	Net Operating Income
$25.00	50,000	$1,250,000	$300,000	$960,000	$(10,000)
$23.75	54,000	$1,282,500	$324,000	$960,000	$ (1,500)
$22.56	58,320	?	?	?	?
$21.43	62,986	?	?	?	?
$20.36	68,025	?	?	?	?
$19.34	73,467	?	?	?	?
$18.37	79,344	?	?	?	?
$17.45	85,692	?	?	?	?
$16.58	92,547	?	?	?	?
$15.75	99.951	?	?	?	?

2. Using the data from the table, construct a chart that shows the net operating income as a function of the selling price. Put the selling price on the *X*-axis and the net operating income on the *Y*-axis. Using the chart, determine the approximate selling price at which net operating income is maximized.
3. Compute the price elasticity of demand for the SpamBlocker software. Based on this calculation, what is the profit-maximizing price?
4. The owners have invested $400,000 in the company and feel that they should be earning at least 10% on these funds. If the absorption costing approach to pricing were used, what would be the target selling price based on the current sales of 50,000 units? What do you think would happen to the net operating income of the company if this price were charged?
5. If the owners of the company are dissatisfied with the net operating income and return on investment at the selling price you computed in (3) above, should they increase the selling price? Explain.

Group Exercises

GEA–11 What's the Relationship between Costs and Prices? Consider two restaurants in the same general area of town. One restaurant is an up-scale dining establishment offering a wide variety of appetizers, soups, entrees, and desserts. The other restaurant is a franchise of a national fast-food chain.

1. What role do costs play in arriving at prices?
2. What are the variable and fixed costs?
3. How are prices determined at these two different establishments?
4. Are the products of both restaurants quality products?
5. What is the product at each restaurant?

Appendix B
Cost of Quality

Learning Objectives

After studying this appendix, you should be able to:

1. Identify the four types of quality costs.
2. Understand the organization, content, and uses of a quality cost report.

Introduction

Companies that develop a reputation for low-quality products generally lose market share and face declining profits. It doesn't do much good to have a product with a high-quality design that is made with high-quality materials if the product falls apart on the first use. One very important aspect of quality is the absence of defects. Defective products result in high warranty costs, but more importantly, they result in dissatisfied customers. People who are dissatisfied with a product are unlikely to buy the product again. They are also likely to tell others about their bad experiences. One study found that "[c]ustomers who have bad experiences tell approximately 11 people about it."[1] This is the worst possible sort of advertising. To prevent such problems, companies have been expending a great deal of effort to reduce defects. The objective is to have high *quality of conformance*.

Quality of Conformance

objective 1

Identify the four types of quality costs.

A product that meets or exceeds its design specifications and is free of defects that mar its appearance or degrade its performance is said to have high **quality of conformance**. Note that if an economy car is free of defects, it can have a quality of conformance that is just as high as a defect-free luxury car. The purchasers of economy cars cannot expect their cars to be as opulently equipped as luxury cars, but they can and do expect them to be free of defects.

Preventing, detecting, and dealing with defects cause costs that are called *quality costs* or the *cost of quality*. The use of the term *quality cost* is confusing to some people. It does not refer to costs such as using a higher-grade leather to make a wallet or using 14K gold instead of gold-plating in jewelry. Instead, the term **quality cost** refers to all of the costs that are incurred to prevent defects or that are incurred as a result of defects occurring.

1. Christopher W. L. Hart, James L. Heskett, and W. Earl Sasser, Jr., "The Profitable Art of Service Recovery," *Harvard Business Review*, July–August 1990, p. 153.

Exhibit B–1 Typical Quality Costs

Prevention Costs	Internal Failure Costs
Systems development	Net cost of scrap
Quality engineering	Net cost of spoilage
Quality training	Rework labor and overhead
Quality circles	Reinspection of reworked products
Statistical process control activities	Retesting of reworked products
Supervision of prevention activities	Downtime caused by quality problems
Quality data gathering, analysis, and reporting	Disposal of defective products
Quality improvement projects	Analysis of the cause of defects in production
Technical support provided to suppliers	Re-entering data because of keying errors
Audits of the effectiveness of the quality system	Debugging software errors
Appraisal Costs	***External Failure Costs***
Test and inspection of incoming materials	Cost of field servicing and handling complaints
Test and inspection of in-process goods	Warranty repairs and replacements
Final product testing and inspection	Repairs and replacements beyond the warranty period
Supplies used in testing and inspection	Product recalls
Supervision of testing and inspection activities	Liability arising from defective products
Depreciation of test equipment	Returns and allowances arising from quality problems
Maintenance of test equipment	Lost sales arising from a reputation for poor quality
Plant utilities in the inspection area	
Field testing and appraisal at customer site	

Quality costs can be broken down into four broad groups. Two of these groups—known as *prevention costs* and *appraisal costs*—are incurred in an effort to keep defective products from falling into the hands of customers. The other two groups of costs—known as *internal failure costs* and *external failure costs*—are incurred because defects are produced despite efforts to prevent them. Examples of specific costs involved in each of these four groups are given in Exhibit B–1.

Several things should be noted about the quality costs shown in the exhibit. First, note that quality costs don't relate to just manufacturing; rather, they relate to all the activities in a company from initial research and development (R&D) through customer service. Second, note that the number of costs associated with quality is very large; therefore, total quality cost can be quite high unless management gives this area special attention. Finally, note how different the costs are in the four groupings. We will now look at each of these groupings more closely.

Prevention Costs

The most effective way to minimize quality costs while maintaining high-quality output is to avoid having quality problems arise in the first place. This is the purpose of **prevention costs**; such costs relate to any activity that reduces the number of defects in products or services. Companies have learned that it is much less costly to prevent a problem from ever happening than it is to find and correct the problem after it has occurred.

Note from Exhibit B–1 that prevention costs include activities relating to quality circles and statistical process control. **Quality circles** consist of small groups of employees that meet on a regular basis to discuss ways to improve the quality of output. Both management and workers are included in these circles. Quality circles are widely used and can be found in manufacturing companies, utilities, health care organizations, banks, and many other organizations.

Statistical process control is a technique that is used to detect whether a process is in or out of control. An out-of-control process results in defective units and may be caused by a miscalibrated machine or some other factor. In statistical process control, workers use charts to monitor the quality of units that pass through their workstations. Using these charts, workers can quickly spot processes that are out of control and that are creating defects. Problems can be immediately corrected and further defects prevented rather than waiting for an inspector to catch the defects later.

Note also from the list of prevention costs in Exhibit B–1 that some companies provide technical support to their suppliers as a way of preventing defects. Particularly in just-in-time (JIT) systems, such support to suppliers is vital. In a JIT system, parts are delivered from suppliers just in time and in just the correct quantity to fill customer orders. There are no stockpiles of parts. If a defective part is received from a supplier, the part cannot be used and the order for the ultimate customer cannot be filled on time. Hence, every part received from a supplier must be free of defects. Consequently, companies that use JIT often require that their suppliers use sophisticated quality control programs such as statistical process control and that their suppliers certify that they will deliver parts and materials that are free of defects.

Focus on Current Practice

Very simple and inexpensive procedures can be used to prevent defects. Yamada Electric had a persistent problem assembling a simple push-button switch. The switch has two buttons, an on button and an off button, with a small spring under each button. Assembly is very simple. A worker inserts the small springs in the device and then installs the buttons. However, the worker sometimes forgets to put in one of the springs. When the customer discovers such a defective switch in a shipment from Yamada, an inspector has to be sent to the customer's plant to check every switch in the shipment. After each such incident, workers are urged to be more careful, and for a while quality improves. But eventually, someone forgets to put in a spring, and Yamada gets into trouble with the customer again. This chronic problem was very embarrassing to Yamada.

Shigeo Shingo, an expert on quality control, suggested a very simple solution. A small dish was placed next to the assembly station. At the beginning of each operation, two of the small springs are taken out of a parts box containing hundreds of springs and placed in the dish. The worker then assembles the switch. If a spring remains on the dish after assembling the switch, the worker immediately realizes a spring has been left out, and the switch is reassembled. This simple change in procedures completely eliminated the problem.[2] ■

Focus on Current Practice

A member of top management from Hewlett-Packard has stated that "the earlier you detect and prevent a defect, the more you can save. If you throw away a defective 2-cent resistor before you use it, you lose 2 cents. If you don't find it until it has been soldered into a computer component, it

2. Shigeo Shingo and Dr. Alan Robinson, editor-in-chief, *Modern Approaches to Manufacturing Improvement: The Shingo System*, (Cambridge, MA: Productivity Press, 1990), pp. 214–16.

may cost $10 to repair the part. If you don't catch the defect until it is in the computer user's hands, the repair will cost hundreds of dollars. Indeed, if a $5,000 computer must be repaired in the field, the expense may exceed the manufacturing cost."[3] ■

Appraisal Costs

Any defective parts and products should be caught as early as possible. **Appraisal costs**, which are sometimes called *inspection costs*, are incurred to identify defective products *before* the products are shipped to customers. Unfortunately, performing appraisal activities doesn't keep defects from happening again, and most managers now realize that maintaining an army of inspectors is a costly (and ineffective) approach to quality control.

Professor John K. Shank of Dartmouth College has aptly stated, "The old-style approach was to say, 'We've got great quality. We have 40 quality control inspectors in the factory.' Then somebody realized that if you need 40 inspectors, it must be a lousy factory. So now the trick is to run a factory without any quality control inspectors; each employee is his or her own quality control person."[4]

Employees in both manufacturing and service functions are increasingly being asked to be responsible for their own quality control. This approach, along with designing products to be easy to manufacture properly, allows quality to be built into products rather than relying on inspection to get the defects out.

Internal Failure Costs

Failure costs are incurred when a product fails to conform to its design specifications. Failure costs can be either internal or external. **Internal failure costs** result from identification of defects during the appraisal process. Such costs include scrap, rejected products, reworking of defective units, and downtime caused by quality problems. It is crucial that defects be discovered before a product is shipped to customers. Of course, the more effective a company's appraisal activities, the greater the chance of catching defects internally and the greater the level of internal failure costs (as compared to external failure costs). Unfortunately, appraisal activities focus on symptoms rather than on causes and they do nothing to reduce the number of defective items. However, appraisal activities do bring defects to the attention of management, which may lead to efforts to increase prevention activities so that the defects do not happen.

External Failure Costs

External failure costs result when a defective product is delivered to a customer. As shown in Exhibit B–1, external failure costs include warranty repairs and replacements, product recalls, liability arising from legal action against a company, and lost sales arising from a reputation for poor quality. Such costs can devastate profits.

In the past, some managers have taken the attitude, "Let's go ahead and ship everything to customers, and we'll take care of any problems under the warranty." This attitude generally results in high external failure costs, customer ill will, and declining market share and profits.

---

3. David A. Garvin, "Product Quality: Profitable at Any Cost," *The New York Times* 134 (March 3, 1985), p. F3. Copyright © 1985 by The New York Times Company. Reprinted by permission.
4. Robert W. Casey, "The Changing World of the CEO," *PPM World* 24, no. 2 (1990), p. 31.

Distribution of Quality Costs

We stated earlier that a company's total quality cost is likely to be very high unless management gives this area special attention. Studies show that quality costs for U.S. companies range between 10% and 20% of total sales, whereas experts say that these costs should be more in the 2% to 4% range. How does a company reduce its total quality cost? The answer lies in how the quality costs are distributed. Refer to the graph in Exhibit B–2, which shows total quality costs as a function of the quality of conformance.

The graph shows that when the quality of conformance is low, total quality cost is high and that most of this cost consists of costs of internal and external failure. A low quality of conformance means that a high percentage of units are defective and hence the company must incur high failure costs. However, as a company spends more and more on prevention and appraisal, the percentage of defective units drops (the percentage of defect-free units increases). This results in lower costs of internal and external failure. Ordinarily, total quality cost drops rapidly as the quality of conformance increases. Thus, a company can reduce its total quality cost by focusing its efforts on prevention and appraisal. The cost savings from reduced defects usually swamp the costs of the additional prevention and appraisal efforts.

The graph in Exhibit B–2 has been drawn so that the total quality cost is minimized when the quality of conformance is less than 100%. However, some experts and managers contend that the total quality cost is not minimized until the quality of conformance is 100% and there are no defects. Indeed, many companies have found that the total quality costs seem to keep dropping even when the quality of conformance approaches 100% and defect rates get as low as 1 in a million units. Others argue that eventually total quality cost increases as the quality of conformance increases. However, in most companies this does not seem to happen until the quality of conformance is very close to 100% and defect rates are very close to zero.

As a company's quality program becomes more refined and as its failure costs begin to fall, prevention activities usually become more effective than appraisal activities. Appraisal can only find defects, whereas prevention can eliminate them. The best way to prevent defects from happening is to design processes that reduce the likelihood of defects and to continually monitor processes using statistical process control methods.

Exhibit B–2 Effect of Quality Costs on Quality of Conformance

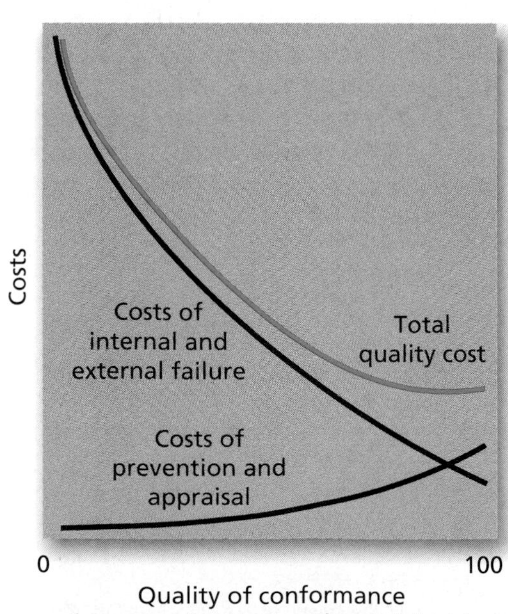

Focus on Current Practice

After returning from a trip to Japan, an executive from a large U.S. company asked the manager of one of the company's plants what percentage of the plant's output made it all the way through the manufacturing process without defects being noted. The plant had never kept this information, and when it was finally compiled, the executive was stunned to find that less than 10% of all products made it through the plant without rework of some type. The company initiated an immediate review of its quality program, and a year after implementing extensive changes, the number of products going through this plant without defects was increased to 60%. The company's goal over time is to increase this figure to 100%.[5] ■

Quality Cost Reports

objective 2
Understand the organization, content, and uses of a quality cost report.

As an initial step in quality improvement programs, companies often construct a *quality cost report* that provides an estimate of the financial consequences of the company's current level of defects. A **quality cost report** details the prevention costs, appraisal costs, and costs of internal and external failures that arise from the company's current level of defective products and services. Managers are often shocked by the magnitude of these costs. A typical quality cost report is shown in Exhibit B–3.

Several things should be noted from the data in the exhibit. First, note that Ventura Company's quality costs are poorly distributed in both years, with most of the costs being traceable to either internal failure or external failure. The external failure costs are particularly high in Year 1 in comparison to other costs.

Second, note that the company increased its spending on prevention and appraisal activities in Year 2. As a result, internal failure costs go up in that year (from $2 million in Year 1 to $3 million in Year 2), but external failure costs drop sharply (from $5.15 million in Year 1 to only $2 million in Year 2). Because of the increase in appraisal activity in Year 2, more defects are being caught inside the company before they are shipped to customers. This results in more cost for scrap, rework, and so forth, but saves huge amounts in warranty repairs, warranty replacements, and other external failure costs.

Third, note that as a result of greater emphasis on prevention and appraisal, *total* quality cost has decreased in Year 2. As continued emphasis is placed on prevention and appraisal in future years, total quality cost should continue to decrease. That is, future increases in prevention and appraisal costs should be more than offset by decreases in failure costs. Moreover, appraisal costs should also decrease as more effort is placed into prevention.

Quality Cost Reports in Graphic Form

As a supplement to the quality cost report shown in Exhibit B–3, companies frequently prepare quality cost information in graphic form. Graphic presentations include pie charts, bar graphs, trend lines, and so forth. The data for Ventura Company from Exhibit B–3 are presented in bar graph form in Exhibit B–4.

The first bar graph in Exhibit B–4 is scaled in terms of dollars of quality cost, and the second is scaled in terms of quality cost as a percentage of sales. In both graphs, the

5. Robert S. Kaplan, "Measuring Manufacturing Performance," *The Accounting Review* 63, no. 4 (October 1983), p. 690.

Exhibit B–3 Quality Cost Report

VENTURA COMPANY
Quality Cost Report
For Years 1 and 2

	Year 2		Year 1	
	Amount	Percent*	Amount	Percent*
Prevention costs:				
Systems development	$ 400,000	0.80%	$ 270,000	0.54%
Quality training	210,000	0.42%	130,000	0.26%
Supervision of prevention activities	70,000	0.14%	40,000	0.08%
Quality improvement projects	320,000	0.64%	210,000	0.42%
Total	1,000,000	2.00%	650,000	1.30%
Appraisal costs:				
Inspection	600,000	1.20%	560,000	1.12%
Reliability testing	580,000	1.16%	420,000	0.84%
Supervision of testing and inspection	120,000	0.24%	80,000	0.16%
Depreciation of test equipment	200,000	0.40%	140,000	0.28%
Total	1,500,000	3.00%	1,200,000	2.40%
Internal failure costs:				
Net cost of scrap	900,000	1.80%	750,000	1.50%
Rework labor and overhead	1,430,000	2.86%	810,000	1.62%
Downtime due to defects in quality	170,000	0.34%	100,000	0.20%
Disposal of defective products	500,000	1.00%	340,000	0.68%
Total	3,000,000	6.00%	2,000,000	4.00%
External failure costs:				
Warranty repairs	400,000	0.80%	900,000	1.80%
Warranty replacements	870,000	1.74%	2,300,000	4.60%
Allowances	130,000	0.26%	630,000	1.26%
Cost of field servicing	600,000	1.20%	1,320,000	2.64%
Total	2,000,000	4.00%	5,150,000	10.30%
Total quality cost	$7,500,000	15.00%	$9,000,000	18.00%

*As a percentage of total sales. We assume that in each year sales totaled $50,000,000.

data are "stacked" upward. That is, appraisal costs are stacked on top of prevention costs, internal failure costs are stacked on top of the sum of prevention costs plus appraisal costs, and so forth. The percentage figures in the second graph show that total quality cost equals 18% of sales in Year 1 and 15% of sales in Year 2, the same as reported earlier in Exhibit B–3.

Data in graphic form help managers to see trends more clearly and to see the magnitude of the various costs in relation to each other. Such graphs are easily prepared using computer graphics packages.

Uses of Quality Cost Information

The information provided by a quality cost report is used by managers in several ways. First, quality cost information helps managers see the financial significance of defects. Managers usually are not aware of the magnitude of their quality costs because these costs cut across departmental lines and are not normally tracked and accumulated by the cost system. Thus, when first presented with a quality cost report, managers often are surprised by the amount of cost attributable to poor quality.

Exhibit B–4 Quality Cost Reports in Graphic Form

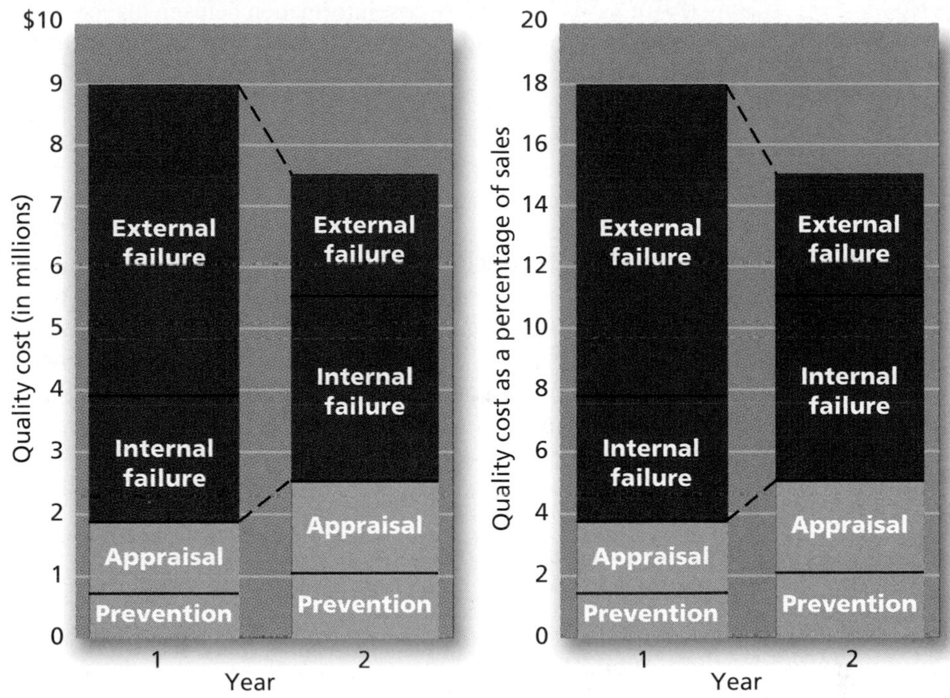

Focus on Current Practice

Sola Optical, a manufacturer of ophthalmic spectacle lenses in Petaluma, California, prepared a cost of quality report similar to the one illustrated in this chapter. The company found that its cost of quality was about 20% of its revenues and about equal to its profits. The report demonstrated that relatively few dollars were spent on defect prevention, that appraisal costs were high, internal failure costs were extremely high, and external failure costs were quite low. This pattern occurred because the Quality Control Department used final inspection to assure only good products were shipped to customers. This resulted in high inspection, rework, and scrap costs, but few problems with defective products being sent to customers. "The Cost of Quality report was successful in alerting management to the magnitude of the costs and was a reasonable baseline against which to measure future performance."[6] ■

Second, quality cost information helps managers identify the relative importance of the quality problems faced by the firm. For example, the quality cost report may show that scrap is a major quality problem or that the company is incurring huge warranty costs. With this information, managers have a better idea of where to focus efforts.

6. Richard K. Youde, "Cost-of-Quality Reporting: How We See It," *Management Accounting,* January 1992, pp. 34–38.

Third, quality cost information helps managers see whether their quality costs are poorly distributed. In general, quality costs should be distributed more toward prevention and appraisal activities and less toward failures.

Counterbalancing these uses, three limitations of quality cost information should be recognized. First, simply measuring and reporting quality costs does not solve quality problems. Problems can be solved only by taking action. Second, results usually lag behind quality improvement programs. Initially, total quality cost may even increase as quality control systems are designed and installed. Decreases in these costs may not begin to occur until the quality program has been in effect for a year or more. And third, the most important quality cost, lost sales arising from customer ill will, is usually omitted from the quality cost report because it is difficult to estimate.

Typically, during the initial years of a quality improvement program, the benefits of compiling a quality cost report outweigh the costs and limitations of the reports. As managers gain experience in balancing prevention and appraisal activities, the need for quality cost reports often diminishes.

International Aspects of Quality

Many of the tools used in quality management today were developed in Japan after World War II. In statistical process control, Japanese companies borrowed heavily from the work of W. Edwards Deming. However, Japanese companies are largely responsible for quality circles, JIT, the idea that quality is everyone's responsibility, and the emphasis on prevention rather than on inspection.

In the 1980s, quality re-emerged as a pivotal factor in the market. Many companies now find that it is impossible to effectively compete without a very strong quality program in place. This is particularly true of companies that wish to compete in the European market.

The ISO 9000 Standards

The International Standards Organization (ISO), based in Geneva, Switzerland, has established quality control guidelines known as the **ISO 9000 standards**. Many companies and organizations in Europe will buy only from ISO 9000 standard-certified suppliers. This means that the suppliers must demonstrate to a certifying agency that:

1. A quality control system is in use, and the system clearly defines an expected level of quality.
2. The system is fully operational and is backed up with detailed documentation of quality control procedures.
3. The intended level of quality is being achieved on a sustained, consistent basis.

The key to receiving certification under the ISO 9000 standards is documentation. It's one thing for a company to say that it has a quality control system in operation, but it's quite a different thing to be able to document the steps in that system. Under ISO 9000, this documentation must be so detailed and precise that if all the employees in a company were suddenly replaced, the new employees could use the documentation to make the product exactly as it was made by the old employees. Even companies with good quality control systems find that it takes up to two years of painstaking work to develop this detailed documentation. But companies often find that compiling this documentation results in improvements in their quality systems.

The ISO 9000 standards have become an international measure of quality. Although the standards were developed to control the quality of goods sold in European countries, they have become widely accepted elsewhere as well. Companies in the United States that export to Europe often expect their own suppliers to comply with the ISO 9000 standards, since these exporters must document the quality of the materials going into their products as part of their own ISO 9000 certification.

The ISO program for certification of quality management programs is not limited to manufacturing companies. The American Institute of Certified Public Accountants was the first professional membership organization in the United States to win recognition under an ISO certification program.[7]

Focus on Current Practice

Over the years, E. I. du Pont de Nemours & Company has been a leader in quality control systems. Despite this emphasis on quality, for many years the engineers at one of Du Pont's plants were unable to control a high defect rate in the output from a molding press that makes plastic connectors for computers. As part of the documentation needed for certification under the ISO 9000 standards, workers on the press were required to detail in writing how they do their jobs. When engineers compared the workers' notes, they found that the workers were inconsistent in the way they calibrated probes that measure press temperature. As a result, the press temperature was often set incorrectly. When this problem was corrected, the defect rate for the press fell from 30% to only 8% of output.[8] ■

Summary

Defects cause costs, which can be classified into prevention costs, appraisal costs, internal failure costs, and external failure costs. Prevention costs are incurred to keep defects from happening. Appraisal costs are incurred to ensure that defective products, once made, are not shipped to customers. Internal failure costs are incurred as a consequence of detecting defective products before they are shipped to customers. External failure costs are the consequences (in terms of repairs, servicing, and lost future business) of delivering defective products to customers. Most experts agree that management effort should be focused on preventing defects. Small investments in prevention can lead to dramatic reductions in appraisal costs and costs of internal and external failure.

Quality costs are summarized on a quality cost report. This report shows the type of quality costs being incurred and their significance and trends. The report helps managers understand the importance of quality costs, spot problem areas, and assess the way in which the quality costs are distributed.

Key Terms for Review

Appraisal costs Costs that are incurred to identify defective products before the products are shipped to customers. (p. 895)

7. *The CPA Letter*, May 1998, p.1.
8. "Want EC Business? You Have Two Choices," *Business Week*, no. 3288 (October 19, 1992), p. 58.

External failure costs Costs that are incurred when a product or service that is defective is delivered to a customer. (p. 895)

Internal failure costs Costs that are incurred as a result of identifying defective products before they are shipped to customers. (p. 895)

ISO 9000 standards Quality control requirements issued by the International Standards Organization that relate to products sold in European countries. (p. 900)

Prevention costs Costs that are incurred to keep defects from occurring. (p. 893)

Quality circles Small groups of employees that meet on a regular basis to discuss ways of improving quality. (p. 893)

Quality cost Costs that are incurred to prevent defective products from falling into the hands of customers or that are incurred as a result of defective units. (p. 892)

Quality cost report A report that details prevention costs, appraisal costs, and the costs of internal and external failures. (p. 897)

Quality of conformance The degree to which a product or service meets or exceeds its design specifications and is free of defects or other problems that mar its appearance or degrade its performance. (p. 892)

Statistical process control A charting technique used to monitor the quality of work being done in a workstation for the purpose of immediately correcting any problems. (p. 893)

Questions

B–1 Costs associated with the quality of conformance can be broken down into four broad groups. What are these four groups and how do they differ?

B–2 In their efforts to reduce the total cost of quality, should companies generally focus on decreasing prevention costs and appraisal costs?

B–3 What is probably the most effective way to reduce a company's total quality costs?

B–4 What are the main uses of quality cost reports?

B–5 Why are managers often unaware of the magnitude of quality costs?

Exercises

EB–1 Listed below are a number of costs that are incurred in connection with a company's quality control system.

a. Product testing.
b. Product recalls.
c. Rework labor and overhead.
d. Quality circles.
e. Downtime caused by defects.
f. Cost of field servicing.
g. Inspection of goods.
h. Quality engineering.
i. Warranty repairs.
j. Statistical process control.
k. Net cost of scrap.
l. Depreciation of test equipment.
m. Returns and allowances arising from poor quality.
n. Disposal of defective products.
o. Technical support to suppliers.
p. Systems development.
q. Warranty replacements.
r. Field testing at customer site.
s. Product design.

Required

1. Classify each of the costs above into one of the following categories: prevention cost, appraisal cost, internal failure cost, or external failure cost.
2. Which of the costs in (1) above are incurred in an effort to keep poor quality of conformance from occurring? Which of the costs in (1) above are incurred because poor quality of conformance has occurred?

EB–2 Listed below are a number of terms relating to quality management:

Appraisal costs	Quality circles
Quality cost report	Prevention costs
Quality of conformance	External failure costs
Internal failure costs	Quality costs

Required Choose the term or terms that most appropriately complete the following statements. The terms can be used more than once. (A fill-in blank can hold more than one word.)

1. A product that has a high rate of defects is said to have a low _____.
2. All of the costs associated with preventing and dealing with defects once they occur are known as _____.
3. In many companies, small groups of employees, known as _____, meet on a regular basis to discuss ways to improve quality.
4. A company incurs _____ and _____ in an effort to keep defects from occurring..
5. A company incurs _____ and _____ because defects have occurred.
6. Of thc four groups of costs associated with quality of conformance, _____ are generally the most damaging to a company.
7. Inspection, testing, and other costs incurred to keep defective products from being shipped to customers are known as _____.
8. _____ are incurred in an effort to eliminate poor product design, defective manufacturing practices, and the providing of substandard service.
9. The costs relating to defects, rejected products, and downtime caused by quality problems are known as _____.
10. When a product that is defective in some way is delivered to a customer, _____ are incurred.
11. Over time a company's total quality costs should decrease if it redistributes its quality costs by placing its greatest emphasis on _____ and _____.
12. One way to ensure that management is aware of the costs associated with quality is to summarize such costs on a _____.

Problems

PB–3 Quality Cost Report In response to intensive foreign competition, the management of Florex Company has attempted over the past year to improve the quality of its products. A statistical process control system has been installed and other steps have been taken to decrease the amount of warranty and other field costs, which have been trending upward over the past several years. Costs relating to quality and quality control over the last two years are given below:

	This Year	Last Year
Inspection	$ 900,000	$ 750,000
Quality engineering	570,000	420,000
Depreciation of test equipment	240,000	210,000
Rework labor	1,500,000	1,050,000
Statistical process control	180,000	—
Cost of field servicing	900,000	1,200,000
Supplies used in testing	60,000	30,000
Systems development	750,000	480,000
Warranty repairs	1,050,000	3,600,000
Net cost of scrap	1,125,000	630,000
Product testing	1,200,000	810,000
Product recalls	750,000	2,100,000
Disposal of defective products	975,000	720,000

Sales have been flat over the past few years, at $75,000,000 per year. A great deal of money has been spent in the effort to upgrade quality, and management is anxious to see whether or not the effort has been effective.

Required

1. Prepare a quality cost report that contains data for both this year and last year. Carry percentage computations to two decimal places.
2. Prepare a bar graph showing the distribution of the various quality costs by category.
3. Prepare a written evaluation to accompany the reports you have prepared in (1) and (2) above. This evaluation should discuss the distribution of quality costs in the company, changes in this distribution that you see taking place, the reasons for changes in costs in the various categories, and any other information that would be of value to management.

PB–4 Quality Cost Report "Maybe the emphasis we've placed on upgrading our quality control system will pay off in the long run, but it doesn't seem to be helping us much right now," said Renee Penretti, president of Halogen Products. "I thought improved quality would give a real boost to sales, but sales have remained flat at $50,000,000 for the last two years."

Halogen Products has seen its market share decline in recent years due to increased foreign competition. An intensive effort to strengthen the quality control system was initiated at the beginning of the current year in the hope that better quality would strengthen the company's competitive position and also reduce warranty and servicing costs. Costs relating to quality and quality control over the last two years are given below:

	This Year	Last Year
Product testing	$ 800,000	$ 490,000
Rework labor	1,000,000	700,000
Systems development	530,000	320,000
Warranty repairs	700,000	2,100,000
Net cost of scrap	620,000	430,000
Supplies used in testing	30,000	20,000
Field servicing	600,000	900,000
Quality engineering	400,000	280,000
Warranty replacements	90,000	300,000
Inspection	600,000	380,000
Product recalls	410,000	1,700,000
Statistical process control	370,000	—
Disposal of defective products	380,000	270,000
Depreciation of testing equipment	170,000	110,000

Required

1. Prepare a quality cost report that contains data for both years. Carry percentage computations to two decimal places.
2. Prepare a bar graph showing the distribution of the various quality costs by category.
3. Prepare a written evaluation to accompany the reports you have prepared in (1) and (2) above. This evaluation should discuss the distribution of quality costs in the company, changes in this distribution that you detect have taken place over the last year, and any other information you believe would be useful to management.

PB–5 Analyzing a Quality Cost Report Mercury, Inc., produces pagers at its plant in Texas. In recent years, the company's market share has been eroded by stiff competition from overseas competitors. Price and product quality are the two key areas in which companies compete in this market.

A year ago, the company's pagers had been ranked low in product quality in a consumer survey. Shocked by this result. Jorge Gomez, Mercury's president, initiated a crash effort to improve product quality. Gomez set up a task force to implement a formal quality improvement program. Included on this task force were representatives from the Engineering, Marketing, Customer Service, Production, and Accounting departments. The broad representation was needed because Gomez believed that this was a companywide program and that all employees should share the responsibility for its success.

After the first meeting of the task force, Holly Elsoe, manager of the Marketing Department, asked John Tran, production manager, what he thought of the proposed program. Tran replied, "I have reservations. Quality is too abstract to be attaching costs to it and then to be holding you and me responsible for cost improvements. I like to work with goals that I can see and count! I'm nervous about having my annual bonus based on a decrease in quality costs; there are too many variables that we have no control over."

Mercury's quality improvement program has now been in operation for one year. The company's most recent quality cost report is shown below.

MERCURY, INC.
Quality Cost Report
(in thousands)

	This Year	Last Year
Prevention costs:		
Machine maintenance	$ 120	$ 70
Training suppliers	10	—
Quality circles	20	—
Total	150	70
Appraisal costs:		
Incoming inspection	40	20
Final testing	90	80
Total	130	100
Internal failure costs:		
Rework	130	50
Scrap	70	40
Total	200	90
External failure costs:		
Warranty repairs	30	90
Customer returns	80	320
Total	110	410
Total quality cost	$ 590	$ 670
Total production cost	$4,800	$4,200

As they were reviewing the report, Elsoe asked Tran what he now thought of the quality improvement program. Tran replied. "I'm relieved that the new quality improvement program hasn't hurt our bonuses, but the program has increased the workload in the Production Department. It is true that customer returns are way down, but the pagers that were returned by customers to retail outlets were rarely sent back to us for rework."

Required

1. Expand the company's quality cost report by showing the costs in both years as percentages of both total production cost and total quality cost. Carry all computations to one decimal place. By analyzing the report, determine if Mercury, Inc.'s quality improvement program has been successful. *List specific evidence to support your answer.*
2. Do you expect the improvement program as it progresses to continue to increase the workload in the Production Department?
3. Jorge Gomez believed that the quality improvement program was essential and that Mercury, Inc., could no longer afford to ignore the importance of product quality. Discuss how Mercury, Inc., could measure the cost of *not* implementing the quality improvement program.

(CMA, adapted)

Group Exercises

GEB–6 TQM and COQ Total quality management, or TQM, was to American companies competing in the nineties what it was for Japanese firms throughout the seventies and eighties. The concept of cost of quality (COQ) gives quality a bottom-line discipline that is at the core of many well-managed quality improvement programs (QIP). With a focus on satisfying the customer, those who view quality as a marathon race stand a greater chance of improving market share than do those who view quality as the latest project with a start date and a completion date.

Required

1. Surveys have shown that when financial managers are asked to estimate the total cost of quality (prior to implementing a QIP), half or more estimate that COQ is less than 5% of sales revenue. The reality is that actual COQ is typically 10% to 20% of sales, and in some cases it has exceeded 60% of sales. Why do you think there is such a large gap between the perception and the reality of the quality problem?
2. Why do you think the cost of poor quality reached such an epidemic level before U.S. companies were motivated to do something about the problem?
3. What function(s) does COQ reporting play in a quality improvement program?
4. For most companies starting a QIP, investments in prevention and appraisal usually result in major cost savings in other areas. Explain this phenomenon.
5. The traditional view of quality is that the total costs of prevention and appraisal plus internal and external failure costs are minimized at a point somewhere above zero defects. Additional investments in prevention beyond this point would result in savings that are less than the additional investment in prevention. An alternative view of quality is that the total costs of the four categories of quality are minimized at zero defects. Additional investments in prevention will always result in larger reductions in appraisal and failure costs. With the zero defects model, the search for quality improvements is continuous. Explain these two viewpoints.

Photo Credits

1-OP: page 3 © Wolfgang Knapp/Thema
P1-1: page 13 Wyatt McSpadden
P1-2: page 17 © Mark Richards/PhotoEdit
P1-3: page 25 © Michael Newman/PhotoEdit
P1-4: page 31 © Martin A. Levick
2-OP: page 43 © Bill Aron/PhotoEdit
P2-1: page 54 © Carlos Angel/Liaison Agency
P2-2a: page 55 © Photofest
P2-2b: page 55 No credit necessary.
P2-3: page 61 Courtesy of Benetton
3-OP: page 85 © Laurence Monneret/ Tony Stone Images
P3-1: page 91 Courtesy of Agricultural Data Systems
P3-2: page 95 © Mike Blank/Tony Stone Images
P3-3: page 112 © Photofest
P3-4: page 113 Courtesy of Andersen Corporation
4-OP: page 147 © Richard Hutchings
P4-1: page 148 © Jim Bryant/Gamma Liaison
P4-2: page 150 © Greenlar/The Image Works
P4-3: page 154 © Allsport
P4-4: page 163 © Jeff Greenberg/PhotoEdit
5-OP: page 189 © Michael A. Keller/ The Stock Market
P5-1: page 195 © Chris Sorensen
P5-2: page 198 © Michael Newman/PhotoEdit
P5-3: page 198 © Luc Novovitch/ Liaison International
P5-4: page 198 © Mark Richards/PhotoEdit
6-OP: page 233 © Joe Sohm/Stock Boston
P6-1: page 237 Courtesy of Elgin Sweeper Co.
P6-2: page 244 Courtesy of *The American*
P6-3: page 247 © Spencer Grant/PhotoEdit
P6-4: page 250 © Martin A. Levick
P6-5: page 252 © Jeff Greenberg/The Image Works
7-OP page 283 © Richard Hutchings
P7-1: page 288 © L. Mulvehill/The Image Works
8-OP: page 321 © Ariel Skelley/The Stock Market
P8-1A: page 327 Courtesy of Super Bakery, Inc.
P8-1B: page 327 © PhotoDisc, Inc.
P8-2: page 331 Courtesy of Dayton Technologies, Inc.
9-OP: page 377 Courtesy of Lucy Carter
P9-1: page 380 Courtesy of Power Express Mortgage Bankers
P9-2: page 381Courtesy of the Repertory Theatre of St. Louis
P9-3: page 383 © The Image Works
P9-4: page 387 © Jose L. Pelaez/The Stock Market
P9-5: page 404 Courtesy of the Toronto Blue Jays
10-OP: page 439 © Photofest
P10-1: page 446 Courtesy of Natuzzi Leather
P10-2: page 463 © General Motors Corp., used with permission.
P10-3: page 467© Jim Pickerell/Tony Stone Images
11-OP: page 503 © Stephen Frisch/Stock Boston
P11-1: page 504 © David Young-Wolff/PhotoEdit
P11-2: page 515 © Michael Newman/PhotoEdit
P11-3: page 522 © Paul Steel/The Stock Market
12-OP: page 551 © MGA/Photri: Michael Philip Manheim
P12-1: page 566 © Photofest
P12-2: page 574 © John Neubauer/PhotoEdit
P12-3: page 576 © Felicia Martinez/PhotoEdit
13-OP: page 615 © 92 Henley & Savage/ The Stock Market
P13-1: page 628 © Tony Freeman/PhotoEdit
P13-2: page 628 Courtesy of Cummins Engine Co.
14-OP: page 667 © Eric Myer Photography
P14-1: page 683 © F. Hoffman/The Image Works
P14-2: page 686 © Ted Horowitz/The Stock Market page 689 *My P14-3*
15-OPA: page 725 © Cassy Cohen/PhotoEdit
P15-1: page 726 © Tony Freeman/PhotoEdit
P15-2: page 726 © Jack Affleck/Vail Associates, Inc.
P15-3: page 733 © Joan Baron/The Stock Market page 736 *My P15-3*
16-OP: page 755 Stock Boston
P16-1: page 757 Chris Sorensen
P16-2: page 772 © Owen Franken/Stock Boston
17-OP: page 791 © Catherine Panchout/ Tony Stone Images
P17-1A: page 792 Courtesy of Wendy's International, Inc.
P17-1B: page 792 © Tom and Michelle Grimm/ Tony Stone Images
P17-2: page 797 © Kathy Ferguson/PhotoEdit
18 OP: page 827 © Don Smetzer/Tony Stone Images
P18-1: page 829 © Sylvain Coffie/Tony Stone Images
P18-2: page 841 © Michael Newman/PhotoEdit
P18-3: page 847 Courtesy of Impact Communications, Inc.

Author Index

Company Index

Subject Index